ALL GLORY TO ŚRĪ GURU AND GAURĀṄGA

ŚRĪMAD BHĀGAVATAM

of

KṚṢṆA-DVAIPĀYANA VYĀSA

नायं श्रियोऽङ्ग उ नितान्तरतेः प्रसादः
स्वर्योषितां नलिनगन्धरुचां कुतोऽन्याः ।
रासोत्सवेऽस्य भुजदण्डगृहीतकण्ठ-
लब्धाशिषां य उदगाद्व्रजवल्लभीनाम् ॥६०॥

nāyaṁ śriyo 'ṅga u nitānta-rateḥ prasādaḥ
svar-yoṣitāṁ nalina-gandha-rucāṁ kuto 'nyāḥ
rāsotsave 'sya bhuja-daṇḍa-gṛhīta-kaṇṭha-
labdhāśiṣāṁ ya udagād vraja-vallabhīnām

(p. 134)

BOOKS by
His Divine Grace
A. C. Bhaktivedanta Swami Prabhupāda

Bhagavad-gītā As It Is
Śrīmad-Bhāgavatam, cantos 1–10 (12 vols.)
Śrī Caitanya-caritāmṛta (17 vols.)
Teachings of Lord Caitanya
The Nectar of Devotion
The Nectar of Instruction
Śrī Īśopaniṣad
Easy Journey to Other Planets
Kṛṣṇa Consciousness: The Topmost Yoga System
Kṛṣṇa, The Supreme Personality of Godhead (3 vols.)
Perfect Questions, Perfect Answers
Teachings of Lord Kapila, the Son of Devahūti
Transcendental Teachings of Prahlāda Mahārāja
Dialectic Spiritualism—A Vedic View of Western Philosophy
Teachings of Queen Kuntī
Kṛṣṇa, the Reservoir of Pleasure
The Science of Self-Realization
The Path of Perfection
Search for Liberation
Life Comes from Life
The Perfection of Yoga
Beyond Birth and Death
On the Way to Kṛṣṇa
Geetār-gan (Bengali)
Vairāgya-vidyā (Bengali)
Buddhi-yoga (Bengali)
Bhakti-ratna-bolī (Bengali)
Rāja-vidyā: The King of Knowledge
Elevation to Kṛṣṇa Consciousness
Kṛṣṇa Consciousness: The Matchless Gift
Back to Godhead magazine (founder)

A complete catalog is available upon request.

Bhaktivedanta Book Trust
3764 Watseka Avenue
Los Angeles, California 90034

Bhaktivedanta Book Trust
P.O. Box 262
Botany
N. S. W. 2019, Australia

ŚRĪMAD BHĀGAVATAM

Tenth Canto
"The Summum Bonum"

(Part Three—Chapters 45-69)

With the Original Sanskrit Text, Its Roman Transliteration, Synonyms, Translation and Elaborate Purports

by disciples of

His Divine Grace
A.C. Bhaktivedanta Swami Prabhupāda
Founder-*Ācārya* of the International Society for Krishna Consciousness

THE BHAKTIVEDANTA BOOK TRUST
Los Angeles · London · Stockholm · Bombay · Sydney

Readers interested in the subject matter of this book
are invited by the International Society for Krishna Consciousness
to correspond with its Secretary at either of the following addresses:

International Society for Krishna Consciousness
P. O. Box 262
Botany
N. S. W. 2019
Australia

International Society for Krishna Consciousness
3764 Watseka Avenue
Los Angeles, California 90034

First Printing, 1988: 5,000 copies

Printed in Singapore

Library of Congress Cataloging in Publication Data (Revised)

Śrīmad-Bhāgavatam.

In English and Sanskrit.
Translation of: Bhāgavatapurāṇa
10th canto, v.2-12th canto by disciples of His Divine Grace A. C. Bhaktivedanta Swami Prabhupāda.
Includes index.
Contents: 1st canto. Creation— 2nd canto. The cosmic manifestation— 3rd canto. The status quo (2 v)— 4th canto. The creation of the fourth order (2 v)— 5th canto. The creative impetus— 6th canto. Prescribed duties for mankind— 7th canto. The science of God— 8th canto. Withdrawal of the cosmic creations— 9th canto. Liberation— 10th canto. The summum bonum (4 v)— 11th canto. General history (2 v)— 12th canto. The age of deterioration.
1. Purāṇas. Bhāgavatapurāṇa—Criticism, interpretation, etc. I. Bhaktivedanta Swami, A. C., 1896-1977.
BL1140.4.B432E5 1987 294.5'925 87-25585
ISBN 0-89213-263-9 (v. 14)

Table of Contents

CHAPTER FORTY-SEVEN
The Song of the Bee

CHAPTER FORTY–EIGHT
Kṛṣṇa Pleases His Devotees

CHAPTER FORTY–NINE
Akrūra's Mission in Hastināpura

CHAPTER FIFTY

Kṛṣṇa Establishes the City of Dvārakā

CHAPTER FIFTY–ONE
The Deliverance of Mucukunda

CHAPTER FIFTY–TWO
Rukmiṇī's Message to Lord Kṛṣṇa

CHAPTER FIFTY–THREE
Kṛṣṇa Kidnaps Rukmiṇī

CHAPTER FIFTY–FOUR
The Marriage of Kṛṣṇa and Rukmiṇī

CHAPTER FIFTY–FIVE
The History of Pradyumna

CHAPTER FIFTY–SIX
The Syamantaka Jewel

CHAPTER FIFTY-SEVEN
Satrājit Murdered, the Jewel Returned

CHAPTER FIFTY-EIGHT
Kṛṣṇa Marries Five Princesses

CHAPTER FIFTY-NINE
The Killing of the Demon Naraka

CHAPTER SIXTY
Lord Kṛṣṇa Teases Queen Rukmiṇī

CHAPTER SIXTY–ONE
Lord Balarāma Slays Rukmī

CHAPTER SIXTY–TWO
The Meeting of Ūṣā and Aniruddha

CHAPTER SIXTY-THREE
Lord Kṛṣṇa Fights with Bāṇāsura

CHAPTER SIXTY-FOUR
The Deliverance of King Nṛga

CHAPTER SIXTY–FIVE
Lord Balarāma Visits Vṛndāvana

CHAPTER SIXTY–SIX
Pauṇḍraka, the False Vāsudeva

CHAPTER SIXTY-SEVEN
Lord Balarāma Slays Dvivida Gorilla

CHAPTER SIXTY-EIGHT
The Marriage of Sāmba

CHAPTER SIXTY–NINE
Nārada Muni Visits Lord Kṛṣṇa's Palaces in Dvārakā

Appendixes

Preface

nama oṁ viṣṇu-pādāya kṛṣṇa-preṣṭhāya bhū-tale
śrīmate bhaktivedānta-svāmin iti nāmine

I offer my most respectful obeisances at the lotus feet of His Divine Grace A. C. Bhaktivedanta Swami Prabhupāda, who is very dear to Lord Kṛṣṇa on this earth, having taken shelter at His lotus feet.

namas te sārasvate deve gaura-vāṇī-pracāriṇe
nirviśeṣa-śūnyavādi-pāścātya-deśa-tāriṇe

I offer my most respectful obeisances unto the lotus feet of His Divine Grace A. C. Bhaktivedanta Swami Prabhupāda, who is the disciple of Śrīla Bhaktisiddhānta Sarasvatī Ṭhākura and who is powerfully distributing the message of Caitanya Mahāprabhu and thus saving the fallen Western countries from impersonalism and voidism.

Śrīmad-Bhāgavatam, with authorized translation and elaborate purports in the English language, is the great work of His Divine Grace Oṁ Viṣṇupāda Paramahaṁsa Parivrājakācārya Aṣṭottara-śata Śrī Śrīmad A. C. Bhaktivedanta Swami Prabhupāda, our beloved spiritual master. Our present publication is a humble attempt by his servants to complete his most cherished work of *Śrīmad-Bhāgavatam*. Just as one may worship the holy Ganges River by offering Ganges water unto the Ganges, similarly, in our attempt to serve our spiritual master, we are offering to him that which he has given to us.

Śrīla Prabhupāda came to America in 1965, at a critical moment in the history of America and the world in general. The story of Śrīla Prabhupāda's arrival and his specific impact on world civilization, and especially Western civilization, has been brilliantly documented by Satsvarūpa dāsa Goswami. From Satsvarūpa Goswami's authorized biography of Śrīla Prabhupāda, called *Śrīla Prabhupāda-līlāmṛta*, the reader can fully understand Śrīla Prabhupāda's purpose, desire and mission in presenting *Śrīmad-Bhāgavatam*. Further, in Śrīla Prabhupāda's own preface to the *Bhāgavatam* (reprinted as the foreword in this volume), he clearly states that this transcendental literature will provoke a cultural revolution in the world, and that is now underway. I do not wish to be redundant by repeating what Śrīla Prabhupāda has so eloquently stated in his preface, or that which has been so abundantly documented by Satsvarūpa Goswami in his authorized biography.

It is necessary to mention, however, that *Śrīmad-Bhāgavatam* is a completely transcendental, liberated sound vibration coming from the spiritual world. And, being absolute, it is not different from the Absolute Truth Himself, Lord Śrī Kṛṣṇa. By understanding *Śrīmad-Bhāgavatam,* consisting of twelve cantos, the reader acquires perfect knowledge, by which he or she may live peacefully and progressively on the earth, attending to all material necessities and simultaneously achieving supreme spiritual liberation. As we have worked to prepare this and other volumes of *Śrīmad-Bhāgavatam,* our intention has always been to faithfully serve the lotus feet of our spiritual master, carefully trying to translate and comment exactly as he would have, thus preserving the unity and spiritual potency of this edition of *Śrīmad-Bhāgavatam.* In other words, by our strictly following the disciplic succession, called in Sanskrit *guru-paramparā,* this edition of the *Bhāgavatam* will continue to be throughout its volumes a liberated work, free from material contamination and capable of elevating the reader to the kingdom of God.

Our method has been to faithfully follow the commentaries of previous *ācāryas* and exercise a careful selectivity of material based on the example and mood of Śrīla Prabhupāda. One may write transcendental literature only by the mercy of the Supreme Personality of Godhead, Śrī Kṛṣṇa, and the authorized, liberated spiritual masters coming in disciplic succession. Thus we humbly fall at the lotus feet of the previous *ācāryas,* offering special gratitude to the great commentators on the *Bhāgavatam,* namely Śrīla Śrīdhara Svāmī, Śrīla Jīva Gosvāmī, Śrīla Viśvanātha Cakravartī Ṭhākura and Śrīla Bhaktisiddhānta Sarasvatī Gosvāmī, the spiritual master of Śrīla Prabhupāda. We also offer our obeisances at the lotus feet of Śrīla Vīrarāghavācārya, Śrīla Vijayadhvaja Ṭhākura and Śrīla Vaṁśīdhara Ṭhākura, whose commentaries have also helped in this work. Additionally, we offer our humble obeisances at the lotus feet of the great *ācārya* Śrīla Madhva, who has made innumerable learned comments on *Śrīmad-Bhāgavatam.* We further offer our humble obeisances at the lotus feet of the Supreme Personality of Godhead, Śrī Kṛṣṇa Caitanya Mahāprabhu, and to all of His eternally liberated followers, headed by Śrīla

Nityānanda Prabhu, Advaita Prabhu, Gadādhara Prabhu, Śrīvāsa Ṭhākura and the six Gosvāmīs, namely Śrīla Rūpa Gosvāmī, Śrīla Sanātana Gosvāmī, Śrīla Raghunātha dāsa Gosvāmī, Śrīla Raghunātha Bhaṭṭa Gosvāmī, Śrīla Jīva Gosvāmī and Śrīla Gopāla Bhaṭṭa Gosvāmī. Finally we offer our most respectful obeisances at the lotus feet of the Absolute Truth, Śrī Śrī Rādhā and Kṛṣṇa, and humbly beg for Their mercy so that this great work of *Śrīmad-Bhāgavatam* can be quickly finished. *Śrīmad-Bhāgavatam* is undoubtedly the most important book in the universe, and the sincere readers of *Śrīmad-Bhāgavatam* will undoubtedly achieve the highest perfection of life, Kṛṣṇa consciousness.

In conclusion, I again remind the reader that *Śrīmad-Bhāgavatam* is the great work of His Divine Grace A. C. Bhaktivedanta Swami Prabhupāda, and that the present volume is the humble attempt of his devoted servants.

Hare Kṛṣṇa

Hridayananda dāsa Goswami

Foreword

We must know the present need of human society. And what is that need? Human society is no longer bounded by geographical limits to particular countries or communities. Human society is broader than in the Middle Ages, and the world tendency is toward one state or one human society. The ideals of spiritual communism, according to *Śrīmad-Bhāgavatam,* are based more or less on the oneness of the entire human society, nay, of the entire energy of living beings. The need is felt by great thinkers to make this a successful ideology. *Śrīmad-Bhāgavatam* will fill this need in human society. It begins, therefore, with an aphorism of Vedānta philosophy, *janmādy asya yataḥ,* to establish the ideal of a common cause.

Human society, at the present moment, is not in the darkness of oblivion. It has made rapid progress in the fields of material comforts, education and economic development throughout the entire world. But there is a pinprick somewhere in the social body at large, and therefore there are large-scale quarrels, even over less important issues. There is need of a clue as to how humanity can become one in peace, friendship and prosperity with a common cause. *Śrīmad-Bhāgavatam* will fill this need, for it is a cultural presentation for the respiritualization of the entire human society.

Śrīmad-Bhāgavatam should be introduced also in the schools and colleges, for it is recommended by the great student-devotee Prahlāda Mahārāja in order to change the demoniac face of society:

kaumāra ācaret prājño
dharmān bhāgavatān iha
durlabhaṁ mānuṣaṁ janma
tad apy adhruvam artha-dam
(*Bhāg.* 7.6.1)

Disparity in human society is due to lack of principles in a godless civilization. There is God, or the Almighty One, from whom everything emanates, by whom everything is maintained and in whom everything is merged to rest. Material science has tried to find the ultimate source of creation very insufficiently, but it is a fact that there is one ultimate source of everything that be. This ultimate source is explained rationally and authoritatively in the beautiful *Bhāgavatam,* or *Śrīmad-Bhāgavatam.*

Śrīmad-Bhāgavatam is the transcendental science not only for knowing the ultimate source of everything but also for knowing our relation with Him and our duty toward perfection of the human society on the basis of this perfect knowledge. It is powerful reading matter in the Sanskrit language, and it is now rendered into English elaborately so that simply by a careful reading one will know God perfectly well, so much so that the reader will be sufficiently educated to defend himself from the onslaught of atheists. Over and above this, the reader will be able to convert others to accepting God as a concrete principle.

Śrīmad-Bhāgavatam begins with the definition of the ultimate source. It is a bona fide commentary on the *Vedānta-sūtra* by the same author, Śrīla Vyāsadeva, and gradually it develops into nine cantos up to the highest state of God realization. The only qualification one needs to study this great book of transcendental knowledge is to proceed step by step cautiously and not jump forward haphazardly, as with an ordinary book. It should be gone through chapter by chapter, one after another. The reading matter is so arranged with the original Sanskrit text, its roman transliteration, synonyms, translation and purports so that one is sure to become a God-realized soul at the end of finishing the first nine cantos.

The Tenth Canto is distinct from the first nine cantos because it deals directly with the transcendental activities of the Personality of Godhead, Śrī Kṛṣṇa. One will be unable to capture the effects of the Tenth Canto without going through the first nine cantos. The book is complete in twelve cantos, each independent, but it is good for all to read them in small installments one after another.

I must admit my frailties in presenting *Śrīmad-Bhāgavatam,* but still I am hopeful of its good reception by the thinkers and leaders of society on the strength of the following statement of *Śrīmad-Bhāgavatam* (1.5.11):

tad-vāg-visargo janatāgha-viplavo
yasmin prati-ślokam abaddhavaty api
nāmāny anantasya yaśo 'ṅkitāni yat
śṛṇvanti gāyanti gṛṇanti sādhavaḥ

"On the other hand, that literature which is full of descriptions of the transcendental glories of the name, fame, forms, pastimes, etc., of the unlimited Supreme Lord is a different creation, full of transcendental words directed toward bringing about a revolution in the impious lives of this world's misdirected civilization. Such transcendental literatures, even though imperfectly composed, are heard, sung and accepted by purified men who are thoroughly honest."

Oṁ tat sat

A. C. Bhaktivedanta Swami

Introduction

"This *Bhāgavata Purāṇa* is as brilliant as the sun, and it has arisen just after the departure of Lord Kṛṣṇa to His own abode, accompanied by religion, knowledge, etc. Persons who have lost their vision due to the dense darkness of ignorance in the age of Kali shall get light from this *Purāṇa.*" (*Śrīmad-Bhāgavatam* 1.3.43)

The timeless wisdom of India is expressed in the *Vedas,* ancient Sanskrit texts that touch upon all fields of human knowledge. Originally preserved through oral tradition, the *Vedas* were first put into writing five thousand years ago by Śrīla Vyāsadeva, "the literary incarnation of God." After compiling the *Vedas,* Vyāsadeva set forth their essence in the aphorisms known as *Vedānta-sūtras. Śrīmad-Bhāgavatam* (*Bhāgavata Purāṇa*) is Vyāsadeva's commentary on his own *Vedānta-sūtras.* It was written in the maturity of his spiritual life under the direction of Nārada Muni, his spiritual master. Referred to as "the ripened fruit of the tree of Vedic literature," *Śrīmad-Bhāgavatam* is the most complete and authoritative exposition of Vedic knowledge.

After compiling the *Bhāgavatam,* Vyāsa imparted the synopsis of it to his son, the sage Śukadeva Gosvāmī. Śukadeva Gosvāmī subsequently recited the entire *Bhāgavatam* to Mahārāja Parīkṣit in an assembly of learned saints on the bank of the Ganges at Hastināpura (now Delhi). Mahārāja Parīkṣit was the emperor of the world and was a great *rājarṣi* (saintly king). Having received a warning that he would die within a week, he renounced his entire kingdom and retired to the bank of the Ganges to fast until death and receive spiritual enlightenment. The *Bhāgavatam* begins with Emperor Parīkṣit's sober inquiry to Śukadeva Gosvāmī: "You are the spiritual master of great saints and devotees. I am therefore begging you to show the way of perfection for all persons, and especially for one who is about to die. Please let me know what a man should hear, chant, remember and worship, and also what he should not do. Please explain all this to me."

Śukadeva Gosvāmī's answer to this question, and numerous other questions posed by Mahārāja Parīkṣit, concerning everything from the nature of the self to the origin of the universe, held the assembled sages in rapt attention continuously for the seven days leading up to the king's death. The sage Sūta Gosvāmī, who was present in that assembly when Śukadeva Gosvāmī first recited *Śrīmad-Bhāgavatam,* later repeated the *Bhāgavatam* before a gathering of sages in the forest of Naimiṣāraṇya. Those sages, concerned about the spiritual welfare of the people in general, had gathered to perform a long, continuous chain of sacrifices to counteract the degrading influence of the incipient age of Kali. In response to the sages' request that he speak the essence of Vedic wisdom, Sūta Gosvāmī repeated from memory the entire eighteen thousand verses of *Śrīmad-Bhāgavatam,* as spoken by Śukadeva Gosvāmī to Mahārāja Parīkṣit.

The reader of *Śrīmad-Bhāgavatam* hears Sūta Gosvāmī relate the questions of Mahārāja Parīkṣit and the answers of Śukadeva Gosvāmī. Also, Sūta Gosvāmī sometimes responds directly to questions put by Śaunaka Ṛṣi, the spokesman for the sages gathered at Naimiṣāraṇya. One therefore simultaneously hears two dialogues: one between Mahārāja Parīkṣit and Śukadeva Gosvāmī on the bank of the Ganges, and another between Sūta Gosvāmī and the sages at Naimiṣāraṇya forest, headed by Śaunaka Ṛṣi. Furthermore, while instructing King Parīkṣit, Śukadeva Gosvāmī often relates historical episodes and gives accounts of lengthy philosophical discussions between such great souls as Nārada Muni and Vasudeva. With this understanding of the history of the *Bhāgavatam,* the reader will easily be able to follow its intermingling of dialogues and events from various sources. Since philosophical wisdom, not chronological order, is most important in the text, one need only be attentive to the subject matter of *Śrīmad-Bhāgavatam* to fully appreciate its profound message.

The translators of this edition compare the *Bhāgavatam* to sugar candy—wherever you taste it, you will find it equally sweet and relishable. Therefore, to taste the sweetness of the *Bhāgavatam,* one may begin by reading any of its volumes. After such an introductory taste, however, the serious reader is best advised to go back to the First Canto and then proceed through the *Bhāgavatam,* canto after canto, in its natural order.

This edition of the *Bhāgavatam* is the first complete English translation of the important text with an elaborate commentary, and it is the first widely available to the English-speaking public. The first twelve volumes (Canto One through Part One of Canto Ten) are the product of the scholarly and devotional effort of His Divine Grace A. C. Bhaktivedanta

His Divine Grace
A. C. Bhaktivedanta Swami Prabhupāda
Founder-Ācārya of the International Society for Krishna Consciousness

PLATE ONE: Śrīmatī Rādhārāṇī became mad with ecstasy while meditating on Her previous association with Kṛṣṇa, and thus when She saw a honeybee She imagined it to be a messenger sent by Her beloved. (*p. 86*)

PLATE TWO: Overwhelmed with the sentiments of love in separation from Kṛṣṇa, Śrīmatī Rādhārāṇī remembered the many intimate moments She had shared with Him in the groves of Vṛndāvana. (*pp. 88-104*)

PLATE THREE: Calling forward the maiden Trivakrā, who was anxious and shy at the prospect of intimacies with Kṛṣṇa, the Lord pulled her by her bangled hand onto the bed. (*pp. 148–49*)

PLATE FOUR: As Lord Kṛṣṇa looked on from a secluded corner of the cave, Mucukunda awoke and angrily cast his glance at Kālayavana, causing his body to burst into flames within a single moment. (*p. 244*)

PLATE FIVE: Jarāsandha having set Pravarṣaṇa Mountain ablaze, Kṛṣṇa and Balarāma jumped off the peak and fell ninety miles to the ground. (*p. 292*)

PLATE SIX: Queen Rukmiṇī felt extremely saddened when Lord Kṛṣṇa teasingly told her, "I am always satisfied within Myself, and thus I care nothing for wives, children and wealth. Why don't you search out a suitable husband?" (*p. 582*)

PLATE SEVEN: Rukmiṇī appeared as enchanting as the Lord's illusory potency. As the assembled kings gazed upon her beauty, she smiled sweetly, her jasmine-bud teeth reflecting the glow of her *bimba*-red lips. Stupefied at the sight of her extraordinary beauty, the kings dropped their weapons and

fell unconscious to the ground from their elephants, chariots and horses. Slowly Rukmiṇī walked forward, expecting the arrival of Kṛṣṇa at any moment. Suddenly she saw Him, and then, while His enemies looked on, the Lord lifted the princess onto His chariot. (*p. 352*)

PLATE EIGHT: To negate the offense he had committed by refusing to give the Syamantaka jewel to King Ugrasena when Kṛṣṇa had asked him to do so, Satrājit presented the Lord with both the jewel and his daughter, Satyabhāmā. (*p. 652*)

PLATE NINE: Once, when Śiva was dancing his *tāṇḍava-nṛtya*, Bāṇāsura satisfied the lord by playing a musical accompaniment with his one thousand arms. (*p. 652*)

PLATE TEN: Nagnajit, the very pious King of Kauśalya, had a lovely daughter named Nāgnajitī. A suitor could win her hand only by subduing seven sharp-horned, vicious bulls. Lord Kṛṣṇa desired to wed Nāgnajitī; so he went to Kauśalya and asked King Nagnajit for her hand. Upon hearing the

conditions He had to meet, the Lord tightened His clothing, expanded Himself into seven forms and easily subdued the bulls, breaking their pride and strength. Then the Lord pulled them with ropes just as a child playfully pulls wooden toy bulls. (*pp. 514, 522-23*)

PLATE ELEVEN: When Lord Balarāma began dragging the river Yamunā with His plow, the river-goddess Kālindī became frightened. Coming before the Lord, she prayed for mercy. (*pp. 769-71*)

PLATE TWELVE: Lord Balarāma angrily dug up Hastināpura with the tip of His plow and began to drag it, intending to cast the entire city into the Ganges. (*p. 854*)

PLATE THIRTEEN: When Lord Kṛṣṇa noticed that Nārada Muni had entered His palace, the Lord rose at once, bowed His head at Nārada's feet and had the sage sit in His own seat. (*p. 874*)

Swami Prabhupāda, the founder-*ācārya* of the International Society for Krishna Consciousness and the world's most distinguished teacher of Indian religious and philosophical thought.

Śrīla Prabhupāda began his *Śrīmad-Bhāgavatam* in mid-1962 in Vṛndavana, India, the land most sacred to Lord Kṛṣṇa. With no assistants and limited funds, but with an abundance of devotion and determination, he was able to publish the First Canto (then in three volumes) by early 1965. After coming to the United States later that year, Śrīla Prabhupāda continued his commentated translation of the *Bhāgavatam,* and over the next twelve years, while developing his growing Kṛṣṇa consciousness movement and traveling incessantly, he produced twenty-seven more volumes. These were all edited, illustrated, typeset, proofread and indexed by his disciples, members of the Bhaktivedanta Book Trust (BBT). Throughout all of these volumes (totaling twelve in the present edition), Śrīla Prabhupāda's pure devotion to Lord Kṛṣṇa, his consummate Sanskrit scholarship and his intimate familiarity with Vedic culture and thought, and with modern life, combine to reveal to the Western reader a magnificent exposition of this important classic.

After Śrīla Prabhupāda's departure from this world in 1977, his monumental work of translating and commenting on *Śrīmad-Bhāgavatam* was continued by his disciples, headed by Hridayānanda dāsa Goswami, Gopīparāṇadhana dāsa Adhikārī and Draviḍa dāsa Brahmacārī—all seasoned BBT workers. Relying on the same Sanskrit editions of *Śrīmad-Bhāgavatam* that Śrīla Prabhupāda had used, Hridayānanda dāsa Goswami and Gopīparāṇadhana dāsa translated the Sanskrit text and added commentary. Then they turned over the manuscript to Draviḍa dāsa for final editing and production. In this way the concluding six volumes were published.

Readers will find this work of value for many reasons. For those interested in the classical roots of Indian civilization, it serves as a vast detailed reservoir of information on virtually every one of its aspects. For students of comparative philosophy and religion, the *Bhāgavatam* offers a penetrating view into the meaning of India's profound spiritual heritage. To sociologists and anthropologists, the *Bhāgavatam* reveals the practical workings of a peaceful, prosperous and scientifically organized Vedic culture, whose institutions were integrated on the basis of a highly developed spiritual world view. Students of literature will discover the *Bhāgavatam* to be a masterpiece of majestic poetry. For students of psychology, the text provides important perspectives on the nature of consciousness, human behavior and the philosophical study of identity. Finally, to those seeking spiritual insight, the *Bhāgavatam* offers simple and practical guidance for attainment of the highest self-knowledge and realization of the Absolute Truth. The entire eighteen-volume text, presented by the Bhaktivedanta Book Trust, promises to occupy a significant place in the intellectual, cultural and spiritual life of modern man for a long time to come.

—The Publishers

CHAPTER FORTY-FIVE

Kṛṣṇa Rescues His Teacher's Son

This chapter describes how Lord Kṛṣṇa consoled Devakī, Vasudeva and Nanda Mahārāja and installed Ugrasena as king. It also relates how Kṛṣṇa and Balarāma completed Their education, retrieved the dead son of Their *guru* and then returned home.

Noting that His parents—Vasudeva and Devakī—had realized His true position as God, Śrī Kṛṣṇa expanded His Yogamāyā to again make them think of Him as their dear child. Then, with Lord Balarāma, Kṛṣṇa approached them and said how unhappy He was that He and they had been unable to enjoy the mutual satisfaction of parents and children who live together. Then He stated, "Even in a lifetime of one hundred years, no son can ever repay the debt he owes his parents, from whom he receives his very body. Any capable son who fails to support his parents will be forced, in the hereafter, to eat his own flesh. Indeed, any person who does not maintain and nourish those under his care—children, wife, spiritual masters, *brāhmaṇas,* elderly parents and so on—is simply a living corpse. It was out of fear of Kaṁsa that We could not serve you, so now please forgive Us." Vasudeva and Devakī, overcome with emotion upon hearing these words of Śrī Kṛṣṇa's, embraced their two sons and in ecstasy shed a torrent of tears.

Having thus satisfied His mother and father, Lord Kṛṣṇa offered Kaṁsa's kingdom to His maternal grandfather, Ugrasena, and then arranged for all His family members who had fled in fear of Kaṁsa to return to their homes. Protected by the mighty arms of Kṛṣṇa and Balarāma, the Yādavas began to enjoy supreme bliss.

Kṛṣṇa and Balarāma next approached Nanda Mahārāja and praised him for having cared so lovingly for Them, another's sons. Kṛṣṇa then said to Nanda, "Dear Father, please return to Vraja. Knowing how much you and Our other relatives are suffering in separation from Us, Balarāma and I will come to see you as soon as We have satisfied your friends here in Mathurā." Kṛṣṇa then worshiped Nanda with various offerings, and Nanda felt overwhelmed with love for his sons. After tearfully embracing

Kṛṣṇa and Balarāma, he took the cowherd men and departed for Vraja.

Next Vasudeva had his priests perform his sons' ritual of second birth, brahminical initiation. Kṛṣṇa and Balarāma then went to Garga Muni to take the vow of *brahmacarya,* celibacy. Afterward, Kṛṣṇa and Balarāma, though omniscient, desired to reside at the school of a spiritual master, and thus They went to live with Sāndīpani Muni at Avantīpura.

To teach the proper way to respect one's *guru,* Kṛṣṇa and Balarāma served Their spiritual master with great devotion, as They would a Deity of the Supreme Lord Himself. Sāndīpani Muni, pleased by Their service, imparted to Them detailed knowledge of all the *Vedas,* together with their six corollaries and the *Upaniṣads.* Kṛṣṇa and Balarāma needed to hear each subject explained only once to assimilate it completely, and thus in sixty-four days They learned the sixty-four traditional arts.

Before taking leave of Their *guru,* the two Lords offered Sāndīpani Muni any gift he desired. The wise Sāndīpani, seeing Their amazing prowess, requested that They bring back his son, who had died in the ocean at Prabhāsa.

Kṛṣṇa and Balarāma mounted a chariot and went to Prabhāsa, where They approached the shore and worshiped the presiding deity of the ocean. Kṛṣṇa asked the ocean to return His spiritual master's son, and the lord of the ocean replied that a demon dwelling within the ocean named Pañcajana had taken the boy away. Hearing this, Śrī Kṛṣṇa entered the ocean, killed that demon and took the shell that had grown from his body. But when Kṛṣṇa did not find His *guru's* son within the demon's belly, He went to the planet of Yamarāja, the lord of death. Yamarāja came forward when he heard Kṛṣṇa blow the Pāñcajanya conchshell and devotedly worshiped Him. Lord Kṛṣṇa then asked Yamarāja for Sāndīpani Muni's son, and Yamarāja immediately gave him to the two Lords.

Kṛṣṇa and Balarāma then returned to Their spiritual master and presented him with his son, requesting him to choose yet another favor. But Sāndīpani Muni replied that by having obtained disciples such as Them, all his desires were fulfilled. He thus instructed Them to return home.

Kṛṣṇa and Balarāma traveled to Their home by chariot, and upon Their arrival all the citizens became unlimitedly ecstatic to see Them, just like persons who have regained a lost treasure.

TEXT 1

श्रीशुक उवाच
पितरावुपलब्धार्थौ विदित्वा पुरुषोत्तमः ।
मा भूदिति निजां मायां ततान जनमोहिनीम् ॥१॥

śrī-śuka uvāca
pitarāv upalabdhārthau
viditvā puruṣottamaḥ
mā bhūd iti nijāṁ māyāṁ
tatāna jana-mohinīm

śrī-śukaḥ uvāca—Śukadeva Gosvāmī said; *pitarau*—His parents; *upalabdha*—having realized; *arthau*—the idea (of His opulent position as God); *viditvā*—knowing; *puruṣa-uttamaḥ*—the Supreme Personality; *mā bhūt iti*—"this should not be"; *nijām*—His personal; *māyām*—illusory potency; *tatāna*—He expanded; *jana*—His devotees; *mohinīm*—which bewilders.

TRANSLATION

Śukadeva Gosvāmī said: Understanding that His parents were becoming aware of His transcendental opulences, the Supreme Personality of Godhead thought that this should not be allowed to happen. Thus He expanded His Yogamāyā, which bewilders His devotees.

PURPORT

If Vasudeva and Devakī would have seen Kṛṣṇa as almighty God, their intense love for Him as their son would have been spoiled. Lord Kṛṣṇa did not want this. Rather, the Lord wanted to enjoy with them the ecstatic love of *vātsalya-rasa,* the relationship between parents and children. As Śrīla Prabhupāda often pointed out, although we normally think of God as the supreme father, in Kṛṣṇa consciousness we can enter into the Lord's pastimes and play the part of His parents, thus intensifying our love for Him.

Śrīla Viśvanātha Cakravartī Ṭhākura points out that the word *jana* may be translated here as "devotees," as in the verse *dīyamānaṁ na gṛhṇanti vinā mat-sevanaṁ janāḥ* (*Bhāg.* 3.29.13). He further explains that *jana* may also be translated as "parents," since *jana* is derived from the verb *jan*, which in the causative form (*janayate*) means "to generate or to give birth to." In this sense of the word (as in *jananī* or *janakau*), the term *jana-mohinī* indicates that the Lord was about to expand His internal illusory potency so that Vasudeva and Devakī would again love Him as their dear child.

TEXT 2

उवाच पितरावेत्य साग्रजः सात्वतर्षभः ।
प्रश्रयावनतः प्रीणन्नम्ब तातेति सादरम् ॥२॥

uvāca pitarāv etya
sāgrajaḥ sātvatarṣabhaḥ
praśrayāvanataḥ prīṇann
amba tāteti sādaram

uvāca—He said; *pitarau*—to His parents; *etya*—approaching them; *sa*—together with; *agra-jaḥ*—His elder brother, Lord Balarāma; *sātvata*—of the Sātvata dynasty; *ṛṣabhaḥ*—the greatest hero; *praśraya*—with humility; *avanataḥ*—bowing down; *prīṇan*—gratifying them; *amba tāta iti*—"My dear mother, My dear father"; *sa-ādaram*—respectfully.

TRANSLATION

Lord Kṛṣṇa, the greatest of the Sātvatas, approached His parents with His elder brother. Humbly bowing His head and gratifying them by respectfully addressing them as "My dear mother" and "My dear father," Kṛṣṇa spoke as follows.

TEXT 3

नास्मत्तो युवयोस्तात नित्योत्कण्ठितयोरपि ।
बाल्यपौगण्डकैशोराः पुत्राभ्यामभवन् क्वचित् ॥३॥

nāsmatto yuvayos tāta
nityotkaṇṭhitayor api
bālya-paugaṇḍa-kaiśorāḥ
putrābhyām abhavan kvacit

na—not; *asmattaḥ*—because of Us; *yuvayoḥ*—for you two; *tāta*—O dear father; *nitya*—always; *utkaṇṭhitayoḥ*—who have been in anxiety; *api*—indeed; *bālya*—(the pleasures of) the toddler age; *paugaṇḍa*—boyhood; *kaiśorāḥ*—and youth; *putrābhyām*—because of your two sons; *abhavan*—there were; *kvacit*—at all.

TRANSLATION

[Lord Kṛṣṇa said:] Dear Father, because of Us, your two sons, you and mother Devakī always remained in anxiety and could never enjoy Our childhood, boyhood or youth.

PURPORT

Śrīla Viśvanātha Cakravartī discusses this verse as follows: "One may object that at this point Lord Kṛṣṇa had not actually passed the *kaiśora* stage [age ten to fifteen], since the women of Mathurā had stated, *kva cāti-sukumārāṅgau kiśorau nāpta-yauvanau:* 'Kṛṣṇa and Balarāma have very tender limbs, being still at the *kiśora* stage, not having reached adolescence.' (*Bhāg.* 10.44.8) The definition of the different stages of growing up is given as follows:

kaumāraṁ pañcamābdāntaṁ
paugaṇḍaṁ daśamāvadhi
kaiśoram ā-pañcadaśād
yauvanaṁ tu tataḥ param

'The *kaumāra* stage lasts until the age of five, *paugaṇḍa* up to age ten and *kaiśora* to age fifteen. From then on, one is known as *yauvana*.' According to this statement, the *kaiśora* period ends at the age of fifteen. Kṛṣṇa was only eleven years old when He killed Kaṁsa, according to Uddhava's words: *ekādaśa-samās tatra gūḍhārciḥ sa-balo 'vasat.* 'Like a covered flame, Lord Kṛṣṇa remained there incognito with Balarāma for eleven years.' (*Bhāg.* 3.2.26) And since Kṛṣṇa and Balarāma never took brahminical initiation in Vraja-bhūmi, it was at the time [of Their going to Mathurā] that Their *kaiśora* stage began rather than ended.

"This objection to Lord Kṛṣṇa's statement in the present verse—that His parents could not enjoy His *kaiśora* stage—is based on ordinary measurement of age. Yet we should consider the following statement [from the *Bhāgavatam* (10.8.26)]:

kālenālpena rājarṣe
rāmaḥ kṛṣṇaś ca go-vraje
aghṛṣṭa-jānubhiḥ padbhir
vicakramatur añjasā

'O King Parīkṣit, within a short time Rāma and Kṛṣṇa began to walk very easily in Gokula on Their legs, by Their own strength, without the need to crawl.' Sometimes we see that the son of a king, even while in his *paugaṇḍa* stage of life, undergoes exceptional physical growth and exhibits activities appropriate to a *kaiśora*. Then what to speak of Lord Kṛṣṇa, whose exceptional growth is established in the *Vaiṣṇava-toṣaṇī, Bhakti-rasāmṛta-sindhu, Ānanda-vṛndāvana-campū* and other works?

"The three years and four months that Lord Kṛṣṇa stayed in Mahāvana were the equivalent of five years for an ordinary child, and thus in that period He completed His *kaumāra* stage of childhood. The period from then to the age of six years and eight months, during which He lived in Vṛndāvana, constitutes His *paugaṇḍa* stage. And the period from the age of six years and eight months through His tenth year, during which time He lived in Nandīśvara [Nandagrāma], constitutes His *kaiśora* stage. Then, at the age of ten years and seven months, on the eleventh lunar day of the dark fortnight of the month of Caitra, He went to Mathurā, and on the fourteenth day thereafter He killed Kaṁsa. Thus He completed His *kaiśora* period at age ten, and He eternally remains at that age. In other words, we should understand that from this point on the Lord remains forever a *kiśora*."

Thus Śrīla Viśvanātha Cakravartī analyzes the intricacies of this verse.

TEXT 4

न लब्धो दैवहतयोर्वासो नौ भवदन्तिके ।
यां बालाः पितृगेहस्था विन्दन्ते लालिता मुदम् ॥४॥

na labdho daiva-hatayor
vāso nau bhavad-antike
yāṁ bālāḥ pitṛ-geha-sthā
vindante lālitā mudam

na—not; *labdhaḥ*—obtained; *daiva*—by fate; *hatayoḥ*—who have been deprived; *vāsaḥ*—residence; *nau*—by Us; *bhavat-antike*—in your presence; *yām*—which; *bālāḥ*—children; *pitṛ*—of their parents; *geha*—in the home; *sthāḥ*—staying; *vindante*—experience; *lālitāḥ*—pampered; *mudam*—happiness.

TRANSLATION

Deprived by fate, We could not live with you and enjoy the pampered happiness most children enjoy in their parents' home.

PURPORT

Here Lord Kṛṣṇa points out that not only did His parents suffer in separation from Him and Balarāma, but the two boys also suffered in separation from Their parents.

TEXT 5

सर्वार्थसम्भवो देहो जनितः पोषितो यतः ।
न तयोर्याति निर्वेशं पित्रोर्मर्त्यः शतायुषा ॥५॥

sarvārtha-sambhavo deho
janitaḥ poṣito yataḥ
na tayor yāti nirveśaṁ
pitror martyaḥ śatāyuṣā

sarva—of all; *artha*—goals of life; *sambhavaḥ*—the source; *dehaḥ*—one's body; *janitaḥ*—born; *poṣitaḥ*—maintained; *yataḥ*—from whom; *na*—not; *tayoḥ*—to them; *yāti*—one achieves; *nirveśam*—repayment of the debt; *pitroḥ*—to the parents; *martyaḥ*—a mortal; *śata*—of one hundred (years); *āyuṣā*—with a life span.

TRANSLATION

With one's body one can acquire all goals of life, and it is one's parents who give the body birth and sustenance. Therefore no mortal man can repay his debt to his parents, even if he serves them for a full lifetime of a hundred years.

PURPORT

Having stated, "Both you, Our parents, and We have suffered because of Our separation," Kṛṣṇa now states that His and Balarāma's religious principles have been spoiled by Their failure to satisfy Their parents.

TEXT 6

यस्तयोरात्मजः कल्प आत्मना च धनेन च ।
वृत्तिं न दद्यात्तं प्रेत्य स्वमांसं खादयन्ति हि ॥६॥

yas tayor ātmajaḥ kalpa
ātmanā ca dhanena ca
vṛttiṁ na dadyāt taṁ pretya
sva-māṁsaṁ khādayanti hi

yaḥ—who; *tayoḥ*—of them; *ātma-jaḥ*—a son; *kalpaḥ*—capable; *ātmanā*—with his physical resources; *ca*—and; *dhanena*—with his wealth; *ca*—also; *vṛttim*—a livelihood; *na dadyāt*—does not give; *tam*—him; *pretya*—after passing away; *sva*—his own; *māṁsam*—flesh; *khādayanti*—they make eat; *hi*—indeed.

TRANSLATION

A son who, though able to do so, fails to provide for his parents with his physical resources and wealth is forced after his death to eat his own flesh.

TEXT 7

मातरं पितरं वृद्धं भार्यां साध्वीं सुतं शिशुम् ।
गुरुं विप्रं प्रपन्नं च कल्पोऽबिभ्रच्छ्वसन्मृतः ॥७॥

mātaraṁ pitaraṁ vṛddhaṁ
bhāryāṁ sādhvīṁ sutaṁ śiśum
guruṁ vipraṁ prapannaṁ ca
kalpo 'bibhrac chvasan-mṛtaḥ

mātaram—one's mother; *pitaram*—and father; *vṛddham*—elderly; *bhāryām*—one's wife; *sādhvīm*—chaste; *sutam*—one's child; *śiśum*—very young; *gurum*—a spiritual master; *vipram*—a *brāhmaṇa; prapannam*—a person who has come to one for shelter; *ca*—and; *kalpaḥ*—able; *abibhrat*—not maintaining; *śvasan*—breathing; *mṛtaḥ*—dead.

TRANSLATION

A man who, though able to do so, fails to support his elderly parents, chaste wife, young child or spiritual master, or who neglects a *brāhmaṇa* or anyone who comes to him for shelter, is considered dead, though breathing.

TEXT 8

तन्नावकल्पयोः कंसान्नित्यमुद्विग्नचेतसोः ।
मोघमेते व्यतिक्रान्ता दिवसा वामनर्चतोः ॥८॥

tan nāv akalpayoḥ kaṁsān
nityam udvigna-cetasoḥ
mogham ete vyatikrāntā
divasā vām anarcatoḥ

tat—therefore; *nau*—of Us two; *akalpayoḥ*—who were unable; *kaṁsāt*—because of Kaṁsa; *nityam*—always; *udvigna*—disturbed; *cetasoḥ*—whose minds; *mogham*—uselessly; *ete*—these; *vyatikrāntāḥ*—spent; *divasāḥ*—days; *vām*—you; *anarcatoḥ*—not honoring.

TRANSLATION

Thus We have wasted all these days, unable as We were to properly honor you because Our minds were always disturbed by fear of Kaṁsa.

PURPORT

Lord Kṛṣṇa continues to bring Vasudeva and Devakī back to their normal parental feelings toward Him and Balarāma. An ordinary child would be afraid of a cruel, tyrannical king like Kaṁsa, and Lord Kṛṣṇa here plays the part of such a child, thus evoking the parental sympathy of Vasudeva and Devakī.

TEXT 9

तत्क्षन्तुमर्हथस्तात मातर्नौ परतन्त्रयोः ।
अकुर्वतोर्वां शुश्रूषां क्लिष्टयोर्दुर्हृदा भृशम् ॥९॥

tat kṣantum arhathas tāta
mātar nau para-tantrayoḥ
akurvator vāṁ śuśrūṣāṁ
kliṣṭayor durhṛdā bhṛśam

tat—that; *kṣantum*—forgive; *arhathaḥ*—you may please; *tāta*—O Father; *mātaḥ*—O Mother; *nau*—on the part of Us; *para-tantrayoḥ*—who are under the control of others; *akurvatoḥ*—not executing; *vām*—your; *śuśrūṣām*—service; *kliṣṭayoḥ*—caused pain; *durhṛdā*—by the hard-hearted (Kaṁsa); *bhṛśam*—greatly.

TRANSLATION

Dear Father and Mother, please forgive Us for not serving you. We are not independent and have been greatly frustrated by cruel Kaṁsa.

PURPORT

According to Sanskrit grammar, the words *para-tantrayoḥ* and *kliṣṭayoḥ* may also refer to Vasudeva and Devakī. Actually, Vasudeva and Devakī were under the control of Providence and were disturbed by the activities of Kaṁsa, whereas Śrī Kṛṣṇa is always the absolute Personality of Godhead.

TEXT 10

श्रीशुक उवाच
इति मायामनुष्यस्य हरेर्विश्वात्मनो गिरा ।
मोहितावंकमारोप्य परिष्वज्यापतुर्मुदम् ॥१०॥

śrī-śuka uvāca
iti māyā-manuṣyasya
harer viśvātmano girā
mohitāv aṅkam āropya
pariṣvajyāpatur mudam

śrī-śukaḥ uvāca—Śukadeva Gosvāmī said; *iti*—thus; *māyā*—by His internal illusory potency; *manuṣyasya*—of Him who appears as a human; *hareḥ*—Lord Śrī Hari; *viśva*—of the universe; *ātmanaḥ*—the Soul; *girā*—by the words; *mohitau*—bewildered; *aṅkam*—upon their laps; *āropya*—raising; *pariṣvajya*—embracing; *āpatuḥ*—they both experienced; *mudam*—joy.

TRANSLATION

Śukadeva Gosvāmī said: Thus beguiled by the words of Lord Hari, the Supreme Soul of the universe, who by His internal illusory potency appeared to be a human, His parents joyfully raised Him up on their laps and embraced Him.

TEXT 11

सिञ्चन्तावश्रुधाराभिः स्नेहपाशेन चावृतौ ।
न किञ्चिदूचतू राजन् बाष्पकण्ठौ विमोहितौ ॥११॥

siñcantāv aśru-dhārābhiḥ
sneha-pāśena cāvṛtau
na kiñcid ūcatū rājan
bāṣpa-kaṇṭhau vimohitau

siñcantau—sprinkling; *aśru*—of tears; *dhārābhiḥ*—with showers; *sneha*—of affection; *pāśena*—by the rope; *ca*—and; *āvṛtau*—enveloped; *na*—not; *kiñcit*—anything; *ūcatuḥ*—they spoke; *rājan*—O King (Parīkṣit); *bāṣpa*—(full of) tears; *kaṇṭhau*—whose throats; *vimohitau*—overwhelmed.

TRANSLATION

Pouring out a shower of tears upon the Lord, His parents, who were bound up by the rope of affection, could not speak. They were overwhelmed, O King, and their throats choked up with tears.

TEXT 12

एवमाश्वास्य पितरौ भगवान् देवकीसुतः ।
मातामहं तूग्रसेनं यदूनामकरोन्नृपम् ॥१२॥

evam āśvāsya pitarau
bhagavān devakī-sutaḥ
mātāmahaṁ tūgrasenaṁ
yadūnām akaron nṛpam

evam—in this way; *āśvāsya*—assuring; *pitarau*—His parents; *bhagavān*—the Supreme Lord; *devakī-sutaḥ*—the son of Devakī; *mātāmaham*—His maternal grandfather; *tu*—and; *ugrasenam*—Ugrasena; *yadūnām*—of the Yadus; *akarot*—He made; *nṛpam*—King.

TRANSLATION

Thus having comforted His mother and father, the Supreme Personality of Godhead, appearing as the son of Devakī, installed His maternal grandfather, Ugrasena, as King of the Yadus.

TEXT 13

आह चास्मान्महाराज प्रजाश्चाज्ञप्तुमर्हसि ।
ययातिशापाद्यदुभिर्नासितव्यं नृपासने ॥१३॥

āha cāsmān mahā-rāja
prajāś cājñaptum arhasi
yayāti-śāpād yadubhir
nāsitavyaṁ nṛpāsane

āha—He (Lord Kṛṣṇa) said; *ca*—and; *asmān*—Us; *mahā-rāja*—O great King; *prajāḥ*—your subjects; *ca*—also; *ājñaptum arhasi*—please command; *yayāti*—by the ancient King Yayāti; *śāpāt*—because of the curse; *yadubhiḥ*—the Yadus; *na āsitavyam*—should not sit; *nṛpa*—royal; *āsane*—on the throne.

TRANSLATION

The Lord told him: O mighty King, We are your subjects, so please command Us. Indeed, because of the curse of Yayāti, no Yadu may sit on the royal throne.

PURPORT

Ugrasena might have told the Lord, "My dear Lord, it is actually You who should sit on the throne." Anticipating this statement, Lord Kṛṣṇa told Ugrasena that because of Yayāti's ancient curse, princes in the Yadu dynasty could technically not sit on the royal throne, and therefore Kṛṣṇa and Balarāma were disqualified. Of course, Ugrasena also could be considered part of the Yadu dynasty, but by the order of the Lord he could sit on the royal throne. In conclusion, these were all pastimes the Supreme Lord enjoyed as He played the part of a human being.

TEXT 14

मयि भृत्य उपासीने भवतो विबुधादयः ।
बलिं हरन्त्यवनताः किमुतान्ये नराधिपाः ॥१४॥

mayi bhṛtya upāsīne
bhavato vibudhādayaḥ
baliṁ haranty avanatāḥ
kim utānye narādhipāḥ

mayi—when I; *bhṛtye*—as a servant; *upāsīne*—am present in attendance; *bhavataḥ*—to you; *vibudha*—the demigods; *ādayaḥ*—and so on; *balim*—tribute; *haranti*—will bring; *avanatāḥ*—bowed down in humility; *kim uta*—what then to speak of; *anye*—other; *nara*—of men; *adhipāḥ*—rulers.

TRANSLATION

Since I am present in your entourage as your personal attendant, all the demigods and other exalted personalities will come with heads bowed to offer you tribute. What, then, to speak of the rulers of men?

PURPORT

Lord Kṛṣṇa again assures Ugrasena that he should confidently take the throne.

TEXTS 15–16

सर्वान् स्वान् ज्ञातिसम्बन्धान् दिग्भ्यः कंसभयाकुलान् ।
यदुवृष्ण्यन्धकमधुदाशार्हकुकुरादिकान् ॥१५॥
सभाजितान् समाश्वास्य विदेशावासकर्शितान् ।
न्यवासयत्स्वगेहेषु वित्तैः सन्तर्प्य विश्वकृत् ॥१६॥

sarvān svān jñāti-sambandhān
digbhyaḥ kaṁsa-bhayākulān
yadu-vṛṣṇy-andhaka-madhu-
dāśārha-kukurādikān

sabhājitān samāśvāsya
videśāvāsa-karśitān
nyavāsayat sva-geheṣu
vittaiḥ santarpya viśva-kṛt

sarvān—all; *svān*—His; *jñāti*—close family members; *sambandhān*—and other relations; *digbhyaḥ*—from all directions; *kaṁsa-bhaya*—by fear of Kaṁsa; *ākulān*—disturbed; *yadu-vṛṣṇi-andhaka-madhu-dāśārha-*

kukura-ādikān—the Yadus, Vṛṣṇis, Andhakas, Madhus, Dāśārhas, Kukuras and so on; *sabhājitān*—shown honor; *samāśvāsya*—consoling them; *videśa*—in foreign regions; *āvāsa*—by living; *karśitān*—made weary; *nyavāsayat*—He settled; *sva*—in their own; *geheṣu*—homes; *vittaiḥ*—with valuable gifts; *santarpya*—gratifying; *viśva*—of the universe; *kṛt*—the maker.

TRANSLATION

The Lord then brought all His close family members and other relatives back from the various places to which they had fled in fear of Kaṁsa. He received the Yadus, Vṛṣṇis, Andhakas, Madhus, Dāśārhas, Kukuras and other clans with due honor, and He also consoled them, for they were weary of living in foreign lands. Then Lord Kṛṣṇa, the creator of the universe, resettled them in their homes and gratified them with valuable gifts.

TEXTS 17–18

कृष्णसंकर्षणभुजैर्गुप्ता लब्धमनोरथाः ।
गृहेषु रेमिरे सिद्धाः कृष्णरामगतज्वराः ॥१७॥
वीक्षन्तोऽहरहः प्रीता मुकुन्दवदनाम्बुजम् ।
नित्यं प्रमुदितं श्रीमत्सदयस्मितवीक्षणम् ॥१८॥

kṛṣṇa-saṅkarṣaṇa-bhujair
guptā labdha-manorathāḥ
gṛheṣu remire siddhāḥ
kṛṣṇa-rāma-gata-jvarāḥ

vīkṣanto 'har ahaḥ prītā
mukunda-vadanāmbujam
nityaṁ pramuditaṁ śrīmat-
sa-daya-smita-vīkṣaṇam

kṛṣṇa-saṅkarṣaṇa—of Kṛṣṇa and Balarāma; *bhujaiḥ*—by the arms; *guptāḥ*—protected; *labdha*—obtaining; *manaḥ-rathāḥ*—their desires; *gṛheṣu*—in their homes; *remire*—they enjoyed; *siddhāḥ*—perfectly fulfilled; *kṛṣṇa-rāma*—because of Kṛṣṇa and Balarāma; *gata*—ceased; *jvarāḥ*—the fever (of material life); *vīkṣantaḥ*—seeing; *ahaḥ ahaḥ*—day after day; *prītāḥ*—loving; *mukunda*—of Lord Kṛṣṇa; *vadana*—the face; *ambujam*—lotuslike; *nityam*—always; *pramuditam*—cheerful; *śrīmat*—beautiful; *sa-daya*—merciful; *smita*—smiling; *vīkṣaṇam*—with glances.

TRANSLATION

The members of these clans, protected by the arms of Lord Kṛṣṇa and Lord Saṅkarṣaṇa, felt that all their desires were fulfilled. Thus they enjoyed perfect happiness while living at home with their families. Because of the presence of Kṛṣṇa and Balarāma, they no longer suffered from the fever of material existence. Every day these loving devotees could see Mukunda's ever-cheerful lotus face, which was decorated with beautiful, merciful smiling glances.

TEXT 19

तत्र प्रवयसोऽप्यासन् युवानोऽतिबलौजसः ।
पिबन्तोऽक्षैर्मुकुन्दस्य मुखाम्बुजसुधां मुहुः ॥१९॥

tatra pravayaso 'py āsan
yuvāno 'ti-balaujasaḥ
pibanto 'kṣair mukundasya
mukhāmbuja-sudhāṁ muhuḥ

tatra—there (in Mathurā); *pravayasaḥ*—the most elderly; *api*—even; *āsan*—were; *yuvānaḥ*—youthful; *ati*—having abundant; *bala*—strength; *ojasaḥ*—and vitality; *pibantaḥ*—drinking; *akṣaiḥ*—with their eyes; *mukundasya*—of Lord Kṛṣṇa; *mukha-ambuja*—of the lotus face; *sudhām*—the nectar; *muhuḥ*—repeatedly.

TRANSLATION

Even the most elderly inhabitants of the city appeared youthful, full of strength and vitality, for with their eyes they constantly drank the elixir of Lord Mukunda's lotus face.

TEXT 20

अथ नन्दं समासाद्य भगवान् देवकीसुतः ।
संकर्षणश्च राजेन्द्र परिष्वज्येदमूचतुः ॥२०॥

atha nandaṁ samāsādya
bhagavān devakī-sutaḥ
saṅkarṣaṇaś ca rājendra
pariṣvajyedam ūcatuḥ

atha—then; *nandam*—Nanda Mahārāja; *samāsādya*—approaching; *bhagavān*—the Supreme Lord; *devakī-sutaḥ*—Kṛṣṇa, the son of Devakī; *saṅkarṣaṇaḥ*—Lord Balarāma; *ca*—and; *rāja-indra*—O exalted King (Parīkṣit); *pariṣvajya*—embracing him; *idam*—this; *ūcatuḥ*—They said.

TRANSLATION

Then, O exalted Parīkṣit, the Supreme Lord Kṛṣṇa, the son of Devakī, along with Lord Balarāma, approached Nanda Mahārāja. The two Lords embraced him and then addressed him as follows.

TEXT 21

पितर्युवाभ्यां स्निग्धाभ्यां पोषितौ लालितौ भृशम् ।
पित्रोरभ्यधिका प्रीतिरात्मजेष्वात्मनोऽपि हि ॥२१॥

pitar yuvābhyāṁ snigdhābhyāṁ
poṣitau lālitau bhṛśam
pitror abhyadhikā prītir
ātmajeṣv ātmano 'pi hi

pitaḥ—O Father; *yuvābhyām*—by you two; *snigdhābhyām*—affectionate; *poṣitau*—maintained; *lālitau*—coddled; *bhṛśam*—thoroughly; *pitroḥ*—for parents; *abhyadhikā*—greater; *prītiḥ*—love; *ātmajeṣu*—for their children; *ātmanaḥ*—than for themselves; *api*—even; *hi*—indeed.

TRANSLATION

[Kṛṣṇa and Balarāma said:] O Father, you and mother Yaśodā have affectionately maintained Us and cared for Us so much! Indeed, parents love their children more than their own lives.

TEXT 22

स पिता सा च जननी यौ पुष्णीतां स्वपुत्रवत् ।
शिशून् बन्धुभिरुत्सृष्टानकल्पैः पोषरक्षणे ॥२२॥

sa pitā sā ca jananī
yau puṣṇītāṁ sva-putra-vat
śiśūn bandhubhir utsṛṣṭān
akalpaiḥ poṣa-rakṣaṇe

saḥ—he; *pitā*—father; *sā*—she; *ca*—and; *jananī*—mother; *yau*—who; *puṣṇītām*—nourish; *sva*—their own; *putra*—sons; *vat*—like; *śiśūn*—children; *bandhubhiḥ*—by their family; *utsṛṣṭān*—abandoned; *akalpaiḥ*—who are unable; *poṣa*—to maintain; *rakṣaṇe*—and protect.

TRANSLATION

They are the real father and mother who care for, as they would their own sons, children abandoned by relatives unable to maintain and protect them.

TEXT 23

यात यूयं व्रजं तात वयं च स्नेहदुःखितान् ।
ज्ञातीन् वो द्रष्टुमेष्यामो विधाय सुहृदां सुखम् ॥२३॥

yāta yūyaṁ vrajaṁ tāta
vayaṁ ca sneha-duḥkhitān
jñātīn vo draṣṭum eṣyāmo
vidhāya suhṛdāṁ sukham

yata—please go; *yūyam*—all of you (cowherds); *vrajam*—to Vraja; *tāta*—My dear father; *vayam*—We; *ca*—and; *sneha*—due to loving affection; *duḥkhitān*—miserable; *jñātīn*—relatives; *vaḥ*—you; *draṣṭum*—to see; *eṣyāmaḥ*—will come; *vidhāya*—after bestowing; *suhṛdām*—to your loving friends; *sukham*—happiness.

TRANSLATION

Now you should all return to Vraja, dear Father. We shall come to see you, Our dear relatives who suffer in separation from Us, as soon as We have given some happiness to your well-wishing friends.

PURPORT

The Lord here indicates His desire to satisfy His dear devotees in Mathurā—Vasudeva, Devakī and other members of the Yadu dynasty—who for so long had been separated from Him during His stay in Vṛndāvana.

TEXT 24

एवं सान्त्वय्य भगवान्नन्दं सव्रजमच्युतः ।
वासोऽलंकारकुप्याद्यैरर्हयामास सादरम् ॥२४॥

evaṁ sāntvayya bhagavān
nandaṁ sa-vrajam acyutaḥ
vāso-'laṅkāra-kupyādyair
arhayām āsa sādaram

evam—in this manner; *sāntvayya*—consoling; *bhagavān*—the Supreme Personality of Godhead; *nandam*—King Nanda; *sa-vrajam*—together with the other men of Vraja; *acyutaḥ*—the infallible Lord; *vāsaḥ*—with clothing; *alaṅkāra*—jewelry; *kupya*—vessels made of metals other than gold or silver; *ādyaiḥ*—and so on; *arhayām āsa*—He honored them; *sa-ādaram*—respectfully.

TRANSLATION

Thus consoling Nanda Mahārāja and the other men of Vraja, the infallible Supreme Lord respectfully honored them with gifts of clothing, jewelry, household utensils and so on.

TEXT 25

इत्युक्तस्तौ परिष्वज्य नन्दः प्रणयविह्वलः ।
पूरयन्नश्रुभिर्नेत्रे सह गोपैर्व्रजं ययौ ॥२५॥

ity uktas tau pariṣvajya
nandaḥ praṇaya-vihvalaḥ
pūrayann aśrubhir netre
saha gopair vrajaṁ yayau

iti—thus; *uktaḥ*—addressed; *tau*—the two of Them; *pariṣvajya*—embracing; *nandaḥ*—Nanda Mahārāja; *praṇaya*—with affection; *vihvalaḥ*—overwhelmed; *pūrayan*—filling; *aśrubhiḥ*—with tears; *netre*—his eyes; *saha*—together with; *gopaiḥ*—the cowherds; *vrajam*—to Vraja; *yayau*—went.

TRANSLATION

Nanda Mahārāja was overwhelmed with affection upon hearing Kṛṣṇa's words, and his eyes brimmed with tears as he embraced the two Lords. Then he went back to Vraja with the cowherd men.

PURPORT

Śrīla Viśvanātha Cakravarti has written an extensive purport to this verse, elaborately analyzing this portion of Lord Kṛṣṇa's pastimes. Just as a man places his valuable gold within fire to reveal its purity, the Lord placed His most beloved devotees, the residents of Vṛndāvana, in the fire of separation from Him in order to manifest their supreme love. This is the essence of Ācārya Viśvanātha's comments.

TEXT 26

अथ शूरसुतो राजन् पुत्रयोः समकारयत् ।
पुरोधसा ब्राह्मणैश्च यथावद्द्विजसंस्कृतिम् ॥२६॥

atha śūra-suto rājan
putrayoḥ samakārayat
purodhasā brāhmaṇaiś ca
yathāvad dvija-saṁskṛtim

atha—then; *śūra-sutaḥ*—the son of Śūrasena (Vasudeva); *rājan*—O King (Parīkṣit); *putrayoḥ*—of his two sons; *samakārayat*—had performed; *purodhasā*—by a priest; *brāhmaṇaiḥ*—by *brāhmaṇas; ca*—and; *yathā-vat*—properly; *dvija-saṁskṛtim*—brahminical initiation.

TRANSLATION

My dear King, then Vasudeva, the son of Śūrasena, arranged for a priest and other *brāhmaṇas* to perform his two sons' second-birth initiation.

TEXT 27

तेभ्योऽदाद्दक्षिणा गावो रुक्ममालाः स्वलंकृताः ।
स्वलंकृतेभ्यः सम्पूज्य सवत्साः क्षौममालिनीः ॥२७॥

tebhyo 'dād dakṣiṇā gāvo
rukma-mālāḥ sv-alaṅkṛtāḥ
sv-alaṅkṛtebhyaḥ sampūjya
sa-vatsāḥ kṣauma-mālinīḥ

tebhyaḥ—to them (the *brāhmaṇas*); *adāt*—he gave; *dakṣiṇāḥ*—gifts in remuneration; *gāvaḥ*—cows; *rukma*—of gold; *mālāḥ*—with necklaces; *su*—well; *alaṅkṛtāḥ*—ornamented; *su-alaṅkṛtebhyaḥ*—to the well-ornamented (*brāhmaṇas*); *sampūjya*—worshiping them; *sa*—having; *vatsāḥ*—calves; *kṣauma*—of linen; *mālinīḥ*—wearing garlands.

TRANSLATION

Vasudeva honored these *brāhmaṇas* by worshiping them and giving them fine ornaments and well-ornamented cows with their calves. All these cows wore gold necklaces and linen wreaths.

TEXT 28

याः कृष्णरामजन्मर्क्षे मनोदत्ता महामतिः ।
ताश्चाददादनुस्मृत्य कंसेनाधर्मतो हृताः ॥२८॥

yāḥ kṛṣṇa-rāma-janmarkṣe
mano-dattā mahā-matiḥ
tāś cādadād anusmṛtya
kaṁsenādharmato hṛtāḥ

yāḥ—which (cows); *kṛṣṇa-rāma*—of Kṛṣṇa and Balarāma; *janma-ṛkṣe*—on the day of birth; *manaḥ*—in his mind; *dattāḥ*—given in charity; *mahā-matiḥ*—the magnanimous (Vasudeva); *tāḥ*—them; *ca*—and; *ādadāt*—he gave; *anusmṛtya*—remembering; *kaṁsena*—by Kaṁsa; *adharmataḥ*—impiously; *hṛtāḥ*—taken away.

TRANSLATION

The magnanimous Vasudeva then remembered the cows he had mentally given away on the occasion of Kṛṣṇa's and Balarāma's birth. Kaṁsa had stolen those cows, and Vasudeva now recovered them and gave them away in charity also.

PURPORT

At the time of Kṛṣṇa's appearance, Vasudeva had been imprisoned by Kaṁsa, who had stolen all his cows. Still, Vasudeva had been so jubilant at the birth of the Lord that he had mentally donated ten thousand of his cows to the *brāhmaṇas.*

Now, upon Kaṁsa's death, Vasudeva took back all his cows from the late King's herd and gave ten thousand of them, according to religious principles, to the worthy *brāhmaṇas.*

TEXT 29

ततश्च लब्धसंस्कारौ द्विजत्वं प्राप्य सुव्रतौ ।
गर्गाद्यदुकुलाचार्याद् गायत्रं व्रतमास्थितौ ॥२९॥

tataś ca labdha-saṁskārau
dvijatvaṁ prāpya su-vratau

gargād yadu-kulācāryād
gāyatraṁ vratam āsthitau

tataḥ—then; *ca*—and; *labdha*—having received; *saṁskārau*—initiation (Kṛṣṇa and Balarāma); *dvijatvam*—twice-born status; *prāpya*—attaining; *su-vratau*—sincere in Their vows; *gargāt*—from Garga Muni; *yadu-kula*—of the Yadu dynasty; *ācāryāt*—from the spiritual master; *gāyatram*—of celibacy; *vratam*—the vow; *āsthitau*—assumed.

TRANSLATION

After attaining twice-born status through initiation, the Lords, sincere in Their vows, took the further vow of celibacy from Garga Muni, the spiritual master of the Yadus.

PURPORT

Both Śrīdhara Svāmī and Viśvanātha Cakravartī Ṭhākura explain the term *gāyatraṁ vratam* as the vow of *brahmacarya,* or celibacy in student life. Kṛṣṇa and Balarāma were playing the part of perfect students on the path of self-realization. Of course, in the modern, degraded age, student life has become a wild, animalistic affair filled with illicit sex and drugs.

TEXTS 30–31

प्रभवौ सर्वविद्यानां सर्वज्ञौ जगदीश्वरौ ।
नान्यसिद्धामलं ज्ञानं गूहमानौ नरेहितैः ॥३०॥
अथो गुरुकुले वासमिच्छन्तावुपजग्मतुः ।
काश्यं सान्दीपनिं नाम ह्यवन्तिपुरवासिनम् ॥३१॥

prabhavau sarva-vidyānāṁ
sarva-jñau jagad-īśvarau
nānya-siddhāmalaṁ jñānaṁ
gūhamānau narehitaiḥ

atho guru-kule vāsam
icchantāv upajagmatuḥ
kāśyaṁ sāndīpaniṁ nāma
hy avanti-pura-vāsinam

prabhavau—They who were the origin; *sarva*—of all varieties; *vidyānām*—of knowledge; *sarva-jñau*—omniscient; *jagat-īśvarau*—the Lords of the universe; *na*—not; *anya*—from any other source; *siddha*—achieved; *amalam*—impeccable; *jñānam*—knowledge; *gūhamānau*—hiding; *nara*—humanlike; *īhitaiḥ*—by Their activities; *atha u*—then; *guru*—of the spiritual master; *kule*—in the school; *vāsam*—residence; *icchantau*—desiring; *upajagmatuḥ*—They approached; *kāśyam*—the native of Kāśi (Benares); *sāndīpanim nāma*—named Sāndīpani; *hi*—indeed; *avanti-pura*—in the city of Avantī (modern Ujjain); *vāsinam*—living.

TRANSLATION

Concealing Their innately perfect knowledge by Their humanlike activities, those two omniscient Lords of the universe, Themselves the origin of all branches of knowledge, next desired to reside at the school of a spiritual master. Thus They approached Sāndīpani Muni, a native of Kāśī living in the city of Avantī.

TEXT 32

यथोपसाद्य तौ दान्तौ गुरौ वृत्तिमनिन्दिताम् ।
ग्राहयन्तावुपेतौ स्म भक्त्या देवमिवादृतौ ॥३२॥

yathopasādya tau dāntau
gurau vṛttim aninditām
grāhayantāv upetau sma
bhaktyā devam ivādṛtau

yathā—fittingly; *upasādya*—obtaining; *tau*—Them; *dāntau*—who were self-controlled; *gurau*—to one's spiritual master; *vṛttim*—service; *aninditām*—irreproachable; *grāhayantau*—making others take to; *upetau*—approaching for service; *sma*—indeed; *bhaktyā*—with devotion; *devam*—the Supreme Lord; *iva*—as if; *ādṛtau*—respected (by the *guru*).

TRANSLATION

Sāndīpani thought very highly of these two self-controlled disciples, whom he had obtained so fortuitously. By serving him as

devotedly as one would serve the Supreme Lord Himself, They showed others an irreproachable example of how to worship the spiritual master.

TEXT 33

तयोर्द्विजवरस्तुष्टः शुद्धभावानुवृत्तिभिः ।
प्रोवाच वेदानखिलान् संगोपनिषदो गुरुः ॥३३॥

tayor dvija-varas tuṣṭaḥ
śuddha-bhāvānuvṛttibhiḥ
provāca vedān akhilān
saṅgopaniṣado guruḥ

tayoḥ—Their; *dvija-varaḥ*—the best of *brāhmaṇas* (Sāndīpani); *tuṣṭaḥ*—satisfied; *śuddha*—pure; *bhāva*—with love; *anuvṛttibhiḥ*—by the submissive acts; *provāca*—he spoke; *vedān*—the *Vedās; akhilān*—all; *sa*—together with; *aṅga*—the (six) corollary literatures; *upaniṣadaḥ*—and the *Upaniṣads; guruḥ*—the spiritual master.

TRANSLATION

That best of *brāhmaṇas,* the spiritual master Sāndīpani, was satisfied with Their submissive behavior, and thus he taught Them the entire *Vedas,* together with their six corollaries and the *Upaniṣads.*

TEXT 34

सरहस्यं धनुर्वेदं धर्मान् न्यायपथांस्तथा ।
तथा चान्वीक्षिकीं विद्यां राजनीतिं च षड्विधाम् ॥३४॥

sa-rahasyaṁ dhanur-vedaṁ
dharmān nyāya-pathāṁs tathā
tathā cānvīkṣikīṁ vidyāṁ
rāja-nītiṁ ca ṣaḍ-vidhām

sa-rahasyam—along with its confidential portion; *dhanuḥ-vedam*—the science of military weapons; *dharmān*—the doctrines of human law;

nyāya—of logic; *pathān*—the methods; *tathā*—also; *tathā ca*—and similarly; *ānvīkṣikīm*—of philosophical debate; *vidyām*—the branch of knowledge; *rāja-nītim*—political science; *ca*—and; *ṣaṭ-vidhām*—in six aspects.

TRANSLATION

He also taught Them the *Dhanur-veda,* with its most confidential secrets; the standard books of law; the methods of logical reasoning and philosophical debate; and the sixfold science of politics.

PURPORT

Śrīla Śrīdhara Svāmī explains that the confidential portion of the *Dhanur-veda,* military science, includes knowledge of the appropriate *mantras* and presiding deities of warfare. *Dharmān* refers to the *Manu-saṁhitā* and other standard lawbooks (*dharma-śāstras*). *Nyāya-pathān* refers to the doctrine of Karma-mīmāṁsā and other such theories. *Ānvīkṣikīm* is knowledge of the techniques of logical argument (*tarka*). The sixfold political science is quite pragmatic and includes (1) *sandhi,* making peace; (2) *vigraha,* war; (3) *yāna,* marching; (4) *āsana,* sitting tight; (5) *dvaidha,* dividing one's forces; and (6) *saṁśaya,* seeking the protection of a more powerful ruler.

TEXTS 35–36

सर्वं नरवरश्रेष्ठौ सर्वविद्याप्रवर्तकौ ।
सकृन्निगदमात्रेण तौ सञ्जगृहतुर्नृप ॥३५॥
अहोरात्रैश्चतुःषष्ट्या संयत्तौ तावतीः कलाः ।
गुरुदक्षिणयाचार्यं छन्दयामासतुर्नृप ॥३६॥

sarvaṁ nara-vara-śreṣṭhau
sarva-vidyā-pravartakau
sakṛn nigada-mātreṇa
tau sañjagṛhatur nṛpa

aho-rātraiś catuḥ-ṣaṣṭyā
saṁyattau tāvatīḥ kalāḥ
guru-dakṣiṇayācāryaṁ
chandayām āsatur nṛpa

sarvam—everything; *nara-vara*—of first-class men; *śreṣṭhau*—the best; *sarva*—of all; *vidyā*—branches of knowledge; *pravartakau*—the initiators; *sakṛt*—once; *nigada*—being related; *mātreṇa*—simply; *tau*—They; *sañjagṛhatuḥ*—fully assimilated; *nṛpa*—O King (Parīkṣit); *ahaḥ*—in days; *rātraiḥ*—and nights; *catuḥ-ṣaṣṭyā*—sixty-four; *saṁyattau*—fixed in concentration; *tāvatīḥ*—that many; *kalāḥ*—arts; *guru-dakṣiṇayā*—with the traditional gift for the spiritual master before one leaves him; *ācāryam*—Their teacher; *chandayām āsatuḥ*—They satisfied; *nṛpa*—O King.

TRANSLATION

O King, those best of persons, Kṛṣṇa and Balarāma, being Themselves the original promulgators of all varieties of knowledge, could immediately assimilate each and every subject after hearing it explained just once. Thus with fixed concentration They learned the sixty-four arts and skills in as many days and nights. Thereafter, O King, They satisfied Their spiritual master by offering him *guru-dakṣiṇā*.

PURPORT

The following list comprises the sixty-four subjects mastered by Lord Kṛṣṇa and Lord Balarāma in sixty-four days. Additional information may be found in Śrīla Prabhupāda's *Kṛṣṇa, the Supreme Personality of Godhead.*

The Lords learned (1) *gītam,* singing; (2) *vādyam,* playing on musical instruments; (3) *nṛtyam,* dancing; (4) *nāṭyam,* drama; (5) *ālekhyam,* painting; (6) *viśeṣaka-cchedyam,* painting the face and body with colored unguents and cosmetics; (7) *taṇḍula-kusuma-bali-vikārāḥ,* preparing auspicious designs on the floor with rice and flowers; (8) *puṣpāstaraṇam,* making a bed of flowers; (9) *daśana-vasanāṅga-rāgāḥ,* coloring one's teeth, clothes and limbs; (10) *maṇi-bhūmikā-karma,* inlaying a floor with jewels; (11) *śayyā-racanam,* covering a bed; (12) *udaka-vādyam,* ringing waterpots; (13) *udaka-ghātaḥ,* splashing with water; (14) *citra-yogāḥ,* mixing colors; (15) *mālya-grathana-vikalpāḥ,* preparing wreaths; (16) *śekharāpīḍa-yojanam,* setting a helmet on the head; (17) *nepathya-yogāḥ,* putting on apparel in a dressing room; (18) *karṇa-patra-bhaṅgāḥ,* decorating the earlobe; (19) *sugandha-yuktiḥ,* applying aromatics; (20) *bhūṣaṇa-yojanam,* decorating with jewelry; (21) *aindrajālam,* jugglery; (22) *kaucumāra-yogāḥ,* the art of disguise; (23) *hasta-lāghavam,* sleight of hand; (24) *citra-śākāpūpa-bhakṣya-vikāra-kriyāḥ,* preparing varieties of salad, bread, cake and other delicious food; (25) *pānaka-rasa-rāgāsava-yojanam,* preparing palatable drinks and tinging draughts with red color; (26) *sūcī-vāya-karma,* needlework and weaving; (27) *sūtra-krīḍā,* making puppets dance by manipulating thin threads; (28) *vīṇā-ḍamaruka-vādyāni,* playing on a lute and a small X-shaped drum; (29) *prahelikā,* making and solving riddles; (29a) *pratimālā,* capping verses, or reciting poems verse for verse as a trial of memory or skill; (30) *durvacaka-yogāḥ,* uttering statements difficult for others to answer; (31) *pustaka-vācanam,* reciting books; and (32) *nāṭikākhyāyikā-darśanam,* enacting short plays and writing anecdotes.

Kṛṣṇa and Balarāma also learned (33) *kāvya-samasyā-pūraṇam,* solving enigmatic verses; (34) *paṭṭikā-vetra-bāṇa-vikalpāḥ,* making a bow from a strip of cloth and a stick; (35) *tarku-karma,* spinning with a spindle; (36) *takṣaṇam,* carpentry; (37) *vāstu-vidyā,* architecture; (38) *raupya-ratna-parīkṣā,* testing silver and jewels; (39) *dhātu-vādaḥ,* metallurgy; (40) *maṇi-rāga-jñānam,* tinging jewels with various colors; (41) *ākara-jñānam,* mineralogy; (42) *vṛkṣāyur-veda-yogāḥ,* herbal medicine; (43) *meṣa-kukkuṭa-lāvaka-yuddha-vidhiḥ,* the art of training and engaging rams, cocks and quails in fighting; (44) *śuka-śārikā-pralāpanam,* knowledge of how to train male and female parrots to speak and to answer the questions of human beings; (45) *utsādanam,* healing a person with ointments; (46) *keśa-mārjana-kauśalam,* hairdressing; (47) *akṣara-muṣṭikā-kathanam,* telling what is written in a book without seeing it, and telling what is hidden in another's fist; (48) *mlecchita-kutarka-vikalpāḥ,* fabricating barbarous or foreign sophistry; (49) *deśa-bhāṣā-jñānam,* knowledge of provincial dialects; (50) *puṣpa-śakaṭikā-nirmiti-jñānam,* knowledge of how to build toy carts with flowers; (51) *yantra-mātṛkā,* composing magic squares, arrangements of numbers adding up to the same total in all directions; (52) *dhāraṇa-mātṛkā,* the use of amulets; (53) *saṁvācyam,* conversation; (54) *mānasī-kāvya-kriyā,* composing verses mentally; (55) *kriyā-vikalpāḥ,* designing a literary work or a medical remedy; (56) *chalitaka-yogāḥ,* building shrines; (57) *abhidhāna-koṣa-cchando-jñānam,* lexicography and the knowledge of poetic meters; (58) *vastra-gopanam,* disguising one kind of cloth to look like another; (59) *dyūta-viśeṣam,* knowledge of various forms of gambling; (60) *ākarṣa-krīḍā,* playing dice; (61) *bālaka-krīḍanakam,* playing with children's toys; (62) *vaināyikī vidyā,* enforcing discipline by mystic power; (63) *vaijayikī vidyā,* gaining victory; and (64) *vaitālikī vidyā,* awakening one's master with music at dawn.

TEXT 37

द्विजस्तयोस्तं महिमानमद्भुतं
संलक्ष्य राजन्नतिमानुषीं मतिम् ।
सम्मन्त्र्य पत्न्या स महार्णवे मृतं
बालं प्रभासे वरयां बभूव ह ॥३७॥

dvijas tayos taṁ mahimānam adbhutaṁ
saṁlakṣya rājann ati-mānuṣīṁ matim
sammantrya patnyā sa mahārṇave mṛtaṁ
bālaṁ prabhāse varayāṁ babhūva ha

dvijaḥ—the learned *brāhmaṇa; tayoḥ*—of the two of Them; *tam*—that; *mahimānam*—greatness; *adbhutam*—amazing; *saṁlakṣya*—observing well; *rājan*—O King; *ati-mānuṣīm*—beyond human capacity; *matim*—intelligence; *sammantrya*—after consulting; *patnyā*—with his wife; *saḥ*—he; *mahā-arṇave*—in the great ocean; *mṛtam*—who had died; *bālam*—his child; *prabhāse*—at the holy place Prabhāsa; *varayām babhūva ha*—he chose.

TRANSLATION

O King, the learned *brāhmaṇa* Sāndīpani carefully considered the two Lords' glorious and amazing qualities and Their superhuman intelligence. Then, after consulting with his wife, he chose as his remuneration the return of his young son, who had died in the ocean at Prabhāsa.

PURPORT

According to Śrīla Viśvanātha Cakravartī, the child was captured by the conchshell demon while playing at the Mahā-śiva-kṣetra.

TEXT 38

तथेत्यथारुह्य महारथौ रथं
प्रभासमासाद्य दुरन्तविक्रमौ ।
वेलामुपव्रज्य निषीदतुः क्षणं
सिन्धुर्विदित्वार्हणमाहरत्तयोः ॥३८॥

tathety athāruhya mahā-rathau rathaṁ
prabhāsam āsādya duranta-vikramau
velām upavrajya niṣīdatuḥ kṣaṇaṁ
sindhur viditvārhaṇam āharat tayoḥ

tathā—so be it; *iti*—saying this; *atha*—then; *āruhya*—mounting; *mahā-rathau*—the two great charioteers; *ratham*—a chariot; *prabhāsam*—Prabhāsa-tīrtha; *āsādya*—reaching; *duranta*—limitless; *vikramau*—whose prowess; *velām*—up to the shore; *upavrajya*—walking; *niṣīdatuḥ*—They sat down; *kṣaṇam*—for a moment; *sindhuḥ*—the (presiding demigod of the) ocean; *viditvā*—recognizing; *arhaṇam*—respectful offering; *āharat*—brought; *tayoḥ*—for Them.

TRANSLATION

"So be it," replied those two great charioteers of limitless might, and They at once mounted Their chariot and set off for Prabhāsa. When They reached that place, They walked up to the shore and sat down. In a moment the deity of the ocean, recognizing Them to be the Supreme Lords, approached Them with offerings of tribute.

PURPORT

Western scholars sometimes think that references in ancient books of wisdom to the deity of the ocean, the deity of the sun and so on reveal a primitive, mythical way of thinking. They sometimes say that primitive men think that the ocean is a god or that the sun and moon are gods. In fact, references such as the word *sindhu* in this verse, meaning "the ocean," indicate the person who governs that aspect of physical nature.

We can give several modern examples. In the United Nations we may say, "The United States votes 'Yes,' the Soviet Union votes 'No.'" We hardly mean that the physical countries or the buildings in them have voted. We mean that a particular person, representing that political and geographical entity, has voted. Yet the newspapers will simply say, "The United States voted, decided, etc." and everyone knows what that means.

Similarly, in business we may say, "A large conglomerate has swallowed up a smaller firm." We hardly mean that the buildings, office equipment and the like have physically swallowed another building full of workers and office equipment. We mean that the empowered authorities have engaged in a particular act on behalf of their respective corporate entities.

Unfortunately, modern scholars are eager to confirm their pet theories that ancient spiritual wisdom is primitive, mythic and largely supplanted by more modern ways of thinking, exemplified by their own eloquent remarks. However, much in modern scholarship must be rethought in the light of Kṛṣṇa consciousness.

TEXT 39

तमाह भगवानाशु गुरुपुत्रः प्रदीयताम् ।
योऽसाविह त्वया ग्रस्तो बालको महतोर्मिणा ॥३९॥

tam āha bhagavān āśu
guru-putraḥ pradīyatām
yo 'sāv iha tvayā grasto
bālako mahatormiṇā

tam—to him; *āha*—said; *bhagavān*—the Supreme Lord; *āśu*—quickly; *guru*—of My spiritual master; *putraḥ*—the son; *pradīyatām*—must be presented; *yaḥ*—who; *asau*—he; *iha*—in this place; *tvayā*—by you; *grastaḥ*—seized; *bālakaḥ*—a young boy; *mahatā*—mighty; *ūrmiṇā*—by your wave.

TRANSLATION

The Supreme Lord Kṛṣṇa addressed the lord of the ocean: Let the son of My *guru* be presented at once—the one you seized here with your mighty waves.

TEXT 40

श्रीसमुद्र उवाच
न चाहार्षमहं देव दैत्यः पञ्चजनो महान् ।
अन्तर्जलचरः कृष्ण शंखरूपधरोऽसुरः ॥४०॥

śrī-samudra uvāca
na cāhārṣam ahaṁ deva
daityaḥ pañcajano mahān
antar-jala-caraḥ kṛṣṇa
śaṅkha-rūpa-dharo 'suraḥ

śrī-samudraḥ uvāca—the ocean personified said; *na*—not; *ca*—and; *ahārṣam*—did take (him) away; *aham*—I; *deva*—O Lord; *daityaḥ*—a descendant of Diti; *pañcajanaḥ*—named Pañcajana; *mahān*—powerful; *antaḥ*—within; *jala*—the water; *caraḥ*—going; *kṛṣṇa*—O Kṛṣṇa; *śaṅkha*—of a conch; *rūpa*—the form; *dharaḥ*—assuming; *asuraḥ*—the demon.

TRANSLATION

The ocean replied: O Lord Kṛṣṇa, it was not I who abducted him, but a demonic descendant of Diti named Pañcajana, who travels in the water in the form of a conch.

PURPORT

Clearly the demon Pañcajana was too powerful for the ocean to control; otherwise the ocean would have prevented such an unlawful act.

TEXT 41

आस्ते तेनाहृतो नूनं तच्छ्रुत्वा सत्वरं प्रभुः ।
जलमाविश्य तं हत्वा नापश्यदुदरेऽर्भकम् ॥४१॥

āste tenāhṛto nūnaṁ
tac chrutvā satvaraṁ prabhuḥ
jalam āviśya taṁ hatvā
nāpaśyad udare 'rbhakam

āste—he is there; *tena*—by him, Pañcajana; *āhṛtaḥ*—taken away; *nūnam*—indeed; *tat*—that; *śrutvā*—hearing; *satvaram*—with haste; *prabhuḥ*—the Lord; *jalam*—the water; *āviśya*—entering; *tam*—him, the demon; *hatvā*—killing; *na apaśyat*—did not see; *udare*—in his abdomen; *arbhakam*—the boy.

TRANSLATION

"Indeed," the ocean said, "that demon has taken him away." Hearing this, Lord Kṛṣṇa entered the ocean, found Pañcajana and killed him. But the Lord did not find the boy within the demon's belly.

TEXTS 42–44

तदंगप्रभवं शंखमादाय रथमागमत् ।
ततः संयमनीं नाम यमस्य दयितां पुरीम् ॥४२॥
गत्वा जनार्दनः शंखं प्रदध्मौ सहलायुधः ।
शंखनिर्ह्रादमाकर्ण्य प्रजासंयमनो यमः ॥४३॥
तयोः सपर्यां महतीं चक्रे भक्त्युपबृंहिताम् ।
उवाचावनतः कृष्णं सर्वभूताशयालयम् ।
लीलामनुष्ययोर्विष्णो युवयोः करवाम किम् ॥४४॥

tad-aṅga-prabhavaṁ śaṅkham
ādāya ratham āgamat
tataḥ saṁyamanīṁ nāma
yamasya dayitāṁ purīm

gatvā janārdanaḥ śaṅkhaṁ
pradadhmau sa-halāyudhaḥ
śaṅkha-nirhrādam ākarṇya
prajā-saṁyamano yamaḥ

tayoḥ saparyāṁ mahatīṁ
cakre bhakty-upabṛṁhitām
uvācāvanataḥ kṛṣṇaṁ
sarva-bhūtāśayālayam
līlā-manuṣyayor viṣṇo
yuvayoḥ karavāma kim

tat—his (the demon's); *aṅga*—from the body; *prabhavam*—grown; *śaṅkham*—the conchshell; *ādāya*—taking; *ratham*—to the chariot; *āgamat*—He returned; *tataḥ*—then; *saṁyamanīm nāma*—known as Saṁyamanī; *yamasya*—of Lord Yamarāja; *dayitām*—beloved; *purīm*—to the city; *gatvā*—going; *jana-ardanaḥ*—Lord Kṛṣṇa, the abode of all persons; *śaṅkham*—the conchshell; *pradadhmau*—blew loudly; *sa*—accompanied by; *hala-āyudhaḥ*—Lord Balarāma, whose weapon is a plow; *śaṅkha*—of the conchshell; *nirhrādam*—the resounding; *ākarṇya*—hearing; *prajā*—of those who take birth; *saṁyamanaḥ*—the restrainer; *yamaḥ*—Yamarāja; tayoḥ—of Them; *saparyām*—worship; *mahatīm*—elaborate; *cakre*—performed; *bhakti*—with devotion; *upabṛṁhitām*—overflowing; *uvāca*—he said; *avanataḥ*—bowing down humbly; *kṛṣṇam*—to Lord Kṛṣṇa; *sarva*—of all; *bhūta*—living beings; *āśaya*—the minds; *ālayam*—whose residence; *līlā*—as Your pastime; *manuṣyayoḥ*—appearing as human beings; *viṣṇo*—O Supreme Lord Viṣṇu; *yuvayoḥ*—for the two of You; *karavāma*—I should do; *kim*—what.

TRANSLATION

Lord Janārdana took the conchshell that had grown around the demon's body and went back to the chariot. Then He proceeded to Saṁyamanī, the beloved capital of Yamarāja, the lord of death. Upon arriving there with Lord Balarāma, He loudly blew His conchshell, and Yamarāja, who keeps the conditioned souls in check, came as soon as he heard the resounding vibration. Yamarāja elaborately worshiped the two Lords with great devotion, and then he addressed Lord Kṛṣṇa, who lives in everyone's heart: "O Supreme Lord Viṣṇu, what shall I do for You and Lord Balarāma, who are playing the part of ordinary humans?"

PURPORT

The conchshell the Lord took from Pañcajana, which is called Pāñcajanya, is the same one He sounded at the beginning of the *Bhagavad-gītā.* According to the *ācāryas,* Pañcajana had become a demon in a way similar to that of Jaya and Vijaya. In other words, though appearing in the form of a demon, he was actually a devotee of the Lord. The *Skanda Purāṇa, Avanti-khaṇḍa,* describes the wonderful things that happened when Lord Kṛṣṇa sounded His conchshell:

asipatra-vanaṁ nāma
śīrṇa-patram ajāyata
rauravaṁ nāma narakam
arauravam abhūt tadā

abhairavaṁ bhairavākhyaṁ
kumbhī-pākam apācakam

"The hell known as Asipatra-vana lost the sharp, swordlike leaves on its trees, and the hell named Raurava became free of its *ruru* beasts. The Bhairava hell lost its fearfulness, and all cooking stopped in the Kumbhīpāka hell."

The *Skanda Purāṇa* further states,

pāpa-kṣayāt tataḥ sarve
vimuktā nārakā narāḥ
padam avyayam āsādya

"Their sinful reactions eradicated, all the inhabitants of hell attained liberation and approached the spiritual world."

TEXT 45

श्रीभगवानुवाच
गुरुपुत्रमिहानीतं निजकर्मनिबन्धनम् ।
आनयस्व महाराज मच्छासनपुरस्कृत: ॥४५॥

śrī-bhagavān uvāca
guru-putram ihānītaṁ
nija-karma-nibandhanam
ānayasva mahā-rāja
mac-chāsana-puraskṛtaḥ

śrī-bhagavān uvāca—the Supreme Lord said; *guru-putram*—the son of My spiritual master; *iha*—here; *ānītam*—brought; *nija*—his own; *karma*—of reactions of past activity; *nibandhanam*—suffering the bondage; *ānayasva*—please bring; *mahā-rāja*—O great King; *mat*—My; *śāsana*—to the command; *puraḥ-kṛtaḥ*—giving first priority.

TRANSLATION

The Supreme Personality of Godhead said: Suffering the bondage of his past activity, My spiritual master's son was brought here to you. O great King, obey My command and bring this boy to Me without delay.

TEXT 46

तथेति तेनोपानीतं गुरुपुत्रं यदूत्तमौ ।
दत्त्वा स्वगुरवे भूयो वृणीष्वेति तमूचतु: ॥४६॥

tatheti tenopānītaṁ
guru-putraṁ yadūttamau
dattvā sva-gurave bhūyo
vṛṇīṣveti tam ūcatuḥ

tathā—so be it; *iti*—(Yamarāja) thus saying; *tena*—by him; *upānītam*—brought forward; *guru-putram*—the spiritual master's son; *yadu-uttamau*—the best of the Yadus, Kṛṣṇa and Balarāma; *dattvā*—giving; *sva-gurave*—to Their *guru;* *bhūyaḥ*—again; *vṛṇīṣva*—please choose; *iti*—thus; *tam*—to him; *ūcatuḥ*—They said.

TRANSLATION

Yamarāja said, "So be it," and brought forth the *guru's* son. Then those two most exalted Yadus presented the boy to Their spiritual master and said to him, "Please select another boon."

TEXT 47

श्रीगुरुरुवाच
सम्यक् सम्पादितो वत्स भवद्भ्यां गुरुनिष्क्रयः ।
को नु युष्मद्विधगुरोः कामानामवशिष्यते ॥४७॥

śrī-gurur uvāca
samyak sampādito vatsa
bhavadbhyāṁ guru-niṣkrayaḥ
ko nu yuṣmad-vidha-guroḥ
kāmānām avaśiṣyate

śrī-guruḥ uvāca—Their spiritual master, Sāndīpani Muni, said; *samyak*—completely; *sampāditaḥ*—fulfilled; *vatsa*—my dear boy; *bhavadbhyām*—by You two; *guru-niṣkrayaḥ*—the remuneration of one's *guru; kaḥ*—which; *nu*—indeed; *yuṣmat-vidha*—of persons like You; *guroḥ*—for the spiritual master; *kāmānām*—of his desires; *avaśiṣyate*—remains.

TRANSLATION

The spiritual master said: My dear boys, You two have completely fulfilled the disciple's obligation to reward his spiritual master. Indeed, with disciples like You, what further desires could a *guru* have?

TEXT 48

गच्छतं स्वगृहं वीरौ कीर्तिर्वामस्तु पावनी ।
छन्दांस्ययातयामानि भवन्त्विह परत्र च ॥४८॥

gacchataṁ sva-gṛhaṁ vīrau
kīrtir vām astu pāvanī
chandāṁsy ayāta-yāmāni
bhavantv iha paratra ca

gacchatam—please go; *sva-gṛham*—to Your home; *vīrau*—O heroes; *kīrtiḥ*—fame; *vām*—Your; *astu*—may it be; *pāvanī*—purifying;

chandāṁsi—Vedic hymns; *ayāta-yāmāni*—ever fresh; *bhavantu*—may there be; *iha*—in this life; *paratra*—in the next life; *ca*—and.

TRANSLATION

O heroes, now please return home. May Your fame sanctify the world, and may the Vedic hymns be ever fresh in Your minds, both in this life and the next.

TEXT 49

गुरुणैवमनुज्ञातौ रथेनानिलरंहसा ।
आयातौ स्वपुरं तात पर्जन्यनिनदेन वै ॥४९॥

guruṇaivam anujñātau
rathenānila-raṁhasā
āyātau sva-puraṁ tāta
parjanya-ninadena vai

guruṇā—by Their spiritual master; *evam*—in this way; *anujñātau*—given leave; *rathena*—in Their chariot; *anila*—like the wind; *raṁhasā*—whose speed; *āyātau*—came; *sva*—to Their own; *puram*—city (Mathurā); *tāta*—my dear (King Parīkṣit); *parjanya*—like a cloud; *ninadena*—whose reverberation; *vai*—indeed.

TRANSLATION

Thus receiving Their *guru's* permission to leave, the two Lords returned to Their city on Their chariot, which moved as swiftly as the wind and resounded like a cloud.

TEXT 50

समनन्दन् प्रजाः सर्वा दृष्ट्वा रामजनार्दनौ ।
अपश्यन्त्यो बह्वहानि नष्टलब्धधना इव ॥५०॥

samanandan prajāḥ sarvā
dṛṣṭvā rāma-janārdanau

apaśyantyo bahv ahāni
naṣṭa-labdha-dhanā iva

samanandan—rejoiced; *prajāḥ*—the citizens; *sarvāḥ*—all; *dṛṣṭvā*—seeing; *rāma-janārdanau*—Balarāma and Kṛṣṇa; *apaśyantyaḥ*—not having seen; *bahu*—for many; *ahāni*—days; *naṣṭa*—lost; *labdha*—and regained; *dhanāḥ*—those whose wealth; *iva*—like.

TRANSLATION

All the citizens rejoiced upon seeing Kṛṣṇa and Balarāma, whom they had not seen for many days. The people felt just like those who have lost their wealth and then regained it.

Thus end the purports of the humble servants of His Divine Grace A. C. Bhaktivedanta Swami Prabhupāda to the Tenth Canto, Forty-fifth Chapter, of the Śrīmad-Bhāgavatam, *entitled "Kṛṣṇa Rescues His Teacher's Son."*

CHAPTER FORTY-SIX

Uddhava Visits Vṛndāvana

This chapter describes how Śrī Kṛṣṇa sent Uddhava to Vraja to relieve the distress of Nanda, Yaśodā and the young *gopīs*.

One day Lord Kṛṣṇa asked His intimate friend Uddhava to take news of Him to Vraja and thus relieve His parents and the *gopīs* of their misery caused by their separation from Him. Riding on a chariot, Uddhava reached Vraja at sunset. He saw the cows returning home to the cowherd village and the calves jumping here and there as their mothers followed slowly behind, weighed down by their heavy milk bags. The cowherd men and women were chanting the glories of Kṛṣṇa and Balarāma, and the village was attractively decorated with burning incense and rows of lamps. All this presented a scene of exceptional transcendental beauty.

Nanda Mahārāja welcomed Uddhava warmly into his home. The cowherd King then worshiped him as nondifferent from Lord Vāsudeva, fed him nicely, seated him comfortably upon a bed and then inquired from him about the welfare of Vasudeva and his sons, Kṛṣṇa and Balarāma. Nanda asked, "Does Kṛṣṇa still remember His friends, the village of Gokula and Govardhana Hill? He protected us from a forest fire, wind and rain, and many other disasters. By remembering His pastimes again and again, we are relieved of all karmic entanglement, and when we see the places marked by His lotus feet, our minds become fully absorbed in thought of Him. Garga Muni told me that Kṛṣṇa and Balarāma have both descended directly from the spiritual world. Just see how They have so easily dispatched Kaṁsa, the wrestlers, the elephant Kuvalayāpīḍa and many other demons!" As Nanda remembered Kṛṣṇa's pastimes, his throat choked up with tears and he could speak no further. Meanwhile, as mother Yaśodā heard her husband speak of Kṛṣṇa, the intense love she felt for her son caused a flood of milk to pour from her breasts and a torrent of tears from her eyes.

Seeing the superexcellent affection Nanda and Yaśodā had for Śrī Kṛṣṇa, Uddhava commented, "You two are indeed most glorious. One who has attained pure love for the Supreme Absolute Truth in His humanlike form has nothing further to accomplish. Kṛṣṇa and Balarāma are present in the hearts of all living beings, just as fire lies dormant within wood. These two Lords see all equally, having no particular friends or enemies. Free from egoism and possessiveness, They have no father, mother, wife or children, are never subject to birth, and have no material body. Only to enjoy spiritual happiness and deliver Their saintly devotees do They appear by Their own sweet will among various species of life, both high and low.

"Lord Kṛṣṇa is not merely the son of you, O Nanda and Yaśodā, but the son of all persons, as well as their mother and father. In fact, He is everyone's dearest relation inasmuch as nothing that is seen or heard in the past, present or future, among the moving or nonmoving, is independent of Him."

Nanda Mahārāja and Uddhava passed the night talking about Kṛṣṇa in this way. Then the cowherd women performed their morning worship and began churning butter, singing the glories of Śrī Kṛṣṇa as they busily pulled the churning ropes. The sounds of churning and singing reverberated into the sky, cleansing the world of all inauspiciousness.

When the sun rose, the *gopīs* saw Uddhava's chariot at the edge of the cowherd village, and they thought that Akrūra might have returned. But just then Uddhava finished his morning duties and presented himself before them.

TEXT 1

श्रीशुक उवाच
वृष्णीनां प्रवरो मन्त्री कृष्णस्य दयितः सखा ।
शिष्यो बृहस्पतेः साक्षादुद्धवो बुद्धिसत्तमः ॥१॥

śrī-śuka uvāca
vṛṣṇīnāṁ pravaro mantrī
kṛṣṇasya dayitaḥ sakhā
śiṣyo bṛhaspateḥ sākṣād
uddhavo buddhi-sattamaḥ

śrī-śukaḥ uvāca—Śukadeva Gosvāmī said; *vṛṣṇīnām*—of the Vṛṣṇis; *pravaraḥ*—the best; *mantrī*—adviser; *kṛṣṇasya*—of Kṛṣṇa; *dayitaḥ*—beloved; *sakhā*—friend; *śiṣyaḥ*—disciple; *bṛhaspateḥ*—of Bṛhaspati, the spiritual master of the demigods; *sākṣāt*—directly; *uddhavaḥ*—Uddhava; *buddhi*—having intelligence; *sat-tamaḥ*—of the highest quality.

TRANSLATION

Śukadeva Gosvāmī said: The supremely intelligent Uddhava was the best counselor of the Vṛṣṇi dynasty, a beloved friend of Lord Śrī Kṛṣṇa and a direct disciple of Bṛhaspati.

PURPORT

The *ācāryas* give various reasons why Lord Kṛṣṇa sent Uddhava to Vṛndāvana. The Lord had promised the residents of Vṛndāvana: *āyāsye,* "I shall return." (*Bhāg.* 10.39.35) Also, in the previous chapter Lord Kṛṣṇa promised Nanda Mahārāja: *draṣṭum eṣyāmaḥ,* "We will come back to see you and mother Yaśodā." (*Bhāg.* 10.45.23) At the same time, the Lord could not break His promise to Śrī Vasudeva and mother Devakī to finally spend some time with them after they had suffered for so many years. Therefore, the Lord decided to send His intimate representative to Vṛndāvana in His place.

The question may be asked, Why did Kṛṣṇa not invite Nanda and Yaśodā to visit Him in Mathurā? According to Śrīla Jīva Gosvāmī, for the Lord to have exchanged loving feelings with Nanda and Yaśodā in the same place and at the same time that He was exchanging them with Vasudeva and Devakī would have created an awkward situation in the Lord's pastimes. Thus Kṛṣṇa did not invite Nanda and Yaśodā to stay with Him in Mathurā. The residents of Vṛndāvana had their own way of understanding Kṛṣṇa, and their feelings could not have been appropriately expressed on a regular basis in the kingly atmosphere of Mathurā.

Śrī Uddhava is described in this verse as *buddhi-sattamaḥ,* "the most intelligent," and thus he could expertly pacify the residents of Vṛndāvana, who were feeling such intense separation from Lord Kṛṣṇa. Then, upon his return to Mathurā, Uddhava would describe to all the members of the Vṛṣṇi dynasty the extraordinary pure love he had seen in Vṛndāvana. Indeed, the love the cowherd men and *gopīs* felt for Kṛṣṇa was far beyond anything the Lord's other devotees had ever experienced, and by hearing about that love all the Lord's devotees would increase their faith and devotion.

As stated in the Third Canto by the Lord Himself, *noddhavo 'ṇv api man-nyūnaḥ:* "Uddhava is not even slightly different from Me." Resembling Kṛṣṇa so much, Uddhava was the perfect person to carry out the Lord's mission in Vṛndāvana. In fact, *Śrī Hari-vaṁśa* states that Uddhava is the son of Vasudeva's brother Devabhāga: *uddhavo devabhāgasya mahā-bhāgaḥ suto 'bhavat.* In other words, he is a cousin-brother of Śrī Kṛṣṇa's.

TEXT 2

तमाह भगवान् प्रेष्ठं भक्तमेकान्तिनं क्वचित् ।
गृहीत्वा पाणिना पाणिं प्रपन्नार्तिहरो हरिः ॥२॥

tam āha bhagavān preṣṭhaṁ
bhaktam ekāntinaṁ kvacit
gṛhītvā pāṇinā pāṇiṁ
prapannārti-haro hariḥ

tam—to him; *āha*—spoke; *bhagavān*—the Supreme Lord; *preṣṭham*—to His most dear; *bhaktam*—devotee; *ekāntinam*—exclusive; *kvacit*—on one occasion; *gṛhītvā*—taking; *pāṇinā*—with His hand; *pāṇim*—(Uddhava's) hand; *prapanna*—of those who surrender; *ārti*—the distress; *haraḥ*—who takes away; *hariḥ*—Lord Hari.

TRANSLATION

The Supreme Lord Hari, who relieves the distress of all who surrender to Him, once took the hand of His fully devoted, dearmost friend Uddhava and addressed him as follows.

TEXT 3

गच्छोद्धव व्रजं सौम्य पित्रोर्नौ प्रीतिमावह ।
गोपीनां मद्वियोगाधिं मत्सन्देशैर्विमोचय ॥३॥

gacchoddhava vrajaṁ saumya
pitror nau prītim āvaha
gopīnāṁ mad-viyogādhiṁ
mat-sandeśair vimocaya

gaccha—please go; *uddhava*—O Uddhava; *vrajam*—to Vraja; *saumya*—O gentle one; *pitroḥ*—to the parents; *nau*—Our; *prītim*—satisfaction; *āvaha*—carry; *gopīnām*—of the *gopīs;* *mat*—from Me; *viyoga*—caused by separation; *ādhim*—of the mental pain; *mat*—brought from Me; *sandeśaiḥ*—by messages; *vimocaya*—relieve them.

TRANSLATION

[Lord Kṛṣṇa said:] Dear gentle Uddhava, go to Vraja and give pleasure to Our parents. And also relieve the *gopīs,* suffering in separation from Me, by giving them My message.

TEXT 4

ता मन्मनस्का मत्प्राणा मदर्थे त्यक्तदैहिकाः ।
मामेव दयितं प्रेष्ठमात्मानं मनसा गताः ।
ये त्यक्तलोकधर्माश्च मदर्थे तान् बिभर्म्यहम् ॥४॥

tā man-manaskā mat-prāṇā
mad-arthe tyakta-daihikāḥ
mām eva dayitaṁ preṣṭham
ātmānaṁ manasā gatāḥ
ye tyakta-loka-dharmāś ca
mad-arthe tān bibharmy aham

tāḥ—they (the *gopīs*); *mat*—absorbed in Me; *manaskāḥ*—their minds; *mat*—fixed upon Me; *prāṇāḥ*—their lives; *mat-arthe*—for My sake; *tyakta*—abandoning; *daihikāḥ*—everything on the bodily platform; *mām*—Me; *eva*—alone; *dayitam*—their beloved; *preṣṭham*—dearmost; *ātmānam*—Self; *manasā gatāḥ*—understood; *ye*—who (the *gopīs,* or anyone); *tyakta*—giving up; *loka*—this world; *dharmāḥ*—religiosity; *ca*—and; *mat-arthe*—for My sake; *tān*—them; *bibharmi*—sustain; *aham*—I.

TRANSLATION

The minds of those *gopīs* are always absorbed in Me, and their very lives are ever devoted to Me. For My sake they have abandoned everything related to their bodies, renouncing ordinary

happiness in this life, as well as religious duties necessary for such happiness in the next life. I alone am their dearmost beloved and, indeed, their very Self. Therefore I take it upon Myself to sustain them in all circumstances.

PURPORT

Here the Lord explains why He wants to send a special message to the *gopīs*. According to the Vaiṣṇava *ācāryas*, the word *daihikāḥ*, "related to the body," refers to husbands, children, homes and so on. The *gopīs* loved Kṛṣṇa so intensely that they could think of nothing else. Since Śrī Kṛṣṇa maintains ordinary devotees engaged in *sādhana-bhakti*, devotional service in practice, He will certainly maintain the *gopīs*, His most exalted devotees.

TEXT 5

मयि ताः प्रेयसां प्रेष्ठे दूरस्थे गोकुलस्त्रियः ।
स्मरन्त्योऽङ्ग विमुह्यन्ति विरहौत्कण्ठ्यविह्वलाः ॥५॥

mayi tāḥ preyasāṁ preṣṭhe
dūra-sthe gokula-striyaḥ
smarantyo 'ṅga vimuhyanti
virahautkaṇṭhya-vihvalāḥ

mayi—I; *tāḥ*—they; *preyasām*—of all objects of endearment; *preṣṭhe*—the most dear; *dūra-sthe*—being far away; *gokula-striyaḥ*—the women of Gokula; *smarantyaḥ*—remembering; *aṅga*—dear (Uddhava); *vimuhyanti*—become stunned; *viraha*—of separation; *autkaṇṭhya*—by the anxiety; *vihvalāḥ*—overwhelmed.

TRANSLATION

My dear Uddhava, for those women of Gokula I am the most cherished object of love. Thus when they remember Me, who am so far away, they are overwhelmed by the anxiety of separation.

PURPORT

Whatever is dear to us becomes an object of our possessiveness. Ultimately the most dear object is our very soul, or our self. Thus things in a favorable relationship to our self also become dear to us, and we try to possess them. According to Śrīla Viśvanātha Cakravartī, among countless millions of such dear things, Śrī Kṛṣṇa is the most dear of all, even dearer than one's own self. The *gopīs* had realized this fact, and thus they were stunned in separation from the Lord because of their intense love for Him. Although they would have given up their lives, they were kept alive by the Lord's transcendental potency.

TEXT 6

धारयन्त्यतिकृच्छ्रेण प्रायः प्राणान् कथञ्चन ।
प्रत्यागमनसन्देशैर्बल्लव्यो मे मदात्मिकाः ॥६॥

dhārayanty ati-kṛcchreṇa
prāyaḥ prāṇān kathañcana
pratyāgamana-sandeśair
ballavyo me mad-ātmikāḥ

dhārayanti—they hold on; *ati-kṛcchreṇa*—with great difficulty; *prāyaḥ*—barely; *prāṇān*—to their lives; *kathañcana*—somehow; *prati-āgamana*—of return; *sandeśaiḥ*—by the promises; *ballavyaḥ*—the cowherd women; *me*—My; *mat-ātmikāḥ*—who are fully dedicated to Me.

TRANSLATION

Simply because I have promised to return to them, My fully devoted cowherd girlfriends struggle to maintain their lives somehow or other.

PURPORT

According to Śrīla Viśvanātha Cakravartī, although the *gopīs* of Vṛndāvana were apparently married, their husbands actually had no contact whatsoever with their supremely attractive qualities of form, taste, fragrance, sound, touch and so on. Rather, their husbands merely presumed, "These are our wives." In other words, by Lord Kṛṣṇa's spiritual potency, the *gopīs* existed entirely for His pleasure, and Kṛṣṇa loved them in the mood of a paramour. In fact, the *gopīs* were manifestations of Kṛṣṇa's internal nature, His supreme pleasure potency, and on the spiritual platform they attracted the Lord by their pure love.

Nanda Mahārāja and mother Yaśodā, Lord Kṛṣṇa's parents in Vṛndāvana, had also attained a most exalted state of love for Kṛṣṇa, and they too could barely maintain their lives in His absence. Thus Uddhava would also give special attention to them.

TEXT 7

श्रीशुक उवाच
इत्युक्त उद्धवो राजन् सन्देशं भर्तुरादृतः ।
आदाय रथमारुह्य प्रययौ नन्दगोकुलम् ॥७॥

śrī-śuka uvāca
ity ukta uddhavo rājan
sandeśaṁ bhartur ādṛtaḥ
ādāya ratham āruhya
prayayau nanda-gokulam

śrī-śukaḥ uvāca—Śukadeva Gosvāmī said; *iti*—thus; *uktaḥ*—spoken to; *uddhavaḥ*—Uddhava; *rājan*—O King (Parīkṣit); *sandeśam*—the message; *bhartuḥ*—of his master; *ādṛtaḥ*—respectfully; *ādāya*—taking; *ratham*—his chariot; *āruhya*—mounting; *prayayau*—went off; *nanda-gokulam*—to the cowherd village of Nanda Mahārāja.

TRANSLATION

Śukadeva Gosvāmī said: Thus addressed, O King, Uddhava respectfully accepted his master's message, mounted his chariot and set off for Nanda-gokula.

TEXT 8

प्राप्तो नन्दव्रजं श्रीमान्निम्लोचति विभावसौ ।
छन्नयानः प्रविशतां पशूनां खुररेणुभिः ॥८॥

prāpto nanda-vrajaṁ śrīmān
nimlocati vibhāvasau
channa-yānaḥ praviśatāṁ
paśūnāṁ khura-reṇubhiḥ

prāptaḥ—reaching; *nanda-vrajam*—the pastures of Nanda Mahārāja; *śrīmān*—the fortunate (Uddhava); *nimlocati*—while it was setting; *vibhāvasau*—the sun; *channa*—invisible; *yānaḥ*—whose passing; *praviśatām*—who were entering; *paśūnām*—of the animals; *khura*—of the hooves; *reṇubhiḥ*—by the dust.

TRANSLATION

The fortunate Uddhava reached Nanda Mahārāja's pastures just as the sun was setting, and since the returning cows and other animals were raising dust with their hooves, his chariot passed unnoticed.

TEXTS 9–13

वासितार्थेऽभियुध्यद्भिर्नादितं शुश्मिभिर्वृषैः ।
धावन्तीभिश्च वास्राभिरुधोभारैः स्ववत्सकान् ॥९॥
इतस्ततो विलङ्घद्भिर्गोवत्सैर्मण्डितं सितैः ।
गोदोहशब्दाभिरवं वेणूनां निःस्वनेन च ॥१०॥
गायन्तीभिश्च कर्माणि शुभानि बलकृष्णयोः ।
स्वलंकृताभिर्गोपीभिर्गोपैश्च सुविराजितम् ॥११॥
अग्न्यर्कातिथिगोविप्रपितृदेवार्चनान्वितैः ।
धूपदीपैश्च माल्यैश्च गोपावासैर्मनोरमम् ॥१२॥
सर्वतः पुष्पितवनं द्विजालिकुलनादितम् ।
हंसकारण्डवाकीर्णैः पद्मषण्डैश्च मण्डितम् ॥१३॥

vāsitārthe 'bhiyudhyadbhir
nāditaṁ śuśmibhir vṛṣaiḥ
dhāvantībhiś ca vāsrābhir
udho-bhāraiḥ sva-vatsakān

itas tato vilaṅghadbhir
go-vatsair maṇḍitaṁ sitaiḥ
go-doha-śabdābhiravaṁ
veṇūnāṁ niḥsvanena ca

gāyantībhiś ca karmāṇi
śubhāni bala-kṛṣṇayoḥ
sv-alaṅkṛtābhir gopībhir
gopaiś ca su-virājitam

agny-arkātithi-go-vipra-
pitṛ-devārcanānvitaiḥ
dhūpa-dīpaiś ca mālyaiś ca
gopāvāsair mano-ramam

sarvataḥ puṣpita-vanaṁ
dvijāli-kula-nāditam
haṁsa-kāraṇḍavākīrṇaiḥ
padma-ṣaṇḍaiś ca maṇḍitam

vāsita—of the fertile (cows); *arthe*—for the sake; *abhiyudhyadbhiḥ*—who were fighting with one another; *nāditam*—resounding; *śuśmibhiḥ*—sexually aroused; *vṛṣaiḥ*—with the bulls; *dhāvantībhiḥ*—running; *ca*—and; *vāsrābhiḥ*—with the cows; *udhaḥ*—by their udders; *bhāraiḥ*—burdened; *sva*—after their own; *vatsakān*—calves; *itaḥ tataḥ*—here and there; *vilaṅghadbhiḥ*—jumping; *go-vatsaiḥ*—by the calves; *maṇḍitam*—adorned; *sitaiḥ*—white; *go-doha*—of the milking of the cows; *śabda*—by the sounds; *abhiravam*—reverberating; *veṇūnām*—of flutes; *niḥsvanena*—with the loud vibration; *ca*—and; *gāyantībhiḥ*—who were singing; *ca*—and; *karmāṇi*—about the deeds; *śubhāni*—auspicious; *bala-kṛṣṇayoḥ*—of Balarāma and Kṛṣṇa; *su*—finely; *alaṅkṛtābhiḥ*—ornamented; *gopībhiḥ*—with the cowherd women; *gopaiḥ*—the cowherd men; *ca*—and; *su-virājitam*—resplendent; *agni*—of the sacrificial fire; *arka*—the sun; *atithi*—guests; *go*—the cows; *vipra*—the *brāhmaṇas; pitṛ*—forefathers; *deva*—and demigods; *arcana*—with worship; *anvitaiḥ*—filled; *dhūpa*—with incense; *dīpaiḥ*—lamps; *ca*—and; *mālyaiḥ*—with flower garlands; *ca*—also; *gopa-āvāsaiḥ*—because of the homes of the cowherds; *manaḥ-ramam*—very attractive; *sarvataḥ*—on all sides; *puṣpita*—flowering;

vanam—with the forest; *dvija*—of birds; *ali*—and bees; *kula*—with the swarms; *nāditam*—resounding; *haṁsa*—with swans; *kāraṇḍava*—and a certain species of duck; *ākīrṇaiḥ*—crowded; *padma-ṣaṇḍaiḥ*—with bowers of lotuses; *ca*—and; *maṇḍitam*—beautified.

TRANSLATION

Gokula resounded on all sides with the sounds of bulls in rut fighting with one another for fertile cows; with the mooing of cows, burdened by their udders, chasing after their calves; with the noise of milking and of the white calves jumping here and there; with the loud reverberation of flute-playing; and with the singing of the all-auspicious deeds of Kṛṣṇa and Balarāma by the cowherd men and women, who made the village resplendent with their wonderfully ornamented attire. The cowherds' homes in Gokula appeared most charming with their abundant paraphernalia for worship of the sacrificial fire, the sun, unexpected guests, the cows, the *brāhmaṇas*, the forefathers and the demigods. On all sides lay the flowering forest, echoing with flocks of birds and swarms of bees and beautified by its lakes crowded with swans, *kāraṇḍava* ducks and bowers of lotuses.

PURPORT

Although Gokula was merged in grief because of separation from Lord Kṛṣṇa, the Lord expanded His internal potency to cover that particular manifestation of Vraja and allow Uddhava to see the normal bustle and joy of Vraja at sunset.

TEXT 14

तमागतं समागम्य कृष्णस्यानुचरं प्रियम् ।
नन्दः प्रीतः परिष्वज्य वासुदेवधियार्चयत् ॥१४॥

tam āgataṁ samāgamya
kṛṣṇasyānucaraṁ priyam
nandaḥ prītaḥ pariṣvajya
vāsudeva-dhiyārcayat

tam—him (Uddhava); *āgatam*—arrived; *samāgamya*—approaching; *kṛṣṇasya*—of Kṛṣṇa; *anucaram*—the follower; *priyam*—dear; *nandaḥ*—Nanda Mahārāja; *prītaḥ*—happy; *pariṣvajya*—embracing; *vāsudeva-dhiyā*—thinking of Lord Vāsudeva; *ārcayat*—worshiped.

TRANSLATION

As soon as Uddhava arrived at Nanda Mahārāja's home, Nanda came forward to meet him. The cowherd King embraced him in great happiness and worshiped him as nondifferent from Lord Vāsudeva.

PURPORT

Uddhava looked just like Nanda's son Kṛṣṇa and gave pleasure to anyone who saw him. Thus although Nanda was absorbed in thoughts of separation from Kṛṣṇa, when he saw Uddhava coming toward his house, he became aware of external events and eagerly went out to embrace his exalted visitor.

TEXT 15

भोजितं परमान्नेन संविष्टं कशिपौ सुखम् ।
गतश्रमं पर्यपृच्छत्पादसंवाहनादिभिः ॥१५॥

bhojitaṁ paramānnena
saṁviṣṭaṁ kaśipau sukham
gata-śramaṁ paryapṛcchat
pāda-saṁvāhanādibhiḥ

bhojitam—fed; *parama-annena*—with first-class food; *saṁviṣṭam*—seated; *kaśipau*—on a nice bed; *sukham*—comfortably; *gata*—relieved; *śramam*—of fatigue; *paryapṛcchat*—he inquired; *pāda*—of his feet; *saṁvāhana*—with massaging; *ādibhiḥ*—and so on.

TRANSLATION

After Uddhava had eaten first-class food, been seated comfortably on a bed and been relieved of his fatigue by a foot massage and other means, Nanda inquired from him as follows.

PURPORT

Śrīla Jīva Gosvāmī mentions that Nanda had a servant massage Uddhava's feet, since Uddhava was Nanda's nephew.

TEXT 16

कच्चिदंग महाभाग सखा नः शूरनन्दनः ।
आस्ते कुशल्यपत्याद्यैर्युक्तो मुक्तः सुहृद्व्रतः ॥१६॥

kaccid aṅga mahā-bhāga
sakhā naḥ śūra-nandanaḥ
āste kuśaly apatyādyair
yukto muktaḥ suhṛd-vrataḥ

kaccit—whether; *aṅga*—my dear; *mahā-bhāga*—O most fortunate one; *sakhā*—the friend; *naḥ*—our; *śūra-nandanaḥ*—the son of King Śūra (Vasudeva); *āste*—lives; *kuśalī*—well; *apatya-ādyaiḥ*—with his children and so on; *yuktaḥ*—joined; *muktaḥ*—freed; *suhṛt*—to his friends; *vrataḥ*—who is devoted.

TRANSLATION

[Nanda Mahārāja said:] My dear most fortunate one, does the son of Śūra fare well, now that he is free and has rejoined his children and other relatives?

TEXT 17

दिष्टया कंसो हतः पापः सानुगः स्वेन पाप्मना ।
साधूनां धर्मशीलानां यदूनां द्वेष्टि यः सदा ॥१७॥

diṣṭyā kaṁso hataḥ pāpaḥ
sānugaḥ svena pāpmanā
sādhūnāṁ dharma-śīlānāṁ
yadūnāṁ dveṣṭi yaḥ sadā

diṣṭyā—by good fortune; *kaṁsaḥ*—King Kaṁsa; *hataḥ*—has been killed; *pāpaḥ*—the sinful; *sa*—along with; *anugaḥ*—his followers (brothers); *svena*—because of his own; *pāpmanā*—sinfulness; *sādhū-nām*—saintly; *dharma-śīlānām*—always righteous in their behavior; *yadūnām*—the Yadus; *dveṣṭi*—hated; *yaḥ*—who; *sadā*—always.

TRANSLATION

Fortunately, because of his own sins, the sinful Kaṁsa has been killed, along with all his brothers. He always hated the saintly and righteous Yadus.

TEXT 18

अपि स्मरति नः कृष्णो मातरं सुहृदः सखीन् ।
गोपान् व्रजं चात्मनाथं गावो वृन्दावनं गिरिम् ॥१८॥

api smarati naḥ kṛṣṇo
mātaraṁ suhṛdaḥ sakhīn
gopān vrajaṁ cātma-nāthaṁ
gāvo vṛndāvanaṁ girim

api—perhaps; *smarati*—remembers; *naḥ*—us; *kṛṣṇaḥ*—Kṛṣṇa; *mātaram*—His mother; *suhṛdaḥ*—His well-wishers; *sakhīn*—and dear friends; *gopān*—the cowherds; *vrajam*—the village of Vraja; *ca*—and; *ātma*—Himself; *nātham*—whose master; *gāvaḥ*—the cows; *vṛndāvanam*—the forest of Vṛndāvana; *girim*—the mountain Govardhana.

TRANSLATION

Does Kṛṣṇa remember us? Does He remember His mother and His friends and well-wishers? Does He remember the cowherds and their village of Vraja, of which He is the master? Does He remember the cows, Vṛndāvana forest and Govardhana Hill?

TEXT 19

अप्यायास्यति गोविन्दः स्वजनान् सकृदीक्षितुम् ।
तर्हि द्रक्ष्याम तद्वक्त्रं सुनसं सुस्मितेक्षणम् ॥१९॥

apy āyāsyati govindaḥ
sva-janān sakṛd īkṣitum
tarhi drakṣyāma tad-vaktraṁ
su-nasaṁ su-smitekṣaṇam

api—whether; *āyāsyati*—will come back; *govindaḥ*—Kṛṣṇa; *sva-janān*—His relatives; *sakṛt*—once; *īkṣitum*—to see; *tarhi*—then; *drakṣyāma*—we may glance upon; *tat*—His; *vaktram*—face; *su-nasam*—with beautiful nose; *su*—beautiful; *smita*—smile; *īkṣaṇam*—and eyes.

TRANSLATION

Will Govinda return even once to see His family? If He ever does, we may then glance upon His beautiful face, with its beautiful eyes, nose and smile.

PURPORT

Now that Kṛṣṇa had become a prince in the great city of Mathurā, Nanda had lost hope that He would come back to live in the simple cowherd village of Vṛndāvana. But he hoped against hope that Kṛṣṇa would come back at least once to visit the simple cowherd folk who had raised Him from birth.

TEXT 20

दावाग्नेर्वातवर्षाच्च वृषसर्पाच्च रक्षिताः ।
दुरत्ययेभ्यो मृत्युभ्यः कृष्णेन सुमहात्मना ॥२०॥

dāvāgner vāta-varṣāc ca
vṛṣa-sarpāc ca rakṣitāḥ
duratyayebhyo mṛtyubhyaḥ
kṛṣṇena su-mahātmanā

dāva-agneḥ—from the forest fire; *vāta*—from the wind; *varṣāt*—and rain; *ca*—also; *vṛṣa*—from the bull; *sarpāt*—from the serpent; *ca*—and; *rakṣitāḥ*—protected; *duratyayebhyaḥ*—insurmountable; *mṛtyubhyaḥ*—from mortal dangers; *kṛṣṇena*—by Kṛṣṇa; *su-mahā-ātmanā*—the very great soul.

TRANSLATION

We were saved from the forest fire, the wind and rain, the bull and serpent demons—from all such insurmountable, deadly dangers—by that very great soul, Kṛṣṇa.

TEXT 21

स्मरतां कृष्णवीर्याणि लीलापांगनिरीक्षितम् ।
हसितं भाषितं चांग सर्वा नः शिथिलाः क्रियाः ॥२१॥

smaratāṁ kṛṣṇa-vīryāṇi
līlāpāṅga-nirīkṣitam
hasitaṁ bhāṣitaṁ cāṅga
sarvā naḥ śithilāḥ kriyāḥ

smaratām—who are remembering; *kṛṣṇa-vīryāṇi*—the valorous deeds of Kṛṣṇa; *līlā*—playful; *apāṅga*—with sidelong glances; *nirīkṣitam*—His looking; *hasitam*—smiling; *bhāṣitam*—speaking; *ca*—and; *aṅga*—my dear (Uddhava); *sarvāḥ*—all; *naḥ*—for us; *śithilāḥ*—slackened; *kriyāḥ*—material activities.

TRANSLATION

As we remember the wonderful deeds Kṛṣṇa performed, His playful sidelong glances, His smiles and His words, O Uddhava, we forget all our material engagements.

TEXT 22

सरिच्छैलवनोद्देशान्मुकुन्दपदभूषितान् ।
आक्रीडानीक्ष्यमाणानां मनो याति तदात्मताम् ॥२२॥

saric-chaila-vanoddeśān
mukunda-pada-bhūṣitān
ākrīḍān īkṣyamāṇānāṁ
mano yāti tad-ātmatām

sarit—the rivers; *śaila*—hills; *vana*—of the forests; *uddeśān*—and the various parts; *mukunda*—of Kṛṣṇa; *pada*—by the feet; *bhūṣitān*—ornamented; *ākrīḍān*—the locations of His play; *īkṣyamāṇānām*—for those who are seeing; *manaḥ*—the mind; *yāti*—attains; *tat-ātmatām*—total absorption in Him.

TRANSLATION

When we see the places where Mukunda enjoyed His sporting pastimes—the rivers, hills and forests He decorated with His feet—our minds become totally absorbed in Him.

TEXT 23

मन्ये कृष्णं च रामं च प्राप्ताविह सुरोत्तमौ ।
सुराणां महदर्थाय गर्गस्य वचनं यथा ॥२३॥

manye kṛṣṇaṁ ca rāmaṁ ca
prāptāv iha surottamau
surāṇāṁ mahad-arthāya
gargasya vacanaṁ yathā

manye—I think; *kṛṣṇam*—Kṛṣṇa; *ca*—and; *rāmam*—Balarāma; *ca*—and; *prāptau*—obtained; *iha*—on this planet; *sura*—of demigods; *uttamau*—two of the most elevated; *surāṇām*—of the demigods; *mahat*—great; *arthāya*—for a purpose; *gargasya*—of the sage Garga; *vacanam*—the statement; *yathā*—as.

TRANSLATION

In my opinion, Kṛṣṇa and Balarāma must be two exalted demigods who have come to this planet to fulfill some great mission of the demigods. Such was foretold by Garga Ṛṣi.

TEXT 24

कंसं नागायुतप्राणं मल्लौ गजपतिं यथा ।
अवधिष्टां लीलयैव पशूनिव मृगाधिपः ॥२४॥

kaṁsaṁ nāgāyuta-prāṇaṁ
mallau gaja-patiṁ yathā
avadhiṣṭāṁ līlayaiva
paśūn iva mṛgādhipaḥ

kaṁsam—Kaṁsa; *nāga*—of elephants; *ayuta*—ten thousand; *prāṇam*—whose vital strength; *mallau*—the two wrestlers (Cāṇūra and Muṣṭika); *gaja-patim*—the king of the elephants (Kuvalayāpīḍa); *yathā*—inasmuch as; *avadhiṣṭām*—the two of Them killed; *līlayā*—as a game; *eva*—simply; *paśūn*—animals; *iva*—as; *mṛga-adhipaḥ*—the lion, king of animals.

TRANSLATION

After all, Kṛṣṇa and Balarāma killed Kaṁsa, who was as strong as ten thousand elephants, as well as the wrestlers Cāṇūra and Muṣṭika and the elephant Kuvalayāpīḍa. They killed them all sportingly, as easily as a lion disposes of small animals.

PURPORT

Here Nanda means to say, "Not only did Garga Muni declare that these boys are divine, but just see what They have done! Everyone is talking about it."

TEXT 25

तालत्रयं महासारं धनुर्यष्टिमिवेभराट् ।
बभञ्जैकेन हस्तेन सप्ताहमदधाद् गिरिम् ॥२५॥

tāla-trayaṁ mahā-sāraṁ
dhanur yaṣṭim ivebha-rāṭ
babhañjaikena hastena
saptāham adadhād girim

tāla-trayam—as long as three palm trees; *mahā-sāram*—extremely solid; *dhanuḥ*—the bow; *yaṣṭim*—a stick; *iva*—as; *ibha-rāṭ*—a royal elephant; *babhañja*—He broke; *ekena*—with one; *hastena*—hand; *sapta-aham*—for seven days; *adadhāt*—held; *girim*—a mountain.

TRANSLATION

With the ease of a royal elephant breaking a stick, Kṛṣṇa broke a powerful, giant bow three *tālas* long. He also held a mountain aloft for seven days with just one hand.

PURPORT

According to Ācārya Viśvanātha, a *tāla* ("palm tree") is a measurement of about sixty *hastas,* or ninety feet. Thus the great bow Kṛṣṇa broke was two hundred seventy feet long.

TEXT 26

प्रलम्बो धेनुकोऽरिष्टस्तृणावर्तो बकादयः ।
दैत्याः सुरासुरजितो हता येनेह लीलया ॥२६॥

pralambo dhenuko 'riṣṭas
tṛṇāvarto bakādayaḥ
daityāḥ surāsura-jito
hatā yeneha līlayā

pralambaḥ dhenukaḥ ariṣṭaḥ—Pralamba, Dhenuka and Ariṣṭa; *tṛṇāvartaḥ*—Tṛṇāvarta; *baka-ādayaḥ*—Baka and others; *daityāḥ*—demons; *sura-asura*—both the demigods and the demons; *jitaḥ*—who conquered; *hatāḥ*—killed; *yena*—by whom; *iha*—here (in Vṛndāvana); *līlayā*—easily.

TRANSLATION

Here in Vṛndāvana, Kṛṣṇa and Balarāma easily destroyed demons like Pralamba, Dhenuka, Ariṣṭa, Tṛṇāvarta and Baka, who had themselves defeated both demigods and other demons.

TEXT 27

श्रीशुक उवाच

इति संस्मृत्य संस्मृत्य नन्दः कृष्णानुरक्तधीः ।
अत्युत्कण्ठोऽभवत्तूष्णीं प्रेमप्रसरविह्वलः ॥२७॥

śrī-śuka uvāca
iti saṁsmṛtya saṁsmṛtya
nandaḥ kṛṣṇānurakta-dhīḥ
aty-utkaṇṭho 'bhavat tūṣṇīṁ
prema-prasara-vihvalaḥ

śrī-śukaḥ uvāca—Śukadeva Gosvāmī said; *iti*—thus; *saṁsmṛtya saṁsmṛtya*—intensely and repeatedly remembering; *nandaḥ*—Nanda Mahārāja; *kṛṣṇa*—to Kṛṣṇa; *anurakta*—completely attracted; *dhīḥ*—whose mind; *ati*—extremely; *utkaṇṭhaḥ*—anxious; *abhavat*—he became; *tūṣṇīm*—silent; *prema*—of his pure love; *prasara*—by the force; *vihvalaḥ*—overcome.

TRANSLATION

Śukadeva Gosvāmī said: Thus intensely remembering Kṛṣṇa again and again, Nanda Mahārāja, his mind completely attached to the Lord, felt extreme anxiety and fell silent, overcome by the strength of his love.

TEXT 28

यशोदा वर्ण्यमानानि पुत्रस्य चरितानि च ।
शृण्वन्त्यश्रूण्यवास्राक्षीत्स्नेहस्नुतपयोधरा ॥२८॥

yaśodā varṇyamānāni
putrasya caritāni ca
śṛṇvanty aśrūṇy avāsrākṣīt
sneha-snuta-payodharā

yaśodā—mother Yaśodā; *varṇyamānāni*—being described; *putrasya*—of her son; *caritāni*—the activities; *ca*—and; *śṛṇvantī*—as she heard; *aśrūṇi*—tears; *avāsrākṣīt*—poured down; *sneha*—out of love; *snuta*—moistened; *payodharā*—her breasts.

TRANSLATION

As mother Yaśodā heard the descriptions of her son's activities, she poured out her tears, and milk flowed from her breasts out of love.

PURPORT

From the very day that Kṛṣṇa had left for Mathurā, mother Yaśodā, though counseled and consoled by hundreds of men and women, could see nothing but the face of her son. She kept her eyes closed to everyone else and cried constantly. Thus she could not recognize Uddhava, treat him with parental affection, ask him any questions or give him any message for her son. She was simply overwhelmed with love for Kṛṣṇa.

TEXT 29

तयोरित्थं भगवति कृष्णे नन्दयशोदयोः ।
वीक्ष्यानुरागं परमं नन्दमाहोद्धवो मुदा ॥२९॥

tayor itthaṁ bhagavati
kṛṣṇe nanda-yaśodayoḥ
vīkṣyānurāgaṁ paramaṁ
nandam āhoddhavo mudā

tayoḥ—of the two of them; *ittham*—like this; *bhagavati*—for the Supreme Personality of Godhead; *kṛṣṇe*—Lord Kṛṣṇa; *nanda-yaśodayoḥ*—of Nanda and Yaśodā; *vīkṣya*—clearly seeing; *anurāgam*—the loving attraction; *paramam*—supreme; *nandam*—to Nanda; *āha*—spoke; *uddhavaḥ*—Uddhava; *mudā*—with joy.

TRANSLATION

Uddhava then joyfully addressed Nanda Mahārāja, having clearly seen the supreme loving attraction he and Yaśodā felt for Kṛṣṇa, the Supreme Personality of Godhead.

PURPORT

If Uddhava had seen Nanda and Yaśodā actually suffering, he would not have reacted with joy. But in fact all emotions on the spiritual platform are transcendental bliss. The so-called anguish of the pure devotees is another form of loving ecstasy. This was clearly seen by Uddhava, and thus he spoke as follows.

TEXT 30

श्रीउद्धव उवाच
युवां श्लाघ्यतमौ नूनं देहिनामिह मानद ।
नारायणेऽखिलगुरौ यत्कृता मतिरीदृशी ॥३०॥

śrī-uddhava uvāca
yuvāṁ ślāghyatamau nūnaṁ
dehināṁ iha māna-da
nārāyaṇe 'khila-gurau
yat kṛtā matir īdṛśī

śrī-uddhavaḥ uvāca—Śrī Uddhava said; *yuvām*—you two; *ślāghya-tamau*—the most praiseworthy; *nūnam*—for certain; *dehinām*—of embodied living beings; *iha*—in this world; *māna-da*—O respectful one; *nārāyaṇe*—for the Supreme Lord Nārāyaṇa; *akhila-gurau*—the spiritual master of all; *yat*—because; *kṛtā*—produced; *matiḥ*—a mentality; *īdṛśī*—like this.

TRANSLATION

Śrī Uddhava said: O respectful Nanda, certainly you and mother Yaśodā are the most praiseworthy persons in the entire world, since you have developed such a loving attitude toward Lord Nārāyaṇa, the spiritual master of all living beings.

PURPORT

Understanding Nanda's mood, as expressed by his statement *manye kṛṣṇaṁ ca rāmaṁ ca prāptāv iha surottamau* ("I think Kṛṣṇa and Rāma must be two exalted demigods"), Uddhava here referred to Kṛṣṇa as Lord Nārāyaṇa.

TEXT 31

एतौ हि विश्वस्य च बीजयोनी
रामो मुकुन्दः पुरुषः प्रधानम् ।
अन्वीय भूतेषु विलक्षणस्य
ज्ञानस्य चेशात इमौ पुराणौ ॥३१॥

etau hi viśvasya ca bīja-yonī
rāmo mukundaḥ puruṣaḥ pradhānam
anvīya bhūteṣu vilakṣaṇasya
jñānasya ceśāta imau purāṇau

etau—these two; *hi*—indeed; *viśvasya*—of the universe; *ca*—and; *bīja*—the seed; *yonī*—and the womb; *rāmaḥ*—Lord Balarāma; *mukundaḥ*—Lord Kṛṣṇa; *puruṣaḥ*—the creating Lord; *pradhānam*—His creative energy; *anvīya*—entering; *bhūteṣu*—within all living beings; *vilakṣaṇasya*—confused or perceiving; *jñānasya*—knowledge; *ca*—and; *īśāte*—control; *imau*—They; *purāṇau*—primeval.

TRANSLATION

These two Lords, Mukunda and Balarāma, are each the seed and womb of the universe, the creator and His creative potency. They enter the hearts of living beings and control their conditioned awareness. They are the primeval Supreme.

PURPORT

The word *vilakṣaṇa* means either "distinctly perceiving" or "confused," depending on how the prefix *vi-* is understood in context. In the case of enlightened souls, *vilakṣaṇa* means "perceiving the correct distinction between the body and the soul," and thus Lord Kṛṣṇa, as indicated by the word *īśāte*, guides the spiritually advancing soul. The other meaning of *vilakṣaṇa*—"confused" or "bewildered"—clearly applies to those who have not understood the difference between the soul and the body, or the distinction between the individual soul and the Supreme Soul. Such bewildered living beings do not go back home, back to Godhead, to the eternal spiritual world, but rather achieve temporary destinations according to the laws of nature.

It is understood from all Vaiṣṇava literature that Śrī Rāma, Balarāma, here accompanying Lord Kṛṣṇa, is nondifferent from Him, being His plenary expansion. The Lord is one, yet He expands Himself, and thus Lord Balarāma in no way compromises the principle of monotheism.

TEXTS 32–33

यस्मिन् जनः प्राणवियोगकाले
क्षणं समावेश्य मनोऽविशुद्धम् ।
निर्हृत्य कर्माशयमाशु याति
परां गतिं ब्रह्ममयोऽर्कवर्णः ॥३२॥
तस्मिन् भवन्तावखिलात्महेतौ
नारायणे कारणमर्त्यमूर्तौ ।
भावं विधत्तां नितरां महात्मन्
किं वावशिष्टं युवयोः सुकृत्यम् ॥३३॥

yasmin janaḥ prāṇa-viyoga-kāle
kṣaṇaṁ samāveśya mano 'viśuddham
nirhṛtya karmāśayam āśu yāti
parāṁ gatiṁ brahma-mayo 'rka-varṇaḥ

tasmin bhavantāv akhilātma-hetau
nārāyaṇe kāraṇa-martya-mūrtau
bhāvaṁ vidhattāṁ nitarāṁ mahātman
kiṁ vāvaśiṣṭaṁ yuvayoḥ su-kṛtyam

yasmin—in whom; *janaḥ*—any person; *prāṇa*—from one's life air; *viyoga*—of separation; *kāle*—at the time; *kṣaṇam*—for a moment; *samāveśya*—absorbing; *manaḥ*—one's mind; *aviśuddham*—impure; *nirhṛtya*—eradicating; *karma*—of the reactions of material work; *āśayam*—all traces; *āśu*—immediately; *yāti*—he goes; *parām*—to the supreme; *gatim*—destination; *brahma-mayaḥ*—in a purely spiritual form; *arka*—like the sun; *varṇaḥ*—whose color; *tasmin*—to Him; *bhavantau*—your good selves; *akhila*—of all; *ātma*—the Supreme Soul; *hetau*—and reason for existence; *nārāyaṇe*—Lord Nārāyaṇa; *kāraṇa*—the cause of everything; *martya*—human; *mūrtau*—in a form; *bhāvam*—pure love; *vidhattām*—have given; *nitarām*—exceedingly; *mahā-ātman*—to the perfectly complete; *kim vā*—then what; *avaśiṣṭam*—remaining; *yuvayoḥ*—for you; *su-kṛtyam*—required pious activity.

TRANSLATION

Anyone, even a person in an impure state, who absorbs his mind in Him for just a moment at the time of death burns up all traces of sinful reactions and immediately attains the supreme transcendental destination in a pure, spiritual form as effulgent as the sun. You two have rendered exceptional loving service to Him, Lord Nārāyaṇa, the Supersoul of all and the cause of all existence, the great soul who, although the original cause of everything, has a humanlike form. What pious deeds could still be required of you?

TEXT 34

आगमिष्यत्यदीर्घेण कालेन व्रजमच्युतः ।
प्रियं विधास्यते पित्रोर्भगवान् सात्वतां पतिः ॥३४॥

āgamiṣyaty adīrgheṇa
kālena vrajam acyutaḥ
priyaṁ vidhāsyate pitror
bhagavān sātvatāṁ patiḥ

āgamiṣyati—He will return; *adīrgheṇa*—not long; *kālena*—in time; *vrajam*—to Vraja; *acyutaḥ*—Kṛṣṇa, the infallible one; *priyam*—satisfaction; *vidhāsyate*—He will give; *pitroḥ*—to His parents; *bhagavān*—the Supreme Lord; *sātvatām*—of the devotees; *patiḥ*—master and protector.

TRANSLATION

Infallible Kṛṣṇa, the Lord of the devotees, will soon return to Vraja to satisfy His parents.

PURPORT

Here Uddhava begins to deliver Lord Kṛṣṇa's message.

TEXT 35

हत्वा कंसं रंगमध्ये प्रतीपं सर्वसात्वताम् ।
यदाह वः समागत्य कृष्णः सत्यं करोति तत् ॥३५॥

hatvā kaṁsaṁ raṅga-madhye
pratīpaṁ sarva-sātvatām
yad āha vaḥ samāgatya
kṛṣṇaḥ satyaṁ karoti tat

hatvā—having killed; *kaṁsam*—Kaṁsa; *raṅga*—the arena; *madhye*—within; *pratīpam*—the enemy; *sarva-sātvatām*—of all the Yadus; *yat*—what; *āha*—He spoke; *vaḥ*—to you; *samāgatya*—by coming back; *kṛṣṇaḥ*—Kṛṣṇa; *satyam*—true; *karoti*—will make; *tat*—that.

TRANSLATION

Having killed Kaṁsa, the enemy of all the Yadus, in the wrestling arena, Kṛṣṇa will now surely fulfill His promise to you by coming back.

TEXT 36

मा खिद्यतं महाभागौ द्रक्ष्यथः कृष्णमन्तिके ।
अन्तर्हृदि स भूतानामास्ते ज्योतिरिवैधसि ॥३६॥

mā khidyataṁ mahā-bhāgau
drakṣyathaḥ kṛṣṇam antike
antar hṛdi sa bhūtānām
āste jyotir ivaidhasi

mā khidyatam—please do not lament; *mahā-bhāgau*—O most fortunate ones; *drakṣyathaḥ*—you will see; *kṛṣṇam*—Kṛṣṇa; *antike*—in the near future; *antaḥ*—within; *hṛdi*—the hearts; *saḥ*—He; *bhūtānām*—of all living beings; *āste*—is present; *jyotiḥ*—fire; *iva*—just as; *edhasi*—within firewood.

TRANSLATION

O most fortunate ones, do not lament. You will see Kṛṣṇa again very soon. He is present in the hearts of all living beings, just as fire lies dormant in wood.

PURPORT

Uddhava understood that Nanda and Yaśodā were very impatient to see Kṛṣṇa, and thus he reassured them that Śrī Kṛṣṇa would come soon.

TEXT 37

न ह्यस्यास्ति प्रियः कश्चिन्नाप्रियो वास्त्यमानिनः ।
नोत्तमो नाधमो वापि समानस्यासमोऽपि वा ॥३७॥

na hy asyāsti priyaḥ kaścin
nāpriyo vāsty amāninaḥ
nottamo nādhamo vāpi
sa-mānasyāsamo 'pi vā

na—not; *hi*—indeed; *asya*—for Him; *asti*—there is; *priyaḥ*—dear; *kaścit*—anyone; *na*—not; *apriyaḥ*—not dear; *vā*—or; *asti*—there is; *amāninaḥ*—who is free from desire for respect; *na*—not; *uttamaḥ*—superior; *na*—not; *adhamaḥ*—inferior; *vā*—or; *api*—also; *sa-mānasya*—for Him who has all respect for others; *āsamaḥ*—completely ordinary; *api*—also; *vā*—or.

TRANSLATION

For Him no one is especially dear or despicable, superior or inferior, and yet He is not indifferent to anyone. He is free from all desire for respect and yet gives respect to all others.

TEXT 38

न माता न पिता तस्य न भार्या न सुतादयः ।
नात्मीयो न परश्चापि न देहो जन्म एव च ॥३८॥

na mātā na pitā tasya
na bhāryā na sutādayaḥ
nātmīyo na paraś cāpi
na deho janma eva ca

na—there is no; *mātā*—mother; *na*—no; *pitā*—father; *tasya*—for Him; *na*—no; *bhāryā*—wife; *na*—no; *suta-ādayaḥ*—children and so forth; *na*—no one; *ātmīyaḥ*—related to Himself; *na*—nor; *paraḥ*—an outsider; *ca api*—also; *na*—no; *dehaḥ*—body; *janma*—birth; *eva*—either; *ca*—and.

TRANSLATION

He has no mother, no father, no wife, children or other relatives. No one is related to Him, and yet no one is a stranger to Him. He has no material body and no birth.

TEXT 39

न चास्य कर्म वा लोके सदसन्मिश्रयोनिषु ।
क्रीडार्थं सोऽपि साधूनां परित्राणाय कल्पते ॥३९॥

na cāsya karma vā loke
sad-asan-miśra-yoniṣu
krīḍārthaṁ so 'pi sādhūnāṁ
paritrāṇāya kalpate

na—there is not; *ca*—and; *asya*—for Him; *karma*—work; *vā*—or; *loke*—in this world; *sat*—pure; *asat*—impure; *miśra*—or mixed; *yoniṣu*—in wombs or species; *krīḍā*—of playing; *artham*—for the sake; *saḥ*—He; *api*—also; *sādhūnām*—of His saintly devotees; *paritrāṇāya*—for the saving; *kalpate*—appears.

TRANSLATION

He has no work to do in this world that would oblige Him to take birth in pure, impure or mixed species of life. Yet to enjoy His pastimes and deliver His saintly devotees, He manifests Himself.

TEXT 40

सत्त्वं रजस्तम इति भजते निर्गुणो गुणान् ।
क्रीडन्नतीतोऽपि गुणैः सृजत्यवति हन्त्यजः ॥४०॥

sattvaṁ rajas tama iti
bhajate nirguṇo guṇān
krīḍann atīto 'pi guṇaiḥ
sṛjaty avati hanty ajaḥ

sattvam—goodness; *rajaḥ*—passion; *tamaḥ*—and ignorance; *iti*—thus called; *bhajate*—He accepts; *nirguṇaḥ*—beyond the material modes; *guṇān*—the modes; *krīḍan*—playing; *atītaḥ*—transcendental; *api*—although; *guṇaiḥ*—using the modes; *sṛjati*—He creates; *avati*—maintains; *hanti*—and destroys; *ajaḥ*—the unborn Lord.

TRANSLATION

Although beyond the three modes of material nature—goodness, passion and ignorance—the transcendental Lord accepts association with them as His play. Thus the unborn Supreme Lord utilizes the material modes to create, maintain and destroy.

PURPORT

As stated in the *Brahma-sūtra* (2.1.34), *loka-vat līlā-kaivalyam:* "The Lord performs His spiritual pastimes as if He were a resident of this world."

Although the Lord does not favor or abuse anyone, we still observe happiness and suffering in this world. The *Gītā* (13.22) states, *kāraṇaṁ guṇa-saṅgo 'sya*: We desire to associate with various qualities of material nature, and thus we must accept the consequences. The Lord provides the field of material nature, in which we exercise our free will. Foolish nondevotees not only attempt to cheat the Lord by trying to exploit His nature, but when they suffer the reaction they blame God for their own misdeeds. This is the shameless position of those who are envious of God.

TEXT 41

यथा भ्रमरिकादृष्ट्या भ्राम्यतीव महीयते ।
चित्ते कर्तरि तत्रात्मा कर्तेवाहंधिया स्मृतः ॥४१॥

yathā bhramarikā-dṛṣṭyā
bhrāmyatīva mahīyate
citte kartari tatrātmā
kartevāhaṁ-dhiyā smṛtaḥ

yathā—as; *bhramarikā*—because of whirling around; *dṛṣṭyā*—in one's vision; *bhrāmyati*—whirling; *iva*—as if; *mahī*—the ground; *iyate*—appears; *citte*—the mind; *kartari*—being the doer; *tatra*—there; *ātmā*—the self; *kartā*—the doer; *iva*—as if; *aham-dhiyā*—because of false ego; *smṛtaḥ*—is thought.

TRANSLATION

Just as a person who is whirling around perceives the ground to be turning, one who is affected by false ego thinks himself the doer, when actually only his mind is acting.

PURPORT

Śrīla Viśvanātha Cakravartī gives a parallel idea: Although our happiness and distress are caused by our own interaction with the material qualities, we perceive the Lord to be their cause.

TEXT 42

युवयोरेव नैवायमात्मजो भगवान् हरिः ।
सर्वेषामात्मजो ह्यात्मा पिता माता स ईश्वरः ॥४२॥

yuvayor eva naivāyam
ātmajo bhagavān hariḥ
sarveṣām ātmajo hy ātmā
pitā mātā sa īśvaraḥ

yuvayoḥ—of you two; *eva*—alone; *na*—not; *eva*—indeed; *ayam*—He; *ātma-jaḥ*—the son; *bhagavān*—the Supreme Personality of Godhead; *hariḥ*—Lord Kṛṣṇa; *sarveṣām*—of all; *ātma-jaḥ*—the son; *hi*—indeed; *ātmā*—the very self; *pitā*—father; *mātā*—mother; *saḥ*—He; *īśvaraḥ*—the controlling Lord.

TRANSLATION

The Supreme Lord Hari is certainly not your son alone. Rather, being the Lord, He is the son, Soul, father and mother of everyone.

TEXT 43

दृष्टं श्रुतं भूतभवद्भविष्यत्
स्थास्नुश्चरिष्णुर्महदल्पकं च ।
विनाच्युताद्वस्तु तरां न वाच्यं
स एव सर्वं परमात्मभूतः ॥४३॥

dṛṣṭaṁ śrutaṁ bhūta-bhavad-bhaviṣyat
sthāsnuś cariṣṇur mahad alpakaṁ ca
vinācyutād vastu tarāṁ na vācyaṁ
sa eva sarvaṁ paramātma-bhūtaḥ

dṛṣṭam—seen; *śrutam*—heard; *bhūta*—past; *bhavat*—present; *bhaviṣyat*—future; *sthāsnuḥ*—stationary; *cariṣṇuḥ*—mobile; *mahat*—large; *alpakam*—small; *ca*—and; *vinā*—apart from; *acyutāt*—the infallible Lord Kṛṣṇa; *vastu*—thing; *tarām*—at all; *na*—is not; *vācyam*—capable of being named; *saḥ*—He; *eva*—alone; *sarvam*—everything; *parama-ātma*—as the Supersoul; *bhūtaḥ*—manifesting.

TRANSLATION

Nothing can be said to exist independent of Lord Acyuta—nothing heard or seen, nothing in the past, present or future, nothing moving or unmoving, great or small. He indeed is everything, for He is the Supreme Soul.

PURPORT

Śri Uddhava is relieving the distress of Nanda and Yaśodā by bringing them to a more philosophical plane. He is explaining that since Lord Kṛṣṇa is everything and is within everything, His pure devotees are always with Him.

TEXT 44

एवं निशा सा ब्रुवतोर्व्यतीता
नन्दस्य कृष्णानुचरस्य राजन् ।
गोप्यः समुत्थाय निरूप्य दीपान्
वास्तून् समभ्यर्च्य दधीन्यमन्थन् ॥४४॥

evaṁ niśā sā bruvator vyatītā
nandasya kṛṣṇānucarasya rājan
gopyaḥ samutthāya nirūpya dīpān
vāstūn samabhyarcya dadhīny amanthan

evam—in this way; *niśā*—the night; *sā*—that; *bruvatoḥ*—as they were both speaking; *vyatītā*—was finished; *nandasya*—Nanda Mahārāja; *kṛṣṇa-anucarasya*—and the servant of Kṛṣṇa (Uddhava); *rājan*—O King (Parīkṣit); *gopyaḥ*—the cowherd women; *samutthāya*—rising from sleep; *nirūpya*—lighting; *dīpān*—lamps; *vāstūn*—the domestic deities; *samabhyarcya*—worshiping; *dadhīni*—curds; *amanthan*—churned.

TRANSLATION

While Kṛṣṇa's messenger continued speaking with Nanda, the night ended, O King. The women of the cowherd village rose from bed and, lighting lamps, worshiped their household deities. Then they began churning the yogurt into butter.

TEXT 45

ता दीपदीप्तैर्मणिभिर्विरेजू
रज्जूर्विकर्षद्भुजकंकणस्रजः ।

चलन्नितम्बस्तनहारकुण्डल-
त्विषत्कपोलारुणकुंकुमाननाः ॥४५॥

tā dīpa-dīptair maṇibhir virejū
rajjūr vikarṣad-bhuja-kaṅkaṇa-srajaḥ
calan-nitamba-stana-hāra-kuṇḍala-
tviṣat-kapolāruṇa-kuṅkumānanāḥ

tāḥ—those women; *dīpa*—by the lamps; *dīptaiḥ*—illumined; *maṇibhiḥ*—with jewels; *virejuḥ*—shone; *rajjūḥ*—the (churning) ropes; *vikarṣat*—pulling; *bhuja*—upon their arms; *kaṅkaṇa*—of bangles; *srajaḥ*—wearing rows; *calan*—moving; *nitamba*—their hips; *stana*—breasts; *hāra*—and necklaces; *kuṇḍala*—due to their earrings; *tviṣat*—glowing; *kapola*—their cheeks; *aruṇa*—reddish; *kuṅkuma*—with *kuṅkuma* powder; *ānanāḥ*—their faces.

TRANSLATION

As they pulled on the churning ropes with their bangled arms, the women of Vraja shone with the splendor of their jewels, which reflected the lamps' light. Their hips, breasts and necklaces moved about, and their faces, anointed with reddish *kuṅkuma*, glowed radiantly with the luster of their earrings reflecting from their cheeks.

TEXT 46

उद्गायतीनामरविन्दलोचनं
व्रजांगनानां दिवमस्पृशद्ध्वनिः ।
दध्नश्च निर्मन्थनशब्दमिश्रितो
निरस्यते येन दिशाममंगलम् ॥४६॥

udgāyatīnām aravinda-locanaṁ
vrajāṅganānāṁ divam aspṛśad dhvaniḥ
dadhnaś ca nirmanthana-śabda-miśrito
nirasyate yena diśām amaṅgalam

udgāyatīnām—who were loudly singing; *aravinda*—like lotuses; *locanam*—(about the Lord) whose eyes; *vraja-aṅganānām*—of the women of Vraja; *divam*—the sky; *aspṛśat*—touched; *dhvaniḥ*—the reverberation; *dadhnaḥ*—of the curds; *ca*—and; *nirmanthana*—of the churning; *śabda*—with the sound; *miśritaḥ*—mixed; *nirasyate*—is dispelled; *yena*—by which; *diśām*—of all directions; *amaṅgalam*—the inauspiciousness.

TRANSLATION

As the ladies of Vraja loudly sang the glories of lotus-eyed Kṛṣṇa, their songs blended with the sound of their churning, ascended to the sky and dissipated all inauspiciousness in every direction.

PURPORT

The *gopīs* were absorbed in thought of Kṛṣṇa and were thus feeling His presence. Therefore they could joyfully sing.

TEXT 47

भगवत्युदिते सूर्ये नन्दद्वारि व्रजौकसः ।
दृष्ट्वा रथं शातकौम्भं कस्यायमिति चाब्रुवन् ॥४७॥

bhagavaty udite sūrye
nanda-dvāri vrajaukasaḥ
dṛṣṭvā rathaṁ śātakaumbhaṁ
kasyāyam iti cābruvan

bhagavati—the lord; *udite*—when he rose; *sūrye*—the sun; *nanda-dvāri*—in the doorway of Nanda Mahārāja's home; *vraja-okasaḥ*—the residents of Vraja; *dṛṣṭvā*—seeing; *ratham*—the chariot; *śātakaumbham*—made of gold; *kasya*—whose; *ayam*—this; *iti*—thus; *ca*—and; *abruvan*—they spoke.

TRANSLATION

When the godly sun had risen, the people of Vraja noticed the golden chariot in front of Nanda Mahārāja's doorway. "Who does this belong to?" they asked.

TEXT 48

अक्रूर आगतः किं वा यः कंसस्यार्थसाधकः ।
येन नीतो मधुपुरीं कृष्णः कमललोचनः ॥४८॥

akrūra āgataḥ kiṁ vā
yaḥ kaṁsasyārtha-sādhakaḥ
yena nīto madhu-purīṁ
kṛṣṇaḥ kamala-locanaḥ

akrūraḥ—Akrūra; *āgataḥ*—has come; *kim vā*—perhaps; *yaḥ*—who; *kaṁsasya*—of King Kaṁsa; *artha*—of the purpose; *sādhakaḥ*—the executor; *yena*—by whom; *nītaḥ*—brought; *madhu-purīm*—to Mathurā City; *kṛṣṇaḥ*—Kṛṣṇa; *kamala*—lotuslike; *locanaḥ*—whose eyes.

TRANSLATION

"Perhaps Akrūra has returned—he who fulfilled Kaṁsa's desire by taking lotus-eyed Kṛṣṇa to Mathurā.

PURPORT

The *gopīs* angrily spoke this statement.

TEXT 49

किं साधयिष्यत्यस्माभिर्भर्तुः प्रीतस्य निष्कृतिम् ।
ततः स्त्रीणां वदन्तीनामुद्धवोऽगात्कृताह्निकः ॥४९॥

kiṁ sādhayiṣyaty asmābhir
bhartuḥ prītasya niṣkṛtim
tataḥ strīṇāṁ vadantīnām
uddhavo 'gāt kṛtāhnikaḥ

kim—whether; *sādhayiṣyati*—will he accomplish; *asmābhiḥ*—with us; *bhartuḥ*—of his master; *prītasya*—who was satisfied with him; *niṣkṛtim*—the funeral ritual; *tataḥ*—then; *strīṇām*—the women; *vadantīnām*—as they were speaking; *uddhavaḥ*—Uddhava; *agāt*—came there; *kṛta*—having performed; *ahnikaḥ*—his early-morning religious duties.

TRANSLATION

"Is he going to use our flesh to offer funeral oblations for his master, who was so satisfied with his service?" As the women were speaking in this way, Uddhava appeared, having finished his early-morning duties.

PURPORT

This verse reveals the bitter disappointment the *gopīs* felt when Akrūra took Kṛṣṇa away. However, they will be pleasantly surprised to see that the unexpected guest is Uddhava.

Thus end the purports of the humble servants of His Divine Grace A. C. Bhaktivedanta Swami Prabhupāda to the Tenth Canto, Forty-sixth Chapter, of the Śrīmad-Bhāgavatam, *entitled "Uddhava Visits Vṛndāvana."*

CHAPTER FORTY–SEVEN

The Song of the Bee

This chapter describes how Uddhava, on the order of Lord Śrī Kṛṣṇa, delivered the Lord's message to the *gopīs,* consoled them and then returned to Mathurā.

When the young maidens of Vraja saw lotus-eyed Uddhava, who wore a yellow garment and attractive earrings, they were astonished at how much he resembled Kṛṣṇa. Thinking "Who is this?" they approached and encircled him. When they realized that Kṛṣṇa must have sent him, they brought him to a secluded place where he could speak to them confidentially.

The *gopīs* then began to remember the pastimes they had enjoyed with Śrī Kṛṣṇa, and putting aside all ordinary propriety and shyness, they loudly wept. One *gopī,* while deeply meditating on Her association with Kṛṣṇa, noticed a bumblebee before Her. Imagining the bee to be a messenger from Him, She said, "Just as bees wander among various flowers, Śrī Kṛṣṇa has abandoned the young girls of Vraja and developed affection for other women." The *gopī* continued to speak in this way, contrasting Her own supposed ill fortune to Her rival lovers' good fortune, all the while glorifying the names, forms, qualities and pastimes of Lord Kṛṣṇa. She then declared that although Kṛṣṇa may have abandoned the *gopīs,* they could not possibly stop remembering Him for even a moment.

Uddhava tried to console the damsels of Vraja, who were so anxious to see Kṛṣṇa once again. Uddhava explained, "While ordinary persons must perform many pious deeds to qualify as servants of Lord Kṛṣṇa, you simple cowherd girls are so extremely fortunate that the Lord has favored you with the very highest degree of pure devotion for Him." Uddhava then related to them the Lord's message.

Quoting Lord Kṛṣṇa, Uddhava said, "'I am the Supreme Soul and supreme shelter of all. By My potencies I create, maintain and destroy the cosmos. I am indeed most dear to you *gopīs*, but to increase your attraction for Me and intensify your remembrance of Me, I left you. After all, when a woman's beloved is far away, she fixes her mind upon him constantly. By incessantly remembering Me, you are sure to regain My association without delay.'"

The *gopīs* then asked Uddhava, "Is Kṛṣṇa happy now that Kaṁsa is dead and He can enjoy the company of His family members and the women of Mathurā? Does He still remember all the pastimes He enjoyed with us, such as the *rāsa* dance? Will Śrī Kṛṣṇa once again appear before us and give us ecstasy, just as Lord Indra, with his rain, gives life back to the forests aggrieved by the summer heat? Although we know that the greatest happiness comes from renunciation, we simply cannot stop hoping to attain Kṛṣṇa, for the marks of His lotus feet are still present throughout the land of Vraja, reminding us of His graceful gait, generous smiles and gentle talks. By all these our hearts have been stolen away."

Having said this, the *gopīs* loudly chanted Lord Kṛṣṇa's names, calling out, "O Govinda, please come and destroy our suffering!" Uddhava then pacified the *gopīs* with statements that dispelled their pain of separation, and they in turn worshiped him as nondifferent from Śrī Kṛṣṇa.

Uddhava stayed in the district of Vraja for several months, giving pleasure to the residents by reminding them about Kṛṣṇa in various ways. Very satisfied at seeing the extent of the *gopīs'* love for the Lord, he declared, "These cowherd girls have perfected their lives by coming to the platform of unalloyed love for Kṛṣṇa. Indeed, even Lord Brahmā is inferior to them. The goddess of fortune herself, who always resides on Kṛṣṇa's chest, could not get the same mercy as that which the *gopīs* obtained during the *rāsa* dance, when Kṛṣṇa embraced their necks with His mighty arms. What, then, to speak of other women! Indeed, I would consider myself most fortunate to take birth as even a bush or creeper that would sometimes be touched by the dust of these *gopīs'* lotus feet."

Finally, Uddhava entreated Nanda Mahārāja and the other cowherd men for permission to go back to Mathurā. Nanda presented him with many gifts and prayed to Uddhava for the ability to always remember Kṛṣṇa. Returning to Mathurā, Uddhava offered Balarāma, Kṛṣṇa and King Ugrasena the gifts sent by Nanda Mahārāja and described to them everything he had experienced in Vraja.

TEXTS 1–2

श्रीशुक उवाच
तं वीक्ष्य कृष्णानुचरं व्रजस्त्रियः
प्रलम्बबाहुं नवकञ्जलोचनम् ।
पीताम्बरं पुष्करमालिनं लसन्-
मुखारविन्दं परिमृष्टकुण्डलम् ॥१॥
सुविस्मिताः कोऽयमपीव्यदर्शनः
कुतश्च कस्याच्युतवेषभूषणः ।
इति स्म सर्वाः परिवव्रुरुत्सुकास्
तमुत्तमःश्लोकपदाम्बुजाश्रयम् ॥२॥

śrī-śuka uvāca
taṁ vīkṣya kṛṣṇānucaraṁ vraja-striyaḥ
pralamba-bāhuṁ nava-kañja-locanam
pītāmbaraṁ puṣkara-mālinaṁ lasan-
mukhāravindaṁ parimṛṣṭa-kuṇḍalam

su-vismitāḥ ko 'yam apīvya-darśanaḥ
kutaś ca kasyācyuta-veṣa-bhūṣaṇaḥ
iti sma sarvāḥ parivavrur utsukās
tam uttamaḥ-śloka-padāmbujāśrayam

śrī-śukaḥ uvāca—Śrī Śukadeva Gosvāmī said; *tam*—him; *vīkṣya*—seeing; *kṛṣṇa-anucaram*—the servant of Lord Kṛṣṇa (Uddhava); *vraja-striyaḥ*—the women of Vraja; *pralamba*—hanging down; *bāhum*—whose arms; *nava*—young; *kañja*—like lotuses; *locanam*—whose eyes; *pīta*—yellow; *ambaram*—wearing a garment; *puṣkara*—of lotuses; *mālinam*—wearing a garland; *lasat*—effulgently glowing; *mukha*—whose face; *aravindam*—lotuslike; *parimṛṣṭa*—polished; *kuṇḍalam*—whose earrings; *su-vismitāḥ*—quite astonished; *kaḥ*—who; *ayam*—this; *apīvya*—handsome; *darśanaḥ*—whose appearance; *kutaḥ*—from where; *ca*—and; *kasya*—belonging to whom; *acyuta*—of Kṛṣṇa; *veṣa*—wearing the clothing; *bhūṣaṇaḥ*—and ornaments; *iti*—saying this; *sma*—indeed;

sarvāḥ—all of them; *parivavruḥ*—surrounded; *utsukāḥ*—eager; *tam*—him; *uttamaḥ-śloka*—of Lord Kṛṣṇa, who is praised by the best poetry; *pada-ambuja*—by the lotus feet; *āśrayam*—who is sheltered.

TRANSLATION

Śukadeva Gosvāmī said: The young women of Vraja became astonished upon seeing Lord Kṛṣṇa's servant, who had long arms, whose eyes resembled a newly grown lotus, who wore a yellow garment and a lotus garland, and whose lotuslike face glowed with brightly polished earrings. "Who is this handsome man?" the *gopīs* asked. "Where has he come from, and whom does he serve? He's wearing Kṛṣṇa's clothes and ornaments!" Saying this, the *gopīs* eagerly crowded around Uddhava, whose shelter was the lotus feet of Lord Uttamaḥśloka, Śrī Kṛṣṇa.

TEXT 3

तं प्रश्रयेणावनताः सुसत्कृतं
सव्रीडहासेक्षणसूनृतादिभिः ।
रहस्यपृच्छन्नुपविष्टमासने
विज्ञाय सन्देशहरं रमापतेः ॥३॥

taṁ praśrayeṇāvanatāḥ su-sat-kṛtaṁ
sa-vrīḍa-hāsekṣaṇa-sūnṛtādibhiḥ
rahasy apṛcchann upaviṣṭam āsane
vijñāya sandeśa-haraṁ ramā-pateḥ

tam—him, Uddhava; *praśrayeṇa*—with humility; *avanatāḥ*—bowed down (the *gopīs*); *su*—properly; *sat-kṛtam*—honored; *sa-vrīḍa*—with shyness; *hāsa*—and smiling; *īkṣaṇa*—by their glances; *sūnṛta*—pleasing words; *ādibhiḥ*—and so forth; *rahasi*—in a secluded place; *apṛcchan*—they inquired; *upaviṣṭam*—who was seated; *āsane*—on a cushion; *vijñāya*—understanding him to be; *sandeśa-haram*—the message carrier; *ramā-pateḥ*—of the master of the goddess of fortune.

TRANSLATION

Bowing their heads in humility, the *gopīs* duly honored Uddhava with their shy, smiling glances and pleasing words. They took him to a quiet place, seated him comfortably and began to question him, for they recognized him to be a messenger from Kṛṣṇa, the master of the goddess of fortune.

PURPORT

The chaste *gopīs* were enlivened to see that a messenger had come from Kṛṣṇa. As Uddhava will discover during his stay in Vṛndāvana, the unique *gopīs* could not think of anything but their beloved Kṛṣṇa.

TEXT 4

जानीमस्त्वां यदुपतेः पार्षदं समुपागतम् ।
भर्त्रेह प्रेषितः पित्रोर्भवान् प्रियचिकीर्षया ॥४॥

jānīmas tvāṁ yadu-pateḥ
pārṣadaṁ samupāgatam
bhartreha preṣitaḥ pitror
bhavān priya-cikīrṣayā

jānīmaḥ—we know; *tvām*—you; *yadu-pateḥ*—of the chief of the Yadus; *pārṣadam*—the personal associate; *samupāgatam*—arrived here; *bhartrā*—by your master; *iha*—here; *preṣitaḥ*—sent; *pitroḥ*—of His parents; *bhavān*—your good self; *priya*—satisfaction; *cikīrṣayā*—wanting to give.

TRANSLATION

[The *gopīs* said:] We know that you are the personal servant of Kṛṣṇa, the chief of the Yadus, and that you have come here on the order of your good master, who desires to give pleasure to His parents.

TEXT 5

अन्यथा गोव्रजे तस्य स्मरणीयं न चक्ष्महे ।
स्नेहानुबन्धो बन्धूनां मुनेरपि सुदुस्त्यजः ॥५॥

anyathā go-vraje tasya
smaraṇīyaṁ na cakṣmahe
snehānubandho bandhūnāṁ
muner api su-dustyajaḥ

anyathā—otherwise; *go-vraje*—in the cow pasture; *tasya*—for Him; *smaraṇīyam*—that which is worth remembering; *na cakṣmahe*—we do not see; *sneha*—of affection; *anubandhaḥ*—the attachment; *bandhūnām*—to relatives; *muneḥ*—for a sage; *api*—even; *su-dustyajaḥ*—very difficult to abandon.

TRANSLATION

We see nothing else He might consider worth remembering in these cow pastures of Vraja. Indeed, the bonds of affection for one's family members are difficult to break, even for a sage.

TEXT 6

अन्येष्वर्थकृता मैत्री यावदर्थविडम्बनम् ।
पुम्भिः स्त्रीषु कृता यद्वत्सुमनःस्विव षट्पदैः ॥६॥

anyeṣv artha-kṛtā maitrī
yāvad-artha-viḍambanam
pumbhiḥ strīṣu kṛtā yadvat
sumanaḥsv iva ṣaṭpadaiḥ

anyeṣu—toward others; *artha*—for some motivation; *kṛtā*—manifested; *maitrī*—friendship; *yāvat*—for as long; *artha*—(as one is fulfilling his) motive; *viḍambanam*—pretense; *pumbhiḥ*—by men; *strīṣu*—for women; *kṛtā*—shown; *yadvat*—as much; *sumanaḥsu*—for flowers; *iva*—as; *ṣaṭ-padaiḥ*—by bees.

TRANSLATION

The friendship shown toward others—those who are not family members—is motivated by personal interest, and thus it is a pretense that lasts only until one's purpose is fulfilled. Such friendship is just like the interest men take in women, or bees in flowers.

PURPORT

Śrīla Viśvanātha Cakravartī Ṭhākura explains here that attractive women, like flowers, possess beauty, fragrance, tenderness, charm and so on. And as bees drink only once of a flower's nectar and then leave it for another, fickle men abandon beautiful and devoted women to pursue other pleasures. This tendency is condemned here by the *gopīs,* who gave their hearts completely to Śrī Kṛṣṇa. The *gopīs* wanted only to exhibit their charms for Lord Kṛṣṇa's pleasure, and in the pain of separation they questioned the motives of His friendship with them.

These are the transcendental pastimes of the Lord. Both Lord Kṛṣṇa and the *gopīs* are completely liberated souls engaged in spiritual loving affairs. By contrast, our so-called loving affairs, being perverted reflections of the perfect loving relationships in the spiritual world, are polluted with lust, greed, pride and so on. Like all liberated souls, the *gopīs*—and certainly Lord Kṛṣṇa Himself—are eternally free of these lower qualities, and their intense loving affairs are motivated exclusively by unalloyed devotion.

TEXT 7

निःस्वं त्यजन्ति गणिका अकल्पं नृपतिं प्रजाः ।
अधीतविद्या आचार्यमृत्विजो दत्तदक्षिणम् ॥७॥

niḥsvaṁ tyajanti gaṇikā
akalpaṁ nṛpatiṁ prajāḥ
adhīta-vidyā ācāryam
ṛtvijo datta-dakṣiṇam

niḥsvam—one without any assets; *tyajanti*—abandon; *gaṇikāḥ*—prostitutes; *akalpam*—incompetent; *nṛ-patim*—a king; *prajāḥ*—citizens;

adhīta-vidyāḥ—those who have completed their education; *ācāryam*—the teacher; *ṛtvijaḥ*—priests; *datta*—(the sacrificer) who has given; *dakṣiṇam*—their remuneration.

TRANSLATION

Prostitutes abandon a penniless man, subjects an incompetent king, students their teacher once they have finished their education, and priests a man who has remunerated them for a sacrifice.

TEXT 8

खगा वीतफलं वृक्षं भुक्त्वा चातिथयो गृहम् ।
दग्धं मृगास्तथारण्यं जारा भुक्त्वा रतां स्त्रियम् ॥८॥

khagā vīta-phalaṁ vṛkṣaṁ
bhuktvā cātithayo gṛham
dagdhaṁ mṛgās tathāraṇyaṁ
jārā bhuktvā ratāṁ striyam

khagāḥ—birds; *vīta*—rid; *phalam*—of its fruits; *vṛkṣam*—a tree; *bhuktvā*—having eaten; *ca*—and; *atithayaḥ*—guests; *gṛham*—a house; *dagdham*—burned down; *mṛgāḥ*—animals; *tathā*—similarly; *araṇyam*—a forest; *jārāḥ*—paramours; *bhuktvā*—having enjoyed; *ratām*—attracted; *striyam*—a woman.

TRANSLATION

Birds abandon a tree when its fruits are gone, guests a house after they have eaten, animals a forest that has burnt down, and a lover the woman he has enjoyed, even though she remains attached to him.

TEXTS 9–10

इति गोप्यो हि गोविन्दे गतवाक्कायमानसाः ।
कृष्णदूते समायाते उद्धवे त्यक्तलौकिकाः ॥९॥

गायन्त्यः प्रियकर्माणि रुदन्त्यश्च गतह्रियः ।
तस्य संस्मृत्य संस्मृत्य यानि कैशोरबाल्ययोः ॥१०॥

iti gopyo hi govinde
gata-vāk-kāya-mānasāḥ
kṛṣṇa-dūte samāyāte
uddhave tyakta-laukikāḥ

gāyantyaḥ priya-karmāṇi
rudantyaś ca gata-hriyaḥ
tasya saṁsmṛtya saṁsmṛtya
yāni kaiśora-bālyayoḥ

iti—thus; *gopyaḥ*—the *gopīs; hi*—indeed; *govinde*—on Govinda; *gata*—focusing; *vāk*—their speech; *kāya*—bodies; *mānasāḥ*—and minds; *kṛṣṇa-dūte*—the messenger of Kṛṣṇa; *samāyāte*—having arrived and joined them; *uddhave*—Uddhava; *tyakta*—putting aside; *laukikāḥ*—worldly affairs; *gāyantyaḥ*—singing; *priya*—of their beloved; *karmāṇi*—about the activities; *rudantyaḥ*—crying; *ca*—and; *gata-hriyaḥ*—forgetting all shyness; *tasya*—His; *saṁsmṛtya saṁsmṛtya*—intensely remembering again and again; *yāni*—which; *kaiśora*—of youth; *bālyayoḥ*—and childhood.

TRANSLATION

Thus speaking, the *gopīs,* whose words, bodies and minds were fully dedicated to Lord Govinda, put aside all their regular work now that Kṛṣṇa's messenger, Śrī Uddhava, had arrived among them. Constantly remembering the activities their beloved Kṛṣṇa had performed in His childhood and youth, they sang about them and cried without shame.

PURPORT

The word *bālyayoḥ* here indicates that ever since their childhood, the *gopīs* had been completely in love with Kṛṣṇa. Thus even though social custom dictated that they not reveal their love to others, they forgot all external considerations and wept openly before Kṛṣṇa's messenger, Uddhava.

TEXT 11

काचिन्मधुकरं दृष्ट्वा ध्यायन्ती कृष्णसंगमम् ।
प्रियप्रस्थापितं दूतं कल्पयित्वेदमब्रवीत् ॥११॥

kācin madhukaraṁ dṛṣṭvā
dhyāyantī kṛṣṇa-saṅgamam
priya-prasthāpitaṁ dūtaṁ
kalpayitvedam abravīt

kācit—one (of the *gopīs*); *madhu-karam*—a honeybee; *dṛṣṭvā*—seeing; *dhyāyantī*—while meditating; *kṛṣṇa-saṅgamam*—on Her association with Kṛṣṇa; *priya*—by Her beloved; *prasthāpitam*—sent; *dūtam*—a messenger; *kalpayitvā*—imagining it; *idam*—the following; *abravīt*—spoke.

TRANSLATION

One of the *gopīs*, while meditating on Her previous association with Kṛṣṇa, saw a honeybee before Her and imagined it to be a messenger sent by Her beloved. Thus She spoke as follows.

PURPORT

Śrīmatī Rādhārāṇī is referred to in this verse as *kācit*, "a certain *gopī*." To establish that this particular *gopī* is in fact Śrīmatī Rādhārāṇī, Śrīla Jīva Gosvāmī quotes the following verses from the *Agni Purāṇa:*

gopyaḥ papracchur ūṣasi
kṛṣṇānucaram uddhavam
hari-līlā-vihārāṁś ca
tatraikāṁ rādhikāṁ vinā

rādhā tad-bhāva-saṁlīnā
vāsanāyā virāmitā
sakhībhiḥ sābhyadhāc chuddha-
vijñāna-guṇa-jṛmbhitam

ijyānte-vāsināṁ veda-
caramāṁśa-vibhāvanaiḥ

"At dawn the *gopīs* inquired from Kṛṣṇa's servant, Uddhava, about the Lord's pastimes and recreation. Only Śrīmatī Rādhārāṇī, immersed in thought of Kṛṣṇa, withdrew Her interest in the talks. Then Rādhā, who is worshiped by the residents of Her Vṛndāvana village, spoke up in the midst of Her girlfriends. Her words were full of pure transcendental knowledge and expressed the ultimate portion of the *Vedas*."

In the *Bhagavad-gītā* (15.15) Lord Kṛṣṇa states, *vedaiś ca sarvair aham eva vedyaḥ*: "By all the *Vedas*, I am to be known." To know Kṛṣṇa is to love Kṛṣṇa, and thus Rādhārāṇī, by Her own example and words, revealed Her supreme love for the Lord.

Having quoted the above verses from the *Agni Purāṇa*, Śrīla Jīva Gosvāmī also quotes the following from the *Nṛsiṁha-tāpanī Upaniṣad* (*Pūrva-khaṇḍa* 2.4): *yaṁ sarve devā namanti mumukṣavo brahma-vādinaś ca*. "All the demigods and all the transcendental philosophers who desire liberation bow down to the Supreme Lord." We should follow suit.

TEXT 12

गोप्युवाच
मधुप कितवबन्धो मा स्पृशाङ्घ्रिं सपत्न्याः
कुचविलुलितमालाकुंकुमश्मश्रुभिर्नः ।
वहतु मधुपतिस्तन्मानिनीनां प्रसादं
यदुसदसि विडम्ब्यं यस्य दूतस्त्वमीदृक् ॥१२॥

gopy uvāca
madhupa kitava-bandho mā spṛśāṅghriṁ sapatnyāḥ
kuca-vilulita-mālā-kuṅkuma-śmaśrubhir naḥ
vahatu madhu-patis tan-māninīnāṁ prasādaṁ
yadu-sadasi viḍambyaṁ yasya dūtas tvam īdṛk

gopī uvāca—the *gopī* said; *madhupa*—O bumblebee; *kitava*—of a cheater; *bandho*—O friend; *mā spṛśa*—please do not touch; *aṅghrim*—the feet; *sapatnyāḥ*—of the lover who is our rival; *kuca*—the breast; *vilulita*—fallen from; *mālā*—from the garland; *kuṅkuma*—with the red cosmetic; *śmaśrubhiḥ*—with the whiskers; *naḥ*—our; *vahatu*—let Him bring; *madhu-patiḥ*—the Lord of the Madhu dynasty; *tat*—His;

māninīnām—to the women; *prasādam*—mercy or kindness; *yadu-sadasi*—in the royal assembly of the Yadus; *viḍambyam*—an object of ridicule or contempt; *yasya*—whose; *dūtaḥ*—messenger; *tvam*—you; *īdṛk*—such.

TRANSLATION

The *gopī* said: O honeybee, O friend of a cheater, don't touch My feet with your whiskers, which are smeared with the *kuṅkuma* that rubbed onto Kṛṣṇa's garland when it was crushed by the breasts of a rival lover! Let Kṛṣṇa satisfy the women of Mathurā. One who sends a messenger like you will certainly be ridiculed in the Yadus' assembly.

PURPORT

Śrīmatī Rādhārāṇī indirectly chastised Kṛṣṇa by chastising the bumblebee, which She took for His messenger. She addressed the bumblebee as *madhupa,* "one who drinks the nectar (of flowers)," and She addressed Kṛṣṇa as *madhu-pati,* "the Lord of Madhu."

Śrīla Viśvanātha Cakravartī points out that this and the following nine verses exemplify ten kinds of impulsive speech spoken by a lover. This verse illustrates the qualities of *prajalpa,* as described by Śrīla Rūpa Gosvāmī in the following verse from his *Ujjvala-nīlamaṇi* (14.182):

asūyerṣyā-mada-yujā
yo 'vadhīraṇa-mudrayā
priyasyākauśalodgāraḥ
prajalpaḥ sa tu kīrtyate

"*Prajalpa* is speech that denigrates the tactlessness of one's lover with expressions of disrespect. It is spoken in a mood of envy, jealousy and pride." Śrīla Viśvanātha Cakravartī points out that the word *kitava-bandho* expresses envy; the phrase from *sapatnyāḥ* to *naḥ,* jealousy; the phrase *mā spṛśa aṅghrim,* pride; and the phrase from *vahatu* to *prasādam,* disrespect, while the phrase from *yadu-sadasi* to the end of the verse decries Kṛṣṇa's tactless treatment of Rādhārāṇī.

TEXT 13

सकृदधरसुधां स्वां मोहिनीं पाययित्वा
सुमनस इव सद्यस्तत्यजेऽस्मान् भवादृक् ।
परिचरति कथं तत्पादपद्मं नु पद्मा
ह्यपि बत हृतचेता ह्युत्तमःश्लोकजल्पैः ॥१३॥

sakṛd adhara-sudhāṁ svāṁ mohinīṁ pāyayitvā
sumanasa iva sadyas tatyaje 'smān bhavādṛk
paricarati kathaṁ tat-pāda-padmaṁ nu padmā
hy api bata hṛta-cetā hy uttamaḥ-śloka-jalpaiḥ

sakṛt—once; *adhara*—of the lips; *sudhām*—the nectar; *svām*—His own; *mohinīm*—bewildering; *pāyayitvā*—making drink; *sumanasaḥ*—flowers; *iva*—like; *sadyaḥ*—suddenly; *tatyaje*—He abandoned; *asmān*—us; *bhavādṛk*—like you; *paricarati*—serves; *katham*—why; *tat*—His; *pāda-padmam*—lotus feet; *nu*—I wonder; *padmā*—Lakṣmī, the goddess of fortune; *hi api*—indeed, because; *bata*—alas; *hṛta*—taken away; *cetāḥ*—her mind; *hi*—certainly; *uttamaḥ-śloka*—of Kṛṣṇa; *jalpaiḥ*—by the false speech.

TRANSLATION

After making us drink the enchanting nectar of His lips only once, Kṛṣṇa suddenly abandoned us, just as you might quickly abandon some flowers. How is it, then, that Goddess Padmā willingly serves His lotus feet? Alas! The answer must certainly be that her mind has been stolen away by His deceitful words.

PURPORT

In this verse Śrīmatī Rādhārāṇī continues to compare Śrī Kṛṣṇa to the bumblebee, and in Her distress She states that the reason the goddess of fortune is constantly devoted to His lotus feet must be that she has been fooled by Kṛṣṇa's promises. According to Śrīla Viśvanātha Cakravartī, this statement of Śrīmatī Rādhārāṇī's illustrates *parijalpa*, as described in *Śrī Ujjvala-nīlamaṇi* (14.184):

prabhor nidayatā-śāṭhya-
cāpalyādy-upapādanāt
sva-vicakṣaṇatā-vyaktir
bhaṅgyā syāt parijalpitam

"*Parijalpa* is that speech which, through various devices, shows one's own cleverness by exposing the mercilessness, duplicity, unreliability and so on of one's Lord."

TEXT 14

किमिह बहु षडङ्घ्रे गायसि त्वं यदूनाम्
अधिपतिमगृहाणामग्रतो नः पुराणम् ।
विजयसखसखीनां गीयतां तत्प्रसंगः
क्षपितकुचरुजस्ते कल्पयन्तीष्टमिष्टाः ॥१४॥

kim iha bahu ṣaḍ-aṅghre gāyasi tvaṁ yadūnām
adhipatim agṛhāṇām agrato naḥ purāṇam
vijaya-sakha-sakhīnāṁ gīyatāṁ tat-prasaṅgaḥ
kṣapita-kuca-rujas te kalpayantīṣṭam iṣṭāḥ

kim—why; *iha*—here; *bahu*—much; *ṣaṭ-aṅghre*—O bee (six-footed one); *gāyasi*—are singing; *tvam*—you; *yadūnām*—of the Yadus; *adhipatim*—about the master; *agṛhāṇām*—who have no home; *agrataḥ*—in front of; *naḥ*—us; *purāṇam*—old; *vijaya*—of Arjuna; *sakha*—of the friend; *sakhīnām*—for the friends; *gīyatām*—should be sung; *tat*—of Him; *prasaṅgaḥ*—the topics; *kṣapita*—relieved; *kuca*—of whose breasts; *rujaḥ*—the pain; *te*—they; *kalpayanti*—will provide; *iṣṭam*—the charity you desire; *iṣṭāḥ*—His beloveds.

TRANSLATION

O bee, why do you sing here so much about the Lord of the Yadus, in front of us homeless people? These topics are old news to us. Better you sing about that friend of Arjuna in front of His new girlfriends, the burning desire in whose breasts He has now relieved. Those ladies will surely give you the charity you are begging.

PURPORT

With the words *agrhāṇām agrato naḥ*, Rādhārāṇī laments that even though She and the other *gopīs* gave up their homes to love Kṛṣṇa in a conjugal relationship, the Lord left them and became a prince in the great royal city of the Yadus. Besides meaning "Arjuna, the victor," the word *vijaya* also directly indicates Śrī Kṛṣṇa, who is always victorious in His endeavors, and besides meaning "old (news)," the word *purāṇam* also indicates that Śrī Kṛṣṇa is glorified in the ancient Vedic scriptures of that name.

In this verse we observe in Rādhārāṇī's mood the seed of jealous anger, which arises from an apparent disdain for Kṛṣṇa, accompanied by a sarcastic sidelong glance directed toward Him. Thus this verse fits the following description of *vijalpa* from the *Ujjvala-nīlamaṇi* (14.186):

vyaktayāsūyayā gūḍha-
māna-mudrāntarālayā
agha-dviṣi kaṭākṣoktir
vijalpo viduṣāṁ mataḥ

"According to learned authorities, *vijalpa* is sarcastic speech that is addressed to the killer of Agha and that openly expresses jealousy while at the same time hinting at one's angry pride."

TEXT 15

दिवि भुवि च रसायां काः स्त्रियस्तद्दुरापाः
कपटरुचिरहासभ्रूविजृम्भस्य याः स्युः ।
चरणरज उपास्ते यस्य भूतिर्वयं का
अपि च कृपणपक्षे ह्युत्तमःश्लोकशब्दः ॥१५॥

divi bhuvi ca rasāyāṁ kāḥ striyas tad-durāpāḥ
kapaṭa-rucira-hāsa-bhrū-vijṛmbhasya yāḥ syuḥ
caraṇa-raja upāste yasya bhūtir vayaṁ kā
api ca kṛpaṇa-pakṣe hy uttamaḥ-śloka-śabdaḥ

divi—in the heavenly region; *bhuvi*—on the earth; *ca*—and; *rasāyām*—in the subterranean sphere; *kāḥ*—what; *striyaḥ*—women;

tat—by Him; *durāpāḥ*—unobtainable; *kapaṭa*—deceptive; *rucira*—charming; *hāsa*—with smiles; *bhrū*—of whose eyebrows; *vijṛmbhasya*—the arching; *yāḥ*—who; *syuḥ*—become; *caraṇa*—of the feet; *rajaḥ*—the dust; *upāste*—worships; *yasya*—whose; *bhūtiḥ*—the goddess of fortune, wife of Lord Nārāyaṇa; *vayam*—we; *kā*—who; *api ca*—nevertheless; *kṛpaṇa-pakṣe*—for those who are wretched; *hi*—indeed; *uttamaḥ-śloka*—the Supreme Lord, who is glorified by the most sublime prayers; *śabdaḥ*—the name.

TRANSLATION

In heaven, on earth or in the subterranean sphere, what women are unavailable to Him? He simply arches His eyebrows and smiles with deceptive charm, and they all become His. The supreme goddess herself worships the dust of His feet, so what is our position in comparison? But at least those who are wretched can chant His name, Uttamaḥśloka.

PURPORT

Śrila Viśvanātha Cakravartī states that Rādhārāṇī's speech, expressing all the feelings of a disappointed lover, indicates an intensity of love for Śrī Kṛṣṇa surpassing even that of the goddess of fortune. While all the *gopīs* are perfectly compatible with Śrī Kṛṣṇa in terms of their beauty, temperament and so on, Śrīmatī Rādhārāṇī is especially so. In Her forlorn state, Rādhārāṇī indicates to Kṛṣṇa, "You are called Uttamaḥśloka because You are merciful to the wretched and fallen, but if You would be merciful to Me, then You would actually deserve this exalted name."

Śrila Viśvanātha Cakravartī further points out that in this verse, Śrīmatī Rādhārāṇī expresses Her spite born of pride, accuses Kṛṣṇa of being a cheater and finds fault with His behavior. Thus this verse contains speech known as *ujjalpa*, as described in the following verse of the *Ujjvala-nīlamaṇi* (14.188):

hareḥ kuhakatākhyānaṁ
garva-garbhitayerṣyayā
sāsūyaś ca tad-ākṣepo
dhīrair ujjalpa īryate

"The declaration of Lord Hari's duplicitous nature in a mood of spite born of pride, together with jealously spoken insults directed against Him, has been termed *ujjalpa* by the wise."

TEXT 16

विसृज शिरसि पादं वेद्म्यहं चाटुकारैर्
अनुनयविदुषस्तेऽभ्येत्य दौत्यैर्मुकुन्दात् ।
स्वकृत इह विसृष्टापत्यपत्यन्यलोका
व्यसृजदकृतचेताः किं नु सन्धेयमस्मिन् ॥१६॥

visṛja śirasi pādaṁ vedmy ahaṁ cāṭu-kārair
anunaya-viduṣas te 'bhyetya dautyair mukundāt
sva-kṛta iha visṛṣṭāpatya-paty-anya-lokā
vyasṛjad akṛta-cetāḥ kiṁ nu sandheyam asmin

visṛja—let go of; *śirasi*—held on your head; *pādam*—My foot; *vedmi*—know; *aham*—I; *cāṭu-kāraiḥ*—with flattering words; *anunaya*—in the art of conciliation; *viduṣaḥ*—who are expert; *te*—of you; *abhyetya*—having learned; *dautyaiḥ*—by acting as a messenger; *mukundāt*—from Kṛṣṇa; *sva*—for His own; *kṛte*—sake; *iha*—in this life; *visṛṣṭa*—who have abandoned; *apatya*—children; *pati*—husbands; *anya-lokāḥ*—and everyone else; *vyasṛjat*—He abandoned; *akṛta-cetāḥ*—ungrateful; *kim nu*—why indeed; *sandheyam*—should I make reconciliation; *asmin*—with Him.

TRANSLATION

Keep your head off My feet! I know what you're doing. You expertly learned diplomacy from Mukunda, and now you come as His messenger with flattering words. But He abandoned those who for His sake alone gave up their children, husbands and all other relations. He's simply ungrateful. Why should I make up with Him now?

PURPORT

According to Śrīla Viśvanātha Cakravartī, this verse illustrates the qualities of *sañjalpa*, as described by Śrīla Rūpa Gosvāmī in the following verse of his *Ujjvala-nīlamaṇi* (14.190):

solluṇṭhayā gahanayā
kayāpy ākṣepa-mudrayā
tasyākṛta-jñatādy-uktiḥ
sañjalpaḥ kathito budhaiḥ

"The learned describe *sañjalpa* as that speech which decries with deep irony and insulting gestures the beloved's ungratefulness and so on." Śrīla Viśvanātha Cakravartī points out that the word *ādi*, "and so on," implies the perception in one's lover of hardheartedness, of an inimical attitude and of a complete lack of love.

TEXT 17

मृगयुरिव कपीन्द्रं विव्यधे लुब्धधर्मा
स्त्रियमकृत विरूपां स्त्रीजितः कामयानाम् ।
बलिमपि बलिमत्त्वावेष्टयद्ध्वाङ्क्षवद्यस्
तदलमसितसख्यैर्दुस्त्यजस्तत्कथार्थः ॥१७॥

mṛgayur iva kapīndraṁ vivyadhe lubdha-dharmā
striyam akṛta virūpāṁ strī-jitaḥ kāma-yānām
balim api balim attvāveṣṭayad dhvāṅkṣa-vad yas
tad alam asita-sakhyair dustyajas tat-kathārthaḥ

mṛgayuḥ—a hunter; *iva*—like; *kapi*—of the monkeys; *indram*—the king; *vivyadhe*—shot; *lubdha-dharmā*—behaving like a cruel hunter; *striyam*—a woman (namely, Śūrpaṇakhā); *akṛta*—made; *virūpām*—disfigured; *strī*—by a woman (Sītā-devī); *jitaḥ*—conquered; *kāma-yānām*—who was impelled by lusty desire; *balim*—King Bali; *api*—also; *balim*—his tribute; *attvā*—consuming; *aveṣṭayat*—bound up; *dhvāṅkṣa-vat*—just like a crow; *yaḥ*—who; *tat*—therefore; *alam*—enough; *asita*—with black Kṛṣṇa; *sakhyaiḥ*—of all kinds of friendship; *dustyajaḥ*—impossible to give up; *tat*—about Him; *kathā*—of the topics; *arthaḥ*—the elaboration.

TRANSLATION

Like a hunter, He cruelly shot the king of the monkeys with arrows. Because He was conquered by a woman, He disfigured

another woman who came to Him with lusty desires. And even after consuming the gifts of Bali Mahārāja, He bound him up with ropes as if he were a crow. So let us give up all friendship with this dark-complexioned boy, even if we can't give up talking about Him.

PURPORT

In *Kṛṣṇa, the Supreme Personality of Godhead,* Śrīla Prabhupāda explains the meaning of this verse as follows: "[Śrīmatī Rādhārāṇī said to the bee,] 'You poor messenger, you are only a less intelligent servant. You do not know much about Kṛṣṇa—how ungrateful and hardhearted He has been, not only in this life but in His previous lives also. We have heard this from Our grandmother Paurṇamāsī. She has informed Us that Kṛṣṇa was born in a *kṣatriya* family previous to this birth and was known as Rāmacandra. In that birth, instead of killing Vālī, an enemy of His friend, in the manner of a *kṣatriya,* He killed him just like a hunter. A hunter takes a secure hiding place and then kills an animal without facing it. So Lord Rāmacandra, as a *kṣatriya,* should have fought with Vālī face to face, but instigated by His friend, He killed him from behind a tree. Thus He deviated from the religious principles of a *kṣatriya.* Also, He was so attracted by the beauty of Sītā that He converted Śūrpaṇakhā, the sister of Rāvaṇa, into an ugly woman by cutting off her nose and ears. Śūrpaṇakhā proposed an intimate relationship with Him, and as a *kṣatriya* He should have satisfied her. But He was so henpecked that He could not forget Sītā-devī and converted Śūrpaṇakhā into an ugly woman. Before that birth as a *kṣatriya,* He took birth as a *brāhmaṇa* boy known as Vāmanadeva and asked charity from Bali Mahārāja. Bali was so magnanimous that he gave Him whatever he had, yet Kṛṣṇa as Vāmanadeva ungratefully arrested him just like a crow and pushed him down to the Pātāla kingdom. We know all about Kṛṣṇa and how ungrateful He is. But here is the difficulty: In spite of His being so cruel and hardhearted, it is very difficult for us to give up talking about Him.'"

Śrīla Viśvanātha Cakravartī points out that this speech of Rādhārāṇī's is called *avajalpa,* as described by Rūpa Gosvāmī in the following verse from the *Ujjvala-nīlamaṇi* (14.192):

harau kāṭhinya-kāmitva-
dhaurtyād āsakty-ayogyatā

yatra serṣyā-bhiyevoktā
so 'vajalpaḥ satāṁ mataḥ

"Saintly persons have concluded that when a lover, impelled by jealousy and fear, declares that Lord Hari is unworthy of her attachment because of His harshness, lustiness and dishonesty, such speech is called *avajalpa.*"

TEXT 18

यदनुचरितलीलाकर्णपीयूषविप्रुट्-
सकृददनविधूतद्वन्द्वधर्मा विनष्टाः ।
सपदि गृहकुटुम्बं दीनमुत्सृज्य दीना
बहव इह विहंगा भिक्षुचर्यां चरन्ति ॥१८॥

yad-anucarita-līlā-karṇa-pīyūṣa-viprut-
sakṛd-adana-vidhūta-dvandva-dharmā vinaṣṭāḥ
sapadi gṛha-kuṭumbaṁ dīnam utsṛjya dīnā
bahava iha vihaṅgā bhikṣu-caryāṁ caranti

yat—whose; *anucarita*—constantly performed activities; *līlā*—of such pastimes; *karṇa*—for the ears; *pīyūṣa*—of the nectar; *viprut*—of a drop; *sakṛt*—just once; *adana*—by the partaking; *vidhūta*—removed entirely; *dvandva*—of duality; *dharmāḥ*—their propensities; *vinaṣṭāḥ*—ruined; *sapadi*—immediately; *gṛha*—their homes; *kuṭumbam*—and families; *dīnam*—wretched; *utsṛjya*—rejecting; *dīnāḥ*—becoming themselves wretched; *bahavaḥ*—many persons; *iha*—here (in Vṛndāvana); *vihaṅgāḥ*—(like) birds; *bhikṣu*—of begging; *caryām*—the livelihood; *caranti*—they pursue.

TRANSLATION

To hear about the pastimes that Kṛṣṇa regularly performs is nectar for the ears. For those who relish just a single drop of that nectar, even once, their dedication to material duality is ruined. Many such persons have suddenly given up their wretched homes and families and, themselves becoming wretched, traveled here to Vṛndāvana to wander about like birds, begging for their living.

PURPORT

Material duality is based on falsely thinking, "This is mine, and that is yours," or "This is our country, and that is yours," or "This is my family, and that is yours," and so on. In fact, there is one Absolute Truth, in which we all exist and to whom everything belongs. His beauty and pleasure are also absolute and infinite, and if one actually hears about this Absolute Truth, called Kṛṣṇa, one's dedication to the illusion of mundane duality is spoiled.

According to the *ācāryas*, and certainly in accord with Sanskrit grammar, the last two words of the second line of this text may also be divided *dharma-avinaṣṭāḥ*. Then the entire line becomes part of a single compound, the meaning of which is that hearing about Kṛṣṇa cleanses one of irreligious duality and thus one is not vanquished (*avinaṣṭa*) by material illusion. The word *dīnāḥ* is then given the alternate reading of *dhīrāḥ*, meaning that one becomes spiritually sober and thus gives up attachment to fleeting material relationships. The word *vihaṅgāḥ*, "birds," would in this case refer to swans, the symbol of essential discrimination.

Śrīlā Viśvanātha Cakravarti quotes Rūpa Gosvāmī as follows in connection with this verse:

bhaṅgyā tyāgaucitī tasya
khagānām api khedanāt
yatra sānuśayaṁ proktā
tad bhaved abhijalpitam

"When a lover indirectly states with remorse that her beloved is fit to be given up, such speech, uttered like the plaintive crying of a bird, is called *abhijalpa*." (*Ujjvala-nīlamaṇi* 14.194)

TEXT 19

वयमृतमिव जिह्मव्याहृतं श्रद्दधानाः
कुलिकरुतमिवाज्ञाः कृष्णवध्वो हरिण्यः ।
ददृशुरसकृदेतत्तन्नखस्पर्शतीव्र-
स्मररुज उपमन्त्रिन् भण्यतामन्यवार्ता ॥१९॥

vayam ṛtam iva jihma-vyāhṛtaṁ śraddadhānāḥ
kulika-rutam ivājñāḥ kṛṣṇa-vadhvo hariṇyaḥ
dadṛśur asakṛd etat tan-nakha-sparśa-tīvra-
smara-ruja upamantrin bhaṇyatām anya-vārtā

vayam—we; *ṛtam*—true; *iva*—as if; *jihma*—deceptive; *vyāhṛtam*—His speech; *śraddadhānāḥ*—trusting; *kulika*—of a hunter; *rutam*—the song; *iva*—as if; *ajñāḥ*—foolish; *kṛṣṇa*—of the black deer; *vadhvaḥ*—wives; *hariṇyaḥ*—the doe; *dadṛśuḥ*—experienced; *asakṛt*—repeatedly; *etat*—this; *tat*—His; *nakha*—of the fingernails; *sparśa*—by the touch; *tīvra*—sharp; *smara*—of lust; *rujaḥ*—the pain; *upamantrin*—O messenger; *bhaṇyatām*—please speak; *anya*—another; *vārtā*—topic.

TRANSLATION

Faithfully taking His deceitful words as true, we became just like the black deer's foolish wives, who trust the cruel hunter's song. Thus we repeatedly felt the sharp pain of lust caused by the touch of His nails. O messenger, please talk about something besides Kṛṣṇa.

PURPORT

Śrīla Viśvanātha Cakravartī categorizes this statement of Śrīmatī Rādhārāṇī's as *ājalpa,* as defined by Śrīla Rūpa Gosvāmī:

jaihmyaṁ tasyārti-datvaṁ ca
nirvedād yatra kīrtitam
bhaṅgyānya-sukha-datvaṁ ca
sa ājalpa udīritaḥ

"A statement spoken in disgust, describing how the male lover is deceitful and brings one misery, and also implying that He gives happiness to others, is known as *ājalpa.*" (*Ujjvala-nīlamaṇi* 14.196)

TEXT 20

प्रियसख पुनरागाः प्रेयसा प्रेषितः किं
वरय किमनुरुन्धे माननीयोऽसि मेऽङ्ग ।

नयसि कथमिहास्मान् दुस्त्यजद्वन्द्वपार्श्वं
सततमुरसि सौम्य श्रीर्वधूः साकमास्ते ॥२०॥

priya-sakha punar āgāḥ preyasā preṣitaḥ kiṁ
varaya kim anurundhe mānanīyo 'si me 'ṅga
nayasi katham ihāsmān dustyaja-dvandva-pārśvaṁ
satatam urasi saumya śrīr vadhūḥ sākam āste

priya—of My beloved; *sakha*—O friend; *punaḥ*—once again; *āgāḥ*—you have come; *preyasā*—by My beloved; *preṣitaḥ*—sent; *kim*—whether; *varaya*—please choose; *kim*—what; *anurundhe*—do you wish; *mānanīyaḥ*—to be honored; *asi*—you are; *me*—by Me; *aṅga*—My dear one; *nayasi*—you are bringing; *katham*—why; *iha*—here; *asmān*—us; *dustyaja*—impossible to give up; *dvandva*—conjugal connection with whom; *pārśvam*—to the side; *satatam*—always; *urasi*—on the chest; *saumya*—O gentle one; *śrīḥ*—the goddess of fortune; *vadhūḥ*—His consort; *sākam*—together with Him; *āste*—is present.

TRANSLATION

O friend of My dear one, has My beloved sent you here again? I should honor you, friend, so please choose whatever boon you wish. But why have you come back here to take us to Him, whose conjugal love is so difficult to give up? After all, gentle bee, His consort is the goddess Śrī, and she is always with Him, staying upon His chest.

PURPORT

In *Kṛṣṇa, the Supreme Personality of Godhead,* Śrīla Prabhupāda explains the context of this verse: "While Rādhārāṇī was talking with the bee and the bee was flying hither and thither, it all of a sudden disappeared from Her sight. She was in full mourning due to separation from Kṛṣṇa and felt ecstasy by talking with the bee. But as soon as the bee disappeared, She became almost mad, thinking that the messenger-bee might have returned to Kṛṣṇa to inform Him all about Her talking against Him. 'Kṛṣṇa must be very sorry to hear it,' She thought. In this way She was overwhelmed by another type of ecstasy.

"In the meantime, the bee, flying hither and thither, appeared before

Her again. She thought, 'Kṛṣṇa is still kind to Me. In spite of the messenger's carrying disruptive messages, He is so kind that He has again sent the bee to take Me to Him.' Śrīmati Rādhārāṇī was very careful this time not to say anything against Kṛṣṇa."

Śrīla Viśvanātha Cakravartī explains that the goddess of fortune, Śrī, has the power to assume many different forms. Thus when Kṛṣṇa enjoys other women, she stays on His chest in the form of a golden line. When He is not consorting with other women, she puts aside this form and gives Him pleasure in Her naturally beautiful form of a young women.

According to Śrīla Viśvanātha Cakravartī, this statement of Śrīmatī Rādhārāṇī's expresses *pratijalpa,* as described by Śrīla Rūpa Gosvāmī:

dustyaja-dvandva-bhāve 'smin
prāptir nārhety anuddhatam
dūta-sammānanenoktaṁ
yatra sa pratijalpakaḥ

"When the lover humbly states that although she is unworthy of attaining her beloved she cannot give up hoping for a conjugal relationship with Him, such words, spoken with respect for her beloved's message, are called *pratijalpa.*" (*Ujjvala-nīlamaṇi* 14.198)

Here Śrīmatī Rādhārāṇī has given up Her harsh feelings and humbly acknowledges the greatness of Śrī Kṛṣṇa.

TEXT 21

अपि बत मधुपुर्यामार्यपुत्रोऽधुनास्ते
स्मरति स पितृगेहान् सौम्य बन्धूंश्च गोपान् ।
क्वचिदपि स कथा नः किंकरीणां गृणीते
भुजमगुरुसुगन्धं मूर्ध्न्यधास्यत्कदा नु ॥२१॥

api bata madhu-puryām ārya-putro 'dhunāste
smarati sa pitṛ-gehān saumya bandhūṁś ca gopān
kvacid api sa kathā naḥ kiṅkarīṇāṁ gṛṇīte
bhujam aguru-sugandhaṁ mūrdhny adhāsyat kadā nu

api—certainly; *bata*—regrettable; *madhu-puryām*—in the city of Mathurā; *ārya-putraḥ*—the son of Nanda Mahārāja; *adhunā*—now;

āste—resides; *smarati*—remembers; *saḥ*—He; *pitṛ-gehān*—the household affairs of His father; *saumya*—O great soul (Uddhava); *bandhūn*—His friends; *ca*—and; *gopān*—the cowherd boys; *kvacit*—sometimes; *api*—or; *saḥ*—He; *kathāḥ*—talks; *naḥ*—of us; *kiṅkarīṇām*—of the maidservants; *gṛṇīte*—relates; *bhujam*—hand; *aguru-su-gandham*—having the fragrance of *aguru; mūrdhni*—on the head; *adhāsyat*—will keep; *kadā*—when; *nu*—maybe.

TRANSLATION

O Uddhava! It is indeed regrettable that Kṛṣṇa resides in Mathurā. Does He remember His father's household affairs and His friends, the cowherd boys? O great soul! Does He ever talk about us, His maidservants? When will He lay on our heads His *aguru*-scented hand?

PURPORT

The translation and word meanings for this verse are taken from Śrīla Prabhupāda's *Caitanya-caritāmṛta* (*Ādi* 6.68).

Śrīla Viśvanātha Cakravartī writes very poetically, with deep spiritual insight, about the emotions expressed in this and the previous nine verses. He interprets Rādhārāṇī's feelings as follows:

Śrīmatī Rādhārāṇī thought, "Since Kṛṣṇa was once satisfied in Vraja but left for Mathurā City, won't He also develop a desire to leave that place and go somewhere else? Mathurā is so close to Vṛndāvana that it's possible He may even come back here.

"Kṛṣṇa is the son of a respectable gentleman, Nanda Mahārāja, so He must be staying in Mathurā because of His sense of obligation to His father, who authorized His going there. On the other hand, while Nanda's whole life is dedicated exclusively to Kṛṣṇa, Nanda is so innocent that he allowed himself to be tricked by the Yadus, who brought Kṛṣṇa to Mathurā. Kṛṣṇa must be thinking, 'Alas, alas! Since even My father could not bring Me back to Vraja, what can I do to return there?' Thus Kṛṣṇa must be impatient to come back here, and so He has sent you, a messenger.

"It is only because Nanda is so innocent that he allowed his son to leave. If Nanda had allowed Kṛṣṇa's mother, the queen of Vraja, to do so, she would have climbed onto Akrūra's chariot and, holding her son by the neck, gone off to Mathurā with Him, followed by all the *gopīs*. But this was not possible.

"Ever since Kṛṣṇa left, Nanda has been stunned by separation from Him, and Nanda's treasury rooms, storehouses, kitchens, sleeping quarters, opulent houses and so on are now vacant. Unswept and uncleansed, they are littered with grass, dust, leaves and cobwebs. Does Kṛṣṇa ever remember His father's houses? And does He sometimes remember Subala and His other friends, who are now lying stunned in other neglected houses?

"The women in Mathurā who now associate with Kṛṣṇa cannot know how to serve Him in the way that pleases Him most. When they see He is not satisfied and ask how they can make Him happy, does He tell them about us *gopīs*?

"Kṛṣṇa must tell them, 'You city ladies cannot please Me as much as the *gopīs* of Vraja. They are most expert in stringing flower garlands, perfuming their bodies with ointments, playing various rhythms and melodies on stringed instruments, dancing and singing in the *rāsa* performance, displaying their beauty, charm and cleverness, and skillfully playing at questions and answers. They are especially expert in the pastimes of meeting one's lover and showing jealous anger and other signs of pure love and affection.' Surely Kṛṣṇa must know this. Therefore He'll probably tell the women of Mathurā, 'My dear women of the Yadu clan, please go back to your families. I no longer desire to associate with you. In fact, I'm going back to Vraja early tomorrow morning.'

"When will Kṛṣṇa speak like this and come back here to place His hand, fragrant with *aguru*, on our heads? Then He will console us, saying, 'O beloveds of My heart, I swear to you that I will never abandon you again and go elsewhere. Indeed, I have not been able to find anyone in all the three worlds with even a trace of your good qualities.'"

Thus Śrīla Viśvanātha Cakravartī interprets the feelings of Śrīmatī Rādhārāṇī. The *ācārya* further explains that the present text displays the speech called *sujalpa*, as described by Rūpa Gosvāmī:

yatrārjavāt sa-gāmbhīryaṁ
sa-dainyaṁ saha-cāpalam
sotkaṇṭhaṁ ca hariḥ pṛṣṭaḥ
sa sujalpo nigadyate

"When, out of honest sincerity, a lover questions Śrī Hari with gravity, humility, unsteadiness and eagerness, such speech is known as *sujalpa*." (*Ujjvala-nīlamaṇi* 14.200)

Concluding this section of Chapter Forty-seven, Śrīla Viśvanātha Cakravartī explains that there are ten divisions of divine madness (*divyonmāda*), which are expressed by the ten divisions of *citra-jalpa*, or variegated speech. Such divine madness is shown in the special pastime of bewilderment, which is itself part of the supreme bliss, *mahā-bhāva*, of Śrīmatī Rādhārāṇī. The *ācārya* quotes the following verses from Rūpa Gosvāmī's *Ujjvala-nīlamaṇi* (14.174, 178–80) to explain these ecstasies:

prāyo vṛndāvaneśvaryāṁ
mohano 'yam udañcati
etasya mohanākhyasya
gatiṁ kām apy upeyuṣaḥ

bhramābhā kāpi vaicitrī
divyonmāda itīryate
udghūrṇā citra-jalpādyās
tad-bhedā bahavo matāḥ

preṣṭhasya suhṛd-āloke
gūḍha-roṣābhijṛmbhitaḥ
bhūri-bhāva-mayo jalpo
yas tīvrotkaṇṭhitāntimaḥ

citra-jalpo daśāṅgo 'yaṁ
prajalpaḥ parijalpitaḥ
vijalpo 'jjalpa-sañjalpaḥ
avajalpo 'bhijalpitam

ājalpaḥ pratijalpaś ca
sujalpaś ceti kīrtitaḥ

"It is virtually only within the princess of Vṛndāvana [Śrīmatī Rādhārāṇī] that the ecstasy of bewilderment arises. She has attained to a special stage of this bewilderment, a wonderful state that resembles delusion. Known as *divyonmāda*, it has many aspects, which come and go unsteadily, and one of these manifestations is *citra-jalpa*. This talk, induced by Her seeing Her beloved's friend, is filled with covered anger and comprises many different ecstasies. It culminates in Her intense, anxious eagerness.

"This *citra-jalpa* has ten divisions, known as *prajalpa, parijalpa, vijalpa, ujjalpa, sañjalpa, avajalpa, abhijalpa, ājalpa, pratijalpa* and *sujalpa.*"

Finally, some authorities say that Kṛṣṇa Himself, eager to drink the sweetness of His beloved's speech, assumed the form of the messenger bee.

TEXT 22

श्रीशुक उवाच
अथोद्धवो निशम्यैवं कृष्णदर्शनलालसाः ।
सान्त्वयन् प्रियसन्देशैर्गोपीरिदमभाषत ॥२२॥

śrī-śuka uvāca
athoddhavo niśamyaivaṁ
kṛṣṇa-darśana-lālasāḥ
sāntvayan priya-sandeśair
gopīr idam abhāṣata

śrī-śukaḥ uvāca—Śukadeva Gosvāmī said; *atha*—then; *uddhavaḥ*—Uddhava; *niśamya*—having heard; *evam*—thus; *kṛṣṇa-darśana*—after the sight of Kṛṣṇa; *lālasāḥ*—who were hankering; *sāntvayan*—pacifying; *priya*—of their beloved; *sandeśaiḥ*—with the messages; *gopīḥ*—to the cowherd girls; *idam*—this; *abhāṣata*—he said.

TRANSLATION

Śukadeva Gosvāmī said: Having heard this, Uddhava then tried to pacify the *gopīs*, who were most eager to see Lord Kṛṣṇa. He thus began relating to them the message of their beloved.

TEXT 23

श्रीउद्धव उवाच
अहो यूयं स्म पूर्णार्था भवत्यो लोकपूजिताः ।
वासुदेवे भगवति यासामित्यर्पितं मनः ॥२३॥

śrī-uddhava uvāca
aho yūyaṁ sma pūrṇārthā
bhavatyo loka-pūjitāḥ
vāsudeve bhagavati
yāsām ity arpitaṁ manaḥ

śrī-uddhavaḥ uvāca—Śrī Uddhava said; *aho*—indeed; *yūyam*—you; *sma*—surely; *pūrṇa*—fulfilled; *arthāḥ*—whose purposes; *bhavatyaḥ*—your good selves; *loka*—by all people; *pūjitāḥ*—worshiped; *vāsudeve bhagavati*—unto Lord Vāsudeva, Kṛṣṇa, the Supreme Personality of Godhead; *yāsām*—whose; *iti*—in this manner; *arpitam*—offered; *manaḥ*—the minds.

TRANSLATION

Śrī Uddhava said: Certainly you *gopīs* are all-successful and are universally worshiped because you have dedicated your minds in this way to the Supreme Personality of Godhead, Vāsudeva.

PURPORT

Although other devotees have certainly surrendered their minds unto the Lord, the *gopīs* are unique in the intensity of their love.

TEXT 24

दानव्रततपोहोमजपस्वाध्यायसंयमैः ।
श्रेयोभिर्विविधैश्चान्यैः कृष्णे भक्तिर्हि साध्यते ॥२४॥

dāna-vrata-tapo-homa-
japa-svādhyāya-saṁyamaiḥ
śreyobhir vividhaiś cānyaiḥ
kṛṣṇe bhaktir hi sādhyate

dāna—by charity; *vrata*—strict vows; *tapaḥ*—austerities; *homa*—fire sacrifices; *japa*—private chanting of *mantras; svādhyāya*—study of Vedic texts; *saṁyamaiḥ*—and regulative principles; *śreyobhiḥ*—by auspicious practices; *vividhaiḥ*—various; *ca*—also; *anyaiḥ*—others; *kṛṣṇe*—to Lord Kṛṣṇa; *bhaktiḥ*—devotional service; *hi*—indeed; *sādhyate*—is realized.

TRANSLATION

Devotional service unto Lord Kṛṣṇa is attained by charity, strict vows, austerities and fire sacrifices, by *japa,* study of Vedic texts, observance of regulative principles and, indeed, by the performance of many other auspicious practices.

PURPORT

Śrīla Viśvanātha Cakravartī explains the processes described here as follows. *Dāna:* donations given to Lord Viṣṇu and His devotees. *Vrata:* observing vows such as Ekādaśī. *Tapas:* renunciation of sense gratification for Kṛṣṇa's sake. *Homa:* fire sacrifices dedicated to Viṣṇu. *Japa:* privately chanting the holy names of the Lord. *Svādhyāya:* study and recitation of Vedic texts such as the *Gopāla-tāpanī Upaniṣad.*

TEXT 25

भगवत्युत्तमःश्लोके भवतीभिरनुत्तमा ।
भक्तिः प्रवर्तिता दिष्टया मुनीनामपि दुर्लभा ॥२५॥

bhagavaty uttamaḥ-śloke
bhavatībhir anuttamā
bhaktiḥ pravartitā diṣṭyā
munīnām api durlabhā

bhagavati—for the Supreme Lord; *uttamaḥ-śloke*—who is glorified in sublime poetry; *bhavatībhiḥ*—by your good selves; *anuttamā*—unexcelled; *bhaktiḥ*—devotion; *pravartitā*—established; *diṣṭyā*—(congratulations on your) good fortune; *munīnām*—for great sages; *api*—even; *durlabhā*—hard to obtain.

TRANSLATION

By your great fortune you have established an unexcelled standard of pure devotion for the Lord, Uttamaḥśloka—a standard even the sages can hardly attain.

PURPORT

The term *pravartitā* indicates that the *gopīs* brought to this world a standard of pure love of God that was previously unknown on the earth. Thus Uddhava congratulates them on their unparalleled contribution to the religious life.

TEXT 26

दिष्टया पुत्रान् पतीन् देहान् स्वजनान् भवनानि च ।
हित्वावृणीत यूयं यत्कृष्णाख्यं पुरुषं परम् ॥२६॥

diṣṭyā putrān patīn dehān
sva-janān bhavanāni ca
hitvāvṛṇīta yūyaṁ yat
kṛṣṇākhyaṁ puruṣaṁ param

diṣṭyā—by good fortune; *putrān*—sons; *patīn*—husbands; *dehān*—bodies; *sva-janān*—relatives; *bhavanāni*—homes; *ca*—and; *hitvā*—leaving; *avṛṇīta*—did choose; *yūyam*—you; *yat*—the fact that; *kṛṣṇa-ākhyam*—named Kṛṣṇa; *puruṣam*—the male personality; *param*—supreme.

TRANSLATION

By your great fortune you have left your sons, husbands, bodily comforts, relatives and homes in favor of the supreme male, who is known as Kṛṣṇa.

PURPORT

Śrīla Viśvanātha Cakravartī explains that the *gopīs* gave up their sense of possessiveness toward these objects. History shows that the *gopīs* remained in Vṛndāvana, living in their houses with their families. However, unlike ordinary persons, they entirely renounced the egoistical sense of possession of sons, husbands and so on. They never tried to enjoy them but rather gave their whole heart and mind to the Supreme Lord, as recommended in the great religious scriptures of the world. Following the example of the *gopīs,* we should love the Supreme Lord with all of our heart, soul and might.

TEXT 27

सर्वात्मभावोऽधिकृतो भवतीनामधोक्षजे ।
विरहेण महाभागा महान्मेऽनुग्रहः कृतः ॥२७॥

sarvātma-bhāvo 'dhikṛto
bhavatīnām adhokṣaje
viraheṇa mahā-bhāgā
mahān me 'nugrahaḥ kṛtaḥ

sarva-ātma—wholehearted; *bhāvaḥ*—love; *adhikṛtaḥ*—claimed by right; *bhavatīnām*—by you; *adhokṣaje*—for the transcendental Lord; *viraheṇa*—through this mood of separation; *mahā-bhāgāḥ*—O most glorious ones; *mahān*—great; *me*—to me; *anugrahaḥ*—mercy; *kṛtaḥ*—done.

TRANSLATION

You have rightfully claimed the privilege of unalloyed love for the transcendental Lord, O most glorious *gopīs.* Indeed, by exhibiting your love for Kṛṣṇa in separation from Him, you have shown me great mercy.

PURPORT

The *gopīs* showed not only Uddhava but the whole world the joy of love of Godhead, and thus they bestowed their mercy on everyone. According to Śrīla Jīva Gosvāmī, because their loving devotion was executed in an appropriate way, their love brought the Supreme Lord under their control. Still, to show the intensity of their love, He apparently left them. But now He again manifested Himself among them, becoming spiritually present through their intense devotion.

TEXT 28

श्रूयतां प्रियसन्देशो भवतीनां सुखावहः ।
यमादायागतो भद्रा अहं भर्तू रहस्करः ॥२८॥

śrūyatāṁ priya-sandeśo
bhavatīnāṁ sukhāvahaḥ
yam ādāyāgato bhadrā
ahaṁ bhartū rahas-karaḥ

śrūyatām—please hear; *priya*—of your beloved; *sandeśaḥ*—the message; *bhavatīnām*—for you; *sukha*—happiness; *āvahaḥ*—bringing; *yam*—which; *ādāya*—carrying; *āgataḥ*—have come; *bhadrāḥ*—good ladies; *aham*—I; *bhartuḥ*—of my master; *rahaḥ*—of confidential duties; *karaḥ*—the executor.

TRANSLATION

My good ladies, now please hear your beloved's message, which I, the confidential servant of my master, have come here to bring you.

TEXT 29

श्रीभगवानुवाच
भवतीनां वियोगो मे न हि सर्वात्मना क्वचित् ।
यथा भूतानि भूतेषु खं वाय्वग्निर्जलं मही ।
तथाहं च मनःप्राणभूतेन्द्रियगुणाश्रयः ॥२९॥

śrī-bhagavān uvāca
bhavatīnāṁ viyogo me
na hi sarvātmanā kvacit
yathā bhūtāni bhūteṣu
khaṁ vāyv-agnir jalaṁ mahī
tathāhaṁ ca manaḥ-prāṇa-
bhūtendriya-guṇāśrayaḥ

śrī-bhagavān uvāca—the Supreme Lord said; *bhavatīnām*—of you women; *viyogaḥ*—separation; *me*—from Me; *na*—is not; *hi*—indeed; *sarva-ātmanā*—from the Soul of all existence; *kvacit*—ever; *yathā*—as; *bhūtāni*—the physical elements; *bhūteṣu*—in all created beings; *kham*—the ether; *vāyu-agniḥ*—air and fire; *jalam*—water; *mahī*—earth;

tathā—so; *aham*—I; *ca*—and; *manaḥ*—of the mind; *prāṇa*—vital air; *bhūta*—material elements; *indriya*—bodily senses; *guṇa*—and of the primal modes of nature; *āśrayaḥ*—present as their shelter.

TRANSLATION

The Supreme Lord said: You are never actually separated from Me, for I am the Soul of all creation. Just as the elements of nature—ether, air, fire, water and earth—are present in every created thing, so I am present within everyone's mind, life air and senses, and also within the physical elements and the modes of material nature.

PURPORT

According to Śrīla Jīva Gosvāmī and Śrīla Viśvanātha Cakravartī, the apparently philosophical language of the Lord's statement conceals a deeper meaning. The Supreme Lord was secretly telling the *gopīs* that He, by way of reciprocating their special love for Him, was present with them, not only as the Soul of all creation but also as their special lover. In this sense of the verse, the word *guṇa* indicates the *gopīs'* special divine qualities, which attracted Śrī Kṛṣṇa, and the word *sarvātmanā,* which we have here translated in reference to Lord Kṛṣṇa Himself (corresponding to the word *me,* which is also in the instrumental case), is also understood in the sense of *sarvathā,* or "completely." In other words, although in one sense Lord Kṛṣṇa was absent, He could never be completely absent, since in His spiritual form He is always in the hearts and minds of the *gopīs.*

In *Kṛṣṇa, the Supreme Personality of Godhead* and other books, Śrīla Prabhupāda has elaborately explained that the reason Lord Kṛṣṇa separated Himself from the *gopīs* was to intensify their love for Him and, as Uddhava noted, to bless other devotees by revealing to them the intensity of the *gopīs'* love. In fact, the Lord was spiritually present with the *gopīs,* since they are His eternal associates.

Śrīla Viśvanātha Cakravartī further points out that foolish persons will conclude that Śrī Kṛṣṇa's use of philosophical language meant that the Lord was trying to bring the *gopīs* to the point of liberation by explaining basic points of Kṛṣṇa conscious philosophy. In truth, the *gopīs* are the most exalted liberated souls, and their pastimes with Śrī Kṛṣṇa must be understood with the help of authorized *ācāryas.* When the *gopīs* came for the *rāsa* dance, Śrī Kṛṣṇa tried to preach *karma-yoga* to them, emphasizing ordinary ethics and morality, but the *gopīs* were beyond that. Similarly, Lord Kṛṣṇa now offers them *jñāna-yoga,* or metaphysical philosophy, but this is also inadequate for the *gopīs,* who have achieved spontaneous, unalloyed love for Śrī Kṛṣṇa.

TEXT 30

आत्मन्येवात्मनात्मानं सृजे हन्म्यनुपालये ।
आत्ममायानुभावेन भूतेन्द्रियगुणात्मना ॥३०॥

ātmany evātmanātmānaṁ
sṛje hanmy anupālaye
ātma-māyānubhāvena
bhūtendriya-guṇātmanā

ātmani—within Myself; *eva*—indeed; *ātmanā*—by Myself; *ātmānam*—Myself; *sṛje*—I create; *hanmi*—I destroy; *anupālaye*—I sustain; *ātma*—My own; *māyā*—of the mystic potency; *anubhāvena*—by the power; *bhūta*—the material elements; *indriya*—the senses; *guṇa*—and the modes of nature; *ātmanā*—comprising.

TRANSLATION

By Myself I create, sustain and withdraw Myself within Myself by the power of My personal energy, which comprises the material elements, the senses and the modes of nature.

PURPORT

Although the Lord is the supreme entity, there is no absolute duality between Him and His creation, since the creation is an extension of His being. This oneness is here emphasized by the Lord.

TEXT 31

आत्मा ज्ञानमयः शुद्धो व्यतिरिक्तोऽगुणान्वयः ।
सुषुप्तिस्वप्नजाग्रद्भिर्मायावृत्तिभिरीयते ॥३१॥

ātmā jñāna-mayaḥ śuddho
vyatirikto 'guṇānvayaḥ
suṣupti-svapna-jāgradbhir
māyā-vṛttibhir īyate

ātmā—the soul; *jñāna-mayaḥ*—comprising transcendental knowledge; *śuddhaḥ*—pure; *vyatiriktaḥ*—separate; *aguṇa-anvayaḥ*—uninvolved in the reactions of the material modes; *suṣupti*—in deep sleep; *svapna*—ordinary sleep; *jāgradbhiḥ*—and waking consciousness; *māyā*—of the material energy; *vṛttibhiḥ*—by the functions; *īyate*—is perceived.

TRANSLATION

Being composed of pure consciousness, or knowledge, the soul is distinct from everything material and is uninvolved in the entanglements of the modes of nature. We can perceive the soul through the three functions of material nature known as wakefulness, sleep and deep sleep.

PURPORT

It is clearly stated here that the soul, *ātmā*, is constituted of pure knowledge, pure consciousness, and is thus ontologically distinct from the material nature. Śrīla Viśvanātha Cakravartī points out that the word *ātmā* may also be taken to mean "the Supreme Soul, Lord Kṛṣṇa." Since the Lord has just explained in the previous verses that all material phenomena are expansions of Himself, the phrase *māyā-vṛttibhir īyate* indicates that by studying this world deeply we will come to the perception of God. From this point of view also, the *gopīs* were advised not to lament.

TEXT 32

येनेन्द्रियार्थान् ध्यायेत मृषा स्वप्नवदुत्थितः ।
तन्निरुन्ध्यादिन्द्रियाणि विनिद्रः प्रत्यपद्यत ॥३२॥

yenendriyārthān dhyāyeta
mṛṣā svapna-vad utthitaḥ

tan nirundhyād indriyāṇi
vinidraḥ pratyapadyata

yena—by which (mind); *indriya*—of the senses; *arthān*—upon the objects; *dhyāyeta*—one meditates; *mṛṣā*—false; *svapna-vat*—like a dream; *utthitaḥ*—arisen from sleep; *tat*—that (mind); *nirundhyāt*—one should bring under control; *indriyāṇi*—the senses; *vinidraḥ*—not sleeping (alert); *pratyapadyata*—they obtain.

TRANSLATION

As a person just arisen from sleep may continue to meditate on a dream even though it is illusory, so by the agency of the mind one meditates on the sense objects, which the senses can then obtain. Therefore one should become fully alert and bring the mind under control.

PURPORT

The verb *pratipad* means "to be perceived or restored." The soul that is *vinidra,* free from the dreamlike condition of material consciousness, is restored to its constitutional position as an eternal servitor of the Lord, Śrī Kṛṣṇa, and thus the soul is directly perceived by pure consciousness.

TEXT 33

एतदन्तः समाम्नायो योगः सांख्यं मनीषिणाम् ।
त्यागस्तपो दमः सत्यं समुद्रान्ता इवापगाः ॥३३॥

etad-antaḥ samāmnāyo
yogaḥ sāṅkhyaṁ manīṣiṇām
tyāgas tapo damaḥ satyaṁ
samudrāntā ivāpagāḥ

etat—having this; *antaḥ*—as its conclusion; *samāmnāyaḥ*—the entire Vedic literature; *yogaḥ*—the standard system of *yoga;* *sāṅkhyam*—the process of Sāṅkhya meditation, by which one learns to discriminate between spirit and matter; *manīṣiṇām*—of the intelligent; *tyāgaḥ*—renunciation; *tapaḥ*—austerity; *damaḥ*—sense control; *satyam*—and honesty; *samudra-antāḥ*—leading to the ocean; *iva*—as; *āpa-gāḥ*—rivers.

TRANSLATION

According to intelligent authorities, this is the ultimate conclusion of all the *Vedas*, as well as all practice of *yoga*, Sāṅkhya, renunciation, austerity, sense control and truthfulness, just as the sea is the ultimate destination of all rivers.

PURPORT

Here the Lord states that all Vedic literature is meant ultimately to bring the soul to the point of controlling the mind and senses and fixing them in transcendental self-realization. Thus processes of so-called *yoga*, mysticism or religion that involve unrestricted sense gratification are not actually spiritual processes but rather convenient ways for foolish people to justify their beastly behavior.

Lord Kṛṣṇa here assures the *gopīs* that by fixing their minds in self-realization, they will realize their spiritual oneness with the Lord. Thus they will no longer suffer the pangs of separation.

TEXT 34

यत्त्वहं भवतीनां वै दूरे वर्ते प्रियो दृशाम् ।
मनसः सन्निकर्षार्थं मदनुध्यानकाम्यया ॥३४॥

yat tv ahaṁ bhavatīnāṁ vai
dūre varte priyo dṛśām
manasaḥ sannikarṣārthaṁ
mad-anudhyāna-kāmyayā

yat—the fact that; *tu*—however; *aham*—I; *bhavatīnām*—from your; *vai*—indeed; *dūre*—far away; *varte*—am situated; *priyaḥ*—who am dear; *dṛśām*—to the eyes; *manasaḥ*—of the mind; *sannikarṣa*—of the attraction; *artham*—for the sake; *mat*—upon Me; *anudhyāna*—for your meditation; *kāmyayā*—out of My desire.

TRANSLATION

But the actual reason why I, the beloved object of your sight, have stayed far away from you is that I wanted to intensify your meditation upon Me and thus draw your minds closer to Me.

PURPORT

Sometimes that which is close to our eyes is far from our heart and mind, and conversely absence makes the heart grow fonder. Although apparently going far away from the *gopīs,* Lord Kṛṣṇa was bringing them closer to Him on the spiritual platform.

TEXT 35

यथा दूरचरे प्रेष्ठे मन आविश्य वर्तते ।
स्त्रीणां च न तथा चेतः सन्निकृष्टेऽक्षिगोचरे ॥३५॥

yathā dūra-care preṣṭhe
mana āviśya vartate
strīṇāṁ ca na tathā cetaḥ
sannikṛṣṭe 'kṣi-gocare

yathā—as; *dūra-care*—being situated far away; *preṣṭhe*—a lover; *manaḥ*—the minds; *āviśya*—becoming absorbed; *vartate*—remain; *strīṇām*—of women; *ca*—and; *na*—not; *tathā*—so; *cetaḥ*—their minds; *sannikṛṣṭe*—when he is near; *akṣi-gocare*—present before their eyes.

TRANSLATION

When her lover is far away, a woman thinks of him more than when he is present before her.

PURPORT

According to Śrīla Viśvanātha Cakravartī, the same holds true for men, who become more absorbed in thinking of a beloved woman when she is far away than when she is present before their eyes.

TEXT 36

मय्यावेश्य मनः कृत्स्नं विमुक्ताशेषवृत्ति यत् ।
अनुस्मरन्त्यो मां नित्यमचिरान्मामुपैष्यथ ॥३६॥

mayy āveśya manaḥ kṛtsnaṁ
vimuktāśeṣa-vṛtti yat
anusmarantyo māṁ nityam
acirān mām upaiṣyatha

mayi—in Me; *āveśya*—absorbing; *manaḥ*—your minds; *kṛtsnam*—entire; *vimukta*—having given up; *aśeṣa*—all; *vṛtti*—its (material) functions; *yat*—because; *anusmarantyaḥ*—remembering; *mām*—Me; *nityam*—constantly; *acirāt*—soon; *mām*—Me; *upaiṣyatha*—you will obtain.

TRANSLATION

Because your minds are totally absorbed in Me and free from all other engagement, you remember Me always, and so you will very soon have Me again in your presence.

TEXT 37

या मया क्रीडता रात्र्यां वनेऽस्मिन् व्रज आस्थिताः ।
अलब्धरासाः कल्याण्यो मापुर्मद्वीर्यचिन्तया ॥३७॥

yā mayā krīḍatā rātryāṁ
vane 'smin vraja āsthitāḥ
alabdha-rāsāḥ kalyāṇyo
māpur mad-vīrya-cintayā

yāḥ—which women; *mayā*—with Me; *krīḍatā*—who was sporting; *rātryām*—at night; *vane*—in the forest; *asmin*—this; *vraje*—in the village of Vraja; *āsthitāḥ*—remaining; *alabdha*—not experiencing; *rāsāḥ*—the *rāsa* dance; *kalyāṇyaḥ*—fortunate; *mā*—Me; *āpuḥ*—they achieved; *mat-vīrya*—upon My valorous pastimes; *cintayā*—by concentration.

TRANSLATION

Although some *gopīs* had to remain in the cowherd village and so could not join the *rāsa* dance to sport with Me at night in the forest, they were nonetheless fortunate. Indeed, they attained Me by thinking of My potent pastimes.

TEXT 38

श्रीशुक उवाच

एवं प्रियतमादिष्टमाकर्ण्य व्रजयोषितः ।
ता ऊचुरुद्धवं प्रीतास्तत्सन्देशागतस्मृतीः ॥३८॥

śrī-śuka uvāca
evaṁ priyatamādiṣṭam
ākarṇya vraja-yoṣitaḥ
tā ūcur uddhavaṁ prītās
tat-sandeśāgata-smṛtīḥ

śrī-śukaḥ uvāca—Śukadeva Gosvāmī said; *evam*—in this fashion; *priya-tama*—given by their beloved (Kṛṣṇa); *ādiṣṭam*—the instructions; *ākarṇya*—hearing; *vraja-yoṣitaḥ*—the women of Vraja; *tāḥ*—they; *ūcuḥ*—said; *uddhavam*—to Uddhava; *prītāḥ*—pleased; *tat*—by that; *sandeśa*—message; *āgata*—having returned; *smṛtīḥ*—their memories.

TRANSLATION

Śukadeva Gosvāmī said: The women of Vraja were pleased to hear this message from their dearmost Kṛṣṇa. His words having revived their memory, they addressed Uddhava as follows.

TEXT 39

गोप्य ऊचुः

दिष्टयाहितो हतः कंसो यदूनां सानुगोऽघकृत् ।
दिष्टयाप्तैर्लब्धसर्वार्थैः कुशल्यास्तेऽच्युतोऽधुना ॥३९॥

gopya ūcuḥ
diṣṭyāhito hataḥ kaṁso
yadūnāṁ sānugo 'gha-kṛt

diṣṭyāptair labdha-sarvārthaiḥ
kuśaly āste 'cyuto 'dhunā

gopyaḥ ūcuḥ—the *gopīs* said; *diṣṭyā*—fortunately; *ahitaḥ*—the enemy; *hataḥ*—has been killed; *kaṁsaḥ*—King Kaṁsa; *yadūnām*—for the Yadus; *sa-anugaḥ*—together with his followers; *agha*—of suffering; *kṛt*—the cause; *diṣṭyā*—fortunately; *āptaiḥ*—with His well-wishers; *labdha*—who have attained; *sarva*—all; *arthaiḥ*—their desires; *kuśalī*—happily; *āste*—is living; *acyutaḥ*—Lord Kṛṣṇa; *adhunā*—at present.

TRANSLATION

The *gopīs* said: It is very good that Kaṁsa, the enemy and persecutor of the Yadus, has now been killed, along with his followers. And it is also very good that Lord Acyuta is living happily in the company of His well-wishing friends and relatives, whose every desire is now fulfilled.

TEXT 40

कच्चिद् गदाग्रजः सौम्य करोति पुरयोषिताम् ।
प्रीतिं नः स्निग्धसव्रीडहासोदारेक्षणार्चितः ॥४०॥

kaccid gadāgrajaḥ saumya
karoti pura-yoṣitām
prītiṁ naḥ snigdha-savrīḍa-
hāsodārekṣaṇārcitaḥ

kaccit—perhaps; *gada-agrajaḥ*—Kṛṣṇa, the elder brother of Gada; *saumya*—O gentle (Uddhava); *karoti*—is giving; *pura*—of the city; *yoṣitām*—for the women; *prītim*—loving happiness; *naḥ*—which belongs to us; *snigdha*—affectionate; *sa-vrīḍa*—and bashful; *hāsa*—with smiles; *udāra*—generous; *īkṣaṇa*—by their glances; *arcitaḥ*—worshiped.

TRANSLATION

Gentle Uddhava, is the elder brother of Gada now bestowing on the city women the pleasure that actually belongs to us? We suppose those ladies worship Him with generous glances full of affectionate, shy smiles.

PURPORT

The name Gadāgraja indicates Kṛṣṇa, the elder brother (*agraja*) of Gada, the first son of Devarakṣitā. She was a sister of Devakī's who was also married to Vasudeva. The *gopīs,* by addressing Kṛṣṇa in this way, indicate that He now thinks of Himself mostly as the son of Devakī, the implication being that His connection with Vṛndāvana has now slackened. Because of intense love, the *gopīs* could not stop thinking of Kṛṣṇa for a moment.

TEXT 41

कथं रतिविशेषज्ञः प्रियश्च पुरयोषिताम् ।
नानुबध्येत तद्वाक्यैर्विभ्रमैश्चानुभाजितः ॥४१॥

kathaṁ rati-viśeṣa-jñaḥ
priyaś ca pura-yoṣitām
nānubadhyetą tad-vākyair
vibhramaiś cānubhājitaḥ

katham—how; *rati*—of conjugal affairs; *viśeṣa*—in all the specific aspects; *jñaḥ*—the expert; *priyaḥ*—the darling; *ca*—and; *pura-yoṣitām*—of the city women; *na anubadhyeta*—will not become bound; *tat*—by their; *vākyaiḥ*—words; *vibhramaiḥ*—bewildering gestures; *ca*—and; *anubhājitaḥ*—constantly worshiped.

TRANSLATION

Śrī Kṛṣṇa is expert in all kinds of conjugal affairs and is the darling of the city women. How can He not become entangled, now that He's constantly adored by their enchanting words and gestures?

PURPORT

According to Śrīdhara Svāmī, each of these verses is spoken by a different *gopī.*

TEXT 42

अपि स्मरति नः साधो गोविन्दः प्रस्तुते क्वचित् ।
गोष्ठिमध्ये पुरस्त्रीणां ग्राम्याः स्वैरकथान्तरे ॥४२॥

api smarati naḥ sādho
govindaḥ prastute kvacit
goṣṭhi-madhye pura-strīṇāṁ
grāmyāḥ svaira-kathāntare

api—moreover; *smarati*—remembers; *naḥ*—us; *sādho*—O pious one; *govindaḥ*—Kṛṣṇa; *prastute*—brought up in discussions; *kvacit*—ever; *goṣṭhi*—the assembly; *madhye*—within; *pura-striṇām*—of the city women; *grāmyāḥ*—village girls; *svaira*—free; *kathā*—conversation; *antare*—during.

TRANSLATION

O saintly one, does Govinda ever remember us during His conversations with the city women? Does He ever mention us village girls as He freely talks with them?

PURPORT

The *gopīs* were so completely in love with Kṛṣṇa, without selfish motive, that even in their great disappointment they never considered giving their love to another. Śrīla Viśvanātha Cakravartī interprets their feelings as follows.

The *gopīs* might say, "Surely Kṛṣṇa has abandoned us because we deserve to be abandoned. Indeed, we are the most insignificant women in the world and have been rejected after having been enjoyed. Still, do we sometimes enter into His memory on account of some good quality of ours, or even because of something we did wrong? Kṛṣṇa must speak very freely with the city women. He and they must sing, joke, make riddles and talk about so many things. Does Kṛṣṇa ever say, 'My dear city women, your sophisticated singing and speech is unknown to the *gopīs* in My home village. They couldn't understand these things.' Does He ever speak about us even in that way?"

TEXT 43

ताः किं निशाः स्मरति यासु तदा प्रियाभिर्
वृन्दावने कुमुदकुन्दशशांकरम्ये ।
रेमे क्वणच्चरणनूपुररासगोष्ठ्याम्
अस्माभिरीडितमनोज्ञकथः कदाचित् ॥४३॥

tāḥ kiṁ niśāḥ smarati yāsu tadā priyābhir
vṛndāvane kumuda-kunda-śaśāṅka-ramye
reme kvaṇac-caraṇa-nūpura-rāsa-goṣṭhyām
asmābhir īḍita-manojña-kathaḥ kadācit

tāḥ—those; *kim*—whether; *niśāḥ*—nights; *smarati*—He remembers; *yāsu*—in which; *tadā*—then; *priyābhiḥ*—with His beloved girlfriends; *vṛndāvane*—in the Vṛndāvana forest; *kumuda*—because of the lotuses; *kunda*—and jasmines; *śaśāṅka*—and because of the moon; *ramye*—attractive; *reme*—He enjoyed; *kvaṇat*—jingling; *caraṇa-nūpura*—(where) the ankle bells; *rāsa-goṣṭhyām*—in the party of the *rāsa* dance; *asmābhiḥ*—with us; *īḍita*—glorified; *manojña*—charming; *kathaḥ*—topics about whom; *kadācit*—ever.

TRANSLATION

Does He recall those nights in the Vṛndāvana forest, lovely with lotus, jasmine and the bright moon? As we glorified His charming pastimes, He enjoyed with us, His beloved girlfriends, in the circle of the *rāsa* dance, which resounded with the music of ankle bells.

PURPORT

Śrīla Viśvanātha Cakravartī gives the following deep realization about this verse: "The *gopīs* knew that no place could be as beautiful as Vṛndāvana. Nowhere else in the universe could one find such a charming scene as the Vṛndāvana forest, which was scented with pious flowers and illumined by the full moon's light reflected from the serene waves of the sacred Yamunā River. No one loved Kṛṣṇa as much as the *gopīs*, and thus no one else could understand Him as well. The *gopīs* rendered intimate service to Kṛṣṇa that only they could perfect. Thus the *gopīs* were distraught to think that Lord Kṛṣṇa was bereft of Vṛndāvana and bereft of their service. Free of all material lust, they were overwhelmed with disappointment because they could not give Kṛṣṇa happiness by their loving service. They simply could not imagine Kṛṣṇa enjoying anywhere else as He did in Vṛndāvana in their company."

TEXT 44

अप्येष्यतीह दाशार्हस्तप्ताः स्वकृतया शुचा ।
सञ्जीवयन्नु नो गात्रैर्यथेन्द्रो वनमम्बुदैः ॥४४॥

apy eṣyatīha dāśārhas
taptāḥ sva-kṛtayā śucā
sañjīvayan nu no gātrair
yathendro vanam ambudaiḥ

api—whether; *eṣyati*—He will come; *iha*—here; *dāśārhaḥ*—Kṛṣṇa, the descendant of Daśārha; *taptāḥ*—who are tormented; *sva-kṛtayā*—by His own doing; *śucā*—with sorrow; *sañjīvayan*—bringing back to life; *nu*—perhaps; *naḥ*—us; *gātraiḥ*—with (the touch of) His limbs; *yathā*—as; *indraḥ*—Lord Indra; *vanam*—a forest; *ambudaiḥ*—with clouds.

TRANSLATION

Will that descendant of Daśārha return here and by the touch of His limbs bring back to life those who are now burning with the grief He Himself has caused? Will He save us in that way, just as Lord Indra brings a forest back to life with his water-bearing clouds?

TEXT 45

कस्मात्कृष्ण इहायाति प्राप्तराज्यो हताहितः ।
नरेन्द्रकन्या उद्वाह्य प्रीतः सर्वसुहृद्वृतः ॥४५॥

kasmāt kṛṣṇa ihāyāti
prāpta-rājyo hatāhitaḥ

narendra-kanyā udvāhya
prītaḥ sarva-suhṛd-vṛtaḥ

kasmāt—why; *kṛṣṇaḥ*—Kṛṣṇa; *iha*—here; *āyāti*—will come; *prāpta*—having attained; *rājyaḥ*—a kingdom; *hata*—having killed; *ahitaḥ*—His enemies; *nara-indra*—of kings; *kanyāḥ*—the daughters; *udvāhya*—after marrying; *prītaḥ*—happy; *sarva*—by all; *suhṛt*—His well-wishers; *vṛtaḥ*—surrounded.

TRANSLATION

But why should Kṛṣṇa come here after winning a kingdom, killing His enemies and marrying the daughters of kings? He's satisfied there, surrounded by all His friends and well-wishers.

TEXT 46

किमस्माभिर्वनौकोभिरन्याभिर्वा महात्मनः ।
श्रीपतेराप्तकामस्य क्रियेतार्थः कृतात्मनः ॥४६॥

kim asmābhir vanaukobhir
anyābhir vā mahātmanaḥ
śrī-pater āpta-kāmasya
kriyetārthaḥ kṛtātmanaḥ

kim—what; *asmābhiḥ*—with us; *vana*—the forest; *okobhiḥ*—whose residence; *anyābhiḥ*—with other women; *vā*—or; *mahā-ātmanaḥ*—for the exalted personality (Kṛṣṇa); *śrī*—of the goddess of fortune; *pateḥ*—for the husband; *āpta-kāmasya*—whose desires are already completely fulfilled; *kriyeta*—is to be served; *arthaḥ*—purpose; *kṛta-ātmanaḥ*—for Him who is complete in Himself.

TRANSLATION

The great soul Kṛṣṇa is the Lord of the goddess of fortune, and He automatically achieves whatever He desires. How can we forest-dwellers or any other women fulfill His purposes when He is already fulfilled within Himself?

PURPORT

Although the *gopīs* lamented that Kṛṣṇa was associating with the city women in Mathurā, they now realize that as the absolute Personality of Godhead, He has no need for any women. It is out of His causeless mercy that He awards His association to His loving devotees.

TEXT 47

परं सौख्यं हि नैराश्यं स्वैरिण्यप्याह पिंगला ।
तज्जानतीनां नः कृष्णे तथाप्याशा दुरत्यया ॥४७॥

paraṁ saukhyaṁ hi nairāśyaṁ
svairiṇy apy āha piṅgalā
taj jānatīnāṁ naḥ kṛṣṇe
tathāpy āśā duratyayā

param—the highest; *saukhyam*—happiness; *hi*—indeed; *nairāśyam*—indifference; *svairiṇī*—unchaste; *api*—although; *āha*—stated; *piṅgalā*—the prostitute Piṅgalā; *tat*—of that; *jānatīnām*—who are aware; *naḥ*—for us; *kṛṣṇe*—focused on Kṛṣṇa; *tathā api*—nevertheless; *āśā*—the hope; *duratyayā*—is impossible to transcend.

TRANSLATION

Indeed, the greatest happiness is to renounce all desires, as even the prostitute Piṅgalā has declared. Yet even though we know this, we cannot give up our hopes of attaining Kṛṣṇa.

PURPORT

The story of Piṅgalā is narrated in the Eleventh Canto, Eighth Chapter, of *Śrīmad-Bhāgavatam.*

TEXT 48

क उत्सहेत सन्त्यक्तुमुत्तमःश्लोकसंविदम् ।
अनिच्छतोऽपि यस्य श्रीरंगान्न च्यवते क्वचित् ॥४८॥

ka utsaheta santyaktum
uttamaḥśloka-saṁvidam
anicchato 'pi yasya śrīr
aṅgān na cyavate kvacit

kaḥ—who; *utsaheta*—can bear; *santyaktum*—to give up; *uttamaḥ-śloka*—with Lord Kṛṣṇa; *saṁvidam*—intimate talks; *anicchataḥ*—not wanted; *api*—even though; *yasya*—whose; *śrīḥ*—the supreme goddess of fortune; *aṅgāt*—the body; *na cyavate*—does not let go of; *kvacit*—ever.

TRANSLATION

Who can bear to give up intimate talks with Lord Uttamaḥśloka? Although He shows no interest in her, Goddess Śrī never moves from her place on His chest.

TEXT 49

सरिच्छैलवनोद्देशा गावो वेणुरवा इमे ।
संकर्षणसहायेन कृष्णेनाचरिताः प्रभो ॥४९॥

saric-chaila-vanoddeśā
gāvo veṇu-ravā ime
saṅkarṣaṇa-sahāyena
kṛṣṇenācaritāḥ prabho

sarit—rivers; *śaila*—hills; *vana-uddeśāḥ*—and areas of the forest; *gāvaḥ*—cows; *veṇu-ravāḥ*—flute sounds; *ime*—all these; *saṅkarṣaṇa*—Lord Balarāma; *sahāyena*—whose companion; *kṛṣṇena*—by Kṛṣṇa; *ācaritāḥ*—utilized; *prabho*—O master (Uddhava).

TRANSLATION

Dear Uddhava Prabhu, when Kṛṣṇa was here in the company of Saṅkarṣaṇa, He enjoyed all these rivers, hills, forests, cows and flute sounds.

TEXT 50

पुनः पुनः स्मारयन्ति नन्दगोपसुतं बत ।
श्रीनिकेतैस्तत्पदकैर्विस्मर्तुं नैव शक्नुमः ॥५०॥

punaḥ punaḥ smārayanti
nanda-gopa-sutaṁ bata
śrī-niketais tat-padakair
vismartuṁ naiva śaknumaḥ

punaḥ punaḥ—again and again; *smārayanti*—they remind; *nanda-gopa-sutam*—of the son of Nanda, the cowherd king; *bata*—certainly; *śrī*—divine; *niketaiḥ*—having markings; *tat*—His; *padakaiḥ*—because of the footprints; *vismartum*—to forget; *na*—not; *eva*—indeed; *śaknumaḥ*—are we able.

TRANSLATION

All these remind us constantly of Nanda's son. Indeed, because we see Kṛṣṇa's footprints, which are marked with divine symbols, we can never forget Him.

TEXT 51

गत्या ललितयोदारहासलीलावलोकनैः ।
माध्व्या गिरा हृतधियः कथं तं विस्मराम हे ॥५१॥

gatyā lalitayodāra-
hāsa-līlāvalokanaiḥ
mādhvyā girā hṛta-dhiyaḥ
kathaṁ taṁ vismarāma he

gatyā—by His gait; *lalitayā*—charming; *udāra*—with generous; *hāsa*—smiles; *līlā*—playful; *avalokanaiḥ*—by His glances; *mādhvyā*—honeylike; *girā*—by His words; *hṛta*—stolen away; *dhiyaḥ*—whose hearts; *katham*—how; *tam*—Him; *vismarāma*—we can forget; *he*—O (Uddhava).

TRANSLATION

O Uddhava, how can we forget Him when our hearts have been stolen away by the charming way He walks, His generous smile and playful glances, and His honeylike words?

TEXT 52

हे नाथ हे रमानाथ व्रजनाथार्तिनाशन ।
मग्नमुद्धर गोविन्द गोकुलं वृजिनार्णवात् ॥५२॥

he nātha he ramā-nātha
vraja-nāthārti-nāśana
magnam uddhara govinda
gokulaṁ vṛjinārṇavāt

he nātha—O master; *he ramā-nātha*—O master of the goddess of fortune; *vraja-nātha*—O master of the cowherd village; *ārti*—of suffering; *nāśana*—O destroyer; *magnam*—submerged; *uddhara*—uplift; *govinda*—O Govinda; *gokulam*—Gokula; *vṛjina*—of distress; *arṇavāt*—from the ocean.

TRANSLATION

O master, O master of the goddess of fortune, O master of Vraja! O destroyer of all suffering, Govinda, please lift Your Gokula out of the ocean of distress in which it is drowning!

PURPORT

Śrīla Viśvanātha Cakravartī presents the following insight into this scene: Someone might propose to the *gopīs,* "Why don't you just go somewhere else? Leave Vṛndāvana, and then you won't have to see these rivers, mountains and forests. Cover your eyes with your garments, use your intelligence to lead your minds to some other thought, and thus forget Kṛṣṇa." The *gopīs* answer this suggestion in the previous verse by stating, "We no longer possess our intelligence, for Kṛṣṇa has taken it away by His supreme beauty and charm."

Now in the present verse the feelings of the *gopīs* become so strong that they disregard Uddhava and, turning toward Mathurā, address Kṛṣṇa Himself with humble cries. They address Kṛṣṇa as Vrajanātha because in the past young Kṛṣṇa performed many inconceivable pastimes to protect His beloved village people, such as lifting Govardhana Hill and destroying many monstrous demons. In this heartrending verse, the *gopīs* cry out to Kṛṣṇa to remember the wonderful, sweet relationship they once enjoyed together as innocent village people. Indeed, Śrī Kṛṣṇa would lovingly take care of His father's cows, and the *gopīs* appealed to Him to remember these duties and return so He could resume them.

TEXT 53

श्रीशुक उवाच
ततस्ताः कृष्णसन्देशैर्व्यपेतविरहज्वराः ।
उद्धवं पूजयां चक्रुर्ज्ञात्वात्मानमधोक्षजम् ॥५३॥

śrī-śuka uvāca
tatas tāḥ kṛṣṇa-sandeśair
vyapeta-viraha-jvarāḥ
uddhavaṁ pūjayāṁ cakrur
jñātvātmānam adhokṣajam

śrī-śukaḥ uvāca—Śrī Śukadeva Gosvāmī said; *tataḥ*—then; *tāḥ*—they; *kṛṣṇa-sandeśaiḥ*—by the messages from Kṛṣṇa; *vyapeta*—removed; *viraha*—of their separation; *jvarāḥ*—the fever; *uddhavam*—Uddhava; *pūjayām cakruḥ*—worshiped; *jñātvā*—recognizing him; *ātmānam*—Himself; *adhokṣajam*—as the Supreme Lord.

TRANSLATION

Śukadeva Gosvāmī continued: Lord Kṛṣṇa's messages having relieved their fever of separation, the *gopīs* then worshiped Uddhava, recognizing him as nondifferent from their Lord, Kṛṣṇa.

PURPORT

Śrīla Śrīdhara Svāmī states that the words *jñātvātmānam adhokṣajam* also indicate that the *gopīs* recognize Lord Kṛṣṇa to be the very soul of their lives and thus spiritually one with them.

TEXT 54

उवास कतिचिन्मासान् गोपीनां विनुदन् शुचः ।
कृष्णलीलाकथां गायन् रमयामास गोकुलम् ॥५४॥

uvāsa katicin māsān
gopīnāṁ vinudan śucaḥ
kṛṣṇa-līlā-kathāṁ gāyan
ramayām āsa gokulam

uvāsa—he resided; *katicit*—for some; *māsān*—months; *gopīnām*—of the cowherd girls; *vinudan*—dispelling; *śucaḥ*—the unhappiness; *kṛṣṇa-līlā*—of the pastimes of Lord Kṛṣṇa; *kathām*—the topics; *gāyan*—singing; *ramayām āsa*—he gave joy; *gokulam*—to Gokula.

TRANSLATION

Uddhava remained there for several months, dispelling the *gopīs'* sorrow by chanting the topics of Lord Kṛṣṇa's pastimes. Thus he brought joy to all the people of Gokula.

PURPORT

The great *ācārya* Jīva Gosvāmī comments in this regard that Uddhava, during his stay in Vṛndāvana, certainly took special care to enliven Kṛṣṇa's foster parents, Nanda and Yaśodā.

TEXT 55

यावन्त्यहानि नन्दस्य व्रजेऽवात्सीत्स उद्धवः ।
व्रजौकसां क्षणप्रायाण्यासन् कृष्णस्य वार्तया ॥५५॥

yāvanty ahāni nandasya
vraje 'vātsīt sa uddhavaḥ
vrajaukasāṁ kṣaṇa-prāyāṇy
āsan kṛṣṇasya vārtayā

yāvanti—for as many; *ahāni*—days; *nandasya*—of King Nanda; *vraje*—in the cowherd village; *avātsīt*—dwelled; *saḥ*—he; *uddhavaḥ*—Uddhava; *vraja-okasām*—for the residents of Vraja; *kṣaṇa-prāyāṇi*—passing like a moment; *āsan*—they were; *kṛṣṇasya*—about Kṛṣṇa; *vārtayā*—because of the discussions.

TRANSLATION

All the days that Uddhava dwelled in Nanda's cowherd village seemed like a single moment to the residents of Vraja, for Uddhava was always discussing Kṛṣṇa.

TEXT 56

सरिद्वनगिरिद्रोणीर्वीक्षन् कुसुमितान् द्रुमान् ।
कृष्णं संस्मारयन् रेमे हरिदासो व्रजौकसाम् ॥५६॥

sarid-vana-giri-droṇīr
vīkṣan kusumitān drumān
kṛṣṇaṁ saṁsmārayan reme
hari-dāso vrajaukasām

sarit—the rivers; *vana*—forests; *giri*—mountains; *droṇīḥ*—and valleys; *vīkṣan*—seeing; *kusumitān*—flowering; *drumān*—the trees; *kṛṣṇam*—about Kṛṣṇa; *saṁsmārayan*—inspiring remembrance; *reme*—he took pleasure; *hari-dāsaḥ*—the servant of Lord Hari; *vraja-okasām*—for the residents of Vraja.

TRANSLATION

That servant of Lord Hari, seeing the rivers, forests, mountains, valleys and flowering trees of Vraja, enjoyed inspiring the inhabitants of Vṛndāvana by reminding them of Lord Kṛṣṇa.

PURPORT

Śrīla Śrīdhara Svāmī points out that as Uddhava wandered about Vṛndāvana, he reminded Vraja's residents of Kṛṣṇa by asking them questions about the pastimes the Lord had performed in each of these places, namely the rivers, forests, mountains and valleys. Thus Uddhava himself enjoyed great transcendental bliss in their association.

TEXT 57

दृष्ट्वैवमादि गोपीनां कृष्णावेशात्मविक्लवम् ।
उद्धवः परमप्रीतस्ता नमस्यन्निदं जगौ ॥५७॥

dṛṣṭvaivam-ādi gopīnāṁ
kṛṣṇāveśātma-viklavam
uddhavaḥ parama-prītas
tā namasyann idaṁ jagau

dṛṣṭvā—seeing; *evam*—such; *ādi*—and more; *gopīnām*—of the *gopīs; kṛṣṇa-āveśa*—their total absorption in thought of Kṛṣṇa; *ātma*—consisting of; *viklavam*—the mental agitation; *uddhavaḥ*—Uddhava; *parama*—supremely; *prītaḥ*—pleased; *tāḥ*—to them; *namasyan*—offering all respect; *idam*—this; *jagau*—sang.

TRANSLATION

Thus seeing how the *gopīs* were always disturbed because of their total absorption in Kṛṣṇa, Uddhava was supremely pleased. Desiring to offer them all respect, he sang as follows.

PURPORT

Viklava, "mental disturbance," should not be confused here with ordinary material distress. It is clearly stated that Uddhava was supremely pleased, and he felt this way because he saw that the *gopīs* had attained the highest state of loving ecstasy. Uddhava was an exalted member of the court in Dvārakā, an important minister in world political affairs, and yet he felt the spiritual urge to offer his obeisances to the glorious *gopīs,* although externally they were mere cowherd girls in an insignificant village called Vṛndāvana. Thus, to explain his feelings he sang the following verses. Śrīla Jīva Gosvāmī states that Uddhava sang these verses daily while he was in Vṛndāvana.

TEXT 58

एताः परं तनुभृतो भुवि गोपवध्वो
गोविन्द एव निखिलात्मनि रूढभावाः ।
वाञ्छन्ति यद् भवभियो मुनयो वयं च
किं ब्रह्मजन्मभिरनन्तकथारसस्य ॥५८॥

etāḥ paraṁ tanu-bhṛto bhuvi gopa-vadhvo
govinda eva nikhilātmani rūḍha-bhāvāḥ
vāñchanti yad bhava-bhiyo munayo vayaṁ ca
kiṁ brahma-janmabhir ananta-kathā-rasasya

etāḥ—these women; *param*—alone; *tanu*—their bodies; *bhṛtaḥ*—maintain successfully; *bhuvi*—on the earth; *gopa-vadhvaḥ*—the young cowherd women; *govinde*—for Lord Kṛṣṇa; *eva*—exclusively; *nikhila*—of all; *ātmani*—the Soul; *rūḍha*—perfected; *bhāvāḥ*—ecstatic loving attraction; *vāñchanti*—they desire; *yat*—which; *bhava*—material existence; *bhiyaḥ*—those who are afraid of; *munayaḥ*—sages; *vayam*—we; *ca*—also; *kim*—what use; *brahma*—as a *brāhmaṇa* or as Lord Brahmā; *janmabhiḥ*—with births; *ananta*—of the unlimited Lord; *kathā*—for the topics; *rasasya*—for one who has a taste.

TRANSLATION

[Uddhava sang:] Among all persons on earth, these cowherd women alone have actually perfected their embodied lives, for they have achieved the perfection of unalloyed love for Lord Govinda. Their pure love is hankered after by those who fear material existence, by great sages, and by ourselves as well. For one who has tasted the narrations of the infinite Lord, what is the use of taking birth as a high-class *brāhmaṇa*, or even as Lord Brahmā himself?

PURPORT

Śrīla Viśvanātha Cakravartī explains that here the term *brahma-janmabhiḥ*, "brahminical births," refers to the threefold birth by (1) seminal parenthood, (2) sacred-thread initiation and (3) sacrificial initiation. These cannot compare to pure Kṛṣṇa consciousness. In fact, Śrī Uddhava, who spoke this verse, took birth as a pure *brāhmaṇa,* but he deprecates this position in comparison to that of the exalted *gopīs.*

TEXT 59

क्वेमाः स्त्रियो वनचरीर्व्यभिचारदुष्टाः
कृष्णे क्व चैष परमात्मनि रूढभावः ।
नन्वीश्वरोऽनुभजतोऽविदुषोऽपि साक्षाच्
छ्रेयस्तनोत्यगदराज इवोपयुक्तः ॥५९॥

kvemāḥ striyo vana-carīr vyabhicāra-duṣṭāḥ
kṛṣṇe kva caiṣa paramātmani rūḍha-bhāvaḥ
nanv īśvaro 'nubhajato 'viduṣo 'pi sākṣāc
chreyas tanoty agada-rāja ivopayuktaḥ

kva—where, in comparison; *imāḥ*—these; *striyaḥ*—women; *vana*—in the forests; *carīḥ*—who wander; *vyabhicāra*—by improper behavior; *duṣṭāḥ*—contaminated; *kṛṣṇe*—for Kṛṣṇa; *kva ca*—and where; *eṣaḥ*—this; *parama-ātmani*—for the Supreme Soul; *rūḍha-bhāvaḥ*—stage of perfect love (known technically as *mahā-bhāva*); *nanu*—certainly; *īśvaraḥ*—the Personality of Godhead; *anubhajataḥ*—to one who constantly worships Him; *aviduṣaḥ*—not learned; *api*—even though; *sākṣāt*—directly; *śreyaḥ*—the highest good; *tanoti*—bestows; *agada*—of medicines; *rājaḥ*—the king (namely, the nectar which the demigods drink for long life); *iva*—as if; *upayuktaḥ*—taken.

TRANSLATION

How amazing it is that these simple women who wander about the forest, seemingly spoiled by improper behavior, have achieved the perfection of unalloyed love for Kṛṣṇa, the Supreme Soul! Still, it is true that the Supreme Lord Himself awards His blessings even to an ignorant worshiper, just as the best medicine works even when taken by a person ignorant of its ingredients.

PURPORT

The use of the word *kva* in the first two lines indicates a sharp contrast between apparently incompatible items, in this case the apparently insignificant and even impure position of the *gopīs,* mentioned in the first line, and their attainment of the highest perfection of life, mentioned in the second. In this regard Śrīla Viśvanātha Cakravartī describes three types of adulterous women. The first is a woman who enjoys both her husband and a lover, being faithful to neither. Both ordinary society and the scriptures condemn this conduct. The second type of adulterous woman is she who abandons her husband to enjoy only with her lover. Society and the scriptures also condemn this behavior, although such a fallen woman may be said to at least have the good quality of dedicating herself to a single man. The last kind of adulterous woman is she who abandons her husband and enjoys in the attitude of being a lover of the Supreme Lord alone. Śrīla Viśvanātha Cakravartī explains that although foolish, common people criticize this position, such behavior is commended by those who are wise in spiritual science. Therefore learned members of society and the revealed scriptures praise such single-minded devotion to the Lord. Such was the *gopīs'* behavior. Thus the term *vyabhicāra-duṣṭāḥ,* "corrupted by deviation," indicates the apparent resemblance between the *gopīs'* behavior and that of ordinary adulterous women.

TEXT 60

नायं श्रियोऽङ्ग उ नितान्तरतेः प्रसादः
स्वर्योषितां नलिनगन्धरुचां कुतोऽन्याः ।
रासोत्सवेऽस्य भुजदण्डगृहीतकण्ठ-
लब्धाशिषां य उदगाद्व्रजवल्लभीनाम् ॥६०॥

nāyaṁ śriyo 'ṅga u nitānta-rateḥ prasādaḥ
svar-yoṣitāṁ nalina-gandha-rucāṁ kuto 'nyāḥ
rāsotsave 'sya bhuja-daṇḍa-gṛhīta-kaṇṭha-
labdhāśiṣāṁ ya udagād vraja-vallabhīnām

na—not; *ayam*—this; *śriyaḥ*—of the goddess of fortune; *aṅge*—on the chest; *u*—alas; *nitānta-rateḥ*—who is very intimately related; *prasādaḥ*—the favor; *svaḥ*—of the heavenly planets; *yoṣitām*—of women; *nalina*—of the lotus flower; *gandha*—having the aroma; *rucām*—and bodily luster; *kutaḥ*—much less; *anyāḥ*—others; *rāsa-utsave*—in the festival of the *rāsa* dance; *asya*—of Lord Śrī Kṛṣṇa; *bhuja-daṇḍa*—by the arms; *gṛhīta*—embraced; *kaṇṭha*—their necks; *labdha-āśiṣām*—who achieved such a blessing; *yaḥ*—which; *udagāt*—became manifest; *vraja-vallabhīnām*—of the beautiful *gopīs,* the transcendental girls of Vrajabhūmi.

TRANSLATION

When Lord Śrī Kṛṣṇa was dancing with the *gopīs* in the *rāsa-līlā,* the *gopīs* were embraced by the arms of the Lord. This transcendental favor was never bestowed upon the goddess of fortune or other consorts in the spiritual world. Indeed, never was such a thing even imagined by the most beautiful girls in the heavenly planets, whose bodily luster and aroma resemble the lotus flower. And what to speak of worldly women who are very beautiful according to material estimation?

PURPORT

The word meanings and translation for this verse are taken from Śrīla Prabhupāda's English rendering of *Caitanya-caritāmṛta* (*Madhya* 8.80).

Śrīla Viśvanātha Cakravartī comments as follows: Lord Kṛṣṇa, the best of all *avatāras,* exists on the highest platform of purity and morality, and thus He always remained praiseworthy by all, even while accepting worldly criticism for His cow-tending, wandering in the forest, taking meals with young monkeys, stealing yogurt, seducing other men's wives, and so on. Similarly, the *gopīs,* who are constituted of the Lord's pleasure potency, achieved the highest standard of purity and auspiciousness, even in comparison to the goddesses of fortune, and thus the *gopīs* are supremely glorious, even though they were criticized by worldly people because they were mere cowherd women living in the forest and behaving in an apparently improper way.

TEXT 61

आसामहो चरणरेणुजुषामहं स्यां
वृन्दावने किमपि गुल्मलतौषधीनाम् ।
या दुस्त्यजं स्वजनमार्यपथं च हित्वा
भेजुर्मुकुन्दपदवीं श्रुतिभिर्विमृग्याम् ॥६१॥

āsām aho caraṇa-reṇu-juṣām ahaṁ syāṁ
vṛndāvane kim api gulma-latauṣadhīnām
yā dustyajaṁ sva-janam ārya-pathaṁ ca hitvā
bhejur mukunda-padavīṁ śrutibhir vimṛgyām

āsām—of the *gopīs; aho*—oh; *caraṇa-reṇu*—the dust of the lotus feet; *juṣām*—devoted to; *aham syām*—let me become; *vṛndāvane*—in Vṛndāvana; *kim api*—any one; *gulma-latā-oṣadhīnām*—among bushes, creepers and herbs; *yā*—they who; *dustyajam*—very difficult to give up; *sva-janam*—family members; *ārya-patham*—the path of chastity; *ca*—and; *hitvā*—giving up; *bhejuḥ*—worshiped; *mukunda-padavīm*—the lotus feet of Mukunda, Kṛṣṇa; *śrutibhiḥ*—by the *Vedas; vimṛgyām*—to be searched for.

TRANSLATION

The *gopīs* of Vṛndāvana have given up the association of their husbands, sons and other family members, who are very difficult to give up, and they have forsaken the path of chastity to take shelter of the lotus feet of Mukunda, Kṛṣṇa, which one should search for by Vedic knowledge. Oh, let me be fortunate enough to be one of the bushes, creepers or herbs in Vṛndāvana, because the *gopīs* trample them and bless them with the dust of their lotus feet.

PURPORT

The word meanings and translation for this verse are taken from Śrīla Prabhupāda's English rendering of *Caitanya-caritāmṛta* (*Antya* 7.47).

Śrī Uddhava here shows the perfect Vaiṣṇava attitude of humility. He does not pray to be equal to the *gopīs* in their exalted stage of love, but rather to take birth as a bush or creeper in Vṛndāvana so that when they walk upon him he will get the dust of their feet and thus be blessed. The shy *gopīs* would never agree to give such blessings to a great personality like Uddhava; therefore he cleverly sought to get such mercy by taking birth as a plant in Vṛndāvana.

TEXT 62

या वै श्रियार्चितमजादिभिराप्तकामैर्
योगेश्वरैरपि यदात्मनि रासगोष्ठ्याम् ।

कृष्णस्य तद् भगवतः चरणारविन्दं
न्यस्तं स्तनेषु विजहुः परिरभ्य तापम् ॥६२॥

yā vai śriyārcitam ajādibhir āpta-kāmair
yogeśvarair api yad ātmani rāsa-goṣṭhyām
kṛṣṇasya tad bhagavataḥ caraṇāravindaṁ
nyastaṁ staneṣu vijahuḥ parirabhya tāpam

yāḥ—who (the *gopīs*); *vai*—indeed; *śriyā*—by the goddess of fortune; *arcitam*—worshiped; *aja*—by unborn Brahmā; *ādibhiḥ*—and other demigods; *āpta-kāmaiḥ*—who have already realized all desires; *yoga-īśvaraiḥ*—masters of mystic power; *api*—even though; *yat*—which; *ātmani*—in the mind; *rāsa*—of the *rāsa* dance; *goṣṭhyām*—in the gathering; *kṛṣṇasya*—of Lord Kṛṣṇa; *tat*—those; *bhagavataḥ*—of the Supreme Lord; *caraṇa-aravindam*—the lotus feet; *nyastam*—placed; *staneṣu*—on their breasts; *vijahuḥ*—they gave up; *parirabhya*—by embracing; *tāpam*—their torment.

TRANSLATION

The goddess of fortune herself, along with Lord Brahmā and all the other demigods, who are masters of yogic perfection, can worship the lotus feet of Kṛṣṇa only within her mind. But during the *rāsa* dance Lord Kṛṣṇa placed His feet upon these *gopīs'* breasts, and by embracing those feet the *gopīs* gave up all distress.

TEXT 63

वन्दे नन्दव्रजस्त्रीणां पादरेणुमभीक्ष्णशः ।
यासां हरिकथोद्गीतं पुनाति भुवनत्रयम् ॥६३॥

vande nanda-vraja-strīṇāṁ
pāda-reṇum abhīkṣṇaśaḥ
yāsāṁ hari-kathodgītaṁ
punāti bhuvana-trayam

vande—I offer my respects; *nanda-vraja*—of the cowherd village of Nanda Mahārāja; *strīṇām*—of the women; *pāda*—of the feet; *reṇum*—to the dust; *abhīkṣṇaśaḥ*—perpetually; *yāsām*—whose; *hari*—of Lord Kṛṣṇa; *kathā*—about the topics; *udgītam*—loud chanting; *punāti*—purifies; *bhuvana-trayam*—the three worlds.

TRANSLATION

I repeatedly offer my respects to the dust from the feet of the women of Nanda Mahārāja's cowherd village. When these *gopīs* loudly chant the glories of Śrī Kṛṣṇa, the vibration purifies the three worlds.

PURPORT

Śrī Uddhava, having established the glories of the *gopīs* in the previous verses, now directly offers his obeisances to them. According to the *Śrī Vaiṣṇava-toṣaṇī*, Śrī Uddhava did not offer such respect even to Lord Kṛṣṇa's queens in Dvārakā.

TEXT 64

श्रीशुक उवाच
अथ गोपीरनुज्ञाप्य यशोदां नन्दमेव च ।
गोपानामन्त्र्य दाशार्हो यास्यन्नारुरुहे रथम् ॥६४॥

śrī-śuka uvāca
atha gopīr anujñāpya
yaśodāṁ nandam eva ca
gopān āmantrya dāśārho
yāsyann āruruhe ratham

śrī-śukaḥ uvāca—Śukadeva Gosvāmī said; *atha*—then; *gopīḥ*—of the *gopīs; anujñāpya*—taking permission; *yaśodām*—of mother Yaśodā; *nandam*—King Nanda; *eva ca*—also; *gopān*—of the cowherds; *āmantrya*—taking leave; *dāśārhaḥ*—Uddhava, descendant of Daśārha; *yāsyan*—being about to leave; *āruruhe*—mounted; *ratham*—his chariot.

TRANSLATION

Śukadeva Gosvāmī said: Uddhava, the descendant of Daśārha, then took permission to leave from the *gopīs* and from mother

Yaśodā and Nanda Mahārāja. He bade farewell to all the cowherd men and, about to depart, mounted his chariot.

TEXT 65

तं निर्गतं समासाद्य नानोपायनपाणयः ।
नन्दादयोऽनुरागेण प्रावोचन्नश्रुलोचनाः ॥६५॥

taṁ nirgataṁ samāsādya
nānopāyana-pāṇayaḥ
nandādayo 'nurāgeṇa
prāvocann aśru-locanāḥ

tam—him (Uddhava); *nirgatam*—gone out; *samāsādya*—approaching; *nānā*—various; *upāyana*—items for worship; *pāṇayaḥ*—in their hands; *nanda-ādayaḥ*—Nanda and the others; *anurāgeṇa*—with affection; *prāvocan*—spoke; *aśru*—with tears; *locanāḥ*—in their eyes.

TRANSLATION

As Uddhava was about to leave, Nanda and the others approached him bearing various items of worship. With tears in their eyes they addressed him as follows.

PURPORT

Śrīla Jīva Gosvāmī points out that Nanda and the cowherd men did not approach Uddhava as a formality, but rather out of spontaneous affection for a dear friend of Kṛṣṇa's.

TEXT 66

मनसो वृत्तयो नः स्युः कृष्णपादाम्बुजाश्रयाः ।
वाचोऽभिधायिनीर्नाम्नां कायस्तत्प्रह्वणादिषु ॥६६॥

manaso vṛttayo naḥ syuḥ
kṛṣṇa-pādāmbujāśrayāḥ
vāco 'bhidhāyinīr nāmnāṁ
kāyas tat-prahvaṇādiṣu

manasaḥ—of the minds; *vṛttayaḥ*—the functions; *naḥ*—our; *syuḥ*—may they be; *kṛṣṇa*—of Kṛṣṇa; *pāda-ambuja*—of the lotus feet; *āśrayāḥ*—taking shelter; *vācaḥ*—our words; *abhidhāyinīḥ*—expressing; *nāmnām*—His names; *kāyaḥ*—our bodies; *tat*—to Him; *prahvaṇa-ādiṣu*—(engaged) in bowing down and so forth.

TRANSLATION

[Nanda and the other cowherds said:] May our mental functions always take shelter of Kṛṣṇa's lotus feet, may our words always chant His names, and may our bodies always bow down to Him and serve Him.

PURPORT

The residents of Vṛndāvana were firmly convinced that even if they could not have direct association with their beloved Kṛṣṇa, they would never be indifferent to Him. They were all topmost pure devotees of the Lord.

TEXT 67

कर्मभिर्भ्राम्यमाणानां यत्र क्वापीश्वरेच्छया ।
मंगलाचरितैर्दानै रतिर्नः कृष्ण ईश्वरे ॥६७॥

karmabhir bhrāmyamāṇānāṁ
yatra kvāpīśvarecchayā
maṅgalācaritair dānai
ratir naḥ kṛṣṇa īśvare

karmabhiḥ—by our fruitive actions; *bhrāmyamāṇānām*—who are made to wander; *yatra kva api*—wherever; *īśvara*—of the Supreme Lord; *icchayā*—by the desire; *maṅgala*—auspicious; *ācaritaiḥ*—because of works; *dānaiḥ*—because of charity; *ratiḥ*—attachment; *naḥ*—our; *kṛṣṇe*—for Kṛṣṇa; *īśvare*—the Lord.

TRANSLATION

Wherever we are made to wander about this world by the Supreme Lord's will, in accordance with the reactions to our

fruitive work, may our good works and charity always grant us love for Lord Kṛṣṇa.

TEXT 68

एवं सभाजितो गोपैः कृष्णभक्त्या नराधिप ।
उद्धवः पुनरागच्छन्मथुरां कृष्णपालिताम् ॥६८॥

evaṁ sabhājito gopaiḥ
kṛṣṇa-bhaktyā narādhipa
uddhavaḥ punar āgacchan
mathurāṁ kṛṣṇa-pālitām

evam—thus; *sabhājitaḥ*—shown honor; *gopaiḥ*—by the cowherds; *kṛṣṇa-bhaktyā*—with devotion for Kṛṣṇa; *nara-adhipa*—O ruler of men (Parīkṣit); *uddhavaḥ*—Uddhava; *punaḥ*—again; *āgacchat*—returned; *mathurām*—to Mathurā; *kṛṣṇa-pālitām*—which was being protected by Lord Kṛṣṇa.

TRANSLATION

[Śukadeva Gosvāmī continued:] O ruler of men, thus honored by the cowherd men with expressions of devotion for Lord Kṛṣṇa, Uddhava went back to the city of Mathurā, which was under Kṛṣṇa's protection.

PURPORT

The word *kṛṣṇa-pālitām* indicates that even though Uddhava became quite attached to the land of Vṛndāvana, he returned to Mathurā because Śrī Kṛṣṇa was personally displaying His transcendental pastimes there.

TEXT 69

कृष्णाय प्रणिपत्याह भक्त्युद्रेकं व्रजौकसाम् ।
वसुदेवाय रामाय राज्ञे चोपायनान्यदात् ॥६९॥

kṛṣṇāya praṇipatyāha
bhakty-udrekaṁ vrajaukasām

vasudevāya rāmāya
rājñe copāyanāny adāt

kṛṣṇāya—to Lord Kṛṣṇa; *praṇipatya*—after falling down to pay homage; *āha*—he told; *bhakti*—of pure devotion; *udrekam*—the abundance; *vraja-okasām*—of the residents of Vraja; *vasudevāya*—to Vasudeva; *rāmāya*—to Lord Balarāma; *rājñe*—to the King (Ugrasena); *ca*—and; *upāyanāni*—the items received in tribute; *adāt*—he gave.

TRANSLATION

After falling down to pay his homage, Uddhava described to Lord Kṛṣṇa the immense devotion of the residents of Vraja. Uddhava also described it to Vasudeva, Lord Balarāma and King Ugrasena and presented to them the gifts of tribute he had brought with him.

Thus end the purports of the humble servants of His Divine Grace A. C. Bhaktivedanta Swami Prabhupāda to the Tenth Canto, Forty-seventh Chapter, of the Śrīmad-Bhāgavatam, *entitled "The Song of the Bee."*

CHAPTER FORTY-EIGHT

Kṛṣṇa Pleases His Devotees

In this chapter Lord Śrī Kṛṣṇa first visits Trivakrā (also known as Kubjā) and enjoys with her, and then He visits Akrūra. The Lord sends Akrūra to Hastināpura to satisfy the Pāṇḍavas.

After Uddhava had related to Śrī Kṛṣṇa the news of Vraja, the Lord went to the home of Trivakrā, which was decorated with diverse ornamentation conducive to sexual enjoyment. Trivakrā welcomed Kṛṣṇa with great respect, giving Him a raised seat and, together with her female companions, worshiping Him. She also offered Uddhava a seat, as befitted his position, but Uddhava simply touched the seat and sat on the floor.

Lord Kṛṣṇa then reclined on an opulent bed as the maidservant Trivakrā elaborately washed and decorated herself. Then she approached Him. Kṛṣṇa invited Trivakrā to the bed and began to enjoy with her in various ways. By embracing Lord Kṛṣṇa, Trivakrā freed herself of the torment of lust. She asked Kṛṣṇa to remain with her for some time, and the considerate Lord promised to fulfill her request in due course. He then returned with Uddhava to His residence. Apart from offering sandal paste to Kṛṣṇa, Trivakrā had never performed any pious acts, yet simply on the strength of the piety of this single act she attained the rare personal association of Śrī Kṛṣṇa.

Śrī Kṛṣṇa next went to Akrūra's house with Lord Baladeva and Uddhava. Akrūra honored the three of them by bowing down and presenting them with suitable sitting places. Then he worshiped Rāma and Kṛṣṇa, washed Their feet and poured the water on his head. Akrūra also offered Them many prayers.

Lord Kṛṣṇa was pleased with Akrūra's prayers. He told him that since he, Akrūra, was in fact Their paternal uncle, Kṛṣṇa and Balarāma should be the recipients of his protection and mercy. Lord Kṛṣṇa then praised Akrūra as a saint and purifier of the sinful, and He asked him to visit Hastināpura to find out how the Pāṇḍavas, deprived of their father, were faring. Finally, the Lord returned home, taking Balarāma and Uddhava with Him.

TEXT 1

श्रीशुक उवाच
अथ विज्ञाय भगवान् सर्वात्मा सर्वदर्शनः ।
सैरन्ध्र्याः कामतप्तायाः प्रियमिच्छन् गृहं ययौ ॥१॥

śrī-śuka uvāca
atha vijñāya bhagavān
sarvātmā sarva-darśanaḥ
sairandhryāḥ kāma-taptāyāḥ
priyam icchan gṛhaṁ yayau

śrī-śukaḥ uvāca—Śrī Śukadeva Gosvāmī said; *atha*—then; *vijñāya*—understanding; *bhagavān*—the Supreme Lord; *sarva*—of all; *ātmā*—the Soul; *sarva*—of everything; *darśanaḥ*—the seer; *sairandhryāḥ*—of the serving girl, Trivakrā; *kāma*—by lust; *taptāyāḥ*—troubled; *priyam*—the satisfaction; *icchan*—wanting; *gṛham*—to her house; *yayau*—He went.

TRANSLATION

Śukadeva Gosvāmī said: Next, after assimilating Uddhava's report, Lord Kṛṣṇa, the Supreme Personality of Godhead, the omniscient Soul of all that be, desired to satisfy the serving girl Trivakrā, who was troubled by lust. Thus He went to her house.

PURPORT

This text gives an interesting insight into the Lord's pastimes. The first line says, *atha vijñāya bhagavān:* "Thus the Lord, understanding [Uddhava's report]. . . ." The second line states that Lord Kṛṣṇa is the Soul of everything (*sarvātmā*) and the seer of everything (*sarva-darśanaḥ*). In other words, although He certainly does not depend on spoken reports from messengers, He plays the part of a human being and listens to news from a messenger—not out of need, as we would do, but in the bliss of His spiritual pastimes, exchanging love with His pure devotee. The word *sarva-darśanaḥ* also indicates that the Lord perfectly understood the feelings of the residents of Vraja and was perfectly reciprocating with them within their hearts. Now, in His external pastimes, He desired to bless Śrīmatī Trivakrā, who was about to be freed from the disease of material lust.

TEXT 2

महार्होपस्करैराढ्यं कामोपायोपबृंहितम् ।
मुक्तादामपताकाभिर्वितानशयनासनैः ।
धूपैः सुरभिभिर्दीपैः स्रग्गन्धैरपि मण्डितम् ॥२॥

mahārhopaskarair āḍhyaṁ
kāmopāyopabṛṁhitam
muktā-dāma-patākābhir
vitāna-śayanāsanaiḥ
dhūpaiḥ surabhibhir dīpaiḥ
srag-gandhair api maṇḍitam

mahā-arha—expensive; *upaskaraiḥ*—with furnishings; *āḍhyam*—rich; *kāma*—of lust; *upāya*—with accoutrements; *upabṛṁhitam*—replete; *muktā-dāma*—with strings of pearls; *patākābhiḥ*—and banners; *vitāna*—with canopies; *śayana*—beds; *āsanaiḥ*—and seats; *dhūpaiḥ*—with incense; *surabhibhiḥ*—fragrant; *dīpaiḥ*—with oil lamps; *srak*—with flower garlands; *gandhaiḥ*—and aromatic sandalwood paste; *api*—also; *maṇḍitam*—decorated.

TRANSLATION

Trivakrā's home was opulently appointed with expensive furnishings and replete with sensual accouterments meant to inspire sexual desire. There were banners, rows of strung pearls, canopies, fine beds and sitting places, and also fragrant incense, oil lamps, flower garlands and aromatic sandalwood paste.

PURPORT

According to Śrīdhara Svāmī, the sensual accoutrements in Trivakrā's house included explicit sexual pictures. Śrīla Viśvanātha Cakravartī adds that her paraphernalia included herbal aphrodisiacs. It is not hard to guess Trivakrā's intention, yet Lord Kṛṣṇa went there to save her from material existence.

TEXT 3

गृहं तमायान्तमवेक्ष्य सासनात्
सद्यः समुत्थाय हि जातसम्भ्रमा ।
यथोपसंगम्य सखीभिरच्युतं
सभाजयामास सदासनादिभिः ॥३॥

gṛhaṁ tam āyāntam avekṣya sāsanāt
sadyaḥ samutthāya hi jāta-sambhramā
yathopasaṅgamya sakhībhir acyutaṁ
sabhājayām āsa sad-āsanādibhiḥ

gṛham—to her house; *tam*—Him; *āyāntam*—arrived; *avekṣya*—seeing; *sā*—she; *āsanāt*—from her seat; *sadyaḥ*—suddenly; *samutthāya*—rising; *hi*—indeed; *jāta-sambhramā*—being in a flurry; *yathā*—properly; *upasaṅgamya*—coming toward; *sakhībhiḥ*—with her female companions; *acyutam*—Lord Kṛṣṇa; *sabhājayām āsa*—respectfully greeted; *sat-āsana*—with an excellent seat; *ādibhiḥ*—and so on.

TRANSLATION

When Trivakrā saw Him arriving at her house, she at once rose from her seat in a flurry. Coming forward graciously with her girlfriends, she respectfully greeted Lord Acyuta by offering Him an excellent seat and other articles of worship.

TEXT 4

तथोद्धवः साधुतयाभिपूजितो
न्यषीददुर्व्यामभिमृश्य चासनम् ।
कृष्णोऽपि तूर्णं शयनं महाधनं
विवेश लोकाचरितान्यनुव्रतः ॥४॥

tathoddhavaḥ sādhutayābhipūjito
nyaṣīdad urvyām abhimṛśya cāsanam
kṛṣṇo 'pi tūrṇaṁ śayanaṁ mahā-dhanaṁ
viveśa lokācaritāny anuvrataḥ

tathā—also; *uddhavaḥ*—Uddhava; *sādhutayā*—as a saintly person; *abhipūjitaḥ*—worshiped; *nyaṣīdat*—sat; *urvyām*—on the ground; *abhimṛśya*—touching; *ca*—and; *āsanam*—the seat; *kṛṣṇaḥ*—Lord Kṛṣṇa; *api*—and; *tūrṇam*—without delay; *śayanam*—a bed; *mahā-dhanam*—very rich; *viveśa*—lay upon; *loka*—of human society; *ācaritāni*—the modes of behavior; *anuvrataḥ*—imitating.

TRANSLATION

Uddhava also received a seat of honor, since he was a saintly person, but he simply touched it and sat on the floor. Then Lord Kṛṣṇa, imitating the manners of human society, quickly made Himself comfortable on an opulent bed.

PURPORT

According to the *ācāryas,* Uddhava felt reverence for his Lord and thus declined to sit on an opulent seat in His presence; rather, he touched the seat with his hand and sat on the floor. Śrīla Viśvanātha Cakravartī adds that Lord Kṛṣṇa made Himself comfortable on a bed located in the inner chambers of Trivakrā's home.

TEXT 5

सा मज्जनालेपदुकूलभूषण-
स्रग्गन्धताम्बूलसुधासवादिभिः ।
प्रसाधितात्मोपससार माधवं
सव्रीडलीलोत्स्मितविभ्रमेक्षितैः ॥५॥

sā majjanālepa-dukūla-bhūṣaṇa-
srag-gandha-tāmbūla-sudhāsavādibhiḥ
prasādhitātmopasasāra mādhavaṁ
sa-vrīḍa-līlotsmita-vibhramekṣitaiḥ

sā—she, Trivakrā; *majjana*—by bathing; *ālepa*—anointing; *dukūla*—dressing in fine garments; *bhūṣaṇa*—with ornaments; *srak*—garlands; *gandha*—perfume; *tāmbūla*—betel nut; *sudhā-āsava*—drinking fragrant liquor; *ādibhiḥ*—and so on; *prasādhita*—prepared; *ātmā*—her body;

upasasāra—she approached; *mādhavam*—Lord Kṛṣṇa; *sa-vrīḍa*—shy; *līlā*—playful; *utsmita*—of her smiles; *vibhrama*—exhibiting the allurement; *īkṣitaiḥ*—with glances.

TRANSLATION

Trivakrā prepared herself by bathing, anointing her body, and dressing in fine garments, by putting on jewelry, garlands and perfume, and also by chewing betel nut, drinking fragrant liquor, and so on. She then approached Lord Mādhava with shy, playful smiles and coquettish glances.

PURPORT

It is clear from this verse that the ways a woman prepares for sexual enjoyment have not changed in thousands of years.

TEXT 6

आहूय कान्तां नवसंगमह्रिया
विशङ्कितां कंकणभूषिते करे ।
प्रगृह्य शय्यामधिवेश्य रामया
रेमेऽनुलेपार्पणपुण्यलेशया ॥६॥

āhūya kāntāṁ nava-saṅgama-hriyā
viśaṅkitāṁ kaṅkaṇa-bhūṣite kare
pragṛhya śayyām adhiveśya rāmayā
reme 'nulepārpaṇa-puṇya-leśayā

āhūya—calling forward; *kāntām*—His beloved; *nava*—new; *saṅgama*—of contact; *hriyā*—with shyness; *viśaṅkitām*—fearful; *kaṅkaṇa*—with bangles; *bhūṣite*—ornamented; *kare*—her two hands; *pragṛhya*—taking hold of; *śayyām*—on the bed; *adhiveśya*—placing her; *rāmayā*—with the beautiful girl; *reme*—He enjoyed; *anulepa*—of ointment; *arpaṇa*—the offering; *puṇya*—of piety; *leśayā*—whose single trace.

TRANSLATION

Calling forward His beloved, who was anxious and shy at the prospect of this new contact, the Lord pulled her by her bangled

hands onto the bed. Thus He enjoyed with that beautiful girl, whose only trace of piety was her having offered ointment to the Lord.

PURPORT

Śrīla Viśvanātha Cakravartī explains that the words *nava-saṅgama-hriyā* indicate that Trivakrā was in fact a virgin girl at this point. She had been a deformed hunchback, and the Lord had recently transformed her into a beautiful girl. Therefore, although clearly lusting after Śrī Kṛṣṇa, she was naturally shy and anxious.

TEXT 7

सानंगतप्तकुचयोरुरसस्तथाक्ष्णोर्
जिघ्रन्त्यनन्तचरणेन रुजो मृजन्ती ।
दोर्भ्यां स्तनान्तरगतं परिरभ्य कान्तम्
आनन्दमूर्तिमजहादतिदीर्घतापम् ॥७॥

sānaṅga-tapta-kucayor urasas tathākṣṇor
jighranty ananta-caraṇena rujo mṛjantī
dorbhyāṁ stanāntara-gataṁ parirabhya kāntam
ānanda-mūrtim ajahād ati-dīrgha-tāpam

sā—she; *anaṅga*—by Cupid; *tapta*—made to burn; *kucayoḥ*—of her breasts; *urasaḥ*—of her chest; *tathā*—and; *akṣṇoḥ*—of her eyes; *jighrantī*—smelling; *ananta*—of Kṛṣṇa, the unlimited Supreme Lord; *caraṇena*—by the feet; *rujaḥ*—the pain; *mṛjantī*—wiping away; *dorbhyām*—with her arms; *stana*—her breasts; *antara-gatam*—between; *parirabhya*—embracing; *kāntam*—her lover; *ānanda*—of all ecstasy; *mūrtim*—the personal manifestation; *ajahāt*—she gave up; *ati*—extremely; *dīrgha*—long-standing; *tāpam*—her distress.

TRANSLATION

Simply by smelling the fragrance of Kṛṣṇa's lotus feet, Trivakrā cleansed away the burning lust Cupid had aroused in her breasts, chest and eyes. With her two arms she embraced between her

breasts her lover, Śrī Kṛṣṇa, the personification of bliss, and thus she gave up her long-standing distress.

TEXT 8

सैवं कैवल्यनाथं तं प्राप्य दुष्प्राप्यमीश्वरम् ।
अंगरागार्पणेनाहो दुर्भगेदमयाचत ॥८॥

saivaṁ kaivalya-nāthaṁ taṁ
prāpya duṣprāpyam īśvaram
aṅga-rāgārpaṇenāho
durbhagedam ayācata

sā—she; *evam*—thus; *kaivalya*—of liberation; *nātham*—the controller; *tam*—Him; *prāpya*—obtaining; *duṣprāpyam*—unobtainable; *īśvaram*—the Supreme Lord; *aṅga-rāga*—body ointment; *arpaṇena*—by offering; *aho*—oh; *durbhagā*—unfortunate; *idam*—this; *ayācata*—she begged.

TRANSLATION

Having thus gotten the hard-to-get Supreme Lord by the simple act of offering Him body ointment, unfortunate Trivakrā submitted to that Lord of freedom the following request.

PURPORT

According to Śrīla Viśvanātha Cakravartī, Śrīmatī Trivakrā prayed to the Lord, "Please enjoy only with me, and not with any other woman." Because Kṛṣṇa was not prepared to grant such a benediction, Trivakrā is described here as unfortunate. Śrīdhara Svāmī adds that although to ordinary eyes she seemed to beg for material sex pleasure, in fact she was a liberated soul at this point.

TEXT 9

सहोष्यतामिह प्रेष्ठ दिनानि कतिचिन्मया ।
रमस्व नोत्सहे त्यक्तुं संगं तेऽम्बुरुहेक्षण ॥९॥

sahoṣyatām iha preṣṭha
dināni katicin mayā
ramasva notsahe tyaktuṁ
saṅgaṁ te 'mburuhekṣaṇa

saha—together; *uṣyatām*—please stay; *iha*—here; *preṣṭha*—O beloved; *dināni*—days; *katicit*—some; *mayā*—with me; *ramasva*—please take pleasure; *na utsahe*—I cannot tolerate; *tyaktum*—giving up; *saṅgam*—association; *te*—Your; *amburuha-īkṣaṇa*—O lotus-eyed one.

TRANSLATION

[Trivakrā said:] O beloved, please stay here with me for a few days more and enjoy. I cannot bear to give up Your association, O lotus-eyed one!

PURPORT

The word *ambu* means "water," and *ruha* means "rising." Thus *amburuha* means "the lotus flower, which rises up from the water." Lord Kṛṣṇa is called *amburuhekṣaṇa*, "the lotus-eyed one." He is the source and embodiment of all beauty, and naturally Trivakrā was attracted to Him. However, the Lord's beauty is spiritual and pure, and His intention was not to gratify Himself with Trivakrā but rather to bring her to the point of pure spiritual existence, Kṛṣṇa consciousness.

TEXT 10

तस्यै कामवरं दत्त्वा मानयित्वा च मानदः ।
सहोद्धवेन सर्वेशः स्वधामागमदृद्धिमत् ॥१०॥

tasyai kāma-varaṁ dattvā
mānayitvā ca māna-daḥ
sahoddhavena sarveśaḥ
sva-dhāmāgamad ṛddhimat

tasyai—to her; *kāma*—of material desire; *varam*—her benediction; *dattvā*—granting; *mānayitvā*—showing her respect; *ca*—and; *māna-daḥ*—He who gives respect to others; *saha uddhavena*—together with

Uddhava; *sarva-īśaḥ*—the Lord of all beings; *sva*—to His own; *dhāma*—residence; *agamat*—went; *ṛddhi-mat*—supremely opulent.

TRANSLATION

Promising her the fulfillment of this lusty desire, considerate Kṛṣṇa, Lord of all beings, paid Trivakrā His respects and then returned with Uddhava to His own supremely opulent residence.

PURPORT

All the *ācāryas* agree that the words *kāma-varaṁ dattvā* indicate that Lord Kṛṣṇa promised Trivakrā He would fulfill her lusty desires.

TEXT 11

दुराराध्यं समाराध्य विष्णुं सर्वेश्वरेश्वरम् ।
यो वृणीते मनोग्राह्यमसत्त्वात्कुमनीष्यसौ ॥११॥

durārādhyaṁ samārādhya
viṣṇuṁ sarveśvareśvaram
yo vṛṇīte mano-grāhyam
asattvāt kumanīṣy asau

durārādhyam—rarely worshiped; *samārādhya*—fully worshiping; *viṣṇum*—Lord Viṣṇu; *sarva*—of all; *īśvara*—controllers; *īśvaram*—the supreme controller; *yaḥ*—who; *vṛṇīte*—chooses as a benediction; *manaḥ*—to the mind; *grāhyam*—that which is accessible, namely sense gratification; *asattvāt*—because of its insignificance; *kumanīṣī*—unintelligent; *asau*—that person.

TRANSLATION

Lord Viṣṇu, the Supreme Lord of all lords, is ordinarily difficult to approach. One who has properly worshiped Him and then chooses the benediction of mundane sense gratification is cer-

tainly of poor intelligence, for he is satisfied with an insignificant result.

PURPORT

It is clear from the commentaries of the *ācāryas* that the story of Trivakrā is to be understood on two levels. On the one hand, she is understood to be a liberated soul, directly associating with the Lord and participating in His pastimes. On the other hand, her conduct is clearly meant to teach a lesson about what not to do in relation with Lord Kṛṣṇa. Since all of the Lord's pastimes are not only blissful but also didactic, there is no real contradiction in this pastime, since Trivakrā's purity and her bad example take place on two distinct levels. Arjuna is also considered a pure devotee, yet by initially disobeying Kṛṣṇa's instruction to fight, he also showed an example of what not to do. However, such "bad examples" always have happy endings in the blissful association of the Absolute Truth, Śrī Kṛṣṇa.

TEXT 12

अक्रूरभवनं कृष्णः सहरामोद्धवः प्रभुः ।
किञ्चिच्चिकीर्षयन् प्रागादक्रूरप्रियकाम्यया ॥१२॥

akrūra-bhavanaṁ kṛṣṇaḥ
saha-rāmoddhavaḥ prabhuḥ
kiñcic cikīrṣayan prāgād
akrūra-priya-kāmyayā

akrūra-bhavanam—the home of Akrūra; *kṛṣṇaḥ*—Kṛṣṇa; *saha*—with; *rāma-uddhavaḥ*—Lord Balarāma and Uddhava; *prabhuḥ*—the Supreme Lord; *kiñcit*—something; *cikīrṣayan*—wanting to have done; *prāgāt*—went; *akrūra*—of Akrūra; *priya*—the satisfaction; *kāmyayā*—desiring.

TRANSLATION

Then Lord Kṛṣṇa, wanting to have some things done, went to Akrūra's house with Balarāma and Uddhava. The Lord also desired to please Akrūra.

PURPORT

The previous incident of Lord Kṛṣṇa's visit to Trivakrā's house, and now His visit to Akrūra's, gives a fascinating glimpse into the daily activities of Śrī Kṛṣṇa in Mathurā City.

TEXTS 13–14

स तान्नरवरश्रेष्ठानाराद्वीक्ष्य स्वबान्धवान् ।
प्रत्युत्थाय प्रमुदितः परिष्वज्याभिनन्द्य च ॥१३॥
ननाम कृष्णं रामं च स तैरप्यभिवादितः ।
पूजयामास विधिवत्कृतासनपरिग्रहान् ॥१४॥

sa tān nara-vara-śreṣṭhān
ārād vīkṣya sva-bāndhavān
pratyutthāya pramuditaḥ
pariṣvajyābhinandya ca

nanāma kṛṣṇaṁ rāmaṁ ca
sa tair apy abhivāditaḥ
pūjayām āsa vidhi-vat
kṛtāsana-parigrahān

saḥ—he (Akrūra); *tān*—them (Kṛṣṇa, Balarāma and Uddhava); *nara-vara*—of illustrious personalities; *śreṣṭhān*—the greatest; *ārāt*—from a distance; *vīkṣya*—seeing; *sva*—his (Akrūra's); *bāndhavān*—relatives; *pratyutthāya*—rising up; *pramuditaḥ*—joyful; *pariṣvajya*—embracing; *abhinandya*—greeting; *ca*—and; *nanāma*—bowed down; *kṛṣṇam rāmam ca*—to Lord Kṛṣṇa and Lord Balarāma; *saḥ*—he; *taiḥ*—by Them; *api*—and; *abhivāditaḥ*—greeted; *pūjayām āsa*—he worshiped; *vidhi-vat*—according to scriptural injunctions; *kṛta*—who had done; *āsana*—of seats; *parigrahān*—acceptance.

TRANSLATION

Akrūra stood up in great joy when he saw them, his own relatives and the greatest of exalted personalities, coming from a distance. After embracing them and greeting them, Akrūra bowed

down to Kṛṣṇa and Balarāma and was greeted by Them in return. Then, when his guests had taken their seats, he worshiped them in accordance with scriptural rules.

PURPORT

Śrīla Jīva Gosvāmī points out that Lord Śrī Kṛṣṇa and the others approached Akrūra in a friendly attitude. At first Akrūra reciprocated that friendly mood, and then, in the course of showing them hospitality, he adopted his natural devotional attitude toward the Lord and thus offered his obeisances to Śrī Kṛṣṇa and Śrī Balarāma.

TEXTS 15–16

पादावनेजनीरापो धारयन् शिरसा नृप ।
अर्हणेनाम्बरैर्दिव्यैर्गन्धस्रग्भूषणोत्तमैः ॥१५॥
अर्चित्वा शिरसानम्य पादावंकगतौ मृजन् ।
प्रश्रयावनतोऽक्रूरः कृष्णरामावभाषत ॥१६॥

pādāvanejanīr āpo
dhārayan śirasā nṛpa
arhaṇenāmbarair divyair
gandha-srag-bhūṣaṇottamaiḥ

arcitvā śirasānamya
pādāv aṅka-gatau mṛjan
praśrayāvanato 'krūraḥ
kṛṣṇa-rāmāv abhāṣata

pāda—Their feet; *avanejanīḥ*—used for bathing; *ā*—all over; *āpaḥ*—the water; *dhārayan*—putting; *śirasā*—on his head; *nṛpa*—O King (Parīkṣit); *arhaṇena*—with gifts; *ambaraiḥ*—clothing; *divyaiḥ*—celestial; *gandha*—fragrant sandalwood paste; *srak*—flower garlands; *bhūṣaṇa*—and ornaments; *uttamaiḥ*—excellent; *arcitvā*—worshiping; *śirasā*—with his head; *ānamya*—bowing down; *pādau*—(Lord Kṛṣṇa's) feet; *aṅka*—on his lap; *gatau*—placed; *mṛjan*—massaging; *praśraya*—with humility; *avanataḥ*—his head lowered; *akrūraḥ*—Akrūra; *kṛṣṇa-rāmau*—to Kṛṣṇa and Balarāma; *abhāṣata*—spoke.

TRANSLATION

O King, Akrūra bathed the feet of Lord Kṛṣṇa and Lord Balarāma and then poured the bath water on his head. He presented Them with gifts of fine clothing, aromatic sandalwood paste, flower garlands and excellent jewelry. After thus worshiping the two Lords, he bowed his head to the floor. He then began to massage Lord Kṛṣṇa's feet, placing them on his lap, and with his head bowed in humility he addressed Kṛṣṇa and Balarāma as follows.

TEXT 17

दिष्टया पापो हतः कंसः सानुगो वामिदं कुलम् ।
भवद्भ्यामुद्धृतं कृच्छ्राद्दुरन्ताच्च समेधितम् ॥१७॥

diṣṭyā pāpo hataḥ kaṁsaḥ
sānugo vām idaṁ kulam
bhavadbhyām uddhṛtaṁ kṛcchrād
durantāc ca samedhitam

diṣṭyā—by good fortune; *pāpaḥ*—sinful; *hataḥ*—killed; *kaṁsaḥ*—Kaṁsa; *sa-anugaḥ*—together with his brothers and other followers; *vām*—of Yours; *idam*—this; *kulam*—dynasty; *bhavadbhyām*—by You two; *uddhṛtam*—delivered; *kṛcchrāt*—from difficulty; *durantāt*—endless; *ca*—and; *samedhitam*—made prosperous.

TRANSLATION

[Akrūra said:] It is our good fortune that You two Lords have killed the evil Kaṁsa and his followers, thus delivering Your dynasty from endless suffering and causing it to flourish.

TEXT 18

युवां प्रधानपुरुषौ जगद्धेतू जगन्मयौ ।
भवद्भ्यां न विना किञ्चित्परमस्ति न चापरम् ॥१८॥

yuvāṁ pradhāna-puruṣau
jagad-dhetū jagan-mayau
bhavadbhyāṁ na vinā kiñcit
param asti na cāparam

yuvām—You two; *pradhāna-puruṣau*—the original persons; *jagat*—of the universe; *hetū*—the causes; *jagat-mayau*—identical with the universe; *bhavadbhyām*—than You; *na*—not; *vinā*—apart from; *kiñcit*—anything; *param*—cause; *asti*—there is; *na ca*—nor; *aparam*—product.

TRANSLATION

You both are the original Supreme Person, the cause of the universe and its very substance. Not the slightest subtle cause or manifest product of creation exists apart from You.

PURPORT

After praising Kṛṣṇa and Balarāma for having saved Their dynasty, Akrūra now points out that the Lord actually has no mundane connection with any social or political institution. He is the original Personality of Godhead, performing His pastimes for the benefit of the entire universe.

TEXT 19

आत्मसृष्टमिदं विश्वमन्वाविश्य स्वशक्तिभिः ।
ईयते बहुधा ब्रह्मन् श्रुतप्रत्यक्षगोचरम् ॥१९॥

ātma-sṛṣṭam idaṁ viśvam
anvāviśya sva-śaktibhiḥ
īyate bahudhā brahman
śruta-pratyakṣa-gocaram

ātma-sṛṣṭam—created by You; *idam*—this; *viśvam*—universe; *anvāviśya*—subsequently entering; *sva*—with Your own; *śaktibhiḥ*—energies; *īyate*—You are perceived; *bahudhā*—manifold; *brahman*—O Supreme; *śruta*—by hearing from scripture; *pratyakṣa*—and by direct perception; *gocaram*—knowable.

TRANSLATION

O Supreme Absolute Truth, with Your personal energies You create this universe and then enter into it. Thus one can perceive You in many different forms by hearing from authorities and by direct experience.

PURPORT

The grammatical agreement of *śruta-pratyakṣa-gocaram,* in the neuter case, with *ātma-sṛṣṭam idaṁ viśvam* indicates that the Supreme Lord, by entering His creation with His potencies, makes Himself perceivable within the universe. Throughout the *Bhāgavatam* and other authorized Vedic literatures, we often find descriptions of the Lord's simultaneous supremacy over all other things and His identity with them. We cannot reasonably draw any other conclusion from Vedic literature than the one powerfully preached by Śrī Caitanya Mahāprabhu: *acintya-bhedābheda-tattva.* That is, the Absolute Truth is greater than and distinct from everything (since He is the omnipotent creator and controller of all), and simultaneously one with everything (since all that exists is the expansion of His own power).

Throughout these chapters of *Śrīmad-Bhāgavatam,* we also observe one of the unique, extraordinary features of this great work. Whether Kṛṣṇa is sending His message to the *gopīs* or accepting the prayers of Akrūra, there is constant philosophical discussion. Throughout the *Bhāgavatam,* the steady combination of fascinating pastimes with persistent spiritual philosophy is an extraordinary feature. We are allowed to glimpse and even to relish the spiritual emotions of the Lord and His liberated associates, and yet we are constantly reminded of their ontological position lest we lapse into a cheap, anthropomorphic vision. Thus it is entirely in character with the work that Akrūra, in his ecstasy, glorifies the Lord with precise philosophical prayers.

TEXT 20

यथा हि भूतेषु चराचरेषु
महृयादयो योनिषु भान्ति नाना ।
एवं भवान् केवल आत्मयोनिष्व्
आत्मात्मतन्त्रो बहुधा विभाति ॥२०॥

yathā hi bhūteṣu carācareṣu
mahy-ādayo yoniṣu bhānti nānā
evaṁ bhavān kevala ātma-yoniṣv
ātmātma-tantro bahudhā vibhāti

yathā—as; *hi*—indeed; *bhūteṣu*—among manifested beings; *cara*—mobile; *acareṣu*—and immobile; *mahī-ādayaḥ*—earth and so on (the primary elements of creation); *yoniṣu*—in species; *bhānti*—manifest; *nānā*—variously; *evam*—so; *bhavān*—You; *kevalaḥ*—one alone; *ātma*—Yourself; *yoniṣu*—in those whose source; *ātmā*—the Supreme Soul; *ātma-tantraḥ*—self-reliant; *bahudhā*—manifold; *vibhāti*—appear.

TRANSLATION

Just as the primary elements—earth and so on—manifest themselves in abundant variety among all the species of mobile and immobile life, so You, the one independent Supreme Soul, appear to be manifold among the variegated objects of Your creation.

TEXT 21

सृजस्यथो लुम्पसि पासि विश्वं
रजस्तमःसत्त्वगुणैः स्वशक्तिभिः ।
न बध्यसे तद्गुणकर्मभिर्वा
ज्ञानात्मनस्ते क्व च बन्धहेतुः ॥२१॥

sṛjasy atho lumpasi pāsi viśvaṁ
rajas-tamaḥ-sattva-guṇaiḥ sva-śaktibhiḥ
na badhyase tad-guṇa-karmabhir vā
jñānātmanas te kva ca bandha-hetuḥ

sṛjasi—You create; *atha u*—and then; *lumpasi*—You destroy; *pāsi*—You protect; *viśvam*—the universe; *rajaḥ*—known as passion; *tamaḥ*—ignorance; *sattva*—and goodness; *guṇaiḥ*—by the modes; *sva-śakti-bhiḥ*—Your personal potencies; *na badhyase*—You are not bound; *tat*—of this world; *guṇa*—by the modes; *karmabhiḥ*—by the material activities; *vā*—or; *jñāna-ātmanaḥ*—who are knowledge itself; *te*—for You; *kva ca*—where at all; *bandha*—of bondage; *hetuḥ*—cause.

TRANSLATION

You create, destroy and also maintain this universe with Your personal energies—the modes of passion, ignorance and goodness—yet You are never entangled by these modes or the activities they generate. Since You are the original source of all knowledge, what could ever cause You to be bound by illusion?

PURPORT

The phrase *jñānātmanas te kva ca bandha-hetuḥ,* "Since You are constituted of knowledge, what could be a cause of bondage for You?" definitely indicates the obvious, that the omniscient Supreme God is never in illusion. Therefore the impersonalistic theory that we are all God but have forgotten and are now in illusion is refuted here in the pages of *Śrīmad-Bhāgavatam.*

TEXT 22

देहाद्युपाधेरनिरूपितत्वाद्
भवो न साक्षान्न भिदात्मनः स्यात् ।
अतो न बन्धस्तव नैव मोक्षः
स्यातां निकामस्त्वयि नोऽविवेकः ॥२२॥

dehādy-upādher anirūpitatvād
bhavo na sākṣān na bhidātmanaḥ syāt
ato na bandhas tava naiva mokṣaḥ
syātāṁ nikāmas tvayi no 'vivekaḥ

deha—of the body; *ādi*—and so on; *upādheḥ*—as material, designative coverings; *anirūpitatvāt*—because of not being determined; *bhavaḥ*—birth; *na*—not; *sākṣāt*—literal; *na*—nor; *bhidā*—duality; *ātmanaḥ*—for the Supreme Soul; *syāt*—exists; *ataḥ*—therefore; *na*—no; *bandhaḥ*—bondage; *tava*—Your; *na eva*—nor, in fact; *mokṣaḥ*—liberation; *syātām*—if they occur; *nikāmaḥ*—by Your sweet will; *tvayi*—concerning You; *naḥ*—our; *avivekaḥ*—erroneous discrimination.

TRANSLATION

Since it has never been demonstrated that You are covered by material, bodily designations, it must be concluded that for You there is neither birth in a literal sense nor any duality. Therefore You never undergo bondage or liberation, and if You appear to, it is only because of Your desire that we see You in that way, or simply because of our lack of discrimination.

PURPORT

Here Akrūra states two reasons why the Lord appears to be covered by a material form, or to take birth like a human being. First, when Lord Kṛṣṇa executes His pastimes, His loving devotees think of Him as their beloved child, friend, lover and so on. In the ecstasy of this loving reciprocation, they do not think of Kṛṣṇa as God. For example, because of her extraordinary love for Him, mother Yaśodā worries that Kṛṣṇa will be injured in the forest. That she feels this way is the desire of the Lord, which is here indicated by the word *nikāmaḥ*. The second reason the Lord may appear material is indicated by the word *avivekaḥ:* Simply because of ignorance, a lack of discrimination, one may misunderstand the position of the Personality of Godhead. In the Eleventh Canto of the *Bhāgavatam*, in Lord Kṛṣṇa's discussion with Śrī Uddhava, the Lord elaborately discusses His transcendental position beyond bondage and liberation. As stated in Vedic literature, *deha-dehi-vibhāgo 'yaṁ neśvare vidyate kvacit:* "There is never a distinction of body and soul in the Supreme Lord." In other words, Śrī Kṛṣṇa's body is eternal, spiritual, omniscient and the reservoir of all pleasure.

TEXT 23

त्वयोदितोऽयं जगतो हिताय
यदा यदा वेदपथः पुराणः ।
बाध्येत पाषण्डपथैरसद्भिस्
तदा भवान् सत्त्वगुणं बिभर्ति ॥२३॥

tvayodito 'yaṁ jagato hitāya
yadā yadā veda-pathaḥ purāṇaḥ
bādhyeta pāṣaṇḍa-pathair asadbhis
tadā bhavān sattva-guṇaṁ bibharti

tvayā—by You; *uditaḥ*—enunciated; *ayam*—this; *jagataḥ*—of the universe; *hitāya*—for the benefit; *yadā yadā*—whenever; *veda*—of the Vedic scriptures; *pathaḥ*—the path (of religiousness); *purāṇaḥ*—ancient; *bādhyeta*—is obstructed; *pāṣaṇḍa*—of atheism; *pathaiḥ*—by those who follow the path; *asadbhiḥ*—wicked persons; *tadā*—at that time; *bhavān*—You; *sattva-guṇam*—the pure mode of goodness; *bibharti*—assume.

TRANSLATION

You originally enunciated the ancient religious path of the *Vedas* for the benefit of the whole universe. Whenever that path becomes obstructed by wicked persons following the path of atheism, You assume one of Your incarnations, which are all in the transcendental mode of goodness.

TEXT 24

स त्वं प्रभोऽद्य वसुदेवगृहेऽवतीर्णः
स्वांशेन भारमपनेतुमिहासि भूमेः ।
अक्षौहिणीशतवधेन सुरेतरांश-
राज्ञाममुष्य च कुलस्य यशो वितन्वन् ॥२४॥

sa tvaṁ prabho 'dya vasudeva-gṛhe 'vatīrṇaḥ
svāṁśena bhāram apanetum ihāsi bhūmeḥ
akṣauhiṇī-śata-vadhena suretarāṁśa-
rājñām amuṣya ca kulasya yaśo vitanvan

saḥ—He; *tvam*—You; *prabho*—O master; *adya*—now; *vasudeva-gṛhe*—in the home of Vasudeva; *avatīrṇaḥ*—have descended; *sva*—with Your own; *aṁśena*—direct expansion (Lord Balarāma); *bhāram*—the burden; *apanetum*—to remove; *iha*—here; *asi*—You are; *bhūmeḥ*—of the earth; *akṣauhiṇī*—of the armies; *śata*—hundreds; *vadhena*—by killing; *sura-itara*—of the opponents of the demigods; *aṁśa*—who are expansions; *rājñām*—of the kings; *amuṣya*—of this; *ca*—and; *kulasya*—dynasty (of the descendants of Yadu); *yaśaḥ*—the fame; *vitanvan*—spreading.

TRANSLATION

You are that very same Supreme Person, my Lord, and You have now appeared in the home of Vasudeva with Your plenary portion. You have done this to relieve the earth's burden by killing hundreds of armies led by kings who are expansions of the demigods' enemies, and also to spread the fame of our dynasty.

PURPORT

The term *suretarāṁśa-rājñām* indicates that the demoniac kings slain by Kṛṣṇa were in fact expansions or incarnations of the enemies of the demigods. This fact is elaborately explained in the *Mahābhārata,* which reveals the specific identities of the demoniac kings.

TEXT 25

अद्येश नो वसतयः खलु भूरिभागा
य: सर्वदेवपितृभूतनृदेवमूर्तिः ।
यत्पादशौचसलिलं त्रिजगत्पुनाति
स त्वं जगद्गुरुरधोक्षज याः प्रविष्टः ॥२५॥

adyeśa no vasatayaḥ khalu bhūri-bhāgā
yaḥ sarva-deva-pitṛ-bhūta-nṛ-deva-mūrtiḥ
yat-pāda-śauca-salilaṁ tri-jagat punāti
sa tvaṁ jagad-gurur adhokṣaja yāḥ praviṣṭaḥ

adya—today; *īśa*—O Lord; *naḥ*—our; *vasatayaḥ*—residence; *khalu*—indeed; *bhūri*—extremely; *bhāgāḥ*—fortunate; *yaḥ*—who; *sarva-deva*—the Supreme Lord; *pitṛ*—the forefathers; *bhūta*—all living creatures; *nṛ*—human beings; *deva*—and the demigods; *mūrtiḥ*—who embody *yat*—whose; *pāda*—feet; *śauca*—which has washed; *salilam*—the water (of the river Ganges); *tri-jagat*—the three worlds; *punāti*—purifies; *saḥ*—He; *tvam*—You; *jagat*—of the universe; *guruḥ*—the spiritual master; *adhokṣaja*—O You who are beyond the purview of the material senses; *yāḥ*—which; *praviṣṭaḥ*—having entered.

TRANSLATION

Today, O Lord, my home has become most fortunate because You have entered it. As the Supreme Truth, You embody the forefathers, ordinary creatures, human beings and demigods, and the water that has washed Your feet purifies the three worlds. Indeed, O transcendent one, You are the spiritual master of the universe.

PURPORT

Śrīla Śrīdhara Svāmī has nicely interpreted Akrūra's feelings as follows:

Akrūra said, "My Lord, although I am a householder, today my home has become more pious than the forests where sages perform austerities. Why? Simply because You have entered my home. Indeed, You are the personification of the deities who preside over the five sacrifices a householder must perform daily to atone for unavoidable violence committed to living beings in the home. You are the spiritual truth behind all these creations, and now You have entered my home."

The five daily sacrifices enjoined for a householder are (1) sacrifice to Brahman by studying the *Vedas,* (2) sacrifice to the forefathers by making offerings to them, (3) sacrifice to all creatures by putting aside a portion of one's meals, (4) sacrifice to human beings by extending hospitality and (5) sacrifice to the demigods by performing fire sacrifices and so on.

TEXT 26

कः पण्डितस्त्वदपरं शरणं समीयाद्
भक्तप्रियादृतगिरः सुहृदः कृतज्ञात् ।
सर्वान् ददाति सुहृदो भजतोऽभिकामान्
आत्मानमप्युपचयापचयौ न यस्य ॥२६॥

kaḥ paṇḍitas tvad aparaṁ śaraṇaṁ samīyād
bhakta-priyād ṛta-giraḥ suhṛdaḥ kṛta-jñāt
sarvān dadāti suhṛdo bhajato 'bhikāmān
ātmānam apy upacayāpacayau na yasya

kaḥ—what; *paṇḍitaḥ*—scholar; *tvat*—other than You; *aparam*—to another; *śaraṇam*—for shelter; *samīyāt*—would go; *bhakta*—to Your devotees; *priyāt*—affectionate; *ṛta*—always true; *giraḥ*—whose words; *suhṛdaḥ*—the well-wisher; *kṛta-jñāt*—grateful; *sarvān*—all; *dadāti*—You give; *suhṛdaḥ*—to Your well-wishing devotees; *bhajataḥ*—who are engaged in worshiping You; *abhikāmān*—desires; *ātmānam*—Yourself; *api*—even; *upacaya*—increase; *apacayau*—or diminution; *na*—never; *yasya*—whose.

TRANSLATION

What learned person would approach anyone but You for shelter, when You are the affectionate, grateful and truthful well-wisher of Your devotees? To those who worship You in sincere friendship You reward everything they desire, even Your own self, yet You never increase or diminish.

PURPORT

This verse describes both the Lord and His devotees as *suhṛdaḥ*, "well-wishers." The Lord is the well-wisher of His devotee, and the devotee lovingly desires all happiness for the Lord. Even in this world, an excess of love may sometimes produce unnecessary solicitude. For example, we often observe that a mother's loving concern for her adult child is not always justified by an actual danger to the child. A grown child may be wealthy, competent and healthy, and yet the mother's loving concern continues. Similarly, a pure devotee always feels loving concern for Lord Kṛṣṇa, as exemplified by mother Yaśodā, who could only think of Kṛṣṇa as her beautiful son.

Lord Kṛṣṇa had promised Akrūra that after killing Kaṁsa He would visit his home, and now the Lord kept His promise. Akrūra recognizes this and glorifies the Lord as *ṛta-giraḥ*, "one who is true to His word." The Lord is *kṛta-jña*, grateful for whatever little worship a devotee offers, and even if the devotee forgets, the Lord does not.

TEXT 27

दिष्टया जनार्दन भवानिह नः प्रतीतो
योगेश्वरैरपि दुरापगतिः सुरेशैः ।
छिन्ध्याशु नः सुतकलत्रधनाप्तगेह-
देहादिमोहरशनां भवदीयमायाम् ॥२७॥

diṣṭyā janārdana bhavān iha naḥ pratīto
yogeśvarair api durāpa-gatiḥ sureśaiḥ
chindhy āśu naḥ suta-kalatra-dhanāpta-geha-
dehādi-moha-raśanāṁ bhavadīya-māyām

diṣṭyā—by fortune; *janārdana*—O Kṛṣṇa; *bhavān*—You; *iha*—here; *naḥ*—by us; *pratītaḥ*—perceivable; *yoga-īśvaraiḥ*—by the masters of mystic *yoga; api*—even; *durāpa-gatiḥ*—a goal hard to achieve; *sura-īśaiḥ*—and by the rulers of the demigods; *chindhi*—please cut; *āśu*—quickly; *naḥ*—our; *suta*—for children; *kalatra*—wife; *dhana*—wealth; *āpta*—worthy friends; *geha*—home; *deha*—body; *ādi*—and so on; *moha*—of delusion; *raśanām*—the ropes; *bhavadīya*—Your own; *māyām*—illusory material energy.

TRANSLATION

It is by our great fortune, Janārdana, that You are now visible to us, for even the masters of *yoga* and the foremost demigods can achieve this goal only with great difficulty. Please quickly cut the ropes of our illusory attachment for children, wife, wealth, influential friends, home and body. All such attachment is simply the effect of Your illusory material energy.

TEXT 28

इत्यर्चितः संस्तुतश्च भक्तेन भगवान् हरिः ।
अक्रूरं सस्मितं प्राह गीर्भिः सम्मोहयन्निव ॥२८॥

ity arcitaḥ saṁstutaś ca
bhaktena bhagavān hariḥ

akrūraṁ sa-smitaṁ prāha
gīrbhiḥ sammohayann iva

iti—thus; *arcitaḥ*—worshiped; *saṁstutaḥ*—profusely glorified; *ca*—and; *bhaktena*—by His devotee; *bhagavān*—the Supreme Lord; *hariḥ*—Kṛṣṇa; *akrūram*—to Akrūra; *sa-smitam*—smiling; *prāha*—He spoke; *gīrbhiḥ*—with His words; *sammohayan*—completely enchanting; *iva*—almost.

TRANSLATION

[Śukadeva Gosvāmī continued:] Thus worshiped and fully glorified by His devotee, the Supreme Lord Hari smilingly addressed Akrūra, completely charming him with His words.

TEXT 29

श्रीभगवानुवाच
त्वं नो गुरुः पितृव्यश्च श्लाघ्यो बन्धुश्च नित्यदा ।
वयं तु रक्ष्याः पोष्याश्च अनुकम्प्याः प्रजा हि वः ॥२९॥

śrī-bhagavān uvāca
tvaṁ no guruḥ pitṛvyaś ca
ślāghyo bandhuś ca nityadā
vayaṁ tu rakṣyāḥ poṣyāś ca
anukampyāḥ prajā hi vaḥ

śrī-bhagavān uvāca—the Supreme Personality of Godhead said; *tvam*—you; *naḥ*—Our; *guruḥ*—spiritual master; *pitṛvyaḥ*—paternal uncle; *ca*—and; *ślāghyaḥ*—praiseworthy; *bandhuḥ*—friend; *ca*—and; *nityadā*—always; *vayam*—We; *tu*—on the other hand; *rakṣyāḥ*—to be protected; *poṣyāḥ*—to be maintained; *ca*—and; *anukampyāḥ*—to be shown compassion; *prajāḥ*—dependents; *hi*—indeed; *vaḥ*—your.

TRANSLATION

The Supreme Lord said: You are Our spiritual master, paternal uncle and praiseworthy friend, and We are like your sons, always dependent on your protection, sustenance and compassion.

TEXT 30

भवद्विधा महाभागा निषेव्या अर्हसत्तमाः ।
श्रेयस्कामैर्नृभिर्नित्यं देवाः स्वार्था न साधवः ॥३०॥

bhavad-vidhā mahā-bhāgā
niṣevyā arha-sattamāḥ
śreyas-kāmair nṛbhir nityaṁ
devāḥ svārthā na sādhavaḥ

bhavat-vidhāḥ—like your good self; *mahā-bhāgāḥ*—most eminent; *niṣevyāḥ*—worthy of being served; *arha*—of those who are worshipable; *sat-tamāḥ*—the most saintly; *śreyaḥ*—the highest good; *kāmaiḥ*—who desire; *nṛbhiḥ*—by men; *nityam*—always; *devāḥ*—the demigods; *sva-arthāḥ*—concerned with their personal interest; *na*—not so; *sādhavaḥ*—saintly devotees.

TRANSLATION

Exalted souls like you are the true objects of service and the most worshipable authorities for those who desire the highest good in life. Demigods are generally concerned with their own interests, but saintly devotees never are.

PURPORT

Whereas demigods may award material benefit, saintly devotees of the Lord have the power to award the real perfection of life, Kṛṣṇa consciousness. Thus Lord Kṛṣṇa reinforces the respectful mood He has adopted here toward His uncle Akrūra.

TEXT 31

न ह्यम्मयानि तीर्थानि न देवा मृच्छिलामयाः ।
ते पुनन्त्युरुकालेन दर्शनादेव साधवः ॥३१॥

na hy am-mayāni tīrthāni
na devā mṛc-chilā-mayāḥ

te punanty uru-kālena
darśanād eva sādhavaḥ

na—not; *hi*—indeed; *ap-mayāni*—made of water; *tīrthāni*—holy places; *na*—such is not the case; *devāḥ*—deities; *mṛt*—of earth; *śilā*—and stone; *mayāḥ*—made; *te*—they; *punanti*—purify; *uru-kālena*—after a long time; *darśanāt*—by being seen; *eva*—only; *sādhavaḥ*—saints.

TRANSLATION

No one can deny that there are holy places with sacred rivers, or that the demigods appear in deity forms made of earth and stone. But these purify the soul only after a long time, whereas saintly persons purify just by being seen.

TEXT 32

स भवान् सुहृदां वै नः श्रेयान् श्रेयश्चिकीर्षया ।
जिज्ञासार्थं पाण्डवानां गच्छस्व त्वं गजाह्वयम् ॥३२॥

sa bhavān suhṛdāṁ vai naḥ
śreyān śreyaś-cikīrṣayā
jijñāsārthaṁ pāṇḍavānāṁ
gacchasva tvaṁ gajāhvayam

saḥ—that person; *bhavān*—you; *suhṛdām*—of the well-wishers; *vai*—certainly; *naḥ*—Our; *śreyān*—the very best; *śreyaḥ*—for their welfare; *cikīrṣayā*—wishing to arrange; *jijñāsā*—of inquiry; *artham*—for the sake; *pāṇḍavānām*—about the sons of Pāṇḍu; *gacchasva*—please go; *tvam*—you; *gaja-āhvayam*—to Gajāhvaya (Hastināpura, the capital of the Kuru dynasty).

TRANSLATION

You are indeed the best of Our friends, so please go to Hastināpura and, as the well-wisher of the Pāṇḍavas, find out how they are doing.

PURPORT

In Sanskrit the imperative "you go" may be rendered by *gacchasva* or *gaccha*. In the second of these cases, the word following *gaccha*, namely *sva*, which is taken in the vocative sense, indicates Kṛṣṇa addressing Akrūra as "Our own." This is in reference to Lord Kṛṣṇa's intimate relationship with His uncle.

TEXT 33

पितर्युपरते बालाः सह मात्रा सुदुःखिताः ।
आनीताः स्वपुरं राज्ञा वसन्त इति शुश्रुम ॥३३॥

pitary uparate bālāḥ
saha mātrā su-duḥkhitāḥ
ānītāḥ sva-puraṁ rājñā
vasanta iti śuśruma

pitari—their father; *uparate*—when he passed away; *bālāḥ*—young boys; *saha*—together with; *mātrā*—their mother; *su*—very; *duḥkhitāḥ*—distressed; *ānītāḥ*—brought; *sva*—to his own; *puram*—capital city; *rājñā*—by the King; *vasante*—they are residing; *iti*—thus; *śuśruma*—We have heard.

TRANSLATION

We have heard that when their father passed away, the young Pāṇḍavas were brought with their anguished mother to the capital city by King Dhṛtarāṣṭra, and that they are now living there.

TEXT 34

तेषु राजाम्बिकापुत्रो भ्रातृपुत्रेषु दीनधीः ।
समो न वर्तते नूनं दुष्पुत्रवशगोऽन्धदृक् ॥३४॥

teṣu rājāmbikā-putro
bhrātṛ-putreṣu dīna-dhīḥ
samo na vartate nūnaṁ
duṣputra-vaśa-go 'ndha-dṛk

teṣu—toward them; *rājā*—the King (Dhṛtarāṣṭra); *ambikā*—of Ambikā; *putraḥ*—the son; *bhrātṛ*—of his brother; *putreṣu*—toward the sons; *dīna-dhīḥ*—whose mind is wretched; *samaḥ*—equally disposed; *na vartate*—is not; *nūnam*—surely; *duḥ*—wicked; *putra*—of his sons; *vaśa-gaḥ*—under the control; *andha*—blinded; *dṛk*—whose vision.

TRANSLATION

Indeed, weak-minded Dhṛtarāṣṭra, the son of Ambikā, has come under the control of his wicked sons, and therefore that blind King is not treating his brother's sons fairly.

TEXT 35

गच्छ जानीहि तद्वृत्तमधुना साध्वसाधु वा ।
विज्ञाय तद्विधास्यामो यथा शं सुहृदां भवेत् ॥३५॥

gaccha jānīhi tad-vṛttam
adhunā sādhv asādhu vā
vijñāya tad vidhāsyāmo
yathā śaṁ suhṛdāṁ bhavet

gaccha—go; *jānīhi*—learn; *tat*—his (Dhṛtarāṣṭra's); *vṛttam*—activity; *adhunā*—at present; *sādhu*—good; *asādhu*—evil; *vā*—or; *vijñāya*—knowing; *tat*—that; *vidhāsyāmaḥ*—We will arrange; *yathā*—so that; *śam*—the benefit; *suhṛdām*—of Our dear ones; *bhavet*—will be.

TRANSLATION

Go and see whether Dhṛtarāṣṭra is acting properly or not. When We find out, We will make the necessary arrangements to help Our dear friends.

TEXT 36

इत्यक्रूरं समादिश्य भगवान् हरिरीश्वरः ।
संकर्षणोद्धवाभ्यां वै ततः स्वभवनं ययौ ॥३६॥

ity akrūraṁ samādiśya
bhagavān harir īśvaraḥ
saṅkarṣaṇoddhavābhyāṁ vai
tataḥ sva-bhavanaṁ yayau

iti—with these words; *akrūram*—Akrūra; *samādiśya*—fully instructing; *bhagavān*—the Personality of Godhead; *hariḥ īśvaraḥ*—Lord Hari; *saṅkarṣaṇa*—with Lord Balarāma; *uddhavābhyām*—and Uddhava; *vai*—indeed; *tataḥ*—then; *sva*—to His own; *bhavanam*—residence; *yayau*—went.

TRANSLATION

[Śukadeva Gosvāmī continued:] Thus fully instructing Akrūra, the Supreme Personality of Godhead Hari then returned to His residence, accompanied by Lord Saṅkarṣaṇa and Uddhava.

Thus end the purports of the humble servants of His Divine Grace A. C. Bhaktivedanta Swami Prabhupāda to the Tenth Canto, Forty-eighth Chapter, of the Śrīmad-Bhāgavatam, *entitled "Kṛṣṇa Pleases His Devotees."*

CHAPTER FORTY-NINE

Akrūra's Mission in Hastināpura

This chapter describes how Akrūra went to Hastināpura, saw Dhṛtarāṣṭra's unfair behavior toward his nephews, the Pāṇḍavas, and then returned to Mathurā.

On the order of Lord Kṛṣṇa, Akrūra went to Hastināpura, where he met the Kauravas and Pāṇḍavas and then set about to find out how Dhṛtarāṣṭra was treating the latter. This task would keep Akrūra in Hastināpura for several months.

Vidura and Kuntīdevī described to Akrūra in detail how Dhṛtarāṣṭra's sons, envious of the exalted qualities of the Pāṇḍavas, had tried to destroy them by various evil means and were contemplating further atrocities. With tearful eyes, Kuntīdevī asked Akrūra, "Do my parents and other relatives, headed by Kṛṣṇa and Balarāma, ever think of me and my sons, and will Kṛṣṇa ever come to console us in our distress?" Then Kuntīdevī began to chant Lord Kṛṣṇa's names for her protection, and she also chanted *mantras* expressing surrender to Him. Akrūra assured Kuntīdevī, "Since your sons were born from demigods like Dharma and Vāyu, there is no reason to expect that any misfortune will befall them; rather, you should be confident that very soon they will receive the greatest possible good fortune."

Akrūra then delivered to Dhṛtarāṣṭra the message from Kṛṣṇa and Balarāma. Akrūra told the King, "You have assumed the royal throne after the death of Pāṇḍu. Seeing all equally, which is the religious duty of kings, you should protect all your subjects and personal relations. By such fair behavior you will gain all fame and good fortune. But if you act otherwise, you will attain only infamy in this life and condemnation to a hellish existence in the next. A living being takes his birth all alone, and alone he gives up his life. Alone he enjoys the fruits of his piety and sin. If one fails to understand the true identity of the self and instead maintains his progeny by indulging in evil deeds, then surely he will go to hell. One should therefore learn to understand the unsteadiness of material existence, which is like a sleeper's dream, a magician's illusion or a flight of fancy, and should thus control his mind in order to remain peaceful and equipoised."

To this Dhṛtarāṣṭra replied, "I cannot hear enough of your beneficial words, O Akrūra, which are like the sweet nectar of immortality. But because the tight knot of affection for my sons has made me biased toward them, your statements cannot become fixed within my mind. No one can transgress the arrangement of the Supreme Lord; His purpose for descending into the Yadu dynasty will inevitably be fulfilled."

Knowing now the mentality of Dhṛtarāṣṭra, Akrūra took permission from his dear relatives and friends and returned to Mathurā, where he related everything to Lord Kṛṣṇa and Lord Balarāma.

TEXTS 1–2

श्रीशुक उवाच

स गत्वा हास्तिनपुरं पौरवेन्द्रयशोऽङ्कितम् ।
ददर्श तत्राम्बिकेयं सभीष्मं विदुरं पृथाम् ॥१॥
सहपुत्रं च बाह्लीकं भारद्वाजं सगौतमम् ।
कर्णं सुयोधनं द्रौणिं पाण्डवान् सुहृदोऽपरान् ॥२॥

śrī-śuka uvāca
sa gatvā hāstinapuraṁ
pauravendra-yaśo-'ṅkitam
dadarśa tatrāmbikeyaṁ
sa-bhīṣmaṁ viduraṁ pṛthām

saha-putraṁ ca bāhlīkaṁ
bhāradvājaṁ sa-gautamam
karṇaṁ suyodhanaṁ drauṇiṁ
pāṇḍavān suhṛdo 'parān

śrī-śukaḥ uvāca—Śukadeva Gosvāmī said; *saḥ*—he (Akrūra); *gatvā*—going; *hāstina-puram*—to Hastināpura; *paurava-indra*—of the rulers of the dynasty of Pūru; *yaśaḥ*—by the glory; *aṅkitam*—decorated; *dadarśa*—he saw; *tatra*—there; *āmbikeyam*—the son of Ambikā (Dhṛtarāṣṭra); *sa*—together with; *bhīṣmam*—Bhīṣma; *viduram*—Vidura; *pṛthām*—Pṛthā (Kuntī, the widow of King Pāṇḍu); *saha-putram*—with his son (namely, Somadatta); *ca*—and; *bāhlīkam*—Mahārāja Bāhlika; *bhāradvājam*—Droṇa; *sa*—and; *gautamam*—Kṛpa; *karṇam*—Karṇa; *suyodhanam*—Duryodhana; *drauṇim*—the son of Droṇa (Aśvatthāmā); *pāṇḍavān*—the sons of Pāṇḍu; *suhṛdaḥ*—friends; *aparān*—other.

TRANSLATION

Śukadeva Gosvāmī said: Akrūra went to Hastināpura, the city distinguished by the glory of the Paurava rulers. There he saw Dhṛtarāṣṭra, Bhīṣma, Vidura and Kuntī, along with Bāhlīka and his son Somadatta. He also saw Droṇācārya, Kṛpācārya, Karṇa, Duryodhana, Aśvatthāmā, the Pāṇḍavas and other close friends.

TEXT 3

यथावदुपसंगम्य बन्धुभिर्गान्दिनीसुतः ।
सम्पृष्टस्तैः सुहृद्वार्तां स्वयं चापृच्छदव्ययम् ॥३॥

yathāvad upasaṅgamya
bandhubhir gāndinī-sutaḥ
sampṛṣṭas taiḥ suhṛd-vārtāṁ
svayaṁ cāpṛcchad avyayam

yathā-vat—appropriately; *upasaṅgamya*—meeting; *bandhubhiḥ*—with his relatives and friends; *gāndinī-sutaḥ*—Akrūra, son of Gāndinī; *sampṛṣṭaḥ*—inquired from; *taiḥ*—by them; *suhṛt*—of their dear ones; *vārtām*—for news; *svayam*—himself; *ca*—in addition; *apṛcchat*—asked; *avyayam*—about their well-being.

TRANSLATION

After Akrūra, the son of Gāndinī, had appropriately greeted all his relatives and friends, they asked him for news of their family members, and he in turn asked about their welfare.

TEXT 4

उवास कतिचिन्मासान् राज्ञो वृत्तविवित्सया ।
दुष्प्रजस्याल्पसारस्य खलच्छन्दानुवर्तिनः ॥४॥

uvāsa katicin māsān
rājño vṛtta-vivitsayā
duṣprajasyālpa-sārasya
khala-cchandānuvartinaḥ

uvāsa—resided; *katicit*—some; *māsān*—months; *rājñaḥ*—of the King (Dhṛtarāṣṭra); *vṛtta*—the activity; *vivitsayā*—with the desire of finding out; *duṣprajasya*—whose sons were wicked; *alpa*—weak; *sārasya*—whose determination; *khala*—of mischievous persons (like Karṇa); *chanda*—the desires; *anuvartinaḥ*—who tended to follow.

TRANSLATION

He remained in Hastināpura for several months to scrutinize the conduct of the weak-willed King, who had bad sons and who was inclined to give in to the whims of mischievous advisers.

TEXTS 5–6

तेज ओजोबलं वीर्यं प्रश्रयादींश्च सद्गुणान् ।
प्रजानुरागं पार्थेषु न सहद्‌भिश्चिकीर्षितम् ॥५॥
कृतं च धार्तराष्ट्रैर्यद् गरदानाद्यपेशलम् ।
आचख्यौ सर्वमेवास्मै पृथा विदुर एव च ॥६॥

teja ojo balaṁ vīryaṁ
praśrayādīṁś ca sad-guṇān
prajānurāgaṁ pārtheṣu
na sahadbhiś cikīrṣitam

kṛtaṁ ca dhārtarāṣṭrair yad
gara-dānādy apeśalam
ācakhyau sarvam evāsmai
pṛthā vidura eva ca

tejaḥ—the influence; *ojaḥ*—skill; *balam*—strength; *vīryam*—bravery; *praśraya*—humility; *ādīn*—and so on; *ca*—and; *sat*—excellent; *guṇān*—qualities; *prajā*—of the citizens; *anurāgam*—the great affection; *pārtheṣu*—for the sons of Pṛthā; *na sahadbhiḥ*—of those who could not tolerate; *cikīrṣitam*—the intentions; *kṛtam*—had been done; *ca*—also; *dhārtarāṣṭraiḥ*—by the sons of Dhṛtarāṣṭra; *yat*—what; *gara*—of poison; *dāna*—the giving; *ādi*—and so on; *apeśalam*—unbecoming; *ācakhyau*—told; *sarvam*—everything; *eva*—indeed; *asmai*—to him (Akrūra); *pṛthā*—Kuntī; *viduraḥ*—Vidura; *eva ca*—both.

TRANSLATION

Kuntī and Vidura described to Akrūra in detail the evil intentions of Dhṛtarāṣṭra's sons, who could not tolerate the great qualities of Kuntī's sons—such as their powerful influence, military skill, physical strength, bravery and humility—or the intense affection the citizens had for them. Kuntī and Vidura also told Akrūra about how the sons of Dhṛtarāṣṭra had tried to poison the Pāṇḍavas and carry out other such plots.

TEXT 7

पृथा तु भ्रातरं प्राप्तमक्रूरमुपसृत्य तम् ।
उवाच जन्मनिलयं स्मरन्त्यश्रुकलेक्षणा ॥७॥

pṛthā tu bhrātaraṁ prāptam
akrūram upasṛtya tam
uvāca janma-nilayaṁ
smaranty aśru-kalekṣaṇā

pṛthā—Kuntī; *tu*—and; *bhrātaram*—her brother (more exactly, the grandson of Vṛṣṇi, her own and Vasudeva's tenth-generation ancestor); *prāptam*—obtained; *akrūram*—Akrūra; *upasṛtya*—approaching; *tam*—him; *uvāca*—she said; *janma*—of her birth; *nilayam*—the home (Mathurā); *smarantī*—remembering; *aśru*—of tears; *kalā*—with traces; *īkṣaṇā*—whose eyes.

TRANSLATION

Kuntīdevī, taking advantage of her brother Akrūra's visit, approached him confidentially. While remembering her birthplace, she spoke with tears in her eyes.

TEXT 8

अपि स्मरन्ति नः सौम्य पितरौ भ्रातरश्च मे ।
भगिन्यौ भ्रातृपुत्राश्च जामयः सख्य एव च ॥८॥

api smaranti naḥ saumya
pitarau bhrātaraś ca me
bhaginyau bhrātṛ-putrāś ca
jāmayaḥ sakhya eva ca

api—whether; *smaranti*—they remember; *naḥ*—us; *saumya*—O gentle one; *pitarau*—parents; *bhrātaraḥ*—brothers; *ca*—and; *me*—my; *bhaginyau*—sisters; *bhrātṛ-putrāḥ*—brother's sons; *ca*—and; *jāmayaḥ*—women of the family; *sakhyaḥ*—girlfriends; *eva ca*—also.

TRANSLATION

[Queen Kuntī said:] O gentle one, do my parents, brothers, sisters, nephews, family women and girlhood friends still remember us?

TEXT 9

भ्रात्रेयो भगवान् कृष्णः शरण्यो भक्तवत्सलः ।
पैतृष्वसेयान् स्मरति रामश्चाम्बुरुहेक्षणः ॥९॥

bhrātreyo bhagavān kṛṣṇaḥ
śaraṇyo bhakta-vatsalaḥ
paitṛ-ṣvasreyān smarati
rāmaś cāmburuhekṣaṇaḥ

bhrātreyaḥ—brother's son; *bhagavān*—the Supreme Lord; *kṛṣṇaḥ*—Kṛṣṇa; *śaraṇyaḥ*—the giver of shelter; *bhakta*—to His devotees; *vatsalaḥ*—compassionate; *paitṛ-svasreyān*—the sons of His father's sister; *smarati*—remembers; *rāmaḥ*—Lord Balarāma; *ca*—and; *amburuha*—like lotus petals; *īkṣaṇaḥ*—whose eyes.

TRANSLATION

Does my nephew Kṛṣṇa, the Supreme Personality and the compassionate shelter of His devotees, still remember His aunt's sons? And does lotus-eyed Rāma remember them also?

TEXT 10

सपत्नमध्ये शोचन्तीं वृकानां हरिणीमिव ।
सान्त्वयिष्यति मां वाक्यैः पितृहीनांश्च बालकान् ॥१०॥

sapatna-madhye śocantīṁ
vṛkānāṁ hariṇīm iva
sāntvayiṣyati māṁ vākyaiḥ
pitṛ-hīnāṁś ca bālakān

sapatna—of enemies; *madhye*—in the midst; *śocantīm*—who is lamenting; *vṛkānām*—of wolves; *hariṇīm*—a doe; *iva*—like; *sāntvayiṣyati*—will He console; *mām*—me; *vākyaiḥ*—with His words; *pitṛ*—of their father; *hīnān*—deprived; *ca*—and; *bālakān*—young boys.

TRANSLATION

Now that I am suffering in the midst of my enemies like a doe in the midst of wolves, will Kṛṣṇa come to console me and my fatherless sons with His words?

TEXT 11

कृष्ण कृष्ण महायोगिन् विश्वात्मन् विश्वभावन ।
प्रपन्नां पाहि गोविन्द शिशुभिश्चावसीदतीम् ॥११॥

kṛṣṇa kṛṣṇa mahā-yogin
viśvātman viśva-bhāvana
prapannāṁ pāhi govinda
śiśubhiś cāvasīdatīm

kṛṣṇa kṛṣṇa—O Kṛṣṇa, Kṛṣṇa; *mahā-yogin*—possessor of the greatest spiritual power; *viśva-ātman*—O Supreme Soul of the universe; *viśva-bhāvana*—O protector of the universe; *prapannām*—a surrendered lady; *pāhi*—please protect; *govinda*—O Govinda; *śiśubhiḥ*—along with my children; *ca*—and; *avasīdatīm*—who am sinking down in distress.

TRANSLATION

Kṛṣṇa, Kṛṣṇa! O great *yogī*! O Supreme Soul and protector of the universe! O Govinda! Please protect me, who have surrendered to You. I and my sons are being overwhelmed by trouble.

PURPORT

"Since Lord Kṛṣṇa maintains the entire universe," thought Kuntīdevī, "surely He can protect our family." The word *avasīdatīm* indicates that Kuntīdevī was overwhelmed by troubles; thus exhausted, she was helplessly taking shelter of Śrī Kṛṣṇa. In her prayers in the First Canto of the *Śrīmad-Bhāgavatam,* Kuntī admits that all these troubles were actually a blessing, for they forced her to always be intensely Kṛṣṇa conscious.

TEXT 12

नान्यत्तव पदाम्भोजात्पश्यामि शरणं नृणाम् ।
बिभ्यतां मृत्युसंसारादीश्वरस्यापवर्गिकात् ॥१२॥

nānyat tava padāmbhojāt
paśyāmi śaraṇaṁ nṛṇām
bibhyatāṁ mṛtyu-saṁsārād
īśvarasyāpavargikāt

na—no; *anyat*—other; *tava*—Your; *pada-ambhojāt*—than the lotus feet; *paśyāmi*—I see; *śaraṇam*—shelter; *nṛṇām*—for men; *bibhyatām*—fearful; *mṛtyu*—of death; *saṁsārāt*—and rebirth; *īśvarasya*—of the Supreme Personality of Godhead; *āpavargikāt*—which give liberation.

TRANSLATION

For persons fearful of death and rebirth, I see no shelter other than Your liberating lotus feet, for You are the Supreme Lord.

TEXT 13

नमः कृष्णाय शुद्धाय ब्रह्मणे परमात्मने ।
योगेश्वराय योगाय त्वामहं शरणं गता ॥१३॥

namaḥ kṛṣṇāya śuddhāya
brahmaṇe paramātmane
yogeśvarāya yogāya
tvām ahaṁ śaraṇaṁ gatā

namaḥ—obeisances; *kṛṣṇāya*—to Kṛṣṇa; *śuddhāya*—the pure; *brahmaṇe*—the Absolute Truth; *parama-ātmane*—the Supersoul; *yoga*—of pure devotional service; *īśvarāya*—the controller; *yogāya*—the source of all knowledge; *tvām*—You; *aham*—I; *śaraṇam*—for shelter; *gatā*—have approached.

TRANSLATION

I offer my obeisances unto You, Kṛṣṇa, the supreme pure, the Absolute Truth and the Supersoul, the Lord of pure devotional service and the source of all knowledge. I have come to You for shelter.

PURPORT

Śrīla Śrīdhara Svāmī has translated the word *yogāya* as "unto Kṛṣṇa, the source of knowledge." The word *yoga* indicates connection and also the means to achieve something. As conscious souls, we have a connection with the Supreme Soul through *bhakti*, or devotion. Through that relationship we experience perfect knowledge of the Supreme Soul. Since the Supreme Soul is the Absolute Truth, perfect knowledge of Him means perfect knowledge of everything. As stated in the *Muṇḍaka Upaniṣad* (1.3), *kasmin bhagavo vijñāte sarvam idaṁ vijñātaṁ bhavati:* When the Absolute is understood, everything is understood. Thus Lord Kṛṣṇa

Himself, by His spiritual potency, establishes our connection with Him, and that connection is the source of all spiritual knowledge. Thus Ācārya Śrīdhara, by his thoughtful translation, stimulates us to deeper understanding of Kṛṣṇa conscious philosophy.

TEXT 14

श्रीशुक उवाच
इत्यनुस्मृत्य स्वजनं कृष्णं च जगदीश्वरम् ।
प्रारुदद्दुःखिता राजन् भवतां प्रपितामही ॥१४॥

śrī-śuka uvāca
ity anusmṛtya sva-janaṁ
kṛṣṇaṁ ca jagad-īśvaram
prārudad duḥkhitā rājan
bhavatāṁ prapitāmahī

śrī-śukaḥ uvāca—Śrī Śukadeva Gosvāmī said; *iti*—as expressed in these words; *anusmṛtya*—remembering; *sva-janam*—her own relatives; *kṛṣṇam*—Kṛṣṇa; *ca*—and; *jagat*—of the universe; *īśvaram*—the Supreme Lord; *prārudat*—she cried loudly; *duḥkhitā*—unhappy; *rājan*—O King (Parīkṣit); *bhavatām*—of your good self; *prapitāmahī*—the great-grandmother.

TRANSLATION

Śukadeva Gosvāmī said: Thus meditating on her family members and also on Kṛṣṇa, the Lord of the universe, your great-grandmother Kuntīdevī began to cry out in grief, O King.

TEXT 15

समदुःखसुखोऽक्रूरो विदुरश्च महायशाः ।
सान्त्वयामासतुः कुन्तीं तत्पुत्रोत्पत्तिहेतुभिः ॥१५॥

sama-duḥkha-sukho 'krūro
viduraś ca mahā-yaśāḥ
sāntvayām āsatuḥ kuntīṁ
tat-putrotpatti-hetubhiḥ

sama—equal (with her); *duḥkha*—in distress; *sukhaḥ*—and happiness; *akrūraḥ*—Akrūra; *viduraḥ*—Vidura; *ca*—and; *mahā-yaśāḥ*—most famous; *sāntvayām āsatuḥ*—the two of them consoled; *kuntīm*—Śrīmatī Kuntīdevī; *tat*—her; *putra*—of the sons; *utpatti*—of the births; *hetubhiḥ*—with explanations about the origins.

TRANSLATION

Both Akrūra, who shared Queen Kuntī's distress and happiness, and the illustrious Vidura consoled the Queen by reminding her of the extraordinary way her sons had taken birth.

PURPORT

Akrūra and Vidura reminded Queen Kuntī that her sons were born of heavenly gods and thus could not be vanquished like ordinary mortals. In fact, an extraordinary victory awaited this most pious family.

TEXT 16

यास्यन् राजानमभ्येत्य विषमं पुत्रलालसम् ।
अवदत्सुहृदां मध्ये बन्धुभिः सौहृदोदितम् ॥१६॥

yāsyan rājānam abhyetya
viṣamaṁ putra-lālasam
avadat suhṛdāṁ madhye
bandhubhiḥ sauhṛdoditam

yāsyan—when he was about to go; *rājānam*—the King (Dhṛtarāṣṭra); *abhyetya*—going up to; *viṣamam*—biased; *putra*—toward his sons; *lālasam*—ardently affectionate; *avadat*—he spoke; *suhṛdām*—relatives; *madhye*—among; *bandhubhiḥ*—by well-wishing relatives (Lord Kṛṣṇa and Lord Balarāma); *sauhṛda*—in friendship; *uditam*—what had been said.

TRANSLATION

The ardent affection King Dhṛtarāṣṭra felt for his sons had made him act unjustly toward the Pāṇḍavas. Just before leaving, Akrūra approached the King, who was seated among his friends

and supporters, and related to him the message that his relatives—Lord Kṛṣṇa and Lord Balarāma—had sent out of friendship.

TEXT 17

अक्रूर उवाच
भो भो वैचित्रवीर्य त्वं कुरूणां कीर्तिवर्धन ।
भ्रातर्युपरते पाण्डावधुनासनमास्थितः ॥१७॥

akrūra uvāca
bho bho vaicitravīrya tvaṁ
kurūṇāṁ kīrti-vardhana
bhrātary uparate pāṇḍāv
adhunāsanam āsthitaḥ

akrūraḥ uvāca—Akrūra said; *bhoḥ bhoḥ*—O my dear, my dear; *vaicitravīrya*—son of Vicitravirya; *tvam*—you; *kurūṇām*—of the Kurus; *kīrti*—the glory; *vardhana*—O you who increase; *bhrātari*—your brother; *uparate*—having passed away; *pāṇḍau*—Mahārāja Pāṇḍu; *adhunā*—now; *āsanam*—the throne; *āsthitaḥ*—have assumed.

TRANSLATION

Akrūra said: O my dear son of Vicitravīrya, O enhancer of the Kurus' glory, your brother Pāṇḍu having passed away, you have now assumed the royal throne.

PURPORT

Akrūra was speaking ironically, since the young sons of Pāṇḍu should actually have been occupying the throne. Upon the death of Pāṇḍu, they were too young to immediately govern and so were put in Dhṛtarāṣṭra's care, but now sufficient time had passed, and their legitimate rights should have been recognized.

TEXT 18

धर्मेण पालयन्नुर्वी प्रजाः शीलेन रञ्जयन् ।
वर्तमानः समः स्वेषु श्रेयः कीर्तिमवाप्स्यसि ॥१८॥

dharmeṇa pālayann urvīṁ
prajāḥ śīlena rañjayan
vartamānaḥ samaḥ sveṣu
śreyaḥ kīrtim avāpsyasi

dharmeṇa—religiously; *pālayan*—protecting; *urvīm*—the earth; *prajāḥ*—the citizens; *śīlena*—by good character; *rañjayan*—delighting; *vartamānaḥ*—remaining; *samaḥ*—equally disposed; *sveṣu*—to your relatives; *śreyaḥ*—perfection; *kīrtim*—glory; *avāpsyasi*—you will achieve.

TRANSLATION

By religiously protecting the earth, delighting your subjects with your noble character, and treating all your relatives equally, you will surely achieve success and glory.

PURPORT

Akrūra told Dhṛtarāṣṭra that even though he had usurped the throne, if he now ruled according to the principles of *dharma* and behaved properly, he could be successful.

TEXT 19

अन्यथा त्वाचरल्ँ लोके गर्हितो यास्यसे तमः ।
तस्मात्समत्वे वर्तस्व पाण्डवेष्वात्मजेषु च ॥१९॥

anyathā tv ācaral̐ loke
garhito yāsyase tamaḥ
tasmāt samatve vartasva
pāṇḍaveṣv ātmajeṣu ca

anyathā—otherwise; *tu*—however; *ācaran*—acting; *loke*—in this world; *garhitaḥ*—condemned; *yāsyase*—you will attain; *tamaḥ*—darkness; *tasmāt*—therefore; *samatve*—in equanimity; *vartasva*—remain situated; *pāṇḍaveṣu*—toward the Pāṇḍavas; *ātma-jeṣu*—toward your sons; *ca*—and.

TRANSLATION

If you act otherwise, however, people will condemn you in this world, and in the next life you will enter the darkness of hell. Remain equally disposed, therefore, toward Pāṇḍu's sons and your own.

PURPORT

Dhṛtarāṣṭra's whole problem was his excessive attachment to his nasty sons. That was the fatal flaw that caused his downfall. There was no lack of good advice from all sides, and Dhṛtarāṣṭra even admitted that the advice was sound, but he could not follow it. One can have clear, practical intelligence when the mind and heart are pure.

TEXT 20

नेह चात्यन्तसंवासः कस्यचित्केनचित्सह ।
राजन् स्वेनापि देहेन किमु जायात्मजादिभिः ॥२०॥

neha cātyanta-saṁvāsaḥ
kasyacit kenacit saha
rājan svenāpi dehena
kim u jāyātmajādibhiḥ

na—not; *iha*—in this world; *ca*—and; *atyanta*—perpetual; *saṁvāsaḥ*—association (dwelling together); *kasyacit*—of anyone; *kenacit saha*—with anyone; *rājan*—O King; *svena*—with one's own; *api*—even; *dehena*—body; *kim u*—what to speak then; *jāyā*—with wife; *ātma-ja*—children; *ādibhiḥ*—and so on.

TRANSLATION

In this world no one has any permanent relationship with anyone else, O King. We cannot stay forever even with our own body, what to speak of our wife, children and the rest.

TEXT 21

एकः प्रसूयते जन्तुरेक एव प्रलीयते ।
एकोऽनुभुंक्ते सुकृतमेक एव च दुष्कृतम् ॥२१॥

ekaḥ prasūyate jantur
eka eva pralīyate
eko 'nubhuṅkte sukṛtam
eka eva ca duṣkṛtam

ekaḥ—alone; *prasūyate*—is born; *jantuḥ*—a living creature; *ekaḥ*—alone; *eva*—also; *pralīyate*—meets his demise; *ekaḥ*—alone; *anubhuṅkte*—enjoys as is due him; *sukṛtam*—his good reactions; *ekaḥ*—alone; *eva ca*—and surely; *duṣkṛtam*—bad reactions.

TRANSLATION

Every creature is born alone and dies alone, and alone one experiences the just rewards of his good and evil deeds.

PURPORT

The term *anubhuṅkte* is significant here. *Bhuṅkte* means "(the living being) experiences," and *anu* means "following," or "in sequence." In other words, we experience happiness and distress according to the moral and spiritual quality of our activities. We are responsible for what we do. Dhṛtarāṣṭra was falsely and obsessively attached to his evil-minded sons, forgetting that he alone would have to suffer for his imprudent behavior.

TEXT 22

अधर्मोपचितं वित्तं हरन्त्यन्येऽल्पमेधसः ।
सम्भोजनीयापदेशैर्जलानीव जलौकसः ॥२२॥

adharmopacitaṁ vittaṁ
haranty anye 'lpa-medhasaḥ

sambhojanīyāpadeśair
jalānīva jalaukasaḥ

adharma—by irreligious means; *upacitam*—gathered; *vittam*—wealth; *haranti*—steal; *anye*—other persons; *alpa-medhasaḥ*—of one who is unintelligent; *sambhojanīya*—as requiring support; *apadeśaiḥ*—by the false designations; *jalāni*—water; *iva*—as; *jala-okasaḥ*—of a resident of the water.

TRANSLATION

In the guise of dear dependents, strangers steal the sinfully acquired wealth of a foolish man, just as the offspring of a fish drink up the water that sustains the fish.

PURPORT

Ordinary people feel they cannot live without their wealth, although their possession of it is circumstantial and temporary. Just as wealth gives life to an ordinary man, water gives life to a fish. One's dear dependents, however, steal one's wealth, just as a fish's offspring drink up the water sustaining the fish. In the words of Śrīla Bhaktivinoda Ṭhākura, this world is "a weird abode."

TEXT 23

पुष्णाति यानधर्मेण स्वबुद्ध्या तमपण्डितम् ।
तेऽकृतार्थं प्रहिण्वन्ति प्राणा रायः सुतादयः ॥२३॥

puṣṇāti yān adharmeṇa
sva-buddhyā tam apaṇḍitam
te 'kṛtārthaṁ prahiṇvanti
prāṇā rāyaḥ sutādayaḥ

puṣṇāti—nourishes; *yān*—which things; *adharmeṇa*—by sinful activity; *sva-buddhyā*—thinking them to be his own; *tam*—him; *apaṇḍitam*—uneducated; *te*—they; *akṛta-artham*—his purposes frustrated; *prahiṇvanti*—abandon; *prāṇāḥ*—life air; *rāyaḥ*—wealth; *suta-ādayaḥ*—children and others.

TRANSLATION

A fool indulges in sin to maintain his life, wealth and children and other relatives, for he thinks, "These things are mine." In the end, however, these very things all abandon him, leaving him frustrated.

PURPORT

In these verses, Akrūra is giving rather frank advice to Dhṛtarāṣṭra. Those who know the story of the *Mahābhārata* will realize how relevant and prophetic these instructions are, and how much Dhṛtarāṣṭra suffered for not accepting them. Although one tenaciously clings to his property, in the end all is lost, and the blundering soul is swept away by the wheel of birth and death.

TEXT 24

स्वयं किल्बिषमादाय तैस्त्यक्तो नार्थकोविदः ।
असिद्धार्थो विशत्यन्धं स्वधर्मविमुखस्तमः ॥२४॥

svayaṁ kilbiṣam ādāya
tais tyakto nārtha-kovidaḥ
asiddhārtho viśaty andhaṁ
sva-dharma-vimukhas tamaḥ

svayam—for himself; *kilbiṣam*—sinful reaction; *ādāya*—taking on; *taiḥ*—by them; *tyaktaḥ*—abandoned; *na*—not; *artha*—the purpose of his life; *kovidaḥ*—knowing properly; *asiddha*—unfulfilled; *arthaḥ*—whose goals; *viśati*—he enters; *andham*—blind; *sva*—his own; *dharma*—to the religious duty; *vimukhaḥ*—indifferent; *tamaḥ*—darkness (of hell).

TRANSLATION

Abandoned by his so-called dependents, ignorant of the actual goal of life, indifferent to his real duty, and having failed to fulfill his purposes, the foolish soul enters the blindness of hell, taking his sinful reactions with him.

PURPORT

It is sadly ironic that materialistic persons, who labor so assiduously to accumulate insurance, security, property and family, enter the darkness of hell equipped with nothing but the painful reactions of their sins. On the other hand, those who cultivate Kṛṣṇa consciousness, spiritual life, while apparently neglecting to accumulate property, a large family and so on, enter the next life enriched with many spiritual assets and thus enjoy the deep pleasures of the soul.

TEXT 25

तस्माल्लोकमिमं राजन् स्वप्नमायामनोरथम् ।
वीक्ष्यायम्यात्मनात्मानं समः शान्तो भव प्रभो ॥२५॥

tasmāl lokam imaṁ rājan
svapna-māyā-manoratham
vīkṣyāyamyātmanātmānaṁ
samaḥ śānto bhava prabho

tasmāt—therefore; *lokam*—world; *imam*—this; *rājan*—O King; *svapna*—as a dream; *māyā*—a magic trick; *manaḥ-ratham*—or a fantasy in the mind; *vīkṣya*—seeing; *āyamya*—bringing under control; *ātmanā*—by intelligence; *ātmānam*—the mind; *samaḥ*—equal; *śāntaḥ*—peaceful; *bhava*—become; *prabho*—my dear master.

TRANSLATION

Therefore, O King, looking upon this world as a dream, a magician's illusion or a flight of fancy, please control your mind with intelligence and become equipoised and peaceful, my lord.

TEXT 26

धृतराष्ट्र उवाच
यथा वदति कल्याणीं वाचं दानपते भवान् ।
तथानया न तृप्यामि मर्त्यः प्राप्य यथामृतम् ॥२६॥

dhṛtarāṣṭra uvāca
yathā vadati kalyāṇīṁ
vācaṁ dāna-pate bhavān
tathānayā na tṛpyāmi
martyaḥ prāpya yathāmṛtam

dhṛtarāṣṭraḥ uvāca—Dhṛtarāṣṭra said; *yathā*—as; *vadati*—speak; *kalyāṇīm*—auspicious; *vācam*—words; *dāna*—of charity; *pate*—O master; *bhavān*—you; *tathā*—so; *anayā*—by this; *na tṛpyāmi*—I am not satiated; *martyaḥ*—a mortal; *prāpya*—attaining; *yathā*—as if; *amṛtam*—the nectar of immortality.

TRANSLATION

Dhṛtarāṣṭra said: O master of charity, I can never be satiated while hearing your auspicious words. Indeed, I am like a mortal who has obtained the nectar of the gods.

PURPORT

In the opinion of Śrīla Viśvanātha Cakravartī, Dhṛtarāṣṭra was in fact proud and felt he already knew everything Akrūra was speaking, but to maintain diplomatic gravity he spoke as a saintly gentleman.

TEXT 27

तथापि सूनृता सौम्य हृदि न स्थीयते चले ।
पुत्रानुरागविषमे विद्युत्सौदामनी यथा ॥२७॥

tathāpi sūnṛtā saumya
hṛdi na sthīyate cale
putrānurāga-viṣame
vidyut saudāmanī yathā

tathā api—nevertheless; *sūnṛtā*—pleasing words; *saumya*—O gentle one; *hṛdi*—in my heart; *na sthīyate*—do not remain steady; *cale*—which is unsteady; *putra*—for my sons; *anurāga*—by affection; *viṣame*—prejudiced; *vidyut*—lightning; *saudāmanī*—in a cloud; *yathā*—as.

TRANSLATION

Even so, gentle Akrūra, because my unsteady heart is prejudiced by affection for my sons, these pleasing words of yours cannot remain fixed there, just as lightning cannot remain fixed in a cloud.

TEXT 28

ईश्वरस्य विधिं को नु विधुनोत्यन्यथा पुमान् ।
भूमेर्भारावताराय योऽवतीर्णो यदोः कुले ॥२८॥

īśvarasya vidhiṁ ko nu
vidhunoty anyathā pumān
bhūmer bhārāvatārāya
yo 'vatīrṇo yadoḥ kule

īśvarasya—of the Supreme Lord; *vidhim*—the law; *kaḥ*—what; *nu*—at all; *vidhunoti*—can shake off; *anyathā*—otherwise; *pumān*—person; *bhūmeḥ*—of the earth; *bhāra*—the burden; *avatārāya*—in order to diminish; *yaḥ*—who; *avatīrṇaḥ*—has descended; *yadoḥ*—of Yadu; *kule*—in the family.

TRANSLATION

Who can defy the injunctions of the Supreme Lord, who has now descended in the Yadu dynasty to diminish the earth's burden?

PURPORT

Naturally, we would like to ask Dhṛtarāṣṭra, "If you know all this, why don't you behave properly?" Of course, this is exactly Dhṛtarāṣṭra's point: he feels that since events have already been set in motion, he is helpless to change them. In fact, events have been set in motion by his attachment and sinful propensities, and therefore he should have taken responsibility for his own acts. Lord Kṛṣṇa clearly states in the *Bhagavad-gītā* (5.15), *nādatte kasyacit pāpam:* "The Supreme Lord does not accept responsibility for anyone's sinful activities." It is a dangerous policy to claim that we are acting improperly because of "destiny" or "fate." We should take up Kṛṣṇa consciousness seriously and create an auspicious future for ourselves and our associates.

Finally, one may argue that, after all, Dhṛtarāṣṭra is involved in the Lord's pastimes and is actually His eternal associate. In answer to this we may say that the Lord's pastimes are not only entertaining but also didactic, and the lesson here is that Dhṛtarāṣṭra should have acted properly. This is what the Lord wanted to teach. Dhṛtarāṣṭra claims that Kṛṣṇa came to relieve the burden of the earth, but the earth's burden is precisely the improper behavior of its inhabitants. So, let us take the lesson the Lord wants to teach here and be instructed for our benefit.

TEXT 29

यो दुर्विमर्शपथया निजमाययेदं
सृष्ट्वा गुणान् विभजते तदनुप्रविष्टः ।
तस्मै नमो दुरवबोधविहारतन्त्र-
संसारचक्रगतये परमेश्वराय ॥२९॥

yo durvimarśa-pathayā nija-māyayedaṁ
sṛṣṭvā guṇān vibhajate tad-anupraviṣṭaḥ
tasmai namo duravabodha-vihāra-tantra-
saṁsāra-cakra-gataye parameśvarāya

yaḥ—who; *durvimarśa*—inconceivable; *pathayā*—whose path; *nija*—by His own; *māyayā*—creative energy; *idam*—this universe; *sṛṣṭvā*—creating; *guṇān*—its modes; *vibhajate*—He distributes; *tat*—within it; *anupraviṣṭaḥ*—entering; *tasmai*—to Him; *namaḥ*—obeisances; *duravabodha*—unfathomable; *vihāra*—of whose pastimes; *tantra*—the purport; *saṁsāra*—of birth and death; *cakra*—the cycle; *gataye*—and liberation (coming from whom); *parama-īśvarāya*—to the supreme controller.

TRANSLATION

I offer my obeisances to Him, the Supreme Personality of Godhead, who creates this universe by the inconceivable activity of His material energy and then distributes the various modes of nature by entering within the creation. From Him, the meaning of

whose pastimes is unfathomable, come both the entangling cycle of birth and death and the process of deliverance from it.

PURPORT

When all is said and done, Dhṛtarāṣṭra was not an ordinary person but an associate of the Supreme Lord, Kṛṣṇa. Certainly an ordinary person could not offer such a learned hymn to the Lord.

TEXT 30

श्रीशुक उवाच
इत्यभिप्रेत्य नृपतेरभिप्रायं स यादवः ।
सुहृद्भिः समनुज्ञातः पुनर्यदुपुरीमगात् ॥३०॥

śrī-śuka uvāca
ity abhipretya nṛpater
abhiprāyaṁ sa yādavaḥ
suhṛdbhiḥ samanujñātaḥ
punar yadu-purīm agāt

śrī-śukaḥ uvāca—Śukadeva Gosvāmī said; *iti*—thus; *abhipretya*—ascertaining; *nṛpateḥ*—of the King; *abhiprāyam*—the mentality; *saḥ*—he; *yādavaḥ*—Akrūra, the descendant of King Yadu; *suhṛdbhiḥ*—by his well-wishers; *samanujñātaḥ*—given permission to leave; *punaḥ*—again; *yadu-purīm*—to the city of the Yadu dynasty; *agāt*—went.

TRANSLATION

Śukadeva Gosvāmī said: Having thus apprised himself of the King's attitude, Akrūra, the descendant of Yadu, took permission from his well-wishing relatives and friends and returned to the capital of the Yādavas.

TEXT 31

शशंस रामकृष्णाभ्यां धृतराष्ट्रविचेष्टितम् ।
पाण्डवान् प्रति कौरव्य यदर्थं प्रेषितः स्वयम् ॥३१॥

śaśaṁsa rāma-kṛṣṇābhyāṁ
dhṛtarāṣṭra-viceṣṭitam
pāṇḍavān prati kauravya
yad-arthaṁ preṣitaḥ svayam

śaśaṁsa—he reported; *rāma-kṛṣṇābhyām*—to Lord Balarāma and Lord Kṛṣṇa; *dhṛtarāṣṭra-viceṣṭitam*—the behavior of King Dhṛtarāṣṭra; *pāṇḍavān prati*—toward the sons of Pāṇḍu; *kauravya*—O descendant of the Kurus (Parīkṣit); *yat*—for which; *artham*—purpose; *preṣitaḥ*—sent; *svayam*—himself.

TRANSLATION

Akrūra reported to Lord Balarāma and Lord Kṛṣṇa how Dhṛtarāṣṭra was behaving toward the Pāṇḍavas. Thus, O descendant of the Kurus, he fulfilled the purpose for which he had been sent.

Thus end the purports of the humble servants of His Divine Grace A. C. Bhaktivedanta Swami Prabhupāda to the Tenth Canto, Forty-ninth Chapter, of the Śrīmad-Bhāgavatam, *entitled "Akrūra's Mission in Hastināpura."*

CHAPTER FIFTY

Kṛṣṇa Establishes the City of Dvārakā

This chapter relates how Lord Kṛṣṇa defeated Jarāsandha seventeen times in battle and then constructed the city of Dvārakā.

After Kaṁsa was killed, his two queens, Asti and Prāpti, went to the home of their father, Jarāsandha, and sorrowfully described to him how Kṛṣṇa had made them widows. Upon hearing this account, King Jarāsandha became angry. He vowed to rid the earth of all the Yādavas, and he gathered an immense army to lay siege to Mathurā. When Śrī Kṛṣṇa saw Jarāsandha attacking, the Lord considered the reasons for His descent to this world and then decided to destroy Jarāsandha's army, which was a burden to the earth.

Two effulgent chariots suddenly appeared, equipped with drivers and furnishings, together with all the Lord's personal weapons. Seeing this, Lord Kṛṣṇa addressed Lord Baladeva, "My dear brother, Jarāsandha is now attacking Mathurā-purī, so please mount Your chariot and let Us go destroy the enemy's army." The two Lords took up Their weapons, mounted Their chariots and went forth from the city.

When Lord Kṛṣṇa came before His opponent's army, He sounded His conchshell, striking fear into His enemies' hearts. King Jarāsandha surrounded Kṛṣṇa and Balarāma with his soldiers, chariots and so on, and the women of the city, having climbed up to the roofs of the palaces, became extremely unhappy because they could not see the Lords. Then Kṛṣṇa twanged His bow and started to rain down a torrent of arrows upon the enemy soldiers. Soon Jarāsandha's unfathomable army had been annihilated.

Then Lord Baladeva arrested Jarāsandha and was about to bind him up with ropes when Śrī Kṛṣṇa had Baladeva release the King. Lord Kṛṣṇa reasoned that Jarāsandha would assemble another army and return again to fight; this would facilitate Kṛṣṇa's goal of removing the earth's burden. Released, Jarāsandha returned to Magadha and vowed to perform austerities with the aim of avenging his defeat. The other kings advised him that his defeat was only a reaction of his *karma*. Thus informed, King Jarāsandha withdrew to his kingdom with a heavy heart.

Śrī Kṛṣṇa rejoined the citizens of Mathurā, who began rejoicing, singing songs of triumph and arranging victory celebrations. The Lord brought all the warriors' jewelry and ornaments that had been picked up from the battlefield and presented them to Mahārāja Ugrasena.

Jarāsandha attacked the Yādavas in Mathurā seventeen times, and each time his armies were totally destroyed. Then, as Jarāsandha prepared to attack for the eighteenth time, a warrior named Kālayavana, who had been searching for a worthy opponent, was sent by Nārada Muni to fight the Yādavas. With thirty million soldiers Kālayavana laid siege to the Yādava capital. Lord Kṛṣṇa looked upon this attack with concern, for He knew that with Jarāsandha's arrival imminent, there was a serious danger that the simultaneous attack of these two enemies might endanger the Yādavas. Therefore the Lord constructed a wonderful city within the sea as a safe haven for the Yādavas; then He brought them all there by His mystic power. This city was fully populated with members of all four social orders, and within it no one felt the pangs of thirst and hunger. The various demigods, headed by Indra, each offered as tribute to Lord Kṛṣṇa the same opulences they had originally obtained from Him to establish their positions of authority.

Once He saw His subjects safely settled, Lord Śrī Kṛṣṇa took permission from Lord Baladeva and went out of Mathurā unarmed.

TEXT 1

श्रीशुक उवाच
अस्तिः प्राप्तिश्च कंसस्य महिष्यौ भरतर्षभ ।
मृते भर्तरि दुःखार्ते ईयतुः स्म पितुर्गृहान् ॥१॥

śrī-śuka uvāca
astiḥ prāptiś ca kaṁsasya
mahiṣyau bharatarṣabha
mṛte bhartari duḥkhārte
īyatuḥ sma pitur gṛhān

śrī-śukaḥ uvāca—Śukadeva Gosvāmī said; *astiḥ prāptiḥ ca*—Asti and Prāpti; *kaṁsasya*—of Kaṁsa; *mahiṣyau*—the queens; *bharata-ṛṣabha*—O hero of the Bhāratas (Parīkṣit); *mṛte*—having been killed; *bhartari*—

their husband; *duḥkha*—with unhappiness; *ārte*—distressed; *īyatuḥ sma*—they went; *pituḥ*—of their father; *gṛhān*—to the house.

TRANSLATION

Śukadeva Gosvāmī said: When Kaṁsa was killed, O heroic descendant of Bharata, his two queens, Asti and Prāpti, went to their father's house in great distress.

TEXT 2

पित्रे मगधराजाय जरासन्धाय दुःखिते ।
वेदयां चक्रतुः सर्वमात्मवैधव्यकारणम् ॥२॥

pitre magadha-rājāya
jarāsandhāya duḥkhite
vedayāṁ cakratuḥ sarvam
ātma-vaidhavya-kāraṇam

pitre—to their father; *magadha-rājāya*—the King of Magadha; *jarāsandhāya*—named Jarāsandha; *duḥkhite*—unhappy; *vedayām cakratuḥ*—they related; *sarvam*—all; *ātma*—their own; *vaidhavya*—of widowhood; *kāraṇam*—the cause.

TRANSLATION

The sorrowful queens told their father, King Jarāsandha of Magadha, all about how they had become widows.

TEXT 3

स तदप्रियमाकर्ण्य शोकामर्षयुतो नृप ।
अयादवीं महीं कर्तुं चक्रे परममुद्यमम् ॥३॥

sa tad apriyam ākarṇya
śokāmarṣa-yuto nṛpa
ayādavīṁ mahīṁ kartuṁ
cakre paramam udyamam

saḥ—he, Jarāsandha; *tat*—that; *apriyam*—unpleasant news; *ākarṇya*—hearing; *śoka*—sorrow; *amarṣa*—and intolerant anger; *yutaḥ*—experiencing; *nṛpa*—O King; *ayādavīm*—devoid of Yādavas; *mahīm*—the earth; *kartum*—to make; *cakre*—he made; *paramam*—extreme; *udyamam*—endeavor.

TRANSLATION

Hearing this odious news, O King, Jarāsandha was filled with sorrow and anger, and he began the greatest possible endeavor to rid the earth of the Yādavas.

TEXT 4

अक्षौहिणीभिर्विंशत्या तिसृभिश्चापि संवृतः ।
यदुराजधानीं मथुरां न्यरुधत्सर्वतो दिशम् ॥४॥

akṣauhiṇībhir viṁśatyā
tisṛbhiś cāpi saṁvṛtaḥ
yadu-rājadhānīṁ mathurāṁ
nyarudhat sarvato diśam

akṣauhiṇībhiḥ—by *akṣauhiṇī* divisions (each consisting of 21,870 soldiers on elephants, 21,870 charioteers, 65,610 cavalrymen and 109,350 infantry soldiers); *viṁśatyā*—twenty; *tisṛbhiḥ ca api*—plus three; *saṁvṛtaḥ*—surrounded; *yadu*—of the dynasty of Yadu; *rājadhānīm*—the royal capital; *mathurām*—Mathurā; *nyarudhat*—he besieged; *sarvataḥ diśam*—on all sides.

TRANSLATION

With a force of twenty-three *akṣauhiṇī* divisions, he laid siege to the Yadu capital, Mathurā, on all sides.

PURPORT

The numbers involved in an *akṣauhiṇī* division are given in the word meanings. An *akṣauhiṇī* was a standard fighting force in ancient times.

TEXTS 5–6

निरीक्ष्य तद्बलं कृष्ण उद्वेलमिव सागरम् ।
स्वपुरं तेन संरुद्धं स्वजनं च भयाकुलम् ॥५॥
चिन्तयामास भगवान् हरिः कारणमानुषः ।
तद्देशकालानुगुणं स्वावतारप्रयोजनम् ॥६॥

nirīkṣya tad-balaṁ kṛṣṇa
udvelam iva sāgaram
sva-puraṁ tena saṁruddhaṁ
sva-janaṁ ca bhayākulam

cintayām āsa bhagavān
hariḥ kāraṇa-mānuṣaḥ
tad-deśa-kālānuguṇaṁ
svāvatāra-prayojanam

nirīkṣya—observing; *tat*—of him (Jarāsandha); *balam*—the military force; *kṛṣṇaḥ*—Lord Kṛṣṇa; *udvelam*—having overflowed its boundaries; *iva*—like; *sāgaram*—an ocean; *sva*—His own; *puram*—city, Mathurā; *tena*—by it; *saṁruddham*—besieged; *sva-janam*—His subjects; *ca*—and; *bhaya*—by fear; *ākulam*—disturbed; *cintayām āsa*—He thought; *bhagavān*—the Supreme Personality of Godhead; *hariḥ*—Lord Hari; *kāraṇa*—the cause of everything; *mānuṣaḥ*—appearing as a human being; *tat*—for that; *deśa*—place; *kāla*—and time; *anuguṇam*—suitable; *sva-avatāra*—of His descent to this world; *prayojanam*—the purpose.

TRANSLATION

Although Lord Kṛṣṇa, the Supreme Personality of Godhead, is the original cause of this world, when He descended to the earth He played the role of a human being. Thus when He saw Jarāsandha's assembled army surrounding His city like a great ocean overflowing its shores, and when He saw how this army was striking fear into His subjects, the Lord considered what His suitable response should be according to the time, place and specific purpose of His current incarnation.

PURPORT

The *ācaryas* point out that the Supreme Godhead did not have to worry about a mortal attack from Jarāsandha and his soldiers. But, as stated here, Śrī Kṛṣṇa was playing the part of a human being (*kāraṇa-mānuṣaḥ*), and He played the part well. This play is called *līlā,* the Lord's enactment of spiritual pastimes for the pleasure of His devotees. Although ordinary persons may be dumbfounded by the Lord's pastimes, the devotees derive tremendous pleasure from His inimitable style of behavior. Thus Śrīla Śrīdhara Svāmī points out that Śrī Kṛṣṇa thought as follows: "How should I defeat Jarāsandha? Should I kill the army but not Jarāsandha, or should I kill Jarāsandha and take the army for Myself? Or perhaps I should just kill both of them." Lord Kṛṣṇa's conclusion is described in the following verses.

TEXTS 7–8

हनिष्यामि बलं ह्येतद् भुवि भारं समाहितम् ।
मागधेन समानीतं वश्यानां सर्वभूभुजाम् ॥७॥
अक्षौहिणीभिः संख्यातं भटाश्वरथकुञ्जरैः ।
मागधस्तु न हन्तव्यो भूयः कर्ता बलोद्यमम् ॥८॥

haniṣyāmi balaṁ hy etad
bhuvi bhāraṁ samāhitam
māgadhena samānītaṁ
vaśyānāṁ sarva-bhūbhujām

akṣauhiṇībhiḥ saṅkhyātaṁ
bhaṭāśva-ratha-kuñjaraiḥ
māgadhas tu na hantavyo
bhūyaḥ kartā balodyamam

haniṣyāmi—I will kill; *balam*—army; *hi*—certainly; *etat*—this; *bhuvi*—upon the earth; *bhāram*—a burden; *samāhitam*—collected; *māgadhena*—by the King of Magadha, Jarāsandha; *samānītam*—brought together; *vaśyānām*—subservient; *sarva*—all; *bhū-bhujām*—of the kings; *akṣauhiṇībhiḥ*—in *akṣauhiṇīs; saṅkhyātam*—counted; *bhaṭa*—(consisting) of foot soldiers; *aśva*—horses; *ratha*—chariots; *kuñjaraiḥ*—and elephants; *māgadhaḥ*—Jarāsandha; *tu*—however; *na hantavyaḥ*—should not be killed; *bhūyaḥ*—again; *kartā*—he will make; *bala*—(to collect) an army; *udyamam*—the endeavor.

TRANSLATION

[The Supreme Lord thought:] Since it is such a burden on the earth, I will destroy Jarāsandha's army, consisting of *akṣauhiṇīs* of foot soldiers, horses, chariots and elephants, which the King of Māgadha has assembled from all subservient kings and brought together here. But Jarāsandha himself should not be killed, since in the future he will certainly assemble another army.

PURPORT

After due consideration, Lord Kṛṣṇa decided that since He had descended to the earth to destroy the demons, and since Jarāsandha was so enthusiastic to bring all the demons to the Lord's front door, it was definitely more efficient to keep Jarāsandha alive and busy.

TEXT 9

एतदर्थोऽवतारोऽयं भूभारहरणाय मे ।
संरक्षणाय साधूनां कृतोऽन्येषां वधाय च ॥९॥

etad-artho 'vatāro 'yaṁ
bhū-bhāra-haraṇāya me
saṁrakṣaṇāya sādhūnāṁ
kṛto 'nyeṣāṁ vadhāya ca

etat—for this; *arthaḥ*—purpose; *avatāraḥ*—descent; *ayam*—this; *bhū*—of the earth; *bhāra*—the burden; *haraṇāya*—for removing; *me*—by Me; *saṁrakṣaṇāya*—for the complete protection; *sādhūnām*—of the saintly; *kṛtaḥ*—done; *anyeṣām*—of others (the nonsaintly); *vadhāya*—for killing; *ca*—and.

TRANSLATION

This is the purpose of My present incarnation—to relieve the earth of its burden, protect the pious and kill the impious.

TEXT 10

अन्योऽपि धर्मरक्षायै देहः संभ्रियते मया ।
विरामायाप्यधर्मस्य काले प्रभवतः क्वचित् ॥१०॥

anyo 'pi dharma-rakṣāyai
dehaḥ sambhriyate mayā
virāmāyāpy adharmasya
kāle prabhavataḥ kvacit

anyaḥ—another; *api*—as well; *dharma*—of religion; *rakṣāyai*—for the protection; *dehaḥ*—body; *sambhriyate*—is assumed; *mayā*—by Me; *virāmāya*—for the stopping; *api*—also; *adharmasya*—of irreligion; *kāle*—in the course of time; *prabhavataḥ*—becoming prominent; *kvacit*—whenever.

TRANSLATION

I also assume other bodies to protect religion and to end irreligion whenever it flourishes in the course of time.

TEXT 11

एवं ध्यायति गोविन्द आकाशात्सूर्यवर्चसौ ।
रथावुपस्थितौ सद्यः ससूतौ सपरिच्छदौ ॥११॥

evaṁ dhyāyati govinda
ākāśāt sūrya-varcasau
rathāv upasthitau sadyaḥ
sa-sūtau sa-paricchadau

evam—in this manner; *dhyāyati*—while He was meditating; *govinde*—Lord Kṛṣṇa; *ākāśāt*—from the sky; *sūrya*—like the sun; *varcasau*—having effulgence; *rathau*—two chariots; *upasthitau*—appeared; *sadyaḥ*—suddenly; *sa*—with; *sūtau*—drivers; *sa*—with; *paricchadau*—equipment.

TRANSLATION

[Śukadeva Gosvāmī continued:] As Lord Govinda was thinking in this way, two chariots as effulgent as the sun suddenly descended from the sky. They were complete with drivers and equipment.

PURPORT

Śrīla Jīva Gosvāmī and Śrīla Viśvanātha Cakravartī agree that the chariots came down from the Lord's own abode, Vaikuṇṭha-loka, the kingdom of God. The faithful devotees of the Lord derive tremendous pleasure by observing the Lord's incomparable technology.

TEXT 12

आयुधानि च दिव्यानि पुराणानि यदृच्छया ।
दृष्ट्वा तानि हृषीकेशः संकर्षणमथाब्रवीत् ॥१२॥

āyudhāni ca divyāni
purāṇāni yadṛcchayā
dṛṣṭvā tāni hṛṣīkeśaḥ
saṅkarṣaṇam athābravīt

āyudhāni—weapons; *ca*—and; *divyāni*—divine; *purāṇāni*—ancient; *yadṛcchayā*—automatically; *dṛṣṭvā*—seeing; *tāni*—them; *hṛṣīkeśaḥ*—Lord Kṛṣṇa; *saṅkarṣaṇam*—to Lord Balarāma; *atha*—then; *abravīt*—He spoke.

TRANSLATION

The Lord's eternal divine weapons also appeared before Him spontaneously. Seeing these, Śrī Kṛṣṇa, Lord of the senses, addressed Lord Saṅkarṣaṇa.

TEXTS 13–14

पश्यार्य व्यसनं प्राप्तं यदूनां त्वावतां प्रभो ।
एष ते रथ आयातो दयितान्यायुधानि च ॥१३॥
एतदर्थं हि नौ जन्म साधूनामीश शर्मकृत् ।
त्रयोविंशत्यनीकाख्यं भूमेर्भारमपाकुरु ॥१४॥

paśyārya vyasanaṁ prāptaṁ
yadūnāṁ tvāvatāṁ prabho
eṣa te ratha āyāto
dayitāny āyudhāni ca

etad-arthaṁ hi nau janma
sādhūnām īśa śarma-kṛt
trayo-viṁśaty-anīkākhyaṁ
bhūmer bhāram apākuru

paśya—please see; *ārya*—respected one; *vyasanam*—the danger; *prāptam*—now present; *yadūnām*—for the Yadus; *tvā*—by You; *avatām*—who are protected; *prabho*—My dear master; *eṣaḥ*—this; *te*—Your; *rathaḥ*—chariot; *āyātaḥ*—has come; *dayitāni*—favorite; *āyudhāni*—weapons; *ca*—and; *etat-artham*—for this purpose; *hi*—indeed; *nau*—Our; *janma*—birth; *sādhūnām*—of the saintly devotees; *īśa*—O Lord; *śarma*—the benefit; *kṛt*—doing; *trayaḥ-viṁśati*—twenty-three; *anīka*—armies; *ākhyam*—in terms of; *bhūmeḥ*—of the earth; *bhāram*—burden; *apākuru*—please remove.

TRANSLATION

[The Supreme Lord said:] My respected elder brother, see this danger which has beset Your dependents, the Yadus! And see, dear master, how Your personal chariot and favorite weapons have come before You. The purpose for which We have taken birth, My Lord, is to secure the welfare of Our devotees. Please now remove from the earth the burden of these twenty-three armies.

TEXT 15

एवं सम्मन्त्र्य दाशार्हौ दंशितौ रथिनौ पुरात् ।
निर्जग्मतुः स्वायुधाढ्यौ बलेनाल्पीयसा वृतौ ॥१५॥

evaṁ sammantrya dāśārhau
daṁśitau rathinau purāt
nirjagmatuḥ svāyudhāḍhyau
balenālpīyasā vṛtau

evam—thus; *sammantrya*—inviting Him; *dāśārhau*—the two descendants of Daśārha (Kṛṣṇa and Balarāma); *daṁśitau*—wearing armor; *rathinau*—riding Their chariots; *purāt*—from the city; *nirjagmatuḥ*—went out; *sva*—Their own; *āyudha*—with weapons; *āḍhyau*—resplendent; *balena*—by a force; *alpīyasā*—very small; *vṛtau*—accompanied.

TRANSLATION

After Lord Kṛṣṇa had thus invited His brother, the two Dāśārhas, Kṛṣṇa and Balarāma, wearing armor and displaying Their resplendent weapons, drove out of the city in Their chariots. Only a very small contingent of soldiers accompanied Them.

TEXT 16

शंखं दध्मौ विनिर्गत्य हरिर्दारुकसारथिः ।
ततोऽभूत्परसैन्यानां हृदि वित्रासवेपथुः ॥१६॥

śaṅkhaṁ dadhmau vinirgatya
harir dāruka-sārathiḥ
tato 'bhūt para-sainyānāṁ
hṛdi vitrāsa-vepathuḥ

śaṅkham—His conchshell; *dadhmau*—blew; *vinirgatya*—upon going out; *hariḥ*—Lord Kṛṣṇa; *dāruka-sārathiḥ*—whose chariot driver was

Dāruka; *tataḥ*—thereupon; *abhūt*—arose; *para*—of the enemy; *sainyānām*—among the soldiers; *hṛdi*—in their hearts; *vitrāsa*—in terror; *vepathuḥ*—trembling.

TRANSLATION

As Lord Kṛṣṇa came out of the city with Dāruka at the reins of His chariot, He blew His conchshell, and the enemy soldiers' hearts began to tremble with fear.

TEXT 17

तावाह मागधो वीक्ष्य हे कृष्ण पुरुषाधम ।
न त्वया योद्धुमिच्छामि बालेनैकेन लज्जया ।
गुप्तेन हि त्वया मन्द न योत्स्ये याहि बन्धुहन् ॥१७॥

tāv āha māgadho vīkṣya
he kṛṣṇa puruṣādhama
na tvayā yoddhum icchāmi
bālenaikena lajjayā
guptena hi tvayā manda
na yotsye yāhi bandhu-han

tau—to the two of Them; *āha*—said; *māgadhaḥ*—Jarāsandha; *vīkṣya*—watching; *he kṛṣṇa*—O Kṛṣṇa; *puruṣa-adhama*—lowest of men; *na*—not; *tvayā*—with You; *yoddhum*—to fight; *icchāmi*—do I want; *bālena*—with a boy; *ekena*—alone; *lajjayā*—shamefully; *guptena*—hidden; *hi*—indeed; *tvayā*—with You; *manda*—O fool; *na yotsye*—I will not fight; *yāhi*—go away; *bandhu*—of relatives; *han*—O killer.

TRANSLATION

Jarāsandha looked at the two of Them and said: O Kṛṣṇa, lowest of men! I do not wish to fight alone with You, since it would be a shame to fight with a mere boy. You fool who keep Yourself hidden, O murderer of Your relatives, go away! I will not fight with You.

PURPORT

Śrīla Śrīdhara Svāmī has interpreted Jarāsandha's words as follows. *Puruṣādhama* can be understood as *puruṣā adhamā yasmāt,* meaning "Kṛṣṇa, to whom all men are inferior." In other words, here Lord Kṛṣṇa is being addressed as "O Puruṣottama, best of living beings." Similarly, the word *guptena,* "hidden," indicates Lord Kṛṣṇa's aspect of being in everyone's heart and invisible to material vision. The words *tvayā manda* can also be divided, according to Sanskrit grammar, as *tvayā amanda.* In this case Jarāsandha is indicating that Kṛṣṇa is not foolish but rather most alert. The word *bandhu* was used by Jarāsandha in the sense of "relative," since Lord Kṛṣṇa killed His maternal uncle, Kaṁsa. However, *bandhu* comes from the verb *bandh,* "to bind," and therefore *bandhu-han* can be understood as "one who destroys the bondage of ignorance." Similarly, the word *yāhi,* "please go," indicates that Lord Kṛṣṇa should approach the living beings and bless them to become Kṛṣṇa conscious.

TEXT 18

तव राम यदि श्रद्धा युध्यस्व धैर्यमुद्वह ।
हित्वा वा मच्छरैश्छिन्नं देहं स्वर्याहि मां जहि ॥१८॥

tava rāma yadi śraddhā
yudhyasva dhairyam udvaha
hitvā vā mac-charaiś chinnaṁ
dehaṁ svar yāhi māṁ jahi

tava—Your; *rāma*—O Balarāma; *yadi*—if; *śraddhā*—confidence; *yudhyasva*—fight; *dhairyam*—courage; *udvaha*—take up; *hitvā*—leaving aside; *vā*—either; *mat*—my; *śaraiḥ*—by the arrows; *chinnam*—cut to pieces; *deham*—Your body; *svaḥ*—to heaven; *yāhi*—go; *mām*—(or else) me; *jahi*—kill.

TRANSLATION

You, Rāma, should gather Your courage and fight with me, if You think You can do it. You may either give up Your body when it is cut to pieces by my arrows, and thus attain to heaven, or else kill me.

PURPORT

According to *ācārya* Śrīdhara Svāmī, Jarāsandha suspected that Lord Balarāma's body was indestructible, and thus he offered what might be a more practical alternative, that Balarāma kill Jarāsandha.

TEXT 19

श्रीभगवानुवाच
न वै शूरा विकत्थन्ते दर्शयन्त्येव पौरुषम् ।
न गृह्णीमो वचो राजन्नातुरस्य मुमूर्षतः ॥१९॥

śrī-bhagavān uvāca
na vai śūrā vikatthante
darśayanty eva pauruṣam
na gṛhṇīmo vaco rājann
āturasya mumūrṣataḥ

śrī-bhagavān uvāca—the Supreme Lord said; *na*—do not; *vai*—indeed; *śūrāḥ*—heroes; *vikatthante*—boast vainly; *darśayanti*—they show; *eva*—simply; *pauruṣam*—their prowess; *na gṛhṇīmaḥ*—We do not accept; *vacaḥ*—the words; *rājan*—O King; *āturasya*—of one who is mentally agitated; *mumūrṣataḥ*—who is about to die.

TRANSLATION

The Supreme Lord said: Real heroes do not simply boast but rather show their prowess in action. We cannot take seriously the words of one who is full of anxiety and who wants to die.

TEXT 20

श्रीशुक उवाच
जरासुतस्तावभिसृत्य माधवौ
महाबलौघेन बलीयसावृणोत् ।
ससैन्ययानध्वजवाजिसारथी
सूर्यानलौ वायुरिवाभ्ररेणुभिः ॥२०॥

śrī-śuka uvāca
jarā-sutas tāv abhisṛtya mādhavau
mahā-balaughena balīyasāvṛṇot
sa-sainya-yāna-dhvaja-vāji-sārathī
sūryānalau vāyur ivābhra-reṇubhiḥ

śrī-śukaḥ uvāca—Śukadeva Gosvāmī said; *jarā-sutaḥ*—the son of Jarā; *tau*—the two of Them; *abhisṛtya*—going up to; *mādhavau*—the descendants of Madhu; *mahā*—great; *bala*—of military prowess; *oghena*—with a flood; *balīyasā*—powerful; *āvṛṇot*—surrounded; *sa*—with; *sainya*—soldiers; *yāna*—chariots; *dhvaja*—flags; *vāji*—horses; *sārathī*—and charioteers; *sūrya*—the sun; *analau*—and a fire; *vāyuḥ*—the wind; *iva*—as; *abhra*—by clouds; *reṇubhiḥ*—and by particles of dust.

TRANSLATION

Śukadeva Gosvāmī said: Just as the wind covers the sun with clouds or a fire with dust, the son of Jarā marched toward the two descendants of Madhu and with his huge assemblage of armies surrounded Them and Their soldiers, chariots, flags, horses and charioteers.

PURPORT

Ācārya Śrīdhara points out that clouds only seem to cover the sun: the sun remains shining in the vast sky. Nor is the potency of fire affected by a thin covering of dust. Similarly, the "covering" of Jarāsandha's military strength was only apparent.

TEXT 21

सुपर्णतालध्वजचिह्नितौ रथाव्
अलक्षयन्त्यो हरिराममयोर्मृधे ।
स्त्रियः पुराट्टालकहर्म्यगोपुरं
समाश्रिताः सम्मुमुहुः शुचार्दिताः ॥२१॥

suparṇa-tāla-dhvaja-cihnitau rathāv
alakṣayantyo hari-rāmayor mṛdhe

striyaḥ purāṭṭālaka-harmya-gopuraṁ
samāśritāḥ sammumuhuḥ śucārditāḥ

suparṇa—with (the symbol of) Garuḍa (the bird who carries Lord Viṣṇu); *tāla*—and the palm tree; *dhvaja*—by the banners; *cihnitau*—marked; *rathau*—the two chariots; *alakṣayantyaḥ*—not identifying; *hari-rāmayoḥ*—of Kṛṣṇa and Balarāma; *mṛdhe*—in the battle; *striyaḥ*—women; *pura*—of the city; *aṭṭālaka*—in the watchtowers; *harmya*—palaces; *gopuram*—and in the gateways; *samāśritāḥ*—having taken positions; *sammumuhuḥ*—fainted; *śucā*—by grief; *arditāḥ*—tormented.

TRANSLATION

The women stood in the watchtowers, palaces and high gates of the city. When they could no longer see Kṛṣṇa's and Balarāma's chariots, identified by banners marked with the emblems of Garuḍa and a palm tree, they were struck with grief and fainted.

PURPORT

The women are especially mentioned here because of their extraordinary attachment to Lord Kṛṣṇa and Lord Balarāma.

TEXT 22

हरिः परानीकपयोमुचां मुहुः
शिलीमुखात्युल्बणवर्षपीडितम् ।
स्वसैन्यमालोक्य सुरासुरार्चितं
व्यस्फूर्जयच्छार्ंगशरासनोत्तमम् ॥२२॥

hariḥ parānīka-payomucāṁ muhuḥ
śilīmukhāty-ulbaṇa-varṣa-pīḍitam
sva-sainyam ālokya surāsurārcitaṁ
vyasphūrjayac chārṅga-śarāsanottamam

hariḥ—Lord Kṛṣṇa; *para*—of the enemy; *anīka*—of the armies; *payaḥ-mucām*—(which were like) clouds; *muhuḥ*—repeatedly;

śilīmukha—of their arrows; *ati*—extremely; *ulbaṇa*—fearsome; *varṣa*—by the rain; *pīḍitam*—pained; *sva*—His own; *sainyam*—army; *ālokya*—seeing; *sura*—by demigods; *asura*—and demons; *arcitam*—worshiped; *vyasphūrjayat*—He twanged; *śārṅga*—known as Śārṅga; *śara-asana*—His bow; *uttamam*—most excellent.

TRANSLATION

Seeing His army tormented by the relentless and savage rain of arrows from the massive opposing forces gathered like clouds about Him, Lord Hari twanged His excellent bow, Śārṅga, which both gods and demons worship.

TEXT 23

गृह्णन्निशंगादथ सन्दधच्छरान्
विकृष्य मुञ्चन् शितबाणपूगान् ।
निघ्नन् रथान् कुञ्जरवाजिपत्तीन्
निरन्तरं यद्वदलातचक्रम् ॥२३॥

gṛhṇan niśaṅgād atha sandadhac charān
vikṛṣya muñcan śita-bāṇa-pūgān
nighnan rathān kuñjara-vāji-pattīn
nirantaraṁ yadvad alāta-cakram

gṛhṇan—taking; *niśaṅgāt*—from His quiver; *atha*—then; *sandadhat*—fixing; *śarān*—arrows; *vikṛṣya*—pulling back; *muñcan*—releasing; *śita*—sharp; *bāṇa*—of arrows; *pūgān*—floods; *nighnan*—striking; *rathān*—chariots; *kuñjara*—elephants; *vāji*—horses; *pattīn*—and infantrymen; *nirantaram*—relentlessly; *yadvat*—just like; *alāta-cakram*—a burning torch whirled around to make a circle of fire.

TRANSLATION

Lord Kṛṣṇa took arrows from His quiver, fixed them on the bowstring, pulled back, and released endless torrents of sharp shafts, which struck the enemy's chariots, elephants, horses and infantrymen. The Lord shooting His arrows resembled a blazing circle of fire.

TEXT 24

निर्भिन्नकुम्भाः करिणो निपेतुर्
अनेकशोऽश्वाः शरवृक्णकन्धराः ।
रथा हताश्वध्वजसूतनायकाः
पदायतश्छिन्नभुजोरुकन्धराः ॥२४॥

nirbhinna-kumbhāḥ kariṇo nipetur
anekaśo 'śvāḥ śara-vṛkṇa-kandharāḥ
rathā hatāśva-dhvaja-sūta-nāyakāḥ
padāyataś chinna-bhujoru-kandharāḥ

nirbhinna—split; *kumbhāḥ*—the protuberances of their foreheads; *kariṇaḥ*—elephants; *nipetuḥ*—fell; *anekaśaḥ*—many at a time; *aśvāḥ*—horses; *śara*—by the arrows; *vṛkṇa*—severed; *kandharāḥ*—whose necks; *rathāḥ*—chariots; *hata*—struck; *aśva*—whose horses; *dhvaja*—flags; *sūta*—drivers; *nāyakāḥ*—and masters; *padāyataḥ*—foot soldiers; *chinna*—cut; *bhuja*—whose arms; *ūru*—thighs; *kandharāḥ*—and shoulders.

TRANSLATION

Elephants fell to the ground, their foreheads split open, cavalry horses fell with severed necks, chariots fell with their horses, flags, drivers and masters all shattered, and foot soldiers collapsed with severed arms, thighs and shoulders.

TEXTS 25–28

सञ्छिद्यमानद्विपदेभवाजिनाम्
अंगप्रसूताः शतशोऽसृगापगाः ।
भुजाहयः पूरुषशीर्षकच्छपा
हतद्विपद्वीपहयग्रहाकुलाः ॥२५॥
करोरुमीना नरकेशशैवला
धनुस्तरंगायुधगुल्मसंकुलाः ।

अच्छूरिकावर्तभयानका महा-
मणिप्रवेकाभरणाश्मशर्कराः ॥२६॥
प्रवर्तिता भीरुभयावहा मृधे
मनस्विनां हर्षकरीः परस्परम् ।
विनिघ्नतारीन्मुषलेन दुर्मदान्
संकर्षणेनापरिमेयतेजसा ॥२७॥
बलं तदंगार्णवदुर्गभैरवं
दुरन्तपारं मगधेन्द्रपालितम् ।
क्षयं प्रणीतं वसुदेवपुत्रयोर्
विक्रीडितं तज्जगदीशयोः परम् ॥२८॥

sañchidyamāna-dvipadebha-vājinām
aṅga-prasūtāḥ śataśo 'sṛg-āpagāḥ
bhujāhayaḥ pūruṣa-śīrṣa-kacchapā
hata-dvipa-dvīpa-haya-grahākulāḥ

karoru-mīnā nara-keśa-śaivalā
dhanus-taraṅgāyudha-gulma-saṅkulāḥ
acchūrikāvarta-bhayānakā mahā-
maṇi-pravekābharaṇāśma-śarkarāḥ

pravartitā bhīru-bhayāvahā mṛdhe
manasvināṁ harṣa-karīḥ parasparam
vinighnatārīn muṣalena durmadān
saṅkarṣaṇenāparimeya-tejasā

balaṁ tad aṅgārṇava-durga-bhairavaṁ
duranta-pāraṁ magadhendra-pālitam
kṣayaṁ praṇītaṁ vasudeva-putrayor
vikrīḍitaṁ taj jagad-īśayoḥ param

sañchidyamāna—being cut to pieces; *dvi-pada*—of the two-legged (humans); *ibha*—elephants; *vājinām*—and horses; *aṅga*—from the limbs; *prasūtāḥ*—flowing; *śataśaḥ*—by the hundreds; *asṛk*—of blood; *āpa-gāḥ*—rivers; *bhuja*—arms; *ahayaḥ*—as the snakes; *pūruṣa*—of men;

śīrṣa—heads; *kacchapāḥ*—as the turtles; *hata*—dead; *dvipa*—with elephants; *dvīpa*—as islands; *haya*—and with horses; *graha*—as crocodiles; *ākulāḥ*—filled; *kara*—hands; *ūru*—and thighs; *mīnāḥ*—as the fish; *nara*—human; *keśa*—hair; *śaivalāḥ*—as the aquatic weeds; *dhanuḥ*—with bows; *taraṅga*—as the waves; *āyudha*—and with weapons; *gulma*—as the clumps of bushes; *saṅkulāḥ*—crowded; *acchūrikā*—chariot wheels; *āvarta*—as the whirlpools; *bhayānakāḥ*—fearful; *mahā-maṇi*—precious gems; *praveka*—excellent; *ābharaṇa*—and ornaments; *aśma*—as the stones; *śarkarāḥ*—and gravel; *pravartitāḥ*—issuing forth; *bhīru*—for the timid; *bhaya-āvahāḥ*—terrifying; *mṛdhe*—on the battlefield; *manasvinām*—for the intelligent; *harṣa-karīḥ*—inspiring joy; *parasparam*—from one to another; *vinighnatā*—who was striking down; *arīn*—His enemies; *muṣalena*—with His plow weapon; *durmadān*—who were furious; *saṅkarṣaṇena*—by Lord Balarāma; *aparimeya*—immeasurable; *tejasā*—whose potency; *balam*—military force; *tat*—that; *aṅga*—my dear (King Parīkṣit); *arṇava*—like the ocean; *durga*—unfathomable; *bhairavam*—and frightening; *duranta*—impossible to cross over; *pāram*—whose limit; *magadha-indra*—by the King of Magadha, Jarāsandha; *pālitam*—overseen; *kṣayam*—to destruction; *praṇītam*—led; *vasudeva-putrayoḥ*—for the sons of Vasudeva; *vikrīḍitam*—play; *tat*—that; *jagat*—of the universe; *īśayoḥ*—for the Lords; *param*—at most.

TRANSLATION

On the battlefield, hundreds of rivers of blood flowed from the limbs of the humans, elephants and horses who had been cut to pieces. In these rivers arms resembled snakes; human heads, turtles; dead elephants, islands; and dead horses, crocodiles. Hands and thighs appeared like fish, human hair like waterweeds, bows like waves, and various weapons like clumps of bushes. The rivers of blood teemed with all of these.

Chariot wheels looked like terrifying whirlpools, and precious gems and ornaments resembled stones and gravel in the rushing red rivers, which aroused fear in the timid, joy in the wise. With the blows of His plow weapon the immeasurably powerful Lord Balarāma destroyed Magadhendra's military force. And though this force was as unfathomable and fearsome as an impassable ocean, for the two sons of Vasudeva, the Lords of the universe, the battle was hardly more than play.

TEXT 29

स्थित्युद्भवान्तं भुवनत्रयस्य यः
समीहितेऽनन्तगुणः स्वलीलया ।
न तस्य चित्रं परपक्षनिग्रहस्
तथापि मर्त्यानुविधस्य वर्ण्यते ॥२९॥

sthity-udbhavāntaṁ bhuvana-trayasya yaḥ
samīhite 'nanta-guṇaḥ sva-līlayā
na tasya citraṁ para-pakṣa-nigrahas
tathāpi martyānuvidhasya varṇyate

sthiti—the maintenance; *udbhava*—creation; *antam*—and annihilation; *bhuvana-trayasya*—of the three worlds; *yaḥ*—who; *samīhite*—effects; *ananta*—unlimited; *guṇaḥ*—whose transcendental qualities; *sva-līlayā*—as His own pastime; *na*—not; *tasya*—for Him; *citram*—wonderful; *para*—opposing; *pakṣa*—of the party; *nigrahaḥ*—the subduing; *tathā api*—nevertheless; *martya*—human beings; *anuvidhasya*—who is imitating; *varṇyate*—it is described.

TRANSLATION

For Him who orchestrates the creation, maintenance and destruction of the three worlds and who possesses unlimited spiritual qualities, it is hardly amazing that He subdues an opposing party. Still, when the Lord does so, imitating human behavior, sages glorify His acts.

PURPORT

The philosopher Aristotle once argued that the Supreme God would hardly take part in human activities, since all ordinary activities are unworthy of such a divine being. Similarly, Śrīla Viśvanātha Cakravartī, who almost certainly never read the works of Aristotle, raises a similar point. Since Śrī Kṛṣṇa creates, maintains and annihilates the entire universe, isn't it an uninteresting mismatch when He fights against Jarāsandha?

The answer is as follows: The Lord plays the part of a human being and, expanding His pleasure potency, creates thrilling transcendental pastimes full of suspense and dynamic action. By the Lord's Yogamāyā potency, He appears exactly like a human being, and thus we may enjoy the spectacle of the Supreme Person acting on the earthly stage. Undoubtedly, stubborn agnostics will argue that since Kṛṣṇa is God, there is no real suspense involved. Such skeptics simply do not understand Kṛṣṇa's attractive potency. Beauty and drama, even on the material stage, possess their own fascinating logic, and similarly we love Kṛṣṇa for His own sake, we appreciate His beauty for its own sake, and we enjoy Kṛṣṇa's pastimes because they are in fact wonderful in and of themselves. In fact, Kṛṣṇa executes His pastimes not for a mundane egotistical purpose but for our pleasure. Thus the presentation of spiritual pastimes is itself an act of love that Kṛṣṇa performs for the infinite spiritual happiness of pure-hearted souls who have transcended material envy of the Godhead.

In this regard, Śrīla Viśvanātha Cakravartī quotes an important verse from the *Gopāla-tāpanī Upaniṣad: narākṛti para-brahma kāraṇa-mānuṣaḥ.* "The Supreme Absolute Truth, for His own purpose, appears in a human-like form, although He is the source of everthing." Similarly, in the *Śrīmad-Bhāgavatam* (10.14.32) we find, *yan-mitraṁ paramānandaṁ pūrṇaṁ brahma sanātanam:* "The source of transcendental bliss, the eternal Supreme Brahman, has become their friend."

TEXT 30

जग्राह विरथं रामो जरासन्धं महाबलम् ।
हतानीकावशिष्टासुं सिंहः सिंहमिवौजसा ॥३०॥

jagrāha virathaṁ rāmo
jarāsandhaṁ mahā-balam
hatānīkāvaśiṣṭāsuṁ
siṁhaḥ siṁham ivaujasā

jagrāha—He seized; *viratham*—who was deprived of his chariot; *rāmaḥ*—Lord Balarāma; *jarāsandham*—Jarāsandha; *mahā*—very; *balam*—strong; *hata*—killed; *anīka*—whose army; *avaśiṣṭa*—remaining; *asum*—whose breath; *siṁhaḥ*—a lion; *siṁham*—another lion; *iva*—as; *ojasā*—forcibly.

TRANSLATION

Jarāsandha, with his chariot lost and all his soldiers dead, was left with only his breath. At that point Lord Balarāma forcibly seized the powerful warrior, just as one lion takes hold of another.

TEXT 31

बध्यमानं हतारातिं पाशैर्वारुणमानुषैः ।
वारयामास गोविन्दस्तेन कार्यचिकीर्षया ॥३१॥

badhyamānaṁ hatārātiṁ
pāśair vāruṇa-mānuṣaiḥ
vārayām āsa govindas
tena kārya-cikīrṣayā

badhyamānam—in the process of being tied up; *hata*—who had killed; *arātim*—his enemies; *pāśaiḥ*—with ropes; *vāruṇa*—those of the demigod Varuṇa; *mānuṣaiḥ*—and those of ordinary humans; *vārayām āsa*—checked Him; *govindaḥ*—Lord Kṛṣṇa; *tena*—by him (Jarāsandha); *kārya*—some need; *cikīrṣayā*—desiring to fulfill.

TRANSLATION

With the divine noose of Varuṇa and other, mortal ropes, Balarāma began tying up Jarāsandha, who had killed so many foes. But Lord Govinda still had a purpose to fulfill through Jarāsandha, and thus He asked Balarāma to stop.

PURPORT

The word *hatārātim* means "who has killed his enemies," or "through whom his enemies would be killed." Śrīla Viśvanātha Cakravartī has provided this thoughtful note.

TEXTS 32–33

स मुक्तो लोकनाथाभ्यां व्रीडितो वीरसम्मतः ।
तपसे कृतसंकल्पो वारितः पथि राजभिः ॥३२॥

वाक्यैः पवित्रार्थपदैर्नयनैः प्राकृतैरपि ।
स्वकर्मबन्धप्राप्तोऽयं यदुभिस्ते पराभवः ॥३३॥

sa mukto loka-nāthābhyāṁ
vrīḍito vīra-sammataḥ
tapase kṛta-saṅkalpo
vāritaḥ pathi rājabhiḥ

vākyaiḥ pavitrārtha-padair
nayanaiḥ prākṛtair api
sva-karma-bandha-prāpto 'yaṁ
yadubhis te parābhavaḥ

saḥ—he, Jarāsandha; *muktaḥ*—freed; *loka-nāthābhyām*—by the two Lords of the universe; *vrīḍitaḥ*—ashamed; *vīra*—by heroes; *sammataḥ*—honored; *tapase*—to perform austerities; *kṛta-saṅkalpaḥ*—having made up his mind; *vāritaḥ*—was stopped; *pathi*—on the road; *rājabhiḥ*—by kings; *vākyaiḥ*—with statements; *pavitra*—purifying; *artha*—having meanings; *padaiḥ*—with words; *nayanaiḥ*—with reasoning; *prākṛtaiḥ*—mundane; *api*—also; *sva*—own; *karma-bandha*—due to the unavoidable reactions of past work; *prāptaḥ*—obtained; *ayam*—this; *yadubhiḥ*—by the Yadus; *te*—your; *parābhavaḥ*—defeat.

TRANSLATION

Jarāsandha, whom fighters had highly honored, was ashamed after being released by the two Lords of the universe, and thus he decided to undergo penances. On the road, however, several kings convinced him with both spiritual wisdom and mundane arguments that he should give up his idea of self-abnegation. They told him, "Your defeat by the Yadus was simply the unavoidable reaction of your past *karma*."

TEXT 34

हतेषु सर्वानीकेषु नृपो बार्हद्रथस्तदा ।
उपेक्षितो भगवता मगधान् दुर्मना ययौ ॥३४॥

hateṣu sarvānīkeṣu
nṛpo bārhadrathas tadā
upekṣito bhagavatā
magadhān durmanā yayau

hateṣu—having been killed; *sarva*—all; *anīkeṣu*—the soldiers of his armies; *nṛpaḥ*—the king; *bārhadrathaḥ*—Jarāsandha, the son of Bṛhadratha; *tadā*—then; *upekṣitaḥ*—neglected; *bhagavatā*—by the Supreme Lord; *magadhān*—to the Magadha kingdom; *durmanāḥ*—depressed; *yayau*—he went.

TRANSLATION

All of his armies having been killed, and himself neglected by the Personality of Godhead, King Jarāsandha, son of Bṛhadratha, then sadly returned to the kingdom of the Magadhas.

TEXTS 35–36

मुकुन्दोऽप्यक्षतबलो निस्तीर्णारिबलार्णवः ।
विकीर्यमाणः कुसुमैस्त्रिदशैरनुमोदितः ॥३५॥
माथुरैरुपसंगम्य विज्वरैर्मुदितात्मभिः ।
उपगीयमानविजयः सूतमागधवन्दिभिः ॥३६॥

mukundo 'py akṣata-balo
nistīrṇāri-balārṇavaḥ
vikīryamāṇaḥ kusumais
tridaśair anumoditaḥ

māthurair upasaṅgamya
vijvarair muditātmabhiḥ
upagīyamāna-vijayaḥ
sūta-māgadha-vandibhiḥ

mukundaḥ—Lord Kṛṣṇa; *api*—and; *akṣata*—unbroken; *balaḥ*—His military force; *nistīrṇa*—having crossed over; *ari*—of His enemy; *bala*—of the armies; *arṇavaḥ*—the ocean; *vikīryamāṇaḥ*—having scattered upon Him; *kusumaiḥ*—flowers; *tridaśaiḥ*—by the demigods; *anumoditaḥ*—congratulated; *māthuraiḥ*—by the people of Mathurā; *upasaṅgamya*—being met; *vijvaraiḥ*—who were relieved of their fever; *mudita-ātmabhiḥ*—who felt great joy; *upagīyamāna*—being sung about; *vijayaḥ*—His victory; *sūta*—by Purāṇic bards; *māgadha*—panegyrists; *vandibhiḥ*—and heralds.

TRANSLATION

Lord Mukunda had crossed the ocean of His enemy's armies with His own military force completely intact. He received congratulations from the denizens of heaven, who showered Him with flowers. The people of Mathurā, relieved of their feverish anxiety and filled with joy, came out to meet Him as professional bards, heralds and panegyrists sang in praise of His victory.

TEXTS 37–38

शंखदुन्दुभयो नेदुर्भेरीतूर्याण्यनेकशः ।
वीणावेणुमृदंगानि पुरं प्रविशति प्रभौ ॥३७॥
सिक्तमार्गां हृष्टजनां पताकाभिरभ्यलंकृताम् ।
निर्घुष्टां ब्रह्मघोषेण कौतुकाबद्धतोरणाम् ॥३८॥

śaṅkha-dundubhayo nedur
bherī-tūryāṇy anekaśaḥ
vīṇā-veṇu-mṛdaṅgāni
puraṁ praviśati prabhau

sikta-mārgāṁ hṛṣṭa-janāṁ
patākābhir abhyalaṅkṛtām
nirghuṣṭāṁ brahma-ghoṣeṇa
kautukābaddha-toraṇām

śaṅkha—conchshells; *dundubhayaḥ*—and kettledrums; *neduḥ*—sounded; *bherī*—drums; *tūryāṇi*—and horns; *anekaśaḥ*—many at once; *vīṇā-veṇu-mṛdaṅgāni*—*vīṇās,* flutes and *mṛdaṅga* drums; *puram*—the city

(Mathurā); *praviśati*—as He entered; *prabhau*—the Lord; *sikta*—sprinkled with water; *mārgām*—its boulevards; *hṛṣṭa*—joyful; *janām*—its citizens; *patākābhiḥ*—with banners; *abhyalaṅkṛtām*—abundantly decorated; *nirghuṣṭām*—resounding; *brahma*—of the *Vedas; ghoṣeṇa*—with chanting; *kautuka*—festive; *ābaddha*—ornaments; *toraṇām*—on its gateways.

TRANSLATION

As the Lord entered His city, conchshells and kettledrums sounded, and many drums, horns, *vīṇās,* flutes and *mṛdaṅgas* played in concert. The boulevards were sprinkled with water, there were banners everywhere, and the gateways were decorated for the celebration. The citizens were elated, and the city resounded with the chanting of Vedic hymns.

TEXT 39

निचीयमानो नारीभिर्माल्यदध्यक्षतांकुरैः ।
निरीक्ष्यमाणः सस्नेहं प्रीत्युत्कलितलोचनैः ॥३९॥

nicīyamāno nārībhir
mālya-dadhy-akṣatāṅkuraiḥ
nirīkṣyamāṇaḥ sa-snehaṁ
prīty-utkalita-locanaiḥ

nicīyamānaḥ—having scattered upon Him; *nārībhiḥ*—by the women; *mālya*—flower garlands; *dadhi*—yogurt; *akṣata*—parched rice; *aṅkuraiḥ*—and sprouts; *nirīkṣyamāṇaḥ*—being looked on; *sa-sneham*—affectionately; *prīti*—out of love; *utkalita*—opened wide; *locanaiḥ*—with eyes.

TRANSLATION

As the women of the city affectionately looked at the Lord, their eyes wide open with love, they scattered flower garlands, yogurt, parched rice and newly grown sprouts upon Him.

PURPORT

All this is taking place as Lord Kṛṣṇa enters the city of Mathurā.

TEXT 40

आयोधनगतं वित्तमनन्तं वीरभूषणम् ।
यदुराजाय तत्सर्वमाहृतं प्रादिशत्प्रभुः ॥४०॥

āyodhana-gataṁ vittam
anantaṁ vīra-bhūṣaṇam
yadu-rājāya tat sarvam
āhṛtaṁ prādiśat prabhuḥ

āyodhana-gatam—fallen on the battlefield; *vittam*—the valuables; *anantam*—countless; *vīra*—of the heroes; *bhūṣaṇam*—the ornaments; *yadu-rājāya*—to the King of the Yadus, Ugrasena; *tat*—that; *sarvam*—all; *āhṛtam*—which was brought; *prādiśat*—presented; *prabhuḥ*—the Lord.

TRANSLATION

Lord Kṛṣṇa then presented to the Yadu king all the wealth that had fallen on the battlefield—namely, the countless ornaments of the dead warriors.

PURPORT

Śrīla Viśvanātha Cakravartī adds that jeweled ornaments had also been collected from the horses and other animals. What might be added here, for the sake of the squeamish, is that Jarāsandha came to Mathurā with the clear intention of slaughtering every last man in the city, including Kṛṣṇa and Balarāma. It is out of the causeless mercy of the Lord that He gives the conditioned souls a taste of their own medicine and thus helps them become more sensitive to the laws of nature and the existence of a Supreme Godhead. Ultimately, Kṛṣṇa awarded Jarāsandha and others killed on the battlefield spiritual liberation. The Lord is strict, but He is not malicious. In fact, He is an ocean of mercy.

TEXT 41

एवं सप्तदशकृत्वस्तावत्यक्षौहिणीबलः ।
युयुधे मागधो राजा यदुभिः कृष्णपालितैः ॥४१॥

evaṁ saptadaśa-kṛtvas
tāvaty akṣauhiṇī-balaḥ
yuyudhe māgadho rājā
yadubhiḥ kṛṣṇa-pālitaiḥ

evam—in this way; *sapta-daśa*—seventeen; *kṛtvaḥ*—times; *tāvati*—even thus (being defeated); *akṣauhiṇī*—consisting of entire divisions; *balaḥ*—His military strength; *yuyudhe*—fought; *māgadhaḥ rājā*—the King of Magadha; *yadubhiḥ*—with the Yadus; *kṛṣṇa-pālitaiḥ*—protected by Kṛṣṇa.

TRANSLATION

Seventeen times the King of Magadha met defeat in this very way. And yet throughout these defeats he fought on with his *akṣauhiṇī* divisions against the forces of the Yadu dynasty, who were protected by Śrī Kṛṣṇa.

TEXT 42

अक्षिण्वंस्तद्बलं सर्वं वृष्णयः कृष्णतेजसा ।
हतेषु स्वेष्वनीकेषु त्यक्तोऽगादरिभिर्नृपः ॥४२॥

akṣiṇvaṁs tad-balaṁ sarvaṁ
vṛṣṇayaḥ kṛṣṇa-tejasā
hateṣu sveṣv anīkeṣu
tyakto 'gād aribhir nṛpaḥ

akṣiṇvan—they destroyed; *tat*—his; *balam*—force; *sarvam*—entire; *vṛṣṇayaḥ*—the Vṛṣṇis; *kṛṣṇa-tejasā*—by the power of Lord Kṛṣṇa; *hateṣu*—when they were dead; *sveṣu*—his; *anīkeṣu*—soldiers; *tyaktaḥ*—abandoned; *agāt*—went away; *aribhiḥ*—by his enemies; *nṛpaḥ*—the King, Jarāsandha.

TRANSLATION

By the power of Lord Kṛṣṇa, the Vṛṣṇis would invariably annihilate all of Jarāsandha's forces, and when all his soldiers had been killed, the King, released by his enemies, would again go away.

TEXT 43

अष्टादशमसंग्राम आगामिनि तदन्तरा ।
नारदप्रेषितो वीरो यवनः प्रत्यदृश्यत ॥४३॥

aṣṭādaśama-saṅgrāma
āgāmini tad-antarā
nārada-preṣito vīro
yavanaḥ pratyadṛśyata

aṣṭā-daśama—the eighteenth; *saṅgrāme*—battle; *āgāmini*—being about to happen; *tat-antarā*—at that instant; *nārada*—by the sage Nārada; *preṣitaḥ*—sent; *vīraḥ*—a fighter; *yavanaḥ*—a barbarian (named Kālayavana); *pratyadṛśyata*—appeared.

TRANSLATION

Just as the eighteenth battle was about to take place, a barbarian warrior named Kālayavana, sent by Nārada, appeared on the battlefield.

TEXT 44

रुरोध मथुरामेत्य तिसृभिर्म्लेच्छकोटिभिः ।
नृलोके चाप्रतिद्वन्द्वो वृष्णीन् श्रुत्वात्मसम्मितान् ॥४४॥

rurodha mathurām etya
tisṛbhir mleccha-koṭibhiḥ
nṛ-loke cāpratidvandvo
vṛṣṇīn śrutvātma-sammitān

rurodha—he besieged; *mathurām*—Mathurā; *etya*—arriving there; *tisṛbhiḥ*—times three; *mleccha*—with barbarians; *koṭibhiḥ*—ten million;

nṛ-loke—among mankind; *ca*—and; *apratidvandvaḥ*—having no suitable rival; *vṛṣṇīn*—the Vṛṣṇis; *śrutvā*—hearing; *ātma*—to himself; *sam-mitān*—comparable.

TRANSLATION

Arriving at Mathurā, this Yavana laid siege to the city with thirty million barbarian soldiers. He had never found a human rival worth fighting, but he had heard that the Vṛṣṇis were his equals.

PURPORT

Śrīla Viśvanātha Cakravartī quotes from the *Viṣṇu Purāṇa* concerning the history of Kālayavana: "Once, Gārgya was ridiculed by his brother-in-law as a eunuch, and when the Yādavas heard this they laughed heartily. Infuriated by their laughter, Gārgya set out for the south, thinking, 'May I have a son who will bring terror to the Yādavas.' He worshiped Lord Mahādeva, eating powdered iron, and after twelve years obtained his desired benediction. Elated, he returned home.

"Later, when the childless King of the Yavanas requested a son from him, Gārgya begot in the Yavana's wife a son, Kālayavana. Kālayavana possessed the fury of Lord Śiva in his aspect as Mahākāla. Once, Kālayavana asked Nārada, 'Who are now the strongest kings on earth?' Nārada replied that the Yadus were. Thus sent by Nārada, Kālayavana appeared at Mathurā."

TEXT 45

तं दृष्ट्वाचिन्तयत्कृष्णः संकर्षणसहायवान् ।
अहो यदूनां वृजिनं प्राप्तं ह्युभयतो महत् ॥४५॥

taṁ dṛṣṭvācintayat kṛṣṇaḥ
saṅkarṣaṇa-sahāyavān
aho yadūnāṁ vṛjinaṁ
prāptaṁ hy ubhayato mahat

tam—him; *dṛṣṭvā*—seeing; *acintayat*—thought; *kṛṣṇaḥ*—Lord Kṛṣṇa; *saṅkarṣaṇa*—by Lord Balarāma; *sahāya-vān*—assisted; *aho*—ah; *yadū-*

nām—for the Yadus; *vṛjinam*—a problem; *prāptam*—arrived; *hi*—indeed; *ubhayataḥ*—from both sides (from Kālayavana and also from Jarāsandha); *mahat*—great.

TRANSLATION

When Lord Kṛṣṇa and Lord Saṅkarṣaṇa saw Kālayavana, Kṛṣṇa thought about the situation and said, "Ah, a great danger now threatens the Yadus from two sides.

PURPORT

We may note here that although Śrī Kṛṣṇa had defeated Jarāsandha seventeen times against tremendous odds, He did not immediately annihilate the army of Kālayavana, thus keeping intact the benediction granted to Gargya by Lord Śiva, as explained in the previous purport.

TEXT 46

यवनोऽयं निरुन्धेऽस्मानद्य तावन्महाबलः ।
मागधोऽप्यद्य वा श्वो वा परश्वो वागमिष्यति ॥४६॥

yavano 'yaṁ nirundhe 'smān
adya tāvan mahā-balaḥ
māgadho 'py adya vā śvo vā
paraśvo vāgamiṣyati

yavanaḥ—foreign barbarian; *ayam*—this; *nirundhe*—is opposing; *asmān*—us; *adya*—today; *tāvat*—as much; *mahā-balaḥ*—greatly powerful; *māgadhaḥ*—Jarāsandha; *api*—also; *adya*—today; *vā*—or; *śvaḥ*—tomorrow; *vā*—or; *para-śvaḥ*—the day after tomorrow; *vā*—or; *āgamiṣyati*—will come.

TRANSLATION

"This Yavana is besieging us already, and the mighty King of Magadha will soon arrive here, if not today then tomorrow or the next day.

TEXT 47

आवयोः युध्यतोरस्य यद्यागन्ता जरासुतः ।
बन्धून् हनिष्यत्यथ वा नेष्यते स्वपुरं बली ॥४७॥

āvayoḥ yudhyator asya
yady āgantā jarā-sutaḥ
bandhūn haniṣyaty atha vā
neṣyate sva-puraṁ balī

āvayoḥ—the two of Us; *yudhyatoḥ*—while fighting; *asya*—with him (Kālayavana); *yadi*—if; *āgantā*—comes; *jarā-sutaḥ*—the son of Jarā; *bandhūn*—Our relatives; *haniṣyati*—he will kill; *atha vā*—or else; *neṣyate*—he will take; *sva*—to his own; *puram*—city; *balī*—strong.

TRANSLATION

"If powerful Jarāsandha comes while We two are busy fighting Kālayavana, Jarāsandha may kill Our relatives or else take them away to his capital.

TEXT 48

तस्मादद्य विधास्यामो दुर्गं द्विपददुर्गमम् ।
तत्र ज्ञातीन् समाधाय यवनं घातयामहे ॥४८॥

tasmād adya vidhāsyāmo
durgaṁ dvipada-durgamam
tatra jñātīn samādhāya
yavanaṁ ghātayāmahe

tasmāt—therefore; *adya*—today; *vidhāsyāmaḥ*—We will construct; *durgam*—a fortress; *dvipada*—to humans; *durgamam*—insurmountable; *tatra*—there; *jñātīn*—Our family members; *samādhāya*—settling; *yavanam*—the barbarian; *ghātayāmahe*—We will kill.

TRANSLATION

"Therefore We will immediately construct a fortress that no human force can penetrate. Let Us settle our family members there and then kill the barbarian king."

TEXT 49

इति सम्मन्त्र्य भगवान् दुर्गं द्वादशयोजनम् ।
अन्तःसमुद्रे नगरं कृत्स्नाद्भुतमचीकरत् ॥४९॥

iti sammantrya bhagavān
durgaṁ dvādaśa-yojanam
antaḥ-samudre nagaraṁ
kṛtsnādbhutam acīkarat

iti—thus; *sammantrya*—consulting; *bhagavān*—the Supreme Personality of Godhead; *durgam*—a fortress; *dvādaśa-yojanam*—twelve *yojanas* (about one hundred miles); *antaḥ*—within; *samudre*—the sea; *nagaram*—a city; *kṛtsna*—with everything; *adbhutam*—wonderful; *acīkarat*—He had made.

TRANSLATION

After thus discussing the matter with Balarāma, the Supreme Personality of Godhead had a fortress twelve *yojanas* in circumference built within the sea. Inside that fort He had a city built containing all kinds of wonderful things.

TEXTS 50–53

दृश्यते यत्र हि त्वाष्ट्रं विज्ञानं शिल्पनैपुणम् ।
रथ्याचत्वरवीथीभिर्यथावास्तु विनिर्मितम् ॥५०॥
सुरद्रुमलतोद्यानविचित्रोपवनान्वितम् ।
हेमशृंगैर्दिविस्पृग्भिः स्फटिकाट्टालगोपुरैः ॥५१॥
राजतारकुटैः कोष्ठैर्हेमकुम्भैरलंकृतैः ।
रत्नकूतैर्गृहैर्हेमैर्महामारकतस्थलैः ॥५२॥

वास्तोष्पतीनां च गृहैर्वल्लभीभिश्च निर्मितम् ।
चातुर्वर्ण्यजनाकीर्णं यदुदेवगृहोल्लसत् ॥५३॥

dṛśyate yatra hi tvāṣṭraṁ
vijñānaṁ śilpa-naipuṇam
rathyā-catvara-vīthībhir
yathā-vāstu vinirmitam

sura-druma-latodyāna-
vicitropavanānvitam
hema-śṛṅgair divi-spṛgbhiḥ
sphaṭikāṭṭāla-gopuraiḥ

rājatārakuṭaiḥ koṣṭhair
hema-kumbhair alaṅkṛtaiḥ
ratna-kūtair gṛhair hemair
mahā-mārakata-sthalaiḥ

vāstoṣpatīnāṁ ca gṛhair
vallabhībhiś ca nirmitam
cātur-varṇya-janākīrṇaṁ
yadu-deva-gṛhollasat

dṛśyate—was seen; *yatra*—wherein; *hi*—indeed; *tvāṣṭram*—of Tvaṣṭā (Viśvakarmā), the architect of the demigods; *vijñānam*—the scientific knowledge; *śilpa*—in architecture; *naipuṇam*—the expertise; *rathyā*—with main avenues; *catvara*—courtyards; *vīthībhiḥ*—and commercial roads; *yathā-vāstu*—on ample plots of land; *vinirmitam*—constructed; *sura*—of the demigods; *druma*—having trees; *latā*—and creepers; *udyāna*—gardens; *vicitra*—splendid; *upavana*—and parks; *anvitam*—containing; *hema*—gold; *śṛṅgaiḥ*—having peaks; *divi*—the sky; *spṛgbhiḥ*—touching; *sphaṭikā*—of crystal quartz; *aṭṭāla*—having upper levels; *gopuraiḥ*—with gateways; *rājata*—of silver; *ārakuṭaiḥ*—and brass; *koṣṭhaiḥ*—with treasury buildings, warehouses and stables; *hema*—gold; *kumbhaiḥ*—by pots; *alaṅkṛtaiḥ*—decorated; *ratna*—jeweled; *kūtaiḥ*—having peaks; *gṛhaiḥ*—with houses; *hemaiḥ*—of gold; *mahā-mārakata*—with precious emeralds; *sthalaiḥ*—having floors; *vāstoḥ*—of the households; *patīnām*—belonging to the presiding deities;

ca—and; *gṛhaiḥ*—with temples; *vallabhībhiḥ*—with watchtowers; *ca*—and; *nirmitam*—constructed; *cātuḥ-varṇya*—of the four occupational orders; *jana*—with people; *ākīrṇam*—filled; *yadu-deva*—of the Lord of the Yadus, Śrī Kṛṣṇa; *gṛha*—by the residences; *ullasat*—beautified.

TRANSLATION

In the construction of that city could be seen the full scientific knowledge and architectural skill of Viśvakarmā. There were wide avenues, commercial roads and courtyards laid out on ample plots of land; there were splendid parks, and also gardens stocked with trees and creepers from the heavenly planets. The gateway towers were topped with golden turrets touching the sky, and their upper levels were fashioned of crystal quartz. The gold-covered houses were adorned in front with golden pots and on top with jeweled roofs, and their floors were inlaid with precious emeralds. Beside the houses stood treasury buildings, warehouses, and stables for fine horses, all built of silver and brass. Each residence had a watchtower, and also a temple for its household deity. Filled with citizens of all four social orders, the city was especially beautified by the palaces of Śrī Kṛṣṇa, the Lord of the Yadus.

PURPORT

Śrīla Śrīdhara Svāmī explains that the state highways (*rathyāḥ*) were in front and the secondary roads (*vīthyaḥ*) behind, and between them were courtyards (*catvarāṇi*). Within these courtyards were surrounding walls, and within the walls stood golden residences, atop which shone crystal watchtowers crowned with golden pots. Thus the buildings were multistoried. The word *vāstu* indicates that the houses and buildings were constructed on ample plots of land, with plenty of room for green areas.

TEXT 54

सुधर्मां पारिजातं च महेन्द्रः प्राहिणोद्धरेः ।
यत्र चावस्थितो मर्त्यो मर्त्यधर्मैर्न युज्यते ॥५४॥

sudharmāṁ pārijātaṁ ca
mahendraḥ prāhiṇod dhareḥ
yatra cāvasthito martyo
martya-dharmair na yujyate

sudharmām—the Sudharmā assembly hall; *pārijātam*—the *pārijāta* tree; *ca*—and; *mahā-indraḥ*—Lord Indra, King of heaven; *prāhiṇot*—delivered; *hareḥ*—to Lord Kṛṣṇa; *yatra*—in which (Sudharmā); *ca*—and; *avasthitaḥ*—situated; *martyaḥ*—a mortal; *martya-dharmaiḥ*—by the laws of mortality; *na yujyate*—is not affected.

TRANSLATION

Lord Indra brought Śrī Kṛṣṇa the Sudharmā assembly hall, standing within which a mortal man is not subject to the laws of mortality. Indra also gave the *pārijāta* tree.

TEXT 55

श्यामैकवर्णान् वरुणो हयान् शुक्लान्मनोजवान् ।
अष्टौ निधिपतिः कोशान् लोकपालो निजोदयान् ॥५५॥

śyāmaika-varṇān varuṇo
hayān śuklān mano-javān
aṣṭau nidhi-patiḥ kośān
loka-pālo nijodayān

śyāma—dark blue; *eka*—exclusively; *varṇān*—colored; *varuṇaḥ*—Varuṇa, ruler of the oceans; *hayān*—horses; *śuklān*—white; *manaḥ*—(as the) mind; *javān*—swift; *aṣṭau*—eight; *nidhi-patiḥ*—the treasurer of the demigods, Kuvera; *kośān*—treasures; *loka-pālaḥ*—the rulers of various planets; *nija*—their own; *udayān*—opulences.

TRANSLATION

Lord Varuṇa offered horses as swift as the mind, some of which were pure dark-blue, others white. The treasurer of the demigods, Kuvera, gave his eight mystic treasures, and the rulers of various planets each presented their own opulences.

PURPORT

Śrila Śrīdhara Svāmī comments as follows on this verse: "The master of the treasury is Kuvera, and the eight treasures are his *nidhis*. These are described as follows:

padmaś caiva mahāpadmo
matsya-kūrmau tathaudakaḥ
nīlo mukundaḥ śaṅkhaś ca
nidhayo 'ṣṭau prakīrtitāḥ

'The eight mystic treasures are called Padma, Mahāpadma, Matsya, Kūrma, Audaka, Nīla, Mukunda and Śaṅkha.'"

TEXT 56

यद्यद् भगवता दत्तमाधिपत्यं स्वसिद्धये ।
सर्वं प्रत्यर्पयामासुर्हरौ भूमिगते नृप ॥५६॥

yad yad bhagavatā dattam
ādhipatyaṁ sva-siddhaye
sarvaṁ pratyarpayām āsur
harau bhūmi-gate nṛpa

yat yat—whatever; *bhagavatā*—by the Supreme Lord; *dattam*—given; *ādhipatyam*—delegated power of control; *sva*—their own; *siddhaye*—for facilitating the exercise of authority; *sarvam*—all; *pratyarpayām āsuḥ*—they offered back; *harau*—to Kṛṣṇa; *bhūmi*—to the earth; *gate*—come; *nṛpa*—O King (Parīkṣit).

TRANSLATION

The Supreme Lord having come to the earth, O King, these demigods now offered Him whatever powers of control He had previously delegated to them for the exercise of their particular authority.

TEXT 57

तत्र योगप्रभावेन नीत्वा सर्वजनं हरिः ।
प्रजापालेन रामेण कृष्णः समनुमन्त्रितः ।
निर्जगाम पुरद्वारात्पद्ममाली निरायुधः ॥५७॥

tatra yoga-prabhāvena
nītvā sarva-janaṁ hariḥ
prajā-pālena rāmeṇa
kṛṣṇaḥ samanumantritaḥ
nirjagāma pura-dvārāt
padma-mālī nirāyudhaḥ

tatra—there; *yoga*—of His mystic potency; *prabhāvena*—by the power; *nītvā*—bringing; *sarva*—all; *janam*—His subjects; *hariḥ*—Lord Kṛṣṇa; *prajā*—of the citizens; *pālena*—by the protector; *rāmeṇa*—Lord Balarāma; *kṛṣṇaḥ*—Lord Kṛṣṇa; *samanumantritaḥ*—advised; *nirjagāma*—went out; *pura*—of the city; *dvārāt*—by the gate; *padma*—of lotus flowers; *mālī*—wearing a garland; *nirāyudhaḥ*—without weapons.

TRANSLATION

After transporting all His subjects to the new city by the power of His mystic Yogamāyā, Lord Kṛṣṇa consulted with Lord Balarāma, who had remained in Mathurā to protect it. Then, wearing a garland of lotuses but bearing no weapons, Lord Kṛṣṇa went out of Mathurā by its main gate.

PURPORT

Śrīla Viśvanātha Cakravartī quotes the following verses from *Śrī Padma Purāṇa, Uttara-khaṇḍa,* to describe how Lord Kṛṣṇa transfered the citizens from Mathurā to Dvārakā:

suṣuptān mathurāyān tu
paurāṁs tatra janārdanaḥ
uddhṛtya sahasā rātrau
dvārakāyāṁ nyaveśayat

prabuddhās te janāḥ sarve
putra-dāra-samanvitāḥ
haima-harmya-tale viṣṭā
vismayaṁ paramaṁ yayuḥ

"In the middle of the night, as the citizens of Mathurā slept, Lord Janārdana suddenly removed them from that city and placed them in Dvārakā. When the men awoke, they were all amazed to find themselves, their children and their wives sitting inside palaces made of gold."

Thus end the purports of the humble servants of His Divine Grace A. C. Bhaktivedanta Swami Prabhupāda to the Tenth Canto, Fiftieth Chapter, of the Śrīmad-Bhāgavatam, *entitled "Kṛṣṇa Establishes the City of Dvārakā."*

CHAPTER FIFTY-ONE

The Deliverance of Mucukunda

This chapter describes how Lord Śrī Kṛṣṇa caused Mucukunda to kill Kālayavana with his harsh glance, and it also relates the conversation between Mucukunda and Lord Kṛṣṇa.

After placing His family members safely within the Dvārakā fortress, Śrī Kṛṣṇa went out of Mathurā. He appeared like the rising moon. Kālayavana saw that Kṛṣṇa's brilliantly effulgent body matched Nārada's description of the Lord, and thus the Yavana knew He was the Personality of Godhead. Seeing that the Lord carried no weapons, Kālayavana put his own weapons aside and ran toward Him from behind, wanting to fight with Him. Śrī Kṛṣṇa ran from the Yavana, staying just barely beyond Kālayavana's grasp at every step and eventually leading him a long distance toward a mountain cave. As Kālayavana ran, he hurled insults at the Lord, but he could not grasp Him, since his stock of impious *karma* was not yet depleted. Śrī Kṛṣṇa entered the cave, whereupon Kālayavana followed after Him and saw a man lying on the ground. Taking him for Śrī Kṛṣṇa, Kālayavana kicked him. The man had been sleeping for a very long time, and now, having been violently awakened, he looked around angrily in all directions and saw Kālayavana. The man stared harshly at him, igniting a fire in Kālayavana's body and in a moment burning him to ashes.

This extraordinary person was a son of Māndhātā's named Mucukunda. He was devoted to brahminical culture and always true to his vow. Previously, he had spent many long years helping to protect the demigods from the demons. When the demigods had eventually obtained Kārttikeya as their protector, they allowed Mucukunda to retire, offering him any boon other than liberation, which only Lord Viṣṇu can bestow. Mucukunda had chosen from the demigods the benediction of being covered by sleep, and thus since then he had been lying asleep within the cave.

Upon Kālayavana's immolation, Śrī Kṛṣṇa showed Himself to Mucukunda, who was struck with wonder at seeing Kṛṣṇa's incomparable beauty. Mucukunda asked Lord Kṛṣṇa who He was and also explained to the Lord his own identity. Mucukunda said, "After growing weary from remaining awake for a long time, I was enjoying my sleep here in this cave when some stranger disturbed me and, suffering the reaction of his sins, was burnt to ashes. O Lord, O vanquisher of all enemies, it is my great fortune that I now have the vision of Your beautiful form."

Lord Śrī Kṛṣṇa then told Mucukunda who He was and offered him a boon. The wise Mucukunda, understanding the futility of material life, asked only that he might be allowed to take shelter of Lord Śrī Kṛṣṇa's lotus feet.

Pleased at this request, the Lord said to Mucukunda, "My devotees are never enticed by material benedictions offered to them; only nondevotees, namely *yogīs* and speculative philosophers, are interested in material benedictions, having mundane desires in their hearts. My dear Mucukunda, you will have perpetual devotion for Me. Now, always remaining surrendered to Me, go perform penances to eradicate the sinful reactions incurred from the killing you had to do in your role as a warrior. In your next life you will become a first-class *brāhmaṇa* and attain Me." Thus the Lord offered Mucukunda His blessings.

TEXTS 1–6

श्रीशुक उवाच

तं विलोक्य विनिष्क्रान्तमुज्जिहानमिवोडुपम् ।
दर्शनीयतमं श्यामं पीतकौशेयवाससम् ॥१॥
श्रीवत्सवक्षसं भ्राजत्कौस्तुभामुक्तकन्धरम् ।
पृथुदीर्घचतुर्बाहुं नवकञ्जारुणेक्षणम् ॥२॥
नित्यप्रमुदितं श्रीमत्सुकपोलं शुचिस्मितम् ।
मुखारविन्दं बिभ्राणं स्फुरन्मकरकुण्डलम् ॥३॥
वासुदेवो ह्ययमिति पुमान् श्रीवत्सलाञ्छनः ।
चतुर्भुजोऽरविन्दाक्षो वनमाल्यतिसुन्दरः ॥४॥
लक्षणैर्नारदप्रोक्तैर्नान्यो भवितुमर्हति ।
निरायुधश्चलन् पद्भ्यां योत्स्येऽनेन निरायुधः ॥५॥
इति निश्चित्य यवनः प्राद्रवद् तं पराङ्मुखम् ।
अन्वधावज्जिघृक्षुस्तं दुरापमपि योगिनाम् ॥६॥

śrī-śuka uvāca
taṁ vilokya viniṣkrāntam
ujjihānam ivoḍupam
darśanīyatamaṁ śyāmaṁ
pīta-kauśeya-vāsasam

śrīvatsa-vakṣasaṁ bhrājat-
kaustubhāmukta-kandharam
pṛthu-dīrgha-catur-bāhuṁ
nava-kañjāruṇekṣaṇam

nitya-pramuditaṁ śrīmat-
su-kapolaṁ śuci-smitam
mukhāravindaṁ bibhrāṇaṁ
sphuran-makara-kuṇḍalam

vāsudevo hy ayam iti
pumān śrīvatsa-lāñchanaḥ
catur-bhujo 'ravindākṣo
vana-māly ati-sundaraḥ

lakṣaṇair nārada-proktair
nānyo bhavitum arhati
nirāyudhaś calan padbhyāṁ
yotsye 'nena nirāyudhaḥ

iti niścitya yavanaḥ
prādravad taṁ parāṅ-mukham
anvadhāvaj jighṛkṣus taṁ
durāpam api yoginām

śrī-śukaḥ uvāca—Śukadeva Gosvāmī said; *tam*—Him; *vilokya*—seeing; *viniṣkrāntam*—coming out; *ujjihānam*—rising; *iva*—as if; *uḍupam*—the moon; *darśanīya-tamam*—the most beautiful to behold; *śyāmam*—dark blue; *pīta*—yellow; *kauśeya*—silk; *vāsasam*—whose garment; *śrīvatsa*—the mark of the goddess of fortune, consisting of a special swirl of hair and belonging to the Supreme Lord alone; *vakṣasam*—upon whose chest; *bhrājat*—brilliant; *kaustubha*—with the gem Kaustubha; *āmukta*—decorated; *kandharam*—whose neck; *pṛthu*—broad; *dīrgha*—and long;

catuḥ—four; *bāhum*—having arms; *nava*—newly grown; *kañja*—like lotuses; *aruṇa*—pink; *īkṣaṇam*—whose eyes; *nitya*—always; *pramuditam*—joyful; *śrīmat*—effulgent; *su*—beautiful; *kapolam*—with cheeks; *śuci*—clean; *smitam*—with a smile; *mukha*—His face; *aravindam*—lotuslike; *bibhrāṇam*—displaying; *sphuran*—glittering; *makara*—shark; *kuṇḍalam*—earrings; *vāsudevaḥ*—Vāsudeva; *hi*—indeed; *ayam*—this; *iti*—thus thinking; *pumān*—person; *śrīvatsa-lāñchanaḥ*—marked with Śrivatsa; *catuḥ-bhujaḥ*—four-armed; *aravinda-akṣaḥ*—lotus-eyed; *vana*—of forest flowers; *mālī*—wearing a garland; *ati*—extremely; *sundaraḥ*—beautiful; *lakṣaṇaiḥ*—by the symptoms; *nārada-proktaiḥ*—told by Nārada Muni; *na*—no; *anyaḥ*—other; *bhavitum arhati*—can He be; *nirāyudhaḥ*—without weapons; *calan*—going; *padbhyām*—by foot; *yotsye*—I will fight; *anena*—with Him; *nirāyudhaḥ*—without weapons; *iti*—thus; *niścitya*—deciding; *yavanaḥ*—the barbarian Kālayavana; *prādravantam*—who was fleeing; *parāk*—turned away; *mukham*—whose face; *anvadhāvat*—he pursued; *jighṛkṣuḥ*—wanting to catch; *tam*—Him; *durāpam*—unattainable; *api*—even; *yoginām*—by mystic *yogīs*.

TRANSLATION

Śukadeva Gosvāmī said: Kālayavana saw the Lord come out from Mathurā like the rising moon. The Lord was most beautiful to behold, with His dark-blue complexion and yellow silk garment. Upon His chest He bore the mark of Śrīvatsa, and the Kaustubha gem adorned His neck. His four arms were sturdy and long. He displayed His ever-joyful lotuslike face, with eyes pink like lotuses, beautifully effulgent cheeks, a pristine smile and glittering shark-shaped earrings. The barbarian thought, "This person must indeed be Vāsudeva, since He possesses the characteristics Nārada mentioned: He is marked with Śrīvatsa, He has four arms, His eyes are like lotuses, He wears a garland of forest flowers, and He is extremely handsome. He cannot be anyone else. Since He goes on foot and unarmed, I will fight Him without weapons." Resolving thus, he ran after the Lord, who turned His back and ran away. Kālayavana hoped to catch Lord Kṛṣṇa, though great mystic *yogīs* cannot attain Him.

PURPORT

Although Kālayavana was seeing Lord Kṛṣṇa with his own eyes, he could not adequately appreciate the beautiful Lord. Thus instead of worshiping Kṛṣṇa, he attacked Him. Similarly, it is not uncommon for modern men to attack Kṛṣṇa in the name of philosophy, "law and order" and even religion.

TEXT 7

हस्तप्राप्तमिवात्मानं हरिणा स पदे पदे ।
नीतो दर्शयता दूरं यवनेशोऽद्रिकन्दरम् ॥७॥

hasta-prāptam ivātmānaṁ
hariṇā sa pade pade
nīto darśayatā dūraṁ
yavaneśo 'dri-kandaram

hasta—in his hands; *prāptam*—reached; *iva*—as if; *ātmānam*—Himself; *hariṇā*—by Lord Kṛṣṇa; *saḥ*—he; *pade pade*—at each step; *nītaḥ*—brought; *darśayatā*—by Him who was showing; *dūram*—far; *yavana-īśaḥ*—the King of the Yavanas; *adri*—in a mountain; *kandaram*—to a cave.

TRANSLATION

Appearing virtually within reach of Kālayavana's hands at every moment, Lord Hari led the King of the Yavanas far away to a mountain cave.

TEXT 8

पलायनं यदुकुले जातस्य तव नोचितम् ।
इति क्षिपन्ननुगतो नैनं प्रापाहताशुभः ॥८॥

palāyanaṁ yadu-kule
jātasya tava nocitam

iti kṣipann anugato
nainaṁ prāpāhatāśubhaḥ

palāyanam—fleeing; *yadu-kule*—in the Yadu dynasty; *jātasya*—who have been born; *tava*—for You; *na*—is not; *ucitam*—proper; *iti*—in these words; *kṣipan*—insulting; *anugataḥ*—in pursuit; *na*—not; *enam*—Him; *prāpa*—reached; *ahata*—not cleansed or eliminated; *aśubhaḥ*—whose sinful reactions.

TRANSLATION

While chasing the Lord, the Yavana cast insults at Him, saying "You took birth in the Yadu dynasty. It's not proper for You to run away!" But still Kālayavana could not reach Lord Kṛṣṇa, because his sinful reactions had not been cleansed away.

TEXT 9

एवं क्षिप्तोऽपि भगवान् प्राविशद् गिरिकन्दरम् ।
सोऽपि प्रविष्टस्तत्रान्यं शयानं ददृशे नरम् ॥९॥

evaṁ kṣipto 'pi bhagavān
prāviśad giri-kandaram
so 'pi praviṣṭas tatrānyaṁ
śayānaṁ dadṛśe naram

evam—thus; *kṣiptaḥ*—insulted; *api*—even though; *bhagavān*—the Supreme Lord; *prāviśat*—entered; *giri-kandaram*—the mountain cave; *saḥ*—he, Kālayavana; *api*—as well; *praviṣṭaḥ*—entering; *tatra*—there; *anyam*—another; *śayānam*—lying; *dadṛśe*—saw; *naram*—man.

TRANSLATION

Although insulted in this way, the Supreme Lord entered the mountain cave. Kālayavana also entered, and there he saw another man lying asleep.

PURPORT

The Lord exhibits here His opulence of renunciation. Determined to execute His plan and give His blessings to Mucukunda, the Lord ignored Kālayavana's insults and calmly proceeded with His program.

TEXT 10

नन्वसौ दूरमानीय शेते मामिह साधुवत् ।
इति मत्वाच्युतं मूढस्तं पदा समताडयत् ॥१०॥

nanv asau dūram ānīya
śete mām iha sādhu-vat
iti matvācyutaṁ mūḍhas
taṁ padā samatāḍayat

nanu—is it so; *asau*—He; *dūram*—a long distance; *ānīya*—bringing; *śete*—is lying down; *mām*—me; *iha*—here; *sādhu-vat*—like a saintly person; *iti*—so; *matvā*—thinking (him); *acyutam*—(to be) Lord Kṛṣṇa; *mūḍhaḥ*—deluded; *tam*—him; *padā*—with his foot; *samatāḍayat*—struck with full force.

TRANSLATION

"So, after leading me such a long distance, now He is lying here like some saint!" Thus thinking the sleeping man to be Lord Kṛṣṇa, the deluded fool kicked him with all his strength.

TEXT 11

स उत्थाय चिरं सुप्तः शनैरुन्मील्य लोचने ।
दिशो विलोकयन् पार्श्वे तमद्राक्षीदवस्थितम् ॥११॥

sa utthāya ciraṁ suptaḥ
śanair unmīlya locane
diśo vilokayan pārśve
tam adrākṣīd avasthitam

saḥ—he; *utthāya*—waking; *ciram*—for a long time; *suptaḥ*—asleep; *śanaiḥ*—slowly; *unmīlya*—opening; *locane*—his eyes; *diśaḥ*—in all directions; *vilokayan*—looking about; *pārśve*—at his side; *tam*—him, Kālayavana; *adrākṣīt*—he saw; *avasthitam*—standing.

TRANSLATION

The man awoke after a long sleep and slowly opened his eyes. Looking all about, he saw Kālayavana standing beside him.

TEXT 12

स तावत्तस्य रुष्टस्य दृष्टिपातेन भारत ।
देहजेनाग्निना दग्धो भस्मसादभवत्क्षणात् ॥१२॥

sa tāvat tasya ruṣṭasya
dṛṣṭi-pātena bhārata
deha-jenāgninā dagdho
bhasma-sād abhavat kṣaṇāt

saḥ—he, Kālayavana; *tāvat*—that much; *tasya*—of him, the awakened man; *ruṣṭasya*—who was angered; *dṛṣṭi*—of the glance; *pātena*—by the casting; *bhārata*—O descendant of Bharata (Parīkṣit Mahārāja); *deha-jena*—generated in his own body; *agninā*—by the fire; *dagdhaḥ*—burned; *bhasma-sāt*—to ashes; *abhavat*—he was; *kṣaṇāt*—in a moment.

TRANSLATION

The awakened man was angry and cast his glance at Kālayavana, whose body burst into flames. In a single moment, O King Parīkṣit, Kālayavana was burnt to ashes.

PURPORT

The man who incinerated Kālayavana with his glance was named Mucukunda. As he will explain to Lord Kṛṣṇa, he had fought for a long time on behalf of the demigods, finally taking as his benediction the right to sleep undisturbed. The *Hari-vaṁśa* explains that he secured the further benediction of being able to destroy anyone who disturbed his sleep. Ācārya Viśvanātha Cakravartī Ṭhākura quotes from the *Śrī Harivaṁśa* as follows:

prasuptaṁ bodhayed yo māṁ
taṁ daheyam ahaṁ surāḥ
cakṣuṣā krodha-dīptena
evam āha punaḥ punaḥ

"Again and again Mucukunda said, 'O demigods, with eyes blazing with anger, may I incinerate anyone who awakens me from sleep.'"

Śrīla Viśvanātha Cakravartī explains that Mucukunda made this rather morbid request to scare Lord Indra, who, Mucukunda thought, might otherwise wake him repeatedly to request his help in fighting Indra's cosmic enemies. Indra's consent to Mucukunda's request is described in *Śrī Viṣṇu Purāṇa* as follows:

proktaś ca devaiḥ saṁsuptaṁ
yas tvām utthāpayiṣyati
deha-jenāgninā sadyaḥ
sa tu bhasmī-kariṣyati

"The demigods declared, 'Whoever awakens you from sleep will suddenly be burnt to ashes by a fire generated from his own body.'"

TEXT 13

श्रीराजोवाच
को नाम स पुमान् ब्रह्मन् कस्य किंवीर्य एव च ।
कस्माद् गुहां गतः शिष्ये किंतेजो यवनार्दनः ॥१३॥

śrī-rājovāca
ko nāma sa pumān brahman
kasya kiṁ-vīrya eva ca
kasmād guhāṁ gataḥ śiṣye
kiṁ-tejo yavanārdanaḥ

śrī-rājā uvāca—the King (Parīkṣit) said; *kaḥ*—who; *nāma*—in particular; *saḥ*—that; *pumān*—person; *brahman*—O *brāhmaṇa* (Śukadeva);

kasya—of which (family); *kim*—having what; *vīryaḥ*—powers; *eva ca*—as also; *kasmāt*—why; *guhām*—in the cave; *gataḥ*—having gone; *śiṣye*—lay down to sleep; *kim*—whose; *tejaḥ*—semen (offspring); *yavana*—of the Yavana; *ardanaḥ*—the destroyer.

TRANSLATION

King Parīkṣit said: Who was that person, O *brāhmaṇa*? To which family did he belong, and what were his powers? Why did that destroyer of the barbarian lie down to sleep in the cave, and whose son was he?

TEXT 14

श्रीशुक उवाच
स इक्ष्वाकुकुले जातो मान्धातृतनयो महान् ।
मुचुकुन्द इति ख्यातो ब्रह्मण्यः सत्यसंगरः ॥१४॥

śrī-śuka uvāca
sa ikṣvāku-kule jāto
māndhātṛ-tanayo mahān
mucukunda iti khyāto
brahmaṇyaḥ satya-saṅgaraḥ

śrī-śukaḥ uvāca—Śukadeva Gosvāmī said; *saḥ*—he; *ikṣvāku-kule*—in the dynasty of Ikṣvāku (grandson of Vivasvān, the sun-god); *jātaḥ*—born; *māndhātṛ-tanayaḥ*—the son of King Māndhātā; *mahān*—the great personality; *mucukundaḥ iti khyātaḥ*—known as Mucukunda; *brahmaṇyaḥ*—devoted to the *brāhmaṇas; satya*—true to his vow; *saṅgaraḥ*—in battle.

TRANSLATION

Śukadeva Gosvāmī said: Mucukunda was the name of this great personality, who was born in the Ikṣvāku dynasty as the son of Māndhātā. He was devoted to brahminical culture and always true to his vow in battle.

TEXT 15

स याचितः सुरगणैरिन्द्राद्यैरात्मरक्षणे ।
असुरेभ्यः परित्रस्तैस्तद्रक्षां सोऽकरोच्चिरम् ॥१५॥

sa yācitaḥ sura-gaṇair
indrādyair ātma-rakṣaṇe
asurebhyaḥ paritrastais
tad-rakṣāṁ so 'karoc ciram

saḥ—he; *yācitaḥ*—requested; *sura-gaṇaiḥ*—by the demigods; *indra-ādyaiḥ*—headed by Lord Indra; *ātma*—their own; *rakṣaṇe*—for protection; *asurebhyaḥ*—of the demons; *paritrastaiḥ*—who were terrified; *tat*—their; *rakṣām*—protection; *saḥ*—he; *akarot*—carried out; *ciram*—for a long time.

TRANSLATION

Begged by Indra and the other demigods to help protect them when they were terrorized by the demons, Mucukunda defended them for a long time.

TEXT 16

लब्ध्वा गुहं ते स्वःपालं मुचुकुन्दमथाब्रुवन् ।
राजन् विरमतां कृच्छ्राद् भवान्नः परिपालनात् ॥१६॥

labdhvā guhaṁ te svaḥ-pālaṁ
mucukundam athābruvan
rājan viramatāṁ kṛcchrād
bhavān naḥ paripālanāt

labdhvā—after obtaining; *guham*—Kārttikeya; *te*—they; *svaḥ*—of heaven; *pālam*—as the protector; *mucukundam*—to Mucukunda; *atha*—then; *abruvan*—said; *rājan*—O King; *viramatām*—please desist; *kṛcchrāt*—troublesome; *bhavān*—your good self; *naḥ*—our; *paripālanāt*—from the guarding.

TRANSLATION

When the demigods obtained Kārttikeya as their general, they told Mucukunda, "O King, you may now give up your troublesome duty of guarding us.

TEXT 17

नरलोकं परित्यज्य राज्यं निहतकण्टकम् ।
अस्मान् पालयतो वीर कामास्ते सर्व उज्झिताः ॥१७॥

nara-lokaṁ parityajya
rājyaṁ nihata-kaṇṭakam
asmān pālayato vīra
kāmās te sarva ujjhitāḥ

nara-lokam—in the world of men; *parityajya*—abandoning; *rājyam*—a kingdom; *nihata*—removed; *kaṇṭakam*—whose thorns; *asmān*—us; *pālayataḥ*—who was protecting; *vīra*—O hero; *kāmāḥ*—desires; *te*—your; *sarve*—all; *ujjhitāḥ*—thrown away.

TRANSLATION

"Abandoning an unopposed kingdom in the world of men, O valiant one, you neglected all your personal desires while engaged in protecting us.

TEXT 18

सुता महिष्यो भवतो ज्ञातयोऽमात्यमन्त्रिणः ।
प्रजाश्च तुल्यकालीना नाधुना सन्ति कालिताः ॥१८॥

sutā mahiṣyo bhavato
jñātayo 'mātya-mantriṇaḥ
prajāś ca tulya-kālīnā
nādhunā santi kālitāḥ

sutāḥ—children; *mahiṣyaḥ*—queens; *bhavataḥ*—your; *jñātayaḥ*—other relatives; *amātya*—ministers; *mantriṇaḥ*—and advisers; *prajāḥ*—subjects; *ca*—and; *tulya-kālīnāḥ*—contemporary; *na*—not; *adhunā*—now; *santi*—are alive; *kālitāḥ*—forced to move on by time.

TRANSLATION

"The children, queens, relatives, ministers, advisers and subjects who were your contemporaries are no longer alive. They have all been swept away by time.

TEXT 19

कालो बलीयान् बलिनां भगवानीश्वरोऽव्ययः ।
प्रजाः कालयते क्रीडन् पशुपालो यथा पशून् ॥१९॥

kālo balīyān balināṁ
bhagavān īśvaro 'vyayaḥ
prajāḥ kālayate krīḍan
paśu-pālo yathā paśūn

kālaḥ—time; *balīyān*—more powerful; *balinām*—than the powerful; *bhagavān īśvaraḥ*—the Supreme Personality of Godhead; *avyayaḥ*—inexhaustible; *prajāḥ*—mortal creatures; *kālayate*—causes to move; *krīḍan*—playing; *paśu-pālaḥ*—a herdsman; *yathā*—as; *paśūn*—domestic animals.

TRANSLATION

"Inexhaustible time, stronger than the strong, is the Supreme Personality of Godhead Himself. Like a herdsman moving his animals along, He moves mortal creatures as His pastime.

PURPORT

The universe is created to gradually rectify the contaminated souls trying to exploit material nature. The Lord moves the conditioned souls along, according to their *karma,* through the various stages of spiritual rectification. Thus the Lord is like a herdsman (the word *paśu-pāla* literally means "protector of animals"), who moves the creatures under his protection to various pastures and watering spots in order to protect them and sustain them. A further analogy is that of a doctor, who moves the patient under his care to various areas of a hospital for diverse kinds of examination and treatment. Similarly, the Lord brings us through the network of material existence in a gradual cleansing process so that we can enjoy our eternal life of bliss and knowledge as His enlightened associates. Thus all of Mucukunda's relatives, friends and co-workers had long ago been swept away by the force of time, which of course is Kṛṣṇa Himself.

TEXT 20

वरं वृणीष्व भद्रं ते ऋते कैवल्यमद्य नः ।
एक एवेश्वरस्तस्य भगवान् विष्णुरव्ययः ॥२०॥

varaṁ vṛṇīṣva bhadraṁ te
ṛte kaivalyam adya naḥ
eka eveśvaras tasya
bhagavān viṣṇur avyayaḥ

varam—a benediction; *vṛṇīṣva*—choose; *bhadram*—all good; *te*—unto you; *ṛte*—except; *kaivalyam*—liberation; *adya*—today; *naḥ*—from us; *ekaḥ*—one; *eva*—only; *īśvaraḥ*—capable; *tasya*—of that; *bhagavān*—the Supreme Lord; *viṣṇuḥ*—Śrī Viṣṇu; *avyayaḥ*—the inexhaustible.

TRANSLATION

"All good fortune to you! Now please choose a benediction from us—anything but liberation, since only the infallible Supreme Lord, Viṣṇu, can bestow that."

TEXT 21

एवमुक्तः स वै देवानभिवन्द्य महायशाः ।
अशयिष्ट गुहाविष्टो निद्रया देवदत्तया ॥२१॥

evam uktaḥ sa vai devān
abhivandya mahā-yaśāḥ

aśayiṣṭa guhā-viṣṭo
nidrayā deva-dattayā

evam—thus; *uktaḥ*—addressed; *saḥ*—he; *vai*—indeed; *devān*—the demigods; *abhivandya*—saluting; *mahā*—great; *yaśāḥ*—whose fame; *aśayiṣṭa*—he lay down; *guhā-viṣṭaḥ*—entering a cave; *nidrayā*—in sleep; *deva*—by the demigods; *dattayā*—given.

TRANSLATION

Addressed thus, King Mucukunda took his respectful leave of the demigods and went to a cave, where he lay down to enjoy the sleep they had granted him.

PURPORT

Śrīla Bhaktisiddhānta Sarasvatī Ṭhākura gives the following lines from an alternate reading of this chapter. These lines are to be inserted between the two halves of this verse:

nidrām eva tato vavre
sa rājā śrama-karṣitaḥ

yaḥ kaścin mama nidrāyā
bhaṅgaṁ kuryād surottamāḥ
sa hi bhasmī-bhaved āśu
tathoktaś ca surais tadā

svāpaṁ yātaṁ yo madhye tu
bodhayet tvām acetanaḥ
sa tvayā dṛṣṭa-mātras tu
bhasmī-bhavatu tat-kṣaṇāt

"The King, exhausted by his labor, then chose sleep as his benediction. He further stated, 'O best of the demigods, may whoever disturbs my sleep be immediately burned to ashes.' The demigods replied, 'So be it,' and told him, 'That insensitive person who wakes you in the middle of your sleep will immediately turn to ashes simply by your seeing him.' "

TEXT 22

यवने भस्मसान्नीते भगवान् सात्वतर्षभः ।
आत्मानं दर्शयामास मुचुकुन्दाय धीमते ॥२२॥

yavane bhasma-sān nīte
bhagavān sātvatarṣabhaḥ
ātmānaṁ darśayām āsa
mucukundāya dhīmate

yavane—after the barbarian; *bhasma-sāt*—into ashes; *nīte*—was turned; *bhagavān*—the Supreme Lord; *sātvata*—of the Sātvata clan; *ṛṣabhaḥ*—the greatest hero; *ātmānam*—Himself; *darśayām āsa*—revealed; *mucukundāya*—to Mucukunda; *dhī-mate*—the intelligent.

TRANSLATION

After the Yavana was burnt to ashes, the Supreme Lord, chief of the Sātvatas, revealed Himself to the wise Mucukunda.

TEXTS 23–26

तमालोक्य घनश्यामं पीतकौशेयवाससम् ।
श्रीवत्सवक्षसं भ्राजत्कौस्तुभेन विराजितम् ॥२३॥
चतुर्भुजं रोचमानं वैजयन्त्या च मालया ।
चारुप्रसन्नवदनं स्फुरन्मकरकुण्डलम् ॥२४॥
प्रेक्षणीयं नृलोकस्य सानुरागस्मितेक्षणम् ।
अपीव्यवयसं मत्तमृगेन्द्रोदारविक्रमम् ॥२५॥
पर्यपृच्छन्महाबुद्धिस्तेजसा तस्य धर्षितः ।
शङ्कितः शनकै राजा दुर्धर्षमिव तेजसा ॥२६॥

tam ālokya ghana-śyāmaṁ
pīta-kauśeya-vāsasam
śrīvatsa-vakṣasaṁ bhrājat-
kaustubhena virājitam

catur-bhujaṁ rocamānaṁ
vaijayantyā ca mālayā
cāru-prasanna-vadanaṁ
sphuran-makara-kuṇḍalam

prekṣaṇīyaṁ nṛ-lokasya
sānurāga-smitekṣaṇam
apīvya-vayasaṁ matta-
mṛgendrodāra-vikramam

paryapṛcchan mahā-buddhis
tejasā tasya dharṣitaḥ
śaṅkitaḥ śanakai rājā
durdharṣam iva tejasā

tam—Him; *ālokya*—looking upon; *ghana*—like a cloud; *śyāmam*—dark blue; *pīta*—yellow; *kauśeya*—silk; *vāsasam*—whose garment; *śrīvatsa*—the Śrīvatsa mark; *vakṣasam*—on whose chest; *bhrājat*—brilliant; *kaustubhena*—with the Kaustubha gem; *virājitam*—glowing; *catuḥ-bhujam*—four-armed; *rocamānam*—beautified; *vaijayantyā*—named Vaijayantī; *ca*—and; *mālayā*—by the flower garland; *cāru*—attractive; *prasanna*—and calm; *vadanam*—whose face; *sphurat*—glittering; *makara*—shaped like sharks; *kuṇḍalam*—whose earrings; *prekṣaṇīyam*—attracting the eyes; *nṛ-lokasya*—of mankind; *sa*—with; *anurāga*—affection; *smita*—smiling; *īkṣaṇam*—whose eyes or glance; *apīvya*—handsome; *vayasam*—whose youthful form; *matta*—angered; *mṛga-indra*—like a lion; *udāra*—noble; *vikramam*—whose walking; *parya-pṛcchat*—he questioned; *mahā-buddhiḥ*—having great intelligence; *tejasā*—by the effulgence; *tasya*—His; *dharṣitaḥ*—overwhelmed; *śaṅkitaḥ*—having doubt; *śanakaiḥ*—slowly; *rājā*—the King; *dur-dharṣam*—unassailable; *iva*—indeed; *tejasā*—with His effulgence.

TRANSLATION

As he gazed at the Lord, King Mucukunda saw that He was dark blue like a cloud, had four arms, and wore a yellow silk garment. On His chest He bore the Śrīvatsa mark and on His neck the brilliantly glowing Kaustubha gem. Adorned with a Vaijayantī

garland, the Lord displayed His handsome, peaceful face, which attracts the eyes of all mankind with its shark-shaped earrings and affectionately smiling glance. The beauty of His youthful form was unexcelled, and He moved with the nobility of an angry lion. The highly intelligent King was overwhelmed by the Lord's effulgence, which showed Him to be invincible. Expressing his uncertainty, Mucukunda hesitantly questioned Lord Kṛṣṇa as follows.

PURPORT

It is significant that Text 24 states, *catur-bhujaṁ rocamānam:* "The Lord was seen in the beauty of His four-armed form." Throughout this great work, we find Lord Kṛṣṇa manifesting His various transcendental forms, most prominently the two-armed form of Kṛṣṇa and the four-armed form of Nārāyaṇa or Viṣṇu. Thus there is no doubt that Kṛṣṇa and Viṣṇu are nondifferent, or that Kṛṣṇa is the original form of the Lord. These things are sometimes misunderstood, but the great *ācāryas,* experts in spiritual science, have clarified the matter for us. God in His original form is not merely the creator, maintainer and destroyer, or the punisher of conditioned souls, but rather the infinitely beautiful Godhead, enjoying in His own right, in His own abode. This is the form of Kṛṣṇa, the same Kṛṣṇa who expands Himself into Viṣṇu forms for the maintenance of our bumbling world.

Śrīla Jīva Gosvāmī mentions that the word *śaṅkitaḥ,* "having some doubt," indicates that Mucukunda was thinking, "Is this indeed the Supreme Lord?" He expresses himself frankly in the following verses.

TEXT 27

श्रीमुचुकुन्द उवाच
को भवानिह सम्प्राप्तो विपिने गिरिगह्वरे ।
पद्भ्यां पद्मपलाशाभ्यां विचरस्युरुकण्टके ॥२७॥

śrī-mucukunda uvāca
ko bhavān iha samprāpto
vipine giri-gahvare
padbhyāṁ padma-palāśābhyāṁ
vicarasy uru-kaṇṭake

śrī-mucukundaḥ uvāca—Śrī Mucukunda said; *kaḥ*—who; *bhavān*—are You; *iha*—here; *samprāptaḥ*—arrived together (with me); *vipine*—in the forest; *giri-gahvare*—in a mountain cave; *padbhyām*—with Your feet; *padma*—of a lotus; *palāśābhyām*—(which are like) the petals; *vicarasi*—You are walking; *uru-kaṇṭake*—which is full of thorns.

TRANSLATION

Śrī Mucukunda said: Who are You who have come to this mountain cave in the forest, having walked on the thorny ground with feet as soft as lotus petals?

TEXT 28

किं स्वित्तेजस्विनां तेजो भगवान् वा विभावसुः ।
सूर्यः सोमो महेन्द्रो वा लोकपालोऽपरोऽपि वा ॥२८॥

kiṁ svit tejasvināṁ tejo
bhagavān vā vibhāvasuḥ
sūryaḥ somo mahendro vā
loka-pālo 'paro 'pi vā

kim svit—perhaps; *tejasvinām*—of all potent beings; *tejaḥ*—the original form; *bhagavān*—powerful lord; *vā*—or else; *vibhāvasuḥ*—the god of fire; *sūryaḥ*—the sun-god; *somaḥ*—the moon-god; *mahā-indraḥ*—the King of heaven; *vā*—or; *loka*—of a planet; *pālaḥ*—the ruler; *aparaḥ*—other; *api vā*—else.

TRANSLATION

Perhaps You are the potency of all potent beings. Or maybe You are the powerful god of fire, or the sun-god, the moon-god, the King of heaven or the ruling demigod of some other planet.

TEXT 29

मन्ये त्वां देवदेवानां त्रयाणां पुरुषर्षभम् ।
यद् बाधसे गुहाध्वान्तं प्रदीपः प्रभया यथा ॥२९॥

manye tvāṁ deva-devānāṁ
trayāṇāṁ puruṣarṣabham
yad bādhase guhā-dhvāntaṁ
pradīpaḥ prabhayā yathā

manye—I consider; *tvām*—You; *deva-devānām*—of the chief of the demigods; *trayāṇām*—three (Brahmā, Viṣṇu and Śiva); *puruṣa*—of the personalities; *ṛṣabham*—the greatest; *yat*—because; *bādhase*—You drive away; *guhā*—of the cave; *dhvāntam*—the darkness; *pradīpaḥ*—a lamp; *prabhayā*—with its light; *yathā*—as.

TRANSLATION

I think You are the Supreme Personality among the three chief gods, since You drive away the darkness of this cave as a lamp dispels darkness with its light.

PURPORT

Śrīla Viśvanātha Cakravartī points out that with His effulgence Lord Kṛṣṇa dispelled not only the darkness of the mountain cave but also the darkness in Mucukunda's heart. In Sanskrit the heart is sometimes metaphorically referred to as *guhā,* "cavern," a deep and secret place.

TEXT 30

शुश्रूषतामव्यलीकमस्माकं नरपुंगव ।
स्वजन्म कर्म गोत्रं वा कथ्यतां यदि रोचते ॥३०॥

śuśrūṣatām avyalīkam
asmākaṁ nara-puṅgava
sva-janma karma gotraṁ vā
kathyatāṁ yadi rocate

śuśrūṣatām—who are eager to hear; *avyalīkam*—truthfully; *asmākam*—to us; *nara*—among men; *pum-gava*—O most eminent; *sva*—Your; *janma*—birth; *karma*—activity; *gotram*—lineage; *vā*—and; *kathyatām*—may it be told; *yadi*—if; *rocate*—it pleases.

TRANSLATION

O best among men, if You like, please truly describe Your birth, activities and lineage to us, who are eager to hear.

PURPORT

When the Supreme Lord descends to this world, He certainly becomes *nara-puṅgava,* the most eminent member of human society. Of course, the Lord is not actually a human being, and Mucukunda's questions will lead to a clarification of this point. Thus the term *śuśrūṣatām,* "to us, who are sincerely eager to hear," indicates that Mucukunda is inquiring in a noble way for his own and others' benefit.

TEXT 31

वयं तु पुरुषव्याघ्र ऐक्ष्वाकाः क्षत्रबन्धवः ।
मुचुकुन्द इति प्रोक्तो यौवनाश्वात्मजः प्रभो ॥३१॥

vayaṁ tu puruṣa-vyāghra
aikṣvākāḥ kṣatra-bandhavaḥ
mucukunda iti prokto
yauvanāśvātmajaḥ prabho

vayam—we; *tu*—on the other hand; *puruṣa*—among men; *vyāghra*—O tiger; *aikṣvākāḥ*—descendants of Ikṣvāku; *kṣatra*—of *kṣatriyas; bandhavaḥ*—family members; *mucukundaḥ*—Mucukunda; *iti*—thus; *proktaḥ*—called; *yauvanāśva*—of Yauvanāśva (Māndhātā, the son of Yuvanāśva); *ātma-jaḥ*—the son; *prabho*—O Lord.

TRANSLATION

As for ourselves, O tiger among men, we belong to a family of fallen *kṣatriyas,* descendants of King Ikṣvāku. My name is Mucukunda, my Lord, and I am the son of Yauvanāśva.

PURPORT

It is common in Vedic culture that a *kṣatriya* will humbly introduce himself as *kṣatra-bandhu,* a mere relative in a *kṣatriya* family, or in other words a fallen *kṣatriya*. In ancient Vedic culture, to claim a particular status on the basis of one's family relations was itself indicative of a fallen position. *Kṣatriyas* and *brāhmaṇas* should be given status according to their merit, by their qualities of work and character. When the caste system in India became degraded, people proudly claimed to be relatives of *kṣatriyas* or *brāhmaṇas*, though in the past such a claim, unaccompanied by tangible qualifications, indicated a fallen position.

TEXT 32

चिरप्रजागरश्रान्तो निद्रयापहतेन्द्रियः ।
शयेऽस्मिन् विजने कामं केनाप्युत्थापितोऽधुना ॥३२॥

cira-prajāgara-śrānto
nidrayāpahatendriyaḥ
śaye 'smin vijane kāmaṁ
kenāpy utthāpito 'dhunā

cira—for a long time; *prajāgara*—because of remaining awake; *śrāntaḥ*—fatigued; *nidrayā*—by sleep; *apahata*—covered over; *indriyaḥ*—my senses; *śaye*—I have been lying; *asmin*—in this; *vijane*—solitary place; *kāmam*—as pleases me; *kena api*—by someone; *utthāpitaḥ*—awakened; *adhunā*—now.

TRANSLATION

I was fatigued after remaining awake for a long time, and my senses were overwhelmed by sleep. Thus I slept comfortably here in this solitary place until, just now, someone woke me.

TEXT 33

सोऽपि भस्मीकृतो नूनमात्मीयेनैव पाप्मना ।
अनन्तरं भवान् श्रीमाल्ँल्लक्षितोऽमित्रशासनः ॥३३॥

so 'pi bhasmī-kṛto nūnam
ātmīyenaiva pāpmanā

anantaraṁ bhavān śrīmāl̐
lakṣito 'mitra-śāsanaḥ

saḥ api—that very person; *bhasmī-kṛtaḥ*—turned to ashes; *nūnam*—indeed; *ātmīyena*—by his own; *eva*—only; *pāpmanā*—sinful *karma; anantaram*—immediately following; *bhavān*—Your good self; *śrīmān*—glorious; *lakṣitaḥ*—observed; *amitra*—of enemies; *śāsanaḥ*—the chastiser.

TRANSLATION

The man who woke me was burned to ashes by the reaction of his sins. Just then I saw You, possessing a glorious appearance and the power to chastise Your enemies.

PURPORT

Kālayavana had declared himself the enemy of Śrī Kṛṣṇa and the Yadu dynasty. Through Mucukunda, Śrī Kṛṣṇa destroyed the opposition of that foolish barbarian.

TEXT 34

तेजसा तेऽविषह्येण भूरि द्रष्टुं न शक्नुमः ।
हतौजसा महाभाग माननीयोऽसि देहिनाम् ॥३४॥

tejasā te 'viṣahyeṇa
bhūri draṣṭuṁ na śaknumaḥ
hataujasā mahā-bhāga
mānanīyo 'si dehinām

tejasā—because of the effulgence; *te*—Your; *aviṣahyeṇa*—unbearable; *bhūri*—much; *draṣṭum*—to see; *na śaknumaḥ*—we are not able; *hata*—diminished; *ojasā*—with our faculties; *mahā-bhāga*—O most opulent one; *mānanīyaḥ*—to be honored; *asi*—You are; *dehinām*—by embodied beings.

TRANSLATION

Your unbearably brilliant effulgence overwhelms our strength, and thus we cannot fix our gaze upon You. O exalted one, You are to be honored by all embodied beings.

TEXT 35

एवं सम्भाषितो राज्ञा भगवान् भूतभावनः ।
प्रत्याह प्रहसन् वाण्या मेघनादगभीरया ॥३५॥

evaṁ sambhāṣito rājñā
bhagavān bhūta-bhāvanaḥ
pratyāha prahasan vāṇyā
megha-nāda-gabhīrayā

evam—thus; *sambhāṣitaḥ*—spoken to; *rājñā*—by the King; *bhagavān*—the Supreme Lord; *bhūta*—of all creation; *bhāvanaḥ*—the origin; *pratyāha*—He replied; *prahasan*—smiling broadly; *vāṇyā*—with words; *megha*—of clouds; *nāda*—like the rumbling; *gabhīrayā*—deep.

TRANSLATION

[Śukadeva Gosvāmī continued:] Thus addressed by the King, the Supreme Personality of Godhead, origin of all creation, smiled and then replied to him in a voice as deep as the rumbling of clouds.

TEXT 36

श्रीभगवानुवाच
जन्मकर्माभिधानानि सन्ति मेऽंग सहस्रशः ।
न शक्यन्तेऽनुसंख्यातुमनन्तत्वान्मयापि हि ॥३६॥

śrī-bhagavān uvāca
janma-karmābhidhānāni
santi me 'ṅga sahasraśaḥ
na śakyante 'nusaṅkhyātum
anantatvān mayāpi hi

śrī-bhagavān uvāca—the Supreme Lord said; *janma*—births; *karma*—activities; *abhidhānāni*—and names; *santi*—there are; *me*—My; *aṅga*—O dear one; *sahasraśaḥ*—by the thousands; *na śakyante*—they cannot; *anusaṅkhyātum*—be enumerated; *anantatvāt*—because of having no limit; *mayā*—by Me; *api hi*—even.

TRANSLATION

The Supreme Lord said: My dear friend, I have taken thousands of births, lived thousands of lives and accepted thousands of names. In fact My births, activities and names are limitless, and thus even I cannot count them.

TEXT 37

क्वचिद् रजांसि विममे पार्थिवान्युरुजन्मभिः ।
गुणकर्माभिधानानि न मे जन्मानि कर्हिचित् ॥३७॥

kvacid rajāṁsi vimame
pārthivāny uru-janmabhiḥ
guṇa-karmābhidhānāni
na me janmāni karhicit

kvacit—at some time; *rajāṁsi*—the particles of dust; *vimame*—one might count; *pārthivāni*—on the earth; *uru-janmabhiḥ*—in many lifetimes; *guṇa*—qualities; *karma*—activities; *abhidhānāni*—and names; *na*—not; *me*—My; *janmāni*—births; *karhicit*—ever.

TRANSLATION

After many lifetimes someone might count the dust particles on the earth, but no one can ever finish counting My qualities, activities, names and births.

TEXT 38

कालत्रयोपपन्नानि जन्मकर्माणि मे नृप ।
अनुक्रमन्तो नैवान्तं गच्छन्ति परमर्षयः ॥३८॥

kāla-trayopapannāni
janma-karmāṇi me nṛpa
anukramanto naivāntaṁ
gacchanti paramarṣayaḥ

kāla—of time; *traya*—in three phases (past, present and future); *upapannāni*—occurring; *janma*—births; *karmāṇi*—and activities; *me*—My; *nṛpa*—O King (Mucukunda); *anukramantaḥ*—enumerating; *na*—not; *eva*—at all; *antam*—the end; *gacchanti*—reach; *parama*—the greatest; *ṛṣayaḥ*—sages.

TRANSLATION

O King, the greatest sages enumerate My births and activities, which take place throughout the three phases of time, but never do they reach the end of them.

TEXTS 39–40

तथाप्यद्यतनान्यंग शृणुष्व गदतो मम ।
विज्ञापितो विरिञ्चेन पुराहं धर्मगुप्तये ।
भूमेर्भारायमाणानामसुराणां क्षयाय च ॥३९॥
अवतीर्णो यदुकुले गृह आनकदुन्दुभेः ।
वदन्ति वासुदेवेति वसुदेवसुतं हि माम् ॥४०॥

tathāpy adyatanāny aṅga
śṛṇuṣva gadato mama
vijñāpito viriñcena
purāhaṁ dharma-guptaye
bhūmer bhārāyamāṇānām
asurāṇāṁ kṣayāya ca

avatīrṇo yadu-kule
gṛha ānakadundubheḥ
vadanti vāsudeveti
vasudeva-sutaṁ hi mām

tathā api—nevertheless; *adyatanāni*—those current; *aṅga*—O friend; *śṛṇuṣva*—just hear; *gadataḥ*—who am speaking; *mama*—from Me; *vijñāpitaḥ*—sincerely requested; *viriñcena*—by Lord Brahmā; *purā*—in the past; *aham*—I; *dharma*—religious principles; *guptaye*—to protect; *bhūmeḥ*—for the earth; *bhārāyamāṇānām*—who are a burden;

asurāṇām—of the demons; *kṣayāya*—for the destruction; *ca*—and; *avatīrṇaḥ*—descended; *yadu*—of Yadu; *kule*—into the dynasty; *gṛhe*—in the home; *ānakadundubheḥ*—of Vasudeva; *vadanti*—people call; *vāsudevaḥ iti*—by the name Vāsudeva; *vasudeva-sutam*—the son of Vasudeva; *hi*—indeed; *mām*—Me.

TRANSLATION

Nonetheless, O friend, I will tell you about My current birth, name and activities. Kindly hear. Some time ago, Lord Brahmā requested Me to protect religious principles and destroy the demons who were burdening the earth. Thus I descended in the Yadu dynasty, in the home of Ānakadundubhi. Indeed, because I am the son of Vasudeva, people call Me Vāsudeva.

TEXT 41

कालनेमिर्हतः कंसः प्रलम्बाद्याश्च सद्द्विषः ।
अयं च यवनो दग्धो राजंस्ते तिग्मचक्षुषा ॥४१॥

kālanemir hataḥ kaṁsaḥ
pralambādyāś ca sad-dviṣaḥ
ayaṁ ca yavano dagdho
rājaṁs te tigma-cakṣuṣā

kālanemiḥ—the demon Kālanemi; *hataḥ*—killed; *kaṁsaḥ*—Kaṁsa; *pralamba*—Pralamba; *ādyāḥ*—and others; *ca*—also; *sat*—of those who are pious; *dviṣaḥ*—envious; *ayam*—this; *ca*—and; *yavanaḥ*—barbarian; *dagdhaḥ*—burned; *rājan*—O King; *te*—your; *tigma*—sharp; *cakṣuṣā*—by the glance.

TRANSLATION

I have killed Kālanemi, reborn as Kaṁsa, as well as Pralamba and other enemies of the pious. And now, O King, this barbarian has been burnt to ashes by your piercing glance.

TEXT 42

सोऽहं तवानुग्रहार्थं गुहामेतामुपागतः ।
प्रार्थितः प्रचुरं पूर्वं त्वयाहं भक्तवत्सलः ॥४२॥

so 'haṁ tavānugrahārthaṁ
guhām etām upāgataḥ
prārthitaḥ pracuraṁ pūrvaṁ
tvayāhaṁ bhakta-vatsalaḥ

saḥ—that same person; *aham*—I; *tava*—your; *anugraha*—of the favoring; *artham*—for the sake; *guhām*—cave; *etām*—this; *upāgataḥ*—approached; *prārthitaḥ*—prayed to; *pracuram*—abundantly; *pūrvam*—before; *tvayā*—by you; *aham*—I; *bhakta*—to My devotees; *vatsalaḥ*—affectionate.

TRANSLATION

Since in the past you repeatedly prayed to Me, I have personally come to this cave to show you mercy, for I am affectionately inclined to My devotees.

PURPORT

It is apparent from this verse that Mucukunda was a devotee of the Supreme Lord. He had prayed for the Lord's association, and now Śrī Kṛṣṇa granted his fervent request.

TEXT 43

वरान् वृणीष्व राजर्षे सर्वान् कामान् ददामि ते ।
मां प्रसन्नो जनः कश्चिन्न भूयोऽर्हति शोचितुम् ॥४३॥

varān vṛṇīṣva rājarṣe
sarvān kāmān dadāmi te
māṁ prasanno janaḥ kaścin
na bhūyo 'rhati śocitum

varān—benedictions; *vṛṇīṣva*—just choose; *rāja-ṛṣe*—O saintly King; *sarvān*—all; *kāmān*—desirable things; *dadāmi*—I give; *te*—to you; *mām*—Me; *prasannaḥ*—having satisfied; *janaḥ*—person; *kaścit*—any; *na bhūyaḥ*—never again; *arhati*—needs; *śocitum*—to lament.

TRANSLATION

Now choose some benedictions from Me, O saintly King. I will fulfill all your desires. One who has satisfied Me need never again lament.

PURPORT

The *ācāryas* explain that we lament when we feel incomplete, when we have lost something or when we fail to achieve something desirable. One who has satisfied Kṛṣṇa and thus attained the Lord's mercy will never be troubled in these ways. Lord Kṛṣṇa is the reservoir of all pleasure, and He enjoys sharing His spiritual bliss with all living beings. We need only cooperate with the Supreme Lord.

TEXT 44

श्रीशुक उवाच
इत्युक्तस्तं प्रणम्याह मुचुकुन्दो मुदान्वितः ।
ज्ञात्वा नारायणं देवं गर्गवाक्यमनुस्मरन् ॥४४॥

śrī-śuka uvāca
ity uktas taṁ praṇamyāha
mucukundo mudānvitaḥ
jñātvā nārāyaṇaṁ devaṁ
garga-vākyam anusmaran

śrī-śukaḥ uvāca—Śukadeva Gosvāmī said; *iti*—thus; *uktaḥ*—addressed; *tam*—to Him; *praṇamya*—after bowing down; *āha*—said; *mucukundaḥ*—Mucukunda; *mudā*—with joy; *anvitaḥ*—filled; *jñātvā*—knowing (Him) to be; *nārāyaṇam devam*—Nārāyaṇa, the Supreme Lord; *garga-vākyam*—the words of the sage Garga; *anusmaran*—remembering.

TRANSLATION

Śukadeva Gosvāmī said: Mucukunda bowed down to the Lord when he heard this. Remembering the words of the sage Garga, he joyfully recognized Kṛṣṇa to be the Supreme Lord, Nārāyaṇa. The King then addressed Him as follows.

PURPORT

Although the Lord here appears as four-handed Nārāyaṇa, we may say that Mucukunda was addressing Śrī Kṛṣṇa. All of this is taking place within the context of *kṛṣṇa-līlā,* the pastimes of Lord Kṛṣṇa. It is well known to Vaiṣṇavas that the four-handed forms of Viṣṇu, or Nārāyaṇa, are expansions of Śrī Kṛṣṇa. Thus within the pastimes of Lord Kṛṣṇa there may also appear *viṣṇu-līlā,* the activities of Viṣṇu. Such are the qualities and activities of the Supreme Godhead. Deeds that for us would be extraordinary and even impossible are commonplace, effortless pastimes for the Supreme Personality of Godhead.

Śrīla Śrīdhara Svāmī informs us that Mucukunda was aware of the prediction of the ancient sage Garga that in the twenty-eighth millennium the Supreme Lord would descend. According to Ācārya Viśvanātha, Garga Muni further informed Mucukunda that he would personally see the Lord. Now it was all happening.

TEXT 45

श्रीमुचुकुन्द उवाच
विमोहितोऽयं जन ईश मायया
त्वदीयया त्वां न भजत्यनर्थदृक् ।
सुखाय दुःखप्रभवेषु सज्जते
गृहेषु योषित्पुरुषश्च वञ्चितः ॥४५॥

śrī-mucukunda uvāca
vimohito 'yaṁ jana īśa māyayā
tvadīyayā tvāṁ na bhajaty anartha-dṛk
sukhāya duḥkha-prabhaveṣu sajjate
gṛheṣu yoṣit puruṣaś ca vañcitaḥ

śrī-mucukundaḥ uvāca—Śrī Mucukunda said; *vimohitaḥ*—bewildered; *ayam*—this; *janaḥ*—person; *īśa*—O Lord; *māyayā*—by the illusory energy; *tvadīyayā*—Your own; *tvām*—You; *na bhajati*—does not worship; *anartha-dṛk*—not seeing one's real benefit; *sukhāya*—for the sake of happiness; *duḥkha*—misery; *prabhaveṣu*—in things that cause; *sajjate*—becomes entangled; *gṛheṣu*—in affairs of family life; *yoṣit*—woman; *puruṣaḥ*—man; *ca*—and; *vañcitaḥ*—cheated.

TRANSLATION

Śrī Mucukunda said: O Lord, the people of this world, both men and women, are bewildered by Your illusory energy. Unaware of their real benefit, they do not worship You but instead seek happiness by entangling themselves in family affairs, which are actually sources of misery.

PURPORT

Mucukunda immediately makes it clear that he is not going to ask the Lord for material blessings. He has advanced, spiritually, far beyond those who try to exploit religion for all kinds of material benefits. *Artha* means "value," and the negation of this word, *anartha*, means "that which is valueless or useless." Thus the term *anartha-dṛk* indicates those whose vision is focused on valueless things, who have not understood what actual *artha*, or value, is. All that glitters is not gold, and Mucukunda here emphatically states that we should not ruin our spiritual chances by entangling ourselves in the fool's gold of bodily relationships. We are meant to love the Lord.

TEXT 46

लब्ध्वा जनो दुर्लभमत्र मानुषं
कथञ्चिदव्यंगमयत्नतोऽनघ ।
पादारविन्दं न भजत्यसन्मतिर्
गृहान्धकूपे पतितो यथा पशुः ॥४६॥

labdhvā jano durlabham atra mānuṣaṁ
kathañcid avyaṅgam ayatnato 'nagha

pādāravindaṁ na bhajaty asan-matir
gṛhāndha-kūpe patito yathā paśuḥ

labdhvā—attaining; *janaḥ*—a person; *durlabham*—rarely obtained; *atra*—in this world; *mānuṣam*—the human form of life; *kathañcit*—somehow or other; *avyaṅgam*—with undistorted limbs (unlike the various animal forms); *ayatnataḥ*—without endeavor; *anagha*—O sinless one; *pāda*—Your feet; *aravindam*—lotuslike; *na bhajati*—he does not worship; *asat*—impure; *matiḥ*—his mentality; *gṛha*—of home; *andha*—blind; *kūpe*—in the well; *patitaḥ*—fallen; *yathā*—as; *paśuḥ*—an animal.

TRANSLATION

That person has an impure mind who, despite having somehow or other automatically obtained the rare and highly evolved human form of life, does not worship Your lotus feet. Like an animal that has fallen into a blind well, such a person has fallen into the darkness of a material home.

PURPORT

Our real home is in the kingdom of God. Despite our tenacious determination to remain in our material home, death will rudely eject us from the theater of material affairs. To stay at home is not bad, nor is it bad to devote ourselves to our loved ones. But we must understand that our real home is eternal, in the spiritual kingdom.

The word *ayatnataḥ* indicates that human life has been automatically awarded to us. We have not constructed our human bodies, and therefore we should not foolishly claim, "This body is mine." The human form is a gift of God and should be used to achieve the perfection of God consciousness. One who does not understand this is *asan-mati,* possessed of dull, mundane understanding.

TEXT 47

ममैष कालोऽजित निष्फलो गतो
राज्यश्रियोन्नद्धमदस्य भूपतेः ।
मर्त्यात्मबुद्धेः सुतदारकोशभूष्व्
आसज्जमानस्य दुरन्तचिन्तया ॥४७॥

mamaiṣa kālo 'jita niṣphalo gato
rājya-śriyonnaddha-madasya bhū-pateḥ
martyātma-buddheḥ suta-dāra-kośa-bhūṣv
āsajjamānasya duranta-cintayā

mama—my; *eṣaḥ*—this; *kālaḥ*—time; *ajita*—O unconquerable one; *niṣphalaḥ*—fruitlessly; *gataḥ*—now gone; *rājya*—by kingdom; *śriyā*—and opulence; *unnaddha*—built up; *madasya*—whose intoxication; *bhū-pateḥ*—a king of the earth; *martya*—the mortal body; *ātma*—as the self; *buddheḥ*—whose mentality; *suta*—to children; *dāra*—wives; *kośa*—treasury; *bhūṣu*—and land; *āsajjamānasya*—becoming attached; *dur-anta*—endless; *cintayā*—with anxiety.

TRANSLATION

I have wasted all this time, O unconquerable one, becoming more and more intoxicated by my domain and opulence as an earthly king. Misidentifying the mortal body as the self, becoming attached to children, wives, treasury and land, I suffered endless anxiety.

PURPORT

Having in the previous verse condemned those who misuse the valuable human form of life for mundane purposes, Mucukunda now admits that he himself falls into this category. He intelligently wants to take advantage of the Lord's association and become a pure devotee once and for all.

TEXT 48

कलेवरेऽस्मिन् घटकुड्यसन्निभे
निरूढमानो नरदेव इत्यहम् ।
वृतो रथेभाश्वपदात्यनीकपैर्
गां पर्यटंस्त्वागणयन् सुदुर्मदः ॥४८॥

kalevare 'smin ghaṭa-kuḍya-sannibhe
nirūḍha-māno nara-deva ity aham

vṛto rathebhāśva-padāty-anīkapair
gāṁ paryaṭaṁs tvāgaṇayan su-durmadaḥ

kalevare—in the body; *asmin*—this; *ghaṭa*—a pot; *kuḍya*—or a wall; *sannibhe*—which is like; *nirūḍha*—exaggerated; *mānaḥ*—whose false identification; *nara-devaḥ*—a god among men (king); *iti*—thus (thinking myself); *aham*—I; *vṛtaḥ*—surrounded; *ratha*—by chariots; *ibha*—elephants; *aśva*—horses; *padāti*—infantry; *anīkapaiḥ*—and generals; *gām*—the earth; *paryaṭan*—traveling; *tvā*—You; *agaṇayan*—not regarding seriously; *su-durmadaḥ*—very much deluded by pride.

TRANSLATION

With deep arrogance I took myself to be the body, which is a material object like a pot or a wall. Thinking myself a god among men, I traveled the earth surrounded by my charioteers, elephants, cavalry, foot soldiers and generals, disregarding You in my deluding pride.

TEXT 49

प्रमत्तमुच्चैरितिकृत्यचिन्तयया
प्रवृद्धलोभं विषयेषु लालसम् ।
त्वमप्रमत्तः सहसाभिपद्यसे
क्षुल्लेलिहानोऽहिरिवाखुमन्तकः ॥४९॥

pramattam uccair itikṛtya-cintayā
pravṛddha-lobhaṁ viṣayeṣu lālasam
tvam apramattaḥ sahasābhipadyase
kṣul-lelihāno 'hir ivākhum antakaḥ

pramattam—thoroughly deluded; *uccaiḥ*—extensive; *iti-kṛtya*—of what needs to be done; *cintayā*—with thought; *pravṛddha*—increased fully; *lobham*—whose greed; *viṣayeṣu*—for sense objects; *lālasam*—hankering; *tvam*—You; *apramattaḥ*—not deluded; *sahasā*—suddenly; *abhipadyase*—confront; *kṣut*—out of thirst; *lelihānaḥ*—licking its fangs; *ahiḥ*—a snake; *iva*—as; *ākhum*—a mouse; *antakaḥ*—death.

TRANSLATION

A man obsessed with thoughts of what he thinks needs to be done, intensely greedy, and delighting in sense enjoyment is suddenly confronted by You, who are ever alert. Like a hungry snake licking its fangs before a mouse, You appear before him as death.

PURPORT

We may note here the contrast between the words *pramattam* and *apramattaḥ*. Those who are trying to exploit the material world are *pramatta:* "deluded, bewildered, maddened by desire." But the Lord is *apramatta:* "alert, sober, and unbewildered." In our madness we may deny God or His laws, but the Lord is sober and will not fail to reward or punish us according to the quality of our activities.

TEXT 50

पुरा रथैर्हेमपरिष्कृतैश्चरन्
मतंगजैर्वा नरदेवसंज्ञितः ।
स एव कालेन दुरत्ययेन ते
कलेवरो विट्कृमिभस्मसंज्ञितः ॥५०॥

purā rathair hema-pariṣkṛtaiś caran
mataṁ-gajair vā nara-deva-saṁjñitaḥ
sa eva kālena duratyayena te
kalevaro viṭ-kṛmi-bhasma-saṁjñitaḥ

purā—previously; *rathaiḥ*—in chariots; *hema*—with gold; *pariṣkṛtaiḥ*—furnished; *caran*—riding; *matam*—fierce; *gajaiḥ*—on elephants; *vā*—or; *nara-deva*—king; *saṁjñitaḥ*—named; *saḥ*—that; *eva*—same; *kālena*—by time; *duratyayena*—unavoidable; *te*—Your; *kalevaraḥ*—body; *viṭ*—as feces; *kṛmi*—worms; *bhasma*—ashes; *saṁjñitaḥ*—named.

TRANSLATION

The body that at first rides high on fierce elephants or chariots adorned with gold and is known by the name "king" is later, by

Your invincible power of time, called "feces," "worms," or "ashes."

PURPORT

In the United States and other materially developed countries, dead bodies are cosmetically disposed of in a tidy ceremonial way, but in many parts of the world old, sickly and injured people die in lonely or neglected places, where dogs and jackals consume their bodies and transform them into stool. And if one is so blessed as to be buried in a coffin, one's body may very well be consumed by worms and other minuscule creatures. Also, many earthly cadavers are burned and thus transformed into ashes. In any case, death is certain, and the ultimate fate of the body is never sublime. That is the real purport of Mucukunda's statement here—that the body, though now called "king," "prince," "beauty queen," "upper-middle class" and so on, will eventually be called "stool," "worms" and "ashes."

Śrīla Śrīdhara Svāmī quotes the following Vedic statement:

yoneḥ sahasrāṇi bahūni gatvā
duḥkhena labdhvāpi ca mānuṣatvam
sukhāvahaṁ ye na bhajanti viṣṇuṁ
te vai manuṣyātmani śatru-bhūtāḥ

"After passing through many thousands of species and undergoing great struggle, the conditioned living entities finally obtain the human form. Thus those human beings who still do not worship Lord Viṣṇu, who can bring them real happiness, have certainly become enemies of both themselves and humanity."

TEXT 51

निर्जित्य दिक्चक्रमभूतविग्रहो
वरासनस्थः समराजवन्दितः ।
गृहेषु मैथुन्यसुखेषु योषितां
क्रीडामृगः पूरुष ईश नीयते ॥५१॥

nirjitya dik-cakram abhūta-vigraho
varāsana-sthaḥ sama-rāja-vanditaḥ

gṛheṣu maithunya-sukheṣu yoṣitāṁ
krīḍā-mṛgaḥ pūruṣa īśa nīyate

nirjitya—having conquered; *dik*—of directions; *cakram*—the whole circle; *abhūta*—nonexistent; *vigrahaḥ*—any conflict for whom; *vara-āsana*—on an exalted throne; *sthaḥ*—seated; *sama*—equal; *rāja*—by kings; *vanditaḥ*—praised; *gṛheṣu*—in residences; *maithunya*—sex; *sukheṣu*—whose happiness; *yoṣitām*—of women; *krīḍā-mṛgaḥ*—a pet animal; *pūruṣaḥ*—the person; *īśa*—O Lord; *nīyate*—is led about.

TRANSLATION

Having conquered the entire circle of directions and being thus free of conflict, a man sits on a splendid throne, receiving praise from leaders who were once his equals. But when he enters the women's chambers, where sex pleasure is found, he is led about like a pet animal, O Lord.

TEXT 52

करोति कर्माणि तपःसुनिष्ठितो
निवृत्तभोगस्तदपेक्षयाददत् ।
पुनश्च भूयासमहं स्वराडिति
प्रवृद्धतर्षो न सुखाय कल्पते ॥५२॥

karoti karmāṇi tapaḥ-suniṣṭhito
nivṛtta-bhogas tad-apekṣayādadat
punaś ca bhūyāsam ahaṁ sva-rāḍ iti
pravṛddha-tarṣo na sukhāya kalpate

karoti—one performs; *karmāṇi*—duties; *tapaḥ*—in the practice of austerities; *su-niṣṭhitaḥ*—very fixed; *nivṛtta*—avoiding; *bhogaḥ*—sense enjoyment; *tat*—with that (position which he already has); *apekṣayā*—in comparison; *ādadat*—assuming; *punaḥ*—further; *ca*—and; *bhūyāsam*—greater; *aham*—I; *sva-rāṭ*—sovereign ruler; *iti*—thus thinking; *pravṛddha*—rampant; *tarṣaḥ*—whose urges; *na*—not; *sukhāya*—happiness; *kalpate*—can attain.

TRANSLATION

A king who desires even greater power than he already has strictly performs his duties, carefully practicing austerity and forgoing sense enjoyment. But he whose urges are so rampant, thinking "I am independent and supreme," cannot attain happiness.

TEXT 53

भवापवर्गो भ्रमतो यदा भवेज्
जनस्य तर्ह्यच्युत सत्समागमः ।
सत्संगमो यर्हि तदैव सद्गतौ
परावरेशे त्वयि जायते मतिः ॥५३॥

bhavāpavargo bhramato yadā bhavej
janasya tarhy acyuta sat-samāgamaḥ
sat-saṅgamo yarhi tadaiva sad-gatau
parāvareśe tvayi jāyate matiḥ

bhava—of material existence; *apavargaḥ*—the cessation; *bhramataḥ*—who has been wandering; *yadā*—when; *bhavet*—occurs; *janasya*—for a person; *tarhi*—at that time; *acyuta*—O infallible Lord; *sat*—of saintly devotees; *samāgamaḥ*—the association; *sat-saṅgamaḥ*—saintly association; *yarhi*—when; *tadā*—then; *eva*—only; *sat*—of the saintly; *gatau*—who is the goal; *para*—of superior (the causes of material creation); *avara*—and inferior (their products); *īśe*—for the Supreme Lord; *tvayi*—Yourself; *jāyate*—is born; *matiḥ*—devotion.

TRANSLATION

When the material life of a wandering soul has ceased, O Acyuta, he may attain the association of Your devotees. And when he associates with them, there awakens in him devotion unto You, who are the goal of the devotees and the Lord of all causes and their effects.

PURPORT

Ācāryas Jīva Gosvāmī and Viśvanātha Cakravartī agree on the following point: Although it is stated here that when material life ceases one attains the association of devotees, in fact it is the association of the Lord's devotees that enables one to transcend material existence. Śrīla Jīva Gosvāmī explains this apparent inversion of sequence by quoting the *Kāvya-prakāśa* (10.153) as follows: *kārya-kāraṇayoś ca paurvāparya-viparyayo vijñeyātiśayoktiḥ syāt sā.* "A statement in which the logical order of a cause and its effect is reversed should be understood as *atiśayokti*, emphasis by extreme assertion." Śrīla Jīva Gosvāmī cites the following commentary on this statement: *kāraṇasya śīghra-kāritāṁ vaktuṁ kāryasya pūrvam uktau.* "To express the swift action of a cause, one may assert the result before the cause."

In this connection Śrīla Viśvanātha Cakravartī points out that the merciful association of the Lord's devotees makes possible our determination to become Kṛṣṇa conscious. And the *ācārya* agrees with Śrīla Jīva Gosvāmī that this verse is an instance of *atiśayokti*.

TEXT 54

मन्ये ममानुग्रह ईश ते कृतो
राज्यानुबन्धापगमो यदृच्छया ।
यः प्रार्थ्यते साधुभिरेकचर्यया
वनं विविक्षद्भिरखण्डभूमिपैः ॥५४॥

manye mamānugraha īśa te kṛto
rājyānubandhāpagamo yadṛcchayā
yaḥ prārthyate sādhubhir eka-caryayā
vanaṁ vivikṣadbhir akhaṇḍa-bhūmi-paiḥ

manye—I think; *mama*—to me; *anugrahaḥ*—mercy; *īśa*—O Lord; *te*—by You; *kṛtaḥ*—done; *rājya*—to kingdom; *anubandha*—of attachment; *apagamaḥ*—the removal; *yadṛcchayā*—spontaneous; *yaḥ*—which; *prārthyate*—is prayed for; *sādhubhiḥ*—saintly; *eka-caryayā*—in solitude; *vanam*—the forest; *vivikṣadbhiḥ*—who desire to enter; *akhaṇḍa*—unlimited; *bhūmi*—of lands; *paiḥ*—by rulers.

TRANSLATION

My Lord, I think You have shown me mercy, since my attachment to my kingdom has spontaneously ceased. Such freedom is prayed for by saintly rulers of vast empires who desire to enter the forest for a life of solitude.

TEXT 55

न कामयेऽन्यं तव पादसेवनाद्
अकिञ्चनप्रार्थ्यतमाद्वरं विभो ।
आराध्य कस्त्वां ह्यपवर्गदं हरे
वृणीत आर्यो वरमात्मबन्धनम् ॥५५॥

na kāmaye 'nyaṁ tava pāda-sevanād
akiñcana-prārthyatamād varaṁ vibho
ārādhya kas tvāṁ hy apavarga-daṁ hare
vṛṇīta āryo varam ātma-bandhanam

na kāmaye—I do not desire; *anyam*—another; *tava*—Your; *pāda*—of the feet; *sevanāt*—than the service; *akiñcana*—by those who want nothing material; *prārthya-tamāt*—which is the favorite object of entreaty; *varam*—boon; *vibho*—O all-powerful one; *ārādhya*—worshiping; *kaḥ*—who; *tvām*—You; *hi*—indeed; *apavarga*—of liberation; *dam*—the bestower; *hare*—O Lord Hari; *vṛṇīta*—would choose; *āryaḥ*—a spiritually advanced person; *varam*—boon; *ātma*—his own; *bandhanam*—(cause of) bondage.

TRANSLATION

O all-powerful one, I desire no boon other than service to Your lotus feet, the boon most eagerly sought by those free of material desire. O Hari, what enlightened person who worships You, the giver of liberation, would choose a boon that causes his own bondage?

PURPORT

The Lord offered Mucukunda anything he desired, but Mucukunda desired only the Lord. This is pure Kṛṣṇa consciousness.

TEXT 56

तस्माद्विसृज्याशिष ईश सर्वतो
रजस्तमःसत्त्वगुणानुबन्धनाः ।
निरञ्जनं निर्गुणमद्वयं परं
त्वां ज्ञाप्तिमात्रं पुरुषं व्रजाम्यहम् ॥५६॥

tasmād visṛjyāśiṣa īśa sarvato
rajas-tamaḥ-sattva-guṇānubandhanāḥ
nirañjanaṁ nirguṇam advayaṁ paraṁ
tvāṁ jñāpti-mātraṁ puruṣaṁ vrajāmy aham

tasmāt—therefore; *visṛjya*—putting aside; *āśiṣaḥ*—desirable objects; *īśa*—O Lord; *sarvataḥ*—entirely; *rajaḥ*—with passion; *tamaḥ*—ignorance; *sattva*—and goodness; *guṇa*—the material modes; *anubandhanāḥ*—entangled; *nirañjanam*—free from mundane designations; *nirguṇam*—transcendental to the material modes; *advayam*—nondual; *param*—supreme; *tvām*—You; *jñāpti-mātram*—pure knowledge; *puruṣam*—the original person; *vrajāmi*—am approaching; *aham*—I.

TRANSLATION

Therefore, O Lord, having put aside all objects of material desire, which are bound to the modes of passion, ignorance and goodness, I am approaching You, the Supreme Personality of Godhead, for shelter. You are not covered by mundane designations; rather, You are the Supreme Absolute Truth, full in pure knowledge and transcendental to the material modes.

PURPORT

The word *nirguṇam* here indicates that the Lord's existence is beyond the qualities of material nature. One might argue that Lord Kṛṣṇa's body is made of material nature, but here the word *advayam* refutes that argument. There is no duality in Lord Kṛṣṇa's existence. His eternal, spiritual body is Kṛṣṇa, and Kṛṣṇa is God.

TEXT 57

चिरमिह वृजिनार्तस्तप्यमानोऽनुतापैर्
अवितृषषडमित्रोऽलब्धशान्तिः कथञ्चित् ।
शरणद समुपेतस्त्वत्पदाब्जं परात्मन्
अभयमृतमशोकं पाहि मापन्नमीश ॥५७॥

ciram iha vṛjinārtas tapyamāno 'nutāpair
avitṛṣa-ṣaḍ-amitro 'labdha-śāntiḥ kathañcit
śaraṇa-da samupetas tvat-padābjaṁ parātman
abhayam ṛtam aśokaṁ pāhi māpannam īśa

ciram—for a long time; *iha*—in this world; *vṛjina*—by disturbances; *ārtaḥ*—distressed; *tapyamānaḥ*—tormented; *anutāpaiḥ*—with remorse; *avitṛṣa*—unsatiated; *ṣaṭ*—six; *amitraḥ*—whose enemies (the five senses and the mind); *alabdha*—not attaining; *śāntiḥ*—peace; *kathañcit*—by some means; *śaraṇa*—of shelter; *da*—O bestower; *samupetaḥ*—who have approached; *tvat*—Your; *pada-abjam*—lotus feet; *para-ātman*—O Supreme Soul; *abhayam*—fearless; *ṛtam*—the truth; *aśokam*—free from sorrow; *pāhi*—please protect; *mā*—me; *āpannam*—who am confronted with dangers; *īśa*—O Lord.

TRANSLATION

For so long I have been pained by troubles in this world and have been burning with lamentation. My six enemies are never satiated, and I can find no peace. Therefore, O giver of shelter, O Supreme Soul, please protect me. O Lord, in the midst of danger I have by good fortune approached Your lotus feet, which are the truth and which thus make one fearless and free of sorrow.

TEXT 58

श्रीभगवानुवाच
सार्वभौम महाराज मतिस्ते विमलोर्जिता ।
वरैः प्रलोभितस्यापि न कामैर्विहता यतः ॥५८॥

śrī-bhagavān uvāca
sārvabhauma mahā-rāja
matis te vimalorjitā
varaiḥ pralobhitasyāpi
na kāmair vihatā yataḥ

śrī-bhagavān uvāca—the Supreme Lord said; *sārvabhauma*—O emperor; *mahā-rāja*—great ruler; *matiḥ*—mind; *te*—Your; *vimala*—spotless; *ūrjitā*—potent; *varaiḥ*—with benedictions; *pralobhitasya*—of (you) who were enticed; *api*—even though; *na*—not; *kāmaiḥ*—by material desires; *vihatā*—spoiled; *yataḥ*—since.

TRANSLATION

The Supreme Lord said: O emperor, great ruler, your mind is pure and potent. Though I enticed You with benedictions, your mind was not overcome by material desires.

TEXT 59

प्रलोभितो वरैर्यत्त्वमप्रमादाय विद्धि तत् ।
न धीरेकान्तभक्तानामाशीर्भिर्भिद्यते क्वचित् ॥५९॥

pralobhito varair yat tvam
apramādāya viddhi tat
na dhīr ekānta-bhaktānām
āśīrbhir bhidyate kvacit

pralobhitaḥ—enticed; *varaiḥ*—with benedictions; *yat*—which fact; *tvam*—you; *apramādāya*—for (showing your) freedom from bewilderment; *viddhi*—please know; *tat*—that; *na*—not; *dhīḥ*—the intelligence; *ekānta*—exclusive; *bhaktānām*—of devotees; *āśīrbhiḥ*—by blessings; *bhidyate*—is diverted; *kvacit*—ever.

TRANSLATION

Understand that I enticed you with benedictions just to prove that you would not be deceived. The intelligence of My unalloyed devotees is never diverted by material blessings.

TEXT 60

युञ्जानानामभक्तानां प्राणायामादिभिर्मनः ।
अक्षीणवासनं राजन् दृश्यते पुनरुत्थितम् ॥६०॥

yuñjānānām abhaktānāṁ
prāṇāyāmādibhir manaḥ
akṣīṇa-vāsanaṁ rājan
dṛśyate punar utthitam

yuñjānānām—who are engaging themselves; *abhaktānām*—of nondevotees; *prāṇāyāma*—with *prāṇāyāma* (yogic breath control); *ādibhiḥ*—and other practices; *manaḥ*—the minds; *akṣīṇa*—not eliminated; *vāsanam*—the last traces of whose material desire; *rājan*—O King (Mucukunda); *dṛśyate*—is seen; *punaḥ*—again; *utthitam*—waking (to thoughts of sense gratification).

TRANSLATION

The minds of nondevotees who engage in such practices as *prāṇāyāma* are not fully cleansed of material desires. Thus, O King, material desires are again seen to arise in their minds.

TEXT 61

विचरस्व महीं कामं मय्यावेशितमानसः ।
अस्त्वेवं नित्यदा तुभ्यं भक्तिर्मय्यनपायिनी ॥६१॥

vicarasva mahīṁ kāmaṁ
mayy āveśita-mānasaḥ
astv evaṁ nityadā tubhyaṁ
bhaktir mayy anapāyinī

vicarasva—wander; *mahīm*—this earth; *kāmam*—at will; *mayi*—in Me; *āveśita*—fixed; *mānasaḥ*—your mind; *astu*—may there be; *evam*—thus; *nityadā*—always; *tubhyam*—for you; *bhaktiḥ*—devotion; *mayi*—to Me; *anapāyinī*—unfailing.

TRANSLATION

Wander this earth at will, with your mind fixed on Me. May you always possess such unfailing devotion for Me.

TEXT 62

क्षात्रधर्मस्थितो जन्तूंन्यवधीर्मृगयादिभिः ।
समाहितस्तत्तपसा जह्यघं मदुपाश्रितः ॥६२॥

kṣātra-dharma-sthito jantūn
nyavadhīr mṛgayādibhiḥ
samāhitas tat tapasā
jahy aghaṁ mad-upāśritaḥ

kṣātra—of the ruling class; *dharma*—in the religious principles; *sthitaḥ*—situated; *jantūn*—living beings; *nyavadhīḥ*—you killed; *mṛgayā*—in the course of hunting; *ādibhiḥ*—and other activities; *samāhitaḥ*—fully concentrated; *tat*—that; *tapasā*—by penances; *jahi*—you should eradicate; *agham*—sinful reaction; *mat*—in Me; *upāśritaḥ*—taking shelter.

TRANSLATION

Because you followed the principles of a *kṣatriya,* you killed living beings while hunting and performing other duties. You must vanquish the sins thus incurred by carefully executing penances while remaining surrendered to Me.

TEXT 63

जन्मन्यनन्तरे राजन् सर्वभूतसुहृत्तमः ।
भूत्वा द्विजवरस्त्वं वै मामुपैष्यसि केवलम् ॥६३॥

janmany anantare rājan
sarva-bhūta-suhṛttamaḥ
bhūtvā dvija-varas tvaṁ vai
mām upaiṣyasi kevalam

janmani—in the birth; *anantare*—immediately following; *rājan*—O King; *sarva*—of all; *bhūta*—living beings; *suhṛt-tamaḥ*—a supreme well-wisher; *bhūtvā*—becoming; *dvija-varaḥ*—an excellent *brāhmaṇa; tvam*—you; *vai*—indeed; *mām*—to Me; *upaiṣyasi*—will come; *kevalam*—exclusively.

TRANSLATION

O King, in your very next life you will become an excellent *brāhmaṇa*, the greatest well-wisher of all creatures, and certainly come to Me alone.

PURPORT

Śrī Kṛṣṇa states in the *Bhagavad-gītā* (5.29), *suhṛdaṁ sarva-bhūtānāṁ jñātvā māṁ śāntim ṛcchati:* "A person attains peace by understanding Me to be the well-wishing friend of all living beings." Lord Kṛṣṇa and His pure devotees work together to rescue the fallen souls from the ocean of illusion. This is the real purport of the Kṛṣṇa consciousness movement.

Thus end the purports of the humble servants of His Divine Grace A. C. Bhaktivedanta Swami Prabhupāda to the Tenth Canto, Fifty-first Chapter, of the Śrīmad-Bhāgavatam, *entitled "The Deliverance of Mucukunda."*

CHAPTER FIFTY-TWO

Rukmiṇī's Message to Lord Kṛṣṇa

This chapter describes how Lord Balarāma and Lord Kṛṣṇa, running as if in fear, went to Dvārakā. Then Lord Kṛṣṇa heard the message of Rukmiṇī from the mouth of a *brāhmaṇa* and chose her as His wife.

King Mucukunda, shown mercy by Lord Śrī Kṛṣṇa, offered obeisances and circumambulated Him. The King then left the cave and saw that humans, animals, trees and plants were all smaller than when he had fallen asleep. From this he could understand that the age of Kali was at hand. Thus, in a mood of detachment from all material association, the King began worshiping the Supreme Lord, Śrī Hari.

Śrī Kṛṣṇa returned to Mathurā, which was still under siege by the barbarian army. He destroyed this army, collected all the valuables the soldiers had been carrying, and set off for Dvārakā. Just then Jarāsandha arrived on the scene with a force of twenty-three *akṣauhiṇīs.* Lord Balarāma and Lord Kṛṣṇa, acting as if fearful, left Their riches aside and ran far away. Because Jarāsandha could not appreciate Their true power, he ran after Them. After running a long way, Rāma and Kṛṣṇa came to a mountain named Pravarṣaṇa and proceeded to climb it. Jarāsandha thought They had hidden inside a cave and looked all over for Them. Unable to find Them, he built fires on all sides of the mountain. As the vegetation on the mountain slopes burst into flame, Kṛṣṇa and Balarāma jumped off the peak. After reaching the ground unseen by Jarāsandha and his followers, They returned to the Dvārakā fort, which floated within the sea. Jarāsandha decided that Rāma and Kṛṣṇa had burned to death in the fire, and he took his army back to his kingdom.

At this point Mahārāja Parīkṣit asked a question, and Śrī Śukadeva Gosvāmī responded to it by beginning to narrate the history of the marriage of Lord Śrī Kṛṣṇa and Rukmiṇī. Rukmiṇī, the young daughter of Bhīṣmaka, King of Vidarbha, had heard of Śrī Kṛṣṇa's beauty, strength and other fine qualities, and she therefore made up her mind that He would be the perfect husband for her. Lord Kṛṣṇa also wanted to marry her. But although Rukmiṇī's other relatives approved of her marriage to Kṛṣṇa, her brother Rukmī was envious of the Lord and thus forbade her to marry Him. Rukmī wanted her to marry Śiśupāla instead. Rukmiṇī unhappily took up her duties in preparation for the marriage, but she also sent a trustworthy *brāhmaṇa* to Kṛṣṇa with a letter.

When the *brāhmaṇa* arrived in Dvārakā, Śrī Kṛṣṇa properly honored him with ritual worship and other tokens of reverence. The Lord then asked the *brāhmaṇa* why he had come. The *brāhmaṇa* opened Rukmiṇī's letter and showed it to Lord Kṛṣṇa, who had the messenger read it to Him. Rukmiṇī-devī wrote, "Ever since I have heard about You, my Lord, I have become completely attracted to You. Without fail please come before my marriage to Śiśupāla and take me away. In accordance with family custom, on the day before my marriage I will visit the temple of goddess Ambikā. That would be the best opportunity for You to appear and easily kidnap me. If You do not show me this favor, I will give up my life by fasting and observing severe vows. Then perhaps in my next life I will be able to obtain You."

After reading Rukmiṇī's letter to Lord Kṛṣṇa, the *brāhmaṇa* took his leave so he might carry out his daily religious duties.

TEXT 1

श्रीशुक उवाच
इत्थं सोऽनुग्रहीतोऽङ्ग कृष्णेनेक्ष्वाकुनन्दनः ।
तं परिक्रम्य सन्नम्य निश्चक्राम गुहामुखात् ॥१॥

śrī-śuka uvāca
itthaṁ so 'nugrahīto 'ṅga
kṛṣṇenekṣvāku-nandanaḥ
taṁ parikramya sannamya
niścakrāma guhā-mukhāt

śrī-śukaḥ uvāca—Śukadeva Gosvāmī said; *ittham*—in this manner; *saḥ*—he; *anugrahītaḥ*—shown mercy; *aṅga*—my dear (Parīkṣit Mahārāja); *kṛṣṇena*—by Lord Kṛṣṇa; *ikṣvāku-nandanaḥ*—Mucukunda, the beloved descendant of Ikṣvāku; *tam*—Him; *parikramya*—circumambulating; *sannamya*—bowing down; *niścakrāma*—he went out; *guhā*—of the cave; *mukhāt*—from the mouth.

TRANSLATION

Śukadeva Gosvāmī said: My dear King, thus graced by Lord Kṛṣṇa, Mucukunda circumambulated Him and bowed down to Him. Then Mucukunda, the beloved descendant of Ikṣvāku, exited through the mouth of the cave.

TEXT 2

संवीक्ष्य क्षुल्लकान्मर्त्यान् पशून् वीरुद्वनस्पतीन् ।
मत्वा कलियुगं प्राप्तं जगाम दिशमुत्तराम् ॥२॥

saṁvīkṣya kṣullakān martyān
paśūn vīrud-vanaspatīn
matvā kali-yugaṁ prāptaṁ
jagāma diśam uttarām

saṁvīkṣya—noticing; *kṣullakān*—tiny; *martyān*—the human beings; *paśūn*—animals; *vīrut*—plants; *vanaspatīn*—and trees; *matvā*—considering; *kali-yugam*—the age of Kali; *prāptam*—having arrived; *jagāma*—he went; *diśam*—to the direction; *uttarām*—northern.

TRANSLATION

Seeing that the size of all the human beings, animals, trees and plants was severely reduced, and thus realizing that the age of Kali was at hand, Mucukunda left for the north.

PURPORT

There are several significant words in this verse. A standard Sanskrit dictionary gives the following English meanings for the word *kṣullaka:* "little, small, low, vile, poor, indigent, wicked, malicious, abandoned, hard, pained, distressed." These are the symptoms of the age of Kali, and all these qualities are said here to apply to men, animals, plants and trees in this age. We who are enamored of ourselves and our environment can perhaps imagine the superior beauty and living conditions available to people in former ages.

The last line of this text, *jagāma diśam uttarām*—"He went toward the north"—can be understood as follows. By traveling north in India, one comes to the world's highest mountains, the Himālayan range. There one can still find many beautiful peaks and valleys, where there are quiet hermitages suitable for austerity and meditation. Thus in Vedic culture "going to the north" indicates renouncing the comforts of ordinary society and going to the Himālayan Mountains to practice serious austerities for spiritual advancement.

TEXT 3

तपःश्रद्धायुतो धीरो निःसंगो मुक्तसंशयः ।
समाधाय मनः कृष्णे प्राविशद् गन्धमादनम् ॥३॥

tapaḥ-śraddhā-yuto dhīro
niḥsaṅgo mukta-saṁśayaḥ
samādhāya manaḥ kṛṣṇe
prāviśad gandhamādanam

tapaḥ—in austerities; *śraddhā*—faith; *yutaḥ*—having; *dhīraḥ*—serious; *niḥsaṅgaḥ*—detached from material association; *mukta*—freed; *saṁśayaḥ*—of doubts; *samādhāya*—fixing in trance; *manaḥ*—his mind; *kṛṣṇe*—upon Lord Kṛṣṇa; *prāviśat*—he entered upon; *gandha-mādanam*—the mountain known as Gandhamādana.

TRANSLATION

The sober King, beyond material association and free of doubt, was convinced of the value of austerity. Absorbing his mind in Lord Kṛṣṇa, he came to Gandhamādana Mountain.

PURPORT

The name Gandhamādana indicates a place of delightful fragrances. Undoubtedly Gandhamādana was filled with the aroma of wild flowers and forest honey, and with other natural scents.

TEXT 4

बदर्याश्रममासाद्य नरनारायणालयम् ।
सर्वद्वन्द्वसहः शान्तस्तपसाराधयद्धरिम् ॥४॥

badary-āśramam āsādya
nara-nārāyaṇālayam
sarva-dvandva-sahaḥ śāntas
tapasārādhayad dharim

badarī-āśramam—the hermitage Badarikāśrama; *āsādya*—reaching; *nara-nārāyaṇa*—of the Supreme Lord's dual incarnation as Nara and Nārāyaṇa; *ālayam*—the residence; *sarva*—all; *dvandva*—dualities; *sahaḥ*—tolerating; *śāntaḥ*—peaceful; *tapasā*—with severe austerities; *ārādhayat*—he worshiped; *harim*—Lord Kṛṣṇa.

TRANSLATION

There he arrived at Badarikāśrama, the abode of Lord Nara-Nārāyaṇa, where, remaining tolerant of all dualities, he peacefully worshiped the Supreme Lord Hari by performing severe austerities.

TEXT 5

भगवान् पुनराव्रज्य पुरीं यवनवेष्टिताम् ।
हत्वा म्लेच्छबलं निन्ये तदीयं द्वारकां धनम् ॥५॥

bhagavān punar āvrajya
purīṁ yavana-veṣṭitām
hatvā mleccha-balaṁ ninye
tadīyaṁ dvārakāṁ dhanam

bhagavān—the Lord; *punaḥ*—once again; *āvrajya*—returning; *purīm*—to His city; *yavana*—by the Yavanas; *veṣṭitām*—surrounded; *hatvā*—killing; *mleccha*—of barbarians; *balam*—the army; *ninye*—He brought; *tadīyam*—their; *dvārakām*—to Dvārakā; *dhanam*—wealth.

TRANSLATION

The Lord returned to Mathurā, which was still surrounded by Yavanas. Then He destroyed the army of barbarians and began taking their valuables to Dvārakā.

PURPORT

It is clear from this verse that Kālayavana alone pursued Lord Kṛṣṇa into the mountain cave. When Kṛṣṇa returned to the besieged city of Mathurā, He eliminated the vast barbarian army.

TEXT 6

नीयमाने धने गोभिर्नृभिश्चाच्युतचोदितैः ।
आजगाम जरासन्धस्त्रयोविंशत्यनीकपः ॥६॥

nīyamāne dhane gobhir
nṛbhiś cācyuta-coditaiḥ
ājagāma jarāsandhas
trayo-viṁśaty-anīka-paḥ

nīyamāne—as it was being taken; *dhane*—the wealth; *gobhiḥ*—by oxen; *nṛbhiḥ*—by men; *ca*—and; *acyuta*—by Lord Kṛṣṇa; *coditaiḥ*—engaged; *ājagāma*—came there; *jarāsandhaḥ*—Jarāsandha; *trayaḥ*—three; *viṁśati*—plus twenty; *anīka*—of armies; *paḥ*—the leader.

TRANSLATION

As the wealth was being carried by oxen and men under Lord Kṛṣṇa's direction, Jarāsandha appeared at the head of twenty-three armies.

TEXT 7

विलोक्य वेगरभसं रिपुसैन्यस्य माधवौ ।
मनुष्यचेष्टामापन्नौ राजन् दुद्रुवतुर्द्रुतम् ॥७॥

vilokya vega-rabhasaṁ
ripu-sainyasya mādhavau
manuṣya-ceṣṭām āpannau
rājan dudruvatur drutam

vilokya—seeing; *vega*—of the waves; *rabhasam*—the fierceness; *ripu*—enemy; *sainyasya*—of the armies; *mādhavau*—the two Mādhavas (Kṛṣṇa and Balarāma); *manuṣya*—humanlike; *ceṣṭām*—behavior; *āpannau*—assuming; *rājan*—O King (Parīkṣit); *dudruvatuḥ*—ran away; *drutam*—quickly.

TRANSLATION

O King, seeing the fierce waves of the enemy's army, the two Mādhavas, imitating human behavior, ran swiftly away.

TEXT 8

विहाय वित्तं प्रचुरमभीतौ भीरुभीतवत् ।
पद्भ्यां पद्मपलाशाभ्यां चेलतुर्बहुयोजनम् ॥८॥

vihāya vittaṁ pracuram
abhītau bhīru-bhīta-vat
padbhyāṁ padma-palāśābhyāṁ
celatur bahu-yojanam

vihāya—abandoning; *vittam*—the riches; *pracuram*—abundant; *abhītau*—actually unafraid; *bhīru*—like cowards; *bhīta-vat*—as if frightened; *padbhyām*—with Their feet; *padma*—of lotuses; *palāśābhyām*—like petals; *celatuḥ*—They went; *bahu-yojanam*—for many *yojanas* (one *yojana* is slightly more than eight miles).

TRANSLATION

Abandoning the abundant riches, fearless but feigning fear, They went many *yojanas* on Their lotuslike feet.

TEXT 9

पलायमानौ तौ दृष्ट्वा मागधः प्रहसन् बली ।
अन्वधावद् रथानीकैरीशयोरप्रमाणवित् ॥९॥

palāyamānau tau dṛṣṭvā
māgadhaḥ prahasan balī
anvadhāvad rathānīkair
īśayor apramāṇa-vit

palāyamānau—who were fleeing; *tau*—Those two; *dṛṣṭvā*—seeing; *māgadhaḥ*—Jarāsandha; *prahasan*—laughing loudly; *balī*—powerful; *anvadhāvat*—he ran after; *ratha*—with charioteers; *anīkaiḥ*—and soldiers; *īśayoḥ*—of the Lords; *apramāṇa-vit*—unaware of the scope.

TRANSLATION

When he saw Them fleeing, powerful Jarāsandha laughed loudly and then pursued Them with charioteers and foot soldiers. He could not understand the exalted position of the two Lords.

TEXT 10

प्रद्रुत्य दूरं संश्रान्तौ तुंगमारुहतां गिरिम् ।
प्रवर्षणाख्यं भगवान्नित्यदा यत्र वर्षति ॥१०॥

pradrutya dūraṁ saṁśrāntau
tuṅgam āruhatāṁ girim
pravarṣaṇākhyaṁ bhagavān
nityadā yatra varṣati

pradrutya—having run with full speed; *dūram*—a long distance; *saṁśrāntau*—exhausted; *tuṅgam*—very high; *āruhatām*—They climbed; *girim*—the mountain; *pravarṣaṇa-ākhyam*—known as Pravarṣaṇa; *bhagavān*—Lord Indra; *nityadā*—always; *yatra*—where; *varṣati*—he rains.

TRANSLATION

Apparently exhausted after fleeing a long distance, the two Lords climbed a high mountain named Pravarṣaṇa, upon which Lord Indra showers incessant rain.

TEXT 11

गिरौ निलीनावाज्ञाय नाधिगम्य पदं नृप ।
ददाह गिरिमेधोभिः समन्तादग्निमुत्सृजन् ॥११॥

girau nilīnāv ājñāya
nādhigamya padaṁ nṛpa
dadāha girim edhobhiḥ
samantād agnim utsṛjan

girau—on the mountain; *nilīnau*—hiding; *ājñāya*—being aware; *na adhigamya*—not finding; *padam*—Their location; *nṛpa*—O King (Parīkṣit); *dadāha*—he set ablaze; *girim*—the mountain; *edhobhiḥ*—with firewood; *samantāt*—on all sides; *agnim*—fire; *utsṛjan*—generating.

TRANSLATION

Although he knew They were hiding on the mountain, Jarasāndha could find no trace of Them. Therefore, O King, he placed firewood on all sides and set the mountain ablaze.

PURPORT

Clearly we are observing one of the Supreme Lord's transcendental pastimes. Although the *Bhāgavatam* states that the two Lords, Kṛṣṇa and Balarāma, were "exhausted," even in Their so-called exhausted state They were able to quickly climb a high mountain and shortly thereafter jump off it to the ground. It would be unwise and illogical to ignore the whole picture the sages are giving us here and instead try to pick apart isolated descriptions. Clearly we are watching the Supreme Personality of Godhead in the midst of His spiritual pastimes; we are not observing an ordinary human being. Lord Kṛṣṇa and Lord Balarāma were still quite young men when this pastime took place, and one can easily see in these descriptions how They must have been enjoying Themselves, eagerly fleeing from the somewhat ridiculous King Jarāsandha, racing up a mountain, jumping off and totally befuddling the constantly failing demon, who somehow or other never lost confidence in himself. Seen without envy or quarrelsomeness, the Lord's pastimes are immensely entertaining.

TEXT 12

तत उत्पत्य तरसा दह्यमानतटादुभौ ।
दशैकयोजनात्तुंगान्निपेततुरधो भुवि ॥१२॥

tata utpatya tarasā
dahyamāna-taṭād ubhau
daśaika-yojanāt tuṅgān
nipetatur adho bhuvi

tataḥ—from it (the mountain); *utpatya*—jumping; *tarasā*—with haste; *dahyamāna*—which were burning; *taṭāt*—whose sides; *ubhau*—the two of Them; *daśa-eka*—eleven; *yojanāt—yojanas; tuṅgāt*—high; *nipetatuḥ*—They fell; *adhaḥ*—down; *bhuvi*—to the ground.

TRANSLATION

The two of Them then suddenly jumped from the burning mountain, which was eleven *yojanas* high, and fell to the ground.

PURPORT

Eleven *yojanas* is approximately ninety miles.

TEXT 13

अलक्ष्यमाणौ रिपुणा सानुगेन यदूत्तमौ ।
स्वपुरं पुनरायातौ समुद्रपरिखां नृप ॥१३॥

alakṣyamāṇau ripuṇā
sānugena yadūttamau
sva-puraṁ punar āyātau
samudra-parikhāṁ nṛpa

alakṣyamāṇau—not being seen; *ripuṇā*—by Their enemy; *sa*—together; *anugena*—with his followers; *yadu*—of the Yadus; *uttamau*—the two most excellent; *sva-puram*—to Their own city (Dvārakā); *punaḥ*—again; *āyātau*—They went; *samudra*—the ocean; *parikhām*—having as its protective moat; *nṛpa*—O King.

TRANSLATION

Unseen by Their opponent or his followers, O King, those two most exalted Yadus returned to Their city of Dvārakā, which had the ocean as a protective moat.

TEXT 14

सोऽपि दग्धाविति मृषा मन्वानो बलकेशवौ ।
बलमाकृष्य सुमहन्मगधान्मागधो ययौ ॥१४॥

so 'pi dagdhāv iti mṛṣā
manvāno bala-keśavau
balam ākṛṣya su-mahan
magadhān māgadho yayau

saḥ—he; *api*—further; *dagdhau*—both burned in the fire; *iti*—thus; *mṛṣā*—falsely; *manvānaḥ*—thinking; *bala-keśavau*—Balarāma and Kṛṣṇa; *balam*—his force; *ākṛṣya*—pulling back; *su-mahat*—huge; *magadhān*—to the kingdom of the Magadhas; *māgadhaḥ*—the King of the Magadhas; *yayau*—went.

TRANSLATION

Jarāsandha, moreover, mistakenly thought that Balarāma and Keśava had burned to death in the fire. Thus he withdrew his vast military force and returned to the Magadha kingdom.

TEXT 15

आनर्ताधिपतिः श्रीमान् रैवतो रैवतीं सुताम् ।
ब्रह्मणा चोदितः प्रादाद् बलायेति पुरोदितम् ॥१५॥

ānartādhipatiḥ śrīmān
raivato raivatīṁ sutām
brahmaṇā coditaḥ prādād
balāyeti puroditam

ānarta—of the Ānarta province; *adhipatiḥ*—the overlord; *śrīmān*—opulent; *raivataḥ*—Raivata; *raivatīm*—named Raivatī; *sutām*—his daughter; *brahmaṇā*—by Lord Brahmā; *coditaḥ*—ordered; *prādāt*—gave; *balāya*—to Balarāma; *iti*—thus; *purā*—previously; *uditam*—mentioned.

TRANSLATION

As ordered by Lord Brahmā, Raivata, the opulent ruler of Ānarta, gave Lord Balarāma his daughter Raivatī in marriage. This has already been discussed.

PURPORT

The topic of Lord Kṛṣṇa's marriage to Rukmiṇī will now be discussed. By way of introduction, a brief mention is made of His brother Baladeva's marriage. This marriage was alluded to in the Ninth Canto of the *Bhāgavatam,* Third Chapter, texts 33–36.

TEXTS 16–17

भगवानपि गोविन्द उपयेमे कुरूद्वह ।
वैदर्भीं भीष्मकसुतां श्रियो मात्रां स्वयंवरे ॥१६॥
प्रमथ्य तरसा राज्ञः शाल्वादींश्चैद्यपक्षगान् ।
पश्यतां सर्वलोकानां तार्क्ष्यपुत्रः सुधामिव ॥१७॥

bhagavān api govinda
upayeme kurūdvaha

vaidarbhīṁ bhīṣmaka-sutāṁ
śriyo mātrāṁ svayaṁ-vare

pramathya tarasā rājñaḥ
śālvādīṁś caidya-pakṣa-gān
paśyatāṁ sarva-lokānāṁ
tārkṣya-putraḥ sudhām iva

bhagavān—the Supreme Lord; *api*—indeed; *govindaḥ*—Kṛṣṇa; *upayeme*—married; *kuru-udvaha*—O hero among the Kurus (Parīkṣit); *vaidarbhīm*—Rukmiṇī; *bhīṣmaka-sutām*—the daughter of King Bhīṣmaka; *śriyaḥ*—of the goddess of fortune; *mātrām*—the plenary portion; *svayam-vare*—by her own choice; *pramathya*—subduing; *tarasā*—by force; *rājñaḥ*—kings; *śālva-ādīn*—Śālva and others; *caidya*—of Śiśupāla; *pakṣa-gān*—the supporters; *paśyatām*—as they looked on; *sarva*—all; *lokānām*—the people; *tārkṣya-putraḥ*—the son of Tārkṣya (Garuḍa); *sudhām*—the nectar of heaven; *iva*—as.

TRANSLATION

O hero among the Kurus, the Supreme Lord Himself, Govinda, married Bhīṣmaka's daughter, Vaidarbhī, who was a direct expansion of the goddess of fortune. The Lord did this by her desire, and in the process He beat down Śālva and other kings who took Śiśupāla's side. Indeed, as everyone watched, Śrī Kṛṣṇa took Rukmiṇī just as Garuḍa boldly stole nectar from the demigods.

PURPORT

Śrīla Jīva Gosvāmī gives the following profound comments on these two verses: The words *śriyo mātrām* indicate that beautiful Rukmiṇī is a direct expansion of the eternal goddess of fortune. Therefore she is worthy to be the bride of the Personality of Godhead. As stated in the *Brahma-saṁhitā* (5.67), *śriyaḥ kāntā kāntaḥ parama-puruṣaḥ:* "In the spiritual world, all the female lovers are goddesses of fortune and the male lover is the Supreme Personality." Thus, Śrīla Jīva Gosvāmī explains, Śrīmatī Rukmiṇī-devī is a plenary portion of Śrīmatī Rādhārāṇī. The *Kārttika-māhātmya* section of the *Padma Purāṇa* states, *kaiśore gopa-kanyās tā yauvane rāja-kanyakāḥ:* "In childhood, Śrī Kṛṣṇa enjoyed with the daughters of cowherd men, and in His adolescence He enjoyed with the daughters of kings." Similarly, in the *Skanda Purāṇa* we find this statement: *rukmiṇī dvāravatyāṁ tu rādhā vṛndāvane vane.* "Rukmiṇī is in Dvārakā what Rādhā is in the forest of Vṛndāvana."

The term *svayaṁ-vare* here means "by one's own choice." Although the word often refers to a formal Vedic ceremony in which an aristocratic girl may select her own husband, here it indicates the informal and indeed unprecedented events surrounding Kṛṣṇa's marriage to Rukmiṇī. In fact, Śrī Kṛṣṇa and Śrīmatī Rukmiṇī chose each other because of their eternal, transcendental love.

TEXT 18

श्रीराजोवाच
भगवान् भीष्मकसुतां रुक्मिणीं रुचिराननाम् ।
राक्षसेन विधानेन उपयेमे इति श्रुतम् ॥१८॥

śrī-rājovāca
bhagavān bhīṣmaka-sutāṁ
rukmiṇīṁ rucirānanām
rākṣasena vidhānena
upayema iti śrutam

śrī-rājā uvāca—the King (Parīkṣit Mahārāja) said; *bhagavān*—the Supreme Lord; *bhīṣmaka-sutām*—the daughter of Bhīṣmaka; *rukmiṇīm*—Śrīmatī Rukmiṇī-devī; *rucira*—charming; *ānanām*—whose face; *rākṣasena*—called Rākṣasa; *vidhānena*—by the method (namely, by kidnapping); *upayeme*—He married; *iti*—thus; *śrutam*—heard.

TRANSLATION

King Parīkṣit said: The Supreme Lord married Rukmiṇī, the beautiful-faced daughter of Bhīṣmaka, in the Rākṣasa style—or so I have heard.

PURPORT

Śrīla Śrīdhara Svāmī quotes the following *smṛti* statement: *rākṣaso yuddha-haraṇāt.* "A Rākṣasa marriage takes place when the bride is stolen from one's rival suitors by force." Similarly, Śukadeva Gosvāmī himself has already said, *rājñaḥ pramathya:* Kṛṣṇa had to beat down opposing kings to take Rukmiṇī.

TEXT 19

भगवन् श्रोतुमिच्छामि कृष्णस्यामिततेजसः ।
यथा मागधशाल्वादीन् जित्वा कन्यामुपाहरत् ॥१९॥

bhagavan śrotum icchāmi
kṛṣṇasyāmita-tejasaḥ
yathā māgadha-śālvādīn
jitvā kanyām upāharat

bhagavan—O lord (Śukadeva Gosvāmī); *śrotum*—to hear; *icchāmi*—I wish; *kṛṣṇasya*—about Kṛṣṇa; *amita*—immeasurable; *tejasaḥ*—whose potency; *yathā*—how; *māgadha-śālva-ādīn*—such kings as Jarāsandha and Śālva; *jitvā*—defeating; *kanyām*—the bride; *upāharat*—He took away.

TRANSLATION

My lord, I wish to hear how the immeasurably powerful Lord Kṛṣṇa took away His bride while defeating such kings as Māgadha and Śālva.

PURPORT

We should not think that Śrī Kṛṣṇa was actually afraid of Jarāsandha. In the very next chapter we will find that Śrī Kṛṣṇa easily defeats Jarāsandha and his soldiers. Thus we should never doubt the supreme prowess of Lord Kṛṣṇa.

TEXT 20

ब्रह्मन् कृष्णकथाः पुण्या माध्वीर्लोकमलापहाः ।
को नु तृप्येत शृण्वानः श्रुतज्ञो नित्यनूतनाः ॥२०॥

brahman kṛṣṇa-kathāḥ puṇyā
mādhvīr loka-malāpahāḥ
ko nu tṛpyeta śṛṇvānaḥ
śruta-jño nitya-nūtanāḥ

brahman—O *brāhmaṇa; kṛṣṇa-kathāḥ*—topics of Kṛṣṇa; *puṇyāḥ*—pious; *mādhvīḥ*—sweet; *loka*—of the world; *mala*—the contamination; *apahāḥ*—which remove; *kaḥ*—who; *nu*—at all; *tṛpyeta*—would become satiated; *śṛṇvānaḥ*—hearing; *śruta*—what is heard; *jñaḥ*—who can understand; *nitya*—always; *nūtanāḥ*—novel.

TRANSLATION

What experienced listener, O *brāhmaṇa*, could ever grow satiated while listening to the pious, charming and ever-fresh topics of Lord Kṛṣṇa, which cleanse away the world's contamination?

TEXT 21

श्रीबादरायणिरुवाच
राजासीद् भीष्मको नाम विदर्भाधिपतिर्महान् ।
तस्य पञ्चाभवन् पुत्राः कन्यैका च वरानना ॥२१॥

śrī-bādarāyaṇir uvāca
rājāsīd bhīṣmako nāma
vidarbhādhipatir mahān
tasya pañcābhavan putrāḥ
kanyaikā ca varānanā

śrī-bādarāyaṇiḥ—Śrī Bādarāyaṇi (Śukadeva, the son of Badarāyaṇa Veda-vyāsa); *uvāca*—said; *rājā*—a king; *āsīt*—there was; *bhīṣmakaḥ nāma*—named Bhīṣmaka; *vidarbha-adhipatiḥ*—ruler of the kingdom Vidarbha; *mahān*—great; *tasya*—his; *pañca*—five; *abhavan*—there were; *putrāḥ*—sons; *kanyā*—daughter; *ekā*—one; *ca*—and; *vara*—exceptionally beautiful; *ānanā*—whose face.

TRANSLATION

Śrī Bādarāyaṇi said: There was a king named Bhīṣmaka, the powerful ruler of Vidarbha. He had five sons and one daughter of lovely countenance.

TEXT 22

रुक्म्यग्रजो रुक्मरथो रुक्मबाहुरनन्तरः ।
रुक्मकेशो रुक्ममाली रुक्मिण्येषा स्वसा सती ॥२२॥

rukmy agrajo rukmaratho
rukmabāhur anantaraḥ
rukmakeśo rukmamālī
rukmiṇy eṣā svasā satī

rukmī—Rukmī; *agra-jaḥ*—the first-born; *rukma-rathaḥ rukma-bāhuḥ*—Rukmaratha and Rukmabāhu; *anantaraḥ*—following him; *rukma-keśaḥ rukma-mālī*—Rukmakeśa and Rukmamālī; *rukmiṇī*—Rukmiṇī; *eṣā*—she; *svasā*—sister; *satī*—of saintly character.

TRANSLATION

Rukmī was the first-born son, followed by Rukmaratha, Rukmabāhu, Rukmakeśa and Rukmamālī. Their sister was the exalted Rukmiṇī.

TEXT 23

सोपश्रुत्य मुकुन्दस्य रूपवीर्यगुणश्रियः ।
गृहागतैर्गीयमानास्तं मेने सदृशं पतिम् ॥२३॥

sopaśrutya mukundasya
rūpa-vīrya-guṇa-śriyaḥ
gṛhāgatair gīyamānās
taṁ mene sadṛśaṁ patim

sā—she; *upaśrutya*—hearing; *mukundasya*—Kṛṣṇa's; *rūpa*—about the beauty; *vīrya*—prowess; *guṇa*—character; *śriyaḥ*—and opulences; *gṛha*—to her family's residence; *āgataiḥ*—by those who came; *gīyamānāḥ*—being sung; *tam*—Him; *mene*—she thought; *sadṛśam*—suitable; *patim*—husband.

TRANSLATION

Hearing of the beauty, prowess, transcendental character and opulence of Mukunda from visitors to the palace who sang His praises, Rukmiṇī decided that He would be the perfect husband for her.

PURPORT

The word *sadṛśam* indicates that Rukmiṇī and Śrī Kṛṣṇa had similar qualities and thus were naturally attracted to each other. King Bhīṣmaka was a pious man, and therefore many spiritually advanced persons must have visited his palace. These saintly persons undoubtedly preached openly about the glories of Śrī Kṛṣṇa.

TEXT 24

तां बुद्धिलक्षणौदार्यरूपशीलगुणाश्रयाम् ।
कृष्णश्च सदृशीं भार्यां समुद्वोढुं मनो दधे ॥२४॥

tāṁ buddhi-lakṣaṇaudārya-
rūpa-śīla-guṇāśrayām
kṛṣṇaś ca sadṛśīṁ bhāryāṁ
samudvoḍhuṁ mano dadhe

tām—her; *buddhi*—of intelligence; *lakṣaṇa*—auspicious bodily markings; *audārya*—magnanimity; *rūpa*—beauty; *śīla*—proper behavior; *guṇa*—and other personal qualities; *āśrayām*—repository; *kṛṣṇaḥ*—Lord Kṛṣṇa; *ca*—and; *sadṛśīm*—suitable; *bhāryām*—wife; *samudvoḍhum*—to marry; *manaḥ*—His mind; *dadhe*—made up.

TRANSLATION

Lord Kṛṣṇa knew that Rukmiṇī possessed intelligence, auspicious bodily markings, beauty, proper behavior and all other good qualities. Concluding that she would be an ideal wife for Him, He made up His mind to marry her.

PURPORT

Just as Lord Kṛṣṇa was described as *sadṛśaṁ patim,* an ideal husband for Rukmiṇī, being just like her, Rukmiṇī is described as *sadṛśīṁ bhāryām,* an ideal wife for Śrī Kṛṣṇa, being just like Him. That is natural, since Śrīmatī Rukmiṇī is Lord Kṛṣṇa's internal potency.

TEXT 25

बन्धूनामिच्छतां दातुं कृष्णाय भगिनीं नृप ।
ततो निवार्य कृष्णद्विड् रुक्मी चैद्यममन्यत ॥२५॥

bandhūnām icchatāṁ dātuṁ
kṛṣṇāya bhaginīṁ nṛpa
tato nivārya kṛṣṇa-dviḍ
rukmī caidyam amanyata

bandhūnām—her family members; *icchatām*—even as they were desiring; *dātum*—to give; *kṛṣṇāya*—to Kṛṣṇa; *bhaginīm*—their sister; *nṛpa*—O King; *tataḥ*—from this; *nivārya*—preventing them; *kṛṣṇa-dviṭ*—hateful of Kṛṣṇa; *rukmī*—Rukmī; *caidyam*—Caidya (Śiśupāla); *amanyata*—considered.

TRANSLATION

Because Rukmī envied the Lord, O King, he forbade his family members to give his sister to Kṛṣṇa, although they wanted to. Instead, Rukmī decided to give Rukmiṇī to Śiśupāla.

PURPORT

Rukmī abused his position as elder brother and acted with impure motives. He would only suffer for his decision.

TEXT 26

तदवेत्यासितापांगी वैदर्भी दुर्मना भृशम् ।
विचिन्त्याप्तं द्विजं कञ्चित्कृष्णाय प्राहिणोद्द्रुतम् ॥२६॥

tad avetyāsitāpāṅgī
vaidarbhī durmanā bhṛśam
vicintyāptaṁ dvijaṁ kañcit
kṛṣṇāya prāhiṇod drutam

tat—that; *avetya*—knowing; *asita*—dark; *apāṅgī*—the corners of whose eyes; *vaidarbhī*—the princess of Vidarbha; *durmanā*—unhappy; *bhṛśam*—very much; *vicintya*—thinking; *āptam*—reliable; *dvijam*—*brāhmaṇa;* *kañcit*—a certain; *kṛṣṇāya*—to Kṛṣṇa; *prāhiṇot*—sent; *drutam*—with haste.

TRANSLATION

Dark-eyed Vaidarbhī was aware of this plan, and it deeply upset her. Analyzing the situation, she quickly sent a trustworthy *brāhmaṇa* to Kṛṣṇa.

TEXT 27

द्वारकां स समभ्येत्य प्रतीहारैः प्रवेशितः ।
अपश्यदाद्यं पुरुषमासीनं काञ्चनासने ॥२७॥

dvārakāṁ sa samabhyetya
pratīhāraiḥ praveśitaḥ
apaśyad ādyaṁ puruṣam
āsīnaṁ kāñcanāsane

dvārakām—at Dvārakā; *saḥ*—he (the *brāhmaṇa*); *samabhyetya*—arriving; *pratīhāraiḥ*—by the gatekeepers; *praveśitaḥ*—brought inside; *apaśyat*—he saw; *ādyam*—the original; *puruṣam*—Supreme Person; *āsīnam*—seated; *kāñcana*—golden; *āsane*—on a throne.

TRANSLATION

Upon reaching Dvārakā, the *brāhmaṇa* was brought inside by the gatekeepers and saw the primeval Personality of Godhead sitting on a golden throne.

TEXT 28

दृष्ट्वा ब्रह्मण्यदेवस्तमवरुह्य निजासनात् ।
उपवेश्यार्हयां चक्रे यथात्मानं दिवौकसः ॥२८॥

dṛṣṭvā brahmaṇya-devas tam
avaruhya nijāsanāt
upaveśyārhayāṁ cakre
yathātmānaṁ divaukasaḥ

dṛṣṭvā—seeing; *brahmaṇya*—who is considerate to the *brāhmaṇas; devaḥ*—the Lord; *tam*—him; *avaruhya*—getting down; *nija*—His own; *āsanāt*—from the throne; *upaveśya*—seating him; *arhayām cakre*—He performed worship; *yathā*—as; *ātmānam*—to Himself; *diva-okasaḥ*—the residents of heaven.

TRANSLATION

Seeing the *brāhmaṇa*, Śrī Kṛṣṇa, Lord of the *brāhmaṇas*, came down from His throne and seated him. Then the Lord worshiped him just as He Himself is worshiped by the demigods.

TEXT 29

तं भुक्तवन्तं विश्रान्तमुपगम्य सतां गतिः ।
पाणिनाभिमृशन् पादावव्यग्रस्तमपृच्छत ॥२९॥

taṁ bhuktavantaṁ viśrāntam
upagamya satāṁ gatiḥ
pāṇinābhimṛśan pādāv
avyagras tam apṛcchata

tam—him; *bhuktavantam*—having eaten; *viśrāntam*—rested; *upagamya*—approaching; *satām*—of saintly devotees; *gatiḥ*—the goal; *pāṇinā*—with His hands; *abhimṛśan*—massaging; *pādau*—his feet; *avyagraḥ*—without agitation; *tam*—of him; *apṛcchata*—He inquired.

TRANSLATION

After the *brāhmaṇa* had eaten and rested, Śrī Kṛṣṇa, the goal of saintly devotees, came forward, and while massaging the *brāhmaṇa's* feet with His own hands, He patiently questioned him as follows.

TEXT 30

कच्चिद्द्विजवरश्रेष्ठ धर्मस्ते वृद्धसम्मतः ।
वर्तते नातिकृच्छ्रेण सन्तुष्टमनसः सदा ॥३०॥

kaccid dvija-vara-śreṣṭha
dharmas te vṛddha-sammataḥ
vartate nāti-kṛcchreṇa
santuṣṭa-manasaḥ sadā

kaccit—whether; *dvija*—of the *brāhmaṇas; vara*—first-class; *śreṣṭha*—O best; *dharmaḥ*—religious principles; *te*—your; *vṛddha*—by senior authorities; *sammataḥ*—sanctioned; *vartate*—are proceeding; *na*—not; *ati*—too much; *kṛcchreṇa*—with difficulty; *santuṣṭa*—fully satisfied; *manasaḥ*—whose mind; *sadā*—always.

TRANSLATION

[The Supreme Lord said:] O best of exalted *brāhmaṇas*, are your religious practices, sanctioned by senior authorities, proceeding without great difficulty? Is your mind always fully satisfied?

PURPORT

Here we have translated the word *dharma* as "religious practice," although this does not fully convey the Sanskrit sense of the word. Kṛṣṇa did not appear within a secular society. The people in Vedic times could hardly imagine a society that did not understand the need to obey God's law. Thus to them the word *dharma* conveyed a sense of duty in general, higher principles, prescribed duty and so on. It was automatically understood that such duties were within a religious context. But religion in those days was not a specific aspect or department of life, but rather a guiding light for all activities. Irreligious life was considered demoniac, and God's hand was seen in everything.

TEXT 31

सन्तुष्टो यर्हि वर्तेत ब्राह्मणो येन केनचित् ।
अहीयमानः स्वाद्धर्मात्स ह्यस्याखिलकामधुक् ॥३१॥

santuṣṭo yarhi varteta
brāhmaṇo yena kenacit
ahīyamānaḥ svād dharmāt
sa hy asyākhila-kāma-dhuk

santuṣṭaḥ—satisfied; *yarhi*—when; *varteta*—carries on; *brāhmaṇaḥ*—a *brāhmaṇa; yena kenacit*—with whatever; *ahīyamānaḥ*—not falling short; *svāt*—of his own; *dharmāt*—religious duty; *saḥ*—those religious principles; *hi*—indeed; *asya*—for him; *akhila*—of everything; *kāma-dhuk*—the mystic cow, milked for fulfillment of any desire.

TRANSLATION

When a *brāhmaṇa* is satisfied with whatever comes his way and does not fall away from his religious duties, those very religious principles become his desire cow, fulfilling all his wishes.

TEXT 32

असन्तुष्टोऽसकृल्लोकानाप्नोत्यपि सुरेश्वरः ।
अकिञ्चनोऽपि सन्तुष्टः शेते सर्वांगविज्वरः ॥३२॥

asantuṣṭo 'sakṛl lokān
āpnoty api sureśvaraḥ
akiñcano 'pi santuṣṭaḥ
śete sarvāṅga-vijvaraḥ

asantuṣṭaḥ—dissatisfied; *asakṛt*—repeatedly; *lokān*—various planets; *āpnoti*—he attains; *api*—even though; *sura*—of the demigods; *īśvaraḥ*—the master; *akiñcanaḥ*—possessing nothing; *api*—even; *santuṣṭaḥ*—satisfied; *śete*—he rests; *sarva*—all; *aṅga*—his limbs; *vijvaraḥ*—free of distress.

TRANSLATION

An unsatisfied *brāhmaṇa* wanders restlessly from one planet to another, even if he becomes King of heaven. But a satisfied *brāhmaṇa*, though he may possess nothing, rests peacefully, all his limbs free of distress.

PURPORT

Those who are unsatisfied feel distress throughout their body, becoming subject to many diseases. A satisfied *brāhmaṇa*, however, though he may possess nothing, is peaceful and calm, and there is no distress within his body or mind.

TEXT 33

विप्रान् स्वलाभसन्तुष्टान् साधून् भूतसुहृत्तमान् ।
निरहंकारिणः शान्तान्नमस्ये शिरसासकृत् ॥३३॥

viprān sva-lābha-santuṣṭān
sādhūn bhūta-suhṛttamān
nirahaṅkāriṇaḥ śāntān
namasye śirasāsakṛt

viprān—to the learned *brāhmaṇas; sva*—their own; *lābha*—by the gain; *santuṣṭān*—satisfied; *sādhūn*—saintly; *bhūta*—of all living beings; *suhṛt-tamān*—the best well-wishing friends; *nirahaṅkāriṇaḥ*—devoid of false ego; *śāntān*—peaceful; *namasye*—I bow down; *śirasā*—with My head; *asakṛt*—again and again.

TRANSLATION

I repeatedly bow My head in respect to those *brāhmaṇas* who are satisfied with their lot. Saintly, prideless and peaceful, they are the best well-wishers of all living beings.

PURPORT

Śrīla Śrīdhara Svāmī explains that *sva-lābha* also means "achieving one's self," or, in other words, self-realization. Thus an advanced *brāhmaṇa* is always satisfied with his spiritual understanding, never depending on material formalities or facilities.

TEXT 34

कच्चिद्वः कुशलं ब्रह्मन् राजतो यस्य हि प्रजाः ।
सुखं वसन्ति विषये पाल्यमानाः स मे प्रियः ॥३४॥

kaccid vaḥ kuśalaṁ brahman
rājato yasya hi prajāḥ
sukhaṁ vasanti viṣaye
pālyamānāḥ sa me priyaḥ

kaccit—whether; *vaḥ*—your; *kuśalam*—well-being; *brahman*—O *brāhmaṇa; rājataḥ*—from the King; *yasya*—whose; *hi*—indeed; *prajāḥ*—subjects; *sukham*—happily; *vasanti*—reside; *viṣaye*—in the state; *pālyamānāḥ*—being protected; *saḥ*—he; *me*—to Me; *priyaḥ*—dear.

TRANSLATION

O *brāhmaṇa*, is your King attending to your welfare? Indeed, that king in whose country the citizens are happy and protected is very dear to Me.

TEXT 35

यतस्त्वमागतो दुर्गं निस्तीर्येह यदिच्छया ।
सर्वं नो ब्रूह्यगुह्यं चेत्किं कार्यं करवाम ते ॥३५॥

yatas tvam āgato durgaṁ
nistīryeha yad-icchayā
sarvaṁ no brūhy aguhyaṁ cet
kiṁ kāryaṁ karavāma te

yataḥ—from which place; *tvam*—you; *āgataḥ*—have come; *durgam*—the impassable sea; *nistīrya*—crossing; *iha*—here; *yat*—with what; *icchayā*—desire; *sarvam*—everything; *naḥ*—to Us; *brūhi*—please tell; *aguhyam*—not secret; *cet*—if; *kim*—what; *kāryam*—work; *karavāma*—may We do; *te*—for you.

TRANSLATION

Whence have you come, crossing the impassable sea, and for what purpose? Explain all this to Us if it is not a secret, and tell Us what We may do for you.

TEXT 36

एवं सम्पृष्टसम्प्रश्नो ब्राह्मणः परमेष्ठिना ।
लीलागृहीतदेहेन तस्मै सर्वमवर्णयत् ॥३६॥

evaṁ sampṛṣṭa-sampraśno
brāhmaṇaḥ parameṣṭhinā
līlā-gṛhīta-dehena
tasmai sarvam avarṇayat

evam—thus; *sampṛṣṭa*—asked; *sampraśnaḥ*—questions; *brāhmaṇaḥ*—the *brāhmaṇa; parameṣṭhinā*—by the Supreme Personality of Godhead; *līlā*—as His pastime; *gṛhīta*—who assumes; *dehena*—His bodies; *tasmai*—to Him; *sarvam*—everything; *avarṇayat*—he related.

TRANSLATION

Thus questioned by the Supreme Personality of Godhead, who incarnates to perform His pastimes, the *brāhmaṇa* told Him everything.

PURPORT

The word *gṛhīta* may be translated as "grasped or caught," and thus, exactly as in English, may also mean "to perceive or understand something." Therefore Lord Kṛṣṇa's transcendental body is perceived, understood or in other words grasped by the devotees when the Lord comes to exhibit His transcendental pastimes. These pastimes are not whimsical but are a part of the complex program, structured and executed by the Lord Himself, for awakening the conditioned souls to their natural love and devotion for Him and bringing them back to Godhead.

TEXT 37

श्रीरुक्मिण्युवाच
श्रुत्वा गुणान् भुवनसुन्दर शृण्वतां ते
निर्विश्य कर्णविवरैर्हरतोऽङ्गतापम् ।
रूपं दृशां दृशिमतामखिलार्थलाभं
त्वय्यच्युताविशति चित्तमपत्रपं मे ॥३७॥

śrī-rukmiṇy uvāca
śrutvā guṇān bhuvana-sundara śṛṇvatāṁ te
nirviśya karṇa-vivarair harato 'ṅga-tāpam
rūpaṁ dṛśāṁ dṛśimatām akhilārtha-lābhaṁ
tvayy acyutāviśati cittam apatrapaṁ me

śrī-rukmiṇī uvāca—Śrī Rukmiṇī said; *śrutvā*—hearing; *guṇān*—the qualities; *bhuvana*—of all the worlds; *sundara*—O beauty; *śṛṇvatām*—for those who hear; *te*—Your; *nirviśya*—having entered; *karṇa*—of the ears; *vivaraiḥ*—by the orifices; *harataḥ*—removing; *aṅga*—of their bodies; *tāpam*—the pain; *rūpam*—the beauty; *dṛśām*—of the sense of sight; *dṛśi-matām*—of those who have eyes; *akhila*—total; *artha*—of the fulfillment of desires; *lābham*—the obtaining; *tvayi*—in You; *acyuta*—O infallible Kṛṣṇa; *āviśati*—is entering; *cittam*—mind; *apatrapam*—shameless; *me*—my.

TRANSLATION

Śrī Rukmiṇī said [in her letter, as read by the *brāhmaṇa*]: O beauty of the worlds, having heard of Your qualities, which enter the ears of those who hear and remove their bodily distress, and having also heard of Your beauty, which fulfills all the visual desires of those who see, I have fixed my shameless mind upon You, O Kṛṣṇa.

PURPORT

Rukmiṇī was a king's daughter, courageous and bold, and furthermore she would rather die than lose Kṛṣṇa. Considering all this, she wrote a frank, explicit letter, begging Kṛṣṇa to come and take her away.

TEXT 38

का त्वा मुकुन्द महती कुलशीलरूप-
विद्यावयोद्रविणधामभिरात्मतुल्यम् ।
धीरा पतिं कुलवती न वृणीत कन्या
काले नृसिंह नरलोकमनोऽभिरामम् ॥३८॥

kā tvā mukunda mahatī kula-śīla-rūpa-
vidyā-vayo-draviṇa-dhāmabhir ātma-tulyam
dhīrā patiṁ kulavatī na vṛṇīta kanyā
kāle nṛ-siṁha nara-loka-mano-'bhirāmam

kā—who; *tvā*—You; *mukunda*—O Kṛṣṇa; *mahatī*—aristocratic; *kula*—in terms of family background; *śīla*—character; *rūpa*—beauty; *vidyā*—knowledge; *vayaḥ*—youth; *draviṇa*—property; *dhāmabhiḥ*—and influence; *ātma*—to Yourself only; *tulyam*—equal; *dhīrā*—who is sober; *patim*—as her husband; *kula-vatī*—of a good family; *na vṛṇīta*—would not choose; *kanyā*—marriageable young lady; *kāle*—at such a time; *nṛ*—among men; *siṁha*—O lion; *nara-loka*—of human society; *manaḥ*—to the minds; *abhirāmam*—who give pleasure.

TRANSLATION

O Mukunda, You are equal only to Yourself in lineage, character, beauty, knowledge, youthfulness, wealth and influence. O lion among men, You delight the minds of all mankind. What aristocratic, sober-minded and marriageable girl of a good family would not choose You as her husband when the proper time has come?

TEXT 39

तन्मे भवान् खलु वृतः पतिरंग जायाम्
आत्मार्पितश्च भवतोऽत्र विभो विधेहि ।
मा वीरभागमभिमर्शतु चैद्य आराद्
गोमायुवन्मृगपतेर्बलिमम्बुजाक्ष ॥३९॥

tan me bhavān khalu vṛtaḥ patir aṅga jāyām
ātmārpitaś ca bhavato 'tra vibho vidhehi
mā vīra-bhāgam abhimarśatu caidya ārād
gomāyu-van mṛga-pater balim ambujākṣa

tat—therefore; *me*—by me; *bhavān*—Your good self; *khalu*—indeed; *vṛtaḥ*—chosen; *patiḥ*—as husband; *aṅga*—dear Lord; *jāyām*—as wife; *ātmā*—myself; *arpitaḥ*—offered; *ca*—and; *bhavataḥ*—to You; *atra*—here; *vibho*—O omnipotent one; *vidhehi*—please accept; *mā*—never; *vīra*—of the hero; *bhāgam*—the portion; *abhimarśatu*—should touch; *caidyaḥ*—Śiśupāla, son of the King of Cedi; *ārāt*—swiftly; *gomāyu-vat*—like a jackal; *mṛga-pateḥ*—belonging to the king of animals, the lion; *balim*—the tribute; *ambuja-akṣa*—O lotus-eyed one.

TRANSLATION

Therefore, my dear Lord, I have chosen You as my husband, and I surrender myself to You. Please come swiftly, O almighty one, and make me Your wife. My dear lotus-eyed Lord, let Śiśupāla never touch the hero's portion like a jackal stealing the property of a lion.

TEXT 40

पूर्तेष्टदत्तनियमव्रतदेवविप्र-
गुर्वर्चनादिभिरलं भगवान् परेशः ।
आराधितो यदि गदाग्रज एत्य पाणिं
गृह्णातु मे न दमघोषसुतादयोऽन्ये ॥४०॥

pūrteṣṭa-datta-niyama-vrata-deva-vipra-
gurv-arcanādibhir alaṁ bhagavān pareśaḥ
ārādhito yadi gadāgraja etya pāṇiṁ
gṛhṇātu me na damaghoṣa-sutādayo 'nye

pūrta—by pious works (such as feeding *brāhmaṇas,* digging wells, etc.); *iṣṭa*—sacrificial performances; *datta*—charity; *niyama*—ritual observances (such as visiting holy places); *vrata*—vows of penance; *deva*—of the demigods; *vipra*—*brāhmaṇas; guru*—and spiritual masters; *arcana*—by worship; *ādibhiḥ*—and by other activities; *alam*—sufficiently; *bhagavān*—the Personality of Godhead; *para*—supreme; *īśaḥ*—controller; *ārādhitaḥ*—rendered devotional service; *yadi*—if; *gada-agrajaḥ*—Kṛṣṇa, the elder brother of Gada; *etya*—coming here; *pāṇim*—the hand; *gṛhṇātu*—may please take; *me*—my; *na*—not; *damaghoṣa-suta*—Śiśupāla, the son of Damaghoṣa; *ādayaḥ*—and so on; *anye*—others.

TRANSLATION

If I have sufficiently worshiped the Supreme Personality of Godhead by pious works, sacrifices, charity, rituals and vows, and also by worshiping the demigods, *brāhmaṇas* and *gurus,* then may Gadāgraja come and take my hand, and not Damaghoṣa's son or anyone else.

PURPORT

The *ācāryas* comment as follows on this verse: "Rukmiṇī felt that no one could obtain Lord Kṛṣṇa by the efforts of a single lifetime. Therefore she earnestly pointed out the pious activities she had performed in that life and previous lives, hoping to convince Śrī Kṛṣṇa to come."

TEXT 41

श्वो भाविनि त्वमजितोद्वहने विदर्भान्
गुप्तः समेत्य पृतनापतिभिः परीतः ।
निर्मथ्य चैद्यमगधेन्द्रबलं प्रसह्य
मां राक्षसेन विधिनोद्वह वीर्यशुल्काम् ॥४१॥

śvo bhāvini tvam ajitodvahane vidarbhān
guptaḥ sametya pṛtanā-patibhiḥ parītaḥ
nirmathya caidya-magadhendra-balaṁ prasahya
māṁ rākṣasena vidhinodvaha vīrya-śulkām

śvaḥ bhāvini—tomorrow; *tvam*—You; *ajita*—O unconquerable one; *udvahane*—at the time of the marriage ceremony; *vidarbhān*—to Vidarbha; *guptaḥ*—unseen; *sametya*—coming; *pṛtanā*—of Your army; *patibhiḥ*—by the leaders; *parītaḥ*—surrounded; *nirmathya*—crushing; *caidya*—of Caidya, Śiśupāla; *magadha-indra*—and the King of Magadha, Jarāsandha; *balam*—the military strength; *prasahya*—by force; *mām*—me; *rākṣasena vidhinā*—in the Rākṣasa style; *udvaha*—take in marriage; *vīrya*—Your prowess; *śulkām*—the payment for whom.

TRANSLATION

O unconquerable one, tomorrow when my marriage ceremony is about to begin, You should arrive unseen in Vidarbha and surround Yourself with the leaders of Your army. Then crush the forces of Caidya and Magadhendra and marry me in the Rākṣasa style, winning me with Your valor.

PURPORT

As Śrīla Prabhupāda points out in *Kṛṣṇa, the Supreme Personality of Godhead,* Rukmiṇī, being born of royal blood, certainly had a brilliant grasp of political affairs. She advised Śrī Kṛṣṇa to enter the city alone and unnoticed and then surround Himself with His military commanders so He could do what was needed. Śrīla Viśvanātha Cakravartī compares the coming fight to the Lord's churning of the ocean to extract the goddess Lakṣmī. Gorgeous Rukmiṇī, the goddess of fortune, would be gained in the coming turbulence.

TEXT 42

अन्तःपुरान्तरचरीमनिहत्य बन्धून्
त्वामुद्वहे कथमिति प्रवदाम्युपायम् ।
पूर्वेद्युरस्ति महती कुलदेवयात्रा
यस्यां बहिर्नववधूर्गिरिजामुपेयात् ॥४२॥

antaḥ-purāntara-carīm anihatya bandhūn
tvām udvahe katham iti pravadāmy upāyam
pūrve-dyur asti mahatī kula-deva-yātrā
yasyāṁ bahir nava-vadhūr girijām upeyāt

antaḥ-pura—the women's quarters of the palace; *antara*—within; *carīm*—moving; *anihatya*—without killing; *bandhūn*—your relatives; *tvām*—you; *udvahe*—I shall carry away; *katham*—how; *iti*—saying such words; *pravadāmi*—I shall explain; *upāyam*—a means; *pūrve-dyuḥ*—on the day before; *asti*—there is; *mahatī*—large; *kula*—of the royal family; *deva*—for the presiding deity; *yātrā*—a ceremonial procession; *yasyām*—in which; *bahiḥ*—outside; *nava*—new; *vadhūḥ*—the bride; *girijām*—goddess Girijā (Ambikā); *upeyāt*—approaches.

TRANSLATION

Since I will be staying within the inner chambers of the palace, You may wonder, "How can I carry you away without killing some of your relatives?" But I shall tell You a way: On the day before the marriage there is a grand procession to honor the royal family's deity, and in this procession the new bride goes outside the city to visit Goddess Girijā.

PURPORT

Clever Rukmiṇī anticipated a possible objection on the part of Śrī Kṛṣṇa. He certainly would not object to subduing rascals like Śiśupāla and Jarāsandha, but He might be reluctant to injure or kill Rukmiṇī's relatives, some of whom might block His way to the palace's inner sanctum, where the women were protected. The procession to or from the temple of Girijā (Durgā) would provide the perfect opportunity for Kṛṣṇa to kidnap Rukmiṇī without harming her relatives.

TEXT 43

यस्याङ्घ्रिपंकजरजःस्नपनं महान्तो
वाञ्छन्त्युमापतिरिवात्मतमोऽपहत्यै ।
यर्ह्यम्बुजाक्ष न लभेय भवत्प्रसादं
जह्यामसून् व्रतकृशान् शतजन्मभिः स्यात् ॥४३॥

yasyāṅghri-paṅkaja-rajaḥ-snapanaṁ mahānto
vāñchanty umā-patir ivātma-tamo-'pahatyai
yarhy ambujākṣa na labheya bhavat-prasādaṁ
jahyām asūn vrata-kṛśān śata-janmabhiḥ syāt

yasya—whose; *aṅghri*—of the feet; *paṅkaja*—lotus; *rajaḥ*—with the dust; *snapanam*—bathing; *mahāntaḥ*—great souls; *vāñchanti*—hanker after; *umā-patiḥ*—Lord Śiva, husband of Goddess Umā; *iva*—just as; *ātma*—their own; *tamaḥ*—of the ignorance; *apahatyai*—to vanquish; *yarhi*—when; *ambuja-akṣa*—O lotus-eyed one; *na labheya*—I cannot obtain; *bhavat*—Your; *prasādam*—mercy; *jahyām*—I should give up; *asūn*—my life airs; *vrata*—by austere penances; *kṛśān*—weakened; *śata*—hundreds; *janmabhiḥ*—after lifetimes; *syāt*—it may be.

TRANSLATION

O lotus-eyed one, great souls like Lord Śiva hanker to bathe in the dust of Your lotus feet and thereby destroy their ignorance. If I cannot obtain Your mercy, I shall simply give up my vital force, which will have become weak from the severe penances I will perform. Then, after hundreds of lifetimes of endeavor, I may obtain Your mercy.

PURPORT

The divine Rukmiṇī's extraordinary dedication to Śrī Kṛṣṇa is possible only on the spiritual platform, not in the fragile world of mundane affection.

TEXT 44

ब्राह्मण उवाच
इत्येते गुह्यसन्देशा यदुदेव मयाहृताः ।
विमृश्य कर्तुं यच्चात्र क्रियतां तदनन्तरम् ॥४४॥

brāhmaṇa uvāca
ity ete guhya-sandeśā
yadu-deva mayāhṛtāḥ

vimṛśya kartuṁ yac cātra
kriyatāṁ tad anantaram

brāhmaṇaḥ uvāca—the *brāhmaṇa* said; *iti*—thus; *ete*—these; *guhya*—confidential; *sandeśāḥ*—messages; *yadu-deva*—O Lord of the Yadus; *mayā*—by me; *āhṛtāḥ*—brought; *vimṛśya*—considering; *kartum*—to be done; *yat*—what; *ca*—and; *atra*—in this matter; *kriyatām*—please do; *tat*—that; *anantaram*—immediately following.

TRANSLATION

The *brāhmaṇa* said: This is the confidential message I have brought with me, O Lord of the Yadus. Please consider what must be done in these circumstances, and do it at once.

PURPORT

When the *brāhmaṇa* arrived, he broke the seal of a confidential letter written in the privacy of Rukmiṇī's quarters and meant only for Lord Kṛṣṇa. By using the term *guhya-sandeśāḥ*, the trustworthy *brāhmaṇa*, personally selected by Rukmiṇī, here affirms that he has not violated the confidentiality of this message. Only Lord Kṛṣṇa has heard it. Since the marriage of Rukmiṇī was fast approaching, Śrī Kṛṣṇa would have to act immediately. The term *yadu-deva* indicates that Lord Kṛṣṇa, as the Lord of the powerful Yadu dynasty, should make His decision and then mobilize His followers if necessary.

Thus end the purports of the humble servants of His Divine Grace A. C. Bhaktivedanta Swami Prabhupāda to the Tenth Canto, Fifty-second Chapter, of the Śrīmad-Bhāgavatam, *entitled "Rukmiṇī's Message to Lord Kṛṣṇa."*

CHAPTER FIFTY–THREE

Kṛṣṇa Kidnaps Rukmiṇī

This chapter describes how Lord Śrī Kṛṣṇa arrived in Kuṇḍina, the capital of Vidarbha, and kidnapped Rukmiṇī in the presence of powerful enemies.

After Lord Kṛṣṇa had heard the *brāhmaṇa* messenger recite Rukmiṇī's letter, the Lord said to him, "I am indeed attracted to Rukmiṇī, and I know of her brother Rukmī's opposition to My marrying her. Therefore I must kidnap her after crushing all the low-class kings, just as one might generate fire from wood by friction." Since the solemnizing of vows between Rukmiṇī and Śiśupāla was scheduled to occur in only three days, Lord Kṛṣṇa had Dāruka ready His chariot at once. Then He immediately set out for Vidarbha, which He reached after one night's travel.

King Bhīṣmaka, trapped by his affection for his son Rukmī, was prepared to give his daughter to Śiśupāla. Bhīṣmaka saw to all the necessary preparations: he had the city decorated in various ways and had its main roads and intersections thoroughly cleansed. Damaghoṣa, the King of Cedi, having also done everything necessary to prepare for his son's marriage, arrived in Vidarbha. King Bhīṣmaka greeted him properly and gave him a place to stay. Many other kings, such as Jarāsandha, Śālva and Dantavakra, also came to witness the occasion. These enemies of Kṛṣṇa had conspired to kidnap the bride if Kṛṣṇa came. They planned to fight Him together and thus guarantee Śiśupāla his bride. Hearing of these plans, Lord Baladeva gathered His entire army and quickly went to Kuṇḍinapura.

On the night before the wedding, Rukmiṇī, about to retire, had still not seen either the *brāhmaṇa* or Kṛṣṇa arrive. In anxiety, she cursed her bad fortune. But just then she felt her left side twitch, a good omen. Indeed, the *brāhmaṇa* shortly appeared and related to her what Kṛṣṇa had said, including His firm promise to kidnap her.

When King Bhīṣmaka heard that Kṛṣṇa and Balarāma had arrived, he went out to greet Them to the accompaniment of triumphant music. He worshiped the Lords with various gifts and then designated residences for

Them. Thus the King showed due respect to the Lords, as he did to each of his numerous royal guests.

The people of Vidarbha, seeing Lord Kṛṣṇa, remarked to one another that He alone would be a suitable husband for Rukmiṇī. They prayed that on the strength of whatever pious credit they had, Kṛṣṇa might win Rukmiṇī's hand.

When the time came for Śrīmatī Rukmiṇī-devī to visit the temple of Śrī Ambikā, she proceeded there surrounded by many guards. After bowing down to the deity, Rukmiṇī prayed to be allowed to have Śrī Kṛṣṇa as her husband. Then she took the hand of a girlfriend and left the Ambikā temple. Seeing her inexpressible beauty, the great heroes present dropped their weapons and fell to the ground unconscious. Rukmiṇī walked with deliberate steps until she noticed Kṛṣṇa. Then, as everyone looked on, Śrī Kṛṣṇa took Rukmiṇī onto His chariot. Like a lion claiming his rightful share from a band of jackals, He drove back all the opposing kings and slowly made His exit, followed by His associates. Jarāsandha and the other kings, unable to bear their defeat and dishonor, loudly condemned themselves, declaring that this defamation was like a petty animal's stealing away what rightfully belongs to the lion.

TEXT 1

श्रीशुक उवाच
वैदर्भ्याः स तु सन्देशं निशम्य यदुनन्दनः ।
प्रगृह्य पाणिना पाणिं प्रहसन्निदमब्रवीत् ॥१॥

śrī-śuka uvāca
vaidarbhyāḥ sa tu sandeśaṁ
niśamya yadu-nandanaḥ
pragṛhya pāṇinā pāṇiṁ
prahasann idam abravīt

śrī-śukaḥ uvāca—Śukadeva Gosvāmī said; *vaidarbhyāḥ*—of the princess of Vidarbha; *saḥ*—He; *tu*—and; *sandeśam*—the confidential message; *niśamya*—hearing; *yadu-nandanaḥ*—Lord Kṛṣṇa, the descendant of Yadu; *pragṛhya*—taking; *pāṇinā*—by His hand; *pāṇim*—the hand (of the *brāhmaṇa* messenger); *prahasan*—smiling; *idam*—this; *abravīt*—said.

TRANSLATION

Śukadeva Gosvāmī said: Thus hearing the confidential message of Princess Vaidarbhī, Lord Yadunandana took the *brāhmaṇa's* hand and, smiling, spoke to him as follows.

TEXT 2

श्रीभगवानुवाच
तथाहमपि तच्चित्तो निद्रां च न लभे निशि ।
वेदाहं रुक्मिणा द्वेषान्ममोद्वाहो निवारितः ॥२॥

śrī-bhagavān uvāca
tathāham api tac-citto
nidrāṁ ca na labhe niśi
vedāhaṁ rukmiṇā dveṣān
mamodvāho nivāritaḥ

śrī-bhagavān uvāca—the Supreme Personality of Godhead said; *tathā*—in the same way; *aham*—I; *api*—also; *tat*—fixed on her; *cittaḥ*—My mind; *nidrām*—sleep; *ca*—and; *na labhe*—I cannot get; *niśi*—at night; *veda*—know; *aham*—I; *rukmiṇā*—by Rukmī; *dveṣāt*—out of enmity; *mama*—My; *udvāhaḥ*—marriage; *nivāritaḥ*—forbidden.

TRANSLATION

The Supreme Lord said: Just as Rukmiṇī's mind is fixed on Me, My mind is fixed on her. I can't even sleep at night. I know that Rukmī, out of envy, has forbidden our marriage.

TEXT 3

तामानयिष्य उन्मथ्य राजन्यापसदान्मृधे ।
मत्परामनवद्यांगीमेधसोऽग्निशिखामिव ॥३॥

tām ānayiṣya unmathya
rājanyāpasadān mṛdhe
mat-parām anavadyāṅgīm
edhaso 'gni-śikhām iva

tām—she; *ānayiṣye*—I will bring here; *unmathya*—churning up; *rājanya*—of the royal order; *apasadān*—unfit members; *mṛdhe*—in battle; *mat*—to Me; *parām*—who is solely dedicated; *anavadya*—unquestionable; *aṅgīm*—the beauty of whose body; *edhasaḥ*—from kindling wood; *agni*—of fire; *śikhām*—the flames; *iva*—as.

TRANSLATION

She has dedicated herself exclusively to Me, and her beauty is flawless. I will bring her here after thrashing those worthless kings in battle, just as one brings a blazing flame out of firewood.

PURPORT

When latent fire is aroused in wood, the fire bursts forth, consuming the wood in the act of manifestation. Similarly, Lord Kṛṣṇa boldly predicted that Rukmiṇī would come forth to take His hand and that in the process the wicked kings would be burned by the fire of Kṛṣṇa's determination.

TEXT 4

श्रीशुक उवाच

उद्वाहर्क्षं च विज्ञाय रुक्मिण्या मधुसूदनः ।
रथः संयुज्यतामाशु दारुकेत्याह सारथिम् ॥४॥

śrī-śuka uvāca
udvāharkṣaṁ ca vijñāya
rukmiṇyā madhusūdanaḥ
rathaḥ saṁyujyatām āśu
dārukety āha sārathim

śrī-śukaḥ uvāca—Śukadeva Gosvāmī said; *udvāha*—of the wedding; *ṛkṣam*—the lunar asterism (the measurement that fixes the exact auspicious time); *ca*—and; *vijñāya*—knowing; *rukmiṇyāḥ*—of Rukmiṇī; *madhusūdanaḥ*—Lord Kṛṣṇa; *rathaḥ*—the chariot; *saṁyujyatām*—should be readied; *āśu*—immediately; *dāruka*—O Dāruka; *iti*—thus; *āha*—He said; *sārathim*—to His driver.

TRANSLATION

Śukadeva Gosvāmī said: Lord Madhusūdana also understood the exact lunar time for Rukmiṇī's wedding. Thus He told His driver, "Dāruka, ready My chariot immediately."

TEXT 5

स चाश्वैः शैब्यसुग्रीवमेघपुष्पबलाहकैः ।
युक्तं रथमुपानीय तस्थौ प्राञ्जलिरग्रतः ॥५॥

sa cāśvaiḥ śaibya-sugrīva-
meghapuṣpa-balāhakaiḥ
yuktaṁ ratham upānīya
tasthau prāñjalir agrataḥ

saḥ—he, Dāruka; *ca*—and; *aśvaiḥ*—with the horses; *śaibya-sugrīva-meghapuṣpa-balāhakaiḥ*—named Śaibya, Sugrīva, Meghapuṣpa and Balāhaka; *yuktam*—yoked; *ratham*—the chariot; *upānīya*—bringing; *tasthau*—stood; *prāñjaliḥ*—with palms joined in reverence; *agrataḥ*—in front.

TRANSLATION

Dāruka brought the Lord's chariot, yoked with the horses named Śaibya, Sugrīva, Meghapuṣpa and Balāhaka. He then stood before Lord Kṛṣṇa with joined palms.

PURPORT

Śrīla Viśvanātha Cakravartī quotes the following text of the *Padma Purāṇa* describing Lord Kṛṣṇa's chariot horses:

śaibyas tu śuka-patrābhaḥ
sugrīvo hema-piṅgalaḥ
meghapuṣpas tu meghābhaḥ
pāṇḍuro hi balāhakaḥ

"Śaibya was green like a parrot's wings, Sugrīva yellow-gold, Meghapuṣpa the color of a cloud, and Balāhaka whitish."

TEXT 6

आरुह्य स्यन्दनं शौरिर्द्विजमारोप्य तूर्णगैः ।
आनर्तादेकरात्रेण विदर्भानगमद्धयैः ॥६॥

āruhya syandanaṁ śaurir
dvijam āropya tūrṇa-gaiḥ
ānartād eka-rātreṇa
vidarbhān agamad dhayaiḥ

āruhya—mounting; *syandanam*—His chariot; *śauriḥ*—Lord Kṛṣṇa; *dvijam*—the *brāhmaṇa; āropya*—placing (on the chariot); *tūrṇa-gaiḥ*—(who were) swift; *ānartāt*—from the district of Ānarta; *eka*—single; *rātreṇa*—in a night; *vidarbhān*—to the Vidarbha kingdom; *agamat*—went; *hayaiḥ*—with His horses.

TRANSLATION

Lord Śauri mounted His chariot and had the *brāhmaṇa* do likewise. Then the Lord's swift horses took them from the Ānarta district to Vidarbha in a single night.

TEXT 7

राजा स कुण्डिनपतिः पुत्रस्नेहवशानुगः ।
शिशुपालाय स्वां कन्यां दास्यन् कर्माण्यकारयत् ॥७॥

rājā sa kuṇḍina-patiḥ
putra-sneha-vaśānugaḥ
śiśupālāya svāṁ kanyāṁ
dāsyan karmāṇy akārayat

rājā—the king; *saḥ*—he, Bhiṣmaka; *kuṇḍina-patiḥ*—master of Kuṇḍina; *putra*—for his son; *sneha*—of affection; *vaśa*—the control; *anugaḥ*—obeying; *śiśupālāya*—to Śiśupāla; *svām*—his; *kanyām*—daughter; *dāsyan*—being about to give; *karmāṇi*—the required duties; *akārayat*—he had done.

TRANSLATION

King Bhīṣmaka, the master of Kuṇḍina, having succumbed to the sway of affection for his son, was about to give his daughter to Śiśupāla. The King saw to all the required preparations.

PURPORT

Śrīla Śrīdhara Svāmī points out in this connection that King Bhīṣmaka had no particular liking for Śiśupāla but rather acted out of attachment for his son Rukmī.

TEXTS 8–9

पुरं सम्मृष्टसंसिक्तमार्गरथ्याचतुष्पथम् ।
चित्रध्वजपताकाभिस्तोरणैः समलंकृतम् ॥८॥
स्रग्गन्धमाल्याभरणैर्विरजोऽम्बरभूषितैः ।
जुष्टं स्त्रीपुरुषैः श्रीमद्गृहैरगुरुधूपितैः ॥९॥

puraṁ sammṛṣṭa-saṁsikta-
mārga-rathyā-catuṣpatham
citra-dhvaja-patākābhis
toraṇaiḥ samalaṅkṛtam

srag-gandha-mālyābharaṇair
virajo-'mbara-bhūṣitaiḥ
juṣṭaṁ strī-puruṣaiḥ śrīmad-
gṛhair aguru-dhūpitaiḥ

puram—the city; *sammṛṣṭa*—thoroughly cleaned; *saṁsikta*—and sprinkled abundantly with water; *mārga*—the main avenues; *rathyā*—commercial roads; *catuḥ-patham*—and intersections; *citra*—variegated; *dhvaja*—on flagpoles; *patākābhiḥ*—with banners; *toraṇaiḥ*—and archways; *samalaṅkṛtam*—decorated; *srak*—with jeweled necklaces; *gandha*—fragrant substances such as sandalwood paste; *mālya*—flower garlands; *ābharaṇaiḥ*—and other ornaments; *virajaḥ*—spotless; *ambara*—in clothing; *bhūṣitaiḥ*—who were arrayed; *juṣṭam*—containing; *strī*—women; *puruṣaiḥ*—and men; *śrī-mat*—opulent; *gṛhaiḥ*—homes; *aguru-dhūpitaiḥ*—aromatic with *aguru* incense.

TRANSLATION

The king had the main avenues, commercial roads and intersections thoroughly cleaned and then sprinkled with water, and he also had the city decorated with triumphant archways and multicolored banners on poles. The men and women of the city, arrayed in spotless raiment and anointed with fragrant sandalwood paste, wore precious necklaces, flower garlands and jeweled ornaments, and their opulent homes were filled with the aroma of *aguru.*

PURPORT

When earthen roads are sprinkled with water, the dust settles down and the road becomes smooth and firm. King Bhīṣmaka thoroughly prepared for the great wedding, setting the scene for Lord Kṛṣṇa's triumphant abduction of beautiful Rukmiṇī-devī.

TEXT 10

पितॄन् देवान् समभ्यर्च्य विप्रांश्च विधिवन्नृप ।
भोजयित्वा यथान्यायं वाचयामास मंगलम् ॥१०॥

pitṝn devān samabhyarcya
viprāṁś ca vidhi-van nṛpa
bhojayitvā yathā-nyāyaṁ
vācayām āsa maṅgalam

pitṝn—the forefathers; *devān*—the demigods; *samabhyarcya*—correctly worshiping; *viprān*—the *brāhmaṇas; ca*—and; *vidhi-vat*—according to prescribed rituals; *nṛpa*—O King (Parīkṣit); *bhojayitvā*—feeding them; *yathā*—as; *nyāyam*—is just; *vācayām āsa*—he had chanted; *maṅgalam*—auspicious *mantras.*

TRANSLATION

O King, in accordance with prescribed rituals, Mahārāja Bhīṣmaka worshiped the forefathers, demigods and *brāhmaṇas,* feeding them all properly. Then He had the traditional *mantras* chanted for the well-being of the bride.

TEXT 11

सुस्नातां सुदतीं कन्यां कृतकौतुकमंगलाम् ।
आहतांशुकयुग्मेन भूषितां भूषणोत्तमैः ॥११॥

su-snātāṁ su-datīṁ kanyāṁ
kṛta-kautuka-maṅgalām
āhatāṁśuka-yugmena
bhūṣitāṁ bhūṣaṇottamaiḥ

su-snātām—properly bathed; *su-datīm*—with spotless teeth; *kanyām*—the bride; *kṛta*—having performed; *kautuka-maṅgalām*—the ceremony of putting on the auspicious marriage necklace; *āhata*—unused; *aṁśuka*—of garments; *yugmena*—with a pair; *bhūṣitām*—adorned; *bhūṣaṇa*—with ornaments; *uttamaiḥ*—most excellent.

TRANSLATION

The bride cleaned her teeth and bathed, after which she put on the auspicious wedding necklace. Then she was dressed in brand-new upper and lower garments and adorned with most excellent jeweled ornaments.

PURPORT

According to Śrīla Viśvanātha Cakravartī, only spotless clothing fresh off the loom should be worn during auspicious ceremonies.

TEXT 12

चक्रुः सामर्ग्यजुर्मन्त्रैर्वध्वा रक्षां द्विजोत्तमाः ।
पुरोहितोऽथर्वविद्वै जुहाव ग्रहशान्तये ॥१२॥

cakruḥ sāma-ṛg-yajur-mantrair
vadhvā rakṣāṁ dvijottamāḥ
purohito 'tharva-vid vai
juhāva graha-śāntaye

cakruḥ—effected; *sāma-ṛg-yajuḥ*—of the *Sāma, Ṛg* and *Yajur Vedas; mantraiḥ*—with chants; *vadhvāḥ*—of the bride; *rakṣām*—the protection; *dvija-uttamāḥ*—first-class *brāhmaṇas; purohitaḥ*—the priest; *atharva-vit*—who was expert in the *mantras* of the *Atharva Veda; vai*—indeed; *juhāva*—poured oblations of ghee; *graha*—the controlling planets; *śāntaye*—to pacify.

TRANSLATION

The best of *brāhmaṇas* chanted *mantras* of the *Ṛg, Sāma* and *Yajur Vedas* for the bride's protection, and the priest learned in the *Atharva Veda* offered oblations to pacify the controlling planets.

PURPORT

Śrīla Viśvanātha Cakravartī points out that the *Atharva Veda* often deals with the pacification of unfavorable planets.

TEXT 13

हिरण्यरूप्यवासांसि तिलांश्च गुडमिश्रितान् ।
प्रादाद्धेनूश्च विप्रेभ्यो राजा विधिविदां वरः ॥१३॥

hiraṇya-rūpya-vāsāṁsi
tilāṁś ca guḍa-miśritān
prādād dhenūś ca viprebhyo
rājā vidhi-vidāṁ varaḥ

hiraṇya—gold; *rūpya*—silver; *vāsāṁsi*—and clothing; *tilān*—sesame seeds; *ca*—and; *guḍa*—with raw sugar; *miśritān*—mixed; *prādāt*—gave; *dhenūḥ*—cows; *ca*—also; *viprebhyaḥ*—to the *brāhmaṇas; rājā*—the king, Bhīṣmaka; *vidhi*—regulative principles; *vidām*—of those who know; *varaḥ*—the best.

TRANSLATION

Outstanding in his knowledge of regulative principles, the King rewarded the *brāhmaṇas* with gold, silver, clothing, cows and sesame seeds mixed with raw sugar.

TEXT 14

एवं चेदिपती राजा दमघोषः सुताय वै ।
कारयामास मन्त्रज्ञैः सर्वमभ्युदयोचितम् ॥१४॥

evaṁ cedi-patī rājā
damaghoṣaḥ sutāya vai
kārayām āsa mantra-jñaiḥ
sarvam abhyudayocitam

evam—in the same way; *cedi-patiḥ*—the lord of Cedi; *rājā damaghoṣaḥ*—King Damaghoṣa; *sutāya*—for his son (Śiśupāla); *vai*—indeed; *kārayām āsa*—had done; *mantra-jñaiḥ*—by expert knowers of *mantras; sarvam*—everything; *abhyudaya*—to his prosperity; *ucitam*—conducive.

TRANSLATION

Rājā Damaghoṣa, lord of Cedi, had also engaged *brāhmaṇas* expert in chanting *mantras* to perform all rituals necessary to assure his son's prosperity.

TEXT 15

मदच्युद्‌भिर्गजानीकैः स्यन्दनैर्हेममालिभिः ।
पत्त्यश्वसंकुलैः सैन्यैः परीतः कुण्डिनं ययौ ॥१५॥

mada-cyudbhir gajānīkaiḥ
syandanair hema-mālibhiḥ
patty-aśva-saṅkulaiḥ sainyaiḥ
parītaḥ kuṇḍinaṁ yayau

mada—liquid secreted from the forehead; *cyudbhiḥ*—exuding; *gaja*—of elephants; *anīkaiḥ*—with hordes; *syandanaiḥ*—with chariots; *hema*—golden; *mālibhiḥ*—decorated with garlands; *patti*—with foot soldiers; *aśva*—and horses; *saṅkulaiḥ*—crowded; *sainyaiḥ*—by armies; *parītaḥ*—accompanied; *kuṇḍinam*—to Kuṇḍina, Bhīṣmaka's capital; *yayau*—he went.

TRANSLATION

King Damaghoṣa traveled to Kuṇḍina accompanied by armies of elephants exuding *mada,* chariots hung with golden chains, and numerous cavalry and infantry soldiers.

TEXT 16

तं वै विदर्भाधिपतिः समभ्येत्याभिपूज्य च ।
निवेशयामास मुदा कल्पितान्यनिवेशने ॥१६॥

taṁ vai vidarbhādhipatiḥ
samabhyetyābhipūjya ca
niveśayām āsa mudā
kalpitānya-niveśane

tam—him, King Damaghoṣa; *vai*—indeed; *vidarbha-adhipatiḥ*—the master of Vidarbha, Bhīṣmaka; *samabhyetya*—going forward to meet; *abhipūjya*—honoring; *ca*—and; *niveśayām āsa*—settled him; *mudā*—with pleasure; *kalpita*—constructed; *anya*—special; *niveśane*—at a place of residence.

TRANSLATION

Bhīṣmaka, the lord of Vidarbha, came out of the city and met King Damaghoṣa, offering him tokens of respect. Bhīṣmaka then settled Damaghoṣa in a residence especially constructed for the occasion.

TEXT 17

तत्र शाल्वो जरासन्धो दन्तवक्रो विदूरथः ।
आजग्मुश्चैद्यपक्षीयाः पौण्ड्रकाद्याः सहस्रशः ॥१७॥

tatra śālvo jarāsandho
dantavakro vidūrathaḥ
ājagmuś caidya-pakṣīyāḥ
pauṇḍrakādyāḥ sahasraśaḥ

tatra—there; *śālvaḥ jarāsandhaḥ dantavakraḥ vidūrathaḥ*—Śālva, Jarāsandha, Dantavakra and Vidūratha; *ājagmuḥ*—came; *caidya*—of Śiśupāla; *pakṣīyāḥ*—taking the side; *pauṇḍraka*—Pauṇḍraka; *ādyāḥ*—and others; *sahasraśaḥ*—by the thousands.

TRANSLATION

Śiśupāla's supporters—Śālva, Jarāsandha, Dantavakra and Vidūratha—all came, along with Pauṇḍraka and thousands of other kings.

PURPORT

Those familiar with the history of Lord Kṛṣṇa's life will immediately recognize the names given in this text. The kings mentioned here maintained a deep animosity toward Śrī Kṛṣṇa and opposed Him in one way or another. But they were all to be frustrated and defeated on the occasion of Śiśupāla's would-be wedding.

TEXTS 18–19

कृष्णरामद्विषो यत्ताः कन्यां चैद्याय साधितुम् ।
यद्यागत्य हरेत्कृष्णो रामाद्यैर्यदुभिर्वृतः ॥१८॥
योत्स्यामः संहतास्तेन इति निश्चितमानसाः ।
आजग्मुर्भूभुजः सर्वे समग्रबलवाहनाः ॥१९॥

kṛṣṇa-rāma-dviṣo yattāḥ
kanyāṁ caidyāya sādhitum
yady āgatya haret kṛṣṇo
rāmādyair yadubhir vṛtaḥ

yotsyāmaḥ saṁhatās tena
iti niścita-mānasāḥ
ājagmur bhū-bhujaḥ sarve
samagra-bala-vāhanāḥ

kṛṣṇa-rāma-dviṣaḥ—those hateful toward Kṛṣṇa and Balarāma; *yattāḥ*—prepared; *kanyām*—the bride; *caidyāya*—for Śiśupāla; *sādhitum*—in order to secure; *yadi*—if; *āgatya*—coming; *haret*—should steal;

kṛṣṇaḥ—Kṛṣṇa; *rāma*—by Balarāma; *ādyaiḥ*—and other; *yadubhiḥ*—Yadus; *vṛtaḥ*—accompanied; *yotsyāmaḥ*—we will fight; *saṁhatāḥ*—joining all together; *tena*—with Him; *iti*—thus; *niścita-mānasāḥ*—having decided; *ājagmuḥ*—came; *bhū-bhujaḥ*—the kings; *sarve*—all; *samagra*—complete; *bala*—with military forces; *vāhanāḥ*—and conveyances.

TRANSLATION

To secure the bride for Śiśupāla, the kings who envied Kṛṣṇa and Balarāma came to the following decision among themselves: "If Kṛṣṇa comes here with Balarāma and the other Yadus to steal the bride, we shall band together and fight Him." Thus those envious kings went to the wedding with their entire armies and a full complement of military conveyances.

PURPORT

The word *saṁhatāḥ*, which normally means "bound tightly together," may also mean "thoroughly struck down" or "killed." Thus although Kṛṣṇa's enemies thought they were unified and strong—*saṁhatāḥ* in the former sense—they could not successfully oppose the Personality of Godhead, and consequently they would be struck down and killed—*saṁhatāḥ* in the latter sense.

TEXTS 20–21

श्रुत्वैतद् भगवान् रामो विपक्षीयनृपोद्यमम् ।
कृष्णं चैकं गतं हर्तुं कन्यां कलहशङ्कितः ॥२०॥
बलेन महता सार्धं भ्रातृस्नेहपरिप्लुतः ।
त्वरितः कुण्डिनं प्रागाद् गजाश्वरथपत्तिभिः ॥२१॥

śrutvaitad bhagavān rāmo
vipakṣīya-nṛpodyamam
kṛṣṇaṁ caikaṁ gataṁ hartuṁ
kanyāṁ kalaha-śaṅkitaḥ

balena mahatā sārdhaṁ
bhrātṛ-sneha-pariplutaḥ

tvaritaḥ kuṇḍinaṁ prāgād
gajāśva-ratha-pattibhiḥ

śrutvā—hearing; *etat*—this; *bhagavān rāmaḥ*—Lord Balarāma; *vipakṣīya*—inimical; *nṛpa*—of the kings; *udyamam*—the preparations; *kṛṣṇam*—Lord Kṛṣṇa; *ca*—and; *ekam*—alone; *gatam*—gone; *hartum*—to take away; *kanyām*—the bride; *kalaha*—a fight; *śaṅkitaḥ*—fearing; *balena*—a force; *mahatā*—mighty; *sārdham*—together with; *bhrātṛ*—for His brother; *sneha*—in affection; *pariplutaḥ*—immersed; *tvaritaḥ*—swiftly; *kuṇḍinam*—to Kuṇḍina; *prāgāt*—went; *gaja*—with elephants; *aśva*—horses; *ratha*—chariots; *pattibhiḥ*—and infantry.

TRANSLATION

When Lord Balarāma heard about these preparations of the inimical kings and how Lord Kṛṣṇa had set off alone to steal the bride, He feared that a fight would ensue. Immersed in affection for His brother, He hurried to Kuṇḍina with a mighty army consisting of infantry and of soldiers riding on elephants, horses and chariots.

TEXT 22

भीष्मकन्या वरारोहा काङ्‌क्षन्त्यागमनं हरेः ।
प्रत्यापत्तिमपश्यन्ती द्विजस्याचिन्तयत्तदा ॥२२॥

bhīṣma-kanyā varārohā
kāṅkṣanty āgamanaṁ hareḥ
pratyāpattim apaśyantī
dvijasyācintayat tadā

bhīṣma-kanyā—the daughter of Bhīṣmaka; *vara-ārohā*—having lovely hips; *kāṅkṣantī*—waiting for; *āgamanam*—the arrival; *hareḥ*—of Kṛṣṇa; *pratyāpattim*—the return; *apaśyantī*—not seeing; *dvijasya*—of the *brāhmaṇa; acintayat*—thought; *tadā*—then.

TRANSLATION

The lovely daughter of Bhīṣmaka anxiously awaited the arrival of Kṛṣṇa, but when she did not see the *brāhmaṇa* return she thought as follows.

TEXT 23

अहो त्रियामान्तरित उद्वाहो मेऽल्पराधसः ।
नागच्छत्यरविन्दाक्षो नाहं वेद्म्यत्र कारणम् ।
सोऽपि नावर्ततेऽद्यापि मत्सन्देशहरो द्विजः ॥२३॥

aho tri-yāmāntarita
udvāho me 'lpa-rādhasaḥ
nāgacchaty aravindākṣo
nāhaṁ vedmy atra kāraṇam
so 'pi nāvartate 'dyāpi
mat-sandeśa-haro dvijaḥ

aho—alas; *tri-yāma*—three *yāmas* (nine hours), i.e., the night; *antaritaḥ*—having ended; *udvāhaḥ*—the marriage; *me*—of me; *alpa*—insufficient; *rādhasaḥ*—whose good fortune; *na āgacchati*—does not come; *aravinda-akṣaḥ*—lotus-eyed Kṛṣṇa; *na*—do not; *aham*—I; *vedmi*—know; *atra*—for this; *kāraṇam*—the reason; *saḥ*—he; *api*—also; *na āvartate*—does not return; *adya api*—even now; *mat*—my; *sandeśa*—of the message; *haraḥ*—the carrier; *dvijaḥ*—the *brāhmaṇa*.

TRANSLATION

[Princess Rukmiṇī thought:] Alas, my wedding is to take place when the night ends! How unlucky I am! Lotus-eyed Kṛṣṇa does not come. I don't know why. And even the *brāhmaṇa* messenger has not yet returned.

PURPORT

It is apparent from this verse, as confirmed by Śrīla Śrīdhara Svāmī, that the present scene takes place before sunrise.

TEXT 24

अपि मय्यनवद्यात्मा दृष्ट्वा किञ्चिज्जुगुप्सितम् ।
मत्पाणिग्रहणे नूनं नायाति हि कृतोद्यमः ॥२४॥

api mayy anavadyātmā
dṛṣṭvā kiñcij jugupsitam
mat-pāṇi-grahaṇe nūnaṁ
nāyāti hi kṛtodyamaḥ

api—perhaps; *mayi*—in me; *anavadya*—faultless; *ātmā*—He whose body and mind; *dṛṣṭvā*—seeing; *kiñcit*—something; *jugupsitam*—contemptible; *mat*—my; *pāṇi*—hand; *grahaṇe*—for the taking; *nūnam*—indeed; *na āyāti*—has not come; *hi*—certainly; *kṛta-udyamaḥ*—even though originally intending to do so.

TRANSLATION

Perhaps the faultless Lord, even while preparing to come here, saw something contemptible in me and therefore has not come to take my hand.

PURPORT

Princess Rukmiṇī boldly invited Śrī Kṛṣṇa to kidnap her. When Rukmiṇī did not see Him come, she naturally feared that He had rejected her proposal, perhaps finding some unacceptable quality in her. As expressed here, the Lord Himself is *anavadya*, faultless, and if He saw some fault in Rukmiṇī she would be an unworthy bride for Him. It was natural for the young princess to feel such anxiety. Furthermore, if Śrī Kṛṣṇa had actually made this decision, it would be natural for the *brāhmaṇa* to fear Rukmiṇī's reaction were he to bring her the news, and that would explain why he had not come.

TEXT 25

दुर्भगाया न मे धाता नानुकूलो महेश्वरः ।
देवी वा विमुखी गौरी रुद्राणी गिरिजा सती ॥२५॥

durbhagāyā na me dhātā
nānukūlo maheśvaraḥ
devī vā vimukhī gaurī
rudrāṇī girijā satī

durbhagāyāḥ—who is unfortunate; *na*—not; *me*—with me; *dhātā*—the creator (Lord Brahmā); *na*—not; *anukūlaḥ*—favorably disposed; *mahā-īśvaraḥ*—the great Lord Śiva; *devī*—the goddess (his consort); *vā*—or; *vimukhī*—turned against; *gaurī*—Gaurī; *rudrāṇī*—the wife of Rudra; *giri-jā*—the adopted daughter of the Himālayan mountain range; *satī*—Satī, who, in her previous life as the daughter of Dakṣa, chose to give up her body.

TRANSLATION

I am extremely unfortunate, for the creator is not favorably disposed toward me, nor is the great Lord Śiva. Or perhaps Śiva's wife, Devī, who is known as Gaurī, Rudrāṇī, Girijā and Satī, has turned against me.

PURPORT

Śrīla Viśvanātha Cakravartī explains that Rukmiṇī might have thought, "Even if Kṛṣṇa wanted to come, He might have been stopped on the path by the creator, Brahmā, who is not favorably inclined toward me. But why should he be unfavorable? Perhaps it is Maheśvara, Lord Śiva, whom on some occasion I did not properly worship and who thus became angry with me. But he is Maheśvara, the great controller, so why would he be angry with such an insignificant and foolish girl as me?

"Perhaps it is Śiva's wife, Gaurī-devī, who is displeased, though I worship her every day. Alas, alas, how have I offended her so that she has turned against me? But after all, she is Rudrāṇī, the wife of Rudra, and her very name means 'one who makes everyone cry.' So perhaps she and Śiva want me to cry. But seeing that I am so miserable, about to give up my life, why don't they soften their attitude? The reason must be that Goddess Devī is Girijā, an adopted daughter, so why should she be soft-hearted? In her incarnation as Satī she gave up her body, so perhaps she now wants me to give up my body also."

Thus the *ācārya,* with realized poetic sensitivity, interprets the various names used in this verse.

TEXT 26

एवं चिन्तयती बाला गोविन्दहृतमानसा ।
न्यमीलयत कालज्ञा नेत्रे चाश्रुकलाकुले ॥२६॥

evaṁ cintayatī bālā
govinda-hṛta-mānasā
nyamīlayata kāla-jñā
netre cāśru-kalākule

evam—in this manner; *cintayatī*—thinking; *bālā*—the young girl; *govinda*—by Kṛṣṇa; *hṛta*—stolen; *mānasā*—whose mind; *nyamīlayata*—she closed; *kāla*—the time; *jñā*—knowing; *netre*—her eyes; *ca*—and; *aśru-kalā*—with tears; *ākule*—brimming.

TRANSLATION

As she thought in this way, the young maiden, whose mind had been stolen by Kṛṣṇa, closed her tear-filled eyes, remembering that there was still time.

PURPORT

Śrīla Śrīdhara Svāmī explains the word *kāla-jñā* as follows: "[Rukmiṇī thought,] 'It is not even the right time yet for Govinda to come,' and thus she felt a bit consoled."

TEXT 27

एवं वध्वाः प्रतीक्षन्त्या गोविन्दागमनं नृप ।
वाम ऊरुर्भुजो नेत्रमस्फुरन् प्रियभाषिणः ॥२७॥

evaṁ vadhvāḥ pratīkṣantyā
govindāgamanaṁ nṛpa
vāma ūrur bhujo netram
asphuran priya-bhāṣiṇaḥ

evam—thus; *vadhvāḥ*—the bride; *pratīkṣantyāḥ*—as she awaited; *govinda-āgamanam*—the arrival of Kṛṣṇa; *nṛpa*—O King (Parīkṣit); *vāmaḥ*—left; *ūruḥ*—her thigh; *bhujaḥ*—arm; *netram*—and eye; *asphuran*—twitched; *priya*—something desirable; *bhāṣiṇaḥ*—bespeaking.

TRANSLATION

O King, as the bride thus awaited the arrival of Govinda, she felt a twitch in her left thigh, arm and eye. This was a sign that something desirable would happen.

TEXT 28

अथ कृष्णविनिर्दिष्टः स एव द्विजसत्तमः ।
अन्तःपुरचरीं देवीं राजपुत्रीं ददर्श ह ॥२८॥

atha kṛṣṇa-vinirdiṣṭaḥ
sa eva dvija-sattamaḥ
antaḥpura-carīṁ devīṁ
rāja-putrīṁ dadarśa ha

atha—then; *kṛṣṇa-vinirdiṣṭaḥ*—ordered by Lord Kṛṣṇa; *saḥ*—that; *eva*—very; *dvija*—of learned *brāhmaṇas; sat-tamaḥ*—the most pure; *antaḥ-pura*—within the inner palace; *carīm*—staying; *devīm*—the goddess, Rukmiṇī; *rāja*—of the king; *putrīm*—the daughter; *dadarśa ha*—saw.

TRANSLATION

Just then that purest of learned *brāhmaṇas*, following Kṛṣṇa's order, came to see the divine Princess Rukmiṇī within the inner chambers of the palace.

PURPORT

According to Śrila Śrīdhara Svāmī, Śrī Kṛṣṇa had reached the gardens outside the city, and out of concern for Rukmiṇī He had instructed the *brāhmaṇa* to tell her of His arrival.

TEXT 29

सा तं प्रहृष्टवदनमव्यग्रात्मगतिं सती ।
आलक्ष्य लक्षणाभिज्ञा समपृच्छच्छुचिस्मिता ॥२९॥

sā taṁ prahṛṣṭa-vadanam
avyagrātma-gatiṁ satī
ālakṣya lakṣaṇābhijñā
samapṛcchac chuci-smitā

sā—she; *tam*—him; *prahṛṣṭa*—filled with joy; *vadanam*—whose face; *avyagra*—unagitated; *ātma*—of whose body; *gatim*—the movement; *satī*—the saintly young woman; *ālakṣya*—noting; *lakṣaṇa*—of symptoms; *abhijñā*—an expert knower; *samapṛcchat*—inquired; *śuci*—pure; *smitā*—with a smile.

TRANSLATION

Noting the *brāhmaṇa's* joyful face and serene movements, saintly Rukmiṇī, who could expertly interpret such symptoms, inquired from him with a pure smile.

TEXT 30

तस्या आवेदयत्प्राप्तं शशंस यदुनन्दनम् ।
उक्तं च सत्यवचनमात्मोपनयनं प्रति ॥३०॥

tasyā āvedayat prāptaṁ
śaśaṁsa yadu-nandanam
uktaṁ ca satya-vacanam
ātmopanayanaṁ prati

tasyāḥ—to her; *āvedayat*—he announced; *prāptam*—as having arrived; *śaśaṁsa*—he related; *yadu-nandanam*—Kṛṣṇa, the child of the Yadus; *uktam*—what He had said; *ca*—and; *satya*—of assurance; *vacanam*—words; *ātma*—with her; *upanayanam*—His marriage; *prati*—concerning.

TRANSLATION

The *brāhmaṇa* announced to her the arrival of Lord Yadunandana and relayed the Lord's promise to marry her.

TEXT 31

तमागतं समाज्ञाय वैदर्भी हृष्टमानसा ।
न पश्यन्ती ब्राह्मणाय प्रियमन्यन्ननाम सा ॥३१॥

tam āgataṁ samājñāya
vaidarbhī hṛṣṭa-mānasā
na paśyantī brāhmaṇāya
priyam anyan nanāma sā

tam—Him, Kṛṣṇa; *āgatam*—arrived; *samājñāya*—fully realizing; *vaidarbhī*—Rukmiṇī; *hṛṣṭa*—gladdened; *mānasā*—her mind; *na paśyantī*—not seeing; *brāhmaṇāya*—to the *brāhmaṇa; priyam*—dear; *anyat*—anything else; *nanāma*—bowed down; *sā*—she.

TRANSLATION

Princess Vaidarbhī was overjoyed to learn of Kṛṣṇa's arrival. Not finding anything at hand suitable to offer the *brāhmaṇa*, she simply bowed down to him.

TEXT 32

प्राप्तौ श्रुत्वा स्वदुहितुरुद्वाहप्रेक्षणोत्सुकौ ।
अभ्ययात्तूर्यघोषेण रामकृष्णौ समर्हणैः ॥३२॥

prāptau śrutvā sva-duhitur
udvāha-prekṣaṇotsukau
abhyayāt tūrya-ghoṣeṇa
rāma-kṛṣṇau samarhaṇaiḥ

prāptau—arrived; *śrutvā*—hearing; *sva*—his; *duhituḥ*—daughter's; *udvāha*—marriage; *prekṣaṇa*—to witness; *utsukau*—eager; *abhyayāt*—he went forward; *tūrya*—of musical instruments; *ghoṣeṇa*—with the resounding; *rāma-kṛṣṇau*—to Balarāma and Kṛṣṇa; *samarhaṇaiḥ*—with abundant offerings.

TRANSLATION

The King, upon hearing that Kṛṣṇa and Balarāma had come and were eager to witness his daughter's wedding, went forth with abundant offerings to greet Them as music resounded.

TEXT 33

मधुपर्कमुपानीय वासांसि विरजांसि सः ।
उपायनान्यभीष्टानि विधिवत्समपूजयत् ॥३३॥

madhu-parkam upānīya
vāsāṁsi virajāṁsi saḥ
upāyanāny abhīṣṭāni
vidhi-vat samapūjayat

madhu-parkam—the traditional mixture of milk and honey; *upānīya*—bearing; *vāsāṁsi*—garments; *virajāṁsi*—spotless; *saḥ*—he; *upāyanāni*—presentations; *abhīṣṭāni*—desirable; *vidhi-vat*—according to scriptural prescriptions; *samapūjayat*—performed worshiped.

TRANSLATION

Presenting Them with *madhu-parka*, new clothing and other desirable gifts, he worshiped Them according to standard rituals.

TEXT 34

तयोर्निवेशनं श्रीमदुपाकल्प्य महामतिः ।
ससैन्ययोः सानुगयोरातिथ्यं विदधे यथा ॥३४॥

tayor niveśanaṁ śrīmad
upākalpya mahā-matiḥ
sa-sainyayoḥ sānugayor
ātithyaṁ vidadhe yathā

tayoḥ—for Them; *niveśanam*—place to stay; *śrī-mat*—opulent; *upākalpya*—arranging; *mahā-matiḥ*—generous; *sa*—together with; *sainyayoḥ*—Their soldiers; *sa*—together with; *anugayoḥ*—Their personal associates; *ātithyam*—hospitality; *vidadhe*—he afforded; *yathā*—properly.

TRANSLATION

Generous King Bhīṣmaka arranged opulent accommodations for the two Lords, and also for Their army and entourage. In this way he afforded Them proper hospitality.

TEXT 35

एवं राज्ञां समेतानां यथावीर्यं यथावयः ।
यथाबलं यथावित्तं सर्वैः कामैः समर्हयत् ॥३५॥

evaṁ rājñāṁ sametānāṁ
yathā-vīryaṁ yathā-vayaḥ
yathā-balaṁ yathā-vittaṁ
sarvaiḥ kāmaiḥ samarhayat

evam—thus; *rājñām*—for the kings; *sametānām*—who had assembled; *yathā*—according; *vīryam*—to their power; *yathā*—according; *vayaḥ*—to their age; *yathā*—according; *balam*—to their strength; *yathā*—according; *vittam*—to their wealth; *sarvaiḥ*—with all; *kāmaiḥ*—desirable things; *samarhayat*—he honored them.

TRANSLATION

Thus it was that Bhīṣmaka gave all desirable things to the kings who had assembled for the occasion, honoring them as befitted their political power, age, physical prowess and wealth.

TEXT 36

कृष्णमागतमाकर्ण्य विदर्भपुरवासिनः ।
आगत्य नेत्राञ्जलिभिः पपुस्तन्मुखपंकजम् ॥३६॥

kṛṣṇam āgatam ākarṇya
vidarbha-pura-vāsinaḥ
āgatya netrāñjalibhiḥ
papus tan-mukha-paṅkajam

kṛṣṇam—Lord Kṛṣṇa; *āgatam*—come; *ākarṇya*—hearing; *vidarbha-pura*—of the capital city of Vidarbha; *vāsinaḥ*—the residents; *āgatya*—coming; *netra*—of their eyes; *añjalibhiḥ*—with the cupped palms; *papuḥ*—they drank; *tat*—His; *mukha*—face; *paṅkajam*—lotus.

TRANSLATION

When the residents of Vidarbha-pura heard that Lord Kṛṣṇa had come, they all went to see Him. With the cupped palms of their eyes they drank the honey of His lotus face.

TEXT 37

अस्यैव भार्या भवितुं रुक्मिण्यर्हति नापरा ।
असावप्यनवद्यात्मा भैष्म्याः समुचितः पतिः ॥३७॥

asyaiva bhāryā bhavituṁ
rukmiṇy arhati nāparā
asāv apy anavadyātmā
bhaiṣmyāḥ samucitaḥ patiḥ

asya—for Him; *eva*—alone; *bhāryā*—wife; *bhavitum*—to be; *rukmiṇī*—Rukmiṇī; *arhati*—deserves; *na aparā*—none other; *asau*—He; *api*—as well; *anavadya*—faultless; *ātmā*—whose bodily form; *bhaiṣmyāḥ*—for the daughter of Bhīṣmaka; *samucitaḥ*—most suitable; *patiḥ*—husband.

TRANSLATION

[The people of the city said:] Rukmiṇī, and no one else, deserves to become His wife, and He also, possessing such flawless beauty, is the only suitable husband for Princess Bhaiṣmī.

PURPORT

According to Śrīla Viśvanātha Cakravartī, this text combines statements made by different citizens. Some pointed out that Rukmiṇī was a suitable wife for Kṛṣṇa, others said that no one else was suitable. Similarly, some stated that Kṛṣṇa was most suitable for Rukmiṇī, and others stated that no one else would be a suitable husband for her.

TEXT 38

किञ्चित्सुचरितं यन्नस्तेन तुष्टस्त्रिलोककृत् ।
अनुगृह्णातु गृह्णातु वैदर्भ्याः पाणिमच्युतः ॥३८॥

kiñcit su-caritaṁ yan nas
tena tuṣṭas tri-loka-kṛt
anugṛhṇātu gṛhṇātu
vaidarbhyāḥ pāṇim acyutaḥ

kiñcit—at all; *su-caritam*—pious work; *yat*—whatever; *naḥ*—our; *tena*—with that; *tuṣṭaḥ*—satisfied; *tri-loka*—of the three worlds; *kṛt*—the creator; *anugṛhṇātu*—may please show mercy; *gṛhṇātu*—may take; *vaidarbhyāḥ*—of Rukmiṇī; *pāṇim*—the hand; *acyutaḥ*—Kṛṣṇa.

TRANSLATION

May Acyuta, the creator of the three worlds, be satisfied with whatever pious work we may have done and show His mercy by taking the hand of Vaidarbhī.

PURPORT

The devoted citizens of Vidarbha lovingly offered their entire stock of pious credit to Princess Rukmiṇī. They were very eager to see her marry Lord Kṛṣṇa.

TEXT 39

एवं प्रेमकलाबद्धा वदन्ति स्म पुरौकसः ।
कन्या चान्तःपुरात्प्रागाद् भटैर्गुप्ताम्बिकालयम् ॥३९॥

evaṁ prema-kalā-baddhā
vadanti sma puraukasaḥ
kanyā cāntaḥ-purāt prāgād
bhaṭair guptāmbikālayam

evam—thus; *prema*—of pure love; *kalā*—by the increase; *baddhāḥ*—bound; *vadanti sma*—they spoke; *pura-okasaḥ*—the residents of the city; *kanyā*—the bride; *ca*—and; *antaḥ-purāt*—from the inner palace; *prāgāt*—went out; *bhaṭaiḥ*—by guards; *guptā*—protected; *ambikā-ālayam*—to the temple of Goddess Ambikā.

TRANSLATION

Bound by their swelling love, the city's residents spoke in this way. Then the bride, protected by guards, left the inner palace to visit the temple of Ambikā.

PURPORT

Śrīla Viśvanātha Cakravartī quotes the *Medinī* dictionary's definition of the word *kalā* as follows: *kalā mūle pravṛddhau syāc chilādāv aṁśa-mātrake.* "The word *kalā* means 'a root,' 'increase,' 'a stone' or 'a mere part.'"

TEXTS 40–41

पद्‌भ्यां विनिर्ययौ द्रष्टुं भवान्याः पादपल्लवम् ।
सा चानुध्यायती सम्यङ् मुकुन्दचरणाम्बुजम् ॥४०॥
यतवाङ् मातृभिः सार्धं सखीभिः परिवारिता ।
गुप्ता राजभटैः शूरैः सन्नद्धैरुद्यतायुधैः ।
मृदंगशंखपणवास्तूर्यभेर्यश्च जघ्निरे ॥४१॥

padbhyāṁ viniryayau draṣṭuṁ
bhavānyāḥ pāda-pallavam
sā cānudhyāyatī samyaṅ
mukunda-caraṇāmbujam

yata-vāṅ mātṛbhiḥ sārdhaṁ
sakhībhiḥ parivāritā

guptā rāja-bhaṭaiḥ śūraiḥ
sannaddhair udyatāyudhaiḥ
mṛdaṅga-śaṅkha-paṇavās
tūrya-bheryaś ca jaghnire

padbhyām—on foot; *viniryayau*—went out; *draṣṭum*—in order to see; *bhavānyāḥ*—of mother Bhavānī; *pāda-pallavam*—the lotus-petal feet; *sā*—she; *ca*—and; *anudhyāyatī*—meditating; *samyak*—totally; *mukunda*—of Kṛṣṇa; *caraṇa-ambujam*—on the lotus feet; *yata-vāk*—maintaining silence; *mātṛbhiḥ*—by her mothers; *sārdham*—accompanied; *sakhībhiḥ*—by her female companions; *parivāritā*—surrounded; *guptā*—guarded; *rāja*—of the King; *bhaṭaiḥ*—by soldiers; *śūraiḥ*—valiant; *sannaddhaiḥ*—armed and ready; *udyata*—upraised; *āyudhaiḥ*—with weapons; *mṛdaṅga-śaṅkha-paṇavāḥ*—clay drums, conchshells and side drums; *tūrya*—wind instruments; *bheryaḥ*—horns; *ca*—and; *jaghnire*— played.

TRANSLATION

Rukmiṇī silently went out on foot to see the lotus feet of the deity Bhavānī. Accompanied by her mothers and girlfriends and protected by the King's valiant soldiers, who held their upraised weapons at the ready, she simply absorbed her mind in the lotus feet of Kṛṣṇa. And all the while *mṛdaṅgas*, conchshells, *paṇavas*, horns and other instruments resounded.

TEXTS 42–43

नानोपहारबलिभिर्वारमुख्याः सहस्रशः ।
स्रग्गन्धवस्त्राभरणैर्द्विजपत्न्यः स्वलंकृताः ॥४२॥
गायन्त्यश्च स्तुवन्तश्च गायका वाद्यवादकाः ।
परिवार्य वधूं जग्मुः सूतमागधवन्दिनः ॥४३॥

nānopahāra-balibhir
vāramukhyāḥ sahasraśaḥ
srag-gandha-vastrābharaṇair
dvija-patnyaḥ sv-alaṅkṛtāḥ

gāyantyaś ca stuvantaś ca
gāyakā vādya-vādakāḥ
parivārya vadhūṁ jagmuḥ
sūta-māgadha-vandinaḥ

nānā—various; *upahāra*—with paraphernalia of worship; *balibhiḥ*—and presents; *vāra-mukhyāḥ*—prominent courtesans; *sahasraśaḥ*—by the thousands; *srak*—with flower garlands; *gandha*—fragrances; *vastra*—clothing; *ābharaṇaiḥ*—and jewelry; *dvija*—of *brāhmaṇas; patnyaḥ*—the wives; *sv-alaṅkṛtāḥ*—well ornamented; *gāyantyaḥ*—singing; *ca*—and; *stuvantaḥ*—offering prayers; *ca*—and; *gāyakāḥ*—singers; *vādya-vādakāḥ*—instrumental musicians; *parivārya*—accompanying; *vadhūm*—the bride; *jagmuḥ*—went; *sūta*—bards; *māgadha*—chroniclers; *vandinaḥ*—and heralds.

TRANSLATION

Behind the bride followed thousands of prominent courtesans bearing various offerings and presents, along with well-adorned *brāhmaṇas'* wives singing and reciting prayers and bearing gifts of garlands, scents, clothing and jewelry. There were also professional singers, musicians, bards, chroniclers and heralds.

PURPORT

Śrīla Viśvanātha Cakravartī explains that from her own quarters up to the temple of Bhavānī, Rukmiṇī went by palanquin and thus was easily protected. Only for the last twelve to fifteen feet, from the palace to the temple area, did she go on foot, with royal bodyguards stationed outside the temple on all sides.

TEXT 44

आसाद्य देवीसदनं धौतपादकराम्बुजा ।
उपस्पृश्य शुचिः शान्ता प्रविवेशाम्बिकान्तिकम् ॥४४॥

āsādya devī-sadanaṁ
dhauta-pāda-karāmbujā

upaspṛśya śuciḥ śāntā
praviveśāmbikāntikam

āsādya—reaching; *devī*—of the goddess; *sadanam*—the residence; *dhauta*—washing; *pāda*—her feet; *kara*—and hands; *ambujā*—lotuslike; *upaspṛśya*—sipping water for purification; *śuciḥ*—sanctified; *śāntā*—peaceful; *praviveśa*—she entered; *ambikā-antikam*—the presence of Ambikā.

TRANSLATION

Upon reaching the goddess's temple, Rukmiṇī first washed her lotus feet and hands and then sipped water for purification. Thus sanctified and peaceful, she came into the presence of mother Ambikā.

TEXT 45

तां वै प्रवयसो बालां विधिज्ञा विप्रयोषितः ।
भवानीं वन्दयां चक्रुर्भवपत्नीं भवान्विताम् ॥४५॥

tāṁ vai pravayaso bālāṁ
vidhi-jñā vipra-yoṣitaḥ
bhavānīṁ vandayāṁ cakrur
bhava-patnīṁ bhavānvitām

tām—her; *vai*—indeed; *pravayasaḥ*—elderly; *bālām*—the young girl; *vidhi*—of ritual injunctions; *jñāḥ*—expert knowers; *vipra*—of *brāhmaṇas; yoṣitaḥ*—the wives; *bhavānīm*—to Goddess Bhavānī; *vandayām cakruḥ*—they led in offering respects; *bhava-patnīm*—the wife of Bhava (Lord Śiva); *bhava-anvitām*—accompanied by Lord Bhava.

TRANSLATION

The older wives of *brāhmaṇas*, expert in the knowledge of rituals, led young Rukmiṇī in offering respects to Bhavānī, who appeared with her consort, Lord Bhava.

PURPORT

According to the *ācāryas*, here the term *bhavānvitām* indicates that in the Ambikā temple visited by Rukmiṇī, the presiding deity was the goddess, whose husband appeared in an accompanying role. Thus the ritual was properly performed by women.

Śrīla Viśvanātha Cakravartī comments that the term *vidhi-jñāḥ* may be understood to mean that since the learned wives of *brāhmaṇas* knew of Rukmiṇī's desire to marry Kṛṣṇa, the verb *vandayāṁ cakruḥ* thus indicates that they prompted her to pray for what she really wanted. In this way, like the goddess Bhavānī, Rukmiṇī could be united with her eternal male companion.

TEXT 46

नमस्ये त्वाम्बिकेऽभीक्ष्णं स्वसन्तानयुतां शिवाम् ।
भूयात्पतिर्मे भगवान् कृष्णस्तदनुमोदताम् ॥४६॥

namasye tvāmbike 'bhīkṣṇaṁ
sva-santāna-yutāṁ śivām
bhūyāt patir me bhagavān
kṛṣṇas tad anumodatām

namasye—I offer my obeisances; *tvā*—to you; *ambike*—O Ambikā; *abhīkṣṇam*—constantly; *sva*—your; *santāna*—children; *yutām*—along with; *śivām*—the wife of Lord Śiva; *bhūyāt*—may He become; *patiḥ*—husband; *me*—my; *bhagavān*—the Supreme Lord; *kṛṣṇaḥ*—Kṛṣṇa; *tat*—that; *anumodatām*—please allow.

TRANSLATION

[Princess Rukmiṇī prayed:] O mother Ambikā, wife of Lord Śiva, I repeatedly offer my obeisances unto you, together with your children. May Lord Kṛṣṇa become my husband. Please grant this!

TEXTS 47–48

अद्भिर्गन्धाक्षतैर्धूपैर्वासःस्रङ्माल्यभूषणैः ।
नानोपहारबलिभिः प्रदीपावलिभिः पृथक् ॥४७॥
विप्रस्त्रियः पतिमतीस्तथा तैः समपूजयत् ।
लवणापूपताम्बूलकण्ठसूत्रफलेक्षुभिः ॥४८॥

adbhir gandhākṣatair dhūpair
vāsaḥ-sraṅ-mālya-bhūṣaṇaiḥ
nānopahāra-balibhiḥ
pradīpāvalibhiḥ pṛthak

vipra-striyaḥ patimatīs
tathā taiḥ samapūjayat
lavaṇāpūpa-tāmbūla-
kaṇṭha-sūtra-phalekṣubhiḥ

adbhiḥ—with water; *gandha*—fragrant substances; *akṣataiḥ*—and whole grains; *dhūpaiḥ*—with incense; *vāsaḥ*—with clothing; *srak*—flower garlands; *mālya*—jeweled necklaces; *bhūṣaṇaiḥ*—and ornaments; *nānā*—with various; *upahāra*—offerings; *balibhiḥ*—and gifts; *pradīpa*—of lamps; *āvalibhiḥ*—with rows; *pṛthak*—separately; *vipra-striyaḥ*—the *brāhmaṇa* ladies; *pati*—husbands; *matīḥ*—having; *tathā*—also; *taiḥ*—with these items; *samapūjayat*—performed worship; *lavaṇa*—with savory preparations; *āpūpa*—cakes; *tāmbūla*—prepared betel nut; *kaṇṭha-sūtra*—sacred threads; *phala*—fruits; *ikṣubhiḥ*—and sugar cane.

TRANSLATION

Rukmiṇī worshiped the goddess with water, scents, whole grains, incense, clothing, garlands, necklaces, jewelry and other prescribed offerings and gifts, and also with arrays of lamps. The married *brāhmaṇa* women each performed worship simultaneously with the same items, also offering savories and cakes, prepared betel nut, sacred threads, fruit and sugar-cane juice.

TEXT 49

तस्यै स्त्रियस्ताः प्रददुः शेषां युयुजुराशिषः ।
ताभ्यो देव्यै नमश्चक्रे शेषां च जगृहे वधूः ॥४९॥

tasyai striyas tāḥ pradaduḥ
śeṣāṁ yuyujur āśiṣaḥ
tābhyo devyai namaś cakre
śeṣāṁ ca jagṛhe vadhūḥ

tasyai—to her, Rukmiṇī; *striyaḥ*—women; *tāḥ*—they; *pradaduḥ*—gave; *śeṣām*—the remnants; *yuyujuḥ*—they bestowed; *āśiṣaḥ*—blessings; *tābhyaḥ*—to them; *devyai*—and to the deity; *namaḥ cakre*—bowed down; *śeṣām*—the remnants; *ca*—and; *jagṛhe*—took; *vadhūḥ*—the bride.

TRANSLATION

The ladies gave the bride the remnants of the offerings and then blessed her. She in turn bowed down to them and the deity and accepted the remnants as *prasādam*.

TEXT 50

मुनिव्रतमथ त्यक्त्वा निश्चक्रामाम्बिकागृहात् ।
प्रगृह्य पाणिना भृत्यां रत्नमुद्रोपशोभिना ॥५०॥

muni-vratam atha tyaktvā
niścakrāmāmbikā-gṛhāt
pragṛhya pāṇinā bhṛtyāṁ
ratna-mudropaśobhinā

muni—of silence; *vratam*—her vow; *atha*—then; *tyaktvā*—giving up; *niścakrāma*—she exited; *ambikā-gṛhāt*—from the temple of Ambikā; *pragṛhya*—holding on; *pāṇinā*—with her hand; *bhṛtyām*—to a maidservant; *ratna*—jeweled; *mudrā*—by a ring; *upaśobhinā*—beautified.

TRANSLATION

The princess then gave up her vow of silence and left the Ambikā temple, holding on to a maidservant with her hand, which was adorned with a jeweled ring.

TEXTS 51–55

तां देवमायामिव धीरमोहिनीं
सुमध्यमां कुण्डलमण्डिताननाम् ।
श्यामां नितम्बार्पितरत्नमेखलां
व्यञ्जत्स्तनीं कुन्तलशङ्कितेक्षणाम् ।

शुचिस्मितां बिम्बफलाधरद्युति-
शोणायमानद्विजकुन्दकुड्मलाम् ॥५१॥
पदा चलन्तीं कलहंसगामिनीं
सिञ्जत्कलानूपुरधामशोभिना ।
विलोक्य वीरा मुमुहुः समागता
यशस्विनस्तत्कृतहृच्छयार्दिताः ॥५२॥
यां वीक्ष्य ते नृपतयस्तदुदारहास-
व्रीडावलोकहृतचेतस उज्झितास्त्राः ।
पेतुः क्षितौ गजरथाश्वगता विमूढा
यात्राच्छलेन हरयेऽर्पयतीं स्वशोभाम् ॥५३॥
सैवं शनैश्चलयती चलपद्मकोशौ
प्राप्तिं तदा भगवतः प्रसमीक्षमाणा ।
उत्सार्य वामकरजैरलकानपांगैः
प्राप्तान् ह्रियैक्षत नृपान् ददृशेऽच्युतं च ॥५४॥
तां राजकन्यां रथमारुरुक्षतीं
जहार कृष्णो द्विषतां समीक्षताम् ॥५५॥

tāṁ deva-māyām iva dhīra-mohinīṁ
su-madhyamāṁ kuṇḍala-maṇḍitānanām
śyāmāṁ nitambārpita-ratna-mekhalāṁ
vyañjat-stanīṁ kuntala-śaṅkitekṣaṇām
śuci-smitāṁ bimba-phalādhara-dyuti-
śoṇāyamāna-dvija-kunda-kuḍmalām

padā calantīṁ kala-haṁsa-gāminīṁ
siñjat-kalā-nūpura-dhāma-śobhinā
vilokya vīrā mumuhuḥ samāgatā
yaśasvinas tat-kṛta-hṛc-chayārditāḥ

yāṁ vīkṣya te nṛpatayas tad-udāra-hāsa-
vrīḍāvaloka-hṛta-cetasa ujjhitāstrāḥ

petuḥ kṣitau gaja-rathāśva-gatā vimūḍhā
yātrā-cchalena haraye 'rpayatīṁ sva-śobhām

saivaṁ śanaiś calayatī cala-padma-kośau
prāptiṁ tadā bhagavataḥ prasamīkṣamāṇā
utsārya vāma-karajair alakān apāṅgaiḥ
prāptān hriyaikṣata nṛpān dadṛśe 'cyutaṁ ca

tāṁ rāja-kanyāṁ ratham ārurukṣatīṁ
jahāra kṛṣṇo dviṣatāṁ samīkṣatām

tām—her; *deva*—of the Supreme Lord; *māyām*—the illusory potency; *iva*—as if; *dhīra*—even those who are sober; *mohinīm*—who bewilders; *su-madhyamām*—whose waist was well-formed; *kuṇḍala*—with earrings; *maṇḍita*—decorated; *ānanām*—whose face; *śyāmām*—uncontaminated beauty; *nitamba*—on whose hips; *arpita*—placed; *ratna*—jewel-studded; *mekhalām*—a belt; *vyañjat*—budding; *stanīm*—whose breasts; *kuntala*—of the locks of her hair; *śaṅkita*—frightened; *īkṣaṇām*—whose eyes; *śuci*—pure; *smitām*—with a smile; *bimba-phala*—like a *bimba* fruit; *adhara*—of whose lips; *dyuti*—by the glow; *śoṇāyamāna*—becoming reddened; *dvija*—whose teeth; *kunda*—jasmine; *kuḍmalām*—like buds; *padā*—with her feet; *calantīm*—walking; *kala-haṁsa*—like that of a royal swan; *gāminīm*—whose gait; *siñjat*—tinkling; *kalā*—skillfully fashioned; *nūpura*—of whose ankle bells; *dhāma*—by the effulgence; *śobhinā*—beautified; *vilokya*—seeing; *vīrāḥ*—the heroes; *mumuhuḥ*—became bewildered; *samāgatāḥ*—assembled; *yaśasvinaḥ*—respectable; *tat*—by this; *kṛta*—generated; *hṛt-śaya*—by the lust; *arditāḥ*—distressed; *yām*—whom; *vīkṣya*—upon seeing; *te*—these; *nṛ-patayaḥ*—kings; *tat*—her; *udāra*—broad; *hāsa*—by the smiles; *vrīḍā*—of shyness; *avaloka*—and the glances; *hṛta*—stolen; *cetasaḥ*—whose minds; *ujjhita*—dropping; *astrāḥ*—their weapons; *petuḥ*—they fell; *kṣitau*—to the ground; *gaja*—on elephants; *ratha*—chariots; *aśva*—and horses; *gatāḥ*—sitting; *vimūḍhāḥ*—fainting; *yātrā*—of the procession; *chalena*—on the pretext; *haraye*—to Lord Hari, Kṛṣṇa; *arpayatīm*—who was offering; *sva*—her own; *śobhām*—beauty; *sā*—she; *evam*—thus; *śanaiḥ*—slowly; *calayatī*—making walk; *cala*—moving; *padma*—of lotus flowers; *kośau*—the two whorls (that is, her feet); *prāptim*—the arrival; *tadā*—then;

bhagavataḥ—of the Supreme Lord; *prasamīkṣamāṇā*—eagerly awaiting; *utsārya*—pushing away; *vāma*—left; *kara-jaiḥ*—with the nails of her hand; *alakān*—her hair; *apāṅgaiḥ*—with sidelong glances; *prāptān*—those present; *hriyā*—with shyness; *aikṣata*—she looked; *nṛpān*—at the kings; *dadṛśe*—she saw; *acyutam*—Kṛṣṇa; *ca*—and; *tām*—her; *rāja-kanyām*—the King's daughter; *ratham*—His chariot; *ārurukṣatīm*—who was ready to mount; *jahāra*—seized; *kṛṣṇaḥ*—Lord Kṛṣṇa; *dviṣatām*—His enemies; *samīkṣatām*—as they looked on.

TRANSLATION

Rukmiṇī appeared as enchanting as the Lord's illusory potency, who enchants even the sober and grave. Thus the kings gazed upon her virgin beauty, her shapely waist, and her lovely face adorned with earrings. Her hips were graced with a jewel-studded belt, her breasts were just budding, and her eyes seemed apprehensive of her encroaching locks of hair. She smiled sweetly, her jasmine-bud teeth reflecting the glow of her *bimba*-red lips. As she walked with the motions of a royal swan, the effulgence of her tinkling ankle bells beautified her feet. Seeing her, the assembled heroes were totally bewildered. Lust tore at their hearts. Indeed, when the kings saw her broad smile and shy glance, they became stupefied, dropped their weapons and fell unconscious to the ground from their elephants, chariots and horses. On the pretext of the procession, Rukmiṇī displayed her beauty for Kṛṣṇa alone. Slowly she advanced the two moving lotus-whorls of her feet, awaiting the arrival of the Supreme Lord. With the fingernails of her left hand she pushed some strands of hair away from her face and shyly looked from the corners of her eyes at the kings standing before her. At that moment she saw Kṛṣṇa. Then, while His enemies looked on, the Lord seized the princess, who was eager to mount His chariot.

PURPORT

According to Śrīla Jīva Gosvāmī, Rukmiṇī was anxious that her locks of hair might impede her vision, since she was most eager to see her beloved Kṛṣṇa. The nondevotees, or demons, are bewildered at seeing the opulences of the Lord and think that His potency is meant for their gross sense gratification. But Rukmiṇī, an expansion of Kṛṣṇa's internal pleasure potency, was meant for the Lord alone.

Śrīla Viśvanātha Cakravartī quotes the following verse to describe the kind of woman known as *śyāmā:*

śīta-kāle bhaved uṣṇo
uṣṇa-kāle tu śītalā
stanau su-kaṭhinau yasyāḥ
sā śyāmā parikīrtitā

"A woman is called *śyāmā* when her breasts are very firm and when someone in her presence feels warm in the winter and cool in the summer."

Śrīla Viśvanātha Cakravartī further points out that since the beautiful form of Rukmiṇī is a manifestation of the Lord's internal energy, the nondevotees cannot perceive her. Thus the heroic kings assembled in Vidarbha were agitated with lust upon seeing the Lord's illusory potency, an expansion of Rukmiṇī. In other words, no one can lust after the Lord's eternal consort, since as soon as one's mind is contaminated with lust, the covering of Māyā separates one from the pristine beauty of the spiritual world and its inhabitants.

Finally, Śrīmatī Rukmiṇī-devī felt shy as she looked from the corners of her eyes at the other kings, for she did not want to meet the glances of those inferior men.

TEXT 56

रथं समारोप्य सुपर्णलक्षणं
राजन्यचक्रं परिभूय माधवः ।
ततो ययौ रामपुरोगमः शनैः
शृगालमध्यादिव भागहृद्धरिः ॥५६॥

rathaṁ samāropya suparṇa-lakṣaṇaṁ
rājanya-cakraṁ paribhūya mādhavaḥ
tato yayau rāma-purogamaḥ śanaiḥ
śṛgāla-madhyād iva bhāga-hṛd dhariḥ

ratham—onto His chariot; *samāropya*—lifting her; *suparṇa*—Garuḍa; *lakṣaṇam*—whose mark; *rājanya*—of kings; *cakram*—the circle; *paribhūya*—defeating; *mādhavaḥ*—Kṛṣṇa; *tataḥ*—from there; *yayau*—went; *rāma*—by Rāma; *puraḥ-gamaḥ*—preceded; *śanaiḥ*—slowly; *śṛgāla*—of jackals; *madhyāt*—from the midst; *iva*—as; *bhāga*—his portion; *hṛt*—removing; *hariḥ*—a lion.

TRANSLATION

Lifting the princess onto His chariot, whose flag bore the emblem of Garuḍa, Lord Mādhava drove back the circle of kings. With Balarāma in the lead, He slowly exited, like a lion removing his prey from the midst of jackals.

TEXT 57

तं मानिनः स्वाभिभवं यशःक्षयं
परे जरासन्धमुखा न सेहिरे ।
अहो धिगस्मान् यश आत्तधन्वनां
गोपैर्हृतं केशरिणां मृगैरिव ॥५७॥

taṁ māninaḥ svābhibhavaṁ yaśaḥ-kṣayaṁ
pare jarāsandha-mukhā na sehire
aho dhig asmān yaśa ātta-dhanvanāṁ
gopair hṛtaṁ keśariṇāṁ mṛgair iva

tam—that; *māninaḥ*—conceited; *sva*—their; *abhibhavam*—defeat; *yaśaḥ*—their honor; *kṣayam*—ruining; *pare*—the enemies; *jarāsandha-mukhāḥ*—headed by Jarasāndha; *na sehire*—could not tolerate; *aho*—ah; *dhik*—condemnation; *asmān*—upon us; *yaśaḥ*—the honor; *ātta-dhanvanām*—of the archers; *gopaiḥ*—by cowherds; *hṛtam*—taken away; *keśariṇām*—of lions; *mṛgaiḥ*—by small animals; *iva*—as if.

TRANSLATION

The kings inimical to the Lord, headed by Jarāsandha, could not tolerate this humiliating defeat. They exclaimed, "Oh, damn us! Though we are mighty archers, mere cowherds have stolen our honor, just as puny animals might steal the honor of lions!"

PURPORT

From the last two verses of this chapter it is clear that the perverted intelligence of demons makes them perceive things in a way exactly opposite to reality. It is clearly stated that Kṛṣṇa stole Rukmiṇī like a lion taking his prey from the midst of jackals. The demons, however, saw *themselves* as lions and Lord Kṛṣṇa as an inferior creature. Without Kṛṣṇa consciousness, life becomes most dangerous.

Thus end the purports of the humble servants of His Divine Grace A. C. Bhaktivedanta Swami Prabhupāda to the Tenth Canto, Fifty-third Chapter, of the Śrīmad-Bhāgavatam, *entitled "Kṛṣṇa Kidnaps Rukmiṇī."*

CHAPTER FIFTY-FOUR

The Marriage of Kṛṣṇa and Rukmiṇī

This chapter descibes how Lord Śrī Kṛṣṇa defeated the opposing kings after kidnapping Rukmiṇī, disfigured Rukmiṇī's brother Rukmī, brought Rukmiṇī to His capital and married her.

As Śrī Kṛṣṇa was taking Princess Rukmiṇī away, the inimical kings gathered their armies and pursued Him. Lord Baladeva and the generals of the Yādava army turned to face these opponents, blocking their advance. The enemy armies then began pouring incessant showers of arrows upon Lord Kṛṣṇa's army. Seeing her husband-to-be's forces under such violent attack, Śrīmatī Rukmiṇī looked at Śrī Kṛṣṇa fearfully. But Kṛṣṇa simply smiled and told her there was nothing to fear because His army would surely destroy the enemy in short order.

Lord Balarāma and the other heroes then began to annihilate the opposing army with *nārāca* arrows. The enemy kings, headed by Jarāsandha, retreated after suffering the destruction of their armies at the hands of the Yādavas.

Jarāsandha consoled Śiśupāla: "Happiness and distress are never permanent and are under the control of the Supreme Lord. Seventeen times Kṛṣṇa defeated me, but in the end I was victorious over Him. Thus seeing that victory and defeat are under the control of destiny and time, I have learned not to succumb to either lamentation or joy. Time now favors the Yādavas, so they have defeated you with only a small army, but in the future time will favor you, and you will surely conquer them." Consoled in this way, Śiśupāla took his followers and returned to his kingdom.

Rukmiṇī's brother Rukmī, who hated Kṛṣṇa, was infuriated by Kṛṣṇa's kidnapping of his sister. So, after vowing before all the kings present that he would not return to Kuṇḍina until Kṛṣṇa had been destroyed and Rukmiṇī rescued, Rukmī set out with his army to attack the Lord. Ignorant of Lord Kṛṣṇa's glories, Rukmī boldly went out to attack Kṛṣṇa in a lone chariot. He approached the Lord, struck Him with arrows and demanded that He release Rukmiṇī. Śrī Kṛṣṇa fended off Rukmī's weapons, breaking them to pieces. Then He raised His sword high and was about to kill Rukmī when Rukmiṇī interceded and fervently pleaded that her brother's life be spared. Lord Kṛṣṇa did not kill Rukmī, but with His sword He shaved off bits of Rukmī's hair here and there, leaving him disfigured. Just then Lord Baladeva appeared on the scene with the Yādava army. Seeing Rukmī disfigured, He gently reproached Kṛṣṇa: "To disfigure such a close family member is as good as killing him; therefore he should not be killed but set free."

Lord Baladeva then told Rukmiṇī that the sorry condition of her brother was only the fruit of his past work, since everyone is responsible for his own happiness and suffering. He further instructed her about the transcendental position of the *jīva* soul and how the illusion of happiness and distress is simply a result of ignorance. Accepting Lord Balarāma's instructions, Rukmiṇī gave up her sorrow.

Rukmī, meanwhile, felt totally frustrated, deprived as he was of all his strength and his will to fight. Since he had vowed not to return home without conquering Kṛṣṇa, Rukmī constructed a city on that very spot and took up residence there in a mood of undiminished anger.

Lord Kṛṣṇa took Rukmiṇī to His capital, Dvārakā, and married her. All the citizens celebrated in lavish style, broadcasting throughout the city accounts of how the Lord had kidnapped Rukmiṇī. Everyone in Dvārakā was delighted to see Lord Kṛṣṇa united with Rukmiṇī.

TEXT 1

श्रीशुक उवाच
इति सर्वे सुसंरब्धा वाहानारुह्य दंशिताः ।
स्वैः स्वैर्बलैः परिक्रान्ता अन्वीयुर्धृतकार्मुकाः ॥१॥

śrī-śuka uvāca
iti sarve su-saṁrabdhā
vāhān āruhya daṁśitāḥ
svaiḥ svair balaiḥ parikrāntā
anvīyur dhṛta-kārmukāḥ

śrī-śukaḥ uvāca—Śukadeva Gosvāmī said; *iti*—thus (speaking); *sarve*—all of them; *su-saṁrabdhāḥ*—greatly angered; *vāhān*—their conveyances; *āruhya*—mounting; *daṁśitāḥ*—wearing armor; *svaiḥ svaiḥ*—each by his own; *balaiḥ*—military force; *parikrāntāḥ*—surrounded; *anvīyuḥ*—they followed; *dhṛta*—holding; *kārmukāḥ*—their bows.

TRANSLATION

Śukadeva Gosvāmī said: Having thus spoken, all those infuriated kings donned their armor and mounted their conveyances. Each king, bow in hand, was surrounded by his own army as he went after Lord Kṛṣṇa.

TEXT 2

तानापतत आलोक्य यादवानीकयूथपाः ।
तस्थुस्तत्सम्मुखा राजन् विस्फूर्ज्य स्वधनूंषि ते ॥२॥

tān āpatata ālokya
yādavānīka-yūthapāḥ
tasthus tat-sammukhā rājan
visphūrjya sva-dhanūṁṣi te

tān—them; *āpatataḥ*—in pursuit; *ālokya*—seeing; *yādava-anīka*—of the Yādava army; *yūtha-pāḥ*—the officers; *tasthuḥ*—stood; *tat*—them; *sammukhāḥ*—directly facing; *rājan*—O King (Parīkṣit); *visphūrjya*—twanging; *sva*—their; *dhanūṁṣi*—bows; *te*—they.

TRANSLATION

The commanders of the Yādava army, seeing the enemy racing to attack, turned to face them and stood firm, O King, twanging their bows.

TEXT 3

अश्वपृष्ठे गजस्कन्धे रथोपस्थेऽस्त्रकोविदाः ।
मुमुचुः शरवर्षाणि मेघा अद्रिष्वपो यथा ॥३॥

aśva-pṛṣthe gaja-skandhe
rathopasthe 'stra-kovidāḥ
mumucuḥ śara-varṣāṇi
meghā adriṣv apo yathā

aśva-pṛṣṭhe—on horseback; *gaja*—of elephants; *skandhe*—on the shoulders; *ratha*—of chariots; *upasthe*—on the seats; *astra*—of weapons;

kovidāḥ—those expert in the use; *mumucuḥ*—released; *śara*—of arrows; *varṣāṇi*—rains; *meghāḥ*—clouds; *adriṣu*—upon mountains; *apaḥ*—water; *yathā*—as.

TRANSLATION

Mounted on the backs of horses, the shoulders of elephants and the seats of chariots, the enemy kings, expert with weapons, rained down arrows upon the Yadus like clouds pouring rain on mountains.

TEXT 4

पत्युर्बलं शरासारैश्छन्नं वीक्ष्य सुमध्यमा ।
सव्रीडमैक्षत्तद्वक्त्रं भयविह्वललोचना ॥४॥

patyur balaṁ śarāsārais
channaṁ vīkṣya su-madhyamā
sa-vrīḍam aikṣat tad-vaktraṁ
bhaya-vihvala-locanā

patyuḥ—of her Lord; *balam*—the army; *śara*—of arrows; *āsāraiḥ*—by heavy rains; *channam*—covered; *vīkṣya*—seeing; *su-madhyamā*—slender-waisted (Rukmiṇī); *sa-vrīḍam*—shyly; *aikṣat*—looked; *tat*—His; *vaktram*—at the face; *bhaya*—with fear; *vihvala*—disturbed; *locanā*—whose eyes.

TRANSLATION

Slender-waisted Rukmiṇī, seeing her Lord's army covered by torrents of arrows, shyly looked at His face with fear-stricken eyes.

TEXT 5

प्रहस्य भगवानाह मा स्म भैर्वामलोचने ।
विनङ्क्ष्यत्यधुनैवैतत्तावकैः शात्रवं बलम् ॥५॥

prahasya bhagavān āha
mā sma bhair vāma-locane

vinaṅkṣyaty adhunaivaitat
tāvakaiḥ śātravaṁ balam

prahasya—laughing; *bhagavān*—the Supreme Lord; *āha*—said; *mā sma bhaiḥ*—do not be afraid; *vāma-locane*—O beautiful-eyed one; *vinaṅkṣyati*—will be destroyed; *adhunā eva*—just now; *etat*—this; *tāvakaiḥ*—by your (army); *śātravam*—of enemies; *balam*—force.

TRANSLATION

In response the Lord laughed and assured her, "Do not be afraid, beautiful-eyed one. This enemy force is about to be destroyed by your soldiers."

PURPORT

To express His great affection for Rukmiṇī, Lord Kṛṣṇa gallantly referred to His own Yādava army as "your men," indicating that the Lord's entire dynasty was now the property of His beloved queen. The Supreme Lord, Kṛṣṇa, desires to share His blissful opulences with all living beings, and thus He sincerely invites them to come back home, back to Godhead. The Kṛṣṇa consciousness movement, introduced throughout the world by Śrīla Prabhupāda on the order of his spiritual master, Śrīla Bhaktisiddhānta Sarasvatī Ṭhākura, who himself preached all over India on the order of his exalted father, Śrīla Bhaktivinoda Ṭhākura, is broadcasting the loving message of Lord Kṛṣṇa: Remember Him, serve Him, return to Him and share in the infinite bounty of the kingdom of God.

TEXT 6

तेषां तद्विक्रमं वीरा गदसंकर्षणादयः ।
अमृष्यमाणा नाराचैर्जघ्नुर्हयगजान् रथान् ॥६॥

teṣāṁ tad-vikramaṁ vīrā
gada-saṅkarṣaṇādayaḥ
amṛṣyamāṇā nārācair
jaghnur haya-gajān rathān

teṣām—by them (the opposing kings); *tat*—that; *vikramam*—show of prowess; *vīrāḥ*—the heroes; *gada*—Gada, the younger brother of Lord Kṛṣṇa; *saṅkarṣaṇa*—Lord Balarāma; *ādayaḥ*—and others; *amṛṣya-māṇāḥ*—not tolerating; *nārācaiḥ*—with arrows made of iron; *jaghnuḥ*—they struck; *haya*—horses; *gajān*—elephants; *rathān*—and chariots.

TRANSLATION

The heroes of the Lord's army, headed by Gada and Saṅkarṣaṇa, could not tolerate the aggression of the opposing kings. Thus with iron arrows they began to strike down the enemy's horses, elephants and chariots.

TEXT 7

पेतुः शिरांसि रथिनामश्विनां गजिनां भुवि ।
सकुण्डलकिरीटानि सोष्णीषाणि च कोटिशः ॥७॥

petuḥ śirāṁsi rathinām
aśvināṁ gajināṁ bhuvi
sa-kuṇḍala-kirīṭāni
soṣṇīṣāṇi ca koṭiśaḥ

petuḥ—fell; *śirāṁsi*—the heads; *rathinām*—of those riding on chariots; *aśvinām*—of those riding horses; *gajinām*—of those riding elephants; *bhuvi*—to the ground; *sa*—with; *kuṇḍala*—earrings; *kirīṭāni*—and helmets; *sa*—with; *uṣṇīṣāṇi*—turbans; *ca*—and; *koṭiśaḥ*—by the millions.

TRANSLATION

The heads of soldiers fighting on chariots, horses and elephants fell to the ground by the millions; some heads wore earrings and helmets, others turbans.

TEXT 8

हस्ताः सासिगदेष्वासाः करभा ऊरवोऽङ्घ्रयः ।
अश्वाश्वतरनागोष्ट्रखरमर्त्यशिरांसि च ॥८॥

hastāḥ sāsi-gadeṣv-āsāḥ
karabhā ūravo 'ṅghrayaḥ
aśvāśvatara-nāgoṣṭra-
khara-martya-śirāṁsi ca

hastāḥ—hands; *sa*—with; *asi*—swords; *gadā*—clubs; *iṣu-āsāḥ*—bows; *karabhāḥ*—fingerless hands; *ūravaḥ*—thighs; *aṅghrayaḥ*—legs; *aśva*—of horses; *aśvatara*—donkeys; *nāga*—elephants; *uṣṭra*—camels; *khara*—wild asses; *martya*—and humans; *śirāṁsi*—heads; *ca*—also.

TRANSLATION

Lying all around were thighs, legs and fingerless hands, along with hands clutching swords, clubs and bows, and also the heads of horses, donkeys, elephants, camels, wild asses and humans.

PURPORT

Karabhāḥ indicates the portion of the hand from the wrist to the base of the fingers. The same word may also indicate an elephant's trunk, and thus in this verse the implication is that the thighs lying on the battlefield resembled the trunks of elephants.

TEXT 9

हन्यमानबलानीका वृष्णिभिर्जयकाङ्क्षिभिः ।
राजानो विमुखा जग्मुर्जरासन्धपुरःसराः ॥९॥

hanyamāna-balānīkā
vṛṣṇibhir jaya-kāṅkṣibhiḥ
rājāno vimukhā jagmur
jarāsandha-puraḥ-sarāḥ

hanyamāna—being killed; *bala-anīkāḥ*—whose armies; *vṛṣṇibhiḥ*—by the Vṛṣṇis; *jaya*—for victory; *kāṅkṣibhiḥ*—who were eager; *rājānaḥ*—the kings; *vimukhāḥ*—discouraged; *jagmuḥ*—left; *jarāsandha-puraḥ-sarāḥ*—headed by Jarāsandha.

TRANSLATION

Seeing their armies being struck down by the Vṛṣṇis, who were eager for victory, the kings headed by Jarāsandha were discouraged and left the battlefield.

PURPORT

Although Śiśupāla had not married Rukmiṇī, he passionately considered her his property, and thus he was devastated, like a man who has lost his beloved wife.

TEXT 10

शिशुपालं समभ्येत्य हृतदारमिवातुरम् ।
नष्टत्विषं गतोत्साहं शुष्यद्वदनमब्रुवन् ॥१०॥

śiśupālaṁ samabhyetya
hṛta-dāram ivāturam
naṣṭa-tviṣaṁ gatotsāhaṁ
śuṣyad-vadanam abruvan

śiśupālam—Śiśupāla; *samabhyetya*—approaching; *hṛta*—stolen; *dāram*—whose wife; *iva*—as if; *āturam*—perturbed; *naṣṭa*—lost; *tviṣam*—whose color; *gata*—gone; *utsāham*—whose enthusiasm; *śuṣyat*—dried up; *vadanam*—whose face; *abruvan*—they addressed.

TRANSLATION

The kings approached Śiśupāla, who was disturbed like a man who has lost his wife. His complexion was drained of color, his enthusiasm was gone, and his face appeared dried up. The kings spoke to him as follows.

TEXT 11

भो भोः पुरुषशार्दूल दौर्मनस्यमिदं त्यज ।
न प्रियाप्रिययो राजन्निष्ठा देहिषु दृश्यते ॥११॥

bho bhoḥ puruṣa-śārdūla
daurmanasyam idaṁ tyaja
na priyāpriyayo rājan
niṣṭhā dehiṣu dṛśyate

bhoḥ bhoḥ—O sir; *puruṣa*—among men; *śārdūla*—O tiger; *daurmanasyam*—depressed state of mind; *idam*—this; *tyaja*—give up; *na*—no; *priya*—of the desirable; *apriyayoḥ*—or the undesirable; *rājan*—O King; *niṣṭhā*—permanence; *dehiṣu*—among embodied beings; *dṛśyate*—is seen.

TRANSLATION

[Jarāsandha said:] Listen, Śiśupāla, O tiger among men, give up your depression. After all, embodied beings' happiness and unhappiness is never seen to be permanent, O King.

TEXT 12

यथा दारुमयी योषित्नृत्यते कुहकेच्छया ।
एवमीश्वरतन्त्रोऽयमीहते सुखदुःखयोः ॥१२॥

yathā dāru-mayī yoṣit
nṛtyate kuhakecchayā
evam īśvara-tantro 'yam
īhate sukha-duḥkhayoḥ

yathā—as; *dāru-mayī*—made of wood; *yoṣit*—a woman; *nṛtyate*—dances; *kuhaka*—of the showman; *icchayā*—by the desire; *evam*—in the same way; *īśvara*—of the Supreme Lord; *tantraḥ*—under the control; *ayam*—this world; *īhate*—endeavors; *sukha*—in joy; *duḥkhayoḥ*—and misery.

TRANSLATION

Just as a puppet in the form of a woman dances by the desire of the puppeteer, so this world, controlled by the Supreme Lord, struggles in both happiness and misery.

PURPORT

By the will of the Supreme Lord, living beings are awarded the proper results of their own activities. One who understands the Absolute Truth surrenders to the Absolute Truth, the Supreme Personality of Godhead, and is no longer considered to be within the material system of existence. Since those endeavoring within the material system, or world, are necessarily trying to exploit the creation of God, they must be subjected to reactions, which are perceived by the conditioned souls as miserable and joyful. In fact, the entire material way of life is a fiasco when seen from the perspective of absolute bliss.

TEXT 13

शौरेः सप्तदशाहं वै संयुगानि पराजितः ।
त्रयोविंशतिभिः सैन्यैर्जिग्ये एकमहं परम् ॥१३॥

śaureḥ sapta-daśāhaṁ vai
saṁyugāni parājitaḥ
trayo-viṁśatibhiḥ sainyair
jigye ekam ahaṁ param

śaureḥ—with Kṛṣṇa; *sapta-daśa*—seventeen; *aham*—I; *vai*—indeed; *saṁyugāni*—battles; *parājitaḥ*—lost; *trayaḥ-viṁśatibhiḥ*—twenty-three; *sainyaiḥ*—with armies; *jigye*—won; *ekam*—one; *aham*—I; *param*—only.

TRANSLATION

In battle with Kṛṣṇa I and my twenty-three armies lost seventeen times; only once did I defeat Him.

PURPORT

Jarāsandha offers his own life as an example of the inevitable happiness and distress of this material world.

TEXT 14

तथाप्यहं न शोचामि न प्रहृष्यामि कर्हिचित् ।
कालेन दैवयुक्तेन जानन् विद्रावितं जगत् ॥१४॥

tathāpy ahaṁ na śocāmi
na prahṛṣyāmi karhicit
kālena daiva-yuktena
jānan vidrāvitaṁ jagat

tathā api—nonetheless; *aham*—I; *na śocāmi*—do not lament; *na prahṛṣyāmi*—do not rejoice; *karhicit*—ever; *kālena*—by time; *daiva*—with fate; *yuktena*—conjoined; *jānan*—knowing; *vidrāvitam*—driven; *jagat*—the world.

TRANSLATION

But still I never lament or rejoice, because I know this world is driven by time and fate.

PURPORT

Having stated that the Supreme Lord controls this world, Jarāsandha explains the specific method of control. It should be remembered that in the Vedic context *kāla,* or time, does not refer merely to a system of measuring planetary movements such as days, weeks, months and years but rather to the *way* things are being moved. Everything is moving according to its destiny, and this destiny is also described as "time," since everyone's destiny is revealed and imposed by the movements of time.

TEXT 15

अधुनापि वयं सर्वे वीरयूथपयूथपाः ।
पराजिताः फल्गुतन्त्रैर्यदुभिः कृष्णपालितैः ॥१५॥

adhunāpi vayaṁ sarve
vīra-yūthapa-yūthapāḥ
parājitāḥ phalgu-tantrair
yadubhiḥ kṛṣṇa-pālitaiḥ

adhunā—now; *api*—even; *vayam*—we; *sarve*—all; *vīra*—of heroes; *yūtha-pa*—of the leaders; *yūtha-pāḥ*—the leaders; *parājitāḥ*—defeated; *phalgu*—meager; *tantraiḥ*—whose entourage; *yadubhiḥ*—by the Yadus; *kṛṣṇa-pālitaiḥ*—protected by Kṛṣṇa.

TRANSLATION

And now all of us, great commanders of military leaders, have been defeated by the Yadus and their small entourage, who are protected by Kṛṣṇa.

TEXT 16

रिपवो जिग्युरधुना काल आत्मानुसारिणि ।
तदा वयं विजेष्यामो यदा कालः प्रदक्षिणः ॥१६॥

ripavo jigyur adhunā
kāla ātmānusāriṇi
tadā vayaṁ vijeṣyāmo
yadā kālaḥ pradakṣiṇaḥ

ripavaḥ—our enemies; *jigyuḥ*—have conquered; *adhunā*—now; *kāle*—the time; *ātma*—them; *anusāriṇi*—favoring; *tadā*—then; *vayam*—we; *vijeṣyāmaḥ*—shall conquer; *yadā*—when; *kālaḥ*—time; *pradakṣiṇaḥ*—turned toward us.

TRANSLATION

Now our enemies have conquered because time favors them, but in the future, when time is auspicious for us, we shall conquer.

TEXT 17

श्रीशुक उवाच
एवं प्रबोधितो मित्रैश्चैद्योऽगात्सानुगः पुरम् ।
हतशेषाः पुनस्तेऽपि ययुः स्वं स्वं पुरं नृपाः ॥१७॥

śrī-śuka uvāca
evaṁ prabodhito mitraiś
caidyo 'gāt sānugaḥ puram
hata-śeṣāḥ punas te 'pi
yayuḥ svaṁ svaṁ puraṁ nṛpāḥ

śrī-śukaḥ uvāca—Śukadeva Gosvāmī said; *evam*—thus; *prabodhitaḥ*—persuaded; *mitraiḥ*—by his friends; *caidyaḥ*—Śiśupāla; *agāt*—went; *sa-*

anugaḥ—with his followers; *puram*—to his city; *hata*—from the killed; *śeṣāḥ*—who remained; *punaḥ*—again; *te*—they; *api*—also; *yayuḥ*—went; *svam svam*—each to his own; *puram*—city; *nṛpāḥ*—kings.

TRANSLATION

Śukadeva Gosvāmī said: Thus persuaded by his friends, Śiśupāla took his followers and went back to his capital. The surviving warriors also returned to their respective cities.

TEXT 18

रुक्मी तु राक्षसोद्वाहं कृष्णद्विडसहन् स्वसुः ।
पृष्ठतोऽन्वगमत्कृष्णमक्षौहिण्या वृतो बली ॥१८॥

rukmī tu rākṣasodvāhaṁ
kṛṣṇa-dviḍ asahan svasuḥ
pṛṣṭhato 'nvagamat kṛṣṇam
akṣauhiṇyā vṛto balī

rukmī—Rukmī; *tu*—however; *rākṣasa*—in the style of demons; *udvāham*—the marriage; *kṛṣṇa-dviṭ*—the hater of Kṛṣṇa; *asahan*—unable to bear; *svasuḥ*—of his sister; *pṛṣṭhataḥ*—from behind; *anvagamat*—he followed; *kṛṣṇam*—Lord Kṛṣṇa; *akṣauhiṇyā*—by an entire *akṣauhiṇī* division; *vṛtaḥ*—surrounded; *balī*—powerful.

TRANSLATION

Powerful Rukmī, however, was especially envious of Kṛṣṇa. He could not bear the fact that Kṛṣṇa had carried off his sister to marry her in the Rākṣasa style. Thus he pursued the Lord with an entire military division.

TEXTS 19–20

रुक्म्यमर्षी सुसंरब्धः शृण्वतां सर्वभूभुजाम् ।
प्रतिजज्ञे महाबाहुर्दंशितः सशरासनः ॥१९॥
अहत्वा समरे कृष्णमप्रत्यूह्य च रुक्मिणीम् ।
कुण्डिनं न प्रवेक्ष्यामि सत्यमेतद् ब्रवीमि वः ॥२०॥

rukmy amarṣī su-saṁrabdhaḥ
śṛṇvatāṁ sarva-bhūbhujām
pratijajñe mahā-bāhur
daṁśitaḥ sa-śarāsanaḥ

ahatvā samare kṛṣṇam
apratyūhya ca rukmiṇīm
kuṇḍinaṁ na pravekṣyāmi
satyam etad bravīmi vaḥ

rukmī—Rukmī; *amarṣī*—intolerant; *su-saṁrabdhaḥ*—extremely angry; *śṛṇvatām*—while they listened; *sarva*—all; *bhū-bhujām*—the kings; *pratijajñe*—he swore; *mahā-bāhuḥ*—mighty-armed; *daṁśitaḥ*—wearing his armor; *sa-śarāsanaḥ*—with his bow; *ahatvā*—without killing; *samare*—in battle; *kṛṣṇam*—Kṛṣṇa; *apratyūhya*—without bringing back; *ca*—and; *rukmiṇīm*—Rukmiṇī; *kuṇḍinam*—the city of Kuṇḍina; *na pravekṣyāmi*—I shall not enter; *satyam*—in truth; *etat*—this; *bravīmi*—I say; *vaḥ*—to all of you.

TRANSLATION

Frustrated and enraged, mighty-armed Rukmī, dressed in armor and wielding his bow, had sworn before all the kings, "I shall not again enter Kuṇḍina if I do not kill Kṛṣṇa in battle and bring Rukmiṇī back with me. I swear this to you."

PURPORT

Rukmī spoke these angry words and then set off to pursue Lord Kṛṣṇa, as described in the following verses.

TEXT 21

इत्युक्त्वा रथमारुह्य सारथिं प्राह सत्वरः ।
चोदयाश्वान् यतः कृष्णः तस्य मे संयुगं भवेत् ॥२१॥

ity uktvā ratham āruhya
sārathiṁ prāha satvaraḥ

codayāśvān yataḥ kṛṣṇaḥ
tasya me saṁyugaṁ bhavet

iti—thus; *uktvā*—speaking; *ratham*—on his chariot; *āruhya*—climbing; *sārathim*—to his driver; *prāha*—said; *satvaraḥ*—quickly; *codaya*—drive; *aśvān*—the horses; *yataḥ*—to where; *kṛṣṇaḥ*—Kṛṣṇa; *tasya*—His; *me*—with me; *saṁyugam*—fight; *bhavet*—must be.

TRANSLATION

Having said this, he had mounted his chariot and told his charioteer, "Drive the horses quickly to where Kṛṣṇa is. He and I must fight.

TEXT 22

अद्याहं निशितैर्बाणैर्गोपालस्य सुदुर्मतेः ।
नेष्ये वीर्यमदं येन स्वसा मे प्रसभं हृता ॥२२॥

adyāhaṁ niśitair bāṇair
gopālasya su-durmateḥ
neṣye vīrya-madaṁ yena
svasā me prasabhaṁ hṛtā

adya—today; *aham*—I; *niśitaiḥ*—sharp; *bāṇaiḥ*—with my arrows; *gopālasya*—of the cowherd; *su-durmateḥ*—whose mentality is most wicked; *neṣye*—I will remove; *vīrya*—in His power; *madam*—the intoxicated pride; *yena*—by which; *svasā*—sister; *me*—my; *prasabham*—violently; *hṛtā*—abducted.

TRANSLATION

"This wicked-minded cowherd boy, infatuated with His prowess, has violently abducted my sister. But today I will remove His pride with my sharp arrows."

PURPORT

Śrīla Śrīdhara Svāmī explains that *gopālasya* actually means "of the protector of the *Vedas*," while *durmateḥ* means "of Him whose beautiful mind is compassionate even toward the wicked." Śrīla Viśvanātha Cakravartī adds that the real meaning of what Rukmī said is that today, fighting with Lord Kṛṣṇa, Rukmī would relieve himself of his pretensions to being a great hero.

TEXT 23

विकत्थमानः कुमतिरीश्वरस्याप्रमाणवित् ।
रथेनैकेन गोविन्दं तिष्ठ तिष्ठेत्यथाह्वयत् ॥२३॥

vikatthamānaḥ kumatir
īśvarasyāpramāṇa-vit
rathenaikena govindaṁ
tiṣṭha tiṣṭhety athāhvayat

vikatthamānaḥ—boasting; *ku-matiḥ*—foolish; *īśvarasya*—of the Supreme Lord; *apramāṇa-vit*—not knowing the dimensions; *rathena ekena*—with a single chariot; *govindam*—to Lord Kṛṣṇa; *tiṣṭha tiṣṭha*—stand and fight; *iti*—so saying; *atha*—then; *āhvayat*—he called.

TRANSLATION

Boasting thus, foolish Rukmī, ignorant of the true extent of the Supreme Lord's power, approached Lord Govinda in his lone chariot and challenged Him, "Just stand and fight!"

PURPORT

It appears from these verses that though Rukmī set out with an entire military division, he personally rushed up to Lord Kṛṣṇa to fight with Him.

TEXT 24

धनुर्विकृष्य सुदृढं जघ्ने कृष्णं त्रिभिः शरैः ।
आह चात्र क्षणं तिष्ठ यदूनां कुलपांसन ॥२४॥

dhanur vikṛṣya su-dṛḍhaṁ
jaghne kṛṣṇaṁ tribhiḥ śaraiḥ
āha cātra kṣaṇaṁ tiṣṭha
yadūnāṁ kula-pāṁsana

dhanuḥ—his bow; *vikṛṣya*—drawing; *su*—very; *dṛḍham*—firmly; *jaghne*—he struck; *kṛṣṇam*—Lord Kṛṣṇa; *tribhiḥ*—with three; *śaraiḥ*—arrows; *āha*—he said; *ca*—and; *atra*—here; *kṣaṇam*—a moment; *tiṣṭha*—stand; *yadūnām*—of the Yadus; *kula*—of the dynasty; *pāṁsana*—O corrupter.

TRANSLATION

Rukmī drew his bow with great strength and struck Lord Kṛṣṇa with three arrows. Then he said, "Stand here for a moment, O defiler of the Yadu dynasty!

PURPORT

Śrīla Śrīdhara Svāmī points out that *kula-pāṁsana* may be understood as a combination of the words *kula-pa,* "O master of the Yadu dynasty," and *aṁsana,* "O expert killer of enemies." The *ācārya* gives the grammatical details that make this interpretation possible.

TEXT 25

यत्र यासि स्वसारं मे मुषित्वा ध्वाङ्क्षवद्धविः ।
हरिष्येऽद्य मदं मन्द मायिनः कूटयोधिनः ॥२५॥

yatra yāsi svasāraṁ me
muṣitvā dhvāṅkṣa-vad dhaviḥ
hariṣye 'dya madaṁ manda
māyinaḥ kūṭa-yodhinaḥ

yatra—wherever; *yāsi*—You go; *svasāram*—sister; *me*—my; *muṣitvā*—having stolen; *dhvāṅkṣa-vat*—like a crow; *haviḥ*—the sacrificial butter; *hariṣye*—I will remove; *adya*—today; *madam*—Your false pride; *manda*—You fool; *māyinaḥ*—of the deceiver; *kūṭa*—cheating; *yodhinaḥ*—of the fighter.

TRANSLATION

"Wherever You go, carrying off my sister like a crow stealing sacrificial butter, I will follow. This very day I shall relieve You of Your false pride, You fool, You deceiver, You cheater in battle!

PURPORT

In his hysterical attack, Rukmī displays the very qualities he attributes to Śrī Kṛṣṇa. Every living being is part and parcel of the Lord and belongs to the Lord. Therefore Rukmī was like a crow trying to steal the sacrificial offering meant for the enjoyment of the Lord.

TEXT 26

यावन्न मे हतो बाणैः शयीथा मुञ्च दारिकाम् ।
स्मयन् कृष्णो धनुश्छित्त्वा षड्भिर्विव्याध रुक्मिणम् ॥२६॥

yāvan na me hato bāṇaiḥ
śayīthā muñca dārikām
smayan kṛṣṇo dhanuś chittvā
ṣaḍbhir vivyādha rukmiṇam

yāvat—while; *na*—not; *me*—my; *hataḥ*—killed; *bāṇaiḥ*—by the arrows; *śayīthāḥ*—you lie down; *muñca*—release; *dārikām*—the girl; *smayan*—smiling; *kṛṣṇaḥ*—Lord Kṛṣṇa; *dhanuḥ*—his bow; *chittvā*—breaking; *ṣaḍbhiḥ*—with six (arrows); *vivyādha*—pierced; *rukmiṇam*—Rukmī.

TRANSLATION

"Release the girl before You are struck dead by my arrows and made to lie down!" In response to this, Lord Kṛṣṇa smiled, and with six arrows He struck Rukmī and broke his bow.

PURPORT

Śrīla Viśvanātha Cakravartī points out that in fact Lord Kṛṣṇa was meant to lie down together with Rukmiṇī on a beautiful bed of flowers, but out of shyness Rukmī did not directly mention this point.

TEXT 27

अष्टभिश्चतुरो वाहान् द्वाभ्यां सूतं ध्वजं त्रिभिः ।
स चान्यद्धनुराधाय कृष्णं विव्याध पञ्चभिः ॥२७॥

aṣṭabhiś caturo vāhān
dvābhyāṁ sūtaṁ dhvajaṁ tribhiḥ
sa cānyad dhanur ādhāya
kṛṣṇaṁ vivyādha pañcabhiḥ

aṣṭabhiḥ—with eight (arrows); *caturaḥ*—the four; *vāhān*—horses; *dvābhyām*—with two; *sūtam*—the chariot driver; *dhvajam*—the flagpole; *tribhiḥ*—with three; *saḥ*—he, Rukmī; *ca*—and; *anyat*—another; *dhanuḥ*—bow; *ādhāya*—taking up; *kṛṣṇam*—Kṛṣṇa; *vivyādha*—pierced; *pañcabhiḥ*—with five.

TRANSLATION

The Lord struck Rukmī's four horses with eight arrows, his chariot driver with two, and the chariot's flag with three. Rukmī grabbed another bow and struck Lord Kṛṣṇa with five arrows.

TEXT 28

तैस्ताडितः शरौघैस्तु चिच्छेद धनुरच्युतः ।
पुनरन्यदुपादत्त तदप्यच्छिनदव्ययः ॥२८॥

tais tāḍitaḥ śaraughais tu
ciccheda dhanur acyutaḥ
punar anyad upādatta
tad apy acchinad avyayaḥ

taiḥ—by these; *tāḍitaḥ*—struck; *śara*—of arrows; *oghaiḥ*—floods; *tu*—although; *ciccheda*—broke; *dhanuḥ*—(Rukmī's) bow; *acyutaḥ*—Lord Kṛṣṇa; *punaḥ*—again; *anyat*—another; *upādatta*—he (Rukmī) picked up; *tat*—that; *api*—also; *acchinat*—broke; *avyayaḥ*—the infallible Lord.

TRANSLATION

Although hit by these many arrows, Lord Acyuta again broke Rukmī's bow. Rukmī picked up yet another bow, but the infallible Lord broke that one to pieces as well.

TEXT 29

परिघं पट्टिशं शूलं चर्मासी शक्तितोमरौ ।
यद्यदायुधमादत्त तत्सर्वं सोऽच्छिनद्धरिः ॥२९॥

parighaṁ paṭṭiśaṁ śūlaṁ
carmāsī śakti-tomarau
yad yad āyudham ādatta
tat sarvaṁ so 'cchinad dhariḥ

parigham—spiked iron bludgeon; *paṭṭiśam*—three-pointed spear; *śūlam*—lance; *carma-asī*—shield and sword; *śakti*—pike; *tomarau*—javelin; *yat yat*—whatever; *āyudham*—weapon; *ādatta*—he took up; *tat sarvam*—all of them; *saḥ*—He; *acchinat*—broke; *hariḥ*—Lord Kṛṣṇa.

TRANSLATION

Iron bludgeon, three-pointed spear, sword and shield, pike, javelin—whatever weapon Rukmī picked up, Lord Hari smashed it to bits.

TEXT 30

ततो रथादवप्लुत्य खड्गपाणिर्जिघांसया ।
कृष्णमभ्यद्रवत्क्रुद्धः पतंग इव पावकम् ॥३०॥

tato rathād avaplutya
khaḍga-pāṇir jighāṁsayā
kṛṣṇam abhyadravat kruddhaḥ
pataṅga iva pāvakam

tataḥ—then; *rathāt*—from his chariot; *avaplutya*—leaping down; *khaḍga*—a sword; *pāṇiḥ*—in his hand; *jighāṁsayā*—with the desire to kill; *kṛṣṇam*—Lord Kṛṣṇa; *abhyadravat*—he ran toward; *kruddhaḥ*—furious; *pataṅgaḥ*—a bird; *iva*—as; *pāvakam*—the wind.

TRANSLATION

Then Rukmī leaped down from his chariot and, sword in hand, rushed furiously toward Kṛṣṇa to kill Him, like a bird flying into the wind.

TEXT 31

तस्य चापततः खड्गं तिलशश्चर्म चेषुभिः ।
छित्त्वासिमाददे तिग्मं रुक्मिणं हन्तुमुद्यतः ॥३१॥

tasya cāpatataḥ khaḍgaṁ
tilaśaś carma ceṣubhiḥ
chittvāsim ādade tigmaṁ
rukmiṇaṁ hantum udyataḥ

tasya—of him; *ca*—and; *āpatataḥ*—who was attacking; *khaḍgam*—the sword; *tilaśaḥ*—into small pieces; *carma*—the shield; *ca*—and; *iṣubhiḥ*—with His arrows; *chittvā*—breaking; *asim*—His sword; *ādade*—He took; *tigmam*—sharp; *rukmiṇam*—Rukmī; *hantum*—to kill; *udyataḥ*—prepared.

TRANSLATION

As Rukmī attacked Him, the Lord shot arrows that broke Rukmī's sword and shield into small pieces. Kṛṣṇa then took up His own sharp sword and prepared to kill Rukmī.

TEXT 32

दृष्ट्वा भ्रातृवधोद्योगं रुक्मिणी भयविह्वला ।
पतित्वा पादयोर्भर्तुरुवाच करुणं सती ॥३२॥

dṛṣṭvā bhrātṛ-vadhodyogaṁ
rukmiṇī bhaya-vihvalā

patitvā pādayor bhartur
uvāca karuṇaṁ satī

dṛṣṭvā—seeing; *bhrātṛ*—her brother; *vadha*—to kill; *udyogam*—the attempt; *rukmiṇī*—Śrīmatī Rukmiṇī; *bhaya*—by fear; *vihvalā*—agitated; *patitvā*—falling; *pādayoḥ*—at the feet; *bhartuḥ*—of her husband; *uvāca*—spoke; *karuṇam*—pathetically; *satī*—saintly.

TRANSLATION

Seeing Lord Kṛṣṇa ready to kill her brother, saintly Rukmiṇī was filled with alarm. She fell at her husband's feet and piteously spoke as follows.

TEXT 33

श्रीरुक्मिण्युवाच
योगेश्वराप्रमेयात्मन् देवदेव जगत्पते ।
हन्तुं नार्हसि कल्याण भ्रातरं मे महाभुज ॥३३॥

śrī-rukmiṇy uvāca
yogeśvarāprameyātman
deva-deva jagat-pate
hantuṁ nārhasi kalyāṇa
bhrātaraṁ me mahā-bhuja

śrī-rukmiṇī uvāca—Śrī Rukmiṇī said; *yoga-īśvara*—O controller of all mystic power; *aprameya-ātman*—O immeasurable one; *deva-deva*—O Lord of lords; *jagat-pate*—O master of the universe; *hantum na arhasi*—please do not kill; *kalyāṇa*—O all-auspicious one; *bhrātaram*—brother; *me*—my; *mahā-bhuja*—O mighty-armed one.

TRANSLATION

Śrī Rukmiṇī said: O controller of all mystic power, immeasurable one, Lord of lords, master of the universe! O all-auspicious and mighty-armed one, please do not kill my brother!

TEXT 34

श्रीशुक उवाच
तया परित्रासविकम्पितांगया
शुचावशुष्यन्मुखरुद्धकण्ठया ।
कातर्यविस्रंसितहेममालया
गृहीतपादः करुणो न्यवर्तत ॥३४॥

śrī-śuka uvāca
tayā paritrāsa-vikampitāṅgayā
śucāvaśuṣyan-mukha-ruddha-kaṇṭhayā
kātarya-visraṁsita-hema-mālayā
gṛhīta-pādaḥ karuṇo nyavartata

śrī-śukaḥ uvāca—Śukadeva Gosvāmī said; *tayā*—by her; *paritrāsa*—in total fear; *vikampita*—trembling; *aṅgayā*—whose limbs; *śucā*—out of sorrow; *avaśuṣyat*—drying up; *mukha*—whose mouth; *ruddha*—and choked; *kaṇṭhayā*—whose throat; *kātarya*—in her agitation; *visraṁsita*—disheveled; *hema*—golden; *mālayā*—whose necklace; *gṛhīta*—held; *pādaḥ*—His feet; *karuṇaḥ*—compassionate; *nyavartata*—He desisted.

TRANSLATION

Śukadeva Gosvāmī said: Rukmiṇī's utter fear caused her limbs to tremble and her mouth to dry up, while her throat choked up out of sorrow. And in her agitation her golden necklace scattered. She grasped Kṛṣṇa's feet, and the Lord, feeling compassionate, desisted.

PURPORT

Śrīla Viśvanātha Cakravartī quotes the "worldly rule" that one's sister is the personification of mercy: *dayāyā bhaginī mūrtiḥ.* Even though Rukmī was wicked and was opposed to his sister's best interest, Rukmiṇī was compassionate toward him, and the Lord shared her compassion.

TEXT 35

चैलेन बद्ध्वा तमसाधुकारिणं
सश्मश्रुकेशं प्रवपन् व्यरूपयत् ।
तावन्ममर्दुः परसैन्यमद्भुतं
यदुप्रवीरा नलिनीं यथा गजाः ॥३५॥

cailena baddhvā tam asādhu-kāriṇaṁ
sa-śmaśru-keśaṁ pravapan vyarūpayat
tāvan mamarduḥ para-sainyam adbhutaṁ
yadu-pravīrā nalinīṁ yathā gajāḥ

cailena—with a strip of cloth; *baddhvā*—tying up; *tam*—him; *asādhu-kāriṇam*—the evil-doer; *sa-śmaśru-keśam*—leaving some of his mustache and hair remaining; *pravapan*—by shaving him; *vyarūpayat*—made him disfigured; *tāvat*—by then; *mamarduḥ*—they had crushed; *para*—opposing; *sainyam*—the army; *adbhutam*—extraordinary; *yadu-pravīrāḥ*—the heroes of the Yadu dynasty; *nalinīm*—a lotus flower; *yathā*—as; *gajāḥ*—elephants.

TRANSLATION

Lord Kṛṣṇa tied up the evil-doer with a strip of cloth. He then proceeded to disfigure Rukmī by comically shaving him, leaving parts of his mustache and hair. By that time the Yadu heroes had crushed the extraordinary army of their opponents, just as elephants crush a lotus flower.

PURPORT

Lord Kṛṣṇa used His same sharp sword to give the wicked Rukmī a peculiar haircut.

TEXT 36

कृष्णान्तिकमुपव्रज्य ददृशुस्तत्र रुक्मिणम् ।
तथाभूतं हतप्रायं दृष्ट्वा संकर्षणो विभुः ।
विमुच्य बद्धं करुणो भगवान् कृष्णमब्रवीत् ॥३६॥

kṛṣṇāntikam upavrajya
dadṛśus tatra rukmiṇam
tathā-bhūtaṁ hata-prāyaṁ
dṛṣṭvā saṅkarṣaṇo vibhuḥ
vimucya baddhaṁ karuṇo
bhagavān kṛṣṇam abravīt

kṛṣṇa—of Kṛṣṇa; *antikam*—the proximity; *upavrajya*—approaching; *dadṛśuḥ*—they (the Yadu soldiers) saw; *tatra*—there; *rukmiṇam*—Rukmī; *tathā-bhūtam*—in such a condition; *hata*—dead; *prāyam*—practically; *dṛṣṭvā*—seeing; *saṅkarṣaṇaḥ*—Balarāma; *vibhuḥ*—the omnipotent; *vimucya*—releasing; *baddham*—the bound-up (Rukmī); *karuṇaḥ*—compassionate; *bhagavān*—the Lord; *kṛṣṇam*—to Kṛṣṇa; *abravīt*—said.

TRANSLATION

As the Yadus approached Lord Kṛṣṇa, they saw Rukmī in this sorry condition, practically dying of shame. When the all-powerful Lord Balarāma saw Rukmī, He compassionately released him and spoke the following to Lord Kṛṣṇa.

TEXT 37

असाध्विदं त्वया कृष्ण कृतमस्मज्जुगुप्सितम् ।
वपनं श्मश्रुकेशानां वैरूप्यं सुहृदो वधः ॥३७॥

asādhv idaṁ tvayā kṛṣṇa
kṛtam asmaj-jugupsitam
vapanaṁ śmaśru-keśānāṁ
vairūpyaṁ suhṛdo vadhaḥ

asādhu—improperly; *idam*—this; *tvayā*—by You; *kṛṣṇa*—O Kṛṣṇa; *kṛtam*—done; *asmat*—for Us; *jugupsitam*—terrible; *vapanam*—the shaving; *śmaśru-keśānām*—of his mustache and hair; *vairūpyam*—the disfigurement; *suhṛdaḥ*—of a family member; *vadhaḥ*—death.

TRANSLATION

[Lord Balarāma said:] My dear Kṛṣṇa, You have acted improperly! This deed will bring shame on Us, for to disfigure a close relative by shaving off his mustache and hair is as good as killing him.

PURPORT

Omniscient Balarāma knew that Rukmī was the guilty party, but to encourage the lamenting Rukmiṇī He decided to gently reproach Śrī Kṛṣṇa.

TEXT 38

मैवास्मान् साध्व्यसूयेथा भ्रातुर्वैरूप्यचिन्तया ।
सुखदुःखदो न चान्योऽस्ति यतः स्वकृतभुक् पुमान् ॥३८॥

maivāsmān sādhvy asūyethā
bhrātur vairūpya-cintayā
sukha-duḥkha-do na cānyo 'sti
yataḥ sva-kṛta-bhuk pumān

mā—please do not; *eva*—indeed; *asmān*—toward Us; *sādhvi*—O saintly lady; *asūyethāḥ*—feel inimical; *bhrātuḥ*—of your brother; *vairūpya*—over the disfigurement; *cintayā*—out of concern; *sukha*—of happiness; *duḥkha*—and unhappiness; *daḥ*—bestower; *na*—not; *ca*—and; *anyaḥ*—anyone else; *asti*—there is; *yataḥ*—since; *sva*—of his own; *kṛta*—action; *bhuk*—the sufferer of the reaction; *pumān*—a man.

TRANSLATION

Saintly lady, please do not be displeased with Us out of anxiety for your brother's disfigurement. No one but oneself is responsible for one's joy and grief, for a man experiences the result of his own deeds.

TEXT 39

बन्धुर्वधार्हदोषोऽपि न बन्धोर्वधमर्हति ।
त्याज्यः स्वेनैव दोषेण हतः किं हन्यते पुनः ॥३९॥

bandhur vadhārha-doṣo 'pi
na bandhor vadham arhati
tyājyaḥ svenaiva doṣeṇa
hataḥ kiṁ hanyate punaḥ

bandhuḥ—a relative; *vadha*—being killed; *arha*—which merits; *doṣaḥ*—whose wrong-doing; *api*—even though; *na*—not; *bandhoḥ*—from a relative; *vadham*—being killed; *arhati*—deserves; *tyājyaḥ*—to be cast out; *svena eva*—by his own; *doṣeṇa*—fault; *hataḥ*—killed; *kim*—why; *hanyate*—is to be killed; *punaḥ*—again.

TRANSLATION

[Again addressing Kṛṣṇa, Balarāma said:] A relative should not be killed even if his wrongdoing warrants capital punishment. Rather, he should be thrown out of the family. Since he has already been killed by his own sin, why kill him again?

PURPORT

To further encourage Lady Rukmiṇī, Balarāma again emphasizes that Kṛṣṇa should not humiliate Rukmī.

TEXT 40

क्षत्रियाणामयं धर्मः प्रजापतिविनिर्मितः ।
भ्रातापि भ्रातरं हन्याद्येन घोरतमस्ततः ॥४०॥

kṣatriyāṇām ayaṁ dharmaḥ
prajāpati-vinirmitaḥ
bhrātāpi bhrātaraṁ hanyād
yena ghoratamas tataḥ

kṣatriyāṇām—of warriors; *ayam*—this; *dharmaḥ*—code of sacred duty; *prajāpati*—by the original progenitor, Lord Brahmā; *vinirmitaḥ*—established; *bhrātā*—a brother; *api*—even; *bhrātaram*—his brother; *hanyāt*—has to kill; *yena*—by which (code); *ghora-tamaḥ*—most terrible; *tataḥ*—therefore.

TRANSLATION

[Turning to Rukmiṇī, Balarāma continued:] The code of sacred duty for warriors established by Lord Brahmā enjoins that one may have to kill even his own brother. That is indeed a most dreadful law.

PURPORT

Lord Balarāma, in the interest of fairness, is giving a complete analysis of the situation. Although one should not kill a relative, there are extenuating circumstances according to military codes. In the American Civil War, which took place in the 1860's, many families were divided between the army of the North and that of the South, and thus fratricidal killing unfortunately became a common affair. Such killing is certainly *ghoratama*, most dreadful. Yet such is the nature of the material world, where duty, honor and so-called justice often create conflict. Only on the spiritual platform, in pure Kṛṣṇa consciousness, can we transcend the unacceptable pain of material existence. Rukmī was maddened by pride and envy and thus could not understand anything about Kṛṣṇa or Kṛṣṇa consciousness.

TEXT 41

राज्यस्य भूमेर्वित्तस्य स्त्रियो मानस्य तेजसः ।
मानिनो?न्यस्य वा हेतोः श्रीमदान्धाः क्षिपन्ति हि ॥४१॥

rājyasya bhūmer vittasya
striyo mānasya tejasaḥ
mānino 'nyasya vā hetoḥ
śrī-madāndhāḥ kṣipanti hi

rājyasya—of kingdom; *bhūmeḥ*—of land; *vittasya*—of wealth; *striyaḥ*—of a woman; *mānasya*—of honor; *tejasaḥ*—of power; *māninaḥ*—those who are proud; *anyasya*—of something else; *vā*—or; *hetoḥ*—for the reason; *śrī*—in their opulence; *mada*—by their intoxication; *andhāḥ*—blinded; *kṣipanti*—they commit insult; *hi*—indeed.

TRANSLATION

[Again Balarāma addressed Kṛṣṇa:] Blinded by conceit with their personal opulences, proud men offend others for the sake of such things as kingdom, land, wealth, women, honor and power.

PURPORT

Lord Kṛṣṇa was originally meant to marry Rukmiṇī. All along this was the best arrangement for all concerned, and yet from the beginning Rukmī had maliciously opposed this beautiful arrangement. When his sister's desire was finally fulfilled and she was taken by Kṛṣṇa, he viciously attacked the Lord with vulgar insults and mortal weapons. In return Lord Kṛṣṇa tied him up and partially clipped his hair and mustache. While certainly humiliating for a puffed-up prince like Rukmī, his punishment was a mere slap on the wrist, considering what he had done.

TEXT 42

तवेयं विषमा बुद्धिः सर्वभूतेषु दुर्हृदाम् ।
यन्मन्यसे सदाभद्रं सुहृदां भद्रमज्ञवत् ॥४२॥

taveyaṁ viṣamā buddhiḥ
sarva-bhūteṣu durhṛdām
yan manyase sadābhadraṁ
suhṛdāṁ bhadram ajña-vat

tava—your; *iyam*—this; *viṣamā*—biased; *buddhiḥ*—attitude; *sarva-bhūteṣu*—toward all living beings; *durhṛdām*—of those who have ill intentions; *yat*—that; *manyase*—you wish; *sadā*—always; *abhadram*—evil; *suhṛdām*—to your well-wishers; *bhadram*—good; *ajña-vat*—like an ignorant person.

TRANSLATION

[To Rukmiṇī Balarāma said:] Your attitude is unfair, for like an ignorant person you wish good to those who are inimical to all living beings and who have done evil to your true well-wishers.

TEXT 43

आत्ममोहो नृणामेव कल्पते देवमायया ।
सुहृद्दुर्हृदुदासीन इति देहात्ममानिनाम् ॥४३॥

ātma-moho nṛṇām eva
kalpate deva-māyayā
suhṛd durhṛd udāsīna
iti dehātma-māninām

ātma—about the self; *mohaḥ*—the bewilderment; *nṛṇām*—of men; *eva*—only; *kalpate*—is effected; *deva*—of the Supreme Lord; *māyayā*—by the illusory, material energy; *suhṛt*—a friend; *durhṛt*—an enemy; *udāsīnaḥ*—a neutral party; *iti*—thus thinking; *deha*—the body; *ātma*—as the self; *māninām*—for those who consider.

TRANSLATION

The Supreme Lord's Māyā makes men forget their real selves, and thus, taking the body for the self, they consider others to be friends, enemies or neutral parties.

TEXT 44

एक एव परो ह्यात्मा सर्वेषामपि देहिनाम् ।
नानेव गृह्यते मूढैर्यथा ज्योतिर्यथा नभः ॥४४॥

eka eva paro hy ātmā
sarveṣām api dehinām
nāneva gṛhyate mūḍhair
yathā jyotir yathā nabhaḥ

ekaḥ—one; *eva*—only; *paraḥ*—the Supreme; *hi*—indeed; *ātmā*—Soul; *sarveṣām*—among all; *api*—and; *dehinām*—embodied beings; *nānā*—many; *iva*—as if; *gṛhyate*—is perceived; *mūḍhaiḥ*—by those who are bewildered; *yathā*—as; *jyotiḥ*—a celestial body; *yathā*—as; *nabhaḥ*—the sky.

TRANSLATION

Those who are bewildered perceive the one Supreme Soul, who resides in all embodied beings, as many, just as one may perceive the light in the sky, or the sky itself, as many.

PURPORT

The last line of this text, *yathā jyotir yathā nabhaḥ,* introduces two analogies in which we perceive one thing to be many. *Jyotiḥ* indicates the light of heavenly bodies such as the sun or moon. Although there is only one moon, we may see the moon reflected in pools, rivers, lakes and buckets of water. Then it would appear as if there were many moons, although there is only one. Similarly, we perceive a divine presence in each living being because the Supreme Lord is present everywhere, although He is one. The second analogy given here, *yathā nabhaḥ,* is that of the sky. If we have a row of sealed clay pots in a room, the sky, or air, is in each pot, although the sky itself is one.

The *Śrīmad-Bhāgavatam* (1.2.32) gives a similar analogy concerning fire and wood:

yathā hy avahito vahnir
dāruṣv ekaḥ sva-yoniṣu
nāneva bhāti viśvātmā
bhūteṣu ca tathā pumān

"The Lord, as the Supersoul, pervades all things, just as fire permeates wood, and so He appears to be of many varieties, though He is the absolute one without a second."

TEXT 45

देह आद्यन्तवानेष द्रव्यप्राणगुणात्मकः ।
आत्मन्यविद्यया क्लृप्तः संसारयति देहिनम् ॥४५॥

deha ādy-antavān eṣa
dravya-prāṇa-guṇātmakaḥ
ātmany avidyayā kḷptaḥ
saṁsārayati dehinam

dehaḥ—the material body; *ādi*—beginning; *anta*—and end; *vān*—having; *eṣaḥ*—this; *dravya*—of the physical elements; *prāṇa*—the senses; *guṇa*—and the primary modes of material nature (goodness, passion and ignorance); *ātmakaḥ*—composed; *ātmani*—on the self; *avidyayā*—by material ignorance; *kḷptaḥ*—imposed; *saṁsārayati*—causes to experience the cycle of birth and death; *dehinam*—an embodied being.

TRANSLATION

This material body, which has a beginning and an end, is composed of the physical elements, the senses and the modes of nature. The body, imposed on the self by material ignorance, causes one to experience the cycle of birth and death.

PURPORT

The material body, composed of various material qualities, elements and so on, attracts and repels the conditioned soul and thus entangles him in material existence. Because of our attraction and repulsion for our own body and other bodies, we establish temporary relationships, dedicate ourselves to great endeavors and sacrifices, concoct imaginary religions, make noble speeches and thoroughly involve ourselves in material illusion. As Shakespeare said, "All the world's a stage." Beyond the somewhat absurd theater of material existence is the real and meaningful world of Kṛṣṇa consciousness, the liberated life of pure souls devoted in loving service to the Supreme Lord.

TEXT 46

नात्मनोऽन्येन संयोगो वियोगश्चासतः सति ।
तद्धेतुत्वात्तत्प्रसिद्धेर्दृग्रूपाभ्यां यथा रवेः ॥४६॥

nātmano 'nyena saṁyogo
viyogaś cāsataḥ sati
tad-dhetutvāt tat-prasiddher
dṛg-rūpābhyāṁ yathā raveḥ

na—not; *ātmanaḥ*—for the self; *anyena*—with anything else; *saṁyogaḥ*—contact; *viyogaḥ*—separation; *ca*—and; *asataḥ*—with that which is insubstantial; *sati*—O discriminating one; *tat*—from it (the self) *hetutvāt*—because of originating; *tat*—by it (the self); *prasiddheḥ*—because of being revealed; *dṛk*—with the sense of vision; *rūpābhyām*—and visible form; *yathā*—as; *raveḥ*—for the sun.

TRANSLATION

O intelligent lady, the soul never undergoes contact with or separation from insubstantial, material objects, because the soul is their very origin and illuminator. Thus the soul resembles the sun, which neither comes in contact with nor separates from the sense of sight and what is seen.

PURPORT

As explained in the previous text, the conditioned soul ignorantly assumes himself to be the material body and thus rotates in the cycle of birth and death. In fact, matter and spirit are co-energies of the original source of everything, the Supreme Lord, who is the Absolute Truth.

As Lord Kṛṣṇa explains in the *Bhagavad-gītā* (7.5), *jīva-bhūtāṁ mahā-bāho yayedaṁ dhāryate jagat.* The material world is sustained by the living beings' desire to exploit it. The material world is like a prison. Criminals are determined to commit crimes, and thus the government finds it necessary to maintain a prison system. Similarly, the Supreme Lord maintains the material universes because the conditioned souls are determined to rebel against Him and try to enjoy without His loving co-operation. Thus here the phrase *tad-dhetutvāt* is used to describe the soul, meaning that the soul is the cause of matter assembling itself into a material body. The term *tat-prasiddheḥ* indicates that the soul is the cause of the body's being perceived, and the same term also indicates that this fact is well known to the enlightened.

Besides its given meaning, the word *ātmanaḥ* in this verse may indicate the Supreme Soul, in which case the term *tad-dhetutvāt* indicates that Lord Kṛṣṇa expands His personal potency and thus manifests the material universe. Since the Lord exists eternally in His pure, spiritual body, He never becomes material, as indicated here.

TEXT 47

जन्मादयस्तु देहस्य विक्रिया नात्मनः क्वचित् ।
कलानामिव नैवेन्दोर्मृतिर्ह्यस्य कुहूरिव ॥४७॥

janmādayas tu dehasya
vikriyā nātmanaḥ kvacit
kalānām iva naivendor
mṛtir hy asya kuhūr iva

janma-ādayaḥ—birth and so on; *tu*—but; *dehasya*—of the body; *vikriyāḥ*—transformations; *na*—not; *ātmanaḥ*—of the self; *kvacit*—ever; *kalānām*—of the phases; *iva*—as; *na*—not; *eva*—indeed; *indoḥ*—of the moon; *mṛtiḥ*—the death; *hi*—indeed; *asya*—of it; *kuhūḥ*—the new moon day; *iva*—as.

TRANSLATION

Birth and other transformations are undergone by the body but never by the self, just as change occurs for the moon's phases but never for the moon, though the new-moon day may be called the moon's "death."

PURPORT

Lord Balarāma here explains how the conditioned souls identify with the body and how this identification should be given up. Certainly every ordinary person considers himself or herself young, middle-aged or old, healthy or sick. But such identification is an illusion, just as the waxing and waning of the moon is an illusion. When we identify ourselves with the material body, we lose our power to understand the soul.

TEXT 48

यथा शयान आत्मानं विषयान् फलमेव च ।
अनुभुंक्तेऽप्यसत्यर्थे तथाप्नोत्यबुधो भवम् ॥४८॥

yathā śayāna ātmānaṁ
viṣayān phalam eva ca

anubhuṅkte 'py asaty arthe
tathāpnoty abudho bhavam

yathā—as; *śayānaḥ*—a sleeping person; *ātmānam*—himself; *viṣayān*—sense objects; *phalam*—the fruits; *eva*—indeed; *ca*—also; *anubhuṅkte*—experiences; *api*—even; *asati arthe*—in that which is not real; *tathā*—so; *āpnoti*—undergoes; *abudhaḥ*—the unintelligent; *bhavam*—material existence.

TRANSLATION

As a sleeping person perceives himself, the objects of sense enjoyment and the fruits of his acts within the illusion of a dream, so one who is unintelligent undergoes material existence.

PURPORT

As stated in *śruti, asaṅgo hy ayaṁ puruṣaḥ:* "The living being has no intimate connection with the material world." This point is explained in the present verse. A similar statement is found in the *Śrīmad-Bhāgavatam* (11.22.56):

arthe 'hy avidyamāne 'pi
saṁsṛtir na nivartate
dhyāyato viṣayān asya
svapne 'narthāgamo yathā

"For one who is meditating on sense gratification, material life, although lacking factual existence, does not go away, just as the unpleasant experiences of a dream do not."

TEXT 49

तस्मादज्ञानजं शोकमात्मशोषविमोहनम् ।
तत्त्वज्ञानेन निर्हृत्य स्वस्था भव शुचिस्मिते ॥४९॥

tasmād ajñāna-jaṁ śokam
ātma-śoṣa-vimohanam
tattva-jñānena nirhṛtya
sva-sthā bhava śuci-smite

tasmāt—therefore; *ajñāna*—out of ignorance; *jam*—born; *śokam*—the lamentation; *ātma*—yourself; *śoṣa*—drying up; *vimohanam*—and bewildering; *tattva*—of the truth; *jñānena*—with knowledge; *nirhṛtya*—dispelling; *sva-sthā*—reinstated in your natural mood; *bhava*—please be; *śuci-smite*—O you whose smile is pure.

TRANSLATION

Therefore, with transcendental knowledge dispel the grief that is weakening and confounding your mind. Please resume your natural mood, O princess of the pristine smile.

PURPORT

Lord Balarāma reminds Śrīmatī Rukmiṇī that she is the eternal goddess of fortune performing pastimes with the Lord in this world and should thus give up her so-called grief.

TEXT 50

श्रीशुक उवाच
एवं भगवता तन्वी रामेण प्रतिबोधिता ।
वैमनस्यं परित्यज्य मनो बुद्ध्या समादधे ॥५०॥

śrī-śuka uvāca
evaṁ bhagavatā tanvī
rāmeṇa pratibodhitā
vaimanasyaṁ parityajya
mano buddhyā samādadhe

śrī-śukaḥ uvāca—Śukadeva Gosvāmī said; *evam*—thus; *bhagavatā*—by the Supreme Lord; *tanvī*—slender-waisted Rukmiṇī; *rāmeṇa*—by Balarāma; *pratibodhitā*—enlightened; *vaimanasyam*—her depression; *parityajya*—giving up; *manaḥ*—her mind; *buddhyā*—by intelligence; *samādadhe*—composed.

TRANSLATION

Śukadeva Gosvāmī said: Thus enlightened by Lord Balarāma, slender Rukmiṇī forgot her depression and steadied her mind by spiritual intelligence.

TEXT 51

प्राणावशेष उत्सृष्टो द्विड्भिर्हतबलप्रभः ।
स्मरन् विरूपकरणं वितथात्ममनोरथः ।
चक्रे भोजकटं नाम निवासाय महत्पुरम् ॥५१॥

prāṇāvaśeṣa utsṛṣṭo
dviḍbhir hata-bala-prabhaḥ
smaran virūpa-karaṇaṁ
vitathātma-manorathaḥ
cakre bhojakaṭaṁ nāma
nivāsāya mahat puram

prāṇa—his life air; *avaśeṣaḥ*—remaining only; *utsṛṣṭaḥ*—expelled; *dviḍbhiḥ*—by his enemies; *hata*—destroyed; *bala*—his strength; *prabhaḥ*—and bodily effulgence; *smaran*—remembering; *virūpa-karaṇam*—his disfigurement; *vitatha*—frustrated; *ātma*—his personal; *manaḥ-rathaḥ*—desires; *cakre*—he made; *bhoja-kaṭam nāma*—named Bhojakaṭa; *nivāsāya*—for his residence; *mahat*—large; *puram*—a city.

TRANSLATION

Left with only his life air, cast out by his enemies and deprived of his strength and bodily radiance, Rukmī could not forget how he had been disfigured. In frustration he constructed for his residence a large city, which he called Bhojakaṭa.

TEXT 52

अहत्वा दुर्मतिं कृष्णमप्रत्यूह्य यवीयसीम् ।
कुण्डिनं न प्रवेक्ष्यामीत्युक्त्वा तत्रावसद् रुषा ॥५२॥

ahatvā durmatiṁ kṛṣṇam
apratyūhya yavīyasīm
kuṇḍinaṁ na pravekṣyāmīty
uktvā tatrāvasad ruṣā

ahatvā—without killing; *durmatim*—evil-minded; *kṛṣṇam*—Kṛṣṇa; *apratyūhya*—without bringing back; *yavīyasīm*—my younger sister; *kuṇḍinam*—Kuṇḍina; *na pravekṣyāmi*—I will not enter; *iti*—such; *uktvā*—having spoken; *tatra*—there (in the same place where he had been disfigured); *avasat*—he took up residence; *ruṣā*—in anger.

TRANSLATION

Because he had promised "I will not reenter Kuṇḍina until I have killed wicked Kṛṣṇa and brought back my younger sister," in a mood of angry frustration Rukmī took up residence at that very place.

PURPORT

Śrīla Viśvanātha Cakravartī explains that the word *bhoja* means "experience" and that *kaṭaḥ*, according to the *Nānārtha-varga* dictionary, means "vow." Thus Bhojakaṭa is the place where Rukmī experienced misery as a result of his vow.

TEXT 53

भगवान् भीष्मकसुतामेवं निर्जित्य भूमिपान् ।
पुरमानीय विधिवदुपयेमे कुरूद्वह ॥५३॥

bhagavān bhīṣmaka-sutām
evaṁ nirjitya bhūmi-pān
puram ānīya vidhi-vad
upayeme kurūdvaha

bhagavān—the Supreme Lord; *bhīṣmaka-sutām*—the daughter of Bhīṣmaka; *evam*—thus; *nirjitya*—defeating; *bhūmi-pān*—the kings; *puram*—to His capital; *ānīya*—bringing; *vidhi-vat*—in accordance with the injunctions of the *Vedas; upayeme*—married; *kuru-udvaha*—O protector of the Kurus.

TRANSLATION

Thus defeating all the opposing kings, the Supreme Personality of Godhead brought the daughter of Bhīṣmaka to His capital and married her according to the Vedic injunctions, O protector of the Kurus.

TEXT 54

तदा महोत्सवो नृणां यदुपुर्यां गृहे गृहे ।
अभूदनन्यभावानां कृष्णे यदुपतौ नृप ॥५४॥

tadā mahotsavo nṛṇāṁ
yadu-puryāṁ gṛhe gṛhe
abhūd ananya-bhāvānāṁ
kṛṣṇe yadu-patau nṛpa

tadā—then; *mahā-utsavaḥ*—great rejoicing; *nṛṇām*—by the people; *yadu-puryām*—in the capital of the Yadus, Dvārakā; *gṛhe gṛhe*—in each and every home; *abhūt*—arose; *ananya-bhāvānām*—who had exclusive love; *kṛṣṇe*—for Kṛṣṇa; *yadu-patau*—the chief of the Yadus; *nṛpa*—O King (Parīkṣit).

TRANSLATION

At that time, O King, there was great rejoicing in all the homes of Yadupurī, whose citizens loved only Kṛṣṇa, chief of the Yadus.

TEXT 55

नरा नार्यश्च मुदिताः प्रमृष्टमणिकुण्डलाः ।
पारिबर्हमुपाजहुर्वरयोश्चित्रवाससोः ॥५५॥

narā nāryaś ca muditāḥ
pramṛṣṭa-maṇi-kuṇḍalāḥ
pāribarham upājahrur
varayoś citra-vāsasoḥ

narāḥ—the men; *nāryaḥ*—women; *ca*—and; *muditāḥ*—joyful; *pra-mṛṣṭa*—polished; *maṇi*—their jewels; *kuṇḍalāḥ*—and earrings; *pāribar-ham*—wedding gifts; *upājahruḥ*—they respectfully presented; *varayoḥ*—to the groom and the bride; *citra*—wonderful; *vāsasoḥ*—whose dress.

TRANSLATION

All the men and women, full of joy and adorned with shining jewels and earrings, brought wedding presents, which they reverently offered to the exquisitely dressed groom and bride.

TEXT 56

सा वृष्णिपुर्युत्तम्भितेन्द्रकेतुभिर्
विचित्रमाल्याम्बररत्नतोरणैः ।
बभौ प्रतिद्वार्युपक्लृप्तमंगलैर्
आपूर्णकुम्भागुरुधूपदीपकैः ॥५६॥

sā vṛṣṇi-pury uttambhitendra-ketubhir
vicitra-mālyāmbara-ratna-toraṇaiḥ
babhau prati-dvāry upakḷpta-maṅgalair
āpūrṇa-kumbhāguru-dhūpa-dīpakaiḥ

sā—that; *vṛṣṇi-purī*—city of the Vṛṣṇis; *uttambhita*—upraised; *indra-ketubhiḥ*—with festive columns; *vicitra*—variegated; *mālya*—having flower garlands; *ambara*—cloth banners; *ratna*—and jewels; *toraṇaiḥ*—with archways; *babhau*—appeared beautiful; *prati*—in every; *dvāri*—doorway; *upakḷpta*—arranged; *maṅgalaiḥ*—with auspicious items; *āpūrṇa*—full; *kumbha*—waterpots; *aguru*—scented with *aguru; dhūpa*—with incense; *dīpakaiḥ*—and lamps.

TRANSLATION

The city of the Vṛṣṇis appeared most beautiful: there were tall, festive columns, and also archways decorated with flower garlands, cloth banners and precious gems. Arrangements of auspicious, full waterpots, *aguru*-scented incense, and lamps graced every doorway.

TEXT 57

सिक्तमार्गा मदच्युद्भिराहूतप्रेष्ठभूभुजाम् ।
गजैर्द्वाःसु परामृष्टरम्भापूगोपशोभिता ॥५७॥

sikta-mārgā mada-cyudbhir
āhūta-preṣṭha-bhūbhujām
gajair dvāḥsu parāmṛṣṭa-
rambhā-pūgopaśobhitā

sikta—sprinkled; *mārgā*—its streets; *mada*—a secretion that flows from the foreheads of excited elephants; *cyudbhiḥ*—exuding; *āhūta*—invited; *preṣṭha*—beloved; *bhū-bhujām*—of the kings; *gajaiḥ*—by the elephants; *dvāḥsu*—in the doorways; *parāmṛṣṭa*—handled; *rambhā*—by plantain trees; *pūga*—and betel-nut trees; *upaśobhitā*—beautified.

TRANSLATION

The city's streets were cleansed by the intoxicated elephants belonging to the beloved kings who were guests at the wedding, and these elephants further enhanced the beauty of the city by placing trunks of plantain and betel-nut trees in all the doorways.

TEXT 58

कुरुसृञ्जयकैकेयविदर्भयदुकुन्तयः ।
मिथो मुमुदिरे तस्मिन् सम्भ्रमात्परिधावताम् ॥५८॥

kuru-sṛñjaya-kaikeya-
vidarbha-yadu-kuntayaḥ
mitho mumudire tasmin
sambhramāt paridhāvatām

kuru-sṛñjaya-kaikeya-vidarbha-yadu-kuntayaḥ—of the members of the Kuru, Sṛñjaya, Kaikeya, Vidarbha, Yadu and Kunti clans; *mithaḥ*—with one another; *mumudire*—they took pleasure; *tasmin*—in that (festivity); *sambhramāt*—out of excitement; *paridhāvatām*—among those who were running about.

TRANSLATION

Those who belonged to the royal families of the Kuru, Sṛñjaya, Kaikeya, Vidarbha, Yadu and Kunti clans joyfully met one another in the midst of the crowds of people excitedly running here and there.

TEXT 59

रुक्मिण्या हरणं श्रुत्वा गीयमानं ततस्ततः ।
राजानो राजकन्याश्च बभूवुर्भृशविस्मिताः ॥५९॥

rukmiṇyā haraṇaṁ śrutvā
gīyamānaṁ tatas tataḥ
rājāno rāja-kanyāś ca
babhūvur bhṛśa-vismitāḥ

rukmiṇyāḥ—of Rukmiṇī; *haraṇam*—about the kidnapping; *śrutvā*—hearing; *gīyamānam*—which was being sung; *tataḥ tataḥ*—all over; *rājānaḥ*—the kings; *rāja-kanyāḥ*—the kings' daughters; *ca*—and; *babhūvuḥ*—became; *bhṛśa*—extremely; *vismitāḥ*—amazed.

TRANSLATION

The kings and their daughters were totally astonished to hear the story of Rukmiṇī's abduction, which was being glorified in song everywhere.

TEXT 60

द्वारकायामभूद् राजन्महामोदः पुरौकसाम् ।
रुक्मिण्या रमयोपेतं दृष्ट्वा कृष्णं श्रियः पतिम् ॥६०॥

dvārakāyām abhūd rājan
mahā-modaḥ puraukasām
rukmiṇyā ramayopetaṁ
dṛṣṭvā kṛṣṇaṁ śriyaḥ patim

dvārakāyām—in Dvārakā; *abhūt*—there was; *rājan*—O King; *mahā-modaḥ*—great joy; *pura-okasām*—for the inhabitants of the city; *rukmiṇyā*—with Rukmiṇī; *ramayā*—the goddess of fortune; *upetam*—joined; *dṛṣṭvā*—seeing; *kṛṣṇam*—Lord Kṛṣṇa; *śriyaḥ*—of all opulence; *patim*—the master.

TRANSLATION

Dvārakā's citizens were overjoyed to see Kṛṣṇa, the Lord of all opulence, united with Rukmiṇī, the goddess of fortune.

Thus end the purports of the humble servants of His Divine Grace A. C. Bhaktivedanta Swami Prabhupāda to the Tenth Canto, Fifty-fourth Chapter, of the Śrīmad-Bhāgavatam, *entitled "The Marriage of Kṛṣṇa and Rukmiṇī."*

CHAPTER FIFTY-FIVE

The History of Pradyumna

This chapter tells how Pradyumna was born as the son of Lord Kṛṣṇa and then kidnapped by the demon Śambara. It also describes how Pradyumna killed Śambara and returned home with a wife.

Kāmadeva (Cupid), an expansion of Lord Vāsudeva, had been burned to ashes by Lord Śiva's anger and was reborn as part and parcel of Pradyumna from the womb of Rukmiṇī. A demon named Śambara, thinking Pradyumna his enemy, kidnapped Him from the maternity room even before He was ten days old. Śambara threw Pradyumna into the ocean and returned to his kingdom. A powerful fish swallowed Pradyumna and was caught by fishermen in a net. They presented the huge fish to Śambara, and when his cooks cut it open they found a child within its belly. The cooks gave the infant to the maidservant Māyāvatī, who was astonished to see Him. Just then Nārada Muni appeared and told her who the infant was. Māyāvatī was actually Kāmadeva's wife, Ratidevī. While waiting for her husband to be reborn in a new body, she had taken employment as a cook in the household of Śambara. Now that she understood who the infant was, she began to feel intense affection for Him. After a very short time, Pradyumna grew to youthful maturity, entrancing all the women with His beauty.

Once, Ratidevī approached Pradyumna and playfully moved her eyebrows in a conjugal mood. Addressing her as His mother, Pradyumna commented that she was putting aside her proper maternal mood and behaving like a passionate girlfriend. Rati then told Pradyumna who they both were. She advised Him to kill Śambara, and to help Him she instructed Him in the mystic *mantras* known as Mahā-māyā. Pradyumna went to Śambara and, after angering him with various insults, challenged him to fight, upon which Śambara angrily took up his club and marched outside. The demon tried various magic spells against Pradyumna, but Pradyumna fended off all of them with the Mahā-māyā *mantras* and then beheaded Śambara with His sword. At that moment Ratidevī appeared in the sky and took Pradyumna away to Dvārakā.

When Pradyumna and His wife entered the inner chambers of Lord Kṛṣṇa's palace, the many beautiful ladies there thought He was Kṛṣṇa Himself, so much did His appearance and dress resemble the Lord's. Out of shyness the ladies ran here and there to hide themselves. But after a little while they noticed small differences in Pradyumna's and Kṛṣṇa's appearances, and once they understood that He was not Lord Kṛṣṇa, they gathered around Him.

When Rukmiṇī-devī saw Pradyumna, she felt overwhelmed with motherly love, and milk began to flow spontaneously from her breasts. Noting that Pradyumna looked exactly like Kṛṣṇa, she became eager to find out who He was. She remembered how one of her sons had been abducted from the maternity room. "If He were still alive," she thought, "He would be the same age as this Pradyumna standing before me." While Rukmiṇī reflected in this way, Lord Kṛṣṇa arrived in the company of Devakī and Vasudeva. Although the Lord understood the situation perfectly well, He remained silent. Then Nārada Muni arrived and explained everything. Everyone was amazed to hear the account and embraced Pradyumna in great ecstasy.

Because Pradyumna's beauty so closely resembled Kṛṣṇa's, the ladies in a maternal relationship with Pradyumna could not help thinking of Him as their conjugal lover. He was, after all, the exact reflection of Śrī Kṛṣṇa, and therefore it was natural for them to see Him in this way.

TEXT 1

श्रीशुक उवाच

कामस्तु वासुदेवांशो दग्धः प्राग् रुद्रमन्युना ।
देहोपपत्तये भूयस्तमेव प्रत्यपद्यत ॥१॥

śrī-śuka uvāca
kāmas tu vāsudevāṁśo
dagdhaḥ prāg rudra-manyunā
dehopapattaye bhūyas
tam eva pratyapadyata

śrī-śukaḥ uvāca—Śukadeva Gosvāmī said; *kāmaḥ*—Cupid; *tu*—and; *vāsudeva*—of Lord Vāsudeva; *aṁśaḥ*—the expansion; *dagdhaḥ*—burned; *prāk*—previously; *rudra*—of Lord Śiva; *manyunā*—by the anger; *deha*—a body; *upapattaye*—in order to obtain; *bhūyaḥ*—again; *tam*—to Him, Lord Vāsudeva; *eva*—indeed; *pratyapadyat*—came back.

TRANSLATION

Śukadeva Gosvāmī said: Kāmadeva [Cupid], an expansion of Vāsudeva, had previously been burned to ashes by Rudra's anger. Now, to obtain a new body, he merged back into the body of Lord Vāsudeva.

PURPORT

In his *Kṛṣṇa-sandarbha* (*Anuccheda* 87), Śrīla Jīva Gosvāmī cites the following verse of the *Gopāla-tāpanī Upaniṣad* (2.40) to prove that the Pradyumna who is the son of Kṛṣṇa and Rukmiṇī is the same Pradyumna who is a member of Lord Kṛṣṇa's eternal fourfold plenary expansion, the *catur-vyūha:*

yatrāsau saṁsthitaḥ kṛṣṇas
tribhiḥ śaktyā samāhitaḥ
rāmāniruddha-pradyumnai
rukmiṇyā sahito vibhuḥ

"There [in Dvārakā] the almighty Lord Kṛṣṇa, endowed with His full potency, resided in the company of His three plenary expansions—Balarāma, Aniruddha and Pradyumna." The *Kṛṣṇa-sandarbha* goes on to explain, with reference to the present verse of the *Śrīmad-Bhāgavatam,* that "the Cupid whom Rudra burned up with his anger is a demigod subordinate to Indra. This demigod Cupid is a partial manifestation of the prototype Cupid, Pradyumna, who is a plenary expansion of Vāsudeva. The demigod Cupid, being unable to attain a new body on his own, entered within the body of Pradyumna. Otherwise Cupid would have had to remain in a perpetual state of disembodiment, a result of Rudra's having incinerated him with his anger."

In his English rendering of the *Śrīmad-Bhāgavatam* (1.14.30 purport), Śrīla Prabhupāda confirms the absolute status of Pradyumna, Lord Kṛṣṇa's first son: "Pradyumna and Aniruddha are also expansions of the Personality of Godhead, and thus They are also *viṣṇu-tattva.* At Dvārakā Lord Vāsudeva is engaged in His transcendental pastimes along with His plenary expansions, namely Saṅkarṣaṇa, Pradyumna and Aniruddha, and therefore each and every one of Them can be addressed as the Personality of Godhead...."

According to Śrīla Śrīdhara Svāmī, Pradyumna took birth from the womb of Rukmiṇī before Śrī Kṛṣṇa's marriage to Jāmbavatī and the Lord's other marriages took place. Subsequently, Pradyumna returned from Śambara's palace. But before Śukadeva Gosvāmī tells of Kṛṣṇa's pastimes with His other wives, he will narrate the entire story of Pradyumna for the sake of continuity.

Śrīla Śrīdhara Svāmī further notes that Kāmadeva, or Cupid, now appearing within Pradyumna, is a portion of Vāsudeva because he is manifest from the element *citta*, consciousness, which is presided over by Vāsudeva, and also because he (Cupid) is the cause of material generation. As the Lord states in the *Bhagavad-gītā* (10.28), *prajanaś cāsmi kandarpaḥ:* "Of progenitors I am Kandarpa [Cupid]."

TEXT 2

स एव जातो वैदर्भ्यां कृष्णवीर्यसमुद्भवः ।
प्रद्युम्न इति विख्यातः सर्वतोऽनवमः पितुः ॥२॥

sa eva jāto vaidarbhyāṁ
kṛṣṇa-vīrya-samudbhavaḥ
pradyumna iti vikhyātaḥ
sarvato 'navamaḥ pituḥ

saḥ—He; *eva*—indeed; *jātaḥ*—taking birth; *vaidarbhyām*—in the daughter of the king of Vidarbha; *kṛṣṇa-vīrya*—from the seed of Lord Kṛṣṇa; *samudbhavaḥ*—generated; *pradyumnaḥ*—Pradyumna; *iti*—thus; *vikhyātaḥ*—known; *sarvataḥ*—in all aspects; *anavamaḥ*—not inferior; *pituḥ*—to His father.

TRANSLATION

He took birth in the womb of Vaidarbhī from the seed of Lord Kṛṣṇa and received the name Pradyumna. In no respect was He inferior to His father.

TEXT 3

तं शम्बरः कामरूपी हृत्वा तोकमनिर्दशम् ।
स विदित्वात्मनः शत्रुं प्रास्योदन्वत्यगाद् गृहम् ॥३॥

taṁ śambaraḥ kāma-rūpī
hṛtvā tokam anirdaśam
sa viditvātmanaḥ śatruṁ
prāsyodanvaty agād gṛham

tam—Him; *śambaraḥ*—the demon Śambara; *kāma*—as he desired; *rūpī*—assuming forms; *hṛtvā*—stealing; *tokam*—the child; *aniḥ-daśam*—not yet ten days old; *saḥ*—he (Śambara); *viditvā*—recognizing; *ātmanaḥ*—his own; *śatrum*—enemy; *prāsya*—throwing; *udanvati*—into the sea; *agāt*—went; *gṛham*—to his home.

TRANSLATION

The demon Śambara, who could assume any form he desired, kidnapped the infant before He was even ten days old. Understanding Pradyumna to be his enemy, Śambara threw Him into the sea and then returned home.

PURPORT

Śrīla Viśvanātha Cakravartī points out that according to the *Viṣṇu Purāṇa*, Pradyumna was kidnapped on the sixth day after His birth.

TEXT 4

तं निर्जगार बलवान्मीनः सोऽप्यपरैः सह ।
वृतो जालेन महता गृहीतो मत्स्यजीविभिः ॥४॥

taṁ nirjagāra balavān
mīnaḥ so 'py aparaiḥ saha
vṛto jālena mahatā
gṛhīto matsya-jīvibhiḥ

tam—Him; *nirjagāra*—swallowed; *bala-vān*—powerful; *mīnaḥ*—a fish; *saḥ*—he (the fish); *api*—and; *aparaiḥ*—others; *saha*—together with; *vṛtaḥ*—enveloped; *jālena*—with a net; *mahatā*—huge; *gṛhītaḥ*—seized; *matsya-jīvibhiḥ*—by fishermen (who gain their livelihood from fish).

TRANSLATION

A powerful fish swallowed Pradyumna, and this fish, along with others, was caught in a huge net and seized by fishermen.

TEXT 5

तं शम्बराय कैवर्ता उपाजहुरुपायनम् ।
सूदा महानसं नीत्वावद्यन् सुधितिनाद्भुतम् ॥५॥

taṁ śambarāya kaivartā
upājahrur upāyanam
sūdā mahānasaṁ nītvā-
vadyan sudhitinādbhutam

tam—it (the fish); *śambarāya*—to Śambara; *kaivartāḥ*—the fishermen; *upājahruḥ*—presented; *upāyanam*—the offering; *sūdāḥ*—the cooks; *mahānasam*—to the kitchen; *nītvā*—bringing; *avadyan*—cut it up; *sudhitinā*—with a butcher knife; *adbhutam*—amazing.

TRANSLATION

The fishermen presented that extraordinary fish to Śambara, who had his cooks bring it to the kitchen, where they began cutting it up with a butcher knife.

TEXT 6

दृष्ट्वा तदुदरे बालं मायावत्यै न्यवेदयन् ।
नारदोऽकथयत्सर्वं तस्याः शंकितचेतसः ।
बालस्य तत्त्वमुत्पत्तिं मत्स्योदरनिवेशनम् ॥६॥

dṛṣṭvā tad-udare bālaṁ
māyāvatyai nyavedayan
nārado 'kathayat sarvaṁ
tasyāḥ śaṅkita-cetasaḥ
bālasya tattvam utpattiṁ
matsyodara-niveśanam

dṛṣṭvā—seeing; *tat*—in its; *udare*—belly; *bālam*—a child; *māyāvatyai*—to Māyāvatī; *nyavedayan*—they gave; *nāradaḥ*—Nārada Muni; *akathayat*—related; *sarvam*—all; *tasyāḥ*—to her; *śaṅkita*—astonished; *cetasaḥ*—whose mind; *bālasya*—of the child; *tattvam*—the facts; *utpattim*—the birth; *matsya*—of the fish; *udara*—in the abdomen; *niveśanam*—the entrance.

TRANSLATION

Seeing a male child in the belly of the fish, the cooks gave the infant to Māyāvatī, who was astonished. Nārada Muni then appeared and explained to her everything about the child's birth and His entering the fish's abdomen.

TEXTS 7–8

सा च कामस्य वै पत्नी रतिर्नाम यशस्विनी ।
पत्युर्निर्दग्धदेहस्य देहोत्पत्तिं प्रतीक्षती ॥७॥
निरूपिता शम्बरेण सा सूदौदनसाधने ।
कामदेवं शिशुं बुद्ध्वा चक्रे स्नेहं तदार्भके ॥८॥

sā ca kāmasya vai patnī
ratir nāma yaśasvinī
patyur nirdagdha-dehasya
dehotpattiṁ pratīkṣatī

nirūpitā śambareṇa
sā sūdaudana-sādhane
kāmadevaṁ śiśuṁ buddhvā
cakre snehaṁ tadārbhake

sā—she; *ca*—and; *kāmasya*—of Cupid; *vai*—in fact; *patnī*—the wife; *ratiḥ nāma*—named Rati; *yaśasvinī*—famous; *patyuḥ*—of her husband; *nirdagdha*—burnt to ashes; *dehasya*—whose body; *deha*—of a body; *utpattim*—the attainment; *pratīkṣatī*—waiting; *nirūpitā*—appointed; *śambareṇa*—by Śambara; *sā*—she; *sūda-odana*—of vegetables and rice; *sādhane*—in the preparation; *kāma-devam*—as Cupid; *śiśum*—the infant; *buddhvā*—understanding; *cakre*—she developed; *sneham*—love; *tadā*—then; *arbhake*—for the child.

TRANSLATION

Māyāvatī was in fact Cupid's renowned wife, Rati. While waiting for her husband to obtain a new body—his previous one having been burnt up—she had been assigned by Śambara to prepare vegetables and rice. Māyāvatī understood that this infant was actually Kāmadeva, and thus she began to feel love for Him.

PURPORT

Śrīla Viśvanātha Cakravartī explains this story as follows: When Cupid's body was burned to ashes, Rati worshiped Lord Śiva to obtain another body for Cupid. Śambara, having also come to Śiva for a benediction, was recognized by the lord first, who told him, "You should now ask for your benediction." Śambara, struck with lust at seeing Rati, replied that he wanted her as his benediction, and Śiva complied. Lord Śiva then consoled the sobbing Rati, telling her, "Go with him, and in his very home you will attain what you desire." Thereupon, Rati bewildered Śambara with her deluding power and, taking the name Māyāvatī, remained in his house untouched.

TEXT 9

नातिदीर्घेण कालेन स कार्ष्णि रूढयौवनः ।
जनयामास नारीणां वीक्षन्तीनां च विभ्रमम् ॥९॥

nāti-dīrgheṇa kālena
sa kārṣṇi rūḍha-yauvanaḥ
janayām āsa nārīṇāṁ
vīkṣantīnāṁ ca vibhramam

na—not; *ati-dīrgheṇa*—very long; *kālena*—after a time; *saḥ*—He; *kārṣṇiḥ*—the son of Kṛṣṇa; *rūḍha*—attaining; *yauvanaḥ*—full youth; *janayām āsa*—generated; *nārīṇām*—for the women; *vīkṣantīnām*—who looked upon Him; *ca*—and; *vibhramam*—enchantment.

TRANSLATION

After a short time, this son of Kṛṣṇa—Pradyumna—attained His full youth. He enchanted all women who gazed upon Him.

TEXT 10

सा तं पतिं पद्मदलायतेक्षणं
प्रलम्बबाहुं नरलोकसुन्दरम् ।
सव्रीडहासोत्तभितभ्रुवेक्षती
प्रीत्योपतस्थे रतिरंग सौरतैः ॥१०॥

sā taṁ patiṁ padma-dalāyatekṣaṇaṁ
pralamba-bāhuṁ nara-loka-sundaram
sa-vrīḍa-hāsottabhita-bhruvekṣatī
prītyopatasthe ratir aṅga saurataiḥ

sā—she; *tam*—Him; *patim*—her husband; *padma*—of a lotus flower; *dala-āyata*—spread wide like the petals; *īkṣaṇam*—whose eyes; *pralamba*—extended; *bāhum*—whose arms; *nara-loka*—of human society; *sundaram*—the greatest object of beauty; *sa-vrīḍa*—bashful; *hāsa*—with a smile; *uttabhita*—upraised; *bhruvā*—and with eyebrows; *īkṣatī*—glancing; *prītyā*—lovingly; *upatasthe*—approached; *ratiḥ*—Rati; *aṅga*—my dear (King Parīkṣit); *sauerataiḥ*—with gestures indicative of conjugal attraction.

TRANSLATION

My dear King, with a bashful smile and raised eyebrows, Māyāvatī exhibited various gestures of conjugal attraction as she lovingly approached her husband, whose eyes were broad like the petals of a lotus, whose arms were very long and who was the most beautiful of men.

PURPORT

Māyāvatī exhibited her conjugal attraction for Pradyumna even before revealing their true identities. Naturally this caused some confusion at first, as described in the following verse.

TEXT 11

तामाह भगवान् कार्ष्णिर्मातस्ते मतिरन्यथा ।
मातृभावमतिक्रम्य वर्तसे कामिनी यथा ॥११॥

tām āha bhagavān kārṣṇir
mātas te matir anyathā
mātṛ-bhāvam atikramya
vartase kāminī yathā

tām—to her; *āha*—said; *bhagavān*—the Lord; *kārṣṇiḥ*—Pradyumna; *mātaḥ*—O mother; *te*—your; *matiḥ*—attitude; *anyathā*—otherwise; *mātṛ-bhāvam*—the mood or affection of a mother; *atikramya*—overstepping; *vartase*—you are acting; *kāminī*—a girlfriend; *yathā*—like.

TRANSLATION

Lord Pradyumna told her, "O mother, your attitude has changed. You are overstepping the proper feelings of a mother and behaving like a lover."

TEXT 12

रतिरुवाच
भवान्नारायणसुतः शम्बरेण हृतो गृहात् ।
अहं तेऽधिकृता पत्नी रतिः कामो भवान् प्रभो ॥१२॥

ratir uvāca
bhavān nārāyaṇa-sutaḥ
śambareṇa hṛto gṛhāt
ahaṁ te 'dhikṛtā patnī
ratiḥ kāmo bhavān prabho

ratiḥ uvāca—Rati said; *bhavān*—You; *nārāyaṇa-sutaḥ*—the son of Lord Nārāyaṇa; *śambareṇa*—by Śambara; *hṛtaḥ*—stolen; *gṛhāt*—from Your home; *aham*—I; *te*—Your; *adhikṛtā*—legitimate; *patnī*—wife; *ratiḥ*—Rati; *kāmaḥ*—Cupid; *bhavān*—You; *prabho*—O master.

TRANSLATION

Rati said: You are the son of Lord Nārāyaṇa and were kidnapped from Your parents' home by Śambara. I, Rati, am Your legitimate wife, O master, because You are Cupid.

TEXT 13

एष त्वानिर्दशं सिन्धावक्षिपच्छम्बरोऽसुरः ।
मत्स्योऽग्रसीत्तदुदरादितः प्राप्तो भवान् प्रभो ॥१३॥

eṣa tvānirdaśaṁ sindhāv
akṣipac chambaro 'suraḥ
matsyo 'grasīt tad-udarād
itaḥ prāpto bhavān prabho

eṣaḥ—he; *tvā*—You; *aniḥ-daśam*—not yet ten days old; *sindhau*—into the sea; *akṣipat*—threw; *śambaraḥ*—Śambara; *asuraḥ*—the demon; *matsyaḥ*—a fish; *agrasīt*—devoured; *tat*—its; *udarāt*—from the belly; *itaḥ*—here; *prāptaḥ*—obtained; *bhavān*—You; *prabho*—O master.

TRANSLATION

That demon, Śambara, threw You into the sea when You were not even ten days old, and a fish swallowed You. Then in this very place we recovered You from the fish's abdomen, O master.

TEXT 14

तमिमं जहि दुर्धर्षं दुर्जयं शत्रुमात्मनः ।
मायाशतविदं तं च मायाभिर्मोहनादिभिः ॥१४॥

tam imaṁ jahi durdharṣaṁ
durjayaṁ śatrum ātmanaḥ
māyā-śata-vidaṁ taṁ ca
māyābhir mohanādibhiḥ

tam imam—him; *jahi*—please kill; *durdharṣam*—who is difficult to approach; *durjayam*—and difficult to conquer; *śatrum*—enemy; *ātmanaḥ*—Your own; *māyā*—magic spells; *śata*—hundreds; *vidam*—who knows; *tam*—him; *ca*—and; *māyābhiḥ*—by magic spells; *mohana-ādibhiḥ*—of bewilderment and so on.

TRANSLATION

Now kill this dreadful Śambara, Your formidable enemy. Although he knows hundreds of magic spells, You can defeat him with bewildering magic and other techniques.

TEXT 15

परिशोचति ते माता कुररीव गतप्रजा ।
पुत्रस्नेहाकुला दीना विवत्सा गौरिवातुरा ॥१५॥

pariśocati te mātā
kurarīva gata-prajā
putra-snehākulā dīnā
vivatsā gaur ivāturā

pariśocati—is crying; *te*—Your; *mātā*—mother (Rukmiṇī); *kurarī iva*—like an osprey; *gata*—gone; *prajā*—whose son; *putra*—for her child; *sneha*—by love; *ākulā*—overwhelmed; *dīnā*—pitiful; *vivatsā*—deprived of its calf; *gauḥ*—a cow; *iva*—as; *āturā*—extremely distressed.

TRANSLATION

Your poor mother, having lost her son, cries for You like a *kurarī* bird. She is overwhelmed with love for her child, just like a cow that has lost its calf.

TEXT 16

प्रभाष्यैवं ददौ विद्यां प्रद्युम्नाय महात्मने ।
मायावती महामायां सर्वमायाविनाशिनीम् ॥१६॥

prabhāṣyaivaṁ dadau vidyāṁ
pradyumnāya mahātmane
māyāvatī mahā-māyāṁ
sarva-māyā-vināśinīm

prabhāṣya—speaking; *evam*—thus; *dadau*—gave; *vidyām*—mystic knowledge; *pradyumnāya*—to Pradyumna; *mahā-ātmane*—the great soul; *māyāvatī*—Māyāvatī; *mahā-māyām*—known as Mahā-māyā; *sarva*—all; *māyā*—deluding spells; *vināśinīm*—which destroys.

TRANSLATION

[Śukadeva Gosvāmī continued:] Speaking thus, Māyāvatī gave to the great soul Pradyumna the mystic knowledge called Mahā-māyā, which vanquishes all other deluding spells.

TEXT 17

स च शम्बरमभ्येत्य संयुगाय समाह्वयत् ।
अविषह्यैस्तमाक्षेपैः क्षिपन् सञ्जनयन् कलिम् ॥१७॥

sa ca śambaram abhyetya
saṁyugāya samāhvayat
aviṣahyais tam ākṣepaiḥ
kṣipan sañjanayan kalim

saḥ—He; *ca*—and; *śambaram*—Śambara; *abhyetya*—approaching; *saṁyugāya*—to battle; *samāhvayat*—called him; *aviṣahyaiḥ*—intolerable; *tam*—him; *ākṣepaiḥ*—with insults; *kṣipan*—reviling; *sañjanayan*—inciting; *kalim*—a fight.

TRANSLATION

Pradyumna approached Śambara and called him to battle, hurling intolerable insults at him to foment a conflict.

TEXT 18

सोऽधिक्षिप्तो दुर्वाचोभिः पदाहत इवोरगः ।
निश्चक्राम गदापाणिरमर्षात्ताम्रलोचनः ॥१८॥

so 'dhikṣipto durvācobhiḥ
padāhata ivoragaḥ
niścakrāma gadā-pāṇir
amarṣāt tāmra-locanaḥ

saḥ—he, Śambara; *adhikṣiptaḥ*—insulted; *durvācobhiḥ*—by harsh words; *padā*—by a foot; *āhataḥ*—struck; *iva*—like; *uragaḥ*—a snake; *niścakrāma*—came out; *gadā*—a club; *pāṇiḥ*—in his hand; *amarṣāt*—out of intolerant anger; *tāmra*—copper-red; *locanaḥ*—whose eyes.

TRANSLATION

Offended by these harsh words, Śambara became as agitated as a kicked snake. He came out, club in hand, his eyes red with rage.

TEXT 19

गदामाविध्य तरसा प्रद्युम्नाय महात्मने ।
प्रक्षिप्य व्यनदन्नादं वज्रनिष्पेषनिष्ठुरम् ॥१९॥

gadām āvidhya tarasā
pradyumnāya mahātmane
prakṣipya vyanadan nādaṁ
vajra-niṣpeṣa-niṣṭhuram

gadām—his club; *āvidhya*—whirling; *tarasā*—swiftly; *pradyumnāya*—at Pradyumna; *mahā-ātmane*—the wise; *prakṣipya*—threw; *vyanadan nādam*—creating a resonance; *vajra*—of lightning; *niṣpeṣa*—the striking; *niṣṭhuram*—as sharp.

TRANSLATION

Śambara whirled his club swiftly about and then hurled it at the wise Pradyumna, producing a sound as sharp as a thunder crack.

TEXT 20

तामापतन्तीं भगवान् प्रद्युम्नो गदया गदाम् ।
अपास्य शत्रवे क्रुद्धः प्राहिणोत्स्वगदां नृप ॥२०॥

tām āpatantīṁ bhagavān
pradyumno gadayā gadām
apāsya śatrave kruddhaḥ
prāhiṇot sva-gadāṁ nṛpa

tām—that; *āpatantīm*—flying toward Him; *bhagavān*—the Supreme Lord; *pradyumnaḥ*—Pradyumna; *gadayā*—with His club; *gadām*—the club; *apāsya*—driving off; *śatrave*—at His enemy; *kruddhaḥ*—angered; *prāhiṇot*—He threw; *sva-gadām*—His own club; *nṛpa*—O King (Parīkṣit).

TRANSLATION

As Śambara's club came flying toward Him, Lord Pradyumna knocked it away with His own. Then, O King, Pradyumna angrily threw His club at the enemy.

TEXT 21

स च मायां समाश्रित्य दैतेयीं मयदर्शितम् ।
मुमुचेऽस्त्रमयं वर्षं कार्ष्णौ वैहायसोऽसुरः ॥२१॥

sa ca māyāṁ samāśritya
daiteyīṁ maya-darśitam
mumuce 'stra-mayaṁ varṣaṁ
kārṣṇau vaihāyaso 'suraḥ

saḥ—he, Śambara; *ca*—and; *māyām*—magic; *samāśritya*—resorting to; *daiteyīm*—demoniac; *maya*—by Maya Dānava; *darśitam*—shown;

mumuce—he released; *astra-mayam*—of weapons; *varṣam*—a rainfall; *kārṣṇau*—upon the son of Kṛṣṇa; *vaihāyasaḥ*—standing in the sky; *asuraḥ*—the demon.

TRANSLATION

Resorting to the black magic of the Daityas taught to him by Maya Dānava, Śambara suddenly appeared in the sky and released a downpour of weapons upon Kṛṣṇa's son.

TEXT 22

बाध्यमानोऽस्त्रवर्षेण रौक्मिणेयो महारथः ।
सत्त्वात्मिकां महाविद्यां सर्वमायोपमर्दिनीम् ॥२२॥

bādhyamāno 'stra-varṣeṇa
raukmiṇeyo mahā-rathaḥ
sattvātmikāṁ mahā-vidyāṁ
sarva-māyopamardinīm

bādhyamānaḥ—harassed; *astra*—of weapons; *varṣeṇa*—by the rain; *raukmiṇeyaḥ*—Pradyumna, son of Rukmiṇī; *mahā-rathaḥ*—the powerful warrior; *sattva-ātmikām*—produced of the mode of goodness; *mahā-vidyām*—(He utilized) the mystic knowledge called Mahā-māyā; *sarva*—all; *māyā*—magic; *upamardinīm*—which overcomes.

TRANSLATION

Harassed by this rain of weapons, Lord Raukmiṇeya, the greatly powerful warrior, made use of the mystic science called Mahā-māyā, which was created from the mode of goodness and which could defeat all other mystic power.

TEXT 23

ततो गौह्यकगान्धर्वपैशाचोरगराक्षसीः ।
प्रायुंक्त शतशो दैत्यः कार्ष्णिर्व्यधमयत्स ताः ॥२३॥

tato gauhyaka-gāndharva-
paiśācoraga-rākṣasīḥ
prāyuṅkta śataśo daityaḥ
kārṣṇir vyadhamayat sa tāḥ

tataḥ—then; *gauhyaka-gāndharva-paiśāca-uraga-rākṣasīḥ*—(weapons) of the Guhyakas, Gandharvas, witches, celestial serpents and Rākṣasas (man-eaters); *prāyuṅkta*—he used; *śataśaḥ*—hundreds; *daityaḥ*—the demon; *kārṣṇiḥ*—Lord Pradyumna; *vyadhamayat*—struck down; *saḥ*—He; *tāḥ*—these.

TRANSLATION

The demon then unleashed hundreds of mystic weapons belonging to the Guhyakas, Gandharvas, Piśācas, Uragas and Rākṣasas, but Lord Kārṣṇi, Pradyumna, struck them all down.

TEXT 24

निशातमसिमुद्यम्य सकिरीटं सकुण्डलम् ।
शम्बरस्य शिरः कायात्ताम्रश्मश्र्वोजसाहरत् ॥२४॥

niśātam asim udyamya
sa-kirīṭaṁ sa-kuṇḍalam
śambarasya śiraḥ kāyāt
tāmra-śmaśrv ojasāharat

niśātam—sharp-edged; *asim*—His sword; *udyamya*—raising; *sa*—with; *kirīṭam*—helmet; *sa*—with; *kuṇḍalam*—earrings; *śambarasya*—of Śambara; *śiraḥ*—the head; *kāyāt*—from his body; *tāmra*—copper-colored; *śmaśru*—whose mustache; *ojasā*—with force; *aharat*—He removed.

TRANSLATION

Drawing His sharp-edged sword, Pradyumna forcefully cut off Śambara's head, complete with red mustache, helmet and earrings.

TEXT 25

आकीर्यमाणो दिविजैः स्तुवद्भिः कुसुमोत्करैः ।
भार्ययाम्बरचारिण्या पुरं नीतो विहायसा ॥२५॥

ākīryamāṇo divi-jaiḥ
stuvadbhiḥ kusumotkaraiḥ
bhāryayāmbara-cāriṇyā
puraṁ nīto vihāyasā

ākīryamāṇaḥ—being showered; *divi-jaiḥ*—by the residents of heaven; *stuvadbhiḥ*—who were offering praise; *kusuma*—of flowers; *utkaraiḥ*—with the scattering; *bhāryayā*—by His wife; *ambara*—in the sky; *cāriṇyā*—who was traveling; *puram*—to the city (Dvārakā); *nītaḥ*—He was brought; *vihāyasā*—through the sky.

TRANSLATION

As the residents of the higher planets showered Pradyumna with flowers and chanted His praises, His wife appeared in the sky and transported Him through the heavens, back to the city of Dvārakā.

TEXT 26

अन्तःपुरवरं राजन् ललनाशतसंकुलम् ।
विवेश पत्न्या गगनाद्विद्युतेव बलाहकः ॥२६॥

antaḥ-pura-varaṁ rājan
lalanā-śata-saṅkulam
viveśa patnyā gaganād
vidyuteva balāhakaḥ

antaḥ-pura—the inner palace; *varam*—most excellent; *rājan*—O King (Parīkṣit); *lalanā*—lovely women; *śata*—with hundreds; *saṅkulam*—crowded; *viveśa*—He entered; *patnyā*—with His wife; *gaganāt*—from the sky; *vidyutā*—with lightning; *iva*—as; *balāhakaḥ*—a cloud.

TRANSLATION

O King, Lord Pradyumna and His wife resembled a cloud accompanied by lightning as they descended from the sky into the inner quarters of Kṛṣṇa's most excellent palace, which were crowded with lovely women.

TEXTS 27–28

तं दृष्ट्वा जलदश्यामं पीतकौशेयवाससम् ।
प्रलम्बबाहुं ताम्राक्षं सुस्मितं रुचिराननम् ॥२७॥
स्वलंकृतमुखाम्भोजं नीलवक्रालकालिभिः ।
कृष्णं मत्वा स्त्रियो ह्रीता निलिल्युस्तत्र तत्र ह ॥२८॥

taṁ dṛṣṭvā jalada-śyāmaṁ
pīta-kauśeya-vāsasam
pralamba-bāhuṁ tāmrākṣaṁ
su-smitaṁ rucirānanam

sv-alaṅkṛta-mukhāmbhojaṁ
nīla-vakrālakālibhiḥ
kṛṣṇaṁ matvā striyo hrītā
nililyus tatra tatra ha

tam—Him; *dṛṣṭvā*—seeing; *jala-da*—like a cloud; *śyāmam*—of dark blue complexion; *pīta*—yellow; *kauśeya*—silk; *vāsasam*—whose dress; *pralamba*—long; *bāhum*—whose arms; *tāmra*—reddish; *akṣam*—whose eyes; *su-smitam*—with a pleasing smile; *rucira*—charming; *ānanam*—face; *su-alaṅkṛta*—nicely decorated; *mukha*—face; *ambhojam*—lotus-like; *nīla*—blue; *vakra*—curling; *ālaka-ālibhiḥ*—with locks of hair; *kṛṣṇam*—Kṛṣṇa; *matvā*—thinking Him; *striyaḥ*—the women; *hrītāḥ*—becoming bashful; *nililyuḥ*—hid themselves; *tatra tatra*—here and there; *ha*—indeed.

TRANSLATION

The women of the palace thought He was Lord Kṛṣṇa when they saw His dark-blue complexion the color of a rain cloud, His

yellow silk garments, His long arms and red-tinged eyes, His charming lotus face adorned with a pleasing smile, His fine ornaments and His thick, curly blue hair. Thus the women became bashful and hid themselves here and there.

TEXT 29

अवधार्य शनैरीषद्वैलक्षण्येन योषितः ।
उपजग्मुः प्रमुदिताः सस्त्रीरत्नं सुविस्मिताः ॥२९॥

avadhārya śanair īṣad
vailakṣaṇyena yoṣitaḥ
upajagmuḥ pramuditāḥ
sa-strī-ratnaṁ su-vismitāḥ

avadhārya—realizing; *śanaiḥ*—gradually; *īṣat*—slight; *vailakṣaṇyena*—by the difference of appearance; *yoṣitaḥ*—the ladies; *upajagmuḥ*—they came near; *pramuditāḥ*—delighted; *sa*—together with; *strī*—of women; *ratnam*—the jewel; *su-vismitāḥ*—very surprised.

TRANSLATION

Gradually, from the slight differences between His appearance and Kṛṣṇa's, the ladies realized He was not the Lord. Delighted and astonished, they approached Pradyumna and His consort, who was a jewel among women.

TEXT 30

अथ तत्रासितापांगी वैदर्भी वल्गुभाषिणी ।
अस्मरत्स्वसुतं नष्टं स्नेहस्नुतपयोधरा ॥३०॥

atha tatrāsitāpāṅgī
vaidarbhī valgu-bhāṣiṇī
asmarat sva-sutaṁ naṣṭaṁ
sneha-snuta-payodharā

atha—then; *tatra*—there; *asita*—black; *apāṅgī*—the corners of whose eyes; *vaidarbhī*—Queen Rukmiṇī; *valgu*—sweet; *bhāṣiṇī*—whose speaking; *asmarat*—remembered; *sva-sutam*—her son; *naṣṭam*—lost; *sneha*—out of love; *snuta*—having become moist; *payaḥ-dharā*—whose breasts.

TRANSLATION

Seeing Pradyumna, sweet-voiced, dark-eyed Rukmiṇī remembered her lost son, and her breasts became moist out of affection.

TEXT 31

को न्वयं नरवैदूर्यः कस्य वा कमलेक्षणः ।
धृतः कया वा जठरे केयं लब्धा त्वनेन वा ॥३१॥

ko nv ayaṁ nara-vaidūryaḥ
kasya vā kamalekṣaṇaḥ
dhṛtaḥ kayā vā jaṭhare
keyaṁ labdhā tv anena vā

kaḥ—who; *nu*—indeed; *ayam*—this; *nara-vaidūryaḥ*—gem among men; *kasya*—whose (son); *vā*—and; *kamala-īkṣaṇaḥ*—lotus-eyed; *dhṛtaḥ*—carried; *kayā*—by what woman; *vā*—and; *jaṭhare*—in her womb; *kā*—who; *iyam*—this woman; *labdhā*—obtained; *tu*—moreover; *anena*—by Him; *vā*—and.

TRANSLATION

[Śrīmatī Rukmiṇī-devī said:] Who is this lotus-eyed jewel among men? What man's son is He, and what woman carried Him in her womb? And who is this woman He has taken as His wife?

TEXT 32

मम चाप्यात्मजो नष्टो नीतो यः सूतिकागृहात् ।
एतत्तुल्यवयोरूपो यदि जीवति कुत्रचित् ॥३२॥

mama cāpy ātmajo naṣṭo
nīto yaḥ sūtikā-gṛhāt
etat-tulya-vayo-rūpo
yadi jīvati kutracit

mama—my; *ca*—and; *api*—also; *ātmajaḥ*—son; *naṣṭaḥ*—lost; *nītaḥ*—taken; *yaḥ*—who; *sūtikā-gṛhāt*—from the maternity room; *etat*—to Him; *tulya*—equal; *vayaḥ*—in age; *rūpaḥ*—and appearance; *yadi*—if; *jīvati*—He is living; *kutracit*—somewhere.

TRANSLATION

If my lost son, who was kidnapped from the maternity room, were still alive somewhere, He would be of the same age and appearance as this young man.

TEXT 33

कथं त्वनेन सम्प्राप्तं सारूप्यं शार्ङ्गधन्वनः ।
आकृत्यावयवैर्गत्या स्वरहासावलोकनैः ॥३३॥

kathaṁ tv anena samprāptaṁ
sārūpyaṁ śārṅga-dhanvanaḥ
ākṛtyāvayavair gatyā
svara-hāsāvalokanaiḥ

katham—how; *tu*—but; *anena*—by Him; *samprāptam*—obtained; *sārūpyam*—the same appearance; *śārṅga-dhanvanaḥ*—as Kṛṣṇa, the wielder of the Śārṅga bow; *ākṛtyā*—in bodily form; *avayavaiḥ*—limbs; *gatyā*—gait; *svara*—tone of voice; *hāsa*—smile; *avalokanaiḥ*—and glance.

TRANSLATION

But how is it that this young man so much resembles my own Lord, Kṛṣṇa, the wielder of Śārṅga, in His bodily form and His limbs, in His gait and the tone of His voice, and in His smiling glance?

TEXT 34

स एव वा भवेन्नूनं यो मे गर्भे धृतोऽर्भकः ।
अमुष्मिन् प्रीतिरधिका वामः स्फुरति मे भुजः ॥३४॥

sa eva vā bhaven nūnaṁ
yo me garbhe dhṛto 'rbhakaḥ
amuṣmin prītir adhikā
vāmaḥ sphurati me bhujaḥ

saḥ—He; *eva*—indeed; *vā*—or else; *bhavet*—must be; *nūnam*—for certain; *yaḥ*—who; *me*—my; *garbhe*—in the womb; *dhṛtaḥ*—was carried; *arbhakaḥ*—child; *amuṣmin*—for Him; *prītiḥ*—affection; *adhikā*—great; *vāmaḥ*—left; *sphurati*—trembles; *me*—my; *bhujaḥ*—arm.

TRANSLATION

Yes, He must be the same child I bore in my womb, since I feel great affection for Him and my left arm is quivering.

TEXT 35

एवं मीमांसमानायां वैदर्भ्यां देवकीसुतः ।
देवक्यानकदुन्दुभ्यामुत्तमःश्लोक आगमत् ॥३५॥

evaṁ mīmāṁsamānāyāṁ
vaidarbhyāṁ devakī-sutaḥ
devaky-ānakadundubhyām
uttamaḥ-śloka āgamat

evam—thus; *mīmāṁsamānāyām*—as she was conjecturing; *vaidarbhyām*—Queen Rukmiṇī; *devakī-sutaḥ*—the son of Devakī; *devakī-ānakadundubhyām*—together with Devakī and Vasudeva; *uttamaḥ-ślokaḥ*—Lord Kṛṣṇa; *āgamat*—came there.

TRANSLATION

As Queen Rukmiṇī conjectured in this way, Lord Kṛṣṇa, the son of Devakī, arrived on the scene with Vasudeva and Devakī.

TEXT 36

विज्ञातार्थोऽपि भगवांस्तूष्णीमास जनार्दनः ।
नारदोऽकथयत्सर्वं शम्बराहरणादिकम् ॥३६॥

vijñātārtho 'pi bhagavāṁs
tūṣṇīm āsa janārdanaḥ
nārado 'kathayat sarvaṁ
śambarāharaṇādikam

vijñāta—understanding fully; *arthaḥ*—the matter; *api*—even though; *bhagavān*—the Supreme Personality of Godhead; *tūṣṇīm*—silent; *āsa*—remained; *janārdanaḥ*—Kṛṣṇa; *nāradaḥ*—Nārada Muni; *akathayat*—recounted; *sarvam*—everything; *śambara*—by Śambara; *āharaṇa*—the kidnapping; *ādikam*—beginning with.

TRANSLATION

Although Lord Janārdana knew perfectly well what had transpired, He remained silent. The sage Nārada, however, explained everything, beginning with Śambara's kidnapping of the child.

TEXT 37

तच्छ्रुत्वा महदाश्चर्यं कृष्णान्तःपुरयोषितः ।
अभ्यनन्दन् बहूनब्दान्नष्टं मृतमिवागतम् ॥३७॥

tac chrutvā mahad āścaryaṁ
kṛṣṇāntaḥ-pura-yoṣitaḥ
abhyanandan bahūn abdān
naṣṭaṁ mṛtam ivāgatam

tat—that; *śrutvā*—hearing; *mahat*—great; *āścaryam*—wonder; *kṛṣṇa-antaḥ-pura*—of Lord Kṛṣṇa's personal residence; *yoṣitaḥ*—the women; *abhyanandan*—they greeted; *bahūn*—for many; *abdān*—years; *naṣṭam*—lost; *mṛtam*—someone dead; *iva*—as if; *āgatam*—returned.

TRANSLATION

When the women of Lord Kṛṣṇa's palace heard this most amazing account, they joyfully greeted Pradyumna, who had been lost for many years but who had now returned as if from the dead.

TEXT 38

देवकी वसुदेवश्च कृष्णरामौ तथा स्त्रियः ।
दम्पती तौ परिष्वज्य रुक्मिणी च ययुर्मुदम् ॥३८॥

devakī vasudevaś ca
kṛṣṇa-rāmau tathā striyaḥ
dampatī tau pariṣvajya
rukmiṇī ca yayur mudam

devakī—Devakī; *vasudevaḥ*—Vasudeva; *ca*—and; *kṛṣṇa-rāmau*—Kṛṣṇa and Balarāma; *tathā*—also; *striyaḥ*—the women; *dam-patī*—man and wife; *tau*—these two; *pariṣvajya*—embracing; *rukmiṇī*—Rukmiṇī; *ca*—and; *yayuḥ mudam*—they became full of joy.

TRANSLATION

Devakī, Vasudeva, Kṛṣṇa, Balarāma and all the women of the palace, especially Queen Rukmiṇī, embraced the young couple and rejoiced.

TEXT 39

नष्टं प्रद्युम्नमायातमाकर्ण्य द्वारकौकसः ।
अहो मृत इवायातो बालो दिष्टचेति हाब्रुवन् ॥३९॥

naṣṭaṁ pradyumnam āyātam
ākarṇya dvārakaukasaḥ
aho mṛta ivāyāto
bālo diṣṭyeti hābruvan

naṣṭam—lost; *pradyumnam*—Pradyumna; *āyātam*—returned; *ākarṇya*—hearing; *dvārakā-okasaḥ*—the residents of Dvārakā; *aho*—ah; *mṛtaḥ*—dead; *iva*—as if; *āyātaḥ*—come back; *bālaḥ*—the child; *diṣṭyā*—by the favor of providence; *iti*—thus; *ha*—indeed; *abruvan*—they spoke.

TRANSLATION

Hearing that lost Pradyumna had come home, the residents of Dvārakā declared, "Ah, providence has allowed this child to return as if from death!"

TEXT 40

यं वै मुहुः पितृसरूपनिजेशभावास्
तन्मातरो यदभजन् रहरूढभावाः ।
चित्रं न तत्खलु रमास्पदबिम्बबिम्बे
कामे स्मरेऽक्षविषये किमुतान्यनार्यः ॥४०॥

yaṁ vai muhuḥ pitṛ-sarūpa-nijeśa-bhāvās
tan-mātaro yad abhajan raha-rūḍha-bhāvāḥ
citraṁ na tat khalu ramāspada-bimba-bimbe
kāme smare 'kṣa-viṣaye kim utānya-nāryaḥ

yam—whom; *vai*—indeed; *muhuḥ*—repeatedly; *pitṛ*—His father; *sarūpa*—who exactly resembled; *nija*—as their own; *īśa*—master; *bhāvāḥ*—who thought of Him; *tat*—His; *mātaraḥ*—mothers; *yat*—inasmuch as; *abhajan*—they worshiped; *raha*—in privacy; *rūḍha*—full-blown; *bhāvāḥ*—whose ecstatic attraction; *citram*—amazing; *na*—not; *tat*—that; *khalu*—indeed; *ramā*—of the goddess of fortune; *āspada*—of the shelter (Lord Kṛṣṇa); *bimba*—of the form; *bimbe*—who was the reflection; *kāme*—lust personified; *smare*—Cupid; *akṣa-viṣaye*—when He was before their eyes; *kim uta*—what then to speak of; *anya*—other; *nāryaḥ*—women.

TRANSLATION

It is not astonishing that the palace women, who should have felt maternal affection for Pradyumna, privately felt ecstatic attraction for Him as if He were their own Lord. After all, the son

exactly resembled His father. Indeed, Pradyumna was a perfect reflection of the beauty of Lord Kṛṣṇa, the shelter of the goddess of fortune, and appeared before their eyes as Cupid Himself. Since even those on the level of His mother felt conjugal attraction for Him, then what to speak of how other women felt when they saw Him?

PURPORT

As Śrīla Viśvanātha Cakravartī explains, whenever the palace women saw Śrī Pradyumna, they immediately remembered their Lord, Śrī Kṛṣṇa. Śrīla Prabhupāda comments as follows in *Kṛṣṇa, the Supreme Personality of Godhead:* "Śrīla Śukadeva Gosvāmī has explained that in the beginning all the residents of the palace, who were all mothers and stepmothers of Pradyumna, mistook Him to be Kṛṣṇa and were all bashful, infected by the desire for conjugal love. The explanation is that Pradyumna's personal appearance was exactly like Kṛṣṇa's, and He was factually Cupid Himself. There was no cause of astonishment, therefore, when the mothers of Pradyumna and other women mistook Him in that way. It is clear from the statement that Pradyumna's bodily characteristics were so similar to Kṛṣṇa's that He was mistaken to be Kṛṣṇa even by His mother."

Thus end the purports of the humble servants of His Divine Grace A. C. Bhaktivedanta Swami Prabhupāda to the Tenth Canto, Fifty-fifth Chapter, of the Śrīmad-Bhāgavatam, *entitled "The History of Pradyumna."*

CHAPTER FIFTY–SIX

The Syamantaka Jewel

This chapter describes how Lord Kṛṣṇa recovered the Syamantaka jewel to allay false accusations against Him and married the daughters of Jāmbavān and Satrājit. By enacting the pastime involving the Syamantaka jewel, the Lord demonstrated the futility of material wealth.

When Śukadeva Gosvāmī mentioned that King Satrājit offended Lord Kṛṣṇa on account of the Syamantaka jewel, King Parīkṣit became curious to hear the details of this incident. Thus Śukadeva Gosvāmī narrated the story.

King Satrājit received the Syamantaka gem by the grace of his best well-wisher, the sun-god, Sūrya. After fastening the gem to a chain, which he then hung around his neck, Satrājit traveled to Dvārakā. The residents, thinking he was the sun-god himself, went to Kṛṣṇa and told Him that Lord Sūrya had come to take His audience. But Kṛṣṇa replied that the man who had come was not Sūrya but King Satrājit, who looked extremely effulgent because he was wearing the Syamantaka jewel.

In Dvārakā Satrājit installed the precious stone on a special altar in his home. Every day the gem produced a large quantity of gold, and it had the additional power of assuring that wherever it was properly worshiped no calamity could occur.

On one occasion Lord Śrī Kṛṣṇa requested Satrājit to give the gem to the King of the Yadus, Ugrasena. But Satrājit refused, obsessed as he was with greed. Shortly thereafter Satrājit's brother Prasena left the city to hunt on horseback, wearing the Syamantaka jewel on his neck. On the road a lion killed Prasena and took the jewel away to a mountain cave, where the king of the bears, Jāmbavān, happened to be living. Jāmbavān killed the lion and gave the jewel to his son to play with.

When King Satrājit's brother did not return, the King presumed that Śrī Kṛṣṇa had killed him for the Syamantaka gem. Lord Kṛṣṇa heard about this rumor circulating among the general populace, and to clear His name He went with some of the citizens to find Prasena. Following his path, they eventually found his body and that of his horse lying on the road. Further on they saw the body of the lion Jāmbavān had killed. Lord Kṛṣṇa told the citizens to remain outside the cave while He went in to investigate.

The Lord entered Jāmbavān's cave and saw the Syamantaka jewel lying next to a child. But when Kṛṣṇa tried to take the jewel, the child's nurse cried out in alarm, bringing Jāmbavān quickly to the scene. Jāmbavān considered Kṛṣṇa an ordinary man and began fighting with Him. For twenty-eight days continuously the two fought, until finally Jāmbavān grew weak from the Lord's blows. Now understanding that Kṛṣṇa was the Supreme Personality of Godhead, Jāmbavān began to praise Him. The Lord touched Jāmbavān with His lotus hand, dispelling his fear, and then explained everything about the jewel. With great devotion Jāmbavān gladly presented the Syamantaka jewel to the Lord, together with his unmarried daughter, Jāmbavatī.

Meanwhile Lord Kṛṣṇa's companions, having waited twelve days for Kṛṣṇa to come out of the cave, returned to Dvārakā despondent. All of Kṛṣṇa's friends and family members became extremely sorrowful and began regularly worshiping Goddess Durgā to assure the Lord's safe return. Even as they performed this worship, Lord Kṛṣṇa entered the city in the company of His new wife. He summoned Satrājit to the royal assembly and, after recounting to him the entire story of the Syamantaka jewel's recovery, gave the jewel back to him. Satrājit accepted the jewel, but with great shame and remorse. He went back to his home, and there he decided to offer Lord Kṛṣṇa not only the jewel but also his daughter so as to atone for the offense he had committed against the Lord's lotus feet. Śrī Kṛṣṇa accepted the hand of Satrājit's daughter, Satyabhāmā, who was endowed with all divine qualities. But the jewel He refused, returning it to King Satrājit.

TEXT 1

श्रीशुक उवाच
सत्राजितः स्वतनयां कृष्णाय कृतकिल्बिषः ।
स्यमन्तकेन मणिना स्वयमुद्यम्य दत्तवान् ॥१॥

śrī-śuka uvāca
satrājitaḥ sva-tanayāṁ
kṛṣṇāya kṛta-kilbiṣaḥ

syamantakena maṇinā
svayam udyamya dattavān

śrī-śukaḥ uvāca—Śukadeva Gosvāmī said; *satrājitaḥ*—King Satrājit; *sva*—his own; *tanayām*—daughter; *kṛṣṇāya*—to Lord Kṛṣṇa; *kṛta*—having committed; *kilbiṣaḥ*—offense; *syamantakena*—known as Syamantaka; *maṇinā*—together with the jewel; *svayam*—personally; *udyamya*—striving; *dattavān*—he gave.

TRANSLATION

Śukadeva Gosvāmī said: Having offended Lord Kṛṣṇa, Satrājit tried as best he could to atone by presenting Him with his daughter and the Syamantaka jewel.

TEXT 2

श्रीराजोवाच
सत्राजितः किमकरोद् ब्रह्मन् कृष्णस्य किल्बिषः ।
स्यमन्तकः कुतस्तस्य कस्माद्दत्ता सुता हरेः ॥२॥

śrī-rājovāca
satrājitaḥ kim akarod
brahman kṛṣṇasya kilbiṣaḥ
syamantakaḥ kutas tasya
kasmād dattā sutā hareḥ

śrī-rājā—the King (Parīkṣit Mahārāja); *uvāca*—said; *satrājitaḥ*—Satrājit; *kim*—what; *akarot*—committed; *brahman*—O *brāhmaṇa; kṛṣṇasya*—against Lord Kṛṣṇa; *kilbiṣaḥ*—offense; *syamantakaḥ*—the Syamantaka jewel; *kutaḥ*—from where; *tasya*—his; *kasmāt*—why; *dattā*—given; *sutā*—his daughter; *hareḥ*—to Lord Hari.

TRANSLATION

Mahārāja Parīkṣit inquired: O *brāhmaṇa*, what did King Satrājit do to offend Lord Kṛṣṇa? Where did he get the Syamantaka jewel, and why did he give his daughter to the Supreme Lord?

TEXT 3

श्रीशुक उवाच
आसीत्सत्राजितः सूर्यो भक्तस्य परमः सखा ।
प्रीतस्तस्मै मणिं प्रादात्स च तुष्टः स्यमन्तकम् ॥३॥

śrī-śuka uvāca
āsīt satrājitaḥ sūryo
bhaktasya paramaḥ sakhā
prītas tasmai maṇiṁ prādāt
sa ca tuṣṭaḥ syamantakam

śrī-śukaḥ uvāca—Śukadeva Gosvāmī said; *āsīt*—was; *satrājitaḥ*—of Satrājit; *sūryaḥ*—the sun-god; *bhaktasya*—who was his devotee; *paramaḥ*—the best; *sakhā*—well-wishing friend; *prītaḥ*—affectionate; *tasmai*—to him; *maṇim*—the jewel; *prādāt*—gave; *saḥ*—he; *ca*—and; *tuṣṭaḥ*—satisfied; *syamantakam*—named Syamantaka.

TRANSLATION

Śukadeva Gosvāmī said: Sūrya, the sun-god, felt great affection for his devotee Satrājit. Acting as his greatest friend, the demigod gave him the jewel called Syamantaka as a token of his satisfaction.

TEXT 4

स तं बिभ्रन्मणिं कण्ठे भ्राजमानो यथा रविः ।
प्रविष्टो द्वारकां राजन् तेजसा नोपलक्षितः ॥४॥

sa taṁ bibhran maṇiṁ kaṇṭhe
bhrājamāno yathā raviḥ
praviṣṭo dvārakāṁ rājan
tejasā nopalakṣitaḥ

saḥ—he, King Satrājit; *tam*—that; *bibhrat*—wearing; *maṇim*—jewel; *kaṇṭhe*—on his neck; *bhrājamānaḥ*—shining brilliantly; *yathā*—like; *raviḥ*—the sun; *praviṣṭaḥ*—having entered; *dvārakām*—the city of Dvārakā; *rājan*—O King (Parīkṣit); *tejasā*—because of the effulgence; *na*—not; *upalakṣitaḥ*—recognized.

TRANSLATION

Wearing the jewel on his neck, Satrājit entered Dvārakā. He shone as brightly as the sun itself, O King, and thus he went unrecognized because of the jewel's effulgence.

TEXT 5

तं विलोक्य जना दूरात् तेजसा मुष्टदृष्टयः ।
दीव्यतेऽक्षैर्भगवते शशंसुः सूर्यशङ्किताः ॥५॥

taṁ vilokya janā dūrāt
tejasā muṣṭa-dṛṣṭayaḥ
dīvyate 'kṣair bhagavate
śaśaṁsuḥ sūrya-śaṅkitāḥ

tam—him; *vilokya*—seeing; *janāḥ*—the people; *dūrāt*—from some distance; *tejasā*—by his effulgence; *muṣṭa*—stolen; *dṛṣṭayaḥ*—their ability to see; *dīvyate*—who was playing; *akṣaiḥ*—with dice; *bhagavate*—to the Supreme Lord, Śrī Kṛṣṇa; *śaśaṁsuḥ*—they reported; *sūrya*—the sun-god; *śaṅkitāḥ*—presuming him.

TRANSLATION

As the people looked at Satrājit from a distance, his brilliance blinded them. They presumed he was the sun-god, Sūrya, and went to tell Lord Kṛṣṇa, who was at that time playing at dice.

TEXT 6

नारायण नमस्तेऽस्तु शंखचक्रगदाधर ।
दामोदरारविन्दाक्ष गोविन्द यदुनन्दन ॥६॥

nārāyaṇa namas te 'stu
śaṅkha-cakra-gadā-dhara
dāmodarāravindākṣa
govinda yadu-nandana

nārāyaṇa—O Lord Nārāyaṇa; *namaḥ*—obeisances; *te*—unto; *astu*—may there be; *śaṅkha*—of the conchshell; *cakra*—disc; *gadā*—and club; *dhara*—O holder; *dāmodara*—O Lord Dāmodara; *aravinda-akṣa*—O lotus-eyed one; *govinda*—O Lord Govinda; *yadu-nandana*—O darling son of the Yadus.

TRANSLATION

[The residents of Dvārakā said:] Obeisances unto You, O Nārāyaṇa, O holder of the conch, disc and club, O lotus-eyed Dāmodara, O Govinda, O cherished descendant of Yadu!

TEXT 7

एष आयाति सविता त्वां दिदृक्षुर्जगत्पते ।
मुष्णन् गभस्तिचक्रेण नृणां चक्षूंषि तिग्मगु: ॥७॥

eṣa āyāti savitā
tvāṁ didṛkṣur jagat-pate
muṣṇan gabhasti-cakreṇa
nṛṇāṁ cakṣūṁṣi tigma-guḥ

eṣaḥ—this; *āyāti*—comes; *savitā*—the sun-god; *tvām*—You; *didṛkṣuḥ*—wanting to see; *jagat-pate*—O Lord of the universe; *muṣṇan*—stealing; *gabhasti*—of his rays; *cakreṇa*—with the circle; *nṛṇām*—of men; *cakṣūṁṣi*—the eyes; *tigma*—intense; *guḥ*—whose radiation.

TRANSLATION

Lord Savitā has come to see You, O Lord of the universe. He is blinding everyone's eyes with his intensely effulgent rays.

TEXT 8

नन्वन्विच्छन्ति ते मार्गं त्रिलोक्यां विबुधर्षभा: ।
ज्ञात्वाद्य गूढं यदुषु द्रष्टुं त्वां यात्यज: प्रभो ॥८॥

nanv anvicchanti te mārgaṁ
tri-lokyāṁ vibudharṣabhāḥ

jñātvādya gūḍhaṁ yaduṣu
draṣṭuṁ tvāṁ yāty ajaḥ prabho

nanu—certainly; *anvicchanti*—they seek out; *te*—Your; *mārgam*—path; *tri-lokyām*—in all the three worlds; *vibudha*—of the wise demigods; *ṛṣabhāḥ*—the most exalted; *jñātvā*—knowing; *adya*—now; *gūḍham*—disguised; *yaduṣu*—among the Yadus; *draṣṭum*—to see; *tvām*—You; *yāti*—comes; *ajaḥ*—the unborn (sun-god); *prabho*—O Lord.

TRANSLATION

The most exalted demigods in the three worlds are certainly anxious to seek You out, O Lord, now that You have hidden Yourself among the Yadu dynasty. Thus the unborn sun-god has come to see You here.

TEXT 9

श्रीशुक उवाच
निशम्य बालवचनं प्रहस्याम्बुजलोचनः ।
प्राह नासौ रविर्देवः सत्राजिन्मणिना ज्वलन् ॥९॥

śrī-śuka uvāca
niśamya bāla-vacanaṁ
prahasyāmbuja-locanaḥ
prāha nāsau ravir devaḥ
satrājin maṇinā jvalan

śrī-śukaḥ uvāca—Śukadeva Gosvāmī said; *niśamya*—hearing; *bāla*—childish; *vacanam*—these words; *prahasya*—smiling broadly; *ambuja*—lotuslike; *locanaḥ*—He whose eyes; *prāha*—said; *na*—not; *asau*—this person; *raviḥ devaḥ*—the sun-god; *satrājit*—King Satrājit; *maṇinā*—because of his jewel; *jvalan*—glowing.

TRANSLATION

Śukadeva Gosvāmī continued: Hearing these innocent words, the lotus-eyed Lord smiled broadly and said, "This is not the sun-god, Ravi, but rather Satrājit, who is glowing because of his jewel."

TEXT 10

सत्राजित्स्वगृहं श्रीमत्कृतकौतुकमंगलम् ।
प्रविश्य देवसदने मणिं विप्रैर्न्यवेशयत् ॥१०॥

satrājit sva-gṛhaṁ śrīmat
kṛta-kautuka-maṅgalam
praviśya deva-sadane
maṇiṁ viprair nyaveśayat

satrājit—Satrājit; *sva*—his; *gṛham*—home; *śrīmat*—opulent; *kṛta*—(where there were) executed; *kautuka*—with festivity; *maṅgalam*—auspicious rituals; *praviśya*—entering; *deva-sadane*—in the temple room; *maṇim*—the jewel; *vipraiḥ*—by learned *brāhmaṇas; nyaveśayat*—he had installed.

TRANSLATION

King Satrājit entered his opulent home, festively executing auspicious rituals. He had qualified *brāhmaṇas* install the Syamantaka jewel in the house's temple room.

TEXT 11

दिने दिने स्वर्णभारानष्टौ स सृजति प्रभो ।
दुर्भिक्षमार्यरिष्टानि सर्पाधिव्याधयोऽशुभाः ।
न सन्ति मायिनस्तत्र यत्रास्तेऽभ्यर्चितो मणिः ॥११॥

dine dine svarṇa-bhārān
aṣṭau sa sṛjati prabho
durbhikṣa-māry-ariṣṭāni
sarpādhi-vyādhayo 'śubhāḥ
na santi māyinas tatra
yatrāste 'bhyarcito maṇiḥ

dine dine—day after day; *svarṇa*—of gold; *bhārān*—*bhāras* (a measure of weight); *aṣṭau*—eight; *saḥ*—it; *sṛjati*—would produce; *prabho*—O master (Parīkṣit Mahārāja); *durbhikṣa*—famine; *māri*—untimely deaths; *ariṣṭāni*—catastrophes; *sarpa*—snake (bites); *ādhi*—mental disorders; *vyādhayaḥ*—diseases; *aśubhāḥ*—inauspicious; *na santi*—there are none; *māyinaḥ*—cheaters; *tatra*—there; *yatra*—where; *āste*—it is present; *abhyarcitaḥ*—properly worshiped; *maṇiḥ*—the gem.

TRANSLATION

Each day the gem would produce eight *bhāras* of gold, my dear Prabhu, and the place in which it was kept and properly worshiped would be free of calamities such as famine or untimely death, and also of evils like snake bites, mental and physical disorders and the presence of deceitful persons.

PURPORT

Śrīla Śrīdhara Svāmī gives the following śāstric reference concerning the *bhāra:*

caturbhir vrīhibhir guñjāṁ
guñjāḥ pañca paṇaṁ paṇān
aṣṭau dharaṇam aṣṭau ca
karṣaṁ tāṁś caturaḥ palam
tulāṁ pala-śataṁ prāhur
bhāraḥ syād viṁśatis tulāḥ

"Four rice grains are called one *guñjā;* five *guñjās,* one *paṇa;* eight *paṇas,* one *karṣa;* four *karṣas,* one *pala;* and one hundred *palas,* one *tulā.* Twenty *tulās* make up one *bhāra.*" Since there are about 3,700 grains of rice in an ounce, the Syamantaka jewel was producing approximately 170 pounds of gold every day.

TEXT 12

स याचितो मणिं क्वापि यदुराजाय शौरिणा ।
नैवार्थकामुकः प्रादाद्याच्ञाभंगमतर्कयन् ॥१२॥

sa yācito maṇiṁ kvāpi
yadu-rājāya śauriṇā

naivārtha-kāmukaḥ prādād
yācñā-bhaṅgam atarkayan

saḥ—he, Satrājit; *yācitaḥ*—requested; *maṇim*—the gem; *kva api*—on one occasion; *yadu-rājāya*—for the king of the Yadus, Ugrasena; *śauriṇā*—by Lord Kṛṣṇa; *na*—not; *eva*—indeed; *artha*—after wealth; *kāmukaḥ*—greedy; *prādāt*—gave; *yācñā*—of the request; *bhaṅgam*—the transgression; *atarkayan*—not considering.

TRANSLATION

On one occasion Lord Kṛṣṇa requested Satrājit to give the jewel to the Yadu king, Ugrasena, but Satrājit was so greedy that he refused. He gave no thought to the seriousness of the offense he committed by denying the Lord's request.

TEXT 13

तमेकदा मणिं कण्ठे प्रतिमुच्य महाप्रभम् ।
प्रसेनो हयमारुह्य मृगायां व्यचरद्वने ॥१३॥

tam ekadā maṇiṁ kaṇṭhe
pratimucya mahā-prabham
praseno hayam āruhya
mṛgāyāṁ vyacarad vane

tam—that; *ekadā*—once; *maṇim*—the jewel; *kaṇṭhe*—on his neck; *pratimucya*—fixing; *mahā*—greatly; *prabham*—effulgent; *prasenaḥ*—Prasena (the brother of Satrājit); *hayam*—a horse; *āruhya*—mounting; *mṛgāyām*—for hunting; *vyacarat*—went about; *vane*—in the forest.

TRANSLATION

Once Satrājit's brother, Prasena, having hung the brilliant jewel about his neck, mounted a horse and went hunting in the forest.

PURPORT

The inauspicious result of Satrājit's refusal of Lord Kṛṣṇa's request is about to manifest.

TEXT 14

प्रसेनं सहयं हत्वा मणिमाच्छिद्य केशरी ।
गिरिं विशन् जाम्बवता निहतो मणिमिच्छता ॥१४॥

prasenaṁ sa-hayaṁ hatvā
maṇim ācchidya keśarī
giriṁ viśan jāmbavatā
nihato maṇim icchatā

prasenam—Prasena; *sa*—along with; *hayam*—his horse; *hatvā*—killing; *maṇim*—the jewel; *ācchidya*—seizing; *keśarī*—a lion; *girim*—(a cave in) a mountain; *viśan*—entering; *jāmbavatā*—by Jāmbavān, the king of the bears; *nihataḥ*—killed; *maṇim*—the jewel; *icchatā*—who wanted.

TRANSLATION

A lion killed Prasena and his horse and took the jewel. But when the lion entered a mountain cave he was killed by Jāmbavān, who wanted the jewel.

TEXT 15

सोऽपि चक्रे कुमारस्य मणिं क्रीडनकं बिले ।
अपश्यन् भ्रातरं भ्राता सत्राजित्पर्यतप्यत ॥१५॥

so 'pi cakre kumārasya
maṇiṁ krīḍanakaṁ bile
apaśyan bhrātaraṁ bhrātā
satrājit paryatapyata

saḥ—he, Jāmbavān; *api*—moreover; *cakre*—made; *kumārasya*—for his child; *maṇim*—the jewel; *krīḍanakam*—a toy; *bile*—in the cave;

apaśyan—not seeing; *bhrātaram*—his brother; *bhrātā*—the brother; *satrājit*—Satrājit; *paryatapyata*—became deeply troubled.

TRANSLATION

Within the cave Jāmbavān let his young son have the Syamantaka jewel as a toy to play with. Meanwhile Satrājit, not seeing his brother return, became deeply troubled.

TEXT 16

प्रायः कृष्णेन निहतो मणिग्रीवो वनं गतः ।
भ्राता ममेति तच्छ्रुत्वा कर्णे कर्णेऽजपन् जनाः ॥१६॥

prāyaḥ kṛṣṇena nihato
maṇi-grīvo vanaṁ gataḥ
bhrātā mameti tac chrutvā
karṇe karṇe 'japan janāḥ

prāyaḥ—probably; *kṛṣṇena*—by Kṛṣṇa; *nihataḥ*—killed; *maṇi*—the jewel; *grīvaḥ*—wearing on his neck; *vanam*—to the forest; *gataḥ*—gone; *bhrātā*—brother; *mama*—my; *iti*—thus saying; *tat*—that; *śrutvā*—hearing; *karṇe karṇe*—in one another's ears; *ajapan*—whispered; *janāḥ*—the people.

TRANSLATION

He said, "Kṛṣṇa probably killed my brother, who went to the forest wearing the jewel on his neck." The general populace heard this accusation and began whispering it in one another's ears.

TEXT 17

भगवांस्तदुपश्रुत्य दुर्यशो लिप्तमात्मनि ।
मार्ष्टुं प्रसेनपदवीमन्वपद्यत नागरैः ॥१७॥

bhagavāṁs tad upaśrutya
duryaśo liptam ātmani
mārṣṭuṁ prasena-padavīm
anvapadyata nāgaraiḥ

bhagavān—the Supreme Lord, Kṛṣṇa; *tat*—that; *upaśrutya*—coming to hear; *duryaśaḥ*—infamy; *liptam*—smeared; *ātmani*—upon Himself; *mārṣṭum*—in order to clean away; *prasena-padavīm*—the path taken by Prasena; *anvapadyata*—He followed; *nāgaraiḥ*—together with people of the city.

TRANSLATION

When Lord Kṛṣṇa heard this rumor, He wanted to remove the stain on His reputation. So He took some of Dvārakā's citizens with Him and set out to retrace Prasena's path.

TEXT 18

हतं प्रसेनं अश्वं च वीक्ष्य केशरिणा वने ।
तं चाद्रिपृष्ठे निहतमृक्षेण ददृशुर्जनाः ॥१८॥

hataṁ prasenaṁ aśvaṁ ca
vīkṣya keśariṇā vane
taṁ cādri-pṛṣṭhe nihatam
ṛkṣeṇa dadṛśur janāḥ

hatam—killed; *prasenam*—Prasena; *aśvam*—his horse; *ca*—and; *vīkṣya*—seeing; *keśariṇā*—by a lion; *vane*—in the forest; *tam*—that (lion); *ca*—also; *adri*—of a mountain; *pṛṣṭhe*—on the side; *nihatam*—killed; *ṛkṣeṇa*—by Ṛkṣa (Jāmbavān); *dadṛśuḥ*—they saw; *janāḥ*—the people.

TRANSLATION

In the forest they found Prasena and his horse, both killed by the lion. Further on they found the lion dead on a mountainside, slain by Ṛkṣa [Jāmbavān].

TEXT 19

ऋक्षराजबिलं भीममन्धेन तमसावृतम् ।
एको विवेश भगवानवस्थाप्य बहिः प्रजाः ॥१९॥

ṛkṣa-rāja-bilaṁ bhīmam
andhena tamasāvṛtam
eko viveśa bhagavān
avasthāpya bahiḥ prajāḥ

ṛkṣa-rāja—of the king of the bears; *bilam*—the cave; *bhīmam*—terrifying; *andhena tamasā*—by blinding darkness; *āvṛtam*—covered; *ekaḥ*—alone; *viveśa*—entered; *bhagavān*—the Supreme Lord; *avasthāpya*—stationing; *bahiḥ*—outside; *prajāḥ*—the citizens.

TRANSLATION

The Lord stationed His subjects outside the terrifying, pitch-dark cave of the king of the bears, and then He entered alone.

TEXT 20

तत्र दृष्ट्वा मणिप्रेष्ठं बालक्रीडनकं कृतम् ।
हर्तुं कृतमतिस्तस्मिन्नवतस्थेऽर्भकान्तिके ॥२०॥

tatra dṛṣṭvā maṇi-preṣṭhaṁ
bāla-krīḍanakaṁ kṛtam
hartuṁ kṛta-matis tasminn
avatasthe 'rbhakāntike

tatra—there; *dṛṣṭvā*—seeing; *maṇi-preṣṭham*—the most precious of jewels; *bāla*—of a child; *krīḍanakam*—the plaything; *kṛtam*—made; *hartum*—to take it away; *kṛta-matiḥ*—deciding; *tasmin*—there; *avatasthe*—He placed Himself; *arbhaka-antike*—near the child.

TRANSLATION

There Lord Kṛṣṇa saw that the most precious of jewels had been made into a child's plaything. Determined to take it away, He approached the child.

TEXT 21

तमपूर्वं नरं दृष्ट्वा धात्री चुक्रोश भीतवत् ।
तच्छ्रुत्वाभ्यद्रवत्क्रुद्धो जाम्बवान् बलिनां वरः ॥२१॥

tam apūrvaṁ naraṁ dṛṣṭvā
dhātrī cukrośa bhīta-vat
tac chrutvābhyadravat kruddho
jāmbavān balināṁ varaḥ

tam—that; *apūrvam*—never before (seen); *naram*—person; *dṛṣṭvā*—seeing; *dhātrī*—the nurse; *cukrośa*—cried out; *bhīta-vat*—afraid; *tat*—that; *śrutvā*—hearing; *abhyadravat*—ran toward; *kruddhaḥ*—angry; *jāmbavān*—Jāmbavān; *balinām*—of the strong; *varaḥ*—the best.

TRANSLATION

The child's nurse cried out in fear upon seeing that extraordinary person standing before them. Jāmbavān, strongest of the strong, heard her cries and angrily ran toward the Lord.

TEXT 22

स वै भगवता तेन युयुधे स्वामिनात्मनः ।
पुरुषं प्राकृतं मत्वा कुपितो नानुभाववित् ॥२२॥

sa vai bhagavatā tena
yuyudhe svāminātmanaḥ
puruṣaṁ prākṛtaṁ matvā
kupito nānubhāva-vit

saḥ—he; *vai*—indeed; *bhagavatā*—with the Lord; *tena*—with Him; *yuyudhe*—fought; *svāminā*—master; *ātmanaḥ*—his own; *puruṣam*—a person; *prākṛtam*—mundane; *matvā*—thinking Him; *kupitaḥ*—angry; *na*—not; *anubhāva*—of His position; *vit*—aware.

TRANSLATION

Unaware of His true position and thinking Him an ordinary man, Jāmbavān angrily began fighting with the Supreme Lord, his master.

PURPORT

The words *puruṣaṁ prākṛtaṁ matvā,* "thinking Him a mundane person," are very significant. So-called Vedic scholars, including most Western ones, enjoy translating the word *puruṣam* as "man" even when the word refers to Lord Kṛṣṇa, and thus their unauthorized translations of Vedic literature are tainted by their materialistic conceptions of the Godhead. However, here it is clearly stated that it was because Jāmbavān misunderstood the Lord's position that he considered Him *prākṛta-puruṣa,* "a mundane person." In other words, the Lord is actually *puruṣottama,* "the ultimate transcendental person."

TEXT 23

द्वन्द्वयुद्धं सुतुमुलमुभयोर्विजिगीषतोः ।
आयुधाश्मद्रुमैर्दोर्भिः क्रव्यार्थे श्येनयोरिव ॥२३॥

dvandva-yuddhaṁ su-tumulam
ubhayor vijigīṣatoḥ
āyudhāśma-drumair dorbhiḥ
kravyārthe śyenayor iva

dvandva—paired; *yuddham*—the fight; *su-tumulam*—very furious; *ubhayoḥ*—between the two of them; *vijigīṣatoḥ*—who both were striving to win; *āyudha*—with weapons; *aśma*—stones; *drumaiḥ*—and trees; *dorbhiḥ*—with their arms; *kravya*—carrion; *arthe*—for the sake; *śyenayoḥ*—between two hawks; *iva*—as if.

TRANSLATION

The two fought furiously in single combat, each determined to win. Contending against each other with various weapons and then with stones, tree trunks and finally their bare arms, they struggled like two hawks battling over a piece of flesh.

TEXT 24

आसीत्तदष्टाविंशाहमितरेतरमुष्टिभिः ।
वज्रनिष्पेषपरुषैरविश्रममहर्निशम् ॥२४॥

āsīt tad aṣṭā-viṁśāham
itaretara-muṣṭibhiḥ
vajra-niṣpeṣa-paruṣair
aviśramam ahar-niśam

āsīt—was; *tat*—that; *aṣṭā-viṁśa*—twenty-eight; *aham*—days; *itara-itara*—with one another's; *muṣṭibhiḥ*—fists; *vajra*—of lightning; *niṣpeṣa*—like the blows; *paruṣaiḥ*—hard; *aviśramam*—without pause; *ahaḥ-niśam*—day and night.

TRANSLATION

The fight went on without rest for twenty-eight days, the two opponents striking each other with their fists, which fell like the cracking blows of lightning.

PURPORT

Śrīla Viśvanātha Cakravartī points out that the fight continued day and night without intermission.

TEXT 25

कृष्णमुष्टिविनिष्पातनिष्पिष्टांगोरुबन्धनः ।
क्षीणसत्त्वः स्विन्नगात्रस्तमाहातीव विस्मितः ॥२५॥

kṛṣṇa-muṣṭi-viniṣpāta-
niṣpiṣṭāṅgoru-bandhanaḥ
kṣīṇa-sattvaḥ svinna-gātras
tam āhātīva vismitaḥ

kṛṣṇa-muṣṭi—of Lord Kṛṣṇa's fists; *viniṣpāta*—by the blows; *niṣpiṣṭa*—pummeled; *aṅga*—of whose body; *uru*—huge; *bandhanaḥ*—the muscles; *kṣīṇa*—diminished; *sattvaḥ*—whose strength; *svinna*—perspiring; *gātraḥ*—whose limbs; *tam*—to Him; *āha*—he spoke; *atīva*—extremely; *vismitaḥ*—astonished.

TRANSLATION

His bulging muscles pummeled by the blows of Lord Kṛṣṇa's fists, his strength faltering and his limbs perspiring, Jāmbavān, greatly astonished, finally spoke to the Lord.

TEXT 26

जाने त्वां सर्वभूतानां प्राण ओजः सहो बलम् ।
विष्णुं पुराणपुरुषं प्रभविष्णुमधीश्वरम् ॥२६॥

jāne tvāṁ sarva-bhūtānāṁ
prāṇa ojaḥ saho balam
viṣṇuṁ purāṇa-puruṣaṁ
prabhaviṣṇum adhīśvaram

jāne—I know; *tvām*—You (to be); *sarva*—of all; *bhūtānām*—living beings; *prāṇaḥ*—the life air; *ojaḥ*—the sensory strength; *sahaḥ*—the mental strength; *balam*—the physical strength; *viṣṇum*—Lord Viṣṇu; *purāṇa*—primeval; *puruṣam*—the Supreme Person; *prabhaviṣṇum*—all-powerful; *adhīśvaram*—the supreme controller.

TRANSLATION

[Jāmbavān said:] I know now that You are the life air and the sensory, mental and bodily strength of all living beings. You are Lord Viṣṇu, the original person, the supreme, all-powerful controller.

TEXT 27

त्वं हि विश्वसृजां स्रष्टा सृष्टानामपि यच्च सत् ।
कालः कलयतामीशः पर आत्मा तथात्मनाम् ॥२७॥

tvaṁ hi viśva-sṛjāṁ sraṣṭā
sṛṣṭānām api yac ca sat
kālaḥ kalayatām īśaḥ
para ātmā tathātmanām

tvam—You; *hi*—indeed; *viśva*—of the universe; *sṛjām*—of the creators; *sraṣṭā*—the creator; *sṛṣṭānām*—of created entities; *api*—also; *yat*—which; *ca*—and; *sat*—underlying substance; *kālaḥ*—the subduer; *kalayatām*—of subduers; *īśaḥ*—the Supreme Lord; *paraḥ ātmā*—the Supreme Soul; *tathā*—also; *ātmanām*—of all souls.

TRANSLATION

You are the ultimate creator of all creators of the universe, and of everything created You are the underlying substance. You are the subduer of all subduers, the Supreme Lord and Supreme Soul of all souls.

PURPORT

As Lord Kapila states in the *Śrīmad-Bhāgavatam* (3.25.42): *mṛtyuś carati mad-bhayāt*. "Death himself moves about out of fear of Me."

TEXT 28

यस्येषदुत्कलितरोषकटाक्षमोक्षैर्
वर्त्मादिशत्क्षुभितनक्रतिमिंगलोऽब्धिः ।
सेतुः कृतः स्वयश उज्ज्वलिता च लंका
रक्षःशिरांसि भुवि पेतुरिषुक्षतानि ॥२८॥

yasyeṣad-utkalita-roṣa-kaṭākṣa-mokṣair
vartmādiśat kṣubhita-nakra-timiṅgalo 'bdhiḥ

setuḥ kṛtaḥ sva-yaśa ujjvalitā ca laṅkā
rakṣaḥ-śirāṁsi bhuvi petur iṣu-kṣatāni

yasya—whose; *īṣat*—slightly; *utkalita*—manifested; *roṣa*—from the anger; *kaṭā-akṣa*—of sidelong glances; *mokṣaiḥ*—because of the release; *vartma*—a way; *ādiśat*—showed; *kṣubhita*—agitated; *nakra*—(in which) the crocodiles; *timiṅgalaḥ*—and huge *timiṅgila* fish; *abdhiḥ*—the ocean; *setuḥ*—a bridge; *kṛtaḥ*—made; *sva*—His own; *yaśaḥ*—fame; *ujjvalitā*—set ablaze; *ca*—and; *laṅkā*—the city of Laṅkā; *rakṣaḥ*—of the demon (Rāvaṇa); *śirāṁsi*—the heads; *bhuvi*—to the ground; *petuḥ*—fell; *iṣu*—by whose arrows; *kṣatāni*—cut off.

TRANSLATION

You are He who impelled the ocean to give way when His sidelong glances, slightly manifesting His anger, disturbed the crocodiles and *timiṅgila* fish within the watery depths. You are He who built a great bridge to establish His fame, who burned down the city of Laṅkā, and whose arrows severed the heads of Rāvaṇa, which then fell to the ground.

TEXTS 29–30

इति विज्ञातविज्ञानमृक्षराजानमच्युतः ।
व्याजहार महाराज भगवान् देवकीसुतः ॥२९॥
अभिमृश्यारविन्दाक्षः पाणिना शंकरेण तम् ।
कृपया परया भक्तं मेघगम्भीरया गिरा ॥३०॥

iti vijñāta-vijñānam
ṛkṣa-rājānam acyutaḥ
vyājahāra mahā-rāja
bhagavān devakī-sutaḥ

abhimṛśyāravindākṣaḥ
pāṇinā śaṁ-kareṇa tam
kṛpayā parayā bhaktaṁ
megha-gambhīrayā girā

iti—thus; *vijñāta-vijñānam*—who had understood the truth; *ṛkṣa*—of the bears; *rājānam*—to the king; *acyutaḥ*—Lord Kṛṣṇa; *vyājahāra*—spoke; *mahā-rāja*—O King (Parīkṣit); *bhagavān*—the Supreme Lord; *devakī-sutaḥ*—the son of Devakī; *abhimṛśya*—touching; *aravinda-akṣaḥ*—lotus-eyed; *pāṇinā*—with His hand; *śam*—auspiciousness; *kareṇa*—which bestows; *tam*—to him; *kṛpayā*—with compassion; *parayā*—great; *bhaktam*—to His devotee; *megha*—like a cloud; *gambhīrayā*—deep; *girā*—in a voice.

TRANSLATION

[Śukadeva Gosvāmī continued:] O King, Lord Kṛṣṇa then addressed the king of the bears, who had understood the truth. The lotus-eyed Personality of Godhead, the son of Devakī, touched Jāmbavān with His hand, which bestows all blessings, and spoke to His devotee with sublime compassion, His grave voice deeply resounding like a cloud.

TEXT 31

मणिहेतोरिह प्राप्ता वयमृक्षपते बिलम् ।
मिथ्याभिशापं प्रमृजन्नात्मनो मणिनामुना ॥३१॥

maṇi-hetor iha prāptā
vayam ṛkṣa-pate bilam
mithyābhiśāpaṁ pramṛjann
ātmano maṇināmunā

maṇi—the jewel; *hetoḥ*—because of; *iha*—here; *prāptāḥ*—have come; *vayam*—we; *ṛkṣa-pate*—O lord of the bears; *bilam*—to the cave; *mithyā*—false; *abhiśāpam*—the accusation; *pramṛjan*—to dispel; *ātmanaḥ*—against Myself; *maṇinā*—with the jewel; *amunā*—this.

TRANSLATION

[Lord Kṛṣṇa said:] It is for this jewel, O lord of the bears, that we have come to your cave. I intend to use the jewel to disprove the false accusations against Me.

TEXT 32

इत्युक्तः स्वां दुहितरं कन्यां जाम्बवतीं मुदा ।
अर्हणार्थं स मणिना कृष्णायोपजहार ह ॥३२॥

ity uktaḥ svāṁ duhitaraṁ
kanyāṁ jāmbavatīṁ mudā
arhaṇārthaṁ sa maṇinā
kṛṣṇāyopajahāra ha

iti—thus; *uktaḥ*—addressed; *svām*—his; *duhitaram*—daughter; *kanyām*—maiden; *jāmbavatīm*—named Jāmbavatī; *mudā*—happily; *arhaṇa-artham*—as a respectful offering; *saḥ*—he; *maṇinā*—with the jewel; *kṛṣṇāya*—to Lord Kṛṣṇa; *upajahāra ha*—presented.

TRANSLATION

Thus addressed, Jāmbavān happily honored Lord Kṛṣṇa by offering Him his maiden daughter, Jāmbavatī, together with the jewel.

TEXT 33

अदृष्ट्वा निर्गमं शौरेः प्रविष्टस्य बिलं जनाः ।
प्रतीक्ष्य द्वादशाहानि दुःखिताः स्वपुरं ययुः ॥३३॥

adṛṣṭvā nirgamaṁ śaureḥ
praviṣṭasya bilaṁ janāḥ
pratīkṣya dvādaśāhāni
duḥkhitāḥ sva-puraṁ yayuḥ

adṛṣṭvā—not seeing; *nirgamam*—the exit; *śaureḥ*—of Lord Kṛṣṇa; *praviṣṭasya*—who had gone inside; *bilam*—the cave; *janāḥ*—the people; *pratīkṣya*—after waiting; *dvādaśa*—twelve; *ahāni*—days; *duḥkhitāḥ*—unhappy; *sva*—their; *puram*—to the city; *yayuḥ*—went.

TRANSLATION

After Lord Śauri had entered the cave, the people of Dvārakā who had accompanied Him had waited twelve days without seeing

Him come out again. Finally they had given up and returned to their city in great sorrow.

TEXT 34

निशम्य देवकी देवी रुक्मिण्यानकदुन्दुभिः ।
सुहृदो ज्ञातयोऽशोचन् बिलात्कृष्णमनिर्गतम् ॥३४॥

niśamya devakī devī
rukmiṇy ānakadundubhiḥ
suhṛdo jñātayo 'śocan
bilāt kṛṣṇam anirgatam

niśamya—hearing; *devakī*—Devakī; *devī rukmiṇī*—the divine Rukmiṇī; *ānakadundubhiḥ*—Vasudeva; *suhṛdaḥ*—friends; *jñātayaḥ*—relatives; *aśocan*—they lamented; *bilāt*—from the cave; *kṛṣṇam*—Kṛṣṇa; *anirgatam*—not come out.

TRANSLATION

When Devakī, Rukmiṇī-devī, Vasudeva and the Lord's other relatives and friends heard that He had not come out of the cave, they all lamented.

TEXT 35

सत्राजितं शपन्तस्ते दुःखिता द्वारकौकसः ।
उपतस्थुश्चन्द्रभागां दुर्गां कृष्णोपलब्धये ॥३५॥

satrājitaṁ śapantas te
duḥkhitā dvārakaukasaḥ
upatasthuś candrabhāgāṁ
durgāṁ kṛṣṇopalabdhaye

satrājitam—Satrājit; *śapantaḥ*—cursing; *te*—they; *duḥkhitāḥ*—sorrowful; *dvārakā-okasaḥ*—the residents of Dvārakā; *upatasthuḥ*—worshiped; *candrabhāgām*—Candrabhāgā; *durgām*—Durgā; *kṛṣṇa-upalabdhaye*—in order to obtain Kṛṣṇa.

TRANSLATION

Cursing Satrājit, the sorrowful residents of Dvārakā approached the Durgā deity named Candrabhāgā and prayed to her for Kṛṣṇa's return.

TEXT 36

तेषां तु देव्युपस्थानात्प्रत्यादिष्टाशिषा स च ।
प्रादुर्बभूव सिद्धार्थः सदारो हर्षयन् हरिः ॥३६॥

teṣāṁ tu devy-upasthānāt
pratyādiṣṭāśiṣā sa ca
prādurbabhūva siddhārthaḥ
sa-dāro harṣayan hariḥ

teṣām—to them; *tu*—but; *devī*—of the demigoddess; *upasthānāt*—after the worship; *pratyādiṣṭa*—granted in response; *āśiṣāḥ*—benediction; *saḥ*—He; *ca*—and; *prādurbabhūva*—appeared; *siddha*—having achieved; *arthaḥ*—His purpose; *sa-dāraḥ*—together with His wife; *harṣayan*—creating joy; *hariḥ*—Lord Kṛṣṇa.

TRANSLATION

When the citizens had finished worshiping the demigoddess, she spoke to them in response, promising to grant their request. Just then Lord Kṛṣṇa, who had achieved His purpose, appeared before them in the company of His new wife, filling them with joy.

TEXT 37

उपलभ्य हृषीकेशं मृतं पुनरिवागतम् ।
सह पत्न्या मणिग्रीवं सर्वे जातमहोत्सवाः ॥३७॥

upalabhya hṛṣīkeśaṁ
mṛtaṁ punar ivāgatam
saha patnyā maṇi-grīvaṁ
sarve jāta-mahotsavāḥ

upalabhya—recognizing; *hṛṣīkeśam*—the Lord of the senses; *mṛtam*—someone dead; *punaḥ*—again; *iva*—as if; *āgatam*—come; *saha*—with; *patnyā*—a wife; *maṇi*—the jewel; *grīvam*—on His neck; *sarve*—all of them; *jāta*—aroused; *mahā*—great; *utsavāḥ*—rejoicing.

TRANSLATION

Seeing Lord Hṛṣīkeśa return as if from death, accompanied by His new wife and wearing the Syamantaka jewel on His neck, all the people were roused to jubilation.

PURPORT

According to Śrīla Viśvanātha Cakravartī, Jāmbavān had placed the jewel on the Lord's neck when he had presented his daughter in marriage.

TEXT 38

सत्राजितं समाहूय सभायां राजसन्निधौ ।
प्राप्तिं चाख्याय भगवान्मणिं तस्मै न्यवेदयत् ॥३८॥

satrājitaṁ samāhūya
sabhāyāṁ rāja-sannidhau
prāptiṁ cākhyāya bhagavān
maṇiṁ tasmai nyavedayat

satrājitam—Satrājit; *samāhūya*—calling; *sabhāyām*—into the royal assembly; *rāja*—of the King (Ugrasena); *sannidhau*—in the presence; *prāptim*—the recovery; *ca*—and; *ākhyāya*—announcing; *bhagavān*—the Supreme Lord; *maṇim*—the jewel; *tasmai*—to him; *nyavedayat*—presented.

TRANSLATION

Lord Kṛṣṇa summoned Satrājit to the royal assembly. There, in the presence of King Ugrasena, Kṛṣṇa announced the recovery of the jewel and then formally presented it to Satrājit.

TEXT 39

स चातिव्रीडितो रत्नं गृहीत्वावाङ्मुखस्ततः ।
अनुतप्यमानो भवनमगमत्स्वेन पाप्मना ॥३९॥

sa cāti-vrīḍito ratnaṁ
gṛhītvāvāṅ-mukhas tataḥ
anutapyamāno bhavanam
agamat svena pāpmanā

saḥ—he, Satrājit; *ca*—and; *ati*—extremely; *vrīḍitaḥ*—ashamed; *ratnam*—the gem; *gṛhītvā*—taking; *avāk*—downward; *mukhaḥ*—his face; *tataḥ*—from there; *anutapyamānaḥ*—feeling remorse; *bhavanam*—to his home; *agamat*—went; *svena*—with his own; *pāpmanā*—sinful behavior.

TRANSLATION

Hanging his head in great shame, Satrājit took the gem and returned home, all the while feeling remorse for his sinful behavior.

TEXTS 40–42

सोऽनुध्यायंस्तदेवाघं बलवद्विग्रहाकुलः ।
कथं मृजाम्यात्मरजः प्रसीदेद्वाच्युतः कथम् ॥४०॥
किं कृत्वा साधु मह्यं स्यान्न शपेद्वा जनो यथा ।
अदीर्घदर्शनं क्षुद्रं मूढं द्रविणलोलुपम् ॥४१॥
दास्ये दुहितरं तस्मै स्त्रीरत्नं रत्नमेव च ।
उपायोऽयं समीचीनस्तस्य शान्तिर्न चान्यथा ॥४२॥

so 'nudhyāyaṁs tad evāghaṁ
balavad-vigrahākulaḥ
kathaṁ mṛjāmy ātma-rajaḥ
prasīded vācyutaḥ katham

kiṁ kṛtvā sādhu mahyaṁ syān
na śaped vā jano yathā

adīrgha-darśanaṁ kṣudraṁ
mūḍhaṁ draviṇa-lolupam

dāsye duhitaraṁ tasmai
strī-ratnaṁ ratnam eva ca
upāyo 'yaṁ samīcīnas
tasya śāntir na cānyathā

saḥ—he; *anudhyāyan*—pondering over; *tat*—that; *eva*—indeed; *agham*—offense; *bala-vat*—with those who are powerful; *vigraha*—about a conflict; *ākulaḥ*—worried; *katham*—how; *mṛjāmi*—will I cleanse; *ātma*—of myself; *rajaḥ*—the contamination; *prasīdet*—may become satisfied; *vā*—or; *acyutaḥ*—Lord Kṛṣṇa; *katham*—how; *kim*—what; *kṛtvā*—doing; *sādhu*—good; *mahyam*—for me; *syāt*—there may be; *na śapet*—may not curse; *vā*—or; *janaḥ*—the people; *yathā*—so as; *adīrgha*—short-ranged; *darśanam*—whose vision; *kṣudram*—petty; *mūḍham*—befooled; *draviṇa*—after wealth; *lolupam*—avaricious; *dāsye*—I will give; *duhitaram*—my daughter; *tasmai*—to Him; *strī*—of women; *ratnam*—the jewel; *ratnam*—the jewel; *eva ca*—as well; *upāyaḥ*—means; *ayam*—this; *samīcīnaḥ*—effective; *tasya*—His; *śāntiḥ*—pacification; *na*—not; *ca*—and; *anyathā*—otherwise.

TRANSLATION

Pondering over his grievous offense and worried about the possibility of conflict with the Lord's mighty devotees, King Satrājit thought, "How can I cleanse myself of my contamination, and how may Lord Acyuta become satisfied with me? What can I do to regain my good fortune and avoid being cursed by the populace for being so short-sighted, miserly, foolish and avaricious? I shall give my daughter, the jewel of all women, to the Lord, together with the Syamantaka jewel. That, indeed, is the only proper way to pacify Him."

TEXT 43

एवं व्यवसितो बुद्ध्या सत्राजित्स्वसुतां शुभाम् ।
मणिं च स्वयमुद्यम्य कृष्णायोपजहार ह ॥४३॥

evaṁ vyavasito buddhyā
satrājit sva-sutāṁ śubhām
maṇiṁ ca svayam udyamya
kṛṣṇāyopajahāra ha

evam—thus; *vyavasitaḥ*—fixing his determination; *buddhyā*—by use of intelligence; *satrājit*—King Satrājit; *sva*—his own; *sutām*—daughter; *śubhām*—fair; *maṇim*—the jewel; *ca*—and; *svayam*—himself; *udyamya*—endeavoring; *kṛṣṇāya*—to Lord Kṛṣṇa; *upajahāra ha*—presented.

TRANSLATION

Having thus intelligently made up his mind, King Satrājit personally arranged to present Lord Kṛṣṇa with his fair daughter and the Syamantaka jewel.

TEXT 44

तां सत्यभामां भगवानुपयेमे यथाविधि ।
बहुभिर्याचितां शीलरूपौदार्यगुणान्विताम् ॥४४॥

tāṁ satyabhāmāṁ bhagavān
upayeme yathā-vidhi
bahubhir yācitāṁ śīla-
rūpaudārya-guṇānvitām

tām—she; *satyabhāmām*—Satyabhāmā; *bhagavān*—the Lord; *upayeme*—married; *yathā-vidhi*—by proper rituals; *bahubhiḥ*—by many men; *yācitām*—asked for; *śīla*—of fine character; *rūpa*—beauty; *audārya*—and magnanimity; *guṇa*—with the qualities; *anvitām*—endowed.

TRANSLATION

The Lord married Satyabhāmā in proper religious fashion. Possessed of excellent behavior, along with beauty, broad-mindedness and all other good qualities, she had been sought by many men.

PURPORT

Śrīla Śrīdhara Svāmī explains that men such as Kṛtavarmā had sought the hand of Satyabhāmā.

TEXT 45

भगवानाह न मणिं प्रतीच्छामो वयं नृप ।
तवास्तां देवभक्तस्य वयं च फलभागिनः ॥४५॥

bhagavān āha na maṇiṁ
pratīcchāmo vayaṁ nṛpa
tavāstāṁ deva-bhaktasya
vayaṁ ca phala-bhāginaḥ

bhagavān—the Supreme Lord; *āha*—said; *na*—not; *maṇim*—the jewel; *pratīcchāmaḥ*—desire back; *vayam*—We; *nṛpa*—O King; *tava*—yours; *āstām*—let it remain; *deva*—of the demigod (the sun-god Sūrya); *bhaktasya*—the devotee's; *vayam*—We; *ca*—also; *phala*—of its fruits; *bhāginaḥ*—enjoyers.

TRANSLATION

The Supreme Personality of Godhead told Satrājit: We do not care to take this jewel back, O King. You are the sun-god's devotee, so let it stay in your possession. Thus We will also enjoy its benefits.

PURPORT

Satrājit should have worshiped Lord Kṛṣṇa, the Supreme God. Thus there is certainly a touch of irony in Lord Kṛṣṇa's saying "After all, you are a devotee of the sun-god." Furthermore, Kṛṣṇa had already acquired Satrājit's greatest treasure, the pure and beautiful Satyabhāmā.

Thus end the purports of the humble servants of His Divine Grace A. C. Bhaktivedanta Swami Prabhupāda to the Tenth Canto, Fifty-sixth Chapter, of the Śrīmad-Bhāgavatam, *entitled "The Syamantaka Jewel."*

CHAPTER FIFTY-SEVEN

Satrājit Murdered, the Jewel Returned

This chapter describes how Lord Kṛṣṇa, after the murder of Satrājit, killed Śatadhanvā and had Akrūra bring the Syamantaka jewel back to Dvārakā.

When Lord Śrī Kṛṣṇa heard that the Pāṇḍavas had supposedly been burned to death in the palace of lac, He went to Hastināpura with Lord Baladeva to maintain the principles of worldly protocol, even though, being omniscient, He knew the report was false. With Kṛṣṇa out of Dvārakā, Akrūra and Kṛtavarmā incited Śatadhanvā to steal the Syamantaka jewel from Satrājit. Bewildered by their words, the sinful Śatadhanvā murdered King Satrājit in his sleep and stole the gem. Queen Satyabhāmā was overcome with grief at the death of her father, and she rushed to Hastināpura to report the sorrowful news to Śrī Kṛṣṇa. Together with Lord Baladeva, Kṛṣṇa then returned to Dvārakā to kill Śatadhanvā.

Śatadhanvā went to Akrūra and Kṛtavarmā to beg for help, but when they refused he left the jewel with Akrūra and fled for his life. Kṛṣṇa and Balarāma pursued him, and Lord Kṛṣṇa beheaded him with His sharp-edged disc. When the Lord could not find the Syamantaka jewel on Śatadhanvā's person, Baladeva told Him that Śatadhanvā must have left it in someone's care. Baladeva further suggested that Kṛṣṇa return to Dvārakā to find the jewel while He, Baladeva, would take the opportunity to visit the King of Videha. Thus Lord Balarāma traveled to Mithilā and remained there for a few years, during which He taught King Duryodhana the art of fighting with a club.

Lord Kṛṣṇa returned to Dvārakā and had the funeral rites performed for Satrājit. When Akrūra and Kṛtavarmā heard how Śatadhanvā had met his death, they fled Dvārakā. Soon many kinds of disturbances—mental, physical and so on—began to afflict Dvārakā, and the citizens concluded that the cause of these troubles must be Akrūra's exile. The city elders explained, "Once there was a drought in Benares, and the king of the region gave his daughter in marriage to Akrūra's father, who was visiting Benares at the time. As a result of this gift, the drought ended." The elders, thinking Akrūra had the same power as his father, declared that Akrūra should be brought back.

Lord Kṛṣṇa knew that Akrūra's exile was not the main cause of the disturbances. Still, He had Akrūra brought back to Dvārakā, and after properly honoring him with worship and greeting him with sweet words, Kṛṣṇa told him, "I know Śatadhanvā left the jewel in your care. Since Satrājit had no sons, his daughter's offspring are the just claimants to whatever property he has left behind. Nonetheless, it would be best for you to keep the troublesome jewel in your care. Just let Me show it once to My relatives." Akrūra presented Kṛṣṇa with the jewel, which shone as brilliantly as the sun, and after the Lord had shown it to His family members He returned it to Akrūra.

TEXT 1

श्रीबादरायणिरुवाच
विज्ञातार्थोऽपि गोविन्दो दग्धानाकर्ण्य पाण्डवान् ।
कुन्तीं च कुल्यकरणे सहरामो ययौ कुरून् ॥१॥

śrī-bādarāyaṇir uvāca
vijñātārtho 'pi govindo
dagdhān ākarṇya pāṇḍavān
kuntīṁ ca kulya-karaṇe
saha-rāmo yayau kurūn

śrī-bādarāyaṇiḥ uvāca—Śrī Śukadeva Gosvāmī, the son of Badarāyaṇa, said; *vijñāta*—aware; *arthaḥ*—of the facts; *api*—although; *govindaḥ*—Lord Kṛṣṇa; *dagdhān*—burned to death; *ākarṇya*—hearing; *pāṇḍavān*—the sons of Pāṇḍu; *kuntīm*—their mother, Kuntī; *ca*—and; *kulya*—family obligations; *karaṇe*—to carry out; *saha-rāmaḥ*—together with Lord Balarāma; *yayau*—went; *kurūn*—to the kingdom of the Kurus.

TRANSLATION

Śrī Bādarāyaṇi said: Although Lord Govinda was fully aware of what had actually occurred, when He heard reports that the Pāṇḍavas and Queen Kuntī had burned to death, He went with Lord Balarāma to the kingdom of the Kurus to fulfill the family obligations expected of Him.

PURPORT

The Lord was quite aware that the Pāṇḍavas had escaped the assassination plot of Duryodhana, although the world heard the false news that the Pāṇḍavas and their mother had perished in the fire.

TEXT 2

भीष्मं कृपं सविदुरं गान्धारीं द्रोणमेव च ।
तुल्यदु:खौ च संगम्य हा कष्टमिति होचतु: ॥२॥

bhīṣmaṁ kṛpaṁ sa-viduraṁ
gāndhārīṁ droṇam eva ca
tulya-duḥkhau ca saṅgamya
hā kaṣṭam iti hocatuḥ

bhīṣmam—Bhīṣma; *kṛpam*—Ācārya Kṛpa; *sa-viduram*—and also Vidura; *gāndhārīm*—Gāndhārī, the wife of Dhṛtarāṣṭra; *droṇam*—Ācārya Droṇa; *eva ca*—as well; *tulya*—equally; *duḥkhau*—sorrowful; *ca*—and; *saṅgamya*—meeting with; *hā*—alas; *kaṣṭam*—how painful; *iti*—thus; *ha ūcatuḥ*—They spoke.

TRANSLATION

The two Lords met with Bhīṣma, Kṛpa, Vidura, Gāndhārī and Droṇa. Showing sorrow equal to theirs, They cried out, "Alas, how painful this is!"

PURPORT

Śrīla Śrīdhara Svāmī points out that those who were involved in the assassination attempt were of course not at all sorry to hear of the Pāṇḍavas' death. The persons specifically mentioned here, however—Bhīṣma, Kṛpa, Vidura, Gāndhārī and Droṇa—were actually unhappy to hear of the supposed tragedy.

TEXT 3

लब्ध्वैतदन्तरं राजन् शतधन्वानमूचतु: ।
अक्रूरकृतवर्माणौ मनि: कस्मान्न गृह्यते ॥३॥

labdhvaitad antaraṁ rājan
śatadhanvānam ūcatuḥ
akrūra-kṛtavarmāṇau
maniḥ kasmān na gṛhyate

labdhvā—achieving; *etat*—this; *antaram*—opportunity; *rājan*—O King (Parīkṣit); *śatadhanvānam*—to Śatadhanvā; *ūcatuḥ*—said; *akrūra-kṛtavarmāṇau*—Akrūra and Kṛtavarmā; *maniḥ*—the jewel; *kasmāt*—why; *na gṛhyate*—should not be taken.

TRANSLATION

Taking advantage of this opportunity, O King, Akrūra and Kṛtavarmā went to Śatadhanvā and said, "Why not take the Syamantaka jewel?

PURPORT

Akrūra and Kṛtavarmā reasoned that since Kṛṣṇa and Balarāma were absent from Dvārakā, Satrājit could be killed and the jewel stolen. Śrīla Śrīdhara Svāmī mentions that these two must have flattered Śatadhanvā, telling him, "You are much braver than we are; so you kill him."

TEXT 4

योऽस्मभ्यं सम्प्रतिश्रुत्य कन्यारत्नं विगर्ह्य नः ।
कृष्णायादान्न सत्राजित्कस्माद् भ्रातरमन्वियात् ॥४॥

yo 'smabhyaṁ sampratiśrutya
kanyā-ratnaṁ vigarhya naḥ
kṛṣṇāyādān na satrājit
kasmād bhrātaram anviyāt

yaḥ—who; *asmabhyam*—to each of us; *sampratiśrutya*—promising; *kanyā*—his daughter; *ratnam*—jewellike; *vigarhya*—contemptuously neglecting; *naḥ*—us; *kṛṣṇāya*—to Kṛṣṇa; *adāt*—gave; *na*—not; *satrājit*—Satrājit; *kasmāt*—why; *bhrātaram*—his brother; *anviyāt*—should follow (in death).

TRANSLATION

"Satrājit promised his jewellike daughter to us but then gave her to Kṛṣṇa instead, contemptuously neglecting us. So why should Satrājit not follow his brother's path?"

PURPORT

Since Satrājit's brother, Prasena, had been violently killed, the implication of "following his brother's path" is obvious. What we have here is an assassination plot.

It is well known that both Akrūra and Kṛtavarmā are exalted, pure devotees of the Supreme Lord, so their unusual behavior requires some explanation. The *ācāryas* provide it as follows: Śrīla Jīva Gosvāmī states that Akrūra, although a first-class, pure devotee of the Lord, was a victim of the anger directed against him by the residents of Gokula because he took Lord Kṛṣṇa away from Vṛndāvana. The *gosvāmī* further states that Kṛtavarmā had associated with Kaṁsa—both of them being members of the Bhoja dynasty—and thus Kṛtavarmā was now suffering from this undesirable association.

Śrīla Viśvanātha Cakravartī offers an alternative explanation: Both Akrūra and Kṛtavarmā were furious with Satrājit because he had insulted Lord Kṛṣṇa and spread false rumors about Him in Dvārakā. Under normal circumstances Akrūra and Kṛtavarmā would have been most pleased that Lord Kṛṣṇa married the beautiful Satyabhāmā. Being pure devotees, they could not actually be unhappy about this match, nor could they become jealous rivals of the Lord. Therefore they had an ulterior motive in behaving like His rivals.

TEXT 5

एवं भिन्नमतिस्ताभ्यां सत्राजितमसत्तमः ।
शयानमवधील्लोभात्स पापः क्षीणजीवितः ॥५॥

evaṁ bhinna-matis tābhyāṁ
satrājitam asattamaḥ
śayānam avadhīl lobhāt
sa pāpaḥ kṣīṇa-jīvitaḥ

evam—thus; *bhinna*—affected; *matiḥ*—whose mind; *tābhyām*—by the two of them; *satrājitam*—Satrājit; *asat-tamaḥ*—the most wicked; *śayānam*—sleeping; *avadhīt*—killed; *lobhāt*—out of greed; *saḥ*—he; *pāpaḥ*—sinful; *kṣīṇa*—diminished; *jīvitaḥ*—whose life span.

TRANSLATION

His mind thus influenced by their advice, wicked Śatadhanvā murdered Satrājit in his sleep simply out of greed. In this way the sinful Śatadhanvā shortened his own life span.

PURPORT

According to Śrīla Viśvanātha Cakravartī, the word *asattamaḥ* indicates that Śatadhanvā was basically evil-minded and a firm hater of Satrājit.

TEXT 6

स्त्रीणां विक्रोशमानानां क्रन्दन्तीनामनाथवत् ।
हत्वा पशून् सौनिकवन्मणिमादाय जग्मिवान् ॥६॥

strīṇāṁ vikrośamānānāṁ
krandantīnām anātha-vat
hatvā paśūn saunika-van
maṇim ādāya jagmivān

strīṇām—as the women; *vikrośamānānām*—called out; *krandantīnām*—and cried; *anātha*—persons who have no protector; *vat*—as if; *hatvā*—having killed; *paśūn*—animals; *saunika*—a butcher; *vat*—like; *maṇim*—the jewel; *ādāya*—taking; *jagmivān*—he went.

TRANSLATION

As the women of Satrājit's palace screamed and helplessly wept, Śatadhanvā took the jewel and left, like a butcher after he has killed some animals.

TEXT 7

सत्यभामा च पितरं हतं वीक्ष्य शुचार्पिता ।
व्यलपत्तात तातेति हा हतास्मीति मुह्यती ॥७॥

satyabhāmā ca pitaraṁ
hataṁ vīkṣya śucārpitā
vyalapat tāta tāteti
hā hatāsmīti muhyatī

satyabhāmā—Queen Satyabhāmā; *ca*—and; *pitaram*—her father; *hatam*—killed; *vīkṣya*—seeing; *śucā-arpitā*—cast into sorrow; *vyalapat*—lamented; *tāta tāta*—O father, O father; *iti*—thus; *hā*—alas; *hatā*—killed; *asmi*—I am; *iti*—thus; *muhyatī*—fainting.

TRANSLATION

When Satyabhāmā saw her dead father, she was plunged into grief. Lamenting "My father, my father! Oh, I am killed!" she fell unconscious.

PURPORT

According to Śrīla Jīva Gosvāmī, Satyabhāmā's anguished feelings and words at the death of her father were prompted by Lord Kṛṣṇa's pastime potency (*līlā-śakti*), to prepare for the Lord's violent reaction against Śatadhanvā.

TEXT 8

तैलद्रोण्यां मृतं प्रास्य जगाम गजसाह्वयम् ।
कृष्णाय विदितार्थाय तप्ताचख्यौ पितुर्वधम् ॥८॥

taila-droṇyāṁ mṛtaṁ prāsya
jagāma gajasāhvayam
kṛṣṇāya viditārthāya
taptācakhyau pitur vadham

taila—of oil; *droṇyām*—in a large vessel; *mṛtam*—the corpse; *prāsya*—putting; *jagāma*—she went; *gaja-sāhvayam*—to Hastināpura, the Kuru capital; *kṛṣṇāya*—to Kṛṣṇa; *vidita-arthāya*—who already was aware of the situation; *taptā*—sorrowful; *ācakhyau*—she related; *pituḥ*—of her father; *vadham*—the killing.

TRANSLATION

Queen Satyabhāmā put her father's corpse in a large vat of oil and went to Hastināpura, where she sorrowfully told Lord Kṛṣṇa, who was already aware of the situation, about her father's murder.

TEXT 9

तदाकर्ण्येश्वरौ राजन्ननुसृत्य नृलोकताम् ।
अहो नः परमं कष्टमित्यस्राक्षौ विलेपतुः ॥९॥

tad ākarṇyeśvarau rājann
anusṛtya nṛ-lokatām
aho naḥ paramaṁ kaṣṭam
ity asrākṣau vilepatuḥ

tat—that; *ākarṇya*—hearing; *īśvarau*—the two Lords; *rājan*—O King (Parikṣit); *anusṛtya*—imitating; *nṛ-lokatām*—the way of human society; *aho*—alas; *naḥ*—for Us; *paramam*—the greatest; *kaṣṭam*—distress; *iti*—thus; *asra*—tearful; *akṣau*—whose eyes; *vilepatuḥ*—They both lamented.

TRANSLATION

When Lord Kṛṣṇa and Lord Balarāma heard this news, O King, They exclaimed, "Alas! This is the greatest tragedy for Us!" Thus imitating the ways of human society, They lamented, Their eyes brimming with tears.

TEXT 10

आगत्य भगवांस्तस्मात्सभार्यः साग्रजः पुरम् ।
शतधन्वानमारेभे हन्तुं हर्तुं मणिं ततः ॥१०॥

āgatya bhagavāṁs tasmāt
sa-bhāryaḥ sāgrajaḥ puram
śatadhanvānam ārebhe
hantuṁ hartuṁ maṇiṁ tataḥ

āgatya—returning; *bhagavān*—the Supreme Personality of Godhead; *tasmāt*—from that place; *sa-bhāryaḥ*—with His wife; *sa-agrajaḥ*—and with His elder brother; *puram*—to His capital; *śatadhanvānam*—Śatadhanvā; *ārebhe*—He prepared; *hantum*—to kill; *hartum*—to take; *maṇim*—the jewel; *tataḥ*—from him.

TRANSLATION

The Supreme Lord returned to His capital with His wife and elder brother. After arriving in Dvārakā, He readied Himself to kill Śatadhanvā and retrieve the jewel from him.

TEXT 11

सोऽपि कृतोद्यमं ज्ञात्वा भीतः प्राणपरीप्सया ।
साहाय्ये कृतवर्माणमयाचत स चाब्रवीत् ॥११॥

so 'pi kṛtodyamaṁ jñātvā
bhītaḥ prāṇa-parīpsayā
sāhāyye kṛtavarmāṇam
ayācata sa cābravīt

saḥ—he (Śatadhanvā); *api*—also; *kṛta-udyamam*—preparing Himself; *jñātvā*—learning; *bhītaḥ*—frightened; *prāṇa*—his life air; *parīpsayā*—wishing to save; *sāhāyye*—for assistance; *kṛtavarmāṇam*—Kṛtavarmā; *ayācata*—he entreated; *saḥ*—he; *ca*—and; *abravīt*—said.

TRANSLATION

Upon learning that Lord Kṛṣṇa was preparing to kill him, Śatadhanvā was struck with fear. To save his life he approached Kṛtavarmā and begged him for help, but Kṛtavarmā replied as follows.

TEXTS 12–13

नाहमीश्वरयोः कुर्यां हेलनं रामकृष्णयोः ।
को नु क्षेमाय कल्पेत तयोर्वृजिनमाचरन् ॥१२॥
कंसः सहानुगोऽपीतो यद्द्वेषात्त्याजितः श्रिया ।
जरासन्धः सप्तदशसंयुगाद्विरथो गतः ॥१३॥

nāham īśvarayoḥ kuryāṁ
helanaṁ rāma-kṛṣṇayoḥ
ko nu kṣemāya kalpeta
tayor vṛjinam ācaran

kaṁsaḥ sahānugo 'pīto
yad-dveṣāt tyājitaḥ śriyā
jarāsandhaḥ saptadaśa-
saṁyugād viratho gataḥ

na—not; *aham*—I; *īśvarayoḥ*—toward the Lords; *kuryām*—can commit; *helanam*—offense; *rāma-kṛṣṇayoḥ*—toward Balarāma and Kṛṣṇa; *kaḥ*—who; *nu*—indeed; *kṣemāya*—good fortune; *kalpeta*—can achieve; *tayoḥ*—to Them; *vṛjinam*—trouble; *ācaran*—causing; *kaṁsaḥ*—King Kaṁsa; *saha*—along with; *anugaḥ*—his followers; *apītaḥ*—dead; *yat*—against whom; *dveṣāt*—because of his hatred; *tyājitaḥ*—abandoned; *śriyā*—by his opulence; *jarāsandhaḥ*—Jarāsandha; *saptadaśa*—seventeen; *saṁyugāt*—resulting from battles; *virathaḥ*—deprived of his chariot; *gataḥ*—became.

TRANSLATION

[Kṛtavarmā said:] I dare not offend the Supreme Lords, Kṛṣṇa and Balarāma. Indeed, how can one who troubles Them expect any good fortune? Kaṁsa and all his followers lost both their wealth and their lives because of enmity toward Them, and after battling Them seventeen times Jarāsandha was left without even a chariot.

PURPORT

Śrīla Śrīdhara Svāmī explains that the word *helanam* indicates acting against the Lords' will, and that *vṛjinam* indicates an offense against the Lords.

TEXT 14

प्रत्याख्यातः स चाक्रूरं पार्ष्णिग्राहमयाचत ।
सोऽप्याह को विरुध्येत विद्वानीश्वरयोर्बलम् ॥१४॥

pratyākhyātaḥ sa cākrūraṁ
pārṣṇi-grāham ayācata
so 'py āha ko virudhyeta
vidvān īśvarayor balam

pratyākhyātaḥ—refused; *saḥ*—he, Śatadhanvā; *ca*—and; *akrūram*—Akrūra; *pārṣṇi-grāham*—for help; *ayācata*—begged; *saḥ*—he, Akrūra; *api*—also; *āha*—said; *kaḥ*—who; *virudhyeta*—can stand against; *vidvān*—knowing; *īśvarayoḥ*—of the two Personalities of Godhead; *balam*—the strength.

TRANSLATION

His appeal refused, Śatadhanvā went to Akrūra and begged him for protection. But Akrūra similarly told him, "Who would oppose the two Personalities of Godhead if he knew Their strength?

TEXT 15

य इदं लीलया विश्वं सृजत्यवति हन्ति च ।
चेष्टां विश्वसृजो यस्य न विदुर्मोहिताजया ॥१५॥

ya idaṁ līlayā viśvaṁ
sṛjaty avati hanti ca
ceṣṭāṁ viśva-sṛjo yasya
na vidur mohitājayā

yaḥ—who; *idam*—this; *līlayā*—as play; *viśvam*—universe; *sṛjati*—creates; *avati*—maintains; *hanti*—destroys; *ca*—and; *ceṣṭām*—purpose; *viśva-sṛjaḥ*—the (secondary) creators of the universe (headed by Lord Brahmā); *yasya*—whose; *na viduḥ*—do not know; *mohitāḥ*—bewildered; *ajayā*—by His eternal deluding potency.

TRANSLATION

"It is the Supreme Lord who creates, maintains and destroys this universe simply as His pastime. The cosmic creators cannot even understand His purpose, bewildered as they are by His illusory Māyā.

PURPORT

The use of the singular *yaḥ,* "He who," indicates that the frequent references to "the two Lords, Kṛṣṇa and Rāma," do not compromise the firm principle of monotheism expressed in the *Śrīmad-Bhāgavatam.* As explained in many Vedic literatures, the one Supreme Lord expands Himself into innumerable forms, yet He remains the one and almighty God. For example, we have this statement in the *Brahma-saṁhitā* (5.33): *advaitam acyutam anādir ananta-rūpam.* "The one Supreme Lord is infallible and beginningless, and He expands Himself into innumerable manifest forms." Out of regard for the spirit of the Lord's pastimes, in which He expands Himself and appears as His own older brother, Balarāma, the *Bhāgavatam* here refers to "the two Lords." But the "bottom line" is that there is one Supreme Godhead, one Absolute Truth, who appears in His original form as Kṛṣṇa.

TEXT 16

यः सप्तहायनः शैलमुत्पाटचैकेन पाणिना ।
दधार लीलया बाल उच्छिलीन्ध्रमिवार्भकः ॥१६॥

yaḥ sapta-hāyanaḥ śailam
utpāṭyaikena pāṇinā
dadhāra līlayā bāla
ucchilīndhram ivārbhakaḥ

yaḥ—who; *sapta*—seven; *hāyanaḥ*—years of age; *śailam*—a mountain; *utpāṭya*—uprooting; *ekena*—with a single; *pāṇinā*—hand; *dadhāra*—held up; *līlayā*—as play; *bālaḥ*—a mere child; *ucchilīndhram*—a mushroom; *iva*—as; *arbhakaḥ*—a boy.

TRANSLATION

"As a child of seven, Kṛṣṇa uprooted an entire mountain and held it aloft as easily as a young boy picks up a mushroom.

TEXT 17

नमस्तस्मै भगवते कृष्णायाद्भुतकर्मणे ।
अनन्तायादिभूताय कूटस्थायात्मने नमः ॥१७॥

namas tasmai bhagavate
kṛṣṇāyādbhuta-karmaṇe
anantāyādi-bhūtāya
kūṭa-sthāyātmane namaḥ

namaḥ—obeisances; *tasmai*—to Him; *bhagavate*—the Supreme Lord; *kṛṣṇāya*—Kṛṣṇa; *adbhuta*—amazing; *karmaṇe*—whose acts; *anantāya*—the unlimited; *ādi-bhūtāya*—the source of all existence; *kūṭa-sthāya*—the immovable center of existence; *ātmane*—the Supreme Soul; *namaḥ*—obeisances.

TRANSLATION

"I offer my obeisances to that Supreme Personality of Godhead, Kṛṣṇa, whose every deed is amazing. He is the Supreme Soul, the unlimited source and fixed center of all existence."

TEXT 18

प्रत्याख्यातः स तेनापि शतधन्वा महामणिम् ।
तस्मिन् न्यस्याश्वमारुह्य शतयोजनगं ययौ ॥१८॥

pratyākhyātaḥ sa tenāpi
śatadhanvā mahā-maṇim
tasmin nyasyāśvam āruhya
śata-yojana-gaṁ yayau

pratyākhyātaḥ—refused; *saḥ*—he; *tena*—by him, Akrūra; *api*—also; *śatadhanvā*—Śatadhanvā; *mahā-maṇim*—the precious jewel; *tasmin*—with him; *nyasya*—leaving; *aśvam*—a horse; *āruhya*—mounting; *śata*—one hundred; *yojana*—*yojanas* (one *yojana* measures about eight miles); *gam*—which could go; *yayau*—he departed.

TRANSLATION

His appeal thus rejected by Akrūra also, Śatadhanvā placed the precious jewel in Akrūra's care and fled on a horse that could travel one hundred *yojanas* [eight hundred miles].

PURPORT

The term *nyasya*, "leaving in the care of," implies Śatadhanvā now believed the jewel was his; thus he was leaving it in the care of a friend. In blunt terms, this is a thief's mentality.

TEXT 19

गरुडध्वजमारुह्य रथं रामजनार्दनौ ।
अन्वयातां महावेगैरश्वै राजन् गुरुद्रुहम् ॥१९॥

garuḍa-dhvajam āruhya
rathaṁ rāma-janārdanau
anvayātāṁ mahā-vegair
aśvai rājan guru-druham

garuḍa-dhvajam—having the emblem of Garuḍa on its flag; *āruhya*—mounting; *ratham*—the chariot; *rāma*—Balarāma; *janārdanau*—and Kṛṣṇa; *anvayātām*—followed; *mahā-vegaiḥ*—very swift; *aśvaiḥ*—by horses; *rājan*—O King (Parīkṣit); *guru*—to Their superior (Satrājit, Their father-in-law); *druham*—the committer of violence.

TRANSLATION

My dear King, Kṛṣṇa and Balarāma mounted Kṛṣṇa's chariot, which flew the flag of Garuḍa and was yoked with tremendously swift horses, and pursued Their elder's murderer.

TEXT 20

मिथिलायामुपवने विसृज्य पतितं हयम् ।
पद्भ्यामधावत्सन्त्रस्तः कृष्णोऽप्यन्वद्रवद् रुषा ॥२०॥

mithilāyām upavane
visṛjya patitaṁ hayam
padbhyām adhāvat santrastaḥ
kṛṣṇo 'py anvadravad ruṣā

mithilāyām—at Mithilā; *upavane*—in a suburban garden; *visṛjya*—abandoning; *patitam*—fallen; *hayam*—his horse; *padbhyām*—on foot; *adhāvat*—he ran; *santrastaḥ*—terrified; *kṛṣṇaḥ*—Lord Kṛṣṇa; *api*—also; *anvadravat*—ran after; *ruṣā*—furiously.

TRANSLATION

In a garden on the outskirts of Mithilā, the horse Śatadhanvā was riding collapsed. Terrified, he abandoned the horse and began to flee on foot, with Kṛṣṇa in angry pursuit.

TEXT 21

पदातेर्भगवांस्तस्य पदातिस्तिग्मनेमिना ।
चक्रेण शिर उत्कृत्य वाससोर्व्यचिनोन्मणिम् ॥२१॥

padāter bhagavāṁs tasya
padātis tigma-neminā
cakreṇa śira utkṛtya
vāsasor vyacinon maṇim

padāteḥ—of him who was on foot; *bhagavān*—the Supreme Lord; *tasya*—his; *padātiḥ*—Himself on foot; *tigma*—sharp; *neminā*—whose edge; *cakreṇa*—with His disc; *śiraḥ*—head; *utkṛtya*—severing; *vāsasoḥ*—within Śatadhanvā's garments (upper and lower); *vyacinot*—He searched for; *maṇim*—the jewel.

TRANSLATION

As Śatadhanvā fled on foot, the Supreme Lord, also going on foot, cut off his head with His sharp-edged disc. The Lord then searched Śatadhanvā's upper and lower garments for the Syamantaka jewel.

TEXT 22

अलब्धमणिरागत्य कृष्ण आहाग्रजान्तिकम् ।
वृथा हतः शतधनुर्मणिस्तत्र न विद्यते ॥२२॥

alabdha-maṇir āgatya
kṛṣṇa āhāgrajāntikam
vṛthā hataḥ śatadhanur
maṇis tatra na vidyate

alabdha—not finding; *maṇiḥ*—the gem; *āgatya*—approaching; *kṛṣṇaḥ*—Lord Kṛṣṇa; *āha*—said; *agra-ja*—of His elder brother; *antikam*—to the proximity; *vṛthā*—uselessly; *hataḥ*—killed; *śatadhanuḥ*—Śatadhanvā; *maṇiḥ*—the jewel; *tatra*—with him; *na vidyate*—is not present.

TRANSLATION

Not finding the jewel, Lord Kṛṣṇa went to His elder brother and said, "We have killed Śatadhanvā uselessly. The jewel isn't here."

TEXT 23

तत आह बलो नूनं स मणिः शतधन्वना ।
कस्मिंश्चित्पुरुषे न्यस्तस्तमन्वेष पुरं व्रज ॥२३॥

tata āha balo nūnaṁ
sa maṇiḥ śatadhanvanā
kasmiṁścit puruṣe nyastas
tam anveṣa puraṁ vraja

tataḥ—then; *āha*—said; *balaḥ*—Lord Balarāma; *nūnam*—certainly; *saḥ*—that; *maṇiḥ*—jewel; *śatadhanvanā*—by Śatadhanvā; *kasmiṁścit*—with some particular; *puruṣe*—person; *nyastaḥ*—left; *tam*—him; *anveṣa*—search out; *puram*—to the city; *vraja*—go.

TRANSLATION

To this Lord Balarāma replied, "Indeed, Śatadhanvā must have placed the jewel in the care of someone. You should return to Our city and find that person.

TEXT 24

अहं वैदेहमिच्छामि द्रष्टुं प्रियतमं मम ।
इत्युक्त्वा मिथिलां राजन् विवेश यदुनन्दनः ॥२४॥

ahaṁ vaideham icchāmi
draṣṭuṁ priyatamaṁ mama
ity uktvā mithilāṁ rājan
viveśa yadu-nandanaḥ

aham—I; *vaideham*—the King of Videha; *icchāmi*—wish; *draṣṭum*—to see; *priya-tamam*—who is most dear; *mama*—to Me; *iti*—thus; *uktvā*—saying; *mithilām*—Mithilā (the capital of the Videha kingdom); *rājan*—O King (Parīkṣit); *viveśa*—entered; *yadu-nandanaḥ*—Lord Balarāma, the descendant of Yadu.

TRANSLATION

"I wish to visit King Videha, who is most dear to Me." O King, having said this, Lord Balarāma, the beloved descendant of Yadu, entered the city of Mithilā.

PURPORT

Kṛṣṇa and Balarāma had finally caught up with Śatadhanvā on the outskirts of Mithilā. Since the king of this city was a dear friend of Balarāma's, the Lord decided to enter the city and spend some time there.

TEXT 25

तं दृष्ट्वा सहसोत्थाय मैथिलः प्रीतमानसः ।
अर्हयामास विधिवदर्हणीयं समर्हणैः ॥२५॥

taṁ dṛṣṭvā sahasotthāya
maithilaḥ prīta-mānasaḥ
arhayām āsa vidhi-vad
arhaṇīyaṁ samarhaṇaiḥ

tam—Him, Lord Balarāma; *dṛṣṭvā*—seeing; *sahasā*—immediately; *utthāya*—rising; *maithilaḥ*—the King of Mithilā; *prīta-mānasaḥ*—feeling affection; *arhayām āsa*—he honored Him; *vidhi-vat*—in accordance with scriptural injunctions; *arhaṇīyam*—worshipable; *samarhaṇaiḥ*—with elaborate paraphernalia of worship.

TRANSLATION

The King of Mithilā immediately rose from his seat when he saw Lord Balarāma approaching. With great love the King honored the supremely worshipable Lord by offering Him elaborate worship, as stipulated by scriptural injunctions.

TEXT 26

उवास तस्यां कतिचिन्मिथिलायां समा विभुः ।
मानितः प्रीतियुक्तेन जनकेन महात्मना ।
ततोऽशिक्षद् गदां काले धार्तराष्ट्रः सुयोधनः ॥२६॥

uvāsa tasyāṁ katicin
mithilāyāṁ samā vibhuḥ
mānitaḥ prīti-yuktena
janakena mahātmanā
tato 'śikṣad gadāṁ kāle
dhārtarāṣṭraḥ suyodhanaḥ

uvāsa—He lived; *tasyām*—there; *katicit*—several; *mithilāyām*—in Mithilā; *samāḥ*—years; *vibhuḥ*—the almighty Lord, Śrī Balarāma; *mānitaḥ*—honored; *prīti-yuktena*—affectionate; *janakena*—by King Janaka (Videha); *mahā-ātmanā*—the great soul; *tataḥ*—then; *aśikṣat*—learned; *gadām*—the club; *kāle*—in time; *dhārtarāṣṭraḥ*—the son of Dhṛtarāṣṭra; *suyodhanaḥ*—Duryodhana.

TRANSLATION

The almighty Lord Balarāma stayed in Mithilā for several years, honored by His affectionate devotee Janaka Mahārāja. During that time Dhṛtarāṣṭra's son Duryodhana learned from Balarāma the art of fighting with a club.

TEXT 27

केशवो द्वारकामेत्य निधनं शतधन्वनः ।
अप्राप्तिं च मणेः प्राह प्रियायाः प्रियकृद्विभुः ॥२७॥

keśavo dvārakām etya
nidhanaṁ śatadhanvanaḥ
aprāptiṁ ca maṇeḥ prāha
priyāyāḥ priya-kṛd vibhuḥ

keśavaḥ—Lord Kṛṣṇa; *dvārakām*—to Dvārakā; *etya*—coming; *nidhanam*—the demise; *śatadhanvanaḥ*—of Śatadhanvā; *aprāptim*—the failure to obtain; *ca*—and; *maṇeḥ*—the jewel; *prāha*—he told; *priyāyāḥ*—of His beloved (Queen Satyabhāmā); *priya*—the pleasure; *kṛt*—doing; *vibhuḥ*—the all-powerful Lord.

TRANSLATION

Lord Keśava arrived in Dvārakā and described the demise of Śatadhanvā and His own failure to find the Syamantaka jewel. He spoke in a way that would please His beloved, Satyabhāmā.

PURPORT

Naturally Queen Satyabhāmā was pleased to hear that her father's murderer had been brought to justice. But her father's Syamantaka jewel still had to be recovered, and thus she was also pleased to hear of Lord Kṛṣṇa's determination to recover it.

TEXT 28

ततः स कारयामास क्रिया बन्धोर्हतस्य वै ।
साकं सुहृद्भिर्भगवान् या याः स्युः साम्परायिकीः ॥२८॥

tataḥ sa kārayām āsa
kriyā bandhor hatasya vai
sākaṁ suhṛdbhir bhagavān
yā yāḥ syuḥ sāmparāyikīḥ

tataḥ—then; *saḥ*—He, Lord Kṛṣṇa; *kārayām āsa*—had done; *kriyā*—the ritual duties; *bandhoḥ*—for His relative (Satrājit); *hatasya*—killed; *vai*—indeed; *sākam*—together with; *suhṛdbhiḥ*—well-wishers; *bhagavān*—the Supreme Lord; *yāḥ yāḥ*—all which; *syuḥ*—there are; *sāmparāyikīḥ*—for the time of one's departure from this world.

TRANSLATION

Lord Kṛṣṇa then had the various funeral rites performed for His deceased relative, Satrājit. The Lord attended the funeral along with well-wishers of the family.

TEXT 29

अक्रूरः कृतवर्मा च श्रुत्वा शतधनोर्वधम् ।
व्यूषतुर्भयवित्रस्तौ द्वारकायाः प्रयोजकौ ॥२९॥

akrūraḥ kṛtavarmā ca
śrutvā śatadhanor vadham
vyūṣatur bhaya-vitrastau
dvārakāyāḥ prayojakau

akrūraḥ kṛtavarmā ca—Akrūra and Kṛtavarmā; *śrutvā*—hearing about; *śatadhanoḥ*—of Śatadhanvā; *vadham*—the killing; *vyūṣatuḥ*—they went into exile; *bhaya-vitrastau*—seized with overwhelming fear; *dvārakāyāḥ*—from Dvārakā; *prayojakau*—the engagers.

TRANSLATION

When Akrūra and Kṛtavarmā, who had originally incited Śatadhanvā to commit his crime, heard that he had been killed, they fled Dvārakā in terror and took up residence elsewhere.

TEXT 30

अक्रूरे प्रोषितेऽरिष्टान्यासन् वै द्वारकौकसाम् ।
शारीरा मानसास्तापा मुहुर्दैविकभौतिकाः ॥३०॥

akrūre proṣite 'riṣṭāny
āsan vai dvārakaukasām
śārīrā mānasās tāpā
muhur daivika-bhautikāḥ

akrūre—Akrūra; *proṣite*—being in exile; *ariṣṭāni*—ill omens; *āsan*—arose; *vai*—indeed; *dvārakā-okasām*—for the residents of Dvārakā; *śārīrāḥ*—caused by the body; *mānasāḥ*—and by the mind; *tāpāḥ*—distresses; *muhuḥ*—repeated; *daivika*—caused by higher powers; *bhautikāḥ*—caused by other creatures.

TRANSLATION

In Akrūra's absence ill omens arose in Dvārakā, and the citizens began to suffer continually from physical and mental distresses, as well as from disturbances caused by higher powers and by creatures of the earth.

PURPORT

The word *daivika* here refers to disturbances caused by supernatural beings. These disturbances often manifest as natural calamities like earthquakes, tidal waves or extreme weather. Nowadays materialistic people attribute these disturbances to earthly causes, not realizing that they constitute punishment at the hands of superior beings. The word *bhautikāḥ* refers to trouble caused by fellow creatures of the earth, such as human beings, animals and insects.

According to Śrīla Śrīdhara Svāmī, Akrūra took the Syamantaka jewel and went to reside in the city of Benares, where he became known as Dānapati, "the master of charity." There he executed fire sacrifices on gold altars with elaborate assemblies of qualified priests.

Some residents of Dvārakā felt that the unusual calamities were due to Akrūra's absence, forgetting (as described in the next verse) that the Supreme Lord's personal presence in Dvārakā precluded that possibility. Because when the Lord comes to earth His pastimes resemble those of human beings, the principle of "familiarity breeds contempt" comes into play. It appears that during the lives of many saintly persons and incarnations of God there always exists a class of people who fail to appreciate, or who only occasionally appreciate, the position of the great souls among them. On the other hand, the fortunate and enlightened souls who recognize the true position of the Lord and His associates are supremely blessed.

TEXT 31

इत्यंगोपदिशन्त्येके विस्मृत्य प्रागुदाहृतम् ।
मुनिवासनिवासे किं घटेतारिष्टदर्शनम् ॥३१॥

ity aṅgopadiśanty eke
vismṛtya prāg udāhṛtam
muni-vāsa-nivāse kiṁ
ghaṭetāriṣṭa-darśanam

iti—thus; *aṅga*—my dear (King Parīkṣit); *upadiśanti*—were proposing; *eke*—some; *vismṛtya*—forgetting; *prāk*—previously; *udāhṛtam*—what had been described; *muni*—of sages; *vāsa*—the residence; *nivāse*—when He is residing; *kim*—how; *ghaṭeta*—can arise; *ariṣṭa*—of calamities; *darśanam*—the appearance.

TRANSLATION

Some men proposed [that the troubles were due to Akrūra's absence], but they had forgotten the glories of the Supreme Lord, which they themselves had so often described. Indeed, how can calamities occur in a place where the Personality of Godhead, the residence of all the sages, resides?

PURPORT

Śrīla Viśvanātha Cakravartī provides the following insight on this verse: In Benares Akrūra became famous for performing sacrifices on golden altars and for his abundant charity to the *brāhmaṇas.* When the citizens of Dvārakā heard about this, some of them gossiped that Kṛṣṇa, considering Akrūra a rival, had sent him into exile. To dispel this new and incredible stain on His reputation, Lord Kṛṣṇa created various calamities in Dvārakā, thus inducing the citizens to call for Akrūra's return, which the Lord then ordered.

TEXT 32

देवेऽवर्षति काशीशः श्वफल्कायागताय वै ।
स्वसुतां गान्दिनीं प्रादात्ततोऽवर्षत्स्म काशिषु ॥३२॥

deve 'varṣati kāśīśaḥ
śvaphalkāyāgatāya vai
sva-sutāṁ gāndinīṁ prādāt
tato 'varṣat sma kāśiṣu

deve—when the demigod, Lord Indra; *avarṣati*—had not been supplying rain; *kāśī-īśaḥ*—the King of Benares; *śvaphalkāya*—to Śvaphalka (Akrūra's father); *āgatāya*—who had come; *vai*—certainly; *sva*—his own; *sutām*—daughter; *gāndinīm*—Gāndinī; *prādāt*—gave; *tataḥ*—then; *avarṣat*—it rained; *sma*—indeed; *kāśiṣu*—in the kingdom of Kāśī.

TRANSLATION

[The elders said:] Previously, when Lord Indra had withheld rain from Kāśī [Benares], the king of that city gave his daughter

Gāndinī to Śvaphalka, who was then visiting him. It soon rained in the kingdom of Kāśī.

PURPORT

Śvaphalka was Akrūra's father, and the citizens felt that the son must have the same power as the father. Śrīla Viśvanātha Cakravartī points out that because of Akrūra's relationship with his maternal grandfather, the King of Kāśī, in a time of difficulty Akrūra went to that city.

TEXT 33

तत्सुतस्तत्प्रभावोऽसावक्रूरो यत्र यत्र ह ।
देवोऽभिवर्षते तत्र नोपतापा न मारिकाः ॥३३॥

tat-sutas tat-prabhāvo 'sāv
akrūro yatra yatra ha
devo 'bhivarṣate tatra
nopatāpā na mārikāḥ

tat—his (Śvaphalka's); *sutaḥ*—son; *tat-prabhāvaḥ*—having his powers; *asau*—he; *akrūraḥ*—Akrūra; *yatra yatra*—wherever; *ha*—indeed; *devaḥ*—Lord Indra; *abhivarṣate*—will provide rain; *tatra*—there; *na*—no; *upatāpāḥ*—painful disturbances; *na*—no; *mārikāḥ*—untimely deaths.

TRANSLATION

Wherever his equally powerful son Akrūra stays, Lord Indra will provide sufficient rain. Indeed, that place will be free of miseries and untimely deaths.

TEXT 34

इति वृद्धवचः श्रुत्वा नैतावदिह कारणम् ।
इति मत्वा समानाय्य प्राहाक्रूरं जनार्दनः ॥३४॥

iti vṛddha-vacaḥ śrutvā
naitāvad iha kāraṇam

iti matvā samānāyya
prāhākrūraṁ janārdanaḥ

iti—thus; *vṛddha*—of the elders; *vacaḥ*—the words; *śrutvā*—having heard; *na*—not; *etāvat*—only this; *iha*—of the matter at hand; *kāraṇam*—the cause; *iti*—thus; *matvā*—thinking; *samānāyya*—having him brought back; *prāha*—said; *akrūram*—to Akrūra; *janārdanaḥ*—Lord Kṛṣṇa.

TRANSLATION

Hearing these words from the elders, Lord Janārdana, though aware that the absence of Akrūra was not the only cause of the evil omens, had him summoned back to Dvārakā and spoke to him.

PURPORT

Since Lord Kṛṣṇa is the supreme controller, it was obviously by His will that certain troubles appeared in the city of Dvārakā. Superficially these evils may have been caused by Akrūra's absence, and also by the absence of the auspicious Syamantaka jewel. But we should recall that Dvārakā is the eternal abode of Lord Kṛṣṇa; it is a city of divine bliss because the Lord resides there. Still, to execute His pastimes as a prince of this world, Lord Kṛṣṇa did the needful and summoned Akrūra.

TEXTS 35–36

पूजयित्वाभिभाष्यैनं कथयित्वा प्रियाः कथाः ।
विज्ञाताखिलचित्तज्ञः स्मयमान उवाच ह ॥३५॥
ननु दानपते न्यस्तस्त्वय्यास्ते शतधन्वना ।
स्यमन्तको मनिः श्रीमान् विदितः पूर्वमेव नः ॥३६॥

pūjayitvābhibhāṣyainaṁ
kathayitvā priyāḥ kathāḥ
vijñātākhila-citta-jñaḥ
smayamāna uvāca ha

nanu dāna-pate nyastas
tvayy āste śatadhanvanā
syamantako maṇiḥ śrīmān
viditaḥ pūrvam eva naḥ

pūjayitvā—honoring; *abhibhāṣya*—greeting; *enam*—him (Akrūra); *kathayitvā*—discussing; *priyāḥ*—pleasant; *kathāḥ*—topics; *vijñāta*—fully aware; *akhila*—of everything; *citta*—(Akrūra's) heart; *jñaḥ*—knowing; *smayamānaḥ*—smiling; *uvāca ha*—He said; *nanu*—surely; *dāna*—of charity; *pate*—O master; *nyastaḥ*—kept; *tvayi*—in your care; *āste*—is present; *śatadhanvanā*—by Śatadhanvā; *syamantakaḥ maṇiḥ*—the Syamantaka jewel; *śrī-mān*—opulent; *viditaḥ*—known; *pūrvam*—beforehand; *eva*—indeed; *naḥ*—by Us.

TRANSLATION

Lord Kṛṣṇa honored Akrūra, greeted him confidentially and spoke pleasant words with him. Then the Lord, who was fully aware of Akrūra's heart by virtue of His being the knower of everything, smiled and addressed him: "O master of charity, surely the opulent Syamantaka jewel was left in your care by Śatadhanvā and is still with you. Indeed, We have known this all along.

PURPORT

Lord Kṛṣṇa's treatment of Akrūra here confirms that he is actually a great devotee of the Lord.

TEXT 37

सत्राजितोऽनपत्यत्वाद् गृह्णीयुर्दुहितुः सुताः ।
दायं निनीयापः पिण्डान् विमुच्यर्णं च शेषितम् ॥३७॥

satrājito 'napatyatvād
gṛhṇīyur duhituḥ sutāḥ
dāyaṁ ninīyāpaḥ piṇḍān
vimucyarṇaṁ ca śeṣitam

satrājitaḥ—of Satrājit; *anapatyatvāt*—because of not having sons; *gṛhṇīyuḥ*—they should take; *duhituḥ*—of his daughter; *sutāḥ*—the sons; *dāyam*—the inheritance; *ninīya*—after presenting; *āpaḥ*—water; *piṇḍān*—and memorial offerings; *vimucya*—after clearing; *ṛṇam*—debts; *ca*—and; *śeṣitam*—remaining.

TRANSLATION

"Since Satrājit had no sons, his daughter's sons should receive his inheritance. They should pay for memorial offerings of water and *piṇḍa*, clear their grandfather's outstanding debts and keep the remainder of the inheritance for themselves.

PURPORT

Śrīla Śrīdhara Svāmī quotes the following *smṛti* injunction regarding inheritance: *patnī duhitaraś caiva pitaro bhrātaras tathā/ tat-sutā gotra-jā bandhuḥ śiṣyāḥ sa-brahmacāriṇaḥ.* "The inheritance goes first to the wife, then [if the wife has passed away] to the daughters, then to the parents, then to the brothers, then to the brothers' sons, then to family members of the same *gotra* as the deceased, and then to his disciples, including *brahmacārīs.*"

Śrīla Viśvanātha Cakravartī adds that since Satrājit had no sons, since his wives were killed together with him, and since his daughter Satyabhāmā was not interested in the Syamantaka jewel, which constituted the inheritance, it rightfully belonged to her sons.

In *Kṛṣṇa, the Supreme Personality of Godhead,* Śrīla Prabhupāda explains, "Lord Kṛṣṇa indicated by this statement that Satyabhāmā was already pregnant and that her son would be the real claimant of the jewel and would certainly take the jewel from [Akrūra if he tried to conceal it]."

TEXTS 38–39

तथापि दुर्धरस्त्वन्यैस्त्वय्यास्तां सुव्रते मणिः ।
किन्तु मामग्रजः सम्यङ् न प्रत्येति मणिं प्रति ॥३८॥
दर्शयस्व महाभाग बन्धूनां शान्तिमावह ।
अव्युच्छिन्ना मखास्तेऽद्य वर्तन्ते रुक्मवेदयः ॥३९॥

tathāpi durdharas tv anyais
tvayy āstāṁ su-vrate maṇiḥ
kintu mām agrajaḥ samyaṅ
na pratyeti maṇiṁ prati

darśayasva mahā-bhāga
bandhūnāṁ śāntim āvaha
avyucchinnā makhās te 'dya
vartante rukma-vedayaḥ

tathā api—nevertheless; *durdharaḥ*—impossible to hold on to; *tu*—but; *anyaiḥ*—by others; *tvayi*—with you; *āstām*—should remain; *su-vrate*—O trustworthy keeper of vows; *maṇiḥ*—the jewel; *kintu*—only; *mām*—Me; *agra-jaḥ*—My elder brother; *samyak*—completely; *na pratyeti*—does not believe; *maṇim prati*—concerning the jewel; *darśayasva*—please show it; *mahā-bhāga*—O most fortunate one; *bandhūnām*—to My relatives; *śāntim*—peace; *āvaha*—bring; *avyucchinnāḥ*—uninterrupted; *makhāḥ*—sacrifices; *te*—your; *adya*—now; *vartante*—are going on; *rukma*—of gold; *vedayaḥ*—whose altars.

TRANSLATION

"Nevertheless, the jewel should remain in your care, O trustworthy Akrūra, because no one else can keep it safely. But please show the jewel just once, since My elder brother does not fully believe what I have told Him about it. In this way, O most fortunate one, you will pacify My relatives. [Everyone knows you have the jewel, for] you are now continually performing sacrifices on altars of gold."

PURPORT

Although technically Satyabhāmā's sons had a right to the jewel, Lord Kṛṣṇa decided to leave the jewel in the care of Akrūra, who was using the jewel's wealth to continually perform religious sacrifices. Indeed, Akrūra's ability to perform such rituals on altars of gold was an indication of the jewel's potency.

TEXT 40

एवं सामभिरालब्धः श्वफल्कतनयो मणिम् ।
आदाय वाससाच्छन्नः ददौ सूर्यसमप्रभम् ॥४०॥

evaṁ sāmabhir ālabdhaḥ
śvaphalka-tanayo maṇim
ādāya vāsasācchannaḥ
dadau sūrya-sama-prabham

evam—thus; *sāmabhiḥ*—with conciliatory words; *ālabdhaḥ*—reproached; *śvaphalka-tanayaḥ*—the son of Śvaphalka; *maṇim*—the Syamantaka jewel; *ādāya*—taking; *vāsasā*—in his garment; *ācchannaḥ*—concealed; *dadau*—he gave; *sūrya*—to the sun; *sama*—equal; *prabham*—in effulgence.

TRANSLATION

Thus shamed by Lord Kṛṣṇa's conciliatory words, the son of Śvaphalka brought out the jewel from where he had concealed it in his clothing and gave it to the Lord. The brilliant gem shone like the sun.

PURPORT

We can see in this chapter how a valuable jewel caused so much intrigue, violence and suffering. This is certainly a good lesson for those who desire a trouble-free spiritual life.

TEXT 41

स्यमन्तकं दर्शयित्वा ज्ञातिभ्यो रज आत्मनः ।
विमृज्य मणिना भूयस्तस्मै प्रत्यर्पयत्प्रभुः ॥४१॥

syamantakaṁ darśayitvā
jñātibhyo raja ātmanaḥ
vimṛjya maṇinā bhūyas
tasmai pratyarpayat prabhuḥ

syamantakam—the Syamantaka jewel; *darśayitvā*—after showing; *jñātibhyaḥ*—to His relatives; *rajaḥ*—the contamination; *ātmanaḥ*—(falsely heaped upon) Himself; *vimṛjya*—wiping away; *maṇinā*—with the jewel; *bhūyaḥ*—again; *tasmai*—to him, Akrūra; *pratyarpayat*—offered it back; *prabhuḥ*—the Supreme Lord.

TRANSLATION

After the almighty Lord had shown the Syamantaka jewel to His relatives, thus dispelling the false accusations against Him, He returned it to Akrūra.

PURPORT

For the second time, doubts about the Lord's reputation occasioned by the Syamantaka jewel are dispelled by the jewel itself. Indeed, for the second time the Lord brought the jewel to Dvārakā to establish His integrity there. This amazing series of incidents demonstrates that even when Lord Kṛṣṇa descends to this world there is a tendency for His "peers" to criticize Him. The whole material world is infected by the faultfinding propensity, and in this chapter the Supreme Lord demonstrates the nature of this undesirable quality.

TEXT 42

यस्त्वेतद् भगवत ईश्वरस्य विष्णोर्
वीर्याढ्यं वृजिनहरं सुमंगलं च ।
आख्यानं पठति शृणोत्यनुस्मरेद्वा
दुष्कीर्तिं दुरितमपोह्य याति शान्तिम् ॥४२॥

yas tv etad bhagavata īśvarasya viṣṇor
vīryāḍhyaṁ vṛjina-haraṁ su-maṅgalaṁ ca
ākhyānaṁ paṭhati śṛṇoty anusmared vā
duṣkīrtiṁ duritam apohya yāti śāntim

yaḥ—whoever; *tu*—indeed; *etat*—this; *bhagavataḥ*—of the Personality of Godhead; *īśvarasya*—the supreme controller; *viṣṇoḥ*—Lord Viṣṇu; *vīrya*—with the prowess; *āḍhyam*—which is rich; *vṛjina*—sinful reactions; *haram*—which removes; *su-maṅgalam*—most auspicious; *ca*—and; *ākhyānam*—narration; *paṭhati*—recites; *śṛṇoti*—hears; *anu-smaret*—remembers; *vā*—or; *duṣkīrtim*—bad reputation; *duritam*—and sins; *apohya*—driving away; *yāti*—he attains; *śāntim*—peace.

TRANSLATION

This narration, rich with descriptions of the prowess of Lord Śrī Viṣṇu, the Supreme Personality of Godhead, removes sinful reactions and bestows all auspiciousness. Anyone who recites, hears or remembers it will drive away his own infamy and sins and attain peace.

Thus end the purports of the humble servants of His Divine Grace A. C. Bhaktivedanta Swami Prabhupāda to the Tenth Canto, Fifty-seventh Chapter, of the Śrīmad-Bhāgavatam, *entitled "Satrājit Murdered, the Jewel Returned."*

CHAPTER FIFTY–EIGHT

Kṛṣṇa Marries Five Princesses

This chapter describes how Lord Kṛṣṇa married five brides, beginning with Kālindī, and went to Indraprastha to visit the Pāṇḍavas.

After the Pāṇḍavas had completed their incognito exile, Lord Kṛṣṇa went with Sātyaki and other Yadus to see them in Indraprastha. The Pāṇḍavas greeted the Lord and embraced Him in great ecstasy. Their new bride, Draupadī, shyly approached Kṛṣṇa and bowed down to Him. Then the Pāṇḍavas properly worshiped and welcomed Sātyaki and the Lord's other companions, offering them sitting places.

Lord Kṛṣṇa paid a visit to Queen Kuntī, and after He had offered her His respects, they inquired from each other about their family members. As Kuntī-devī recalled the various miseries Duryodhana had inflicted upon her and her sons, she remarked that Kṛṣṇa was their only protector. "You are the well-wisher of the entire universe," she said, "yet even though You are free from all delusion of 'mine' and 'another's,' You nonetheless reside within the hearts of those who meditate on You constantly, and from within their hearts You destroy all their miseries." Then Yudhiṣṭhira told Kṛṣṇa, "Only because we executed many pious acts are we able to see Your lotus feet, which even great *yogīs* find it impossible to attain." Honored by King Yudhiṣṭhira, Śrī Kṛṣṇa happily remained as a guest in Indraprastha for several months.

One day, Kṛṣṇa and Arjuna went hunting in the forest. While bathing in the Yamunā River, they saw a charming young maiden. On Kṛṣṇa's request Arjuna went up to the girl and asked who she was. The beautiful maiden replied, "I am Kālindī, the daughter of the sun-god. Hoping to attain Lord Viṣṇu as my husband, I have been performing severe austerities. I will accept no one else as my husband, and until He marries me I will remain in the Yamunā, living in a house my father built for me here." After Arjuna reported all this to Kṛṣṇa, the omniscient Lord took Kālindī onto His chariot, and then the three of them returned to Yudhiṣṭhira's residence.

Later the Pāṇḍavas requested Kṛṣṇa to build them a city, and He did so by having Viśvakarmā, the architect of the demigods, construct one that was extremely attractive. The Lord satisfied His beloved devotees by remaining with them there for some time. Then, to please Agni, the fire-god, Kṛṣṇa arranged to offer him the Khāṇḍava forest. The Lord asked Arjuna to burn down the forest and accompanied him as his charioteer. Agni was so satisfied with the offering that he presented Arjuna with the Gāṇḍīva bow, a team of horses, a chariot, two inexhaustible quivers, and armor. While the Khāṇḍava forest burned, Arjuna saved a demon named Maya from the blaze. Maya Dānava reciprocated by building Arjuna a splendid palace. In this building Duryodhana would later get a good drenching after mistaking the surface of a pond for a solid floor, thus embarrassing himself.

Next Lord Kṛṣṇa took permission from Arjuna and His other relatives and went back to Dvārakā with His entourage. There He married Kālindī. Some time later He went to Avantīpura, where, in the presence of many kings, He abducted the King of Avantī's sister, Mitravindā, who was very much attracted to Him.

In the kingdom of Ayodhyā lived a devout king named Nagnajit. He had an extraordinarily beautiful, marriageable daughter named Satyā, or Nāgnajitī. The girl's relatives had laid down the stipulation that any man who could subdue a certain group of seven ferocious bulls would win her hand. When Kṛṣṇa heard about this princess, He went to Ayodhyā with a large contingent of soldiers. King Nagnajit greeted Him hospitably and joyfully worshiped Him with various offerings. When Satyā saw Kṛṣṇa, she immediately desired Him as her husband, and King Nagnajit, understanding his daughter's intentions, informed Lord Kṛṣṇa of his own wish that the Lord and his daughter be married. The King affectionately told the Lord, "You alone would be a suitable husband for my daughter, and if You subdue the seven bulls You may certainly marry her."

Lord Kṛṣṇa then manifested Himself in seven separate forms and subdued the seven bulls. King Nagnajit duly presented his daughter to the Lord, together with a dowry of abundant gifts, and the Lord took Satyā onto His chariot for the journey back to Dvārakā. Just then the rival kings who had been defeated by the bulls tried to attack Lord Kṛṣṇa. But Arjuna easily beat them back, and Kṛṣṇa proceeded with Nāgnajitī to Dvārakā.

Subsequently Śrī Kṛṣṇa married Bhadrā after abducting her from her *svayaṁ-vara* ceremony, and He also married Lakṣmaṇā, the royal daughter of the King of Madra.

TEXT 1

श्रीशुक उवाच
एकदा पाण्डवान् द्रष्टुं प्रतीतान् पुरुषोत्तमः ।
इन्द्रप्रस्थं गतः श्रीमान् युयुधानादिभिर्वृतः ॥१॥

śrī-śuka uvāca
ekadā pāṇḍavān draṣṭuṁ
pratītān puruṣottamaḥ
indraprasthaṁ gataḥ śrīmān
yuyudhānādibhir vṛtaḥ

śrī-śukaḥ uvāca—Śukadeva Gosvāmī said; *ekadā*—once; *pāṇḍavān*—the sons of Pāṇḍu; *draṣṭum*—to see; *pratītān*—visible; *puruṣa-uttamaḥ*—the Supreme Personality of Godhead; *indraprastham*—to Indraprastha, the Pāṇḍavas' capital; *gataḥ*—went; *śrī-mān*—the possessor of all opulence; *yuyudhāna-ādibhir*—by Yuyudhāna (Sātyaki) and others; *vṛtaḥ*—accompanied.

TRANSLATION

Śukadeva Gosvāmī said: Once, the supremely opulent Personality of Godhead went to Indraprastha to visit the Pāṇḍavas, who had again appeared in public. Accompanying the Lord were Yuyudhāna and other associates.

PURPORT

Almost everyone except Lord Kṛṣṇa and Lord Balarāma had thought the Pāṇḍavas perished in the fire set by Duryodhana in the house of lac. Now the Pāṇḍavas had appeared again in public, and Kṛṣṇa was paying them a visit.

TEXT 2

दृष्ट्वा तमागतं पार्था मुकुन्दमखिलेश्वरम् ।
उत्तस्थुर्युगपद्वीराः प्राणा मुख्यमिवागतम् ॥२॥

dṛṣṭvā tam āgataṁ pārthā
mukundam akhileśvaram

uttasthur yugapad vīrāḥ
prāṇā mukhyam ivāgatam

dṛṣṭvā—seeing; *tam*—Him; *āgatam*—arrived; *pārthāḥ*—the sons of Pṛthā (Kuntī); *mukundam*—Kṛṣṇa; *akhila*—of everything; *īśvaram*—the Lord; *uttasthuḥ*—they stood up; *yugapat*—all at once; *vīrāḥ*—heroes; *prāṇāḥ*—the senses; *mukhyam*—their chief, the vital air; *iva*—as; *āgatam*—returned.

TRANSLATION

When the Pāṇḍavas saw that Lord Mukunda had arrived, those heroic sons of Pṛthā all stood up at once, like the senses responding to the return of the life air.

PURPORT

The metaphor used here is quite poetic. When a person is unconscious, the senses do not function. But when consciousness returns to the body, all the senses spring to life at once and begin functioning. Similarly, the Pāṇḍavas all stood up at once, enlivened to receive their Lord, Śrī Kṛṣṇa.

TEXT 3

परिष्वज्याच्युतं वीरा अंगसंगहतैनसः ।
सानुरागस्मितं वक्त्रं वीक्ष्य तस्य मुदं ययुः ॥३॥

pariṣvajyācyutaṁ vīrā
aṅga-saṅga-hatainasaḥ
sānurāga-smitaṁ vaktraṁ
vīkṣya tasya mudaṁ yayuḥ

pariṣvajya—embracing; *acyutam*—Lord Kṛṣṇa; *vīrāḥ*—the heroes; *aṅga*—with His body; *saṅga*—by the contact; *hata*—destroyed; *enasaḥ*—all their sinful reactions; *sa-anurāga*—affectionate; *smitam*—with a smile; *vaktram*—face; *vīkṣya*—looking upon; *tasya*—His; *mudam*—joy; *yayuḥ*—they experienced.

TRANSLATION

The heroes embraced Lord Acyuta, and the touch of His body freed them of sin. Looking at His affectionate, smiling face, they were overwhelmed with joy.

PURPORT

Śrīla Jīva Gosvāmī explains that since the Pāṇḍavas were never sinful, the term *enasaḥ* here refers to the suffering caused by separation from Kṛṣṇa. That unhappiness was now vanquished by the Lord's return.

TEXT 4

युधिष्ठिरस्य भीमस्य कृत्वा पादाभिवन्दनम् ।
फाल्गुनं परिरभ्याथ यमाभ्यां चाभिवन्दितः ॥४॥

yudhiṣṭhirasya bhīmasya
kṛtvā pādābhivandanam
phālgunaṁ parirabhyātha
yamābhyāṁ cābhivanditaḥ

yudhiṣṭhirasya bhīmasya—to Yudhiṣṭhira and Bhīma; *kṛtvā*—after offering; *pāda*—at their feet; *abhivandanam*—obeisances; *phālgunam*—Arjuna; *parirabhya*—firmly embracing; *atha*—then; *yamābhyām*—by the twin brothers, Nakula and Sahadeva; *ca*—and; *abhivanditaḥ*—greeted respectfully.

TRANSLATION

After the Lord bowed down at the feet of Yudhiṣṭhira and Bhīma and firmly embraced Arjuna, He accepted obeisances from the twin brothers, Nakula and Sahadeva.

PURPORT

Externally Kṛṣṇa was the Pāṇḍavas' cousin, and their relationship was just like that between cousin-brothers. Because Yudhiṣṭhira and Bhīma were externally senior to Kṛṣṇa, the Lord bowed down at their feet, whereas He embraced His peer Arjuna and accepted obeisances from the younger brothers, Nakula and Sahadeva. Sometimes inexperienced devotees think it is sinful to honor or bow down to an elder brother in Kṛṣṇa consciousness. But from Lord Kṛṣṇa's example here we may conclude that offering all respects to a senior brother in Kṛṣṇa consciousness is not sinful.

TEXT 5

परमासन आसीनं कृष्णा कृष्णमनिन्दिता ।
नवोढा व्रीडिता किञ्चिच्छनैरेत्याभ्यवन्दत ॥५॥

paramāsana āsīnaṁ
kṛṣṇā kṛṣṇam aninditā
navoḍhā vrīḍitā kiñcic
chanair etyābhyavandata

parama—exalted; *āsane*—on a seat; *āsīnam*—sitting; *kṛṣṇā*—Draupadī; *kṛṣṇam*—Kṛṣṇa; *aninditā*—blameless; *nava*—newly; *ūḍhā*—married; *vrīḍitā*—shy; *kiñcit*—somewhat; *śanaiḥ*—slowly; *etya*—approaching; *abhyavandata*—offered her obeisances.

TRANSLATION

Faultless Draupadī, the Pāṇḍavas' newly married wife, slowly and somewhat timidly approached Lord Kṛṣṇa, who sat on an exalted seat, and offered Him her obeisances.

PURPORT

Śrīmatī Draupadī was so devoted to Kṛṣṇa that she herself was called Kṛṣṇā, which is the feminine form of the name, and Arjuna was also called Kṛṣṇa because of his devotion to the Lord. Similarly, the devotees of the modern Kṛṣṇa consciousness movement are often called "the Kṛṣṇas." So it appears that the custom of addressing Kṛṣṇa's devotees by His name has a long history.

TEXT 6

तथैव सात्यकिः पार्थैः पूजितश्चाभिवन्दितः ।
निषसादासनेऽन्ये च पूजिताः पर्युपासत ॥६॥

tathaiva sātyakiḥ pārthaiḥ
pūjitaś cābhivanditaḥ
niṣasādāsane 'nye ca
pūjitāḥ paryupāsata

tathā eva—similarly; *sātyakiḥ*—Sātyaki; *pārthaiḥ*—by the sons of Pṛthā; *pūjitaḥ*—worshiped; *ca*—and; *abhivanditaḥ*—welcomed; *niṣasāda*—sat down; *āsane*—on a seat; *anye*—the others; *ca*—also; *pūjitāḥ*—worshiped; *paryupāsata*—sat around.

TRANSLATION

Sātyaki also accepted a seat of honor after receiving worship and welcome from the Pāṇḍavas, and the Lord's other companions, being duly honored, sat down in various places.

TEXT 7

पृथां समागत्य कृताभिवादनस्
तयातिहार्दार्द्रदृशाभिरम्भितः ।
आपृष्टवांस्तां कुशलं सहस्नुषां
पितृष्वसारं परिपृष्टबान्धवः ॥७॥

pṛthāṁ samāgatya kṛtābhivādanas
tayāti-hārdārdra-dṛśābhirambhitaḥ
āpṛṣṭavāṁs tāṁ kuśalaṁ saha-snuṣāṁ
pitṛ-ṣvasāraṁ paripṛṣṭa-bāndhavaḥ

pṛthām—to Queen Kuntī; *samāgatya*—going; *kṛta*—offering; *abhivādanaḥ*—His obeisances; *tayā*—by her; *ati*—extreme; *hārda*—with affection; *ardra*—wet; *dṛśā*—whose eyes; *abhirambhitaḥ*—embraced;

āpṛṣṭavān—He asked; *tām*—from her; *kuśalam*—about her welfare; *saha*—together; *snuṣām*—with her daughter-in-law, Draupadī; *pitṛ*—of His father, Vasudeva; *svasāram*—the sister; *paripṛṣṭa*—inquired in detail; *bāndhavaḥ*—about their relatives (living in Dvārakā).

TRANSLATION

The Lord then went to see His aunt, Queen Kuntī. He bowed down to her and she embraced Him, her eyes moist with great affection. Lord Kṛṣṇa inquired from her and her daughter-in-law, Draupadī, about their welfare, and they in turn questioned Him at length about His relatives [in Dvārakā].

PURPORT

Viśvanātha Cakravartī Ṭhākura envisions that as Lord Kṛṣṇa was sitting on His seat, He saw His aunt Kuntī approaching in great eagerness to see Him. He then rose at once, quickly went up to her and offered His obeisances. Her eyes moistened with extreme love, she embraced Him and smelled His head.

TEXT 8

**तमाह प्रेमवैक्लव्यरुद्धकण्ठाश्रुलोचना ।
स्मरन्ती तान् बहून् क्लेशान् क्लेशापायात्मदर्शनम् ॥८॥**

tam āha prema-vaiklavya-
ruddha-kaṇṭhāśru-locanā
smarantī tān bahūn kleśān
kleśāpāyātma-darśanam

tam—to Him; *āha*—she said; *prema*—of love; *vaiklavya*—due to the distress; *ruddha*—choking; *kaṇṭhā*—whose throat; *aśru*—(filled) with tears; *locanā*—whose eyes; *smarantī*—remembering; *tān*—those; *bahūn*—many; *kleśān*—pains; *kleśa*—of pain; *apāya*—for the dispelling; *ātma*—Himself; *darśanam*—who shows.

TRANSLATION

So overcome by love that her throat choked up and her eyes filled with tears, Queen Kuntī remembered the many troubles she and her sons had endured. Thus she addressed Lord Kṛṣṇa, who appears before His devotees to drive away their distress.

TEXT 9

तदैव कुशलं नोऽभूत्सनाथास्ते कृता वयम् ।
ज्ञातीन्नः स्मरता कृष्ण भ्राता मे प्रेषितस्त्वया ॥९॥

tadaiva kuśalaṁ no 'bhūt
sa-nāthās te kṛtā vayam
jñātīn naḥ smaratā kṛṣṇa
bhrātā me preṣitas tvayā

tadā—at that time; *eva*—only; *kuśalam*—well-being; *naḥ*—our; *abhūt*—arose; *sa*—with; *nāthāḥ*—a protector; *te*—by You; *kṛtāḥ*—made; *vayam*—we; *jñātīn*—Your relatives; *naḥ*—us; *smaratā*—who remembered; *kṛṣṇa*—O Kṛṣṇa; *bhrātā*—brother (Akrūra); *me*—my; *preṣitaḥ*—sent; *tvayā*—by You.

TRANSLATION

[Queen Kuntī said:] My dear Kṛṣṇa, our welfare was assured only when You remembered us, Your relatives, and gave us Your protection by sending my brother to visit us.

TEXT 10

न तेऽस्ति स्वपरभ्रान्तिर्विश्वस्य सुहृदात्मनः ।
तथापि स्मरतां शश्वत् क्लेशान् हंसि हृदि स्थितः ॥१०॥

na te 'sti sva-para-bhrāntir
viśvasya suhṛd-ātmanaḥ
tathāpi smaratāṁ śaśvat
kleśān haṁsi hṛdi sthitaḥ

na—not; *te*—for You; *asti*—there is; *sva*—of one's own; *para*—and of others'; *bhrāntiḥ*—delusion; *viśvasya*—of the universe; *suhṛt*—for the well-wisher; *ātmanaḥ*—and Soul; *tathā api*—nonetheless; *smaratām*—of those who remember; *śaśvat*—continuously; *kleśān*—the sufferings; *haṁsi*—You destroy; *hṛdi*—in the heart; *sthitaḥ*—situated.

TRANSLATION

For You, the well-wishing friend and Supreme Soul of the universe, there is never any illusion of "us" and "them." Yet even so, residing within the hearts of all, You eradicate the sufferings of those who remember You constantly.

PURPORT

The intelligent Queen Kuntī here points out that even though Lord Kṛṣṇa is dealing with her affectionately as a relative, He is not compromising His position as the well-wishing Soul of the universe. In other words, the Lord doesn't play favorites. As He says in the *Bhagavad-gītā* (9.29), *samo 'haṁ sarva-bhūteṣu:* "I am equal to everyone." So while the Lord reciprocates with all souls, it is natural that those who love Him intensely receive His special attention, for they want Him and nothing else.

TEXT 11

युधिष्ठिर उवाच
किं न आचरितं श्रेयो न वेदाहमधीश्वर ।
योगेश्वराणां दुर्दर्शो यन्नो दृष्टः कुमेधसाम् ॥११॥

yudhiṣṭhira uvāca
kiṁ na ācaritaṁ śreyo
na vedāham adhīśvara
yogeśvarāṇāṁ durdarśo
yan no dṛṣṭaḥ ku-medhasām

yudhiṣṭhiraḥ uvāca—Yudhiṣṭhira said; *kim*—what; *naḥ*—by us; *ācaritam*—performed; *śreyaḥ*—pious work; *na veda*—do not know; *aham*—I; *adhīśvara*—O supreme controller; *yoga*—of mystic *yoga;*

īśvarāṇām—by the masters; *durdarśaḥ*—rarely seen; *yat*—that; *naḥ*—by us; *dṛṣṭaḥ*—seen; *ku-medhasām*—who are unintelligent.

TRANSLATION

King Yudhiṣṭhira said: O supreme controller, I do not know what pious deeds we fools have done so that we can see You, whom the masters of yogic perfection rarely see.

TEXT 12

इति वै वार्षिकान्मासान् राज्ञा सोऽभ्यर्थितः सुखम् ।
जनयन्नयनानन्दमिन्द्रप्रस्थौकसां विभुः ॥१२॥

iti vai vārṣikān māsān
rājñā so 'bhyarthitaḥ sukham
janayan nayanānandam
indraprasthaukasāṁ vibhuḥ

iti—thus; *vai*—indeed; *vārṣikān*—of the rainy season; *māsān*—the months; *rājñā*—by the King; *saḥ*—He; *abhyarthitaḥ*—invited; *sukham*—happily; *janayan*—generating; *nayana*—for the eyes; *ānandam*—bliss; *indraprastha-okasām*—of the residents of Indraprastha; *vibhuḥ*—the almighty Lord.

TRANSLATION

Requested by the King to stay with them, the almighty Lord remained happily in Indraprastha during the months of the rainy season, giving joy to the eyes of the city's residents.

PURPORT

If possible, the readers of the *Bhāgavatam* should try to correctly chant the Sanskrit verses, which are exquisitely poetic.

TEXTS 13–14

एकदा रथमारुह्य विजयो वानरध्वजम् ।
गाण्डीवं धनुरादाय तूणौ चाक्षयसायकौ ॥१३॥

साकं कृष्णेन सन्नद्धो विहर्तुं विपिनं महत् ।
बहुव्यालमृगाकीर्णं प्राविशत्परवीरहा ॥१४॥

ekadā ratham āruhya
vijayo vānara-dhvajam
gāṇḍīvaṁ dhanur ādāya
tūṇau cākṣaya-sāyakau

sākaṁ kṛṣṇena sannaddho
vihartuṁ vipinaṁ mahat
bahu-vyāla-mṛgākīrṇaṁ
prāviśat para-vīra-hā

ekadā—once; *ratham*—his chariot; *āruhya*—mounting; *vijayaḥ*—Arjuna; *vānara*—the monkey (Hanumān); *dhvajam*—on whose flag; *gāṇḍīvam*—named Gāṇḍiva; *dhanuḥ*—his bow; *ādāya*—taking up; *tūṇau*—his two quivers; *ca*—and; *akṣaya*—inexhaustible; *sāyakau*—whose arrows; *sākam*—together; *kṛṣṇena*—with Lord Kṛṣṇa; *sannaddhaḥ*—wearing armor; *vihartum*—to sport; *vipinam*—a forest; *mahat*—large; *bahu*—with many; *vyāla-mṛga*—beasts of prey; *ākīrṇam*—filled; *prāviśat*—entered; *para*—enemy; *vīra*—of heroes; *hā*—the killer.

TRANSLATION

Once Arjuna, the slayer of powerful enemies, donned his armor, mounted his chariot flying the flag of Hanumān, took up his bow and his two inexhaustible quivers, and went to sport with Lord Kṛṣṇa in a large forest filled with fierce animals.

PURPORT

This incident must have taken place after the burning of the Khāṇḍava forest, since Arjuna was now using the Gāṇḍiva bow and other weapons he had acquired during that incident.

TEXT 15

तत्राविध्यच्छरैर्व्याघ्रान् शूकरान्महिषान् रुरून् ।
शरभान् गवयान् खड्गान् हरिणान् शशशल्लकान् ॥१५॥

tatrāvidhyac charair vyāghrān
śūkarān mahiṣān rurūn
śarabhān gavayān khaḍgān
hariṇān śaśa-śallakān

tatra—there; *avidhyat*—he shot; *śaraiḥ*—with his arrows; *vyāghrān*—tigers; *śūkarān*—boars; *mahiṣān*—wild buffalo; *rurūn*—a species of antelope; *śarabhān*—a species of deer; *gavayān*—a wild oxlike mammal; *khaḍgān*—rhinoceroses; *hariṇān*—black deer; *śaśa*—rabbits; *śallakān*—and porcupines.

TRANSLATION

With his arrows Arjuna shot tigers, boars and buffalo in that forest, along with *rurus, śarabhas, gavayas,* rhinoceroses, black deer, rabbits and porcupines.

TEXT 16

तान्निन्युः किंकरा राज्ञे मेध्यान् पर्वण्युपागते ।
तृट्परीतः परिश्रान्तो बिभत्सुर्यमुनामगात् ॥१६॥

tān ninyuḥ kiṅkarā rājñe
medhyān parvaṇy upāgate
tṛṭ-parītaḥ pariśrānto
bibhatsur yamunām agāt

tān—them; *ninyuḥ*—carried; *kiṅkarāḥ*—servants; *rājñe*—to the King; *medhyān*—fit to be offered in sacrifice; *parvaṇi*—a special occasion; *upāgate*—approaching; *tṛṭ*—by thirst; *parītaḥ*—overcome; *pariśrāntaḥ*—fatigued; *bibhatsuḥ*—Arjuna; *yamunām*—to the Yamunā River; *agāt*—went.

TRANSLATION

A crew of servants carried to King Yudhiṣṭhira the slain animals fit to be offered in sacrifice on some special occasion. Then, feeling thirsty and tired, Arjuna went to the bank of the Yamunā.

PURPORT

As Śrīla Prabhupāda often explained, the *kṣatriyas,* or warriors, would hunt in the forest for several purposes: to practice their fighting skills, to control the population of ferocious beasts, who were a threat to human beings, and to provide animals for Vedic sacrifices. The killed animals would be given new bodies by the power of the sacrifices. Since priests no longer have that power, the sacrifices would now constitute mere killing and are thus forbidden.

In the Fourth Canto of the *Śrīmad-Bhāgavatam* we find that the great sage Nārada severely chastised King Prācīnabarhiṣat for abusing this principle of authorized hunting. In fact, the King had become like modern sportsmen, who cruelly kill animals as a so-called hobby.

TEXT 17

तत्रोपस्पृश्य विशदं पीत्वा वारि महारथौ ।
कृष्णौ ददृशतुः कन्यां चरन्तीं चारुदर्शनाम् ॥१७॥

tatropaspṛśya viśadaṁ
pītvā vāri mahā-rathau
kṛṣṇau dadṛśatuḥ kanyāṁ
carantīṁ cāru-darśanām

tatra—there; *upaspṛśya*—taking bath; *viśadam*—clear; *pītvā*—drinking; *vāri*—the water; *mahā-rathau*—great chariot warriors; *kṛṣṇau*—the two Kṛṣṇas; *dadṛśatuḥ*—saw; *kanyām*—a maiden; *carantīm*—walking; *cāru-darśanām*—charming to see.

TRANSLATION

After the two Kṛṣṇas bathed there, they drank the river's clear water. The great warriors then saw an attractive young girl walking nearby.

TEXT 18

तामासाद्य वरारोहां सुद्विजां रुचिराननाम् ।
पप्रच्छ प्रेषितः सख्या फाल्गुनः प्रमदोत्तमाम् ॥१८॥

tām āsādya varārohāṁ
su-dvijāṁ rucirānanām
papraccha preṣitaḥ sakhyā
phālgunaḥ pramadottamām

tām—her; *āsādya*—approaching; *varā*—excellent; *ārohām*—whose hips; *su*—fine; *dvijām*—whose teeth; *rucira*—attractive; *ānanām*—whose face; *papraccha*—inquired; *preṣitaḥ*—sent; *sakhyā*—by his friend, Śrī Kṛṣṇa; *phālgunaḥ*—Arjuna; *pramadā*—the woman; *uttamām*—extraordinary.

TRANSLATION

Sent by his friend, Arjuna approached the exceptional young woman, who possessed beautiful hips, fine teeth and a lovely face, and inquired from her as follows.

PURPORT

Kṛṣṇa wanted Arjuna to see the deep devotion of this girl, and thus He urged him to make the initial inquiries.

TEXT 19

का त्वं कस्यासि सुश्रोणि कुतो वा किं चिकीर्षसि ।
मन्ये त्वां पतिमिच्छन्तीं सर्वं कथय शोभने ॥१९॥

kā tvaṁ kasyāsi su-śroṇi
kuto vā kiṁ cikīrṣasi
manye tvāṁ patim icchantīṁ
sarvaṁ kathaya śobhane

kā—who; *tvam*—you; *kasya*—whose; *asi*—are you; *su-śroṇi*—O you with the beautiful waist; *kutaḥ*—from where; *vā*—or; *kim*—what; *cikīrṣasi*—do you desire to do; *manye*—I think; *tvām*—you; *patim*—a husband; *icchantīm*—seeking; *sarvam*—everything; *kathaya*—please tell; *śobhane*—O beautiful one.

TRANSLATION

[Arjuna said:] Who are you, O fine-waisted lady? Whose daughter are you, and where do you come from? What are you doing here? I think you must be looking for a husband. Please explain everything, O beautiful one.

TEXT 20

श्रीकालिन्द्युवाच
अहं देवस्य सवितुर्दुहिता पतिमिच्छती ।
विष्णुं वरेण्यं वरदं तपः परममास्थितः ॥२०॥

śrī-kālindy uvāca
ahaṁ devasya savitur
duhitā patim icchatī
viṣṇuṁ vareṇyaṁ vara-daṁ
tapaḥ paramam āsthitaḥ

śrī-kālindī uvāca—Śrī Kālindī said; *aham*—I; *devasya*—of the demigod; *savituḥ*—Savitā (the sun-god); *duhitā*—the daughter; *patim*—as my husband; *icchatī*—desiring; *viṣṇum*—Lord Viṣṇu; *vareṇyam*—the most choice; *vara-dam*—bestower of one's choice; *tapaḥ*—in austerities; *paramam*—extreme; *āsthitaḥ*—engaged.

TRANSLATION

Śrī Kālindī said: I am the daughter of the sun-god. I desire to get as my husband the most excellent and munificent Lord Viṣṇu, and to that end I am performing severe penances.

PURPORT

As Śrīla Viśvanātha Cakravartī points out, Śrīmatī Kālindī correctly understood that Lord Viṣṇu, being the source of all benedictions, is the supreme husband and can thus fulfill all the desires of His wife.

TEXT 21

नान्यं पतिं वृणे वीर तमृते श्रीनिकेतनम् ।
तुष्यतां मे स भगवान्मुकुन्दोऽनाथसंश्रयः ॥२१॥

nānyaṁ patiṁ vṛṇe vīra
tam ṛte śrī-niketanam
tuṣyatāṁ me sa bhagavān
mukundo 'nātha-saṁśrayaḥ

na—no; *anyam*—other; *patim*—husband; *vṛṇe*—will I choose; *vīra*—O hero; *tam*—Him; *ṛte*—except for; *śrī*—of the goddess of fortune; *niketanam*—the abode; *tuṣyatām*—may please be satisfied; *me*—with me; *saḥ*—He; *bhagavān*—the Supreme Lord; *mukundaḥ*—Kṛṣṇa; *anātha*—of those who have no master; *saṁśrayaḥ*—the shelter.

TRANSLATION

I will accept no husband other than Him, the abode of the goddess of fortune. May that Mukunda, the Supreme Personality, the shelter of the helpless, be pleased with me.

PURPORT

The beautiful Kālindī here reveals some apprehension. She insists that she will not accept any husband except Lord Kṛṣṇa, and she states that He is the shelter for those who have no other master. Since she will accept no other shelter, Kṛṣṇa must give her shelter. Also, she says, *tuṣyatāṁ me sa bhagavān:* "May that Supreme Lord be pleased with me." This is her prayer.

As Śrīla Viśvanātha Cakravartī points out, although Kālindī is a young, helpless girl staying in a secluded place, she is not afraid. This staunch faith in and devotion for Lord Kṛṣṇa is ideal Kṛṣṇa consciousness, and Śrīmatī Kālindī's desire will soon be fulfilled.

TEXT 22

कालिन्दीति समाख्याता वसामि यमुनाजले ।
निर्मिते भवने पित्रा यावदच्युतदर्शनम् ॥२२॥

kālindīti samākhyātā
vasāmi yamunā-jale
nirmite bhavane pitrā
yāvad acyuta-darśanam

kālindī—Kālindī; *iti*—thus; *samākhyātā*—named; *vasāmi*—I am living; *yamunā-jale*—in the water of the Yamunā; *nirmite*—built; *bhavane*—in a mansion; *pitrā*—by my father; *yāvat*—until; *acyuta*—of Lord Kṛṣṇa; *darśanam*—the seeing.

TRANSLATION

I am known as Kālindī, and I live in a mansion my father built for me within the water of the Yamunā. There I will stay until I meet Lord Acyuta.

PURPORT

Since Kālindī was a beloved child of the sun-god himself, who would dare disturb her? From this incident we can appreciate the beautiful spiritual processes executed in previous ages by great souls. Unlike the so-called love in worldly "love affairs," beautiful Kālindī's love for Lord Kṛṣṇa was pure and perfect. Even though Kālindī was a tender young girl, her determination to marry Kṛṣṇa was so strong that she arranged for her father to build her a house in the Yamunā where she could perform severe austerities until the day her beloved came.

TEXT 23

तथावदद् गुडाकेशो वासुदेवाय सोऽपि ताम् ।
रथमारोप्य तद्विद्वान् धर्मराजमुपागमत् ॥२३॥

tathāvadad guḍākeśo
vāsudevāya so 'pi tām
ratham āropya tad-vidvān
dharma-rājam upāgamat

tathā—thus; *avadat*—said; *guḍākeśaḥ*—Arjuna; *vāsudevāya*—to Lord Kṛṣṇa; *saḥ*—He; *api*—and; *tām*—her; *ratham*—on His chariot; *āropya*—taking up; *tat*—of all this; *vidvān*—already aware; *dharma-rājam*—to King Yudhiṣṭhira; *upāgamat*—He went.

TRANSLATION

[Śukadeva Gosvāmī continued:] Arjuna repeated all this to Lord Vāsudeva, who was already aware of it. The Lord then took Kālindī onto His chariot and went back to see King Yudhiṣṭhira.

TEXT 24

यदैव कृष्णः सन्दिष्टः पार्थानां परमाद्भुतम् ।
कारयामास नगरं विचित्रं विश्वकर्मणा ॥२४॥

yadaiva kṛṣṇaḥ sandiṣṭaḥ
pārthānāṁ paramādbhutam
kārayām āsa nagaraṁ
vicitraṁ viśvakarmaṇā

yadā eva—when; *kṛṣṇaḥ*—Lord Kṛṣṇa; *sandiṣṭaḥ*—requested; *pārthānām*—for the sons of Pṛthā; *parama*—most; *adbhutam*—amazing; *kārayām āsa*—He had constructed; *nagaram*—a city; *vicitram*—full of variety; *viśvakarmaṇā*—by Viśvakarmā, the architect of the demigods.

TRANSLATION

[Describing a previous incident, Śukadeva Gosvāmī said:] Upon the request of the Pāṇḍavas, Lord Kṛṣṇa had Viśvakarmā build them a most wonderful and amazing city.

PURPORT

Śrīla Viśvanātha Cakravartī mentions that this city was constructed before the burning of the Khāṇḍava forest and hence before the Lord found His bride Kālindī.

TEXT 25

भगवांस्तत्र निवसन् स्वानां प्रियचिकीर्षया ।
अग्नये खाण्डवं दातुमर्जुनस्यास सारथिः ॥२५॥

bhagavāṁs tatra nivasan
svānāṁ priya-cikīrṣayā
agnaye khāṇḍavaṁ dātum
arjunasyāsa sārathiḥ

bhagavān—the Supreme Lord; *tatra*—there; *nivasan*—residing; *svānām*—for His own (devotees); *priya*—pleasure; *cikīrṣayā*—desiring to give; *agnaye*—to Agni, the demigod of fire; *khāṇḍavam*—the Khāṇḍava forest; *dātum*—in order to give; *arjunasya*—of Arjuna; *āsa*—He became; *sārathiḥ*—the chariot driver.

TRANSLATION

The Supreme Lord stayed in that city for some time to please His devotees. On one occasion, Śrī Kṛṣṇa wanted to give the Khāṇḍava forest as a gift to Agni, and so the Lord became Arjuna's charioteer.

PURPORT

Śrīla Jīva Gosvāmī explains the sequence of events that occurred during Lord Kṛṣṇa's stay with the Pāṇḍavas. He states that first the Khāṇḍava forest was burned, then Kālindī was found, then the city was constructed, and then the assembly hall was presented to the Pāṇḍavas.

TEXT 26

सोऽग्निस्तुष्टो धनुरदाद्धयान् श्वेतान् रथं नृप ।
अर्जुनायाक्षयौ तूणौ वर्म चाभेद्यमस्त्रिभिः ॥२६॥

so 'gnis tuṣṭo dhanur adād
dhayān śvetān rathaṁ nṛpa
arjunāyākṣayau tūṇau
varma cābhedyam astribhiḥ

saḥ—that; *agniḥ*—Lord Agni; *tuṣṭaḥ*—pleased; *dhanuḥ*—a bow; *adāt*—gave; *hayān*—horses; *śvetān*—white; *ratham*—a chariot; *nṛpa*—O King (Parīkṣit); *arjunāya*—to Arjuna; *akṣayau*—inexhaustible; *tūṇau*—two quivers; *varma*—armor; *ca*—and; *abhedyam*—unbreakable; *astribhiḥ*—by wielders of weapons.

TRANSLATION

Being pleased, O King, Lord Agni presented Arjuna with a bow, a set of white horses, a chariot, a pair of inexhaustible quivers, and armor that no fighter could pierce with weapons.

TEXT 27

मयश्च मोचितो वह्नेः सभां सख्य उपाहरत् ।
यस्मिन् दुर्योधनस्यासीज्जलस्थलदृशिभ्रमः ॥२७॥

mayaś ca mocito vahneḥ
sabhāṁ sakhya upāharat
yasmin duryodhanasyāsīj
jala-sthala-dṛśi-bhramaḥ

mayaḥ—the demon named Maya; *ca*—and; *mocitaḥ*—delivered; *vahneḥ*—from the fire; *sabhām*—an assembly hall; *sakhye*—to his friend, Arjuna; *upāharat*—presented; *yasmin*—in which; *duryodhanasya*—of Duryodhana; *āsīt*—there was; *jala*—of water; *sthala*—and dry ground; *dṛśi*—in seeing; *bhramaḥ*—confusion.

TRANSLATION

When the demon Maya was saved from the fire by his friend Arjuna, Maya presented him with an assembly hall, in which Duryodhana would later mistake water for a solid floor.

TEXT 28

स तेन समनुज्ञातः सुहृद्भिश्चानुमोदितः ।
आययौ द्वारकां भूयः सात्यकिप्रमुखैर्वृतः ॥२८॥

sa tena samanujñātaḥ
suhṛdbhiś cānumoditaḥ
āyayau dvārakāṁ bhūyaḥ
sātyaki-pramukhair vṛtaḥ

saḥ—He, Lord Kṛṣṇa; *tena*—by him, Arjuna; *samanujñātaḥ*—given leave; *su-hṛdbhiḥ*—by His well-wishers; *ca*—and; *anumoditaḥ*—allowed; *āyayau*—He went; *dvārakām*—to Dvārakā; *bhūyaḥ*—again; *sātyaki-pramukhaiḥ*—by those headed by Sātyaki; *vṛtaḥ*—accompanied.

TRANSLATION

Then Lord Kṛṣṇa, given leave by Arjuna and other well-wishing relatives and friends, returned to Dvārakā with Sātyaki and the rest of His entourage.

TEXT 29

अथोपयेमे कालिन्दीं सुपुण्यर्त्वृक्ष ऊर्जिते ।
वितन्वन् परमानन्दं स्वानां परममंगलः ॥२९॥

athopayeme kālindīṁ
su-puṇya-rtv-ṛkṣa ūrjite
vitanvan paramānandaṁ
svānāṁ parama-maṅgalaḥ

atha—then; *upayeme*—He married; *kālindīm*—Kālindī; *su*—very; *puṇya*—auspicious; *ṛtu*—the season; *ṛkṣe*—and the lunar asterism; *ūrjite*—(on a day) when the configuration of the sun and other heavenly bodies was good; *vitanvan*—spreading; *parama*—the greatest; *ānandam*—pleasure; *svānām*—for His devotees; *parama*—supremely; *maṅgalaḥ*—auspicious.

TRANSLATION

The supremely auspicious Lord then married Kālindī on a day when the season, the lunar asterism and the configurations of the sun and other heavenly bodies were all propitious. In this way He brought the greatest pleasure to His devotees.

TEXT 30

विन्ध्यानुविन्ध्यावावन्त्यौ दुर्योधनवशानुगौ ।
स्वयंवरे स्वभगिनीं कृष्णे सक्तां न्यषेधताम् ॥३०॥

vindyānuvindyāv āvantyau
duryodhana-vaśānugau
svayaṁ-vare sva-bhaginīṁ
kṛṣṇe saktāṁ nyaṣedhatām

vindya-anuvindyau—Vindya and Anuvindya; *āvantyau*—dual kings of Avantī; *duryodhana-vaśa-anugau*—subservient to Duryodhana; *svayam-vare*—in the ceremony of choosing her own husband; *sva*—their; *bhaginīm*—sister; *kṛṣṇe*—to Kṛṣṇa; *saktām*—who was attracted; *nyaṣedhatām*—they forbade.

TRANSLATION

Vindya and Anuvindya, who shared the throne of Avantī, were followers of Duryodhana's. When the time came for their sister [Mitravindā] to select her husband in the *svayaṁ-vara* ceremony, they forbade her to choose Kṛṣṇa, although she was attracted to Him.

PURPORT

The feelings of enmity between the Kurus and the Pāṇḍavas were so strong that Mitravindā's brothers, out of friendship for Duryodhana, forbade the young maiden to accept Kṛṣṇa as her husband.

TEXT 31

राजाधिदेव्यास्तनयां मित्रविन्दां पितृष्वसुः ।
प्रसह्य हृतवान् कृष्णो राजन् राज्ञां प्रपश्यताम् ॥३१॥

rājādhidevyās tanayāṁ
mitravindāṁ pitṛ-ṣvasuḥ
prasahya hṛtavān kṛṣṇo
rājan rājñāṁ prapaśyatām

rājādhidevyāḥ—of Queen Rājādhidevī; *tanayām*—the daughter; *mitravindām*—Mitravindā; *pitṛ*—of His father; *svasuḥ*—of the sister; *prasahya*—forcibly; *hṛtavān*—took away; *kṛṣṇaḥ*—Lord Kṛṣṇa; *rājan*—O King (Parīkṣit); *rājñām*—the kings; *prapaśyatām*—as they watched.

TRANSLATION

My dear King, Lord Kṛṣṇa forcibly took away Princess Mitravindā, the daughter of His aunt Rājādhidevī, before the eyes of the rival kings.

TEXT 32

**नग्नजिन्नाम कौशल्य आसीद् राजातिधार्मिकः ।
तस्य सत्याभवत्कन्या देवी नाग्नजिती नृप ॥३२॥**

*nagnajin nāma kauśalya
āsīd rājāti-dhārmikaḥ
tasya satyābhavat kanyā
devī nāgnajitī nṛpa*

nagnajit—Nagnajit; *nāma*—named; *kauśalyaḥ*—ruler of Kauśalya (Ayodhyā); *āsīt*—there was; *rājā*—a king; *ati*—very; *dhārmikaḥ*—religious; *tasya*—his; *satyā*—Satyā; *abhavat*—there was; *kanyā*—a daughter; *devī*—lovely; *nāgnajitī*—also called Nāgnajiti; *nṛpa*—O King.

TRANSLATION

O King, Nagnajit, the very pious King of Kauśalya, had a lovely daughter named Satyā, or Nāgnajitī.

TEXT 33

**न तां शेकुर्नृपा वोढुमजित्वा सप्तगोवृषान् ।
तीक्ष्णशृंगान् सुदुर्धर्षान् वीर्यगन्धासहान् खलान् ॥३३॥**

*na tāṁ śekur nṛpā voḍhum
ajitvā sapta-go-vṛṣān
tīkṣṇa-śṛṅgān su-durdharṣān
vīrya-gandhāsahān khalān*

na—not; *tām*—her; *śekuḥ*—were able; *nṛpāḥ*—kings; *voḍhum*—to marry; *ajitvā*—without defeating; *sapta*—seven; *go-vṛṣān*—bulls;

tīkṣṇa—sharp; *śṛṅgān*—whose horns; *su*—very; *durdharṣān*—uncontrollable; *vīrya*—of warriors; *gandha*—the smell; *asahān*—not tolerating; *khalān*—vicious.

TRANSLATION

The kings who came as suitors were not allowed to marry her unless they could subdue seven sharp-horned bulls. These bulls were extremely vicious and uncontrollable, and they could not tolerate even the smell of warriors.

TEXT 34

तां श्रुत्वा वृषजिल्लभ्यां भगवान् सात्वतां पतिः ।
जगाम कौशल्यपुरं सैन्येन महता वृतः ॥३४॥

tāṁ śrutvā vṛṣa-jil-labhyāṁ
bhagavān sātvatāṁ patiḥ
jagāma kauśalya-puraṁ
sainyena mahatā vṛtaḥ

tām—of her; *śrutvā*—hearing; *vṛṣa*—the bulls; *jit*—by him who conquers; *labhyām*—attainable; *bhagavān*—the Supreme Lord; *sātvatām*—of the Vaiṣṇavas; *patiḥ*—master; *jagāma*—went; *kauśalya-puram*—to the capital of the Kauśalya kingdom; *sainyena*—by an army; *mahatā*—large; *vṛtaḥ*—surrounded.

TRANSLATION

When the Supreme Personality of Godhead, the master of the Vaiṣṇavas, heard of the princess who was to be won by the conqueror of the bulls, He went to the capital of Kauśalya with a large army.

TEXT 35

स कोशलपतिः प्रीतः प्रत्युत्थानासनादिभिः ।
अर्हणेनापि गुरुणा पूजयन् प्रतिनन्दितः ॥३५॥

sa kośala-patiḥ prītaḥ
pratyutthānāsanādibhiḥ
arhaṇenāpi guruṇā
pūjayan pratinanditaḥ

saḥ—he; *kośala-patiḥ*—the lord of Kośala; *prītaḥ*—pleased; *pratyutthāna*—by standing up; *āsana*—offering a seat; *ādibhiḥ*—and so on; *arhaṇena*—and with offerings; *api*—also; *guruṇā*—substantial; *pūjayan*—worshiping; *pratinanditaḥ*—was greeted in return.

TRANSLATION

The King of Kośala, pleased to see Lord Kṛṣṇa, worshiped Him by rising from his throne and offering Him a seat of honor and substantial gifts. Lord Kṛṣṇa also greeted the King respectfully.

TEXT 36

वरं विलोक्याभिमतं समागतं
नरेन्द्रकन्या चकमे रमापतिम् ।
भूयादयं मे पतिराशिषोऽनलः
करोतु सत्या यदि मे धृतो व्रतः ॥३६॥

varaṁ vilokyābhimataṁ samāgataṁ
narendra-kanyā cakame ramā-patim
bhūyād ayaṁ me patir āśiṣo 'nalaḥ
karotu satyā yadi me dhṛto vrataḥ

varam—suitor; *vilokya*—seeing; *abhimatam*—agreeable; *samāgatam*—arrived; *narendra*—of the King; *kanyā*—the daughter; *cakame*—desired; *ramā*—of the goddess of fortune; *patim*—the husband; *bhūyāt*—may become; *ayam*—He; *me*—my; *patiḥ*—husband; *āśiṣaḥ*—hopes; *analaḥ*—the fire; *karotu*—may it make; *satyāḥ*—true; *yadi*—if; *me*—by me; *dhṛtaḥ*—sustained; *vrataḥ*—my vows.

TRANSLATION

When the King's daughter saw that most agreeable suitor arrive, she immediately desired to have Him, the Lord of Goddess

Ramā. She prayed, "May He become my husband. If I have kept my vows, may the sacred fire bring about the fulfillment of my hopes.

TEXT 37

यत्पादपंकजरजः शिरसा बिभर्ति
श्रीरब्जजः सगिरिशः सह लोकपालैः ।
लीलातनुः स्वकृतसेतुपरीप्सया यः
कालेऽदधत्स भगवान्मम केन तुष्येत् ॥३७॥

yat-pāda-paṅkaja-rajaḥ śirasā bibharti
śrīr abja-jaḥ sa-giriśaḥ saha loka-pālaiḥ
līlā-tanuḥ sva-kṛta-setu-parīpsayā yaḥ
kāle 'dadhat sa bhagavān mama kena tuṣyet

yat—whose; *pāda*—of the feet; *paṅkaja*—lotuslike; *rajaḥ*—the dust; *śirasā*—on her head; *bibharti*—holds; *śrīḥ*—the goddess of fortune; *abja-jaḥ*—Lord Brahmā, who was born from a lotus flower; *sa*—together with; *giri-śaḥ*—Lord Śiva, the master of Mount Kailāsa; *saha*—together with; *loka*—of the planets; *pālaiḥ*—the various rulers; *līlā*—as His pastime; *tanuḥ*—a body; *sva*—by Himself; *kṛta*—created; *setu*—the codes of religion; *parīpsayā*—with the desire to protect; *yaḥ*—who; *kāle*—in course of time; *adadhat*—has assumed; *saḥ*—He; *bhagavān*—the Supreme Personality of Godhead; *mama*—with me; *kena*—on account of what; *tuṣyet*—may be pleased.

TRANSLATION

"Goddess Lakṣmī, Lord Brahmā, Lord Śiva and the rulers of the various planets place the dust of His lotus feet on their heads, and to protect the codes of religion, which He has created, He assumes pastime incarnations at various times. How may that Supreme Personality of Godhead become pleased with me?"

TEXT 38

अर्चितं पुनरित्याह नारायण जगत्पते ।
आत्मानन्देन पूर्णस्य करवाणि किमल्पकः ॥३८॥

arcitaṁ punar ity āha
nārāyaṇa jagat-pate
ātmānandena pūrṇasya
karavāṇi kim alpakaḥ

arcitam—to Him who had been worshiped; *punaḥ*—further; *iti*—as follows; *āha*—he (King Nagnajit) said; *nārāyaṇa*—O Nārāyaṇa; *jagat*—of the universe; *pate*—O Lord; *ātma*—within Himself; *ānandena*—with pleasure; *pūrṇasya*—for Him who is full; *karavāṇi*—may I do; *kim*—what; *alpakaḥ*—insignificant.

TRANSLATION

King Nagnajit first worshiped the Lord properly and then addressed Him: "O Nārāyaṇa, Lord of the universe, You are full in Your own spiritual pleasure. Therefore what can this insignificant person do for You?"

TEXT 39

श्रीशुक उवाच
तमाह भगवान् हृष्टः कृतासनपरिग्रहः ।
मेघगम्भीरया वाचा सस्मितं कुरुनन्दन ॥३९॥

śrī-śuka uvāca
tam āha bhagavān hṛṣṭaḥ
kṛtāsana-parigrahaḥ
megha-gambhīrayā vācā
sa-smitaṁ kuru-nandana

śrī-śukaḥ uvāca—Śukadeva Gosvāmī said; *tam*—to him; *āha*—said; *bhagavān*—the Supreme Lord; *hṛṣṭaḥ*—pleased; *kṛta*—having done; *āsana*—of a seat; *parigrahaḥ*—the acceptance; *megha*—like a cloud; *gambhīrayā*—deep; *vācā*—in a voice; *sa*—with; *smitam*—a smile; *kuru*—of the Kurus; *nandana*—O beloved descendant.

TRANSLATION

Śukadeva Gosvāmī said: O beloved descendant of Kuru, the Supreme Lord was pleased, and after accepting a comfortable seat

He smiled and addressed the King in a voice as deep as the rumbling of a cloud.

TEXT 40

श्रीभगवानुवाच
नरेन्द्र याच्ञा कविभिर्विगर्हिता
राजन्यबन्धोर्निजधर्मवर्तिनः ।
तथापि याचे तव सौहृदेच्छया
कन्यां त्वदीयां न हि शुल्कदा वयम् ॥४०॥

śrī-bhagavān uvāca
narendra yācñā kavibhir vigarhitā
rājanya-bandhor nija-dharma-vartinaḥ
tathāpi yāce tava sauhṛdecchayā
kanyāṁ tvadīyāṁ na hi śulka-dā vayam

śrī-bhagavān uvāca—the Supreme Personality of Godhead said; *nara-indra*—O ruler of men; *yācñā*—begging; *kavibhiḥ*—by learned authorities; *vigarhitā*—condemned; *rājanya*—of the royal order; *bandhoḥ*—for a member; *nija*—in his own; *dharma*—religious standards; *vartinaḥ*—who is situated; *tathā api*—nevertheless; *yāce*—I am begging; *tava*—with you; *sauhṛda*—for friendship; *icchayā*—out of desire; *kanyām*—daughter; *tvadīyām*—your; *na*—not; *hi*—indeed; *śulka-dāḥ*—givers of payment; *vayam*—We.

TRANSLATION

The Supreme Lord said: O ruler of men, learned authorities condemn begging for a person in the royal order who is executing his religious duties. Even so, desiring your friendship, I ask you for your daughter, though We offer no gifts in exchange.

TEXT 41

श्रीराजोवाच
कोऽन्यस्तेऽभ्यधिको नाथ कन्यावर इहेप्सितः ।
गुणैकधाम्नो यस्यांगे श्रीर्वसत्यनपायिनी ॥४१॥

śrī-rājovāca
ko 'nyas te 'bhyadhiko nātha
kanyā-vara ihepsitaḥ
guṇaika-dhāmno yasyāṅge
śrīr vasaty anapāyinī

śrī-rājā uvāca—the King, Nagnajit, said; *kaḥ*—who; *anyaḥ*—other; *te*—to You; *abhyadhikaḥ*—superior; *nātha*—O master; *kanyā*—for my daughter; *varaḥ*—groom; *iha*—in this world; *īpsitaḥ*—desirable; *guṇa*—of transcendental qualities; *eka*—only; *dhāmnaḥ*—who is the abode; *yasya*—on whose; *aṅge*—body; *śrīḥ*—the goddess of fortune; *vasati*—resides; *anapāyinī*—never leaving.

TRANSLATION

The King said: My Lord, who could be a better husband for my daughter than You, the exclusive abode of all transcendental qualities? On Your body the goddess of fortune herself resides, never leaving You for any reason.

TEXT 42

किन्त्वस्माभिः कृतः पूर्वं समयः सात्वतर्षभ ।
पुंसां वीर्यपरीक्षार्थं कन्यावरपरीप्सया ॥४२॥

kintv asmābhiḥ kṛtaḥ pūrvaṁ
samayaḥ sātvatarṣabha
puṁsāṁ vīrya-parīkṣārthaṁ
kanyā-vara-parīpsayā

kintu—but; *asmābhiḥ*—by us (her family); *kṛtaḥ*—made; *pūrvam*—previously; *samayaḥ*—a stipulation; *sātvata-ṛṣabha*—O chief of the Sātvatas; *puṁsām*—of the men (who came as suitors); *vīrya*—the prowess; *parīkṣā*—of testing; *artham*—for the purpose; *kanyā*—for my daughter; *vara*—the husband; *parīpsayā*—with the desire of finding.

TRANSLATION

But to ascertain the proper husband for my daughter, O chief of the Sātvatas, we previously set a condition to test the prowess of her suitors.

PURPORT

According to Śrīla Viśvanātha Cakravartī, the King's actual purpose in setting up the test was to obtain Śrī Kṛṣṇa as his son-in-law, since only He could subdue the bulls. Without such a test it would have been difficult for Nagnajit to refuse the many apparently qualified princes and kings who came to ask for his daughter's hand in marriage.

TEXT 43

सप्तैते गोवृषा वीर दुर्दान्ता दुरवग्रहाः ।
एतैर्भग्नाः सुबहवो भिन्नगात्रा नृपात्मजाः ॥४३॥

saptaite go-vṛṣā vīra
durdāntā duravagrahāḥ
etair bhagnāḥ su-bahavo
bhinna-gātrā nṛpātmajāḥ

sapta—seven; *ete*—these; *go-vṛṣāḥ*—bulls; *vīra*—O hero; *durdāntāḥ*—wild; *duravagrahāḥ*—unbreakable; *etaiḥ*—by them; *bhagnāḥ*—defeated; *su-bahavaḥ*—very many; *bhinna*—broken; *gātrāḥ*—their limbs; *nṛpa*—of kings; *ātma-jāḥ*—sons.

TRANSLATION

These seven wild bulls are impossible to tame, O hero. They have defeated many princes, breaking their limbs.

TEXT 44

यदिमे निगृहीताः स्युस्त्वयैव यदुनन्दन ।
वरो भवानभिमतो दुहितुर्मे श्रियःपते ॥४४॥

yad ime nigṛhītāḥ syus
tvayaiva yadu-nandana
varo bhavān abhimato
duhitur me śriyaḥ-pate

yat—if; *ime*—they; *nigṛhītāḥ*—subdued; *syuḥ*—become; *tvayā*—by You; *eva*—indeed; *yadu-nandana*—O descendant of Yadu; *varaḥ*—groom; *bhavān*—You; *abhimataḥ*—approved; *duhituḥ*—for the daughter; *me*—my; *śriyaḥ*—of the goddess of fortune; *pate*—O husband.

TRANSLATION

If You can subdue them, O descendant of Yadu, You will certainly be the appropriate bridegroom for my daughter, O Lord of Śrī.

TEXT 45

एवं समयमाकर्ण्य बद्ध्वा परिकरं प्रभुः ।
आत्मानं सप्तधा कृत्वा न्यगृह्णाल्लीलयैव तान् ॥४५॥

evaṁ samayam ākarṇya
baddhvā parikaraṁ prabhuḥ
ātmānaṁ saptadhā kṛtvā
nyagṛhṇāl līlayaiva tān

evam—thus; *samayam*—the condition; *ākarṇya*—hearing; *baddhvā*—tightening; *parikaram*—His clothing; *prabhuḥ*—the Lord; *ātmānam*—Himself; *saptadhā*—as seven; *kṛtvā*—making; *nyagṛhṇāt*—He subdued; *līlayā*—like play; *eva*—simply; *tān*—them.

TRANSLATION

Upon hearing these terms, the Lord tightened His clothing, expanded Himself into seven forms and easily subdued the bulls.

PURPORT

According to Śrīla Śrīdhara Svāmī, Lord Kṛṣṇa expanded Himself into seven forms not only to playfully defeat the seven bulls but also to show Princess Satyā that she would not have to compete with His other queens, since He could enjoy with all of them simultaneously.

TEXT 46

बद्ध्वा तान् दामभिः शौरिर्भग्नदर्पान् हतौजसः ।
व्यकर्षल्लीलया बद्धान् बालो दारुमयान् यथा ॥४६॥

baddhvā tān dāmabhiḥ śaurir
bhagna-darpān hataujasaḥ
vyakarṣal līlayā baddhān
bālo dāru-mayān yathā

baddhvā—tying up; *tān*—them; *dāmabhiḥ*—with ropes; *śauriḥ*—Lord Kṛṣṇa; *bhagna*—broken; *darpān*—their pride; *hata*—lost; *ojasaḥ*—their strength; *vyakarṣat*—He dragged; *līlayā*—playfully; *baddhān*—tied up; *bālaḥ*—a boy; *dāru*—of wood; *mayān*—made; *yathā*—as.

TRANSLATION

Lord Śauri tied up the bulls, whose pride and strength were now broken, and pulled them with ropes just as a child playfully pulls wooden toy bulls.

TEXT 47

ततः प्रीतः सुतां राजा ददौ कृष्णाय विस्मितः ।
तां प्रत्यगृह्णाद् भगवान् विधिवत्सदृशीं प्रभुः ॥४७॥

tataḥ prītaḥ sutāṁ rājā
dadau kṛṣṇāya vismitaḥ
tāṁ pratyagṛhṇād bhagavān
vidhi-vat sadṛśīṁ prabhuḥ

tataḥ—then; *prītaḥ*—pleased; *sutām*—his daughter; *rājā*—the King; *dadau*—gave; *kṛṣṇāya*—to Kṛṣṇa; *vismitaḥ*—astonished; *tām*—she; *pratyagṛhṇāt*—accepted; *bhagavān*—the Supreme Person; *vidhi-vat*—in accordance with Vedic prescriptions; *sadṛśīm*—compatible; *prabhuḥ*—the Supreme Lord.

TRANSLATION

Then King Nagnajit, pleased and astonished, presented his daughter to Lord Kṛṣṇa. The Supreme Personality of Godhead accepted this suitable bride in the proper Vedic fashion.

PURPORT

The word *sadṛśīm* indicates that the lovely princess was a fitting bride for the Lord because she possessed wonderful transcendental qualities that complemented His. As Śrīla Jīva Gosvāmī points out, the word *vismitaḥ* indicates that King Nagnajit was certainly astonished at the many extraordinary events suddenly taking place in his life.

TEXT 48

राजपत्न्यश्च दुहितुः कृष्णं लब्ध्वा प्रियं पतिम् ।
लेभिरे परमानन्दं जातश्च परमोत्सवः ॥४८॥

rāja-patnyaś ca duhituḥ
kṛṣṇaṁ labdhvā priyaṁ patim
lebhire paramānandaṁ
jātaś ca paramotsavaḥ

rāja—of the King; *patnyaḥ*—the wives; *ca*—and; *duhituḥ*—of his daughter; *kṛṣṇam*—Kṛṣṇa; *labdhvā*—obtaining; *priyam*—dear; *patim*—husband; *lebhire*—they experienced; *parama*—the greatest; *ānandam*—ecstasy; *jātaḥ*—there arose; *ca*—and; *parama*—the greatest; *utsavaḥ*—festivity.

TRANSLATION

The King's wives felt the greatest ecstasy upon attaining Lord Kṛṣṇa as the dear husband of the royal princess, and a mood of great festivity arose.

TEXT 49

शंखभेर्यानका नेदुर्गीतवाद्यद्विजाशिषः ।
नरा नार्यः प्रमुदिताः सुवासःस्रगलंकृताः ॥४९॥

śaṅkha-bhery-ānakā nedur
gīta-vādya-dvijāśiṣaḥ
narā nāryaḥ pramuditāḥ
suvāsaḥ-srag-alaṅkṛtāḥ

śaṅkha—conchshells; *bherī*—horns; *ānakāḥ*—and drums; *neduḥ*—resounded; *gīta*—songs; *vādya*—instrumental music; *dvija*—of the *brāhmaṇas; āśiṣaḥ*—and blessings; *narāḥ*—men; *nāryaḥ*—women; *pramuditāḥ*—joyful; *su-vāsaḥ*—with fine clothing; *srak*—and garlands; *alaṅkṛtāḥ*—decorated.

TRANSLATION

Conchshells, horns and drums resounded, along with vocal and instrumental music and the sounds of *brāhmaṇas* invoking blessings. The joyful men and women adorned themselves with fine clothing and garlands.

TEXTS 50–51

दशधेनुसहस्राणि पारिबर्हमदाद्विभुः ।
युवतीनां त्रिसाहस्रं निष्कग्रीवसुवाससम् ॥५०॥
नवनागसहस्राणि नागाच्छतगुणान् रथान् ।
रथाच्छतगुणानश्वानश्वाच्छतगुणान्नरान् ॥५१॥

daśa-dhenu-sahasrāṇi
pāribarham adād vibhuḥ
yuvatīnāṁ tri-sāhasraṁ
niṣka-grīva-suvāsasam

nava-nāga-sahasrāṇi
nāgāc chata-guṇān rathān
rathāc chata-guṇān aśvān
aśvāc chata-guṇān narān

daśa—ten; *dhenu*—of cows; *sahasrāṇi*—thousands; *pāribarham*—wedding gift; *adāt*—gave; *vibhuḥ*—the powerful (King Nagnajit);

yuvatīnām—of young women; *tri-sāhasram*—three thousand; *niṣka*—golden ornaments; *grīva*—on whose necks; *su*—excellent; *vāsasam*—whose dress; *nava*—nine; *nāga*—of elephants; *sahasrāṇi*—thousands; *nāgāt*—than the elephants; *śata-guṇān*—one hundred times more (nine hundred thousand); *rathān*—chariots; *rathāt*—than the chariots; *śata-guṇān*—one hundred times more (ninety million); *aśvān*—horses; *aśvāt*—than the horses; *śata-guṇān*—one hundred times more (nine billion); *narān*—men.

TRANSLATION

As the dowry, powerful King Nagnajit gave ten thousand cows, three thousand young maidservants wearing golden ornaments on their necks and bedecked in fine clothing, nine thousand elephants, a hundred times as many chariots as elephants, a hundred times as many horses as chariots, and a hundred times as many manservants as horses.

TEXT 52

दंपती रथमारोप्य महत्या सेनया वृतौ ।
स्नेहप्रक्लिन्नहृदयो यापयामास कोशलः ॥५२॥

dampatī ratham āropya
mahatyā senayā vṛtau
sneha-praklinna-hṛdayo
yāpayām āsa kośalaḥ

dam-patī—the couple; *ratham*—their chariot; *āropya*—having them mount; *mahatyā*—by a large; *senayā*—army; *vṛtau*—accompanied; *sneha*—with affection; *praklinna*—melting; *hṛdayaḥ*—his heart; *yāpayām āsa*—sent them off; *kośalaḥ*—the King of Kośala.

TRANSLATION

The King of Kośala, his heart melting with affection, had the bride and groom seated on their chariot, and then he sent them on their way surrounded by a great army.

TEXT 53

श्रुत्वैतद् रुरुधुर्भूपा नयन्तं पथि कन्यकाम् ।
भग्नवीर्याः सुदुर्मर्षा यदुभिर्गोवृषैः पुरा ॥५३॥

śrutvaitad rurudhur bhūpā
nayantaṁ pathi kanyakām
bhagna-vīryāḥ su-durmarṣā
yadubhir go-vṛṣaiḥ purā

śrutvā—hearing; *etat*—this; *rurudhuḥ*—they obstructed; *bhū-pāḥ*—the kings; *nayantam*—who was taking; *pathi*—along the road; *kanyakām*—His bride; *bhagna*—broken; *vīryāḥ*—whose strength; *su*—very; *durmarṣāḥ*—intolerant; *yadubhiḥ*—by the Yadus; *go-vṛṣaiḥ*—by the bulls; *purā*—before.

TRANSLATION

When the intolerant kings who had been rival suitors heard what had happened, they tried to stop Lord Kṛṣṇa on the road as He took His bride home. But just as the bulls had broken the kings' strength before, the Yadu warriors broke it now.

TEXT 54

तानस्यतः शरव्रातान् बन्धुप्रियकृदर्जुनः ।
गाण्डीवी कालयामास सिंहः क्षुद्रमृगानिव ॥५४॥

tān asyataḥ śara-vrātān
bandhu-priya-kṛd arjunaḥ
gāṇḍīvī kālayām āsa
siṁhaḥ kṣudra-mṛgān iva

tān—them; *asyataḥ*—throwing; *śara*—of arrows; *vrātān*—multitudes; *bandhu*—his friend (Lord Kṛṣṇa); *priya*—to please; *kṛt*—acting; *arjunaḥ*—Arjuna; *gāṇḍīvī*—the possessor of the bow Gāṇḍīva; *kālayām āsa*—drove them away; *siṁhaḥ*—a lion; *kṣudra*—insignificant; *mṛgān*—animals; *iva*—as.

TRANSLATION

Arjuna, wielder of the Gāṇḍiva bow, was always eager to please his friend Kṛṣṇa, and thus he drove back those opponents, who were shooting torrents of arrows at the Lord. He did this just as a lion drives away insignificant animals.

TEXT 55

पारिबर्हमुपागृह्य द्वारकामेत्य सत्यया ।
रेमे यदूनामृषभो भगवान् देवकीसुतः ॥५५॥

pāribarham upāgṛhya
dvārakām etya satyayā
reme yadūnām ṛṣabho
bhagavān devakī-sutaḥ

pāribarham—the dowry; *upāgṛhya*—taking; *dvārakām*—at Dvārakā; *etya*—arriving; *satyayā*—with Satyā; *reme*—enjoyed; *yadūnām*—of the Yadus; *ṛṣabhaḥ*—the chief; *bhagavān*—the Supreme Lord; *devakī-sutaḥ*—the son of Devakī.

TRANSLATION

Lord Devakī-suta, the chief of the Yadus, then took His dowry and Satyā to Dvārakā and continued to live there happily.

TEXT 56

श्रुतकीर्तेः सुतां भद्रां उपयेमे पितृष्वसुः ।
कैकेयीं भ्रातृभिर्दत्तां कृष्णः सन्तर्दनादिभिः ॥५६॥

śrutakīrteḥ sutāṁ bhadrāṁ
upayeme pitṛ-ṣvasuḥ
kaikeyīṁ bhrātṛbhir dattāṁ
kṛṣṇaḥ santardanādibhiḥ

śrutakīrteḥ—of Śrutakīrti; *sutām*—the daughter; *bhadrām*—named Bhadrā; *upayeme*—married; *pitṛ-svasuḥ*—of His father's sister; *kaikeyīm*—the princess of Kaikeya; *bhrātṛbhiḥ*—by her brothers; *dattām*—given; *kṛṣṇaḥ*—Lord Kṛṣṇa; *santardana-ādibhiḥ*—headed by Santardana.

TRANSLATION

Bhadrā was a princess of the Kaikeya kingdom and the daughter of Lord Kṛṣṇa's paternal aunt Śrutakīrti. The Lord married Bhadrā when her brothers, headed by Santardana, offered her to Him.

TEXT 57

सुतां च मद्राधिपतेर्लक्ष्मणां लक्षणैर्युताम् ।
स्वयंवरे जहारैकः स सुपर्णः सुधामिव ॥५७॥

sutāṁ ca madrādhipater
lakṣmaṇāṁ lakṣaṇair yutām
svayaṁ-vare jahāraikaḥ
sa suparṇaḥ sudhām iva

sutām—the daughter; *ca*—and; *madra-adhipateḥ*—of the ruler of Madra; *lakṣmaṇām*—Lakṣmaṇā; *lakṣaṇaiḥ*—with all good qualities; *yutām*—endowed; *svayam-vare*—during her ceremony to choose a husband; *jahāra*—took away; *ekaḥ*—alone; *saḥ*—He, Lord Kṛṣṇa; *suparṇaḥ*—Garuḍa; *sudhām*—nectar; *iva*—as.

TRANSLATION

Then the Lord married Lakṣmaṇā, the daughter of the King of Madra. Kṛṣṇa appeared alone at her *svayaṁ-vara* ceremony and took her away, just as Garuḍa once stole the demigods' nectar.

TEXT 58

अन्याश्चैवंविधा भार्याः कृष्णस्यासन् सहस्रशः ।
भौमं हत्वा तन्निरोधादाहृताश्चारुदर्शनाः ॥५८॥

anyāś caivaṁ-vidhā bhāryāḥ
kṛṣṇasyāsan sahasraśaḥ
bhaumaṁ hatvā tan-nirodhād
āhṛtāś cāru-darśanāḥ

anyāḥ—other; *ca*—and; *evam-vidhāḥ*—just like these; *bhāryāḥ*—wives; *kṛṣṇasya*—of Kṛṣṇa; *āsan*—became; *sahasraśaḥ*—by the thousands; *bhaumam*—(the demon) Bhauma; *hatvā*—after killing; *tat*—by him, Bhauma; *nirodhāt*—from their captivity; *āhṛtāḥ*—taken; *cāru*—beautiful; *darśanāḥ*—whose appearance.

TRANSLATION

Lord Kṛṣṇa also acquired thousands of other wives equal to these when He killed Bhaumāsura and freed the beautiful maidens the demon was holding captive.

Thus end the purports of the humble servants of His Divine Grace A. C. Bhaktivedanta Swami Prabhupāda to the Tenth Canto, Fifty-eighth Chapter, of the Śrīmad-Bhāgavatam, *entitled "Kṛṣṇa Marries Five Princesses."*

CHAPTER FIFTY-NINE

The Killing of the Demon Naraka

This chapter tells how Lord Kṛṣṇa killed Narakāsura, the son of the earth-goddess, and married the thousands of maidens the demon had kidnapped. It also describes how the Lord stole the *pārijāta* tree from heaven and how He behaved like an ordinary householder in each of His palaces.

After Narakāsura stole Lord Varuṇa's umbrella, mother Aditi's earrings, and the playground of the demigods known as Maṇi-parvata, Indra went to Dvārakā and described the demon's transgressions to Lord Kṛṣṇa. Together with Queen Satyabhāmā, the Lord mounted His carrier Garuḍa and traveled to the capital of Narakāsura's kingdom. On a field outside the city He decapitated the demon Mura with His disc. Then He fought Mura's seven sons and sent them all to the abode of death, after which Narakāsura himself entered the battlefield on the back of an elephant. Naraka threw his *śakti* lance at Śrī Kṛṣṇa, but the weapon proved ineffective, and the Lord cut the demon's entire army to pieces. Finally, with His sharp-edged disc Kṛṣṇa cut off Narakāsura's head.

The earth-goddess, Pṛthivī, then approached Lord Kṛṣṇa and gave Him the various items Narakāsura had stolen. She offered prayers to the Lord and presented Naraka's frightened son at Lord Kṛṣṇa's lotus feet. After pacifying the demon's son, Kṛṣṇa entered Narakāsura's palace, where He found sixteen thousand one hundred young women. As soon as they caught sight of the Lord, they all decided to accept Him as their husband. The Lord sent them to Dvārakā along with a great quantity of treasure and then went with Queen Satyabhāmā to the abode of Indra. There He returned Aditi's earrings, and Indra and his wife, Śacī-devī, worshiped Him. On Satyabhāmā's request, Lord Kṛṣṇa uprooted the heavenly *pārijāta* tree and put it on the back of Garuḍa. After defeating Indra and the other demigods who opposed His taking of the tree, Kṛṣṇa returned with Queen Satyabhāmā to Dvārakā, where He planted it in a garden adjacent to Satyabhāmā's palace.

Indra had originally come to Lord Kṛṣṇa offering obeisances and begging Him to kill Narakāsura, but afterwards, when his business had been accomplished, he quarreled with the Lord. The demigods are prone to anger because they become intoxicated with pride in their opulences.

The infallible Supreme Lord manifested Himself in sixteen thousand one hundred separate forms and married each of the sixteen thousand one hundred brides in a different temple. He took up the required activities of household life just like an ordinary person, accepting various kinds of service from each of His many wives.

TEXT 1

श्रीराजोवाच
यथा हतो भगवता भौमो येन च ताः स्त्रियः ।
निरुद्धा एतदाचक्ष्व विक्रमं शार्ंगधन्वनः ॥१॥

śrī-rājovāca
yathā hato bhagavatā
bhaumo yena ca tāḥ striyaḥ
niruddhā etad ācakṣva
vikramaṁ śārṅga-dhanvanaḥ

śrī-rājā uvāca—the King (Parīkṣit) said; *yathā*—how; *hataḥ*—killed; *bhagavatā*—by the Supreme Lord; *bhaumaḥ*—Narakāsura, the son of Bhūmi, goddess of the earth; *yena*—by whom; *ca*—and; *tāḥ*—these; *striyaḥ*—women; *niruddhāḥ*—captured; *etat*—this; *ācakṣva*—please tell; *vikramam*—adventure; *śārṅga-dhanvanaḥ*—of Lord Kṛṣṇa, the possessor of the bow Śārṅga.

TRANSLATION

[King Parīkṣit said:] How was Bhaumāsura, who kidnapped so many women, killed by the Supreme Lord? Please narrate this adventure of Lord Śārṅgadhanvā's.

TEXTS 2–3

श्रीशुक उवाच
इन्द्रेण हतछत्रेण हतकुण्डलबन्धुना ।
हतामराद्रिस्थानेन ज्ञापितो भौमचेष्टितम् ।
सभार्यो गरुडारूढः प्राग्ज्योतिषपुरं ययौ ॥२॥

गिरिदुर्गैः शस्त्रदुर्गैर्जलाग्न्यनिलदुर्गमम् ।
मुरपाशायुतैर्घोरैर्दृढैः सर्वत आवृतम् ॥३॥

śrī-śuka uvāca
indreṇa hṛta-chatreṇa
hṛta-kuṇḍala-bandhunā
hṛtāmarādri-sthānena
jñāpito bhauma-ceṣṭitam
sa-bhāryo garuḍārūḍhaḥ
prāg-jyotiṣa-puraṁ yayau

giri-durgaiḥ śastra-durgair
jalāgny-anila-durgamam
mura-pāśāyutair ghorair
dṛḍhaiḥ sarvata āvṛtam

śrī-śukaḥ uvāca—Śukadeva Gosvāmī said; *indreṇa*—by Lord Indra; *hṛta-chatreṇa*—who had suffered the theft of (Varuṇa's) umbrella; *hṛta-kuṇḍala*—the theft of the earrings; *bandhunā*—of his relative (his mother Aditi); *hṛta*—and the theft; *amara-adri*—on the mountain of the demigods (Mandara); *sthānena*—of the special location (the recreational area at its peak, known as Maṇi-parvata); *jñāpitaḥ*—informed; *bhauma-ceṣṭitam*—of the activities of Bhauma; *sa*—together with; *bhāryaḥ*—His wife (Satyabhāmā); *garuḍa-ārūḍhaḥ*—riding on the giant bird Garuḍa; *prāg-jyotiṣa-puram*—to the city of Prāgjyotiṣa-pura, Bhauma's capital (still existing today as Tejpur in Assam); *yayau*—He went; *giri*—consisting of mountains; *durgaiḥ*—by fortifications; *śastra*—consisting of weapons; *durgaiḥ*—by fortifications; *jala*—of water; *agni*—fire; *anila*—and wind; *durgamam*—made inaccessible by fortifications; *mura-pāśa*—by a dangerous wall of cables; *ayutaiḥ*—tens of thousands; *ghoraiḥ*—fearsome; *dṛḍhaiḥ*—and strong; *sarvataḥ*—on all sides; *āvṛtam*—surrounded.

TRANSLATION

Śukadeva Gosvāmī said: After Bhauma had stolen the earrings belonging to Indra's mother, along with Varuṇa's umbrella and the demigods' playground at the peak of Mandara mountain, Indra went to Lord Kṛṣṇa and informed Him of these misdeeds. The Lord, taking His wife Satyabhāmā with Him, then rode on

Garuḍa to Prāgjyotiṣa-pura, which was surrounded on all sides by fortifications consisting of hills, unmanned weapons, water, fire and wind, and by obstructions of *mura-pāśa* wire.

PURPORT

The *ācāryas* have explained in various plausible ways why Lord Kṛṣṇa took His wife Satyabhāmā with Him. Śrīla Śrīdhara Svāmī begins by saying that the Lord wanted to give His adventurous wife a novel experience and thus took her to the scene of this extraordinary battle. Also, Lord Kṛṣṇa had once granted the blessing to Bhūmi, the earth-goddess, that He would not kill her demoniac son without her permission. Since Bhūmi is an expansion of Satyabhāmā, the latter could authorize Kṛṣṇa to do the needful with the unusually nasty Bhaumāsura.

Finally, Satyabhāmā had been miffed when Nārada Muni brought a celestial *pārijāta* flower to Queen Rukmiṇī. To pacify Satyabhāmā, Lord Kṛṣṇa had promised her, "I'll give you a whole tree of these flowers," and thus the Lord scheduled this procurement of a heavenly tree within His itinerary.

Even nowadays devoted husbands take their wives shopping, and thus Lord Kṛṣṇa took Satyabhāmā to the heavenly planets to get a heavenly tree, as well as to retrieve the goods Bhaumāsura had stolen and return them to their rightful owners.

Śrīla Viśvanātha Cakravartī notes that in the heat of battle Queen Satyabhāmā would naturally become anxious for Lord Kṛṣṇa's safety and pray for the battle to end. Thus she would readily give permission to Kṛṣṇa to kill the son of her expansion, Bhūmi.

TEXT 4

गदया निर्बिभेदाद्रीन् शस्त्रदुर्गाणि सायकैः ।
चक्रेणाग्निं जलं वायुं मुरपाशांस्तथासिना ॥४॥

gadayā nirbibhedādrīn
śastra-durgāṇi sāyakaiḥ
cakreṇāgniṁ jalaṁ vāyuṁ
mura-pāśāṁs tathāsinā

gadayā—with His club; *nirbibheda*—He broke through; *adrīn*—the hills; *śastra-durgāṇi*—the weapon obstacles; *sāyakaiḥ*—with His arrows; *cakreṇa*—with His disc; *agnim*—the fire; *jalam*—water; *vāyum*—and wind; *mura-pāśān*—the cable obstructions; *tathā*—similarly; *asinā*—with His sword.

TRANSLATION

With His club the Lord broke through the rock fortifications; with His arrows, the weapon fortifications; with His disc, the fire, water and wind fortifications; and with His sword, the *mura-pāśa* cables.

TEXT 5

शंखनादेन यन्त्राणि हृदयानि मनस्विनाम् ।
प्राकारं गदया गुर्व्या निर्बिभेद गदाधरः ॥५॥

śaṅkha-nādena yantrāṇi
hṛdayāni manasvinām
prākāraṁ gadayā gurvyā
nirbibheda gadādharaḥ

śaṅkha—of His conchshell; *nādena*—with the resounding; *yantrāṇi*—the mystic talismans; *hṛdayāni*—the hearts; *manasvinām*—of the brave warriors; *prākāram*—the ramparts; *gadayā*—with His club; *gurvyā*—heavy; *nirbibheda*—He broke; *gadādharaḥ*—Lord Kṛṣṇa.

TRANSLATION

With the sound of His conchshell Lord Gadādhara then shattered the magic seals of the fortress, along with the hearts of its brave defenders, and with His heavy club He demolished the surrounding earthen ramparts.

TEXT 6

पाञ्चजन्यध्वनिं श्रुत्वा युगान्ताशनिभीषणम् ।
मुरः शयान उत्तस्थौ दैत्यः पञ्चशिरा जलात् ॥६॥

pāñcajanya-dhvaniṁ śrutvā
yugāntāśani-bhīṣaṇam
muraḥ śayāna uttasthau
daityaḥ pañca-śirā jalāt

pāñcajanya—of Pāñcajanya, Lord Kṛṣṇa's conchshell; *dhvanim*—the vibration; *śrutvā*—hearing; *yuga*—of the universal era; *anta*—at the end; *aśani*—(like the sound) of lightning; *bhīṣaṇam*—terrifying; *muraḥ*—Mura; *śayānaḥ*—sleeping; *uttasthau*—stood up; *daityaḥ*—the demon; *pañca-śirāḥ*—five-headed; *jalāt*—from the water (of the moat surrounding the fortress).

TRANSLATION

The five-headed demon Mura, who slept at the bottom of the city's moat, awoke and rose up out of the water when he heard the vibration of Lord Kṛṣṇa's Pāñcajanya conchshell, a sound as terrifying as the thunder at the end of the cosmic age.

TEXT 7

त्रिशूलमुद्यम्य सुदुर्निरीक्षणो
युगान्तसूर्यानलरोचिरुल्बणः ।
ग्रसंस्त्रिलोकीमिव पञ्चभिर्मुखैर्
अभ्यद्रवत्तार्क्ष्यसुतं यथोरगः ॥७॥

tri-śūlam udyamya su-durnirīkṣaṇo
yugānta-sūryānala-rocir ulbaṇaḥ
grasaṁs tri-lokīm iva pañcabhir mukhair
abhyadravat tārkṣya-sutaṁ yathoragaḥ

tri-śūlam—his trident; *udyamya*—raising; *su*—very; *durnirīkṣaṇaḥ*—difficult to look at; *yuga-anta*—at the end of a millennium; *sūrya*—of the sun; *anala*—(like) the fire; *rociḥ*—whose effulgence; *ulbaṇaḥ*—terrible; *grasan*—swallowing; *tri-lokīm*—the three worlds; *iva*—as if; *pañcabhiḥ*—with his five; *mukhaiḥ*—mouths; *abhyadravat*—he attacked; *tārkṣya-sutam*—Garuḍa, the son of Tārkṣya; *yathā*—as; *uragaḥ*—a snake.

TRANSLATION

Shining with the blinding, terrible effulgence of the sun's fire at the end of a millennium, Mura seemed to be swallowing up the three worlds with his five mouths. He lifed up his trident and fell upon Garuḍa, the son of Tārkṣya, like an attacking snake.

TEXT 8

आविध्य शूलं तरसा गरुत्मते
निरस्य वक्त्रैर्व्यनदत्स पञ्चभिः ।
स रोदसी सर्वदिशोऽम्बरं महान्
आपूरयन्नण्डकटाहमावृणोत् ॥८॥

āvidhya śūlaṁ tarasā garutmate
nirasya vaktrair vyanadat sa pañcabhiḥ
sa rodasī sarva-diśo 'mbaraṁ mahān
āpūrayann aṇḍa-kaṭāham āvṛṇot

āvidhya—whirling about; *śūlam*—his trident; *tarasā*—with great force; *garutmate*—at Garuḍa; *nirasya*—throwing it; *vaktraiḥ*—with his mouths; *vyanadat*—roared; *saḥ*—he; *pañcabhiḥ*—five; *saḥ*—that; *rodasī*—the earth and sky; *sarva*—all; *diśaḥ*—the directions; *ambaram*—outer space; *mahān*—the great (roar); *āpūrayan*—filling; *aṇḍa*—of the egglike covering of the universe; *kaṭāham*—the pot; *āvṛṇot*—covered.

TRANSLATION

Mura whirled his trident and then hurled it fiercely at Garuḍa, roaring from all five mouths. The sound filled the earth and sky, all directions and the limits of outer space, until it reverberated against the very shell of the universe.

TEXT 9

तदापतद्वै त्रिशिखं गरुत्मते
हरिः शराभ्यामभिनत्त्रिधोजसा ।

मुखेषु तं चापि शरैरताडयत्
तस्मै गदां सोऽपि रुषा व्यमुञ्चत ॥९॥

tadāpatad vai tri-śikhaṁ garutmate
hariḥ śarābhyām abhinat tridhojasā
mukheṣu taṁ cāpi śarair atāḍayat
tasmai gadāṁ so 'pi ruṣā vyamuñcata

tadā—then; *āpatat*—flying; *vai*—indeed; *tri-śikham*—the trident; *garutmate*—toward Garuḍa; *hariḥ*—Lord Kṛṣṇa; *śarābhyām*—with two arrows; *abhinat*—broke; *tridhā*—into three pieces; *ojasā*—forcefully; *mukheṣu*—on his faces; *tam*—him, Mura; *ca*—and; *api*—also; *śaraiḥ*—with arrows; *atāḍayat*—He struck; *tasmai*—at Him, Lord Kṛṣṇa; *gadām*—his club; *saḥ*—he, Mura; *api*—and; *ruṣā*—in anger; *vyamuñcata*—released.

TRANSLATION

Then with two arrows Lord Hari struck the trident flying toward Garuḍa and broke it into three pieces. Next the Lord hit Mura's faces with several arrows, and the demon angrily hurled his club at the Lord.

TEXT 10

तामापतन्तीं गदया गदां मृधे
गदाग्रजो निर्बिभिदे सहस्रधा ।
उद्यम्य बाहूनभिधावतोऽजितः
शिरांसि चक्रेण जहार लीलया ॥१०॥

tām āpatantīṁ gadayā gadāṁ mṛdhe
gadāgrajo nirbibhide sahasradhā
udyamya bāhūn abhidhāvato 'jitaḥ
śirāṁsi cakreṇa jahāra līlayā

tām—that; *āpatantīm*—flying toward; *gadayā*—with His club; *gadām*—the club; *mṛdhe*—on the battleground; *gada-agrajaḥ*—Lord Kṛṣṇa, the elder brother of Gada; *nirbibhide*—broke; *sahasradhā*—into thousands of pieces; *udyamya*—raising; *bāhūn*—his arms; *abhidhāvataḥ*—of the one running at him; *ajitaḥ*—unconquerable Lord Kṛṣṇa; *śirāṁsi*—the heads; *cakreṇa*—with His disc; *jahāra*—removed; *līlayā*—easily.

TRANSLATION

As Mura's club sped toward Him on the battlefield, Lord Gadāgraja intercepted it with His own and broke it into thousands of pieces. Mura then raised his arms high and rushed at the unconquerable Lord, who easily sliced off his heads with His disc weapon.

TEXT 11

व्यसुः पपाताम्भसि कृत्तशीर्षो
निकृत्तशृंगोऽद्रिरिवेन्द्रतेजसा ।
तस्यात्मजाः सप्त पितुर्वधातुराः
प्रतिक्रियामर्षजुषः समुद्यताः ॥११॥

vyasuḥ papātāmbhasi kṛtta-śīrṣo
nikṛtta-śṛṅgo 'drir ivendra-tejasā
tasyātmajāḥ sapta pitur vadhāturāḥ
pratikriyāmarṣa-juṣaḥ samudyatāḥ

vyasuḥ—lifeless; *papāta*—he fell; *ambhasi*—into the water; *kṛtta*—severed; *śīrṣaḥ*—his heads; *nikṛtta*—cut off; *śṛṅgaḥ*—whose peak; *adriḥ*—a mountain; *iva*—as if; *indra*—of Lord Indra; *tejasā*—by the power (that is, by his thunderbolt); *tasya*—his, Mura's; *ātma-jāḥ*—sons; *sapta*—seven; *pituḥ*—of their father; *vadha*—by the killing; *āturāḥ*—very distressed; *pratikriyā*—for retribution; *amarṣa*—fury; *juṣaḥ*—feeling; *samudyatāḥ*—aroused to action.

TRANSLATION

Lifeless, Mura's decapitated body fell into the water like a mountain whose peak has been severed by the power of Lord Indra's thunderbolt. The demon's seven sons, enraged by their father's death, prepared to retaliate.

TEXT 12

ताम्रोऽन्तरिक्षः श्रवणो विभावसुर्
वसुर्नभस्वानरुणश्च सप्तमः ।
पीठं पुरस्कृत्य चमूपतिं मृधे
भौमप्रयुक्ता निरगन् धृतायुधाः ॥१२॥

tāmro 'ntarikṣaḥ śravaṇo vibhāvasur
vasur nabhasvān aruṇaś ca saptamaḥ
pīṭhaṁ puraskṛtya camū-patiṁ mṛdhe
bhauma-prayuktā niragan dhṛtāyudhāḥ

tāmraḥ antarikṣaḥ śravaṇaḥ vibhāvasuḥ—Tāmra, Antarikṣa, Śravaṇa and Vibhāvasu; *vasuḥ nabhasvān*—Vasu and Nabhasvān; *aruṇaḥ*—Aruṇa; *ca*—and; *saptamaḥ*—the seventh; *pīṭham*—Pīṭha; *puraḥ-kṛtya*—putting at the head; *camū-patim*—their commander in chief; *mṛdhe*—on the battlefield; *bhauma*—by Bhaumāsura; *prayuktāḥ*—engaged; *niragan*—they came out (of the fortress); *dhṛta*—carrying; *āyudhāḥ*—weapons.

TRANSLATION

Ordered by Bhaumāsura, Mura's seven sons—Tāmra, Antarikṣa, Śravaṇa, Vibhāvasu, Vasu, Nabhasvān and Aruṇa—followed their general, Pīṭha, onto the battlefield bearing their weapons.

TEXT 13

प्रायुञ्जतासाद्य शरानसीन् गदाः
शक्त्यृष्टिशूलान्यजिते रुषोल्बणाः ।
तच्छस्त्रकूटं भगवान् स्वमार्गणैर्
अमोघवीर्यस्तिलशश्चकर्त ह ॥१३॥

prāyuñjatāsādya śarān asīn gadāḥ
śakty-ṛṣṭi-śūlāny ajite ruṣolbaṇāḥ
tac-chastra-kūṭaṁ bhagavān sva-mārgaṇair
amogha-vīryas tilaśaś cakarta ha

prāyuñjata—they used; *āsādya*—attacking; *śarān*—arrows; *asīn*—swords; *gadāḥ*—clubs; *śakti*—spears; *ṛṣti*—lances; *śūlāni*—and tridents; *ajite*—against Lord Kṛṣṇa, the unconquerable; *ruṣā*—angrily; *ulbaṇāḥ*—fierce; *tat*—their; *śastra*—of weapons; *kūṭam*—the mountain; *bhagavān*—the Supreme Lord; *sva*—with His own; *mārgaṇaiḥ*—arrows; *amogha*—never frustrated; *vīryaḥ*—whose prowess; *tilaśaḥ*—into particles the size of sesame seeds; *cakarta ha*—He cut.

TRANSLATION

These fierce warriors furiously attacked invincible Lord Kṛṣṇa with arrows, swords, clubs, spears, lances and tridents, but the Supreme Lord, with unfailing prowess, cut this mountain of weapons into tiny pieces with His arrows.

TEXT 14

तान् पीठमुख्याननयद्यमक्षयं
निकृत्तशीर्षोरुभुजाङ्घ्रिवर्मणः ।
स्वानीकपानच्युतचक्रसायकैस्
तथा निरस्तान्नरको धरासुतः ।
निरीक्ष्य दुर्मर्षण आस्रवन्मदैर्
गजैः पयोधिप्रभवैर्निराक्रमात् ॥१४॥

tān pīṭha-mukhyān anayad yama-kṣayaṁ
nikṛtta-śīrṣoru-bhujāṅghri-varmaṇaḥ
svānīka-pān acyuta-cakra-sāyakais
tathā nirastān narako dharā-sutaḥ
nirīkṣya durmarṣaṇa āsravan-madair
gajaiḥ payodhi-prabhavair nirākramāt

tān—them; *pīṭha-mukhyān*—headed by Pīṭha; *anayat*—He sent; *yama*—of Yamarāja, the lord of death; *kṣayam*—to the abode; *nikṛtta*—cut off; *śīrṣa*—their heads; *ūru*—thighs; *bhuja*—arms; *aṅghri*—legs; *varmaṇaḥ*—and armor; *sva*—his; *anīka*—of the army; *pān*—the leaders; *acyuta*—of Lord Kṛṣṇa; *cakra*—by the disc; *sāyakaiḥ*—and arrows; *tathā*—thus; *nirastān*—removed; *narakaḥ*—Bhauma; *dharā*—of the goddess of the earth; *sutaḥ*—the son; *nirīkṣya*—seeing; *durmarṣaṇaḥ*—unable to tolerate; *āsravat*—exuding; *madaiḥ*—a viscous secretion produced from the foreheads of excited elephants; *gajaiḥ*—with elephants; *payaḥ-dhi*—from the ocean of milk; *prabhavaiḥ*—born; *nirākramāt*—he came out.

TRANSLATION

The Lord severed the heads, thighs, arms, legs and armor of these opponents led by Pīṭha and sent them all to the abode of Yamarāja. Narakāsura, the son of the earth, could not contain his fury when he saw the fate of his military leaders. Thus he went out of the citadel with elephants born from the Milk Ocean who were exuding *mada* from their foreheads out of excitement.

TEXT 15

दृष्ट्वा सभार्यं गरुडोपरि स्थितं
सूर्योपरिष्टात्सतडिद् घनं यथा ।
कृष्णं स तस्मै व्यसृजच्छतघ्नीं
योधाश्च सर्वे युगपच्च विव्यधुः ॥१५॥

dṛṣṭvā sa-bhāryaṁ garuḍopari sthitaṁ
sūryopariṣṭāt sa-taḍid ghanaṁ yathā
kṛṣṇaṁ sa tasmai vyasṛjac chata-ghnīṁ
yodhāś ca sarve yugapac ca vivyadhuḥ

dṛṣṭvā—seeing; *sa-bhāryam*—with His wife; *garuḍa-upari*—upon Garuḍa; *sthitam*—sitting; *sūrya*—the sun; *upariṣṭāt*—higher than; *sa-taḍit*—with lightning; *ghanam*—a cloud; *yathā*—like; *kṛṣṇam*—Lord Kṛṣṇa; *saḥ*—he, Bhauma; *tasmai*—at Him; *vyasṛjat*—released; *śata-ghnīm*—Śataghnī (the name of his *śakti* spear); *yodhāḥ*—his soldiers; *ca*—and; *sarve*—all; *yugapat*—simultaneously; *ca*—and; *vivyadhuḥ*—attacked.

TRANSLATION

Lord Kṛṣṇa and His wife, mounted upon Garuḍa, looked like a cloud with lightning sitting above the sun. Seeing the Lord,

Bhauma released his Śataghnī weapon at Him, whereupon all of Bhauma's soldiers simultaneously attacked with their weapons.

TEXT 16

तद् भौमसैन्यं भगवान् गदाग्रजो
विचित्रवाजैर्निशितैः शिलीमुखैः ।
निकृत्तबाहूरुशिरोध्रविग्रहं
चकार तर्ह्येव हताश्वकुञ्जरम् ॥१६॥

tad bhauma-sainyaṁ bhagavān gadāgrajo
vicitra-vājair niśitaiḥ śilīmukhaiḥ
nikṛtta-bāhūru-śirodhra-vigrahaṁ
cakāra tarhy eva hatāśva-kuñjaram

tat—that; *bhauma-sainyam*—army of Bhaumāsura; *bhagavān*—the Supreme Lord; *gadāgrajaḥ*—Kṛṣṇa; *vicitra*—variegated; *vājaiḥ*—whose feathers; *niśitaiḥ*—sharp; *śilīmukhaiḥ*—with arrows; *nikṛtta*—cut off; *bāhu*—with arms; *ūru*—thighs; *śiraḥ-dhra*—and necks; *vigraham*—whose bodies; *cakāra*—made; *tarhi eva*—at that same moment; *hata*—killed; *aśva*—the horses; *kuñjaram*—and elephants.

TRANSLATION

At that moment Lord Gadāgraja shot His sharp arrows at Bhaumāsura's army. These arrows, displaying variegated feathers, soon reduced that army to a mass of bodies with severed arms, thighs and necks. The Lord similarly killed the opposing horses and elephants.

TEXTS 17–19

यानि योधैः प्रयुक्तानि शस्त्रास्त्राणि कुरूद्वह ।
हरिस्तान्यच्छिनत्तीक्ष्णैः शरैरेकैकशस्त्रिभिः ॥१७॥

उह्यमानः सुपर्णेन पक्षाभ्यां निघ्नता गजान् ।
गुरुत्मता हन्यमानास्तुण्डपक्षनखेर्गजाः ॥१८॥
पुरमेवाविशन्नार्ता नरको युध्ययुध्यत ॥१९॥

yāni yodhaiḥ prayuktāni
śastrāstrāṇi kurūdvaha
haris tāny acchinat tīkṣṇaiḥ
śarair ekaikaśas tribhiḥ

uhyamānaḥ suparṇena
pakṣābhyāṁ nighnatā gajān
gurutmatā hanyamānās
tuṇḍa-pakṣa-nakher gajāḥ

puram evāviśann ārtā
narako yudhy ayudhyata

yāni—those which; *yodhaiḥ*—by the warriors; *prayuktāni*—used; *śastra*—cutting weapons; *astrāṇi*—and missile weapons; *kuru-udvaha*—O hero of the Kurus (King Parīkṣit); *hariḥ*—Lord Kṛṣṇa; *tāni*—them; *acchinat*—cut to pieces; *tīkṣṇaiḥ*—sharp; *śaraiḥ*—with arrows; *eka-ekaśaḥ*—each one; *tribhiḥ*—with three; *uhyamānaḥ*—being carried; *suparṇena*—by him of the great wings (Garuḍa); *pakṣābhyām*—with both his wings; *nighnatā*—who was striking; *gajān*—the elephants; *gurutmatā*—by Garuḍa; *hanyamānāḥ*—being beaten; *tuṇḍa*—with his beak; *pakṣa*—wings; *nakheḥ*—and talons; *gajāḥ*—the elephants; *puram*—into the city; *eva*—indeed; *āviśann*—going back inside; *ārtāḥ*—distressed; *narakaḥ*—Naraka (Bhauma); *yudhi*—in the battle; *ayudhyata*—continued fighting.

TRANSLATION

Lord Hari then struck down all the missiles and weapons the enemy soldiers threw at Him, O hero of the Kurus, destroying each and every one with three sharp arrows. Meanwhile Garuḍa, as he carried the Lord, struck the enemy's elephants with his wings. Beaten by Garuda's wings, beak and talons, the elephants fled back into the city, leaving Narakāsura alone on the battlefield to oppose Kṛṣṇa.

TEXT 20

**दृष्ट्वा विद्रावितं सैन्यं गरुडेनार्दितं स्वकं ।
तं भौमः प्राहरच्छक्त्या वज्रः प्रतिहतो यतः ।
नाकम्पत तया विद्धो मालाहत इव द्विपः ॥२०॥**

dṛṣṭvā vidrāvitaṁ sainyaṁ
garuḍenārditaṁ svakaṁ
taṁ bhaumaḥ prāharac chaktyā
vajraḥ pratihato yataḥ
nākampata tayā viddho
mālāhata iva dvipaḥ

dṛṣṭvā—seeing; *vidrāvitam*—driven away; *sainyam*—the army; *garuḍena*—by Garuḍa; *arditam*—tormented; *svakam*—his; *tam*—him, Garuḍa; *bhaumaḥ*—Bhaumāsura; *prāharat*—struck; *śaktyā*—with his spear; *vajraḥ*—the thunderbolt (of Lord Indra); *pratihataḥ*—counteracted; *yataḥ*—by which; *na akampata*—he (Garuḍa) was not shaken; *tayā*—by it; *viddhaḥ*—struck; *mālā*—by a flower garland; *āhataḥ*—hit; *iva*—like; *dvipaḥ*—an elephant.

TRANSLATION

Seeing his army driven back and tormented by Garuḍa, Bhauma attacked him with his spear, which had once defeated Lord Indra's thunderbolt. But though struck by that mighty weapon, Garuḍa was not shaken. Indeed, he was like an elephant hit with a flower garland.

TEXT 21

**शूलं भौमोऽच्युतं हन्तुमाददे वितथोद्यमः ।
तद्विसर्गात्पूर्वमेव नरकस्य शिरो हरिः ।
अपाहरद् गजस्थस्य चक्रेण क्षुरनेमिना ॥२१॥**

śūlaṁ bhaumo 'cyutaṁ hantum
ādade vitathodyamaḥ

tad-visargāt pūrvam eva
narakasya śiro hariḥ
apāharad gaja-sthasya
cakreṇa kṣura-neminā

śūlam—his trident; *bhaumaḥ*—Bhauma; *acyutam*—Lord Kṛṣṇa; *hantum*—to kill; *ādade*—took up; *vitatha*—frustrated; *udyamaḥ*—whose endeavors; *tat*—its; *visargāt*—release; *pūrvam*—before; *eva*—even; *narakasya*—of Bhauma; *śiraḥ*—the head; *hariḥ*—Lord Kṛṣṇa; *apāharat*—removed; *gaja*—on his elephant; *sthasya*—who was seated; *cakreṇa*—with His disc; *kṣura*—razor-sharp; *neminā*—whose edge.

TRANSLATION

Bhauma, frustrated in all his attempts, took up his trident to kill Lord Kṛṣṇa. But even before he could release it, the Lord cut off his head with His razor-sharp *cakra* as the demon sat atop his elephant.

PURPORT

According to Śrīla Viśvanātha Cakravartī, as Bhauma raised his invincible trident, Satyabhāmā, sitting on Garuḍa with the Lord, said to Kṛṣṇa, "Kill him right away," and Kṛṣṇa did just that.

TEXT 22

सकुण्डलं चारुकिरीटभूषणं
बभौ पृथिव्यां पतितं समुज्ज्वलम् ।
हा हेति साध्वित्यृषयः सुरेश्वरा
माल्यैर्मुकुन्दं विकिरन्त ईडिरे ॥२२॥

sa-kuṇḍalaṁ cāru-kirīṭa-bhūṣaṇaṁ
babhau pṛthivyāṁ patitaṁ samujjvalam
hā heti sādhv ity ṛṣayaḥ sureśvarā
mālyair mukundaṁ vikiranta īḍire

sa—together with; *kuṇḍalam*—earrings; *cāru*—attractive; *kirīṭa*—with a helmet; *bhūṣaṇam*—decorated; *babhau*—shone; *pṛthivyām*—on the ground; *patitam*—fallen; *samujjvalam*—brilliant; *hā hā iti*—"alas, alas!"; *sādhu iti*—"excellent!"; *ṛṣayaḥ*—the sages; *sura-īśvarāḥ*—and the chief demigods; *mālyaiḥ*—with flower garlands; *mukundam*—Lord Kṛṣṇa; *vikirantaḥ*—showering; *īḍire*—they worshiped.

TRANSLATION

Fallen on the ground, Bhaumāsura's head shone brilliantly, decorated as it was with earrings and an attractive helmet. As cries of "Alas, alas!" and "Well done!" arose, the sages and principal demigods worshiped Lord Mukunda by showering Him with flower garlands.

TEXT 23

ततश्च भूः कृष्णमुपेत्य कुण्डले
प्रतप्तजाम्बूनदरत्नभास्वरे ।
सवैजयन्त्या वनमालयार्पयत्
प्राचेतसं छत्रमथो महामणिम् ॥२३॥

tataś ca bhūḥ kṛṣṇam upetya kuṇḍale
pratapta-jāmbūnada-ratna-bhāsvare
sa-vaijayantyā vana-mālayārpayat
prācetasaṁ chatram atho mahā-maṇim

tataḥ—then; *ca*—and; *bhūḥ*—the goddess of the earth; *kṛṣṇam*—Lord Kṛṣṇa; *upetya*—approaching; *kuṇḍale*—the two earrings (belonging to Aditi); *pratapta*—glowing; *jāmbūnada*—gold; *ratna*—with jewels; *bhāsvare*—shining; *sa*—together with; *vaijayantyā*—named Vaijayantī; *vana-mālayā*—and with a flower garland; *arpayat*—presented; *prācetasam*—of Varuṇa; *chatram*—the umbrella; *atha u*—then; *mahā-maṇim*—Maṇi-parvata, the peak of Mandara Mountain.

TRANSLATION

The goddess of the earth then approached Lord Kṛṣṇa and presented Him with Aditi's earrings, which were made of glowing

gold inlaid with shining jewels. She also gave Him a Vaijayantī flower garland, Varuṇa's umbrella and the peak of Mandara Mountain.

TEXT 24

अस्तौषीदथ विश्वेशं देवी देववरार्चितम् ।
प्राञ्जलिः प्रणता राजन् भक्तिप्रवणया धिया ॥२४॥

astauṣīd atha viśveśaṁ
devī deva-varārcitam
prāñjaliḥ praṇatā rājan
bhakti-pravaṇayā dhiyā

astauṣīt—praised; *atha*—then; *viśva*—of the universe; *īśam*—the Lord; *devī*—the goddess; *deva*—of demigods; *vara*—by the best; *arcitam*—who is worshiped; *prāñjaliḥ*—folding her palms; *praṇatā*—bowed down; *rājan*—O King (Parīkṣit); *bhakti*—of devotion; *pravaṇayā*—full; *dhiyā*—with a mentality.

TRANSLATION

O King, after bowing down to Him and then standing with joined palms, the goddess, her mind filled with devotion, began to praise the Lord of the universe, whom the best of demigods worship.

TEXT 25

भूमिरुवाच
नमस्ते देवदेवेश शंखचक्रगदाधर ।
भक्तेच्छोपात्तरूपाय परमात्मन्नमोऽस्तु ते ॥२५॥

bhūmir uvāca
namas te deva-deveśa
śaṅkha-cakra-gadā-dhara
bhaktecchopātta-rūpāya
paramātman namo 'stu te

bhūmiḥ uvāca—the earth-goddess said; *namaḥ*—obeisances; *te*—unto You; *deva-deva*—of the lords of the demigods; *īśa*—O Lord; *śaṅkha*—of the conchshell; *cakra*—disc; *gadā*—and club; *dhara*—O holder; *bhakta*—of Your devotees; *icchā*—by the desire; *upātta*—who have assumed; *rūpāya*—Your forms; *parama-ātman*—O Supreme Soul; *namaḥ*—obeisances; *astu*—let there be; *te*—unto You.

TRANSLATION

Goddess Bhūmi said: Obeisances unto You, O Lord of the chief demigods, O holder of the conchshell, disc and club. O Supreme Soul within the heart, You assume Your various forms to fulfill Your devotees' desires. Obeisances unto You.

TEXT 26

नमः पंकजनाभाय नमः पंकजमालिने ।
नमः पंकजनेत्राय नमस्ते पंकजाङ्घ्रये ॥२६॥

namaḥ paṅkaja-nābhāya
namaḥ paṅkaja-māline
namaḥ paṅkaja-netrāya
namas te paṅkajāṅghraye

namaḥ—all respectful obeisances; *paṅkaja-nābhāya*—unto the Lord who has a specific depression resembling a lotus flower in the center of His abdomen; *namaḥ*—obeisances; *paṅkaja-māline*—one who is always decorated with a garland of lotus flowers; *namaḥ*—obeisances; *paṅkaja-netrāya*—one whose glance is as cooling as a lotus flower; *namaḥ te*—respectful obeisances unto You; *paṅkaja-aṅghraye*—unto You, the soles of whose feet are engraved with lotus flowers (and who are therefore said to possess lotus feet).

TRANSLATION

My respectful obeisances are unto You, O Lord, whose abdomen is marked with a depression like a lotus flower, who are always decorated with garlands of lotus flowers, whose glance is as cool as the lotus and whose feet are engraved with lotuses.

PURPORT

Queen Kuntī offered this same prayer, which is found in First Canto of the *Śrīmad-Bhāgavatam*, Chapter 8, Text 22. The synonyms and translation given here are taken from Śrīla Prabhupāda's rendering of that text.

We may also note that although Kuntī's prayer occurs early in the *Bhāgavatam*, she offered it many years after the incident described here.

TEXT 27

नमो भगवते तुभ्यं वासुदेवाय विष्णवे ।
पुरुषायादिबीजाय पूर्णबोधाय ते नमः ॥२७॥

namo bhagavate tubhyaṁ
vāsudevāya viṣṇave
puruṣāyādi-bījāya
pūrṇa-bodhāya te namaḥ

namaḥ—obeisances; *bhagavate*—to the Supreme Godhead; *tubhyam*—unto You; *vāsudevāya*—Lord Vāsudeva, the shelter of all created beings; *viṣṇave*—all-pervading Lord Viṣṇu; *puruṣāya*—the primeval person; *ādi*—original; *bījāya*—the seed; *pūrṇa*—full; *bodhāya*—knowledge; *te*—to You; *namaḥ*—obeisances.

TRANSLATION

Obeisances unto You, the Supreme Lord Vāsudeva, Viṣṇu, the primeval person, the original seed. Obeisances unto You, the omniscient one.

TEXT 28

अजाय जनयित्रेऽस्य ब्रह्मणेऽनन्तशक्तये ।
परावरात्मन् भूतात्मन् परमात्मन्नमोऽस्तु ते ॥२८॥

ajāya janayitre 'sya
brahmaṇe 'nanta-śaktaye
parāvarātman bhūtātman
paramātman namo 'stu te

ajāya—to the unborn; *janayitre*—the progenitor; *asya*—of this (universe); *brahmaṇe*—the Absolute; *ananta*—unlimited; *śaktaye*—whose energies; *para*—of the superior; *avara*—and the inferior; *ātman*—O Soul; *bhūta*—of the material creation; *ātman*—O Soul; *parama-ātman*—O Supreme Soul, who are all-pervading; *namaḥ*—obeisances; *astu*—may there be; *te*—unto You.

TRANSLATION

Obeisances unto You of unlimited energies, the unborn progenitor of this universe, the Absolute. O Soul of the high and the low, O Soul of the created elements, O all-pervading Supreme Soul, obeisances unto You.

TEXT 29

त्वं वै सिसृक्षुरज उत्कटं प्रभो
तमो निरोधाय बिभर्ष्यसंवृतः ।
स्थानाय सत्त्वं जगतो जगत्पते
कालः प्रधानं पुरुषो भवान् परः ॥२९॥

tvaṁ vai sisṛkṣur aja utkaṭaṁ prabho
tamo nirodhāya bibharṣy asaṁvṛtaḥ
sthānāya sattvaṁ jagato jagat-pate
kālaḥ pradhānaṁ puruṣo bhavān paraḥ

tvam—You; *vai*—indeed; *sisṛkṣuḥ*—desiring to create; *ajaḥ*—unborn; *utkaṭam*—prominent; *prabho*—O master; *tamaḥ*—the mode of ignorance; *nirodhāya*—for annihilation; *bibharṣi*—You assume; *asaṁvṛtaḥ*—uncovered; *sthānāya*—for maintenance; *sattvam*—the mode of goodness; *jagataḥ*—of the universe; *jagat-pate*—O Lord of the universe; *kālaḥ*—time; *pradhānam*—material nature (in its original, undifferentiated state); *puruṣaḥ*—the creator (who interacts with material nature); *bhavān*—You; *paraḥ*—distinct.

TRANSLATION

Desiring to create, O unborn master, You increase and then assume the mode of passion. You do likewise with the mode of

ignorance when You wish to annihilate the universe and with goodness when You wish to maintain it. Nonetheless, You remain uncovered by these modes. You are time, the *pradhāna*, and the *puruṣa*, O Lord of the universe, yet still You are separate and distinct.

PURPORT

The word *jagataḥ* in the third line of this verse indicates that the functions of creation, maintenance and annihilation are here mentioned in a cosmic context.

The word *utkaṭam* indicates that when a particular function is being carried out, whether universal creation, maintenance or annihilation, the particular material quality associated with that function becomes predominant.

TEXT 30

अहं पयो ज्योतिरथानिलो नभो
मात्राणि देवा मन इन्द्रियाणि ।
कर्ता महानित्यखिलं चराचरं
त्वय्यद्वितीये भगवन्नयं भ्रमः ॥३०॥

ahaṁ payo jyotir athānilo nabho
mātrāṇi devā mana indriyāṇi
kartā mahān ity akhilaṁ carācaraṁ
tvayy advitīye bhagavann ayaṁ bhramaḥ

aham—myself (earth); *payaḥ*—water; *jyotiḥ*—fire; *atha*—and; *anilaḥ*—air; *nabhaḥ*—ether; *mātrāṇi*—the various sense objects (corresponding to each of the five gross elements); *devāḥ*—the demigods; *manaḥ*—the mind; *indriyāṇi*—the senses; *kartā*—"the doer," false ego; *mahān*—the total material energy (*mahat-tattva*); *iti*—thus; *akhilam*—everything; *cara*—moving; *acaram*—and nonmoving; *tvayi*—within You; *advitīye*—who has no second; *bhagavan*—O Lord; *ayam*—this; *bhramaḥ*—illusion.

TRANSLATION

This is illusion: that earth, water, fire, air, ether, sense objects, demigods, mind, the senses, false ego and the total material

energy exist independent of You. In fact, they are all within You, my Lord, who are one without a second.

PURPORT

The earth-goddess, in her prayers, directly touches upon the subtleties of transcendental philosophy, clarifying that although the Supreme Lord is unique and distinct from His creation, His creation has no independent existence and always rests within Him. Thus the Lord and His creation are simultaneously one and different, as explained by Śrī Caitanya Mahāprabhu five hundred years ago.

To say that everything is God, without any distinction, is meaningless, since nothing can act like God. Dogs, shoes and human beings are hardly omnipotent or omniscient, nor do they create the universe. On the other hand, there is a real sense in which all things are one, for everything is part of the same supreme, absolute reality. Lord Caitanya has given the very useful analogy of the sun and the sun rays. The sun and its sunshine are one reality, for the sun is the celestial body that shines. On the other hand, one can certainly distinguish between the sun globe and the sun rays. Thus God's simultaneous oneness with and difference from His creation is the final and satisfying explanation of reality. All that exists is the Lord's potency, and yet He endows the superior potency, the living beings, with free will so that they can become responsible for the moral and spiritual quality of their decisions and activities.

This entire transcendental science is clearly and rationally explained in the *Śrīmad-Bhāgavatam*.

TEXT 31

तस्यात्मजोऽयं तव पादपंकजं
भीतः प्रपन्नार्तिहरोपसादितः ।
तत्पालयैनं कुरु हस्तपंकजं
शिरस्यमुष्याखिलकल्मषापहम् ॥३१॥

tasyātmajo 'yaṁ tava pāda-paṅkajaṁ
bhītaḥ prapannārti-haropasāditaḥ
tat pālayainaṁ kuru hasta-paṅkajaṁ
śirasy amuṣyākhila-kalmaṣāpaham

tasya—of him (Bhaumāsura); *ātma-jaḥ*—son; *ayam*—this; *tava*—Your; *pāda*—feet; *paṅkajam*—lotuslike; *bhītaḥ*—afraid; *prapanna*—of those who take shelter; *ārti*—the distress; *hara*—O You who remove; *upasāditaḥ*—has approached; *tat*—therefore; *pālaya*—please protect; *enam*—him; *kuru*—place; *hasta-paṅkajam*—Your lotus hand; *śirasi*—on the head; *amuṣya*—his; *akhila*—all; *kalmaṣa*—sins; *apaham*—which eradicates.

TRANSLATION

Here is the son of Bhaumāsura. Frightened, he is approaching Your lotus feet, since You remove the distress of all who seek refuge in You. Please protect him. Place Your lotus hand, which dispels all sins, upon his head.

PURPORT

Here the earth-goddess seeks protection for her grandson, who has been frightened by all the terribly violent events that just took place.

TEXT 32

श्रीशुक उवाच
इति भूम्यर्थितो वाग्भिर्भगवान् भक्तिनम्रया ।
दत्त्वाभयं भौमगृहं प्राविशत्सकलर्द्धिमत् ॥३२॥

śrī-śuka uvāca
iti bhūmy-arthito vāgbhir
bhagavān bhakti-namrayā
dattvābhayaṁ bhauma-gṛhaṁ
prāviśat sakalarddhimat

śrī-śukaḥ uvāca—Śukadeva Gosvāmī said; *iti*—thus; *bhūmi*—by goddess Bhūmi; *arthitaḥ*—prayed to; *vāgbhiḥ*—in those words; *bhagavān*—the Supreme Lord; *bhakti*—with devotion; *namrayā*—humble; *dattvā*—giving; *abhayam*—fearlessness; *bhauma-gṛham*—the residence of Bhaumāsura; *prāviśat*—He entered; *sakala*—all; *ṛddhi*—with opulences; *mat*—endowed.

TRANSLATION

Śukadeva Gosvāmī said: Thus entreated by Goddess Bhūmi in words of humble devotion, the Supreme Lord bestowed fearlessness upon her grandson and then entered Bhaumāsura's palace, which was filled with all manner of riches.

TEXT 33

तत्र राजन्यकन्यानां षट्सहस्राधिकायुतम् ।
भौमाहृतानां विक्रम्य राजभ्यो ददृशे हरिः ॥३३॥

tatra rājanya-kanyānāṁ
ṣaṭ-sahasrādhikāyutam
bhaumāhṛtānāṁ vikramya
rājabhyo dadṛśe hariḥ

tatra—there; *rājanya*—of the royal order; *kanyānām*—of maidens; *ṣaṭ-sahasra*—six thousand; *adhika*—more than; *ayutam*—ten thousand; *bhauma*—by Bhauma; *āhṛtānām*—taken; *vikramya*—by force; *rājabhyaḥ*—from kings; *dadṛśe*—saw; *hariḥ*—Lord Kṛṣṇa.

TRANSLATION

There Lord Kṛṣṇa saw sixteen thousand royal maidens, whom Bhauma had taken by force from various kings.

PURPORT

Śrīla Śrīdhara Svāmī provides evidence from the sage Parāśara, as quoted in the *Viṣṇu Purāṇa* (5.29.31), to the effect that there were actually 16,100 royal maidens imprisoned in Bhauma's palace:

kanyā-pure sa kanyānāṁ
ṣoḍaśātulya-vikramaḥ
śatādhikāni dadṛśe
sahasrāṇi mahā-mate

"Within the maidens' quarters, O wise one, that Lord of unequaled prowess found 16,100 princesses."

Another relevant verse from the *Viṣṇu Purāṇa* (5.29.9) is as follows:

deva-siddhāsurādīnāṁ
nṛpānāṁ ca janārdana
hṛtvā hi so 'suraḥ kanyā
rurodha nija-mandire

"The demon [Bhaumāsura] kidnapped the unmarried daughters of demigods, *siddhas, asuras* and kings, O Janārdana, and imprisoned them in his palace."

TEXT 34

तं प्रविष्टं स्त्रियो वीक्ष्य नरवर्यं विमोहिताः ।
मनसा वव्रिरेऽभीष्टं पतिं दैवोपसादितम् ॥३४॥

taṁ praviṣṭaṁ striyo vīkṣya
nara-varyaṁ vimohitāḥ
manasā vavrire 'bhīṣṭaṁ
patiṁ daivopasāditam

tam—Him; *praviṣṭam*—entered; *striyaḥ*—the women; *vīkṣya*—seeing; *nara*—of men; *varyam*—the most excellent; *vimohitāḥ*—enchanted; *manasā*—in their minds; *vavrire*—chose; *abhīṣṭam*—desirable; *patim*—as their husband; *daiva*—by fate; *upasāditam*—brought.

TRANSLATION

The women became enchanted when they saw that most excellent of males enter. In their minds they each accepted Him, who had been brought there by destiny, as their chosen husband.

TEXT 35

भूयात्पतिरयं मह्यं धाता तदनुमोदताम् ।
इति सर्वाः पृथक्कृष्णे भावेन हृदयं दधुः ॥३५॥

bhūyāt patir ayaṁ mahyaṁ
dhātā tad anumodatām
iti sarvāḥ pṛthak kṛṣṇe
bhāvena hṛdayaṁ dadhuḥ

bhūyāt—may become; *patiḥ*—husband; *ayam*—He; *mahyam*—my; *dhātā*—providence; *tat*—that; *anumodatām*—may please grant; *iti*—thus; *sarvāḥ*—all of them; *pṛthak*—individually; *kṛṣṇe*—in Kṛṣṇa; *bhāvena*—with the idea; *hṛdayam*—their hearts; *dadhuḥ*—placed.

TRANSLATION

With the thought "May providence grant that this man become my husband," each and every princess absorbed her heart in contemplation of Kṛṣṇa.

TEXT 36

ताः प्राहिणोद् द्वारवतीं सुमृष्टविरजोऽम्बराः ।
नरयानैर्महाकोशान् रथाश्वान् द्रविणं महत् ॥३६॥

tāḥ prāhiṇod dvāravatīṁ
su-mṛṣṭa-virajo-'mbarāḥ
nara-yānair mahā-kośān
rathāśvān draviṇaṁ mahat

tāḥ—them; *prāhiṇot*—He sent; *dvāravatīm*—to Dvārakā; *su-mṛṣṭa*—well cleaned; *virajaḥ*—spotless; *ambarāḥ*—with clothes; *nara-yānaiḥ*—by human conveyances (palanquins); *mahā*—great; *kośān*—treasures; *ratha*—chariots; *aśvān*—and horses; *draviṇam*—wealth; *mahat*—extensive.

TRANSLATION

The Lord had the princesses arrayed in clean, spotless garments and then sent them in palanquins to Dvārakā, together with great treasures of chariots, horses and other valuables.

TEXT 37

ऐरावतकुलेभांश्च चतुर्दन्तांस्तरस्विनः ।
पाण्डुरांश्च चतुःषष्टिं प्रेरयामास केशवः ॥३७॥

airāvata-kulebhāṁś ca
catur-dantāṁs tarasvinaḥ
pāṇḍurāṁś ca catuḥ-ṣaṣṭiṁ
prerayām āsa keśavaḥ

airāvata—of Airāvata, Lord Indra's carrier; *kula*—from the family; *ibhān*—elephants; *ca*—also; *catuḥ*—four; *dantān*—having tusks; *tarasvinaḥ*—swift; *pāṇḍurān*—white; *ca*—and; *catuḥ-ṣaṣṭim*—sixty-four; *prerayām āsa*—dispatched; *keśavaḥ*—Lord Kṛṣṇa.

TRANSLATION

Lord Kṛṣṇa also dispatched sixty-four swift white elephants, descendants of Airāvata, who each sported four tusks.

TEXTS 38–39

गत्वा सुरेन्द्रभवनं दत्त्वादित्यै च कुण्डले ।
पूजितस्त्रिदशेन्द्रेण महेन्द्र्याण्या च सप्रियः ॥३८॥
चोदितो भार्ययोत्पाट्य पारिजातं गरुत्मति ।
आरोप्य सेन्द्रान् विबुधान्निर्जित्योपानयत्पुरम् ॥३९॥

gatvā surendra-bhavanaṁ
dattvādityai ca kuṇḍale
pūjitas tridaśendreṇa
mahendryāṇyā ca sa-priyaḥ

codito bhāryayotpāṭya
pārijātaṁ garutmati
āropya sendrān vibudhān
nirjityopānayat puram

gatvā—going; *sura*—of the demigods; *indra*—of the King; *bhavanam*—to the abode; *dattvā*—giving; *adityai*—to Aditi, the mother of Indra; *ca*—and; *kuṇḍale*—her earrings; *pūjitaḥ*—worshiped; *tridaśa*—of the thirty (chief demigods); *indreṇa*—by the chief; *mahā-indryāṇyā*—by the wife of Lord Indra; *ca*—and; *sa*—together with; *priyaḥ*—His beloved (Queen Satyabhāmā); *coditaḥ*—urged; *bhāryayā*—by His wife; *utpāṭya*—uprooting; *pārijātam*—the *pārijāta* tree; *garutmati*—on Garuḍa; *āropya*—placing; *sa-indrān*—including Indra; *vibudhān*—the demigods; *nirjitya*—defeating; *upānayat*—He brought; *puram*—to His city.

TRANSLATION

The Lord then went to the abode of Indra, the demigods' king, and gave mother Aditi her earrings; there Indra and his wife worshiped Kṛṣṇa and His beloved consort Satyabhāmā. Then, at Satyabhāmā's behest the Lord uprooted the heavenly *pārijāta* tree and put it on the back of Garuḍa. After defeating Indra and all the other demigods, Kṛṣṇa brought the *pārijāta* to His capital.

TEXT 40

स्थापितः सत्यभामाया गृहोद्यानोपशोभनः ।
अन्वगुर्भ्रमराः स्वर्गात्तद्गन्धासवलम्पटाः ॥४०॥

sthāpitaḥ satyabhāmāyā
gṛhodyānopaśobhanaḥ
anvagur bhramarāḥ svargāt
tad-gandhāsava-lampaṭāḥ

sthāpitaḥ—established; *satyabhāmāyāḥ*—of Satyabhāmā; *gṛha*—of the residence; *udyāna*—the garden; *upaśobhanaḥ*—beautifying; *anvaguḥ*—followed; *bhramarāḥ*—bees; *svargāt*—from heaven; *tat*—for its; *gandha*—fragrance; *āsava*—and sweet sap; *lampaṭāḥ*—greedy.

TRANSLATION

Once planted, the *pārijāta* tree beautified the garden of Queen Satyabhāmā's palace. Bees followed the tree all the way from heaven, greedy for its fragrance and sweet sap.

TEXT 41

ययाच आनम्य किरीटकोटिभिः
पादौ स्पृशन्नच्युतमर्थसाधनम् ।
सिद्धार्थ एतेन विगृह्यते महान्
अहो सुराणां च तमो धिगाढ्यताम् ॥४१॥

yayāca ānamya kirīṭa-koṭibhiḥ
pādau spṛśann acyutam artha-sādhanam
siddhārtha etena vigṛhyate mahān
aho surāṇāṁ ca tamo dhig āḍhyatām

yayāca—he (Lord Indra) begged; *ānamya*—bowing down; *kirīṭa*—of his crown; *koṭibhiḥ*—with the tips; *pādau*—His feet; *spṛśan*—touching; *acyutam*—to Lord Kṛṣṇa; *artha*—his (Indra's) purpose; *sādhanam*—who fulfilled; *siddha*—fulfilled; *arthaḥ*—whose purpose; *etena*—with Him; *vigṛhyate*—He quarrels; *mahān*—the great soul; *aho*—indeed; *surāṇām*—of the demigods; *ca*—and; *tamaḥ*—the ignorance; *dhik*—damnation; *āḍhyatām*—upon their wealth.

TRANSLATION

Even after Indra had bowed down to Lord Acyuta, touched His feet with the tips of his crown and begged the Lord to fulfill his desire, that exalted demigod, having achieved his purpose, chose to fight with the Supreme Lord. What ignorance there is among the gods! To hell with their opulence!

PURPORT

It is well known that material wealth and power tend to produce arrogance, and thus an opulent life can often be the royal road to hell.

TEXT 42

अथो मुहूर्त एकस्मिन्नानागारेषु ताः स्त्रियः ।
यथोपयेमे भगवान् तावद्रूपधरोऽव्ययः ॥४२॥

atho muhūrta ekasmin
nānāgāreṣu tāḥ striyaḥ
yathopayeme bhagavān
tāvad-rūpa-dharo 'vyayaḥ

atha u—and then; *muhūrte*—at the auspicious time; *ekasmin*—same; *nānā*—various; *āgāreṣu*—in residences; *tāḥ*—those; *striyaḥ*—women; *yathā*—properly; *upayeme*—married; *bhagavān*—the Supreme Lord; *tāvat*—that many; *rūpa*—forms; *dharaḥ*—assuming; *avyayaḥ*—the imperishable one.

TRANSLATION

Then the imperishable Supreme Personality, assuming a separate form for each bride, duly married all the princesses simultaneously, each in her own palace.

PURPORT

As Śrīla Śrīdhara Svāmī explains, here the word *yathā* indicates that each marriage was duly performed. This means that the entire company of the Lord's relatives, including His mother Devakī, appeared in each and every palace and attended each and every wedding. Since all these weddings took place simultaneously, this event was surely a manifestation of the Lord's inconceivable potency.

When Lord Kṛṣṇa does things, He does them in style. So it is not astonishing that the Lord simultaneously appeared in 16,100 wedding ceremonies taking place in 16,100 royal palaces, accompanied in each palace by all His relatives. Indeed, this is the way one would expect the Supreme Personality of Godhead to do things. After all, He is not an ordinary human being.

Śrīla Śrīdhara Svāmī further explains that on this particular occasion the Lord manifested His original form in each of His palaces. In other words, to take part in the wedding vows, He manifested identical forms (*prakāśa*) in all the palaces.

TEXT 43

गृहेषु तासामनपाय्यतर्क्कृन्
निरस्तसाम्यातिशयेष्ववस्थितः ।

रेमे रमाभिर्निजकामसम्प्लुतो
यथेतरो गार्हकमेधिकांश्चरन् ॥४३॥

gṛheṣu tāsām anapāyy atarka-kṛn
nirasta-sāmyātiśayeṣv avasthitaḥ
reme ramābhir nija-kāma-sampluto
yathetaro gārhaka-medhikāṁś caran

gṛheṣu—in the residences; *tāsām*—their; *anapāyī*—never leaving; *atarka*—inconceivable; *kṛt*—performing deeds; *nirasta*—which refuted; *sāmya*—equality; *atiśayeṣu*—and superiority; *avasthitaḥ*—remaining; *reme*—He enjoyed; *ramābhiḥ*—with the pleasing women; *nija*—His own; *kāma*—in the pleasure; *samplutaḥ*—absorbed; *yathā*—as; *itaraḥ*—any other man; *gārhaka-medhikān*—the duties of household life; *caran*—carrying out.

TRANSLATION

The Lord, performer of the inconceivable, constantly remained in each of His queens' palaces, which were unequaled and unexcelled by any other residence. There, although fully satisfied within Himself, He enjoyed with His pleasing wives, and like an ordinary husband He carried out His household duties.

PURPORT

The word *atarka-kṛt* is significant here. *Tarka* means "logic," and *atarka* means "that which is beyond logic." The Lord can perform (*kṛt*) that which is beyond mundane logic and hence inconceivable. Still, the Lord's activities can be appreciated and understood to a significant extent by those who surrender unto Him. This is the secret of *bhakti,* loving devotion to the Supreme Lord.

Śrīla Śrīdhara Svāmī comments that the Lord was always at home except for when He had to go out to do ordinary household duties. And Śrīla Viśvanātha Cakravartī points out that since in the Vaikuṇṭha planets Lord Nārāyaṇa enjoys with only one goddess of fortune and in Dvārakā Kṛṣṇa enjoys with thousands of queens, Dvārakā must be considered superior to Vaikuṇṭha. In this regard Śrīla Viśvanātha Cakravartī also quotes the following passage from the *Skanda Purāṇa:*

ṣoḍaśaiva sahasrāṇi
gopyas tatra samāgatāḥ
haṁsa eva mataḥ kṛṣṇaḥ
paramātmā janārdanaḥ

tasyaitāḥ śaktayo devi
ṣoḍaśaiva prakīrtitāḥ
candra-rūpī mataḥ kṛṣṇaḥ
kalā-rūpās tu tāḥ smṛtāḥ

sampūrṇa-maṇḍalā tāsāṁ
mālinī ṣoḍaśī kalā
ṣoḍaśaiva kalā yāsu
gopī-rūpā varāṅgane

ekaikaśas tāḥ sambhinnāḥ
sahasreṇa pṛthak pṛthak

"At that place sixteen thousand *gopīs* were assembled with Kṛṣṇa, who is considered the Supreme, the Supersoul, the shelter of all living beings. These *gopīs* are His renowned sixteen potencies, O goddess. Kṛṣṇa is like the moon, the *gopīs* are like its phases, and the full contingent of *gopīs* is like the full sequence of the moon's sixteen phases. Each of these sixteen divisions of *gopīs*, my dear Varāṅganā, is subdivided into one thousand parts."

Śrīla Viśvanātha Cakravartī further quotes the *Kārttika-māhātmya* section of the *Padma Purāṇa: kaiśore gopa-kanyās tā yauvane rāja-kanyakāḥ*. "Those who were the daughters of cowherds in their early youth became royal princesses in their maturity." The *ācārya* adds, "Therefore just as the Lord of Dvārakā is a plenary expansion of the supremely complete Lord of Śrī Vṛndāvana, so His principal queens are full expansions of His supremely complete pleasure potencies, the *gopīs*."

TEXT 44

इत्थं रमापतिमवाप्य पतिं स्त्रियस्ता
ब्रह्मादयोऽपि न विदुः पदवीं यदीयाम् ।

भेजुर्मुदाविरतमेधितयानुराग-
हासावलोकनवसंगमजल्पलज्जाः ॥४४॥

ittham ramā-patim avāpya patiṁ striyas tā
brahmādayo 'pi na viduḥ padavīṁ yadīyām
bhejur mudāviratam edhitayānurāga-
hāsāvaloka-nava-saṅgama-jalpa-lajjāḥ

ittham—in this manner; *ramā-patim*—the Lord of the goddess of fortune; *avāpya*—obtaining; *patim*—as their husband; *striyaḥ*—the women; *tāḥ*—they; *brahmā-ādayaḥ*—Lord Brahmā and other demigods; *api*—even; *na viduḥ*—do not know; *padavīm*—the means of attaining; *yadīyām*—whom; *bhejuḥ*—partook of; *mudā*—with pleasure; *aviratam*—incessantly; *edhitayā*—increasing; *anurāga*—loving attraction; *hāsa*—smiling; *avaloka*—glances; *nava*—ever fresh; *saṅgama*—association; *jalpa*—playful conversations; *lajjāḥ*—and shyness.

TRANSLATION

Thus those women obtained as their husband the husband of the goddess of fortune, although even great demigods like Brahmā do not know how to approach Him. With ever-increasing pleasure they experienced loving attraction for Him, exchanged smiling glances with Him and reciprocated with Him in ever-fresh intimacy, replete with joking and feminine shyness.

TEXT 45

प्रत्युद्गमासनवरार्हणपादशौच-
ताम्बूलविश्रमणवीजनगन्धमाल्यैः ।
केशप्रसारशयनस्नपनोपहार्यैः
दासीशता अपि विभोर्विदधुः स्म दास्यम् ॥४५॥

pratyudgamāsana-varārhaṇa-pāda-śauca-
tāmbūla-viśramaṇa-vījana-gandha-mālyaiḥ
keśa-prasāra-śayana-snapanopahāryaiḥ
dāsī-śatā api vibhor vidadhuḥ sma dāsyam

pratyudgama—by approaching; *āsana*—offering a seat; *vara*—first class; *arhaṇa*—worship; *pāda*—His feet; *śauca*—washing; *tāmbūla*—(offering) betel-nut preparation; *viśramaṇa*—helping Him to relax (by massaging His feet); *vījana*—fanning; *gandha*—(offering) fragrant substances; *mālyaiḥ*—and flower garlands; *keśa*—His hair; *prasāra*—by dressing; *śayana*—putting to bed; *snapana*—bathing; *upahāryaiḥ*—and by presenting gifts; *dāsī*—maidservants; *śatāḥ*—having hundreds; *api*—although; *vibhoḥ*—for the almighty Lord; *vidadhuḥ sma*—they executed; *dāsyam*—service.

TRANSLATION

Although the Supreme Lord's queens each had hundreds of maidservants, they chose to personally serve the Lord by approaching Him humbly, offering Him a seat, worshiping Him with excellent paraphernalia, bathing and massaging His feet, giving Him *pān* to chew, fanning Him, anointing Him with fragrant sandalwood paste, adorning Him with flower garlands, dressing His hair, arranging His bed, bathing Him, and presenting Him with various gifts.

Thus end the purports of the humble servants of His Divine Grace A. C. Bhaktivedanta Swami Prabhupāda to the Tenth Canto, Fifty-ninth Chapter, of the Śrīmad-Bhāgavatam, *entitled "The Killing of the Demon Naraka."*

CHAPTER SIXTY

Lord Kṛṣṇa Teases Queen Rukmiṇī

This chapter describes how Lord Kṛṣṇa provoked anger in Queen Rukmiṇī with joking words and then consoled her, thus demonstrating the opulence of a lovers' quarrel.

One day Lord Kṛṣṇa sat at ease in Queen Rukmiṇī's bedroom while she and her maidservants attended to Him in various ways. Rukmiṇī always responded to Śrī Kṛṣṇa's moods, whatever they might be. On this occasion the Lord looked at Rukmiṇī, whose beauty was faultless, and began to tease her: "Previously many wealthy kings, worthy of you in their appearance and character, wanted to marry you. In fact, your father and brother intended to give you in marriage to Śiśupāla. Why, then, did you accept such an unsuitable husband as Me, who once renounced My kingdom and fled to the sea in fear of Jarāsandha? Besides, I transgress worldly morality, and because I own nothing I am dear to other paupers. Certainly the well-to-do would not worship one such as Me.

"When a man and a woman share the same social class, influence, physical beauty and so on, marriage or friendship can flourish between them. But out of shortsightedness you have accepted a husband who lacks every good quality and is glorified by beggars. Better you had married some prominent warrior; then you might have been happy in this life and the next. Your brother Rukmī and kings like Śiśupāla all hate Me, and it was only to cut down their pride that I kidnapped you. But as for such things as body, home, wife and children, I'm indifferent to them, being the self-satisfied Personality of Godhead, transcendental to all material affairs."

Śrī Kṛṣṇa stopped speaking, having destroyed Queen Rukmiṇī's confidence that she was her husband's favorite. She began to cry, and soon she became stunned in extreme fear, pain and sadness and fell unconscious. Lord Kṛṣṇa saw that she had misunderstood His joking, and thus He felt compassion for her. He picked her up from the floor and, caressing her face, consoled her: "I know you are totally attached to Me. It was only out of eagerness to see your lotus face adorned with a frown that I teased you. To joke with one's beloved is the highest enjoyment for householders."

These words dispelled Rukmiṇī's fear of rejection. Seeing that Kṛṣṇa had spoken only in jest, she said, "What You said about the two of us being mismatched is actually true. After all, no one is equal to You, the omnipotent master of the three principal deities—Brahmā, Viṣṇu and Śiva." Rukmiṇī went on to show how everything Kṛṣṇa had said denigrating Himself was actually glorification.

Lord Kṛṣṇa then spoke to Rukmiṇī with deep affection: "I did not intend to agitate your mind with My joking words; rather, I wanted to demonstrate the strength of your chastity. Anyone who prays to Me for sense gratification and happiness in family life is simply deluded by My illusory energy, Māyā. Such a person will take a low birth. Ordinary women with corrupt desires cannot possibly worship Me faithfully, as you have done. At the time of your marriage you showed no interest in any of the royal suitors; rather, you sent a *brāhmaṇa* messenger for Me. Thus you are certainly the most beloved of all My consorts."

In this way the Lord of the universe, Śrī Kṛṣṇa, took pleasure in joking with the goddess of fortune in her form as Rukmiṇī, and in a similar fashion He fulfilled all the duties of a householder in each palace of His other queens.

TEXT 1

श्रीबादरायणिरुवाच
कर्हिचित्सुखमासीनं स्वतल्पस्थं जगद्गुरुम् ।
पतिं पर्यचरद् भैष्मी व्यजनेन सखीजनैः ॥१॥

śrī-bādarāyaṇir uvāca
karhicit sukham āsīnaṁ
sva-talpa-sthaṁ jagad-gurum
patiṁ paryacarad bhaiṣmī
vyajanena sakhī-janaiḥ

śrī-bādarāyaṇiḥ—Śukadeva Gosvāmī, the son of Bādarāyaṇa Vedavyāsa; *uvāca*—said; *karhicit*—on one occasion; *sukham*—comfortably; *āsīnam*—sitting; *sva*—on her; *talpa*—bed; *stham*—situated; *jagat*—of the universe; *gurum*—the spiritual master; *patim*—her husband; *paryacarat*—served; *bhaiṣmī*—Rukmiṇī; *vyajanena*—by fanning; *sakhī-janaiḥ*—together with her female companions.

TRANSLATION

Śrī Bādarāyaṇi said: Once, in the company of her maidservants, Queen Rukmiṇī was personally serving her husband, the spiritual master of the universe, by fanning Him as He relaxed on her bed.

PURPORT

Śrīla Viśvanātha Cakravartī poetically notes that in this chapter Rukmiṇī-devī is like fragrant camphor crushed on the grinding stone of Lord Kṛṣṇa's speech. In other words, the lovely, chaste qualities of Rukmiṇī will become manifest as a result of Lord Kṛṣṇa's apparently insensitive words, just as camphor's fragrance becomes manifest when granules of camphor are crushed by a grinding stone. The *ācārya* further points out that Rukmiṇī is personally serving the Lord because He is *jagad-gurum*, the spiritual master of the universe, and *patim*, her husband.

TEXT 2

यस्त्वेतल्लीलया विश्वं सृजत्यत्त्यवतीश्वरः ।
स हि जातः स्वसेतूनां गोपीथाय यदुष्वजः ॥२॥

yas tv etal līlayā viśvaṁ
sṛjaty atty avatīśvaraḥ
sa hi jātaḥ sva-setūnāṁ
gopīthāya yaduṣv ajaḥ

yaḥ—who; *tu*—and; *etat*—this; *līlayā*—as His play; *viśvam*—universe; *sṛjati*—sends forth; *atti*—devours; *avati*—protects; *īśvaraḥ*—the supreme controller; *saḥ*—He; *hi*—indeed; *jātaḥ*—born; *sva*—His own; *setūnām*—of the laws; *gopīthāya*—for the protection; *yaduṣu*—among the Yadus; *ajaḥ*—the unborn Lord.

TRANSLATION

The unborn Personality of Godhead, the supreme controller, who creates, maintains and then devours this universe simply as His play, took birth among the Yadus to preserve His own laws.

PURPORT

As stated in the Sixth Canto of the *Śrīmad-Bhāgavatam* (6.3.19), *dharmaṁ tu sākṣād bhagavat-praṇītam:* "Religion is the law established by God." The word *setu* means a "boundary" or "limit," as in the case of a dike. Earth is raised up on both sides of a river or canal so that the water will not deviate from its proper path. Similarly, God establishes laws so that people who follow them can peacefully progress along the path back home, back to Godhead. These laws, which are meant to guide human behavior, are thus called *setu.*

A further note on the word *setu:* Earth that is raised up to separate agricultural fields, or to form a causeway or bridge, is also called *setu.* Thus in the Ninth Canto the *Bhāgavatam* uses the word *setu* to indicate the bridge Lord Rāmacandra built to Śrī Lanka. Since the laws of God act as a bridge to take us from material life to liberated, spiritual life, this additional sense of the word *setu* certainly enriches its use here.

TEXTS 3–6

तस्मिनन्तर्गृहे भ्राजन्मुक्तादामविलम्बिना ।
विराजिते वितानेन दीपैर्मणिमयैरपि ॥३॥
मल्लिकादामभिः पुष्पैर्द्विरेफकुलनादिते ।
जालरन्ध्रप्रविष्टैश्च गोभिश्चन्द्रमसोऽमलैः ॥४॥
पारिजातवनामोदवायुनोद्यानशालिना ।
धूपैरगुरुजै राजन् जालरन्ध्रविनिर्गतैः ॥५॥
पयःफेननिभे शुभ्रे पर्यंके कशिपूत्तमे ।
उपतस्थे सुखासीनं जगतामीश्वरं पतिम् ॥६॥

tasmin antar-gṛhe bhrājan-
muktā-dāma-vilambinā
virājite vitānena
dīpair maṇi-mayair api

mallikā-dāmabhiḥ puṣpair
dvirepha-kula-nādite

jāla-randhra-praviṣṭaiś ca
gobhiś candramaso 'malaiḥ

pārijāta-vanāmoda-
vāyunodyāna-śālinā
dhūpair aguru-jai rājan
jāla-randhra-vinirgataiḥ

payaḥ-phena-nibhe śubhre
paryaṅke kaśipūttame
upatasthe sukhāsīnaṁ
jagatām īśvaraṁ patim

tasmin—in that; *antaḥ-gṛhe*—private part of the palace; *bhrājat*—brilliant; *muktā*—of pearls; *dāma*—with strings; *vilambinā*—hanging; *virājite*—resplendent; *vitānena*—with a canopy; *dīpaiḥ*—with lamps; *maṇi*—of jewels; *mayaiḥ*—made; *api*—also; *mallikā*—of jasmines; *dāmabhiḥ*—with garlands; *puṣpaiḥ*—with flowers; *dvirepha*—of bees; *kula*—with a swarm; *nādite*—resounding; *jāla*—of the lattice windows; *randhra*—through the small holes; *praviṣṭaiḥ*—which entered; *ca*—and; *gobhiḥ*—with the rays; *candramasaḥ*—of the moon; *amalaiḥ*—spotless; *pārijāta*—of *pārijāta* trees; *vana*—of the grove; *āmoda*—(carrying) the fragrance; *vāyunā*—by the wind; *udyāna*—of a garden; *śālinā*—bringing the presence; *dhūpaiḥ*—with incense; *aguru*—from *aguru* perfume; *jaiḥ*—produced; *rājan*—O King (Parīkṣit); *jāla-randhra*—through the holes of the lattice windows; *vinirgataiḥ*—exiting; *payaḥ*—of milk; *phena*—the foam; *nibhe*—resembling; *śubhre*—shining; *paryaṅke*—on the bed; *kaśipu*—on a pillow; *uttame*—excellent; *upatasthe*—she served; *sukha*—comfortably; *āsīnam*—seated; *jagatām*—of all the worlds; *īśvaram*—the supreme controller; *patim*—her husband.

TRANSLATION

Queen Rukmiṇī's quarters were extremely beautiful, boasting a canopy hung with brilliant strings of pearls, as well as effulgent jewels serving as lamps. Garlands of jasmine and other flowers hung here and there, attracting swarms of humming bees, and the spotless rays of the moon shone through the holes of the lattice

windows. As *aguru* incense drifted out of the window holes, my dear King, the breeze wafting the scent of the *pārijāta* grove carried the mood of a garden into the room. There the Queen served her husband, the Supreme Lord of all the worlds, as He reclined upon an opulent pillow on her bed, which was as soft and white as the foam of milk.

PURPORT

According to Śrīla Śrīdhara Svāmī, Rukmiṇī's palace was quite famous then, as now, and these descriptions give a glimpse into its opulence. Śrīla Viśvanātha Cakravartī adds that the word *amalaiḥ* in this verse may also be read *aruṇaiḥ*, which would indicate that when this pastime took place the moon had just risen, bathing the entire palace in beautiful ruddy moonshine.

TEXT 7

वालव्यजनमादाय रत्नदण्डं सखीकरात् ।
तेन वीजयती देवी उपासां चक्र ईश्वरम् ॥७॥

vāla-vyajanam ādāya
ratna-daṇḍaṁ sakhī-karāt
tena vījayatī devī
upāsāṁ cakra īśvaram

vāla—of (yak's) hair; *vyajanam*—a fan; *ādāya*—taking; *ratna*—jeweled; *daṇḍam*—the handle of which; *sakhī*—of her maidservant; *karāt*—from the hand; *tena*—with it; *vījayatī*—fanning; *devī*—the goddess; *upāsām cakre*—she worshiped; *īśvaram*—her master.

TRANSLATION

From her maidservant's hand Goddess Rukmiṇī took a yak-hair fan with a jeweled handle, and then she began to worship her master by fanning Him.

TEXT 8

सोपाच्युतं क्वणयती मणिनूपुराभ्यां
रेजेऽङ्गुलीयवलयव्यजनाग्रहस्ता ।

वस्त्रान्तगूढकुचकुंकुमशोणहार-
भासा नितम्बधृतया च परार्ध्यकाञ्च्या ॥८॥

sopācyutaṁ kvaṇayatī maṇi-nūpurābhyāṁ
reje 'ṅgulīya-valaya-vyajanāgra-hastā
vastrānta-gūḍha-kuca-kuṅkuma-śoṇa-hāra-
bhāsā nitamba-dhṛtayā ca parārdhya-kāñcyā

sā—she; *upa*—next to; *acyutam*—Lord Kṛṣṇa; *kvaṇayatī*—making sound; *maṇi*—jeweled; *nūpurābhyām*—from her ankle bells; *reje*—appeared beautiful; *aṅgulīya*—with rings; *valaya*—bangles; *vyajana*—and the fan; *agra-hastā*—in her hand; *vastra*—of her garment; *anta*—by the end; *gūḍha*—concealed; *kuca*—from her breasts; *kuṅkuma*—by the vermilion powder; *śoṇa*—reddened; *hāra*—of her necklace; *bhāsā*—with the glow; *nitamba*—on her hips; *dhṛtayā*—worn; *ca*—and; *parārdhya*—priceless; *kāñcyā*—with a belt.

TRANSLATION

Her hand adorned with rings, bangles and the *cāmara* fan, Queen Rukmiṇī looked resplendent standing near Lord Kṛṣṇa. Her jeweled ankle-bells tinkled, and her necklace glittered, reddened by the *kuṅkuma* from her breasts, which were covered by the end of her *sārī*. On her hips she wore a priceless belt.

PURPORT

Śrīla Viśvanātha Cakravartī points out that as Queen Rukmiṇī fanned her Lord with broad strokes, the jewels and gold on her beautiful limbs resounded with her effort.

TEXT 9

तां रूपिणीं श्रियमनन्यगतिं निरीक्ष्य
या लीलया धृततनोरनुरूपरूपा ।
प्रीतः स्मयन्नलककुण्डलनिष्ककण्ठ-
वक्त्रोल्लसत्स्मितसुधां हरिराबभाषे ॥९॥

tāṁ rūpiṇīṁ śriyam ananya-gatiṁ nirīkṣya
yā līlayā dhṛta-tanor anurūpa-rūpā
prītaḥ smayann alaka-kuṇḍala-niṣka-kaṇṭha-
vaktrollasat-smita-sudhāṁ harir ābabhāṣe

tām—her; *rūpiṇīm*—appearing in person; *śriyam*—the goddess of fortune; *ananya*—having no other; *gatim*—goal; *nirīkṣya*—seeing; *yā*—she who; *līlayā*—as His pastime; *dhṛta*—of Him who assumes; *tanoḥ*—bodies; *anurūpa*—corresponding; *rūpā*—whose forms; *prītaḥ*—pleased; *smayan*—smiling; *alaka*—with locks of hair; *kuṇḍala*—earrings; *niṣka*—neck ornament; *kaṇṭha*—on her throat; *vaktra*—face; *ullasat*—bright and happy; *smita*—smile; *sudhām*—nectar; *hariḥ*—Lord Kṛṣṇa; *ābabhāṣe*—spoke.

TRANSLATION

As He contemplated her, the goddess of fortune herself, who desires only Him, Lord Kṛṣṇa smiled. The Lord assumes various forms to enact His pastimes, and He was pleased that the form the goddess of fortune had assumed was just suitable for her to serve as His consort. Her charming face was adorned with curling hair, earrings, a locket on her neck, and the nectar of her bright, happy smile. The Lord then spoke to Her as follows.

PURPORT

Śrīla Śrīdhara Svāmī has quoted an interesting verse, spoken by Śrī Parāśara in the *Viṣṇu Purāṇa:*

devatve deva-deheyaṁ
manuṣyatve ca mānuṣī
viṣṇor dehānurūpāṁ vai
karoty eṣātmanas tanum

"When the Lord appears as a demigod, she [the goddess of fortune] takes the form of a demigoddess, and when He appears as a human being, she takes a humanlike form. Thus the body she assumes matches the one Lord Viṣṇu takes."

Śrīla Viśvanātha Cakravartī adds that as Lord Kṛṣṇa is even more beautiful than the Lord of Vaikuṇṭha, Lord Kṛṣṇa's consort Rukmiṇī-devī is even more attractive than the goddess of fortune in the Vaikuṇṭha world.

TEXT 10

श्रीभगवानुवाच
राजपुत्रीप्सिता भूपैर्लोकपालविभूतिभिः ।
महानुभावैः श्रीमद्भी रूपौदार्यबलोर्जितैः ॥१०॥

śrī-bhagavān uvāca
rāja-putrīpsitā bhūpair
loka-pāla-vibhūtibhiḥ
mahānubhāvaiḥ śrīmadbhī
rūpaudārya-balorjitaiḥ

śrī-bhagavān uvāca—the Supreme Lord said; *rāja-putri*—O princess; *īpsitā*—(you were) desired; *bhū-paiḥ*—by kings; *loka*—of planets; *pāla*—like the rulers; *vibhūtibhiḥ*—whose powers; *mahā*—great; *anubhāvaiḥ*—whose influence; *śrī-madbhiḥ*—opulent; *rūpa*—with beauty; *audārya*—generosity; *bala*—and physical strength; *ūrjitaiḥ*—abundantly endowed.

TRANSLATION

The Supreme Lord said: My dear princess, you were sought after by many kings as powerful as the rulers of planets. They were all abundantly endowed with political influence, wealth, beauty, generosity and physical strength.

TEXT 11

तान् प्राप्तानर्थिनो हित्वा चैद्यादीन् स्मरदुर्मदान् ।
दत्ता भ्रात्रा स्वपित्रा च कस्मान्नो ववृषेऽसमान् ॥११॥

tān prāptān arthino hitvā
caidyādīn smara-durmadān
dattā bhrātrā sva-pitrā ca
kasmān no vavṛṣe 'samān

tān—them; *prāptān*—at hand; *arthinaḥ*—suitors; *hitvā*—rejecting; *caidya*—Śiśupāla; *ādīn*—and others; *smara*—by Cupid; *durmadān*—maddened; *dattā*—given; *bhrātrā*—by your brother; *sva*—your; *pitrā*—father; *ca*—and; *kasmāt*—why; *naḥ*—Us; *vavṛṣe*—you chose; *asamān*—unequal.

TRANSLATION

Since your brother and father offered you to them, why did you reject the King of Cedi and all those other suitors, who stood before you, maddened by Cupid? Why, instead, did you choose Us, who are not at all your equal?

TEXT 12

राजभ्यो बिभ्यतः सुभ्रु समुद्रं शरणं गतान् ।
बलवद्भिः कृतद्वेषान् प्रायस्त्यक्तनृपासनान् ॥१२॥

rājabhyo bibhyataḥ su-bhru
samudraṁ śaraṇaṁ gatān
balavadbhiḥ kṛta-dveṣān
prāyas tyakta-nṛpāsanān

rājabhyaḥ—of the kings; *bibhyataḥ*—afraid; *su-bhru*—O lovely-browed one; *samudram*—to the ocean; *śaraṇam*—for shelter; *gatān*—gone; *bala-vadbhiḥ*—toward those who are powerful; *kṛta-dveṣān*—having showed enmity; *prāyaḥ*—for the most part; *tyakta*—having abandoned; *nṛpa*—of a king; *āsanān*—the seat.

TRANSLATION

Terrified of these kings, O lovely-browed one, We took shelter in the ocean. We have become enemies of powerful men, and We practically abandoned Our royal throne.

PURPORT

Śrīla Viśvanātha Cakravartī comments on this verse as follows: "The Lord's mentality here can be understood as follows: 'When I gave Rukmiṇī a single flower from the heavenly *pārijāta* tree, Satyabhāmā showed such a torrent of fury that I could not pacify her even by bowing down at her feet. Only when I gave her a whole *pārijāta* tree was she satisfied. Rukmiṇī, however, did not display any anger even when she saw Me give Satyabhāmā the whole tree. So how can I enjoy the nectar of angry words from this wife, who never feels jealousy, who is supremely sober and who always speaks pleasingly?' Thus considering, the Supreme Lord decided, 'If I speak like this to her, I will be able to provoke her anger.' This is how some authorities explain Kṛṣṇa's speech to Rukmiṇī."

According to the *ācārya,* here the words *balavadbhiḥ kṛta-dveṣān prāyaḥ* indicate that Lord Kṛṣṇa opposed almost all the contemporary kings during His incarnation, befriending only a few, such as the Pāṇḍavas and loyal members of His dynasty. Of course, as stated in the beginning of the Tenth Canto, Lord Kṛṣṇa appeared specifically because the earth was overburdened by innumerable bogus kings and He wanted to remove this burden.

Finally Śrīla Viśvanātha Cakrvartī points out that the word *tyakta-nṛpāsanān,* "giving up the king's throne," indicates that after Lord Kṛṣṇa killed Kaṁsa He humbly gave the royal throne to His grandfather Ugrasena, although the Lord Himself was entitled to it.

TEXT 13

अस्पष्टवर्त्मनां पुंसामलोकपथमीयुषाम् ।
आस्थिताः पदवीं सुभ्रु प्रायः सीदन्ति योषितः ॥१३॥

aspaṣṭa-vartmanāṁ puṁsām
aloka-patham īyuṣām
āsthitāḥ padavīṁ su-bhru
prāyaḥ sīdanti yoṣitaḥ

aspaṣṭa—uncertain; *vartmanām*—whose behavior; *puṁsām*—of men; *aloka*—not acceptable to ordinary society; *patham*—way; *īyuṣām*—who take to; *āsthitāḥ*—following; *padavīm*—the path; *su-bhru*—O you whose eyebrows are beautiful; *prāyaḥ*—usually; *sīdanti*—suffer; *yoṣitaḥ*—women.

TRANSLATION

O fine-browed lady, women are usually destined to suffer when they stay with men whose behavior is uncertain and who pursue a path not approved by society.

TEXT 14

निष्किञ्चना वयं शश्वन्निष्किञ्चनजनप्रियाः ।
तस्मात्प्रायेण न ह्याढ्या मां भजन्ति सुमध्यमे ॥१४॥

niṣkiñcanā vayaṁ śaśvan
niṣkiñcana-jana-priyāḥ
tasmāt prāyeṇa na hy āḍhyā
māṁ bhajanti su-madhyame

niṣkiñcanāḥ—having no possessions; *vayam*—We; *śaśvat*—always; *niṣkiñcana-jana*—to those who have no possessions; *priyāḥ*—very dear; *tasmāt*—therefore; *prāyeṇa*—usually; *na*—not; *hi*—indeed; *āḍhyāḥ*—the rich; *mām*—Me; *bhajanti*—worship; *su-madhyame*—O fine-waisted one.

TRANSLATION

We have no material possessions, and We are dear to those who similarly have nothing. Therefore, O slender one, the wealthy hardly ever worship Me.

PURPORT

Like the Lord, His devotees are uninterested in material sense gratification, being awakened to the superior pleasure of Kṛṣṇa consciousness. Those who are intoxicated by material wealth cannot appreciate the supreme wealth of the kingdom of God.

TEXT 15

ययोरात्मसमं वित्तं जन्मैश्वर्याकृतिर्भवः ।
तयोर्विवाहो मैत्री च नोत्तमाधमयोः क्वचित् ॥१५॥

yayor ātma-samaṁ vittaṁ
janmaiśvaryākṛtir bhavaḥ
tayor vivāho maitrī ca
nottamādhamayoḥ kvacit

yayoḥ—of which two; *ātma-samam*—equal to oneself; *vittam*—property; *janma*—birth; *aiśvarya*—influence; *ākṛtiḥ*—and physical appearance; *bhavaḥ*—posterity; *tayoḥ*—of them; *vivāhaḥ*—marriage; *maitrī*—friendship; *ca*—and; *na*—not; *uttama*—of a superior; *adhama-yoḥ*—and an inferior; *kvacit*—ever.

TRANSLATION

Marriage and friendship are proper between two people who are equal in terms of their wealth, birth, influence, physical appearance and capacity for good progeny, but never between a superior and an inferior.

PURPORT

Persons of superior and inferior qualities may live together in a relationship of master and servant or teacher and student, but marriage and friendship are proper only between those of equal status. The word *bhava,* in the context of marriage, indicates that a couple should have a similar capacity to produce good offspring.

Lord Kṛṣṇa here presents Himself as materially unqualified. In fact, the Lord does not have any material qualities: He lives in pure spiritual existence. Thus all the Lord's opulences are eternal and not of the flimsy mundane sort.

TEXT 16

वैदर्भ्येतदविज्ञाय त्वयादीर्घसमीक्षया ।
वृता वयं गुणैर्हीना भिक्षुभिः श्लाघिता मुधा ॥१६॥

vaidarbhy etad avijñāya
tvayādīrgha-samīkṣayā
vṛtā vayaṁ guṇair hīnā
bhikṣubhiḥ ślāghitā mudhā

vaidarbhi—O princess of Vidarbha; *etat*—this; *avijñāya*—not knowing; *tvayā*—by you; *adīrgha-samīkṣayā*—without long-range vision; *vṛtāḥ*—chosen; *vayam*—We; *guṇaiḥ*—of good qualities; *hīnāḥ*—devoid; *bhikṣubhiḥ*—by beggars; *ślāghitāḥ*—praised; *mudhā*—out of their bewilderment.

TRANSLATION

O Vaidarbhī, not being farsighted, you didn't realize this, and therefore you chose Us as your husband, even though We have no good qualities and are glorified only by deluded beggars.

TEXT 17

अथात्मनोऽनुरूपं वै भजस्व क्षत्रियर्षभम् ।
येन त्वमाशिषः सत्या इहामुत्र च लप्स्यसे ॥१७॥

athātmano 'nurūpaṁ vai
bhajasva kṣatriyarṣabham
yena tvam āśiṣaḥ satyā
ihāmutra ca lapsyase

atha—now; *ātmanaḥ*—for yourself; *anurūpam*—suitable; *vai*—indeed; *bhajasva*—please accept; *kṣatriya-ṛṣabham*—a first-class man of the royal order; *yena*—by whom; *tvam*—you; *āśiṣaḥ*—hopes; *satyāḥ*—becoming fulfilled; *iha*—in this life; *amutra*—in the next life; *ca*—also; *lapsyase*—will obtain.

TRANSLATION

Now you should definitely accept a more suitable husband, a first-class man of the royal order who can help you achieve everything you want, both in this life and the next.

PURPORT

Lord Kṛṣṇa continues to tease His beautiful wife, trying to provoke her loving anger.

TEXT 18

चैद्यशाल्वजरासन्धदन्तवक्रादयो नृपाः ।
मम द्विषन्ति वामोरु रुक्मी चापि तवाग्रजः ॥१८॥

caidya-śālva-jarāsandha-
dantavakrādayo nṛpāḥ
mama dviṣanti vāmoru
rukmī cāpi tavāgrajaḥ

caidya-śālva-jarāsandha-dantavakra-ādayaḥ—Caidya (Śiśupāla), Śālva, Jarāsandha, Dantavakra and others; *nṛpāḥ*—kings; *mama*—Me; *dviṣanti*—hate; *vāma-ūru*—O beautiful-thighed one; *rukmī*—Rukmī; *ca api*—as well; *tava*—your; *agra-jaḥ*—older brother.

TRANSLATION

Kings like Śiśupāla, Śālva, Jarāsandha and Dantavakra all hate Me, O beautiful-thighed one, and so does your elder brother Rukmī.

TEXT 19

तेषां वीर्यमदान्धानां दृप्तानां स्मयनुत्तये ।
आनितासि मया भद्रे तेजोपहरतासताम् ॥१९॥

teṣāṁ vīrya-madāndhānāṁ
dṛptānāṁ smaya-nuttaye
ānitāsi mayā bhadre
tejopaharatāsatām

teṣām—of them; *vīrya*—with their power; *mada*—by the intoxication; *andhānām*—blinded; *dṛptānām*—proud; *smaya*—the arrogance; *nuttaye*—to dispel; *ānitā asi*—you were taken in marriage; *mayā*—by Me; *bhadre*—good woman; *tejaḥ*—the strength; *upaharatā*—removing; *asatām*—of the wicked.

TRANSLATION

It was to dispel the arrogance of these kings that I carried you away, My good woman, for they were blinded by the intoxication of power. My purpose was to curb the strength of the wicked.

TEXT 20

**उदासीना वयं नूनं न स्त्र्यपत्यार्थकामुकाः ।
आत्मलब्ध्यास्महे पूर्णा गेहयोर्ज्योतिरक्रियाः ॥२०॥**

udāsīnā vayaṁ nūnaṁ
na stry-apatyārtha-kāmukāḥ
ātma-labdhyāsmahe pūrṇā
gehayor jyotir-akriyāḥ

udāsīnāḥ—indifferent; *vayam*—We; *nūnam*—indeed; *na*—not; *strī*—for wives; *apatya*—children; *artha*—and wealth; *kāmukāḥ*—hankering; *ātma-labdhyā*—by being self-satisfied; *āsmahe*—We remain; *pūrṇāḥ*—complete; *gehayoḥ*—to body and home; *jyotiḥ*—like a fire; *akriyāḥ*—engaged in no activity.

TRANSLATION

We care nothing for wives, children and wealth. Always satisfied within Ourselves, We do not work for body and home, but like a light, We merely witness.

TEXT 21

श्रीशुक उवाच
**एतावदुक्त्वा भगवानात्मानं वल्लभामिव ।
मन्यमानामविश्लेषात्तद्दर्पघ्न उपारमत् ॥२१॥**

śrī-śuka uvāca
etāvad uktvā bhagavān
ātmānaṁ vallabhām iva
manyamānām aviśleṣāt
tad-darpa-ghna upāramat

śrī-śukaḥ uvāca—Śukadeva Gosvāmī said; *etāvat*—this much; *uktvā*—saying; *bhagavān*—the Supreme Lord; *ātmānam*—herself; *vallabhām*—His beloved; *iva*—as; *manyamānām*—thinking; *aviśleṣāt*—because of (His) never being separated (from her); *tat*—that; *darpa*—of the pride; *ghnaḥ*—the destroyer; *upāramat*—desisted.

TRANSLATION

Śukadeva Gosvāmī said: Rukmiṇī had thought herself especially beloved by the Lord because He never left her company. By saying these things to her He vanquished her pride, and then He stopped speaking.

TEXT 22

इति त्रिलोकेशपतेस्तदात्मनः
प्रियस्य देव्यश्रुतपूर्वमप्रियम् ।
आश्रुत्य भीता हृदि जातवेपथुश्
चिन्तां दुरन्तां रुदती जगाम ह ॥२२॥

iti trilokeśa-pates tadātmanaḥ
priyasya devy aśruta-pūrvam apriyam
āśrutya bhītā hṛdi jāta-vepathuś
cintāṁ durantāṁ rudatī jagāma ha

iti—thus; *tri-loka*—of the three worlds; *īśa*—of the lords; *pateḥ*—of the master; *tadā*—then; *ātmanaḥ*—of her own; *priyasya*—beloved; *devī*—the goddess, Rukmiṇī; *aśruta*—never heard; *pūrvam*—previously; *apriyam*—unpleasantness; *āśrutya*—hearing; *bhītā*—frightened; *hṛdi*—in her heart; *jāta*—born; *vepathuḥ*—trembling; *cintām*—anxiety; *durantām*—terrible; *rudatī*—sobbing; *jagāma ha*—she experienced.

TRANSLATION

Goddess Rukmiṇī had never before heard such unpleasantries from her beloved, the Lord of universal rulers, and she became frightened. A tremor arose in her heart, and in terrible anxiety she began to cry.

TEXT 23

पदा सुजातेन नखारुणश्रिया
भुवं लिखन्त्यश्रुभिरञ्जनासितैः ।
आसिञ्चती कुंकुमरूषितौ स्तनौ
तस्थावधोमुख्यतिदुःखरुद्धवाक् ॥२३॥

padā su-jātena nakhāruṇa-śriyā
bhuvaṁ likhanty aśrubhir añjanāsitaiḥ
āsiñcatī kuṅkuma-rūṣitau stanau
tasthāv adho-mukhy ati-duḥkha-ruddha-vāk

padā—with her foot; *su-jātena*—very tender; *nakha*—of its nails; *aruṇa*—reddish; *śriyā*—having the effulgence; *bhuvam*—the earth; *likhantī*—scratching; *aśrubhiḥ*—with her tears; *añjana*—because of her eye shadow; *asitaiḥ*—which were black; *āsiñcatī*—sprinkling; *kuṅkuma*—with *kuṅkuma* powder; *rūṣitau*—red; *stanau*—breasts; *tasthau*—she stood still; *adhaḥ*—downward; *mukhī*—her face; *ati*—extreme; *duḥkha*—due to the sorrow; *ruddha*—checked; *vāk*—her speech.

TRANSLATION

With her tender foot, effulgent with the reddish glow of her nails, she scratched the ground, and tears darkened by her eye makeup sprinkled her *kuṅkuma*-reddened breasts. There she stood, face downward, her voice choked up by extreme sorrow.

TEXT 24

तस्याः सुदुःखभयशोकविनष्टबुद्धेर्
हस्ताच्छ्लथद्वलयतो व्यजनं पपात ।
देहश्च विक्लवधियः सहसैव मुह्यन्
रम्भेव वायुविहतो प्रविकीर्य केशान् ॥२४॥

tasyāḥ su-duḥkha-bhaya-śoka-vinaṣṭa-buddher
hastāc chlathad-valayato vyajanaṁ papāta
dehaś ca viklava-dhiyaḥ sahasaiva muhyan
rambheva vāyu-vihato pravikīrya keśān

tasyāḥ—her; *su-duḥkha*—by the great unhappiness; *bhaya*—fear; *śoka*—and remorse; *vinaṣṭa*—spoiled; *buddheḥ*—whose intelligence; *hastāt*—from the hand; *ślathat*—slipping; *valayataḥ*—whose bangles; *vyajanam*—the fan; *papāta*—fell; *dehaḥ*—her body; *ca*—also; *viklava*—disrupted; *dhiyaḥ*—whose mind; *sahasā eva*—suddenly; *muhyan*—

fainting; *rambhā*—a plantain tree; *iva*—as if; *vāyu*—by the wind; *vihataḥ*—blown down; *pravikīrya*—scattering; *keśān*—her hair.

TRANSLATION

Rukmiṇī's mind was overwhelmed with unhappiness, fear and grief. Her bangles slipped from her hand, and her fan fell to the ground. In her bewilderment she suddenly fainted, her hair scattering all about as her body fell to the ground like a plantain tree blown over by the wind.

PURPORT

Shocked by Lord Kṛṣṇa's words, Rukmiṇī could not understand that the Lord was only teasing, and thus she displayed these ecstatic symptoms of grief, which Śrīla Viśvanātha Cakravartī characterizes as *sāttvika* ecstasies ranging from "becoming stunned" to "dissolution."

TEXT 25

तद् दृष्ट्वा भगवान् कृष्णः प्रियायाः प्रेमबन्धनम् ।
हास्यप्रौढिमजानन्त्याः करुणः सोऽन्वकम्पत ॥२५॥

tad dṛṣṭvā bhagavān kṛṣṇaḥ
priyāyāḥ prema-bandhanam
hāsya-prauḍhim ajānantyāḥ
karuṇaḥ so 'nvakampata

tat—this; *dṛṣṭvā*—seeing; *bhagavān*—the Supreme Lord; *kṛṣṇaḥ*—Kṛṣṇa; *priyāyāḥ*—of His beloved; *prema*—by pure love of God; *bandhanam*—the bondage; *hāsya*—of His joking; *prauḍhim*—the full import; *ajānantyāḥ*—who could not comprehend; *karuṇaḥ*—merciful; *saḥ*—He; *anvakampata*—felt compassion.

TRANSLATION

Seeing that His beloved was so bound to Him in love that she could not understand the full meaning of His teasing, merciful Lord Kṛṣṇa felt compassion for her.

TEXT 26

पर्यंकादवरुह्याशु तामुत्थाप्य चतुर्भुजः ।
केशान् समुह्य तद्वक्त्रं प्रामृजत्पद्मपाणिना ॥२६॥

paryaṅkād avaruhyāśu
tām utthāpya catur-bhujaḥ
keśān samuhya tad-vaktraṁ
prāmṛjat padma-pāṇinā

paryaṅkāt—from the bed; *avaruhya*—stepping down; *āśu*—quickly; *tām*—her; *utthāpya*—picking up; *catur-bhujaḥ*—displaying four arms; *keśān*—her hair; *samuhya*—gathering; *tat*—her; *vaktram*—face; *prāmṛjat*—He wiped; *padma-pāṇinā*—with His lotus hand.

TRANSLATION

The Lord quickly got down from the bed. Manifesting four arms, He picked her up, gathered her hair and caressed her face with His lotus hand.

PURPORT

The Lord manifested four hands so He could do all of these things simultaneously.

TEXTS 27–28

प्रमृज्याश्रुकले नेत्रे स्तनौ चोपहतौ शुचा ।
आश्लिष्य बाहुना राजननन्यविषयां सतीम् ॥२७॥
सान्त्वयामास सान्त्वज्ञः कृपया कृपणां प्रभुः ।
हास्यप्रौढिभ्रमच्चित्तामतदर्हां सतां गतिः ॥२८॥

pramṛjyāśru-kale netre
stanau copahatau śucā
āśliṣya bāhunā rājan
ananya-viṣayāṁ satīm

sāntvayām āsa sāntva-jñaḥ
kṛpayā kṛpaṇāṁ prabhuḥ
hāsya-prauḍhi-bhramac-cittām
atad-arhāṁ satāṁ gatiḥ

pramṛjya—wiping; *aśru-kale*—filled with tears; *netre*—her eyes; *stanau*—her breasts; *ca*—and; *upahatau*—disarrayed; *śucā*—by her sorrowful tears; *āśliṣya*—embracing her; *bāhunā*—with His arm; *rājan*—O King (Parīkṣit); *ananya*—no other; *viṣayām*—whose object of desire; *satīm*—chaste; *sāntvayām āsa*—He consoled; *sāntva*—of ways of consoling; *jñaḥ*—the expert knower; *kṛpayā*—compassionately; *kṛpaṇām*—pitiable; *prabhuḥ*—the Supreme Lord; *hāsya*—of His joking; *prauḍhi*—by the cleverness; *bhramat*—becoming bewildered; *cittām*—whose mind; *atat-arhām*—not deserving that; *satām*—of pure devotees; *gatiḥ*—the goal.

TRANSLATION

Wiping her tear-filled eyes and her breasts, which were stained by tears of grief, the Supreme Lord, the goal of His devotees, embraced His chaste wife, who desired nothing but Him, O King. Expert in the art of pacification, Śrī Kṛṣṇa tenderly consoled pitiable Rukmiṇī, whose mind was bewildered by His clever joking and who did not deserve to suffer so.

TEXT 29

श्रीभगवानुवाच
मा मा वैदर्भ्यसूयेथा जाने त्वां मत्परायणाम् ।
त्वद्वचः श्रोतुकामेन क्ष्वेल्याचरितमंगने ॥२९॥

śrī-bhagavān uvāca
mā mā vaidarbhy asūyethā
jāne tvāṁ mat-parāyaṇām
tvad-vacaḥ śrotu-kāmena
kṣvelyācaritam aṅgane

śrī-bhagavān uvāca—the Supreme Lord said; *mā*—do not; *mā*—with Me; *vaidarbhi*—O Vaidarbhī; *asūyethāḥ*—be displeased; *jāne*—I know;

tvām—you; *mat*—to Me; *parāyaṇām*—fully dedicated; *tvat*—your; *vacaḥ*—words; *śrotu*—to hear; *kāmena*—desiring; *kṣvelyā*—in jest; *ācaritam*—acted; *aṅgane*—My dear lady.

TRANSLATION

The Supreme Lord said: O Vaidarbhī, do not be displeased with Me. I know that you are fully devoted to Me. I only spoke in jest, dear lady, because I wanted to hear what you would say.

PURPORT

According to Śrīla Viśvanātha Cakravartī, Lord Kṛṣṇa spoke the present verse because He thought that lovely Rukmiṇī might be afraid He would again say something to disturb her, or that she might be angry at what He had done.

TEXT 30

मुखं च प्रेमसंरम्भस्फुरिताधरमीक्षितुम् ।
कटाक्षेपारुणापांगं सुन्दरभ्रुकुटीतटम् ॥३०॥

mukhaṁ ca prema-saṁrambha-
sphuritādharam īkṣitum
kaṭā-kṣepāruṇāpāṅgaṁ
sundara-bhru-kuṭī-taṭam

mukham—the face; *ca*—and; *prema*—of love; *saṁrambha*—by the agitation; *sphurita*—trembling; *adharam*—with lips; *īkṣitum*—to see; *kaṭā*—of sidelong glances; *kṣepa*—by the throwing; *aruṇa*—reddish; *apāṅgam*—corners of the eyes; *sundara*—beautiful; *bhru*—of the eyebrows; *kuṭī*—the furrowing; *taṭam*—on the edges.

TRANSLATION

I also wanted to see your face with lips trembling in loving anger, the reddish corners of your eyes throwing sidelong glances and the line of your beautiful eyebrows knit in a frown.

PURPORT

Śrīla Viśvanātha Cakravartī explains here that normally, by the Lord's transcendental desire, His pure devotees reciprocate with Him in such a way that they satisfy His spiritual desires. But Rukmiṇī's love was so strong that her unique mood predominated in this situation, and thus instead of becoming angry she fainted and fell to the ground. Far from displeasing Kṛṣṇa, however, she increased His transcendental ecstasy by exhibiting her all-encompassing love for Him.

TEXT 31

अयं हि परमो लाभो गृहेषु गृहमेधिनाम् ।
यन्नर्मैरीयते यामः प्रियया भीरु भामिनि ॥३१॥

ayaṁ hi paramo lābho
gṛheṣu gṛha-medhinām
yan narmair īyate yāmaḥ
priyayā bhīru bhāmini

ayam—this; *hi*—indeed; *paramaḥ*—the greatest; *lābhaḥ*—gain; *gṛheṣu*—in family life; *gṛha-medhinām*—for worldly householders; *yat*—which; *narmaiḥ*—with joking words; *īyate*—is spent; *yāmaḥ*—time; *priyayā*—with one's beloved; *bhīru*—O timid one; *bhāmini*—O temperamental one.

TRANSLATION

The greatest pleasure worldly householders can enjoy at home is to spend time joking with their beloved wives, My dear timid and temperamental one.

PURPORT

The word *bhāmini* indicates an angry, passionate, temperamental woman. Since lovely Rukmiṇī did not become angry despite all provocation, the Lord is still speaking facetiously.

TEXT 32

श्रीशुक उवाच
सैवं भगवता राजन् वैदर्भी परिसान्त्विता ।
ज्ञात्वा तत्परिहासोक्तिं प्रियत्यागभयं जहौ ॥३२॥

śrī-śuka uvāca
saivaṁ bhagavatā rājan
vaidarbhī parisāntvitā
jñātvā tat-parihāsoktiṁ
priya-tyāga-bhayaṁ jahau

śrī-śukaḥ uvāca—Śukadeva Gosvāmī said; *sā*—she; *evam*—thus; *bhagavatā*—by the Supreme Personality of Godhead; *rājan*—O King; *vaidarbhī*—Queen Rukmiṇī; *parisāntvitā*—fully pacified; *jñātvā*—understanding; *tat*—His; *parihāsa*—spoken in jest; *uktim*—words; *priya*—by her beloved; *tyāga*—of rejection; *bhayam*—her fear; *jahau*—gave up.

TRANSLATION

Śukadeva Gosvāmī said: O King, Queen Vaidarbhī was fully pacified by the Supreme Personality of Godhead and understood that His words had been spoken in jest. Thus she gave up her fear that her beloved would reject her.

TEXT 33

बभाष ऋषभं पुंसां वीक्षन्ती भगवन्मुखम् ।
सव्रीडहासरुचिरस्निग्धापांगेन भारत ॥३३॥

babhāṣa ṛṣabhaṁ puṁsāṁ
vīkṣantī bhagavan-mukham
sa-vrīḍa-hāsa-rucira-
snigdhāpāṅgena bhārata

babhāṣa—she spoke; *ṛṣabham*—to the most eminent; *puṁsām*—of males; *vīkṣantī*—looking upon; *bhagavat*—of the Supreme Lord; *mukham*—the face; *sa-vrīḍa*—shy; *hāsa*—with a smile; *rucira*—charming; *snigdha*—affectionate; *apāṅgena*—and with glances; *bhārata*—O descendant of Bharata.

TRANSLATION

Smiling bashfullly as she cast charming, affectionate glances upon the face of the Lord, the best of males, Rukmiṇī spoke the following, O descendant of Bharata.

TEXT 34

श्रीरुक्मिण्युवाच
नन्वेवमेतदरविन्दविलोचनाह
यद्वै भवान् भगवतोऽसदृशी विभूम्नः ।
क्व स्वे महिम्न्यभिरतो भगवांस्त्र्यधीशः
क्वाहं गुणप्रकृतिरज्ञगृहीतपादा ॥३४॥

śrī-rukmiṇy uvāca
nanv evam etad aravinda-vilocanāha
yad vai bhavān bhagavato 'sadṛśī vibhūmnaḥ
kva sve mahimny abhirato bhagavāṁs try-adhīśaḥ
kvāhaṁ guṇa-prakṛtir ajña-gṛhīta-pādā

śrī-rukmiṇī uvāca—Śrī Rukmiṇī said; *nanu*—well; *evam*—so be it; *etat*—this; *aravinda-vilocana*—O lotus-eyed one; *āha*—said; *yat*—which; *vai*—indeed; *bhavān*—You; *bhagavataḥ*—to the Supreme Lord; *asadṛśī*—unequal; *vibhūmnaḥ*—to the almighty; *kva*—where, in comparison; *sve*—in His own; *mahimni*—glory; *abhirataḥ*—taking pleasure; *bhagavān*—the Supreme Lord; *tri*—of the three (principal deities, namely Brahmā, Viṣṇu and Śiva); *adhīśaḥ*—the controller; *kva*—and where; *aham*—myself; *guṇa*—of material qualities; *prakṛtiḥ*—whose character; *ajña*—by foolish persons; *gṛhīta*—taken hold of; *pādā*—whose feet.

TRANSLATION

Śrī Rukmiṇī said: Actually, what You have said is true, O lotus-eyed one. I am indeed unsuitable for the almighty Personality of Godhead. What comparison is there between that Supreme Lord, who is master of the three primal deities and who delights in His own glory, and myself, a woman of mundane qualities whose feet are grasped by fools?

PURPORT

Śrīla Śrīdhara Svāmī lists the faults Lord Kṛṣṇa had described in Himself that He claimed disqualified Him from being Rukmiṇī's husband. These include incompatability, fearfulness, taking shelter in the ocean, quarreling with the powerful, abandoning His kingdom, uncertainty as to His identity, acting against ordinary standards of behavior, having no good qualities, being praised falsely by beggars, aloofness, and lack of desire for family life. The Lord claimed that Rukmiṇī had failed to recognize these bad qualities in Him. Now she begins to respond to all the Lord's statements.

First she responds to Śrī Kṛṣṇa's statement in Text 11 of this chapter: *kasmān no vavṛṣe 'samān.* "Why did you select Us, who are not equal to you?" Here Śrīmatī Rukmiṇī-devī says that she and Kṛṣṇa are certainly not equal, for no one can be equal to the Supreme Lord. Śrīla Viśvanātha Cakravartī further points out that in her extreme humility Rukmiṇī is identifying herself with the Lord's external energy, which in fact is her expansion, Rukmiṇī being the goddess of fortune.

TEXT 35

सत्यं भयादिव गुणेभ्य उरुक्रमान्तः
शेते समुद्र उपलम्भनमात्र आत्मा ।
नित्यं कदिन्द्रियगणैः कृतविग्रहस्त्वं
त्वत्सेवकैर्नृपपदं विधुतं तमोऽन्धम् ॥३५॥

satyaṁ bhayād iva guṇebhya urukramāntaḥ
śete samudra upalambhana-mātra ātmā
nityaṁ kad-indriya-gaṇaiḥ kṛta-vigrahas tvaṁ
tvat-sevakair nṛpa-padaṁ vidhutaṁ tamo 'ndham

satyam—true; *bhayāt*—out of fear; *iva*—as if; *guṇebhyaḥ*—of the material modes; *urukrama*—O You who perform transcendental feats; *antaḥ*—within; *śete*—You have lain down; *samudre*—in the ocean; *upalambhana-mātraḥ*—pure awareness; *ātmā*—the Supreme Soul; *nityam*—always; *kat*—bad; *indriya-gaṇaiḥ*—against all the material senses; *kṛta-vigrahaḥ*—battling; *tvam*—You; *tvat*—Your; *sevakaiḥ*—

by the servants; *nṛpa*—of a king; *padam*—the position; *vidhutam*—rejected; *tamaḥ*—darkness; *andham*—blind.

TRANSLATION

Yes, my Lord Urukrama, You lay down within the ocean as if afraid of the material modes, and thus in pure consciousness You appear within the heart as the Supersoul. You are always battling against the foolish material senses, and indeed even Your servants reject the privilege of royal dominion, which leads to the blindness of ignorance.

PURPORT

In Text 12 Lord Kṛṣṇa said, *rājabhyo bibhyataḥ su-bhru samudraṁ śaraṇaṁ gatān:* "Out of fear of the kings, We took shelter in the ocean." Here Śrīmatī Rukmiṇī-devī points out that the actual rulers of this world are the *guṇas*, the material modes of nature, which impel all living beings to act. Śrīla Viśvanātha Cakravartī points out that because Lord Kṛṣṇa fears that His devotee will come under the influence of the modes of nature and become entangled in sense gratification, He enters the internal ocean of their hearts, where He remains as the omniscient Supersoul (*upalambhana-mātra ātmā*). Thus He protects His devotees. The word *upalambhana-mātraḥ* also indicates that the Lord is the object of meditation for His devotees.

In Text 12 Lord Kṛṣṇa also said, *balavadbhiḥ kṛta-dveṣān:* "We created enmity with the powerful." Here Śrīmatī Rukmiṇī-devī points out that it is the material senses which are actually powerful in this world. The Supreme Lord has taken up the battle against sense gratification on the part of His devotees, and thus He is constantly trying to help them in their struggle for spiritual purity. When the devotees become free of unwanted material habits, the Lord reveals Himself to them, and then the eternal loving relationship between the Lord and His devotees becomes an irrevocable fact.

In the same verse Kṛṣṇa stated, *tyakta-nṛpāsanān:* "We renounced the royal throne." But here Śrīmatī Rukmiṇī-devī points out that the position of political supremacy in this world usually implicates so-called powerful leaders in darkness and blindness. As the saying goes, "Power corrupts." Thus even the Lord's loving servants tend to shy away from political intrigue and power politics. The Lord Himself, being completely satisfied in His own spiritual bliss, would hardly be interested in occupying mundane political positions. Thus Śrīmatī Rukmiṇī-devī correctly interprets the Lord's actions as evidence of His supreme transcendental nature.

TEXT 36

त्वत्पादपद्ममकरन्दजुषां मुनीनां
वर्त्मास्फुटं नृपशुभिर्ननु दुर्विभाव्यम् ।
यस्मादलौकिकमिवेहितमीश्वरस्य
भूमंस्तवेहितमथो अनु ये भवन्तम् ॥३६॥

tvat-pāda-padma-makaranda-juṣāṁ munīnāṁ
vartmāsphuṭaṁ nṛ-paśubhir nanu durvibhāvyam
yasmād alaukikam ivehitam īśvarasya
bhūmaṁs tavehitam atho anu ye bhavantam

tvat—Your; *pāda*—of the feet; *padma*—lotuslike; *makaranda*—the honey; *juṣām*—who relish; *munīnām*—for sages; *vartma*—(Your) path; *asphuṭam*—not apparent; *nṛ*—in human form; *paśubhiḥ*—by animals; *nanu*—certainly, then; *durvibhāvyam*—impossible to comprehend; *yasmāt*—because; *alaukikam*—supramundane; *iva*—as if; *īhitam*—the activities; *īśvarasya*—of the Supreme Lord; *bhūman*—O all-powerful one; *tava*—Your; *īhitam*—activities; *atha u*—therefore; *anu*—following; *ye*—who; *bhavantam*—You.

TRANSLATION

Your movements, inscrutable even for sages who relish the honey of Your lotus feet, are certainly incomprehensible for human beings who behave like animals. And just as Your activities are transcendental, O all-powerful Lord, so too are those of Your followers.

PURPORT

Here Queen Rukmiṇī replies to Lord Kṛṣṇa's statement in Text 13:

aspaṣṭa-vartmanāṁ puṁsām
aloka-patham īyuṣām

āsthitāḥ padavīṁ su-bhru
prāyaḥ sīdanti yoṣitaḥ

"O fine-browed lady, women are usually destined to suffer when they stay with men whose behavior is uncertain and who pursue a path not approved by society."

In the present verse Rukmiṇī is taking the term *aloka-patham* to mean "unworldly path." Those who are entangled in worldly behavior are trying to enjoy this world more or less like animals. Even if such people are "culturally advanced," they should simply be considered sophisticated or polished animals. Śrīmati Rukmiṇī-devī points out that because the Lord's activities are always transcendental, they are *aspaṣṭa*, or "unclear," to ordinary people, and even the sages trying to know the Lord cannot perfectly understand these activities.

TEXT 37

निष्किञ्चनो ननु भवान्न यतोऽस्ति किञ्चिद्
यस्मै बलिं बलिभुजोऽपि हरन्त्यजाद्याः ।
न त्वा विदन्त्यसुतृपोऽन्तकमाढ्यतान्धाः
प्रेष्ठो भवान् बलिभुजामपि तेऽपि तुभ्यम् ॥३७॥

niṣkiñcano nanu bhavān na yato 'sti kiñcid
yasmai baliṁ bali-bhujo 'pi haranty ajādyāḥ
na tvā vidanty asu-tṛpo 'ntakam āḍhyatāndhāḥ
preṣṭho bhavān bali-bhujām api te 'pi tubhyam

niṣkiñcanaḥ—without possessions; *nanu*—indeed; *bhavān*—You; *na*—not; *yataḥ*—beyond whom; *asti*—there is; *kiñcit*—anything; *yasmai*—to whom; *balim*—tribute; *bali*—of tribute; *bhujaḥ*—the enjoyers; *api*—even; *haranti*—carry; *aja-ādyāḥ*—headed by Brahmā; *na*—not; *tvā*—You; *vidanti*—know; *asu-tṛpaḥ*—persons satisfied in the body; *antakam*—as death; *āḍhyatā*—by their status of wealth; *andhāḥ*—blinded; *preṣṭhaḥ*—the most dear; *bhavān*—You; *bali-bhujām*—for the great enjoyers of tribute; *api*—even; *te*—they; *api*—also; *tubhyam*—(are dear) to You.

TRANSLATION

You possess nothing because there is nothing beyond You. Even the great enjoyers of tribute—Brahmā and other demigods—pay tribute to You. Those who are blinded by their wealth and absorbed in gratifying their senses do not recognize You in the form of death. But to the gods, the enjoyers of tribute, You are the most dear, as they are to You.

PURPORT

Here Śrīmatī Rukmiṇī-devī replies to Lord Kṛṣṇa's statement in Text 14:

niṣkiñcanā vayaṁ śaśvan
niṣkiñcana-jana-priyāḥ
tasmāt prāyeṇa na hy āḍhyā
māṁ bhajanti su-madhyame

"We have no material possessions, and We are dear to those who similarly have nothing. Therefore, O slender one, the wealthy hardly ever worship Me."

Queen Rukmiṇī begins her statement by saying *niṣkiñcano nanu,* "You are indeed *niṣkiñcana.*" The word *kiñcana* means "something," and the prefix *nir*—or, as it appears here, *niṣ*—indicates negation. Thus in the ordinary sense *niṣkiñcana* means "one who does not have something," or, in other words, "one who has nothing."

But in the present verse Queen Rukmiṇī states that Lord Kṛṣṇa "possesses nothing" not because He is a pauper but because He Himself *is* everything. In other words, since Kṛṣṇa is the Absolute Truth, all that exists is within Him. There is no second thing, something outside the Lord's existence, for Him to possess. For example, a man may possess a house or a car or a child or money, but these things do not become the man: they exist outside of him. We say he possesses them merely in the sense that he has control over them. But the Lord does not merely control His creation: His creation actually exists within Him. Thus there is nothing outside of Him that He can possess in the way that we possess external objects.

The *ācāryas* explain *niṣkiñcana* in the following way: To state that a person possesses something implies that he does not possess everything.

In other words, if we say that a man owns some property, we imply that he does not own all property but rather some specific property. A standard American dictionary defines the word *some* as "a certain indefinite or unspecified number, quantity, etc., as distinguished from the rest." The Sanskrit word *kiñcana* conveys this sense of a partial amount of the total. Thus Lord Kṛṣṇa is called *niṣkiñcana* to refute the idea that He possesses merely a certain amount of beauty, fame, wealth, intelligence and other opulences. Rather, He possesses infinite beauty, infinite intelligence, infinite wealth and so on. This is so because He is the Absolute Truth.

Śrīla Prabhupāda begins his introduction to the First Canto, Volume One, of the *Śrīmad-Bhāgavatam* with the following statement, which is quite relevant to our present discussion: "The conception of God and the conception of the Absolute Truth are not on the same level. The *Śrīmad-Bhāgavatam* hits on the target of the Absolute Truth. The conception of God indicates the controller, whereas the conception of the Absolute Truth indicates the *summum bonum,* or the ultimate source of all energies." Here Śrīla Prabhupāda touches upon a fundamental philosophical point. God is commonly defined as "the supreme being," and the dictionary defines *supreme* as (1) highest in rank, power, authority, etc; (2) highest in quality, achievement, performance, etc; (3) highest in degree; and (4) final, ultimate. None of these definitions adequately indicates absolute existence.

For example, we may say that a particular American is supremely wealthy in the sense that he is wealthier than any other American, or we may speak of the Supreme Court as the highest court in the land, although it certainly does not have absolute authority in all political and social matters, since it shares authority in these fields with the legislature and the president. In other words, the word *supreme* indicates the best in a hierarchy, and thus the supreme being may merely be understood as the best or greatest of all beings but not as the very source of all other beings and, indeed, of everything that exists. Thus Śrīla Prabhupāda specifically points out that the concept of the Absolute Truth, Kṛṣṇa, is higher than the concept of a supreme being, and this point is essential to a clear understanding of Vaiṣṇava philosophy.

Lord Kṛṣṇa is not merely a supreme being: He is the absolute being, and that is exactly the point His wife is making. Thus the word *niṣkiñcana* indicates not that Kṛṣṇa possesses *no* opulence but rather *all* opulence. In that sense she accepts His definition of Himself as *niṣkiñcana.*

In Text 14 Lord Kṛṣṇa also stated, *niṣkiñcana-jana-priyaḥ:* "I am dear to those who have nothing." Here, however, Queen Rukmiṇī points out that the demigods, the wealthiest souls in the universe, regularly make offerings to the Supreme Lord. We may assume that the demigods, being the Lord's appointed representatives, know that everything belongs to Him in the sense that everything is part of Him, as explained above. Therefore the statement *niṣkiñcana-jana-priyāḥ* is correct in the sense that since nothing exists except the Lord and His potencies, no matter how wealthy the Lord's worshipers appear to be they are in fact offering Him nothing but His own energy as a loving act. The same idea is exemplified when one worships the Ganges River by offering Ganges water, or when a child gets money from his father on the father's birthday and buys him a gift. The father is paying for his own present, but what he is really interested in is his child's love. Similarly, the Supreme Lord manifests the cosmos, and then the conditioned souls collect various items of the Lord's creation. Pious souls offer some of the best items from their collection back to the Lord as a sacrifice and thus purify themselves. Since the whole cosmos and everything in it is simply the Lord's energy, we may say that those who worship the Lord possess nothing.

In more conventional terms, people who are proud of their great wealth do not bow down to God. Queen Rukmiṇī also mentions these fools. Satisfied with their temporary bodies, they do not understand the divine power of death, which stalks them. The demigods, however, who are by far the wealthiest living beings, regularly offer sacrifice to the Supreme Lord, and thus the Lord is most dear to them, as stated here.

TEXT 38

त्वं वै समस्तपुरुषार्थमयः फलात्मा
यद्वाञ्छया सुमतयो विसृजन्ति कृत्स्नम् ।
तेषां विभो समुचितो भवतः समाजः
पुंसः स्त्रियाश्च रतयोः सुखदुःखिनोर्न ॥३८॥

tvaṁ vai samasta-puruṣārtha-mayaḥ phalātmā
yad-vāñchayā su-matayo visṛjanti kṛtsnam
teṣāṁ vibho samucito bhavataḥ samājaḥ
puṁsaḥ striyāś ca ratayoḥ sukha-duḥkhinor na

tvam—You; *vai*—indeed; *samasta*—all; *puruṣa*—of human life; *artha*—of the goals; *mayaḥ*—comprising; *phala*—of the ultimate goal; *ātmā*—the very Self; *yat*—for whom; *vāñchayā*—out of desire; *su-matayaḥ*—intelligent persons; *visṛjanti*—discard; *kṛtsnam*—everything; *teṣām*—for them; *vibho*—O omnipotent one; *samucitaḥ*—appropriate; *bhavataḥ*—Your; *samājaḥ*—association; *puṁsaḥ*—of a man; *striyāḥ*—and a women; *ca*—and; *ratayoḥ*—who are attracted to each other in mutual lust; *sukha-duḥkhinoḥ*—who experience material happiness and distress; *na*—not.

TRANSLATION

You are the embodiment of all human goals and are Yourself the final aim of life. Desiring to attain You, O all-powerful Lord, intelligent persons abandon everything else. It is they who are worthy of Your association, not men and women absorbed in the pleasure and grief resulting from their mutual lust.

PURPORT

Here Queen Rukmiṇī refutes Lord Kṛṣṇa's statement in Text 15:

yayor ātma-samaṁ vittaṁ
janmaiśvaryākṛtir bhavaḥ
tayor vivāho maitrī ca
nottamādhamayoḥ kvacit

"Marriage and friendship are proper between two people who are equal in terms of their wealth, birth, influence, physical appearance and capacity for good progeny, but never between a superior and an inferior." In fact, only those who have given up all such material conceptions of sense gratification and have taken exclusively to the Lord's loving service can understand who their real friend and companion is—Lord Śrī Kṛṣṇa Himself.

TEXT 39

त्वं न्यस्तदण्डमुनिभिर्गदितानुभाव
आत्मात्मदश्च जगतामिति मे वृतोऽसि ।

हित्वा भवद्भ्रुव उदीरितकालवेग-
ध्वस्ताशिषोऽब्जभवनाकपतीन् कुतोऽन्ये ॥३९॥

tvaṁ nyasta-daṇḍa-munibhir gaditānubhāva
ātmātma-daś ca jagatām iti me vṛto 'si
hitvā bhavad-bhruva udīrita-kāla-vega-
dhvastāśiṣo 'bja-bhava-nāka-patīn kuto 'nye

tvam—You; *nyasta*—who have renounced; *daṇḍa*—the *sannyāsī's* staff; *munibhiḥ*—by sages; *gadita*—spoken of; *anubhāvaḥ*—whose prowess; *ātmā*—the Supreme Soul; *ātma*—Your own self; *daḥ*—who give away; *ca*—also; *jagatām*—of all the worlds; *iti*—thus; *me*—by me; *vṛtaḥ*—chosen; *asi*—You have been; *hitvā*—rejecting; *bhavat*—Your; *bhruvaḥ*—from the eyebrows; *udīrita*—generated; *kāla*—of time; *vega*—by the impulses; *dhvasta*—destroyed; *āśiṣaḥ*—whose hopes; *abja*—lotus-born (Lord Brahmā); *bhava*—Lord Śiva; *nāka*—of heaven; *patīn*—the masters; *kutaḥ*—what then of; *anye*—others.

TRANSLATION

Knowing that great sages who have renounced the *sannyāsī's daṇḍa* proclaim Your glories, that You are the Supreme Soul of all the worlds, and that You are so gracious that You give away even Your own self, I chose You as my husband, rejecting Lord Brahmā, Lord Śiva and the rulers of heaven, whose aspirations are all frustrated by the force of time, which is born from Your eyebrows. What interest, then, could I have in any other suitors?

PURPORT

This is Queen Rukmiṇī's refutation of Lord Kṛṣṇa's statement in Text 16. There the Lord Kṛṣṇa said, *bhikṣubhiḥ ślāghitā mudhā:* "I am glorified by beggars." But Queen Rukmiṇī points out that those so-called beggars are actually sages in the *paramahaṁsa* stage of life—*sannyāsīs* who have reached the highest level of spiritual advancement and thus given up the *sannyāsī* rod. Lord Kṛṣṇa also made two specific accusations against His wife in Text 16. He said, *vaidarbhy etad avijñāya*—"My dear Vaidarbhī, you were not aware of the situation"—and *tvayādīrgha-samīkṣayā*—"because you lack foresight." In the present verse, Rukmiṇī's statement *iti me vṛto 'si* indicates "I chose You as my husband because You possess the above-mentioned qualities. It was not a blind choice at all." Rukmiṇī further mentions that she passed over lesser personalities like Brahmā, Śiva and the rulers of heaven because she saw that even though, materially speaking, they are great personalities, they are frustrated by the powerful waves of time, which emanate from the eyebrows of Lord Kṛṣṇa. Therefore, far from lacking foresight, Rukmiṇī chose Lord Kṛṣṇa after an exhaustive appraisal of the entire cosmic situation. Thus she lovingly rebukes her husband here.

Śrīla Viśvanātha Cakravartī interprets Rukmiṇī's mood as follows: "My dear husband, Your accusation that I lack foresight indicates that You did know of my deep insight into the situation. Actually, I chose You because I knew of Your true glories."

TEXT 40

जाड्यं वचस्तव गदाग्रज यस्तु भूपान्
विद्राव्य शार्ङ्गनिनदेन जहर्थ मां त्वम् ।
सिंहो यथा स्वबलिमीश पशून् स्वभागं
तेभ्यो भयाद्यदुदधिं शरणं प्रपन्नः ॥४०॥

jāḍyaṁ vacas tava gadāgraja yas tu bhūpān
vidrāvya śārṅga-ninadena jahartha māṁ tvam
siṁho yathā sva-balim īśa paśūn sva-bhāgaṁ
tebhyo bhayād yad udadhiṁ śaraṇaṁ prapannaḥ

jāḍyam—foolishness; *vacaḥ*—words; *tava*—Your; *gadāgraja*—O Gadāgraja; *yaḥ*—who; *tu*—even; *bhū-pān*—the kings; *vidrāvya*—driving away; *śārṅga*—of Śārṅga, Your bow; *ninadena*—by the resounding; *jahartha*—took away; *mām*—me; *tvam*—You; *siṁhaḥ*—a lion; *yathā*—as; *sva*—Your own; *balim*—tribute; *īśa*—O Lord; *paśūn*—animals; *sva-bhāgam*—his own share; *tebhyaḥ*—of them; *bhayāt*—out of fear; *yat*—that; *udadhim*—of the ocean; *śaraṇam prapannaḥ*—took shelter.

TRANSLATION

My Lord, as a lion drives away lesser animals to claim his proper tribute, You drove off the assembled kings with the resounding

twang of Your Śārṅga bow and then claimed me, Your fair share. Thus it is sheer foolishness, my dear Gadāgraja, for You to say You took shelter in the ocean out of fear of those kings.

PURPORT

In Text 12 of this chapter Lord Kṛṣṇa said, *rājabhyo bibhyataḥ su-bhru samudraṁ śaraṇaṁ gatān:* "Terrified of those kings, We went to the ocean for shelter." According to the *ācāryas,* Lord Kṛṣṇa finally provoked Rukmiṇī's anger by glorifying other men who might have been her husband, and thus in an agitated mood she here tells Him that she is not ignorant but rather that He has spoken foolishly. She states, "Like a lion You abducted me in the presence of those kings and drove them away with Your Śārṅga bow, so it is simply foolishness to say that out of fear of those same kings You went to the ocean." According to Śrīla Viśvanātha Cakravartī, as Queen Rukmiṇī spoke these words she frowned and cast angry sidelong glances at the Lord.

TEXT 41

यद्वाञ्छया नृपशिखामणयोऽङगवैन्य-
जायन्तनाहुषगयादय ऐक्यपत्यम् ।
राज्यं विसृज्य विविशुर्वनमम्बुजाक्ष
सीदन्ति तेऽनुपदवीं त इहास्थिताः किम् ॥४१॥

yad-vāñchayā nṛpa-śikhāmaṇayo 'ṅga-vainya-
jāyanta-nāhuṣa-gayādaya aikya-patyam
rājyaṁ visṛjya viviśur vanam ambujākṣa
sīdanti te 'nupadavīṁ ta ihāsthitāḥ kim

yat—for whom; *vāñchayā*—out of desire; *nṛpa*—of kings; *śikhā-maṇayaḥ*—the crown jewels; *aṅga-vainya-jāyanta-nāhuṣa-gaya-ādayaḥ*—Aṅga (the father of Vena), Vainya (Pṛthu, the son of Vena), Jāyanta (Bharata), Nāhuṣa (Yayāti), Gaya and others; *aikya*—exclusive; *pat-yam*—having sovereignty; *rājyam*—their kingdoms; *visṛjya*—abandoning; *viviśuḥ*—entered; *vanam*—the forest; *ambuja-akṣa*—O lotus-eyed one; *sīdanti*—suffer frustration; *te*—Your; *anupadavīm*—on the path; *te*—they; *iha*—in this world; *āsthitāḥ*—fixed; *kim*—whether.

TRANSLATION

Wanting Your association, the best of kings—Aṅga, Vainya, Jāyanta, Nāhuṣa, Gaya and others—abandoned their absolute sovereignty and entered the forest to seek You out. How could those kings suffer frustration in this world, O lotus-eyed one?

PURPORT

Here Queen Rukmiṇī refutes the ideas put forth by Lord Kṛṣṇa in Text 13. In fact Śrīmatī Rukmiṇī-devī repeats Lord Kṛṣṇa's own words. The Lord said, *āsthitāḥ padavīṁ su-bhru prāyaḥ sīdanti yoṣitaḥ:* "Women who follow My path generally suffer." Here Rukmiṇī-devī says, *sīdanti te 'nupadavīṁ ta ihāsthitāḥ kim:* "Why should those fixed on Your path suffer in this world?" She gives the example of many great kings who renounced their powerful sovereignty to enter the forest, where they performed austerities and worshiped the Lord, intensely desiring His transcendental association. Thus, according to Śrīla Viśvanātha Cakravartī, Śrīmatī Rukmiṇī-devī here intends to tell Śrī Kṛṣṇa, "You have said that I, a king's daughter, am unintelligent and frustrated because I married You. But how can You accuse all these great enlightened kings of being unintelligent? They were the wisest of men, yet they gave up everything to follow You and were certainly not frustrated by the result. Indeed, they achieved the perfection of Your association."

TEXT 42

कान्यं श्रयेत तव पादसरोजगन्धम्
आघ्राय सन्मुखरितं जनतापवर्गम् ।
लक्ष्म्यालयं त्वविगणय्य गुणालयस्य
मर्त्या सदोरुभयमर्थविविक्तदृष्टिः ॥४२॥

kānyaṁ śrayeta tava pāda-saroja-gandham
āghrāya san-mukharitaṁ janatāpavargam
lakṣmy-ālayaṁ tv avigaṇayya guṇālayasya
martyā sadoru-bhayam artha-vivikta-dṛṣṭiḥ

kā—what woman; *anyam*—another man; *śrayeta*—would take shelter of; *tava*—Your; *pāda*—of the feet; *saroja*—of the lotus; *gandham*—the aroma; *āghrāya*—having smelled; *sat*—by great saints; *mukharitam*—described; *janatā*—for all people; *apavargam*—bestowing liberation; *lakṣmī*—of the goddess of fortune; *ālayam*—the place of residence; *tu*—but; *aviganayya*—not taking seriously; *guṇa*—of all transcendental qualities; *ālayasya*—of the abode; *martyā*—mortal; *sadā*—always; *uru*—great; *bhayam*—one who has fear; *artha*—her best interest; *vivikta*—ascertaining; *dṛṣṭiḥ*—whose insight.

TRANSLATION

The aroma of Your lotus feet, which is glorified by great saints, awards people liberation and is the abode of Goddess Lakṣmī. What woman would take shelter of any other man after savoring that aroma? Since You are the abode of transcendental qualities, what mortal woman with the insight to distinguish her own true interest would disregard that fragrance and depend instead on someone who is always subject to terrible fear?

PURPORT

In Text 16 Lord Kṛṣṇa claimed that He was *guṇair hīnāḥ*, "bereft of all good qualities." To refute this claim, the devoted Rukmiṇī here states that the Lord is *guṇālaya*, "the abode of all good qualities." In a single moment the so-called powerful men of this world can be reduced to utter helplessness and confusion. Indeed, destruction is the inevitable fate of all powerful masculine bodies. The Lord, however, has an eternal, spiritual body that is omnipotent and infinitely beautiful, and thus, as Queen Rukmiṇī argues here, how could any sane, enlightened woman take shelter of anyone but the Supreme Lord, Kṛṣṇa?

TEXT 43

तं त्वानुरूपमभजं जगतामधीशम्
आत्मानमत्र च परत्र च कामपूरम् ।
स्यान्मे तवाङ्घ्रिररणं सृतिभिर्भ्रमन्त्या
यो वै भजन्तमुपयात्यनृतापवर्गः ॥४३॥

taṁ tvānurūpam abhajaṁ jagatām adhīśam
ātmānam atra ca paratra ca kāma-pūram
syān me tavāṅghrir araṇaṁ sṛtibhir bhramantyā
yo vai bhajantam upayāty anṛtāpavargaḥ

tam—Him; *tvā*—Yourself; *anurūpam*—suitable; *abhajam*—I have chosen; *jagatām*—of all the worlds; *adhīśam*—the ultimate master; *ātmānam*—the Supreme Soul; *atra*—in this life; *ca*—and; *paratra*—in the next life; *ca*—also; *kāma*—of desires; *pūram*—the fulfiller; *syāt*—may they be; *me*—for me; *tava*—Your; *aṅghriḥ*—feet; *araṇam*—shelter; *sṛtibhiḥ*—by the various movements (from one species of life to another); *bhramantyāḥ*—who has been wandering; *yaḥ*—which (feet); *vai*—indeed; *bhajantam*—their worshiper; *upayāti*—approach; *anṛta*—from untruth; *apavargaḥ*—freedom.

TRANSLATION

Because You are suitable for me, I have chosen You, the master and Supreme Soul of all the worlds, who fulfill our desires in this life and the next. May Your feet, which give freedom from illusion by approaching their worshiper, give shelter to me, who have been wandering from one material situation to another.

PURPORT

An alternate reading for the word *sṛtibhiḥ* is *śrutibhiḥ,* in which case the idea Rukmiṇī expresses is this: "I have been bewildered by hearing from various religious scriptures about numerous rituals and ceremonies with their promises of fruitive results." Śrīla Śrīdhara Svāmī gives this explanation, while Śrīla Jīva Gosvāmī and Śrīla Viśvanātha Cakravartī give an additional idea Rukmiṇī might express with the word *śrutibhiḥ:* "My dear Lord Kṛṣṇa, I was bewildered by hearing about Your various incarnations. I heard that when You descended as Rāma You abandoned Your wife, Sītā, and that in this life You abandoned the *gopīs.* Thus I was bewildered."

It is understood that Śrīmatī Rukmiṇī-devī is the eternally liberated consort of Lord Kṛṣṇa, but in these verses she humbly plays the part of a mortal woman taking shelter of the Supreme Lord.

TEXT 44

तस्याः स्युरच्युत नृपा भवतोपदिष्टाः
स्त्रीणां गृहेषु खरगोश्वविडालभृत्याः ।
यत्कर्णमूलमरिकर्षण नोपयायाद्
युष्मत्कथा मृडविरिञ्चसभासु गीता ॥४४॥

tasyāḥ syur acyuta nṛpā bhavatopadiṣṭāḥ
strīṇāṁ gṛheṣu khara-go-śva-viḍāla-bhṛtyāḥ
yat-karṇa-mūlam ari-karṣaṇa nopayāyād
yuṣmat-kathā mṛḍa-viriñca-sabhāsu gītā

tasyāḥ—of her; *syuḥ*—let them become (the husbands); *acyuta*—O infallible Kṛṣṇa; *nṛpāḥ*—kings; *bhavatā*—by You; *upadiṣṭāḥ*—mentioned; *strīṇām*—of women; *gṛheṣu*—in the homes; *khara*—as asses; *go*—oxen; *śva*—dogs; *viḍāla*—cats; *bhṛtyāḥ*—and slaves; *yat*—whose; *karṇa*—of the ear; *mūlam*—the core; *ari*—Your enemies; *karṣaṇa*—O You who vex; *na*—never; *upayāyāt*—come near; *yuṣmat*—concerning You; *kathā*—discussions; *mṛḍa*—of Lord Śiva; *viriñca*—and Lord Brahmā; *sabhāsu*—in the scholarly assemblies; *gītā*—sung.

TRANSLATION

O infallible Kṛṣṇa, let each of the kings You named become the husband of a woman whose ears have never heard Your glories, which are sung in the assemblies of Śiva and Brahmā. After all, in the households of such women these kings live like asses, oxen, dogs, cats and slaves.

PURPORT

According to Śrīla Śrīdhara Svāmī, these fiery words of Queen Rukmiṇī's are a response to Lord Kṛṣṇa's opening statement, found in Text 10 of the chapter. The Supreme Lord had said, "My dear princess, You were sought after by many kings as powerful as the rulers of planets. They were all abundantly endowed with political influence, wealth, beauty, generosity and physical strength." According to Śrīdhara Svāmī, Queen Rukmiṇī here speaks with anger, pointing her index finger at the Lord. She compares the so-called great princes to asses because they carry many material burdens, to oxen because they are always distressed while performing their occupational duties, to dogs because their wives disrespect them, to cats because they are selfish and cruel, and to slaves because they are servile in family affairs. Such kings may appear desirable to a foolish woman who has not heard or understood the glories of Śrī Kṛṣṇa.

Śrīla Viśvanātha Cakravartī adds that such kings are like asses because their wives sometimes kick them, like dogs because they behave inimically toward outsiders in order to protect their homes, and like cats because they eat the remnants left by their wives.

TEXT 45

त्वक्श्मश्रुरोमनखकेशपिनद्धमन्तर्
मांसास्थिरक्तकृमिविट्कफपित्तवातम् ।
जीवच्छवं भजति कान्तमतिर्विमूढा
या ते पदाब्जमकरन्दमजिघ्रती स्त्री ॥४५॥

tvak-śmaśru-roma-nakha-keśa-pinaddham antar
māṁsāsthi-rakta-kṛmi-viṭ-kapha-pitta-vātam
jīvac-chavaṁ bhajati kānta-matir vimūḍhā
yā te padābja-makarandam ajighratī strī

tvak—with skin; *śmaśru*—whiskers; *roma*—bodily hair; *nakha*—nails; *keśa*—and hair on the head; *pinaddham*—covered; *antaḥ*—inside; *māṁsa*—flesh; *asthi*—bones; *rakta*—blood; *kṛmi*—worms; *viṭ*—stool; *kapha*—mucus; *pitta*—bile; *vātam*—and air; *jīvat*—living; *śavam*—a corpse; *bhajati*—worships; *kānta*—as husband or lover; *matiḥ*—whose idea; *vimūḍhā*—totally bewildered; *yā*—who; *te*—Your; *pada-abja*—of the lotus feet; *makarandam*—the honey; *ajighratī*—not smelling; *strī*—woman.

TRANSLATION

A woman who fails to relish the fragrance of the honey of Your lotus feet becomes totally befooled, and thus she accepts as her husband or lover a living corpse covered with skin, whiskers, nails, head-hair and body-hair and filled with flesh, bones, blood, parasites, feces, mucus, bile and air.

PURPORT

Here Lord Kṛṣṇa's chaste wife makes a quite unequivocal statement about material sense gratification based on the physical body. Śrīla Viśvanātha Cakravartī comments as follows on this verse: On the authority of the statement *sa vai patiḥ syād akuto-bhayaḥ svayam*—"He indeed should become one's husband who can remove all fear"—Śrī Kṛṣṇa is the real husband for all women at all times. Thus a woman who worships someone else as her husband simply worships a dead body.

Śrīla Viśvanātha Cakravartī comments further: Rukmiṇī thus considered that although the sweetness of Lord Kṛṣṇa's lotus feet is well known, and although He possesses an eternal body full of knowledge and bliss, foolish women reject Him. An ordinary husband's body is covered on the outside by skin and hair; otherwise, being filled with blood, feces, flesh, bile and so on, it would be overwhelmed with flies and other vermin attracted by its bad smell and other offensive qualities.

Those who have no practical experience of the beauty and purity of Kṛṣṇa or of Kṛṣṇa consciousness may be confused by such uncompromising denunciations of material, bodily gratification. But those who are enlightened in Kṛṣṇa consciousness will be enlivened and enthused by such absolutely truthful statements.

TEXT 46

अस्त्वम्बुजाक्ष मम ते चरणानुराग
आत्मन् रतस्य मयि चानतिरिक्तदृष्टेः ।
यर्ह्यस्य वृद्धय उपात्तरजोऽतिमात्रो
मामीक्षसे तदु ह नः परमानुकम्पा ॥४६॥

astv ambujākṣa mama te caraṇānurāga
ātman ratasya mayi cānatirikta-dṛṣṭeḥ
yarhy asya vṛddhaya upātta-rajo-'ti-mātro
mām īkṣase tad u ha naḥ paramānukampā

astu—may there be; *ambuja-akṣa*—O lotus-eyed one; *mama*—my; *te*—Your; *caraṇa*—for the feet; *anurāgaḥ*—steady attraction; *ātman*—in Yourself; *ratasya*—who take Your pleasure; *mayi*—toward me; *ca*—and;

anatirikta—not much; *dṛṣṭeḥ*—whose glance; *yarhi*—when; *asya*—of this universe; *vṛddhaye*—for the increase; *upātta*—assuming; *rajaḥ*—of the mode of passion; *ati-mātraḥ*—an abundance; *mām*—at me; *īkṣase*—You look; *tat*—that; *u ha*—indeed; *naḥ*—for us; *parama*—the greatest; *anukampā*—show of mercy.

TRANSLATION

O lotus-eyed one, though You are satisfied within Yourself and thus rarely turn Your attention toward me, please bless me with steady love for Your feet. It is when You assume a predominance of passion in order to manifest the universe that You glance upon me, showing me what is indeed Your greatest mercy.

PURPORT

In Text 20 of this chapter Lord Kṛṣṇa stated, "Always satisfied within Ourselves, We care nothing for wives, children and wealth." Here Rukmiṇī-devī humbly replies, "Yes, You take pleasure within Yourself and therefore rarely look at me."

In this regard Śrīla Viśvanātha Cakravartī points out that Lord Kṛṣṇa had already declared His love for Rukmiṇī (*Bhāg.* 10.53.2): *tathāham api tac-citto nidrāṁ ca na labhe niśi.* "I am also thinking about her—so much so that I cannot sleep at night." Lord Kṛṣṇa is satisfied within Himself, and if we remember that Śrīmatī Rukmiṇī-devī is His internal potency, we can understand that His loving affairs with her are expressions of His pure spiritual happiness.

Here, however, Queen Rukmiṇī humbly identifies herself with the Lord's external energy, which is her expansion. Therefore she says, "Though You do not often look at me, when You are ready to manifest the material universe and thus begin to work through the material quality of passion, which is Your potency, You glance at me. In this way You show me Your greatest mercy." Thus Ācārya Viśvanātha explains that Goddess Rukmiṇī's statement can be understood in two ways. And of course the Vaiṣṇavas, after thoroughly understanding the philosophy of Kṛṣṇa from the bona fide *ācāryas,* simply relish these loving affairs between the Lord and His exalted devotees.

TEXT 47

नैवालीकमहं मन्ये वचस्ते मधुसूदन ।
अम्बाया एव हि प्रायः कन्यायाः स्याद् रतिः क्वचित् ॥४७॥

naivālīkam ahaṁ manye
vacas te madhusūdana
ambāyā eva hi prāyaḥ
kanyāyāḥ syād ratiḥ kvacit

na—not; *eva*—indeed; *alīkam*—false; *aham*—I; *manye*—think; *vacaḥ*—words; *te*—Your; *madhu-sūdana*—O killer of Madhu; *ambāyāḥ*—of Ambā; *eva hi*—certainly; *prāyaḥ*—generally; *kanyāyāḥ*—the maiden; *syāt*—arose; *ratiḥ*—attraction (to Śālva); *kvacit*—once.

TRANSLATION

Actually, I don't consider Your words false, Madhusūdana. Quite often an unmarried girl is attracted to a man, as in the case of Ambā.

PURPORT

Having refuted everything Lord Kṛṣṇa said, Śrīmatī Rukmiṇī, in a gracious frame of mind, now praises the truthfulness of His statements. In other words, she accepts that Lord Kṛṣṇa used her as an example to elucidate ordinary female psychology. The King of Kāśī had three daughters—Ambā, Ambālikā and Ambikā—and Ambā was attracted to Śālva. This story is narrated in the *Mahābhārata*.

TEXT 48

व्यूढायाश्चापि पुंश्चल्या मनोऽभ्येति नवं नवम् ।
बुधोऽसतीं न बिभृयात्तां बिभ्रदुभयच्युतः ॥४८॥

vyūḍhāyāś cāpi puṁścalyā
mano 'bhyeti navaṁ navam
budho 'satīṁ na bibhṛyāt
tāṁ bibhrad ubhaya-cyutaḥ

vyūḍhāyāḥ—of a woman who is married; *ca*—and; *api*—even; *puṁścalyāḥ*—promiscuous; *manaḥ*—the mind; *abhyeti*—is attracted; *navam navam*—to newer and newer (lovers); *budhaḥ*—one who is intelligent; *asatīm*—an unchaste woman; *na bibhṛyāt*—should not maintain; *tām*—her; *bibhrat*—maintaining; *ubhaya*—from both (good fortune in this world and in the next); *cyutaḥ*—fallen.

TRANSLATION

The mind of a promiscuous woman always hankers for new lovers, even if she is married. An intelligent man should not keep such an unchaste wife, for if he does he will lose his good fortune both in this life and the next.

TEXT 49

श्रीभगवानुवाच
साध्व्येतच्छ्रोतुकामैस्त्वं राजपुत्रि प्रलम्भिता ।
मयोदितं यदन्वात्थ सर्वं तत्सत्यमेव हि ॥४९॥

śrī-bhagavān uvāca
sādhvy etac-chrotu-kāmais tvaṁ
rāja-putri pralambhitā
mayoditaṁ yad anvāttha
sarvaṁ tat satyam eva hi

śrī-bhagavān uvāca—the Supreme Lord said; *sādhvi*—O saintly lady; *etat*—this; *śrotu*—to hear; *kāmaiḥ*—(by Us) who wanted; *tvam*—you; *rāja-putri*—O princess; *pralambhitā*—fooled; *mayā*—by Me; *uditam*—spoken; *yat*—what; *anvāttha*—you replied to; *sarvam*—all; *tat*—that; *satyam*—correct; *eva hi*—indeed.

TRANSLATION

The Supreme Lord said: O saintly lady, O princess, We deceived you only because We wanted to hear you speak like this. Indeed, everything you said in reply to My words is most certainly true.

TEXT 50

यान् यान् कामयसे कामान्मय्यकामाय भामिनि ।
सन्ति ह्येकान्तभक्तायास्तव कल्याणि नित्यदा ॥५०॥

yān yān kāmayase kāmān
mayy akāmāya bhāmini
santi hy ekānta-bhaktāyās
tava kalyāṇi nityadā

yān yān—whatever; *kāmayase*—you hanker for; *kāmān*—benedictions; *mayi*—to Me; *akāmāya*—for freedom from desire; *bhāmini*—O fair one; *santi*—they are; *hi*—indeed; *eka-anta*—exclusively; *bhaktāyāḥ*—who is devoted; *tava*—for you; *kalyāṇi*—O auspicious one; *nityadā*—always.

TRANSLATION

Whatever benedictions you hope for in order to become free of material desires are ever yours, O fair and noble lady, for you are My unalloyed devotee.

TEXT 51

उपलब्धं पतिप्रेम पातिव्रत्यं च तेऽनघे ।
यद्वाक्यैश्चाल्यमानाया न धीर्मय्यपकर्षिता ॥५१॥

upalabdhaṁ pati-prema
pāti-vratyaṁ ca te 'naghe
yad vākyaiś cālyamānāyā
na dhīr mayy apakarṣitā

upalabdham—perceived; *pati*—for one's husband; *prema*—pure love; *pāti*—toward one's husband; *vratyam*—adherence to vows of chastity; *ca*—and; *te*—your; *anaghe*—O sinless one; *yat*—inasmuch as; *vākyaiḥ*—with words; *cālyamānāyāḥ*—being disturbed; *na*—not; *dhīḥ*—your mind; *mayi*—attached to Me; *apakarṣitā*—dragged away.

TRANSLATION

O sinless one, I have now seen firsthand the pure love and chaste attachment you have for your husband. Even though shaken by My words, your mind could not be pulled away from Me.

PURPORT

Śrīla Viśvanātha Cakravartī quotes the following verse describing the pure love between Rukmiṇī and Kṛṣṇa:

sarvathā dhvaṁsa-rahitaṁ
saty api dhvaṁsa-kāraṇe
yad bhāva-bandhanaṁ yūnoḥ
sa premā parikīrtitaḥ

"When the affectionate bond between a young man and a young woman can never be destroyed, even when there is every cause for the destruction of that relationship, the attachment between them is said to be pure love." This is the nature of the eternal loving affairs between Lord Kṛṣṇa and His pure conjugal associates.

TEXT 52

ये मां भजन्ति दाम्पत्ये तपसा व्रतचर्यया ।
कामात्मानोऽपवर्गेशं मोहिता मम मायया ॥५२॥

ye māṁ bhajanti dāmpatye
tapasā vrata-caryayā
kāmātmāno 'pavargeśaṁ
mohitā mama māyayā

ye—those who; *mām*—Me; *bhajanti*—worship; *dāmpatye*—for status in household life; *tapasā*—by penances; *vrata*—of vows; *caryayā*—and by the execution; *kāma-ātmānaḥ*—lusty by nature; *apavarga*—of liberation; *īśam*—the controller; *mohitāḥ*—bewildered; *mama*—My; *māyayā*—by the illusory, material energy.

TRANSLATION

Although I have the power to award spiritual liberation, lusty persons worship Me with penance and vows in order to get My blessings for their mundane family life. Such persons are bewildered by My illusory energy.

PURPORT

The word *dāmpatye* indicates the relationship between husband and wife. Lusty and bewildered persons worship the Supreme Lord to enhance this relationship, though they know He can free them from their useless attachment to temporary things.

TEXT 53

मां प्राप्य मानिन्यपवर्गसम्पदं
वाञ्छन्ति ये सम्पद एव तत्पतिम् ।
ते मन्दभागा निरयेऽपि ये नृणां
मात्रात्मकत्वात्निरयः सुसंगमः ॥५३॥

māṁ prāpya māniny apavarga-sampadaṁ
vāñchanti ye sampada eva tat-patim
te manda-bhāgā niraye 'pi ye nṛṇāṁ
mātrātmakatvāt nirayaḥ su-saṅgamaḥ

mām—Myself; *prāpya*—obtaining; *mānini*—O reservoir of love; *apavarga*—of liberation; *sampadam*—the treasure; *vāñchanti*—they desire; *ye*—who; *sampadaḥ*—(material) treasures; *eva*—only; *tat*—of such; *patim*—the master; *te*—they; *manda-bhāgāḥ*—less fortunate; *niraye*—in hell; *api*—even; *ye*—which; *nṛṇām*—for persons; *mātrā-ātmakatvāt*—because they are absorbed in sense gratification; *nirayaḥ*—hell; *su-saṅgamaḥ*—appropriate.

TRANSLATION

O supreme reservoir of love, unfortunate are they who even after obtaining Me, the Lord of both liberation and material riches, hanker only for material treasures. These worldly gains

can be found even in hell. Since such persons are obsessed with sense gratification, hell is a fitting place for them.

PURPORT

It stands to reason that since Lord Kṛṣṇa is the source of all pleasure and all opulence, He Himself is the supreme pleasure and the most opulent. Therefore our real self-interest is to always engage in the loving service of Lord Kṛṣṇa. As Prahlāda Mahārāja says (*Bhāg*. 7.5.31), *na te viduḥ svārtha-gatiṁ hi viṣṇum:* "The ignorant do not know that their actual self-interest lies in attaining the Supreme Lord, Viṣṇu [Kṛṣṇa]."

According to Śrīla Viśvanātha Cakravartī, one can easily obtain female association and other sense pleasures even in hell. We have practical experience that even such creatures as hogs, dogs and pigeons have ample opportunity to enjoy sex. It is unfortunate that modern human beings, who have a golden opportuntity to become Kṛṣṇa conscious, prefer to enjoy like dogs and cats. And this goes on in the name of material progress.

TEXT 54

दिष्टया गृहेश्वर्यसकृन्मयि त्वया
कृतानुवृत्तिर्भवमोचनी खलैः ।
सुदुष्करासौ सुतरां दुराशिषो
ह्यसुंभराया निकृतिं जुषः स्त्रियाः ॥५४॥

diṣṭyā gṛheśvary asakṛn mayi tvayā
kṛtānuvṛttir bhava-mocanī khalaiḥ
su-duṣkarāsau sutarāṁ durāśiṣo
hy asuṁ-bharāyā nikṛtiṁ juṣaḥ striyāḥ

diṣṭyā—fortunately; *gṛha*—of the house; *īśvari*—O mistress; *asakṛt*—constantly; *mayi*—to Me; *tvayā*—by you; *kṛtā*—done; *anuvṛttiḥ*—faithful service; *bhava*—from material existence; *mocanī*—which gives liberation; *khalaiḥ*—for those who are envious; *su-duṣkarā*—very difficult to do; *asau*—it; *sutarām*—especially; *durāśiṣaḥ*—whose intentions are wicked; *hi*—indeed; *asum*—her life air; *bharāyāḥ*—who (only) maintains; *nikṛtim*—deception; *juṣaḥ*—who indulges in; *striyāḥ*—for a woman.

TRANSLATION

Fortunately, O mistress of the house, you have always rendered Me faithful devotional service, which liberates one from material existence. This service is very difficult for the envious to perform, especially for a woman whose intentions are wicked, who lives only to gratify her bodily demands, and who indulges in duplicity.

PURPORT

Śrīla Jīva Gosvāmī poses the following question: Since devotional service easily awards one liberation, isn't it possible that everyone will be liberated and the world will no longer exist? The great *ācārya* answers that there is no such danger, since it is very difficult for envious, duplicitous, sensuous persons to faithfully serve the Supreme Personality of Godhead, and there is no shortage of such people in the world.

TEXT 55

न त्वादृशीं प्रणयिनीं गृहिणीं गृहेषु
पश्यामि मानिनि यया स्वविवाहकाले ।
प्राप्तान्नृपान्न विगणय्य रहोहरो मे
प्रस्थापितो द्विज उपश्रुतसत्कथस्य ॥५५॥

na tvādṛśīṁ praṇayinīṁ gṛhiṇīṁ gṛheṣu
paśyāmi mānini yayā sva-vivāha-kāle
prāptān nṛpān na vigaṇayya raho-haro me
prasthāpito dvija upaśruta-sat-kathasya

na—not; *tvādṛśīm*—like you; *praṇayinīm*—loving; *gṛhiṇīm*—wife; *gṛheṣu*—in My residences; *paśyāmi*—do I see; *mānini*—O respectful one; *yayā*—by whom; *sva*—of her own; *vivāha*—marriage; *kāle*—at the time; *prāptān*—arrived; *nṛpān*—kings; *na vigaṇayya*—disregarding; *rahaḥ*—of a confidential message; *haraḥ*—the carrier; *me*—to Me; *prasthāpitaḥ*—sent; *dvijaḥ*—a *brāhmaṇa; upaśruta*—overheard; *sat*—true; *kathasya*—narrations about whom.

TRANSLATION

In all My palaces I can find no other wife as loving as you, O most respectful one. When you were to be married, you disregarded all the kings who had assembled to seek your hand, and simply because you had heard authentic accounts concerning Me, you sent a *brāhmaṇa* to Me with your confidential message.

TEXT 56

भ्रातुर्विरूपकरणं युधि निर्जितस्य
प्रोद्वाहपर्वणि च तद्वधमक्षगोष्ठ्याम् ।
दुःखं समुत्थमसहोऽस्मदयोगभीत्या
नैवाब्रवीः किमपि तेन वयं जितास्ते ॥५६॥

bhrātur virūpa-karaṇaṁ yudhi nirjitasya
prodvāha-parvaṇi ca tad-vadham akṣa-goṣṭhyām
duḥkhaṁ samuttham asaho 'smad-ayoga-bhītyā
naivābravīḥ kim api tena vayaṁ jitās te

bhrātuḥ—of your brother; *virūpa-karaṇam*—the disfigurement; *yudhi*—in battle; *nirjitasya*—who was defeated; *prodvāha*—of the marriage ceremony (of Rukmiṇī's grandson, Aniruddha); *parvaṇi*—on the appointed day; *ca*—and; *tat*—his; *vadham*—killing; *akṣa-goṣṭhyām*—during a gambling match; *duḥkham*—sorrow; *samuttham*—fully experienced; *asahaḥ*—intolerable; *asmat*—from Us; *ayoga*—of separation; *bhītyā*—out of fear; *na*—not; *eva*—indeed; *abravīḥ*—did you speak; *kim api*—anything; *tena*—by that; *vayam*—We; *jitāḥ*—conquered; *te*—by you.

TRANSLATION

When your brother, who had been defeated in battle and then disfigured, was later killed during a gambling match on Aniruddha's wedding day, you felt unbearable grief, yet out of fear of losing Me you spoke not a word. By this silence you have conquered Me.

PURPORT

Here Lord Kṛṣṇa refers to an event that will be described in the next chapter. Thus Kṛṣṇa's talks with Rukmiṇī must have taken place after the marriage of Aniruddha.

TEXT 57

दूतस्त्वयात्मलभने सुविविक्तमन्त्रः
प्रस्थापितो मयि चिरायति शून्यमेतत् ।
मत्वा जिहास इदमंगमनन्ययोग्यं
तिष्ठेत तत्त्वयि वयं प्रतिनन्दयामः ॥५७॥

dūtas tvayātma-labhane su-vivikta-mantraḥ
prasthāpito mayi cirāyati śūnyam etat
matvā jihāsa idam aṅgam ananya-yogyaṁ
tiṣṭheta tat tvayi vayaṁ pratinandayāmaḥ

dūtaḥ—the messenger; *tvayā*—by you; *ātma*—Myself; *labhane*—for obtaining; *su-vivikta*—very confidential; *mantraḥ*—whose advice; *prasthāpitaḥ*—sent; *mayi*—when I; *cirāyati*—delayed; *śūnyam*—empty; *etat*—this (world); *matvā*—thinking; *jihāse*—you wanted to give up; *idam*—this; *aṅgam*—body; *ananya*—for no one else; *yogyam*—suited; *tiṣṭheta*—may stand; *tat*—that; *tvayi*—in you; *vayam*—We; *pratinandayāmaḥ*—respond by rejoicing.

TRANSLATION

When you sent the messenger with your most confidential plan and yet I delayed going to you, you began to see the whole world as void and wanted to quit your body, which could never have been given to anyone but Me. May this greatness of yours remain with you always; I can do nothing to reciprocate except joyfully thank you for your devotion.

PURPORT

Śrīmatī Rukmiṇī-devī had no intention whatsoever of accepting any other husband but Lord Kṛṣṇa, as she stated in her message to the Lord

(*Bhāg*. 10.52.43): *yarhy ambujākṣa na labheya bhavat-prasādaṁ / jahyām asūn vrata-kṛśān śata-janmabhiḥ syāt.* "If I cannot obtain Your mercy, I shall simply give up my vital force, which will have become weak from the severe penances I will perform. Then, after hundreds of lifetimes of endeavor, I may obtain Your mercy." The *Śrīmad-Bhāgavatam* firmly establishes the unique glories of Queen Rukmiṇī-devī.

TEXT 58

श्रीशुक उवाच
एवं सौरतसंलापैर्भगवान् जगदीश्वरः ।
स्वरतो रमया रेमे नरलोकं विडम्बयन् ॥५८॥

śrī-śuka uvāca
evaṁ saurata-saṁlāpair
bhagavān jagad-īśvaraḥ
sva-rato ramayā reme
nara-lokaṁ viḍambayan

śrī-śukaḥ uvāca—Śukadeva Gosvāmī said; *evam*—in this way; *saurata*—conjugal; *saṁlāpaiḥ*—by conversations; *bhagavān*—the Supreme Lord; *jagat*—of the universe; *īśvaraḥ*—the master; *sva*—in Himself; *rataḥ*—taking pleasure; *ramayā*—with Ramā, the goddess of fortune (that is, with Queen Rukmiṇī); *reme*—He enjoyed; *nara-lokam*—the world of humans; *viḍambayan*—imitating.

TRANSLATION

Śukadeva Gosvāmī said: And so the self-satisfied Supreme Lord of the universe enjoyed with the goddess of fortune, engaging her in lovers' talks and thus imitating the ways of human society.

PURPORT

The word *viḍambayan* means "imitating" and also "ridiculing." The Lord acted like a husband of this world, but His pastimes are transcendental and expose the perverted nature of mundane activities aimed at bodily sense gratification.

TEXT 59

**तथान्यासामपि विभुर्गृहेषु गृहवानिव ।
आस्थितो गृहमेधीयान् धर्मान् लोकगुरुर्हरिः ॥५९॥**

tathānyāsām api vibhur
gṛheṣu gṛhavān iva
āsthito gṛha-medhīyān
dharmān loka-gurur hariḥ

tathā—similarly; *anyāsām*—of the other (queens); *api*—also; *vibhuḥ*—the almighty Supreme Lord; *gṛheṣu*—in the residences; *gṛha-vān*—a householder; *iva*—as if; *āsthitaḥ*—carried out; *gṛha-medhīyān*—of a pious householder; *dharmān*—the religious duties; *loka*—of all the worlds; *guruḥ*—the spiritual master; *hariḥ*—Lord Kṛṣṇa.

TRANSLATION

The almighty Lord Hari, preceptor of all the worlds, similarly behaved like a conventional householder in the palaces of His other queens, performing the religious duties of a family man.

Thus end the purports of the humble servants of His Divine Grace A. C. Bhaktivedanta Swami Prabhupāda to the Tenth Canto, Sixtieth Chapter, of the Śrīmad-Bhāgavatam, *entitled "Lord Kṛṣṇa Teases Queen Rukmiṇī."*

CHAPTER SIXTY-ONE

Lord Balarāma Slays Rukmī

This chapter lists Lord Śrī Kṛṣṇa's sons, grandsons and other progeny. It also describes how Lord Balarāma killed Rukmī at Aniruddha's marriage ceremony and how Lord Kṛṣṇa arranged for His sons and daughters to be married.

Not understanding the full truth about Śrī Kṛṣṇa, each of His wives thought that since He remained constantly in her palace she must be His favorite wife. They were all entranced by the Lord's beauty and His loving conversations with them, but they could not agitate His mind with the charming gestures of their eyebrows or by any other means. Having attained as their husband Lord Kṛṣṇa, whom even demigods like Brahmā find it difficult to know in truth, the Lord's queens were always eager to associate with Him. Thus, although each of them had millions of maidservants, they would personally render Him menial service.

Each of Lord Kṛṣṇa's wives had ten sons, who in turn each fathered many sons and grandsons. In the womb of Rukmī's daughter Rukmavatī, Pradyumna fathered Aniruddha. Though Śrī Kṛṣṇa had disrespected Rukmī, to please his sister Rukmī gave his daughter in marriage to Pradyumna, and his granddaughter to Aniruddha. Balī, the son of Kṛtavarmā, married Rukmiṇī's daughter Cārumatī.

At Aniruddha's wedding, Lord Baladeva, Śrī Kṛṣṇa and other Yādavas went to Rukmī's palace in the city of Bhojakaṭa. After the ceremony, Rukmī challenged Lord Baladeva to a game of dice. In the first match Rukmī defeated Baladeva, whereupon the King of Kaliṅga laughed at the Lord, displaying all his teeth. Lord Baladeva won the next match, but Rukmī refused to concede defeat. A voice then spoke from the sky, announcing that Baladeva had in fact won. But Rukmī, encouraged by the wicked kings, offended Lord Baladeva by saying that while He was certainly expert at tending cows, He knew nothing of playing dice. Thus insulted, Lord Baladeva angrily struck Rukmī dead with His club. The King of Kaliṅga tried to flee, but Lord Baladeva seized him and knocked out all his teeth. Then the other offensive kings, their arms, thighs and heads wounded by Baladeva's blows, fled in all directions, bleeding profusely. Śrī Kṛṣṇa expressed neither approval nor disapproval of His brother-in-law's death, fearing He would jeopardize His loving ties with either Rukmiṇī or Baladeva.

Lord Baladeva and the other Yādavas then seated Aniruddha and His bride on a fine chariot, and they all set off for Dvārakā.

TEXT 1

श्रीशुक उवाच
एकैकशस्ताः कृष्णस्य पुत्रान् दशदशाबलाः ।
अजीजनन्ननवमान् पितुः सर्वात्मसम्पदा ॥१॥

śrī-śuka uvāca
ekaikaśas tāḥ kṛṣṇasya
putrān daśa-daśābalāḥ
ajījanann anavamān
pituḥ sarvātma-sampadā

śrī-śukaḥ uvāca—Śrī Śukadeva Gosvāmī said; *eka-ekaśaḥ*—each one of them; *tāḥ*—they; *kṛṣṇasya*—of Lord Kṛṣṇa; *putrān*—sons; *daśa-daśa*—ten each; *abalāḥ*—the wives; *ajījanan*—gave birth to; *anavamān*—not inferior; *pituḥ*—to their father; *sarva*—in all; *ātma*—His personal; *sampadā*—opulences.

TRANSLATION

Śukadeva Gosvāmī said: Each of Lord Kṛṣṇa's wives gave birth to ten sons, who were not less than their father, having all His personal opulence.

PURPORT

Lord Kṛṣṇa had 16,108 wives, and thus this verse indicates that the Lord begot 161,080 sons.

TEXT 2

गृहादनपगं वीक्ष्य राजपुत्र्योऽच्युतं स्थितम् ।
प्रेष्ठं न्यमंसत स्वं स्वं न तत्तत्त्वविदः स्त्रियः ॥२॥

gṛhād anapagaṁ vīkṣya
rāja-putryo 'cyutaṁ sthitam
preṣṭhaṁ nyamaṁsata svaṁ svaṁ
na tat-tattva-vidaḥ striyaḥ

gṛhāt—from their palaces; *anapagam*—never going out; *vīkṣya*—seeing; *rāja-putryaḥ*—daughters of kings; *acyutam*—Lord Kṛṣṇa; *sthitam*—remaining; *preṣṭham*—most dear; *nyamaṁsata*—they considered; *svam svam*—each their own; *na*—not; *tat*—about Him; *tattva*—the truth; *vidaḥ*—knowing; *striyaḥ*—the women.

TRANSLATION

Because each of these princesses saw that Lord Acyuta never left her palace, each thought herself the Lord's favorite. These women did not understand the full truth about Him.

PURPORT

Śrīla Viśvanātha Cakravartī Ṭhākura notes that Lord Kṛṣṇa would leave the palaces only with the permission of His wives, and thus each one considered herself His favorite.

TEXT 3

चार्वब्जकोशवदनायतबाहुनेत्र-
सप्रेमहासरसवीक्षितवल्गुजल्पैः ।
सम्मोहिता भगवतो न मनो विजेतुं
स्वैर्विभ्रमैः समशकन् वनिता विभूम्नः ॥३॥

cārv-abja-kośa-vadanāyata-bāhu-netra-
sa-prema-hāsa-rasa-vīkṣita-valgu-jalpaiḥ
sammohitā bhagavato na mano vijetuṁ
svair vibhramaiḥ samaśakan vanitā vibhūmnaḥ

cāru—beautiful; *abja*—of a lotus; *kośa*—(like) the whorl; *vadana*—by His face; *āyata*—extended; *bāhu*—by His arms; *netra*—and eyes; *sa-prema*—loving; *hāsa*—of laughter; *rasa*—in the mood; *vīkṣita*—by His glances; *valgu*—attractive; *jalpaiḥ*—and by His conversations; *sammohitāḥ*—totally bewildered; *bhagavataḥ*—of the Supreme Lord; *na*—not; *manaḥ*—the mind; *vijetum*—to conquer; *svaiḥ*—with their own; *vibhramaiḥ*—allurements; *samaśakan*—were able; *vanitāḥ*—the women; *vibhūmnaḥ*—of the perfectly complete.

TRANSLATION

The Supreme Lord's wives were fully enchanted by His lovely, lotuslike face, His long arms and large eyes, His loving glances imbued with laughter, and His charming talks with them. But with all their charms these ladies could not conquer the mind of the all-powerful Lord.

PURPORT

The previous verse stated that Lord Kṛṣṇa's queens could not understand the truth of the Lord. This truth is explained in the present verse. The Lord is all-powerful, full in Himself, with infinite opulence.

TEXT 4

स्मायावलोकलवदर्शितभावहारि-
भ्रूमण्डलप्रहितसौरतमन्त्रशौण्डैः ।
पत्न्यस्तु षोडशसहस्रमनंगबाणैर्
यस्येन्द्रियं विमथितुं करणैर्न शेकुः ॥४॥

smāyāvaloka-lava-darśita-bhāva-hāri-
bhrū-maṇḍala-prahita-saurata-mantra-śauṇḍaiḥ
patnyas tu ṣoḍaśa-sahasram anaṅga-bāṇair
yasyendriyaṁ vimathituṁ karaṇair na śekuḥ

smāya—with concealed laughter; *avaloka*—of glances; *lava*—by the traces; *darśita*—displayed; *bhāva*—by the intentions; *hāri*—enchanting; *bhrū*—of the eyebrows; *maṇḍala*—by the arch; *prahita*—sent forth; *saurata*—romantic; *mantra*—of messages; *śauṇḍaiḥ*—with the manifestations of boldness; *patnyaḥ*—wives; *tu*—but; *ṣoḍaśa*—sixteen; *sahasram*—thousand; *anaṅga*—of Cupid; *bāṇaiḥ*—with the arrows;

yasya—whose; *indriyam*—senses; *vimathitum*—to agitate; *karaṇaiḥ*—and by (other) means; *na śekuḥ*—were unable.

TRANSLATION

The arched eyebrows of these sixteen thousand queens enchantingly expressed those ladies' secret intentions through coyly smiling sidelong glances. Thus their eyebrows boldly sent forth conjugal messages. Yet even with these arrows of Cupid, and with other means as well, they could not agitate Lord Kṛṣṇa's senses.

TEXT 5

इत्थं रमापतिमवाप्य पतिं स्त्रियस्ता
ब्रह्मादयोऽपि न विदुः पदवीं यदीयाम् ।
भेजुर्मुदाविरतमेधितयानुराग-
हासावलोकनवसंगमलालसाद्यम् ॥५॥

ittham ramā-patim avāpya patiṁ striyas tā
brahmādayo 'pi na viduḥ padavīṁ yadīyām
bhejur mudāviratam edhitayānurāga-
hāsāvaloka-nava-saṅgama-lālasādyam

ittham—in this manner; *ramā-patim*—the Lord of the goddess of fortune; *avāpya*—obtaining; *patim*—as their husband; *striyaḥ*—the women; *tāḥ*—they; *brahma-ādayaḥ*—Lord Brahmā and other demigods; *api*—even; *na viduḥ*—do not know; *padavīm*—the means of attaining; *yadīyām*—whom; *bhejuḥ*—partook of; *mudā*—with pleasure; *aviratam*—incessantly; *edhitayā*—increasing; *anurāga*—loving attraction; *hāsa*—smiling; *avaloka*—glances; *nava*—ever-fresh; *saṅgama*—for intimate association; *lālasa*—eagerness; *ādyam*—beginning with.

TRANSLATION

Thus these women obtained as their husband the master of the goddess of fortune, although even great demigods like Brahmā do not know how to approach Him. With ever-increasing pleasure, they felt loving attraction for Him, exchanged smiling glances

with Him, eagerly anticipated associating with Him in ever-fresh intimacy and enjoyed in many other ways.

PURPORT

This text describes the intense conjugal attraction the queens felt for Lord Kṛṣṇa.

TEXT 6

प्रत्युद्गमासनवरार्हणपादशौच-
ताम्बूलविश्रमणवीजनगन्धमाल्यैः ।
केशप्रसारशयनस्नपनोपहार्यैः
दासीशता अपि विभोर्विदधुः स्म दास्यम् ॥६॥

pratyudgamāsana-varārhaṇa-pāda-śauca-
tāmbūla-viśramaṇa-vījana-gandha-mālyaiḥ
keśa-prasāra-śayana-snapanopahāryaiḥ
dāsī-śatā api vibhor vidadhuḥ sma dāsyam

pratyudgama—by approaching; *āsana*—offering a seat; *vara*—first class; *arhaṇa*—worship; *pāda*—His feet; *śauca*—washing; *tāmbūla*—(offering) betel nut; *viśramaṇa*—helping Him to relax (by massaging His feet); *vījana*—fanning; *gandha*—(offering) fragrant substances; *mālyaiḥ*—and flower garlands; *keśa*—His hair; *prasāra*—by dressing; *śayana*—arranging His bed; *snapana*—bathing Him; *upahāryaiḥ*—and by presenting gifts; *dāsī*—maidservants; *śatāḥ*—having hundreds; *api*—although; *vibhoḥ*—for the almighty Lord; *vidadhuḥ sma*—they executed; *dāsyam*—service.

TRANSLATION

Although the Supreme Lord's queens each had hundreds of maidservants, they chose to personally serve the Lord by approaching Him humbly, offering Him a seat, worshiping Him with excellent paraphernalia, bathing and massaging His feet, giving Him *pān* to chew, fanning Him, anointing Him with fragrant sandal-

wood paste, adorning Him with flower garlands, dressing His hair, arranging His bed, bathing Him and presenting Him with various gifts.

PURPORT

Śrīla Śrīdhara Svāmī explains that Śukadeva Gosvāmī is so eager to describe these glorious pastimes of the Lord with His queens that he has repeated these verses. That is, Text 5 of this chapter is almost identical with Text 44 of the fifty-ninth chapter in this canto, and Text 6 is identical with Text 45 of that chapter. Śrīla Viśvanātha Cakravartī explains that the term *varārhaṇa* ("excellent offerings") indicates that the queens offered the Lord palmfuls of flowers (*puṣpāñjali*) and palmfuls of jewels (*ratnāñjali*).

TEXT 7

तासां या दशपुत्राणां कृष्णस्त्रीणां पुरोदिताः ।
अष्टौ महिष्यस्तत्पुत्रान् प्रद्युम्नादीन् गृणामि ते ॥७॥

tāsāṁ yā daśa-putrāṇāṁ
kṛṣṇa-strīṇāṁ puroditāḥ
aṣṭau mahiṣyas tat-putrān
pradyumnādīn gṛṇāmi te

tāsām—among those; *yāḥ*—who; *daśa*—having ten; *putrāṇām*—sons; *kṛṣṇa-strīṇām*—wives of Lord Kṛṣṇa; *purā*—previously; *uditāḥ*—mentioned; *aṣṭau*—eight; *mahiṣyaḥ*—chief queens; *tat*—their; *putrān*—sons; *pradyumna-ādīn*—headed by Pradyumna; *gṛṇāmi*—I shall recite; *te*—for you.

TRANSLATION

Among Lord Kṛṣṇa's wives, each of whom had ten sons, I previously mentioned eight principal queens. I shall now recite for you the names of those eight queens' sons, headed by Pradyumna.

TEXTS 8–9

चारुदेष्णः सुदेष्णश्च चारुदेहश्च वीर्यवान् ।
सुचारुश्चारुगुप्तश्च भद्रचारुस्तथापरः ॥८॥
चारुचन्द्रो विचारुश्च चारुश्च दशमो हरेः ।
प्रद्युम्नप्रमुखा जाता रुक्मिण्यां नावमाः पितुः ॥९॥

cārudeṣṇaḥ sudeṣṇaś ca
cārudehaś ca vīryavān
sucāruś cāruguptaś ca
bhadracārus tathāparaḥ

cārucandro vicāruś ca
cāruś ca daśamo hareḥ
pradyumna-pramukhā jātā
rukmiṇyāṁ nāvamāḥ pituḥ

cārudeṣṇaḥ sudeṣṇaḥ ca—Cārudeṣṇa and Sudeṣṇa; *cārudehaḥ*—Cārudeha; *ca*—and; *vīrya-vān*—powerful; *sucāruḥ cāruguptaḥ ca*—Sucāru and Cārugupta; *bhadracāruḥ*—Bhadracāru; *tathā*—also; *aparaḥ*—another; *cārucandraḥ vicāruḥ ca*—Cārucandra and Vicāru; *cāruḥ*—Cāru; *ca*—also; *daśamaḥ*—the tenth; *hareḥ*—by Lord Hari; *pradyumna-pramukhāḥ*—headed by Pradyumna; *jātāḥ*—begotten; *rukmiṇyām*—in Rukmiṇī; *na*—not; *avamāḥ*—inferior; *pituḥ*—to their father.

TRANSLATION

The first son of Queen Rukmiṇī was Pradyumna, and also born of her were Cārudeṣṇa, Sudeṣṇa and the powerful Cārudeha, along with Sucāru, Cārugupta, Bhadracāru, Cārucandra, Vicāru and Cāru, the tenth. None of these sons of Lord Hari was less than his father.

TEXTS 10–12

भानुः सुभानुः स्वर्भानुः प्रभानुर्भानुमांस्तथा ।
चन्द्रभानुर्बृहद्भानुरतिभानुस्तथाष्टमः ॥१०॥

श्रीभानुः प्रतिभानुश्च सत्यभामात्मजा दश ।
साम्बः सुमित्रः पुरुजिच्छतजिच्च सहस्रजित् ॥११॥
विजयश्चित्रकेतुश्च वसुमान् द्रविडः क्रतुः ।
जाम्बवत्याः सुता ह्येते साम्बाद्याः पितृसम्मताः ॥१२॥

bhānuḥ subhānuḥ svarbhānuḥ
prabhānur bhānumāṁs tathā
candrabhānur bṛhadbhānur
atibhānus tathāṣṭamaḥ

śrībhānuḥ pratibhānuś ca
satyabhāmātmajā daśa
sāmbaḥ sumitraḥ purujic
chatajic ca sahasrajit

vijayaś citraketuś ca
vasumān draviḍaḥ kratuḥ
jāmbavatyāḥ sutā hy ete
sāmbādyāḥ pitṛ-sammatāḥ

bhānuḥ subhānuḥ svarbhānuḥ—Bhānu, Subhānu and Svarbhānu; *prabhānuḥ bhānumān*—Prabhānu and Bhānumān; *tathā*—also; *candrabhānuḥ bṛhadbhānuḥ*—Candrabhānu and Bṛhadbhānu; *atibhānuḥ*—Atibhānu; *tathā*—also; *aṣṭamaḥ*—the eighth; *śrībhānuḥ*—Śrībhānu; *pratibhānuḥ*—Pratibhānu; *ca*—and; *satyabhāmā*—of Satyabhāmā; *ātmajāḥ*—the sons; *daśa*—ten; *sāmbaḥ sumitraḥ purujit śatajit ca sahasrajit*—Sāmba, Sumitra, Purujit, Śatajit and Sahasrajit; *vijayaḥ citraketuḥ ca*—Vijaya and Citraketu; *vasumān draviḍaḥ kratuḥ*—Vasumān, Draviḍa and Kratu; *jāmbavatyāḥ*—of Jāmbavatī; *sutāḥ*—sons; *hi*—indeed; *ete*—these; *sāmba-ādyāḥ*—headed by Sāmba; *pitṛ*—by their father; *sammatāḥ*—favored.

TRANSLATION

The ten sons of Satyabhāmā were Bhānu, Subhānu, Svarbhānu, Prabhānu, Bhānumān, Candrabhānu, Bṛhadbhānu, Atibhānu (the eighth), Śrībhānu and Pratibhānu. Sāmba, Sumitra, Purujit, Śatajit, Sahasrajit, Vijaya, Citraketu, Vasumān, Draviḍa and Kratu

were the sons of Jāmbavatī. These ten, headed by Sāmba, were their father's favorites.

PURPORT

Śrīla Jīva Gosvāmī translates the compound *pitṛ-sammatāḥ* in this verse as "highly regarded by their father." The word also indicates that these sons, like the others already mentioned, were regarded as being just like their glorious father, Lord Kṛṣṇa.

TEXT 13

वीरश्चन्द्रोऽश्वसेनश्च चित्रगुर्वेगवान् वृषः ।
आमः शंकुर्वसुः श्रीमान् कुन्तिर्नाग्नजितेः सुताः ॥१३॥

vīraś candro 'śvasenaś ca
citragur vegavān vṛṣaḥ
āmaḥ śaṅkur vasuḥ śrīmān
kuntir nāgnajiteḥ sutāḥ

vīraḥ candraḥ aśvasenaḥ ca—Vīra, Candra and Aśvasena; *citraguḥ vegavān vṛṣaḥ*—Citragu, Vegavān and Vṛṣa; *āmaḥ śaṅkuḥ vasuḥ*—Āma, Śaṅku and Vasu; *śrī-mān*—opulent; *kuntiḥ*—Kunti; *nāgnajiteḥ*—of Nāgnajiti; *sutāḥ*—the sons.

TRANSLATION

The sons of Nāgnajitī were Vīra, Candra, Aśvasena, Citragu, Vegavān, Vṛṣa, Āma, Śaṅku, Vasu and the opulent Kunti.

TEXT 14

श्रुतः कविर्वृषो वीरः सुबाहुर्भद्र एकलः ।
शान्तिर्दर्शः पूर्णमासः कालिन्द्याः सोमकोऽवरः ॥१४॥

śrutaḥ kavir vṛṣo vīraḥ
subāhur bhadra ekalaḥ
śāntir darśaḥ pūrṇamāsaḥ
kālindyāḥ somako 'varaḥ

śrutaḥ kaviḥ vṛṣaḥ vīraḥ—Śruta, Kavi, Vṛṣa and Vīra; *subāhuḥ*—Subāhu; *bhadraḥ*—Bhadra; *ekalaḥ*—one of them; *śāntiḥ darśaḥ pūrṇamāsaḥ*—Śānti, Darśa and Pūrṇamāsa; *kālindyāḥ*—of Kālindī; *somakaḥ*—Somaka; *avaraḥ*—the youngest.

TRANSLATION

Śruta, Kavi, Vṛṣa, Vīra, Subāhu, Bhadra, Śānti, Darśa and Pūrṇamāsa were sons of Kālindī. Her youngest son was Somaka.

TEXT 15

प्रघोषो गात्रवान् सिंहो बलः प्रबल ऊर्धगः ।
माद्र्याः पुत्रा महाशक्तिः सह ओजोऽपराजितः ॥१५॥

praghoṣo gātravān siṁho
balaḥ prabala ūrdhagaḥ
mādryāḥ putrā mahāśaktiḥ
saha ojo 'parājitaḥ

praghoṣaḥ gātravān siṁhaḥ—Praghoṣa, Gātravān and Siṁha; *balaḥ prabalaḥ ūrdhagaḥ*—Bala, Prabala and Ūrdhaga; *mādryāḥ*—of Mādrā; *putrāḥ*—sons; *mahāśaktiḥ sahaḥ ojaḥ aparājitaḥ*—Mahāśakti, Saha, Oja and Aparājita.

TRANSLATION

Mādrā's sons were Praghoṣa, Gātravān, Siṁha, Bala, Prabala, Ūrdhaga, Mahāśakti, Saha, Oja and Aparājita.

PURPORT

Mādrā is also known as Lakṣmaṇā.

TEXT 16

वृको हर्षोऽनिलो गृध्रो वर्धनोन्नाद एव च ।
महांसः पावनो वह्निर्मित्रविन्दात्मजाः क्षुधिः ॥१६॥

vṛko harṣo 'nilo gṛdhro
vardhanonnāda eva ca
mahāṁsaḥ pāvano vahnir
mitravindātmajāḥ kṣudhiḥ

vṛkaḥ harṣaḥ anilaḥ gṛdhraḥ—Vṛka, Harṣa, Anila and Gṛdhra; *vardhana-unnādaḥ*—Vardhana and Unnāda; *eva ca*—also; *mahāṁsaḥ pāvanaḥ vahniḥ*—Mahāṁsa, Pāvana and Vahni; *mitravindā*—of Mitravindā; *ātmajāḥ*—sons; *kṣudhiḥ*—Kṣudhi.

TRANSLATION

Mitravindā's sons were Vṛka, Harṣa, Anila, Gṛdhra, Vardhana, Unnāda, Mahāṁsa, Pāvana, Vahni and Kṣudhi.

TEXT 17

संग्रामजिद् बृहत्सेनः शूरः प्रहरणोऽरिजित् ।
जयः सुभद्रो भद्राया वाम आयुश्च सत्यकः ॥१७॥

saṅgrāmajid bṛhatsenaḥ
śūraḥ praharaṇo 'rijit
jayaḥ subhadro bhadrāyā
vāma āyuś ca satyakaḥ

saṅgrāmajit bṛhatsenaḥ—Saṅgrāmajit and Bṛhatsena; *śūraḥ praharaṇaḥ arijit*—Śūra, Praharaṇa and Arijit; *jayaḥ subhadraḥ*—Jaya and Subhadra; *bhadrāyāḥ*—of Bhadrā (Śaibyā); *vāmaḥ āyuś ca satyakaḥ*—Vāma, Āyur and Satyaka.

TRANSLATION

Saṅgrāmajit, Bṛhatsena, Śūra, Praharaṇa, Arijit, Jaya and Subhadra were the sons of Bhadrā, together with Vāma, Āyur and Satyaka.

TEXT 18

दीप्तिमांस्ताम्रतप्ताद्या रोहिण्यास्तनया हरेः ।
प्रद्युम्नाच्चानिरुद्धोऽभूद् रुक्मवत्यां महाबलः ।
पुत्र्यां तु रुक्मिणो राजन्नाम्ना भोजकटे पुरे ॥१८॥

dīptimāṁs tāmrataptādyā
rohiṇyās tanayā hareḥ
pradyumnāc cāniruddho 'bhūd
rukmavatyāṁ mahā-balaḥ
putryāṁ tu rukmiṇo rājan
nāmnā bhojakaṭe pure

dīptimān tāmratapta-ādyāḥ—Dīptimān, Tāmratapta and others; *rohiṇyāḥ*—of Rohiṇī (chief of the remaining 16,100 queens); *tanayāḥ*—sons; *hareḥ*—of Lord Kṛṣṇa; *pradyumnāt*—from Pradyumna; *ca*—and; *aniruddhaḥ*—Aniruddha; *abhūt*—was born; *rukmavatyām*—in Rukmavatī; *mahā-balaḥ*—greatly powerful; *putryām*—in the daughter; *tu*—indeed; *rukmiṇaḥ*—of Rukmī; *rājan*—O King (Parīkṣit); *nāmnā*—by name; *bhojakaṭe pure*—in the city of Bhojakaṭa (Rukmī's domain).

TRANSLATION

Dīptimān, Tāmratapta and others were the sons of Lord Kṛṣṇa and Rohiṇī. Lord Kṛṣṇa's son Pradyumna fathered the greatly powerful Aniruddha in the womb of Rukmavatī, the daughter of Rukmī. O King, this took place while they were living in the city of Bhojakaṭa.

PURPORT

Lord Kṛṣṇa's eight principal queens are Rukmiṇī, Satyabhāmā, Jāmbavatī, Nāgnajitī, Kālindī, Lakṣmaṇā, Mitravindā and Bhadrā. Having mentioned all their sons, Śukadeva Gosvāmī now refers to the sons of the other 16,100 queens by mentioning the two principal sons of Queen Rohiṇī, the foremost of the remaining queens.

TEXT 19

एतेषां पुत्रपौत्राश्च बभूवुः कोटिशो नृप ।
मातरः कृष्णजातीनां सहस्राणि च षोडश ॥१९॥

eteṣāṁ putra-pautrāś ca
babhūvuḥ koṭiśo nṛpa
mātaraḥ kṛṣṇa-jātīnāṁ
sahasrāṇi ca ṣoḍaśa

eteṣām—of these; *putra*—sons; *pautrāḥ*—and grandsons; *ca*—and; *babhūvuḥ*—were born; *koṭiśaḥ*—by the tens of millions; *nṛpa*—O King; *mātaraḥ*—the mothers; *kṛṣṇa-jātīnām*—of the descendants of Lord Kṛṣṇa; *sahasrāṇi*—thousands; *ca*—and; *ṣoḍaśa*—sixteen.

TRANSLATION

My dear King, the sons and grandsons of Lord Kṛṣṇa's children numbered in the tens of millions. Sixteen thousand mothers gave rise to this dynasty.

TEXT 20

श्रीराजोवाच
कथं रुक्म्यरिपुत्राय प्रादाद्दुहितरं युधि ।
कृष्णेन परिभूतस्तं हन्तुं रन्ध्रं प्रतीक्षते ।
एतदाख्याहि मे विद्वन् द्विषोर्वैवाहिकं मिथः ॥२०॥

śrī-rājovāca
kathaṁ rukmy ari-putrāya
prādād duhitaraṁ yudhi
kṛṣṇena paribhūtas taṁ
hantuṁ randhraṁ pratīkṣate
etad ākhyāhi me vidvan
dviṣor vaivāhikaṁ mithaḥ

śrī-rājā uvāca—the King said; *katham*—how; *rukmī*—Rukmī; *ari*—of his enemy; *putrāya*—to the son; *prādāt*—gave; *duhitaram*—his daughter; *yudhi*—in battle; *kṛṣṇena*—by Kṛṣṇa; *paribhūtaḥ*—defeated; *tam*—Him (Lord Kṛṣṇa); *hantum*—to kill; *randhram*—the opportunity; *pratīkṣate*—he was waiting for; *etat*—this; *ākhyāhi*—please explain; *me*—to me; *vidvan*—O learned one; *dviṣoḥ*—of the two enemies; *vaivāhikam*—the marital arrangement; *mithaḥ*—between them.

TRANSLATION

King Parīkṣit said: How could Rukmī give his daughter to his enemy's son? After all, Rukmī had been defeated by Lord Kṛṣṇa in battle and was waiting for an opportunity to kill Him. Please explain this to me, O learned one—how these two inimical parties became united through marriage.

TEXT 21

अनागतमतीतं च वर्तमानमतीन्द्रियम् ।
विप्रकृष्टं व्यवहितं सम्यक् पश्यन्ति योगिनः ॥२१॥

anāgatam atītaṁ ca
vartamānam atīndriyam
viprakṛṣṭaṁ vyavahitaṁ
samyak paśyanti yoginaḥ

anāgatam—not yet happened; *atītam*—past; *ca*—also; *vartamānam*—present; *atīndriyam*—beyond the purview of the senses; *viprakṛṣṭam*—distant; *vyavahitam*—blocked by obstacles; *samyak*—perfectly; *paśyanti*—see; *yoginaḥ*—mystic *yogīs*.

TRANSLATION

Mystic *yogīs* can perfectly see that which has not yet happened, as well as things in the past or present, beyond the senses, remote or blocked by physical obstacles.

PURPORT

Here King Parīkṣit encourages Śukadeva Gosvāmī to explain why Rukmī gave his daughter to Lord Kṛṣṇa's son Pradyumna. The King stresses that since great *yogīs* like Śukadeva Gosvāmī know everything, the sage must also know this and should explain it to the anxious King.

TEXT 22

श्रीशुक उवाच
वृतः स्वयंवरे साक्षादनंगोऽंगयुतस्तया ।
राज्ञः समेतान्निर्जित्य जहारैकरथो युधि ॥२२॥

śrī-śuka uvāca
vṛtaḥ svayaṁ-vare sākṣād
anaṅgo 'ṅga-yutas tayā
rājñaḥ sametān nirjitya
jahāraika-ratho yudhi

śrī-śukaḥ uvāca—Śukadeva Gosvāmī said; *vṛtaḥ*—chosen; *svayam-vare*—in her *svayaṁ-vara* ceremony; *sākṣāt*—manifest; *anaṅgaḥ*—Cupid; *aṅga-yutaḥ*—incarnate; *tayā*—by her; *rājñaḥ*—the kings; *sametān*—assembled; *nirjitya*—defeating; *jahāra*—He took her away; *eka-rathaḥ*—having only one chariot; *yudhi*—in battle.

TRANSLATION

Śrī Śukadeva Gosvāmī said: At her *svayaṁ-vara* ceremony, Rukmavatī herself chose Pradyumna, who was the re-embodiment of Cupid. Then, although He fought alone on a single chariot, Pradyumna defeated the assembled kings in battle and took her away.

TEXT 23

यद्यप्यनुस्मरन् वैरं रुक्मी कृष्णावमानितः ।
व्यतरद् भागिनेयाय सुतां कुर्वन् स्वसुः प्रियम् ॥२३॥

yady apy anusmaran vairaṁ
rukmī kṛṣṇāvamānitaḥ
vyatarad bhāgineyāya
sutāṁ kurvan svasuḥ priyam

yadi api—although; *anusmaran*—always remembering; *vairam*—his enmity; *rukmī*—Rukmī; *kṛṣṇa*—by Lord Kṛṣṇa; *avamānitaḥ*—insulted; *vyatarat*—granted; *bhāgineyāya*—to his sister's son; *sutām*—his daughter; *kurvan*—doing; *svasuḥ*—of his sister; *priyam*—the pleasing.

TRANSLATION

Though Rukmī always remembered his enmity toward Lord Kṛṣṇa, who had insulted him, in order to please his sister he sanctioned his daughter's marriage to his nephew.

PURPORT

The answer to King Parīkṣit's question is given here. Ultimately Rukmī approved his daughter's marriage to Pradyumna in order to please his sister, Rukmiṇī.

TEXT 24

रुक्मिण्यास्तनयां राजन् कृतवर्मसुतो बली ।
उपयेमे विशालाक्षीं कन्यां चारुमतीं किल ॥२४॥

rukmiṇyās tanayāṁ rājan
kṛtavarma-suto balī
upayeme viśālākṣīṁ
kanyāṁ cārumatīṁ kila

rukmiṇyāḥ—of Rukmiṇī; *tanayām*—the daughter; *rājan*—O King; *kṛtavarma-sutaḥ*—the son of Kṛtavarmā; *balī*—named Balī; *upayeme*—married; *viśāla*—broad; *akṣīm*—whose eyes; *kanyām*—young, innocent girl; *cārumatīm*—named Cārumatī; *kila*—indeed.

TRANSLATION

O King, Balī, the son of Kṛtavarmā, married Rukmiṇī's young daughter, large-eyed Cārumatī.

PURPORT

Śrīla Śrīdhara Svāmī explains that each of the Lord's queens had one daughter, and that this mention of Cārumati's marriage is an indirect reference to the marriages of all these princesses.

TEXT 25

दौहित्रायानिरुद्धाय पौत्रीं रुक्म्याददाद्धरेः ।
रोचनां बद्धवैरोऽपि स्वसुः प्रियचिकीर्षया ।
जानन्नधर्मं तद्यौनं स्नेहपाशानुबन्धनः ॥२५॥

dauhitrāyāniruddhāya
pautrīṁ rukmy ādadād dhareḥ
rocanāṁ baddha-vairo 'pi
svasuḥ priya-cikīrṣayā
jānann adharmaṁ tad yaunaṁ
sneha-pāśānubandhanaḥ

dauhitrāya—to his daughter's son; *aniruddhāya*—Aniruddha; *pautrīm*—his granddaughter; *rukmī*—Rukmī; *ādadāt*—gave; *hareḥ*—toward Lord Kṛṣṇa; *rocanām*—named Rocanā; *baddha*—bound; *vairaḥ*—in enmity; *api*—although; *svasuḥ*—his sister; *priya-cikīrṣayā*—wanting to please; *jānan*—knowing; *adharmam*—irreligion; *tat*—that; *yaunam*—marriage; *sneha*—of affection; *pāśa*—by the ropes; *anu-bandhanaḥ*—whose bondage.

TRANSLATION

Rukmī gave his granddaughter Rocanā to his daughter's son, Aniruddha, despite Rukmī's relentless feud with Lord Hari. Although Rukmī considered this marriage irreligious, he wanted to please his sister, bound as he was by the ropes of affection.

PURPORT

Śrīla Śrīdhara Svāmī explains that according to worldly standards one should not give one's beloved granddaughter to the grandson of one's bitter enemy. Thus we find the following injunction: *dviṣad-annaṁ na bhoktavyaṁ dviṣantaṁ naiva bhojayet.* "One should not eat an enemy's food or feed an enemy." There is also the following prohibition: *asvargyaṁ loka-vidviṣṭaṁ dharmam apy ācaren na tu.* "One should not execute religious injunctions if they will obstruct one's journey to heaven, or if they are odious to human society."

It should be pointed out here that Lord Kṛṣṇa is not really the enemy of anyone. As the Lord states in the *Bhagavad-gītā* (5.29), *suhṛdaṁ sarva-bhūtānāṁ jñātvā māṁ śāntim ṛcchati:* "One achieves peace by understanding that I am the well-wishing friend of every living being." Although Lord Kṛṣṇa is everyone's friend, Rukmī could not appreciate this fact and considered Lord Kṛṣṇa his enemy. Still, out of affection for his sister, he gave his granddaughter to Aniruddha.

Finally, we should note that, contrary to the prohibition quoted above, one may not give up the basic principles of spiritual life merely because such principles are unpopular with people in general. As Lord Kṛṣṇa states in the *Gītā* (18.66), *sarva-dharmān parityajya mām ekaṁ śaraṇaṁ vraja.* The last word in spiritual duties is to surrender to the Supreme Lord, and that duty takes precedence over all secondary injunctions. Moreover, in this age Śrī Caitanya Mahāprabhu has kindly presented a sublime process that will attract all sincere people to come to the point of surrendering to the Lord. By following Lord Caitanya's blissful process of chanting, dancing, feasting and discussing spiritual philosophy, anyone can easily go back home, back to Godhead, for an eternal life of bliss and knowledge.

Still, someone may argue that the members of the Kṛṣṇa consciousness movement should not practice in the Western countries those ceremonies or activities that displease people in general. We respond that even in the Western countries, when people are properly informed of the activities of the Kṛṣṇa consciousness movement, they generally appreciate this great spiritual institution. Those who are especially envious of God will not appreciate any type of religious movement, and since such persons are themselves little better than animals, they cannot impede the great Kṛṣṇa consciousness movement, just as the envious Rukmī could not impede the performance of Lord Kṛṣṇa's pure pastimes.

TEXT 26

तस्मिन्नभ्युदये राजन् रुक्मिणी रामकेशवौ ।
पुरं भोजकटं जग्मुः साम्बप्रद्युम्नकादयः ॥२६॥

tasminn abhyudaye rājan
rukmiṇī rāma-keśavau

puraṁ bhojakaṭaṁ jagmuḥ
sāmba-pradyumnakādayaḥ

tasmin—on the occasion of that; *abhyudaye*—happy event; *rājan*—O King; *rukmiṇī*—Rukmiṇī; *rāma-keśavau*—Balarāma and Kṛṣṇa; *puram*—to the city; *bhojakaṭam*—Bhojakaṭa; *jagmuḥ*—went; *sāmba-pradyumnaka-ādayaḥ*—Sāmba, Pradyumna and others.

TRANSLATION

On the joyous occasion of that marriage, O King, Queen Rukmiṇī, Lord Balarāma, Lord Kṛṣṇa and several of the Lord's sons, headed by Sāmba and Pradyumna, went to the city of Bhojakaṭa.

TEXTS 27–28

तस्मिन्निवृत्त उद्वाहे कालिंगप्रमुखा नृपाः ।
दृप्तास्ते रुक्मिणं प्रोचुर्बलमक्षैर्विनिर्जय ॥२७॥
अनक्षज्ञो ह्ययं राजन्नपि तद्व्यसनं महत् ।
इत्युक्तो बलमाहूय तेनाक्षैरुक्म्यदीव्यत ॥२८॥

tasmin nivṛtta udvāhe
kāliṅga-pramukhā nṛpāḥ
dṛptās te rukmiṇaṁ procur
balam akṣair vinirjaya

anakṣa-jño hy ayaṁ rājann
api tad-vyasanaṁ mahat
ity ukto balam āhūya
tenākṣair rukmy adīvyata

tasmin—when that; *nivṛtte*—was finished; *udvāhe*—the marriage ceremony; *kāliṅga-pramukhāḥ*—headed by the ruler of Kaliṅga; *nṛpāḥ*—kings; *dṛptāḥ*—arrogant; *te*—they; *rukmiṇam*—to Rukmī; *procuḥ*—spoke; *balam*—Balarāma; *akṣaiḥ*—with dice; *vinirjaya*—you should defeat; *anakṣa-jñaḥ*—not expert in gambling with dice; *hi*—indeed; *ayam*—He; *rājan*—O King; *api*—although; *tat*—with that; *vyasanam*—

His fascination; *mahat*—great; *iti*—thus; *uktaḥ*—addressed; *balam*—Lord Balarāma; *āhūya*—inviting; *tena*—with Him; *akṣaiḥ*—at dice; *rukmī*—Rukmī; *adīvyata*—played.

TRANSLATION

After the wedding, a group of arrogant kings headed by the King of Kaliṅga told Rukmī, "You should defeat Balarāma at dice. He's not expert at dice, O King, but still He's quite addicted to it." Thus advised, Rukmī challenged Balarāma and began a gambling match with Him.

TEXT 29

शतं सहस्रमयुतं रामस्तत्राददे पणम् ।
तं तु रुक्म्यजयत्तत्र कालिंगः प्राहसद् बलम् ।
दन्तान् सन्दर्शयन्नुच्चैर्नामृष्यत्तद्धलायुधः ॥२९॥

śataṁ sahasram ayutaṁ
rāmas tatrādade paṇam
taṁ tu rukmy ajayat tatra
kāliṅgaḥ prāhasad balam
dantān sandarśayann uccair
nāmṛṣyat tad dhalāyudhaḥ

śatam—one hundred; *sahasram*—one thousand; *ayutam*—ten thousand; *rāmaḥ*—Lord Balarāma; *tatra*—in that (match); *ādade*—accepted; *paṇam*—wager; *tam*—that; *tu*—but; *rukmī*—Rukmī; *ajayat*—won; *tatra*—thereupon; *kāliṅgaḥ*—the King of Kaliṅga; *prāhasat*—laughed loudly; *balam*—at Lord Balarāma; *dantān*—his teeth; *sandarśayan*—showing; *uccaiḥ*—openly; *na amṛṣyat*—did not forgive; *tat*—this; *hala-āyudhaḥ*—Balarāma, the carrier of the plow weapon.

TRANSLATION

In that match Lord Balarāma first accepted a wager of one hundred coins, then one thousand, then ten thousand. Rukmī won this first round, and the King of Kaliṅga laughed loudly at

Lord Balarāma, showing all his teeth. Lord Balarāma could not tolerate this.

PURPORT

Śrīla Viśvanātha Cakravartī explains that the wagers consisted of gold coins. Lord Balarāma inwardly became quite angry when He saw the gross offense of the King of Kaliṅga.

TEXT 30

ततो लक्षं रुक्म्यगृह्णाद् ग्लहं तत्राजयद् बलः ।
जितवानहमित्याह रुक्मी कैतवमाश्रितः ॥३०॥

tato lakṣaṁ rukmy agṛhṇād
glahaṁ tatrājayad balaḥ
jitavān aham ity āha
rukmī kaitavam āśritaḥ

tataḥ—then; *lakṣam*—one hundred thousand; *rukmī*—Rukmī; *agṛhṇāt*—accepted; *glaham*—a bet; *tatra*—in that; *ajayat*—won; *balaḥ*—Lord Balarāma; *jitavān*—have won; *aham*—I; *iti*—thus; *āha*—said; *rukmī*—Rukmī; *kaitavam*—deception; *āśritaḥ*—resorting to.

TRANSLATION

Next Rukmī accepted a bet of one hundred thousand coins, which Lord Balarāma won. But Rukmī tried to cheat, declaring "I'm the winner!"

TEXT 31

मन्युना क्षुभितः श्रीमान् समुद्र इव पर्वणि ।
जात्यारुणाक्षोऽतिरुषा न्यर्बुदं ग्लहमाददे ॥३१॥

manyunā kṣubhitaḥ śrīmān
samudra iva parvaṇi
jātyāruṇākṣo 'ti-ruṣā
nyarbudaṁ glaham ādade

manyunā—by anger; *kṣubhitaḥ*—agitated; *śrī-mān*—possessing beauty, or the beautiful goddess of fortune; *samudraḥ*—the ocean; *iva*—like; *parvaṇi*—on the full-moon day; *jātyā*—by nature; *aruṇa*—reddish; *akṣaḥ*—whose eyes; *ati*—extreme; *ruṣā*—with anger; *nyarbudam*—of one hundred million; *glaham*—a wager; *ādade*—accepted.

TRANSLATION

Shaking with anger like the ocean on the full-moon day, handsome Lord Balarāma, His naturally reddish eyes even redder in His fury, accepted a wager of one hundred million gold coins.

TEXT 32

तं चापि जितवान् रामो धर्मेण छलमाश्रितः ।
रुक्मी जितं मयात्रेमे वदन्तु प्राश्निका इति ॥३२॥

taṁ cāpi jitavān rāmo
dharmeṇa chalam āśritaḥ
rukmī jitaṁ mayātreme
vadantu prāśnikā iti

tam—that; *ca api*—also; *jitavān*—won; *rāmaḥ*—Lord Balarāma; *dharmeṇa*—fairly; *chalam*—deceit; *āśritaḥ*—resorting to; *rukmī*—Rukmī; *jitam*—won; *mayā*—by me; *atra*—in this regard; *ime*—these; *vadantu*—may speak; *prāśnikāḥ*—witnesses; *iti*—thus.

TRANSLATION

Lord Balarāma fairly won this wager also, but Rukmī again resorted to cheating and declared, "I have won! Let these witnesses here say what they saw."

PURPORT

Rukmī undoubtedly had his friends in mind when he called for the witnesses to speak. But even as his witnesses prepared to aid their cheating friend, a wonderful event took place, as described in the next verse.

TEXT 33

तदाब्रवीन्नभोवाणी बलेनैव जितो ग्लहः ।
धर्मतो वचनेनैव रुक्मी वदति वै मृषा ॥३३॥

tadābravīn nabho-vāṇī
balenaiva jito glahaḥ
dharmato vacanenaiva
rukmī vadati vai mṛṣā

tadā—then; *abravīt*—spoke; *nabhaḥ*—in the sky; *vāṇī*—a voice; *balena*—by Lord Balarāma; *eva*—indeed; *jitaḥ*—won; *glahaḥ*—the wager; *dharmataḥ*—fairly; *vacanena*—with words; *eva*—certainly; *rukmī*—Rukmī; *vadati*—speaks; *vai*—indeed; *mṛṣā*—duplicitous.

TRANSLATION

Just then a voice from the sky declared, "Balarāma has fairly won this wager. Rukmī is surely lying."

TEXT 34

तामनादृत्य वैदर्भो दुष्टराजन्यचोदितः ।
संकर्षणं परिहसन् बभाषे कालचोदितः ॥३४॥

tām anādṛtya vaidarbho
duṣṭa-rājanya-coditaḥ
saṅkarṣaṇaṁ parihasan
babhāṣe kāla-coditaḥ

tām—that (voice); *anādṛtya*—disregarding; *vaidarbhaḥ*—Rukmī, Prince of Vidarbha; *duṣṭa*—wicked; *rājanya*—by the kings; *coditaḥ*—urged on; *saṅkarṣaṇam*—to Lord Balarāma; *parihasan*—ridiculing; *babhāṣe*—he spoke; *kāla*—by the force of time; *coditaḥ*—impelled.

TRANSLATION

Urged on by the wicked kings, Rukmī ignored the divine voice.

In fact destiny itself was urging Rukmī on, and thus he ridiculed Lord Balarāma as follows.

TEXT 35

नैवाक्षकोविदा यूयं गोपाला वनगोचराः ।
अक्षैर्दीव्यन्ति राजानो बाणैश्च न भवादृशाः ॥३५॥

naivākṣa-kovidā yūyaṁ
gopālā vana-gocarāḥ
akṣair dīvyanti rājāno
bāṇaiś ca na bhavādṛśāḥ

na—not; *eva*—indeed; *akṣa*—in playing at dice; *kovidāḥ*—expert; *yūyam*—You; *gopālāḥ*—cowherds; *vana*—in the forest; *gocarāḥ*—ranging about; *akṣaiḥ*—with dice; *dīvyanti*—play; *rājānaḥ*—kings; *bāṇaiḥ*—with arrows; *ca*—and; *na*—not; *bhavādṛśāḥ*—the likes of You.

TRANSLATION

[Rukmī said:] You cowherds who wander about the forests know nothing about dice. Playing with dice and sporting with arrows are only for kings, not for the likes of You.

TEXT 36

रुक्मिणैवमधिक्षिप्तो राजभिश्चोपहासितः ।
क्रुद्धः परिघमुद्यम्य जघ्ने तं नृम्णसंसदि ॥३६॥

rukmiṇaivam adhikṣipto
rājabhiś copahāsitaḥ
kruddhaḥ parigham udyamya
jaghne taṁ nṛmṇa-saṁsadi

rukmiṇā—by Rukmī; *evam*—in this manner; *adhikṣiptaḥ*—insulted; *rājabhiḥ*—by the kings; *ca*—and; *upahāsitaḥ*—laughed at; *kruddhaḥ*—angered; *parigham*—His club; *udyamya*—raising; *jaghne*—He struck dead; *tam*—him; *nṛmṇa-saṁsadi*—in the auspicious assembly.

TRANSLATION

Thus insulted by Rukmī and ridiculed by the kings, Lord Balarāma was provoked to anger. In the midst of the auspicious wedding assembly, He raised His club and struck Rukmī dead.

TEXT 37

कलिंगराजं तरसा गृहीत्वा दशमे पदे ।
दन्तानपातयत्क्रुद्धो योऽहसद्विवृतैर्द्विजैः ॥३७॥

kaliṅga-rājaṁ tarasā
gṛhītvā daśame pade
dantān apātayat kruddho
yo 'hasad vivṛtair dvijaiḥ

kaliṅga-rājam—the King of Kaliṅga; *tarasā*—quickly; *gṛhītvā*—seizing; *daśame*—on his tenth; *pade*—step (as he tried to run away); *dantān*—his teeth; *apātayat*—He knocked out; *kruddhaḥ*—angry; *yaḥ*—who; *ahasat*—laughed; *vivṛtaiḥ*—with openly displayed; *dvijaiḥ*—teeth.

TRANSLATION

The King of Kaliṅga, who had laughed at Lord Balarāma and shown his teeth, tried to run away, but the furious Lord quickly seized him on his tenth step and knocked out all his teeth.

TEXT 38

अन्ये निर्भिन्नबाहूरुशिरसो रुधिरोक्षिताः ।
राजानो दुद्रुवुर्भीता बलेन परिघार्दिताः ॥३८॥

anye nirbhinna-bāhūru-
śiraso rudhirokṣitāḥ
rājāno dudruvur bhītā
balena parighārditāḥ

anye—others; *nirbhinna*—broken; *bāhu*—their arms; *ūru*—thighs; *śirasaḥ*—and heads; *rudhira*—with blood; *ukṣitāḥ*—drenched; *rājānaḥ*—kings; *dudruvuḥ*—fled; *bhītāḥ*—frightened; *balena*—by Lord Balarāma; *parigha*—with His club; *arditāḥ*—tormented.

TRANSLATION

Tormented by Lord Balarāma's club, the other kings fled in fear, their arms, thighs and heads broken and their bodies drenched in blood.

TEXT 39

निहते रुक्मिणि श्याले नाब्रवीत्साध्वसाधु वा ।
रुक्मिणीबलयो राजन् स्नेहभंगभयाद्धरिः ॥३९॥

nihate rukmiṇi śyāle
nābravīt sādhv asādhu vā
rukmiṇī-balayo rājan
sneha-bhaṅga-bhayād dhariḥ

nihate—being killed; *rukmiṇi*—Rukmī; *śyāle*—His brother-in-law; *na abravīt*—did not say; *sādhu*—good; *asādhu*—not good; *vā*—or; *rukmiṇī-balayoḥ*—of Rukmiṇī and Balarāma; *rājan*—O King; *sneha*—the affection; *bhaṅga*—of breaking; *bhayāt*—out of fear; *hariḥ*—Lord Kṛṣṇa.

TRANSLATION

When His brother-in-law Rukmī was slain, Lord Kṛṣṇa neither applauded nor protested, O King, for He feared jeopardizing His affectionate ties with either Rukmiṇī or Balarāma.

TEXT 40

ततोऽनिरुद्धं सह सूर्यया वरं
रथं समारोप्य ययुः कुशस्थलीम् ।
रामादयो भोजकटाद्दशार्हाः
सिद्धाखिलार्था मधुसूदनाश्रयाः ॥४०॥

tato 'niruddhaṁ saha sūryayā varaṁ
rathaṁ samāropya yayuḥ kuśasthalīm
rāmādayo bhojakaṭād daśārhāḥ
siddhākhilārthā madhusūdanāśrayāḥ

tataḥ—then; *aniruddham*—Aniruddha; *saha*—together with; *sūryayā*—His bride; *varam*—the groom; *ratham*—on His chariot; *samāropya*—placing; *yayuḥ*—they went; *kuśasthalīm*—to Kuśasthalī (Dvārakā); *rāma-ādayaḥ*—headed by Lord Balarāma; *bhojakaṭāt*—from Bhojakaṭa; *daśārhāḥ*—the descendants of Daśārha; *siddha*—fulfilled; *akhila*—all; *arthāḥ*—whose purposes; *madhusūdana*—of Lord Kṛṣṇa; *āśrayāḥ*—under the shelter.

TRANSLATION

Then the descendants of Daśārha, headed by Lord Balarāma, seated Aniruddha and His bride on a fine chariot and set off from Bhojakaṭa for Dvārakā. Having taken shelter of Lord Madhusūdana, they had fulfilled all their purposes.

PURPORT

Even though Rukmiṇī was very dear to all the Dāśārhas, her brother Rukmī had constantly opposed and insulted Kṛṣṇa since Rukmiṇī's wedding. Thus, Śrīla Viśvanātha Cakravartī explains, the associates of Lord Kṛṣṇa could hardly lament Rukmī's sudden demise.

Thus end the purports of the humble servants of His Divine Grace A. C. Bhaktivedanta Swami Prabhupāda to the Tenth Canto, Sixty-first Chapter, of the Śrīmad-Bhāgavatam, *entitled "Lord Balarāma Slays Rukmī."*

CHAPTER SIXTY-TWO

The Meeting of Ūṣā and Aniruddha

This chapter recounts the meeting of Aniruddha and Ūṣā, and also Aniruddha's battle with Bāṇāsura.

Of the one hundred sons of King Bali, the oldest was Bāṇāsura. He was a great devotee of Lord Śiva, who favored Bāṇa so much that even demigods like Indra would serve him. Bāṇāsura once satisfied Śiva by playing musical instruments with his one thousand hands while Śiva danced his *tāṇḍava-nṛtya.* In response, Śiva offered Bāṇa whatever benediction he chose, and Bāṇa asked Śiva to become the guardian of his city.

One day when Bāṇa was feeling an urge to do battle, he told Lord Śiva: "Except for you, in the whole world there is no warrior strong enough to fight me. Therefore these thousand arms you've given me are merely a heavy burden." Angered by these words, Lord Śiva replied, "Your pride will be crushed in battle when you meet my equal. Indeed, your chariot flag will fall to the ground, broken."

Bāṇāsura's daughter, Ūṣā, once had an encounter with a lover in her sleep. Several nights in a row this occurred, until one night she failed to see Him in her dreams. She suddenly awoke, speaking aloud to Him in a state of agitation, but when she noticed her maidservants around her, she felt embarrassed. Ūṣā's companion Citralekhā asked her who she had been addressing, and Ūṣā told her everything. Hearing of Ūṣā's dream-lover, Citralekhā tried to relieve her friend's distress by drawing pictures of Gandharvas and other celestial personalities, as well as various men of the Vṛṣṇi dynasty. Citralekhā asked Ūṣā to pick out the man she had seen in her dreams, and Ūṣā pointed to the picture of Aniruddha. Citralekha, who had mystic powers, knew at once that the young man her friend had pointed out was Lord Kṛṣṇa's grandson Aniruddha. Then, using her mystic powers, Citralekhā flew through the sky to Dvārakā, found Aniruddha and brought Him back with her to Śoṇitapura, Bāṇāsura's capital. There she presented Him to Ūṣā.

Having obtained the man of her desires, Ūṣā began serving Him very affectionately within her private quarters, which were supposed to be strictly off limits to men. After some time the female guards of the inner palace noticed symptoms of sexual activity on Ūṣā's person, and they went to Bāṇāsura to inform him. Greatly disturbed, Bāṇāsura rushed to his daughter's apartments with many armed guards and, to his great surprise, saw Aniruddha there. As the guards attacked Him, Aniruddha took up His club and succeeded in killing a few before the powerful Bāṇa could capture Him with his mystic *nāga-pāśa* ropes, filling Ūṣā with lamentation.

TEXT 1

श्रीराजोवाच
बाणस्य तनयामूषामुपयेमे यदूत्तमः ।
तत्र युद्धमभूद् घोरं हरिशंकरयोर्महत् ।
एतत्सर्वं महायोगिन् समाख्यातुं त्वमर्हसि ॥१॥

śrī-rājovāca
bāṇasya tanayām ūṣām
upayeme yadūttamaḥ
tatra yuddham abhūd ghoraṁ
hari-śaṅkarayor mahat
etat sarvaṁ mahā-yogin
samākhyātuṁ tvam arhasi

śrī-rājā uvāca—the King (Parīkṣit Mahārāja) said; *bāṇasya*—of the demon Bāṇa; *tanayām*—the daughter; *ūṣām*—named Ūṣā; *upayeme*—married; *yadu-uttamaḥ*—the best of the Yadus (Aniruddha); *tatra*—in connection with that; *yuddham*—a battle; *abhūt*—occurred; *ghoram*—fearsome; *hari-śaṅkarayoḥ*—between Lord Hari (Kṛṣṇa) and Lord Śaṅkara (Śiva); *mahat*—great; *etat*—this; *sarvam*—all; *mahā-yogin*—O great mystic; *samākhyātum*—to explain; *tvam*—you; *arhasi*—deserve.

TRANSLATION

King Parīkṣit said: The best of the Yadus married Bāṇāsura's daughter, Ūṣā, and as a result a great, fearsome battle occurred between Lord Hari and Lord Śaṅkara. Please explain everything about this incident, O most powerful of mystics.

TEXT 2

श्रीशुक उवाच
बाणः पुत्रशतज्येष्ठो बलेरासीन्महात्मनः ।
येन वामनरूपाय हरयेऽदायि मेदिनी ॥
तस्यौरसः सुतो बाणः शिवभक्तिरतः सदा ।
मान्यो वदान्यो धीमांश्च सत्यसन्धो दृढव्रतः ।
शोणिताख्ये पुरे रम्ये स राज्यमकरोत्पुरा ॥
तस्य शम्भोः प्रसादेन किंकरा इव तेऽमराः ।
सहस्रबाहुर्वाद्येन ताण्डवेऽतोषयन्मृडम् ॥२॥

śrī-śuka uvāca
bāṇaḥ putra-śata-jyeṣṭho
baler āsīn mahātmanaḥ
yena vāmana-rūpāya
haraye 'dāyi medinī

tasyaurasaḥ suto bāṇaḥ
śiva-bhakti-rataḥ sadā
mānyo vadānyo dhīmāṁś ca
satya-sandho dṛḍha-vrataḥ
śoṇitākhye pure ramye
sa rājyam akarot purā

tasya śambhoḥ prasādena
kiṅkarā iva te 'marāḥ
sahasra-bāhur vādyena
tāṇḍave 'toṣayan mṛḍam

śrī-śukaḥ uvāca—Śukadeva Gosvāmī said; *bāṇaḥ*—Bāṇa; *putra*—of sons; *śata*—one hundred; *jyeṣṭhaḥ*—the oldest; *baleḥ*—of Mahārāja Bali; *āsīt*—was; *mahā-ātmanaḥ*—of the great soul; *yena*—by whom (Bali); *vāmana-rūpāya*—in the form of the dwarf, Vāmanadeva; *haraye*—to the Supreme Lord Hari; *adāyi*—was given; *medinī*—the earth; *tasya*—his; *aurasaḥ*—from the semen; *sutaḥ*—the son; *bāṇaḥ*—Bāṇa; *śiva-bhakti*—in devotion for Lord Śiva; *rataḥ*—fixed; *sadā*—always; *mānyaḥ*—respectable; *vadānyaḥ*—magnanimous; *dhī-mān*—intelligent; *ca*—and;

satya-sandhaḥ—truthful; *dṛḍha-vrataḥ*—firm in his vows; *śoṇita-ākhye*—known as Śoṇita; *pure*—in the city; *ramye*—charming; *saḥ*—he; *rājyam akarot*—made his kingdom; *purā*—in the past; *tasya*—upon him; *śambhoḥ*—of Lord Śambhu (Śiva); *prasādena*—by the pleasure; *kiṅkarāḥ*—servants; *iva*—as if; *te*—they; *amarāḥ*—the demigods; *sahasra*—one thousand; *bāhuḥ*—having arms; *vādyena*—with the playing of musical instruments; *tāṇḍave*—while he (Lord Śiva) was dancing his *tāṇḍava-nṛtya; atoṣayat*—he satisfied; *mṛḍam*—Lord Śiva.

TRANSLATION

Śukadeva Gosvāmī said: Bāṇa was the oldest of the hundred sons fathered by the great saint Bali Mahārāja, who gave the whole earth in charity to Lord Hari when He appeared as Vāmanadeva. Bāṇāsura, born from Bali's semen, became a great devotee of Lord Śiva. His behavior was always respectable, and he was generous, intelligent, truthful and firm in his vows. The beautiful city of Śoṇitapura was under his dominion. Because Lord Śiva had favored him, the very demigods waited on Bāṇāsura like menial servants. Once, when Śiva was dancing his *tāṇḍava-nṛtya,* Bāṇa especially satisfied the lord by playing a musical accompaniment with his one thousand arms.

TEXT 3

भगवान् सर्वभूतेशः शरण्यो भक्तवत्सलः ।
वरेण छन्दयामास स तं वव्रे पुराधिपम् ॥३॥

bhagavān sarva-bhūteśaḥ
śaraṇyo bhakta-vatsalaḥ
vareṇa chandayām āsa
sa taṁ vavre purādhipam

bhagavān—the lord; *sarva*—of all; *bhūta*—created beings; *īśaḥ*—the master; *śaraṇyaḥ*—the giver of shelter; *bhakta*—to his devotees; *vatsalaḥ*—compassionate; *vareṇa*—with a choice of benedictions; *chandayām āsa*—gratified him; *saḥ*—he, Bāṇa; *tam*—him, Lord Śiva; *vavre*—chose; *pura*—of his city; *adhipam*—as the guardian.

TRANSLATION

The lord and master of all created beings, the compassionate refuge of his devotees, gladdened Bāṇāsura by offering him the benediction of his choice. Bāṇa chose to have him, Lord Śiva, as the guardian of his city.

TEXT 4

स एकदाह गिरिशं पार्श्वस्थं वीर्यदुर्मदः ।
किरीटेनार्कवर्णेन संस्पृशंस्तत्पदाम्बुजम् ॥४॥

sa ekadāha giriśaṁ
pārśva-sthaṁ vīrya-durmadaḥ
kirīṭenārka-varṇena
saṁspṛśaṁs tat-padāmbujam

saḥ—he, Bāṇāsura; *ekadā*—once; *āha*—said; *giri-śam*—to Lord Śiva; *pārśva*—at his side; *stham*—present; *vīrya*—by his strength; *durmadaḥ*—intoxicated; *kirīṭena*—with his helmet; *arka*—like the sun; *varṇena*—whose color; *saṁspṛśan*—touching; *tat*—his, Lord Śiva's; *pada-ambujam*—lotus feet.

TRANSLATION

Bāṇāsura was intoxicated with his strength. One day, when Lord Śiva was standing beside him, Bāṇāsura touched the lord's lotus feet with his helmet, which shone like the sun, and spoke to him as follows.

TEXT 5

नमस्ये त्वां महादेव लोकानां गुरुमीश्वरम् ।
पुंसामपूर्णकामानां कामपूरामराङ्घ्रिपम् ॥५॥

namasye tvāṁ mahā-deva
lokānāṁ gurum īśvaram
puṁsām apūrṇa-kāmānāṁ
kāma-pūrāmarāṅghripam

namasye—I bow down; *tvām*—to you; *mahā-deva*—O greatest of gods; *lokānām*—of the worlds; *gurum*—to the spiritual master; *īśvaram*—to the controller; *puṁsām*—for men; *apūrṇa*—unfulfilled; *kāmānām*—whose desires; *kāma-pūra*—fulfilling desires; *amara-aṅghripam*—(like) a tree of heaven.

TRANSLATION

[Bāṇāsura said:] O Lord Mahādeva, I bow down to you, the spiritual master and controller of the worlds. You are like the heavenly tree that fulfills the desires of those whose desires are unfulfilled.

TEXT 6

दोःसहस्रं त्वया दत्तं परं भाराय मेऽभवत् ।
त्रिलोक्यां प्रतियोद्धारं न लभे त्वदृते समम् ॥६॥

doḥ-sahasraṁ tvayā dattaṁ
paraṁ bhārāya me 'bhavat
tri-lokyāṁ pratiyoddhāraṁ
na labhe tvad ṛte samam

doḥ—the arms; *sahasram*—one thousand; *tvayā*—by you; *dattam*—given; *param*—only; *bhārāya*—a burden; *me*—for me; *abhavat*—have become; *tri-lokyām*—in the three worlds; *pratiyoddhāram*—an opposing fighter; *na labhe*—I do not find; *tvat*—you; *ṛte*—except for; *samam*—equal.

TRANSLATION

These one thousand arms you bestowed upon me have become merely a heavy burden. Besides you, I find no one in the three worlds worthy to fight.

PURPORT

According to the *ācāryas,* Bāṇāsura's subtle implication here is this: "And so when I have defeated you, Lord Śiva, my world conquest will be complete and my desire for battle satisfied."

TEXT 7

कण्डूत्या निभृतैर्दोर्भिर्युयुत्सुर्दिग्गजानहम् ।
आद्यायां चूर्णयन्नद्रीन् भीतास्तेऽपि प्रदुद्रुवुः ॥७॥

kaṇḍūtyā nibhṛtair dorbhir
yuyutsur dig-gajān aham
ādyāyāṁ cūrṇayann adrīn
bhītās te 'pi pradudruvuḥ

kaṇḍūtyā—with itching; *nibhṛtaiḥ*—filled; *dorbhiḥ*—with my arms; *yuyutsuḥ*—eager to fight; *dik*—of the directions; *gajān*—the elephants; *aham*—I; *ādya*—O primeval one; *ayām*—went; *cūrṇayan*—crushing to powder; *adrīn*—mountains; *bhītāḥ*—frightened; *te*—they; *api*—even; *pradudruvuḥ*—ran away.

TRANSLATION

Eager to fight with the elephants who rule the directions, O primeval lord, I went forth, pulverizing mountains with my arms, which were itching for battle. But even those great elephants fled in fear.

TEXT 8

तच्छ्रुत्वा भगवान् क्रुद्धः केतुस्ते भज्यते यदा ।
त्वद्दर्पघ्नं भवेन्मूढ संयुगं मत्समेन ते ॥८॥

tac chrutvā bhagavān kruddhaḥ
ketus te bhajyate yadā
tvad-darpa-ghnaṁ bhaven mūḍha
saṁyugaṁ mat-samena te

tat—that; *śrutvā*—hearing; *bhagavān*—the lord; *kruddhaḥ*—angry; *ketuḥ*—flag; *te*—your; *bhajyate*—is broken; *yadā*—when; *tvat*—your; *darpa*—pride; *ghnam*—destroyed; *bhavet*—will be; *mūḍha*—O fool; *saṁyugam*—battle; *mat*—to me; *samena*—with Him who is equal; *te*—your.

TRANSLATION

Hearing this, Lord Śiva became angry and replied, "Your flag will be broken, fool, when you have done battle with one who is my equal. That fight will vanquish your conceit."

PURPORT

Lord Śiva could have immediately chastised Bāṇāsura and personally destroyed his pride, but since Bāṇāsura had been such a faithful servant of his, Śiva did not do so.

TEXT 9

इत्युक्तः कुमतिर्हृष्टः स्वगृहं प्राविशन्नृप ।
प्रतीक्षन् गिरिशादेशं स्ववीर्यनशनं कुधीः ॥९॥

ity uktaḥ kumatir hṛṣṭaḥ
sva-gṛhaṁ prāviśan nṛpa
pratīkṣan giriśādeśaṁ
sva-vīrya-naśanaṁ kudhīḥ

iti—thus; *uktaḥ*—spoken to; *ku-matiḥ*—foolish; *hṛṣṭaḥ*—delighted; *sva*—his own; *gṛham*—home; *prāviśat*—entered; *nṛpa*—O King (Parīkṣit); *pratīkṣan*—waiting for; *giriśa*—of Lord Śiva; *ādeśam*—prediction; *sva-vīrya*—of his prowess; *naśanam*—the destruction; *ku-dhīḥ*—unintelligent.

TRANSLATION

Thus advised, unintelligent Bāṇāsura was delighted. The fool then went home, O King, to wait for that which Lord Giriśa had predicted: the destruction of his prowess.

PURPORT

Here Bāṇāsura is described as *ku-dhī* ("having bad intelligence") and *ku-mati* ("foolish") because he completely misunderstood the actual situation. This demon was so arrogant that he was convinced no one could defeat him. He was delighted to hear that someone as powerful as Lord Śiva would come to fight with him and satisfy his itching for battle. Even though Śiva had said that this person would break Bāṇa's flag and destroy his prowess, the demon was too foolish to take this statement seriously and eagerly awaited the fight.

At the present moment materialistic people are delighted by the many unprecedented facilities for sense gratification. Although it is clear that death, both individual and collective, is quickly approaching them, modern sense gratifiers are oblivious to their inevitable destruction. As stated in the *Bhāgavatam* (2.1.4), *paśyann api na paśyati:* Even though their imminent destruction is apparent, they are too blind to see it, being intoxicated by sex enjoyment and family attachment. Similarly, Bāṇāsura was intoxicated with his material prowess and could not believe that he was about to be cut down to size.

TEXT 10

तस्योषा नाम दुहिता स्वप्ने प्राद्युम्निना रतिम् ।
कन्यालभत कान्तेन प्रागदृष्टश्रुतेन सा ॥१०॥

tasyoṣā nāma duhitā
svapne prādyumninā ratim
kanyālabhata kāntena
prāg adṛṣṭa-śrutena sā

tasya—his; *ūṣā nāma*—named Ūṣā; *duhitā*—daughter; *svapne*—in a dream; *prādyumninā*—with the son of Pradyumna (Aniruddha); *ratim*—an amorous encounter; *kanyā*—the unmarried maiden; *alabhata*—obtained; *kāntena*—with her lover; *prāk*—previously; *adṛṣṭa*—never seen; *śrutena*—or heard of; *sā*—she.

TRANSLATION

In a dream Bāṇa's daughter, the maiden Ūṣā, had an amorous encounter with the son of Pradyumna, though she had never before seen or heard of her lover.

PURPORT

The incidents now described will lead up to the fight predicted by Lord Śiva. Śrīla Viśvanātha Cakravartī Ṭhākura quotes the following verses from the *Viṣṇu Purāṇa*, which explain Ūṣā's dream:

ūṣā bāṇa-sutā vipra
pārvatīṁ śambhunā saha
krīḍantīm upalakṣyoccaiḥ
spṛhāṁ cakre tad-āśrayām

"O *brāhmaṇa,* when Ūṣā, the daughter of Bāṇa, happened to see Pārvatī playing with her husband, Lord Śambhu, Ūṣā intensely desired to experience the same feelings."

tataḥ sakala-citta-jñā
gaurī tām āha bhāvinīm
alam atyartha-tāpena
bhartrā tvam api raṁsyase

"At that time Goddess Gaurī [Pārvatī], who knows everyone's heart, told the sensitive young girl, 'Don't be so disturbed! You will have a chance to enjoy with your own husband.'"

ity uktā sā tadā cakre
kadeti matim ātmanaḥ
ko vā bhartā mamety enāṁ
punar apy āha pārvatī

"Hearing this, Ūṣā thought to herself, 'But when? And who will my husband be?' In response, Pārvatī addressed her once more."

vaiśākha-śukla-dvādaśyāṁ
svapne yo 'bhibhavaṁ tava
kariṣyati sa te bhartā
rāja-putri bhaviṣyati

"'The man who approaches you in your dream on the twelfth lunar day of the bright fortnight of the month Vaiśākha will become your husband, O princess.'"

TEXT 11

सा तत्र तमपश्यन्ती क्वासि कान्तेति वादिनी ।
सखीनां मध्य उत्तस्थौ विह्वला व्रीडिता भृशम् ॥११॥

sā tatra tam apaśyantī
kvāsi kānteti vādinī
sakhīnāṁ madhya uttasthau
vihvalā vrīḍitā bhṛśam

sā—she; *tatra*—there (in her dream); *tam*—Him; *apaśyantī*—not seeing; *kva*—where; *asi*—are you; *kānta*—my lover; *iti*—thus; *vādinī*—speaking; *sakhīnām*—of her girlfriends; *madhye*—in the midst; *uttasthau*—arose; *vihvalā*—disturbed; *vrīḍitā*—embarrassed; *bhṛśam*—greatly.

TRANSLATION

Losing sight of Him in her dream, Ūṣā suddenly sat up in the midst of her girlfriends, crying out "Where are You, my lover?" She was greatly disturbed and embarrassed.

PURPORT

Coming to her senses and remembering that she was surrounded by her girlfriends, Ūṣā was naturally very embarrassed to have cried out in that way. At the same time she was disturbed by attachment to the beloved man who had appeared in her dream.

TEXT 12

बाणस्य मन्त्री कुम्भाण्डश्चित्रलेखा च तत्सुता ।
सख्यपृच्छत्सखीमूषां कौतूहलसमन्विता ॥१२॥

bāṇasya mantrī kumbhāṇḍaś
citralekhā ca tat-sutā
sakhy apṛcchat sakhīm ūṣāṁ
kautūhala-samanvitā

bāṇasya—of Bāṇa; *mantrī*—the minister; *kumbhāṇḍaḥ*—Kumbhāṇḍa; *citralekhā*—Citralekhā; *ca*—and; *tat*—his; *sutā*—daughter; *sakhī*—the girlfriend; *apṛcchat*—she asked; *sakhīm*—her girlfriend; *ūṣām*—Ūṣā; *kautūhala*—with curiosity; *samanvitā*—full.

TRANSLATION

Bāṇāsura had a minister named Kumbhāṇḍa, whose daughter was Citralekhā. A companion of Ūṣā's, she was filled with curiosity, and thus she inquired from her friend.

TEXT 13

कं त्वं मृगयसे सुभ्रु कीदृशस्ते मनोरथः ।
हस्तग्राहं न तेऽद्यापि राजपुत्र्युपलक्षये ॥१३॥

kaṁ tvaṁ mṛgayase su-bhru
kīdṛśas te manorathaḥ
hasta-grāhaṁ na te 'dyāpi
rāja-putry upalakṣaye

kam—who; *tvam*—you; *mṛgayase*—are looking for; *su-bhru*—O beautiful-browed one; *kīdṛśaḥ*—of what sort; *te*—your; *manaḥ-rathaḥ*—hankering; *hasta*—of the hand; *grāham*—a taker; *na*—not; *te*—your; *adya api*—up until now; *rāja-putri*—O princess; *upalakṣaye*—do I see.

TRANSLATION

[Citralekhā said:] Who are you searching for, O fine-browed one? What is this hankering you're feeling? Until now, O princess, I haven't seen any man take your hand in marriage.

TEXT 14

दृष्टः कश्चिन्नरः स्वप्ने श्यामः कमललोचनः ।
पीतवासा बृहद्बाहुर्योषितां हृदयंगमः ॥१४॥

dṛṣṭaḥ kaścin naraḥ svapne
śyāmaḥ kamala-locanaḥ
pīta-vāsā bṛhad-bāhur
yoṣitāṁ hṛdayaṁ-gamaḥ

dṛṣṭaḥ—seen; *kaścit*—a certain; *naraḥ*—man; *svapne*—in my dream; *śyāmaḥ*—dark blue; *kamala*—lotuslike; *locanaḥ*—whose eyes; *pīta*—yellow; *vāsāḥ*—whose clothing; *bṛhat*—mighty; *bāhuḥ*—whose arms; *yoṣitām*—of women; *hṛdayam*—the hearts; *gamaḥ*—touching.

TRANSLATION

[Ūṣā said:] In my dream I saw a certain man who had a dark-blue complexion, lotus eyes, yellow garments and mighty arms. He was the kind who touches women's hearts.

TEXT 15

तमहं मृगये कान्तं पाययित्वाधरं मधु ।
क्वापि यातः स्पृहयतीं क्षिप्त्वा मां वृजिनार्णवे ॥१५॥

tam ahaṁ mṛgaye kāntaṁ
pāyayitvādharaṁ madhu
kvāpi yātaḥ spṛhayatīṁ
kṣiptvā māṁ vṛjinārṇave

tam—Him; *aham*—I; *mṛgaye*—am seeking; *kāntam*—lover; *pāyayitvā*—having made drink; *ādharam*—of His lips; *madhu*—the honey; *kva api*—somewhere; *yātaḥ*—has gone; *spṛhayatīm*—hankering for Him; *kṣiptvā*—having thrown; *mām*—me; *vṛjina*—of distress; *arṇave*—in the ocean.

TRANSLATION

It is that lover I search for. After making me drink the honey of His lips, He has gone elsewhere, and thus He has thrown me, hankering fervently for Him, into the ocean of distress.

TEXT 16

चित्रलेखोवाच
व्यसनं तेऽपकर्षामि त्रिलोक्यां यदि भाव्यते ।
तमानेष्ये वरं यस्ते मनोहर्ता तमादिश ॥१६॥

citralekhovāca
vyasanaṁ te 'pakarṣāmi
tri-lokyāṁ yadi bhāvyate
tam āneṣye varaṁ yas te
mano-hartā tam ādiśa

citralekhā uvāca—Citralekhā said; *vyasanam*—distress; *te*—your; *apakarṣāmi*—I will take away; *tri-lokyām*—within the three worlds; *yadi*—if; *bhāvyate*—He is to be found; *tam*—Him; *āneṣye*—I will bring; *varam*—husband-to-be; *yaḥ*—who; *te*—your; *manaḥ*—of the heart; *hartā*—the thief; *tam*—Him; *ādiśa*—please point out.

TRANSLATION

Citralekhā said: I will remove your distress. If He is to be found anywhere in the three worlds, I will bring this future husband of yours who has stolen your heart. Please show me who He is.

PURPORT

Interestingly, the name Citralekhā indicates a person skilled in the art of drawing or painting. *Citra* means "excellent" or "variegated," and *lekhā* means "the art of drawing or painting." Citralekhā, as described in the following verse, will now utilize the talent indicated by her name.

TEXT 17

इत्युक्त्वा देवगन्धर्वसिद्धचारणपन्नगान् ।
दैत्यविद्याधरान् यक्षान्मनुजांश्च यथालिखत् ॥१७॥

ity uktvā deva-gandharva-
siddha-cāraṇa-pannagān

daitya-vidyādharān yakṣān
manujāṁś ca yathālikhat

iti—thus; *uktvā*—saying; *deva-gandharva*—demigods and Gandharvas; *siddha-cāraṇa-pannagān*—Siddhas, Cāraṇas and Pannagas; *daitya-vidyādharān*—demons and Vidyādharas; *yakṣān*—Yakṣas; *manu-jān*—humans; *ca*—also; *yathā*—accurately; *alikhat*—she drew.

TRANSLATION

Saying this, Citralekhā proceeded to draw accurate pictures of various demigods, Gandharvas, Siddhas, Cāraṇas, Pannagas, Daityas, Vidyādharas, Yakṣas and humans.

TEXTS 18–19

मनुजेषु च सा वृष्णीन् शूरमानकदुन्दुभिम् ।
व्यलिखद् रामकृष्णौ च प्रद्युम्नं वीक्ष्य लज्जिता ॥१८॥
अनिरुद्धं विलिखितं वीक्ष्योषावाङ्मुखी ह्रिया ।
सोऽसावसाविति प्राह स्मयमाना महीपते ॥१९॥

manujeṣu ca sā vṛṣṇīn
śūram ānakadundubhim
vyalikhad rāma-kṛṣṇau ca
pradyumnaṁ vīkṣya lajjitā

aniruddhaṁ vilikhitaṁ
vīkṣyoṣāvāṅ-mukhī hriyā
so 'sāv asāv iti prāha
smayamānā mahī-pate

manujeṣu—among the humans; *ca*—and; *sā*—she (Citralekhā); *vṛṣṇīn*—the Vṛṣṇis; *śūram*—Śūrasena; *ānakadundubhim*—Vasudeva; *vyalikhat*—drew; *rāma-kṛṣṇau*—Balarāma and Kṛṣṇa; *ca*—and; *pradyumnam*—Pradyumna; *vīkṣya*—seeing; *lajjitā*—becoming shy;

aniruddham—Aniruddha; *vilikhitam*—drawn; *vīkṣya*—seeing; *ūṣā*—Ūṣā; *avāk*—bending down; *mukhī*—her head; *hriyā*—out of embarrassment; *saḥ asau asau iti*—"That's the one! That's the one!"; *prāha*—she said; *smayamānā*—smiling; *mahī-pate*—O King.

TRANSLATION

O King, among the humans, Citralekhā drew pictures of the Vṛṣṇis, including Śūrasena, Ānakadundubhi, Balarāma and Kṛṣṇa. When Ūṣā saw the picture of Pradyumna she became bashful, and when she saw Aniruddha's picture she bent her head down in embarrassment. Smiling, she exclaimed, "He's the one! It's Him!"

PURPORT

Śrīla Viśvanātha Cakravartī gives this further insight: When Ūṣā saw the picture of Pradyumna, she became bashful because she thought, "This is my father-in-law." Then she saw the picture of her lover, Aniruddha, and cried out in joy.

TEXT 20

चित्रलेखा तमाज्ञाय पौत्रं कृष्णस्य योगिनी ।
ययौ विहायसा राजन् द्वारकां कृष्णपालिताम् ॥२०॥

citralekhā tam ājñāya
pautraṁ kṛṣṇasya yoginī
yayau vihāyasā rājan
dvārakāṁ kṛṣṇa-pālitām

citralekhā—Citralekhā; *tam*—Him; *ājñāya*—recognizing; *pautram*—as the grandson; *kṛṣṇasya*—of Lord Kṛṣṇa; *yoginī*—female mystic; *yayau*—she went; *vihāyasā*—by the mystic skyways; *rājan*—O King; *dvārakām*—to Dvārakā; *kṛṣṇa-pālitām*—protected by Kṛṣṇa.

TRANSLATION

Citralekhā, endowed with mystic powers, recognized Him as Kṛṣṇa's grandson [Aniruddha]. My dear King, she then traveled

by the mystic skyway to Dvārakā, the city under Lord Kṛṣṇa's protection.

TEXT 21

तत्र सुप्तं सुपर्यंके प्राद्युम्निं योगमास्थिता ।
गृहीत्वा शोणितपुरं सख्यै प्रियमदर्शयत् ॥२१॥

tatra suptaṁ su-paryaṅke
prādyumniṁ yogam āsthitā
gṛhītvā śoṇita-puraṁ
sakhyai priyam adarśayat

tatra—there; *suptam*—asleep; *su*—excellent; *paryaṅke*—on a bed; *prādyumnim*—the son of Pradyumna; *yogam*—mystic power; *āsthitā*—using; *gṛhītvā*—taking Him; *śoṇita-puram*—to Śoṇitapura Bāṇāsura's capital; *sakhyai*—to her girlfriend, Ūṣā; *priyam*—her beloved; *adarśayat*—she showed.

TRANSLATION

There she found Pradyumna's son Aniruddha sleeping upon a fine bed. With her yogic power she took Him away to Śoṇitapura, where she presented her girlfriend Ūṣā with her beloved.

PURPORT

Śrīla Viśvanātha Cakravartī comments as follows on this verse: "It is stated here that Citralekhā resorted to mystic power (*yogam āsthitā*). As explained in the *Hari-vaṁśa* and other literatures, she needed to employ her powers because when she arrived at Dvārakā she found herself unable to enter Lord Kṛṣṇa's city. At that time Śrī Nārada Muni instructed her in the mystic art of entering. Some authorities also say that Citralekhā is herself an expansion of Yogamāyā."

TEXT 22

सा च तं सुन्दरवरं विलोक्य मुदितानना ।
दुष्प्रेक्ष्ये स्वगृहे पुम्भी रेमे प्राद्युम्निना समम् ॥२२॥

sā ca taṁ sundara-varaṁ
vilokya muditānanā
duṣprekṣye sva-gṛhe pumbhī
reme prādyumninā samam

sā—she; *ca*—and; *tam*—Him; *sundara-varam*—the most beautiful man; *vilokya*—beholding; *mudita*—joyful; *ānanā*—her face; *duṣprekṣye*—which was not to be seen; *sva*—in her own; *gṛhe*—quarters; *pumbhiḥ*—by men; *reme*—she enjoyed; *prādyumninā samam*—together with the son of Pradyumna.

TRANSLATION

When Ūṣā beheld Him, the most beautiful of men, her face lit up with joy. She took the son of Pradyumna to her private quarters, which men were forbidden even to see, and there enjoyed with Him.

TEXTS 23–24

परार्ध्यवासःस्रग्गन्धधूपदीपासनादिभिः ।
पानभोजनभक्ष्यैश्च वाक्यैः शुश्रूषणार्चितः ॥२३॥
गूढः कन्यापुरे शश्वत्प्रवृद्धस्नेहया तया ।
नाहर्गणान् स बुबुधे ऊषयापहृतेन्द्रियः ॥२४॥

parārdhya-vāsaḥ-srag-gandha-
dhūpa-dīpāsanādibhiḥ
pāna-bhojana-bhakṣyaiś ca
vākyaiḥ śuśrūṣaṇārcitaḥ

gūḍhaḥ kanyā-pure śaśvat-
pravṛddha-snehayā tayā
nāhar-gaṇān sa bubudhe
ūṣayāpahṛtendriyaḥ

parārdhya—priceless; *vāsaḥ*—with garments; *srak*—garlands; *gandha*—fragrances; *dhūpa*—incense; *dīpa*—lamps; *āsana*—sitting places; *ādibhiḥ*—and so on; *pāna*—with beverages; *bhojana*—food that is chewed; *bhakṣyaiḥ*—food that is not chewed; *ca*—also; *vākyaiḥ*—with words; *śuśrūṣaṇa*—by faithful service; *arcitaḥ*—worshiped; *gūḍhaḥ*—kept hidden; *kanyā-pure*—in the quarters for unmarried girls; *śaśvat*—continuously; *pravṛddha*—greatly increasing; *snehayā*—whose affection; *tayā*—by her; *na*—not; *ahaḥ-gaṇān*—the days; *saḥ*—He; *bubudhe*—noticed; *ūṣayā*—by Ūṣā; *apahṛta*—diverted; *indriyaḥ*—His senses.

TRANSLATION

Ūṣā worshiped Aniruddha with faithful service, offering Him priceless garments, along with garlands, fragrances, incense, lamps, sitting places and so on. She also offered Him beverages, all types of food, and sweet words. As He thus remained hidden in the young ladies' quarters, Aniruddha did not notice the passing of the days, for His senses were captivated by Ūṣā, whose affection for Him ever increased.

TEXTS 25–26

तां तथा यदुवीरेण भुज्यमानां हतव्रताम् ।
हेतुभिर्लक्षयां चक्रुराप्रीतां दुरवच्छदैः ॥२५॥
भटा आवेदयां चक्रू राजंस्ते दुहितुर्वयम् ।
विचेष्टितं लक्षयाम कन्यायाः कुलदूषणम् ॥२६॥

tāṁ tathā yadu-vīreṇa
bhujyamānāṁ hata-vratām
hetubhir lakṣayāṁ cakrur
āprītāṁ duravacchadaiḥ

bhaṭā āvedayāṁ cakrū
rājaṁs te duhitur vayam
viceṣṭitaṁ lakṣayāma
kanyāyāḥ kula-dūṣaṇam

tām—her; *tathā*—thus; *yadu-vīreṇa*—by the hero of the Yadus; *bhujyamānām*—being enjoyed; *hata*—broken; *vratām*—whose (virgin) vow; *hetubhiḥ*—by symptoms; *lakṣayām cakruḥ*—they ascertained; *ā-prītām*—who was extremely happy; *duravacchadaiḥ*—impossible to disguise; *bhaṭāḥ*—the female guards; *āvedayām cakruḥ*—announced; *rājan*—O King; *te*—your; *duhituḥ*—of the daughter; *vayam*—we; *viceṣṭitam*—improper behavior; *lakṣayāmaḥ*—have noted; *kanyāyāḥ*—of an unmarried girl; *kula*—the family; *dūṣaṇam*—besmirching.

TRANSLATION

The female guards eventually noticed unmistakable symptoms of romantic involvement in Ūṣā, who, having broken her maiden vow, was being enjoyed by the Yadu hero and showing signs of conjugal happiness. The guards went to Bāṇāsura and told him, "O King, we have detected in your daughter the kind of improper behavior that spoils the reputation of a young girl's family.

PURPORT

Śrīla Viśvanātha Cakravartī has defined the word *bhaṭāḥ* as "female guards," whereas Jīva Gosvāmī defines it as "eunuchs and others." Grammatically, the word can function both ways.

The guards feared that if Bāṇāsura found out about Ūṣā's activities from some other source, he would severely punish them, and thus they personally informed him that his young daughter was no longer innocent.

TEXT 27

अनपायिभिरस्माभिर्गुप्तायाश्च गृहे प्रभो ।
कन्याया दूषणं पुम्भिर्दुष्प्रेक्ष्याया न विद्महे ॥२७॥

anapāyibhir asmābhir
guptāyāś ca gṛhe prabho
kanyāyā dūṣaṇaṁ pumbhir
duṣprekṣyāyā na vidmahe

anapāyibhiḥ—who have never gone away; *asmābhiḥ*—by us; *guptāyāḥ*—of her who has been well guarded; *ca*—and; *gṛhe*—within the palace; *prabho*—O master; *kanyāyāḥ*—of the maiden; *dūṣaṇam*—the polluting; *pumbhiḥ*—by men; *duṣprekṣyāyāḥ*—impossible to be seen; *na vidmahe*—we do not understand.

TRANSLATION

"We have been carefully watching over her, never leaving our posts, O master, so we cannot understand how this maiden, whom no man can even see, has been corrupted within the palace."

PURPORT

The *ācāryas* explain that the word *anapāyibhiḥ* can mean either "never going away" or "never deluded." Also, if we take the alternate reading *duṣpreṣyāyāḥ* instead of *duṣprekṣyāyāḥ,* the guards refer to Ūṣā as "she whose wicked girlfriend has been sent on a mission."

TEXT 28

ततः प्रव्यथितो बाणो दुहितुः श्रुतदूषणः ।
त्वरितः कन्यकागारं प्राप्तोऽद्राक्षीद्यदूद्वहम् ॥२८॥

tataḥ pravyathito bāṇo
duhituḥ śruta-dūṣaṇaḥ
tvaritaḥ kanyakāgāraṁ
prāpto 'drākṣīd yadūdvaham

tataḥ—then; *pravyathitaḥ*—very agitated; *bāṇaḥ*—Bāṇāsura; *duhituḥ*—of his daughter; *śruta*—having heard of; *dūṣaṇaḥ*—the corruption; *tvaritaḥ*—quickly; *kanyakā*—of the unmarried girls; *āgāram*—the quarters; *prāptaḥ*—reaching; *adrākṣīt*—he saw; *yadu-udvaham*—the most eminent of the Yadus.

TRANSLATION

Very agitated to hear of his daughter's corruption, Bāṇāsura rushed at once to the maidens' quarters. There he saw the pride of the Yadus, Aniruddha.

TEXTS 29–30

कामात्मजं तं भुवनैकसुन्दरं
श्यामं पिशंगाम्बरमम्बुजेक्षणम् ।
बृहद्भुजं कुण्डलकुन्तलत्विषा
स्मितावलोकेन च मण्डिताननम् ॥२९॥
दीव्यन्तमक्षैः प्रिययाभिनृम्णया
तदंगसंगस्तनकुंकुमस्रजम् ।
बाह्वोर्दधानं मधुमल्लिकाश्रितां
तस्याग्र आसीनमवेक्ष्य विस्मितः ॥३०॥

kāmātmajaṁ taṁ bhuvanaika-sundaraṁ
śyāmaṁ piśaṅgāmbaram ambujekṣaṇam
bṛhad-bhujaṁ kuṇḍala-kuntala-tviṣā
smitāvalokena ca maṇḍitānanam

dīvyantam akṣaiḥ priyayābhinṛmṇayā
tad-aṅga-saṅga-stana-kuṅkuma-srajam
bāhvor dadhānaṁ madhu-mallikāśritāṁ
tasyāgra āsīnam avekṣya vismitaḥ

kāma—of Cupid (Pradyumna); *ātmajam*—the son; *tam*—Him; *bhuvana*—of all the worlds; *eka*—the exclusive; *sundaram*—beauty; *śyāmam*—dark blue in complexion; *piśaṅga*—yellow; *ambaram*—whose clothing; *ambuja*—like lotuses; *īkṣaṇam*—whose eyes; *bṛhat*—mighty; *bhujam*—whose arms; *kuṇḍala*—of His earrings; *kuntala*—and of the locks of His hair; *tviṣā*—with the glow; *smita*—smiling; *avalokena*—with glances; *ca*—also; *maṇḍita*—ornamented; *ānanam*—whose face; *dīvyantam*—playing; *akṣaiḥ*—with dice; *priyayā*—along with His beloved; *abhinṛmṇayā*—all-auspicious; *tat*—with her; *aṅga*—physical; *saṅga*—because of the contact; *stana*—from her breasts; *kuṅkuma*—having the *kuṅkuma; srajam*—a flower garland; *bāhvoḥ*—between His arms; *dadhānam*—wearing; *madhu*—springtime; *mallikā*—of jasmines; *āśritām*—composed; *tasyāḥ*—of her; *agre*—in the front; *āsīnam*—sitting; *avekṣya*—seeing; *vismitaḥ*—amazed.

TRANSLATION

Bāṇāsura saw before him Cupid's own son, possessed of unrivaled beauty, with dark-blue complexion, yellow garments, lotus eyes and formidable arms. His face was adorned with effulgent earrings and hair, and also with smiling glances. As He sat opposite His most auspicious lover, playing with her at dice, there hung between His arms a garland of spring jasmines that had been smeared with *kuṅkuma* powder from her breasts when He had embraced her. Bāṇāsura was astonished to see all this.

PURPORT

Bāṇāsura was amazed at Aniruddha's boldness: the prince was calmly sitting in the young girl's quarters, playing with Bāṇa's supposedly unmarried daughter! In the context of the strict Vedic culture, this was an unbelievable thing to witness.

TEXT 31

स तं प्रविष्टं वृतमाततायिभिर्
भटैरनीकैरवलोक्य माधवः ।
उद्यम्य मौर्वं परिघं व्यवस्थितो
यथान्तको दण्डधरो जिघांसया ॥३१॥

sa taṁ praviṣṭaṁ vṛtam ātatāyibhir
bhaṭair anīkair avalokya mādhavaḥ
udyamya maurvaṁ parighaṁ vyavasthito
yathāntako daṇḍa-dharo jighāṁsayā

saḥ—He, Aniruddha; *tam*—him, Bāṇāsura; *praviṣṭam*—entered; *vṛtam*—surrounded; *ātatāyibhiḥ*—who were carrying weapons; *bhaṭaiḥ*—by guards; *anīkaiḥ*—numerous; *avalokya*—seeing; *mādhavaḥ*—Aniruddha; *udyamya*—raising; *maurvam*—made of *muru* iron; *parigham*—His club; *vyavasthitaḥ*—standing firm; *yathā*—like; *antakaḥ*—death personified; *daṇḍa*—the rod of punishment; *dharaḥ*—bearing; *jighāṁsayā*—ready to strike.

TRANSLATION

Seeing Bāṇāsura enter with many armed guards, Aniruddha raised His iron club and stood resolute, ready to strike anyone who attacked Him. He resembled death personified holding his rod of punishment.

PURPORT

The club was not made of ordinary iron but of a special kind called *muru.*

TEXT 32

जिघृक्षया तान् परितः प्रसर्पतः
शुनो यथा शूकरयूथपोऽहनत् ।
ते हन्यमाना भवनाद्विनिर्गता
निर्भिन्नमूर्धोरुभुजाः प्रदुद्रुवुः ॥३२॥

jighṛkṣayā tān paritaḥ prasarpataḥ
śuno yathā śūkara-yūthapo 'hanat
te hanyamānā bhavanād vinirgatā
nirbhinna-mūrdhoru-bhujāḥ pradudruvuḥ

jighṛkṣayā—wanting to grab Him; *tān*—them; *paritaḥ*—on all sides; *prasarpataḥ*—approaching; *śunaḥ*—dogs; *yathā*—as; *śūkara*—of hogs; *yūtha*—of a group; *paḥ*—the leader; *ahanat*—He struck; *te*—they; *hanyamānāḥ*—being struck; *bhavanāt*—from the palace; *vinirgatāḥ*—went out; *nirbhinna*—broken; *mūrdha*—their heads; *ūru*—thighs; *bhujāḥ*—and arms; *pradudruvuḥ*—they fled.

TRANSLATION

As the guards converged on Him from all sides, trying to capture Him, Aniruddha struck them just as the leader of a pack of boars strikes back at dogs. Hit by His blows, the guards fled the palace, running for their lives with shattered heads, thighs and arms.

TEXT 33

तं नागपाशैर्बलिनन्दनो बली
घ्नन्तं स्वसैन्यं कुपितो बबन्ध ह ।
ऊषा भृशं शोकविषादविह्वला
बद्धं निशम्याश्रुकलाक्ष्यरौत्सीत् ॥३३॥

taṁ nāga-pāśair bali-nandano balī
ghnantaṁ sva-sainyaṁ kupito babandha ha
ūṣā bhṛśaṁ śoka-viṣāda-vihvalā
baddhaṁ niśamyāśru-kalākṣy arautsīt

tam—Him; *nāga-pāśaiḥ*—with the mystic *nāga* noose; *bali-nandanaḥ*—the son of Bali (Bāṇāsura); *balī*—powerful; *ghnantam*—as He was striking; *sva*—at his own; *sainyam*—army; *kupitaḥ*—angered; *babandha ha*—he captured; *Ūṣā*—Ūṣā; *bhṛśam*—extremely; *śoka*—by sorrow; *viṣāda*—and discouragement; *vihvalā*—overwhelmed; *baddham*—captured; *niśamya*—hearing; *aśru-kalā*—with teardrops; *akṣī*—in her eyes; *arautsīt*—cried.

TRANSLATION

But even as Aniruddha was striking down the army of Bāṇa, that powerful son of Bali angrily caught Him with the mystic *nāga-pāśa* ropes. When Ūṣā heard of Aniruddha's capture, she was overwhelmed with grief and depression; her eyes filled with tears, and she wept.

PURPORT

The *ācāryas* explain that Bāṇāsura could not actually capture the powerful grandson of Lord Kṛṣṇa. However, the Lord's *līlā-śakti,* or pastime potency, allowed this to happen so that the events described in the next chapter could take place.

Thus end the purports of the humble servants of His Divine Grace A. C. Bhaktivedanta Swami Prabhupāda to the Tenth Canto, Sixty-second Chapter, of the Śrīmad-Bhāgavatam, *entitled "The Meeting of Ūṣā and Aniruddha."*

CHAPTER SIXTY-THREE

Lord Kṛṣṇa Fights with Bāṇāsura

This chapter describes the battle between Lord Kṛṣṇa and Lord Śiva, as well as Śiva's glorification of Kṛṣṇa after the Lord had cut off Bāṇāsura's arms.

When Aniruddha did not return from Śoṇitapura, His family and friends passed the four months of the rainy season in extreme distress. When they finally heard from Nārada Muni how Aniruddha had been captured, a large army of the best Yādava warriors, under Kṛṣṇa's protection, set off for Bāṇāsura's capital and laid siege to it. Bāṇāsura fiercely opposed them with his own army of equal size. To help Bāṇāsura, Lord Śiva, accompanied by Kārtikeya and a horde of mystic sages, took up arms against Balarāma and Kṛṣṇa. Bāṇa began fighting against Sātyaki, and Bāṇa's son fought against Sāmba. All the demigods assembled in the sky to witness the battle. With His arrows Lord Kṛṣṇa harassed the followers of Lord Śiva, and by putting Lord Śiva into a state of confusion He was able to destroy Bāṇāsura's army. Kārtikeya was so strongly beaten by Pradyumna that he fled the battlefield, while the remnants of Bāṇāsura's army, harried by the blows of Lord Balarāma's club, scattered in all directions.

Enraged to see his army's destruction, Bāṇāsura rushed Kṛṣṇa to attack Him. But the Lord immediately killed Bāṇa's chariot driver and broke his chariot and bow, and then He sounded His Pāñcajanya conchshell. Next Bāṇāsura's mother, trying to save her son, appeared naked in front of Lord Kṛṣṇa, who averted His face to avoid looking at her. Seeing his chance, Bāṇa fled into his city.

After Lord Kṛṣṇa had thoroughly defeated the ghosts and hobgoblins fighting under Lord Śiva, the Śiva-jvara weapon—a personification of fever with three heads and three legs—approached Lord Kṛṣṇa to fight Him. Seeing the Śiva-jvara, Kṛṣṇa released His Viṣṇu-jvara. The Śiva-jvara was overwhelmed by the Viṣṇu-jvara; having nowhere else to turn for shelter, the Śiva-jvara began to address Lord Kṛṣṇa, glorifying Him and asking for mercy. Lord Kṛṣṇa was pleased with the Śiva-jvara, and after the Lord had promised him freedom from fear, the Śiva-jvara bowed down to Him and departed.

Next Bāṇāsura returned and attacked Lord Śrī Kṛṣṇa again, wielding all kinds of weapons in his thousand hands. But Lord Kṛṣṇa took His Sudarśana disc and began cutting off all the demon's arms. Lord Śiva approached Kṛṣṇa to pray for Bāṇāsura's life, and when the Lord agreed to spare him, He spoke as follows to Śiva: "Bāṇāsura does not deserve to die, since he was born in the family of Prahlāda Mahārāja. I have severed all but four of Bāṇa's arms just to destroy his false pride, and I have annihilated his army because they were a burden to the earth. Henceforward he will be free from old age and death, and remaining fearless in all circumstances, he will be one of your principal attendants."

Assured he had nothing to fear, Bāṇāsura then offered his obeisances to Lord Kṛṣṇa and had Ūṣā and Aniruddha seated on their wedding chariot and brought before the Lord. Kṛṣṇa then set off for Dvārakā with Aniruddha and His bride leading the procession. When the newlyweds arrived at the Lord's capital, they were honored by the citizens, the Lord's relatives and the *brāhmaṇas.*

TEXT 1

श्रीशुक उवाच

अपश्यतां चानिरुद्धं तद्बन्धूनां च भारत ।
चत्वारो वार्षिका मासा व्यतीयुरनुशोचताम् ॥१॥

śrī-śuka uvāca
apaśyatāṁ cāniruddhaṁ
tad-bandhūnāṁ ca bhārata
catvāro vārṣikā māsā
vyatīyur anuśocatām

śrī-śukaḥ uvāca—Śukadeva Gosvāmī said; *apaśyatām*—who did not see; *ca*—and; *aniruddham*—Aniruddha; *tat*—His; *bandhūnām*—for the relatives; *ca*—and; *bhārata*—O descendant of Bharata (Parīkṣit Mahārāja); *catvāraḥ*—four; *vārṣikāḥ*—of the rainy season; *māsāḥ*—the months; *vyatīyuḥ*—passed; *anuśocatām*—who were lamenting.

TRANSLATION

Śukadeva Gosvāmī said: O descendant of Bharata, the relatives of Aniruddha, not seeing Him return, continued to lament as the four rainy months passed.

TEXT 2

नारदात्तदुपाकर्ण्य वार्तां बद्धस्य कर्म च ।
प्रययुः शोणितपुरं वृष्णयः कृष्णदैवताः ॥२॥

nāradāt tad upākarṇya
vārtāṁ baddhasya karma ca
prayayuḥ śoṇita-puraṁ
vṛṣṇayaḥ kṛṣṇa-daivatāḥ

nāradāt—from Nārada; *tat*—that; *upākarṇya*—hearing; *vārtām*—news; *baddhasya*—about Him who was captured; *karma*—actions; *ca*—and; *prayayuḥ*—they went; *śoṇita-puram*—to Śoṇitapura; *vṛṣṇayaḥ*—the Vṛṣṇis; *kṛṣṇa*—Lord Kṛṣṇa; *daivatāḥ*—having as their worshipable Deity.

TRANSLATION

After hearing from Nārada the news of Aniruddha's deeds and His capture, the Vṛṣṇis, who worshiped Lord Kṛṣṇa as their personal Deity, went to Śoṇitapura.

TEXTS 3–4

प्रद्युम्नो युयुधानश्च गदः साम्बोऽथ सारणः ।
नन्दोपनन्दभद्राद्या रामकृष्णानुवर्तिनः ॥३॥
अक्षौहिणीभिर्द्वादशभिः समेताः सर्वतो दिशम् ।
रुरुधुर्बाणनगरं समन्तात्सात्वतर्षभाः ॥४॥

pradyumno yuyudhānaś ca
gadaḥ sāmbo 'tha sāraṇaḥ
nandopananda-bhadrādyā
rāma-kṛṣṇānuvartinaḥ

akṣauhiṇībhir dvādaśabhiḥ
sametāḥ sarvato diśam
rurudhur bāṇa-nagaraṁ
samantāt sātvatarṣabhāḥ

pradyumnaḥ yuyudhānaḥ ca—Pradyumna and Yuyudhāna (Sātyaki); *gadaḥ sāmbaḥ atha sāraṇaḥ*—Gada, Sāmba and Sāraṇa; *nanda-upananda-bhadra*—Nanda, Upananda and Bhadra; *ādyāḥ*—and others; *rāma-kṛṣṇa-anuvartinaḥ*—following Balarāma and Kṛṣṇa; *akṣauhiṇībhiḥ*—with military divisions; *dvādaśabhiḥ*—twelve; *sametāḥ*—assembled; *sarvataḥ diśam*—on all sides; *rurudhuḥ*—they besieged; *bāṇa-nagaram*—Bāṇāsura's city; *samantāt*—totally; *sātvata-ṛṣabhāḥ*—the chiefs of the Sātvatas.

TRANSLATION

With Lord Balarāma and Lord Kṛṣṇa in the lead, the chiefs of the Sātvata clan—Pradyumna, Sātyaki, Gada, Sāmba, Sāraṇa, Nanda, Upananda, Bhadra and others—converged with an army of twelve divisions and laid siege to Bāṇāsura's capital, completely surrounding the city on all sides.

TEXT 5

भज्यमानपुरोद्यानप्राकाराट्टालगोपुरम् ।
प्रेक्षमाणो रुषाविष्टस्तुल्यसैन्योऽभिनिर्ययौ ॥५॥

bhajyamāna-purodyāna-
prākārāṭṭāla-gopuram
prekṣamāṇo ruṣāviṣṭas
tulya-sainyo 'bhiniryayau

bhajyamāna—being broken; *pura*—of the city; *udyāna*—the gardens; *prākāra*—elevated walls; *aṭṭāla*—watchtowers; *gopuram*—and gateways;

prekṣamāṇaḥ—seeing; *ruṣā*—with anger; *āviṣṭaḥ*—filled; *tulya*—equal; *sainyaḥ*—with an army; *abhiniryayau*—went out toward them.

TRANSLATION

Bāṇāsura became filled with anger upon seeing them destroy his city's suburban gardens, ramparts, watchtowers and gateways, and thus he went out to confront them with an army of equal size.

TEXT 6

बाणार्थे भगवान् रुद्रः ससुतः प्रमथैर्वृतः ।
आरुह्य नन्दिवृषभं युयुधे रामकृष्णयोः ॥६॥

bāṇārthe bhagavān rudraḥ
sa-sutaḥ pramathair vṛtaḥ
āruhya nandi-vṛṣabhaṁ
yuyudhe rāma-kṛṣṇayoḥ

bāṇa-arthe—for Bāṇa's sake; *bhagavān rudraḥ*—Lord Śiva; *sa-sutaḥ*—together with his son (Kārtikeya, the general of the demigods' army); *pramathaiḥ*—by the Pramathas (mystic sages who always attend Lord Śiva, appearing in a multitude of forms); *vṛtaḥ*—accompanied; *āruhya*—riding; *nandi*—on Nandi; *vṛṣabham*—his bull; *yuyudhe*—he fought; *rāma-kṛṣṇayoḥ*—with Balarāma and Kṛṣṇa.

TRANSLATION

Lord Rudra, accompanied by his son Kārtikeya and the Pramathas, came riding on Nandi, his bull carrier, to fight Balarāma and Kṛṣṇa on Bāṇa's behalf.

PURPORT

Śrīla Śrīdhara Svāmī states that the word *bhagavān* is used here to indicate that Lord Śiva is by nature all-knowing and thus well aware of Lord Kṛṣṇa's greatness. Still, although Śiva knew Lord Kṛṣṇa would defeat him, he joined the battle against Him to demonstrate the glories of the Supreme Personality of Godhead.

Śrīla Viśvanātha Cakravartī Ṭhākura states that Lord Śiva entered the battle for two reasons: first, to increase Lord Kṛṣṇa's pleasure and enthusiasm; and second, to demonstrate that the Lord's incarnation as Kṛṣṇa, although enacting humanlike pastimes, is superior to other *avatāras*, such as Lord Rāmacandra. Śrīla Viśvanātha Cakravartī further states in this regard that Yogamāyā, Lord Kṛṣṇa's internal potency, bewildered Lord Śiva just as she had bewildered Brahmā. In support of this statement, the *ācārya* cites the phrase *brahma-rudrādi-mohanam* from *Bhakti-rasāmṛta-sindhu*. Of course, Yogamāyā's job is to make fine arrangements for the Lord's pastimes, and thus Śiva became enthusiastic to battle the Supreme Lord, Kṛṣṇa.

TEXT 7

आसीत्सुतुमुलं युद्धमद्भुतं रोमहर्षणम् ।
कृष्णशंकरयो राजन् प्रद्युम्नगुहयोरपि ॥७॥

āsīt su-tumulaṁ yuddham
adbhutaṁ roma-harṣaṇam
kṛṣṇa-śaṅkarayo rājan
pradyumna-guhayor api

āsīt—there occurred; *su-tumulam*—very tumultuous; *yuddham*—a fight; *adbhutam*—astonishing; *roma-harṣaṇam*—causing bodily hair to stand on end; *kṛṣṇa-śaṅkarayoḥ*—between Lord Kṛṣṇa and Lord Śiva; *rājan*—O King (Parīkṣit); *pradyumna-guhayoḥ*—between Pradyumna and Kārtikeya; *api*—also.

TRANSLATION

A most astonishing, tumultuous and hair-raising battle then commenced, with Lord Kṛṣṇa matched against Lord Śaṅkara, and Pradyumna against Kārtikeya.

TEXT 8

कुम्भाण्डकूपकर्णाभ्यां बलेन सह संयुगः ।
साम्बस्य बाणपुत्रेण बाणेन सह सात्यकेः ॥८॥

kumbhāṇḍa-kūpakarṇābhyāṁ
balena saha saṁyugaḥ
sāmbasya bāṇa-putreṇa
bāṇena saha sātyakeḥ

kumbhāṇḍa-kūpakarṇābhyām—by Kumbhāṇḍa and Kūpakarṇa; *balena saha*—with Lord Balarāma; *saṁyugaḥ*—a fight; *sāmbasya*—of Sāmba; *bāṇa-putreṇa*—with the son of Bāṇa; *bāṇena saha*—with Bāṇa; *sātyakeḥ*—of Sātyaki.

TRANSLATION

Lord Balarāma fought with Kumbhāṇḍa and Kūpakarṇa, Sāmba with Bāṇa's son, and Sātyaki with Bāṇa.

TEXT 9

ब्रह्मादयः सुराधीशा मुनयः सिद्धचारणाः ।
गन्धर्वाप्सरसो यक्षा विमानैर्द्रष्टुमागमन् ॥९॥

brahmādayaḥ surādhīśā
munayaḥ siddha-cāraṇāḥ
gandharvāpsaraso yakṣā
vimānair draṣṭum āgaman

brahma-ādayaḥ—headed by Lord Brahmā; *sura*—of the demigods; *adhīśāḥ*—the rulers; *munayaḥ*—great sages; *siddha-cāraṇāḥ*—the Siddha and Cāraṇa demigods; *gandharva-apsarasaḥ*—the Gandharvas and Apsarās; *yakṣāḥ*—the Yakṣas; *vimānaiḥ*—in airplanes; *draṣṭum*—to see; *āgaman*—came.

TRANSLATION

Brahmā and the other ruling demigods, along with Siddhas, Cāraṇas and great sages, as well as Gandharvas, Apsarās and Yakṣas, all came in their celestial airplanes to watch.

TEXTS 10–11

शंकरानुचरान् शौरिर्भूतप्रमथगुह्यकान् ।
डाकिनीर्यातुधानांश्च वेतालान् सविनायकान् ॥१०॥
प्रेतमातृपिशाचांश्च कुष्माण्डान् ब्रह्मराक्षसान् ।
द्रावयामास तीक्ष्णाग्रैः शरैः शार्ङ्गधनुश्च्युतैः ॥११॥

śaṅkarānucarān śaurir
bhūta-pramatha-guhyakān
ḍākinīr yātudhānāṁś ca
vetālān sa-vināyakān

preta-mātṛ-piśācāṁś ca
kuṣmāṇḍān brahma-rākṣasān
drāvayām āsa tīkṣṇāgraiḥ
śaraiḥ śārṅga-dhanuś-cyutaiḥ

śaṅkara—of Lord Śiva; *anucarān*—the followers; *śauriḥ*—Lord Kṛṣṇa; *bhūta-pramatha*—Bhūtas and Pramathas; *guhyakān*—Guhyakas (servants of Kuvera who help him guard the treasury of heaven); *ḍākinīḥ*—female demons who attend Goddess Kālī; *yātudhānān*—man-eating demons, also known as Rākṣasas; *ca*—and; *vetālān*—vampires; *sa-vināyakān*—together with Vināyakas; *preta*—ghosts; *mātṛ*—maternal demons; *piśācān*—meat-eating demons who live in the middle regions of outer space; *ca*—also; *kuṣmāṇḍān*—followers of Lord Śiva who engage in breaking the meditation of *yogīs; brahma-rākṣasān*—the demoniac spirits of *brāhmaṇas* who have died sinfully; *drāvayām āsa*—He drove away; *tīkṣṇa-agraiḥ*—sharp-pointed; *śaraiḥ*—with His arrows; *śārṅga-dhanuḥ*—from His bow, named Śārṅga; *cyutaiḥ*—discharged.

TRANSLATION

With sharp-pointed arrows discharged from His bow Śārṅga, Lord Kṛṣṇa drove away the various followers of Lord Śiva—Bhūtas, Pramathas, Guhyakas, Ḍākinīs, Yātudhānas, Vetālas, Vināyakas, Pretas, Mātās, Piśācas, Kuṣmāṇḍas and Brahma-rākṣasas.

TEXT 12

पृथग्विधानि प्रायुंक्त पिणाक्यस्त्राणि शार्गिणे ।
प्रत्यस्त्रैः शमयामास शांर्गपाणिरविस्मितः ॥१२॥

pṛthag-vidhāni prāyuṅkta
piṇāky astrāṇi śārṅgiṇe
praty-astraiḥ śamayām āsa
śārṅga-pāṇir avismitaḥ

pṛthak-vidhāni—of various kinds; *prāyuṅkta*—engaged; *piṇākī*—Lord Śiva, the holder of the trident; *astrāṇi*—weapons; *śārṅgiṇe*—against Lord Kṛṣṇa, the holder of Śārṅga; *prati-astraiḥ*—with counterweapons; *śamayām āsa*—neutralized them; *śārṅga-pāṇiḥ*—the carrier of Śārṅga; *avismitaḥ*—not perplexed.

TRANSLATION

Lord Śiva, wielder of the trident, shot various weapons at Lord Kṛṣṇa, wielder of Śārṅga. But Lord Kṛṣṇa was not in the least perplexed: He neutralized all these weapons with appropriate counterweapons.

TEXT 13

ब्रह्मास्त्रस्य च ब्रह्मास्त्रं वायव्यस्य च पार्वतम् ।
आग्नेयस्य च पार्जन्यं नैजं पाशुपतस्य च ॥१३॥

brahmāstrasya ca brahmāstraṁ
vāyavyasya ca pārvatam
āgneyasya ca pārjanyaṁ
naijaṁ pāśupatasya ca

brahma-astrasya—of the *brahmāstra; ca*—and; *brahma-astram*—a *brahmāstra; vāyavyasya*—of the wind weapon; *ca*—and; *pārvatam*—a mountain weapon; *āgneyasya*—of the fire weapon; *ca*—and; *pārjanyam*—a rain weapon; *naijam*—His own weapon (the *nārāyaṇāstra*); *pāśupatasya*—of Lord Śiva's own *pāśupatāstra; ca*—and.

TRANSLATION

Lord Kṛṣṇa counteracted a *brahmāstra* with another *brahmāstra,* a wind weapon with a mountain weapon, a fire weapon with a rain weapon, and Lord Śiva's personal *pāśupatāstra* weapon with His own personal weapon, the *nārāyaṇāstra.*

TEXT 14

मोहयित्वा तु गिरिशं जृम्भणास्त्रेण जृम्भितम् ।
बाणस्य पृतनां शौरिर्जघानासिगदेषुभिः ॥१४॥

mohayitvā tu giriśaṁ
jṛmbhaṇāstreṇa jṛmbhitam
bāṇasya pṛtanāṁ śaurir
jaghānāsi-gadeṣubhiḥ

mohayitvā—bewildering; *tu*—then; *giriśam*—Lord Śiva; *jṛmbhaṇa-astreṇa*—with a yawning weapon; *jṛmbhitam*—made to yawn; *bāṇasya*—of Bāṇa; *pṛtanām*—the army; *śauriḥ*—Lord Kṛṣṇa; *jaghāna*—struck; *asi*—with His sword; *gadā*—club; *iṣubhiḥ*—and arrows.

TRANSLATION

After bewildering Lord Śiva by making him yawn with a yawning weapon, Lord Kṛṣṇa proceeded to strike down Bāṇāsura's army with His sword, club and arrows.

TEXT 15

स्कन्दः प्रद्युम्नबाणौघैरर्द्यमानः समन्ततः ।
असृग् विमुञ्चन् गात्रेभ्यः शिखिनापाक्रमद् रणात् ॥१५॥

skandaḥ pradyumna-bāṇaughair
ardyamānaḥ samantataḥ
asṛg vimuñcan gātrebhyaḥ
śikhināpākramad raṇāt

skandaḥ—Kārtikeya; *pradyumna-bāṇa*—of Pradyumna's arrows; *oghaiḥ*—by the torrents; *ardyamānaḥ*—distressed; *samantataḥ*—on all sides; *asṛk*—blood; *vimuñcan*—exuding; *gātrebhyaḥ*—from his limbs; *śikhinā*—on his peacock carrier; *apākramat*—went away; *raṇāt*—from the battlefield.

TRANSLATION

Lord Kārtikeya was distressed by the flood of Pradyumna's arrows raining down from all sides, and thus he fled the battlefield on his peacock as blood poured from his limbs.

TEXT 16

कुम्भाण्डकूपकर्णश्च पेततुर्मुषलार्दितौ ।
दुद्रुवुस्तदनीकानि हतनाथानि सर्वतः ॥१६॥

kumbhāṇḍa-kūpakarṇaś ca
petatur muṣalārditau
dudruvus tad-anīkāni
hata-nāthāni sarvataḥ

kumbhāṇḍa-kūpakarṇaḥ ca—Kumbhāṇḍa and Kūpakarṇa; *petatuḥ*—fell; *muṣala*—by the club (of Lord Balarāma); *arditau*—distressed; *dudruvuḥ*—fled; *tat*—their; *anīkāni*—armies; *hata*—killed; *nāthāni*—whose leaders; *sarvataḥ*—in all directions.

TRANSLATION

Kumbhāṇḍa and Kūpakarṇa, tormented by Lord Balarāma's club, fell down dead. When the soldiers of these two demons saw that their leaders had been killed, they scattered in all directions.

TEXT 17

विशीर्यमाणं स्वबलं दृष्ट्वा बाणोऽत्यमर्षितः ।
कृष्णमभ्यद्रवत्संख्ये रथी हित्वैव सात्यकिम् ॥१७॥

viśīryamāṇaṁ sva-balaṁ
dṛṣṭvā bāṇo 'ty-amarṣitaḥ
kṛṣṇam abhyadravat saṅkhye
rathī hitvaiva sātyakim

viśīryamāṇam—being torn apart; *sva*—his; *balam*—military force; *dṛṣṭvā*—seeing; *bāṇaḥ*—Bāṇāsura; *ati*—extremely; *amarṣitaḥ*—infuriated; *kṛṣṇam*—Lord Kṛṣṇa; *abhyadravat*—he attacked; *saṅkhye*—on the battlefield; *rathī*—riding on his chariot; *hitvā*—leaving aside; *eva*—indeed; *sātyakim*—Sātyaki.

TRANSLATION

Bāṇāsura was furious to see his entire military force being torn apart. Leaving his fight with Sātyaki, he charged across the battlefield on his chariot and attacked Lord Kṛṣṇa.

TEXT 18

धनूंष्याकृष्य युगपद् बाणः पञ्चशतानि वै ।
एकैकस्मिन् शरौ द्वौ द्वौ सन्दधे रणदुर्मदः ॥१८॥

dhanūṁṣy ākṛṣya yugapad
bāṇaḥ pañca-śatāni vai
ekaikasmin śarau dvau dvau
sandadhe raṇa-durmadaḥ

dhanūṁṣi—bows; *ākṛṣya*—pulling back; *yugapat*—simultaneously; *bāṇaḥ*—Bāṇa; *pañca-śatāni*—five hundred; *vai*—indeed; *eka-ekasmin*—upon each one; *śarau*—arrows; *dvau dvau*—two for each; *sandadhe*—he fixed; *raṇa*—due to the fighting; *durmadaḥ*—mad with pride.

TRANSLATION

Excited to a frenzy by the fighting, Bāṇa simultaneously pulled taut all the strings of his five hundred bows and fixed two arrows on each string.

TEXT 19

तानि चिच्छेद भगवान् धनूंषि युगपद्धरिः ।
सारथिं रथमश्वांश्च हत्वा शंखमपूरयत् ॥१९॥

tāni ciccheda bhagavān
dhanūṁṣi yugapad dhariḥ
sārathiṁ ratham aśvāṁś ca
hatvā śaṅkham apūrayat

tāni—these; *ciccheda*—split; *bhagavān*—the Supreme Lord; *dhanūṁṣi*—bows; *yugapat*—all at once; *hariḥ*—Śrī Kṛṣṇa; *sārathim*—the chariot driver; *ratham*—the chariot; *aśvān*—the horses; *ca*—and; *hatvā*—after hitting; *śaṅkham*—His conchshell; *apūrayat*—He filled.

TRANSLATION

Lord Śrī Hari split every one of Bāṇāsura's bows simultaneously, and also struck down his chariot driver, chariot and horses. The Lord then sounded His conchshell.

TEXT 20

तन्माता कोटरा नाम नग्ना मुक्तशिरोरुहा ।
पुरोऽवतस्थे कृष्णस्य पुत्रप्राणरिरक्षया ॥२०॥

tan-mātā koṭarā nāma
nagnā mukta-śiroruhā
puro 'vatasthe kṛṣṇasya
putra-prāṇa-rirakṣayā

tat—his (Bāṇāsura's); *mātā*—mother; *koṭarā nāma*—named Koṭarā; *nagnā*—naked; *mukta*—loosened; *śiraḥ-ruhā*—her hair; *puraḥ*—in front; *avatasthe*—stood; *kṛṣṇasya*—of Kṛṣṇa; *putra*—her son's; *prāṇa*—life; *rirakṣayā*—hoping to save.

TRANSLATION

Just then Bāṇāsura's mother, Koṭarā, desiring to save her son's life, appeared before Lord Kṛṣṇa naked and with her hair undone.

TEXT 21

ततस्तिर्यङ्मुखो नग्नामनिरीक्षन् गदाग्रजः ।
बाणश्च तावद्विरथश्छिन्नधन्वाविशत्पुरम् ॥२१॥

tatas tiryaṅ-mukho nagnām
anirīkṣan gadāgrajaḥ
bāṇaś ca tāvad virathaś
chinna-dhanvāviśat puram

tataḥ—then; *tiryak*—turned away; *mukhaḥ*—His face; *nagnām*—the naked woman; *anirīkṣan*—not looking at; *gadāgrajaḥ*—Lord Kṛṣṇa; *bāṇaḥ*—Bāṇa; *ca*—and; *tāvat*—with that opportunity; *virathaḥ*—deprived of his chariot; *chinna*—broken; *dhanvā*—his bow; *āviśat*—entered; *puram*—the city.

TRANSLATION

Lord Gadāgraja turned His face away to avoid seeing the naked woman, and Bāṇāsura—deprived of his chariot, his bow shattered—took the opportunity to flee into his city.

TEXT 22

विद्राविते भूतगणे ज्वरस्तु त्रिशिरास्त्रिपात् ।
अभ्यधावत दाशार्हं दहन्निव दिशो दश ॥२२॥

vidrāvite bhūta-gaṇe
jvaras tu tri-śirās tri-pāt
abhyadhāvata dāśārhaṁ
dahann iva diśo daśa

vidrāvite—having been driven away; *bhūta-gaṇe*—all the followers of Lord Śiva; *jvaraḥ*—the personification of fever who serves him, Lord Śiva; *tu*—but; *tri*—three; *śirāḥ*—having heads; *tri*—three; *pāt*—having feet; *abhyadhāvata*—ran toward; *dāśārham*—Lord Kṛṣṇa; *dahan*—burning; *iva*—as if it were; *diśaḥ*—the directions; *daśa*—ten.

TRANSLATION

After Lord Śiva's followers had been driven away, the Śiva-jvara, who had three heads and three feet, pressed forward to attack Lord Kṛṣṇa. As the Śiva-jvara approached, he seemed to burn everything in the ten directions.

PURPORT

Śrīla Viśvanātha Cakravartī quotes the following description of the Śiva-jvara:

jvaras tri-padas tri-śirāḥ
ṣaḍ-bhujo nava-locanaḥ
bhasma-praharaṇo raudraḥ
kālāntaka-yamopamaḥ

"The terrible Śiva-jvara had three legs, three heads, six arms and nine eyes. Showering ashes, he resembled Yamarāja at the time of universal annihilation."

TEXT 23

अथ नारायणः देवः तं दृष्ट्वा व्यसृजज्ज्वरम् ।
माहेश्वरो वैष्णवश्च युयुधाते ज्वरावुभौ ॥२३॥

atha nārāyaṇaḥ devaḥ
taṁ dṛṣṭvā vyasṛjaj jvaram
māheśvaro vaiṣṇavaś ca
yuyudhāte jvarāv ubhau

atha—thereupon; *nārāyaṇaḥ devaḥ*—Lord Nārāyaṇa (Kṛṣṇa); *tam*—him (the Śiva-jvara); *dṛṣṭvā*—seeing; *vyasṛjat*—released; *jvaram*—His personified fever (of extreme cold, as opposed to the extreme heat of the Śiva-jvara); *māheśvaraḥ*—of Lord Maheśvara; *vaiṣṇavaḥ*—of Lord Viṣṇu; *ca*—and; *yuyudhāte*—fought; *jvarau*—the two fevers; *ubhau*—against each other.

TRANSLATION

Seeing this personified weapon approach, Lord Nārāyaṇa then released His own personified fever weapon, the Viṣṇu-jvara. The Śiva-jvara and Viṣṇu-jvara thus battled each other.

TEXT 24

माहेश्वरः समाक्रन्दन् वैष्णवेन बलार्दितः ।
अलब्ध्वाभयमन्यत्र भीतो माहेश्वरो ज्वरः ।
शरणार्थी हृषीकेशं तुष्टाव प्रयताञ्जलिः ॥२४॥

māheśvaraḥ samākrandan
vaiṣṇavena balārditaḥ
alabdhvābhayam anyatra
bhīto māheśvaro jvaraḥ
śaraṇārthī hṛṣīkeśaṁ
tuṣṭāva prayatāñjaliḥ

māheśvaraḥ—(the fever weapon) of Lord Śiva; *samākrandan*—crying out; *vaiṣṇavena*—of the Vaiṣṇava-jvara; *bala*—by the strength; *arditaḥ*—tormented; *alabdhvā*—not obtaining; *abhayam*—fearlessness; *anyatra*—elsewhere; *bhītaḥ*—frightened; *māheśvaraḥ jvaraḥ*—the Māheśvara-jvara; *śaraṇa*—for shelter; *arthī*—hankering; *hṛṣīkeśam*—Lord Kṛṣṇa, the master of everyone's senses; *tuṣṭāva*—he praised; *prayata-añjaliḥ*—with palms joined in supplication.

TRANSLATION

The Śiva-jvara, overwhelmed by the strength of the Viṣṇu-jvara, cried out in pain. But finding no refuge, the frightened Śiva-jvara approached Lord Kṛṣṇa, the master of the senses, hoping to attain His shelter. Thus with joined palms he began to praise the Lord.

PURPORT

As pointed out by Śrīla Viśvanātha Cakravartī, it is significant that the Śiva-jvara had to leave the side of his master, Lord Śiva, and directly take shelter of the Supreme Personality of Godhead, Lord Kṛṣṇa.

TEXT 25

ज्वर उवाच
नमामि त्वानन्तशक्तिं परेशं
सर्वात्मानं केवलं ज्ञप्तिमात्रम् ।
विश्वोत्पत्तिस्थानसंरोधहेतुं
यत्तद् ब्रह्म ब्रह्मलिंगं प्रशान्तम् ॥२५॥

jvara uvāca
namāmi tvānanta-śaktiṁ pareśaṁ
sarvātmānaṁ kevalaṁ jñapti-mātram
viśvotpatti-sthāna-saṁrodha-hetuṁ
yat tad brahma brahma-liṅgaṁ praśāntam

jvaraḥ uvāca—the fever weapon (of Lord Śiva) said; *namāmi*—I bow down; *tvā*—to You; *ananta*—unlimited; *śaktim*—whose potencies; *para*—Supreme; *īśam*—the Lord; *sarva*—of all; *ātmānam*—the Soul; *kevalam*—pure; *jñapti*—of consciousness; *mātram*—the totality; *viśva*—of the universe; *utpatti*—of the creation; *sthāna*—maintenance; *saṁrodha*—and dissolution; *hetum*—the cause; *yat*—which; *tat*—that; *brahma*—Absolute Truth; *brahma*—by the *Vedas; liṅgam*—indirect reference to whom; *praśāntam*—perfectly peaceful.

TRANSLATION

The Śiva-jvara said: I bow down to You of unlimited potencies, the Supreme Lord, the Supersoul of all beings. You possess pure and complete consciousness and are the cause of cosmic creation, maintenance and dissolution. Perfectly peaceful, You are the Absolute Truth to whom the *Vedas* indirectly refer.

PURPORT

Previously the Śiva-jvara felt himself to be unlimitedly powerful and thus attempted to burn Śrī Kṛṣṇa. But now he himself has been burned, and understanding that Śrī Kṛṣṇa is the Supreme Lord, he humbly approaches to bow down and offer praise to the Absolute Truth.

According to the *ācāryas*, the word *sarvātmānam* indicates that Lord Śrī Kṛṣṇa is the Supersoul, the giver of consciousness to all living beings. Kṛṣṇa confirms this in the *Bhagavad-gītā* (15.15): *mataḥ smṛtir jñānam apohanaṁ ca.* "From Me come remembrance, knowledge and forgetfulness."

In his commentary Śrīla Viśvanātha Cakravartī emphasizes that the Śiva-jvara has realized in many ways Lord Kṛṣṇa's supremacy over his own master, Lord Śiva. Thus the Śiva-jvara addresses Kṛṣṇa as *ananta-śakti,* "possessor of unlimited potency"; *pareśa,* "the supreme controller"; and *sarvātmā,* "the Supersoul of all beings"—even of Lord Śiva.

The words *kevalaṁ jñapti-mātram* indicate that Lord Kṛṣṇa possesses pure omniscience. According to our limited understanding, we act in this world, but Lord Kṛṣṇa, with His unlimited understanding, performs infinite works of creation, maintenance and annihilation. As Śrīla Jīva Gosvāmī points out, even the functions of the gross elements, such as air, depend on Him. The *Taittirīya Upaniṣad* (2.8.1) confirms this: *bhīṣāsmād vātaḥ pavate.* "Out of fear of Him, the wind blows." Thus Lord Śrī Kṛṣṇa is the ultimate object of worship for all living beings.

TEXT 26

कालो दैवं कर्म जीवः स्वभावो
द्रव्यं क्षेत्रं प्राण आत्मा विकारः ।
तत्सङ्घातो बीजरोहप्रवाहस्
त्वन्मायैषा तन्निषेधं प्रपद्ये ॥२६॥

kālo daivaṁ karma jīvaḥ svabhāvo
dravyaṁ kṣetraṁ prāṇa ātmā vikāraḥ
tat-saṅghāto bīja-roha-pravāhas
tvan-māyaiṣā tan-niṣedhaṁ prapadye

kālaḥ—time; *daivam*—destiny; *karma*—the reactions of material work; *jīvaḥ*—the individual living entity; *svabhāvaḥ*—his propensities; *dravyam*—the subtle forms of matter; *kṣetram*—the body; *prāṇaḥ*—the life air; *ātmā*—the false ego; *vikāraḥ*—the transformations (of the eleven senses); *tat*—of all this; *saṅghātaḥ*—the aggregate (as the subtle body); *bīja*—of seed; *roha*—and sprout; *pravāhaḥ*—the constant flow; *tvat*—Your; *māyā*—material illusory energy; *eṣā*—this; *tat*—of it; *niṣedham*—the negation (You); *prapadye*—I am approaching for shelter.

TRANSLATION

Time; fate; *karma;* the *jīva* and his propensities; the subtle material elements; the material body; the life air; false ego; the various senses; and the totality of these as reflected in the living being's subtle body—all this constitutes your material illusory energy, *māyā,* an endless cycle like that of seed and plant. I take shelter of You, the negation of this *māyā.*

PURPORT

The word *bīja-roha-pravāha* is explained as follows: The conditioned soul accepts a material body, with which he attempts to enjoy the material world. That body is the seed (*bīja*) of future material existence because when a person acts with that body he creates further reactions (*karma*), which grow (*roha*) into the obligation to accept another material body. In other words, material life is a chain of actions and reactions. The simple decision to surrender to the Supreme Lord releases the conditioned soul from this futile repetition of material growth and reaction.

According to Śrīla Śrīdhara Svāmī, the words *tan-niṣedhaṁ prapadye* indicate that the Supreme Personality of Godhead, Lord Kṛṣṇa, is *niṣedhāvadhi-bhūtam,* "the limit of negation." In other words, after all illusion is negated, the Absolute Truth remains.

The process of education may be succinctly described as a way of eradicating ignorance through the attainment of knowledge. Through inductive, deductive and intuitive means, we attempt to refute the specious, the illusory and the imperfect and elevate ourselves to a platform of full knowledge. Ultimately, when all illusion is negated, that which remains firmly in place is the Absolute Truth, the Supreme Personality of Godhead.

In the previous text, the Śiva-jvara described the Supreme Lord as *sarvātmānaṁ kevalaṁ jñapti-mātram,* "pure, concentrated spiritual consciousness." Now the Śiva-jvara concludes his philosophical description of the Lord by saying in this text that the various aspects of material existence are also potencies of the Supreme Lord.

Śrīla Viśvanātha Cakravartī mentions that the Supreme Lord's own body and senses, as implied here by the word *tan-niṣedham,* are nondifferent from the Lord's pure spiritual existence. The Lord's body and senses are not external to Him, nor do they cover Him, but rather the Lord is identical with His spiritual form and senses. The full Absolute Truth, unlimited in fascinating diversity, is Lord Śrī Kṛṣṇa.

TEXT 27

नानाभावैर्लीलयैवोपपन्नैर्
देवान् साधून् लोकसेतून् बिभर्षि ।
हंस्युन्मार्गान् हिंसया वर्तमानान्
जन्मैतत्ते भारहाराय भूमेः ॥२७॥

nānā-bhāvair līlayaivopapannair
devān sādhūn loka-setūn bibharṣi
haṁsy unmārgān hiṁsayā vartamānān
janmaitat te bhāra-hārāya bhūmeḥ

nānā—various; *bhāvaiḥ*—with intentions; *līlayā*—as pastimes; *eva*—indeed; *upapannaiḥ*—assumed; *devān*—the demigods; *sādhūn*—the saintly sages; *loka*—of the world; *setūn*—the codes of religion; *bibharṣi*—You maintain; *haṁsi*—You kill; *ut-mārgān*—those who stray beyond the path; *hiṁsayā*—by violence; *vartamānān*—living; *janma*—birth; *etat*—this; *te*—Your; *bhāra*—the burden; *hārāya*—to relieve; *bhūmeḥ*—of the earth.

TRANSLATION

With various intentions, You perform pastimes to maintain the demigods, the saintly persons and the codes of religion for this world. By these pastimes You also kill those who stray from the

right path and live by violence. Indeed, your present incarnation is meant to relieve the earth's burden.

PURPORT

As Lord Kṛṣṇa states in the *Bhagavad-gītā* (9.29),

samo 'haṁ sarva-bhūteṣu
na me dveṣyo 'sti na priyaḥ
ye bhajanti tu māṁ bhaktyā
mayi te teṣu cāpy aham

"I envy no one, nor am I partial to anyone. I am equal to all. But whoever renders service unto Me in devotion is a friend—is in Me—and I am also a friend to him."

The demigods and sages (*devān sādhūn*) are dedicated to executing the will of the Supreme Lord. The demigods act as cosmic administrators, and the sages, by their teachings and their good example, illumine the path of self-realization and holiness. But those who transgress the natural law, the law of God, and live by committing violence against others are vanquished by the Supreme Lord in His various pastime incarnations. As the Lord states in the *Bhagavad-gītā* (4.11), *ye yathā māṁ prapadyante tāṁs tathaiva bhajāmy aham.* He is impartial, but He responds appropriately to the actions of the living beings.

TEXT 28

तप्तोऽहं ते तेजसा दुःसहेन
शान्तोग्रेणात्युल्बणेन ज्वरेण ।
तावत्तापो देहिनां तेऽङ्घ्रिमूलं
नो सेवेरन् यावदाशानुबद्धाः ॥२८॥

tapto 'haṁ te tejasā duḥsahena
śāntogreṇāty-ulbaṇena jvareṇa
tāvat tāpo dehināṁ te 'ṅghri-mūlaṁ
no severan yāvad āśānubaddhāḥ

taptaḥ—burned; *aham*—I; *te*—Your; *tejasā*—by the power; *duḥsahena*—insufferable; *śānta*—cold; *ugreṇa*—yet burning; *ati*—extremely; *ulbaṇena*—terrible; *jvareṇa*—fever; *tāvat*—for so long; *tāpaḥ*—the burning torment; *dehinām*—of embodied souls; *te*—Your; *aṅghri*—of the feet; *mūlam*—the sole; *na*—do not; *u*—indeed; *severan*—serve; *yāvat*—as long as; *āśā*—in material desires; *anubaddhāḥ*—continuously bound.

TRANSLATION

I am tortured by the fierce power of Your terrible fever weapon, which is cold yet burning. All embodied souls must suffer as long as they remain bound to material ambitions and thus averse to serving Your feet.

PURPORT

In the previous verse, the Śiva-jvara stated that those who live by violence will suffer similar violence at the hands of the Lord. But here he further states that those who do not surrender to the Supreme Lord are especially liable to punishment. Although the Śiva-jvara himself had acted violently up till now, since he has surrendered to the Lord and rectified himself, he hopes to receive the Lord's mercy. In other words, he has now become the Lord's devotee.

TEXT 29

श्रीभगवानुवाच
त्रिशिरस्ते प्रसन्नोऽस्मि व्येतु ते मज्ज्वराद् भयम् ।
यो नौ स्मरति संवादं तस्य त्वन्न भवेद् भयम् ॥२९॥

śrī-bhagavān uvāca
tri-śiras te prasanno 'smi
vyetu te maj-jvarād bhayam
yo nau smarati saṁvādaṁ
tasya tvan na bhaved bhayam

śrī-bhagavān uvāca—the Supreme Lord said; *tri-śiraḥ*—O three-headed one; *te*—with you; *prasannaḥ*—satisfied; *asmi*—I am; *vyetu*—may it go away; *te*—your; *mat*—My; *jvarāt*—of the fever weapon; *bhayam*—fear; *yaḥ*—whoever; *nau*—our; *smarati*—remembers; *saṁvādam*—the conversation; *tasya*—for him; *tvat*—of you; *na bhavet*—there will not be; *bhayam*—fear.

TRANSLATION

The Supreme Lord said: O three-headed one, I am pleased with you. May your fear of My fever weapon be dispelled, and may whoever remembers our conversation here have no reason to fear you.

PURPORT

Here the Lord accepts the Śiva-jvara as His devotee and gives him his first order—that he should never frighten, by hot fever, those who faithfully hear this pastime of the Lord's.

TEXT 30

इत्युक्तोऽच्युतमानम्य गतो माहेश्वरो ज्वरः ।
बाणस्तु रथमारूढः प्रागाद्योत्स्यन् जनार्दनम् ॥३०॥

ity ukto 'cyutam ānamya
gato māheśvaro jvaraḥ
bāṇas tu ratham ārūḍhaḥ
prāgād yotsyan janārdanam

iti—thus; *uktaḥ*—addressed; *acyutam*—to Kṛṣṇa, the infallible Supreme Lord; *ānamya*—bowing down; *gataḥ*—went; *māheśvaraḥ*—of Lord Śiva; *jvaraḥ*—the fever weapon; *bāṇaḥ*—Bāṇāsura; *tu*—but; *ratham*—his chariot; *ārūḍhaḥ*—riding; *prāgāt*—came forward; *yotsyan*—intending to fight; *janārdanam*—Lord Kṛṣṇa.

TRANSLATION

Thus addressed, the Māheśvara-jvara bowed down to the infallible Lord and went away. But Bāṇāsura then appeared, riding forth on his chariot to fight Lord Kṛṣṇa.

TEXT 31

ततो बाहुसहस्रेण नानायुधधरोऽसुरः ।
मुमोच परमक्रुद्धो बाणांश्चक्रायुधे नृप ॥३१॥

tato bāhu-sahasreṇa
nānāyudha-dharo 'suraḥ
mumoca parama-kruddho
bāṇāṁś cakrāyudhe nṛpa

tataḥ—thereupon; *bāhu*—with his arms; *sahasreṇa*—one thousand; *nānā*—numerous; *āyudha*—weapons; *dharaḥ*—carrying; *asuraḥ*—the demon; *mumoca*—released; *parama*—supremely; *kruddhaḥ*—angry; *bāṇān*—arrows; *cakra-āyudhe*—at Him whose weapon is the disc; *nṛpa*—O King (Parīkṣit).

TRANSLATION

Carrying numerous weapons in his thousand hands, O King, the terribly infuriated demon shot many arrows at Lord Kṛṣṇa, the carrier of the disc weapon.

TEXT 32

तस्यास्यतोऽस्त्राण्यसकृच्चक्रेण क्षुरनेमिना ।
चिच्छेद भगवान् बाहून् शाखा इव वनस्पतेः ॥३२॥

tasyāsyato 'strāṇy asakṛc
cakreṇa kṣura-neminā
ciccheda bhagavān bāhūn
śākhā iva vanaspateḥ

tasya—of him; *asyataḥ*—who was throwing; *astrāṇi*—weapons; *asakṛt*—repeatedly; *cakreṇa*—with His disc; *kṣura*—razor-sharp; *neminā*—whose circumference; *ciccheda*—cut off; *bhagavān*—the Supreme Lord; *bāhūn*—the arms; *śākhāḥ*—branches; *iva*—as if; *vanaspateḥ*—of a tree.

TRANSLATION

As Bāṇa continued hurling weapons at Him, the Supreme Lord began using His razor-sharp *cakra* to cut off Bāṇāsura's arms as if they were tree branches.

TEXT 33

बाहुषु छिद्यमानेषु बाणस्य भगवान् भवः ।
भक्तानुकम्प्युपव्रज्य चक्रायुधमभाषत ॥३३॥

bāhuṣu chidyamāneṣu
bāṇasya bhagavān bhavaḥ
bhaktānukampy upavrajya
cakrāyudham abhāṣata

bāhuṣu—the arms; *chidyamāneṣu*—as they were being severed; *bāṇasya*—of Bāṇāsura; *bhagavān bhavaḥ*—the great Lord Śiva; *bhakta*—toward his devotee; *anukampī*—compassionate; *upavrajya*—approaching; *cakra-āyudham*—to Lord Kṛṣṇa, wielder of the disc weapon; *abhāṣata*—he spoke.

TRANSLATION

Lord Śiva felt compassion for his devotee Bāṇāsura, whose arms were being cut off, and thus he approached Lord Cakrāyudha [Kṛṣṇa] and spoke to Him as follows.

TEXT 34

श्रीरुद्र उवाच
त्वं हि ब्रह्म परं ज्योतिर्गूढं ब्रह्मणि वाङ्मये ।
यं पश्यन्त्यमलात्मान आकाशमिव केवलम् ॥३४॥

śrī-rudra uvāca
tvaṁ hi brahma paraṁ jyotir
gūḍhaṁ brahmaṇi vāṅ-maye
yaṁ paśyanty amalātmāna
ākāśam iva kevalam

śrī-rudraḥ uvāca—Lord Śiva said; *tvam*—You; *hi*—alone; *brahma*—the Absolute Truth; *param*—supreme; *jyotiḥ*—light; *gūḍham*—hidden; *brahmaṇi*—in the Absolute; *vāk-maye*—in its form of language (the *Vedas*); *yam*—whom; *paśyanti*—they see; *amala*—spotless; *ātmānaḥ*—whose hearts; *ākāśam*—the sky; *iva*—like; *kevalam*—pure.

TRANSLATION

Śrī Rudra said: You alone are the Absolute Truth, the supreme light, the mystery hidden within the verbal manifestation of the Absolute. Those whose hearts are spotless can see You, for You are uncontaminated, like the sky.

PURPORT

The Absolute Truth is the source of all light and is therefore the supreme light, self-luminous. This Absolute Truth is explained confidentially in the *Vedas* and is therefore difficult for an ordinary reader to understand. The following statements quoted by Śrīla Jīva Gosvāmī from the *Gopāla-tāpanī Upaniṣad* show how the Vedic sounds occasionally reveal the Absolute: *Te hocur upāsanam etasya parātmano govindasyākhilādhāriṇo brūhi* (*Pūrva-khaṇḍa* 17): "They [the four Kumāras] said [to Brahmā], 'Please tell us how to worship Govinda, the Supreme Soul and the foundation of all that exists.'" *Cetanaś cetanānām* (*Pūrva-khaṇḍa* 21): "He is the chief of all living beings." And *taṁ ha devam ātma-vṛtti-prakāśam* (*Pūrva-khaṇḍa* 23): "One realizes that Supreme Godhead by first realizing one's own self." The great *ācārya* Jīva Gosvāmī also quotes a verse from the *Śrīmad-Bhāgavatam* (1.10.48)—*gūḍhaṁ paraṁ brahma manuṣya-liṅgam*—which refers to "the Supreme Truth concealed in a humanlike form."

Since the Lord is pure, why do some people perceive Kṛṣṇa's form and activities as impure? Ācārya Jīva explains that those whose own hearts are impure cannot understand the pure Lord. Śrīla Viśvanātha Cakravartī further quotes the Lord's own instruction to Arjuna in *Śrī Hari-vaṁśa:*

tat-paraṁ paramaṁ brahma
sarvaṁ vibhajate jagat
mamaiva tad ghanaṁ tejo
jñātum arhasi bhārata

"Superior to that [total material nature] is the Supreme Brahman, from which this entire creation expands. O descendant of Bharata, you should know that the Supreme Brahman consists of My concentrated effulgence."

Thus, to save his devotee, Śiva now glorifies the Supreme Lord, Kṛṣṇa, his eternal worshipable master. The Lord's bewildering potency induced Śiva to fight with Lord Kṛṣṇa, but now the fight is over, and to save his devotee Lord Śiva offers these beautiful prayers.

TEXTS 35–36

नाभिर्नभोऽग्निर्मुखमम्बु रेतो
द्यौः शीर्षमाशाः श्रुतिरङ्घ्रिरुर्वी ।
चन्द्रो मनो यस्य दृगर्क आत्मा
अहं समुद्रो जठरं भुजेन्द्रः ॥३५॥
रोमाणि यस्यौषधयोऽम्बुवाहाः
केशा विरिञ्चो धिषणा विसर्गः ।
प्रजापतिर्हृदयं यस्य धर्मः
स वै भवान् पुरुषो लोककल्पः ॥३६॥

nābhir nabho 'gnir mukham ambu reto
dyauḥ śīrṣam āśāḥ śrutir aṅghrir urvī
candro mano yasya dṛg arka ātmā
ahaṁ samudro jaṭharaṁ bhujendraḥ

romāṇi yasyauṣadhayo 'mbu-vāhāḥ
keśā viriñco dhiṣaṇā visargaḥ
prajā-patir hṛdayaṁ yasya dharmaḥ
sa vai bhavān puruṣo loka-kalpaḥ

nābhiḥ—the navel; *nabhaḥ*—the sky; *agniḥ*—fire; *mukham*—the face; *ambu*—water; *retaḥ*—the semen; *dyauḥ*—heaven; *śīrṣam*—the head; *āśāḥ*—the directions; *śrutiḥ*—the sense of hearing; *aṅghriḥ*—the foot; *urvī*—the earth; *candraḥ*—the moon; *manaḥ*—the mind; *yasya*—whose; *dṛk*—sight; *arkaḥ*—the sun; *ātmā*—self-awareness; *aham*—I (Śiva); *samudraḥ*—the ocean; *jaṭharam*—the abdomen; *bhuja*—the arm;

indraḥ—Indra; *romāṇi*—the hairs on the body; *yasya*—whose; *oṣadhayaḥ*—herbal plants; *ambu-vāhāḥ*—water-bearing clouds; *keśāḥ*—the hairs on the head; *viriñcaḥ*—Lord Brahmā; *dhiṣaṇā*—the discriminating intelligence; *visargaḥ*—the genitals; *prajā-patiḥ*—the progenitor of mankind; *hṛdayam*—the heart; *yasya*—whose; *dharmaḥ*—religion; *saḥ*—He; *vai*—indeed; *bhavān*—Your good self; *puruṣaḥ*—the primeval creator; *loka*—the worlds; *kalpaḥ*—produced from whom.

TRANSLATION

The sky is Your navel, fire Your face, water Your semen, and heaven Your head. The cardinal directions are Your sense of hearing, herbal plants the hairs on Your body, and water-bearing clouds the hair on Your head. The earth is Your foot, the moon Your mind, and the sun Your vision, while I am Your ego. The ocean is Your abdomen, Indra Your arm, Lord Brahmā Your intelligence, the progenitor of mankind Your genitals, and religion Your heart. You are indeed the original *puruṣa*, creator of the worlds.

PURPORT

Śrīla Śrīdhara Svāmī explains that just as the tiny bugs living inside a fruit cannot comprehend the fruit, so we tiny living beings cannot understand the Supreme Absolute Truth, in whom we exist. It is difficult to understand the cosmic manifestation of the Lord, what to speak of His transcendental form as Śrī Kṛṣṇa. Therefore we should surrender in Kṛṣṇa consciousness, and the Lord Himself will help us understand.

TEXT 37

तवावतारोऽयमकुण्ठधामन्
धर्मस्य गुप्त्यै जगतो हिताय ।
वयं च सर्वे भवतानुभाविता
विभावयामो भुवनानि सप्त ॥३७॥

tavāvatāro 'yam akuṇṭha-dhāman
dharmasya guptyai jagato hitāya

vayaṁ ca sarve bhavatānubhāvitā
vibhāvayāmo bhuvanāni sapta

tava—Your; *avatāraḥ*—descent; *ayam*—this; *akuṇṭha*—unrestricted; *dhāman*—O You whose power; *dharmasya*—of justice; *guptyai*—for the protection; *jagataḥ*—of the universe; *hitāya*—for the benefit; *vayam*—we; *ca*—also; *sarve*—all; *bhavatā*—by You; *anubhāvitāḥ*—enlightened and authorized; *vibhāvayāmaḥ*—we manifest and develop; *bhuvanāni*—the worlds; *sapta*—seven.

TRANSLATION

Your current descent into the material realm, O Lord of unrestricted power, is meant for upholding the principles of justice and benefiting the entire universe. We demigods, each depending on Your grace and authority, develop the seven planetary systems.

PURPORT

As Lord Śiva glorifies Lord Kṛṣṇa a doubt may arise, since, apparently, Lord Kṛṣṇa is standing before Lord Śiva as a historical personality with a humanlike body. However, it is out of the Lord's causeless mercy that He appears to us in a form visible to our mundane eyes. If we want to understand the Absolute Truth, Śrī Kṛṣṇa, we must hear from recognized authorities in Kṛṣṇa consciousness, such as Lord Kṛṣṇa Himself in the *Bhagavad-gītā*, or from Lord Śiva, a recognized Vaiṣṇava authority, who here glorifies the Supreme Personality of Godhead.

TEXT 38

त्वमेक आद्यः पुरुषोऽद्वितीयस्
तुर्यः स्वदृग् धेतुरहेतुरीशः ।
प्रतीयसेऽथापि यथाविकारं
स्वमायया सर्वगुणप्रसिद्ध्यै ॥३८॥

tvam eka ādyaḥ puruṣo 'dvitīyas
turyaḥ sva-dṛg dhetur ahetur īśaḥ

pratīyase 'thāpi yathā-vikāraṁ
sva-māyayā sarva-guṇa-prasiddhyai

tvam—You; *ekaḥ*—one; *ādyaḥ*—original; *puruṣaḥ*—Supreme Person; *advitīyaḥ*—without a second; *turyaḥ*—transcendental; *sva-dṛk*—self-manifesting; *hetuḥ*—the cause; *ahetuḥ*—having no cause; *īśaḥ*—the supreme controller; *pratīyase*—You are perceived; *atha api*—nonetheless; *yathā*—according to; *vikāram*—various transformations; *sva*—by Your own; *māyayā*—illusory potency; *sarva*—of all; *guṇa*—material qualities; *prasiddhyai*—for the complete manifestation.

TRANSLATION

You are the original person, one without a second, transcendental and self-manifesting. Uncaused, you are the cause of all, and You are the ultimate controller. You are nonetheless perceived in terms of the transformations of matter effected by Your illusory energy—transformations You sanction so that the various material qualities can fully manifest.

PURPORT

The *ācāryas* comment as follows on this verse: Śrīla Śrīdhara Svāmī explains that the term *ādyaḥ puruṣaḥ*, "the original *puruṣa,*" indicates that Lord Kṛṣṇa expands Himself as Mahā-Viṣṇu, the first of the three *puruṣas* who take charge of cosmic manifestation. The Lord is *eka advitīyaḥ,* "one without a second," because there is no one equal to the Lord or different from Him. No one is completely equal to the Supreme Godhead, and yet because all the living beings are expansions of the potency of the Godhead, no one is qualitatively different from Him. Śrī Caitanya Mahāprabhu nicely explains this inconceivable situation by stating that the Absolute Truth and the living beings are qualitatively one but quantitatively different. The Absolute possesses infinite spiritual consciousness, whereas the living beings possess infinitesimal consciousness, which is subject to being covered by illusion.

Śrīla Jīva Gosvāmī, commenting on the term *ādyaḥ puruṣaḥ,* quotes from the *Sātvata-tantra: viṣṇos tu trīṇi rūpāṇi.* "There are three forms of Viṣṇu [for cosmic manifestation, etc.]." Śrīla Jīva Gosvāmī also quotes a statement of the Lord's from *śruti: pūrvam evāham ihāsam.* "In the beginning I alone existed in this world." This statement describes the form of the Lord called the *puruṣa-avatāra,* who exists before the cosmic manifestation. Śrīla Jīva Gosvāmī also quotes the following *śruti-mantra: tat-puruṣasya puruṣatvam,* which means "Such constitutes the Lord's status as *puruṣa.*" Actually, Lord Kṛṣṇa is the essence of the *puruṣa* incarnation because He is *turīya,* as described in the present verse. Jīva Gosvāmī explains the term *turīya* (literally "the fourth") by quoting Śrīdhara Svāmī's commentary to the *Bhāgavatam* verse 11.15.16:

virāṭ hiraṇyagarbhaś ca
kāraṇaṁ cety upādhayaḥ
īśasya yat tribhir hīnaṁ
turīyaṁ tad vidur budhāḥ

"The Lord's universal form, His Hiraṇyagarbha form and the primeval causal manifestation of material nature are all relative conceptions, but because the Lord Himself is not covered by these three, intelligent authorities call Him 'the fourth.'"

According to Śrīla Viśvanātha Cakravartī, the word *turīya* indicates that the Lord is the fourth member of the quadruple expansion of Godhead called the Catur-vyūha. In other words, Lord Kṛṣṇa is Vāsudeva.

Lord Kṛṣṇa is *sva-dṛk*—that is, He alone can perceive Himself perfectly—because He is infinite spiritual existence, infinitely pure. He is *hetu,* the cause of everything, and yet He is *ahetu,* without cause. Therefore He is *īśa,* the supreme controller.

The last two lines of this verse are of special philosophical significance. Why is the Lord perceived differently by different persons, although He is one? A partial explanation is given here. By the agency of Māyā, the Lord's external potency, material nature is in a constant state of transformation, *vikāra.* In one sense, then, material nature is "unreal," *asat.* But because God is the supreme reality, and because He is present within all things and all things are His potency, material objects and energies possess a degree of reality. Therefore some people see one aspect of material energy and think, "This is reality," while other people see a different aspect of material energy and think, "No, that is reality." Being conditioned souls, we are covered by different configurations of material nature, and thus we describe the Supreme Truth or the Supreme Lord in terms of our corrupted vision. Yet even the covering qualities of material nature, such as our conditioned intelligence, mind and senses, are real (being the potency of the Supreme Lord), and therefore through all things we can perceive, in a more or less subjective way, the Supreme Personality of Godhead. That is why the present verse states, *pratīyase:* "You are perceived." Furthermore, without the manifestation of material nature's covering qualities, the creation could not fulfill its purpose—namely, to allow the conditioned souls to make their best attempt to enjoy without God so that they will finally understand the futility of such an illusory notion.

TEXT 39

यथैव सूर्यः पिहितश्छायया स्वया
छायां च रूपाणि च सञ्चकास्ति ।
एवं गुणेनापिहितो गुणांस्त्वम्
आत्मप्रदीपो गुणिनश्च भूमन् ॥३९॥

yathaiva sūryaḥ pihitaś chāyayā svayā
chāyāṁ ca rūpāṇi ca sañcakāsti
evaṁ guṇenāpihito guṇāṁs tvam
ātma-pradīpo guṇinaś ca bhūman

yathā eva—just as; *sūryaḥ*—the sun; *pihitaḥ*—covered; *chāyayā*—by the shade; *svayā*—its own; *chāyām*—the shade; *ca*—and; *rūpāṇi*—visible forms; *ca*—also; *sañcakāsti*—illuminates; *evam*—similarly; *guṇena*—by the material quality (of false ego); *apihitaḥ*—covered; *guṇān*—the qualities of matter; *tvam*—You; *ātma-pradīpaḥ*—self-luminous; *guṇinaḥ*—the possessors of these qualities (the living entities); *ca*—and; *bhūman*—O almighty one.

TRANSLATION

O almighty one, just as the sun, though hidden by a cloud, illuminates the cloud and all other visible forms as well, so You, although hidden by the material qualities, remain self-luminous and thus reveal all those qualities, along with the living entities who possess them.

PURPORT

Here Lord Śiva further clarifies the idea expressed in the final two lines of the previous verse. The analogy of the clouds and the sun is appropriate. With its energy the sun creates clouds, which cover our vision of the sun. Yet it is the sun that allows us to see the clouds and all other things as well. Similarly, the Lord expands His illusory potency and thus prevents us from directly seeing Him. Yet it is God alone who reveals to us His covering potency—namely, the material world—and thus the Lord is *ātma-pradīpa,* "self-luminous." It is the reality of His existence that makes all things visible.

TEXT 40

यन्मायामोहितधिय: पुत्रदारगृहादिषु ।
उन्मज्जन्ति निमज्जन्ति प्रसक्ता वृजिनार्णवे ॥४०॥

yan-māyā-mohita-dhiyaḥ
putra-dāra-gṛhādiṣu
unmajjanti nimajjanti
prasaktā vṛjinārṇave

yat—of whom; *māyā*—by the illusory energy; *mohita*—bewildered; *dhiyaḥ*—their intelligence; *putra*—with regard to children; *dāra*—wife; *gṛha*—home; *ādiṣu*—and so on; *unmajjanti*—they rise to the surface; *nimajjanti*—they become submerged; *prasaktāḥ*—fully entangled; *vṛjina*—of misery; *arṇave*—in the ocean.

TRANSLATION

Their intelligence bewildered by Your *māyā,* fully attached to children, wife, home and so on, persons immersed in the ocean of material misery sometimes rise to the surface and sometimes sink down.

PURPORT

Śrīla Śrīdhara Svāmī explains that "rising in the ocean of misery" indicates elevation to higher species, such as demigods, and that "being submerged" refers to degradation to lower species—even to immobile forms of life such as trees. As stated in the *Vāyu Purāṇa, viparyayaś ca bhavati brahmatva-sthāvaratvayoḥ:* "The living being rotates between the position of Brahmā and that of an unmoving creature."

Śrīla Jīva Gosvāmī points out that Śiva, having glorified the Lord, now pursues his original intention of securing the Lord's grace for Bāṇāsura. Thus in this and the following four verses, Lord Śiva instructs Bāṇa on his actual position in relation to the Lord. Śiva's appeal to the Lord for compassion toward Bāṇa appears in Text 45.

TEXT 41

देवदत्तमिमं लब्ध्वा नृलोकमजितेन्द्रियः ।
यो नाद्रियेत त्वत्पादौ स शोच्यो ह्यात्मवञ्चकः ॥४१॥

deva-dattam imaṁ labdhvā
nṛ-lokam ajitendriyaḥ
yo nādriyeta tvat-pādau
sa śocyo hy ātma-vañcakaḥ

deva—by the Supreme Lord; *dattam*—given; *imam*—this; *labdhvā*—attaining; *nṛ*—of human beings; *lokam*—the world; *ajita*—uncontrolled; *indriyaḥ*—his senses; *yaḥ*—who; *na ādriyeta*—will not honor; *tvat*—Your; *pādau*—feet; *saḥ*—he; *śocyaḥ*—pitiable; *hi*—indeed; *ātma*—of himself; *vañcakaḥ*—a cheater.

TRANSLATION

One who has attained this human form of life as a gift from God, yet who fails to control his senses and honor Your feet, is surely to be pitied, for he is only cheating himself.

PURPORT

Lord Śiva here condemns those who refuse to engage in the devotional service of the Supreme Lord.

TEXT 42

यस्त्वां विसृजते मर्त्य आत्मानं प्रियमीश्वरम् ।
विपर्ययेन्द्रियार्थार्थं विषमत्त्यमृतं त्यजन् ॥४२॥

yas tvāṁ visṛjate martya
ātmānaṁ priyam īśvaram
viparyayendriyārthārthaṁ
viṣam atty amṛtaṁ tyajan

yaḥ—who; *tvām*—You; *visṛjate*—rejects; *martyaḥ*—mortal man; *ātmānam*—his true Self; *priyam*—dearmost; *īśvaram*—Lord; *viparyaya*—which are just the opposite; *indriya-artha*—of sense objects; *artham*—for the sake; *viṣam*—poison; *atti*—he eats; *amṛtam*—nectar; *tyajan*—avoiding.

TRANSLATION

That mortal who rejects You—his true Self, dearmost friend, and Lord—for the sake of sense objects, whose nature is just the opposite, refuses nectar and instead consumes poison.

PURPORT

The person described above is pitiable because he rejects that which is actually dear, the Lord, and accepts that which is not dear and is ungodly: temporary sense gratification, which leads to suffering and bewilderment.

TEXT 43

अहं ब्रह्माथ विबुधा मुनयश्चामलाशयाः ।
सर्वात्मना प्रपन्नास्त्वामात्मानं प्रेष्ठमीश्वरम् ॥४३॥

ahaṁ brahmātha vibudhā
munayaś cāmalāśayāḥ
sarvātmanā prapannās tvām
ātmānaṁ preṣṭham īśvaram

aham—I; *brahmā*—Brahmā; *atha*—and also; *vibudhāḥ*—the demigods; *munayaḥ*—the sages; *ca*—and; *amala*—pure; *āśayāḥ*—whose consciousness; *sarva-ātmanā*—wholeheartedly; *prapannāḥ*—surrendered; *tvām*—unto You; *ātmānam*—the Self; *preṣṭham*—the dearmost; *īśvaram*—the Lord.

TRANSLATION

I, Lord Brahmā, the other demigods and the pure-minded sages have all surrendered wholeheartedly unto You, our dearmost Self and Lord.

TEXT 44

तं त्वा जगत्स्थित्युदयान्तहेतुं
समं प्रशान्तं सुहृदात्मदैवम् ।
अनन्यमेकं जगदात्मकेतं
भवापवर्गाय भजाम देवम् ॥४४॥

taṁ tvā jagat-sthity-udayānta-hetuṁ
samaṁ praśāntaṁ suhṛd-ātma-daivam
ananyam ekaṁ jagad-ātma-ketaṁ
bhavāpavargāya bhajāma devam

tam—Him; *tvā*—You; *jagat*—of the universe; *sthiti*—of the maintenance; *udaya*—the rise; *anta*—and the demise; *hetum*—the cause; *samam*—equipoised; *praśāntam*—perfectly at peace; *suhṛt*—the friend; *ātma*—Self; *daivam*—and worshipable Lord; *ananyam*—without a second; *ekam*—unique; *jagat*—of all the worlds; *ātma*—and all souls; *ketam*—the shelter; *bhava*—of material life; *apavargāya*—for the cessation; *bhajāma*—let us worship; *devam*—the Supreme Lord.

TRANSLATION

Let us worship You, the Supreme Lord, to be freed from material life. You are the maintainer of the universe and the cause of its creation and demise. Equipoised and perfectly at peace, You are the true friend, Self and worshipable Lord. You are one without a second, the shelter of all the worlds and all souls.

PURPORT

Śrīla Śrīdhara Svāmī states that the Lord is a true friend because He sets one's proper intelligence into motion if one desires to know the truth about God and the soul. Śrīla Jīva Gosvāmī and Śrīla Viśvanātha Cakravartī both emphasize that the term *bhavāpavargāya* indicates the highest liberation of pure love of Godhead, characterized by unalloyed devotional service unto the Lord.

Śrīla Viśvanātha Cakravartī also explains that the Supreme Lord is *samam,* "perfectly objective and balanced," whereas other living beings, having an incomplete grasp of reality, cannot be perfectly objective. Those who surrender unto the Lord also become fully objective by taking shelter of His supreme consciousness.

TEXT 45

अयं ममेष्टो दयितोऽनुवर्ती
मयाभयं दत्तममुष्य देव ।
सम्पाद्यतां तद् भवतः प्रसादो
यथा हि ते दैत्यपतौ प्रसादः ॥४५॥

ayaṁ mameṣṭo dayito 'nuvartī
mayābhayaṁ dattam amuṣya deva
sampādyatāṁ tad bhavataḥ prasādo
yathā hi te daitya-patau prasādaḥ

ayam—this; *mama*—my; *iṣṭaḥ*—favored; *dayitaḥ*—very dear; *anuvartī*—follower; *mayā*—by me; *abhayam*—fearlessness; *dattam*—given; *amuṣya*—his; *deva*—O Lord; *sampādyatām*—please let it be granted; *tat*—therefore; *bhavataḥ*—Your; *prasādaḥ*—grace; *yathā*—as; *hi*—indeed; *te*—Your; *daitya*—of the demons; *patau*—for the chief (Prahlāda); *prasādaḥ*—grace.

TRANSLATION

This Bāṇāsura is my dear and faithful follower, and I have awarded him freedom from fear. Therefore, my Lord, please grant him Your mercy, just as You showed mercy to Prahlāda, the lord of the demons.

PURPORT

Lord Śiva feels inclined to help Bāṇāsura because the demon showed great devotion to Lord Śiva when he provided musical accompaniment for Śiva's *tāṇḍava* dance. Another reason Bāṇa is an object of Lord Śiva's favor is that he is a descendant of the great devotees Prahlāda and Bali.

TEXT 46

श्रीभगवानुवाच
यदात्थ भगवंस्त्वं नः करवाम प्रियं तव ।
भवतो यद्व्यवसितं तन्मे साध्वनुमोदितम् ॥४६॥

śrī-bhagavān uvāca
yad āttha bhagavaṁs tvaṁ naḥ
karavāma priyaṁ tava
bhavato yad vyavasitaṁ
tan me sādhv anumoditam

śrī-bhagavān uvāca—the Supreme Lord said; *yat*—what; *āttha*—have spoken; *bhagavan*—O lord; *tvam*—you; *naḥ*—to Us; *karavāma*—We should do; *priyam*—the gratifying; *tava*—of you; *bhavataḥ*—by you; *yat*—what; *vyavasitam*—determined; *tat*—that; *me*—by Me; *sādhu*—well; *anumoditam*—agreed with.

TRANSLATION

The Supreme Lord said: My dear lord, for your pleasure We must certainly do what you have requested of Us. I fully agree with your conclusion.

PURPORT

We should not think it strange that the Supreme Lord, Kṛṣṇa, here addresses Lord Śiva as *bhagavān*, "lord." All living beings are part and parcel of the Lord, qualitatively one with Him, and Lord Śiva is an especially powerful, pure entity who possesses many of the Supreme Lord's qualities. Just as a father is happy to share his riches with a beloved son, so the Supreme Lord happily invests pure living beings with some of His potency and opulence. And just as a father proudly and happily observes the good qualities of his children, the Lord is most happy to glorify the pure living beings who are powerful in Kṛṣṇa consciousness. Thus the Supreme Lord is pleased to glorify Lord Śiva by addressing him as *bhagavān*.

TEXT 47

अवध्योऽयं ममाप्येष वैरोचनिसुतोऽसुरः ।
प्रह्रादाय वरो दत्तो न वध्यो मे तवान्वयः ॥४७॥

avadhyo 'yaṁ mamāpy eṣa
vairocani-suto 'suraḥ
prahrādāya varo datto
na vadhyo me tavānvayaḥ

avadhyaḥ—not to be killed; *ayam*—he; *mama*—by Me; *api*—indeed; *eṣaḥ*—this; *vairocani-sutaḥ*—son of Vairocani (Bali); *asuraḥ*—demon; *prahrādāya*—to Prahlāda; *varaḥ*—the benediction; *dattaḥ*—given; *na vadhyaḥ*—not to be killed; *me*—by Me; *tava*—your; *anvayaḥ*—descendants.

TRANSLATION

I will not kill this demonic son of Vairocani, for I gave Prahlāda Mahārāja the benediction that I would not kill any of his descendants.

TEXT 48

दर्पोपशमनायास्य प्रवृक्णा बाहवो मया ।
सूदितं च बलं भूरि यच्च भारायितं भुवः ॥४८॥

darpopaśamanāyāsya
pravṛkṇā bāhavo mayā
sūditaṁ ca balaṁ bhūri
yac ca bhārāyitaṁ bhuvaḥ

darpa—the false pride; *upaśamanāya*—for subduing; *asya*—his; *pravṛkṇāḥ*—severed; *bāhavaḥ*—arms; *mayā*—by Me; *sūditam*—slain;

ca—and; *balam*—the military force; *bhūri*—huge; *yat*—which; *ca*—and; *bhārāyitam*—having become a burden; *bhuvaḥ*—for the earth.

TRANSLATION

It was to subdue Bāṇāsura's false pride that I severed his arms. And I slew his mighty army because it had become a burden upon the earth.

TEXT 49

चत्वारोऽस्य भुजाः शिष्टा भविष्यत्यजरामरः ।
पार्षदमुख्यो भवतो न कुतश्चिद्भयोऽसुरः ॥४९॥

catvāro 'sya bhujāḥ śiṣṭā
bhaviṣyaty ajarāmaraḥ
pārṣada-mukhyo bhavato
na kutaścid-bhayo 'suraḥ

catvāraḥ—four; *asya*—his; *bhujāḥ*—arms; *śiṣṭāḥ*—remaining; *bhaviṣyati*—will be; *ajara*—unaging; *amaraḥ*—and immortal; *pārṣada*—an associate; *mukhyaḥ*—principal; *bhavataḥ*—of yourself; *na kutaścit-bhayaḥ*—having no fear on any account; *asuraḥ*—the demon.

TRANSLATION

This demon, who still has four arms, will be immune to old age and death, and he will serve as one of your principal attendants. Thus he will have nothing to fear on any account.

TEXT 50

इति लब्ध्वाभयं कृष्णं प्रणम्य शिरसासुरः ।
प्राद्युम्निं रथमारोप्य सवध्वो समुपानयत् ॥५०॥

iti labdhvābhayaṁ kṛṣṇaṁ
praṇamya śirasāsuraḥ

prādyumniṁ ratham āropya
sa-vadhvo samupānayat

iti—thus; *labdhvā*—attaining; *abhayam*—freedom from fear; *kṛṣṇam*—to Lord Kṛṣṇa; *praṇamya*—bowing down; *śirasā*—with his head; *asuraḥ*—the demon; *prādyumnim*—Aniruddha, the son of Pradyumna; *ratham*—on His chariot; *āropya*—placing; *sa-vadhvaḥ*—with His wife; *samupānayat*—he brought them forward.

TRANSLATION

Thus attaining freedom from fear, Bāṇāsura offered obeisances to Lord Kṛṣṇa by touching his head to the ground. Bāṇa then seated Aniruddha and His bride on their chariot and brought them before the Lord.

TEXT 51

अक्षौहिण्या परिवृतं सुवासःसमलंकृतम् ।
सपत्नीकं पुरस्कृत्य ययौ रुद्रानुमोदितः ॥५१॥

akṣauhiṇyā parivṛtaṁ
su-vāsaḥ-samalaṅkṛtam
sa-patnīkaṁ puras-kṛtya
yayau rudrānumoditaḥ

akṣauhiṇyā—by a full military division; *parivṛtam*—surrounded; *su*—fine; *vāsaḥ*—whose clothing; *samalaṅkṛtam*—and adorned with ornaments; *sa-patnīkam*—Aniruddha with His wife; *puraḥ-kṛtya*—putting in front; *yayau*—He (Lord Kṛṣṇa) went; *rudra*—by Lord Śiva; *anumoditaḥ*—given leave.

TRANSLATION

At the front of the party Lord Kṛṣṇa then placed Aniruddha and His bride, both beautifully adorned with fine clothes and ornaments, and surrounded them with a full military division. Thus Lord Kṛṣṇa took His leave of Lord Śiva and departed.

TEXT 52

स्वराजधानीं समलंकृतां ध्वजैः
सतोरणैरुक्षितमार्गचत्वराम् ।
विवेश शंखानकदुन्दुभिस्वनैर्
अभ्युद्यतः पौरसुहृद्द्विजातिभिः ॥५२॥

sva-rājadhānīṁ samalaṅkṛtāṁ dhvajaiḥ
sa-toraṇair ukṣita-mārga-catvarām
viveśa śaṅkhānaka-dundubhi-svanair
abhyudyataḥ paura-suhṛd-dvijātibhiḥ

sva—His own; *rājadhānīm*—capital; *samalaṅkṛtām*—fully decorated; *dhvajaiḥ*—with flags; *sa*—and with; *toraṇaiḥ*—victory arches; *ukṣita*—sprinkled with water; *mārga*—whose avenues; *catvarām*—and crossroads; *viveśa*—He entered; *śaṅkha*—of conchshells; *ānaka*—side drums; *dundubhi*—and kettledrums; *svanaiḥ*—with the resounding; *abhyudyataḥ*—greeted respectfully; *paura*—by the people of the city; *suhṛt*—by His relatives; *dvijātibhiḥ*—and by the *brāhmaṇas.*

TRANSLATION

The Lord then entered His capital. The city was lavishly decorated with flags and victory arches, and its avenues and crossways were all sprinkled with water. As concshells, *ānakas* and *dundubhi* drums resounded, the Lord's relatives, the *brāhmaṇas* and the general populace all came forward to greet Him respectfully.

TEXT 53

य एवं कृष्णविजयं शंकरेण च संयुगम् ।
संस्मरेत्प्रातरुत्थाय न तस्य स्यात्पराजयः ॥५३॥

ya evaṁ kṛṣṇa-vijayaṁ
śaṅkareṇa ca saṁyugam
saṁsmaret prātar utthāya
na tasya syāt parājayaḥ

yaḥ—whoever; *evam*—thus; *kṛṣṇa-vijayam*—the victory of Lord Kṛṣṇa; *śaṅkareṇa*—with Lord Śaṅkara; *ca*—and; *saṁyugam*—battle; *saṁsmaret*—remembers; *prātaḥ*—at dawn; *utthāya*—rising from sleep; *na*—not; *tasya*—for him; *syāt*—there will be; *parājayaḥ*—defeat.

TRANSLATION

Whoever rises early in the morning and remembers Lord Kṛṣṇa's victory in His battle with Lord Śiva will never experience defeat.

Thus end the purports of the humble servants of His Divine Grace A. C. Bhaktivedanta Swami Prabhupāda to the Tenth Canto, Sixty-third Chapter, of the Śrīmad-Bhāgavatam, *entitled "Lord Kṛṣṇa Fights with Bāṇāsura."*

CHAPTER SIXTY-FOUR

The Deliverance of King Nṛga

This chapter describes how Śrī Kṛṣṇa released King Nṛga from a curse and instructed the royal order on the great danger of taking a *brāhmaṇa's* property.

One day Sāmba and other young boys of the Yādava dynasty went to the forest to play, and after playing for a long time they became very thirsty and began looking for water. Inside a dry well they found an amazing creature: a huge lizard resembling a hill. The boys felt sorry for it and tried to pull it out. But after several attempts with leather thongs and ropes, they saw that they would not be able to rescue the creature, and thus they went to Lord Kṛṣṇa and told Him what had happened. The Lord accompanied them to the well and, extending His left hand, easily lifted the lizard out. By the touch of Lord Kṛṣṇa's hand the creature transformed at once into a demigod. Then Lord Kṛṣṇa asked, "Who are you, and how did you assume such a lowly form?

The divine being replied, "My name was King Nṛga, son of Ikṣvāku, and I was famous for giving charity. Indeed, I gave away countless cows to numerous *brāhmaṇas.* But on one occasion a cow belonging to a first-class *brāhmaṇa* wandered into my herd. Unaware of this, I gave this cow in charity to a different *brāhmaṇa.* When the cow's previous owner saw the second *brāhmaṇa* taking this cow away, the first *brāhmaṇa* claimed the cow as his and began arguing with the second *brāhmaṇa.* After quarreling for some time they approached me, and I implored them to each take one hundred thousand cows in exchange for that one cow, and to please forgive me for the offense I had unknowingly committed. But neither *brāhmaṇa* would accept my proposal, and the matter remained unsettled.

"Shortly thereafter I died and was taken by the Yamadūtas to the court of Yamarāja. Yama asked me which I preferred to do first: suffer the results of my sins or enjoy the results of my pious acts. I decided to suffer my sinful reactions first, and thus I assumed the body of a lizard."

After King Nṛga had told his story, he offered prayers to Lord Kṛṣṇa and then mounted a celestial airplane, which transported him to heaven.

Lord Kṛṣṇa then instructed His personal associates, as well as the general mass of people, on the dangers of stealing a *brāhmaṇa's* property. Finally, the Lord returned to His palace.

TEXT 1

श्रीबादरायणिरुवाच
एकदोपवनं राजन् जग्मुर्यदुकुमारकाः ।
विहर्तुं साम्बप्रद्युम्नचारुभानुगदादयः ॥१॥

śrī-bādarāyaṇir uvāca
ekadopavanaṁ rājan
jagmur yadu-kumārakāḥ
vihartuṁ sāmba-pradyumna-
cāru-bhānu-gadādayaḥ

śrī-bādarāyaṇiḥ—the son of Badarāyaṇa (Śukadeva Gosvāmī); *uvāca*—said; *ekadā*—one day; *upavanam*—to a small forest; *rājan*—O King (Parikṣit); *jagmuḥ*—went; *yadu-kumārakāḥ*—boys of the Yadu dynasty; *vihartum*—to play; *sāmba-pradyumna-cāru-bhānu-gada-ādayaḥ*—Sāmba, Pradyumna, Cāru, Bhānu, Gada and others.

TRANSLATION

Śrī Bādarāyaṇi said: O King, one day Sāmba, Pradyumna, Cāru, Bhānu, Gada and other young boys of the Yadu dynasty went to a small forest to play.

PURPORT

Śrīla Śrīdhara Svāmī states that the story of King Nṛga, narrated in this chapter, is meant to give sober instructions to all proud kings. Through this incident Lord Kṛṣṇa also gave serious lessons to the members of His own family who had become proud of their opulences.

TEXT 2

क्रीडित्वा सुचिरं तत्र विचिन्वन्तः पिपासिताः ।
जलं निरुदके कूपे ददृशुः सत्त्वमद्भुतम् ॥२॥

krīḍitvā su-ciraṁ tatra
vicinvantaḥ pipāsitāḥ
jalaṁ nirudake kūpe
dadṛśuḥ sattvam adbhutam

krīḍitvā—after playing; *su-ciram*—for a long time; *tatra*—there; *vicinvantaḥ*—looking for; *pipāsitāḥ*—thirsty; *jalam*—water; *nirudake*—waterless; *kūpe*—in a well; *dadṛśuḥ*—they saw; *sattvam*—a creature; *adbhutam*—amazing.

TRANSLATION

After playing for a long time, they became thirsty. As they searched for water, they looked inside a dry well and saw a peculiar creature.

TEXT 3

कृकलासं गिरिनिभं वीक्ष्य विस्मितमानसाः ।
तस्य चोद्धरणे यत्नं चक्रुस्ते कृपयान्विताः ॥३॥

kṛkalāsaṁ giri-nibhaṁ
vīkṣya vismita-mānasāḥ
tasya coddharaṇe yatnaṁ
cakrus te kṛpayānvitāḥ

kṛkalāsam—a lizard; *giri*—a mountain; *nibham*—resembling; *vīkṣya*—looking at; *vismita*—astonished; *mānasāḥ*—whose minds; *tasya*—of it; *ca*—and; *uddharaṇe*—in the lifting up; *yatnam*—effort; *cakruḥ*—made; *te*—they; *kṛpayā anvitāḥ*—feeling compassion.

TRANSLATION

The boys were astonished to behold this creature, a lizard who looked like a hill. They felt sorry for it and tried to lift it out of the well.

TEXT 4

चर्मजैस्तान्तवैः पाशैर्बद्ध्वा पतितमर्भकाः ।
नाशक्नुरन् समुद्धर्तुं कृष्णायाचख्युरुत्सुकाः ॥४॥

carma-jais tāntavaiḥ pāśair
baddhvā patitam arbhakāḥ
nāśaknuran samuddhartuṁ
kṛṣṇāyācakhyur utsukāḥ

carma-jaiḥ—made of leather; *tāntavaiḥ*—and made of spun thread; *pāśaiḥ*—with ropes; *baddhvā*—attaching; *patitam*—the fallen creature; *arbhakāḥ*—the boys; *na aśaknuran*—they were not able; *samuddhartum*—to lift out; *kṛṣṇāya*—to Lord Kṛṣṇa; *ācakhyuḥ*—they reported; *utsukāḥ*—excitedly.

TRANSLATION

They caught on to the trapped lizard with leather thongs and then with woven ropes, but still they could not lift it out. So they went to Lord Kṛṣṇa and excitedly told Him about the creature.

PURPORT

Śrīla Jīva Gosvāmī explains that because in this chapter the Yadu boys, even Śrī Pradyumna, are described as quite young, this must be an early pastime.

TEXT 5

तत्रागत्यारविन्दाक्षो भगवान् विश्वभावनः ।
वीक्ष्योज्जहार वामेन तं करेण स लीलया ॥५॥

tatrāgatyāravindākṣo
bhagavān viśva-bhāvanaḥ
vīkṣyojjahāra vāmena
taṁ kareṇa sa līlayā

tatra—there; *āgatya*—going; *aravinda-akṣaḥ*—lotus-eyed; *bhagavān*—the Supreme Lord; *viśva*—of the universe; *bhāvanaḥ*—the maintainer; *vīkṣya*—seeing; *ujjahāra*—picked up; *vāmena*—left; *tam*—it; *kareṇa*—with His hand; *saḥ*—He; *līlayā*—easily.

TRANSLATION

The lotus-eyed Supreme Lord, maintainer of the universe, went to the well and saw the lizard. Then with His left hand He easily lifted it out.

TEXT 6

स उत्तमःश्लोककराभिमृष्टो
विहाय सद्यः कृकलासरूपम् ।
सन्तप्तचामीकरचारुवर्णः
स्वर्ग्यद्भुतालंकरणाम्बरस्रक् ॥६॥

sa uttamaḥ-śloka-karābhimṛṣṭo
vihāya sadyaḥ kṛkalāsa-rūpam
santapta-cāmīkara-cāru-varṇaḥ
svargy adbhutālaṅkaraṇāmbara-srak

saḥ—it; *uttamaḥ-śloka*—of the glorious Lord; *kara*—by the hand; *abhimṛṣṭaḥ*—touched; *vihāya*—giving up; *sadyaḥ*—immediately; *kṛkalāsa*—of a lizard; *rūpam*—the form; *santapta*—molten; *cāmīkara*—of gold; *cāru*—beautiful; *varṇaḥ*—whose complexion; *svargī*—a resident of heaven; *adbhuta*—amazing; *alaṅkaraṇa*—whose ornaments; *ambara*—clothing; *srak*—and garlands.

TRANSLATION

Touched by the hand of the glorious Supreme Lord, the being at once gave up its lizard form and assumed that of a resident of heaven. His complexion was beautifully colored like molten gold, and he was adorned with wonderful ornaments, clothes and garlands.

TEXT 7

पप्रच्छ विद्वानपि तन्निदानं
जनेषु विख्यापयितुं मुकुन्दः ।

कस्त्वं महाभाग वरेण्यरूपो
देवोत्तमं त्वां गणयामि नूनम् ॥७॥

papraccha vidvān api tan-nidānaṁ
janeṣu vikhyāpayituṁ mukundaḥ
kas tvaṁ mahā-bhāga vareṇya-rūpo
devottamaṁ tvāṁ gaṇayāmi nūnam

papraccha—He asked; *vidvān*—well aware; *api*—although; *tat*—of this; *nidānam*—the cause; *janeṣu*—among people in general; *vikhyāpayitum*—to make it known; *mukundaḥ*—Lord Kṛṣṇa; *kaḥ*—who; *tvam*—you; *mahā-bhāga*—O fortunate one; *vareṇya*—excellent; *rūpaḥ*—whose form; *deva-uttamam*—an exalted demigod; *tvām*—You; *gaṇayāmi*—I should consider; *nūnam*—certainly.

TRANSLATION

Lord Kṛṣṇa understood the situation, but to inform people in general He inquired as follows: "Who are you, O greatly fortunate one? Seeing your excellent form, I think you must surely be an exalted demigod.

TEXT 8

दशामिमां वा कतमेन कर्मणा
सम्प्रापितोऽस्यतदर्हः सुभद्र ।
आत्मानमाख्याहि विवित्सतां नो
यन्मन्यसे नः क्षममत्र वक्तुम् ॥८॥

daśām imāṁ vā katamena karmaṇā
samprāpito 'sy atad-arhaḥ su-bhadra
ātmānam ākhyāhi vivitsatāṁ no
yan manyase naḥ kṣamam atra vaktum

daśām—condition; *imām*—to this; *vā*—and; *katamena*—by what; *karmaṇā*—action; *samprāpitaḥ*—brought; *asi*—you are; *atat-arhaḥ*—not deserving it; *su-bhadra*—O good soul; *ātmānam*—yourself; *ākhyāhi*—please explain; *vivitsatām*—who are eager to know; *naḥ*—to us; *yat*—if;

manyase—you think; *naḥ*—to us; *kṣamam*—proper; *atra*—here; *vaktum*—to speak.

TRANSLATION

"By what past activity were you brought to this condition? It seems you did not deserve such a fate, O good soul. We are eager to know about you, so please inform us about yourself—if, that is, you think this the proper time and place to tell us."

TEXT 9

श्रीशुक उवाच
इति स्म राजा सम्पृष्टः कृष्णेनानन्तमूर्तिना ।
माधवं प्रणिपत्याह किरीटेनार्कवर्चसा ॥९॥

śrī-śuka uvāca
iti sma rājā sampṛṣṭaḥ
kṛṣṇenānanta-mūrtinā
mādhavaṁ praṇipatyāha
kirīṭenārka-varcasā

śrī-śukaḥ uvāca—Śukadeva Gosvāmī said; *iti*—thus; *sma*—indeed; *rājā*—the King; *sampṛṣṭaḥ*—questioned; *kṛṣṇena*—by Lord Kṛṣṇa; *ananta*—unlimited; *mūrtinā*—whose forms; *mādhavam*—to Him, Lord Mādhava; *praṇipatya*—bowing down; *āha*—he spoke; *kirīṭena*—with his helmet; *arka*—like the sun; *varcasā*—whose brilliance.

TRANSLATION

Śukadeva Gosvāmī said: Thus questioned by Kṛṣṇa, whose forms are unlimited, the King, his helmet as dazzling as the sun, bowed down to Lord Mādhava and replied as follows.

TEXT 10

नृग उवाच
नृगो नाम नरेन्द्रोऽहमिक्ष्वाकुतनयः प्रभो ।
दानिष्वाख्यायमानेषु यदि ते कर्णमस्पृशम् ॥१०॥

nṛga uvāca
nṛgo nāma narendro 'ham
ikṣvāku-tanayaḥ prabho
dāniṣv ākhyāyamāneṣu
yadi te karṇam aspṛśam

nṛgaḥ uvāca—King Nṛga said; *nṛgaḥ nāma*—named Nṛga; *nara-indraḥ*—a ruler of men; *aham*—I; *ikṣvāku-tanayaḥ*—a son of Ikṣvāku; *prabho*—O Lord; *dāniṣu*—among men of charity; *ākhyāyamāneṣu*—when being enumerated; *yadi*—perhaps; *te*—Your; *karṇam*—ear; *aspṛśam*—I have touched.

TRANSLATION

King Nṛga said: I am a king known as Nṛga, the son of Ikṣvāku. Perhaps, Lord, You have heard of me when lists of charitable men were recited.

PURPORT

The *ācāryas* point out here that although a tentative expression is used—"perhaps You have heard of me"—the implication is that there is no doubt.

TEXT 11

किं नु तेऽविदितं नाथ सर्वभूतात्मसाक्षिणः ।
कालेनाव्याहतदृशो वक्ष्येऽथापि तवाज्ञया ॥११॥

kiṁ nu te 'viditaṁ nātha
sarva-bhūtātma-sākṣiṇaḥ
kālenāvyāhata-dṛśo
vakṣye 'thāpi tavājñayā

kim—what; *nu*—indeed; *te*—to You; *aviditam*—unknown; *nātha*—O master; *sarva*—of all; *bhūta*—beings; *ātma*—of the intelligence; *sākṣiṇaḥ*—to the witness; *kālena*—by time; *avyāhata*—undisturbed;

dṛśaḥ—whose vision; *vakṣye*—I will speak; *atha api*—nevertheless; *tava*—Your; *ājñayā*—by the order.

TRANSLATION

What could possibly be unknown to You, O master? With vision undisturbed by time, You witness the minds of all living beings. Nevertheless, on Your order I will speak.

PURPORT

Since the Lord knows everything, there is no need to inform Him about anything. Still, to fullfill the Lord's purpose King Nṛga will speak.

TEXT 12

यावत्यः सिकता भूमेर्यावत्यो दिवि तारकाः ।
यावत्यो वर्षधाराश्च तावतीरददं स्म गाः ॥१२॥

yāvatyaḥ sikatā bhūmer
yāvatyo divi tārakāḥ
yāvatyo varṣa-dhārāś ca
tāvatīr adadaṁ sma gāḥ

yāvatyaḥ—as many; *sikatāḥ*—grains of sand; *bhūmeḥ*—belonging to the earth; *yāvatyaḥ*—as many; *divi*—in the sky; *tārakāḥ*—stars; *yāvatyaḥ*—as many; *varṣa*—of a rainfall; *dhārāḥ*—drops; *ca*—and; *tāvatīḥ*—that many; *adadam*—I gave; *sma*—indeed; *gāḥ*—cows.

TRANSLATION

I gave in charity as many cows as there are grains of sand on the earth, stars in the heavens, or drops in a rain shower.

PURPORT

The idea here is that the King gave innumerable cows in charity.

TEXT 13

पयस्विनीस्तरुणीः शीलरूप-
गुणोपपन्नाः कपिला हेमशृंगीः ।
न्यायार्जिता रूप्यखुराः सवत्सा
दुकूलमालाभरणा ददावहम् ॥१३॥

payasvinīs taruṇīḥ śīla-rūpa-
guṇopapannāḥ kapilā hema-śṛṅgīḥ
nyāyārjitā rūpya-khurāḥ sa-vatsā
dukūla-mālābharaṇā dadāv aham

payaḥ-vinīḥ—having milk; *taruṇīḥ*—young; *śīla*—with good behavior; *rūpa*—beauty; *guṇa*—and other qualities; *upapannāḥ*—endowed; *kapilāḥ*—brown; *hema*—gold; *śṛṅgīḥ*—with horns; *nyāya*—fairly; *arjitāḥ*—earned; *rūpya*—silver; *khurāḥ*—with hooves; *sa-vatsāḥ*—together with their calves; *dukūla*—fine cloth; *mālā*—with garlands; *ābharaṇāḥ*—adorned; *dadau*—gave; *aham*—I.

TRANSLATION

Young, brown, milk-laden cows, who were well behaved, beautiful and endowed with good qualities, who were all acquired honestly, and who had gilded horns, silver-plated hooves and decorations of fine ornamental cloths and garlands—such were the cows, along with their calves, that I gave in charity.

TEXTS 14–15

स्वलंकृतेभ्यो गुणशीलवद्भ्यः
सीदत्कुटुम्बेभ्य ऋतव्रतेभ्यः ।
तपःश्रुतब्रह्मवदान्यसद्भ्यः
प्रादां युवभ्यो द्विजपुंगवेभ्यः ॥१४॥
गोभूहिरण्यायतनाश्वहस्तिनः
कन्याः सदासीस्तिलरूप्यशय्याः ।

वासांसि रत्नानि परिच्छदान् रथान्
इष्टं च यज्ञैश्चरितं च पूर्तम् ॥१५॥

sv-alaṅkṛtebhyo guṇa-śīlavadbhyaḥ
sīdat-kuṭumbebhya ṛta-vratebhyaḥ
tapaḥ-śruta-brahma-vadānya-sadbhyaḥ
prādāṁ yuvabhyo dvija-puṅgavebhyaḥ

go-bhū-hiraṇyāyatanāśva-hastinaḥ
kanyāḥ sa-dāsīs tila-rūpya-śayyāḥ
vāsāṁsi ratnāni paricchadān rathān
iṣṭaṁ ca yajñaiś caritaṁ ca pūrtam

su—well; *alaṅkṛtebhyaḥ*—who were ornamented; *guṇa*—good qualities; *śīla*—and character; *vadbhyaḥ*—who possessed; *sīdat*—distressed; *kuṭumbebhyaḥ*—whose families; *ṛta*—to truth; *vratebhyaḥ*—dedicated; *tapaḥ*—for austerity; *śruta*—well known; *brahma*—in the *Vedas; vadānya*—vastly learned; *sadbhyaḥ*—saintly; *prādām*—I gave; *yuvabhyaḥ*—who were young; *dvija*—to *brāhmaṇas; pum-gavebhyaḥ*—most exceptional; *go*—cows; *bhū*—land; *hiraṇya*—gold; *āyatana*—houses; *aśva*—horses; *hastinaḥ*—and elephants; *kanyāḥ*—marriageable daughters; *sa*—with; *dāsīḥ*—maidservants; *tila*—sesame; *rūpya*—silver; *śayyāḥ*—and beds; *vāsāṁsi*—clothing; *ratnāni*—jewels; *paricchadān*—furniture; *rathān*—chariots; *iṣṭam*—worship executed; *ca*—and; *yajñaiḥ*—by Vedic fire sacrifices; *caritam*—done; *ca*—and; *pūrtam*—pious works.

TRANSLATION

I first honored the *brāhmaṇas* who were recipients of my charity by decorating them with fine ornaments. Those most exalted *brāhmaṇas,* whose families were in need, were young and possessed of excellent character and qualities. They were dedicated to truth, famous for their austerity, vastly learned in the Vedic scriptures and saintly in their behavior. I gave them cows, land, gold and houses, along with horses, elephants and marriageable girls with maidservants, as well as sesame, silver, fine beds, clothing, jewels, furniture and chariots. In addition, I performed Vedic sacrifices and executed various pious welfare activities.

TEXT 16

कस्यचिद्द्विजमुख्यस्य भ्रष्टा गौर्मम गोधने ।
सम्पृक्ताविदुषा सा च मया दत्ता द्विजातये ॥१६॥

kasyacid dvija-mukhyasya
bhraṣṭā gaur mama go-dhane
sampṛktāviduṣā sā ca
mayā dattā dvijātaye

kasyacit—of a certain; *dvija*—*brāhmaṇa; mukhyasya*—first class; *bhraṣṭā*—lost; *gauḥ*—a cow; *mama*—my; *go-dhane*—in the herd; *sampṛktā*—becoming mixed; *aviduṣā*—who was unaware; *sā*—she; *ca*—and; *mayā*—by me; *dattā*—given; *dvi-jātaye*—to (another) *brāhmaṇa.*

TRANSLATION

Once a cow belonging to a certain first-class *brāhmaṇa* wandered away and entered my herd. Unaware of this, I gave that cow in charity to a different *brāhmaṇa.*

PURPORT

Śrīla Śrīdhara Svāmī explains that the term *dvija-mukhya,* "first-class *brāhmaṇa,*" here indicates a *brāhmaṇa* who has stopped accepting charity and would thus refuse to accept even one hundred thousand cows in exchange for the cow that had been improperly given away.

TEXT 17

तां नीयमानां तत्स्वामी दृष्ट्वोवाच ममेति तम् ।
ममेति परिग्राह्याह नृगो मे दत्तवानिति ॥१७॥

tāṁ nīyamānāṁ tat-svāmī
dṛṣṭvovāca mameti tam
mameti parigrāhy āha
nṛgo me dattavān iti

tām—she, the cow; *nīyamānām*—being led away; *tat*—her; *svāmī*—master; *dṛṣṭvā*—seeing; *uvāca*—said; *mama*—mine; *iti*—thus; *tam*—to him; *mama*—mine; *iti*—thus; *parigrāhī*—he who had accepted the gift; *āha*—said; *nṛgaḥ*—King Nṛga; *me*—to me; *dattavān*—gave; *iti*—thus.

TRANSLATION

When the cow's first owner saw her being led away, he said, "She is mine!" The second *brāhmaṇa*, who had accepted her as a gift, replied, "No, she's mine! Nṛga gave her to me."

TEXT 18

विप्रौ विवदमानौ मामूचतुः स्वार्थसाधकौ ।
भवान् दातापहर्तेति तच्छ्रुत्वा मेऽभवद् भ्रमः ॥१८॥

viprau vivadamānau mām
ūcatuḥ svārtha-sādhakau
bhavān dātāpaharteti
tac chrutvā me 'bhavad bhramaḥ

viprau—the two *brāhmaṇas; vivadamānau*—arguing; *mām*—to me; *ūcatuḥ*—said; *sva*—their own; *artha*—interest; *sādhakau*—fulfilling; *bhavān*—you, sir; *dātā*—giver; *apahartā*—taker; *iti*—thus; *tat*—this; *śrutvā*—hearing; *me*—my; *abhavat*—there arose; *bhramaḥ*—consternation.

TRANSLATION

As the two *brāhmaṇas* argued, each trying to fulfill his own purpose, they came to me. One of them said, "You gave me this cow," and the other said, "But you stole her from me." Hearing this, I was bewildered.

TEXTS 19–20

अनुनीतावुभौ विप्रौ धर्मकृच्छ्रगतेन वै ।
गवां लक्षं प्रकृष्टानां दास्याम्येषा प्रदीयताम् ॥१९॥

भवन्तावनुगृह्णीतां किंकरस्याविजानतः ।
समुद्धरतं मां कृच्छ्रात्पतन्तं निरयेऽशुचौ ॥२०॥

anunītāv ubhau viprau
dharma-kṛcchra-gatena vai
gavāṁ lakṣaṁ prakṛṣṭānāṁ
dāsyāmy eṣā pradīyatām

bhavantāv anugṛhṇītāṁ
kiṅkarasyāvijānataḥ
samuddharataṁ māṁ kṛcchrāt
patantaṁ niraye 'śucau

anunītau—humbly requested; *ubhau*—both; *viprau*—the two *brāhmaṇas; dharma*—of religious duty; *kṛcchra*—a difficult situation; *gatena*—by (me) who was in; *vai*—indeed; *gavām*—of cows; *lakṣam*—a lakh (one hundred thousand); *prakṛṣṭānām*—best quality; *dāsyāmi*—I will give; *eṣā*—this one; *pradīyatām*—please give; *bhavantau*—the two of you; *anugṛhṇītām*—should please show mercy; *kiṅkarasya*—to your servant; *avijānataḥ*—who was unaware; *samuddharatam*—please save; *mām*—me; *kṛcchrāt*—from danger; *patantam*—falling; *niraye*—into hell; *aśucau*—unclean.

TRANSLATION

Finding myself in a terrible dilemma concerning my duty in the situation, I humbly entreated both the *brāhmaṇas:* "I will give one hundred thousand of the best cows in exchange for this one. Please give her back to me. Your good selves should be merciful to me, your servant. I did not know what I was doing. Please save me from this difficult situation, or I'll surely fall into a filthy hell."

TEXT 21

नाहं प्रतीच्छे वै राजन्नित्युक्त्वा स्वाम्यपाक्रमत् ।
नान्यद् गवामप्ययुतमिच्छामीत्यपरो ययौ ॥२१॥

nāhaṁ pratīcche vai rājann
ity uktvā svāmy apākramat

nānyad gavām apy ayutam
icchāmīty aparo yayau

na—not; *aham*—I; *pratīcche*—want; *vai*—indeed; *rājan*—O King; *iti*—thus; *uktvā*—saying; *svāmī*—the owner; *apākramat*—went away; *na*—not; *anyat*—in addition; *gavām*—of cows; *api*—even; *ayutam*—ten thousand; *icchāmi*—I want; *iti*—thus saying; *aparaḥ*—the other (*brāhmaṇa*); *yayau*—left.

TRANSLATION

The present owner of the cow said, "I don't want anything in exchange for this cow, O King," and went away. The other *brāhmaṇa* declared, "I don't want even ten thousand more cows [than you are offering]," and he too went away.

PURPORT

In *Kṛṣṇa, the Supreme Personality of Godhead,* Śrīla Prabhupāda comments, "Thus disagreeing with the King's proposal, both *brāhmaṇas* left the palace in anger, thinking that their lawful position had been usurped."

TEXT 22

एतस्मिन्नन्तरे यामैर्दूतैर्नीतो यमक्षयम् ।
यमेन पृष्टस्तत्राहं देवदेव जगत्पते ॥२२॥

etasminn antare yāmair
dūtair nīto yama-kṣayam
yamena pṛṣṭas tatrāhaṁ
deva-deva jagat-pate

etasmin—at this; *antare*—opportunity; *yāmaiḥ*—of Yamarāja, the lord of death; *dūtaiḥ*—by the messengers; *nītaḥ*—taken; *yama-kṣayam*—to the abode of Yamarāja; *yamena*—by Yamarāja; *pṛṣṭaḥ*—questioned; *tatra*—there; *aham*—I; *deva-deva*—O Lord of lords; *jagat*—of the universe; *pate*—O master.

TRANSLATION

O Lord of lords, O master of the universe, the agents of Yamarāja, taking advantage of the opportunity thus created, later carried me to his abode. There Yamarāja himself questioned me.

PURPORT

According to the *ācāryas,* the King's performance of fruitive activities had previously been flawless. But now an inadvertent descrepancy had arisen, and so when the King died the Yamadūtas took him to the abode of Yamarāja, called Saṁyamanī.

TEXT 23

पूर्वं त्वमशुभं भुङ्क्ष उताहो नृपते शुभम् ।
नान्तं दानस्य धर्मस्य पश्ये लोकस्य भास्वतः ॥२३॥

pūrvaṁ tvam aśubhaṁ bhuṅkṣa
utāho nṛpate śubham
nāntaṁ dānasya dharmasya
paśye lokasya bhāsvataḥ

pūrvam—first; *tvam*—you; *aśubham*—impious reactions; *bhuṅkṣe*—wish to experience; *uta āha u*—or else; *nṛ-pate*—O King; *śubham*—pious reactions; *na*—not; *antam*—the end; *dānasya*—of charity; *dharmasya*—religious; *paśye*—I see; *lokasya*—of the world; *bhāsvataḥ*—shining.

TRANSLATION

[Yamarāja said:] My dear King, do you wish to experience the results of your sins first, or those of your piety? Indeed, I see no end to the dutiful charity you have performed, or to your consequent enjoyment in the radiant heavenly planets.

TEXT 24

पूर्वं देवाशुभं भुञ्ज इति प्राह पतेति सः ।
तावदद्राक्षमात्मानं कृकलासं पतन् प्रभो ॥२४॥

pūrvaṁ devāśubhaṁ bhuñja
iti prāha pateti saḥ
tāvad adrākṣam ātmānaṁ
kṛkalāsaṁ patan prabho

pūrvam—first; *deva*—O lord; *aśubham*—the sinful reactions; *bhuñje*—I will experience; *iti*—thus saying; *prāha*—said; *pata*—fall; *iti*—thus; *saḥ*—he; *tāvat*—just then; *adrākṣam*—I saw; *ātmānam*—myself; *kṛkalāsam*—a lizard; *patan*—falling; *prabho*—O master.

TRANSLATION

I replied, "First, my lord, let me suffer my sinful reactions," and Yamarāja said, "Then fall!" At once I fell, and while falling I saw myself becoming a lizard, O master.

TEXT 25

ब्रह्मण्यस्य वदान्यस्य तव दासस्य केशव ।
स्मृतिर्नाद्यापि विध्वस्ता भवत्सन्दर्शनार्थिनः ॥२५॥

brahmaṇyasya vadānyasya
tava dāsasya keśava
smṛtir nādyāpi vidhvastā
bhavat-sandarśanārthinaḥ

brahmaṇyasya—who was devoted to the *brāhmaṇas; vadānyasya*—who was generous; *tava*—Your; *dāsasya*—of the servant; *keśava*—O Kṛṣṇa; *smṛtiḥ*—the memory; *na*—not; *adya*—today; *api*—even; *vidhvastā*—lost; *bhavat*—Your; *sandarśana*—audience; *arthinaḥ*—who hankered for.

TRANSLATION

O Keśava, as Your servant I was devoted to the *brāhmaṇas* and generous to them, and I always hankered for Your audience. Therefore even till now I have never forgotten [my past life].

PURPORT

Śrīla Jīva Gosvāmī comments on this verse as follows: "Since King Nṛga openly declared that he had two outstanding qualities—namely devotion to the *brāhmaṇas,* and generosity—it is clear that he possessed these qualities only partially, since someone who is truly pure would not boast about them. It is also clear that King Nṛga considered such piety to be a separate goal, desirable for its own sake. Thus he did not fully appreciate pure devotional service to Lord Kṛṣṇa. Kṛṣṇa had not been the only goal of Nṛga's life, as He was for Ambarīṣa Mahārāja, even in the stage of regulative practice. Nor do we find that King Nṛga overcame obstacles like those Ambarīṣa did when Durvāsā Muni became angry at him. Still, we can conclude that since Nṛga was able to see the Lord for some reason or another, he must have had the good quality of sincerely desiring the Lord's association."

Śrīla Prabhupāda confirms the above analysis in *Kṛṣṇa, the Supreme Personality of Godhead:* "On the whole, [Nṛga] had not developed Kṛṣṇa consciousness. The Kṛṣṇa conscious person develops love of God, Kṛṣṇa, not love for pious or impious activities; therefore he is not subjected to the results of such action. As stated in the *Brahma-saṁhitā,* a devotee, by the grace of the Lord, does not become subjected to the resultant reactions of fruitive activities."

Śrīla Viśvanātha Cakravartī offers the following commentary: "When Nṛga mentioned 'one who hankered to have Your audience,' he was referring to an incident concerning a certain great devotee King Nṛga had once met. This devotee was very eager to acquire a temple for a most beautiful Deity of the Supreme Lord, and he also wanted copies of such scriptures as the *Bhagavad-gītā* and *Śrīmad-Bhāgavatam.* Being very generous, Nṛga arranged for these things, and the devotee was so satisfied that he blessed the King: 'My dear King, may you have the audience of the Supreme Lord.' From that time on, Nṛga desired to see the Lord."

TEXT 26

स त्वं कथं मम विभोऽक्षिपथः परात्मा
योगेश्वरैः श्रुतिदृशामलहृद्विभाव्यः ।
साक्षादधोक्षज उरुव्यसनान्धबुद्धेः
स्यान्मेऽनुदृश्य इह यस्य भवापवर्गः ॥२६॥

sa tvaṁ kathaṁ mama vibho 'kṣi-pathaḥ parātmā
yogeśvaraiḥ śruti-dṛśāmala-hṛd-vibhāvyaḥ
sākṣād adhokṣaja uru-vyasanāndha-buddheḥ
syān me 'nudṛśya iha yasya bhavāpavargaḥ

saḥ—He; *tvam*—Yourself; *katham*—how; *mama*—to me; *vibho*—O almighty one; *akṣi-pathaḥ*—visible; *para-ātmā*—the Supreme Soul; *yoga*—of mystic *yoga; īśvaraiḥ*—by masters; *śruti*—of the scriptures; *dṛśā*—by the eye; *amala*—spotless; *hṛt*—within their hearts; *vibhāvyaḥ*—to be meditated upon; *sākṣāt*—directly visible; *adhokṣaja*—O transcendental Lord, who cannot be seen by material senses; *uru*—severe; *vyasana*—by troubles; *andha*—blinded; *buddheḥ*—whose intelligence; *syāt*—it may be; *me*—for me; *anudṛśyaḥ*—to be perceived; *iha*—in this world; *yasya*—whose; *bhava*—of material life; *apavargaḥ*—cessation.

TRANSLATION

O almighty one, how is it that my eyes see You here before me? You are the Supreme Soul, whom the greatest masters of mystic *yoga* can meditate upon within their pure hearts only by employing the spiritual eye of the *Vedas*. Then how, O transcendental Lord, are You directly visible to me, since my intelligence has been blinded by the severe tribulations of material life? Only one who has finished his material entanglement in this world should be able to see You.

PURPORT

Even in the body of a lizard, King Nṛga could remember his previous life. And now that he had the opportunity to see the Lord, he could understand that he had received special mercy from the Personality of Godhead.

TEXTS 27–28

देवदेव जगन्नाथ गोविन्द पुरुषोत्तम ।
नारायण हृषीकेश पुण्यश्लोकाच्युताव्यय ॥२७॥
अनुजानीहि मां कृष्ण यान्तं देवगतिं प्रभो ।
यत्र क्वापि सतश्चेतो भूयान्मे त्वत्पदास्पदम् ॥२८॥

deva-deva jagan-nātha
govinda puruṣottama
nārāyaṇa hṛṣīkeśa
puṇya-ślokācyutāvyaya

anujānīhi māṁ kṛṣṇa
yāntaṁ deva-gatiṁ prabho
yatra kvāpi sataś ceto
bhūyān me tvat-padāspadam

deva-deva—O Lord of lords; *jagat*—of the universe; *nātha*—O master; *go-vinda*—O Lord of the cows; *puruṣa-uttama*—O Supreme Personality; *nārāyaṇa*—O foundation of all living beings; *hṛṣīkeśa*—O master of the senses; *puṇya-śloka*—O You who are glorified in transcendental poetry; *acyuta*—O infallible one; *avyaya*—O undiminishing one; *anujānīhi*—please give leave; *mām*—to me; *kṛṣṇa*—O Kṛṣṇa; *yāntam*—who am going; *deva-gatim*—to the world of the demigods; *prabho*—O master; *yatra kva api*—wherever; *sataḥ*—residing; *cetaḥ*—the mind; *bhūyāt*—may it be; *me*—my; *tvat*—Your; *pada*—of the feet; *āspadam*—whose shelter.

TRANSLATION

O Devadeva, Jagannātha, Govinda, Puruṣottama, Nārāyaṇa, Hṛṣīkeśa, Puṇyaśloka, Acyuta, Avyaya! O Kṛṣṇa, please permit me to depart for the world of the demigods. Wherever I live, O master, may my mind always take shelter of Your feet.

PURPORT

Śrīla Viśvanātha Cakravartī comments as follows on this verse: His faith emboldened upon receiving the Lord's mercy and thus attaining the status of servitude, King Nṛga properly glorifies the Lord by chanting His names and then asks the Lord's permission to take his leave. The spirit of his prayer is as follows: "You are Devadeva, God even of the gods, and Jagannātha, the master of the universe, so please be my master. O Govinda, please make me Your property with the same merciful glance You use to enchant the cows. You can do this because You are Puruṣottama, the supreme form of Godhead. O Nārāyaṇa, since You are the foundation of the living entities, please be my support, even though I am a bad living entity. O Hṛṣīkeśa, please make my senses Your own. O Puṇyaśloka, now You have become famous as the deliverer of Nṛga. O Acyuta, please never be lost to my mind. O Avyaya, You will never diminish in my mind." Thus the great *Bhāgavatam* commentator Śrīla Viśvanātha Cakravartī explains the purport of these verses.

TEXT 29

नमस्ते सर्वभावाय ब्रह्मणेऽनन्तशक्तये ।
कृष्णाय वासुदेवाय योगानां पतये नमः ॥२९॥

namas te sarva-bhāvāya
brahmaṇe 'nanta-śaktaye
kṛṣṇāya vāsudevāya
yogānāṁ pataye namaḥ

namaḥ—obeisances; *te*—to You; *sarva-bhāvāya*—the source of all beings; *brahmaṇe*—the Supreme Absolute Truth; *ananta*—unlimited; *śaktaye*—the possessor of potencies; *kṛṣṇāya*—to Kṛṣṇa; *vāsudevāya*—the son of Vasudeva; *yogānām*—of all processes of *yoga; pataye*—to the Lord; *namaḥ*—obeisances.

TRANSLATION

I offer my repeated obeisances unto You, Kṛṣṇa, the son of Vasudeva. You are the source of all beings, the Supreme Absolute Truth, the possessor of unlimited potencies, the master of all spiritual disciplines.

PURPORT

Śrīla Śrīdhara Svāmī comments that King Nṛga here offers his obeisances to Brahman—that is, the Absolute Truth—who is unchanged in spite of performing activities. Since ancient times, Western philosophers have puzzled over the question of how God can be unchanging and yet perform activities. Śrīdhara Svāmī states that this doubt is answered here by the term *ananta-śaktaye*, which describes the Lord as "the possessor of unlimited potency." Thus through the Lord's infinite potencies He can perform innumerable activities without changing His essential nature.

The King further offers his obeisances to Śrī Kṛṣṇa, the possesser of the form of eternal bliss and the supreme goal of life. The holy name of Kṛṣṇa is analyzed in a verse from the *Mahābhārata* (*Udyoga-parva* 71.4), which Śrīla Prabhupāda quotes in his *Caitanya-caritāmṛta* (*Madhya* 9.30, purport):

kṛṣir bhū-vācakaḥ śabdo
ṇaś ca nirvṛti-vācakaḥ
tayor aikyaṁ paraṁ brahma
kṛṣṇa ity abhidhīyate

"'The word *kṛṣ* is the attractive feature of the Lord's existence, and *ṇa* means 'spiritual pleasure.' When the verb *kṛṣ* is added to *ṇa*, it becomes *kṛṣṇa,* which indicates the Absolute Truth.'"

King Nṛga offers the above prayers as he is about to leave the personal assocaition of the Supreme Lord.

TEXT 30

इत्युक्त्वा तं परिक्रम्य पादौ स्पृष्ट्वा स्वमौलिना ।
अनुज्ञातो विमानाग्र्यमारुहत्पश्यतां नृणाम् ॥३०॥

ity uktvā taṁ parikramya
pādau spṛṣṭvā sva-maulinā
anujñāto vimānāgryam
āruhat paśyatāṁ nṛṇām

iti—thus; *uktvā*—having spoken; *tam*—Him; *parikramya*—circumambulating; *pādau*—His feet; *spṛṣṭvā*—touching; *sva*—with his; *maulinā*—crown; *anujñātaḥ*—given leave; *vimāna*—a celestial airplane; *agryam*—excellent; *āruhat*—he boarded; *paśyatām*—as they watched; *nṛṇām*—humans.

TRANSLATION

Having spoken thus, Mahārāja Nṛga circumambulated Lord Kṛṣṇa and touched his crown to the Lord's feet. Granted permis-

sion to depart, King Nṛga then boarded a wonderful celestial airplane as all the people present looked on.

TEXT 31

कृष्णः परिजनं प्राह भगवान् देवकीसुतः ।
ब्रह्मण्यदेवो धर्मात्मा राजन्याननुशिक्षयन् ॥३१॥

kṛṣṇaḥ parijanaṁ prāha
bhagavān devakī-sutaḥ
brahmaṇya-devo dharmātmā
rājanyān anuśikṣayan

kṛṣṇaḥ—Lord Kṛṣṇa; *parijanam*—His personal associates; *prāha*—addressed; *bhagavān*—the Supreme Personality; *devakī-sutaḥ*—son of Devakī; *brahmaṇya*—devoted to the *brāhmaṇas; devaḥ*—God; *dharma*—of religion; *ātmā*—the soul; *rājanyān*—the royal class; *anuśikṣayan*—in effect instructing.

TRANSLATION

The Supreme Personality of Godhead—Lord Kṛṣṇa, the son of Devakī—who is especially devoted to the *brāhmaṇas* and who embodies the essence of religion, then spoke to His personal associates and thus instructed the royal class in general.

TEXT 32

दुर्जरं बत ब्रह्मस्वं भुक्तमग्नेर्मनागपि ।
तेजीयसोऽपि किमुत राज्ञां ईश्वरमानिनाम् ॥३२॥

durjaraṁ bata brahma-svaṁ
bhuktam agner manāg api
tejīyaso 'pi kim uta
rājñāṁ īśvara-māninām

durjaram—indigestible; *bata*—indeed; *brahma*—of a *brāhmaṇa; svam*—the property; *bhuktam*—consumed; *agneḥ*—than fire; *manāk*—a little;

api—even; *tejīyasaḥ*—for one who is more intensely potent; *api*—even; *kim uta*—what then to speak of; *rājñām*—for kings; *īśvara*—controllers; *māninām*—who presume themselves.

TRANSLATION

[Lord Kṛṣṇa said:] How indigestible is the property of a *brāhmaṇa,* even when enjoyed just slightly and by one more potent than fire! What then to speak of kings who try to enjoy it, presuming themselves lords.

PURPORT

Even those made powerful by austerity, mystic *yoga* and so on cannot enjoy property stolen from a *brāhmaṇa,* and what to speak of others.

TEXT 33

नाहं हालाहलं मन्ये विषं यस्य प्रतिक्रिया ।
ब्रह्मस्वं हि विषं प्रोक्तं नास्य प्रतिविधिर्भुवि ॥३३॥

nāhaṁ hālāhalaṁ manye
viṣaṁ yasya pratikriyā
brahma-svaṁ hi viṣaṁ proktaṁ
nāsya pratividhir bhuvi

na—not; *aham*—I; *hālāhalam*—the poison named *hālāhala,* which Lord Śiva is famous for having drunk without toxic effects; *manye*—I consider; *viṣam*—poison; *yasya*—of which; *pratikriyā*—counteraction; *brahma-svam*—a *brāhmaṇa's* property; *hi*—indeed; *viṣam*—poison; *proktam*—called; *na*—not; *asya*—for it; *pratividhiḥ*—antidote; *bhuvi*—in the world.

TRANSLATION

I do not consider *hālāhala* to be real poison, because it has an antidote. But a *brāhmaṇa's* property, when stolen, can truly be called poison, for it has no antidote in this world.

PURPORT

One who takes a *brāhmaṇa's* property, thinking to enjoy it, has actually taken the most deadly poison.

TEXT 34

हिनस्ति विषमत्तारं वह्निरद्भिः प्रशाम्यति ।
कुलं समूलं दहति ब्रह्मस्वारणिपावकः ॥३४॥

hinasti viṣam attāraṁ
vahnir adbhiḥ praśāmyati
kulaṁ sa-mūlaṁ dahati
brahma-svāraṇi-pāvakaḥ

hinasti—destroys; *viṣam*—poison; *attāram*—the one who ingests; *vahniḥ*—fire; *adbhiḥ*—with water; *praśāmyati*—is extinguished; *kulam*—one's family; *sa-mūlam*—to the root; *dahati*—burns; *brahma-sva*—a *brāhmaṇa's* property; *araṇi*—whose kindling wood; *pāvakaḥ*—the fire.

TRANSLATION

Poison kills only the person who ingests it, and an ordinary fire may be extinguished with water. But the fire generated from the kindling wood of a *brāhmaṇa's* property burns the thief's entire family down to the root.

PURPORT

Śrīla Viśvanātha Cakravartī compares the fire ignited by stealing a *brāhmaṇa's* property to the fire that blazes within the cavity of an old tree. Such a fire cannot be put out even with the water of numerous rainfalls. Rather, it burns the whole tree from within, all the way down to the roots in the ground. Similarly, the fire ignited by stealing a *brāhmaṇa's* property is the most deadly and should be avoided at all costs.

TEXT 35

ब्रह्मस्वं दुरनुज्ञातं भुक्तं हन्ति त्रिपूरुषम् ।
प्रसह्य तु बलाद् भुक्तं दश पूर्वान् दशापरान् ॥३५॥

brahma-svaṁ duranujñātaṁ
bhuktaṁ hanti tri-pūruṣam
prasahya tu balād bhuktaṁ
daśa pūrvān daśāparān

brahma-svam—a *brāhmaṇa's* property; *duranujñātam*—not given proper permission; *bhuktam*—enjoyed; *hanti*—destroys; *tri*—three; *pūruṣam*—persons; *prasahya*—by force; *tu*—but; *balāt*—resorting to external power (of the government, etc.); *bhuktam*—enjoyed; *daśa*—ten; *pūrvān*—previous; *daśa*—ten; *aparān*—subsequent.

TRANSLATION

If a person enjoys a *brāhmaṇa's* property without receiving due permission, that property destroys three generations of his family. But if he takes it by force or gets the government or other outsiders to help him usurp it, then ten generations of his ancestors and ten generations of his descendants are all destroyed.

PURPORT

According to Śrīla Śrīdhara Svāmī, *tri-pūruṣa* refers to oneself, one's sons and one's grandsons.

TEXT 36

राजानो राजलक्ष्म्यान्धा नात्मपातं विचक्षते ।
निरयं येऽभिमन्यन्ते ब्रह्मस्वं साधु बालिशाः ॥३६॥

rājāno rāja-lakṣmyāndhā
nātma-pātaṁ vicakṣate
nirayaṁ ye 'bhimanyante
brahma-svaṁ sādhu bāliśāḥ

rājānaḥ—members of the kingly class; *rāja*—royal; *lakṣmyā*—by opulence; *andhāḥ*—blinded; *na*—do not; *ātma*—their own; *pātam*—fall; *vicakṣate*—foresee; *nirayam*—hell; *ye*—who; *abhimanyante*—hanker for; *brahma-svam*—a *brāhmaṇa's* property; *sādhu*—as appropriate; *bāliśāḥ*—childish.

TRANSLATION

Members of the royal order, blinded by royal opulence, fail to foresee their own downfall. Childishly hankering to enjoy a *brāhmaṇa's* property, they are actually hankering to go to hell.

TEXTS 37–38

गृह्णन्ति यावतः पांशून् क्रन्दतामश्रुबिन्दवः ।
विप्राणां हृतवृत्तीनां वदान्यानां कुटुम्बिनाम् ॥३७॥
राजानो राजकुल्याश्च तावतोऽब्दान्निरंकुशाः ।
कुम्भीपाकेषु पच्यन्ते ब्रह्मदायापहारिणः ॥३८॥

gṛhṇanti yāvataḥ pāṁśūn
krandatām aśru-bindavaḥ
viprāṇāṁ hṛta-vṛttīnāṁ
vadānyānāṁ kuṭumbinām

rājāno rāja-kulyāś ca
tāvato 'bdān niraṅkuśāḥ
kumbhī-pākeṣu pacyante
brahma-dāyāpahāriṇaḥ

gṛhṇanti—touch; *yāvataḥ*—as many; *pāṁśūn*—particles of dust; *krandatām*—who are crying; *aśru-bindavaḥ*—teardrops; *viprāṇām*—of *brāhmaṇas; hṛta*—taken away; *vṛttīnām*—whose means of support; *vadānyānām*—generous; *kuṭumbinām*—family men; *rājānaḥ*—the kings; *rāja-kulyāḥ*—other members of the royal families; *ca*—also; *tāvataḥ*—that many; *abdān*—years; *niraṅkuśāḥ*—uncontrolled; *kumbhī-pākeṣu*—in the hell known as Kumbhīpāka; *pacyante*—they are cooked; *brahma-dāya*—of the *brāhmaṇa's* share; *apahāriṇaḥ*—the usurpers.

TRANSLATION

For as many years as there are particles of dust touched by the tears of generous *brāhmaṇas* who have dependent families and whose property is stolen, uncontrolled kings who usurp a *brāhmaṇa's* property are cooked, along with their royal families, in the hell known as Kumbhīpāka.

TEXT 39

स्वदत्तां परदत्तां वा ब्रह्मवृत्तिं हरेच्च यः ।
षष्टिवर्षसहस्राणि विष्ठायां जायते कृमिः ॥३९॥

sva-dattāṁ para-dattāṁ vā
brahma-vṛttiṁ harec ca yaḥ
ṣaṣṭi-varṣa-sahasrāṇi
viṣṭhāyāṁ jāyate kṛmiḥ

sva—by himself; *dattām*—given; *para*—by another; *dattām*—given; *vā*—or; *brahma-vṛttim*—a *brāhmaṇa's* property; *haret*—steals; *ca*—and; *yaḥ*—who; *ṣaṣṭi*—sixty; *varṣa*—of years; *sahasrāṇi*—thousands; *viṣṭhāyām*—in feces; *jāyate*—is born; *kṛmiḥ*—a worm.

TRANSLATION

Whether it be his own gift or someone else's, a person who steals a *brāhmaṇa's* property will take birth as a worm in feces for sixty thousand years.

TEXT 40

न मे ब्रह्मधनं भूयाद्यद् गृध्वाल्पायुषो नराः ।
पराजिताश्च्युता राज्याद् भवन्त्युद्वेजिनोऽहयः ॥४०॥

na me brahma-dhanaṁ bhūyād
yad gṛdhvālpāyuṣo narāḥ
parājitāś cyutā rājyād
bhavanty udvejino 'hayaḥ

na—not; *me*—to Me; *brahma*—of *brāhmaṇas; dhanam*—the wealth; *bhūyāt*—may it come; *yat*—which; *gṛdhvā*—desiring; *alpa-āyuṣaḥ*—short-lived; *narāḥ*—men; *parājitāḥ*—defeated; *cyutāḥ*—deprived; *rājyāt*—of kingdom; *bhavanti*—become; *udvejinaḥ*—creators of distress; *ahayaḥ*—snakes.

TRANSLATION

I do not desire *brāhmaṇas'* wealth. Those who lust after it become short-lived and are defeated. They lose their kingdoms and become snakes, who trouble others.

TEXT 41

विप्रं कृतागसमपि नैव द्रुह्यत मामकाः ।
घ्नन्तं बहु शपन्तं वा नमस्कुरुत नित्यशः ॥४१॥

vipraṁ kṛtāgasam api
naiva druhyata māmakāḥ
ghnantaṁ bahu śapantaṁ vā
namas-kuruta nityaśaḥ

vipram—a learned *brāhmaṇa; kṛta*—having committed; *āgasam*—sin; *api*—even; *na*—not; *eva*—indeed; *druhyata*—do not treat inimically; *māmakāḥ*—O My followers; *ghnantam*—striking physically; *bahu*—repeatedly; *śapantam*—cursing; *vā*—or; *namaḥ-kuruta*—you should offer obeisances; *nityaśaḥ*—always.

TRANSLATION

My dear followers, never treat a learned *brāhmaṇa* harshly, even if he has sinned. Even if he attacks you physically or repeatedly curses you, always continue to offer him obeisances.

PURPORT

Lord Kṛṣṇa offers this instruction not only to His personal associates but to all those who claim to be followers of the Supreme Personality of Godhead.

TEXT 42

यथाहं प्रणमे विप्राननुकालं समाहितः ।
तथा नमत यूयं च योऽन्यथा मे स दण्डभाक् ॥४२॥

yathāhaṁ praṇame viprān
anukālaṁ samāhitaḥ
tathā namata yūyaṁ ca
yo 'nyathā me sa daṇḍa-bhāk

yathā—as; *aham*—I; *praṇame*—bow down; *viprān*—to *brāhmaṇas; anu-kālam*—all the time; *samāhitaḥ*—carefully; *tathā*—so; *namata*—should bow down; *yūyam*—all of you; *ca*—also; *yaḥ*—one who; *anyathā*—(does) otherwise; *me*—by Me; *saḥ*—he; *daṇḍa*—for punishment; *bhāk*—a candidate.

TRANSLATION

Just as I always carefully bow down to *brāhmaṇas*, so all of you should likewise bow down to them. I will punish anyone who acts otherwise.

TEXT 43

ब्राह्मणार्थो ह्यपहृतो हर्तारं पातयत्यधः ।
अजानन्तमपि ह्येनं नृगं ब्राह्मणगौरिव ॥४३॥

brāhmaṇārtho hy apahṛto
hartāraṁ pātayaty adhaḥ
ajānantam api hy enaṁ
nṛgaṁ brāhmaṇa-gaur iva

brāhmaṇa—of a *brāhmaṇa; arthaḥ*—the property; *hi*—indeed; *apahṛtaḥ*—taken away; *hartāram*—the taker; *pātayati*—causes to fall; *adhaḥ*—down; *ajānantam*—unaware; *api*—even; *hi*—indeed; *enam*—this person; *nṛgam*—King Nṛga; *brāhmaṇa*—of the *brāhmaṇa; gauḥ*—the cow; *iva*—as.

TRANSLATION

When a *brāhmaṇa's* property is stolen, even unknowingly, it certainly causes the person who takes it to fall down, just as the *brāhmaṇa's* cow did to Nṛga.

PURPORT

The Lord here demonstrates that His instructions are not theoretical but practical, as seen concretely in the case of Nṛga Mahārāja.

TEXT 44

एवं विश्राव्य भगवान्मुकुन्दो द्वारकौकसः ।
पावनः सर्वलोकानां विवेश निजमन्दिरम् ॥४४॥

evaṁ viśrāvya bhagavān
mukundo dvārakaukasaḥ
pāvanaḥ sarva-lokānāṁ
viveśa nija-mandiram

evam—thus; *viśrāvya*—making hear; *bhagavān*—the Supreme Lord; *mukundaḥ*—Kṛṣṇa; *dvārakā-okasaḥ*—the residents of Dvārakā; *pāvanaḥ*—the purifier; *sarva*—of all; *lokānām*—the worlds; *viveśa*—He entered; *nija*—His; *mandiram*—palace.

TRANSLATION

Having thus instructed the residents of Dvārakā, Lord Mukunda, purifier of all the worlds, entered His palace.

Thus end the purports of the humble servants of His Divine Grace A. C. Bhaktivedanta Swami Prabhupāda to the Tenth Canto, Sixty-fourth Chapter, of the Śrīmad-Bhāgavatam, *entitled "The Deliverance of King Nṛga."*

CHAPTER SIXTY-FIVE

Lord Balarāma Visits Vṛndāvana

This chapter relates how Lord Balarāma went to Gokula, enjoyed the company of the cowherd girls and dragged the Yamunā River.

One day Lord Balarāma went to Gokula to see His relatives and friends. When He arrived there, the elder *gopīs* and Lord Kṛṣṇa's parents, Nanda and Yaśodā, who had all been in great anxiety for a long time, embraced Him and blessed Him. Lord Balarāma offered appropriate respects and greetings to each of His worshipable elders according to age, friendship and family relation. After Gokula's residents and Lord Balarāma had inquired about each other's welfare, the Lord rested from His journey.

In a short while the young *gopīs* came to Lord Balarāma and questioned Him about Kṛṣṇa's well-being. They asked, "Does Kṛṣṇa still remember His parents and friends, and will He be coming to Gokula to visit them? For Kṛṣṇa's sake we gave up everything—even our fathers, mothers and other relatives—but now He has abandoned us. How could we help but put our faith in Kṛṣṇa's words after seeing His sweetly smiling face and thus being overwhelmed by the urges of Cupid? Still, if Kṛṣṇa can spend His days in separation from us, why can't we tolerate separation from Him? So there is no reason to keep talking about Him." In this manner the *gopīs* remembered Śrī Kṛṣṇa's charming talks, enchanting glances, playful gestures and loving embraces, and as a result they began to cry. Lord Balarāma consoled them by conveying the attractive messages Kṛṣṇa had given Him for them.

Lord Balarāma stayed in Gokula for two months, sporting with the *gopīs* in the groves on the Yamunā's shore. The demigods who witnessed these pastimes played kettledrums in the heavens and showered down flower petals, while the celestial sages recited Balarāma's glories.

One day Lord Balarāma became intoxicated by drinking some *vāruṇī* liquor and began wandering about the forest in the company of the *gopīs*. He called out to the Yamunā, "Come near so I and the *gopīs* can enjoy sporting in your waters." But the Yamunā ignored His command. Lord Balarāma then started to pull the Yamunā with the end of His plow, splitting her into hundreds of tributaries. Trembling out of fright, the goddess Yamunā appeared, fell down at Lord Balarāma's feet and prayed for forgiveness. The Lord let her go and then entered her waters with His girlfriends to sport for some time. When they rose from the water, the goddess Kānti presented Lord Balarāma with beautiful ornaments, clothing and garlands. Even today the Yamunā River flows through the many channels cut by Lord Baladeva's plow, the signs of His having subdued her.

While Lord Balarāma played, His mind became enchanted by the *gopīs'* pastimes. Thus the many nights He spent in their company seemed to Him like a single night.

TEXT 1

श्रीशुक उवाच
बलभद्रः कुरुश्रेष्ठ भगवान् रथमास्थितः ।
सुहृद्दिदृक्षुरुत्कण्ठः प्रययौ नन्दगोकुलम् ॥१॥

śrī-śuka uvāca
balabhadraḥ kuru-śreṣtha
bhagavān ratham āsthitaḥ
suhṛd-didṛkṣur utkaṇṭhaḥ
prayayau nanda-gokulam

śrī-śukaḥ uvāca—Śukadeva Gosvāmī said; *balabhadraḥ*—Lord Balarāma; *kuru-śreṣtha*—O best of the Kurus (King Parīkṣit); *bhagavān*—the Supreme Lord; *ratham*—on His chariot; *āsthitaḥ*—mounted; *suhṛt*—His well-wishing friends; *didṛkṣuḥ*—wishing to see; *utkaṇṭhaḥ*—eager; *prayayau*—traveled; *nanda-gokulam*—to the cowherd village of Nanda Mahārāja.

TRANSLATION

Śukadeva Gosvāmī said: O best of the Kurus, once Lord Balarāma, eager to visit His well-wishing friends, mounted His chariot and traveled to Nanda Gokula.

PURPORT

As Śrīla Jīva Gosvāmī points out, Lord Balarāma's journey to Śrī Vṛndāvana is also described in the *Hari-vaṁśa* (*Viṣṇu-parva* 46.10):

kasyacid atha kālasya
smṛtvā gopeṣu sauhṛdam
jagāmaiko vrajaṁ rāmaḥ
kṛṣṇasyānumate sthitaḥ

"Remembering the deep friendship He once enjoyed with the cowherd folk, Lord Rāma went alone to Vraja, having taken Lord Kṛṣṇa's permission." The simple residents of Vṛndāvana were aggrieved that Lord Kṛṣṇa had gone to live elsewhere, so Lord Balarāma went there to console them.

Śrīla Viśvanātha Cakravartī Ṭhākura addresses the question of why Lord Kṛṣṇa, the great ocean of pure love, did not also go to Vraja. In explanation the *ācārya* provides the following two verses:

preyasīḥ prema-vikhyātāḥ
pitarāv ati-vatsalau
prema-vaśyaś ca kṛṣṇas tāṁs
tyaktvā naḥ katham eṣyati

iti matvaiva yadavaḥ
pratyabadhnan harer gatau
vraja-prema-pravardhi sva-
līlādhīnatvam īyuṣaḥ

"The Yadus thought, 'The Lord's beloved girlfriends are famous for their pure, ecstatic love, and His parents are extremely affectionate toward Him. Lord Kṛṣṇa is controlled by pure love, so if He goes to see them, how will He be able to leave them and come back to us?' With this in mind, the Yadus prevented Lord Hari from going, knowing that He becomes subservient to the pastimes in which He reciprocates the ever-increasing love of the inhabitants of Vraja."

TEXT 2

परिष्वक्तश्चिरोत्कण्ठैर्गोपैर्गोपीभिरेव च ।
रामोऽभिवाद्य पितरावाशीर्भिरभिनन्दितः ॥२॥

pariṣvaktaś cirotkaṇṭhair
gopair gopībhir eva ca

rāmo 'bhivādya pitarāv
āśīrbhir abhinanditaḥ

pariṣvaktaḥ—embraced; *cira*—for a long time; *utkaṇṭhaiḥ*—who had been in anxiety; *gopaiḥ*—by the cowherd men; *gopībhiḥ*—by the cowherd women; *eva*—indeed; *ca*—also; *rāmaḥ*—Lord Balarāma; *abhivādya*—offering respects; *pitarau*—to His parents (Nanda and Yaśodā); *āśīrbhiḥ*—with prayers; *abhinanditaḥ*—joyfully greeted.

TRANSLATION

Having long suffered the anxiety of separation, the cowherd men and their wives embraced Lord Balarāma. The Lord then offered respects to His parents, and they joyfully greeted Him with prayers.

PURPORT

Śrīla Viśvanātha Cakravartī gives the following verse regarding this situation:

nityānanda-svarūpo 'pi
prema-tapto vrajaukasām
yayau kṛṣṇam api tyaktvā
yas taṁ rāmaṁ muhuḥ stumaḥ

"Let us repeatedly glorify Lord Balarāma. Although He is the original personality of eternal bliss, Nityānanda, He felt pained by His love for the residents of Vraja, and thus He went to see them, even at the cost of leaving Lord Kṛṣṇa."

TEXT 3

चिरं नः पाहि दाशार्ह सानुजो जगदीश्वरः ।
इत्यारोप्यांकमालिंग्य नेत्रैः सिषिचतुर्जलैः ॥३॥

ciraṁ naḥ pāhi dāśārha
sānujo jagad-īśvaraḥ
ity āropyāṅkam āliṅgya
netraiḥ siṣicatur jalaiḥ

ciram—for a long time; *naḥ*—us; *pāhi*—please protect; *dāśārha*—O descendant of Daśārha; *sa*—together with; *anujaḥ*—Your younger brother; *jagat*—of the universe; *īśvaraḥ*—the Lord; *iti*—thus saying; *āropya*—raising; *aṅkam*—onto their laps; *āliṅgya*—embracing; *netraiḥ*—from their eyes; *siṣicatuḥ*—they moistened; *jalaiḥ*—with the water.

TRANSLATION

[Nanda and Yaśodā prayed,] "O descendant of Daśārha, O Lord of the universe, may You and Your younger brother Kṛṣṇa ever protect us." Saying this, they raised Śrī Balarāma onto their laps, embraced Him and moistened Him with tears from their eyes.

PURPORT

Śrīla Jīva Gosvāmī comments on this verse as follows: "Nanda and Yaśodā prayed to Śrī Balarāma, 'May You, along with Your younger brother, protect us.' Thus they expressed their respect for the fact that He is the elder brother, and they also showed how much they considered Him their own son."

TEXTS 4–6

गोपवृद्धांश्च विधिवद्यविष्ठैरभिवन्दितः ।
यथावयो यथासख्यं यथासम्बन्धमात्मनः ॥४॥
समुपेत्याथ गोपालान् हास्यहस्तग्रहादिभिः ।
विश्रान्तं सुखमासीनं पप्रच्छुः पर्युपागताः ॥५॥
पृष्टाश्चानामयं स्वेषु प्रेमगद्गदया गिरा ।
कृष्णे कमलपत्राक्षे संन्यस्ताखिलराधसः ॥६॥

gopa-vṛddhāṁś ca vidhi-vad
yaviṣṭhair abhivanditaḥ
yathā-vayo yathā-sakhyaṁ
yathā-sambandham ātmanaḥ

samupetyātha gopālān
hāsya-hasta-grahādibhiḥ
viśrāntaṁ sukham āsīnaṁ
papracchuḥ paryupāgatāḥ

pṛṣṭāś cānāmayaṁ sveṣu
prema-gadgadayā girā
kṛṣṇe kamala-patrākṣe
sannyastākhila-rādhasaḥ

gopa—of the cowherds; *vṛddhān*—the elders; *ca*—and; *vidhi-vat*—in accordance with Vedic injunctions; *yaviṣṭhaiḥ*—by those who were younger; *abhivanditaḥ*—respectfully greeted; *yathā-vayaḥ*—according to age; *yathā-sakhyam*—according to friendship; *yathā-sambandham*—according to family relationship; *ātmanaḥ*—with Himself; *samupetya*—going up to; *atha*—then; *gopālān*—the cowherd men; *hāsya*—with smiles; *hasta-graha*—taking of their hands; *ādibhiḥ*—and on; *viśrāntam*—rested; *sukham*—comfortably; *āsīnam*—seated; *papracchuḥ*—they asked; *paryupāgatāḥ*—having gathered on all sides; *pṛṣṭāḥ*—questioned; *ca*—and; *anāmayam*—about health; *sveṣu*—in regard to their dear friends; *prema*—out of love; *gadgadayā*—faltering; *girā*—with voices; *kṛṣṇe*—for Kṛṣṇa; *kamala*—of a lotus; *patra*—(like) petals; *akṣe*—whose eyes; *sannyasta*—having dedicated; *akhila*—all; *rādhasaḥ*—material possessions.

TRANSLATION

Lord Balarāma then paid proper respects to the elder cowherd men, and the younger ones all greeted Him respectfully. He met them all with smiles, handshakes and so on, dealing personally with each one according to age, degree of friendship, and family relationship. Then, after resting, the Lord accepted a comfortable seat, and they all gathered around Him. With voices faltering out of love for Him, those cowherds, who had dedicated everything to lotus-eyed Kṛṣṇa, asked about the health of their dear ones [in Dvārakā], and Balarāma in turn asked about the cowherds' welfare.

TEXT 7

कच्चिन्नो बान्धवा राम सर्वे कुशलमासते ।
कच्चित्स्मरथ नो राम यूयं दारसुतान्विताः ॥७॥

kaccin no bāndhavā rāma
sarve kuśalam āsate

kaccit smaratha no rāma
yūyaṁ dāra-sutānvitāḥ

kaccit—whether; *naḥ*—our; *bāndhavāḥ*—relatives; *rāma*—O Balarāma; *sarve*—all; *kuśalam*—well; *āsate*—are; *kaccit*—whether; *smaratha*—remember; *naḥ*—us; *rāma*—O Rāma; *yūyam*—all of you; *dāra*—with wives; *suta*—and children; *anvitāḥ*—together.

TRANSLATION

[The cowherds said:] O Rāma, are all our relatives doing well? And Rāma, do all of you, with your wives and children, still remember us?

TEXT 8

दिष्टया कंसो हतः पापो दिष्टया मुक्ताः सुहृज्जनाः ।
निहत्य निर्जित्य रिपून् दिष्टया दुर्गं समाश्रिताः ॥८॥

diṣṭyā kaṁso hataḥ pāpo
diṣṭyā muktāḥ suhṛj-janāḥ
nihatya nirjitya ripūn
diṣṭyā durgaṁ samāśritāḥ

diṣṭyā—by good fortune; *kaṁsaḥ*—Kaṁsa; *hataḥ*—killed; *pāpaḥ*—sinful; *diṣṭyā*—by good fortune; *muktāḥ*—freed; *suhṛt-janāḥ*—dear relatives; *nihatya*—killing; *nirjitya*—conquering; *ripūn*—enemies; *diṣṭyā*—by good fortune; *durgam*—a fortress; *samāśritāḥ*—taken shelter of.

TRANSLATION

It is our great fortune that sinful Kaṁsa has been killed and our dear relatives freed. And it is also our good fortune that our relatives have killed and defeated their enemies and found complete security in a great fortress.

TEXT 9

गोप्यो हसन्त्यः पप्रच्छू रामसन्दर्शनादृताः ।
कच्चिदास्ते सुखं कृष्णः पुरस्त्रीजनवल्लभः ॥९॥

gopyo hasantyaḥ papracchū
rāma-sandarśanādṛtāḥ
kaccid āste sukhaṁ kṛṣṇaḥ
pura-strī-jana-vallabhaḥ

gopyaḥ—the young cowherd girls; *hasantyaḥ*—smiling; *papracchuḥ*—asked; *rāma*—of Lord Balarāma; *sandarśana*—by the personal audience; *ādṛtāḥ*—honored; *kaccit*—whether; *āste*—is living; *sukham*—happily; *kṛṣṇaḥ*—Kṛṣṇa; *pura*—of the city; *strī-jana*—of the women; *vallabhaḥ*—the darling.

TRANSLATION

[Śukadeva Gosvāmī continued:] Honored to have the personal audience of Lord Balarāma, the young *gopīs* smiled and asked Him, "Is Kṛṣṇa, the darling of the city women, living happily?

PURPORT

According to the *ācāryas*, Lord Kṛṣṇa's beloved girlfriends were smiling with divine madness, since they were feeling extreme unhappiness in separation from their beloved Kṛṣṇa. Lord Rāma deeply respected their great love for Śrī Kṛṣṇa, His younger brother, and thus the term *rāma-sandarśanādṛtāḥ* carries the meaning that Balarāma honored the *gopīs*, as well as the given meaning, that they honored Him.

TEXT 10

कच्चित्स्मरति वा बन्धून् पितरं मातरं च सः ।
अप्यसौ मातरं द्रष्टुं सकृदप्यागमिष्यति ।
अपि वा स्मरतेऽस्माकमनुसेवां महाभुजः ॥१०॥

kaccit smarati vā bandhūn
pitaraṁ mātaraṁ ca saḥ
apy asau mātaraṁ draṣṭuṁ
sakṛd apy āgamiṣyati
api vā smarate 'smākam
anusevāṁ mahā-bhujaḥ

kaccit—whether; *smarati*—remembers; *vā*—or; *bandhūn*—His family members; *pitaram*—His father; *mātaram*—His mother; *ca*—and; *saḥ*—He; *api*—also; *asau*—Himself; *mātaram*—His mother; *draṣṭum*—to see; *sakṛt*—once; *api*—even; *āgamiṣyati*—will come; *api*—indeed; *vā*—or; *smarate*—He remembers; *asmākam*—our; *anusevām*—steady service; *mahā*—mighty; *bhujaḥ*—whose arms.

TRANSLATION

"Does He remember His family members, especially His father and mother? Do you think He will ever come back even once to see His mother? And does mighty-armed Kṛṣṇa remember the service we always did for Him?

PURPORT

Śrīla Viśvanātha Cakravartī comments that the *gopīs* would render service to Lord Kṛṣṇa by stringing flower garlands, skillfully using perfumes, and constructing fans, beds and canopies out of flower petals. By these simple acts of love, the *gopīs* rendered the greatest service to the Supreme Personality of Godhead.

TEXTS 11–12

मातरं पितरं भ्रातॄन् पतीन् पुत्रान् स्वसॄनपि ।
यदर्थे जहिम दाशार्ह दुस्त्यजान् स्वजनान् प्रभो ॥११॥
ता नः सद्यः परित्यज्य गतः सञ्छिन्नसौहृदः ।
कथं नु तादृशं स्त्रीभिर्न श्रद्धीयेत भाषितम् ॥१२॥

mātaraṁ pitaraṁ bhrātṝn
patīn putrān svasṝn api
yad-arthe jahima dāśārha
dustyajān sva-janān prabho

tā naḥ sadyaḥ parityajya
gataḥ sañchinna-sauhṛdaḥ
kathaṁ nu tādṛśaṁ strībhir
na śraddhīyeta bhāṣitam

mātaram—mother; *pitaram*—father; *bhrātṝn*—brothers; *patīn*—husbands; *putrān*—children; *svasṝn*—sisters; *api*—also; *yat*—of whom; *arthe*—for the sake; *jahima*—we abandoned; *dāśārha*—O descendant of Dāśārha; *dustyajān*—difficult to give up; *sva-janān*—own people; *prabho*—O Lord; *tāḥ*—these women; *naḥ*—ourselves; *sadyaḥ*—suddenly; *parityajya*—rejecting; *gataḥ*—gone away; *sañchinna*—having broken off; *sauhṛdaḥ*—friendship; *katham*—how; *nu*—indeed; *tādṛśam*—such; *strībhiḥ*—by women; *na śraddhīyeta*—would not be trusted; *bhāṣitam*—words spoken.

TRANSLATION

"For Kṛṣṇa's sake, O descendant of Dāśārha, we abandoned our mothers, fathers, brothers, husbands, children and sisters, even though these family relations are difficult to give up. But now, O Lord, that same Kṛṣṇa has suddenly abandoned us and gone away, breaking off all affectionate ties with us. And yet how could any woman fail to trust His promises?

TEXT 13

कथं नु गृह्णन्त्यनवस्थितात्मनो
वचः कृतघ्नस्य बुधाः पुरस्त्रियः ।
गृह्णन्ति वै चित्रकथस्य सुन्दर-
स्मितावलोकोच्छ्वसितस्मरातुराः ॥१३॥

kathaṁ nu gṛhṇanty anavasthitātmano
vacaḥ kṛta-ghnasya budhāḥ pura-striyaḥ
gṛhṇanti vai citra-kathasya sundara-
smitāvalokocchvasita-smarāturāḥ

katham—how; *nu*—indeed; *gṛhṇanti*—do they accept; *anavasthita*—unsteady; *ātmanaḥ*—of Him whose heart; *vacaḥ*—the words; *kṛta-ghnasya*—who is ungrateful; *budhāḥ*—intelligent; *pura*—of the city; *striyaḥ*—women; *gṛhṇanti*—they accept; *vai*—indeed; *citra*—wonderful; *kathasya*—whose narrations; *sundara*—beautifully; *smita*—smiling; *avaloka*—by the glances; *ucchvasita*—brought to life; *smara*—by lust; *āturāḥ*—agitated.

TRANSLATION

"How can intelligent city women possibly trust the words of one whose heart is so unsteady and who is so ungrateful? They must believe Him because He speaks so wonderfully, and also because His beautiful smiling glances arouse their lust.

PURPORT

According to Śrīdhara Svāmī, some *gopīs* speak the first two lines of this verse, and others reply in the second two lines.

TEXT 14

किं नस्तत्कथया गोप्यः कथाः कथयतापराः ।
यात्यस्माभिर्विना कालो यदि तस्य तथैव नः ॥१४॥

kiṁ nas tat-kathayā gopyaḥ
kathāḥ kathayatāparāḥ
yāty asmābhir vinā kālo
yadi tasya tathaiva naḥ

kim—what (use); *naḥ*—for us; *tat*—about Him; *kathayā*—with discussion; *gopyaḥ*—O *gopīs; kathāḥ*—topics; *kathayata*—please narrate; *aparāḥ*—other; *yāti*—it passes; *asmābhiḥ*—us; *vinā*—without; *kālaḥ*—time; *yadi*—if; *tasya*—His; *tathā eva*—in the very same way; *naḥ*—ours.

TRANSLATION

"Why bother talking about Him, dear *gopīs*? Please talk of something else. If He passes His time without us, then we shall similarly pass ours [without Him]."

PURPORT

Śrīla Śrīdhara Svāmī points out that the *gopīs* here subtly indicate that Lord Kṛṣṇa spends His time happily without them whereas they are most unhappy without their Lord. This is the difference between Him and them. Śrīla Viśvanātha Cakravartī adds the following commentary: "Considering themselves different from other women, the *gopīs* thought as follows: 'If other women are together with their lovers, they live, and if they are separated, they die. But we neither live nor die. This is the fate Providence has written on our foreheads. What remedy can we find?' "

TEXT 15

इति प्रहसितं शौरेर्जल्पितं चारुवीक्षितम् ।
गतिं प्रेमपरिष्वंगं स्मरन्त्यो रुरुदुः स्त्रियः ॥१५॥

iti prahasitaṁ śaurer
jalpitaṁ cāru-vīkṣitam
gatiṁ prema-pariṣvaṅgaṁ
smarantyo ruruduḥ striyaḥ

iti—thus speaking; *prahasitam*—the laughter; *śaureḥ*—of Lord Kṛṣṇa; *jalpitam*—the pleasing conversations; *cāru*—attractive; *vīkṣitam*—the glances; *gatim*—the walking; *prema*—loving; *pariṣvaṅgam*—the embrace; *smarantyaḥ*—remembering; *ruruduḥ*—cried; *striyaḥ*—the women.

TRANSLATION

While speaking these words, the young cowherd women remembered Lord Śauri's laughter, His pleasing conversations with them, His attractive glances, His style of walking and His loving embraces. Thus they began to cry.

PURPORT

Śrīla Viśvanātha Cakravartī comments as follows: "The *gopīs* thought, 'The Kṛṣṇa moon, after piercing our hearts with the darts of His nectarean laughter, went away. So how will the city women not die when He does the same to them?' Overwhelmed with these thoughts, the young cowherd girls began to cry, even in the presence of Śrī Baladeva."

TEXT 16

संकर्षणस्ताः कृष्णस्य सन्देशैर्हृदयंगमैः ।
सान्त्वयामास भगवान्नानानुनयकोविदः ॥१६॥

saṅkarṣaṇas tāḥ kṛṣṇasya
sandeśair hṛdayaṁ-gamaiḥ
sāntvayām āsa bhagavān
nānānunaya-kovidaḥ

saṅkarṣaṇaḥ—Lord Balarāma, the supreme attractor; *tāḥ*—them; *kṛṣṇasya*—of Lord Kṛṣṇa; *sandeśaiḥ*—by the confidential messages; *hṛdayam*—the heart; *gamaiḥ*—touching; *sāntvayām āsa*—consoled; *bhagavān*—the Supreme Lord; *nānā*—of various kinds; *anunaya*—in conciliation; *kovidaḥ*—expert.

TRANSLATION

The Supreme Lord Balarāma, the attractor of all, being expert at various kinds of conciliation, consoled the *gopīs* by relaying to them the confidential messages Lord Kṛṣṇa had sent with Him. These messages deeply touched the *gopīs'* hearts.

PURPORT

Śrīla Jīva Gosvāmī quotes the following verse from *Śrī Viṣṇu Purāṇa* (5.24.20), which describes the messages Lord Balarāma brought from Kṛṣṇa for the *gopīs:*

sandeśaiḥ sāma-madhuraiḥ
prema-garbhair agarvitaiḥ
rāmeṇāśvāsitā gopyaḥ
kṛṣṇasyāti-manoharaiḥ

"Lord Balarāma consoled the *gopīs* by giving them Lord Kṛṣṇa's most charming messages, which expressed sweet conciliation, which were inspired by His pure love for them, and which were without a tinge of pride." Śrīla Jīva Gosvāmī also comments that the use of the name Saṅkarṣaṇa here implies that Balarāma attracted Lord Kṛṣṇa to appear in His mind and in this way showed Śrī Kṛṣṇa to the *gopīs*. Thus Balarāma consoled Śrī Kṛṣṇa's beloved girlfriends.

Śrīla Viśvanātha Cakravartī comments that Lord Kṛṣṇa sent various messages. Some instructed the *gopīs* in transcendental knowledge, others were conciliatory, and still others revealed the Lord's power. Besides its given meaning, the word *hṛdayaṁ-gamaiḥ* also indicates that these messages were confidential.

TEXT 17

द्वौ मासौ तत्र चावात्सीन्मधुं माधवमेव च ।
रामः क्षपासु भगवान् गोपीनां रतिमावहन् ॥१७॥

dvau māsau tatra cāvātsīn
madhuṁ mādhavam eva ca
rāmaḥ kṣapāsu bhagavān
gopīnāṁ ratim āvahan

dvau—two; *māsau*—months; *tatra*—there (in Gokula); *ca*—and; *avātsīt*—resided; *madhum*—Madhu (the first month of the Vedic calendar, at the time of the spring equinox); *mādhavam*—Mādhava (the second month); *eva*—indeed; *ca*—also; *rāmaḥ*—Balarāma; *kṣapāsu*—during the nights; *bhagavān*—the Supreme Lord; *gopīnām*—to the *gopīs;* *ratim*—conjugal pleasure; *āvahan*—bringing.

TRANSLATION

Lord Balarāma, the Personality of Godhead, resided there for the two months of Madhu and Mādhava, and during the nights He gave His cowherd girlfriends conjugal pleasure.

PURPORT

Śrīla Śrīdhara Svāmī states that the *gopīs* who enjoyed conjugal affairs with Śrī Balarāma during His visit to Gokula had not taken part in Śrī Kṛṣṇa's *rāsa* dance, being too young at the time. Śrīla Jīva Gosvāmī confirms this statement by quoting a phrase from the *Bhāgavatam* (10.15.8)—*gopyo 'ntareṇa bhujayoḥ*—which indicates that there are particular *gopīs* who act as Lord Balarāma's girlfriends. Furthermore, Jīva Gosvāmī states that during the Holī festivities celebrated when Kṛṣṇa killed Śaṅkhacūḍa, the *gopīs* Lord Balarāma enjoyed with were different from the ones Lord Kṛṣṇa enjoyed with. Śrīla Viśvanātha Cakravartī agrees with this explanation.

TEXT 18

पूर्णचन्द्रकलामृष्टे कौमुदीगन्धवायुना ।
यमुनोपवने रेमे सेविते स्त्रीगणैर्वृतः ॥१८॥

pūrṇa-candra-kalā-mṛṣṭe
kaumudī-gandha-vāyunā
yamunopavane reme
sevite strī-gaṇair vṛtaḥ

pūrṇa—full; *candra*—of the moon; *kalā*—by the rays; *mṛṣṭe*—bathed; *kaumudī*—of lotus flowers that open in the moonlight; *gandha*—(bearing) the fragrance; *vāyunā*—by the wind; *yamunā*—of the Yamunā River; *upavane*—in a garden; *reme*—He enjoyed; *sevite*—served; *strī*—women; *gaṇaiḥ*—by many; *vṛtaḥ*—accompanied.

TRANSLATION

In the company of numerous women, Lord Balarāma enjoyed in a garden by the Yamunā River. This garden was bathed in the rays of the full moon and caressed by breezes bearing the fragrance of night-blooming lotuses.

PURPORT

Śrīla Viśvanātha Cakravartī explains that Lord Balarāma's conjugal pastimes took place in a small forest alongside the Yamunā, a place known as Śrīrāma-ghaṭṭa, which is far from the site of Śrī Kṛṣṇa's *rāsa* dance.

TEXT 19

वरुणप्रेषिता देवी वारुणी वृक्षकोटरात् ।
पतन्ती तद्वनं सर्वं स्वगन्धेनाध्यवासयत् ॥१९॥

varuṇa-preṣitā devī
vāruṇī vṛkṣa-koṭarāt
patantī tad vanaṁ sarvaṁ
sva-gandhenādhyavāsayat

varuṇa—by Varuṇa, the demigod of the ocean; *preṣitā*—sent; *devī*—divine; *vāruṇī*—the Vāruṇī liquor; *vṛkṣa*—of a tree; *koṭarāt*—from the hollow; *patantī*—flowing; *tat*—that; *vanam*—forest; *sarvam*—entire; *sva*—with its own; *gandhena*—aroma; *adhyavāsayat*—made even more fragrant.

TRANSLATION

Sent by the demigod Varuṇa, the divine Vāruṇī liquor flowed from a tree hollow and made the entire forest even more fragrant with its sweet aroma.

PURPORT

Śrīla Śrīdhara Svāmī explains that Vāruṇī is a liquor distilled from honey. Śrīla Viśvanātha Cakravartī adds that the goddess Vāruṇī, the daughter of Varuṇa, is the presiding deity of that particular divine liquor. The *ācārya* also quotes the following statement from *Śrī Hari-vaṁśa: samīpaṁ preṣitā pitrā varuṇena tavānagha.* Here the goddess Vāruṇī says to Lord Balarāma: "My father, Varuṇa, has sent me to You, O sinless one."

TEXT 20

तं गन्धं मधुधाराया वायुनोपहृतं बलः ।
आघ्रायोपगतस्तत्र ललनाभिः समं पपौ ॥२०॥

taṁ gandhaṁ madhu-dhārāyā
vāyunopahṛtaṁ balaḥ
āghrāyopagatas tatra
lalanābhiḥ samaṁ papau

tam—that; *gandham*—fragrance; *madhu*—of honey; *dhārāyāḥ*—of the flood; *vāyunā*—by the breeze; *upahṛtam*—brought near; *balaḥ*—Lord Balarāma; *āghrāya*—smelling; *upagataḥ*—having approached; *tatra*—there; *lalanābhiḥ*—with the young women; *samam*—together; *papau*—drank.

TRANSLATION

The wind carried to Balarāma the fragrance of that flood of sweet liquor, and when He smelled it He went [to the tree]. There He and His female companions drank.

TEXT 21

उपगीयमानो गन्धर्वैर्वनिताशोभिमण्डले ।
रेमे करेणुयूथेशो माहेन्द्र इव वारणः ॥२१॥

upagīyamāno gandharvair
vanitā-śobhi-maṇḍale
reme kareṇu-yūtheśo
māhendra iva vāraṇaḥ

upagīyamānaḥ—being praised in song; *gandharvaiḥ*—by Gandharvas; *vanitā*—by young women; *śobhi*—beautified; *maṇḍale*—in the circle; *reme*—He enjoyed; *kareṇu*—of she-elephants; *yūtha*—of a herd; *īśaḥ*—the master; *māhā-indraḥ*—of Lord Indra; *iva*—just like; *vāraṇaḥ*—the elephant (named Airāvata).

TRANSLATION

As the Gandharvas sang His glories, Lord Balarāma enjoyed within the brilliant circle of young women. He appeared just like Indra's elephant, the lordly Airāvata, enjoying in the company of she-elephants.

TEXT 22

नेदुर्दुन्दुभयो व्योम्नि ववृषुः कुसुमैर्मुदा ।
गन्धर्वा मुनयो रामं तद्वीर्यैरीडिरे तदा ॥२२॥

nedur dundubhayo vyomni
vavṛṣuḥ kusumair mudā
gandharvā munayo rāmaṁ
tad-vīryair īḍire tadā

neduḥ—resounded; *dundubhayaḥ*—kettledrums; *vyomni*—in the sky; *vavṛṣuḥ*—rained down; *kusumaiḥ*—with flowers; *mudā*—with joy; *gandharvāḥ*—the Gandharvas; *munayaḥ*—the great sages; *rāmam*—Lord Balarāma; *tat-vīryaiḥ*—with His heroic deeds; *īḍire*—praised; *tadā*—then.

TRANSLATION

At that time kettledrums resounded in the sky, the Gandharvas joyfully rained down flowers, and the great sages praised Lord Balarāma's heroic deeds.

TEXT 23

उपगीयमानचरितो वनिताभिर्हलायुधः ।
वनेषु व्यचरत्क्षीवो मदविह्वललोचनः ॥२३॥

upagīyamāna-carito
vanitābhir halāyudhaḥ
vaneṣu vyacarat kṣīvo
mada-vihvala-locanaḥ

upagīyamāna—being sung; *caritaḥ*—His pastimes; *vanitābhiḥ*—with the women; *halāyudhaḥ*—Lord Balarāma; *vaneṣu*—among the forests; *vyacarat*—wandered; *kṣīvaḥ*—inebriated; *mada*—by the intoxication; *vihvala*—overcome; *locanaḥ*—His eyes.

TRANSLATION

As His deeds were sung, Lord Halāyudha wandered as if inebriated among the various forests with His girlfriends. His eyes rolled from the effects of the liquor.

TEXTS 24–25

स्रग्व्येककुण्डलो मत्तो वैजयन्त्या च मालया ।
बिभ्रत्स्मितमुखाम्भोजं स्वेदप्रालेयभूषितम् ॥२४॥

स आजुहाव यमुनां जलक्रीडार्थमीश्वरः ।
निजं वाक्यमनादृत्य मत्त इत्यापगां बलः ।
अनागतां हलाग्रेण कुपितो विचकर्ष ह ॥२५॥

sragvy eka-kuṇḍalo matto
vaijayantyā ca mālayā
bibhrat smita-mukhāmbhojaṁ
sveda-prāleya-bhūṣitam

sa ājuhāva yamunāṁ
jala-krīḍārtham īśvaraḥ
nijaṁ vākyam anādṛtya
matta ity āpagāṁ balaḥ
anāgatāṁ halāgreṇa
kupito vicakarṣa ha

srak-vī—having a garland; *eka*—with one; *kuṇḍalaḥ*—earring; *mattaḥ*—intoxicated with joy; *vaijayantyā*—named Vaijayantī; *ca*—and; *mālayā*—with the garland; *bibhrat*—displaying; *smita*—smiling; *mukha*—His face; *ambhojam*—lotuslike; *sveda*—of perspiration; *prāleya*—with the snow; *bhūṣitam*—decorated; *saḥ*—He; *ājuhāva*—called for; *yamunām*—the Yamunā River; *jala*—in the water; *krīḍā*—of playing; *artham*—for the purpose; *īśvaraḥ*—the Supreme Lord; *nijam*—His; *vākyam*—words; *anādṛtya*—disregarding; *mattaḥ*—intoxicated; *iti*—thus (thinking); *āpa-gām*—the river; *balaḥ*—Lord Balarāma; *anāgatām*—who did not come; *hala*—of His plow weapon; *agreṇa*—with the tip; *kupitaḥ*—angry; *vicakarṣa ha*—He dragged.

TRANSLATION

Intoxicated with joy, Lord Balarāma sported flower garlands, including the famous Vaijayantī. He wore a single earring, and beads of perspiration decorated His smiling lotus face like snowflakes. The Lord then summoned the Yamunā River so that He could play in her waters, but she disregarded His command, thinking He was drunk. This angered Balarāma, and He began dragging the river with the tip of His plow.

TEXT 26

पापे त्वं मामवज्ञाय यन्नायासि मयाहुता ।
नेष्ये त्वां लांगलाग्रेण शतधा कामचारिणीम् ॥२६॥

pāpe tvaṁ mām avajñāya
yan nāyāsi mayāhutā
neṣye tvāṁ lāṅgalāgreṇa
śatadhā kāma-cāriṇīm

pāpe—O sinful one; *tvam*—you; *mām*—Me; *avajñāya*—disrespecting; *yat*—because; *na āyāsi*--you do not come; *mayā*—by Me; *āhutā*—called; *neṣye*—I will bring; *tvām*—you; *lāṅgala*—of My plow; *agreṇa*—with the tip; *śatadhā*—in a hundred parts; *kāma*—by whim; *cāriṇīm*—who moves.

TRANSLATION

[Lord Balarāma said:] O sinful one disrespecting Me, you do not come when I call you but rather move only by your own whim. Therefore with the tip of My plow I shall bring you here in a hundred streams!

TEXT 27

एवं निर्भर्त्सिता भीता यमुना यदुनन्दनम् ।
उवाच चकिता वाचं पतिता पादयोर्नृप ॥२७॥

evaṁ nirbhartsitā bhītā
yamunā yadu-nandanam
uvāca cakitā vācaṁ
patitā pādayor nṛpa

evam—thus; *nirbhartsitā*—scolded; *bhītā*—afraid; *yamunā*—the presiding goddess of the river Yamunā; *yadu-nandanam*—to the beloved descendant of Yadu, Lord Balarāma; *uvāca*—spoke; *cakitā*—trembling; *vācam*—words; *patitā*—fallen; *pādayoḥ*—at His feet; *nṛpa*—O King (Parīkṣit).

TRANSLATION

[Śukadeva Gosvāmī continued:] Thus scolded by the Lord, O King, the frightened river-goddess Yamunā came and fell at the feet of Śrī Balarāma, the beloved descendant of Yadu. Trembling, she spoke to Him the following words.

PURPORT

According to Śrīla Jīva Gosvāmī, the goddess who appeared before Lord Balarāma is an expansion of Śrīmatī Kālindī, one of Lord Kṛṣṇa's queens in Dvārakā. Śrīla Jīva Gosvāmī calls her a "shadow" of Kālindī, and Śrīla Viśvanātha Cakravartī confirms that she is an expansion of Kālindī, not Kālindī herself. Śrīla Jīva Gosvāmī also gives evidence from *Śrī Hari-vaṁśa*—in the statement *pratyuvācārṇava-vadhūm*—that Goddess Yamunā is the wife of the ocean. The *Hari-vaṁśa* therefore also refers to her as *sāgarāṅganā.*

TEXT 28

राम राम महाबाहो न जाने तव विक्रमम् ।
यस्यैकांशेन विधृता जगती जगतः पते ॥२८॥

rāma rāma mahā-bāho
na jāne tava vikramam
yasyaikāṁśena vidhṛtā
jagatī jagataḥ pate

rāma rāma—O Rāma, Rāma; *mahā-bāho*—O mighty-armed one; *na jāne*—I do not appreciate; *tava*—Your; *vikramam*—prowess; *yasya*—whose; *eka*—one; *aṁśena*—by a portion; *vidhṛtā*—is sustained; *jagatī*—the earth; *jagataḥ*—of the universe; *pate*—O master.

TRANSLATION

[Goddess Yamunā said:] Rāma, Rāma, O mighty-armed one! I know nothing of Your prowess. With a single portion of Yourself You hold up the earth, O Lord of the universe.

PURPORT

The phrase *ekāṁśena* ("with a single portion") refers to the Lord's expansion as Śeṣa. This is confirmed by the *ācāryas*.

TEXT 29

परं भावं भगवतो भगवन्मामजानतीम् ।
मोक्तुमर्हसि विश्वात्मन् प्रपन्नां भक्तवत्सल ॥२९॥

paraṁ bhāvaṁ bhagavato
bhagavan mām ajānatīm
moktum arhasi viśvātman
prapannāṁ bhakta-vatsala

param—supreme; *bhāvam*—the status; *bhagavataḥ*—of the Personality of Godhead; *bhagavan*—O Supreme Lord; *mām*—me; *ajānatīm*—not knowing; *moktum arhasi*—please release; *viśva*—of the universe; *ātman*—O soul; *prapannām*—surrendered; *bhakta*—to Your devotees; *vatsala*—O You who are compassionate.

TRANSLATION

My Lord, please release me. O soul of the universe, I didn't understand Your position as the Supreme Godhead, but now I have surrendered unto You, and You are always kind to Your devotees.

TEXT 30

ततो व्यमुञ्चद्यमुनां याचितो भगवान् बलः ।
विजगाह जलं स्त्रीभिः करेणुभिरिवेभराट् ॥३०॥

tato vyamuñcad yamunāṁ
yācito bhagavān balaḥ
vijagāha jalaṁ strībhiḥ
kareṇubhir ivebha-rāṭ

tataḥ—then; *vyamuñcat*—released; *yamunām*—the Yamunā; *yācitaḥ*—begged; *bhagavān*—the Supreme Lord; *balaḥ*—Balarāma; *vijagāha*—He submerged Himself; *jalam*—in the water; *strībhiḥ*—with the women; *kareṇubhiḥ*—with his she-elephants; *iva*—as; *ibha*—of elephants; *rāṭ*—the king.

TRANSLATION

[Śukadeva Gosvāmī continued:] Thereupon Lord Balarāma released the Yamunā and, like the king of the elephants with his entourage of she-elephants, entered the river's water with His female companions.

TEXT 31

कामं विहृत्य सलिलादुत्तीर्णायासिताम्बरे ।
भूषणानि महार्हाणि ददौ कान्तिः शुभां स्रजम् ॥३१॥

kāmaṁ vihṛtya salilād
uttīrṇāyāsitāmbare
bhūṣaṇāni mahārhāṇi
dadau kāntiḥ śubhāṁ srajam

kāmam—as pleased Him; *vihṛtya*—having played; *salilāt*—from the water; *uttīrṇāya*—to Him who had risen; *asita*—blue; *ambare*—a pair of garments (upper and lower); *bhūṣaṇāni*—ornaments; *mahā*—greatly; *arhāṇi*—valuable; *dadau*—gave; *kāntiḥ*—Goddess Kānti; *śubhām*—splendidly beautiful; *srajam*—a necklace.

TRANSLATION

The Lord played in the water to His full satisfaction, and when He came out Goddess Kānti presented Him with blue garments, precious ornaments and a brilliant necklace.

PURPORT

Śrīla Śrīdhara Svāmī quotes from the *Viṣṇu Purāṇa* to show that the Goddess Kānti mentioned here is actually Lakṣmī, the goddess of fortune:

varuṇa-prahitā cāsmai
mālām amlāna-paṅkajām
samudrābhe tathā vastre
nīle lakṣmīr ayacchata

"Sent by Varuṇa, Goddess Lakṣmī then presented Him with a garland of unfading lotuses and a pair of garments colored blue like the ocean."

The great *Bhāgavatam* commentator Śrīla Śrīdhara Svāmī also quotes the following statment from *Śrī Hari-vaṁśa,* spoken by Goddess Lakṣmī to Lord Balarāma:

jātarūpa-mayaṁ caikaṁ
kuṇḍalaṁ vajra-bhūṣaṇam
ādi-padmaṁ ca padmākhyaṁ
divyaṁ śravaṇa-bhūṣaṇam
devemāṁ pratigṛhṇīṣva
paurāṇīṁ bhūṣaṇa-kriyām

"O Lord, please accept as divine ornaments for Your ears this single gold earring studded with diamonds and this primeval lotus called Padma. Kindly accept them, for this act of adornment is traditional."

Śrīla Viśvanātha Cakravartī further points out that Goddess Lakṣmī is the consort of the Lord's plenary expansion Saṅkarṣaṇa who belongs to the second *vyūha.*

TEXT 32

वसित्वा वाससी नीले मालामामुच्य काञ्चनीम् ।
रेजे स्वलंकृतो लिप्तो माहेन्द्र इव वारणः ॥३२॥

vasitvā vāsasī nīle
mālām āmucya kāñcanīm
reje sv-alaṅkṛto lipto
māhendra iva vāraṇaḥ

vasitvā—dressing Himself; *vāsasī*—in the two garments; *nīle*—blue; *mālām*—the necklace; *āmucya*—putting on; *kāñcanīm*—golden; *reje*—He appeared resplendent; *su*—excellently; *alaṅkṛtaḥ*—ornamented;

liptaḥ—anointed; *māhā-indraḥ*—of Mahendra, the King of heaven; *iva*—like; *vāraṇaḥ*—the elephant.

TRANSLATION

Lord Balarāma dressed Himself in the blue garments and put on the gold necklace. Anointed with fragrances and beautifully adorned, He appeared as resplendent as Indra's royal elephant.

PURPORT

Anointed with sandalwood paste and other pure, fragrant substances, Balarāma resembled Airāvata, the great elephant of Lord Indra.

TEXT 33

अद्यापि दृश्यते राजन् यमुनाकृष्टवर्त्मना ।
बलस्यानन्तवीर्यस्य वीर्यं सूचयतीव हि ॥३३॥

adyāpi dṛśyate rājan
yamunākṛṣṭa-vartmanā
balasyānanta-vīryasya
vīryaṁ sūcayatīva hi

adya—today; *api*—even; *dṛśyate*—is seen; *rājan*—O King (Parīkṣit); *yamunā*—the Yamunā River; *ākṛṣṭa*—pulled; *vartmanā*—whose currents; *balasya*—of Lord Balarāma; *ananta*—unlimited; *vīryasya*—whose potency; *vīryam*—the prowess; *sūcayatī*—indicating; *iva*—as; *hi*—indeed.

TRANSLATION

Even today, O King, one can see how the Yamunā flows through the many channels created when it was dragged by the unlimitedly powerful Lord Balarāma. Thus she demonstrates His prowess.

TEXT 34

एवं सर्वा निशा याता एकेव रमतो व्रजे ।
रामस्याक्षिप्तचित्तस्य माधुर्यैर्व्रजयोषिताम् ॥३४॥

evaṁ sarvā niśā yātā
ekeva ramato vraje
rāmasyākṣipta-cittasya
mādhuryair vraja-yoṣitām

evam—in this manner; *sarvāḥ*—all; *niśāḥ*—the nights; *yātāḥ*—passed; *ekā*—one; *iva*—as if; *ramataḥ*—who was enjoying; *vraje*—in Vraja; *rāmasya*—for Lord Balarāma; *ākṣipta*—enchanted; *cittasya*—whose mind; *mādhuryaiḥ*—by the exquisite charm and beauty; *vraja-yoṣitām*—of the women of Vraja.

TRANSLATION

Thus for Lord Balarāma all the nights passed like a single night as He enjoyed in Vraja, His mind enchanted by the exquisite charm and beauty of Vraja's young ladies.

PURPORT

Lord Balarāma was enchanted by the charming pastimes of the beautiful young ladies of Vraja. Thus each night was a completely new experience, and all the nights passed as if they were a single night.

Thus end the purports of the humble servants of His Divine Grace A. C. Bhaktivedanta Swami Prabhupāda to the Tenth Canto, Sixty-fifth Chapter, of the Śrīmad-Bhāgavatam, *entitled "Lord Balarāma Visits Vṛndāvana."*

CHAPTER SIXTY–SIX

Pauṇḍraka, the False Vāsudeva

This chapter relates how Lord Kṛṣṇa went to Kāśī (present-day Benares) and killed Pauṇḍraka and Kāśirāja, and how the Lord's Sudarśana disc defeated a demon, incinerated the city of Kāśī and killed Sudakṣiṇa.

While Lord Baladeva was visiting Vraja, King Pauṇḍraka of Karūṣa, encouraged by fools, announced that he was the real Vāsudeva. Thus he challenged Lord Kṛṣṇa with the following message: "Since I alone am the true Personality of Godhead, You should give up Your false claim to this position, as well as my divine symbols, and take shelter of me. If You do not, then prepare for battle."

When Ugrasena and the members of his royal assembly heard Pauṇḍraka's foolish boast, they all laughed heartily. Śrī Kṛṣṇa then told Pauṇḍraka's messenger to convey a message to his master: "O fool, I will force you to give up the so-called Sudarśana disc and the other divine symbols of Mine you have dared to assume. And when you lie down on the battlefield, you will become the shelter of dogs."

Lord Kṛṣṇa then went to Kāśī. Pauṇḍraka, seeing the Lord preparing for battle, quickly came out of the city to confront Him with his army. His friend Kāśirāja followed him, leading the rear guard. Just as the fire of universal devastation destroys every living being in all directions, so Lord Kṛṣṇa annihilated the armies of Pauṇḍraka and Kāśirāja. Then, after chastising Pauṇḍraka, the Lord beheaded both him and Kāśirāja with His Sudarśana disc. Thereafter, He returned to Dvārakā. Because Pauṇḍraka had constantly meditated on the Supreme Lord, even dressing like Him, he gained liberation.

When Kṛṣṇa beheaded Kāśirāja, the King's head flew into his city, and when his queens, sons and other relatives saw it, they all began to lament. At that time a son of Kāśirāja's named Sudakṣiṇa, wanting to avenge his father's death, began worshiping Lord Śiva with the intention of destroying his father's killer. Gratified by Sudakṣiṇa's worship, Lord Śiva offered him a choice of benedictions, and Sudakṣiṇa asked for a means to kill the one who had slain his father. Lord Śiva advised him to worship the

Dakṣiṇāgni fire with black magic rituals. This Sudakṣiṇa did, with the result that a fearsome demon with a body of flames appeared from the pit of the sacrificial fire. The demon rose up carrying a fiery trident and at once set off for Dvārakā.

The residents of Lord Kṛṣṇa's capital became terrified as the demon approached the city, but Lord Kṛṣṇa assured them of protection and dispatched His Sudarśana *cakra* to oppose the magic creation of Lord Śiva. The Sudarśana overpowered the demon, who then returned to Vārāṇasī and burned Sudakṣiṇa to ashes, together with his priests. The Sudarśana disc, following the demon, entered Vārāṇasī and burned the entire city to the ground. Then the Lord's disc returned to His side in Dvārakā.

TEXT 1

श्रीशुक उवाच
नन्दव्रजं गते रामे करूषाधिपतिर्नृप ।
वासुदेवोऽहमित्यज्ञो दूतं कृष्णाय प्राहिणोत् ॥१॥

śrī-śuka uvāca
nanda-vrajaṁ gate rāme
karūṣādhipatir nṛpa
vāsudevo 'ham ity ajño
dūtaṁ kṛṣṇāya prāhiṇot

śrī-śukaḥ uvāca—Śukadeva Gosvāmī said; *nanda*—of Nanda Mahārāja; *vrajam*—to the cowherd village; *gate*—having gone; *rāme*—Lord Balarāma; *karūṣa-adhipatiḥ*—the ruler of Karūṣa (Pauṇḍraka); *nṛpa*—O King (Parīkṣit); *vāsudevaḥ*—the Supreme Lord, Vāsudeva; *aham*—I; *iti*—thus thinking; *ajñaḥ*—foolish; *dūtam*—a messenger; *kṛṣṇāya*—to Lord Kṛṣṇa; *prāhiṇot*—sent.

TRANSLATION

Śukadeva Gosvāmī said: O King, while Lord Balarāma was away visiting Nanda's village of Vraja, the ruler of Karūṣa, foolishly thinking "I am the Supreme Lord, Vāsudeva," sent a messenger to Lord Kṛṣṇa.

PURPORT

Since Lord Rāma had gone to Nanda-vraja, Pauṇḍraka foolishly thought that Lord Kṛṣṇa would be alone and therefore easy to challenge. Thus he dared to send his crazy message to the Lord.

TEXT 2

त्वं वासुदेवो भगवानवतीर्णो जगत्पतिः ।
इति प्रस्तोभितो बालैर्मेन आत्मानमच्युतम् ॥२॥

tvaṁ vāsudevo bhagavān
avatīrṇo jagat-patiḥ
iti prastobhito bālair
mena ātmānam acyutam

tvam—you; *vāsudevaḥ*—Vāsudeva; *bhagavān*—the Supreme Lord; *avatīrṇaḥ*—descended; *jagat*—of the universe; *patiḥ*—the master; *iti*—thus; *prastobhitaḥ*—emboldened with flattery; *bālaiḥ*—by childish men; *mene*—he imagined; *ātmānam*—himself; *acyutam*—the infallible Lord.

TRANSLATION

Pauṇḍraka was emboldened by the flattery of childish men, who told him, "You are Vāsudeva, the Supreme Lord and master of the universe, who have now descended to the earth." Thus he imagined himself to be the infallible Personality of Godhead.

PURPORT

Pauṇḍraka foolishly accepted the flattery of ignorant persons.

TEXT 3

दूतं च प्राहिणोन्मन्दः कृष्णायाव्यक्तवर्त्मने ।
द्वारकायां यथा बालो नृपो बालकृतोऽबुधः ॥३॥

dūtaṁ ca prāhiṇon mandaḥ
kṛṣṇāyāvyakta-vartmane

dvārakāyāṁ yathā bālo
nṛpo bāla-kṛto 'budhaḥ

dūtam—a messenger; *ca*—and; *prāhiṇot*—he sent; *mandaḥ*—slow-witted; *kṛṣṇāya*—to Lord Kṛṣṇa; *avyakta*—inscrutable; *vartmane*—whose path; *dvārakāyām*—at Dvārakā; *yathā*—as; *bālaḥ*—a boy; *nṛpaḥ*—king; *bāla*—by children; *kṛtaḥ*—made; *abudhaḥ*—unintelligent.

TRANSLATION

Thus slow-witted King Pauṇḍraka sent a messenger to the inscrutable Lord Kṛṣṇa at Dvārakā. Pauṇḍraka was acting just like an unintelligent child whom other children are pretending is a king.

PURPORT

According to Śrīla Viśvanātha Cakravartī Ṭhākura, the reason Śukadeva Gosvāmī here mentions for the second time that Pauṇḍraka sent a message to Lord Kṛṣṇa is that the great sage is astonished at Pauṇḍraka's extreme foolishness.

TEXT 4

दूतस्तु द्वारकामेत्य सभायामास्थितं प्रभुम् ।
कृष्णं कमलपत्राक्षं राजसन्देशमब्रवीत् ॥४॥

dūtas tu dvārakām etya
sabhāyām āsthitaṁ prabhum
kṛṣṇaṁ kamala-patrākṣaṁ
rāja-sandeśam abravīt

dūtaḥ—the messenger; *tu*—then; *dvārakām*—at Dvārakā; *etya*—arriving; *sabhāyām*—in the royal assembly; *āsthitam*—present; *prabhum*—to the almighty Lord; *kṛṣṇam*—Kṛṣṇa; *kamala*—of a lotus; *patra*—(like) the petals; *akṣam*—whose eyes; *rāja*—of his King; *sandeśam*—the message; *abravīt*—spoke.

TRANSLATION

Arriving in Dvārakā, the messenger found lotus-eyed Kṛṣṇa in His royal assembly and relayed the King's message to that almighty Lord.

TEXT 5

वासुदेवोऽवतीर्णोऽहमेक एव न चापरः ।
भूतानामनुकम्पार्थं त्वं तु मिथ्याभिधां त्यज ॥५॥

vāsudevo 'vatīrṇo 'ham
eka eva na cāparaḥ
bhūtānām anukampārthaṁ
tvaṁ tu mithyābhidhāṁ tyaja

vāsudevaḥ—Lord Vāsudeva; *avatīrṇaḥ*—descended to this world; *aham*—I; *ekaḥ eva*—the only one; *na*—not; *ca*—and; *aparaḥ*—anyone else; *bhūtānām*—to the living beings; *anukampā*—of showing mercy; *artham*—for the purpose; *tvam*—You; *tu*—however; *mithyā*—false; *abhidhām*—designation; *tyaja*—give up.

TRANSLATION

[On Pauṇḍraka's behalf, the messenger said:] I am the one and only Lord Vāsudeva, and there is no other. It is I who have descended to this world to show mercy to the living beings. Therefore give up Your false name.

PURPORT

Inspired by Goddess Sarasvatī, Śrīla Viśvanātha Cakravartī gives the real import of these two verses: "I am not Vāsudeva incarnate, but rather You alone, and no one else, are Vāsudeva. Since You have descended to show mercy to the living beings, please make me give up my false designation, which is like that of an oyster claiming to be silver." The Supreme Lord will certainly comply with this request.

TEXT 6

यानि त्वमस्मच्चिह्नानि मौढ्याद् बिभर्षि सात्वत ।
त्यक्त्वैहि मां त्वं शरणं नो चेद्देहि ममाहवम् ॥६॥

yāni tvam asmac-cihnāni
mauḍhyād bibharṣi sātvata
tyaktvaihi māṁ tvaṁ śaraṇaṁ
no ced dehi mamāhavam

yāni—which; *tvam*—You; *asmat*—our; *cihnāni*—symbols; *mauḍhyāt*—out of delusion; *bibharṣi*—carry; *sātvata*—O chief of the Sātvatas; *tyaktvā*—giving up; *ehi*—come; *mām*—to me; *tvam*—You; *śaraṇam*—for shelter; *na*—not; *u*—otherwise; *cet*—if; *dehi*—give; *mama*—me; *āhavam*—battle.

TRANSLATION

O Sātvata, give up my personal symbols, which out of foolishness You now carry, and come to me for shelter. If You do not, then You must give me battle.

PURPORT

Śrīla Viśvanātha Cakravartī again interprets Pauṇḍraka's words according to the inspiration of Sarasvatī, the goddess of learning. Thus they may be understood to mean "Out of foolishness I have assumed an imitation conchshell, disc, lotus and club, and You are maintaining these by allowing me to use them. You have not yet subdued me and gotten rid of these imitation symbols. Therefore please mercifully come and liberate me by forcing me to give them up. Give me battle, and grant me liberation by killing me."

TEXT 7

श्रीशुक उवाच
कत्थनं तदुपाकर्ण्य पौण्ड्रकस्याल्पमेधसः ।
उग्रसेनादयः सभ्या उच्चकैर्जहसुस्तदा ॥७॥

śrī-śuka uvāca
katthanaṁ tad upākarṇya
pauṇḍrakasyālpa-medhasaḥ
ugrasenādayaḥ sabhyā
uccakair jahasus tadā

śrī-śukaḥ uvāca—Śukadeva Gosvāmī said; *katthanam*—boasting; *tat*—that; *upākarṇya*—hearing; *pauṇḍrakasya*—of Pauṇḍraka; *alpa*—small; *medhasaḥ*—whose intelligence; *ugrasena-ādayaḥ*—headed by King Ugrasena; *sabhyāḥ*—the members of the assembly; *uccakaiḥ*—loudly; *jahasuḥ*—laughed; *tadā*—then.

TRANSLATION

Śukadeva Gosvāmī said: King Ugrasena and the other members of the assembly laughed loudly when they heard this vain boasting of unintelligent Pauṇḍraka.

TEXT 8

उवाच दूतं भगवान् परिहासकथामनु ।
उत्स्रक्ष्ये मूढ चिह्नानि यैस्त्वमेवं विकत्थसे ॥८॥

uvāca dūtaṁ bhagavān
parihāsa-kathām anu
utsrakṣye mūḍha cihnāni
yais tvam evaṁ vikatthase

uvāca—said; *dūtam*—to the messenger; *bhagavān*—the Supreme Lord; *parihāsa*—joking; *kathām*—discussion; *anu*—after; *utsrakṣye*—I will throw; *mūḍha*—O fool; *cihnāni*—the symbols; *yaiḥ*—about which; *tvam*—you; *evam*—in this way; *vikatthase*—are boasting.

TRANSLATION

The Personality of Godhead, after enjoying the jokes of the assembly, told the messenger [to relay a message to his master:] "You fool, I will indeed let loose the weapons you boast of in this way.

PURPORT

The Sanskrit word *utsrakṣye* means "I will hurl, throw, let loose, abandon, etc." Foolish Pauṇḍraka demanded that Lord Kṛṣṇa give up His powerful weapons, such as the disc and the club, and here the Lord replies, *utsrakṣye mūḍha cihnāni:* "Yes, fool, I will indeed let loose these weapons when we meet on the battlefield."

In *Kṛṣṇa, the Supreme Personality of Godhead,* Śrīla Prabhupāda nicely describes this scene as follows: "When all the members of the royal assembly, including King Ugrasena, heard this message sent by Pauṇḍraka, they laughed very loudly for a considerable time. After enjoying the loud laughter of all the members of the assembly, Kṛṣṇa replied to the messenger as follows: 'O messenger of Pauṇḍraka, you may carry My message to your master. He is a foolish rascal. I directly call him a rascal, and I refuse to follow his instructions. I shall never give up the symbols of Vāsudeva, especially My disc. I shall use this disc to kill not only King Pauṇḍraka but all his followers also. I shall destroy this Pauṇḍraka and his foolish associates, who merely constitute a society of cheaters and the cheated.'"

TEXT 9

मुखं तदपिधायाज्ञ कंकगृध्रवटैर्वृतः ।
शयिष्यसे हतस्तत्र भविता शरणं शुनाम् ॥९॥

mukhaṁ tad apidhāyājña
kaṅka-gṛdhra-vaṭair vṛtaḥ
śayiṣyase hatas tatra
bhavitā śaraṇaṁ śunām

mukham—face; *tat*—that; *apidhāya*—being covered; *ajña*—O ignorant man; *kaṅka*—by herons; *gṛdhra*—vultures; *vaṭaiḥ*—and *vaṭa* birds; *vṛtaḥ*—surrounded; *śayiṣyase*—you will lie; *hataḥ*—killed; *tatra*—thereupon; *bhavitā*—you will become; *śaraṇam*—shelter; *śunām*—for dogs.

TRANSLATION

"When you lie dead, O fool, your face covered by vultures, herons and *vaṭa* birds, you will become the shelter of dogs."

PURPORT

Pauṇḍraka foolishly told the Supreme Lord to come to him for shelter, but here Lord Kṛṣṇa tells him, "You are not My shelter, but rather you will become the shelter of dogs when they happily feast on your dead body."

Śrīla Prabhupāda vividly describes this scene as follows: "[Lord Kṛṣṇa told Pauṇḍraka, 'When I shall destroy you,] foolish King, you will have to conceal your face in disgrace, and when your head is severed from your body by My disc, you will be surrounded by meat-eating birds like vultures, hawks and eagles. At that time, instead of becoming My shelter, as you have demanded, you will be subjected to the mercy of these lowborn birds. At that time your body will be thrown to the dogs, who will eat it with great pleasure.'"

TEXT 10

इति दूतस्तमाक्षेपं स्वामिने सर्वमाहरत् ।
कृष्णोऽपि रथमास्थाय काशीमुपजगाम ह ॥१०॥

iti dūtas tam ākṣepaṁ
svāmine sarvam āharat
kṛṣṇo 'pi ratham āsthāya
kāśīm upajagāma ha

iti—thus addressed; *dūtaḥ*—the messenger; *tam*—those; *ākṣepam*—insults; *svāmine*—to his master; *sarvam*—entire; *āharat*—carried; *kṛṣṇaḥ*—Lord Kṛṣṇa; *api*—and; *ratham*—His chariot; *āsthāya*—riding; *kāśīm*—to Vārāṇasī; *upajagāma ha*—went near.

TRANSLATION

When the Lord had thus spoken, the messenger conveyed His insulting reply to his master in its entirety. Lord Kṛṣṇa then mounted His chariot and went to the vicinity of Kāśī.

PURPORT

In *Kṛṣṇa,* Śrīla Prabhupāda describes this incident as follows: "The messenger carried the words of Lord Kṛṣṇa to his master, Pauṇḍraka, who patiently heard all these insults. Without waiting any longer, Lord

Śrī Kṛṣṇa immediately started out in His chariot to punish the rascal Pauṇḍraka. Because at that time the King of Karūṣa [Pauṇḍraka] was living with his friend the King of Kāśī, Kṛṣṇa surrounded the whole city of Kāśī."

TEXT 11

पौण्ड्रकोऽपि तदुद्योगमुपलभ्य महारथः ।
अक्षौहिणीभ्यां संयुक्तो निश्चक्राम पुराद्द्रुतम् ॥११॥

pauṇḍrako 'pi tad-udyogam
upalabhya mahā-rathaḥ
akṣauhiṇībhyāṁ saṁyukto
niścakrāma purād drutam

pauṇḍrakaḥ—Pauṇḍraka; *api*—and; *tat*—His; *udyogam*—preparations; *upalabhya*—noticing; *mahā-rathaḥ*—the mighty warrior; *akṣauhiṇībhyām*—by two full military divisions; *saṁyuktaḥ*—joined; *niścakrāma*—went out; *purāt*—from the city; *drutam*—quickly.

TRANSLATION

Upon observing Lord Kṛṣṇa's preparations for battle, the mighty warrior Pauṇḍraka quickly went out of the city with two full military divisions.

TEXTS 12–14

तस्य काशीपतिर्मित्रं पार्ष्णिग्राहोऽन्वयान्नृप ।
अक्षौहिणीभिस्तिसृभिरपश्यत्पौण्ड्रकं हरिः ॥१२॥
शंखार्यसिगदाशार्ंगश्रीवत्साद्युपलक्षितम् ।
बिभ्राणं कौस्तुभमणिं वनमालाविभूषितम् ॥१३॥
कौशेयवाससी पीते वसानं गरुडध्वजम् ।
अमूल्यमौल्याभरणं स्फुरन्मकरकुण्डलम् ॥१४॥

tasya kāśī-patir mitraṁ
pārṣṇi-grāho 'nvayān nṛpa

akṣauhiṇībhis tisṛbhir
apaśyat pauṇḍrakaṁ hariḥ

śaṅkhāry-asi-gadā-śārṅga-
śrīvatsādy-upalakṣitam
bibhrāṇaṁ kaustubha-maṇiṁ
vana-mālā-vibhūṣitam

kauśeya-vāsasī pīte
vasānaṁ garuḍa-dhvajam
amūlya-mauly-ābharaṇaṁ
sphuran-makara-kuṇḍalam

tasya—his (Pauṇḍraka's); *kāśī-patiḥ*—the master of Kāśī; *mitram*—friend; *pārṣṇi-grāhaḥ*—as the rear guard; *anvayāt*—followed; *nṛpa*—O King (Parīkṣit); *akṣauhiṇībhiḥ*—with divisions; *tisṛbhiḥ*—three; *apaśyat*—saw; *pauṇḍrakam*—Pauṇḍraka; *hariḥ*—Lord Kṛṣṇa; *śaṅkha*—with conchshell; *ari*—disc; *asi*—sword; *gadā*—club; *śārṅga*—Śārṅga bow; *śrīvatsa*—with the Śrīvatsa sign of hair on His chest; *ādi*—and other symbols; *upalakṣitam*—marked; *bibhrāṇam*—bearing; *kaustubha-maṇim*—the Kaustubha gem; *vana-mālā*—with a garland of forest flowers; *vibhūṣitam*—decorated; *kauśeya*—of fine silk; *vāsasī*—a pair of garments; *pīte*—yellow; *vasānam*—wearing; *garuḍa-dhvajam*—his banner marked with the image of Garuḍa; *amūlya*—valuable; *mauli*—a crown; *ābharaṇam*—whose ornament; *sphurat*—gleaming; *makara*—shark-shaped; *kuṇḍalam*—with earrings.

TRANSLATION

Pauṇḍraka's friend, the King of Kāśī, followed behind, O King, leading the rear guard with three *akṣauhiṇī* divisions. Lord Kṛṣṇa saw that Pauṇḍraka was carrying the Lord's own insignia, such as the conchshell, disc, sword and club, and also an imitation Śārṅga bow and Śrīvatsa mark. He wore a mock Kaustubha gem, was decorated with a garland of forest flowers and was dressed in upper and lower garments of fine yellow silk. His banner bore the image of Garuḍa, and he wore a valuable crown and gleaming, shark-shaped earrings.

PURPORT

Śrīla Prabhupāda comments in *Kṛṣṇa:* "When the two kings came before Lord Kṛṣṇa to oppose Him, Kṛṣṇa saw Pauṇḍraka face to face for the first time."

TEXT 15

दृष्ट्वा तमात्मनस्तुल्यं वेषं कृत्रिममास्थितम् ।
यथा नटं रंगगतं विजहास भृशं हरिः ॥१५॥

dṛṣṭvā tam ātmanas tulyaṁ
veṣaṁ kṛtrimam āsthitam
yathā naṭaṁ raṅga-gataṁ
vijahāsa bhṛśaṁ hariḥ

dṛṣṭvā—seeing; *tam*—him; *ātmanaḥ*—to His own; *tulyam*—equal; *veṣam*—in dress; *kṛtrimam*—imitation; *āsthitam*—arrayed; *yathā*—like; *naṭam*—an actor; *raṅga*—a stage; *gatam*—entered upon; *vijahāsa*—laughed; *bhṛśam*—strongly; *hariḥ*—Lord Kṛṣṇa.

TRANSLATION

Lord Hari laughed heartily when He saw how the King had dressed up in exact imitation of His own appearance, just like an actor on a stage.

PURPORT

Śrīla Prabhupāda describes this scene as follows: "On the whole, [Pauṇḍraka's] dress and makeup were clearly imitation. Anyone could understand that he was just like someone on a stage playing the part of Vāsudeva in false dress. When Lord Śrī Kṛṣṇa saw Pauṇḍraka imitating His posture and dress, He could not check His laughter, and thus He laughed with great satisfaction."

Śrīla Jīva Gosvāmī points out that it was a benediction from Lord Śiva that enabled Pauṇḍraka to imitate the Lord's dress and appearance exactly—a fact gleaned from the *Uttara-khaṇḍa* of *Śrī Padma Purāṇa.*

TEXT 16

शूलैर्गदाभिः परिघैः शक्त्यृष्टिप्रासतोमरैः ।
असिभिः पट्टिशैर्बाणैः प्राहरन्नरयो हरिम् ॥१६॥

śūlair gadābhiḥ parighaiḥ
śakty-ṛṣṭi-prāsa-tomaraiḥ
asibhiḥ paṭṭiśair bāṇaiḥ
prāharann arayo harim

śūlaiḥ—with tridents; *gadābhiḥ*—clubs; *parighaiḥ*—and bludgeons; *śakti*—pikes; *ṛṣṭi*—a kind of sword; *prāsa*—long, barbed darts; *tomaraiḥ*—and lances; *asibhiḥ*—with swords; *paṭṭiśaiḥ*—with axes; *bāṇaiḥ*—and with arrows; *prāharan*—attacked; *arayaḥ*—the enemies; *harim*—Lord Kṛṣṇa.

TRANSLATION

The enemies of Lord Hari attacked Him with tridents, clubs, bludgeons, pikes, *ṛṣṭis*, barbed darts, lances, swords, axes and arrows.

TEXT 17

कृष्णस्तु तत्पौण्ड्रककाशिराजयोर्
बलं गजस्यन्दनवाजिपत्तिमत् ।
गदासिचक्रेषुभिरार्दयद् भृशं
यथा युगान्ते हुतभुक् पृथक् प्रजाः ॥१७॥

kṛṣṇas tu tat pauṇḍraka-kāśirājayor
balaṁ gaja-syandana-vāji-patti-mat
gadāsi-cakreṣubhir ārdayad bhṛśaṁ
yathā yugānte huta-bhuk pṛthak prajāḥ

kṛṣṇaḥ—Lord Kṛṣṇa; *tu*—however; *tat*—that; *pauṇḍraka-kāśirājayoḥ*—of Pauṇḍraka and the King of Kāśī; *balam*—military force; *gaja*—elephants; *syandana*—chariots; *vāji*—horses; *patti*—and infantry;

mat—consisting of; *gadā*—with His club; *asi*—sword; *cakra*—disc; *iṣubhiḥ*—and arrows; *ārdayat*—tormented; *bhṛśam*—fiercely; *yathā*—as; *yuga*—of an age of universal history; *ante*—at the end; *huta-bhuk*—the fire (of universal annihilation); *pṛthak*—of different kinds; *prajāḥ*—living entities.

TRANSLATION

But Lord Kṛṣṇa fiercely struck back at the army of Pauṇḍraka and Kāśirāja, which consisted of elephants, chariots, cavalry and infantry. The Lord tormented His enemies with His club, sword, Sudarśana disc and arrows, just as the fire of annihilation torments the various kinds of creatures at the end of a cosmic age.

PURPORT

Śrīla Prabhupāda comments as follows in *Kṛṣṇa:* "The soldiers on the side of King Pauṇḍraka began to shower their weapons upon Kṛṣṇa. The weapons, including various kinds of tridents, clubs, poles, lances, swords, daggers and arrows, came flying in waves, and Kṛṣṇa counteracted them. He smashed not only the weapons but also the soldiers and assistants of Pauṇḍraka, just as during the dissolution of this universe the fire of devastation burns everything to ashes. The elephants, chariots, horses and infantry belonging to the opposite party were scattered by the weapons of Kṛṣṇa."

TEXT 18

आयोधनं तद् रथवाजिकुञ्जर-
द्विपत्खरोष्ट्रैररिणावखण्डितैः ।
बभौ चितं मोदवहं मनस्विनाम्
आक्रीडनं भूतपतेरिवोल्बणम् ॥१८॥

āyodhanaṁ tad ratha-vāji-kuñjara-
dvipat-kharoṣṭrair ariṇāvakhaṇḍitaiḥ
babhau citaṁ moda-vahaṁ manasvinām
ākrīḍanaṁ bhūta-pater ivolbaṇam

āyodhanam—battlefield; *tat*—that; *ratha*—with the chariots; *vāji*—horses; *kuñjara*—elephants; *dvipat*—two-legged (humans); *khara*—mules; *uṣṭraiḥ*—and camels; *ariṇā*—by His disc; *avakhaṇḍitaiḥ*—cut to pieces; *babhau*—shone; *citam*—spread; *moda*—pleasure; *vaham*—bringing; *manasvinām*—to the wise; *ākrīḍanam*—the playground; *bhūta-pateḥ*—of the lord of ghostly spirits, Lord Śiva; *iva*—as if; *ulba-ṇam*—horrible.

TRANSLATION

The battlefield, strewn with the dismembered chariots, horses, elephants, humans, mules and camels that had been cut to pieces by the Lord's disc weapon, shone like the gruesome playground of Lord Bhūtapati, giving pleasure to the wise.

PURPORT

Śrīla Prabhupāda describes this scene as follows: "Although the devastated battlefield appeared like the dancing place of Lord Śiva at the time of the dissolution of the world, the warriors who were on the side of Kṛṣṇa were very much encouraged by seeing this, and they fought with greater strength."

TEXT 19

अथाह पौण्ड्रकं शौरिर्भो भो पौण्ड्रक यद् भवान् ।
दूतवाक्येन मामाह तान्यस्त्राण्युत्सृजामि ते ॥१९॥

athāha pauṇḍrakaṁ śaurir
bho bho pauṇḍraka yad bhavān
dūta-vākyena mām āha
tāny astraṇy utsṛjāmi te

atha—then; *āha*—said; *pauṇḍrakam*—to Pauṇḍraka; *śauriḥ*—Lord Kṛṣṇa; *bhoḥ bhoḥ pauṇḍraka*—My dear Pauṇḍraka; *yat*—those which; *bhavān*—your good self; *dūta*—of the messenger; *vākyena*—through the words; *mām*—to Me; *āha*—spoke about; *tāni*—those; *astrāṇi*—weapons; *utsṛjāmi*—I am releasing; *te*—unto you.

TRANSLATION

Lord Kṛṣṇa then addressed Pauṇḍraka: My dear Pauṇḍraka, the very weapons you spoke of through your messenger, I now release unto you.

PURPORT

Śrīla Prabhupāda writes as follows in *Kṛṣṇa:* "At this time Lord Kṛṣṇa told Pauṇḍraka, 'Pauṇḍraka, you requested Me to give up the symbols of Lord Viṣṇu, specifically My disc. Now I will give it up to you. Be careful! You falsely declare yourself to be Vāsudeva, imitating Myself. Therefore no one is a greater fool than you.' From this statement of Kṛṣṇa's it is clear that any rascal who advertises himself as God is the greatest fool in human society."

TEXT 20

त्याजयिष्येऽभिधानं मे यत्त्वयाज्ञ मृषा धृतम् ।
व्रजामि शरणं तेऽद्य यदि नेच्छामि संयुगम् ॥२०॥

tyājayiṣye 'bhidhānaṁ me
yat tvayājña mṛṣā dhṛtam
vrajāmi śaraṇaṁ te 'dya
yadi necchāmi saṁyugam

tyājayiṣye—I will make (you) renounce; *abhidhānam*—designation; *me*—My; *yat*—which; *tvayā*—by you; *ajña*—O fool; *mṛṣā*—falsely; *dhṛtam*—assumed; *vrajāmi*—I will go; *śaraṇam*—to the shelter; *te*—your; *adya*—today; *yadi*—if; *na icchāmi*—I do not desire; *saṁyugam*—battle.

TRANSLATION

O fool, now I shall make you renounce My name, which you have falsely assumed. And I will certainly take shelter of you if I do not wish to fight you.

PURPORT

Śrīla Prabhupāda writes as follows: "Now, Pauṇḍraka, I shall force you to give up this false representation. You wanted Me to surrender unto you. Now this is your opportunity. We shall now fight, and if I am defeated and you become victorious, I shall certainly surrender unto you."

TEXT 21

इति क्षिप्त्वा शितैर्बाणैर्विरथीकृत्य पौण्ड्रकम् ।
शिरोऽवृश्चद् रथांगेन वज्रेणेन्द्रो यथा गिरेः ॥२१॥

iti kṣiptvā śitair bāṇair
virathī-kṛtya pauṇḍrakam
śiro 'vṛścad rathāṅgena
vajreṇendro yathā gireḥ

iti—with these words; *kṣiptvā*—deriding; *śitaiḥ*—sharp; *bāṇaiḥ*—with His arrows; *virathī*—chariotless; *kṛtya*—making; *pauṇḍrakam*—Pauṇḍraka; *śiraḥ*—his head; *avṛścat*—He cut off; *ratha-aṅgena*—with His Sudarśana disc; *vajreṇa*—with his thunderbolt weapon; *indraḥ*—Lord Indra; *yathā*—as; *gireḥ*—of a mountain.

TRANSLATION

Having thus derided Pauṇḍraka, Lord Kṛṣṇa destroyed his chariot with His sharp arrows. The Lord then cut off his head with the Sudarśana disc, just as Lord Indra lops off a mountain peak with his thunderbolt weapon.

TEXT 22

तथा काशिपतेः कायाच्छिर उत्कृत्य पत्रिभिः ।
न्यपातयत्काशिपुर्यां पद्मकोशमिवानिलः ॥२२॥

tathā kāśi-pateḥ kāyāc
chira utkṛtya patribhiḥ
nyapātayat kāśi-puryāṁ
padma-kośam ivānilaḥ

tathā—similarly; *kāśi-pateḥ*—of the King of Kāśī; *kāyāt*—from his body; *śiraḥ*—the head; *utkṛtya*—severing; *patribhiḥ*—with His arrows; *nyapātayat*—He sent it flying; *kāśi-puryām*—into the city of Kāśī; *padma*—of a lotus; *kośam*—the flower cup; *iva*—as; *anilaḥ*—the wind.

TRANSLATION

With His arrows, Lord Kṛṣṇa similarly severed Kāśirāja's head from his body, sending it flying into Kāśī city like a lotus flower thrown by the wind.

PURPORT

Śrīla Viśvanātha Cakravartī explains why Kṛṣṇa threw Kāśirāja's head into the city: "As he went off to battle, the King of Kāśī had promised the citizens: 'My dear residents of Kāśī, today I will bring the enemy's head into the midst of the city. Have no doubt of this.' The King's sinful queens had also boasted to their maids-in-waiting: 'Today our master will certainly bring the head of the Lord of Dvārakā.' Therefore the Supreme Lord threw the King's head into the city to astonish the inhabitants."

TEXT 23

एवं मत्सरिणं हत्वा पौण्ड्रकं ससखं हरिः ।
द्वारकामाविशत्सिद्धैर्गीयमानकथामृतः ॥२३॥

evaṁ matsariṇaṁ hatvā
pauṇḍrakaṁ sa-sakhaṁ hariḥ
dvārakām āviśat siddhair
gīyamāna-kathāmṛtaḥ

evam—thus; *matsariṇam*—envious; *hatvā*—killing; *pauṇḍrakam*—Pauṇḍraka; *sa*—together with; *sakham*—his friend; *hariḥ*—Lord Kṛṣṇa; *dvārakām*—Dvārakā; *āviśat*—He entered; *siddhaiḥ*—by the mystics of heaven; *gīyamāna*—being sung; *kathā*—narrations about Him; *amṛtaḥ*—nectarean.

TRANSLATION

Having thus killed envious Pauṇḍraka and his ally, Lord Kṛṣṇa returned to Dvārakā. As He entered the city, the Siddhas of heaven chanted His immortal, nectarean glories.

TEXT 24

स नित्यं भगवद्ध्यानप्रध्वस्ताखिलबन्धनः ।
बिभ्राणश्च हरे राजन् स्वरूपं तन्मयोऽभवत् ॥२४॥

sa nityaṁ bhagavad-dhyāna-
pradhvastākhila-bandhanaḥ
bibhrāṇaś ca hare rājan
svarūpaṁ tan-mayo 'bhavat

saḥ—he (Pauṇḍraka); *nityam*—constant; *bhagavat*—upon the Supreme Lord; *dhyāna*—by his meditation; *pradhvasta*—completely shattered; *akhila*—all; *bandhanaḥ*—whose bondage; *bibhrāṇaḥ*—assuming; *ca*—and; *hareḥ*—of Lord Kṛṣṇa; *rājan*—O King (Parīkṣit); *svarūpam*—the personal form; *tat-mayaḥ*—absorbed in consciousness of Him; *abhavat*—he became.

TRANSLATION

By constantly meditating upon the Supreme Lord, Pauṇḍraka shattered all his material bonds. Indeed, by imitating Lord Kṛṣṇa's appearance, O King, he ultimately became Kṛṣṇa conscious.

PURPORT

Śrīla Prabhupāda writes as follows in *Kṛṣṇa:* "As far as Pauṇḍraka was concerned, somehow or other he was always thinking of Vāsudeva by falsely dressing himself in that way, and therefore Pauṇḍraka achieved *sārūpya*, one of the five kinds of liberation, and was thus promoted to the Vaikuṇṭha planets, where the devotees have the same bodily features as Viṣṇu, with four hands holding the four symbols. Factually, his meditation was concentrated on the Viṣṇu form, but because he thought himself to be Lord Viṣṇu, he was offensive. After being killed by Kṛṣṇa, however, that offense was also mitigated. Thus he was given *sārūpya* liberation, and he attained the same form as the Lord."

TEXT 25

शिरः पतितमालोक्य राजद्वारे सकुण्डलम् ।
किमिदं कस्य वा वक्त्रमिति संशिशिरे जनाः ॥२५॥

śiraḥ patitam ālokya
rāja-dvāre sa-kuṇḍalam
kim idaṁ kasya vā vaktram
iti saṁśiśire janāḥ

śiraḥ—the head; *patitam*—fallen; *ālokya*—seeing; *rāja-dvāre*—at the gate of the royal palace; *sa-kuṇḍalam*—with earrings; *kim*—what; *idam*—is this; *kasya*—whose; *vā*—or; *vaktram*—head; *iti*—thus; *saṁśiśire*—expressed doubt; *janāḥ*—the people.

TRANSLATION

Seeing a head decorated with earrings lying at the gate of the royal palace, the people present were puzzled. Some of them asked, "What is this?" and others said, "It is a head, but whose is it?"

PURPORT

Śrīla Prabhupāda writes as follows: "When the head of the King of Kāśī was thrown through the city gate, people gathered and were astonished to see that wonderful thing. When they found out that there were earrings on it, they could understand that it was someone's head. They conjectured as to whose head it might be. Some thought it was Kṛṣṇa's head because Kṛṣṇa was the enemy of Kāśirāja, and they calculated that the King of Kāśī might have thrown Kṛṣṇa's head into the city so that the people might take pleasure in the enemy's having been killed. But it was finally detected that the head was not Kṛṣṇa's but that of Kāśirāja himself."

TEXT 26

राज्ञः काशीपतेर्ज्ञात्वा महिष्यः पुत्रबान्धवाः ।
पौराश्च हा हता राजन्नाथ नाथेति प्रारुदन् ॥२६॥

rājñaḥ kāśi-pater jñātvā
mahiṣyaḥ putra-bāndhavāḥ
paurāś ca hā hatā rājan
nātha nātheti prārudan

rājñaḥ—of the King; *kāśi-pateḥ*—the lord of Kāśi; *jñātvā*—recognizing; *mahiṣyaḥ*—his queens; *putra*—his sons; *bāndhavāḥ*—and other relatives; *paurāḥ*—the citizens of the city; *ca*—and; *hā*—alas; *hatāḥ*—(we are) killed; *rājan*—O King (Parīkṣit); *nātha nātha*—O master, master; *iti*—thus; *prārudan*—they cried out loud.

TRANSLATION

My dear King, when they recognized it as the head of their King—the lord of Kāśī—his queens, sons and other relatives, along with all the citizens of the city, began to cry pitifully: "Alas, we are killed! O my lord, my lord!"

TEXTS 27–28

सुदक्षिणस्तस्य सुतः कृत्वा संस्थाविधिं पतेः ।
निहत्य पितृहन्तारं यास्याम्यपचितिं पितुः ॥२७॥
इत्यात्मनाभिसन्धाय सोपाध्यायो महेश्वरम् ।
सुदक्षिणोऽर्चयामास परमेण समाधिना ॥२८॥

sudakṣiṇas tasya sutaḥ
kṛtvā saṁsthā-vidhiṁ pateḥ
nihatya pitṛ-hantāraṁ
yāsyāmy apacitiṁ pituḥ

ity ātmanābhisandhāya
sopādhyāyo maheśvaram

su-dakṣiṇo 'rcayām āsa
parameṇa samādhinā

sudakṣiṇaḥ—named Sudakṣiṇa; *tasya*—his (Kāśirāja's); *sutaḥ*—son; *kṛtvā*—executing; *saṁsthā-vidhim*—the funeral rituals; *pateḥ*—of his father; *nihatya*—by killing; *pitṛ*—of my father; *hantāram*—the killer; *yāsyāmi*—I will achieve; *apacitim*—revenge; *pituḥ*—for my father; *iti*—thus; *ātmanā*—with his intelligence; *abhisandhāya*—deciding; *sa*—with; *upādhyāyaḥ*—priests; *mahā-īśvaram*—the great Lord Śiva; *su-dakṣiṇaḥ*—being very charitable; *arcayām āsa*—he worshiped; *parameṇa*—with great; *samādhinā*—attention.

TRANSLATION

After the King's son Sudakṣiṇa had performed the obligatory funeral rituals for his father, he resolved within his mind: "Only by killing my father's murderer can I avenge his death." Thus the charitable Sudakṣiṇa, together with his priests, began worshiping Lord Maheśvara with great attention.

PURPORT

Śrīla Prabhupāda writes, "The lord of the kingdom of Kāśī is Viśvanātha (Lord Śiva). The temple of Lord Viśvanātha is still existing in Vārāṇasī, and many thousands of pilgrims still gather daily in that temple."

TEXT 29

प्रीतोऽविमुक्ते भगवांस्तस्मै वरमदाद्विभुः ।
पितृहन्तृवधोपायं स वव्रे वरमीप्सितम् ॥२९॥

prīto 'vimukte bhagavāṁs
tasmai varam adād vibhuḥ
pitṛ-hantṛ-vadhopāyaṁ
sa vavre varam īpsitam

prītaḥ—satisfied; *avimukte*—at Avimukta, an especially holy area within the district of Kāśī; *bhagavān*—Lord Śiva; *tasmai*—to him;

varam—a choice of benedictions; *adāt*—gave; *vibhuḥ*—the powerful demigod; *pitṛ*—of his father; *hantṛ*—the killer; *vadha*—to slay; *upāyam*—the means; *saḥ*—he; *vavre*—chose; *varam*—as his benediction; *īpsitam*—desired.

TRANSLATION

Satisfied by the worship, the powerful Lord Śiva appeared in the sacred precinct of Avimukta and offered Sudakṣiṇa his choice of benedictions. The prince chose as his benediction a means to slay his father's killer.

TEXTS 30–31

दक्षिणाग्निं परिचर ब्राह्मणैः सममृत्विजम् ।
अभिचारविधानेन स चाग्निः प्रमथैर्वृतः ॥३०॥
साधयिष्यति संकल्पमब्रह्मण्ये प्रयोजितः ।
इत्यादिष्टस्तथा चक्रे कृष्णायाभिचरन् व्रती ॥३१॥

dakṣiṇāgniṁ paricara
brāhmaṇaiḥ samam ṛtvijam
abhicāra-vidhānena
sa cāgniḥ pramathair vṛtaḥ

sādhayiṣyati saṅkalpam
abrahmaṇye prayojitaḥ
ity ādiṣṭas tathā cakre
kṛṣṇāyābhicaran vratī

dakṣiṇa-agnim—to the Dakṣiṇa fire; *paricara*—you should render service; *brāhmaṇaiḥ—brāhmaṇas; samam*—together with; *ṛtvijam*—the original priest; *abhicāra-vidhānena*—with the ritual known as *abhicāra* (meant for killing or otherwise harming an enemy); *saḥ*—that; *ca*—and; *agniḥ*—fire; *pramathaiḥ*—by the Pramathas (powerful mystics who are in Lord Śiva's retinue and who assume many different forms); *vṛtaḥ*—surrounded; *sādhayiṣyati*—it will accomplish; *saṅkalpam*—your intention; *abrahmaṇye*—against one who is inimical to *brāhmaṇas;*

prayojitaḥ—utilized; *iti*—so; *ādiṣṭaḥ*—instructed; *tathā*—in that way; *cakre*—he did; *kṛṣṇāya*—against Lord Kṛṣṇa; *abhicaran*—intending to do harm; *vratī*—observing the required vows.

TRANSLATION

Lord Śiva told him, "Accompanied by *brāhmaṇas*, serve the Dakṣiṇāgni fire—the original priest—following the injunctions of the *abhicāra* ritual. Then the Dakṣiṇāgni fire, together with many Pramathas, will fulfill your desire if you direct it against someone inimical to the *brāhmaṇas*." So instructed, Sudakṣiṇa strictly observed the ritualistic vows and invoked the *abhicāra* against Lord Kṛṣṇa.

PURPORT

It is clearly stated here that the powerful Dakṣiṇāgni fire could be directed only against someone unfavorable to brahminical culture. Lord Kṛṣṇa, however, is most favorable to the *brāhmaṇas* and in fact maintains the brahminical culture. Lord Śiva thus knew that if Sudakṣiṇa attempted to direct the power of this ritual against Lord Kṛṣṇa, Sudakṣiṇa himself would perish.

TEXT 32–33

ततोऽग्निरुत्थितः कुण्डान्मूर्तिमानतिभीषणः ।
तप्तताम्रशिखाश्मश्रुरंगारोद्गारिलोचनः ॥३२॥
दंष्ट्रोग्रभ्रुकुटीदण्डकठोरास्यः स्वजिह्वया ।
आलिहन् सृक्वणी नग्नो विधुन्वंस्त्रिशिखं ज्वलत् ॥३३॥

tato 'gnir utthitaḥ kuṇḍān
mūrtimān ati-bhīṣaṇaḥ
tapta-tāmra-śikhā-śmaśrur
aṅgārodgāri-locanaḥ

daṁṣṭrogra-bhru-kuṭī-daṇḍa-
kaṭhorāsyaḥ sva-jihvayā

ālihan sṛkvaṇī nagno
vidhunvaṁs tri-śikhaṁ jvalat

tataḥ—then; *agniḥ*—the fire; *utthitaḥ*—rose up; *kuṇḍāt*—from the sacrificial altar pit; *mūrti-mān*—assuming a personal form; *ati*—extremely; *bhīṣaṇaḥ*—fearsome; *tapta*—molten; *tāmra*—(like) copper; *śikhā*—the tuft of hair on whose head; *śmaśruḥ*—and whose beard; *aṅgāra*—hot cinders; *udgāri*—emitting; *locanaḥ*—whose eyes; *daṁṣṭra*—with his teeth; *ugra*—terrible; *bhru*—of the eyebrows; *kuṭī*—of the furrowing; *daṇḍa*—and with the arch; *kaṭhora*—harsh; *āsyaḥ*—whose face; *sva*—his; *jihvayā*—with the tongue; *ālihan*—licking; *sṛkvaṇī*—both corners of his mouth; *nagnaḥ*—naked; *vidhunvan*—shaking; *tri-śikham*—his trident; *jvalat*—ablaze.

TRANSLATION

Thereupon the fire rose up out of the altar pit, assuming the form of an extremely fearsome, naked person. The fiery creature's beard and tuft of hair were like molten copper, and his eyes emitted blazing hot cinders. His face looked most frightful with its fangs and terrible arched and furrowed brows. As he licked the corners of his mouth with his tongue, the demon shook his flaming trident.

TEXT 34

पद्भ्यां तालप्रमाणाभ्यां कम्पयन्नवनीतलम् ।
सोऽभ्यधावद्वृतो भूतैर्द्वारकां प्रदहन् दिशः ॥३४॥

padbhyāṁ tāla-pramāṇābhyāṁ
kampayann avanī-talam
so 'bhyadhāvad vṛto bhūtair
dvārakāṁ pradahan diśaḥ

padbhyām—with his legs; *tāla*—of palm trees; *pramāṇābhyām*—whose measure; *kampayan*—shaking; *avanī*—of the earth; *talam*—the surface; *saḥ*—he; *abhyadhāvat*—ran; *vṛtaḥ*—accompanied; *bhūtaiḥ*—by ghostly spirits; *dvārakām*—toward Dvārakā; *pradahan*—burning up; *diśaḥ*—the directions.

TRANSLATION

On legs as tall as palm trees, the monster raced toward Dvārakā in the company of ghostly spirits, shaking the ground and burning the world in all directions.

TEXT 35

तमाभिचारदहनमायान्तं द्वारकौकसः ।
विलोक्य तत्रसुः सर्वे वनदाहे मृगा यथा ॥३५॥

tam ābhicāra-dahanam
āyāntaṁ dvārakaukasaḥ
vilokya tatrasuḥ sarve
vana-dāhe mṛgā yathā

tam—him; *ābhicāra*—created by the *abhicāra* ritual; *dahanam*—the fire; *āyāntam*—approaching; *dvārakā-okasaḥ*—the residents of Dvārakā; *vilokya*—seeing; *tatrasuḥ*—became frightened; *sarve*—all; *vana-dāhe*—when there is a forest fire; *mṛgāḥ*—animals; *yathā*—as.

TRANSLATION

Seeing the approach of the fiery demon created by the *abhicāra* ritual, the residents of Dvārakā were all struck with fear, like animals terrified by a forest fire.

TEXT 36

अक्षैः सभायां क्रीडन्तं भगवन्तं भयातुराः ।
त्राहि त्राहि त्रिलोकेश वह्नेः प्रदहतः पुरम् ॥३६॥

akṣaiḥ sabhāyāṁ krīḍantaṁ
bhagavantaṁ bhayāturāḥ
trāhi trāhi tri-lokeśa
vahneḥ pradahataḥ puram

akṣaiḥ—with dice; *sabhāyām*—in the royal court; *krīḍantam*—playing; *bhagavantam*—to the Personality of Godhead; *bhaya*—with fear; *āturāḥ*—agitated; *trāhi trāhi*—(they said) "Save us! Save us!"; *tri*—three; *loka*—of the worlds; *īśa*—O Lord; *vahneḥ*—from the fire; *pradahataḥ*—which is burning up; *puram*—the city.

TRANSLATION

Distraught with fear, the people cried out to the Supreme Personality of Godhead, who was then playing at dice in the royal court: "Save us! Save us, O Lord of the three worlds, from this fire burning up the city!"

TEXT 37

श्रुत्वा तज्जनवैक्लव्यं दृष्ट्वा स्वानां च साध्वसम् ।
शरण्यः सम्प्रहस्याह मा भैष्टेत्यवितास्म्यहम् ॥३७॥

śrutvā taj jana-vaiklavyaṁ
dṛṣṭvā svānāṁ ca sādhvasam
śaraṇyaḥ samprahasyāha
mā bhaiṣṭety avitāsmy aham

śrutvā—hearing; *tat*—this; *jana*—of the populace; *vaiklavyam*—agitation; *dṛṣṭvā*—seeing; *svānām*—of His own men; *ca*—and; *sādhvasam*—the disturbed condition; *śaraṇyaḥ*—the best source of shelter; *samprahasya*—loudly laughing; *āha*—said; *mā bhaiṣṭa*—do not fear; *iti*—thus; *avitā asmi*—will give protection; *aham*—I.

TRANSLATION

When Lord Kṛṣṇa heard the people's agitation and saw that even His own men were disturbed, that most worthy giver of shelter simply laughed and told them, "Do not fear; I shall protect you."

TEXT 38

सर्वस्यान्तर्बहिःसाक्षी कृत्यां माहेश्वरीं विभुः ।
विज्ञाय तद्विघातार्थं पार्श्वस्थं चक्रमादिशत् ॥३८॥

sarvasyāntar-bahiḥ-sākṣī
kṛtyāṁ māheśvarīṁ vibhuḥ
vijñāya tad-vighātārthaṁ
pārśva-sthaṁ cakram ādiśat

sarvasya—everyone; *antaḥ*—within; *bahiḥ*—and without; *sākṣī*—the witness; *kṛtyām*—the manufactured creature; *māhā-īśvarīm*—of Lord Śiva; *vibhuḥ*—the almighty Supreme Lord; *vijñāya*—fully understanding; *tat*—him; *vighāta*—of defeating; *artham*—for the purpose; *pārśva*—at His side; *stham*—standing; *cakram*—His disc; *ādiśat*—He ordered.

TRANSLATION

The almighty Lord, the internal and external witness of all, understood that the monster had been produced by Lord Śiva from the sacrificial fire. To defeat the demon, Kṛṣṇa dispatched His disc weapon, who was waiting at His side.

PURPORT

Śrīla Viśvanātha Cakravartī comments that Lord Kṛṣṇa, playing the part of a king, was absorbed in a gambling match and did not want to be disturbed by such an insignificant matter as the attack of a fiery demon. So He simply dispatched His *cakra* weapon and ordered him to take the necessary steps.

TEXT 39

तत्सूर्यकोटिप्रतिमं सुदर्शनं
जाज्वल्यमानं प्रलयानलप्रभम् ।
स्वतेजसा खं ककुभोऽथ रोदसी
चक्रं मुकुन्दास्त्रमथाग्निमार्दयत् ॥३९॥

tat sūrya-koṭi-pratimaṁ sudarśanaṁ
jājvalyamānaṁ pralayānala-prabham
sva-tejasā khaṁ kakubho 'tha rodasī
cakraṁ mukundāstram athāgnim ārdayat

tat—that; *sūrya*—of suns; *koṭi*—millions; *pratimam*—resembling; *sudarśanam*—Sudarśana; *jājvalyamānam*—blazing with fire; *pralaya*—of universal annihilation; *anala*—(like) the fire; *prabham*—whose effulgence; *sva*—his own; *tejasā*—with heat; *kham*—the sky; *kakubhaḥ*—the directions; *atha*—and; *rodasī*—heaven and earth; *cakram*—the disc; *mukunda*—of Lord Kṛṣṇa; *astram*—the weapon; *atha*—also; *agnim*—the fire (created by Sudakṣiṇa); *ārdayat*—tormented.

TRANSLATION

That Sudarśana, the disc weapon of Lord Mukunda, blazed forth like millions of suns. His effulgence blazed like the fire of universal annihilation, and with his heat he pained the sky, all the directions, heaven and earth, and also the fiery demon.

TEXT 40

कृत्यानलः प्रतिहतः स रथांगपाणेर्
अस्त्रौजसा स नृप भग्नमुखो निवृत्तः ।
वाराणसीं परिसमेत्य सुदक्षिणं तं
सर्त्विग्जनं समदहत्स्वकृतोऽभिचारः ॥४०॥

kṛtyānalaḥ pratihataḥ sa rathāṅga-pāṇer
astraujasā sa nṛpa bhagna-mukho nivṛttaḥ
vārāṇasīṁ parisametya sudakṣiṇaṁ taṁ
sartvig-janaṁ samadahat sva-kṛto 'bhicāraḥ

kṛtyā—produced by mystic power; *analaḥ*—the fire; *pratihataḥ*—frustrated; *saḥ*—he; *ratha-aṅga-pāṇeḥ*—of Lord Kṛṣṇa, who holds the Sudarśana disc in His hand; *astra*—of the weapon; *ojasā*—by the power; *saḥ*—he; *nṛpa*—O King; *bhagna-mukhaḥ*—turning away; *nivṛttaḥ*—having desisted; *vārāṇasīm*—the city of Vārāṇasi; *parisametya*—approaching on all sides; *sudakṣiṇam*—Sudakṣiṇa; *tam*—him; *sa*—together with; *ṛtvik-janam*—his priests; *samadahat*—burned to death; *sva*—by himself (Sudakṣiṇa); *kṛtaḥ*—created; *abhicāraḥ*—meant for doing violence.

TRANSLATION

Frustrated by the power of Lord Kṛṣṇa's weapon, O King, the fiery creature produced by black magic turned his face away and retreated. Created for violence, the demon then returned to Vārāṇasī, where he surrounded the city and then burned Sudakṣiṇa and his priests to death, even though Sudakṣiṇa was his creator.

PURPORT

Śrīla Prabhupāda comments as follows: "Having failed to set fire to Dvārakā, [the fiery demon] went back to Vārāṇasi, the kingdom of Kāśirāja. As a result of his return, all the priests who had helped instruct the black art of *mantras*, along with their employer, Sudakṣiṇa, were burned into ashes by the glaring effulgence of the fiery demon. According to the methods of black-art *mantras* instructed in the *tantra*, if the *mantra* fails to kill the enemy, then, because it must kill someone, it kills the original creator. Sudakṣiṇa was the originator, and the priests assisted him; therefore all of them were burned to ashes. This is the way of the demons: the demons create something to kill God, but by the same weapon the demons themselves are killed."

TEXT 41

चक्रं च विष्णोस्तदनुप्रविष्टं
वाराणसीं साट्टसभालयापणाम् ।
सगोपुराट्टालककोष्ठसंकुलां
सकोशहस्त्यश्वरथान्नशालिनीम् ॥४१॥

cakraṁ ca viṣṇos tad-anupraviṣṭaṁ
vārāṇasīṁ sāṭṭa-sabhālayāpaṇām
sa-gopurāṭṭālaka-koṣṭha-saṅkulām
sa-kośa-hasty-aśva-rathānna-śālinīm

cakram—the disc; *ca*—and; *viṣṇoḥ*—of Lord Viṣṇu; *tat*—it (the fire demon); *anupraviṣṭam*—entering in pursuit; *vārāṇasīm*—Vārāṇasī; *sa*—with; *aṭṭa*—raised porches; *sabhā*—its assembly halls; *ālaya*—

residences; *āpaṇām*—and marketplaces; *sa*—with; *gopura*—gateways; *aṭṭālaka*—watchtowers; *koṣṭha*—and warehouses; *saṅkulām*—crowded; *sa*—with; *kośa*—banks; *hasti*—for elephants; *aśva*—horses; *ratha*—chariots; *anna*—and grains; *śālinīm*—with the buildings.

TRANSLATION

Lord Viṣṇu's disc also entered Vārāṇasī, in pursuit of the fiery demon, and proceeded to burn the city to the ground, including all its assembly halls and residential palaces with raised porches, its numerous marketplaces, gateways, watchtowers, warehouses and treasuries, and all the buildings housing elephants, horses, chariots and grains.

TEXT 42

दग्ध्वा वाराणसीं सर्वां विष्णोश्चक्रं सुदर्शनम् ।
भूयः पार्श्वमुपातिष्ठत्कृष्णस्याक्लिष्टकर्मणः ॥४२॥

dagdhvā vārāṇasīṁ sarvāṁ
viṣṇoś cakraṁ sudarśanam
bhūyaḥ pārśvam upātiṣṭhat
kṛṣṇasyākliṣṭa-karmaṇaḥ

dagdhvā—having burned; *vārāṇasīm*—Vārāṇasī; *sarvām*—all; *viṣṇoḥ*—of Lord Viṣṇu; *cakram*—the disc; *sudarśanam*—Sudarśana; *bhūyaḥ*—once again; *pārśvam*—the side; *upātiṣṭhat*—went to; *kṛṣṇasya*—of Kṛṣṇa; *akliṣṭa*—without trouble or fatigue; *karmaṇaḥ*—whose actions.

TRANSLATION

After burning down the entire city of Vārāṇasī, Lord Viṣṇu's Sudarśana *cakra* returned to the side of Śrī Kṛṣṇa, whose actions are effortless.

TEXT 43

य एनं श्रावयेन्मर्त्य उत्तमःश्लोकविक्रमम् ।
समाहितो वा शृणुयात्सर्वपापैः प्रमुच्यते ॥४३॥

ya enaṁ śrāvayen martya
uttamaḥ-śloka-vikramam
samāhito vā śṛṇuyāt
sarva-pāpaiḥ pramucyate

yaḥ—one who; *enam*—this; *śrāvayet*—causes others to hear; *martyaḥ*—a mortal human; *uttamaḥ-śloka*—of Lord Kṛṣṇa, who is praised in the best transcendental verses; *vikramam*—the heroic pastime; *samāhitaḥ*—with concentration; *vā*—or; *śṛṇuyāt*—hears; *sarva*—from all; *pāpaiḥ*—sins; *pramucyate*—becomes released.

TRANSLATION

Any mortal who recounts this heroic pastime of Lord Uttamaḥ-śloka's, or who simply hears it attentively, will become freed from all sins.

Thus end the purports of the humble servants of His Divine Grace A. C. Bhaktivedanta Swami Prabhupāda to the Tenth Canto, Sixty-sixth Chapter, of the Śrīmad-Bhāgavatam, *entitled "Pauṇḍraka, the False Vāsudeva."*

CHAPTER SIXTY–SEVEN

Lord Balarāma Slays Dvivida Gorilla

This chapter describes how Lord Baladeva enjoyed the company of the young girls of Vraja on Raivataka Mountain and killed the ape Dvivida there.

Narakāsura, a demon whom Lord Kṛṣṇa killed, had a friend named Dvivida, an ape. Dvivida wanted to avenge the death of his friend, so he set fire to the homes of the cowherds, devastated Lord Kṛṣṇa's province of Ānarta and flooded coastal lands by churning the ocean's water with his mighty arms. The rascal then tore down the trees in the *āśramas* of great sages and even passed stool and urine on their sacrificial fires. He kidnapped men and women and imprisoned them in mountain caves, which he sealed off with boulders. After thus disrupting the entire land and polluting many young women of respectable families, Dvivida came upon Raivataka Mountain, where he found Lord Baladeva enjoying in the company of a bevy of attractive women. Ignoring Lord Baladeva, who was apparently intoxicated from drinking Vāruṇī liquor, Dvivida displayed his anus to the women right in front of the Lord and further insulted them by making crude gestures with his eyebrows and passing stool and urine.

Dvivida's outrageous behavior angered Lord Baladeva, and He threw a stone at the ape. But Dvivida managed to dodge it. He then ridiculed Lord Baladeva and tugged at the women's dresses. Seeing this audacity, Lord Baladeva decided to kill Dvivida. Thus He took up His club and His plow weapon. Powerful Dvivida then armed himself by pulling up a *śāla* tree from the ground, and with this tree he struck the Lord on the head. Lord Baladeva, however, remained unmoved and smashed the tree trunk to pieces. Dvivida uprooted another tree, and yet another and another, until the forest was denuded. But although he struck Baladeva on the head with one tree after another, the Lord simply broke all the trees to pieces. Then the foolish ape started throwing a barrage of stones. Lord Baladeva crushed them all to powder, after which Dvivida charged the Lord and hit Him on the chest with his fists, infuriating Him. Putting aside His club and plow weapons, Lord Balarāma then struck Dvivida's throat and shoulder, at which point the ape vomited blood and fell down dead.

Having killed Dvivida, Lord Baladeva set off for Dvārakā as demigods and sages showered flowers from the sky and offered Him praises, prayers and obeisances.

TEXT 1

श्रीराजोवाच

भूयोऽहं श्रोतुमिच्छामि रामस्याद्‌भुतकर्मणः ।
अनन्तस्याप्रमेयस्य यदन्यत्कृतवान् प्रभुः ॥१॥

śrī-rājovāca
bhūyo 'haṁ śrotum icchāmi
rāmasyādbhuta-karmaṇaḥ
anantasyāprameyasya
yad anyat kṛtavān prabhuḥ

śrī-rājā—the glorious King (Parīkṣit); *uvāca*—said; *bhūyaḥ*—further; *aham*—I; *śrotum*—to hear; *icchāmi*—wish; *rāmasya*—of Lord Balarāma; *adbhuta*—amazing; *karmaṇaḥ*—whose activities; *anantasya*—unlimited; *aprameyasya*—immeasurable; *yat*—what; *anyat*—else; *kṛtavān*—did; *prabhuḥ*—the Lord.

TRANSLATION

The glorious King Parīkṣit said: I wish to hear further about Śrī Balarāma, the unlimited and immeasurable Supreme Lord, whose activities are all astounding. What else did He do?

TEXT 2

श्रीशुक उवाच

नरकस्य सखा कश्चिद् द्विविदो नाम वानरः ।
सुग्रीवसचिवः सोऽथ भ्राता मैन्दस्य वीर्यवान् ॥२॥

śrī-śuka uvāca
narakasya sakhā kaścid
dvivido nāma vānaraḥ
sugrīva-sacivaḥ so 'tha
bhrātā maindasya vīryavān

śrī-śukaḥ uvāca—Śukadeva Gosvāmī said; *narakasya*—of the demon Naraka; *sakhā*—friend; *kaścit*—a certain; *dvividaḥ*—Dvivida; *nāma*—by name; *vānaraḥ*—an ape; *sugrīva*—King Sugrīva; *sacivaḥ*—whose adviser; *saḥ*—he; *atha*—also; *bhrātā*—the brother; *maindasya*—of Mainda; *vīrya-vān*—powerful.

TRANSLATION

Śrī Śukadeva Gosvāmī said: There was an ape named Dvivida who was a friend of Narakāsura's. This powerful Dvivida, the brother of Mainda, had been instructed by King Sugrīva.

PURPORT

Śrīla Jīva Gosvāmī points out some interesting facts about the ape Dvivida. Although Dvivida was an associate of Lord Rāmacandra's, he later became corrupted by bad association with the demon Naraka, as stated here: *narakasya sakhā*. This bad association was the reaction for an offense Dvivida had committed when, being proud of his strength, he disrespected Lord Rāmacandra's brother Lakṣmaṇa and others. Those who worship Lord Rāmacandra sometimes chant hymns addressed to Mainda and Dvivida, who are attendant deities of the Lord. According to Śrīla Jīva Gosvāmī, the Mainda and Dvivida mentioned in this verse are empowered expansions of these deities, who are residents of Lord Rāmacandra's Vaikuṇṭha domain.

Śrīla Viśvanātha Cakravartī Ṭhākura concurs with Śrīla Jīva Gosvāmī's view that Dvivida was ruined by bad association, which was a punishment for his having disrespected Śrīmān Lakṣmaṇa. Śrīla Viśvanātha Cakravartī states, however, that the Mainda and Dvivida mentioned here are actually the eternally liberated devotees addressed as attendant deities during the worship of Lord Rāmacandra. The Lord arranged their degradation, he says, to show the evil of the bad association that results from offending great personalities. Thus Śrīla Viśvanātha Cakravartī compares the fall of Dvivida and Mainda to that of Jaya and Vijaya.

TEXT 3

सख्युः सोऽपचितिं कुर्वन् वानरो राष्ट्रविप्लवम् ।
पुरग्रामाकरान् घोषानदहद्वह्निमुत्सृजन् ॥३॥

sakhyuḥ so 'pacitiṁ kurvan
vānaro rāṣṭra-viplavam
pura-grāmākarān ghoṣān
adahad vahnim utsṛjan

sakhyuḥ—of his friend (Naraka, whom Lord Kṛṣṇa had killed); *saḥ*—he; *apacitim*—repayment of his debt; *kurvan*—doing; *vānaraḥ*—the ape; *rāṣṭra*—of the kingdom; *viplavam*—creating great disturbance; *pura*—the cities; *grāma*—villages; *ākarān*—and mines; *ghoṣān*—cowherd communities; *adahat*—he burned; *vahnim*—fire; *utsṛjan*—spreading about.

TRANSLATION

To avenge the death of his friend [Naraka], the ape Dvivida ravaged the land, setting fires that burned cities, villages, mines and cowherd dwellings.

PURPORT

Kṛṣṇa had killed Dvivida's friend Naraka, and to retaliate the ape intended to destroy Lord Kṛṣṇa's flourishing kingdom. In *Kṛṣṇa* Śrīla Prabhupāda writes, "His first business was to set fires in villages, towns, and industrial and mining places, as well as the residential quarters of the mercantile men who were busy dairy farming and protecting cows."

TEXT 4

क्वचित्स शैलानुत्पाट्य तैर्देशान् समचूर्णयत् ।
आनर्तान् सुतरामेव यत्रास्ते मित्रहा हरिः ॥४॥

kvacit sa śailān utpāṭya
tair deśān samacūrṇayat
ānartān sutarām eva
yatrāste mitra-hā hariḥ

kvacit—once; *saḥ*—he, Dvivida; *śailān*—mountains; *utpāṭya*—tearing up; *taiḥ*—with them; *deśān*—all the kingdoms; *samacūrṇayat*—he devastated; *ānartān*—the province of the Ānarta people (in which Dvārakā is situated); *sutarām eva*—especially; *yatra*—where; *āste*—is present; *mitra*—of his friend; *hā*—the killer; *hariḥ*—Kṛṣṇa.

TRANSLATION

Once Dvivida tore up a number of mountains and used them to devastate all the neighboring kingdoms, especially the province of Ānarta, wherein dwelt his friend's killer, Lord Hari.

TEXT 5

क्वचित्समुद्रमध्यस्थो दोर्भ्यामुत्क्षिप्य तज्जलम् ।
देशान्नागायुतप्राणो वेलाकूले न्यमज्जयत् ॥५॥

kvacit samudra-madhya-stho
dorbhyām utkṣipya taj-jalam
deśān nāgāyuta-prāṇo
velā-kūle nyamajjayat

kvacit—once; *samudra*—of the ocean; *madhya*—in the midst; *sthaḥ*—standing; *dorbhyām*—with his arms; *utkṣipya*—churning up; *tat*—its; *jalam*—water; *deśān*—the kingdoms; *nāga*—elephants; *ayuta*—(like) ten thousand; *prāṇaḥ*—whose vital strength; *velā*—of the coast; *kūle*—upon the shore; *nyamajjayat*—he caused to drown.

TRANSLATION

Another time he entered the ocean and, with the strength of ten thousand elephants, churned up its water with his arms and thus submerged the coastal regions.

TEXT 6

आश्रमानृषिमुख्यानां कृत्वा भग्नवनस्पतीन् ।
अदूषयच्छकृन्मूत्रैरग्नीन् वैतानिकान् खलः ॥६॥

āśramān ṛṣi-mukhyānāṁ
kṛtvā bhagna-vanaspatīn

adūṣayac chakṛn-mūtrair
agnīn vaitānikān khalaḥ

āśramān—the spiritual communities; *ṛṣi*—of sages; *mukhyānām*—exalted; *kṛtvā*—making; *bhagna*—broken; *vanaspatīn*—whose trees; *adūṣayat*—he contaminated; *śakṛt*—with stool; *mūtraiḥ*—and urine; *agnīn*—the fires; *vaitānikān*—sacrificial; *khalaḥ*—wicked.

TRANSLATION

The wicked ape tore down the trees in the hermitages of exalted sages and contaminated their sacrificial fires with his feces and urine.

TEXT 7

पुरुषान् योषितो दृप्तः क्ष्माभृद्द्रोणीगुहासु सः ।
निक्षिप्य चाप्यधाच्छैलैः पेशष्कारीव कीटकम् ॥७॥

puruṣān yoṣito dṛptaḥ
kṣmābhṛd-droṇī-guhāsu saḥ
nikṣipya cāpyadhāc chailaiḥ
peśaṣkārīva kīṭakam

puruṣān—men; *yoṣitaḥ*—and women; *dṛptaḥ*—audacious; *kṣmā-bhṛt*—of a mountain; *droṇī*—within a valley; *guhāsu*—inside caves; *saḥ*—he; *nikṣipya*—casting; *ca*—and; *apyadhāt*—sealed; *śailaiḥ*—with large stones; *peśaṣkārī*—a wasp; *iva*—as; *kīṭakam*—a small insect.

TRANSLATION

Just as a wasp imprisons smaller insects, he arrogantly threw both men and women into caves in a mountain valley and sealed the caves shut with boulders.

TEXT 8

एवं देशान् विप्रकुर्वन् दूषयंश्च कुलस्त्रियः ।
श्रुत्वा सुललितं गीतं गिरिं रैवतकं ययौ ॥८॥

evaṁ deśān viprakurvan
dūṣayaṁś ca kula-striyaḥ
śrutvā su-lalitaṁ gītaṁ
giriṁ raivatakaṁ yayau

evam—thus; *deśān*—the various kingdoms; *viprakurvan*—disturbing; *dūṣayan*—contaminating; *ca*—and; *kula*—of respectable families; *striyaḥ*—the women; *śrutvā*—hearing; *su-lalitam*—very sweet; *gītam*—song; *girim*—to the mountain; *raivatakam*—named Raivataka; *yayau*—he went.

TRANSLATION

Once, while Dvivida was thus engaged in harassing the neighboring kingdoms and polluting women of respectable families, he heard very sweet singing coming from Raivataka Mountain. So he went there.

TEXTS 9–10

तत्रापश्यद्यदुपतिं रामं पुष्करमालिनम् ।
सुदर्शनीयसर्वांगं ललनायूथमध्यगम् ॥९॥
गायन्तं वारुणीं पीत्वा मदविह्वललोचनम् ।
विभ्राजमानं वपुषा प्रभिन्नमिव वारणम् ॥१०॥

tatrāpaśyad yadu-patiṁ
rāmaṁ puṣkara-mālinam
sudarśanīya-sarvāṅgaṁ
lalanā-yūtha-madhya-gam

gāyantaṁ vāruṇīṁ pītvā
mada-vihvala-locanam
vibhrājamānaṁ vapuṣā
prabhinnam iva vāraṇam

tatra—there; *apaśyat*—he saw; *yadu-patim*—the Lord of the Yadus; *rāmam*—Balarāma; *puṣkara*—of lotus flowers; *mālinam*—wearing a garland; *su-darśanīya*—most attractive; *sarva*—all; *aṅgam*—whose limbs;

lalanā—of women; *yūtha*—of a bevy; *madhya-gam*—in the midst; *gāyantam*—singing; *vāruṇīm*—the *vāruṇī* liquor; *pītvā*—drinking; *mada*—with intoxication; *vihvala*—unsteady; *locanam*—whose eyes; *vibhrājamānam*—brilliantly glowing; *vapuṣā*—with His body; *prabhinnam*—in rut; *iva*—as; *vāraṇam*—an elephant.

TRANSLATION

There he saw Śrī Balarāma, the Lord of the Yadus, adorned with a garland of lotuses and appearing most attractive in every limb. He was singing amidst a crowd of young women, and since He had drunk *vāruṇī* liquor, His eyes rolled as if He were intoxicated. His body shone brilliantly as He behaved like an elephant in rut.

TEXT 11

दुष्टः शाखामृगः शाखामारूढः कम्पयन् द्रुमान् ।
चक्रे किलकिलाशब्दमात्मानं सम्प्रदर्शयन् ॥११॥

duṣṭaḥ śākhā-mṛgaḥ śākhām
ārūḍhaḥ kampayan drumān
cakre kilakilā-śabdam
ātmānaṁ sampradarśayan

duṣṭaḥ—mischievous; *śākhā-mṛgaḥ*—the ape ("the animal who lives on branches"); *śākhām*—a branch; *ārūḍhaḥ*—having climbed; *kampayan*—shaking; *drumān*—trees; *cakre*—he made; *kilakilā-śabdam*—the sound *kilakilā; ātmānam*—himself; *sampradarśayan*—showing.

TRANSLATION

The mischievous ape climbed a tree branch and then revealed his presence by shaking the trees and making the sound *kilakilā*.

PURPORT

The word *śākhā-mṛga* indicates that the ape Dvivida, like ordinary apes, was naturally inclined to climb trees. Śrīla Prabhupāda writes, "This gorilla by the name Dvivida could climb up on the trees and jump from one branch to another. Sometimes he would jerk the branches, creating a particular type of sound—*kilakilā*—so that Lord Balarāma was greatly distracted from the pleasing atmosphere."

TEXT 12

तस्य धार्ष्ट्यं कपेर्वीक्ष्य तरुण्यो जातिचापलाः ।
हास्यप्रिया विजहसुर्बलदेवपरिग्रहाः ॥१२॥

tasya dhārṣṭyaṁ kaper vīkṣya
taruṇyo jāti-cāpalāḥ
hāsya-priyā vijahasur
baladeva-parigrahāḥ

tasya—of him; *dhārṣṭyam*—the impudence; *kapeḥ*—of the ape; *vīkṣya*—seeing; *taruṇyaḥ*—the young women; *jāti*—by nature; *cāpalāḥ*—not serious; *hāsya-priyāḥ*—fond of laughter; *vijahasuḥ*—laughed loudly; *baladeva-parigrahāḥ*—the consorts of Lord Baladeva.

TRANSLATION

When Lord Baladeva's consorts saw the ape's impudence, they began to laugh. They were, after all, young girls who were fond of joking and prone to silliness.

TEXT 13

ता हेलयामास कपिर्भ्रूक्षेपैर्सम्मुखादिभिः ।
दर्शयन् स्वगुदं तासां रामस्य च निरीक्षितः ॥१३॥

tā helayām āsa kapir
bhrū-kṣepair sammukhādibhiḥ
darśayan sva-gudaṁ tāsām
rāmasya ca nirīkṣitaḥ

tāḥ—them (the girls); *helayām āsa*—ridiculed; *kapiḥ*—the ape; *bhrū*—of his eyebrows; *kṣepaiḥ*—with odd gestures; *sammukha*—by standing right in front of them; *ādibhiḥ*—and so on; *darśayan*—showing;

sva—his; *gudam*—anus; *tāsām*—to them; *rāmasya*—as Lord Balarāma; *ca*—and; *nirīkṣitaḥ*—was watching.

TRANSLATION

Even as Lord Balarāma looked on, Dvivida insulted the girls by making odd gestures with his eyebrows, coming right in front of them, and showing them his anus.

PURPORT

Śrīla Prabhupāda writes, "The gorilla was so rude that even in the presence of Balarāma he began to show the lower part of his body to the women, and sometimes he would come forward to show his teeth while moving his eyebrows." Śrīla Viśvanātha Cakravartī states that Dvivida would come right up to the women and move about, urinate and so on.

TEXTS 14–15

तं ग्राव्णा प्राहरत्क्रुद्धो बलः प्रहरतां वरः ।
स वञ्चयित्वा ग्रावाणं मदिराकलशं कपिः ॥१४॥
गृहीत्वा हेलयामास धूर्तस्तं कोपयन् हसन् ।
निर्भिद्य कलशं दुष्टो वासांस्यास्फालयद् बलम् ।
कदर्थीकृत्य बलवान् विप्रचक्रे मदोद्धतः ॥१५॥

taṁ grāvṇā prāharat kruddho
balaḥ praharatāṁ varaḥ
sa vañcayitvā grāvāṇam
madirā-kalaśaṁ kapiḥ

gṛhītvā helayām āsa
dhūrtas taṁ kopayan hasan
nirbhidya kalaśaṁ duṣṭo
vāsāṁsy āsphālayad balam
kadarthī-kṛtya balavān
vipracakre madoddhataḥ

tam—at him, Dvivida; *grāvṇā*—a rock; *prāharat*—threw; *kruddhaḥ*—angry; *balaḥ*—Lord Balarāma; *praharatām*—of throwers of weapons;

varaḥ—the best; *saḥ*—he, Dvivida; *vañcayitvā*—avoiding; *grāvāṇam*—the rock; *madirā*—of liquor; *kalaśam*—the pot; *kapiḥ*—the ape; *gṛhītvā*—seizing; *helayām āsa*—made fun of; *dhūrtaḥ*—the rascal; *tam*—Him, Lord Balarāma; *kopayan*—angering; *hasan*—laughing; *nirbhidya*—breaking; *kalaśam*—the pot; *duṣṭaḥ*—wicked; *vāsāṁsi*—the garments (of the girls); *āsphālayat*—he pulled at; *balam*—Lord Balarāma; *kadarthī-kṛtya*—disrespecting; *bala-vān*—powerful; *vipracakre*—he insulted; *mada*—by false pride; *uddhataḥ*—puffed up.

TRANSLATION

Angered, Lord Balarāma, the best of fighters, hurled a rock at him, but the cunning ape dodged the rock and grabbed the Lord's pot of liquor. Further infuriating Lord Balarāma by laughing and by ridiculing Him, wicked Dvivida then broke the pot and offended the Lord even more by pulling at the girls' clothing. Thus the powerful ape, puffed up with false pride, continued to insult Śrī Balarāma.

TEXT 16

तं तस्याविनयं दृष्ट्वा देशांश्च तदुपद्रुतान् ।
क्रुद्धो मुषलमादत्त हलं चारिजिघांसया ॥१६॥

taṁ tasyāvinayaṁ dṛṣṭvā
deśāṁś ca tad-upadrutān
kruddho muṣalam ādatta
halaṁ cāri-jighāṁsayā

tam—that; *tasya*—his; *avinayam*—rudeness; *dṛṣṭvā*—seeing; *deśān*—the kingdoms; *ca*—and; *tat*—by him; *upadrutān*—disrupted; *kruddhaḥ*—angry; *muṣalam*—His club; *ādatta*—took; *halam*—His plow; *ca*—and; *ari*—the enemy; *jighāṁsayā*—intending to kill.

TRANSLATION

Lord Balarāma saw the ape's rude behavior and thought of the disruptions he had created in the surrounding kingdoms. Thus the Lord angrily took up His club and His plow weapon, having decided to put His enemy to death.

PURPORT

The word *avinayam* means "without humility." Dvivida, completely lacking in modesty and humility, shamelessly performed the most wicked activities. Lord Balarāma knew of the great disturbances Dvivida had caused to people in general, apart from the vulgar behavior the ape was exhibiting in the Lord's own presence. The offensive ape would now have to die.

TEXT 17

द्विविदोऽपि महावीर्यः शालमुद्यम्य पाणिना ।
अभ्येत्य तरसा तेन बलं मूर्धन्यताडयत् ॥१७॥

dvivido 'pi mahā-vīryaḥ
śālam udyamya pāṇinā
abhyetya tarasā tena
balaṁ mūrdhany atāḍayat

dvividaḥ—Dvivida; *api*—also; *mahā*—great; *vīryaḥ*—whose potency; *śālam*—a *śāla* tree; *udyamya*—lifting up; *pāṇinā*—with his hand; *abhyetya*—approaching; *tarasā*—swiftly; *tena*—with it; *balam*—Lord Balarāma; *mūrdhani*—on the head; *atāḍayat*—he struck.

TRANSLATION

Mighty Dvivida also came forward to do battle. Uprooting a *śāla* tree with one hand, he rushed toward Balarāma and struck Him on the head with the tree trunk.

TEXT 18

तं तु संकर्षणो मूर्ध्नि पतन्तमचलो यथा ।
प्रतिजग्राह बलवान् सुनन्देनाहनच्च तम् ॥१८॥

taṁ tu saṅkarṣaṇo mūrdhni
patantam acalo yathā
pratijagrāha balavān
sunandenāhanac ca tam

tam—that (tree trunk); *tu*—but; *saṅkarṣaṇaḥ*—Lord Balarāma; *mūrdhni*—on His head; *patantam*—falling; *acalaḥ*—an unmoving mountain; *yathā*—like; *pratijagrāha*—took hold of; *bala-vān*—powerful; *sunandena*—with Sunanda, His club; *ahanat*—He struck; *ca*—and; *tam*—him, Dvivida.

TRANSLATION

But Lord Saṅkarṣaṇa remained as motionless as a mountain and simply grabbed the log as it fell upon His head. He then struck Dvivida with His club, named Sunanda.

TEXTS 19–21

मूषलाहतमस्तिष्को विरेजे रक्तधारया ।
गिरिर्यथा गैरिकया प्रहारं नानुचिन्तयन् ॥१९॥
पुनरन्यं समुत्क्षिप्य कृत्वा निष्पत्रमोजसा ।
तेनाहनत्सुसंक्रुद्धस्तं बलः शतधाच्छिनत् ॥२०॥
ततोऽन्येन रुषा जघ्ने तं चापि शतधाच्छिनत् ॥२१॥

mūṣalāhata-mastiṣko
vireje rakta-dhārayā
girir yathā gairikayā
prahāraṁ nānucintayan

punar anyaṁ samutkṣipya
kṛtvā niṣpatram ojasā
tenāhanat su-saṅkruddhas
taṁ balaḥ śatadhācchinat

tato 'nyena ruṣā jaghne
taṁ cāpi śatadhācchinat

mūṣala—by the club; *āhata*—struck; *mastiṣkaḥ*—his skull; *vireje*—he appeared brilliant; *rakta*—of blood; *dhārayā*—with the downpour; *giriḥ*—a mountain; *yathā*—like; *gairikayā*—with red oxide; *prahāram*—the blow; *na*—not; *anucintayan*—regarding seriously; *punaḥ*—again;

anyam—another (tree); *samutkṣipya*—uprooting; *kṛtvā*—making; *niṣpatram*—devoid of leaves; *ojasā*—forcefully; *tena*—with it; *ahanat*—he struck; *su-saṅkruddhaḥ*—totally angered; *tam*—it; *balaḥ*—Lord Balarāma; *śatadhā*—into hundreds of pieces; *acchinat*—shattered; *tataḥ*—then; *anyena*—with another; *ruṣā*—furiously; *jaghne*—smashed; *tam*—it; *ca*—and; *api*—also; *śatadhā*—into hundreds of pieces; *acchinat*—He broke.

TRANSLATION

Struck on the skull by the Lord's club, Dvivida became brilliantly decorated by the outpour of blood, like a mountain beautified by red oxide. Ignoring the wound, Dvivida uprooted another tree, stripped it of leaves by brute force and struck the Lord again. Now enraged, Lord Balarāma shattered the tree into hundreds of pieces, upon which Dvivida grabbed yet another tree and furiously hit the Lord again. This tree, too, the Lord smashed into hundreds of pieces.

TEXT 22

एवं युध्यन् भगवता भग्ने भग्ने पुनः पुनः ।
आकृष्य सर्वतो वृक्षान्निर्वृक्षमकरोद्वनम् ॥२२॥

evaṁ yudhyan bhagavatā
bhagne bhagne punaḥ punaḥ
ākṛṣya sarvato vṛkṣān
nirvṛkṣam akarod vanam

evam—in this way; *yudhyan*—(Dvivida) fighting; *bhagavatā*—by the Lord; *bhagne bhagne*—being repeatedly broken; *punaḥ punaḥ*—again and again; *ākṛṣya*—pulling out; *sarvataḥ*—from everywhere; *vṛkṣān*—trees; *nirvṛkṣam*—treeless; *akarot*—he made; *vanam*—the forest.

TRANSLATION

Thus fighting the Lord, who again and again demolished the trees He was attacked with, Dvivida kept on uprooting trees from all sides until the forest was left treeless.

TEXT 23

ततोऽमुञ्चच्छिलावर्षं बलस्योपर्यमर्षितः ।
तत्सर्वं चूर्णयामास लीलया मुषलायुधः ॥२३॥

tato 'muñcac chilā-varṣaṁ
balasyopary amarṣitaḥ
tat sarvaṁ cūrṇayām āsa
līlayā muṣalāyudhaḥ

tataḥ—then; *amuñcat*—he released; *śilā*—of stones; *varṣam*—a rain; *balasya upari*—on top of Lord Balarāma; *amarṣitaḥ*—frustrated; *tat*—that; *sarvam*—all; *cūrṇayām āsa*—pulverized; *līlayā*—easily; *muṣala-āyudhaḥ*—the wielder of the club.

TRANSLATION

The angry ape then released a rain of stones upon Lord Balarāma, but the wielder of the club easily pulverized them all.

PURPORT

Śrīla Prabhupāda writes, "When no more trees were available, Dvivida took help from the hills and threw large pieces of stone, like rainfall, upon the body of Balarāma. Lord Balarāma, in a great sporting mood, began to smash those big pieces of stone into mere pebbles." Even today there are many sports wherein people enjoy striking a ball or similar object with a stick or bat. This sporting propensity exists originally in the Supreme Personality of Godhead, who playfully (*līlayā*) pulverized the deadly boulders hurled at Him by the powerful Dvivida.

TEXT 24

स बाहू तालसंकाशौ मुष्टीकृत्य कपीश्वरः ।
आसाद्य रोहिणीपुत्रं ताभ्यां वक्षस्यरूरुजत् ॥२४॥

sa bāhū tāla-saṅkāśau
muṣṭī-kṛtya kapīśvaraḥ

āsādya rohiṇī-putraṁ
tābhyāṁ vakṣasy arūrujat

saḥ—he; *bāhū*—both his arms; *tāla*—palm trees; *saṅkāśau*—as big as; *muṣṭī*—into fists; *kṛtya*—making; *kapi*—of apes; *īśvaraḥ*—the most powerful; *āsādya*—confronting; *rohiṇī-putram*—the son of Rohiṇī, Balarāma; *tābhyām*—with them; *vakṣasi*—upon His chest; *arūrujat*—he beat.

TRANSLATION

Dvivida, the most powerful of apes, now clenched his fists at the end of his palm-tree-sized arms, came before Lord Balarāma and beat his fists against the Lord's body.

TEXT 25

यादवेन्द्रोऽपि तं दोर्भ्यां त्यक्त्वा मुषललांगले ।
जत्रावभ्यर्दयत्क्रुद्धः सोऽपतद् रुधिरं वमन् ॥२५॥

yādavendro 'pi taṁ dorbhyāṁ
tyaktvā muṣala-lāṅgale
jatrāv abhyardayat kruddhaḥ
so 'patad rudhiraṁ vaman

yādava-indraḥ—Balarāma, the Lord of the Yādavas; *api*—and; *tam*—him; *dorbhyām*—with His hands; *tyaktvā*—throwing aside; *muṣala-lāṅgale*—His club and plow; *jatrau*—on the collarbone; *abhyardayat*—hammered; *kruddhaḥ*—angry; *saḥ*—he, Dvivida; *apatat*—fell; *rudhiram*—blood; *vaman*—vomiting.

TRANSLATION

The furious Lord of the Yādavas then threw aside His club and plow and with His bare hands hammered a blow upon Dvivida's collarbone. The ape collapsed, vomiting blood.

PURPORT

In *Kṛṣṇa*, Śrīla Prabhupāda writes, "This time Lord Balarāma became most angry. Since the gorilla was striking Him with his hands, He would not strike him back with His own weapons, the club or the plow. Simply with His fists He began to strike the collarbone of the gorilla. This striking proved to be fatal to Dvivida."

TEXT 26

चकम्पे तेन पतता सटंकः सवनस्पतिः ।
पर्वतः कुरुशार्दूल वायुना नौरिवाम्भसि ॥२६॥

cakampe tena patatā
sa-ṭaṅkaḥ sa-vanaspatiḥ
parvataḥ kuru-śārdūla
vāyunā naur ivāmbhasi

cakampe—shook; *tena*—because of him; *patatā*—as he fell; *sa*—together with; *ṭaṅkaḥ*—its cliffs; *sa*—together with; *vanaspatiḥ*—its trees; *parvataḥ*—the mountain; *kuru-śārdūla*—O tiger among the Kurus (Parīkṣit Mahārāja); *vāyunā*—by the wind; *nauḥ*—a boat; *iva*—as if; *ambhasi*—on the water.

TRANSLATION

When he fell, O tiger among the Kurus, Raivataka Mountain shook, along with its cliffs and trees, like a wind-tossed boat at sea.

PURPORT

The word *ṭaṅka* here indicates not only the mountain cliffs but also the fissures and other spots where water had accumulated. All these mountainous areas shook and trembled when Dvivida fell.

TEXT 27

जयशब्दो नमःशब्दः साधु साध्विति चाम्बरे ।
सुरसिद्धमुनीन्द्राणामासीत्कुसुमवर्षिणाम् ॥२७॥

jaya-śabdo namaḥ-śabdaḥ
sādhu sādhv iti cāmbare
sura-siddha-munīndrāṇām
āsīt kusuma-varṣiṇām

jaya-śabdaḥ—the sound of *jaya* ("Victory!"); *namaḥ-sabdaḥ*—the sound of *namaḥ* ("Obeisances!"); *sādhu sādhu iti*—the exclamation "Excellent! Well done!"; *ca*—and; *ambare*—in the sky; *sura*—of the demigods; *siddha*—advanced mystics; *muni-indrāṇām*—and great sages; *āsīt*—there were; *kusuma*—flowers; *varṣiṇām*—who were pouring down.

TRANSLATION

In the heavens the demigods, perfect mystics and great sages cried out, "Victory to You! Obeisances to You! Excellent! Well done!" and showered flowers upon the Lord.

TEXT 28

एवं निहत्य द्विविदं जगद्व्यतिकरावहम् ।
संस्तूयमानो भगवान् जनैः स्वपुरमाविशत् ॥२८॥

evaṁ nihatya dvividaṁ
jagad-vyatikarāvaham
saṁstūyamāno bhagavān
janaiḥ sva-puram āviśat

evam—thus; *nihatya*—having killed; *dvividam*—Dvivida; *jagat*—to the world; *vyatikara*—disturbance; *āvaham*—who brought; *saṁstūyamānaḥ*—being glorified with the chanting of prayers; *bhagavān*—the Supreme Lord; *janaiḥ*—by the people; *sva*—His; *puram*—city (Dvārakā); *āviśat*—He entered.

TRANSLATION

Having thus killed Dvivida, who had disturbed the whole world, the Supreme Lord returned to His capital as the people along the way chanted His glories.

Thus end the purports of the humble servants of His Divine Grace A. C. Bhaktivedanta Swami Prabhupāda to the Tenth Canto, Sixty-seventh Chapter, of the Śrīmad-Bhāgavatam, *entitled "Lord Balarāma Slays Dvivida Gorilla."*

CHAPTER SIXTY-EIGHT

The Marriage of Sāmba

This chapter describes how the Kauravas captured Sāmba and how Lord Baladeva dragged the city of Hastināpura to secure his release.

Sāmba, the darling son of Jāmbavatī, kidnapped Duryodhana's daughter Lakṣmaṇā from her *svayaṁ-vara* assembly. In response, the Kauravas joined forces to arrest him. After Sāmba held them off single-handedly for some time, six warriors of the Kaurava party deprived him of his chariot, broke his bow to pieces, seized him, tied him up and brought both him and Lakṣmaṇā back to Hastināpura.

When King Ugrasena heard of Sāmba's capture, he called upon the Yādavas to retaliate. Angered, they prepared to fight, but Lord Balarāma pacified them, hoping to avoid a quarrel between the Kuru and Yadu dynasties. The Lord set off for Hastināpura, together with several *brāhmaṇas* and Yādava elders.

The party of Yādavas set up camp in a garden outside the city, and Lord Balarāma sent Uddhava to ascertain King Dhṛtarāṣṭra's frame of mind. When Uddhava appeared in the Kaurava court and announced Lord Balarāma's arrival, the Kauravas worshiped Uddhava and went to see the Lord, taking auspicious items to offer Him. The Kauravas honored Balarāma with rituals and items of respect, but when He conveyed Ugrasena's demand that they release Sāmba, they became angry. "It is very amazing," they said, "that the Yādavas are trying to give orders to the Kauravas. This is like a shoe trying to climb atop one's head. It is from us alone that the Yādavas have obtained their royal thrones, and yet now they are presuming themselves our equals. No longer will we extend to them royal privileges."

Having said this, the Kaurava nobles went inside their city, and Lord Baladeva decided that the only way to deal with those who are maddened by false prestige is through brute punishment. Thus He took His plow weapon and, intending to rid the earth of all the Kurus, began dragging Hastināpura toward the Ganges. Seeing that their city was in imminent danger of falling into the river, the terrified Kauravas quickly brought

Sāmba and Lakṣmaṇā before Lord Balarāma and began to glorify Him. Then they prayed, "O Lord, please forgive us, who were so ignorant of Your true identity."

Baladeva assured the Kauravas He would not harm them, and Duryodhana presented various wedding gifts to his daughter and new son-in-law. Then Duryodhana, extending his greetings to the Yādavas, requested Lord Baladeva to return to Dvārakā with Sāmba and Lakṣmaṇā.

TEXT 1

श्रीशुक उवाच
दुर्योधनसुतां राजन् लक्ष्मणां समितिंजयः ।
स्वयंवरस्थामहरत्साम्बो जाम्बवतीसुतः ॥१॥

śrī-śuka uvāca
duryodhana-sutāṁ rājan
lakṣmaṇāṁ samitiṁ-jayaḥ
svayaṁvara-sthām aharat
sāmbo jāmbavatī-sutaḥ

śrī-śukaḥ uvāca—Śukadeva Gosvāmī said; *duryodhana-sutām*—the daughter of Duryodhana; *rājan*—O King (Parīkṣit); *lakṣmaṇām*—named Lakṣmaṇā; *samitim-jayaḥ*—victorious in battle; *svayam-vara*—in her *svayaṁ-vara* ceremony; *sthām*—situated; *aharat*—stole; *sāmbaḥ*—Sāmba; *jāmbavatī-sutaḥ*—the son of Jāmbavatī.

TRANSLATION

Śukadeva Gosvāmī said: O King, Jāmbavatī's son Sāmba, ever victorious in battle, kidnapped Duryodhana's daughter Lakṣmaṇā from her *svayaṁ-vara* ceremony.

PURPORT

In *Kṛṣṇa*, Śrīla Prabhupāda explains this event as follows: "Duryodhana, the son of Dhṛtarāṣṭra, had a marriageable daughter by the name of Lakṣmaṇā. She was a very highly qualified girl of the Kuru dynasty, and many princes wanted to marry her. In such cases the *svayaṁ-vara* ceremony is held so that the girl may select her husband according to her own choice. In Lakṣmaṇā's *svayaṁ-vara* assembly, when the girl was to select her husband, Sāmba appeared. He was the son of Kṛṣṇa by Jāmbavatī, one of the chief wives of Lord Kṛṣṇa. This son Sāmba is so named because, being a very bad child, he always lived close to his mother. The name Sāmba indicates that this son was very much his mother's pet. *Ambā* means "mother," and *sa* means "with." So this special name was given to him because he always remained with his mother. He was also known as Jāmbavatī-suta for the same reason. As previously explained, all the sons of Kṛṣṇa were as qualified as their great father, Lord Kṛṣṇa. Sāmba wanted the daughter of Duryodhana, Lakṣmaṇā, although she was not inclined to have him. Therefore Sāmba kidnapped Lakṣmaṇā by force from the *svayaṁ-vara* ceremony."

TEXT 2

कौरवाः कुपिता ऊचुर्दुर्विनीतोऽयमर्भकः ।
कदर्थीकृत्य नः कन्यामकामामहरद् बलात् ॥२॥

kauravāḥ kupitā ūcur
durvinīto 'yam arbhakaḥ
kadarthī-kṛtya naḥ kanyām
akāmām aharad balāt

kauravāḥ—the Kurus; *kupitāḥ*—angered; *ūcuḥ*—said; *durvinītaḥ*—ill-behaved; *ayam*—this; *arbhakaḥ*—boy; *kadarthī-kṛtya*—insulting; *naḥ*—us; *kanyām*—the maiden; *akāmām*—unwilling; *aharat*—has taken; *balāt*—by force.

TRANSLATION

The angry Kurus said: This ill-behaved boy has offended us, forcibly kidnapping our unmarried daughter against her will.

TEXT 3

बध्नीतेमं दुर्विनीतं किं करिष्यन्ति वृष्णयः ।
येऽस्मत्प्रसादोपचितां दत्तां नो भुञ्जते महीम् ॥३॥

badhnītemaṁ durvinītaṁ
kiṁ kariṣyanti vṛṣṇayaḥ

ye 'smat-prasādopacitāṁ
dattāṁ no bhuñjate mahīm

badhnīta—arrest; *imam*—him; *durvinītam*—ill-behaved; *kim*—what; *kariṣyanti*—will they do; *vṛṣṇayaḥ*—the Vṛṣṇis; *ye*—who; *asmat*—of us; *prasāda*—by the grace; *upacitām*—acquired; *dattām*—bestowed; *naḥ*—our; *bhuñjate*—are enjoying; *mahīm*—the land.

TRANSLATION

Arrest this ill-behaved Sāmba! What will the Vṛṣṇis do? By our grace they are ruling land that we have granted them.

TEXT 4

निगृहीतं सुतं श्रुत्वा यद्येष्यन्तीह वृष्णयः ।
भग्नदर्पाः शमं यान्ति प्राणा इव सुसंयताः ॥४॥

nigṛhītaṁ sutaṁ śrutvā
yady eṣyantīha vṛṣṇayaḥ
bhagna-darpāḥ śamaṁ yānti
prāṇā iva su-saṁyatāḥ

nigṛhītam—captured; *sutam*—their son; *śrutvā*—hearing; *yadi*—if; *eṣyanti*—they will come; *iha*—here; *vṛṣṇayaḥ*—the Vṛṣṇis; *bhagna*—broken; *darpāḥ*—whose pride; *śamam*—pacification; *yānti*—they will attain; *prāṇāḥ*—the senses; *iva*—as; *su*—properly; *saṁyatāḥ*—brought under control.

TRANSLATION

If the Vṛṣṇis come here when they learn that their son has been captured, we will break their pride. Thus they'll become subdued, like bodily senses brought under strict control.

TEXT 5

इति कर्णः शलो भूरिर्यज्ञकेतुः सुयोधनः ।
साम्बमारेभिरे योद्धुं कुरुवृद्धानुमोदिताः ॥५॥

iti karṇaḥ śalo bhūrir
yajñaketuḥ suyodhanaḥ
sāmbam ārebhire yoddhuṁ
kuru-vṛddhānumoditāḥ

iti—saying this; *karṇaḥ śalaḥ bhūriḥ*—Karṇa, Śala and Bhūri (Saumadatti); *yajñaketuḥ suyodhanaḥ*—Yajñaketu (Bhūriśravā) and Duryodhana; *sāmbam*—against Sāmba; *ārebhire*—they set out; *yoddhum*—to fight; *kuru-vṛddha*—by the elder of the Kurus (Bhīṣma); *anumoditāḥ*—sanctioned.

TRANSLATION

After saying this and having their plan sanctioned by the senior member of the Kuru dynasty, Karṇa, Śala, Bhūri, Yajñaketu and Suyodhana set out to attack Sāmba.

PURPORT

Śrīla Viśvanātha Cakravartī Ṭhākura explains that the elder of the Kurus mentioned here is Bhīṣma, who gave permission to the younger men as follows: "Since this maiden has now been touched by Sāmba, she cannot take any other husband. He must become her husband. Nonetheless, you should arrest him and tie him up to make a statement about his impropriety and our own prowess. But in no case should he be killed." The *ācārya* also adds that Bhīṣma accompanied the five warriors mentioned in this verse.

TEXT 6

दृष्ट्वानुधावतः साम्बो धार्तराष्ट्रान्महारथः ।
प्रगृह्य रुचिरं चापं तस्थौ सिंह इवैकलः ॥६॥

dṛṣṭvānudhāvataḥ sāmbo
dhārtarāṣṭrān mahā-rathaḥ
pragṛhya ruciraṁ cāpaṁ
tasthau siṁha ivaikalaḥ

dṛṣṭvā—seeing; *anudhāvataḥ*—who were rushing toward him; *sāmbaḥ*—Sāmba; *dhārtarāṣṭrān*—the followers of Dhṛtarāṣṭra; *mahā-rathaḥ*—the great chariot-fighter; *pragṛhya*—seizing; *ruciram*—beautiful; *cāpam*—his bow; *tasthau*—he stood; *siṁhaḥ*—a lion; *iva*—like; *ekalaḥ*—all alone.

TRANSLATION

Seeing Duryodhana and his companions rushing toward him, Sāmba, the great chariot-fighter, took up his splendid bow and stood alone like a lion.

TEXT 7

तं ते जिघृक्षवः क्रुद्धास्तिष्ठ तिष्ठेति भाषिणः ।
आसाद्य धन्विनो बाणैः कर्णाग्रण्यः समाकिरन् ॥७॥

taṁ te jighṛkṣavaḥ kruddhās
tiṣṭha tiṣṭheti bhāṣiṇaḥ
āsādya dhanvino bāṇaiḥ
karṇāgraṇyaḥ samākiran

tam—him; *te*—they; *jighṛkṣavaḥ*—determined to capture; *kruddhāḥ*—angry; *tiṣṭha tiṣṭha iti*—"Stand there! Stand there!"; *bhāṣiṇaḥ*—saying; *āsādya*—confronting; *dhanvinaḥ*—the bowmen; *bāṇaiḥ*—with their arrows; *karṇa-agraṇyaḥ*—those headed by Karṇa; *samākiran*—showered him.

TRANSLATION

Determined to capture him, the angry bowmen led by Karṇa shouted at Sāmba, "Stand and fight! Stand and fight!" They came straight for him and showered him with arrows.

TEXT 8

सोऽपविद्धः कुरुश्रेष्ठ कुरुभिर्यदुनन्दनः ।
नामृष्यत्तदचिन्त्यार्भः सिंह क्षुद्रमृगैरिव ॥८॥

so 'paviddhaḥ kuru-śreṣṭha
kurubhir yadu-nandanaḥ
nāmṛṣyat tad acintyārbhaḥ
siṁha kṣudra-mṛgair iva

saḥ—he; *apaviddhaḥ*—unjustly attacked; *kuru-śreṣṭha*—O best of the Kurus (Parīkṣit Mahārāja); *kurubhiḥ*—by the Kurus; *yadu-nandanaḥ*—the dear son of the Yadu dynasty; *na amṛṣyat*—did not tolerate; *tat*—it; *acintya*—of the inconceivable Lord, Kṛṣṇa; *arbhaḥ*—the child; *siṁhaḥ*—a lion; *kṣudra*—insignificant; *mṛgaiḥ*—by animals; *iva*—as.

TRANSLATION

O best of the Kurus, as Kṛṣṇa's son Sāmba was being unjustly harassed by the Kurus, that darling of the Yadu dynasty did not tolerate their attack, any more than a lion would tolerate an attack by puny animals.

PURPORT

Commenting on the word *acintyārbha,* Śrīla Prabhupāda writes in *Kṛṣṇa,* "Sāmba, the glorious son of the Yadu dynasty, [was] endowed with inconceivable potencies as the son of Lord Kṛṣṇa."

TEXTS 9–10

विस्फूर्ज्य रुचिरं चापं सर्वान् विव्याध सायकैः ।
कर्णादीन् षड् रथान् वीरस्तावद्‌भिर्युगपत्पृथक् ॥९॥
चतुर्भिश्चतुरो वाहानेकैकेन च सारथीन् ।
रथिनश्च महेष्वासांस्तस्य तत्तेऽभ्यपूजयन् ॥१०॥

visphūrjya ruciraṁ cāpaṁ
sarvān vivyādha sāyakaiḥ
karṇādīn ṣaḍ rathān vīras
tāvadbhir yugapat pṛthak

caturbhiś caturo vāhān
ekaikena ca sārathīn

rathinaś ca maheṣvāsāṁs
tasya tat te 'bhyapūjayan

visphūrjya—twanging; *ruciram*—attractive; *cāpam*—his bow; *sarvān*—all of them; *vivyādha*—he pierced; *sāyakaiḥ*—with his arrows; *karṇa-ādīn*—Karṇa and the others; *ṣaṭ*—six; *rathān*—the chariots; *vīraḥ*—the hero, Sāmba; *tāvadbhiḥ*—with as many; *yugapat*—simultaneously; *pṛthak*—each individually; *caturbhiḥ*—with four (arrows); *caturaḥ*—the four; *vāhān*—horses (of each chariot); *eka-ekena*—with one each; *ca*—and; *sārathīn*—the chariot drivers; *rathinaḥ*—the warriors commanding the chariots; *ca*—and; *mahā-iṣu-āsān*—great bowmen; *tasya*—his; *tat*—that; *te*—they; *abhyapūjayan*—honored.

TRANSLATION

Twanging his wonderful bow, heroic Sāmba struck with arrows the six warriors headed by Karṇa. He pierced the six chariots with as many arrows, each team of four horses with four arrows, and each chariot driver with a single arrow, and he similarly struck the great bowmen who commanded the chariots. The enemy warriors congratulated Sāmba for this display of prowess.

PURPORT

Śrīla Prabhupāda comments, "While Sāmba was so diligently fighting alone with the six great warriors, they all appreciated the inconceivable potency of the boy. Even in the midst of fighting, they admitted frankly that this boy Sāmba was wonderful."

TEXT 11

तं तु ते विरथं चक्रुश्चत्वारश्चतुरो हयान् ।
एकस्तु सारथिं जघ्ने चिच्छेदान्यः शरासनम् ॥११॥

taṁ tu te virathaṁ cakruś
catvāraś caturo hayān
ekas tu sārathiṁ jaghne
cicchedānyaḥ śarāsanam

tam—him; *tu*—but; *te*—they; *viratham*—deprived of his chariot; *cakruḥ*—made; *catvāraḥ*—four; *caturaḥ*—four of them; *hayān*—horses; *ekaḥ*—one; *tu*—and; *sārathim*—the chariot driver; *jaghne*—struck; *cicheda*—split; *anyaḥ*—another; *śara-asanam*—his bow.

TRANSLATION

But they forced him down from his chariot, and thereupon four of them struck his four horses, one of them struck down his chariot driver, and another broke his bow.

TEXT 12

तं बद्ध्वा विरथीकृत्य कृच्छ्रेण कुरवो युधि ।
कुमारं स्वस्य कन्यां च स्वपुरं जयिनोऽविशन् ॥१२॥

taṁ baddhvā virathī-kṛtya
kṛcchreṇa kuravo yudhi
kumāraṁ svasya kanyāṁ ca
sva-puraṁ jayino 'viśan

tam—him; *baddhvā*—binding up; *virathī-kṛtya*—having deprived him of his chariot; *kṛcchreṇa*—with difficulty; *kuravaḥ*—the Kurus; *yudhi*—in the fight; *kumāram*—the young boy; *svasya*—their own; *kanyām*—girl; *ca*—and; *sva-puram*—their city; *jayinaḥ*—victorious; *aviśan*—entered.

TRANSLATION

Having deprived Sāmba of his chariot during the fight, the Kuru warriors tied him up with great difficulty and then returned victorious to their city, taking the young boy and their princess.

TEXT 13

तच्छ्रुत्वा नारदोक्तेन राजन् सञ्जातमन्यवः ।
कुरून् प्रत्युद्यमं चक्रुरुग्रसेनप्रचोदिताः ॥१३॥

tac chrutvā nāradoktena
rājan sañjāta-manyavaḥ

kurūn praty udyamaṁ cakrur
ugrasena-pracoditāḥ

tat—this; *śrutvā*—hearing; *nārada*—of Nārada Muni; *uktena*—through the statements; *rājan*—O King (Parīkṣit); *sañjāta*—awakened; *manyavaḥ*—whose anger; *kurūn*—the Kurus; *prati*—against; *udyamam*—preparations for war; *cakruḥ*—they made; *ugrasena*—by King Ugrasena; *pracoditāḥ*—urged on.

TRANSLATION

O King, when the Yādavas heard news of this from Śrī Nārada, they became angry. Urged on by King Ugrasena, they prepared for war against the Kurus.

PURPORT

Śrīla Prabhupāda writes, "The great sage Nārada immediately carried the news to the Yadu dynasty that Sāmba was arrested and told them the whole story. The members of the Yadu dynasty became very angry at Sāmba's being arrested, and improperly so by six warriors. Now with the permission of thc head of the Yadu dynasty's King, Ugrasena, they prepared to attack the capital city of the Kuru dynasty."

TEXTS 14–15

सान्त्वयित्वा तु तान् रामः सन्नद्धान् वृष्णिपुंगवान् ।
नैच्छत्कुरूणां वृष्णीनां कलिं कलिमलापहः ॥१४॥
जगाम हास्तिनपुरं रथेनादित्यवर्चसा ।
ब्राह्मणैः कुलवृद्धैश्च वृतश्चन्द्र इव ग्रहैः ॥१५॥

sāntvayitvā tu tān rāmaḥ
sannaddhān vṛṣṇi-puṅgavān
naicchat kurūṇāṁ vṛṣṇīnāṁ
kaliṁ kali-malāpahaḥ

jagāma hāstina-puraṁ
rathenāditya-varcasā

brāhmaṇaiḥ kula-vṛddhaiś ca
vṛtaś candra iva grahaiḥ

sāntvayitvā—calming; *tu*—but; *tān*—them; *rāmaḥ*—Lord Balarāma; *sannaddhān*—suited in armor; *vṛṣṇi-puṅgavān*—the heroes of the Vṛṣṇi dynasty; *na aicchat*—He did not want; *kurūṇām vṛṣṇīnām*—between the Kurus and the Vṛṣṇis; *kalim*—a quarrel; *kali*—of the age of quarrel; *mala*—the contamination; *apahaḥ*—He who removes; *jagāma*—He went; *hāstina-puram*—to Hastināpura; *rathena*—with His chariot; *āditya*—(like) the sun; *varcasā*—whose effulgence; *brāhmaṇaiḥ*—by *brāhmaṇas; kula*—of the family; *vṛddhaiḥ*—by elders; *ca*—and; *vṛtaḥ*—surrounded; *candraḥ*—the moon; *iva*—as; *grahaiḥ*—by the seven planets.

TRANSLATION

Lord Balarāma, however, cooled the tempers of the Vṛṣṇi heroes, who had already put on their armor. He who purifies the age of quarrel did not want a quarrel between the Kurus and Vṛṣṇis. Thus, accompanied by *brāhmaṇas* and family elders, He went to Hastināpura on His chariot, which was as effulgent as the sun. As He went, He appeared like the moon surrounded by the ruling planets.

TEXT 16

गत्वा गजाह्वयं रामो बाह्योपवनमास्थितः ।
उद्धवं प्रेषयामास धृतराष्ट्रं बुभुत्सया ॥१६॥

gatvā gajāhvayaṁ rāmo
bāhyopavanam āsthitaḥ
uddhavaṁ preṣayām āsa
dhṛtarāṣṭraṁ bubhutsayā

gatvā—going; *gajāhvayam*—to Hastināpura; *rāmaḥ*—Lord Balarāma; *bāhya*—outside; *upavanam*—in a garden; *āsthitaḥ*—He stayed; *uddhavam*—Uddhava; *preṣayām āsa*—He sent; *dhṛtarāṣṭram*—about Dhṛtarāṣṭra; *bubhutsayā*—desiring to find out.

TRANSLATION

Upon arriving at Hastināpura, Lord Balarāma remained in a garden outside the city and sent Uddhava ahead to probe King Dhṛtarāṣṭra's intentions.

PURPORT

Śrīla Prabhupāda writes, "When Lord Balarāma reached the precints of the city of Hastināpura, He did not enter but stationed Himself in a camp outside the city in a small garden house. Then He asked Uddhava to see the leaders of the Kuru dynasty and inquire from them whether they wanted to fight with the Yadu dynasty or to make a settlement."

TEXT 17

सोऽभिवन्द्याम्बिकापुत्रं भीष्मं द्रोणं च बाह्लिकम् ।
दुर्योधनं च विधिवद् राममागतमब्रवीत् ॥१७॥

so 'bhivandyāmbikā-putraṁ
bhīṣmaṁ droṇaṁ ca bāhlikam
duryodhanaṁ ca vidhi-vad
rāmam āgatam abravīt

saḥ—he, Uddhava; *abhivandya*—offering respects; *ambikā-putram*—to Dhṛtarāṣṭra, the son of Ambikā; *bhīṣmam droṇam ca*—to Bhīṣma and Droṇa; *bāhlikam duryodhanam ca*—and to Bāhlika and Duryodhana; *vidhi-vat*—according to scriptural injunctions; *rāmam*—Lord Balarāma; *āgatam*—has arrived; *abravīt*—he said.

TRANSLATION

After he had offered proper respects to the son of Ambikā [Dhṛtarāṣṭra] and to Bhīṣma, Droṇa, Bāhlika and Duryodhana, Uddhava informed them that Lord Balarāma had arrived.

PURPORT

Śrīla Viśvanātha Cakravartī points out that there is no reference here to Uddhava offering respect to Yudhiṣṭhira and his associates, since at that time the Pāṇḍavas were staying in Indraprastha.

TEXT 18

तेऽतिप्रीतास्तमाकर्ण्य प्राप्तं रामं सुहृत्तमम् ।
तमर्चयित्वाभिययुः सर्वे मंगलपाणयः ॥१८॥

te 'ti-prītās tam ākarṇya
prāptaṁ rāmaṁ suhṛt-tamam
tam arcayitvābhiyayuḥ
sarve maṅgala-pāṇayaḥ

te—they; *ati*—extremely; *prītāḥ*—pleased; *tam*—Him; *ākarṇya*—hearing; *prāptam*—arrived; *rāmam*—Balarāma; *suhṛt-tamam*—their dearest friend; *tam*—him, Uddhava; *arcayitvā*—after worshiping; *abhiyayuḥ*—went forth; *sarve*—all of them; *maṅgala*—auspicious offerings; *pāṇayaḥ*—in their hands.

TRANSLATION

Overjoyed to hear that Balarāma, their dearmost friend, had come, they first honored Uddhava and then went forth to meet the Lord, carrying auspicious offerings in their hands.

PURPORT

In *Kṛṣṇa,* Śrīla Prabhupāda writes, "The leaders of the Kuru dynasty, especially Dhṛtarāṣṭra and Duryodhana, were very joyful because they knew very well that Lord Balarāma was a great well-wisher of their family. There were no bounds to their joy on hearing the news, and so immediately they welcomed Uddhava. In order to properly receive Lord Balarāma, they all took in their hands auspicious paraphernalia for His reception and went to see Him outside the city door."

TEXT 19

तं संगम्य यथान्यायं गामर्घ्यं च न्यवेदयन् ।
तेषां ये तत्प्रभावज्ञाः प्रणेमुः शिरसा बलम् ॥१९॥

taṁ saṅgamya yathā-nyāyaṁ
gām arghyaṁ ca nyavedayan

teṣāṁ ye tat-prabhāva-jñāḥ
praṇemuḥ śirasā balam

tam—Him; *saṅgamya*—going up to; *yathā*—as; *nyāyam*—proper; *gām*—cows; *arghyam*—*arghya* water; *ca*—and; *nyavedayan*—they presented; *teṣām*—among them; *ye*—those who; *tat*—His; *prabhāva*—power; *jñāḥ*—knowing; *praṇemuḥ*—they bowed down; *śirasā*—with their heads; *balam*—to Lord Balarāma.

TRANSLATION

They approached Lord Balarāma and worshiped Him with gifts of cows and *arghya*, as was fitting. Those among the Kurus who understood His true power bowed down to Him, touching their heads to the ground.

PURPORT

The *ācāryas* explain that even the elders, like Bhīṣmadeva, also bowed down to Lord Baladeva.

TEXT 20

बन्धून् कुशलिनः श्रुत्वा पृष्ट्वा शिवमनामयम् ।
परस्परमथो रामो बभाषेऽविक्लवं वचः ॥२०॥

bandhūn kuśalinaḥ śrutvā
pṛṣṭvā śivam anāmayam
parasparam atho rāmo
babhāṣe 'viklavaṁ vacaḥ

bandhūn—their relatives; *kuśalinaḥ*—doing well; *śrutvā*—hearing; *pṛṣṭvā*—inquiring; *śivam*—about their welfare; *anāmayam*—and health; *parasparam*—among one another; *atha u*—thereupon; *rāmaḥ*—Lord Balarāma; *babhāṣe*—spoke; *aviklavam*—forthrightly; *vacaḥ*—words.

TRANSLATION

After both parties had heard that their relatives were doing well and both had inquired into each other's welfare and health, Lord Balarāma forthrightly spoke to the Kurus as follows.

PURPORT

Śrīla Prabhupāda writes, "They all exchanged words of reception by asking one another of their welfare. When such formality was finished, Lord Balarāma, in a great voice and very patiently, submitted before them the following words for their consideration."

TEXT 21

उग्रसेनः क्षितेशेशो यद्व आज्ञापयत्प्रभुः ।
तदव्यग्रधियः श्रुत्वा कुरुध्वमविलम्बितम् ॥२१॥

ugrasenaḥ kṣiteśeśo
yad va ājñāpayat prabhuḥ
tad avyagra-dhiyaḥ śrutvā
kurudhvam avilambitam

ugrasenaḥ—King Ugrasena; *kṣita*—of the earth; *īśa*—of rulers; *īśaḥ*—the ruler; *yat*—what; *vaḥ*—of you; *ājñāpayat*—has demanded; *prabhuḥ*—our master; *tat*—that; *avyagra-dhiyaḥ*—with undivided attention; *śrutvā*—hearing; *kurudhvam*—you should do; *avilambitam*—without delay.

TRANSLATION

[Lord Balarāma said:] King Ugrasena is our master and the ruler of kings. With undivided attention you should hear what he has ordered you to do, and then you should do it at once.

TEXT 22

यद्यूयं बहवस्त्वेकं जित्वाधर्मेण धार्मिकम् ।
अबध्नीताथ तन्मृष्ये बन्धूनामैक्यकाम्यया ॥२२॥

yad yūyaṁ bahavas tv ekaṁ
jitvādharmeṇa dhārmikam
abadhnītātha tan mṛṣye
bandhūnām aikya-kāmyayā

yat—that; *yūyam*—all of you; *bahavaḥ*—being many; *tu*—but; *ekam*—one person; *jitvā*—defeating; *adharmeṇa*—against religious principles; *dhārmikam*—one who follows religious principles; *abadhnīta*—you bound up; *atha*—even so; *tat*—that; *mṛṣye*—I am tolerating; *bandhūnām*—among relatives; *aikya*—for unity; *kāmyayā*—with the desire.

TRANSLATION

[King Ugrasena has said:] Even though by irreligious means several of you defeated a single opponent who follows the religious codes, still I am tolerating this for the sake of unity among family members.

PURPORT

Here Ugrasena implies that the Kurus should immediately bring Sāmba and present him to Lord Balarāma.

TEXT 23

वीर्यशौर्यबलोन्नद्धमात्मशक्तिसमं वचः ।
कुरवो बलदेवस्य निशम्योचुः प्रकोपिताः ॥२३॥

vīrya-śaurya-balonnaddham
ātma-śakti-samaṁ vacaḥ
kuravo baladevasya
niśamyocuḥ prakopitāḥ

vīrya—with potency; *śaurya*—courage; *bala*—and strength; *unnaddham*—filled; *ātma*—to His own; *śakti*—power; *samam*—appropriate; *vacaḥ*—the words; *kuravaḥ*—the Kauravas; *baladevasya*—of Lord Baladeva; *niśamya*—hearing; *ūcuḥ*—they spoke; *prakopitāḥ*—angered.

TRANSLATION

Upon hearing these words of Lord Baladeva's, which were full of potency, courage and strength and were appropriate to His transcendental power, the Kauravas became furious and spoke as follows.

TEXT 24

अहो महच्चित्रमिदं कालगत्या दुरत्यया ।
आरुरुक्षत्युपानद्वै शिरो मुकुटसेवितम् ॥२४॥

aho mahac citram idaṁ
kāla-gatyā duratyayā
āruruksaty upānad vai
śiro mukuṭa-sevitam

aho—oh; *mahat*—great; *citram*—wonder; *idam*—this; *kāla*—of time; *gatyā*—by the movement; *duratyayā*—unavoidable; *āruruksati*—wants to climb on top; *upānat*—a shoe; *vai*—indeed; *śiraḥ*—the head; *mukuṭa*—with a crown; *sevitam*—ornamented.

TRANSLATION

[The Kuru nobles said:] Oh, how amazing this is! The force of time is indeed insurmountable: a lowly shoe now wants to climb on the head that bears the royal crown.

PURPORT

By the words *kāla-gatyā duratyayā,* "the insurmountable movement of time," the intolerant Kurus allude to the degraded age of Kali, which was about to begin. Here the Kurus indicate that the fallen age of Kali had indeed already begun, since they claim that now "the shoe wants to climb on the head that bears the royal crown." In other words, they thought that the lowly Yadus now wanted to rise above the royal Kurus.

TEXT 25

एते यौनेन सम्बद्धाः सहशय्यासनाशनाः ।
वृष्णयस्तुल्यतां नीता अस्मद्दत्तनृपासनाः ॥२५॥

ete yaunena sambaddhāḥ
saha-śayyāsanāśanāḥ
vṛṣṇayas tulyatāṁ nītā
asmad-datta-nṛpāsanāḥ

ete—these; *yaunena*—by marital relation; *sambaddhāḥ*—connected; *saha*—sharing; *śayyā*—beds; *āsana*—seats; *aśanāḥ*—and meals; *vṛṣṇayaḥ*—the Vṛṣṇis; *tulyatām*—to equality; *nītāḥ*—brought; *asmat*—by us; *datta*—given; *nṛpa-āsanāḥ*—whose thrones.

TRANSLATION

It is because these Vṛṣṇis are bound to us by marital ties that we have granted them equality, allowing them to share our beds, seats and meals. Indeed, it is we who have given them their royal thrones.

TEXT 26

चामरव्यजने शंखमातपत्रं च पाण्डुरम् ।
किरीटमासनं शय्यां भुञ्जतेऽस्मदुपेक्षया ॥२६॥

cāmara-vyajane śaṅkham
ātapatraṁ ca pāṇḍuram
kirīṭam āsanaṁ śayyāṁ
bhuñjate 'smad-upekṣayā

cāmara—of yak-tail hair; *vyajane*—pair of fans; *śaṅkham*—conchshell; *ātapatram*—umbrella; *ca*—and; *pāṇḍuram*—white; *kirīṭam*—crown; *āsanam*—throne; *śayyām*—royal bed; *bhuñjate*—they enjoy; *asmat*—by our; *upekṣayā*—overlooking.

TRANSLATION

Only because we looked the other way could they enjoy the pair of yak-tail fans and the conchshell, white umbrella, throne, and royal bed.

PURPORT

Śrīla Prabhupāda writes that the Kurus were thinking, "They [the Yadus] should not have used such royal paraphernalia in our presence, but we did not check them due to our family relationships." By using the words *asmad-upekṣayā*, the Kurus mean to say, "They were able to use these royal insignia because we did not take the matter seriously." As explained by Śrīla Viśvanātha Cakravartī, the Kurus thought, "Showing concern about their use of these items would have been a sign of respect, but in fact we do not have such respect for them.... Since they are of inferior families, they are not to be respected, and so we pay no regard to them."

TEXT 27

अलं यदूनां नरदेवलाञ्छनैर्
दातुः प्रतीपैः फणिनामिवामृतम् ।
येऽस्मत्प्रसादोपचिता हि यादवा
आज्ञापयन्त्यद्य गतत्रपा बत ॥२७॥

alaṁ yadūnāṁ naradeva-lāñchanair
dātuḥ pratīpaiḥ phaṇinām ivāmṛtam
ye 'smat-prasādopacitā hi yādavā
ājñāpayanty adya gata-trapā bata

alam—enough; *yadūnām*—for the Yadus; *nara-deva*—of kings; *lāñchanaiḥ*—with the symbols; *dātuḥ*—for the giver; *pratīpaiḥ*—adverse; *phaṇinām*—for snakes; *iva*—just like; *amṛtam*—nectar; *ye*—who; *asmat*—our; *prasāda*—by the grace; *upacitāḥ*—made prosperous; *hi*—indeed; *yādavāḥ*—the Yadus; *ājñāpayanti*—are ordering; *adya*—now; *gata-trapāḥ*—having lost shame; *bata*—indeed.

TRANSLATION

No longer should the Yadus be allowed to use these royal symbols, which now cause trouble for those who gave them, like milk fed to poisonous snakes. Having prospered by our grace, these Yādavas have now lost all shame and are daring to command us!

TEXT 28

कथमिन्द्रोऽपि कुरुभिर्भीष्मद्रोणार्जुनादिभिः ।
अदत्तमवरुन्धीत सिंहग्रस्तमिवोरणः ॥२८॥

katham indro 'pi kurubhir
bhīṣma-droṇārjunādibhiḥ
adattam avarundhīta
siṁha-grastam ivoraṇaḥ

katham—how; *indraḥ*—Lord Indra; *api*—even; *kurubhiḥ*—by the Kurus; *bhīṣma-droṇa-arjuna-ādibhiḥ*—Bhīṣma, Droṇa, Arjuna and others; *adattam*—not given; *avarundhīta*—would usurp; *siṁha*—by a lion; *grastam*—that which has been seized; *iva*—as; *uraṇaḥ*—a sheep.

TRANSLATION

How would even Indra dare usurp anything that Bhīṣma, Droṇa, Arjuna or the other Kurus have not given him? It would be like a lamb claiming the lion's kill.

TEXT 29

श्रीबादरायणिरुवाच
जन्मबन्धुश्रियोन्नद्धमदास्ते भरतर्षभ ।
आश्राव्य रामं दुर्वाच्यमसभ्याः पुरमाविशन् ॥२९॥

śrī-bādarāyaṇir uvāca
janma-bandhu-śriyonnaddha-
madās te bharatarṣabha
āśrāvya rāmaṁ durvācyam
asabhyāḥ puram āviśan

śrī-bādarāyaṇiḥ uvāca—Śukadeva Gosvāmī said; *janma*—of birth; *bandhu*—and relationships; *śriyā*—by the opulences; *unnaddha*—made great; *madāḥ*—whose intoxication; *te*—they; *bharata-ṛṣabha*—O best of the descendants of Bharata; *āśrāvya*—making hear; *rāmam*—Lord Balarāma; *durvācyam*—their harsh words; *asabhyāḥ*—rude men; *puram*—the city; *āviśan*—entered.

TRANSLATION

Śrī Bādarāyaṇi said: O best of the Bhāratas, after the arrogant Kurus, thoroughly puffed up by the opulence of their high birth

and relations, had spoken these harsh words to Lord Balarāma, they turned and went back to their city.

TEXT 30

दृष्ट्वा कुरूणां दौःशील्यं श्रुत्वावाच्यानि चाच्युतः ।
अवोचत्कोपसंरब्धो दुष्प्रेक्ष्यः प्रहसन्मुहुः ॥३०॥

dṛṣṭvā kurūṇāṁ dauḥśīlyaṁ
śrutvāvācyāni cācyutaḥ
avocat kopa-saṁrabdho
duṣprekṣyaḥ prahasan muhuḥ

dṛṣṭvā—seeing; *kurūṇām*—of the Kurus; *dauḥśīlyam*—the bad character; *śrutvā*—hearing; *avācyāni*—words not to be spoken; *ca*—and; *acyutaḥ*—infallible Lord Balarāma; *avocat*—He said; *kopa*—with anger; *saṁrabdhaḥ*—enraged; *duṣprekṣyaḥ*—difficult to look at; *prahasan*—laughing; *muhuḥ*—repeatedly.

TRANSLATION

Seeing the bad character of the Kurus and hearing their nasty words, the infallible Lord Balarāma became filled with rage. His countenance frightful to behold, He laughed repeatedly and spoke as follows.

TEXT 31

नूनं नानामदोन्नद्धाः शान्तिं नेच्छन्त्यसाधवः ।
तेषां हि प्रशमो दण्डः पशूनां लगुडो यथा ॥३१॥

nūnaṁ nānā-madonnaddhāḥ
śāntiṁ necchanty asādhavaḥ
teṣāṁ hi praśamo daṇḍaḥ
paśūnāṁ laguḍo yathā

nūnam—certainly; *nānā*—by various; *mada*—by passions; *unnaddhāḥ*—puffed up; *śāntim*—peace; *na icchanti*—they do not desire; *asādhavaḥ*—

scoundrels; *teṣām*—their; *hi*—indeed; *praśamaḥ*—pacification; *daṇḍaḥ*—physical punishment; *paśūnām*—for animals; *laguḍaḥ*—a stick; *yathā*—as.

TRANSLATION

[Lord Balarāma said:] "Clearly the many passions of these scoundrels have made them so proud that they do not want peace. Then let them be pacified by physical punishment, as animals are with a stick.

TEXTS 32–33

अहो यदून् सुसंरब्धान् कृष्णं च कुपितं शनैः ।
सान्त्वयित्वाहमेतेषां शममिच्छन्निहागतः ॥३२॥
त इमे मन्दमतयः कलहाभिरताः खलाः ।
तं मामवज्ञाय मुहुर्दुर्भाषान्मानिनोऽब्रुवन् ॥३३॥

aho yadūn su-saṁrabdhān
kṛṣṇaṁ ca kupitaṁ śanaiḥ
sāntvayitvāham eteṣāṁ
śamam icchann ihāgataḥ

ta ime manda-matayaḥ
kalahābhiratāḥ khalāḥ
taṁ māṁ avajñāya muhur
durbhāṣān mānino 'bruvan

aho—ah; *yadūn*—the Yadus; *su-saṁrabdhān*—boiling with rage; *kṛṣṇam*—Kṛṣṇa; *ca*—also; *kupitam*—angry; *śanaiḥ*—gradually; *sāntvayitvā*—having calmed; *aham*—I; *eteṣām*—for these (Kauravas); *śamam*—peace; *icchan*—desiring; *iha*—here; *āgataḥ*—came; *te ime*—those very ones (the Kurus); *manda-matayaḥ*—dull-headed; *kalaha*—to quarrel; *abhiratāḥ*—addicted; *khalāḥ*—wicked; *tam*—Him; *mām*—Myself; *avajñāya*—disrespecting; *muhuḥ*—repeatedly; *durbhāṣān*—harsh words; *māninaḥ*—being conceited; *abruvan*—they have spoken.

TRANSLATION

"Ah, only gradually was I able to calm the furious Yadus and Lord Kṛṣṇa, who was also enraged. Desiring peace for these Kauravas, I came here. But they are so dull-headed, fond of quarrel and mischievous by nature that they have repeatedly disrespected Me. Out of conceit they dared to address Me with harsh words!

TEXT 34

नोग्रसेनः किल विभुर्भोजवृष्ण्यन्धकेश्वरः ।
शक्रादयो लोकपाला यस्यादेशानुवर्तिनः ॥३४॥

nograsenaḥ kila vibhur
bhoja-vṛṣṇy-andhakeśvaraḥ
śakrādayo loka-pālā
yasyādeśānuvartinaḥ

na—not; *ugrasenaḥ*—King Ugrasena; *kila*—indeed; *vibhuḥ*—fit to command; *bhoja-vṛṣṇi-andhaka*—of the Bhojas, Vṛṣṇis and Andhakas; *īśvaraḥ*—the lord; *śakra-ādayaḥ*—Indra and other demigods; *loka*—of planets; *pālāḥ*—the rulers; *yasya*—of whose; *ādeśa*—orders; *anu-vartinaḥ*—followers.

TRANSLATION

"King Ugrasena, the lord of the Bhojas, Vṛṣṇis and Andhakas, is not fit to command, when Indra and other planetary rulers obey his orders?

TEXT 35

सुधर्माक्रम्यते येन पारिजातोऽमराङ्घ्रिपः ।
आनीय भुज्यते सोऽसौ न किलाध्यासनार्हणः ॥३५॥

sudharmākramyate yena
pārijāto 'marāṅghripaḥ

ānīya bhujyate so 'sau
na kilādhyāsanārhaṇaḥ

sudharmā—Sudharmā, the royal council-chamber of heaven; *ākramyate*—occupies; *yena*—by whom (Lord Kṛṣṇa); *pārijātaḥ*—known as *pārijāta; amara*—of the immortal demigods; *aṅghripaḥ*—the tree; *ānīya*—being brought; *bhujyate*—is enjoyed; *saḥ asau*—that same person; *na*—not; *kila*—indeed; *adhyāsana*—an elevated seat; *arhaṇaḥ*—deserving.

TRANSLATION

"That same Kṛṣṇa who occupies the Sudharmā assembly hall and for His enjoyment took the *pārijāta* tree from the immortal demigods—that very Kṛṣṇa is indeed not fit to sit on a royal throne?

PURPORT

Here Lord Balarāma angrily states, "Never mind the Yadus—these rascal Kauravas even dare to insult Lord Kṛṣṇa!"

TEXT 36

यस्य पादयुगं साक्षाच्छ्रीरुपास्तेऽखिलेश्वरी ।
स नार्हति किल श्रीशो नरदेवपरिच्छदान् ॥३६॥

yasya pāda-yugaṁ sākṣāc
chrīr upāste 'khileśvarī
sa nārhati kila śrīśo
naradeva-paricchadān

yasya—whose; *pāda-yugam*—two feet; *sākṣāt*—herself; *śrīḥ*—the goddess of fortune; *upāste*—worships; *akhila*—of the whole universe; *īśvarī*—the ruler; *saḥ*—He; *na arhati*—does not deserve; *kila*—indeed; *śrī-īśaḥ*—the master of the goddess of fortune; *nara-deva*—of a human king; *paricchadān*—the paraphernalia.

TRANSLATION

"The goddess of fortune herself, ruler of the entire universe, worships His feet. And the master of the goddess of fortune does not deserve the paraphernalia of a mortal king?

TEXT 37

यस्याङ्घ्रिपंकजरजोऽखिललोकपालैर्
मौल्युत्तमैर्धृतमुपासिततीर्थतीर्थम् ।
ब्रह्मा भवोऽहमपि यस्य कलाः कलायाः
श्रीश्चोद्वहेम चिरमस्य नृपासनं क्व ॥३७॥

yasyāṅghri-paṅkaja-rajo 'khila-loka-pālair
mauly-uttamair dhṛtam upāsita-tīrtha-tīrtham
brahmā bhavo 'ham api yasya kalāḥ kalāyāḥ
śrīś codvahema ciram asya nṛpāsanaṁ kva

yasya—whose; *aṅghri*—of the feet; *paṅkaja*—lotuslike; *rajaḥ*—the dust; *akhila*—of all; *loka*—worlds; *pālaiḥ*—by the rulers; *mauli*—on their helmets; *uttamaiḥ*—exalted; *dhṛtam*—held; *upāsita*—worshipable; *tīrtha*—of holy places; *tīrtham*—the source of holiness; *brahmā*—Lord Brahmā; *bhavaḥ*—Lord Śiva; *aham*—I; *api*—also; *yasya*—whose; *kalāḥ*—portions; *kalāyāḥ*—of a portion; *śrīḥ*—the goddess of fortune; *ca*—also; *udvahema*—carry carefully; *ciram*—constantly; *asya*—His; *nṛpa-āsanam*—king's throne; *kva*—where.

TRANSLATION

"The dust of Kṛṣṇa's lotus feet, which is the source of holiness for all places of pilgrimage, is worshiped by all the great demigods. The principal deities of all planets are engaged in His service, and they consider themselves most fortunate to take the dust of the lotus feet of Kṛṣṇa on their crowns. Great demigods like Lord Brahmā and Lord Śiva, and even the goddess of fortune and I, are simply parts of His spiritual identity, and we also

carefully carry that dust on our heads. And still Kṛṣṇa is not fit to use the royal insignia or even sit on the royal throne?

PURPORT

The above translation is based on Śrīla Prabhupāda's *Kṛṣṇa, The Supreme Personality of Godhead.* According to Śrīla Śrīdhara Svāmī, the place of pilgrimage especially referred to here is the Ganges River. The Ganges water is inundating the whole world, and since it is emanating from Kṛṣṇa's lotus feet, its banks have turned into great places of pilgrimage.

TEXT 38

भुञ्जते कुरुभिर्दत्तं भूखण्डं वृष्णयः किल ।
उपानहः किल वयं स्वयं तु कुरवः शिरः ॥३८॥

bhuñjate kurubhir dattaṁ
bhū-khaṇḍaṁ vṛṣṇayaḥ kila
upānahaḥ kila vayaṁ
svayaṁ tu kuravaḥ śiraḥ

bhuñjate—they enjoy; *kurubhiḥ*—by the Kurus; *dattam*—granted; *bhū*—of land; *khaṇḍam*—a limited parcel; *vṛṣṇayaḥ*—the Vṛṣṇis; *kila*—indeed; *upānahaḥ*—shoes; *kila*—indeed; *vayam*—we; *svayam*—themselves; *tu*—however; *kuravaḥ*—the Kurus; *śiraḥ*—the head.

TRANSLATION

"We Vṛṣṇis enjoy only whatever small parcel of land the Kurus allow us? And we are indeed shoes, whereas the Kurus are the head?

TEXT 39

अहो ऐश्वर्यमत्तानां मत्तानामिव मानिनाम् ।
असम्बद्धा गिरो रुक्षाः कः सहेतानुशासिता ॥३९॥

aho aiśvarya-mattānāṁ
mattānām iva māninām

asambaddhā giro rukṣāḥ
kaḥ sahetānuśāsitā

aho—ah; *aiśvarya*—with their ruling power; *mattānām*—of those who are mad; *mattānām*—of those who are physically intoxicated; *iva*—as if; *māninām*—who are proud; *asambaddhāḥ*—incoherent and absurd; *giraḥ*—words; *rukṣāḥ*—harsh; *kaḥ*—who; *saheta*—can tolerate; *anuśāsitā*—commander.

TRANSLATION

"Just see how these puffed-up Kurus are intoxicated with their so-called power, like ordinary drunken men! What actual ruler, with the power to command, would tolerate their foolish, nasty words?

TEXT 40

अद्य निष्कौरवं पृथ्वीं करिष्यामीत्यमर्षितः ।
गृहीत्वा हलमुत्तस्थौ दहन्निव जगत्त्रयम् ॥४०॥

adya niṣkauravaṁ pṛthvīṁ
kariṣyāmīty amarṣitaḥ
gṛhītvā halam uttasthau
dahann iva jagat-trayam

adya—today; *niṣkauravam*—devoid of Kauravas; *pṛthvīm*—the earth; *kariṣyāmi*—I shall make; *iti*—thus speaking; *amarṣitaḥ*—angry; *gṛhītvā*—taking; *halam*—His plow; *uttasthau*—He stood; *dahan*—burning; *iva*—as if; *jagat*—the worlds; *trayam*—three.

TRANSLATION

"Today I shall rid the earth of the Kauravas!" declared the furious Balarāma. Thus He took His plow weapon and rose up as if to set the three worlds ablaze.

TEXT 41

लांगलाग्रेण नगरमुद्विदार्य गजाह्वयम् ।
विचकर्ष स गंगायां प्रहरिष्यन्नमर्षितः ॥४१॥

lāṅgalāgreṇa nagaram
udvidārya gajāhvayam
vicakarṣa sa gaṅgāyāṁ
prahariṣyann amarṣitaḥ

lāṅgala—of His plow; *agreṇa*—with the tip; *nagaram*—the city; *udvidārya*—tearing up; *gajāhvayam*—Hastināpura; *vicakarṣa*—dragged; *saḥ*—He; *gaṅgāyām*—in the Ganges; *prahariṣyan*—about to cast it; *amarṣitaḥ*—enraged.

TRANSLATION

The Lord angrily dug up Hastināpura with the tip of His plow and began to drag it, intending to cast the entire city into the Ganges.

PURPORT

Śrīla Prabhupāda writes as follows: "Lord Balarāma seemed so furious that He looked as if He could burn the whole cosmic creation to ashes. He stood up steadily and, taking His plow in His hand, began striking the earth with it. In this way the whole city of Hastināpura was separated from the earth. Lord Balarāma then began to drag the city toward the flowing water of the river Ganges. Because of this, there was a great tremor throughout Hastināpura, as if there had been an earthquake, and it seemed that the whole city would be dismantled."

Śrīla Viśvanātha Cakravartī states that by the Lord's desire His plow had increased in size, and that as Balarāma began dragging Hastināpura toward the water, He ordered the Ganges, "Except for Sāmba, you should attack and kill everyone in the city with your water." Thus He would fulfill His promise to rid the earth of the Kauravas while making sure that nothing bad would happen to Sāmba.

TEXTS 42–43

जलयानमिवाघूर्णं गंगायां नगरं पतत् ।
आकृष्यमाणमालोक्य कौरवाः जातसम्भ्रमाः ॥४२॥
तमेव शरणं जग्मुः सकुटुम्बा जिजीविषवः ।
सलक्ष्मणं पुरस्कृत्य साम्बं प्राञ्जलयः प्रभुम् ॥४३॥

jala-yānam ivāghūrṇaṁ
gaṅgāyāṁ nagaraṁ patat
ākṛṣyamāṇam ālokya
kauravāḥ jāta-sambhramāḥ

tam eva śaraṇaṁ jagmuḥ
sa-kuṭumbā jijīviṣavaḥ
sa-lakṣmaṇaṁ puras-kṛtya
sāmbaṁ prāñjalayaḥ prabhum

jala-yānam—a raft; *iva*—as if; *āghūrṇam*—tumbling about; *gaṅgāyām*—into the Ganges; *nagaram*—the city; *patat*—falling; *ākṛṣyamāṇam*—being dragged; *ālokya*—seeing; *kauravāḥ*—the Kauravas; *jāta*—becoming; *sambhramāḥ*—excited and bewildered; *tam*—to Him, Lord Balarāma; *eva*—indeed; *śaraṇam*—for shelter; *jagmuḥ*—they went; *sa*—with; *kuṭumbāḥ*—their families; *jijīviṣavaḥ*—wanting to remain alive; *sa*—with; *lakṣmaṇam*—Lakṣmaṇā; *puraḥ-kṛtya*—placing in front; *sāmbam*—Sāmba; *prāñjalayaḥ*—with palms joined in supplication; *prabhum*—to the Lord.

TRANSLATION

Seeing that their city was tumbling about like a raft at sea as it was being dragged away, and that it was about to fall into the Ganges, the Kauravas became terrified. To save their lives they approached the Lord for shelter, taking their families with them. Placing Sāmba and Lakṣmaṇā in front, they joined their palms in supplication.

PURPORT

The city of Hastināpura began to roll about like a raft in a stormy sea. The frightened Kauravas, to quickly appease the Lord, immediately brought Sāmba and Lakṣmaṇā and placed them in front.

TEXT 44

राम रामाखिलाधार प्रभावं न विदाम ते ।
मूढानां नः कुबुद्धीनां क्षन्तुमर्हस्यतिक्रमम् ॥४४॥

rāma rāmākhilādhāra
prabhāvaṁ na vidāma te
mūḍhānāṁ naḥ ku-buddhīnāṁ
kṣantum arhasy atikramam

rāma rāma—O Rāma, Rāma; *akhila*—of everything; *ādhāra*—O foundation; *prabhāvam*—power; *na vidāma*—we do not know; *te*—Your; *mūḍhānām*—of befooled persons; *naḥ*—us; *ku*—bad; *buddhīnām*—whose understanding; *kṣantum arhasi*—You should please forgive; *atikramam*—the offense.

TRANSLATION

[The Kauravas said:] O Rāma, Rāma, foundation of everything! We know nothing of Your power. Please excuse our offense, for we are ignorant and misguided.

TEXT 45

स्थित्युत्पत्त्यप्ययानां त्वमेको हेतुर्निराश्रयः ।
लोकान् क्रीडनकानीश क्रीडतस्ते वदन्ति हि ॥४५॥

sthity-utpatty-apyayānāṁ tvam
eko hetur nirāśrayaḥ
lokān krīḍanakān īśa
krīḍatas te vadanti hi

sthiti—of maintenance; *utpatti*—creation; *apyayānām*—and destruction; *tvam*—You; *ekaḥ*—alone; *hetuḥ*—the cause; *nirāśrayaḥ*—without any other basis; *lokān*—the worlds; *krīḍanakān*—playthings; *īśa*—O Lord; *krīḍataḥ*—who are playing; *te*—Your; *vadanti*—they say; *hi*—indeed.

TRANSLATION

You alone cause the creation, maintenance and annihilation of the cosmos, and of You there is no prior cause. Indeed, O Lord, authorities say that the worlds are mere playthings for You as You perform Your pastimes.

TEXT 46

त्वमेव मूर्ध्नीदमनन्त लीलया
भूमण्डलं बिभर्षि सहस्रमूर्धन् ।
अन्ते च यः स्वात्मनिरुद्धविश्वः
शेषेऽद्वितीयः परिशिष्यमाणः ॥४६॥

tvam eva mūrdhnīdam ananta līlayā
bhū-maṇḍalaṁ bibharṣi sahasra-mūrdhan
ante ca yaḥ svātma-niruddha-viśvaḥ
śeṣe 'dvitīyaḥ pariśiṣyamāṇaḥ

tvam—You; *eva*—alone; *mūrdhni*—on Your head; *idam*—this; *ananta*—O unlimited one; *līlayā*—easily, as a pastime; *bhū*—of the earth; *maṇḍalam*—the globe; *bibharṣi*—(You) carry; *sahasra-mūrdhan*—O thousand-headed Lord; *ante*—in the end; *ca*—and; *yaḥ*—the one who; *sva*—Your own; *ātma*—within the body; *niruddha*—having withdrawn; *viśvaḥ*—the universe; *śeṣe*—You lie; *advitīyaḥ*—without a second; *pariśiṣyamāṇaḥ*—remaining.

TRANSLATION

O unlimited one of a thousand heads, as Your pastime You carry this earthly globe upon one of Your heads. At the time of annihilation You withdraw the entire universe within Your body and, remaining all alone, lie down to rest.

TEXT 47

कोपस्तेऽखिलशिक्षार्थं न द्वेषान्न च मत्सरात् ।
बिभ्रतो भगवन् सत्त्वं स्थितिपालनतत्परः ॥४७॥

kopas te 'khila-śikṣārthaṁ
na dveṣān na ca matsarāt
bibhrato bhagavan sattvaṁ
sthiti-pālana-tatparaḥ

kopaḥ—anger; *te*—Your; *akhila*—of everyone; *śikṣā*—for the instruction; *artham*—meant; *na*—not; *dveṣāt*—out of hatred; *na ca*—nor; *matsarāt*—out of envy; *bibhrataḥ*—of You who are sustaining; *bhagavan*—O Supreme Lord; *sattvam*—the mode of goodness; *sthiti*—maintenance; *pālana*—and protection; *tat-paraḥ*—having as its intent.

TRANSLATION

Your anger is meant for instructing everyone; it is not a manifestation of hatred or envy. O Supreme Lord, You sustain the pure mode of goodness, and You become angry only to maintain and protect this world.

PURPORT

The Kurus admit that Lord Balarāma's anger was entirely appropriate and in fact was meant for their benefit. As Śrīla Viśvanātha Cakravartī puts it, the Kurus meant to say, "Because You exhibited this anger, we have now become civilized, whereas previously we were wicked and could not see You, blinded as we were by pride."

TEXT 48

नमस्ते सर्वभूतात्मन् सर्वशक्तिधराव्यय ।
विश्वकर्मन्नमस्तेऽस्तु त्वां वयं शरणं गताः ॥४८॥

namas te sarva-bhūtātman
sarva-śakti-dharāvyaya
viśva-karman namas te 'stu
tvāṁ vayaṁ śaraṇaṁ gatāḥ

namaḥ—obeisances; *te*—to You; *sarva*—of all; *bhūta*—beings; *ātman*—O Soul; *sarva*—of all; *śakti*—energies; *dhara*—O holder; *avyaya*—O undepletable one; *viśva*—of the universe; *karman*—O maker; *namaḥ*—obeisances; *te*—to You; *astu*—let there be; *tvām*—to You; *vayam*—we; *śaraṇam*—for shelter; *gatāḥ*—have come.

TRANSLATION

We bow down to You, O Soul of all beings, O wielder of all potencies, O tireless maker of the universe! Offering You obeisances, we take shelter of You.

PURPORT

The Kauravas clearly realized that their lives and destinies were in the hands of the Lord.

TEXT 49

श्रीशुक उवाच
एवं प्रपन्नैः संविग्नैर्वेपमानायनैर्बलः ।
प्रसादितः सुप्रसन्नो मा भैष्टेत्यभयं ददौ ॥४९॥

śrī-śuka uvāca
evaṁ prapannaiḥ saṁvignair
vepamānāyanair balaḥ
prasāditaḥ su-prasanno
mā bhaiṣṭety abhayaṁ dadau

śrī-śukaḥ uvāca—Śukadeva Gosvāmī said; *evam*—thus; *prapannaiḥ*—by those who were surrendering; *saṁvignaiḥ*—greatly distressed; *vepamāna*—shaking; *ayanaiḥ*—whose place of residence; *balaḥ*—Lord Balarāma; *prasāditaḥ*—propitiated; *su*—very; *prasannaḥ*—calm and gracious; *mā bhaiṣṭa*—do not be afraid; *iti*—thus saying; *abhayam*—relief from fear; *dadau*—He gave.

TRANSLATION

Śukadeva Gosvāmī said: Thus propitiated by the Kurus, whose city was trembling and who were surrendering to Him in great distress, Lord Balarāma became very calm and kindly disposed toward them. "Do not be afraid," He said, and took away their fear.

TEXTS 50–51

दुर्योधनः पारिबर्हं कुञ्जरान् षष्टिहायनान् ।
ददौ च द्वादशशतान्ययुतानि तुरंगमान् ॥५०॥

रथानां षट्सहस्राणि रौक्माणां सूर्यवर्चसाम् ।
दासीनां निष्ककण्ठीनां सहस्रं दुहितृवत्सलः ॥५१॥

duryodhanaḥ pāribarhaṁ
kuñjarān ṣaṣṭi-hāyanān
dadau ca dvādaśa-śatāny
ayutāni turaṅgamān

rathānāṁ ṣaṭ-sahasrāṇi
raukmāṇāṁ sūrya-varcasām
dāsīnāṁ niṣka-kaṇṭhīnāṁ
sahasraṁ duhitṛ-vatsalaḥ

duryodhanaḥ—Duryodhana; *pāribarham*—as a dowry; *kuñjarān*—elephants; *ṣaṣṭi*—sixty; *hāyanān*—years old; *dadau*—gave; *ca*—and; *dvādaśa*—twelve; *śatāni*—hundred; *ayutāni*—tens of thousands; *turaṅgamān*—horses; *rathānām*—of chariots; *ṣaṭ-sahasrāṇi*—six thousand; *raukmāṇām*—golden; *sūrya*—(like) the sun; *varcasām*—whose effulgence; *dāsīnām*—of maidservants; *niṣka*—jeweled lockets; *kaṇṭhīnām*—on whose throats; *sahasram*—one thousand; *duhitṛ*—for his daughter; *vatsalaḥ*—having fatherly affection.

TRANSLATION

Duryodhana, being very affectionate to his daughter, gave as her dowry 1,200 sixty-year-old elephants, 120,000 horses, 6,000 golden chariots shining like the sun, and 1,000 maidservants with jeweled lockets on their necks.

TEXT 52

प्रतिगृह्य तु तत्सर्वं भगवान् सात्वतर्षभः ।
ससुतः सस्नुषः प्रायात्सुहृद्भिरभिनन्दितः ॥५२॥

pratigṛhya tu tat sarvaṁ
bhagavān sātvatarṣabhaḥ
sa-sutaḥ sa-snuṣaḥ prāyāt
suhṛdbhir abhinanditaḥ

pratigṛhya—accepting; *tu*—and; *tat*—that; *sarvam*—all; *bhagavān*—the Supreme Lord; *sātvata*—of the Yādavas; *ṛṣabhaḥ*—the chief; *sa*—with; *sutaḥ*—His son; *sa*—and with; *snuṣaḥ*—His daughter-in-law; *prāyāt*—He departed; *su-hṛdbhiḥ*—by His well-wishers (the Kurus); *abhinanditaḥ*—bid farewell.

TRANSLATION

The Supreme Lord, chief of the Yādavas, accepted all these gifts and then departed with His son and daughter-in-law as His well-wishers bid Him farewell.

TEXT 53

ततः प्रविष्टः स्वपुरं हलायुधः
समेत्य बन्धूननुरक्तचेतसः ।
शशंस सर्वं यदुपुंगवानां
मध्ये सभायां कुरुषु स्वचेष्टितम् ॥५३॥

tataḥ praviṣṭaḥ sva-puraṁ halāyudhaḥ
sametya bandhūn anurakta-cetasaḥ
śaśaṁsa sarvaṁ yadu-puṅgavānām
madhye sabhāyāṁ kuruṣu sva-ceṣṭitam

tataḥ—then; *praviṣṭaḥ*—having entered; *sva*—His; *puram*—city; *hala-āyudhaḥ*—Lord Balarāma, who has a plow weapon; *sametya*—meeting; *bandhūn*—His relatives; *anurakta*—attached to Him; *cetasaḥ*—whose hearts; *śaśaṁsa*—He related; *sarvam*—everything; *yadu-puṅgavānām*—of the leaders of the Yadus; *madhye*—in the midst; *sabhāyām*—of the assembly; *kuruṣu*—among the Kurus; *sva*—His own; *ceṣṭitam*—action.

TRANSLATION

Then Lord Halāyudha entered His city [Dvārakā] and met His relatives, whose hearts were all bound to him in loving attachment. In the assembly hall He reported to the Yadu leaders everything about His dealings with the Kurus.

TEXT 54

अद्यापि च पुरं ह्येतत्सूचयद् रामविक्रमम् ।
समुन्नतं दक्षिणतो गंगायामनुदृश्यते ॥५४॥

adyāpi ca puraṁ hy etat
sūcayad rāma-vikramam
samunnataṁ dakṣiṇato
gaṅgāyām anudṛśyate

adya—today; *api*—even; *ca*—and; *puram*—city; *hi*—indeed; *etat*—this; *sūcayat*—showing the signs of; *rāma*—of Lord Balarāma; *vikramam*—the prowess; *samunnatam*—prominently elevated; *dakṣiṇataḥ*—on the southern side; *gaṅgāyām*—by the Ganges; *anudṛśyate*—is seen.

TRANSLATION

Even today the city of Hastināpura is visibly elevated on its southern side along the Ganges, thus showing the signs of Lord Balarāma's prowess.

PURPORT

Śrīla Prabhupāda writes as follows: "For the most part it was the practice of the *kṣatriya* kings to inaugurate some kind of fighting between the parties of the bride and bridegroom before the marriage. When Sāmba forcibly took away Lakṣmaṇā, the elderly members of the Kuru dynasty were pleased to see that he was actually the suitable match for her. In order to see his personal strength, however, they fought with him, and without any respect for the regulations of fighting, they all arrested him. When the Yadu dynasty decided to release Sāmba from the confinement of the Kurus, Lord Balarāma came personally to settle the matter, and as a powerful *kṣatriya* He ordered them to free Sāmba immediately. The Kauravas became superficially insulted by this order, so they challenged Lord Balarāma's power. They simply wanted to see Him exhibit His inconceivable strength. Thus with great pleasure they handed over their daughter to Sāmba, and the whole matter was settled. Duryodhana, being affectionate toward his daughter Lakṣmaṇā, had her married to Sāmba in great pomp.... Balarāma was very satisfied after His great reception from the side of the Kurus, and accompanied by the newly married couple, He started toward His capital city of Dvārakā.

"Lord Balarāma triumphantly reached Dvārakā, where He met with many citizens who were all His devotees and friends. When they all assembled, Lord Balarāma narrated the whole story of the marriage, and they were astonished to hear how Balarāma had made the city of Hastināpura tremble."

Thus end the purports of the humble servants of His Divine Grace A. C. Bhaktivedanta Swami Prabhupāda to the Tenth Canto, Sixty-eighth Chapter, of the Śrīmad-Bhāgavatam, *entitled "The Marriage of Sāmba."*

CHAPTER SIXTY–NINE

Nārada Muni Visits Lord Kṛṣṇa's Palaces in Dvārakā

This chapter relates how Nārada Muni was amazed to see the household pastimes of Lord Śrī Kṛṣṇa, and how he offered prayers to the Lord.

After killing the demon Naraka, Lord Kṛṣṇa had simultaneously married sixteen thousand maidens, and sage Nārada wanted to observe the Lord's diverse activities in this unique family situation. Thus he went to Dvārakā. Nārada entered one of the sixteen thousand palaces and saw Goddess Rukmiṇī personally rendering menial service to Śrī Kṛṣṇa, despite her being in the company of thousands of maidservants. As soon as Lord Kṛṣṇa noticed Nārada, He got up from His bed, offered obeisances to the sage and seated him on His own seat. Then the Lord bathed Nārada's feet and sprinkled the water on His own head. Such was the exemplary behavior of the Lord.

After conversing with the Lord for a short while, Nārada went to another of His palaces, where the sage saw Śrī Kṛṣṇa playing at dice with His queen and Uddhava. Going from there to another palace, he found Lord Kṛṣṇa coddling His infant children. In another palace he saw Him preparing to take a bath; in another, performing fire sacrifices; in another, feeding *brāhmaṇas*; and in another, eating the remnants left by *brāhmaṇas.* In one palace the Lord was performing noontime rituals; in another, quietly chanting the Gāyatrī *mantra*; in another, sleeping on His bed; in another, consulting with His ministers; and in yet another, playing in the water with His female companions. Somewhere the Lord was giving charity to *brāhmaṇas,* in another place He was joking and laughing with His consort, in yet another place He was meditating on the Supersoul, somewhere He was serving His spiritual masters, in another place He was arranging for the marriages of His sons and daughters, somewhere else He was going out to hunt animals, and elsewhere He was moving about in disguise to find out what the citizens were thinking.

Having seen all this, Nārada addressed Lord Kṛṣṇa: "Only because I have served Your lotus feet can I understand these varieties of Your Yogamāyā potency, which ordinary living beings bewildered by illusion cannot begin to perceive. Thus I am most fortunate, and I simply desire to travel all over the three worlds chanting the glories of Your pastimes, which purify all the worlds."

Śrī Kṛṣṇa asked Nārada not to be confused by his vision of the Lord's transcendental opulences, and He described to him the purposes of His appearances in this world. He then honored the sage properly, according to religious principles, and Nārada departed, continuously meditating on the Supreme Personality of Godhead.

TEXTS 1–6

श्रीशुक उवाच
नरकं निहतं श्रुत्वा तथोद्वाहं च योषिताम् ।
कृष्णेनैकेन बह्वीनां तद्दिदृक्षुः स्म नारदः ॥१॥
चित्रं बतैतदेकेन वपुषा युगपत्पृथक् ।
गृहेषु द्व्यष्टसाहस्रं स्त्रिय एक उदावहत् ॥२॥
इत्युत्सुको द्वारवतीं देवर्षिर्द्रष्टुमागमत् ।
पुष्पितोपवनारामद्विजालिकुलनादिताम् ॥३॥
उत्फुल्लेन्दीवराम्भोजकह्लारकुमुदोत्पलैः ।
छुरितेषु सरःसूच्चैः कूजितां हंससारसैः ॥४॥
प्रासादलक्षैर्नवभिर्जुष्टां स्फाटिकराजतैः ।
महामरकतप्रख्यैः स्वर्णरत्नपरिच्छदैः ॥५॥
विभक्तरथ्यापथचत्वरापणैः
शालासभाभी रुचिरां सुरालयैः ।
संसिक्तमार्गांगनवीथिदेहलीं
पतत्पताकध्वजवारितातपाम् ॥६॥

śrī-śuka uvāca
narakaṁ nihataṁ śrutvā
tathodvāhaṁ ca yoṣitām

kṛṣṇenaikena bahvīnāṁ
tad-didṛkṣuḥ sma nāradaḥ

citraṁ bataitad ekena
vapuṣā yugapat pṛthak
gṛheṣu dvy-aṣṭa-sāhasraṁ
striya eka udāvahat

ity utsuko dvāravatīṁ
devarṣir draṣṭum āgamat
puṣpitopavanārāma-
dvijāli-kula-nāditām

utphullendīvarāmbhoja-
kahlāra-kumudotpalaiḥ
churiteṣu saraḥsūccaiḥ
kūjitāṁ haṁsa-sārasaiḥ

prāsāda-lakṣair navabhir
juṣṭāṁ sphāṭika-rājataiḥ
mahā-marakata-prakhyaiḥ
svarṇa-ratna-paricchadaiḥ

vibhakta-rathyā-patha-catvarāpaṇaiḥ
śālā-sabhābhī rucirāṁ surālayaiḥ
saṁsikta-mārgāṅgana-vīthi-dehalīṁ
patat-patāka-dhvaja-vāritātapām

śrī-śukaḥ uvāca—Śukadeva Gosvāmī said; *narakam*—the demon Naraka; *nihatam*—killed; *śrutvā*—hearing; *tathā*—also; *udvāham*—the marriage; *ca*—and; *yoṣitām*—with women; *kṛṣṇena*—by Lord Kṛṣṇa; *ekena*—one; *bahvīnām*—with many; *tat*—that; *didṛkṣuḥ*—wanting to see; *sma*—indeed; *nāradaḥ*—Nārada; *citram*—wonderful; *bata*—ah; *etat*—this; *ekena*—with a single; *vapuṣā*—body; *yugapat*—simultaneously; *pṛthak*—separate; *gṛheṣu*—in residences; *dvi*—two times; *aṣṭa*—eight; *sāhasram*—thousand; *striyaḥ*—women; *ekaḥ*—alone; *udāvahat*—He married; *iti*—thus; *utsukaḥ*—eager; *dvāravatīm*—to Dvārakā; *deva*—of the demigods; *ṛṣiḥ*—the sage, Nārada; *draṣṭum*—to see; *āgamat*—came; *puṣpita*—flowery; *upavana*—in parks; *ārāma*—and pleasure gardens;

dvija—of birds; *ali*—and bees; *kula*—with flocks and swarms; *nāditām*—resounding; *utphulla*—blooming; *indīvara*—with blue lotuses; *ambhoja*—day-blooming lotuses; *kahlāra*—white esculent lotuses; *kumuda*—moonlight-blooming lotuses; *utpalaiḥ*—and water lilies; *churiteṣu*—filled; *saraḥsu*—within lakes; *uccaiḥ*—loudly; *kūjitām*—filled with the calling; *haṁsa*—by swans; *sārasaiḥ*—and cranes; *prāsāda*—with palaces; *lakṣaiḥ*—hundreds of thousands; *navabhiḥ*—nine; *juṣṭām*—adorned; *sphāṭika*—made of crystal glass; *rājataiḥ*—and silver; *mahā-marakata*—with great emeralds; *prakhyaiḥ*—splendorous; *svarṇa*—of gold; *ratna*—and jewels; *paricchadaiḥ*—whose furnishings; *vibhakta*—systematically divided; *rathyā*—with main avenues; *patha*—roads; *catvara*—intersections; *āpaṇaiḥ*—and marketplaces; *śālā-sabhābhiḥ*—with assembly houses; *rucirām*—charming; *sura*—of the demigods; *ālayaiḥ*—with temples; *saṁsikta*—sprinkled with water; *mārga*—whose roads; *aṅgana*—courtyards; *vīthi*—commercial streets; *dehalīm*—and patios; *patat*—flying; *patāka*—with banners; *dhvaja*—by the flagpoles; *vārita*—warded off; *ātapām*—the heat of the sun.

TRANSLATION

Śukadeva Gosvāmī said: Hearing that Lord Kṛṣṇa had killed Narakāsura and had alone married many brides, Nārada Muni desired to see the Lord in this situation. He thought, "It is quite amazing that in a single body Lord Kṛṣṇa simultaneously married sixteen thousand women, each in a separate palace." Thus the sage of the demigods eagerly went to Dvārakā.

The city was filled with the sounds of birds and bees flying about the parks and pleasure gardens, while its lakes, crowded with blooming *indīvara, ambhoja, kahlāra, kumuda* and *utpala* lotuses, resounded with the calls of swans and cranes. Dvārakā boasted nine hundred thousand royal palaces, all constructed with crystal and silver and splendorously decorated with huge emeralds. Inside these palaces, the furnishings were bedecked with gold and jewels. Traffic moved along a well laid-out system of boulevards, roads, intersections and marketplaces, and many assembly houses and temples of demigods graced the charming city. The roads, courtyards, commercial streets and residential patios were all sprinkled with water and shaded from the sun's heat by banners waving from flagpoles.

PURPORT

In *Kṛṣṇa,* Śrīla Prabhupāda beautifully describes the city of Dvārakā as follows: "Being inquisitive as to how Kṛṣṇa was managing His household affairs with so many wives, Nārada desired to see these pastimes and so set out to visit Kṛṣṇa's different homes. When Nārada arrived in Dvārakā, he saw that the gardens and parks were full of various flowers of different colors and orchards that were overloaded with a variety of fruits. Beautiful birds were chirping, and peacocks were delightfully crowing. There were tanks and ponds full of blue and red lotus flowers, and some of these sites were filled with varieties of lilies. The lakes were full of nice swans and cranes, whose voices resounded everywhere. In the city there were as many as 900,000 great palaces built of first-class marble, with gates and doors made of silver. The posts of the houses and palaces were bedecked with jewels such as touchstone, sapphires and emeralds, and the floors gave off a beautiful luster. The highways, lanes, streets, crossings and marketplaces were all beautifully decorated. The whole city was full of residential homes, assembly houses and temples, all of different architectural beauty. All of this made Dvārakā a glowing city. The big avenues, crossings, lanes and streets, and also the thresholds of every residential house, were very clean. On both sides of every path there were bushes, and at regular intervals there were large trees that shaded the avenues so that the sunshine would not bother the passersby."

TEXTS 7–8

तस्यामन्तःपुरं श्रीमदर्चितं सर्वधिष्ण्यपैः ।
हरेः स्वकौशलं यत्र त्वष्ट्रा कार्त्स्न्येन दर्शितम् ॥७॥
तत्र षोडशभिः सद्मसहस्रैः समलंकृतम् ।
विवेशैकतमं शौरेः पत्नीनां भवनं महत् ॥८॥

tasyām antaḥ-puraṁ śrīmad
arcitaṁ sarva-dhiṣṇya-paiḥ
hareḥ sva-kauśalaṁ yatra
tvaṣṭrā kārtsnyena darśitam

tatra ṣoḍaśabhiḥ sadma-
sahasraiḥ samalaṅkṛtam

viveśaikatamaṁ śaureḥ
patnīnāṁ bhavanaṁ mahat

tasyām—in that (Dvārakā); *antaḥ-puram*—the private royal precinct; *śrī-mat*—opulent; *arcitam*—worshiped; *sarva*—all; *dhiṣṇya*—of the various planetary systems; *paiḥ*—by the maintainers; *hareḥ*—of Lord Hari; *sva*—his own; *kauśalam*—expertise; *yatra*—where; *tvaṣṭrā*—by Tvaṣṭā (Viśvakarmā, the architect of heaven); *kārtsnyena*—completely; *darśitam*—shown; *tatra*—there; *ṣoḍaśabhiḥ*—with sixteen; *sadma*—of residences; *sahasraiḥ*—thousands; *samalaṅkṛtam*—beautified; *viveśa*—(Nārada) entered; *ekatamam*—one of them; *śaureḥ*—Lord Kṛṣṇa's; *patnīnām*—of the wives; *bhavanam*—palace; *mahat*—great.

TRANSLATION

In the city of Dvārakā was a beautiful private quarter worshiped by the planetary rulers. This district, where the demigod Viśvakarmā had shown all his divine skill, was the residential area of Lord Hari, and thus it was gorgeously decorated by the sixteen thousand palaces of Lord Kṛṣṇa's queens. Nārada Muni entered one of these immense palaces.

PURPORT

Śrīla Jīva Gosvāmī points out that Tvaṣṭā, Viśvakarmā, manifested the expertise of the Supreme Lord, and thus he was able to build such exquisite palaces. Śrīla Prabhupāda writes, "The great kings and princes of the world used to visit these palaces just to worship [Lord Kṛṣṇa]. The architectural plans were made personally by Viśvakarmā, the engineer of the demigods, and in the construction of the palaces he exhibited all of his talents and ingenuity."

TEXTS 9–12

विष्टब्धं विद्रुमस्तम्भैर्वैदूर्यफलकोत्तमैः ।
इन्द्रनीलमयैः कुड्यैर्जगत्या चाहतत्विषा ॥९॥
वितानैर्निर्मितैस्त्वष्ट्रा मुक्तादामविलम्बिभिः ।
दान्तैरासनपर्यंकैर्मण्युत्तमपरिष्कृतैः ॥१०॥

दासीभिर्निष्ककण्ठीभिः सुवासोभिरलंकृतम् ।
पुम्भिः सकञ्चुकोष्णीषसुवस्त्रमणिकुण्डलैः ॥११॥
रत्नप्रदीपनिकरद्युतिभिर्निरस्त-
ध्वान्तं विचित्रवलभीषु शिखण्डिनोऽङ्ग ।
नृत्यन्ति यत्र विहितागुरुधूपमक्षैर्
निर्यान्तमीक्ष्य घनबुद्धय उन्नदन्तः ॥१२॥

viṣṭabdhaṁ vidruma-stambhair
vaidūrya-phalakottamaiḥ
indranīla-mayaiḥ kuḍyair
jagatyā cāhata-tviṣā

vitānair nirmitais tvaṣṭrā
muktā-dāma-vilambibhiḥ
dāntair āsana-paryaṅkair
maṇy-uttama-pariṣkṛtaiḥ

dāsībhir niṣka-kaṇṭhībhiḥ
su-vāsobhir alaṅkṛtam
pumbhiḥ sa-kañcukoṣṇīṣa-
su-vastra-maṇi-kuṇḍalaiḥ

ratna-pradīpa-nikara-dyutibhir nirasta-
dhvāntaṁ vicitra-valabhīṣu śikhaṇḍino 'ṅga
nṛtyanti yatra vihitāguru-dhūpam akṣair
niryāntam īkṣya ghana-buddhaya unnadantaḥ

viṣṭabdham—supported; *vidruma*—of coral; *stambhaiḥ*—by pillars; *vaidūrya*—of *vaidūrya* gems; *phalaka*—with decorative coverings; *uttamaiḥ*—excellent; *indranīla-mayaiḥ*—bedecked with sapphires; *kuḍyaiḥ*—with walls; *jagatyā*—with a floor; *ca*—and; *ahata*—constant; *tviṣā*—whose effulgence; *vitānaiḥ*—with canopies; *nirmitaiḥ*—constructed; *tvaṣṭrā*—by Viśvakarmā; *muktā-dāma*—of strands of pearls; *vilambibhiḥ*—with hangings; *dāntaiḥ*—of ivory; *āsana*—with seats; *paryaṅkaiḥ*—and beds; *maṇi*—with jewels; *uttama*—most excellent; *pariṣkṛtaiḥ*—decorated; *dāsībhiḥ*—with maidservants; *niṣka*—lockets;

kaṇṭhībhiḥ—upon whose throats; *su-vāsobhiḥ*—well-dressed; *alaṅkṛtam*—adorned; *pumbhiḥ*—with men; *sa-kañcuka*—wearing armor; *uṣṇīṣa*—turbans; *su-vastra*—fine clothing; *maṇi*—jeweled; *kuṇḍalaiḥ*—and earrings; *ratna*—jewel-bedecked; *pradīpa*—of lamps; *nikara*—many; *dyutibhiḥ*—with the light; *nirasta*—dispelled; *dhvāntam*—darkness; *vicitra*—variegated; *valabhīṣu*—on the ridges of the roof; *śikhaṇḍinaḥ*—peacocks; *aṅga*—my dear (King Parīkṣit); *nṛtyanti*—dance; *yatra*—wherein; *vihita*—placed; *aguru*—of *aguru; dhūpam*—incense; *akṣaiḥ*—through the small holes in the latticed windows; *niryāntam*—going out; *īkṣya*—seeing; *ghana*—a cloud; *buddhayaḥ*—thinking it to be; *unnadantaḥ*—crying loudly.

TRANSLATION

Supporting the palace were coral pillars decoratively inlaid with *vaidūrya* gems. Sapphires bedecked the walls, and the floors glowed with perpetual brilliance. In that palace Tvaṣṭā had arranged canopies with hanging strands of pearls; there were also seats and beds fashioned of ivory and precious jewels. In attendance were many well-dressed maidservants bearing lockets on their necks, and also armor-clad guards with turbans, fine uniforms and jeweled earrings. The glow of numerous jewel-studded lamps dispelled all darkness in the palace. My dear King, on the ornate ridges of the roof danced loudly crying peacocks, who saw the fragrant *aguru* incense escaping through the holes of the latticed windows and mistook it for a cloud.

PURPORT

Śrīla Prabhupāda writes, "There was so much incense and fragrant gum burning that the scented fumes were coming out of the windows. The peacocks . . . became illusioned by the fumes, mistaking them for clouds, and began dancing jubilantly. There were many maidservants, all of whom were decorated with gold necklaces, bangles and beautiful *sārīs*. There were also many male servants, who were nicely decorated in cloaks and turbans and jeweled earrings. Beautiful as they were, the servants were all engaged in different household duties."

TEXT 13

तस्मिन् समानगुणरूपवयःसुवेष-
दासीसहस्रयुतयानुसवं गृहिण्या ।
विप्रो ददर्श चमरव्यजनेन रुक्म-
दण्डेन सात्वतपतिं परिवीजयन्त्या ॥१३॥

tasmin samāna-guṇa-rūpa-vayaḥ-su-veṣa-
dāsī-sahasra-yutayānusavaṁ gṛhiṇyā
vipro dadarśa camara-vyajanena rukma-
daṇḍena sātvata-patiṁ parivījayantyā

tasmin—therein; *samāna*—equal; *guṇa*—whose personal qualities; *rūpa*—beauty; *vayaḥ*—youth; *su-veṣa*—and fine dress; *dāsī*—by maid-servants; *sahasra*—a thousand; *yutayā*—joined; *anusavam*—at every moment; *gṛhiṇyā*—together with His wife; *vipraḥ*—the learned *brāhmaṇa* (Nārada); *dadarśa*—saw; *camara*—of yak-tail; *vyajanena*—with a fan; *rukma*—gold; *daṇḍena*—whose handle; *sātvata-patim*—the Lord of the Sātvatas, Śrī Kṛṣṇa; *parivījayantyā*—fanning.

TRANSLATION

In that palace the learned *brāhmaṇa* saw the Lord of the Sātvatas, Śrī Kṛṣṇa, together with His wife, who fanned Him with a gold-handled yak-tail fan. She personally served Him in this way, even though she was constantly attended by a thousand maid-servants equal to her in personal character, beauty, youth and fine dress.

TEXT 14

तं सन्निरीक्ष्य भगवान् सहसोत्थितश्री-
पर्यंकतः सकलधर्मभृतां वरिष्ठः ।
आनम्य पादयुगलं शिरसा किरीट-
जुष्टेन साञ्जलिरवीविशदासने स्वे ॥१४॥

taṁ sannirīkṣya bhagavān sahasotthita-śrī-
paryaṅkataḥ sakala-dharma-bhṛtāṁ variṣṭhaḥ
ānamya pāda-yugalaṁ śirasā kirīṭa-
juṣṭena sāñjalir avīviśad āsane sve

tam—him (Nārada); *sannirīkṣya*—noticing; *bhagavān*—the Supreme Lord; *sahasā*—immediately; *utthita*—rising; *śrī*—of the goddess of fortune, Queen Rukmiṇī; *paryaṅkataḥ*—from the bed; *sakala*—all; *dharma*—of religion; *bhṛtām*—of the upholders; *variṣṭhaḥ*—the best; *ānamya*—bowing down; *pāda-yugalam*—to his two feet; *śirasā*—with His head; *kirīṭa*—with a crown; *juṣṭena*—fitted; *sa-añjaliḥ*—with joined palms; *avīviśat*—had him sit down; *āsane*—on the seat; *sve*—His own.

TRANSLATION

The Supreme Lord is the greatest upholder of religious principles. Thus when He noticed Nārada, He rose at once from Goddess Śrī's bed, bowed His crowned head at Nārada's feet and, joining His palms, had the sage sit in His own seat.

TEXT 15

तस्यावनिज्य चरणौ तदपः स्वमूर्ध्ना
बिभ्रज्जगद्गुरुतमोऽपि सतां पतिर्हि ।
ब्रह्मण्यदेव इति यद् गुणनाम युक्तं
तस्यैव यच्चरणशौचमशेषतीर्थम् ॥१५॥

tasyāvanijya caraṇau tad-apaḥ sva-mūrdhnā
bibhraj jagad-gurutamo 'pi satāṁ patir hi
brahmaṇya-deva iti yad guṇa-nāma yuktaṁ
tasyaiva yac-caraṇa-śaucam aśeṣa-tīrtham

tasya—his; *avanijya*—washing; *caraṇau*—the feet; *tat*—that; *apaḥ*—water; *sva*—His own; *mūrdhnā*—on the head; *bibhrat*—carrying; *jagat*—of the entire universe; *guru-tamaḥ*—the supreme spiritual master; *api*—even though; *satām*—of the saintly devotees; *patiḥ*—the master;

hi—indeed; *brahmaṇya*—who favors the *brāhmaṇas; devaḥ*—the Lord; *iti*—thus called; *yat*—since; *guṇa*—based on His quality; *nāma*—the name; *yuktam*—fitting; *tasya*—His; *eva*—indeed; *yat*—whose; *caraṇa*—of the feet; *śaucam*—the bathing; *aśeṣa*—complete; *tīrtham*—holy shrine.

TRANSLATION

The Lord bathed Nārada's feet and then put the water on His own head. Although Lord Kṛṣṇa is the supreme spiritual authority of the universe and the master of His devotees, it was proper for Him to behave in this way, for His name is Brahmaṇya-deva, "the Lord who favors the *brāhmaṇas*." Thus Śrī Kṛṣṇa honored the sage Nārada by bathing his feet, even though the water that bathes the Lord's own feet becomes the Ganges, the ultimate holy shrine.

PURPORT

Since Lord Kṛṣṇa's own lotus feet are the source of the most holy Ganges, the Lord did not have to purify Himself by bathing Nārada Muni's feet. Rather, as Śrīla Prabhupāda explains, "Lord Kṛṣṇa in Dvārakā enjoyed the pastimes of a perfect human being. When, therefore, He washed the feet of the sage Nārada and took the water on His head, Nārada did not object, knowing well that the Lord did so to teach everyone how to respect saintly persons."

TEXT 16

सम्पूज्य देवऋषिवर्यमृषिः पुराणो
नारायणो नरसखो विधिनोदितेन ।
वाण्याभिभाष्य मितयामृतमिष्टया तं
प्राह प्रभो भगवते करवाम हे किम् ॥१६॥

sampūjya deva-ṛṣi-varyam ṛṣiḥ purāṇo
nārāyaṇo nara-sakho vidhinoditena
vāṇyābhibhāṣya mitayāmṛta-miṣṭayā taṁ
prāha prabho bhagavate karavāma he kim

sampūjya—fully worshiping; *deva*—among the demigods; *ṛṣi*—the sage; *varyam*—greatest; *ṛṣiḥ*—the sage; *purāṇaḥ*—primeval; *nārāyaṇaḥ*—Lord Nārāyaṇa; *nara-sakhaḥ*—the friend of Nara; *vidhinā*—by scripture; *uditena*—enjoined; *vāṇyā*—with speech; *abhibhāṣya*—conversing; *mitayā*—measured; *amṛta*—with nectar; *miṣṭayā*—sweet; *tam*—him, Nārada; *prāha*—He addressed; *prabho*—O master; *bhagavate*—for the lord; *karavāma*—We may do; *he*—O; *kim*—what.

TRANSLATION

After fully worshiping the great sage of the demigods according to Vedic injunctions, Lord Kṛṣṇa, who is Himself the original sage—Nārāyaṇa, the friend of Nara—conversed with Nārada, and the Lord's measured speech was as sweet as nectar. Finally the Lord asked Nārada, "What may We do for you, Our lord and master?"

PURPORT

In this verse the words *nārāyaṇo nara-sakhaḥ* indicate that Kṛṣṇa is Himself the Supreme Lord, Nārāyaṇa, who appeared as the friend of the sage Nara. In other words, Lord Kṛṣṇa is *ṛṣiḥ purāṇaḥ,* the original and supreme spiritual master. Nevertheless, following the Vedic injunctions (*vidhinoditena*) that a *kṣatriya* should worship the *brāhmaṇas,* Lord Kṛṣṇa happily worshiped His pure devotee Nārada Muni.

TEXT 17

श्रीनारद उवाच
नैवाद्भुतं त्वयि विभोऽखिललोकनाथे
मैत्री जनेषु सकलेषु दमः खलानाम् ।
निःश्रेयसाय हि जगत्स्थितिरक्षणाभ्यां
स्वैरावतार उरुगाय विदाम सुष्ठु ॥१७॥

śrī-nārada uvāca
naivādbhutaṁ tvayi vibho 'khila-loka-nāthe
maitrī janeṣu sakaleṣu damaḥ khalānām

niḥśreyasāya hi jagat-sthiti-rakṣaṇābhyāṁ
svairāvatāra urugāya vidāma suṣṭhu

śrī-nāradaḥ uvāca—Śrī Nārada said; *na*—not; *eva*—at all; *adbhutam*—surprising; *tvayi*—for You; *vibho*—O almighty one; *akhila*—of all; *loka*—worlds; *nāthe*—for the ruler; *maitrī*—friendship; *janeṣu*—toward people; *sakaleṣu*—all; *damaḥ*—the subduing; *khalānām*—of the envious; *niḥśreyasāya*—for the highest benefit; *hi*—indeed; *jagat*—of the universe; *sthiti*—by maintenance; *rakṣaṇābhyām*—and protection; *svaira*—freely chosen; *avatāraḥ*—descent; *uru-gāya*—O You who are praised universally; *vidāma*—we know; *suṣṭhu*—well.

TRANSLATION

Śrī Nārada said: O almighty Lord, it is no surprise that You, the ruler of all worlds, show friendship for all people and yet subdue the envious. As we well know, You descend by Your sweet will in order to bestow the highest good on this universe by maintaining and protecting it. Thus Your glories are widely sung.

PURPORT

As pointed out by Śrīla Viśvanātha Cakravartī, all living beings are in fact servants of the Lord. The *ācārya* quotes the following verse from the *Padma Purāṇa* to elucidate:

a-kāreṇocyate viṣṇuḥ
śrīr u-kāreṇa kathyate
ma-kāras tu tayor dāsaḥ
pañca-viṁśaḥ prakīrtitaḥ

"[In the *mantra oṁ,*] the letter *a* signifies Lord Viṣṇu, the letter *u* signifies the goddess Śrī, and the letter *m* refers to their servant, who is the twenty-fifth element." The twenty-fifth element is the *jīva,* the living being. Every living being is a servant of the Lord, and the Lord is the true friend of every living being. Thus even when the Lord chastises envious persons like Jarāsandha, such punishment amounts to real friendship, since both the Lord's chastisement and His blessing are for the benefit of the living being.

TEXT 18

दृष्टं तवाङ्घ्रियुगलं जनतापवर्गं
ब्रह्मादिभिर्हृदि विचिन्त्यमगाधबोधैः ।
संसारकूपपतितोत्तरणावलम्बं
ध्यायंश्चराम्यनुगृहाण यथा स्मृतिः स्यात् ॥१८॥

dṛṣṭaṁ tavāṅghri-yugalaṁ janatāpavargaṁ
brahmādibhir hṛdi vicintyam agādha-bodhaiḥ
saṁsāra-kūpa-patitottaraṇāvalambaṁ
dhyāyaṁś carāmy anugṛhāṇa yathā smṛtiḥ syāt

dṛṣṭam—seen; *tava*—Your; *aṅghri*—of feet; *yugalam*—pair; *janatā*—for Your devotees; *apavargam*—the source of liberation; *brahma-ādibhiḥ*—by persons such as Lord Brahmā; *hṛdi*—within the heart; *vicintyam*—meditated upon; *agādha*—unfathomable; *bodhaiḥ*—whose intelligence; *saṁsāra*—of material life; *kūpa*—in the well; *patita*—of those who are fallen; *uttaraṇa*—for deliverance; *avalambam*—the shelter; *dhyāyan*—constantly thinking; *carāmi*—I may travel; *anugṛhāṇa*—please bless me; *yathā*—so that; *smṛtiḥ*—remembrance; *syāt*—may be.

TRANSLATION

Now I have seen Your feet, which grant liberation to Your devotees, which even Lord Brahmā and other great personalities of unfathomable intelligence can only meditate upon within their hearts, and which those who have fallen into the well of material existence resort to for deliverance. Please favor me so that I may constantly think of You as I travel about. Please grant Me the power to remember You.

PURPORT

Lord Kṛṣṇa had asked Nārada Muni, "What can We do for you?" and here Nārada answers. Nārada Muni is a pure devotee of Lord Kṛṣṇa, and thus his request is sublime.

TEXT 19

ततोऽन्यदाविशद् गेहं कृष्णपत्न्याः स नारदः ।
योगेश्वरेश्वरस्यांग योगमायाविवित्सया ॥१९॥

tato 'nyad āviśad gehaṁ
kṛṣṇa-patnyāḥ sa nāradaḥ
yogeśvareśvarasyāṅga
yoga-māyā-vivitsayā

tataḥ—then; *anyat*—another; *āviśat*—entered; *geham*—residence; *kṛṣṇa-patnyāḥ*—of a wife of Lord Kṛṣṇa; *saḥ*—he; *nāradaḥ*—Nārada Muni; *yoga-īśvara*—of the masters of mystic power; *īśvarasya*—of the supreme master; *aṅga*—my dear King; *yoga-māyā*—the spiritual power of bewilderment; *vivitsayā*—with the desire of knowing.

TRANSLATION

Nārada then entered the palace of another of Lord Kṛṣṇa's wives, my dear King. He was eager to witness the spiritual potency possessed by the master of all masters of mystic power.

TEXTS 20–22

दीव्यन्तमक्षैस्तत्रापि प्रियया चोद्धवेन च ।
पूजितः परया भक्त्या प्रत्युत्थानासनादिभिः ॥२०॥
पृष्टश्चाविदुषेवासौ कदायातो भवानिति ।
क्रियते किं नु पूर्णानामपूर्णैरस्मदादिभिः ॥२१॥
अथापि ब्रूहि नो ब्रह्मन् जन्मैतच्छोभनं कुरु ।
स तु विस्मित उत्थाय तूष्णीमन्यदगाद् गृहम् ॥२२॥

dīvyantam akṣais tatrāpi
priyayā coddhavena ca
pūjitaḥ parayā bhaktyā
pratyutthānāsanādibhiḥ

pṛṣṭaś cāviduṣevāsau
kadāyāto bhavān iti
kriyate kiṁ nu pūrṇānām
apūrṇair asmad-ādibhiḥ

athāpi brūhi no brahman
janmaitac chobhanaṁ kuru
sa tu vismita utthāya
tūṣṇīm anyad agād gṛham

dīvyantam—playing; *akṣaiḥ*—with dice; *tatra*—there; *api*—indeed; *priyayā*—with His beloved; *ca*—and; *uddhavena*—with Uddhava; *ca*—also; *pūjitaḥ*—he was worshiped; *parayā*—with transcendental; *bhaktyā*—devotion; *pratyutthāna*—by His standing up from His sitting place; *āsana*—by His offering him a seat; *ādibhiḥ*—and so on; *pṛṣṭaḥ*—questioned; *ca*—and; *aviduṣā*—by one who was in ignorance; *iva*—as if; *asau*—he, Nārada; *kadā*—when; *āyātaḥ*—arrived; *bhavān*—your good self; *iti*—thus; *kriyate*—is intended to be done; *kim*—what; *nu*—indeed; *pūrṇānām*—by those who are full; *apūrṇaiḥ*—with those who are not full; *asmat-ādibhiḥ*—such as Ourself; *atha api*—nonetheless; *brūhi*—please tell; *naḥ*—Us; *brahman*—O *brāhmaṇa; janma*—Our birth; *etat*—this; *śobhanam*—auspicious; *kuru*—please make; *saḥ*—he, Nārada; *tu*—but; *vismitaḥ*—astonished; *utthāya*—standing up; *tūṣṇīm*—silently; *anyat*—to another; *agāt*—went; *gṛham*—palace.

TRANSLATION

There he saw the Lord playing at dice with His beloved consort and His friend Uddhava. Lord Kṛṣṇa worshiped Nārada by standing up, offering him a seat, and so on, and then, as if He did not know, asked him, "When did you arrive? What can needy persons like Us do for those who are full in themselves? In any case, My dear *brāhmaṇa*, please make My life auspicious." Thus addressed, Nārada was astonished. He simply stood up silently and went to another palace.

PURPORT

In *Kṛṣṇa*, Śrīla Prabhupāda explains that when Nārada arrived at the second palace, "Lord Kṛṣṇa acted as if He did not know what had happened in the palace of Rukmiṇī." Nārada understood that Lord Kṛṣṇa was simultaneously present in both palaces, performing different activities, so "he simply left the palace silently, in great astonishment over the Lord's activities."

TEXT 23

तत्राप्यचष्ट गोविन्दं लालयन्तं सुतान् शिशून् ।
ततोऽन्यस्मिन् गृहेऽपश्यन्मज्जनाय कृतोद्यमम् ॥२३॥

tatrāpy acaṣṭa govindaṁ
lālayantaṁ sutān śiśūn
tato 'nyasmin gṛhe 'paśyan
majjanāya kṛtodyamam

tatra—there; *api*—and; *acaṣṭa*—he saw; *govindam*—Lord Kṛṣṇa; *lālayantam*—coddling; *sutān*—His children; *śiśūn*—infant; *tataḥ*—then; *anyasmin*—in another; *gṛhe*—palace; *apaśyat*—he saw (Him); *majjanāya*—for taking bath; *kṛta-udyamam*—preparing.

TRANSLATION

This time Nāradajī saw that Lord Kṛṣṇa was engaged as an affectionate father petting His small children. From there he entered another palace and saw Lord Kṛṣṇa preparing to take His bath.

PURPORT

This translation is from Śrīla Prabhupāda's *Kṛṣṇa, The Supreme Personality of Godhead.*

Śrīla Viśvanātha Cakravartī comments that in virtually all the palaces Nārada visited, Lord Kṛṣṇa worshiped and honored him.

TEXT 24

जुह्वन्तं च वितानाग्नीन् यजन्तं पञ्चभिर्मखैः ।
भोजयन्तं द्विजान् क्वापि भुञ्जानमवशेषितम् ॥२४॥

juhvantaṁ ca vitānāgnīn
yajantaṁ pañcabhir makhaiḥ
bhojayantaṁ dvijān kvāpi
bhuñjānam avaśeṣitam

juhvantam—offering oblations; *ca*—and; *vitāna-agnīn*—to the sacrificial fires; *yajantam*—worshiping; *pañcabhiḥ*—five; *makhaiḥ*—with the obligatory rituals; *bhojayantam*—feeding; *dvijān*—*brāhmaṇas; kva api*—somewhere; *bhuñjānam*—eating; *avaśeṣitam*—remnants.

TRANSLATION

In one place the Lord was offering oblations into the sacrificial fires; in another, worshiping through the five *mahā-yajñas;* in another, feeding *brāhmaṇas;* and in yet another, eating the remnants of food left by *brāhmaṇas.*

PURPORT

The five *mahā-yajñas,* or great sacrifices, are defined as follows: *pāṭho homaś cātithīnāṁ saparyā tarpaṇaṁ baliḥ*—"reciting the *Vedas,* offering oblations into the sacrificial fire, waiting on guests, making offerings to the forefathers, and offering [a share of one's food] to living entities in general."

Śrīla Prabhupāda comments as follows on these sacrifices: "In another palace Kṛṣṇa was found performing the *pañca-yajña* sacrifice, which is compulsory for a householder. This *yajña* is also known as *pañca-sūnā.* Knowingly or unknowingly, everyone, specifically the householder, is committing five kinds of sinful activities. When we receive water from a water pitcher, we kill many germs that are in it. Similarly, when we use a grinding machine or take foodstuffs, we kill many germs. When sweeping the floor or igniting a fire, we kill many germs. When we walk on the street we kill many ants and other insects. Consciously or unconsciously, in all our different activities we are killing. Therefore it is incumbent upon every householder to perform the *pañca-sūnā* sacrifice to rid himself of the reactions to such sinful activities."

Śrīla Viśvanātha Cakravartī, in his commentary on this verse, again points out that all the different times of the day were occurring simultaneously in Lord Kṛṣṇa's palaces. Thus Nārada saw a fire sacrifice—a morning ritual—and at about the same time he saw Lord Kṛṣṇa feeding the *brāhmaṇas* and accepting their remnants—a noontime activity.

TEXT 25

क्वापि सन्ध्यामुपासीनं जपन्तं ब्रह्म वाग्यतम् ।
एकत्र चासिचर्माभ्यां चरन्तमसिवर्त्मसु ॥२५॥

kvāpi sandhyām upāsīnaṁ
japantaṁ brahma vāg-yatam
ekatra cāsi-carmābhyāṁ
carantam asi-vartmasu

kva api—somewhere; *sandhyām*—the rituals of sunset; *upāsīnam*—worshiping; *japantam*—quietly chanting; *brahma*—the Vedic *mantra* (Gāyatrī); *vāk-yatam*—controlling His speech; *ekatra*—in one place; *ca*—and; *asi*—with sword; *carmābhyām*—and shield; *carantam*—moving about; *asi-vartmasu*—in the corridors set aside for sword practice.

TRANSLATION

Somewhere Lord Kṛṣṇa was observing the rituals for worship at sunset by refraining from speech and quietly chanting the Gāyatrī *mantra*, and elsewhere He was moving about with sword and shield in the areas set aside for sword practice.

PURPORT

According to Śrīla Viśvanātha Cakravartī, the words *sandhyām upāsīnam* indicate sunset rituals, whereas the words *asi-carmābhyāṁ carantam* refer to sword practice, which takes place at dawn.

TEXT 26

अश्वैर्गजै रथैः क्वापि विचरन्तं गदाग्रजम् ।
क्वचिच्छयानं पर्यंके स्तूयमानं च वन्दिभिः ॥२६॥

aśvair gajai rathaiḥ kvāpi
vicarantaṁ gadāgrajam
kvacic chayānaṁ paryaṅke
stūyamānaṁ ca vandibhiḥ

aśvaiḥ—on horses; *gajaiḥ*—on elephants; *rathaiḥ*—on chariots; *kva api*—somewhere; *vicarantam*—riding; *gada-agrajam*—Lord Kṛṣṇa, the elder brother of Gada; *kvacit*—somewhere; *śayānam*—lying; *paryaṅke*—on His bed; *stūyamānam*—being praised; *ca*—and; *vandibhiḥ*—by bards.

TRANSLATION

In one place Lord Gadāgraja was riding on horses, elephants and chariots, and in another place He was resting on His bed while bards recited His glories.

PURPORT

Śrīla Viśvanātha Cakravartī points out that riding on horses and elephants is a noon activity, whereas one lies down during the latter part of night.

TEXT 27

मन्त्रयन्तं च कस्मिंश्चिन्मन्त्रिभिश्चोद्धवादिभिः ।
जलक्रीडारतं क्वापि वारमुख्याबलावृतम् ॥२७॥

mantrayantaṁ ca kasmiṁścin
mantribhiś coddhavādibhiḥ
jala-krīḍā-rataṁ kvāpi
vāramukhyābalāvṛtam

mantrayantam—consulting; *ca*—and; *kasmiṁścit*—somewhere; *mantribhiḥ*—with advisers; *ca*—and; *uddhava-ādibhiḥ*—Uddhava and others; *jala*—watery; *krīḍā*—in sports; *ratam*—engaged; *kva api*—somewhere; *vāra-mukhyā*—by royal dancing girls; *abalā*—and other women; *vṛtam*—accompanied.

TRANSLATION

Somewhere He was consulting with royal ministers like Uddhava, and somewhere else He was enjoying in the water, surrounded by many society girls and other young women.

PURPORT

This translation is based on Śrīla Prabhupāda's *Kṛṣṇa.*

According to Śrīla Viśvanātha Cakravartī, Lord Kṛṣṇa met with His counselors around dusk and enjoyed water sports in the afternoon.

TEXT 28

कुत्रचिद्द्विजमुख्येभ्यो ददतं गाः स्वलंकृताः ।
इतिहासपुराणानि शृण्वन्तं मंगलानि च ॥२८॥

kutracid dvija-mukhyebhyo
dadataṁ gāḥ sv-alaṅkṛtāḥ
itihāsa-purāṇāni
śṛṇvantaṁ maṅgalāni ca

kutracit—somewhere; *dvija*—to *brāhmaṇas; mukhyebhyaḥ*—excellent; *dadatam*—giving; *gāḥ*—cows; *su*—well; *alaṅkṛtāḥ*—ornamented; *itihāsa*—epic histories; *purāṇāni*—and the *Purāṇas; śṛṇvantam*—hearing; *maṅgalāni*—auspicious; *ca*—and.

TRANSLATION

Somewhere He was giving well-decorated cows to exalted *brāhmaṇas*, and elsewhere he was listening to the auspicious narration of epic histories and *Purāṇas.*

PURPORT

Śrīla Viśvanātha Cakravartī informs us that giving cows in charity occurs in the morning, while hearing the histories takes place in the afternoon.

TEXT 29

**हसन्तं हासकथया कदाचित्प्रियया गृहे ।
क्वापि धर्मं सेवमानमर्थकामौ च कुत्रचित् ॥२९॥**

*hasantaṁ hāsa-kathayā
kadācit priyayā gṛhe
kvāpi dharmaṁ sevamānam
artha-kāmau ca kutracit*

hasantam—laughing; *hāsa-kathayā*—with joking conversation; *kadācit*—at one time; *priyayā*—with His beloved; *gṛhe*—in the palace; *kva api*—somewhere; *dharmam*—religiosity; *sevamānam*—practicing; *artha*—economic development; *kāmau*—sense gratification; *ca*—and; *kutracit*—somewhere.

TRANSLATION

Somewhere Lord Kṛṣṇa was found enjoying the company of a particular wife by exchanging joking words with her. Somewhere else He was found engaged, along with His wife, in religious ritualistic functions. Somewhere Kṛṣṇa was found engaged in matters of economic development, and somewhere else He was found enjoying family life according to the regulative principles of the *śāstras*.

PURPORT

This translation is based on Śrīla Prabhupāda's *Kṛṣṇa*.

Joking conversations take place during the nighttime, whereas religious rituals, economic development and family enjoyment occur during both the day and the night.

TEXT 30

**ध्यायन्तमेकमासीनं पुरुषं प्रकृतेः परम् ।
शुश्रूषन्तं गुरून् क्वापि कामैर्भोगैः सपर्यया ॥३०॥**

dhyāyantam ekam āsīnaṁ
puruṣaṁ prakṛteḥ param
śuśrūṣantaṁ gurūn kvāpi
kāmair bhogaiḥ saparyayā

dhyāyantam—meditating; *ekam*—alone; *āsīnam*—sitting; *puruṣam*—on the Supreme Personality of Godhead; *prakṛteḥ*—to material nature; *param*—transcendental; *śuśrūṣantam*—rendering menial service; *gurūn*—to His elders; *kva api*—somewhere; *kāmaiḥ*—desirable; *bhogaiḥ*—with objects of enjoyment; *saparyayā*—and with worship.

TRANSLATION

Somewhere He was sitting alone, meditating on the Supreme Personality of Godhead, who is transcendental to material nature, and somewhere He was rendering menial service to His elders, offering them desirable things and reverential worship.

PURPORT

Śrīla Prabhupāda comments, "Meditation, as recommended in authorized scripture, is meant for concentrating one's mind on the Supreme Personality of Godhead, Viṣṇu. Lord Kṛṣṇa is Himself the original Viṣṇu, but because He played the part of a human being, He taught us definitely by His personal behavior what is meant by meditation."

This activity of meditation indicates the *brāhma-muhūrta*, the early-morning hours before sunrise.

TEXT 31

कुर्वन्तं विग्रहं कैश्चित्सन्धिं चान्यत्र केशवम् ।
कुत्रापि सह रामेण चिन्तयन्तं सतां शिवम् ॥३१॥

kurvantaṁ vigrahaṁ kaiścit
sandhiṁ cānyatra keśavam
kutrāpi saha rāmeṇa
cintayantaṁ satāṁ śivam

kurvantam—making; *vigraham*—war; *kaiścit*—with certain persons; *sandhim*—reconciliation; *ca*—and; *anyatra*—elsewhere; *keśavam*—Lord Kṛṣṇa; *kutra api*—somewhere; *saha*—together; *rāmeṇa*—with Lord Balarāma; *cintayantam*—thinking; *satām*—of the saintly; *śivam*—the welfare.

TRANSLATION

In one place He was planning battles in consultation with some of His advisers, and in another place He was making peace. Somewhere Lord Keśava and Lord Balarāma were together pondering the welfare of the pious.

TEXT 32

पुत्राणां दुहितॄणां च काले विध्युपयापनम् ।
दारैर्वरैस्तत्सदृशैः कल्पयन्तं विभूतिभिः ॥३२॥

putrāṇāṁ duhitṝṇāṁ ca
kāle vidhy-upayāpanam
dārair varais tat-sadṛśaiḥ
kalpayantaṁ vibhūtibhiḥ

putrāṇām—of sons; *duhitṝṇām*—of daughters; *ca*—and; *kāle*—at the suitable time; *vidhi*—according to religious principles; *upayāpanam*—getting them married; *dāraiḥ*—with wives; *varaiḥ*—and with husbands; *tat*—for them; *sadṛśaiḥ*—compatible; *kalpayantam*—so arranging; *vibhūtibhiḥ*—in terms of opulences.

TRANSLATION

Nārada saw Lord Kṛṣṇa engaged in getting His sons and daughters married to suitabe brides and bridegrooms at the appropriate time, and the marriage ceremonies were being performed with great pomp.

PURPORT

This translation is based on Śrīla Prabhupāda's *Kṛṣṇa.*

The word *kāle* here means that Kṛṣṇa arranged for His sons and daughters to be married when each of them reached the proper age.

TEXT 33

प्रस्थापनोपनयनैरपत्यानां महोत्सवान् ।
वीक्ष्य योगेश्वरेशस्य येषां लोका विसिस्मिरे ॥३३॥

prasthāpanopanayanair
apatyānāṁ mahotsavān
vīkṣya yogeśvareśasya
yeṣāṁ lokā visismire

prasthāpana—with sending away; *upanayanaiḥ*—and bringing home; *apatyānām*—of the children; *mahā*—great; *utsavān*—holiday celebrations; *vīkṣya*—seeing; *yoga-īśvara*—of the masters of *yoga; īśasya*—of the supreme master; *yeṣām*—whose; *lokāḥ*—the people; *visismire*—were amazed.

TRANSLATION

Nārada observed how Śrī Kṛṣṇa, the master of all *yoga* masters, arranged to send away His daughters and sons-in-law, and also to receive them home again, at the time of great holiday celebrations. All the citizens were astonished to see these celebrations.

TEXT 34

यजन्तं सकलान् देवान् क्वापि क्रतुभिरूर्जितैः ।
पूर्तयन्तं क्वचिद्धर्मं कूर्पाराममठादिभिः ॥३४॥

yajantaṁ sakalān devān
kvāpi kratubhir ūrjitaiḥ
pūrtayantaṁ kvacid dharmaṁ
kūrpārāma-maṭhādibhiḥ

yajantam—worshiping; *sakalān*—all; *devān*—the demigods; *kva api*—somewhere; *kratubhiḥ*—with sacrifices; *ūrjitaiḥ*—full-blown; *pūrtayantam*—fulfilling by civil service; *kvacit*—somewhere; *dharmam*—religious obligation; *kūrpa*—with wells; *ārāma*—public parks; *maṭha*—monasteries; *ādibhiḥ*—and so on.

TRANSLATION

Somewhere He was worshiping all the demigods with elaborate sacrifices, and elsewhere He was fulfilling His religious obligations by doing public welfare work, such as the construction of wells, public parks and monasteries.

TEXT 35

चरन्तं मृगयां क्वापि हयमारुह्य सैन्धवम् ।
घ्नन्तं तत्र पशून्मेध्यान् परीतं यदुपुंगवैः ॥३५॥

carantaṁ mṛgayāṁ kvāpi
hayam āruhya saindhavam
ghnantaṁ tatra paśūn medhyān
parītaṁ yadu-puṅgavaiḥ

carantam—traveling; *mṛgayām*—on a hunting expedition; *kva api*—somewhere; *hayam*—His horse; *āruhya*—mounting; *saindhavam*—of the Sindh country; *ghnantam*—killing; *tatra*—there; *paśūn*—animals; *medhyān*—offerable in sacrifice; *parītam*—surrounded; *yadu-puṅgavaiḥ*—by the most heroic Yadus.

TRANSLATION

In another place He was on a hunting expedition. Mounted on His Sindhī horse and accompanied by the most heroic of the Yadus, He was killing animals meant for offering in sacrifice.

PURPORT

Śrīla Prabhupāda comments, "According to Vedic regulations, the *kṣatriyas* were allowed to kill prescribed animals on certain occasions, either to maintain peace in the forests or to offer the animals in the sacrificial fire. *Kṣatriyas* are allowed to practice this killing art because they have to kill their enemies mercilessly to maintain peace in society."

TEXT 36

अव्यक्तलिंगं प्रकृतिष्वन्तःपुरगृहादिषु ।
क्वचिच्चरन्तं योगेशं तत्तद्भावबुभुत्सया ॥३६॥

avyakta-liṅgaṁ prakṛtiṣv
antaḥ-pura-gṛhādiṣu
kvacic carantaṁ yogeśaṁ
tat-tad-bhāva-bubhutsayā

avyakta—hidden; *liṅgam*—His identity; *prakṛtiṣu*—among His ministers; *antaḥ-pura*—of the royal precincts; *gṛha-ādiṣu*—among the residences, etc.; *kvacit*—somewhere; *carantam*—moving about; *yoga-īśam*—the Lord of mystic power; *tat-tat*—of each of them; *bhāva*—the mentalities; *bubhutsayā*—with the desire to know.

TRANSLATION

Somewhere Kṛṣṇa, the Lord of mystic power, was moving about in disguise among the homes of ministers and other citizens in order to understand what each of them was thinking.

PURPORT

Although Lord Kṛṣṇa is all-knowing, while executing His pastimes as a typical monarch He sometimes traveled about incognito to acquire necessary information about His kingdom.

TEXT 37

अथोवाच हृषीकेशं नारदः प्रहसन्निव ।
योगमायोदयं वीक्ष्य मानुषीमीयुषो गतिम् ॥३७॥

athovāca hṛṣīkeśaṁ
nāradaḥ prahasann iva
yoga-māyodayaṁ vīkṣya
mānuṣīm īyuṣo gatim

atha—thereupon; *uvāca*—said; *hṛṣīkeśam*—to Lord Kṛṣṇa; *nāradaḥ*—Nārada; *prahasan*—laughing; *iva*—mildly; *yoga-māyā*—of His spiritual bewildering potencies; *udayam*—the unfolding; *vīkṣya*—having seen; *mānuṣīm*—human; *īyuṣaḥ*—who was assuming; *gatim*—ways.

TRANSLATION

Having thus seen this display of the Lord's Yogamāyā, Nārada mildly laughed and then addressed Lord Hṛṣīkeśa, who was adopting the behavior of a human being.

PURPORT

According to Śrila Viśvanātha Cakravartī, Nārada fully understood the Lord's omniscience, and thus when he saw the Lord trying to find out the mood of His ministers, moving about in disguise, Nārada could not help laughing. But remembering the Lord's supreme position, he somewhat constrained his laughter.

TEXT 38

विदाम योगमायास्ते दुर्दर्शा अपि मायिनाम् ।
योगेश्वरात्मन्निर्भाता भवत्पादनिषेवया ॥३८॥

vidāma yoga-māyās te
durdarśā api māyinām
yogeśvarātman nirbhātā
bhavat-pāda-niṣevayā

vidāma—we know; *yoga-māyāḥ*—the mystic potencies; *te*—Your; *durdarśāḥ*—impossible to see; *api*—even; *māyinām*—for great mystics; *yoga-īśvara*—O Lord of all mystic power; *ātman*—O Supreme Soul; *nirbhātāḥ*—perceived; *bhavat*—Your; *pāda*—to the feet; *niṣevayā*—by service.

TRANSLATION

[Nārada said:] Now we understand Your mystic potencies, which are difficult to comprehend, even for great mystics, O

Supreme Soul, master of all mystic power. Only by serving Your feet have I been able to perceive Your powers.

PURPORT

According to the *ācāryas,* this verse indicates that even great mystics like Lord Brahmā and Lord Śiva cannot fully comprehend the mystic power of the Supreme Lord.

TEXT 39

अनुजानीहि मां देव लोकांस्ते यशसाप्लुतान् ।
पर्यटामि तवोद्गायन् लीला भुवनपावनीः ॥३९॥

anujānīhi māṁ deva
lokāṁs te yaśasāplutān
paryaṭāmi tavodgāyan
līlā bhuvana-pāvanīḥ

anujānīhi—please give leave; *mām*—to me; *deva*—O Lord; *lokān*—the worlds; *te*—Your; *yaśasā*—with the fame; *āplutān*—flooded; *paryaṭāmi*—I will wander; *tava*—Your; *udgāyan*—loudly singing; *līlāḥ*—the pastimes; *bhuvana*—all the planetary systems; *pāvanīḥ*—which purify.

TRANSLATION

O Lord, please give me Your leave. I will wander about the worlds, which are flooded with Your fame, loudly singing about Your pastimes, which purify the universe.

PURPORT

Even Nārada Muni was bewildered to see Lord Kṛṣṇa's amazing pastimes as a human being. Therefore, with the words *anujānīhi māṁ deva* he requests permission to return to his normal service of traveling and preaching. Inspired by what he has seen, he wants to preach widely the glories of the Supreme Personality of Godhead, Śrī Kṛṣṇa.

TEXT 40

श्रीभगवानुवाच
ब्रह्मन् धर्मस्य वक्ताहं कर्ता तदनुमोदिता ।
तच्छिक्षयन् लोकमिममास्थितः पुत्र मा खिदः ॥४०॥

śrī-bhagavān uvāca
bráhman dharmasya vaktāhaṁ
kartā tad-anumoditā
tac chikṣayan lokam imam
āsthitaḥ putra mā khidaḥ

śrī-bhagavān uvāca—the Supreme Lord said; *brahman*—O *brāhmaṇa; dharmasya*—of religion; *vaktā*—the speaker; *aham*—I; *kartā*—the executor; *tat*—of it; *anumoditā*—the sanctioner; *tat*—it; *śikṣayan*—teaching; *lokam*—to the world; *imam*—in this; *āsthitaḥ*—situated; *putra*—O son; *mā khidaḥ*—do not be disturbed.

TRANSLATION

The Supreme Personality of Godhead said: O *brāhmaṇa*, I am the speaker of religion, its performer and sanctioner. I observe religious principles to teach them to the world, My child, so do not be disturbed.

PURPORT

Śrīla Jīva Gosvāmī explains that Lord Kṛṣṇa wanted to dispel Nārada's distress, which the sage felt because he saw Lord Kṛṣṇa worshiping the demigods and even Nārada himself. Śrīla Viśvanātha Cakravartī explains Lord Kṛṣṇa's feelings as follows: "As I state in the *Bhagavad-gītā, yad yad ācarati śreṣṭhas tat tad evetaro janaḥ:* ['Whatever a great person does, ordinary people follow.'] Thus I bathed your feet today in order to help propagate the principles of religion. In the past, before I began My pastimes of directly teaching religious principles, you came and offered prayers to Me after I had killed the Keśī demon, but I simply listened to your elaborate prayers and glorification and did nothing to honor you. Just remember this and consider.

"Do not think that you have committed an offense by allowing Me to bathe your feet today and accept the water as holy remnants. Just as a son does not offend his father by touching him with his foot while sitting on the father's lap, so you should understand that in the same way, My son, you have not offended Me."

TEXT 41

श्रीशुक उवाच
इत्याचरन्तं सद्धर्मान् पावनान् गृहमेधिनाम् ।
तमेव सर्वगेहेषु सन्तमेकं ददर्श ह ॥४१॥

śrī-śuka uvāca
ity ācarantaṁ sad-dharmān
pāvanān gṛha-medhinām
tam eva sarva-geheṣu
santam ekaṁ dadarśa ha

śrī-śukaḥ uvāca—Śukadeva Gosvāmī said; *iti*—thus; *ācarantam*—performing; *sat*—spiritual; *dharmān*—the principles of religion; *pāvanān*—purifying; *gṛha-medhinām*—for householders; *tam*—Him; *eva*—indeed; *sarva*—in all; *geheṣu*—the palaces; *santam*—present; *ekam*—in one form; *dadarśa ha*—he saw.

TRANSLATION

Śukadeva Gosvāmī said: Thus in every palace Nārada saw the Lord in His same personal form, executing the transcendental principles of religion that purify those engaged in household affairs.

PURPORT

In this verse Śukadeva Gosvāmī repeats what the Lord has Himself explained. As Śrīla Prabhupāda writes in *Kṛṣṇa,* "The Supreme Personality of Godhead was engaged in His so-called household affairs in order to teach people how one can sanctify one's household life although he may be attached to the imprisonment of material existence. Actually, one is obliged to continue the term of material existence because of household life. But the Lord, being very kind upon householders, demonstrated the path of sanctifying ordinary household life. Because Kṛṣṇa is the center of all activities, a Kṛṣṇa conscious householder's life is transcendental to Vedic injunctions and is automatically sanctified."

As stated in Text 2 of this chapter, all the Lord's activities in the many palaces were performed by the Lord's single spiritual form (*ekena vapuṣā*), which manifested in many places at once. This vision was revealed to Nārada because of his desire to see it and the Lord's desire to show it to him. Śrīla Viśvanātha Cakravartī points out that the other residents of Dvārakā could see Kṛṣṇa only in the particular part of the city they themselves occupied, and not anywhere else, even if they would sometimes go to another precinct on some business. Thus the Lord gave a special view of His pastimes to His beloved devotee Nārada Muni.

TEXT 42

कृष्णस्यानन्तवीर्यस्य योगमायामहोदयम् ।
मुहुर्दृष्ट्वा ऋषिरभूद्विस्मितो जातकौतुकः ॥४२॥

kṛṣṇasyānanta-vīryasya
yoga-māyā-mahodayam
muhur dṛṣṭvā ṛṣir abhūd
vismito jāta-kautukaḥ

kṛṣṇasya—of Lord Kṛṣṇa; *ananta*—unlimited; *vīryasya*—whose prowess; *yoga-māyā*—of the mystic, deluding energy; *mahā*—elaborate; *udayam*—the manifestation; *muhuḥ*—repeatedly; *dṛṣṭvā*—having witnessed; *ṛṣiḥ*—the sage, Nārada; *abhūt*—became; *vismitaḥ*—amazed; *jāta-kautukaḥ*—filled with wonder.

TRANSLATION

Having repeatedly seen the vast mystic display of Lord Kṛṣṇa, whose power is unlimited, the sage was amazed and filled with wonder.

TEXT 43

इत्यर्थकामधर्मेषु कृष्णेन श्रद्धितात्मना ।
सम्यक् सभाजितः प्रीतस्तमेवानुस्मरन् ययौ ॥४३॥

ity artha-kāma-dharmeṣu
kṛṣṇena śraddhitātmanā
samyak sabhājitaḥ prītas
tam evānusmaran yayau

iti—thus; *artha*—with items of utility for economic development; *kāma*—of sense gratification; *dharmeṣu*—and of religiosity; *kṛṣṇena*—by Lord Kṛṣṇa; *śraddhita*—faithful; *ātmanā*—whose heart; *samyak*—thoroughly; *sabhājitaḥ*—honored; *prītaḥ*—pleased; *tam*—Him; *eva*—indeed; *anusmaran*—always remembering; *yayau*—he went.

TRANSLATION

Lord Kṛṣṇa greatly honored Nārada, faithfully presenting him with gifts related to economic prosperity, sense gratification and religious duties. Thus fully satisfied, the sage departed, constantly remembering the Lord.

PURPORT

As Śrīla Prabhupāda points out in *Kṛṣṇa,* the phrase *artha-kāma-dharmeṣu* indicates that Lord Kṛṣṇa was behaving like an ordinary householder deeply concerned with economic development, sense gratification and religious duties. Nārada could understand the Lord's purpose, and he was most pleased by Śrī Kṛṣṇa's exemplary behavior. Thus fully enlivened in his pure Kṛṣṇa consciousness, he departed.

TEXT 44

एवं मनुष्यपदवीमनुवर्तमानो
नारायणोऽखिलभवाय गृहीतशक्तिः ।
रेमे ऽंग षोडशसहस्रवरांगनानां
सव्रीडसौहृदनिरीक्षणहासजुष्टः ॥४४॥

evaṁ manuṣya-padavīm anuvartamāno
nārāyaṇo 'khila-bhavāya gṛhīta-śaktiḥ
reme 'ṅga ṣoḍaśa-sahasra-varāṅganānāṁ
sa-vrīḍa-sauhṛda-nirīkṣaṇa-hāsa-juṣṭaḥ

evam—thus; *manuṣya*—of human beings; *padavīm*—the path; *anuvartamānaḥ*—following; *nārāyaṇaḥ*—the Supreme Lord, Nārāyaṇa; *akhila*—of everyone; *bhavāya*—for the welfare; *gṛhīta*—having manifested; *śaktiḥ*—His potencies; *reme*—He enjoyed; *aṅga*—my dear (King Parīkṣit); *ṣoḍaśa*—sixteen; *sahasra*—thousand; *vara*—most excellent; *aṅganānām*—of women; *sa-vrīḍa*—shy; *sauhṛda*—and affectionate; *nirīkṣaṇa*—by the glances; *hāsa*—and laughter; *juṣṭaḥ*—satisfied.

TRANSLATION

In this way Lord Nārāyaṇa imitated the ways of ordinary humans, manifesting His divine potencies for the benefit of all beings. Thus He enjoyed, dear King, in the company of His sixteen thousand exalted consorts, who served the Lord with their shy, affectionate glances and laughter.

TEXT 45

यानीह विश्वविलयोद्भववृत्तिहेतुः
कर्माण्यनन्यविषयाणि हरिश्चकार ।
यस्त्वंग गायति शृणोत्यनुमोदते वा
भक्तिर्भवेद् भगवति ह्यपवर्गमार्गे ॥४५॥

yānīha viśva-vilayodbhava-vṛtti-hetuḥ
karmāṇy ananya-viṣayāṇi hariś cakāra
yas tv aṅga gāyati śṛṇoty anumodate vā
bhaktir bhaved bhagavati hy apavarga-mārge

yāni—which; *iha*—in this world; *viśva*—of the universe; *vilaya*—of the destruction; *udbhava*—creation; *vṛtti*—and maintenance; *hetuḥ*—He who is the cause; *karmāṇi*—activities; *ananya*—of no one else; *viṣayāṇi*—the engagements; *hariḥ*—Lord Kṛṣṇa; *cakāra*—performed; *yaḥ*—whoever; *tu*—indeed; *aṅga*—my dear King; *gāyati*—chants; *śṛṇoti*—hears; *anumodate*—approves; *vā*—or; *bhaktiḥ*—devotion; *bhavet*—arises; *bhagavati*—for the Supreme Lord; *hi*—indeed; *apavarga*—liberation; *mārge*—the path toward whom.

TRANSLATION

Lord Hari is the ultimate cause of universal creation, maintenance and destruction. My dear King, anyone who chants about, hears about or simply appreciates the extraordinary activities He performed in this world, which are impossible to imitate, will surely develop devotion for the Supreme Lord, the bestower of liberation.

PURPORT

Śrīla Viśvanātha Cakravartī has given various meanings for the word *ananya-viṣayāṇi*. This term may indicate that the Lord performed activities in Dvārakā that were unusual even for His plenary expansions, to say nothing of others. Or the term can be understood to indicate that the Lord performed these activities for the sake of His pure, exclusive devotees. In any case, one who recites or hears accounts of these pastimes will certainly be engaged in Kṛṣṇa consciousness and, as Śrīla Prabhupāda writes, "certainly find it very easy to traverse the path of liberation and taste the nectar of the lotus feet of Lord Kṛṣṇa." Śrīla Prabhupāda further points out that the word *anumodate* here indicates that one who "supports a preacher of the Kṛṣṇa consciousness movement" will also receive the benefits mentioned here.

Thus end the purports of the humble servants of His Divine Grace A. C. Bhaktivedanta Swami Prabhupāda to the Tenth Canto, Sixty-ninth Chapter, of the Śrīmad-Bhāgavatam, *entitled "Nārada Muni Visits Lord Kṛṣṇa's Palaces in Dvārakā."*

Appendixes

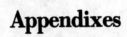

His Divine Grace A. C. Bhaktivedanta Swami Prabhupāda

His Divine Grace A. C. Bhaktivedanta Swami Prabhupāda appeared in this world in 1896 in Calcutta, India. He first met his spiritual master, Śrīla Bhaktisiddhānta Sarasvatī Gosvāmī, in Calcutta in 1922. Bhaktisiddhānta Sarasvatī, a prominent religious scholar and the founder of sixty-four Gauḍīya Maṭhas (Vedic institutes), liked this educated young man and convinced him to dedicate his life to teaching Vedic knowledge. Śrīla Prabhupāda became his student, and eleven years later (1933) at Allahabad he became his formally initiated disciple.

At their first meeting, in 1922, Śrīla Bhaktisiddhānta Sarasvatī Ṭhākura requested Śrīla Prabhupāda to broadcast Vedic knowledge through the English language. In the years that followed, Śrīla Prabhupāda wrote a commentary on the *Bhagavad-gītā,* assisted the Gauḍīya Maṭha in its work and, in 1944, started *Back to Godhead,* an English fortnightly magazine. Maintaining the publication was a struggle. Single-handedly, Śrīla Prabhupāda edited it, typed the manuscripts, checked the galley proofs and even distributed the individual copies. Once begun, the magazine never stopped; it is now being continued by his disciples in the West and is published in over thirty languages.

Recognizing Śrīla Prabhupāda's philosophical learning and devotion, the Gauḍīya Vaiṣṇava Society honored him in 1947 with the title "Bhaktivedanta." In 1950, at the age of fifty-four, Śrīla Prabhupāda retired from married life, adopting the *vānaprastha* (retired) order to devote more time to his studies and writing. Śrīla Prabhupāda traveled to the holy city of Vṛndāvana, where he lived in very humble circumstances in the historic medieval temple of Rādhā-Dāmodara. There he engaged for several years in deep study and writing. He accepted the renounced order of life (*sannyāsa*) in 1959. At Rādhā-Dāmodara, Śrīla Prabhupāda began work on his life's masterpiece: a multivolume commentated translation of the eighteen-thousand-verse *Śrīmad-Bhāgavatam* (*Bhāgavata Purāṇa*). He also wrote *Easy Journey to Other Planets.*

After publishing three volumes of the *Bhāgavatam,* Śrīla Prabhupāda

spiritual master. Subsequently, His Divine Grace wrote more than sixty volumes of authoritative translations, commentaries and summary studies of the philosophical and religious classics of India.

When he first arrived by freighter in New York City, Śrīla Prabhupāda was practically penniless. Only after almost a year of great difficulty did he establish the International Society for Krishna Consciousness, in July of 1966. Before his passing away on November 14, 1977, he guided the Society and saw it grow to a worldwide confederation of more than one hundred *āśramas*, schools, temples, institutes and farm communities.

In 1968, Śrīla Prabhupāda created New Vrindaban, an experimental Vedic community in the hills of West Virginia. Inspired by the success of New Vrindaban, now a thriving farm community of more than two thousand acres, his students have since founded several similar communities in the United States and abroad.

In 1972, His Divine Grace introduced the Vedic system of primary and secondary education in the West by founding the Gurukula school in Dallas, Texas. Since then, under his supervision, his disciples have established children's schools throughout the United States and the rest of the world, with the principal educational center now located in Vṛndāvana, India.

Śrīla Prabhupāda also inspired the construction of several large international cultural centers in India. The center at Śrīdhāma Māyāpur in West Bengal is the site for a planned spiritual city, an ambitious project for which construction will extend over the next decade. In Vṛndāvana, India, are the magnificent Kṛṣṇa-Balarāma Temple and International Guesthouse, and Śrīla Prabhupāda Memorial and Museum. There is also a major cultural and educational center in Bombay. Other centers are planned in a dozen important locations on the Indian subcontinent.

Śrīla Prabhupāda's most significant contribution, however, is his books. Highly respected by the academic community for their authority, depth and clarity, they are used as standard textbooks in numerous college courses. His writings have been translated into over fifty languages. The Bhaktivedanta Book Trust, established in 1972 to publish the works of His Divine Grace, has thus become the world's largest publisher of books in the field of Indian religion and philosophy.

In just twelve years, in spite of his advanced age, Śrīla Prabhupāda circled the globe fourteen times on lecture tours that took him to six continents. In spite of such a vigorous schedule, Śrīla Prabhupāda continued to write prolifically. His writings constitute a veritable library of Vedic philosophy, religion, literature and culture.

References

The purports of *Śrīmad-Bhāgavatam* are all confirmed by standard Vedic authorities. The following authentic scriptures are cited in this volume. For specific page references, consult the general index.

Agni Purāṇa

Atharva Veda

Bhagavad-gītā

Brahma-saṁhitā

Brahma-sūtra (*Vedānta-sūtra*)

Caitanya-caritāmṛta

Gopāla-tāpanī Upaniṣad

Hari-vaṁśa

Kāvya-prakāśa

Kṛṣṇa-sandarbha

Kṛṣṇa, the Supreme Personality of Godhead

Mahābhārata

Mundaka Upaniṣad

Medinī dictionary

Nānārtha-varga dictionary

Nṛsiṁha-tāpanī Upaniṣad

Padma Purāṇa

Sātvata-tantra

Skanda Purāṇa

Śrīmad-Bhagavatam

Taittirīya Upaniṣad

Ujjvala-nīlamaṇi

Vāyu Purāṇa

Viṣṇu Purāṇa

GLOSSARY

A

Ācārya—an ideal teacher, who teaches by his personal example; a spiritual master.

Akṣauhiṇī—a military division consisting of 21,870 chariots, 21,870 elephants, 109,350 infantrymen and 65,610 horses.

Arghya—a ceremonious offering, in a conchshell, of water and other auspicious items.

Asura—a person opposed to the service of the Lord.

Avatāra—a descent, or incarnation, of the Supreme Lord.

B

Bali Mahārāja—a king who became a great devotee by surrendering everything to Vāmanadeva, the Lord's dwarf-*brāhmaṇa* incarnation.

Bhaktivinoda Ṭhākura—(1838-1915) the great-grandfather of the present-day Kṛṣṇa consciousness movement. He was the spiritual master of Śrīla Gaurakiśora dāsa Bābājī and father of Śrīla Bhaktisiddhānta Sarasvatī.

Brahmacarya—celibate student life; the first order of Vedic spiritual life.

Brāhmaṇa—a person wise in Vedic knowledge, fixed in goodness and knowledgeable of Brahman, the Absolute Truth; a member of the first Vedic social order.

Brahmāstra—a nuclear weapon produced by chanting *mantras.*

D

Dvārakā—the island kingdom of Lord Kṛṣṇa, lying off the west coast of India, where He performed pastimes five thousand years ago.

E

Ekādaśī—a special day for increased remembrance of Kṛṣṇa that comes on the eleventh day after both the full and new moon. Abstinence from grains and beans is prescribed.

G

Gopīs—Kṛṣṇa's cowherd girlfriends, who are His most surrendered and confidential devotees.

H

Hari-vaṁśa—the appendix to the *Mahābhārata.* It is a summary of Kṛṣṇa's pastimes by Śrīla Vyāsadeva.

J

Jīva (jīvātmā)—the living entity, who is an eternal individual soul, part and parcel of the Supreme Lord.

Jīva Gosvāmī—one of the six Vaiṣṇava spiritual masters who directly followed Lord Caitanya Mahāprabhu and systematically presented His teachings.

K

Karma—material, fruitive activity and its reactions; also, fruitive actions performed in accordance with Vedic injunctions.

Karma-mīmāṁsā—one of the six main Vedic philosophies. It states that the subtle laws of nature reward or punish one according to how one acts, without reference to an independent God.

Kaustubha gem—a jewel worn by Lord Viṣṇu, or Kṛṣṇa, on His chest.

Kṣatriya—a warrior or administrator; the second Vedic social order.

M

Mahābhārata—Vyāsadeva's epic history of greater India, which includes the events of the Kurukṣetra war and the narration of *Bhagavad-gītā.*

Mantra—a transcendental sound or Vedic hymn that can deliver the mind from illusion.

Mathurā—Lord Kṛṣṇa's abode, surrounding Vṛndāvana, where He took birth and to which He later returned after performing His childhood pastimes in Vṛndāvana.

N

Nārada Muni—a pure devotee of the Lord who travels throughout the universes in his eternal body, glorifying devotional service. He is the spiritual master of Vyāsadeva and of many other great devotees.

P

Pārijāta flower—a wonderful flower found in the heavenly planets.

Pātālaloka—the lowest of the universe's fourteen planetary systems; also, the lower planets in general.

Prasādam—the Lord's mercy; food or other items spiritualized by being first offered to the Supreme Lord.

R

Rākṣasas—man-eating demons.

Rāsa dance—Lord Kṛṣṇa's pleasure dance with the cowherd maidens of Vṛndāvana. It is a pure exchange of spiritual love between the Lord and His most advanced, confidential servitors.

Rūpa Gosvāmī—the chief of the six Vaiṣṇava spiritual masters who directly followed Lord Caitanya Mahāprabhu and systematically presented His teachings.

S

Siddha—a perfected person, or mystic; a demigod from Siddhaloka.

Sītā—the eternal consort of Lord Rāmacandra.

Śrīdhara Svāmī—the author of the earliest extant Vaiṣṇava commentaries on *Bhagavad-gītā* and *Śrīmad-Bhāgavatam*.

Śrīvatsa—the sign of the goddess of fortune on the chest of Lord Viṣṇu, or Nārāyaṇa.

T

Tāṇḍava-nṛtya—Lord Śiva's dance, which he performs at the time of universal devastation, and at other times also.

U

Upaniṣads—108 philosophical works that appear within the *Vedas*.

V

Vaijayantī—a garland containing flowers of five colors and reaching down to the knees. It is worn by Lord Kṛṣṇa.

Varuṇa—the demigod in charge of the oceans.

Vedas—the four original revealed scriptures (*Ṛg, Sāma, Atharva* and *Yajur*).

Viśvanātha Cakravartī Ṭhākura—a great Vaiṣṇava spiritual master in the line of Lord Caitanya Mahāprabhu, and a commentator on *Śrīmad-Bhāgavatam* and *Bhagavad-gītā*.

Y

Yadu (Yādava) dynasty—the dynasty in which Lord Kṛṣṇa appeared.

Yavana—a low-class person, generally a meat-eater; a barbarian.

Yoga—spiritual discipline undergone to link oneself with the Supreme.

Yogamāyā—the internal, spiritual energy of the Supreme Lord; also, its personification as Kṛṣṇa's younger sister.

Sanskrit Pronunciation Guide

Throughout the centuries, the Sanskrit language has been written in a variety of alphabets. The mode of writing most widely used throughout India, however, is called *devanāgarī*, which means, literally, the writing used in "the cities of the demigods." The *devanāgarī* alphabet consists of forty-eight characters: thirteen vowels and thirty-five consonants. Ancient Sanskrit grammarians arranged this alphabet according to practical linguistic principles, and this order has been accepted by all Western scholars. The system of transliteration used in this book conforms to a system that scholars in the last fifty years have accepted to indicate the pronunciation of each Sanskrit sound.

Vowels

अ a आ ā इ i ई ī उ u ऊ ū ऋ ṛ

ॠ ṝ ऌ ḷ ए e ऐ ai ओ o औ au

Consonants

Gutturals:	क ka	ख kha	ग ga	घ gha	ङ ṅa
Palatals:	च ca	छ cha	ज ja	झ jha	ञ ña
Cerebrals:	ट ṭa	ठ ṭha	ड ḍa	ढ ḍha	ण ṇa
Dentals:	त ta	थ tha	द da	ध dha	न na
Labials:	प pa	फ pha	ब ba	भ bha	म ma
Semivowels:	य ya	र ra	ल la	व va	
Sibilants:	श śa	ष ṣa	स sa		

Aspirate: ह ha Anusvāra: ं ṁ Visarga: ः ḥ

Numerals

० -0 १-1 २-2 ३-3 ४-4 ५-5 ६-6 ७-7 ८-8 ९-9

The vowels are written as follows after a consonant:

ा ā ि i ी ī ु u ू ū ृ ṛ ॄ ṝ े e ै ai ो o ौ au

For example: क ka का kā कि ki की kī कु ku कू kū

कृ kṛ कॄ kṝ के ke कै kai को ko कौ kau

Generally two or more consonants in conjunction are written together in a special form, as for example: क्ष kṣa त्र tra

The vowel "a" is implied after a consonant with no vowel symbol.

The symbol virāma (्) indicates that there is no final vowel: क्

The vowels are pronounced as follows:

a — as in **but**

ā — as in **far** but held twice as long as **a**

ai — as in **aisle**

au — as in **how**

e — as in **they**

i — as in **pin**

ī — as in **pique** but held twice as long as **i**

ḷ — as in **lree**

o — as in **go**

ṛ — as in **rim**

ṝ — as in **reed** but held twice as long as **ṛ**

u — as in **push**

ū — as in **rule** but held twice as long as **u**

The consonants are pronounced as follows:

Gutturals
(pronounced from the throat)

k — as in **kite**

kh — as in **Eckhart**

g — as in **give**

gh — as in **dig-hard**

ṅ — as in **sing**

Labials
(pronounced with the lips)

p — as in **pine**

ph — as in **up-hill** (not **f**)

b — as in **bird**

bh — as in **rub-hard**

m — as in **mother**

Cerebrals
(pronounced with tip of tongue against roof of mouth)

ṭ — as in **t**ub
ṭh — as in ligh**t-h**eart
ḍ — as in **d**ove
ḍh — as in re**d-h**ot
ṇ — as in si**ng**

Dentals
(pronounced as cerebrals but with tongue against teeth)

t — as in **t**ub
th — as in ligh**t-h**eart
d — as in **d**ove
dh — as in re**d-h**ot
n — as in **n**ut

Aspirate

h — as in **h**ome

Anusvāra

ṁ — a resonant nasal sound like in the French word *bo***n**

Palatals
(pronounced with middle of tongue against palate)

c — as in **ch**air
ch — as in staun**ch-h**eart
j — as in **j**oy
jh — as in he**dgeh**og
ñ — as in ca**ny**on

Semivowels

y — as in **y**es
r — as in **r**un
l — as in **l**ight
v — as in **v**ine, except when preceded in the same syllable by a consonant, then like in s**w**an

Sibilants

ś — as in the German word s*prechen*
ṣ — as in **sh**ine
s — as in **s**un

Visarga

ḥ — a final **h**-sound: **aḥ** is pronounced like **aha**; **iḥ** like **ihi**

There is no strong accentuation of syllables in Sanskrit, or pausing between words in a line, only a flowing of short and long (twice as long as the short) syllables. A long syllable is one whose vowel is long (**ā, ai, au, e, ī, o, ṝ, ū**) or whose short vowel is followed by more than one consonant (including **ḥ** and **ṁ**). Aspirated consonants (consonants followed by an **h**) count as single consonants.

Index of Sanskrit Verses

This index constitutes a complete listing of the first and third lines of each of the Sanskrit poetry verses of this volume of *Śrīmad-Bhāgavatam*, arranged in English alphabetical order. The first column gives the Sanskrit transliteration; the second, the chapter-verse reference. Apostrophes are alphabetized as *a*'s.

B

H

I

J

K

L

R

S

T

Index of Verses Quoted

This index lists the verses quoted in the purports and footnotes of this volume of *Śrīmad-Bhāgavatam*. Numerals in boldface type refer to the first or third lines of verses quoted in full; numerals in roman type refer to partially quoted verses.

General Index

Numerals in boldface type indicate references to translations of the verses of *Śrīmad-Bhāgavatam*.

A

Abhicāra ritual, **800, 802**
Abhidhāna-koṣa-cchando-jñānam defined, 29
Abhijalpa defined, 97
Absolute Truth
compared with God (conception), 597
knowledge of, 181-82
Kṛṣṇa as, 97, **181, 277,** 596, 597, **691,** 694, **700, 739**
material duality &, 97
as negation of illusion, 693
as one, 470
oneness & difference of, 158
as self-luminous, 700
as source of light, 700
transcendence via surrender to, 366
Vedas explain, confidentially, 700
See also: Kṛṣṇa; Supreme Lord
Ācāryas. See: Spiritual master; *specific* ācāryas
A. C. Bhaktivedanta Swami Prabhupāda. *See:* Prabhupāda, Śrila
Acintya-bhedābheda-tattva explained, 158
Acyuta, Lord. *See:* Kṛṣṇa
Ādi defined, 94
Aditi, **559**
Advayam explained, 277
Ādyaḥ puruṣaḥ defined, 704
Agha, 91
Agni, **510-11**
Agni Purāṇa quoted on Rādhārāṇi, 87
Agraja defined, 119
Aguru incense, **324, 572, 872**
Ahetu defined, 705
Aindrajālam defined, 28
Airāvata, **558**
Balarāma compared to, **767**
Ajalpa defined, 98
Ākara-jñānam defined, 28
Ākarṣa-krīḍā defined, 29
Akrūra
arrival of, in Hastināpura, **175**
behavior of, explained, 463
charity by, 480, 481, **484**
conspiracy by, **462-63**
departure of, from Hastināpura, **194**
Dhṛtarāṣṭra approached by, **183-84**
Dhṛtarāṣṭra's answer to, **191-94**
Dvārakā fled by, **479**
father of, **175, 482**
fear by, **479**
Gokula's residents angry toward, 463
gopīs' mood toward, **75-76**
instructions of, as prophetic, 189
Kṛṣṇa & Balarāma informed by, **195**
Kṛṣṇa & Balarāma visit house of, **153-72**
Kṛṣṇa honors, **484**
Kṛṣṇa leaves jewel in care of, **486**
Kṛṣṇa respectful to, **167-68**
Kṛṣṇa's & Balarāma's relationship with, 155
Kṛṣṇa's promise to, 165
Kṛṣṇa's relationship with, 155, **167,** 168, 170
Kṛṣṇa's request to, **169-71**
Kṛṣṇa summons, to Dvārakā, 483
Kuntī & Vidura inform, **177**
Kuntī's distress shared by, **183**
Kuntī's questions to, **178-79**
Kuntī's relation to, **177**
as Lord's devotee, 463, 484

B

C

D

E

F

K

L

M

O

P

Q

T

U

V